THE ANNUAL REGISTER

Vol. 239

ANNUAL REGISTER ADVISORY BOARD

CHAIRMAN

H. V. HODSON

EDITOR

ALAN J. DAY

ASSISTANT EDITOR

VERENA HOFFMAN

JAMES BISHOP
Editor-in-Chief, The Illustrated London News

FRANK E. CLOSE
Deputy Chief Scientist, Rutherford Appleton University
NOMINATED BY
THE BRITISH ASSOCIATION FOR THE ADVANCEMENT OF SCIENCE

M. R. D. FOOT
Formerly Professor of Modern History, University of Manchester
NOMINATED BY
THE ROYAL HISTORICAL SOCIETY

MICHAEL KASER
*Emeritus Fellow of St Antony's College, Oxford,
and Honorary Professor, University of Birmingham*
NOMINATED BY
THE ROYAL INSTITUTE OF INTERNATIONAL AFFAIRS

ALASTAIR NIVEN
Director of Literature, British Council
NOMINATED BY
THE BRITISH COUNCIL

RICHARD O'BRIEN
Principal, Global Business Network
NOMINATED BY
THE ROYAL ECONOMIC SOCIETY

Popperfoto/Reuter

Icons of an Era

New York, 18 June: Diana, Princess of Wales, meets Mother Teresa of Calcutta at the Missionaries of Charity's residence in the Bronx. They were later to die in the same week, the Princess at the age of 36 in a Paris car crash on 31 August, Mother Teresa in Calcutta on 5 September at the age of 87.

Popperfoto/Reuter

Arrival and Departure

[Top] London, 2 May: Britain's new Prime Minister, Tony Blair, arrives at 10 Downing Street with his wife Cherie, the day after the Labour Party's general election triumph.
[Bottom] Hong Kong, 30 June/1 July: The Chinese flag is raised by soldiers of the People's Liberation Army, as 156 years of British colonial rule come to an end.

THE ANNUAL REGISTER

A Record of World Events
1997

Edited by
ALAN J. DAY

assisted by
VERENA HOFFMAN

FIRST EDITED IN 1758
BY EDMUND BURKE

Keesing's Worldwide, LLC

THE ANNUAL REGISTER 1997
Published by Keesing's Worldwide, LLC, 7979 Old Georgetown Road, #900,
Bethesda, MD 20814, United States of America

ISBN 1-886994-13-7

© Keesing's Worldwide, LLC 1998
All rights reserved; no part of this publication may be reproduced,
stored in a retrieval system, or transmitted in any form or by any
means, electronic, mechanical, photocopying, recording or otherwise
without either the prior written permission of the Publishers or a licence
permitting restricted copying issued by the Copyright Licensing Agency,
90 Tottenham Court Road, London, W1P 9HE

British Library Cataloguing in Publication Data
The Annual Register—1997
 1. History—Periodicals
 909.82'8'05   D410

ISBN 1-886994-13-7

Library of Congress Catalog Card Number: 4-17979

Set in Times Roman by
THE MIDLANDS BOOK TYPESETTING COMPANY, LOUGHBOROUGH

Printed in Great Britain by
BPC WHEATONS LTD, EXETER

describing him as a much-needed 'breath of fresh air' with his concern for national renewal in the next millenium.

The early dissolution of parliament forced the government to drop plans which it claimed would have paved the way for a grammar school in every large town. But Labour agreed to facilitate the passage of other clauses in the Education Bill (notably those designed to improve discipline). The matter of most concern to the electors (48 per cent), according to pollsters, was job insecurity, followed at some distance by crime, education and health, in that order. The economy and Europe were fifth equal at 14 per cent. Other polls indicated that—while many electors did not expect a Labour government to do much to improve their lives, and even more expected taxes to rise—this would not help the Tories. There was a strong feeling that government assurances and promises could not be trusted, which served to neutralize the fact that the so-called 'feel-good factor' and optimism on the economy were at roughly the same level as at the start of the 1992 election, when the Tories were six points clear in the polls. The public remained impervious to a number of independent reports (including some from abroad) which emphasized the increased competitiveness of the economy.

During the campaign, Mr Major again raised the spectre of a return to industrial warfare under a Labour government—a point made even more vehemently by Lady Thatcher with accompanying reminders of the trials and tribulations of the 1970s. Mr Blair retorted that, under Labour, union legislation would be more restrictive than virtually anywhere else in the Western world. Earlier, he had continued his courtship of business leaders with the promise of a seat for the Confederation of British Industry (CBI) on a high-level committee to prepare for Britain's presidency of the EU in 1998. Labour sources said that the unions would not be represented. A threat by the National Union of Teachers (NUT) to take a militant line at its conference at the end of March met an unequivocal warning from David Blunkett (the shadow Education Secretary) that a Labour government would not be intimidated.

Meanwhile, political 'sleaze' had emerged as a major issue. It was hotly debated as to whether Mr Major had timed the dissolution of parliament on 21 March to avoid publication until after the election of the report of the Downey inquiry (see AR 1996, p. 28) into 'sleaze' allegations against a number of MPs, mostly Tories. Mr Major furiously accused Mr Blair of double standards, and charged both the Labour and Liberal Democrat leaders of hijacking parliament with a stage-managed row to divert attention from good employment figures. A brief interim report had been issued by Sir Gordon Downey on 20 March. This cleared most of the MPs under suspicion, but at least four of the rest were accused of serious wrongdoing. The *Sunday Telegraph* of 23 March carried a cartoon of the houses of parliament with a large notice suspended from Big Ben reading 'Closed for Disinfecting'. The opposition parties were also calling for tougher powers for parliament's standards watchdog. On 26 March Tim Smith, one of the Tory MPs accused of taking cash for asking parliamentary questions, resigned. Over the weekend of 29–30 March some leading Tories called upon two other Tory MPs—Neil Hamilton and Piers Merchant, both the subjects of various

Meanwhile, Mr Brown warned that Labour would not accept the new Tory pension plan: it was too risky and costly. Labour intended to supplement the existing state pension with a second 'stake-holder' private pension. Experts were divided over the scale of the projected state-funded pension crisis in the next century. OECD figures suggested that Britain would in any case be significantly cushioned from a demographic time-bomb by private pension assets (£650,000 million), which were nearly four times larger than those of Germany, and more than the rest of Europe combined.

The government fell victim to claims that a meat hygiene report had been suppressed in December 1995. The report in question had identified unhygienic practices which could cause the spread of the E.coli bacterium, one recent outbreak in western Scotland having claimed 20 lives (see AR 1996, p. 36). The head of the inquiry into the latter outbreak said that he had not received all the data in the meat hygiene report. Labour announced on 7 March that it would set up an independent food standards agency which would operate 'openly and transparently'. The government followed this on 11 March with the promise of tighter controls on meat hygiene amid allegations that ministers had been warned several times of a 'potential time-bomb' because of falling standards.

On 8 March Sir George Gardiner, a Euro-sceptic Tory MP who had been deselected by his constituency party, announced that he was resigning the Tory whip and would contest the Reigate constituency for the Referendum Party. Mr Major, he said, had been guilty of an unparalleled abdication of national leadership. On 12 March nearly 100 pro-European Tory MPs (including 17 former ministers) publicized their strong support for British membership of the EU following a warning from 23 senior industrialists of the damage being done to British business by 'extreme Euro-scepticism'.

By this time many stalwart grassroots Tories were criticizing their party's current election strategy. They pressed for an end to the party's in-fighting at Westminster, and clung to the hope that the electorate would finally wake up to the success of government economic policies as reflected in the good figures on unemployment and inflation. An independent think-tank, the Social Market Foundation, argued in March that Britain's relative decline in the 1950s, 1960s and 1970s had been halted and that the potential for economic growth was greater than ever.

4. THE GENERAL ELECTION: LANDSLIDE TO LABOUR

ON 17 March Prime Minister Major announced that the general election would be held on 1 May, thus ensuring a six-and-a-half week campaign, the longest of the century. Despite Labour's unprecedented lead of nearly 30 per cent in the opinion polls, he insisted that the election was 'winnable' and that Labour was straddling 'a chasm of credibility'. To vote for it would be 'a leap into the dark'. Lady Thatcher promised to back him to the hilt. In contrast, *The Sun* newspaper, a strong Tory supporter in 1992, immediately declared for Mr Blair, the main party leaders earned plaudits for their knockabout performances in the debate, Mr Major making much of Labour and 'the West Lothian question'— how Scottish MPs could be allowed a role in English issues whereas the opposite would not apply. But 'if answer came there none' from the Labour benches (or none that anyone could detect), *The Times* agreed with those who asked why, if Mr Major could argue that an Ulster assembly 'would provide the surest foundation' for maintaining Ulster's place in the UK, the same did not apply to Scotland.

On 23 February, the same day that the cabinet was putting the finishing touches to the Tory election manifesto, Sir Edward Heath stated that he saw no threat to the country from Labour's plans for devolution and a minimum wage. Lord Jenkins of Hillhead warned two days later that, if Mr Major persisted with his rigid opposition to devolution and if a future Tory government took an anti-European line, there was a real danger of 'Scottish independence within ten years, an outcome which I would regard as a great misfortune for those on both sides of the border'. Scots, he argued, could not fail to be impressed by the recent economic success of the Irish Republic and by its commitment to the EU.

Labour easily won the Wirral South by-election on 27 February with a swing of no less than 17 per cent. It was estimated that a comparable swing in a general election would leave the Tories with only 124 seats in the next parliament. Mr Major conceded that if public opinion did not change there would be a Labour government, and Britain could be just weeks away from 'a midsummer nightmare'. Meanwhile, the Tories ensured continuing Ulster Unionist support by means of an agreement on 27 February to increase the powers of the special parliamentary committee which dealt with Northern Ireland.

After four months of talks, Labour and the Liberal Democrats on 5 March announced plans (in the event of a change of government) for a national referendum on reforms to the electoral system and to the House of the Lords, as well as Scottish and Welsh devolution. A freedom of information act was also promised. On the same day Mr Major, perhaps with an eye to the Eurosceptic vote, said that entry into the European exchange-rate mechanism (ERM) had been a political mistake (see AR 1990, p. 33). He also unveiled an ambitious and controversial plan under which everyone would have a personal pension scheme by around the year 2040. The plan was welcomed by life companies but not by those who recalled the difficulties which had arisen from the Tories' earlier efforts to encourage private pensions. These were still far from resolution, the whole affair being condemned by *The Times* on 8 March as 'daylight robbery, literally', and as an outrage which had brutally affected over half a million people. The City's watchdog was reprimanded by the Treasury and told to take decisive action in this '£4 billion' scandal, while the Treasury select committee in the Commons complained on 10 March of the 'snail-like' progress in making restitution. The Barings affair was also still rumbling on with another (the ninth) of the company's former directors being disciplined on 11 March by the Securities and Futures Authority of the City of London (see AR 1995, p. 12).

still more alarmed by Mr Brown's warning on 31 January that there would be no blank cheque for public-sector workers after it was disclosed that pay review bodies had been recommending above-inflation rises for 1.3 million in that sector.

Commentators noted that either party could, in government, find ways to increase revenue while honouring its promises on direct taxes simply (for instance) by alterations to tax reliefs and exemptions. Mr Brown himself stressed the importance of the windfall tax and the shortfalls in the collection of many other taxes. The Bishop of Liverpool, however, was among those to protest at Labour's failure to increase taxes to help the poor. Politicians were too intent on wooing 'comfortable Britain'. By 25 January, renewed signs of unrest were emerging among Labour's ranks about Mr Blair's alleged authoritarian approach. However, on 29 January the Labour national executive committee (NEC), with only one dissident, approved sweeping changes to the party structure to prevent damaging internal conflicts under a Labour government. Gains in power by the Labour leader would be balanced by ordinary party members securing more say in policy-making. Veteran left-winger Tony Benn described the new moves as 'the Americanization' of the party so that the annual conference 'would become a rally for the leadership'.

The EU itself entered the election fray on 3 February, when the Commission issued a report on jobs in Britain which, while acknowledging the government's success against unemployment, urged a reversal of some of its policies against job protection—advice which appeared to favour some of Labour's proposed policies. It described greater wage inequality as an 'unambiguous' trend in Britain. Mr Major on 31 January unveiled Tory plans to give people a bigger 'stake' in the nation's wealth through a massive expansion of share ownership and the greater use of personal pensions. Both should become part of an employee's normal employment package.

The election battle was stepped up in the Commons in the week beginning 17 February. It began with Labour's censure motion against the Agriculture Minister, Douglas Hogg, for his alleged mishandling of the BSE crisis (see AR 1996, p. 23). Labour had earlier hinted at hopes that the government might be defeated on this issue, only to mishandle their assault by failing to consult the other parties from the start. Much hinged on the Ulster Unionists, who finally abstained, the censure motion being defeated by 320 votes to 307. Labour, however, had brought the BSE issue back into prominence. One million cattle had already been slaughtered, another 100,000 were scheduled for selective culling, and sections of the beef industry were still suffering from much-reduced prices. On 19 February both the British government and the European Commission were forcefully accused by the European Parliament of mishandling the BSE crisis, but by the middle of March it seemed that the embattled Mr Hogg would survive the savage criticism directed at his handling of the affair.

The devolution debate on 20 February was prefaced by angry exchanges. Mr Ashdown claimed that without constitutional change the United Kingdom would be 'blown apart', in contrast to the Tory argument that devolution would split the UK by creating 'unsustainable constitutional anomalies for the future'. Both slogan 'It would all end in tears' (that is, if Labour won the forthcoming election), a theme reiterated by Mr Major the following day when he declared that the key issues would be the economy, Europe and Labour's constitutional reform proposals. He did, however, hint that he might consider 'cautious incremental' reform of the House of Lords. Mr Blair retorted that his was the party of the centre and that its programme would entail no increase in personal taxation. Only the commitment to get 250,000 unemployed youngsters back into work would require extra money, which would come from the proposed windfall tax on privatized public utilities; the rest would be financed through the redeployment of existing resources. Labour stepped up its pressure on the government by suspending pairing arrangements with the Tories and by waging a guerrilla war in committees as well as in the Commons. The Tories, however, easily surmounted the first expected trial of strength, a financial vote on 14 January. Death then struck at the voting strength of each of the main parties in turn. Iain Mills (Tory MP for West Meriden) died suddenly on 16 January, but the loss of his vote was almost immediately balanced by the death of Martin Redmond (Labour, Don Valley), leaving the government with the same number of seats as all the other parties combined.

The two main parties were finally able to reach agreement on 16 January over the plans for the Millennium Exhibition at Greenwich to celebrate the year 2000. The organizers had warned of serious problems unless they could be assured of continuity from one ministry to another. The new Labour government finally approved the controversial project on 19 June, but only in return for certain changes to ensure that the outcome was truly exciting, would provide durable and useful legacies, and would require no additional government money. Debate and uncertainty also followed the government's announcement on 22 January that it was to spend £60 million on a new royal yacht to replace the ageing *Britannia*. There had been no prior agreement with Labour, and the latter speedily decided that it would not fund the ship if it came to power. By 26 January some senior Tories were accusing ministers of having misjudged the public mood. It was also understood that the Queen was upset that she had been dragged into a political row. Prince Charles, it was said, had not been consulted and would have preferred private funding. The new Labour government stated in August that it was considering several options.

On 24 January Mr Blair declared that more was needed than the reform of the welfare state, adding that he wanted to refound it with the emphasis on practical needs rather than on new principles. He favoured emphasis on positive action rather than the negative provision of benefits. Four days earlier Gordon Brown, in a landmark speech, had announced that he aimed to impose a two-year freeze on government spending at the level announced in Mr Clarke's last budget. He sent the same message to local councils and to public sector employees, and underlined Labour's determination not to raise either the basic or higher rates of income tax. Additional public spending would have to come from savings elsewhere. The Labour leaders were determined to blunt Tory election campaign warnings of high taxes under Labour. Union and left-wing MPs were

3. A GOVERNMENT RUNNING OUT OF TIME

ON 7 January *The Times* bleakly predicted that the Ulster Unionists would probably protect Mr Major in any vote of confidence until May (the latest date for an election), but feared that Tory morale would be sapped by the experience of minority government, adding: 'The new year has begun, but there is little sign yet of a new spirit abroad.' Labour was able to ambush the Tories with a tied vote as early as 27 January. The Tories also added to their own problems. On 2 January the Health Secretary, Stephen Dorrell, called for a renegotiation of Britain's relationship with the European Union (EU) to prevent it developing into a superstate. It was also thought that he favoured a replacement of the current 'wait and see' policy on the single European currency with a definite decision to rule out entry in the next parliament. Some commentators began to sniff the first hints of a post-election leadership battle.

Mr Major claimed on 7 January that no sensible person believed it possible for Britain to leave the EU. Five days later he announced that he would propose more ideas for a multi-speed Europe with additional opt-outs, yet with each state retaining a veto to ensure that an inner core or circle of members could not proceed at their own pace regardless of the interests and needs of others. The European Commission emphatically signalled its opposition to any demand of this kind. Mr Blair was equally fearful of the emergence of an inner core, as this would leave Britain on the sidelines. Malcolm Rifkind, the Foreign Secretary, stated on 23 January that he believed that the future of the EU lay somewhere between the two poles of federation and a free trade area. Mr Major, in a further bid to reunite his party, suggested that British participation in the single currency in 1999 was 'very unlikely'. He subsequently added that he would not like to see a British government lose control of interest rates. The Chancellor of the Exchequer, Kenneth Clarke, said much the same on 26 January, but provocatively surmised that Britain could still be in the first wave of states to join the single currency. Mr Rifkind, however, asserted on 19 February that the cabinet was 'on balance hostile' to monetary union. With Labour spokesman Gordon Brown on the following day warning of increasingly difficult hurdles to entry to monetary union by 1999, it seemed that there was not much to choose between the thinking of the two main parties.

Earlier, on 5 January, Mr Major had fiercely attacked the Labour and Liberal Democrat parties for advancing plans for radical constitutional change, including devolution and reform of the House of Lords. He was also critical of their interest in a freedom of information act and changes to parliamentary procedure. The two opposition parties, however, were still some way from full agreement. Labour refused to go forward with its 'hands tied' when Paddy Ashdown insisted that Liberal Democrat support for Labour's programme was dependent on its acceptance of electoral reform. For his part, Mr Blair seemed disinclined to do more than tinker with the voting system and strengthen individual rights.

The Tories unveiled an ambitious poster campaign on 6 January with the to be confirmed was the growth of personal saving among a large proportion of the public following the economic woes of the early and mid-1990s. The recession in those years, fears of job insecurity and official warnings of the need to make personal provision to ensure adequate pensions in the next century (not to mention the new costs of higher education) were resulting in savings in excess of 10 per cent of income (excluding the huge windfalls from the flotation of several building societies). This was double the rate in the 1980s' boom. Much uncertainty, however, continued to surround the actual strength of high-street spending. Figures in mid-September reported the lowest unemployment figures for 17 years.

A serious train crash at Southall (west London) on 19 September resulted in a final death toll of seven and numerous injuries. This revived fears that little had been done to improve rail safety despite the recommendations following the Clapham disaster nine years earlier. The question was also raised whether private companies were putting profits before safety.

During the year there were a number of interesting contributions to the debate on social change. *The End of Order*, by Francis Fukuyama, discussed the decline of the old-fashioned family, while Andrew Adonis and Stephen Pollard, in *A Class Act: the Myth of Britain's Classless Society*, examined the rise of a 'super-class' (a new meritocracy) since the mid-1960s. Lord Bauer, in *Class on the Brain,* argued that inequality was the inevitable outcome of an open-market economy and was a more powerful engine for economic growth than Keynesian demand management. 'Differences and distinctions', he claimed, promoted rather than restricted talent and offered the inducement that there was 'something to go for at all levels of society'. On 5 October Alan Clark, a former political supporter of Lady Thatcher and recently restored to the Commons for the Conservative Party, suggested on television that great damage to the traditional social fabric of Britain had resulted from Thatcherite policies despite their political and economic successes. A month later, in *Dark Heart: the Shocking Truth about Hidden Britain*, Nick Davies claimed that the underclass already comprised about one quarter of the population. Finally, a report (commissioned by the Major government in 1995) recommended in December that the existing classification of people according to six occupational groups should be replaced by an eight-category division to reflect the growing complexity of society. David Rose, the leader of this review, claimed that under Mr Major, despite his dream of a classless society, class differences had been intensified by a more flexible labour market in which fewer people could look forward to a job for life.

In what was described as the biggest revolution in broadcasting since the introduction of colour television in the 1960s, the two largest ITV companies (Granada and Carlton) were given the right (in June) to begin broadcasting on 15 commercial digital terrestrial channels from 1998 (see also XVI.1.vi). One enthusiast said that this decision would put Britain 'at the head of the worldwide digital television revolution'.

primary schools. On 11 February the Education Secretary announced plans to sack incompetent teachers—the first time this had been contemplated since the Victorian era.

On 2 June the new Prime Minister, Mr Blair, outlined his government's plans to help jobless and single parents to develop the necessary skills to find their way into employment. There would be tough sanctions against those who wilfully declined the opportunities provided for them. Nevertheless, success in the creation of one nation and rescue of the 'forgotten people', so that everyone developed 'the will to win', would also require help from the rest of the community. Soon afterwards Harriet Harman (the incoming Social Security Secretary and Minister for Women) announced new plans to advance the cause of equality for women (not least in facilitating their promotion to top jobs), to provide child-care to enable women to work, and also to arrange for the splitting of pensions in the event of divorce.

On 2 July the Chancellor of the Exchequer outlined the government's 'new deal' for a quarter of a million young people who had been unemployed for six months. Those who refused to take one of the three types of job on offer, or to embark on full-time study in an approved course, would be penalized with up to a month's loss of benefits. Mr Brown said bluntly that there would be no fifth option: to sign on for benefit meant 'signing up for work'. He also looked to all businesses and voluntary organizations to cooperate in a bid to end youth unemployment within five years. He had earmarked £3,500 million for the scheme, which would be gradually introduced in 1998. On 14 August a high-powered Whitehall task-force was set up and charged with the coordination of efforts to reduce social inequality. It would, said Peter Mandelson (Minister without Portfolio), 'harness the full power of government to take on the biggest social crisis of our times'. Roy Hattersley, a former deputy leader of the Labour Party and cabinet minister, struck a different note, claiming that Labour was no longer fighting for greater equality, given its refusal to raise taxes.

New calculations published in August suggested that the average take-home pay of British workers now exceeded that in all EU countries except Germany. The figures applied to 1994, but in the interval taxes had risen in Germany compared with Britain. Overall, taxes took 38 per cent of earnings in Britain on average, compared with an EU average of 46 per cent. It was said that Labour's general election claims that British workers stood 12th in the EU league had failed to take account of tax differences. A set of figures released in August showed that a half-century of inflation had shrunk the pound to a 20th of its value in 1947. The average male manual worker, however, was two-and-a-half times better off in real terms, with weekly earnings of £300. Comparisons, admittedly, were complicated by new products, tastes and aspirations, while some costs (from vehicle licences to houses) had risen 100-fold or more. Many employees were also having to work longer hours. Meanwhile, although it seemed that progress had been made towards greater equality for women since the 1970s, there had been only a tiny rise in men's share of housework: 'husbands have, in effect, one job whereas they [wives] have two'. Another trend which appeared since 1979), after senior judges and lawyers had argued that it would give the police excessive freedom in the use of bugging devices and the 'burgling' of homes and offices during surveillance operations. Mr Howard said on 9 February, with the agreement of Labour, that chief constables would be required to seek authorization from independent commissioners, except in emergency cases. Yet more controversy was generated by further Home Office legal proposals, which included curbs on the right to trial by jury. On 14 March the Lord Chief Justice attacked both the government and Labour for using the reform of criminal justice to score political points. He asked for a return to 'a more measured and bipartisan approach'.

The Churches, meanwhile, implicitly criticized both main parties for their emphasis on crime, while both Anglican archbishops, in their Easter messages, called for a fairer division of Britain's resources and opportunities. The Archbishop of Canterbury, Dr George Carey, spoke of 'a profound confusion about the moral rules which underpin a just and good society'. A report entitled *Unemployment and the Future of Work,* produced by representatives from 11 Christian denominations and published on 8 April, earned much applause as a cogent and constructive document. The Child Poverty Action Group claimed in mid-April (during the election campaign) that one child in three now lived in poverty compared with one in ten in 1979.

On 13 February the then shadow Chancellor of the Exchequer, Gordon Brown, announced that a Labour government would devote at least £3,000 million to combat unemployment and the danger of the emergence of an American-type 'underclass'. He claimed that the scheme could be 'comfortably financed' by a new tax on the windfall profits of privatized public utilities. This was followed by a tough statement about Labour's 'zero tolerance' policy on anti-social behaviour in public places. The party had already threatened a strong line against aggressive beggars. On 8 April Mr Straw (then shadow Home Secretary) argued that a comprehensive approach was needed to confront crime and the causes of crime. He was looking at Scotland's speedier handling of court cases, its youth justice system and the recent successful onslaught on petty crime by the Strathclyde police. Having taken office as Home Secretary of the new Labour government, Mr Straw on 25 September announced the biggest shake-up in youth justice for 50 years. His proposals included curfews for children under ten, as well as orders to make mothers and fathers attend parenting classes and to take responsibility for unruly children in other ways. He was determined to break 'the excuse culture' with a raft of measures to bring home to parents and children what constituted tolerable norms of behaviour.

The Chief Inspector of Schools, in his annual report published on 4 February, recorded a drop in the proportion of unsatisfactory lessons from 18 to 16 per cent in 1995–96, while the number of incompetent teachers had fallen by one-sixth to 13,000. He also claimed that the pressure for improved results was bringing a change in the culture of education, in that 'progressive' methods were beginning to lose ground. The latest analysis (February) from school inspectors, however, suggested a decline in performance in the 'three Rs' in that hereditary monarchy, like the government, existed only with the consent of the people. The royal family, she acknowledged, had to endeavour to interpret correctly, and respond to, the wishes of the public if the monarchy was to survive. The special lunch in Whitehall was described as a 'people's banquet', the 350 guests including numerous commoners as well as members of European royal families both regnant and deposed. The Queen's determination to modernize the Royal Family's image was clearly reflected in a new-look Christmas broadcast, in which special reference was made to the tragic death of the Princess of Wales.

Meanwhile, Prince Charles's popularity, as a result of a new approach to his public appearances, had begun to rival that of Mr Blair, according to a MORI poll. The New Year honours list included awards for leading figures in Diana's funeral arrangements, as well as more generous provision throughout the education sector, from university principals to a street-crossing patroller. Perhaps as a symbol of calmer waters ahead for the monarchy, work was completed in November on the restoration of Windsor Castle after the disastrous fire five years earlier (see AR 1992, p. 32).

2. SOCIAL TRENDS BEFORE AND AFTER THE ELECTION

EARLY in the year, controversy continued to surround the then Conservative government's determination to punish more offenders with imprisonment, the prison population having risen towards a record 60,000 inmates. Douglas Hurd, a former Conservative Home Secretary and presently chairman of the Prison Reform Trust, warned on 14 January that 'prison could be an expensive way of making bad people worse'. He also regretted that change was being pressed during the run-up to an election. The Lord Chief Justice on 27 January described the Home Office's plans to reduce the sentencing discretion given to judges as 'irremediably flawed'. Over the next fortnight the incumbent Home Secretary, Michael Howard, suffered two defeats at the hands of the Lords. Nevertheless, Mr Howard on 13 February said that he was determined to press on against moves which would drive 'a coach and horses' through his legislation. Following the change of government, the High Court ruled in August that the Home Office had been unlawful with respect to the practice of sending young female offenders (aged between 15 and 21) to adult prisons before decisions were taken as to where they should serve their sentences. The same ruling was taken to apply to young male offenders. On 12 November the new Home Secretary, Jack Straw, signalled a retreat from Conservative insistence on the efficacy of prison sentences by announcing that 3,000 prisoners were to be freed early, though they would be subject to electronic monitoring. The necessary legislation was expected to take effect in 1998. Judges and magistrates were also urged to make greater use of electronic tagging and community service for non-violent offenders.

On 20 January the House of Lords defeated the Conservative government's Police Bill by 209 votes to 145 (one of the heaviest defeats suffered by ministers the ancient goddess of hunting was, in the end, the most hunted person of the modern age'. He also pledged that his family would ensure that 'her beloved boys' William and Harry would be familiarized with the wider world outside royalty, 'so that their souls are not simply immersed by duty and tradition but can sing openly', as Diana had planned. Applause in response to his words spread from outside the abbey to the congregation within.

Earlier, as it became apparent that the numbers wishing to watch the funeral in person would far exceed original expectations, the route of the procession was considerably lengthened to four miles. It was estimated that around two million people lined the route of the funeral procession to Westminster or watched the passage of the hearse to the Spencer family home in Northamptonshire, many throwing flowers as the vehicle passed. Despite the huge numbers, there were few calls on the police and emergency services. A one-minute silence was also observed, the whole country coming virtually to a standstill until after the conclusion of the ceremony in London.

Talks between the Queen and Mr Blair were followed by an announcement on 7 September by the latter that the monarchy would change and modernize for the people of Prince William's generation. The government was planning to create a lasting memorial for Diana's life and work. Mr Blair added that her true legacy would be achieved if the country kept alive her spirit of compassion and human sympathy. He also confirmed that he had discussed plans with the late Princess for her to have become an informal ambassador for Britain. Donations to her Memorial Fund were believed to have topped the £100 million mark in four days. Early opinion polls reported much criticism of the royal family's initial handling of the aftermath of Diana's death, and strong support for Prince William, not Prince Charles, as the next monarch. Sections of the press were apologetic about the treatment Diana had received, and hopes were raised that the two princes would not be exposed to intrusive media behaviour, at least from British photographers. On 17 September newspaper editors promised to support rigorous privacy reforms and to help to put an end to 'deplorable practices' by sections of the press. At the end of the year, a revised code of conduct drawn up by the Press Complaints Commission gave some hope that such practices would cease.

Amid suggestions that Diana's influence might be even greater after her death than before, it was reported that the Prime Minister was anxious to impress upon the Queen the lessons that might be learned from the public's reaction to the tragedy. Wider discussion of the future of the monarchy in the light of the extraordinary impact of Diana in recent years was also considered likely. Indeed, Prince Charles on 29 October, during a visit to Swaziland, fully acknowledged the need for change. During his ensuing South African tour the Prince paid tribute to his former wife's charity work and her opposition to landmines. He also seemed anxious to establish a new and good working relationship with the media.

The Queen and the Duke of Edinburgh celebrated their golden wedding anniversary on 20 November. The Queen took the opportunity to state frankly son of Mohammed al-Fayed, the Egyptian owner of London's Harrods department store.

The sudden death of the Princess and Dodi Fayed on 31 August in a car crash in Paris led to the temporary suspension of party campaigning over devolution for Scotland and Wales (see I.6; I.8; I.9). Amid the grief over the loss of Diana, who was widely described as the 'People's Princess' (not least by Mr Blair in a moving tribute on the Sunday morning of her death), there were many calls for tougher privacy laws in view of the alleged conduct of 'paparazzi' freelance photographers before and after the fatal crash. Seven photographers were investigated by the French authorities on manslaughter charges, although it subsequently seemed unlikely that their pursuit of the Princess had been the direct cause of the crash. It was revealed that the dead driver of the Princess's car, an al-Fayed employee, had drunk more than three times the French legal limit and that the car had been travelling at around 100 miles an hour when it crashed in an underpass alongside the River Seine. Still under investigation at year's end was the possible role of another car, as yet untraced, in causing the fatal crash.

The story of Diana's death was front-page news around the world, especially in the United States. In Spain *El Mundo*'s headline ran: 'Diana is wept for across five continents. There has been nothing like it since Kennedy.' In Britain there were huge queues to record tributes in books of remembrance, while 'a swelling sea' of floral tributes materialized at the gates of Kensington Palace, the residence of the late Princess and her children. Indeed, the public became more than a passive presence, as pressure mounted on the royal family to make an early return to London from its seclusion at Balmoral in Scotland. Downing Street began to take a hand in the preparations for the funeral and the management of the proceedings in general. The Queen was persuaded to broadcast on the evening of 5 September, while protocol was broken with the flying of the Union flag at half-mast over Buckingham Palace on the day of the funeral (6 September).

Although no longer a full member of the royal family, Diana was given what was in many ways a *de facto* state funeral, her body being borne on a gun carriage of the King's Troop of Royal Horse Artillery. But the occasion also developed into what was described as a unique 'people's funeral' for a unique person who had established a remarkable rapport with ordinary people in so many countries in addition to Britain. Some 500 workers from her many charities took part in the later stages of the procession to Westminster Abbey. As suggested, many were informally dressed. Others who joined the procession included the Prince of Wales and the Princes William and Harry, who paid simple tribute to their departed mother with gun-carriage flowers for 'Mummy'.

Diana's brother, Earl Spencer, in his tribute during the funeral service, fiercely criticized those of the media who had harried the Princess, seeing the explanation as being 'that genuine goodness is threatening to those at the opposite end of the moral spectrum'. 'It is a point to remember', he continued, 'that of all the ironies about Diana perhaps the greatest was that a girl given the name of

I UNITED KINGDOM

CAPITAL: London   AREA: 244,100 sq km   POPULATION: 58,800,000 ('96)
OFFICIAL LANGUAGES: English; Welsh in Wales
POLITICAL SYSTEM: parliamentary democracy
HEAD OF STATE: Queen Elizabeth II (since Feb '52)
RULING PARTY: Labour Party (since May '97)
HEAD OF GOVERNMENT: Tony Blair, Prime Minister (since May '97); *for cabinet list see* xix.7
MAIN IGO MEMBERSHIPS (non-UN): NATO, CWTH, EU, WEU, OSCE, CE, OECD, G-7
CURRENCY: pound sterling (end-'97 £1=US$1.64
GNP PER CAPITA: US$18,700 ('95) or US$19,260 ('95) by PPP calculation

THE year in Britain was notable for two major events. On 1 May a general election resulted in a landslide victory (in terms of seats won) for the Labour Party, which thus returned to office under the youthful leadership of Tony Blair (43) after 18 years of Conservative government. Four months later Diana, Princess of Wales (36), was killed in a Paris car crash on 31 August, less than a year after her divorce from Prince Charles had become absolute (see AR 1996, p. 9). Elements of the national mood which swept Labour to power, although with a different focus, could be discerned in the massive outpouring of public grief which Diana's death provoked. The culmination was a hugely emotional funeral in London on 6 September that was followed by most people in Britain and by hundreds of millions around the world (see also Editorial and XX: Obituary).

1. DEATH OF THE 'PEOPLE'S PRINCESS'

THE Princess of Wales was rarely out of the headlines in the first half of the year. There were reports early in January that both she and her former husband intended to put past unpleasantness behind them in the interest of their children, the Princes William and Henry (Harry). The Princess excited some controversy in mid-January during a trip to Angola when she called for a worldwide ban on anti-personnel landmines. Some Tories complained that she was straying into the public arena and questioned her suitability as a roving good-will ambassador, although the Foreign Secretary said that there was little difference between government policy and what the Princess had said. (For the subsequent international draft treaty banning anti-personnel landmines, see XII.2; XIX.5.)

In July Prince Charles publicized his longstanding relationship with Camilla Parker-Bowles by hosting a 50th birthday party in her honour at Highgrove, his country residence. The Archbishop of Canterbury, questioned in Australia, said that the Church of England would face a major crisis if the Prince remarried, possibly stretching to disestablishment of the Church. The Princess of Wales complained to a French newspaper on 26 August of her 'ferocious' treatment by the British press, asserting that she would have left Britain long ago had it not been for her children. By then the British and other media were in a feeding frenzy over Diana's new relationship, said to be a serious one, with Dodi Fayed, succession was universally accepted. Not only kingship but all degrees of nobility passed automatically from father to son (occasionally to daughter) or to some more distant heir in the line of blood. Even legislative power followed the same descent. Estates large and small passed normally to the deceased owner's children or to other next of kin. Death duties diminished this hereditary transfer of wealth, but it persists unassailed in principle. The aspect that has been attacked for generations is the hereditary principle in political power and privilege. In Britain the House of Lords with its great majority of hereditary peers has been seen as an anachronism. Prime Minister Macmillan's introduction of life peerages fended off the assault, but the days of hereditary voting rights in a House of Parliament are now numbered.

Hereditary chance and opportunity will not then be extinguished. Democratic republics, too, have their dynasties: the Kennedy family in the United States, for instance, or the Nehru succession in India—Motilal, Jawaharlal, Indira, Rajiv and now possibly Sonia, widow of Rajiv. Family motive and opportunity give heredity durable strength. Heredity as a principle of succession in authority and power has its philosophical defenders. It ensures continuity where breaches of succession might be divisive and dangerous. Heirs to high place are brought up to shoulder its responsibilities as well as its privileges. Prince William knows that in due course he will be King, and that this requires sound judgment and restraint, which are not easily learnt, as well as knowledge of the constitution and its still evolving history. The blood line carries virtues of character and temperament. Inheritance by birth is a near-universal practice in private and social affairs. The principle is instinctive in human society. It is, however, only a framework, not an inflexible construction. Within the frame, ability and ambition should be able to mount to power and wealth, whatever their hereditary starting-point.

One peak they cannot climb without revolutionary violence is a royal throne. Monarchy and heredity march together. Monarchies may be overthrown, or reduced to impotence, but so long as they exist the core of their continuity is hereditary descent. That fact lays a heavy responsibility upon the potential heirs and their tutors and advisers. A monarchy must change its outlook and behaviour as its subjects and the world around them change. As the millennium draws near, every monarchy must adapt to a world radically altered during a single long reign.

London, January 1998

gulf between fervid public emotion and rightful royal reserve. If a lesson had to be learnt, it was that a modern monarchy must be attuned to the common will of its people, or it is in peril.

The event raised questions about the nature of royalty and of monarchy which is royalty's fount. Monarchy may hang by a thin historical thread of hereditary descent, but it is essentially continuous. Its high personnel—kings and queens regnant and their immediate descendants—know what they are from childhood. Bar occasional abdications or, more often, political overthrows, monarchs reign for their lifetime, and their families meanwhile play royal parts. The wives and children of elected presidents may have an active public role during the president's tenure, but when that ends they lose their special status. In monarchies, royal families have public parts to play throughout and beyond a reign.

The history of monarchy is stained with blood and oppression; but, if we had to bear all the sins of our forefathers, which of us should see salvation? In all Western countries which retain this form of state structure, it is nowadays constitutional monarchy: that is to say, in all political and economic affairs executive power belongs to democratically-elected governments; the sovereign has none, only the right to be informed and consulted. But the King or Queen is not thereby reduced to a cypher. He or she is the focus of national loyalty, transcending political differences. He or she represents the whole nation in a more comprehensive and secure way than any passing elected President or Prime Minister. As a symbol of national cohesion, he or she is unique.

In greater or less degree this account holds good for all monarchs still heads of state in the West. The King of Spain has the special esteem of his people for the active part he played in the restoration of democracy after the regime of General Franco. None of those other Western sovereigns, however, enjoys anything like the international status of the Queen of Great Britain and Northern Ireland. She is also head of state of all the remaining British colonial territories, and of such former dominions as have not become republics. She has also the unique status and title of Head of the Commonwealth. As such, she exerts no political authority, but she signifies in her person the mutual concern and fellowship of all the Commonwealth countries. Again, monarchy shows its power to display solidarity beyond the rivalries of politics.

Since the majority of member states of the Commonwealth are themselves republics, the logical deduction would be that the members should elect a republican Head of the Commonwealth itself. To imagine, however, how such an election would proceed, and its likely outcome—persons holding that office each for a short term, facing disappointed rivals, racial prejudices, political intrigues and the dissent of defeated minorities—reveals how such a process would soon destroy the sense of community and soon the reality of the Commonwealth itself. No more eloquently than at this high level does monarchy proclaim its power to unite and reconcile political and cultural fractions of a community.

Heredity is at the heart of monarchy. In past centuries the principle of hereditary

THE ANNUAL REGISTER

FOR THE YEAR 1997

EDITORIAL

MONARCHY AND THE HEREDITARY PRINCIPLE

MONARCHY, as a principle of national government, suffered some vicissitudes in 1997, without conceding any loss to republicanism. Hereditary monarchy was once the rule among heads of state all over the world. Now it survives in no more than 25 independent nations (excluding the Commonwealth countries which retain the British monarch as titular head of state). Of these, nine are in Europe, two of whom head the very small states of Monaco and Liechtenstein; five are in the Middle East, including the powerful Kings of Jordan and Saudi Arabia; the Emperor of Japan alone reigns in the Far East; the rest are in Africa and South Asia. Bar the Arab potentates, these heads of state are for the most part constitutional monarchs, without independent political power. Viewed globally, therefore, monarchy would seem at first sight to be an anachronism, a faded and feeble institution, surviving by historical sentiment and public inertia. A somewhat different picture emerges, however, from a closer look at the British monarchy, which underwent a traumatic experience in 1997.

A modern monarch has to be both regal and popular, in a class apart but in tune with the feelings of the mass of his or her subjects. These two requisites were polarized by the tragic death of Diana, Princess of Wales. The unprecedented display of public grief contrasted with the sorrowful but undemonstrative reaction of Her Majesty the Queen, coincidentally absent from the capital at Balmoral with her family.

Princess Diana had been full of grace and compassion, but she had first become a glittering star, pursued everywhere by photographers and media men, because she was married to the heir to the British throne. The pursuit had begun when she travelled the world with Prince Charles, consorting with heads of state and government; it was greatly intensified after their divorce.

For a few days after her death it seemed that the contrast between public sentiment and royal propriety had widened so far that the affectionate esteem in which the monarchy had been held by most of its subjects was in serious danger. Then the dilemma was resolved. Reconciliation between throne and people, signalled by the flying of the Union Jack at half-mast on Buckingham Palace, was ratified by the Princess's state funeral, attended by the Queen and watched by millions on television. Those who advised the Queen, not least the Prince of Wales, the father of Princess Diana's two young sons, whose brave conduct strengthened public affection, saved the monarchy from a yawning

EXTRACTS FROM PAST VOLUMES

200 years ago

1797. *The Fall of Venice.* Thus fell, after a splendid existence of fourteen centuries, the splendid republic of Venice. No modern state had risen, from such small beginnings, to a situation of equal prosperity. It was with sincere regret that every nation in Europe beheld its fall. The celebrity it had long enjoyed, on a multiplicity of accounts, interested people in its preservation. Without inquiring how far the French could claim a right to doom it so unmercifully to destruction, they only considered that it had submitted with honour to the present period, and had maintained its reputation unimpaired amidst a variety of dangers and trials, that had reduced it sometimes to the last extremity.

150 years ago

1847. *Jenny Lind in London.* [4 May] It is difficult to convey an idea of the enthusiasm which prevailed among every rank of the public; the crush at the doors of the theatre on every night of her performance was terrific; the tickets of admission were sold by the dealers at enormous prices; portraits of the fair songstress, and statuettes, were in every window; vendors of new articles of taste and luxury sought to give them an adventitious attraction, by calling them by her name; and, finally, enormous parties were made up in the most distant cities of the kingdom, which, by hiring an entire railway train, were enabled to share in the fashionable enthusiasm at a reasonable expenditure of money and time.

100 years ago

1897. *Conference of Colonial Premiers.* The presence of the colonial premiers in this country [*for Queen Victoria's golden jubilee*] not only permitted Mr Chamberlain to obtain accurate views of the attitude of the various colonies to the mother country, but helped to make the representatives better acquainted with their respective aims, and to form the basis of a more general understanding. There was in some quarters a fear lest under the outburst of enthusiasm, or artificially created goodwill, some premature step in the direction of imperial federation might be taken by Mr Chamberlain. More cautious political advisers, on the other hand, argued that until more complete local federation had taken place among the colonial groups it was unwise to hurry on a movement which needed the hearty acquiescence of all affected to make it a success.

50 years ago

1947. *Partition of India.* In the Indian Union, after the first slaughter had abated, the most dangerous problem arose in Delhi, where thousands of refugees from Pakistan influenced the minds of local Hindus and Sikhs. Panic-stricken, the Delhi Muslims fled, after some days of disorder and outrage at the beginning of September; and pending their transfer elsewhere had to be accommodated in improvised camps, notably the famous Purana Quila. In this ancient fort, where six months previously the Indian representatives had proudly taken the lead in the first Asian Relations Conference of old and new states of Asia, 50,000 destitute refugees were encamped by mid-September.

PREFACE

THE long Cold War division of Europe at least made life easier for editors of reference books, in that coverage of the Old Continent could sensibly be divided into 'Eastern Europe' and 'Western Europe', i.e. between states that were under communist rule and those that were not. It did not matter that some countries of 'Western Europe' were located well to the east of some of those of 'Eastern Europe': the terms had political meaning rather than geographical precision. The post-1989 demise of communist rule and the emergence of new democracies in 'Eastern Europe' (some of them new countries) has eroded the validity of this convenient means of classification. Indeed, under decisions taken in 1997, three states of 'Eastern Europe' (the Czech Republic, Hungary and Poland) will become members of NATO in 1999, while the same three plus Estonia and Slovenia were selected as prospective members of the European Union (EU). For these and other reasons, many in 'Eastern Europe' object to any continuance of what they consider to be an outmoded differentiation between their part of Europe and 'Western Europe', pointing out, for example, that Prague, the Czech capital, lies to the west of Vienna, capital of EU member Austria.

Nevertheless, this 239th volume of *The Annual Register* continues the AR's long-established practice of separating coverage of Europe into two parts defined by the former Cold War division. The rationale is that, while the old Iron Curtain frontier no longer exists in political/military terms, it still marks a clear dividing line between established free-market democracies and states in the process of transition from one-party state socialism. At the same time, in recognition of changing circumstances, what used to be the AR's 'Eastern Europe' section has been renamed 'Central and Eastern Europe' and its content has been reorganized into three sub-sections which, it is hoped, reflect existing political realities better than the previous arrangement. It is recognized that further change will become necessary in future volumes, as plans for NATO and EU enlargement come to fruition.

Another innovation in this AR volume is the inclusion, in the section on international organizations, of reports on the Francophone Community and the Community of Portuguese-Speaking Countries. The former was given a new institutional identity in 1997 and the latter was founded in 1996, both joining the long-established Commonwealth as groupings of states based essentially on language and colonial history. Also deserving of mention is this volume's expansion the Environment chapter, in recognition of the increasing importance of environmental issues in most parts of the world, and the inclusion in the Statistics section of a new table showing the performance of European Union member states against the Maastricht criteria for participation in a single European currency.

ABBREVIATIONS OF NON-UN INTERNATIONAL ORGANIZATIONS

AC	Arctic Council
ACP	African, Caribbean and Pacific states associated with EU
ACS	Association of Caribbean States
AL	Arab League
ALADI	Latin American Integration Association
AMU	Arab Maghreb Union
ANZUS	Australia-New Zealand-US Security Treaty
AP	Amazon Pact
APEC	Asia-Pacific Economic Cooperation
ASEAN	Association of South-East Asian Nations
Benelux	Belgium-Netherlands-Luxembourg Economic Union
BSEC	Black Sea Economic Cooperation
CA	Andean Community
Caricom	Caribbean Community and Common Market
CBSS	Council of the Baltic Sea States
CE	Council of Europe
CEEAC	Economic Community of Central African States
CEFTA	Central European Free Trade Agreement (Visegrad Group)
CEI	Central European Initiative
CIS	Commonwealth of Independent States
COMESA	Common Market of Eastern and Southern Africa
CP	Colombo Plan
CPLP	Community of Portuguese-Speaking Countries
CWTH	The Commonwealth
EBRD	European Bank for Reconstruction and Development
ECO	Economic Cooperation Organization
ECOWAS	Economic Community of West African States
EEA	European Economic Area
EFTA	European Free Trade Association
EU	European Union
G–7	Group of Seven
GCC	Gulf Cooperation Council
IOC	Indian Ocean Commission
Mercosur	Southern Common Market
NAFTA	North American Free Trade Agreement
NAM	Non-Aligned Movement
NATO	North Atlantic Treaty Organization
NC	Nordic Council
OAPEC	Organization of Arab Petroleum Exporting Countries
OAS	Organization of American States
OAU	Oganization of African Unity
OECD	Organization for Economic Cooperation and Development
OECS	Organization of Eastern Caribbean States
OIC	Organization of the Islamic Conference
OPEC	Organization of the Petroleum Exporting Countries
OSCE	Organization for Security and Cooperation in Europe
PFP	Partnership for Peace
SAARC	South Asian Association for Regional Cooperation
SADC	Southern African Development Community
SELA	Latin American Economic System
SPC	Secretariat of the Pacific Community
SPF	South Pacific Forum
UEMOA	West African Economic and Monetary Union
WEU	Western European Union

PART XVIII	
INTERNATIONAL ECONOMY	**Victor Keegan,** Assistant Editor, *The Guardian*
STATISTICS	**Sue Sparks,** Former member of the Statistical Department, *Financial Times*
PART XX	
OBITUARY	**H. V. Hodson,** Former editor of *The Annual Register*; editor, *The Sunday Times*, 1950–61; Provost of the Ditchley Foundation, 1961–71
MAPS	**MJL Graphics,** N. Yorks, YO14 9BE

ACKNOWLEDGEMENTS

THE Advisory Board again gratefully acknowledges its debt to a number of institutions for their help with sources, references and documents, notably the UK Foreign and Commonwealth Office, the UN Secretariat, the Commonwealth Secretariat, the NATO Secretariat and the Council of Europe. Acknowledgement is also due to the principal sources for the national and IGO data sections (showing the situation as at end-1997 unless otherwise stated), namely *Keesing's Record of World Events* (Keesing's Worldwide), *Worldwide Government Directory* (Keesing's Worldwide), *World Development Report* (Oxford University Press for the World Bank) and the *Financial Times* (London). The Board and the bodies which nominate its members disclaim responsibility for any opinions expressed or the accuracy of facts recorded in this volume.

CONTRIBUTORS

PART XII
DEFENCE, DISARMAMENT AND SECURITY

Donald Kerr, Military Information Specialist; Former Information Officer, International Institute for Strategic Studies (IISS), London.

PART XIII
RELIGION

Geoffrey Parrinder, MA, PhD, DD, Emeritus Professor of the Comparative Study of Religions, University of London

PART XIV
MEDICAL, SCIENTIFIC AND INDUSTRIAL RESEARCH
INFORMATION TECHNOLOGY

ENVIRONMENT

Martin Redfern, Deputy Science Editor, BBC World Service
David Powell, A director of Electronic Publishing Services Ltd and Interactive Media Publications Ltd
Richard Black, Journalist and broadcaster specializing in scientific and environmental affairs

PART XV
INTERNATIONAL LAW

EUROPEAN COMMUNITY LAW

LAW IN THE UK

LAW IN THE USA

Christine Gray, MA, PhD, Fellow in Law, St John's College, Cambridge
N. March Hunnings, LLM, PhD, Editor, *Encyclopedia of European Union Law: Constitutional Texts*
David Ibbetson, MA, PhD, Fellow and Tutor in Law, Magdalen College, Oxford
Robert J. Spjut, ID, LLM, Member of the State Bars of California and Florida

PART XVI
OPERA

MUSIC

BALLET/DANCE

THEATRE
CINEMA
TV & RADIO
VISUAL ARTS
ARCHITECTURE
LITERATURE

Charles Osborne, Author; opera critic, *The Jewish Chronicle*
Francis Routh, Composer and author; founder director of the Redcliffe Concerts
Jane Pritchard, Archivist, Rambert Dance Company and English National Ballet
Jeremy Kingston, Theatre critic, *The Times*
Derek Malcolm, Film critic, *The Guardian*
Raymond Snoddy, Media Editor, *The Times*
David Cohen, MA, independent art critic and lecturer
Paul Finch, Editor, *The Architects' Journal*
Alastair Niven, Director of Literature, British Council; formerly Literature Director of the Arts Council of England

PART XVII
SPORT

Tony Pawson, OBE, Sports writer, *The Observer*; cricket, football and fly-fishing international

CONTRIBUTORS xi

PART X

AUSTRALIA	**James Jupp,** MSc (Econ), PhD, FASSA, Director, Centre for Immigration and Multicultural Studies, Australian National University, Canberra
PAPUA NEW GUINEA	**Norman MacQueen** (see Pt.IX, Indonesia & Philippines)
NEW ZEALAND, PACIFIC ISLAND STATES	**Stephen Levine,** PhD, Associate Professor and Head of School, School of Political Science and International Relations, Victoria University of Wellington

PART XI

UNITED NATIONS	**David Travers,** BA (Wales), Lecturer in Politics and International Relations, Lancaster University; Specialist Adviser on UN to House of Commons' Foreign Affairs Committee
COMMONWEALTH	**Derek Ingram,** Consultant Editor of *Gemini News Service*; author and writer on the Commonwealth
FRANCOPHONE COMMUNITY	**Kaye Whiteman** (see Pt. VI, Ch. 3)
COMMUNITY OF PORTUGUESE-SPEAKING COUNTRIES	**Antonio de Figueiredo** (see Pt. II, Portugal)
NON-ALIGNED MOVEMENT AND GROUP OF 77	**Peter Willetts,** PhD, Reader in International Relations, The City University, London
ORGANIZATION OF THE ISLAMIC CONFERENCE	**Darren Sagar,** MA, Deputy Editor, *Keesing's Record of World Events*
EUROPEAN UNION	**Michael Berendt,** Expert on affairs of the European Union
COUNCIL OF EUROPE	**Colin Lee,** MA, Former Secretary to UK delegation to Parliamentary Assembly of the Council of Europe
ORGANIZATION FOR SECURITY AND COOPERATION IN EUROPE	**Adrian G.V. Hyde-Price,** BSc(Econ), PhD, Lecturer, Department of Politics, University of Southampton
EUROPEAN BANK FOR RECONSTRUCTION AND DEVELOPMENT	**Michael Kaser,** MA, DLitt, DSocSc, Emeritus Fellow of St Antony's College, Oxford, and Honorary Professor, University of Birmingham
NORDIC/BALTIC/ARCTIC ORGANIZATIONS	**David Smith** (see Pt. II, Nordic Countries)
OTHER EUROPEAN ORGANIZATIONS	**Stefan Krause,** MA, Free University of Berlin
ARAB ORGANIZATIONS	**George Joffé** (see Pt. V, Saudi Arabia, etc.)
AFRICAN ORGANIZATIONS AND CONFERENCES	**Kaye Whiteman** (see Pt. VI, Ch. 3)
ASIA-PACIFIC ORGANIZATIONS	**Darren Sagar,** (see above)
AMERICAN ORGANIZATIONS	**Peter Calvert** (see Pt. IV, Latin America)
CARIBBEAN ORGANIZATIONS	**Kirk Meighoo** (see Pt. IV, Caribbean)

CONTRIBUTORS

NIGERIA	**Guy Arnold,** Freelance writer specializing in Africa and North-South affairs
SIERRA LEONE, THE GAMBIA, LIBERIA	**Arnold Hughes,** BA, Director, Centre of West African Studies, The University of Birmingham
CHAPTER 3 (SENEGAL to EQUATORIAL GUINEA)	**Kaye Whiteman,** Publisher, *West Africa*

PART VII

CHAPTER 1 (ZAÏRE TO ANGOLA)	**Robin Hallett,** MA, Writer and lecturer on African affairs
ZAMBIA, MALAWI	**Robin Hallett** (see above)
ZIMBABWE	**R. W. Baldock,** BA, PhD, Senior Editor, Yale University Press; writer on African affairs
NAMIBIA, BOTSWANA, LESOTHO, SWAZILAND, SOUTH AFRICA	**Greg Mills,** MA, PhD, National Director, South African Institute of International Affairs

PART VIII

IRAN	**Keith McLachlan,** BA, PhD, Emeritus Professor, School of Oriental and African Studies, University of London
AFGHANISTAN	**D.S. Lewis,** PhD, Editor, *Keesing's Record of World Events*
CENTRAL ASIAN REPUBLICS	**Shirin Akiner,** PhD, Director, Central Asia Research Forum, School of Oriental and African Studies, University of London
INDIA, BANGLADESH, NEPAL, BHUTAN	**Peter Lyon,** BSc(Econ), PhD, Reader in International Relations and Academic Secretary, Institute of Commonwealth Studies, University of London; Editor, *The Round Table*, the Commonwealth journal of international affairs
PAKISTAN	**David Taylor,** Senior Lecturer in Politics with reference to South Asia, School of Oriental and African Studies, University of London
SRI LANKA	**Charles Gunawardena,** former Director of Information, Commonwealth Secretariat, London
SEYCHELLES, MAURITIUS, MALDIVES	**Harry Drost,** Writer on European and Third World affairs; editor, *The World's News Media*
MADAGASCAR AND COMOROS	**Kaye Whiteman** (see Pt. VI, Ch. 3)

PART IX

MYANMAR (BURMA), THAILAND, VIETNAM, CAMBODIA, LAOS	**Jonathan Rigg,** PhD, Reader in South-East Asian Geography, University of Durham
MALAYSIA, BRUNEI, SINGAPORE	**Michael Leifer,** BA, PhD, Professor of International Relations, London School of Economics and Political Science
INDONESIA, PHILIPPINES	**Norman MacQueen,** Senior Lecturer in Political Science, University of Dundee
CHINA, HONG KONG, TAIWAN	**Robert F. Ash,** MSc(Econ), PhD, Director, EU-China Academic Network and Senior Lecturer in Economics, School of Oriental and African Studies, University of London
JAPAN	**Ian Nish,** Emeritus Professor of International History, London School of Economics and Political Science
KOREA, MONGOLIA	**Alan Sanders,** FIL, Former lecturer in Mongolian Studies, School of Oriental and African Studies, University of London

CONTRIBUTORS ix

PART III

POLAND	**A. Kemp-Welch,** BSc(Econ), PhD, Dean, School of Economic and Social Studies, University of East Anglia
BALTIC REPUBLICS	**John Hiden,** Professor of Modern European History and Director, Baltic Research Unit, University of Bradford
CZECH REPUBLIC, SLOVAKIA	**Sharon Fisher,** MA, Analyst specializing in East European political and economic affairs
HUNGARY	**George Schöpflin,** Joint Lecturer in East European Political Institutions, London School of Economics and School of Slavonic and East European Studies, University of London
ROMANIA	**Gabriel Partos,** Eastern Europe Analyst, BBC World Service
BULGARIA	**Stephen Ashley,** MA, DPhil, Senior Talks Writer, BBC World Service
ALBANIA	**Richard Crampton,** PhD, Professor of East European History, and Fellow of St Edmund Hall, University of Oxford,
EX-YUGOSLAV REPUBLICS	**John B. Allcock,** MA, PhD, Head of Research Unit in South-East European Studies, University of Bradford
RUSSIA, BELARUS, UKRAINE, MOLDOVA AND CAUCASUS	**Stephen White,** DPhil, Professor of Politics, University of Glasgow

PART IV

USA	**Neil A. Wynn,** MA, PhD, Reader in History and American Studies, University of Glamorgan
CANADA	**David M.L. Farr,** Professor Emeritus of History, Carleton University, Ottawa
LATIN AMERICA	**Peter Calvert,** AM, MA, PhD, Professor of Comparative and International Politics, University of Southampton
THE CARIBBEAN	**Kirk Meighoo,** Department of Politics, University of Durham

PART V

ISRAEL	**Joel Peters,**, BSc, DPhil, Lecturer in International Relations, University of Reading
ARAB WORLD, EGYPT, JORDAN, SYRIA, LEBANON, IRAQ	**Christopher Gandy,** Formerly UK Diplomatic Service; writer on Middle Eastern affairs
SAUDI ARABIA, YEMEN, ARAB STATES OF THE GULF	**George Joffé,** Director of Studies, Royal Institute of International Affairs
SUDAN	**Ahmed al-Shahi,** DPhil, Social anthropologist and independent researcher
LIBYA, TUNISIA, ALGERIA, MOROCCO, WESTERN SAHARA	**R. I. Lawless,** PhD, Emeritus Reader in Modern Middle Eastern Studies, University of Durham

PART VI

HORN OF AFRICA	**Christopher Clapham,** MA, DPhil, Professor of Politics and International Relations, University of Lancaster
KENYA, TANZANIA, UGANDA	**William Tordoff,** MA, PhD, Emeritus Professor of Government, University of Manchester
GHANA	**D.G. Austin** (see Pt. III, Malta)

CONTRIBUTORS

EXTRACTS FROM PAST VOLUMES	**M.R.D. Foot,** Former Professor of Modern History, University of Manchester

PART I

UNITED KINGDOM, SCOTLAND	**C.J. Bartlett** FRHistS, FRSE, Professor Emeritus of International History, University of Dundee
WALES	**Gwyn Jenkins,** MA, Keeper of Manuscripts and Records, National Library of Wales, Aberystwyth
NORTHERN IRELAND	**Sydney Elliott,** BA, PhD, Senior Lecturer in Politics, The Queen's University, Belfast

PART II

GERMANY	**Tanya Joseph,** MA, Freelance writer on European affairs
FRANCE	**Martin Harrison,** Professor of Politics, University of Keele
ITALY	**Stephen Gundle,** Senior Lecturer in Italian, Royal Holloway, University of London
BELGIUM, NETHERLANDS LUXEMBOURG	**J.D. McLachlan,** Writer on Belgium, Luxembourg and the Netherlands
REPUBLIC OF IRELAND	**Louis McRedmond,** MA, BL, Journalist, historian and broadcaster
NORDIC COUNTRIES	**David Smith,** PhD, Lecturer in Contemporary History and International Relations; member of Baltic Research Unit, University of Bradford
AUSTRIA	**Angela Gillon,** Researcher in West European affairs
SWITZERLAND	**Hans Hirter,** PhD, Editor, *Année Politique Suisse*. University of Berne
EUROPEAN MINI-STATES	**Tanya Joseph** (see above)
SPAIN, GIBRALTAR	**Richard Gillespie,** PhD, Professor of Iberian and Latin American Studies, University of Portsmouth
PORTUGAL	**Antonio de Figueiredo,** Knight Commander of Portugal's Order of Freedom; Portuguese author, freelance journalist and broadcaster
MALTA	**D.G. Austin,** Emeritus Professor of Government, University of Manchester
GREECE	**Richard Clogg,** MA, St Antony's College, Oxford
CYPRUS	**Robert McDonald,** Freelance writer and broadcaster; author on Greece, Cyprus and Turkey
TURKEY	**A.J.A. Mango,** BA, PhD, Orientalist and writer on current affairs in Turkey and the Near East

CONTENTS

XII	DEFENCE, DISARMAMENT AND SECURITY	
1	NATO and European Security	436
2	Arms Control	440
3	Defence Expenditure and Procurement	443
4	Non-Traditional Threats	445

XIII	RELIGION	447

XIV	THE SCIENCES	
1	Scientific, Medical and Industrial Research	454
2	Information Technology	460
3	The Environment	464

XV	THE LAW	
1	i International Law 472 ii European Community Law 476	472
2	Law in the United Kingdom	479
3	United States Law	484

XVI	THE ARTS	
1	i Opera 487 ii Music 489 iii Ballet & Dance 493 iv Theatre 496 v Cinema 501 vi Television & Radio 504	487
2	i Visual Arts 507 ii Architecture 512	507
3	Literature	516

XVII	SPORT	522

XVIII	ECONOMIC AND SOCIAL AFFAIRS	
1	The International Economy	532
2	Economic and Social Data	540

XIX	DOCUMENTS AND REFERENCE	
1	NATO-Russia Founding Act	555
2	Council of Europe Action Plan	559
3	Commonwealth Summit Declarations	561
4	Hanoi Declaration of Francophone Community	565
5	UN Landmines Convention	566
6	Kyoto Climate Change Protocol	568
7	UK Labour Cabinet	572
8	US Democratic Administration	573

XX	OBITUARY	574

XXI	CHRONICLE OF PRINCIPAL EVENTS IN 1997	589
	INDEX	600

MAPS AND TABLES

Caspian Sea Oil Pipelines	301
European Union and NATO Enlargement	409
Defence Spending by Region	445
El Niño Weather Distortions	468
1998 World Cup Draw	524

CONTENTS

V	MIDDLE EAST AND NORTH AFRICA	
1	Israel	202
2	i Arab World and Palestinians 206 ii Egypt 209 iii Jordan 211	
	iv Syria 213 v Lebanon 215 vi Iraq 217	206
3	i Saudi Arabia 220 ii Yemen 222 iii Arab States of the Gulf 224	220
4	i Sudan 228 ii Libya 231 iii Tunisia 233 iv Algeria 234	
	v Morocco 237 vi Western Sahara 239	228

VI	EQUATORIAL AFRICA	
1	i Horn of Africa 240 ii Kenya 244 iii Tanzania 246 iv Uganda 247	240
2	i Ghana 249 ii Nigeria 250 iii Sierra Leone 253 iv The Gambia 254	
	v Liberia 255	249
3	i West African Francophone States 256 ii Central African Franc	
	Zone States 262	256

VII	CENTRAL AND SOUTHERN AFRICA	
1	i Democratic Republic of Congo 268 ii Burundi and Rwanda 271	
	iii Guinea-Bissau and Cape Verde 273 iv São Tomé & Príncipe 274	
	v Mozambique 274 vi Angola 275	268
2	i Zambia 277 ii Malawi 279 iii Zimbabwe 280 iv Botswana,	
	Lesotho, Namibia and Swaziland 282	277
3	South Africa	289

VIII	SOUTH ASIA AND INDIAN OCEAN	
1	i Iran 293 ii Afghanistan 295 iii Central Asian Republics 298	293
2	i India 305 ii Pakistan 310 iii Bangladesh 313 iv Nepal 316	
	v Bhutan 317 vi Sri Lanka 318	305
3	i Mauritius 320 ii Seychelles, Comoros and Maldives 322	
	iii Madagascar 325	320

IX	SOUTH-EAST AND EAST ASIA	
1	i Myanmar (Burma) 326 ii Thailand 327 iii Malaysia 329	
	iv Brunei 330 v Singapore 331 vi Indonesia 332 vii Philippines 335	
	viii Vietnam 337 ix Cambodia 338 x Laos 340	326
2	i China 341 ii Hong Kong SAR 350 iii Taiwan 353 iv Japan 356	
	v South Korea 360 vi North Korea 362 vii Mongolia 364	341

X	AUSTRALASIA AND THE PACIFIC	
1	i Australia 367 ii Papua New Guinea 371	367
2	i New Zealand 373 ii Pacific Island States 376	373

XI	INTERNATIONAL ORGANIZATIONS	
1	United Nations	380
2	i The Commonwealth 391 ii Francophone and Lusophone Communities 393	
	iii Non-Aligned Movement and Group of 77 397 iv Organization of the Islamic	
	Conference 399	391
3	European Union	402
4	i Council of Europe 411 ii Organization for Security and	
	Cooperation in Europe 413 iii European Bank for Reconstruction	
	and Development 416 iv Nordic, Baltic and Arctic Organizations 418	
	v Other European Organizations 420	411
5	i Arab Organizations 423 ii African Organizations 425	
	iii Asia-Pacific Organizations 428 iv American Organizations 433	423

CONTENTS

CONTRIBUTORS	viii
IGO ABBREVIATIONS	xiv
PREFACE TO 239th VOLUME	xv
EXTRACTS FROM 1797, 1847, 1897 AND 1947 VOLUMES	xvi
EDITORIAL: 'MONARCHY AND THE HEREDITARY PRINCIPLE'	1

I UNITED KINGDOM

1	Death of the 'People's Princess'	4
2	Social Trends Before and After the Election	7
3	A Government Running Out of Time	11
4	The General Election: Landslide to Labour	15
5	Labour in Power	21
6	Devolution and Other Labour Policies	29
7	International Relations	34
8	Scotland	37
9	Wales	40
10	Northern Ireland	42

II WESTERN AND SOUTHERN EUROPE

1   i Germany 49   ii France 52   iii Italy 57   iv Belgium 61
    v The Netherlands 63   vi Luxembourg 64   vii Ireland 65   49
2   i Denmark 69   ii Iceland 70   iii Norway 72   iv Sweden 74   v Finland 76
    vi Austria 78   vii Switzerland 80   viii European Mini-States 83   69
3   i Spain 86   ii Gibraltar 89   iii Portugal 90   iv Malta 93   v Greece 95
    vi Cyprus 97   vii Turkey 101   86

III CENTRAL AND EASTERN EUROPE

1   i Poland 104   ii Baltic Republics 106   iii Czech Republic 110   iv Slovakia 112
    v Hungary 114   vi Romania 116   vii Bulgaria 119   104
2   i Albania 122   ii Bosnia & Hercegovina 125   iii Croatia 129   iv Macedonia 131
    v Slovenia 132   vi Yugoslavia 133   122
3   i Russia 135   ii Belarus, Ukraine, Moldova 140   iii Armenia, Georgia,
    Azerbaijan 143   135

IV AMERICAS AND THE CARIBBEAN

1   United States of America   145
2   Canada   160
3   Latin America: i Argentina 166   ii Bolivia 168   iii Brazil 168   iv Chile 170
    v Colombia 171   vi Ecuador 173   vii Paraguay 174   viii Peru 175   ix Uruguay 177
    x Venezuela 177   xi Cuba 178   xii Dominican Republic and Haiti 179
    xiii Central America and Panama 180   xiv Mexico 183   166
4   Caribbean: i Jamaica 186   ii Guyana 187   iii Trinidad & Tobago 189
    iv Barbados 190   v Belize 191   vi Grenada 192   vii The Bahamas 193
    viii Windward & Leeward Islands 194   ix UK Dependencies 196
    x Suriname 198   xi Netherlands Antilles and Aruba 200
    xii US Dependencies 201   186

media allegations—to do the same. Both men, however, were strongly supported by their constituency organizations. Mr Major later said that he would back the expulsion of MPs from parliament and the Tory Party only if the charges against them were upheld. He thus accepted Mr Hamilton's right to stand for re-election. Labour and the Liberal Democrats, however, agreed that their candidates in Mr Hamilton's Tatton constituency should stand aside in favour of an independent anti-corruption candidate. On 6 April Martin Bell, a BBC war correspondent, accepted this challenge (and went on to win a comprehensive victory). Mr Merchant, though re-elected, finally resigned from parliament on 14 October following further press allegations about his private life.

Tory attempts to portray Labour as being too willing to cooperate with the EU did not earn many dividends. In return, Mr Cook claimed that Labour would restore British influence in the EU, whereas the Tory approach meant that the national interest would be deposited at 'the exit door'. Nevertheless, the Labour shadow Foreign Secretary took a Euro-sceptic line on the single currency in the course of an elaborately-worded statement on 6 April. In effect, he said that if Britain did not join in the first wave, it was unlikely to do so in the coming parliament. Both Mr Major and Mr Cook took a strong stand on 14 April on the subject of EU trawlers in British fishing grounds.

The Tory election manifesto was published on 2 April, Mr Major lavishly promising to make Britain 'the best place in the world to live'. Measures were outlined to protect and promote family life. Action was promised on education, crime and decayed housing estates; wealth and welfare should go hand-in-hand. Labour's manifesto, published on 3 April, was less bullish. Most of the party's programme had already been set out, at least in broad terms. Mr Blair stressed the need for a new beginning under a government the people could trust. 'New Labour' was making substantial commitments, but not promising that it would revolutionize people's lives overnight. 'If we can deliver them, we can come back in the elections after next and say, "Trust us again because we kept our promises".' In short, he was thinking of at least two consecutive terms in office. Failure would mean that 'we blow our place in history'.

Mr Major described Labour's manifesto as 'more of a con-trick than a contract'. Critics in all parties (including some Labour left-wingers in Scotland) detected continuing uncertainty in Labour's policy on devolution. The Liberal Democrats claimed that on one grave issue after another Labour offered no solutions, whereas their party was promising specific action on education and health. Mr Brown conceded that there was a £1,500 million hole in the expenditure plans to which Labour was committed, and the party was evidently looking to the sell-off of further public assets to help foot the bill. Speaking in the City of London on 7 April, Mr Blair said that 'where there was no overriding reason for preferring the public provision of goods and services', then the presumption of his government would be that economic activity was best left to the private sector. His statement provoked Tory derision and some misgiving on the left of his own party.

For a brief period, in the second week of April, Labour's huge poll lead no longer seemed set in stone, amid reports of numerous 'don't knows' and waverers. Over the weekend of 12–13 April the media trumpeted claims of Labour U-turns on policy and 'wobbles' in the party's election strategy. Some even suggested that Mr Blair was no longer projecting so strong or so reassuring an image. On the Tory side there was aggressive campaigning, notably from Mr Major, Michael Heseltine and Lady Thatcher. Labour's 'wobble' was sufficiently serious for Mr Blair himself to signal the need for more 'passion, vision and conviction' and to declare his intention to take the election by the 'scruff of the neck'.

Meanwhile, a large election rally by Sir James Goldsmith's Referendum Party was marked by rhetoric more aggressive than any so far heard in the campaign. The 'German-dominated super-state' was variously described as the greatest threat to British sovereignty since 1940, 1588 or even 1066. In addition, more than 120 Tory MPs (including the party's deputy chairman, five vice-chairmen, the chairman of the 1922 committee of backbenchers and two junior ministers) all came out against the single currency. Several other ministers dropped hints to similar effect. Mr Major immediately changed his campaign agenda for 16 April to make two passionate appeals (including a broadcast to the public) that he should not be sent 'naked into the conference chamber' or be required to negotiate for Britain with his hands tied. The British nation would still be free to decide for or against the single currency once the outcome of the talks was known. Both Labour and the Liberal Democrats accused him of weak leadership when he failed to sack the errant ministers. It was around this time, according to later reports, that Mr Major privately acknowledged the inevitability of defeat. On 18 April the Tories claimed that Mr Blair was too inexperienced and weak to defend British sovereignty at EU summits. But already the thoughts of many Tories were turning to the future of the party on the assumption that it to be was consigned to the opposition benches.

The line-up of the press during the election showed a marked shift from that of 1992. Of the tabloid papers, with a readership of about 18 million, only the *Daily Mail* of the top four remained loyal to the Tories. *The Sun* joined *The Mirror* in supporting Labour, while the *Daily Express* was best described as neutral. The *News of the World* also favoured Mr Blair, whereas *The Times* on 29 April advised its readers only to support candidates who were opposed to further European integration. It agreed that Labour had become an electable party, but thought that to cast a vote for it would be an act of faith. The Tories, the newspaper concluded, had collapsed in 'body and spirit'.

The Home Office on 25 April announced unprecedented security measures for polling day as the IRA again disrupted motorway traffic and two bombs were set off next to an electricity pylon beside the M6. No less than 45,000 polling stations and 600 counting centres required surveillance. In a new campaign launched on 26 March, the IRA had been causing considerable road, rail and air transport chaos and confusion, not to mention economic disruption, with a series of incidents involving small explosive devices and hoax telephone calls. A scare at Aintree on 5 April compelled a two-day postponement of the Grand

I.4. THE GENERAL ELECTION: LANDSLIDE TO LABOUR

National horse race (see also Part XVII). The Sinn Féin leader, Gerry Adams, said on 20 April that he looked forward to the election of a new government which would resume the peace process.

Although the polls had almost consistently pointed to a massive Labour victory, the result on 1 May was still a shock to most people. There was a 10.5 per cent swing to Labour, giving the new government an overall majority of 177 seats, the largest since 1945. The results are set out in the table below (comparable 1992 figures being given in parentheses where appropriate):

	Seats	% of votes
Labour Party	418 (271)	44.4[1] (34.7)
Conservative Party	165 (336)	31.5[1] (41.9)
Liberal Democrats	46 (20)	17.2[1] (17.9)
Referendum Party	0 (–)	2.7[1]
UK Independence Party	0 (0)	0.3[1]
Independent	1 (0)	0.1[1]
Scottish National Party	6 (3)	21.9[2]
Plaid Cymru	4 (4)	9.7[3]
Ulster Unionist Party	10 (9)	32.7[4]
Social Democratic and Labour Party	3 (4)	24.1[4]
Sinn Féin	2 (0)	16.1[4]
Democratic Unionist Party	2 (3)	12.3[4]
UK Unionist Party	1 (1)	1.6[4]
Speaker	1 (1)	
Total	659 (651)	

[1] Share of votes cast on the British mainland
[2] Share of votes cast in Scotland
[3] Share of votes cast in Wales
[4] Share of votes cast in Northern Ireland

The turnout of 73.1 per cent (against 77.7 per cent in 1992) was the lowest since 1945. Participation was especially poor in inner city constituencies, although even marginal and fiercely contested seats were not immune from the trend. Less than 50 per cent of the electorate believed that there were 'really important differences between the parties'. Nor did voters appear to have been greatly swayed by Europe *per se* (despite Euro-sceptic efforts to make it a big issue), save insofar as it had been seen as a major example of Tory divisions. Although 'Black Wednesday' (Britain's enforced exit from the ERM in September 1992— see AR 1992, pp. 22–5) had soon been followed by an economic recovery, the polls had consistently shown electors giving more credence to Labour as the guardian of the economy (for the first time since polling began). There had also been the 1992 'broken promise' of no tax increases. Voters, moreover, had not been deterred from voting Labour despite a wide expectation of tax rises. Public dissatisfaction persisted over education and the National Health Service (NHS), while the job insecurity experienced by many stood in stark contrast to the stories of 'sleaze' and 'fat cats' among the wealthy and privileged. Meanwhile, Labour had done much to reinvent itself and thus confirm the feeling that it was 'time for a change'. Some of the biggest anti-Tory swings occurred in the most prosperous regions. The Tories finished with fewer seats than at any time since 1906, and their smallest share of the vote since 1832. This was humiliation as well as defeat.

Among the most notable Tory losers were Michael Portillo (the Defence Secretary and a certain contender for the Tory leadership had he survived), Malcolm Rifkind (Foreign Secretary, also a likely contestant), Michael Forsyth (Scottish Secretary of State) and Sir Marcus Fox (chairman of the 1922 committee). The Tories were left with no seats in Scotland and Wales, and only in the south-east of England (excluding London) did their share of the vote rise above two-fifths, and then only to 41 per cent (a fall of 13 points since 1992). The local council elections which took place on the same day provided the Tories with some consolation, in that they made significant gains (from a very low base) east of a line drawn from Lincolnshire to Hampshire. Labour won Cumbria, while the Liberal Democrats suffered setbacks in three southern counties but took control of Newbury and Torbay.

On the day after polling (2 May), Mr Major not only tendered his government's resignation to the Queen but also announced that he would stand down as Conservative Party leader as soon as possible. Any possibility of Mr Heseltine being among the contenders for the succession ended on 3 May when health problems once again intervened (following his heart attack in 1993); but there was no shortage of other candidates (see I.5). It was estimated that the 165 Tory MPs could be roughly divided into three groups. About 45 per cent were traditional Tories who would be loyal to whoever succeeded Mr Major; if most of these had reservations on the question of Europe, they were not dogmatists. About 30 per cent were reckoned to belong to the hardline right-wing Euro-sceptics; and the remaining 25 per cent were 'one-nation' pro-Europeans.

Mr Blair's cabinet included John Prescott as Deputy Prime Minister and Secretary of State for the Environment, Transport and the Regions; Lord Irvine of Lairg as Lord Chancellor; Gordon Brown as Chancellor of the Exchequer; Robin Cook as Foreign Secretary; Jack Straw as Home Secretary; David Blunkett as Education and Employment Secretary; Margaret Beckett as President of the Board of Trade; and Donald Dewar and Dr Marjorie (Mo) Mowlam as Secretaries of State for Scotland and Northern Ireland respectively. Peter Mandelson was appointed to the post of Minister without Portfolio with the task of ensuring that policy commitments were turned into action. This was described as the most influential post outside the cabinet. Mr Mandelson was one of the creators of 'New Labour' and had been the manager of Mr Blair's election campaign. In an interesting move reflecting the strength of Labour's new ties with the business community, Sir David Simon, chairman of British Petroleum, was appointed Minister of Trade and Competitiveness in Europe (and was made a life peer). A number of other senior businessmen became involved with the new government in various ways.

5. LABOUR IN POWER

THE new government lost no time in setting out its position on Europe, the issue which had done so much damage to the Tories. The new minister responsible, Doug Henderson, promised the EU a fresh start. Britain, he said, would soon sign up to the EU's Social Chapter, although, in company with the Foreign Secretary, he warned that nothing would be agreed which reduced British competitiveness. The government was ready to accept some extension of qualified majority voting in certain areas, but the national veto was sacrosanct on defence, justice and crucial domestic questions. It was also determined to retain the existing border controls.

At his first meeting with EU leaders on 23 May, Mr Blair, while taking a positive attitude on Europe, stressed the need to concentrate on job-creation and other matters which directly affected people, rather than on further institutional development. He warned of serious political difficulties in Britain if adherence to the Social Chapter began to impose higher business costs. On 5 June the government threatened to ban beef imports from countries which had less stringent BSE controls than Britain. Six weeks later it promised the EU that it would crack down on Britain's beef exports if they breached the world ban, while reiterating its warnings on imported beef. British controls were also being extended to sheep suspected of having scrapie (a form of brain disease). At a European Socialist Party conference in Malmö (Sweden) on 6 June, Mr Blair insisted that 'flexibility' was the economic path which the left must take 'to modernize or die'.

On 6 May the base interest rate was raised by a quarter of a point, to 6.25 per cent, in response to fears that the economy was growing too quickly. This had been widely expected, but there was general surprise when Mr Brown announced one of the biggest changes in economic policy-making this century—the transfer of the government's power to set interest rates to the Bank of England. The governor of the bank would act with a nine-member committee, four of whom would be nominated by the Chancellor of the Exchequer, who retained, for the time being, the power to set the inflation rate target. Mr Brown denied that the historic change was a step towards signing up to a single European currency. Experts believed that the move was designed to remove what had been an area of serious vulnerability for previous Labour governments, namely doubts in the financial markets about Labour's commitment to the fight against inflation. But Mr Brown would still have to fulfil his promises to be tough on spending and borrowing. The Bank of England exercised its new power for the first time on 6 June by applying a 0.25 increase in the base rate.

The new Chancellor had more surprises in store. On 20 May he announced that a strengthened new supervisory body, later named the Financial Services Authority (FSA), would replace the current watchdog system to protect investors and shareholders. The Bank of England would lose its supervisory role over other banks. Mr Brown said that there had been too many failures and scandals in recent years under the existing regulatory system. At the same time, he promised that the government would follow a long-term economic strategy and work with business to increase national dynamism and adaptability. On 25 June Labour's NEC showed its determination to fight scandal in its own ranks when it suspended two MPs from holding any party office pending an inquiry into allegations of improper conduct on their part.

Earlier, on 8 May, Mr Blair had demanded discipline and hard work at his first cabinet meeting, which approved an all-action programme of 22 bills to become law in a parliamentary session projected to run from 14 May to the autumn of 1998. Ministers also agreed to forego for one year the ministerial pay rises announced by the previous government. No time was lost in putting down markers for speedy action. Thus on 11 May the government promised a new action plan to tackle the problem of 'Gulf War syndrome' (illness allegedly arising from service in the 1991 Gulf War—see AR 1996, p. 32). On 14 May the Economic Secretary to the Treasury, Helen Liddell, ordered senior executives from 24 pension companies to report back to the Treasury within a month on plans to speed up compensation to victims of the £4,000 million pension mis-selling scandal of 1988–94. Ms Liddell added that, if they failed to convince the government, this would be taken into account in its reform of financial services regulation. Six weeks later she publicly condemned two companies for their part in what she described as 'one of the worst scandals in financial services this century'.

The Education and Employment Secretary, Mr Blunkett, showed similar urgency when he issued a warning that action would be taken against 'failing' schools even before new legislation was implemented. The Chief Inspector of Schools announced on 15 July that a new grading scheme for teachers would be introduced in September. About 16 per cent of the lessons observed by inspectors in 1996 fell into the unsatisfactory category. A big question-mark was being placed against the future of several thousand teachers. The government also acted swiftly on the demand for a firearms ban following the Dunblane school massacre (see AR 1996, p. 7). In the crucial vote on 11 June, the Commons voted for a total ban on handguns by a majority of 211.

There was also action in other policy areas. On welfare, Mr Blair said that people were no longer prepared to fund an unreformed system which offered rising costs combined with increasing poverty and social division. Life in 1997, he remarked, bore little resemblance to Britain in 1947 when the welfare state was launched. The Social Security Secretary, Harriet Harman, added on 17 July that there would be a review of pension provisions which would focus on the proposed 'stake-holder' pension and a separate citizenship pension for those people (especially women) who for various reasons were unable to afford additional pension cover. In education, the assisted places scheme for public-school entrance would be scrapped, as would the internal market in the NHS. Queue-jumping by patients of fund-holding doctors would be ended from April 1998, when hospitals would be required to admit patients solely on the basis of medical need. A White Paper on the future of the 'people's lottery' (21 July) promised to broaden the list of beneficiaries, notably by the inclusion of health, education and the environment in the descriptors of eligible activities. The regulator would be given additional powers over the lottery operator, currently Camelot. It was conceded that a profit-making company might receive the licence when it came up for renewal in 2001—this representing a departure from the Labour manifesto pledge to award the new licence to a non-profit-making body. Ministers also promised additional action on youth and long-term unemployment and on a national house-building programme. Environmentalists were pleased by the announcement on 2 September of the government's intention to take strong action against radioactive and chemical pollution of the sea.

On 19 May Mr Prescott spelt out the government's determination to protect the environment from over-abstraction of water from vulnerable areas, and to ensure that water companies greatly reduced the current high wastage levels. He was speaking at a conference called in response to the problems caused by three years of below-average rainfall. Water companies were warned on 15 July that legal wastage rates would be reduced to 15 per cent (reports showing that some companies were currently wasting twice that amount). The scandal of high profits and water shortages had to stop, asserted Mr Prescott. He had also spoken earlier in general terms of his determination to push through a programme against urban pollution and traffic congestion. The decision of Railtrack at the end of in July to accept more supervision from the Rail Regulator was seen as an acknowledgement by the company that concessions on its part were needed to prevent more government control of its investment programme.

On 12 May, in the fight for the Tory leadership, Kenneth Clarke dramatically claimed that the position on the single currency adopted by the other five candidates would drive the Conservative Party to 'the political fringe both at home and in European politics'. Further controversy was excited by the former Prisons Minister, Ann Widdecombe, who accused Michael Howard, one of the candidates and former Home Secretary, of mishandling the sacking of Derek Lewis as head of the prison service in October 1995 (see AR 1995, p. 28), and also of 'semantic prestidigitation' in defending his actions. The youngest candidate, 36-year-old William Hague, called for a radical overhaul of the party and for more influence for its grassroots members. He also advocated a drive to increase party membership, which had reportedly halved in the last five years and now stood at less than the 420,000 members credited to Labour. Young recruits were especially needed, said Mr Hague, given an estimate that the average age of remaining members was 64. Lady Thatcher intervened on 1 June to urge that only one right-wing candidate should stand in the second round, to prevent Mr Clarke gaining an unstoppable momentum. Mr Heseltine, who had set in motion the events which led to Lady Thatcher's downfall in 1990 (see AR 1990, pp. 38–41), endorsed Mr Clarke, as did Sir Norman Fowler (a former party chairman), while Stephen Dorrell (one of the initial candidates) withdrew from the race to throw his weight behind Mr Clarke. It was increasingly evident that the Tories were still profoundly split, and were continuing to fight old battles at a time when, ironically, it seemed less and less likely that Britain would join the single currency in 1999.

In the leadership contest, Mr Clarke topped the first ballot of Tory MPs on 10 June, winning 49 votes, followed by Mr Hague (41 votes). John Redwood (27 votes) narrowly headed the three right-wing contenders, whereupon the other two, Peter Lilley (24) and Mr Howard (23), came out in favour of Mr Hague, arguing that he alone had a realistic chance of defeating Mr Clarke. The latter narrowly headed the second ballot on 17 June, with 64 votes against 62 for Mr Hague and 38 for Mr Redwood, who was therefore eliminated. Mr Redwood then surprisingly gave his backing to Mr Clarke, the claim being that a Clarke-Redwood axis would mend Tory divisions. Lady Thatcher promptly intervened in favour of Mr Hague, who won the final ballot on 19 June by 92 votes to 70 for Mr Clarke, thus becoming the youngest Tory leader since the Younger Pitt in 1783. Many Tory MPs, it seemed, were upset by the Clarke-Redwood alliance (the historically-minded recalling the displacement of the notorious Fox-North coalition by Pitt in 1784). Mr Hague promised to reunite the party, underlining this intention by choosing Mr Redwood as his shadow Secretary of Trade and Industry. Mr Clarke promised his full support to Mr Hague, but only as a backbencher. Mr Lilley and Mr Howard became shadow Chancellor and Foreign Secretary respectively. Lord Parkinson, to the surprise of many, returned to the party chairmanship he had held in 1981–83. Although the leftish Mr Dorrell secured the education portfolio, the new team was seen as primarily right-wing and Euro-sceptic. There was a footnote to the contest when on 10 July four former cabinet ministers (Messrs Portillo, Rifkind, Forsyth and Norman Lamont, who had all failed to secure election to the Commons in May) declined Mr Major's offer to give them life peerages in his resignation honours list. All evidently still had political ambitions at the highest level.

Meanwhile, Mr Blair had attended his first EU summit, held in Amsterdam on 17 June. To the dismay of other leaders, the Prime Minister insisted that for the time being the EU could not develop its own defence role because it lacked the common 'strategic perspective' needed for it to act as a defence organization; instead, he called for an explicit acknowledgement of NATO's continuing importance. Mr Blair reiterated his concern that new jobs should be the first concern of the EU, and was able to ensure that Britain retained full control of its political asylum and immigration policy as well as the retention of its existing border controls. He showed some flexibility on the question of more majority voting and the development of a two-speed Europe; but whether anything of real substance had been conceded to Britain on fishing quotas remained to be seen. The resulting Treaty of Amsterdam was, in any case, considered to be a meagre achievement. Britain, however, had accepted the EU's Social Chapter, and on this occasion at least Mr Blair had shown more flexibility than his predecessor.

Mr Hague, in his first major speech as Tory leader, put Europe at the centre of his early moves against Labour. Speaking at Perth on 27 June, he challenged Mr Blair to hold a referendum on the Amsterdam Treaty, claiming that it had seriously eroded Britain's ability to use the veto in defence of her interests in the EU. In contrast, Mr Clarke on 1 July had no time for a referendum: together with Chris Patten (the former governor of Hong Kong) he urged the Tories to drop their 'obsession' with Europe and move towards the centre ground in British politics. Mr Hague made an early move to stamp his authority on the Tory party when, on 23 July, he launched the biggest internal shake-up for more than 50 years. His plans included new disciplinary plans to expel or suspend MPs guilty of gross misconduct, a ban on foreign donations to party funds, and central control of the party machine under a new constitution which he hoped would be completed by April 1998. Mr Hague also promised that the party structure as a whole would be democratized to meet recent grassroots criticism and also to try to reverse the disastrous decline in party membership.

On budget day (2 July), the Chancellor's financial statement and budget report recorded that since 1973 the British economy had been growing more slowly than in the post-war period and more slowly than any of its major competitors. In 1996–97 growth had been led by the service sector; construction had shown more vigour since the middle of 1996, manufacturing in the first quarter of 1997 standing 2 per cent higher than a year earlier. Some rise in inflation was expected, but the 1998 target of 2.5 per cent was still thought attainable. Against this background, Mr Brown introduced his first budget (complete with a new red box, replacing the one that had been used since 1860). His central aim, he said, was to ensure that Britain was equipped to meet the challenge of a fast-changing global economy. To this end, it was necessary to unlock the talent and energy of all the people. Adequate long-term investment required long-term confidence, and this was dependent on stability in monetary and fiscal policies. Since 1980 British investment had been among the lowest (in relation to GDP) of the major industrialized countries. A tax strategy which favoured personal saving (especially among the half of the population who rarely saved at all) and long-term company investment was essential. To assist the latter, he was cutting corporation tax by 2 per cent to a record low of only 31 per cent (and to 21 per cent for small companies). He intended to borrow only for investment and to meet current spending from taxation. The public debt would be held at a stable level in relation to national income, and he planned to follow a five-year deficit reduction plan. The national debt had doubled in the 1990s, resulting in a current annual interest charge of £25,000 million—more than the education budget.

The Chancellor intended to raise additional revenue through a one-off £4,800 million (net) tax on the 'windfall' profits of the privatized utility companies. Another £2,300 million would be obtained from the abolition of pension scheme tax credits. The second measure was described by one critic as the biggest attack on pensions provision since that mounted by the late Robert Maxwell (see AR 1995, p. 31). Tax relief on mortgage interest was cut to 10 per cent, while that on private medical insurance was abolished. There were significant increases in duties on petrol and diesel fuel, spirits and tobacco, but VAT on domestic fuel was reduced from 8 to 5 per cent. The NHS and schools would share an extra £3,500 million between them, the former being allocated the largest hospital building programme since its inception. Meanwhile, the windfall tax would fund the government's new welfare-to-work programme over the next two years. This would include payments of £75 a week to employers for each job created for the long-term unemployed (see also I.2).

Reactions to the budget included City fears of an early rise in interest rates given its belief that too little had been done to slow booming consumer demand. On the other hand, many businessmen were alarmed by the effects of a high pound on exports and warned of possible job losses. They argued that interest rate rises to dampen consumer demand would push the pound still higher. Against the German mark, sterling stood at a five-year high of DM2.9305 on the day of the budget. Mr Brown subsequently reaffirmed (30 July) his commitment to a steady course for the economy as the best guarantee of long-term sustainable growth. He was not going to tinker just because of current economic indicators such as a high pound. He insisted that no autumn budget was being considered. When the base rate rose to 7 per cent on 7 August, there were hopes that foreign-exchange dealers would accept that no more increases were likely in the near future. Any balance-of-payments worries were, for the time being, dispelled by reports that the nation's current account had been almost in balance in 1996 thanks to record financial services earnings.

Meanwhile, if many businessmen were impressed by the corporation tax concessions, others were very disturbed by the loss of pension fund tax credits, which it was estimated would cost £50,000 million in pension contributions over the next ten years. The Chancellor dismissed as 'nonsense' claims that many people would have to increase their savings, but it was suggested that the Treasury had perhaps been unduly influenced by the huge surpluses in the biggest pension funds. Many others had much less fat. Mr Hague accused Labour of breaking its election promises not to raise taxes, and Mr Ashdown warned that the Liberal Democrats would also vote against the budget because, while the increases for the NHS and education were welcome, they were not enough. At the end of August, in an interesting new development, the Tories and the Trades Union Congress (TUC) began what was expected to become a regular series of talks. This balanced Labour's recent contacts with business.

Labour spelt out its intentions on education in a White Paper on 7 July. Among its major themes were the modernization of comprehensive secondary schools and the opening-up of 'access to new technologies for all'. Many ideas were set out to improve the teaching profession and to make provision for both the brightest and those with special needs. Home/school contracts would cover discipline, homework and attendance, and these would be reinforced by an 'assertive discipline' policy of rewards and sanctions. While local authorities would receive more money, they would also be subject to closer inspection. The worst-performing schools would, if necessary, be closed and re-launched under new senior teachers.

The Dearing Report on the future of higher education appeared on 23 July. This included radical proposals on the payment by students of tuition fees and on work experience as part of degree courses, and gave more emphasis to the development of the 'key skills' demanded by employers. There should also be radical changes in the academic profession with the aim of improving examining and course standards. Dearing expected the current intake of 30 per cent of young people to rise to 45 per cent, the main growth coming in one- or two-year courses. These proposals were accepted in the main by the Education Secretary. Generous terms would cover future long-term repayment of loans, but the average student was likely to incur debts in excess of £10,000. Mr Blunkett insisted that the changes were necessary to provide more funding for the university sector, which he described as being in a state of crisis. The Teaching and Higher Education Bill began its passage through parliament in December, amid claims that university autonomy was under serious threat from central government and that more than half of the institutions would be in the red in 2000.

On 22 July Mr Blair announced the establishment of a new cabinet committee which would include Liberal Democrat representatives. Its agenda would embrace issues of mutual interest, notably the constitution. For the Labour left, Mr Benn said that this marked 'the beginning of the end of the Labour Party', while Mr Hattersley, once regarded as being on the right of the party, said that Labour was no longer 'a force for a more equal society'.

The government's detailed plans for an Edinburgh parliament, representing a dramatic shift of power and influence to Scotland, were published on 24 July. The White Paper set out proposals for a 129-member assembly to be elected in 1999 and inaugurated in the year 2000. Electors would have two votes, the first for a constituency member (73 in number) and the second for a party list (56 members), the latter to be elected by proportional representation. The assembly would have the power to increase or decrease the basic rate of income tax by 3p in the pound, although this provision would be revised in the light of future circumstances. The necessary legislation would define the powers to be retained by Westminster (foreign, defence and security policies, and matters relating to the constitution). The number of Scottish MPs in Westminster would be reduced from 72 to about 60, though not until around 2004. The Liberal Democrats were strongly supportive, and there was some praise, too, from the Scottish National Party (SNP). The Tories were less enthusiastic. Their spokesman, Michael Ancram, forecast 'grave instability and long-term constitutional turmoil', while on 27 July Mr Hague reiterated his view that devolution was a 'fundamental mistake'. At the same time, however, the Tory leader made it clear that, if the Scottish and Welsh peoples voted for devolution, a future Conservative government would not challenge those verdicts.

The Downey Report on parliamentary sleaze had been published on 3 July and had severely censured Neil Hamilton and four other former Conservative MPs (see also I.3). Had they still been in the Commons, its findings would almost certainly have led to their expulsion. Mr Hamilton, however, continued to protest his innocence in the face of the Downey conclusion that there had been mounting and compelling evidence which seriously damaged the ex-MP's credibility. In other developments, the Labour NEC on 30 July suspended the entire Doncaster district party in response to various allegations of misconduct, four senior councillors having already been suspended. Speculation surrounded a number of other Labour councils. Indeed, the last few days in July and the beginning of August proved to be the worst week so far of the Blair government. Tory questioning of the propriety of Lord Simon of Highbury, the new European Trade and Competitiveness Minister, continuing to hold shares in BP led to a statement on 5 August that the minister was selling the shares and donating the £350,000 profit to charity. On 31 July a by-election in Uxbridge saw the Tories hold the seat by 3,766 votes (in a 55 per cent turnout), this being their first by-election success for eight and a half years.

At first, the suicide of Gordon McMaster, Labour MP for Paisley South, on 28 July was thought to be connected with the controversies and many problems surrounding the West Renfrewshire Labour Party. Although this interpretation was subsequently discounted, a special Labour task-force was set up to investigate the various allegations rife in the region. On 2 August the Foreign Secretary, Mr Cook, announced that he was parting from his wife to live with his Commons secretary, with whom he had been having a secret affair. The Tories therefore began their summer holidays in rather better spirits than had at one time seemed likely. For its part, Labour promised to set up an independent panel to vet its candidates. Preparations were also afoot for a nationwide campaign to replace many of the current Labour local councillors with younger 'Blairite' professionals, as a response to claims of widespread inefficiency and other failings in Renfrewshire and elsewhere.

On 1 August 57 new working life peers were named, 31 of them (including some leading industrialists) to serve on the Labour benches to reduce the Tory majority in that House. Five Tory and 11 Liberal Democrat working peers were named at the same time. Mr Blair returned from holiday on 26 August, saying that the government had to focus on the 'the big picture' of education, health and devolution, this being an apparent reaction to signs of confusion and division among ministers in his absence.

Progress was made towards a possible first meeting between Mr Blair and Mr Adams of Sinn Féin, as well as on the creation of an international commission for the decommissioning of arms in Northern Ireland (see also I.10). As early as 25 June, following his visit to the United States (see I.7), Mr Blair had delivered an ultimatum to the IRA by announcing plans to begin detailed talks on Ulster's future in September—with or without Sinn Féin. This was in effect a warning that the latter would not be party to the peace negotiations unless a ceasefire was in being by the end of July. The Prime Minister expressed the hope that an agreement could be put to the people of Northern Ireland in a referendum in the early summer of 1998. Sinn Féin and the IRA agreed on 18–19 July to a renewal of the ceasefire, with effect from 20 July. Two Protestant parties thereupon stepped out of the peace process, while the dominant Ulster Unionists rejected the latest Anglo-Irish disarmament plan, arguing on 23 July that it contained no cast-iron guarantees that the IRA would disarm during the peace talks. London and Dublin insisted that the talks would begin on 15 September as planned. Six days before that date Sinn Féin formally renounced the use of force to achieve political ends. Agreement to participate in the talks was not forthcoming from the Ulster Unionists until 24 September, when the party conceded that there could be no absolute guarantee of some IRA disarmament during the talks. The two other Unionist parties, representing about 40 per cent of the Unionist vote, condemned the agreement and continued to boycott the talks. The UK Prime Minister and Mr Adams duly met on 11 December, the former stressing that Northern Ireland now faced an historic choice: violence and despair or peace and progress. Mr Adams said that 'all the hurt and grief and division which has come from British involvement in Irish affairs has to end'. The Democratic Unionist leader, Dr Ian Paisley, said that the two men had been 'dancing on the grave of the Ulster dead'.

6. DEVOLUTION AND OTHER LABOUR POLICIES

ON 11 September Scotland voted overwhelmingly for devolution (see I.8), whereupon Mr Blair hastened to Wales to appeal for a similar verdict. The outcome, however, was a disappointing winning margin of only 0.6 per cent, with barely half the electorate choosing to vote (see I.9). The Tories claimed that the result had sounded the death knell of Labour plans for English regional assemblies. They did, however, accept devolution as the way forward for Scotland. Mr Prescott conceded that the regional issue could not be reopened in England until after another election.

The Liberal Democrats claimed on 17 September that they had reached agreement with Labour to press ahead with the first steps towards proportional representation for elections to Westminster. This was confirmed on 1 December when Mr Blair announced the formation of a commmission headed by Lord Jenkins of Hillhead to devise a replacement for the present voting system. At the same time, many Liberal Democrats feared that Mr Ashdown's overall strategy might produce such a degree of cooperation with Labour as to cloud the identity of their party. Indeed, the Liberal Democrat leader was forced to confront critics and sceptics head-on at the autumn party conference. Risks, he argued, had to be taken to win 'real prizes' even if at times that meant compromises over policy. He claimed on 25 September that the conference was a 'genuine watershed' for the party. Even so, much use was made of the phrase 'constructive opposition' in dealings with the Labour government to emphasize the separate identity of the Liberal Democrats. The conference also called for a royal commission on voluntary euthanasia, a subject which was beginning to attract more public attention.

Meanwhile, opposition leader Mr Hague came under under fire both for his criticism of Mr Blair's involvement in the preparations for the funeral of the Princess of Wales and for some of his plans to revitalize the Conservative Party. Tension was also reported in the cabinet as ministers differed over the question of recent salary increases, while some unions seemed to be flexing their muscles in response to the government's determination to restrain public-sector pay rises.

The Prime Minister bluntly told the trade unions at their conference in Brighton on 10 September that they had to jettison old dogmas, traditions and methods and join the real world. Above all, there had to be employment flexibility. On 29 September Mr Brown reiterated the government's determination to limit public-sector pay increases to 3 per cent, warning that the clampdown on public spending would continue for two or even three years.

At the Labour Party's annual conference in Brighton, elections to the NEC on 29 September resulted in the rejection of Mr Mandelson and the success of one of the heroes of the left, Ken Livingstone. Nevertheless, 'old Labour' efforts to defer the leadership's sweeping reforms of the party's policy-making structures were overwhelmingly defeated. Mr Blair left no-one in any doubt in his conference speech on 30 September that he would press on with his existing programme. He called for an all-out effort to make Britain the best country in the world in terms of education, health, welfare and for the reversal of the crisis in family life—as demonstrated, for instance, by nearly 100,000 teenage pregnancies a year. Britain should become 'the model 21st-century nation, a beacon to the world'. This would, he warned, require all-round effort and sacrifices. William Rees-Mogg, a former editor of *The Times*, described the new Prime Minister's address as more than a speech, rather an 'historic statement of intent'. Deputy leader John Prescott ended the conference in lighter vein, but warned delegates of the need to cherish the party's grassroots. The current problems of the Tories, he asserted, showed what happened when these were neglected: Labour had to make sure it won two full terms in office.

The Tories met in Blackpool in early October in the gloomy knowledge that their party's debts were approaching £8 million, that many corporate donors had withdrawn their support, and that Young Conservative strength had fallen to perhaps less than 3,000. The Tory rank and file wasted no time in condemning 'sleaze' and disloyalty in the parliamentary party, demanding a bigger say in leadership elections and greater powers to throw out errant MPs. Lord Archer was applauded when he called for party members to have a 50 per cent share in choosing future leaders. An overhaul of all Tory policies was promised, including a thorough party modernization to make it more responsive to the needs and demands of the British people. The party would listen to all interest groups in developing 'a programme for Britain'. In a surprising fringe address, Mr Portillo seemed to soften his previous right-wing policy prescriptions by calling for the party to shed its arrogance and 'vulgar' image and to show more tolerance in such matters as single mothers.

In his conference address on 10 October, Mr Hague impressed many with a speech in which he scored badly-needed positive points on his own behalf, after his somewhat shaky start as party leader. He called for a new party of tolerance and compassion to remove the images of 'sleaze' and social unconcern which had so influenced the electorate on 1 May. This was well-received in general terms, but difficulties could be expected when it came to the small print on matters such as his interest in a reduction in the age of consenting homosexuals. More problems had also arisen over the single European currency, on which Mr Hague on 9 October hardened his line by announcing that he would oppose it at the next general election. Three days earlier, however, Mr Clarke had agreed to become leader of the Tory Reform Group, which was broadly pro-Europe and left-of-centre in its sympathies. Thus, while delegates left the conference in rather better spirits than expected, the party clearly had a long way to go before it could be said to be projecting a new sense of unity and purpose.

Labour was by no means immune from divisions over Europe. In mid-October the government ran into serious difficulties over the single currency, some being of its own making due to ambiguous comments from various sources, leading to the inevitable media speculation. Consequent market nervousness and falls in the stock market were exacerbated when Hong Kong began to share the financial turmoil of the 'Asian tiger' economies (see XVIII.1). A statement by Mr Brown on 20 October—the tenth anniversary of the 'Black Monday' stock market collapse (see AR 1987, p. 31)—did not help matters. At the same time, Mr Blair was assuring the German Chancellor that Britain would not 'sabotage' a single currency, although it would be sticking to sterling in the short term.

Parliament reassembled on 27 October and was told by the Chancellor that the government endorsed the principle of European monetary union. Britain, said Mr Brown, should prepare intensively for membership early in the 'next parliament', assuming that it was then seen to be in the economic interest of Britain and given public approval in a referendum. Britain would also have to meet key economic tests such as lower inflation and the fiscal rules and deficit reduction plans set out in the EU's 'stability pact'. Mr Lilley, for the Conservatives, accused Mr Brown of continuing the dithering policy which had unleashed the current woes on the stock market. The shadow cabinet had already effectively decided (on 22 October) to oppose participation in the single currency for the next ten years. In contrast, spokesmen for the TUC, the CBI and the Liberal Democrats, as well as Mr Clarke and Sir Edward Heath, were fearful that Labour might prove too slow in making a positive decision. Those worried by the economic ill-effects of a strong pound were particularly anxious to join as soon as the single currency had proved its viability and attractions.

The blunt anti-EU stance of the Tory leadership quickly provoked the resignations of two shadow ministers, namely Ian Taylor and David Curry. They were promptly supported by Mr Clarke, Mr Heseltine, Lord (Douglas) Hurd and Sir Leon Brittan (a European commissioner). Civil war among the Tories had broken out once again, some obervers suggesting that this state of affairs was likely to persist until monetary union had proved itself a success or failure, or until a referendum had been held on the subject. Mr Hague said on 3 November that he was willing to let the monetary rebels go: the sooner they went the sooner the party could be offer a clear message to electors. But the CBI warned on 5 November that Mr Hague was risking a ten-year rift with business if he persisted in his current stance. Its claims of strong support among its members, however, were weakened when it was revealed that only one in three had responded to the survey, and that a majority of small businessmen were opposed to the single currency.

On 10–11 November both Mr Blair and Mr Brown again urged British business to prepare for membership of the single currency, together delivering their most positive endorsement of that project to date. In contrast, Mr Hague was likening its proponents to 'lemmings'. A fifth rise in the base interest rate since the election (to 7.5 per cent) was a reminder of one of the several areas in which convergence would be necessary before the economy was sufficiently in line with the main continental members of the EU for Britain to opt for the single currency. Mr Blair's prime concern at the special EU 'jobs summit' in Luxembourg on 20–21 November was to ensure that all 15 member states (including Britain) had a say in economic policy, and not only the 'inner circle' of single currency participant states. Intense, even angry, exchanges eventually yielded what the Italian Premier described on 12 December as a 'nice compromise'. This promised that all 15 EU Finance Ministers, forming the EU's ECOFIN Council, would take part in EMU discussions when 'common interests' were at issue. Mr Blair argued that ECOFIN was 'the only decision-making body'; but it seemed likely that the matter was far from settled, especially given the difficulty of defining the meaning of 'common interests'.

In early November the Commons inquiry into breaches of parliamentary standards finally reported critically with respect to Neil Hamilton. Mr Hague said on 8 November that the former MP would 'never again be able to be on a Conservative candidates' list'. Two days later Labour found itself in deep trouble when it was advised by the public standards watchdog to return a £1 million donation from the head of Formula One motor racing in Britain (see also XVII: Sport). This development coincided with an outcry over the government's decision to exempt Formula One racing from a tobacco sponsorship ban. On 11 November a badly-shaken government promised a comprehensive reform of the way Britain's political parties would be funded in the future, while on 16 November Mr Blair appeared on television to apologize to the electorate and to attempt in other ways to repair his image. He admitted that the issues had not been well handled. He also challenged the Tories to match Labour's openness on financial donors, offering to publish details of Labour benefactors since 1992 if other parties did the same.

Attention was diverted from Labour's embarrassments by a disastrous Tory performance in the re-run of the Winchester election on 20 November, after a small irregularity had been discovered in the processing of the ballot papers in the general election. Having taken the seat from the Tories by only two votes in May, the Liberal Democrat candidate romped home with a 21,556-vote majority, helped by tactical voting by Labour supporters. On the same day, the Tories only narrowly held Beckenham, the seat from which Piers Merchant had been forced to resign earlier in the year. Even worse for the Tories was the decision of Peter Temple-Morris to sit as an independent after his strong pro-European views had led to his loss of the party whip on 21 November. He won immediate

I.6 DEVOLUTION AND OTHER LABOUR POLICIES

backing from Mr Heseltine, while Mr Patten called on Mr Hague to take a less 'nationalistic' and more pragmatic approach to Europe.

In a new departure, Mr Brown delivered the government's first 'pre-budget report' on 25 November. The main emphasis was laid on the need for restraint in wage claims and public spending, although the Chancellor expected the same moderation to be shown by business leaders. It would, he warned, be the worst form of short-termism to 'pay ourselves more today at the cost of fewer jobs tomorrow and lower living standards in the very near future'. At the same time, he provided £400 million to help pensioners' winter fuel costs and £300 million to establish child-care clubs to assist the working single parents of a million children. The latter initiative was related to the growing pressure from some 50 Labour backbenchers against the benefit cutbacks to single parents from April 1998. On 8 December Mr Blair launched the government's Social Exclusion Unit with the task of easing the plight of the disadvantaged within two years. The unit would have no funds of its own but would co-ordinate Whitehall action on truancy, homelessness and poor housing. There were many critics of the absence of additional money.

The vote on 10 December on benefit cuts to single parents resulted in a government victory of 457 votes to 107, but 47 Labour MPs defied their whips and 14 more abstained. In addition, five junior ministers resigned or were dismissed for not voting for the cuts. The government was sufficiently impressed by the threat of further trouble to signal over the following weekend that there would be more emphasis on carrots than sticks to encourage all categories of welfare claimants to seek work. Ministers, however, would continue the long-term search for means to trim the rising social security bill, but on a more cautious and consultative basis. Mr Blair stressed again that no-one in real need would be denied benefits.

Meanwhile, the Chief Secretary to the Treasury, Alistair Darling, had been warning ministers that the current two-year clampdown on spending might in fact last to the end of the present parliament. Any surplus money would go to health and education. However, a White Paper published on 9 December announced a capping of the £35,000 million health budget at the start of a ten-year programme to phase out the internal market and GP fundholding in the NHS as set up by the Conservatives. Reforms were also promised to make the service once again 'the envy of the world'.

Even so, the Prime Minister was warned of the possibility of a party crisis over the benefits question when Mr Blunkett (the Education and Employment Secretary) challenged Treasury plans to reduce spending. Mr Blair responded on 21 December by taking personal charge of the moves to reform the welfare system, asserting that change was inevitable. The following day Mr Brown added that the 'true defenders of the welfare state' were those prepared to reform it. There would, however, be 'no indiscriminate slash and burn exercise'.

At the beginning of December the government found itself in dispute with the livestock industry as farmers blockaded several ports to prevent the entry of cheap beef imports from the Irish Republic. On 15 December Britain imposed a unilateral ban on imports of EU beef which did not meet British safety standards (the EU having voted to introduce comparable checks only from April 1998). Meanwhile, domestic producers were further outraged by the decision on health grounds to ban the sale of beef on the bone from 16 December (BSE having been detected in bone marrow). Ministers promised a comprehensive inquiry into all aspects of the BSE crisis amid signs that the unease over meat products might spread to lamb. Reports were circulating that many farmers were facing growing financial problems. The government announced a one-off £85 million emergency package for agriculture; but it was evident that in the longer term the aim was to reduce the number of farmers. In October farming leaders had been warning that the nation's uplands faced a serious risk of depopulation as low incomes (and the hardness of life in such areas) were likely to drive a large proportion of the next generation off the land. Vast areas could become wildernesses resembling those in the heart of France and Spain.

The Scottish Devolution Bill was published on 18 December. Mr Dewar, the Scottish Secretary, claimed that the measure would boost Scottish self-confidence and give the United Kingdom 'a new constitutional foundation, binding Scotland into the UK and giving her the opportunity to take responsibility for her own affairs'.

7. INTERNATIONAL RELATIONS

THE biggest deployment of British naval strength since the Gulf War began on 13 January as 21 ships sailed from Portsmouth on a seven-and-a-half-month 'showing the flag' tour of the Asia-Pacific region. Any connections with the handover of Hong Kong to China at the end of June were denied, though the visits to 34 countries would include naval exercises. A spokesman said the tour was a demonstration of British concern for the stability and health of a huge region in which Britain had major commercial and political interests. At the same time, the Prime Minister, during a visit to Pakistan, met anti-narcotic forces deployed in the Khyber Pass against smugglers from Afghanistan. Britain provided some training and other assistance to the 100,000-strong force, which was trying to police this dangerous border against a drugs operation estimated to be worth more than £20,000 million a year. Robin Cook announced on 28 August that there would be a big increase in the involvement of MI6 in the fight against the drug barons, with special attention being paid to the money-laundering systems which lay at the heart of 'this scourge' against humanity. MI5 would also be active in the United Kingdom insofar as resources could be spared from its counter-terrorist role. Other activities by British servicemen included assistance in August to the people of Montserrat in response to a massive volcanic eruption. Unfortunately, the scale and purpose of British financial aid soon became a matter of serious political controversy on the island and in Britain (see IV.4.ix).

It was reported on 28 January that Spain had proposed that it should share the sovereignty of Gibraltar with Britain for up to 100 years, after which the

Rock would revert to Spain (see also II.3.ii). Detailed proposals were included to try to win the confidence of the people of Gibraltar. The then Foreign Secretary, Mr Rifkind, responded that the proposal would not be acceptable to Gibraltarians and urged Spain to approach the question with the same imagination as Argentina was showing over the Falklands/Malvinas. Gibraltar once again damaged Anglo-Spanish relations when Britain threatened on 9 July to veto Spain's entry into NATO's military structure unless its restrictions on air traffic in Gibraltar were lifted.

On 12 February the Iranian '15 Khordad Foundation' increased the reward for the murder of the writer Salman Rushdie, by $500,000 to $2.5 million. The Foreign Office denounced the move, calling upon the Iranian President to condemn the bounty. Security sources, however, said that Mr Rushdie would never be free from the threat to his life, even if Tehran officially lifted the *fatweh*. Scotland Yard's protection of the author had already cost over £7 million. On the following day, Britain announced that it would participate in an energy fair in Tehran in April despite American sanctions against Iran. The Department of Trade and Industry was anxious to promote British business interests.

On 12 May Mr Cook presented his 'mission statement' as Foreign and Commonwealth Secretary in the new Labour government. He promised a stronger stand on human rights, arms control and disarmament, as well as strict control of Britain's arms sales. NATO remained the core of security policy. On Europe he emphasized the need to remove the last internal trade barriers, and to press rapidly ahead with EU enlargement. He also wished to strengthen both the Commonwealth and the United Nations. On 21 May Mr Cook announced that Britain would take a bigger part in international talks to ban the use of anti-personnel mines (see XII.2), and also take interim steps against British manufacture and use, except in special circumstances. During a tour of South-East Asia at the end of August, the Foreign Secretary spoke out forcefully on behalf of human rights. There was room for debate about implementation but not the principle. Only Myanmar (Burma) was publicly condemned, though Mr Cook also spoke to a leader of the East Timor movement for independence from Indonesia. In Malaysia his hosts stressed the importance of different cultural values and their need to deal with human rights problems in their own way.

President Clinton's visit to London on 29 May was presented as the start of a a new phase in the Anglo-American special relationship. Mr Blair said that he and the US leader belonged to a generation which preferred 'reason to doctrine' and 'ideals to ideology'. Mr Clinton urged the IRA to lay down their guns permanently, and told Sinn Féin that it would have to make concessions. He fully supported the stance of the British government on Northern Ireland. Both leaders expressed their determination to wage war on unemployment and the growth of an underclass. They promised new initiatives, especially through the G-7 group of leading industrial nations.

On 3 June Britain accepted an outline deal which would permit the EU to run its foreign policy partly through majority decision-making rather than unanimity; but the government also insisted on a number of exceptions where an 'emergency brake' could be applied for reasons of national interest. The veto would also stand with reference to immigration. Mr Blair attended the 'summit of eight' (the G-7 countries plus Russia) in Denver (USA) on 20–22 June, winning promises from world leaders, including President Yeltsin, to hold China to its promises to maintain democracy and the rule of law in Hong Kong after the return of the colony to Chinese rule (see also IX.2.ii). Indeed, British satisfaction at this conference was dented only by North American and Japanese lack of vigour in implementing the environmental agreement reached at Rio de Janeiro in 1992. The British Prime Minister returned to this subject in his UN speech on the 23 June, when he called on world leaders to save the planet for their children and grandchildren. Britain itself aimed to cut greenhouse gas emissions by a fifth within 13 years. Mr Blair also used his US visit to urge Americans to stop giving money to Sinn Féin and thus supporting terrorism in Ulster.

Meanwhile, in London, his International Development Secretary, Clare Short, was announcing radical changes to Britain's overseas aid spending. The link with commercial considerations (including arms sales) would be broken, the £2,000 million annual budget being devoted to the poorest countries in Africa. Mr Cook on 25 June took a strong line on Nigeria, currently suspended from Commonwealth membership (see XI.2.i), saying that Britain would veto any move for readmission until that country had made serious progress in the restoration of democracy.

On 30 June Britain handed over its last major colony, Hong Kong, to China (see IX.2.ii). The Chinese President promised to preserve Hong Kong's social and legal systems fundamentally unchanged, committing Beijing to allowing democracy to develop in a manner suitable to the Hong Kong reality. Mr Blair warned that Hong Kong would be 'destroyed' if anything was done to undermine the 1984 Joint Declaration (see AR 1984, pp. 515–24), adding that he viewed the immediate future with 'trepidation and apprehension'. Meanwhile, a dispute had erupted between Chris Patten (the last Governor) and some British critics, including former ministers and diplomats, over the wisdom of his experiment in democracy in the colony and whether a more conciliatory policy should have been pursued towards China in recent years.

Mr Cook on 29 July warned all three factions in Bosnia that more vigour and honesty were needed on their part if they were to continue to receive Western aid. He also said that NATO was determined to persist in its efforts to arrest war criminals. The following day Britain vetoed an IMF loan to Croatia because of its prevarication in implementing the Dayton peace agreement. On 20 August British troops seized police stations in Banja Luka to foil a possible coup against the current Bosnian Serb government. They were also needed to help stabilize the situation in the run-up to, and during, the Bosnian Serb municipal elections in September. During a visit to Bosnia at the end of November, Mr Blair underlined his determination to bring war criminals to justice. He added that British troops would not be withdrawn in the near future.

The government announced on 19 September that, while Britain could no longer serve as a 'world policeman', its armed forces would still be able to 'make a difference'. The Defence Secretary, George Robertson, said that Britain would retain major defence roles in NATO, the Gulf and the Near East, adding that he was trying to allay service fears that British forces were becoming no more than peace-keeping militias. Although the pressure for economy continued, a renewal of tension between the United States and Iraq in November brought strong support for the Americans from Mr Blair. He insisted that Britain's determination to stand firm against the 'still dangerous dictator' Saddam Husain was unshakeable. He later declared that Anglo-American military action could not be ruled out even if other countries declined to take part. Reinforcements to the Gulf included an aircraft carrier, which was to have her complement of aircraft reinforced by Harrier ground-attack fighters. RAF Tornados were already present in the Gulf. Intense diplomatic activity, by the Russians in particular, brought some reduction in tension on 20 November, though Mr Cook insisted that no concessions had been made to Iraq.

The Queen's visit to Pakistan and India in the middle of October was not without incident. The Foreign Secretary, who accompanied her, was accused of bias towards Pakistan following a report that he had offered mediation on the Kashmir question—regarded as a purely internal matter as far as New Delhi was concerned. For many Indian commentators, Mr Cook's reported initiative indicated that even Labour retained remnants of the mentality associated with the British Empire at its peak. On the other hand, the government was able to make some progress at the Commonwealth heads of government meeting in Edinburgh at the end of October towards its aim of a more dynamic multilateral approach to trade and investment—though smaller member states stressed their vulnerability to sweeping trade liberalization.

8. SCOTLAND

THE Tories made an early start to their campaign against devolution with warnings that it would bring a 'tartan tax'. There was also a running battle over the costs of Scottish local council services, the government claiming that these were between 30 and 37 per cent higher than in England. A report published by the Scottish Office on 14 February, however, put the figure at only 18 per cent. This did not satisfy spokesmen for the councils, while the Convention of Scottish Local Authorities (COSLA) was arguing that Tory cuts in local government spending were hitting the whole economy and causing the loss of more jobs than the 12,000 created by Locate in Scotland in 1996. The Liberal Democrats later highlighted the much higher average council tax payments in Scotland compared with England.

The government was embarrassed on 10 February when Mr Dorrell, then Health Secretary, appeared to suggest that a future Tory ministry might abolish a Scottish parliament. The Scottish Secretary, however, insisted that such a parliament would not be 'just for Christmas—it's for life'. There were further exchanges between the Tories and the then opposition parties as to whether devolution would lead to the break-up of the UK. Labour insisted that a Scottish parliament would not have any powers to move towards independence, prompting a Scottish National Party (SNP) comment that the assembly would be more like a parish council.

Scotland's Conservatives made a disastrous start to the general election campaign when on 24 March Allan Stewart, a former minister and the Tory MP with the largest majority in Scotland, resigned for family reasons and an earlier personal indiscretion. Five days later Sir Michael Hirst, the Scottish chairman, also resigned over a previous incident and amid talk of internal party divisions and plots. At the end of a keenly-contested campaign, Labour emerged triumphant with no fewer than 56 seats (and 45.6 per cent of the Scottish vote), the Liberal Democrats with 10 seats (13 per cent), the SNP with six (22 per cent) and the Tories none (17.5 per cent). The SNP took second place in more than two-thirds of the constituencies, but had picked up only a few votes overall compared with 1992.

The bill paving the way for a Scottish devolution referendum began its passage through the Commons on 21 May. A Tory amendment to block the bill was defeated the following day by 251 votes. Only six out of some 900 delegates at the Conservative Party conference in Perth on 27 June backed a call for a rethink of their current opposition to devolution. The conference did, however, vote for a review of the party's structure in response to its lack of representation in Westminster and meagre representation (82 seats) on local councils.

The Devolution White Paper was published on 24 July, public interest being reflected in the sale of 500 copies in the first two hours in one Glasgow bookshop. Donald Dewar, the new Labour Scottish Secretary and architect of the proposals, had designed a blueprint which allayed many Scottish Labour fears that the home rule ideal might be seriously diluted (for details see I.5). The SNP agreed that most of what had been demanded by the Scottish Constitutional Convention had been secured. The campaign for 'yes' and 'no' votes intensified from the end of August with some leading businessmen disputing claims that Scotland would be better off economically with its own parliament. Mr Dewar and the Scottish CBI held talks which were described as 'constructive' despite reservations among some businessmen. The Liberal Democrat leader, Paddy Ashdown, argued that devolution with tax powers would not only give Scotland greater control over its affairs (at home and in the EU) but would also 'blaze the trail' for constitutional reform across Britain. The SNP stressed the economic and political gains. Other critics pointed to the one billion pounds spent by previous Tory governments on policies not wanted by the majority of Scots—notably the poll tax.

Mr Blair visited Scotland on 8 September, insisting that the people had nothing to fear from home rule or an assembly with tax-varying powers. Mr Brown said it was hoped to have the parliament up and running in the year 2000. The tax-raising powers, it seemed, would be operable from 2002. For the Conservatives, Mr Hague claimed on 9 September that the whole future of the United Kingdom hung on the referendum. Supporters of devolution, however, paid more attention to Lady Thatcher's visit, it being widely reckoned that her unpopularity in Scotland would boost the 'yes' vote. In general, the Tory 'no, no' campaign (i.e. to both the assembly and to tax-varying powers) was considered negative and unimaginative.

In the referendum on 11 September, around 1.5 million Scottish voters (74.3 per cent) voted 'yes' to a Scottish parliament, while 1.34 million (63.5 per cent) opted for tax-varying powers. The turnout averaged 60 per cent. Only in Orkney did fewer than half (47.4 per cent) vote 'yes' on taxation, though there was also considerable scepticism in Shetland and the Borders (where the vote in favour was 51.6 and 50.7 per cent respectively). At the SNP conference, Alex Salmond claimed that the referendum outcome was a demonstration of renewed Scottish confidence, judging that Scotland had taken the first 'decisive' step towards independence. He was less happy when the conference voted for a post-independence referendum on the future of the monarchy. The SNP also promised to use the new Scottish parliament as a vehicle for a referendum on Trident nuclear submarines. Early in November two prominent left-wing Tories defected to the Liberal Democrats, disillusioned by current Tory thinking and the failure to elect Kenneth Clarke as leader. Nor were party tensions much relieved when a reform package was unveiled on 13 December. The proposals were subject to approval by the next party conference (in March 1998).

Apathy rather than the faction fighting among Labour members in West Scotland appeared to explain the swing of 11 per cent to the SNP in the Paisley South by-election on 6 November. Labour retained the seat with a greatly reduced majority in a low poll. However, many observers believed that 'new Labour' had much to do before it was firmly established in Scotland.

Overall there were highly promising figures of inward investment, which stood at the highest level since 1981.The most exciting new development was the promise of an American-backed plant at Livingston to design next-generation computer chips. Many spin-offs to the economy of central Scotland were expected, coupled with hopes that Scotland would be placed at the forefront of electronics research and development. Plans for a £3,000 million semiconductor plant in Fife, however, were put in some doubt when Hyundai (the firm in question) was caught up in the economic crisis which wracked South Korea late in the year (see IX.2.v). Yarrow shipbuilders, while reporting good long-term prospects with warship orders to the year 2003, announced further job losses, a third of the work-force having been shed inside 12 months. Lack of orders was also putting the Kvaerner Govan yard at risk. Rosyth was strengthened by a nuclear submarine refit contract awarded by the new Labour government early in May. The Ministry of Defence tried to allay renewed fears that Rosyth would become a long-term radioactive dump with an assurance that decommissioned nuclear submarines would be removed early in the next century.

Dismay at education cuts (involving planned school closures and the loss of 500 teachers) and other economies led to public demonstrations in Glasgow early in the year. In February the transport group National Express made a successful bid for Scotrail with its 3,500 employees and an annual turnover of nearly £400 million. Plans to revive the canal links between the Clyde and the Forth and Edinburgh were given a £32 million boost (nearly half the total expected cost) by the Millenium Commission. The scheme was intended to help both the environment and tourism. There were claims that the Highlands and Islands now had the fastest-growing population in Europe, showing an increase in the last ten years of 2.6 per cent per annum compared with a fall 3.4 per cent in Scotland as a whole. Significant increases in economic activity in recent years included Barmac's creation of many new jobs at its oil yards in the Moray Firth.

The revival of the Gaelic culture also continued. This included an increasing range of television programmes. In June Scottish Media announced a merger of STV and Grampian television, adding that it hoped to loosen ties with ITV and develop a service with more Scottish dimensions as devolution gathered momentum. The end of the year found many Scottish farmers calling for government action to assist their crisis-hit industry.

Scottish universities faced major changes arising from the Dearing Report into higher education (see I.5). The four-year honours degree was likely to be affected by a proposed revitalization of the old three-year ordinary degree. Concern was expressed by some as to the effect of the new tuition fees on student entries from other parts of the British Isles—given the honours norm of four years in Scotland.

9. WALES

IN an historic, and ultimately dramatic, referendum held on 18 September, the Welsh people voted in favour of an elected assembly which would give the nation a greater degree of autonomy than it had experienced since the Middle Ages. Although a far cry from the full self-government sought by Welsh nationalists, and despite lacking many of the powers to be given to the Scottish parliament (see I.6; I.8), many saw the assembly, which would meet for the first time in May 1999, as a symbol which would reaffirm Welsh nationality and bring self-confidence to the Welsh people.

The referendum followed the publication in July of the new Labour government's white paper, *A Voice for Wales*. It proposed that a 60-strong Welsh assembly, elected partly through proportional representation, would take over responsibility from the Secretary of State for Wales for the spending of the annual budget (currently £7,000 million) set by Whitehall. However, unlike the Scottish parliament, it would have no tax-varying powers nor would it be able to make or amend laws. Many of the unelected quangos—a target of criticism for many years—would be abolished or reformed. Although the proposals resembled those which had been decisively rejected by 4 to 1 in a previous referendum in 1979, this time, with Labour in the ascendancy and only the Conservatives and a few dissident socialists opposing, it was believed that there would be a comfortable margin of victory for the government. In the event, the scare tactics employed by opponents of devolution in 1979 were resurrected and the government found it hard to raise enthusiasm in some quarters and to overcome old prejudices and apathy.

When the results were announced, county by county, in the early hours of 19 September, it appeared for a long time that the government's proposals would be rejected. However, a final massive majority in Carmarthen gave it a dramatic victory by the narrowest of margins. The final result was 559,419 (50.3 per cent) in favour of the government's proposals and 552,698 (49.7 per cent) opposed, on a low turnout of 50.3 per cent. Although much was made of the east-west split in the voting pattern, the divisions in Wales were rather more complex and, considering the massive rejection of devolution in 1979, the government's narrow success was a greater achievement than some critics acknowledged.

The result of the referendum was a personal triumph for Ron Davies, who had become Secretary of State for Wales following the general election in May. Though vilified by the London press and attacked by a few dissident Labour MPs, he remained resolute over devolution and many welcomed his emphasis on the building of a new 'inclusive' political ethos in Wales. The Government of Wales bill, to set up what was now to be called the National Assembly for Wales, was published in November, but at the same time a dispute arose over the new body's location. To widespread consternation, Cardiff city council's financial demands for the purchase of the lease of the City Hall, Mr Davies's favoured option, proved excessive, and this led to calls that the assembly should be situated outside the capital. Two new options were proposed in December: a new building in Cardiff or the use of the Guildhall in Swansea, with meetings also being held, using video-conferencing facilities, in Aberystwyth, Bangor, Mold and Cardiff. A decision was expected early in 1998.

Labour's stunning victory in the general election in May had paved the way for the proposed new political structure in Wales. Labour won 34 of the 40 Welsh seats and, for the first time since 1906, the Conservatives failed to return a single member of parliament in Wales. Plaid Cymru (the Welsh National Party) retained its four seats, while Richard Livesey regained Brecon and Radnor for the Liberal Democrats, who thus won two seats in Wales. Soon to become leader of the Conservative Party, William Hague, the Secretary of State for Wales until the election, returned to his Richmond (Yorkshire) seat with one consolation from his period in Wales. In December he married Ffion Jenkins, a Welsh-speaking former civil servant, who had taught him the words of the Welsh national anthem when he was appointed Secretary of State in 1995.

The new government argued that Wales's image as a 'low cost' nation, fostered by the previous government, was an economic strategy doomed to failure. It claimed that high-investment, high-skill economies were more successful than ones which depended on lower wage and social costs and asserted that it intended to modernize the Welsh economy by establishing partnerships between the public and private sectors and by promoting better education and training. As in the past, a crucial aspect of this strategy would be the success of the Welsh Development Agency (WDA) in enticing new industries to Wales. In November the new Secretary of State was able to stave off an attempt by the Department of

Trade and Industry to impose a right of veto on the WDA's efforts to attract foreign investment.

The most economically-disadvantaged parts of Wales received disappointing news in August when it was announced that the Gulf oil refinery at Milford Haven, Pembrokeshire, was to close—this in an area where one in four males was already unemployed. At the same time, the fashion group Laura Ashley, an important employer in rural Wales, stated that it was closing its factories at Machynlleth and Caernarfon, with the loss of 190 jobs.

One sector of the economy, livestock farmers, became increasingly bitter during the year, as prices fell and as the problems over BSE persisted. The strong pound led to cheap imports of foreign meat, with the result that in early December irate farmers attempted to blockade Welsh ports, including Holyhead, where 40 tonnes of beef-burgers from an Irish lorry were tossed into the sea. The limited compensation paid by the government to farmers later in the month only partly defused the situation.

Earlier in the year, a tribunal chaired by Sir Ronald Waterhouse QC began a long and disturbing examination of allegations that there had been widespread abuse of children in the care of local authorities in north Wales. The tribunal heard evidence that over 300 victims had suffered physical and sexual assaults by as many as 148 people.

In sport, the highlight of the year was Glamorgan's outstanding achievement in winning the county cricket championship for the first time since 1969. The dangers of physical contact sports were once again demonstrated when the Welsh rugby captain, Gwyn Jones, suffered a serious neck injury in a club match in December.

10. NORTHERN IRELAND

THE year opened with the imminent UK general elections entering political calculations and with no immediate prospect of a restoration of the ceasefire rescinded by the IRA in February 1996 (see AR 1996, pp. 38–9). Terrorist incidents in January included bombings and mortar attacks—a juxtaposition of 'events' with soft statements from the republican Sinn Féin that was described by Sir Patrick Mayhew, then Northern Ireland Secretary, as 'hard deeds and honeyed words'.

On 13 January the Chief Constable warned of 'very dangerous times' and attributed two bombing incidents in Belfast and Londonderry (Derry) to loyalists. This development called into question the participation in peace talks of the Ulster Democratic Party (UDP) and the Progressive Unionist Party (PUP), the political 'advisers' of the loyalist paramilitary Ulster Defence Association (UDA) and Ulster Volunteer Force (UVF) respectively. When the plenary session of the talks reopened on 27 January, the view of the UK Minister of State, Michael Ancram, that the UDP and PUP had not 'demonstrably dishonoured' the Mitchell Principles (see AR 1996, p. 38), prevailed. However, the plenaries broke down on the second day and discussion returned to bilaterals.

In a statement issued on 7 February, the IRA dismissed speculation that it would call a new ceasefire in advance of the UK elections. Its determination was seen in the planting a 1,000-pound bomb in Strabane on 10 February (although it did not explode) and the killing of a British Army corporal at Bessbrook two days later. There was strong condemnation from the United States and indications that the new Secretary of State, Madeleine Albright, was firmly behind the Major government's line of demanding a credible ceasefire before Sinn Féin could participate in talks. When invitations for the St Patrick's Day celebrations were issued from the White House, Sinn Féin was excluded. Sinn Féin's hope that changes of government in Britain and Ireland might bring policy change was diminished by strong statements from Tony Blair (British Labour leader) and Bertie Ahern (leader of Fianna Fáil in the Republic) supporting the existing London-Dublin line.

In a move intended to reduce sectarian tensions surrounding the Northern Ireland 'marching season', the UK government on 26 March announced the creation of an independent five-member Parades Commission with powers to ban or re-route marches. The new body had been recommended in the report of the North Commission published on 30 January, but implementation had been delayed by unionist opposition to the transfer to it of powers hitherto exercised by the Royal Ulster Constabulary (RUC) and the Secretary of State. The moderate nationalist Social Democratic and Labour Party (SDLP) accepted a seat on the new commission, while expressing concern that the RUC could appeal against its decisions.

Despite some significant anti-terrorist security successes in the first quarter, the shooting of a woman police officer in Londonderry on 10 April highlighted the continuing IRA threat. Two weeks later the *Belfast Telegraph* claimed that a *de facto* IRA ceasefire existed in Northern Ireland, although it was clear that the British mainland was not included. Before and after Easter the IRA carried out a major campaign of transport and other disruption on the mainland, by planting some small bombs and by telephoning warnings of non-existent bombs. By 29 April there had been eight days of severe dislocation, including the postponement of the Grand National horse race at Aintree because of an IRA bomb threat (see also XVII: Sport).

A record number of 125 candidates contested the 18 Northern Ireland seats—one more than in 1992—in the UK general elections on 1 May. A major focus of the campaign was competition between the SDLP and Sinn Féin for the Catholic nationalist vote, the SDLP leader, John Hume, having earlier rebuffed a Sinn Féin offer of an electoral alliance. In a turnout that declined to 67.3 per cent, the aggregate nationalist share of 40.2 per cent (317,736 votes) was the highest ever. Sinn Féin polled its highest popular vote in modern elections (126,921, or 16.1 per cent) and replaced the Democratic Unionists (DUP) as the third largest party. Sinn Féin president Gerry Adams recaptured the West Belfast seat he had held in 1983–92, while Martin McGuinness (vice-president) took the hotly-contested Mid Ulster seat from the DUP. The

SDLP also registered its highest-ever vote (190,815, or 24.1 per cent), although its Commons representation fell from four to three seats.

On the unionist side, the main Ulster Unionist Party (UUP), led by David Trimble, maintained its relative ascendancy among Protestant voters, increasing its seat tally from nine to ten, although its share of the vote fell slightly from 34.5 per cent in 1992 to 32.7 per cent (258,349 votes). The hardline DUP led by Dr Ian Paisley slipped from 13.1 to 12.3 per cent (107,348 votes) and its representation from three seats to two, while the independent UK Unionist, Robert McCartney, retained the North Down seat he had won in a 1995 by-election. The non-sectarian Alliance Party (with 8 per cent of the vote) again failed to win a seat, although its leader, Lord (John) Alderdice, was now a life peer in the upper chamber at Westminster.

Adhering to Sinn Féin's 'abstentionist' policy, Mr Adams and Mr McGuinness subsequently declined to swear an oath of allegiance to the crown and were therefore disqualified from taking their seats. An attempt by the two MPs to obtain office and other facilities at Westminster was rebuffed on 14 May by Speaker Boothroyd.

The landslide election victory of the Labour Party on 1 May changed the Northern Ireland political landscape greatly, not least in that Dr Marjorie (Mo) Mowlam was appointed by incoming Prime Minister Blair to head the Labour team of ministers for the province. The first deaths under the new administration—the murder of an RUC man on 10 May, claimed by Irish National Liberation Army (INLA), and of a Catholic from Bellaghy on 13 May, attributed to the Loyalist Volunteer Force (LVF), occurred even before the Queen's Speech. Delivered on 14 May, the speech recorded the government's commitment to 'seek reconciliation and a political settlement which has broad support, working in cooperation with the Irish government'. The tone of the new administration was set by Mr Blair on a visit to Belfast on 16 May, during which he laid emphasis on the principle of consent and said that his agenda was 'not a united Ireland'.

District council elections on 21 May confirmed the relative party positions in the general election. Sinn Féin confirmed its status as the third-largest party, depriving the SDLP of overall control in Londonderry and the Unionists of control in Strabane, Cookstown and Belfast. Fermanagh joined Dungannon in having no overall control, while Belfast gained its first-ever Catholic lord mayor in the person of Alban Maginness of the SDLP. As a result of the poll, only two of the 26 councils were controlled by single parties. Also significant for Northern Ireland was the general election in the Republic on 6 June (see II.1.vii) and the change of government to a Fianna Fáil/Progressive Democrat coalition under Bertie Ahern, who regarded himself as a spokesman for Northern nationalists.

On a visit to London in late May, President Clinton gave full support to the Blair government's approach, condemning the mentality which said 'we'll talk when we're happy and shoot when we're not'. However, hopes of a speedy post-election IRA ceasefire were dashed by the shooting dead of two RUC officers by the IRA in Lurgan on 16 June and by an attack on the RUC in North Belfast on 27 June. The government responded by deciding that the LVF and the Continuity Army Council (an IRA breakaway faction) should be added to the list of banned organizations.

Joint British and Irish proposals on arms decommissioning were presented to the talks plenary on 24 June. They envisaged a parallel process of talks and decommissioning, the latter process to be supervised by an international commission. The next day Mr Blair set the time-frame for substantive talks to begin on 15 September and to be completed in May 1998. He also detailed recent contacts with Sinn Féin at the level of officials, seeking to dispel unionist unease that these were amounting to separate negotiations. Nevertheless, the DUP claimed that the proposals had been agreed in advance with Sinn Féin, while the UUP wrote to Mr Blair that it had 'serious problems' with them.

The problem of contentious parades dominated the agenda from the last week in June, as Dr Mowlam strove to defuse possible further violence by convening proximity talks at Hillsborough Castle. The delicate problem was compounded by a visit by Mr Ahern to sensitive areas in the North, during which he enraged unionists by backing Catholic residents' opposition to Orange marches through nationalist areas. He made some amends at his first meeting with Mr Blair on 3 July, when he went out of his way to praise the efforts of Dr Mowlam to avert a repeat of the 1996 Drumcree confrontation near Portadown (see AR 1996, p. 40). For their part, the mainstream unionists strongly condemned an LVF threat to take revenge on civilians in the Republic if the Drumcree parade was banned.

Dr Mowlam saw both sides separately on 4 July, after troops and police had put a ring of steel around Portadown the previous evening. The decision late the following day to permit the Orangemen to march to a Protestant church in Drumcree sparked five days of serious violence throughout nationalist areas, at an estimated cost of £10 million in damage. With nationalist attitudes hardening towards other Orange parades scheduled for 12 July (anniversary of the 1690 Battle of the Boyne), some 400 extra British troops were flown in to support the RUC, amid every appearance of a looming major crisis. Late on 10 July, however, the Orange Order suddenly announced that four contentious parades would be cancelled or relocated, thus pulling an ominous situation back from the brink and enabling the main parades to pass off peacefully.

The full text of the decommissioning document was placed before the talks on 16 July. When only one question was permitted about what previously had been described as 'proposals', the DUP and the UK Unionists walked out of the talks. The UUP was also unhappy, especially when a government letter to Sinn Féin on 9 July did not require decommissioning during talks but only 'due progress'. In contrast, the changes, especially on decommissioning, were welcomed by Mr Hume and Mr Adams, who said in a joint statement on 17 July that 'considerable progress' had been made towards restoring the peace process.

On 19 July the IRA suddenly announced the 'unequivocal restoration' of its August 1994 ceasefire, calling 'a complete cessation of military operations from 12 mid-day Sunday 20 July 1997'. Since restoration of the ceasefire was the sole condition for Sinn Féin entry into talks, the party was able to take up office accommodation at Stormont Castle two days later and to begin meeting other delegations and the Irish government. However, strong criticism of the ceasefire was expressed by hardline republican groups, while the unionist parties generally portrayed the cessation as another tactical ploy.

Whereas the UDP and the PUP were content with the government's proposals on decommissioning, both the DUP and the UK Unionists withdrew from the talks on 21 July in protest against what they saw as a surrender to the IRA. At a meeting with Mr Blair the following day, the DUP proposed a new talks format, but without success. For the UUP, Mr Trimble accused the government of 'duplicity' and of giving 'secret promises' to Sinn Féin, pointing out that Mr McGuinness had interpreted the decommissioning proposals as meaning that 'not one bullet' had to be surrendered. Nevertheless, although the participating unionist parties rejected the decommissioning paper on 23 July, Mr Trimble said that the UUP would not walk out of the talks but would engage in consultations during the summer. In contrast to the unionist disunity, Mr Ahern, Mr Hume and Mr Adams met in Dublin on 25 July and expressed joint satisfaction at the terms of Sinn Féin's re-entry into the peace process.

Continuity IRA bombs, an LVF riot in the Maze prison and attacks on prison officers' homes served to maintain a tense situation during the summer political recess, the IRA ceasefire notwithstanding. Nevertheless, there were signs of reductions in the level of official security, and from 11 August army patrols in Belfast wore regimental berets instead of helmets. On 29 August the UK government published a reasoned justification for the readmission of Sinn Féin into the peace process, at the same time issuing formal invitations to talks the following month. The main uncertainty at this stage was whether the UUP would participate, after its consultations with, among others, the Catholic Primate.

Sinn Féin signed the Mitchell Principles on 9 September, although a senior IRA figure, in an interview published in *An Phoblacht* two days later, fuelled unionist suspicions by asserting that the 'IRA would have problems' with sections of the document. After the UUP executive had on 13 September left tactics to Mr Trimble and his team, the UK and Irish Prime Ministers sought to ensure UUP participation by issuing a joint statement on consent and decommissioning. After further intensive exchanges, the UUP and the small loyalist parties entered the talks on 17 September, two days after they had formally commenced under the chairmanship of Senator George Mitchell (USA). Even then, the UUP sought the expulsion of Sinn Féin on the basis of the *An Phoblacht* interview, but this demand was rejected by the British and Irish governments.

The UUP's decision to join the peace talks brought criticism not only from Dr Paisley, who claimed that Mr Trimble was in breach of his party's electoral mandate, but also from the UK Unionists and from elements within the UUP itself, notably William Thompson MP. The DUP leader and Mr McCartney proceeded to arrange a series of public meetings throughout Northern Ireland to explain their rejection of the peace process and its direction.

Within the talks, an agreement on 24 September to create two subcommittees, one on arms decommissioning and the other on confidence-building measures, enabled discussion to move away from procedural matters. It was subsequently confirmed that the international commission on decommissioning would be chaired by General John de Chastelain, a former chief of the Canadian defence staff. A complication when the talks resumed on 7 October was the resignation of the main Irish negotiator, Ray Burke, as the Republic's Foreign Minister, over a political donations scandal (see II.1.vii). His successor, David Andrews, became much sought-after for media interviews after telling the BBC on 10 October that a united Ireland would not be achievable within his lifetime. On 13 October Mr Blair visited Belfast to meet the parties at the talks, his encounter with Mr Adams, behind closed doors, being the UK government's first official contact with Sinn Féin since 1921.

Tensions within the participating loyalist parties with paramilitary connections were apparent when the PUP stayed away from a UDA-organized rally to mark the third anniversary of the loyalist ceasefire of 13 October 1994. On 23 October the Combined Loyalist Military Command (CLMC), which had called the ceasefire, was formally disbanded, reportedly because of divisions over the peace process. Strains were also apparent within the republican movement, impelling Mr McGuinness to tell a Sinn Féin rally in Coalisland on 5 October that the party was going to the negotiating table to 'smash the union', not to accept any version of the status quo. The Chief Constable's assessment was that the IRA ceasefire was holding firm, but he pointed to the Continuity IRA, the INLA and the LVF as major threats to peace. On 6 November the *Irish Independent* broke the story of a split in the IRA in County Louth, while six days later the *Irish Times* claimed that 35 members from a key South Armagh battalion had broken away in opposition to the peace process. Despite IRA denials of a split published in *An Phoblacht* on 14 November, the ceasefire seemed less secure.

Despite the continuing uncertainties, Dr Mowlam made a point of presenting Northern Ireland as 'edging towards normality'. By mid-November the Parachute Regiment had reportedly been withdrawn from north Belfast; patrolling in republican areas had been cut; and military patrols no longer occurred in Belfast city centre and the markets area, nor in Londonderry and Newry. On 21 November 250 paratroops were pictured leaving the province, while on 26 November troops were withdrawn from republican west Belfast in what was described as 'a calculated risk'. Republicans responded to these steps by urging the complete demilitarization of Northern Ireland and the release of 'political prisoners'.

A meeting between Mr Trimble and Prime Minister Ahern on 20 November, at a secret location in London, seemed to improve relations between Dublin and the unionists. However, when Mr Andrews told Radio Ulster on 29 November that future cross-border bodies would have a secretariat with 'strong executive functions not unlike a government', all unionists parties (and the Alliance Party) reacted negatively. Although Mr Ahern sought to repair the damage by stating that his Foreign Minister had gone beyond the Irish government's 'own line', unionist doubts about the peace process were reinforced. Efforts by Senator Mitchell to establish the substantive content of the talks made some progress in December, but no comprehensive agenda had been agreed when the process was adjourned for Christmas.

It was nevertheless clear that relations between London and Dublin were good and that the two governments were determined to drive the process forward. Reform of the RUC, the Emergency Provisions Act and parades legislation were all presented as part of the agenda for change. By this stage, however, many unionists were convinced that the two governments would do anything to maintain the IRA ceasefire and to keep Sinn Féin in the talks, such concerns being communicated to Mr Trimble by four Unionist MPs on 22 December. The following day, morever, loyalist prisoners issued a formal warning that they would review their support for talks after Christmas because of what they saw as their republican agenda.

In this volatile atmosphere, INLA prisoners in the Maze on 27 December shot dead the LVF leader, Billy Wright, who was also an inmate. The fact that the assassins had acquired two guns brought security at the prison—already an issue since the escape of a republican prisoner on 11 December—under further intense scrutiny, as the UUP called for the resignation Dr Mowlam and her prisons advisers. In the inevitable retaliation, the LVF claimed responsibility for the murder of a Catholic on 28 December near Dungannon, while the INLA warned of further attacks on prominent loyalists. Another killing on 31 December, bringing the 1997 death total to 20, added to the sense of regression, amid unassuaged unionist doubts about the viability of the peace process.

The Northern Ireland economy continued to expand for most of 1997. With GDP growing by 3.1 per cent (and manufacturing output by 4.6 per cent), unemployment continued to fall, by 14,100 over the year, to a December total of 60,200 (7.8 per cent). One result of the economic progress was the lowest number of bankruptcies and liquidations for five years—465 compared with 557 in 1996, a fall of 16.5 per cent—the main casualties being in services and retailing. The most exposed sector was again agriculture, where the restrictions on beef exports, limited intervention and the high value of the pound sterling seriously affected farm incomes. The strong pound also impacted negatively on exporters and their employment levels. Despite the progress achieved in 1997, Coopers & Lybrand warned that reduced public spending would slow growth and that there was a danger of recession locally.

II WESTERN AND SOUTHERN EUROPE

1. GERMANY—FRANCE—ITALY—BELGIUM—THE NETHERLANDS—LUXEMBOURG—IRELAND

i. GERMANY

CAPITAL: Berlin   AREA: 357,000 sq km   POPULATION: 82,000,000 ('96)
OFFICIAL LANGUAGE: German
POLITICAL SYSTEM: federal parliamentary democracy
HEAD OF STATE: President Roman Herzog (since July '94)
RULING PARTIES: Christian Democratic Union (CDU), Christian Social Union (CSU) & Free Democratic Party (FDP)
HEAD OF GOVERNMENT: Helmut Kohl (CDU), Federal Chancellor (since Oct '82)
MAIN IGO MEMBERSHIPS (non-UN): NATO, EU, WEU, OSCE, CE, CBSS, AC, OECD, G-7
CURRENCY: Deutsche Mark (end-'97 £1=DM2.96, US$1=DM1.80)
GNP PER CAPITA: US$27,510 ('95) or US$20,070 ('95) by PPP calculation

GERMAN politics were dominated in 1997 by economic matters, as the government attempted to overhaul the country's complex tax system and to qualify for membership of the European economic and monetary union (EMU), involving a single European currency, against a background of rising unemployment.

Announcing what he described as the most sweeping tax reform for 50 years, Finance Minister Theo Waigel said in January that from January 1999 the government wanted to cut the top and bottom rates of income tax from 53 and 25.9 per cent to 39 per cent and 15 per cent respectively. Corporation tax would be cut in 1998 from 47 to 35 per cent and the solidarity surcharge (the tax added to income and corporation tax to help finance eastern Germany) was to be reduced 2 points to 5.5 per cent. Herr Waigel said that some of the consequent loss of revenue of more than DM80,000 million per year would be offset by the abolition of a wide range of tax concessions, the taxation of certain overtime earnings for the first time and the taxation of some pensions and life insurance policies.

Although the reforms were passed by the *Bundestag* (lower house of the bicameral federal parliament) in late June, on 4 July the opposition-dominated *Bundesrat* (upper house) rejected them. The Social Democratic Party (SPD) described the plans as 'fiscally unsolid, socially unbalanced and economically off-target'. The government made repeated attempts during the remainder of 1997 to reach a compromise with the opposition. However, with no real prospect of reaching an agreement, in late 1997 it effectively abandoned the principal elements of the tax reform package until after the September 1998 elections.

On 15 May Herr Waigel announced controversial plans to use the country's gold and foreign exchange reserves to support deteriorating public finances and allow Germany to qualify for EMU from the planned starting-date of 1 January 1999. Under the plans, the reserves would be revalued and the resulting profits used to reduce federal government debt, ensuring that it remained below 60 per cent of GDP as specified by the Maastricht EMU criteria. The announcement provoked a storm of anger. Opposition demands for Herr Waigel's resignation were supported by economic experts and by much of the normally supportive press. The SPD accused the government of bringing the euro (the European single currency) into disrepute. In an unprecedented move, on 28 May the Bundesbank rejected the revaluation plan. Otmar Issing, the bank's chief economist, said that the government was in a desperate situation of its own making, accused it of creative accounting and warned that the scheme threatened the independence of the bank.

With opposition calls for Herr Waigel's resignation growing, on 3 June Finance Ministry officials announced that the government and Bundesbank had agreed that the revaluation of the reserves would still take place but that the proceeds would not be transferred to the government until 1998, too late to help Germany to qualify for EMU. In spite of the government's reversal, the opposition SPD pressed ahead with its motion of no confidence in Herr Waigel. Although the beleaguered Finance Minister survived the vote by a margin of 17 votes (328 to 311), many believed that the government had been badly damaged by the whole affair.

Figures for February released on 6 March indicated that headline unemployment had reached a post-war record high of 4,670,000, or 12.2 per cent of the labour force. The rise prompted trade union leaders to demand a delay in the 1999 launch of the single currency unless major job-creation elements were introduced into the revised Maastricht Treaty. Union concern increased on 7 March when the government announced plans to reduce coal subsidies to DM5,500 million by 2005. The cut, which would result in the closure of ten of the country's 19 pits over that period and the loss of 50,000 mining jobs, was intended to keep Germany on course for the EMU public-spending targets, and was met with predictable fury. Miners in all western German pits went on strike immediately the plans became known. The protests soon reached Bonn, where miners and their supporters blockaded the headquarters of the ruling Christian Democratic Union (CDU) and Free Democrats (FDP) and blocked access to roads and motorways. By 11 March 20,000 miners were involved in an effective siege of Bonn, paralysing the city. After order had been restored in the city on 12 March, as the miners withdrew to Cologne, intensive negotiations between mining unions and the government resulted in a compromise deal hailed as a victory by the miners. Although subsidies would still be reduced over the following eight years, the phasing of the cuts was changed so that only one pit would be closed by the end of the century. Moreover, although 46,000 jobs would eventually go, most of the losses would come through early retirement and retraining schemes.

Although the miners were placated, at least temporarily, unemployment continued to increase month by month. As the year ended, fears grew that seasonally-adjusted unemployment could reach a peak of 5 million by the end of winter, dealing a serious blow to Chancellor Kohl's re-election chances. On 3 April, during a television interview to mark his 67th birthday, Herr Kohl had ended months of speculation when he announced that he would seek an unprecedented fifth term in the 1998 general elections. The Chancellor, who was already Germany's longest-serving post-war head of government, having come into office in October 1982, made it clear that he wanted to oversee the introduction of the planned European single currency, further EU integration and the eastern expansion of NATO. In a further important announcement in October, Herr Kohl ended 15 years of equivocation when, for the first time, he confirmed the position of Wolfgang Schäuble, the CDU parliamentary leader, as his heir apparent. The well-respected Herr Schäuble, confined to a wheelchair since a 1990 assassination attempt, was 12 years Herr Kohl's junior. He was regarded by the SPD as a formidable opponent, while many disaffected elements within the CDU believed that under his leadership the party would stand a better chance of retaining power than under Herr Kohl.

Marcus Wolf (74), the former head of the East German secret police (Stasi), was found guilty of abduction and assault on 27 May, the charges relating to his conduct under the old East German regime. He was given a two-year suspended sentence and ordered to donate DM50,000 to charity. The presiding judge made clear that Herr Wolf, who had run the East German foreign intelligence network for 33 years, had been tried for criminal, not political, offences. Herr Wolf had been found guilty of treason in 1993, but the conviction had been overturned in 1995. In another echo from the past, the former East German head of state, Egon Krenz (60), was sentenced to six-and-a-half years imprisonment on 25 August for the deaths of people shot while trying to flee over the Berlin Wall. Herr Krenz and two other former East German Socialist Unity Party (SED) politburo members had been convicted on four specimen counts of manslaughter. The Berlin court found that, while Herr Krenz had not actually shot the victims, he had shaped the shoot-to-kill orders.

In a report published on 3 July, Amnesty International reported a 'worrying pattern' of brutality among the German police. Amnesty said that officers were often motivated by racism and that since its previous report in 1995 there had been more than 40 fresh allegations of ill-treatment by the police. This was seen as confirming the organization's 1995 conclusion that cases of police ill-treatment were not 'isolated incidents' but amounted to 'a clear pattern of abuse'. Almost concurrently, Defence Minister Volker Rühe pledged on 6 July to punish soldiers who had been involved in staging mock executions and rapes in a privately-made video. Shocking photographs from the film, made at a military training centre in April 1996, had been published in *Bild am Sonntag,* and the tape was later broadcast on television. Herr Rühe was forced to act again in December after a series of damaging press reports linking well-known neo-Nazi Manfred Röder with the military. The Röder revelations came a week after the announcement of disciplinary procedures against six paratroopers who had unfurled pre-war military banners and pinned up pictures of Hitler during a barracks drinking session.

Relations between Germany and the United States were strained during 1997 as a result of Germany's attitude to the US-based Church of Scientology. In its annual survey of global human rights published in January, the US State Department accused the German government of operating a 'campaign of harassment and intimidation' against the Church of Scientology. The issue had already come to public attention after 34 high-profile US actors, film directors and producers and authors accused the German government of discriminating against the group, likening the plight of Scientologists to that suffered by Jews under Nazi Germany. The accusation was published as an open letter to Chancellor Kohl in a full-page advertisement in the *International Herald Tribune* on 9 January, the signatories including Dustin Hoffman, Oliver Stone and Gore Vidal. The letter claimed that Scientologists were banned from German political parties and excluded from jobs in public service, also that their children were expelled from schools. Observers noted that there was some truth in the accusations: German political parties had supported moves to curb the activities of the group on the grounds that it was not founded on religious principles, while in some conservative *Länder* Scientologists were barred from public employment. On 6 June the Interior Ministry announced that it was placing the Church of Scientology under nationwide observation by federal and state counter-intelligence agents on the grounds that sufficient suspicion existed of the anti-democratic intent of the group. A legal challenge to the decision by the organization was rejected in December.

ii. FRANCE

CAPITAL: Paris   AREA: 544,000 sq km   POPULATION: 58,370,000 ('96)
OFFICIAL LANGUAGE: French
POLITICAL SYSTEM: presidential parliamentary democracy
RULING PARTIES: Rally for the Republic (RPR) holds presidency; Socialist Party (PS), French Communist Party (PCF), Greens and other groups form government
HEAD OF STATE & GOVERNMENT: President Jacques Chirac (RPR), since May '95
PRIME MINISTER: Lionel Jospin (PS), since June '97
MAIN IGO MEMBERSHIPS (non-UN): NATO, EU, WEU, OSCE, CE, OECD, G-7, Francophonie
CURRENCY: franc (end-'97 £1=F9.90, US$1=F6.04)
GNP PER CAPITA: US$24,990 ('95) or US$21,030 ('95) by PPP calculation

THE year began inauspiciously. Though it had embarked on many reforms, the government of Alain Juppé had failed to reduce unemployment and the economy had been hard hit by a recent lorry drivers' strike (see AR 1996, p. 47). In addition, the government was dogged by an aura of corruption, featuring a continuing trickle of accusations and trials involving senior politicians, leading businessmen and the president of a national television network. Yet no party emerged unscathed: April brought fresh revelations about phone-tapping during the Mitterrand presidency. Documentation on hundreds of illegal taps by his 'black cell' came to light in a suburban garage, before being spirited from view under the cloak of national security. In the autumn, moreover, the conviction of a former Socialist minister and chairman of the Assembly's finance committee for offences relating to party finance sent a shiver through the whole political class.

President Jacques Chirac was repeatedly urged to drop the deeply unpopular M. Juppé, who was contested within his nominally massive majority as well as by the official opposition. In February the Prime Minister's Rally for the Republic (RPR) did badly in a crucial municipal election in Vitrolles (near Marseille), even though the former National Front (FN) mayor had been barred from standing for breaking election law and the former Socialist mayor had been accused of misusing municipal funds. Despite PS calls for anti-FN unity, the outcome was that the FN candidate, Catherine Mégret, was elected mayor with 52.5 per cent of the second-round vote.

One legacy of the 1996 truckers' strike was the heightened expectations of other groups. In January and February transport workers staged one-day strikes for a cut in the working week from 39 to 35 hours (without loss of pay) and for retirement on full pension at 55. For good measure, bus and Paris metro workers demanded a 32-hour week. The government was also wrestling with the perpetually thorny issue of immigration. In February, its proposals sparked leftwing protests, fanned by a dawn raid by police on a Paris church where some 200 illegal immigrants had taken refuge. While 100,000 people demonstrated in Paris, provincial rallies were less well supported. The parties of the left were slow to commit themselves whole-heartedly to the cause, sensing that the public, linking immigration with unemployment and crime, favoured tougher measures and was hostile to legitimizing immigrants currently outside the law. Many government backbenchers echoed such criticism, not least because they feared losing support to the National Front.

Renault's decision in March to shed jobs in France and close its main plant in Belgium created further controversy. There were also strikes and demonstrations against the pegging of health expenditure at only 1.7 per cent above 1996 levels. Yet March also brought hints that the economy was picking up: trade was booming and interest rates were the lowest for 35 years. Although unemployment remained stubbornly high, the rate of rise was slowing. There was even an improvement in M. Chirac's and M. Juppé's dismal popularity. Talk of dumping the Prime Minister evaporated, for the time being. In April, however, a leaked Finance Ministry memorandum predicted budget deficits of 3.8 per cent in 1997 and 4.5 per cent in 1998. Without corrective action, France would therefore be unable to join in EU economic and monetary union (EMU) and the launching of a single European currency in 1999.

Although the government parties held 80 per cent of the seats in the Assembly, their ranks were so riven by policy divisions and personal feuds that President Chirac called an election for May-June to allow the people to 'express themselves clearly on the scale and pace of change over the next five years'. The government, he said, was seeking support for unspecified measures to strengthen the economy, improve social conditions and strengthen his hand in Europe.

It appeared that the President was prepared to lose up to 150 seats in order to achieve a more disciplined, if greatly reduced, majority. Even though the left seemed disorganized and roused little enthusiasm, this was an astonishing gamble. M. Juppé promised tax cuts and lower social security charges, but his hand was weakened by hints from the Elysée Palace that he would be dropped after the election. The Socialists hastily negotiated joint candidacies with the Greens and Radical-Socialists in over 100 seats and a looser agreement with the Communists. Their leader, Lionel Jospin, took a critical line on the single currency, pressed for 'a more social Europe' and promised to create 700,000 state-subsidized jobs for young people and to introduce a 35-hour working week without loss of pay.

A record 6,300 candidates stood (compared with 5,169 in 1993), partly because of new election subsidies. But even this wealth of choice failed to enthuse many voters. A third stayed at home, while many of those who did vote backed minor or fringe parties. President Chirac's gamble failed. After heavy setbacks for the centre-right in the first ballot on 25 May, M. Juppé announced that he would resign after the second ballot, irrespective of the outcome. This effectively left the government parties to face the run-off balloting without a leader or a clear policy direction.

Unsurprisingly, in the second ballot on 1 June the mainstream centre-right suffered its worst defeat under the Fifth Republic, as the left emerged victorious on a scale that no-one could have imagined only a few weeks earlier. In fact, a majority of first-ballot votes had supported one or other of the centre-right and right-wing parties. However, the pariah status of the FN, and its decision to maintain candidates even where this would hand victory to the left, contrasted sharply with the readiness of left-wing voters to 'vote usefully' in the second round. Thus was the victory of the left ensured. M. Chirac, whose failure to honour his 1995 presidential campaign pledges had been a major factor in the government's defeat, now had to call on M. Jospin to form a government and to accept the much-diminished status of a 'cohabiting' president. The official results of the election were as follows (comparable 1993 figures in parentheses):

	Seats	First round %
Socialist Party	241 (54)	23.4 (17.6)
Rally for the Republic	134 (247)	15.7 (20.4)
National Front	1 (0)	14.9 (12.4)
Union for French Democracy	108 (213)	14.2 (19.1)
French Communist Party	38 (23)	9.9 (9.2)
Greens	7 (0)	6.8 (4.0)
Radical Socialists	12 (–)	1.4 (–)
Other Right	14 (24)	6.6 (4.9)
Other Left	21 (16)	2.8 (3.6)
Other Extreme Left	0 (0)	2.5 (–)
Other Extreme Right	0 (0)	0.1 (–)
Independents	1 (0)	1.1 (–)
Total	577 (577)	

With only 15 senior and 12 other ministers, the new government was the smallest for many years. Comprising 19 Socialists, three Communists, 3 Radical Socialists, one Citizens' Movement member and one Green, it included eight women, five at senior level. It moved quickly to increase the minimum wage by 4 per cent (disappointing many supporters), to close the technically-troubled Super-Phénix fast-breeder reactor near Grenoble, and to abandon the widening of the Rhine-Rhône canal. It promised a million new subsidized homes over five years and the renovation of 100,000 others, an ending of ministerial interference in judicial proceedings, an independent authority to oversee phone-tapping, and the granting of residence papers to up to 40,000 unauthorized immigrants.

Hard decisions were needed if France was to qualify for the single European currency. The autumn budget imposed F32,000 million in additional taxation, mostly on companies, though motorists and wealthier households would also pay more. Government expenditure would fall fractionally in real terms, with less for defence and more for education, employment, health and welfare. The 1998 deficit would be down to 3.0 per cent, meeting a key Maastricht criterion—albeit at the cost, critics complained, of damaging industry's competitiveness. Proposals for introducing the 35-hour week proved highly controversial. Ministers were divided but felt bound to try to honour their election commitment. Negotiations with the employers broke down, however, and the head of their national organization was replaced by a hardliner committed to all-out opposition. There was less opposition to a scheme to create 350,000 new public-sector jobs and to encourage employers to take on young workers. Nevertheless, even with an 80 per cent subsidy, the response from the private sector was poor.

Notwithstanding earlier left-wing opposition to privatization, the Jospin government went ahead with a highly successful sale of a 20 per cent stake in France-Télécom. Privatization of the troubled GAN-CIC banking/insurance group was also to proceed, as a condition of EU approval of a F20,000 million recapitalization plan. The new government also agreed to sell off the defence manufacturing group Thomson-CSF, while retaining a 33 per cent controlling interest. On the other hand, Communist opposition blocked the privatization of Air France, whose president resigned. The unhappy saga of Crédit Lyonnais, the nationalized bank with debts of anything up to F170,000 million, was still unresolved after three rescue packages.

A new Immigration Bill angered not only the left, by failing to repeal earlier legislation outright, but also the right, by allowing more immigrants to remain. However, the government won credit in November for its speedy settlement of a truckers' strike sparked by frustration at the failure to honour fully the 1996 settlement.

In the party political arena, there was a changing of the guard. The outgoing Prime Minister, M. Juppé, was replaced as chairman of the RPR by Philippe Séguin, while François Léotard became leader of the Union for French Democracy (UDF), sidelining former President Valéry Giscard d'Estaing. However, the right remained as divided as ever about how to meet the challenge from the National Front. M. Jospin, who had earlier contemplated abandoning politics, was now seen as an effective and relatively popular leader, fully in command of his party at its November congress. With the Maastricht targets within sight, inflation at

1.2 per cent, real incomes rising, GDP about 2.7 per cent up on 1996 and unemployment, while appallingly high at 12.2 per cent, slightly down from its peak, there seemed to be grounds for quiet economic optimism, for the moment at least.

Apologies became the fashion. The Communist Party apologized to former officials who had been expelled for denouncing Stalin's crimes. And at a ceremony at Drancy, site of a wartime deportation camp, French bishops read a message of repentance to French Jews for the Church's behaviour during the war. The FN leader, Jean-Marie Le Pen, denounced this action as 'scandalous'. He was later fined heavily for reiterating that the Holocaust was a mere 'detail' of history. Something of the nature of that 'detail' emerged in the long-delayed trial of Maurice Papon on charges of crimes against humanity when he was a senior Vichy official involved in the deportation of Jews to the death camps. Not only M. Papon, but also France as a whole, were thus confronted with further evidence of some of the more painful episodes in recent French history.

The principal focuses of external policy were Europe and Africa. In January troop reinforcements were dispatched to the Central African Republic following fighting between French troops and local mutineers (see also VI.3.ii). Having failed to get agreement on the sending of a multinational force to Zaïre to halt the anti-Mobutu rebellion, France was accused of attempting to engineer a coup to forestall the rebel victory (see VII.1.i). Years of supporting President Mobutu ended in humiliation. M. Jospin condemned earlier French policy in Africa as 'a combination of interference and ignorance'. While sharing its predecessors' fear of anglophone 'hegemony' in Africa, the new government announced cuts of 40 per cent in French troops deployed in Africa (involving the closure of two bases) and also called for the closure of the President's 'Africa cell'. In response, President Chirac accepted that Africa could no longer be a presidential 'reserved area' and told French ambassadors that interference in Africa must stop. However, the scale of French interests in countries such as Congo (Brazzaville) made total disengagement difficult. In the worst crisis of all, in Algeria (see V.4.iv), the policy of public anguish and tacit support for the Algiers government continued.

There were other tensions between the President and the new government in the foreign affairs and defence arenas. M. Jospin criticized the President's 'lack of combativeness' at the Denver G-7 and Amsterdam EU summits. However, the Prime Minister rapidly modified the Euro-sceptical tone of his election campaign and accepted the Treaty of Amsterdam, stability pact and all (see also XI.3). Relations with Bonn were initially difficult over French advocacy of ambitious EU employment policies. They eased once the German government was persuaded that France was committed to EMU and the concomitant constraints on public finance. Despite occasional disagreements, the relationship with Germany remained the focal point of external policy. On most issues, including French insistence on conditions for rejoining the command structure of NATO, the broad consensus on foreign policy was unaffected by the change of government. In September President Chirac accepted that he and M. Jospin must 'act in concert' on foreign affairs and defence, while insisting that he should have the last word if there were disagreement. However, the appointment as Foreign Minister of Hubert Védrine, a veteran of an earlier 'cohabitation' government and a strong supporter of the euro, meant that this perception of the relationship between President and government was not seriously tested in the latter part of the year.

iii. ITALY

CAPITAL: Rome   AREA: 301,000 sq km   POPULATION: 57,400,000 ('96)
OFFICIAL LANGUAGE: Italian
POLITICAL SYSTEM: parliamentary democracy
HEAD OF STATE: President Oscar Luigi Scalfaro (since May '92)
RULING PARTIES: Olive Tree coalition
HEAD OF GOVERNMENT: Romano Prodi, Prime Minister (since June '96)
MAIN IGO MEMBERSHIPS (non-UN): NATO, EU, WEU, OSCE, CE, CEI, OECD, G-7
CURRENCY: lira (end-'97 £1=Lit2,908.47, US$1=Lit1,772.70)
GNP PER CAPITA: US$19,020 ('95) or US$19,870 ('95) by PPP calculation

THE year was dominated by economic questions as the left-of-centre Olive Tree coalition, headed by Professor Romano Prodi, continued the battle to reduce the country's deficit in order to meet the Maastricht conditions for participation in European monetary union and the single currency. By December it was clear that Italy would achieve a deficit within 3 per cent of GNP in 1997. For much of the year, however, the matter had been in doubt.

In April the European Commission voiced scepticism about Italy's chances of meeting the target, and members of the government suspected that Chancellor Kohl of Germany wished to keep the country out of the first round. Opponents of Italian entry regarded methods such as the one-off Euro tax levied in 1996 (and to be refunded in part) as questionable; they also pointed out that the national debt remained at over 120 per cent of output, whereas Maastricht specified that it should stand at 60 per cent or less. Even the leading industrialist Cesare Romiti of Fiat and Foreign Minister Lamberto Dini wondered if the effort to fulfil the Maastricht criteria at the expense of all other considerations would not ultimately create more problems than it solved. Despite such doubts, the government remained committed to immediate participation in the single currency, for economic and political reasons as well as reasons of national prestige.

The government was assisted in its endeavours by a favourable economic situation. With the annual inflation rate falling to 1.5 per cent by December, the Bank of Italy was able to reduce the discount rate in stages to 5.5 per cent, the lowest since 1972. Moreover, the continuing relative weakness of the lira aided exports, while internal production and consumption remained buoyant, due in part to the financial inducements which the government offered to Italians to exchange their old motor vehicles for new ones. Also significant was the government's success in containing spending and introducing promptly a special package to correct a larger-than-predicted 1996 deficit. The latter included spending cuts, postponement of public-sector retirements, measures to combat tax evasion and the bringing forward of the payment date of some business taxes. Although the package was finally approved by parliament in May, neither industry nor the trade unions were happy with aspects of it. In March the unions held a large demonstration in Rome calling for more action on unemployment. In April the Confindustria employers' organization held, for the first time in its history, a series of rallies complaining about the tax burden faced by business and criticizing the government for its concessions to the left.

The most controversial issue remained welfare and pension reform. Italy's public debt was aggravated by one of the most generous pension systems in the world. Although both President Scalfaro and the leader of the Democratic Party of the Left (PDS), Massimo D'Alema, spoke of the need to tackle this question, the erosion of privileges and expectations proved to be difficult. Following various government initiatives on youth unemployment, negotiations with the unions began in July and reached what was hailed as an historic conclusion in November. The measures agreed included the abolition of public-sector pension privileges, raising the minimum retirement age from 1998, and introduction in 2002 (instead of the previously-agreed 2006) of a minimum pensionable age of 57. Manual workers were exempt from these innovations.

Before this outcome was reached, a serious breach occurred in the government's parliamentary majority, as Communist Refoundation (RC) threatened to withdraw its support, forcing Professor Prodi to hand in his resignation on 9 October. The RC had refused to accept the 1998 budget, which was to have included abolition of the option of retirement after 35 years of contributions (regardless of age). In addition, they were hostile to welfare reform and demanded redistribution of wealth and a reduction in the length of the working week. Under pressure from public opinion, RC eventually backed down and agreed to vote for the budget, and to sustain the Prodi ministry at least until the end of 1998, in return for government support for the introduction of a 35-hour week by the year 2000. This undertaking, from which small businesses would be exempt, horrified employers; but it meant that on 13 October the centre-left coalition was reborn.

Privatization remained a difficult issue. Previously it had been seen as necessary to render public enterprises economically viable and efficient, but actual progress had been slow due to the resistance of state managers and the lack of enthusiasm of some political forces of both right and left. In January the appointment of Guido Rossi, a former president of the Milan stock market's board of control, to the presidency of the telecommunications holding company STET was seen as a sign of renewed commitment to reform. Yet in April the European Commission expressed its dissatisfaction with the pace of both privatization and the liberalization of the telephone market. Events appeared to turn for the better when a Telecom Italia share launch—the first British-style privatization—persuaded 1.5 million Italians but few foreign investors to buy shares. However, in September Signor Rossi resigned, allegedly after having faced obstacles to his efforts to overhaul the management of Telecom and oust longstanding managers with political links.

This fuelled foreign speculation that Italian-style privatizations might not lead to the creation of genuinely independent companies.

While the balance in the area of economic reform was generally positive, political reform remained problematic. As president of the bicameral commission on institutional reform, Signor D'Alema emerged as a figure of stature. Although critics complained that some of the measures were incoherent and reflected political compromise, he received credit for winning the backing of the opposition for his commission's broad proposals. There was broad agreement, for example, over the proposal to give new powers to the regions (including the power to choose their own electoral system and form of government), turning Italy into a semi-federal system. An area of greater contention was the form of government that the Italian state itself would have. Signor D'Alema was known to prefer a strengthened prime minister combined with a two-round voting system. However, in the bicameral commission the Northern League decided, for tactical reasons of its own, to back the Freedom Pole's preferred alternative of a semi-presidential system. Under this scheme, the President would be elected directly and would have the power to dissolve parliament and to call referendums, although he (or she) would have to be nominated by politicians and would not have direct governmental responsibilities.

The issue of justice remained controversial following the long-running investigations into political corruption which had been launched by Milan magistrates in 1992. The inquiries had led to the downfall of the old political elite, many of whose members were tried and sentenced. The issue was included among the topics to be addressed by the bicameral commission at the insistence of the Freedom Pole. The main reason for this was the legal difficulties of the opposition Forza Italia leader, Silvio Berlusconi, who first received notification that he was under investigation in 1994, while he was still Prime Minister (see AR 1994, p. 62). The television mogul turned politician had always maintained his innocence of all charges, claiming that attempts to incriminate him were the result of a plot by left-wing judges. The position of the opposition, combined with the feeling among other politicians that it was time for the judges to reduce their profile and turn their attentions elsewhere, led to widespread support for proposals to reform the system of regulating judges. Although the bicameral commission in the end rejected proposals to separate the judiciary into investigative and judicial branches, it approved the separation of the Supreme Council of the Judiciary into two sections, a move which was seen by critics as a premise of the former and therefore the source of a potential attack on the independence of judges.

Antonio Di Pietro, the former magistrate who symbolized the Milan investigations, was vociferous in his criticism of the commission's proposals. Still a widely-admired figure despite attempts to discredit him, he made a return to politics following his sudden resignation from government in 1996. Elected to a Senate seat in a Tuscany by-election, he pledged his loyalty to the Olive Tree alliance while also seeking to form a parliamentary group of his own. Thereafter Signor Di Pietro continued to make forceful defence of the activities of the Milan pool of judges in the face of continued criticism from Forza Italia. These reached a crescendo in December when Signor Berlusconi received his first conviction for the submission of falsified accounts (a charge which dated back to the 1980s) and when the judges forwarded to parliament a request for permission to arrest his former lawyer (and Defence Minister in the 1994 government), Cesare Previti, on charges of judicial corruption. Signor Berlusconi regarded these actions as a further instalment in the assault on his person and threatened to block the workings of the bicameral commission if Signor Previti's arrest was approved. At the end of the year parliament had still not voted on the matter.

In general it was not a happy year for the opposition parties. Despite tensions within the left—in particular between RC, the unions and the PDS—and some jostling for position by the small centre parties belonging to the coalition, the Olive Tree alliance maintained a high degree of support in the country. During the year two rounds of local elections were held. In April-May the right-wing Freedom Pole took the post of mayor of Milan from the Northern League, while the centre-left held Turin, Trieste and numerous smaller centres. In November left-of-centre mayors and city councils were re-elected with greatly increased majorities in Rome, Venice and Naples (where Antonio Bassolino scored a remarkable 73 per cent). Only in Palermo was the left-of-centre majority reduced. Although these victories were assisted by the right's failure to field heavyweight candidates, they were also seen as the result of good administration.

Seven referendums were held in June on issues ranging from the abolition of the state's golden share in privatized companies to the abolition of the Ministry of Agriculture. In keeping with a long-term downward trend in participation in such consultations, just 33 per cent of the electorate voted. As a result, the outcomes were invalid since the quorum of 50 per cent was not achieved.

Several international questions gave cause for concern, notably the Albanian internal crisis which exploded in March (see III.1.vii). By agreement with the Albanian government, Italian troops were sent to Albania to protect Italian citizens and airlift them to safety. In the absence of prompt European Union action, Foreign Minister Dini mediated between the Albanian government and the opposition and brokered an agreement to form a broad government, hold new elections and declare an amnesty. Although this intervention, motivated by fears of an exodus of refugees and more general geo-political considerations, reflected Italy's good standing with both sides, it bore little fruit since the signatories lacked credibility. This was demonstrated just a few days later when the Albanian regime collapsed and rebels entered Tirana, provoking the feared exodus to Italy. When the former Austrian Chancellor, Franz Vranitzky, was appointed special UN representative for Albania, Italy was forced to reflect ruefully that not only had it lacked the strength to impose its mediated solution but that it had failed to persuade its European partners of the gravity of the crisis or to gain backing for its attempt to manage it.

Italy was also involved in sustained diplomatic opposition to a reform of the United Nations which would have seen Germany and Japan join the Security Council as permanent members without right of veto (see XII.1). Fearful that this would reduce Italy to the status of a third-class power, Signor Dini led an alliance of medium-sized regional powers in seeking to block these moves. Conscious that no significant international posts were currently held by Italians, the government promoted the candidature of former Prime Minister Giuliano Amato for the presidency of either the European Commission or the imminent European Central Bank. Feelings of disquiet at the country's lack of influence increased when the 2004 Olympics were awarded to Athens despite a strong campaign in favour of Rome.

There was shock and dismay when allegations of murder, rape and torture by Italian soldiers in Somalia in the early 1990s appeared in the press in June. Launched by former soldiers who took part in the UN peace-keeping mission, the claims found apparent confirmation in the accounts of Somali eye-witnesses. Despite the protestations of the military authorities, a commission was set up under a prominent judge to investigate the allegations. In August the commission reported its findings that one case of torture and two of rape had occurred. It also found that the military command was ignorant of these facts and was therefore absolved of blame.

iv. BELGIUM

QCAPITAL: Brussels   AREA: 30,500 sq km   POPULATION: 10,100,000 ('96)
OFFICIAL LANGUAGES: French, Flemish & German
POLITICAL SYSTEM: federal parliamentary democracy based on language communities
HEAD OF STATE: King Albert II (since Aug '93)
RULING PARTIES: Christian People's Party (CVP/Flemish), Christian Social Party (PSC/Walloon), Socialist Party (SP/Flemish) & Socialist Party (PS/Walloon)
HEAD OF GOVERNMENT: Jean-Luc Dehaene (CVP), Prime Minister (since March '92)
MAIN IGO MEMBERSHIPS (non-UN): NATO, EU, WEU, Benelux, OSCE, CE, OECD, Francophonie
CURRENCY: Belgian franc (end-'97 £1=BF61.03, US$1=BF37.20)
GNP PER CAPITA: US$24,710 ('95) or US$21,660 ('95) by PPP calculation

THE coalition government's cohesion was shaken early in the year by public discontent about the high level of unemployment that had resulted largely from spending cuts intended to ensure that Belgium would qualify for the first wave of entry to the EU's single currency as part of economic and monetary union (EMU). To this was added undiminished public anger at the government's mishandling of the investigations into high-level corruption, and into the Dutroux paedophile murders. There were mass demonstrations in February at the closures of the Clabecq steel works and Renault's Vilvorde car plant, both resulting in large job losses.

In April, the atmosphere of political crisis was heightened when the parliamentary commission investigating the Dutroux scandal produced its report condemning major failures by the police and the judiciary which might have added to the number of children killed. The commission's recommendations for sweeping corrective action, including unifying the three separate police forces into a single entity, were at the time accepted by an embarrassed parliament. The legislature also found itself obliged to set up a further investigation into individual responsibilities for failures and into whether the accused had been protected by senior police officers and, possibly, judges.

Simultaneously, the government came under more pressure as the Walloon wing of the Socialist Party—a partner in the coalition—faced renewed police inquiries into the involvement of some of its senior officers in alleged bribery, years earlier, by the Dassault aircraft company in return for government contracts. Two senior members of the party were arrested in January, and in March Guy Spitaels, the party's former president, was indicted on bribery charges after his parliamentary immunity had been lifted. Though the Walloon Socialist Party's continuing role within the coalition government began to look problematic, the Prime Minister, Jean-Luc Dehaene, decided to make no changes, thus avoiding the need either to re-model the coalition or to call a general election.

In October the government announced a plan to merge only two of the three police forces, leaving the communal force under the control of local authorities. Public dissatisfaction at this and most other aspects of the official response to the paedophile scandal, and at the continuing defence industry bribery scandal, further eroded support for the coalition. The opposition Liberals and the Green parties were clear gainers, being seen as having clean hands and thus as credible partners in any new coalition.

Economically, 1997 was a good year. The public deficit was reduced as the austerity programme took effect, enabling Belgium to meet the Maastricht convergence criteria for EMU. Moreover, the pace of economic growth quickened as the year progressed. The strong trend in exports, particularly to the United States and Germany, boosted industrial production and took average capacity utilization in manufacturing to over 80 per cent. However, the construction sector was depressed, with building starts continuing to fall. Investment in machinery and equipment was encouraged by the high utilization rates of existing capacity. Retail sales were sluggish, falling in volume terms. The better trend in the main areas of the economy had still to be reflected in any fall in unemployment by the year-end, though the situation had ceased to worsen. Inflation was modest throughout the year, averaging under 2 per cent. Limited wage rises and some increase in industrial productivity helped to maintain cost competitiveness.

The year ended in an uneasy calm, with the government's popularity at a low ebb amid a general sense that necessary structural reforms were being deferred. The parliamentary opposition parties tacitly supported the government's relative quiescence and were careful to do nothing that might endanger Belgium becoming a founder member of the single European currency.

v. THE NETHERLANDS

CAPITAL: Amsterdam   AREA: 37,000 sq km   POPULATION: 15,520,000 ('96)
OFFICIAL LANGUAGE: Dutch POLITICAL SYSTEM: parliamentary democracy
HEAD OF STATE: Queen Beatrix (since April '80)
RULING PARTIES: Labour Party (PvdA), People's Party for Freedom and Democracy (VVD) &
  Democrats 66 (D66)
HEAD OF GOVERNMENT: Wim Kok (PvdA), Prime Minister (since Aug '94)
MAIN IGO MEMBERSHIPS (non-UN): NATO, EU, WEU, Benelux, OSCE, CE, OECD
CURRENCY: guilder (end-'97 £1=f3.34, US$1=f2.03)
GNP PER CAPITA: US$24,000 ('95) or US$19,950 ('95) by PPP calculation

BY May, with general elections only 12 months ahead, the political parties were manoeuvring to seek electoral advantage. The coalition parties—the Labour Party (PvdA), the right-of-centre Liberals and the centrist Democrats 66 (D66)—sought to differentiate their policies while at the same time maintaining a semblance of partnership. A significant development was the appointment of new leaders by the PvdA, by D66 and by the opposition Christian Democratic Appeal.

This was later followed by publication of the parties' election manifestos, none of which contained radical proposals and together were very similar on major issues. This concurrence reflected the parliamentary consensus of the coalition parties, which had very wide popular support, judging by public opinion polls.

Inter-party differences were more apparent on local issues, as was the case with official plans to merge a number of urban centres, together with their suburbs, into urban provinces. The cabinet proposed that Amsterdam, Rotterdam and The Hague should become urban provinces, and that the city boundaries of Eindhoven and Utrecht should be extended to incorporate outlying areas, with the cities of Hengelo and Enschede being merged. However, objections from the cities affected and from their members of parliament caused the government to modify its plans. On 21 May it was made clear that only the status of Rotterdam and Eindhoven would be changed.

In the second half of the year, immigration became an even more vexed issue when it was revealed that only 20 per cent of naturalized foreigners had surrendered their original nationality on acquiring Dutch citizenship. This was widely interpreted as showing lack of commitment to their new country and led to introduction in October of a requirement that existing nationality must be given up on becoming a Dutch citizen. There were also signs that official policy towards asylum seekers was hardening when 1,000 Iranian and 600 Somali asylum seekers were deported.

In May, the Netherlands was deemed by the EU Finance Ministers to have met the Maastricht convergence criteria by reducing its public deficit to below 3 per cent of GDP. The strong performance of the economy allowed the government to announce in September that the 1998 budget would provide for both cuts in personal income tax and increased public spending, while simultaneously reducing the ratio of deficit to GDP. Unsurprisingly, the budget was generally welcomed, though there were criticisms from the parliamentary opposition that the government had taken advantage of the favourable economic environment to avoid difficult decisions on institutional reform or infrastructure investment that might undermine the popularity of the coalition parties ahead of the general elections.

In the economy as a whole, economic growth accelerated in 1997, driven mainly by investment spending. Private consumption, though strong, showed a smaller increase even though surveys of consumer confidence yielded extremely buoyant results. Exports were affected by an epidemic of swine fever from February onwards, which had the effect of cutting 1997's GDP growth rate by 0.5 per cent when one-third of the 15 million pig population was slaughtered. Manufacturing production grew fast during the year, though lagging behind growth in investment and consumer demand. This caused an increase in inflationary pressure and a surge in prices towards the end of the year. Unemployment continued to fall, and led the main trade union federation to put in demands for pay increases ahead of inflation.

In October, the regulatory framework of the Amsterdam Stock Exchange came under scrutiny when the biggest fraud in its 600-year history was discovered, leading to arrests of senior figures, managers and brokers on charges of fraud. Proposals were made in November for new regulatory measures and licensing of brokers.

Proposals to lower national carbon dioxide emissions by the year 2000 to 3 per cent below the 1990 level were put before parliament at the end of the year. The main driving factor was to be an increase in energy prices, while a lowering of the national speed limit from 120 to 100 kilometres per hour also came under consideration.

vi. LUXEMBOURG

CAPITAL: Luxembourg   AREA: 3,000 sq km   POPULATION: 410,000 ('96)
OFFICIAL LANGUAGE: Letzeburgish
POLITICAL SYSTEM: parliamentary democracy
HEAD OF STATE: Grand Duke Jean (since Nov '64)
RULING PARTIES: Christian Social People's Party (PCS) & Luxembourg Socialist Workers' Party (LSAP)
HEAD OF GOVERNMENT: Jean-Claude Juncker (PCS), Prime Minister (since Jan '95)
MAIN IGO MEMBERSHIPS (non-UN): NATO, EU, WEU, Benelux, OSCE, CE, OECD, Francophonie
CURRENCY: Luxembourg franc (end-'97 £1=LF61.03,US$1=LF37.20)
GNP PER CAPITA: US$41,210 ('95) or US$37,930 ('95) by PPP calculation

ACCUSATIONS by the Belgian and German governments that the Luxembourg banking system was permitting large-scale tax evasion by their citizens with bank accounts in the Grand Duchy assumed serious proportions during 1997. Pressure from EU partners for the government to introduce a withholding tax on capital income received by non-residents was increasingly difficult to withstand. But such a move had the potential to cause a capital flight, threatening

Luxembourg's financial sector (providing one third of government revenue). Throughout the year, the government sought to temporize and to seek alternative solutions. It was aided in this policy by holding the EU presidency from July to December.

The economic recovery accelerated during 1997, led by fast growth in the dominant steel industry, which was operating at 85 per cent of capacity by the third quarter. The construction sector, including housing, also recovered from the previous year's recession. The annual inflation rate stayed at around 1.5 per cent for much of the year, among the lowest in Europe. On the other hand, unemployment rose to 3.5 per cent of the resident workforce, which was very high by Luxembourg standards. By the end of the year, Luxembourg was in full compliance with all the Maastricht criteria for membership of the planned single European currency.

Despite opposition from the public sector trade unions, the government made clear that it intended to reform the public-sector pension scheme which offered generous benefits not fully funded by contributions. Agreement on the planned radical changes had not been reached at year's end. Also in the social sphere, increasing use of drugs led the government to propose new legislation to combat hard drugs but partially to decriminalize use of cannabis and to legalize methadone substitution programmes.

vii. REPUBLIC OF IRELAND

CAPITAL: Dublin   AREA: 70,280 sq km   POPULATION: 3,600,000 ('96)
OFFICIAL LANGUAGES: Irish & English
POLITICAL SYSTEM: parliamentary democracy
HEAD OF STATE: President Mary McAleese (since Nov '97)
RULING PARTIES: coalition of Fianna Fáil (FF) & Progressive Democrats (PD)
HEAD OF GOVERNMENT: Bertie Ahern (FF), Prime Minister/Taoiseach (since June '97)
MAIN IGO MEMBERSHIPS (non-UN): EU, OSCE, CE, OECD
CURRENCY: punt (end-'97 £1=IR£1.15, US$1=IR£0.70)
GNP PER CAPITA: US$14,710 ('95) or US$15,680 ('95) by PPP calculation

IT was the year of the 'Celtic Tiger', the cliché repeatedly invoked to describe the Irish economic buoyancy which continued unchecked throughout 1997. Tax revenue soared while inflation was held to some 1.5 per cent. For the first time in nearly 30 years, Exchequer funds were sufficient by 31 December to meet proposed outgoings for the year ahead without resort to borrowing. Unemployment fell so far that industrial enterprises had difficulty in filling new jobs and concerted efforts were made to lure home Irish emigrants working abroad, especially those with professional or scientific qualifications. Economic growth overall in 1997 exceeded 10 per cent. Analysts agreed that three factors lay behind this remarkable upsurge. First, educational policy had ensured that a high proportion of school-leavers went on to third-level training: the resultant skilled workforce proved powerfully attractive for inward investment from Europe and North America. Second, European Union funding had been wisely used to improve the economic infrastructure. Third, successive agreements between government, trade unions and employers had generated an exceptional degree of wage restraint and minimal disturbance in industrial relations.

Against this background, the demand grew clamorous in 1997 for a reduction in the high level of taxation. The trade unions added their voice to that of business, arguing that the workers' restraint had played a major role in creating the new prosperity, out of which they deserved to be rewarded by a substantial cut in taxes. Corporation and income taxes were accordingly reduced in the January and December budgets. Increases in social welfare payments, substantial by Irish standards, were also announced but failed to satisfy lobbyists seeking relief for the people living in drug-plagued suburban ghettos, the long-term unemployed, the itinerants, the physically and mentally handicapped. The media reflected the widely-shared opinion that prosperity should no longer circulate only through the limited circle of the already reasonably secure sectors of the population. Meanwhile, staff reductions in several computer component plants and the complete closure of a plant in County Tipperary served as reminders that foreign investment could be a shifting sand on which to build economic success.

Recurrent crises for the beef industry, occasioned by BSE-related regulations in external markets and the blockade in December by British farmers of meat imports from Ireland that were cheap in Britain because of the strength of sterling, also underscored how vulnerable was Irish prosperity to developments outside Irish control. This hardened the existing determination to participate in the proposed EU monetary union and single currency, which would copper-fasten Irish involvement in European forward planning. Prosperity, however, created a problem. Despite its comparative weakness against sterling (itself a boost for Irish exports), the punt remained well above the average of its permitted exchange rate against other currencies in the existing European Monetary System (EMS). The Central Bank of Ireland hinted, and economic commentators asserted, that the rate against the Deutschmark would have to fall if Irish participation in the common currency was to receive EU approval. By the year's end speculative selling of the punt was beginning to bring this about without regulatory intervention by the Central Bank.

The general election held on 6 June resulted in a change of government. An alliance of Fianna Fáil and the Progressive Democrats ousted the 'rainbow coalition' of Fine Gael, Labour and the Democratic Left. Fine Gael, led by the outgoing Taoiseach (Prime Minister), John Bruton, was the only major party to win a significant increase in its vote, but insufficient to offset a disastrous result for Labour, which lost nearly half the seats it had dramatically won in 1992 (see AR 1992, p. 68). The full results for the 166 lower house seats were as follows (1992 figures in parentheses):

	Seats won	% of first preferences
Fianna Fáil	77 (68)	39.3 (39.1)
Fine Gael	54 (45)	27.9 (24.5)
Labour Party	17 (33)	10.4 (19.3)
Progressive Democrats	4 (10)	4.7 (4.7)
Democratic Left	4 (4)	2.5 (2.8)
Green Alliance	2 (1)	2.8 (n/a)
Sinn Féin	1 (0)	2.5 (n/a)
Others	7 (5)	9.9 (n/a)

It was generally agreed, not least within Labour itself, that the outcome reflected dissatisfaction with Labour's decision in 1992 to enter a coalition with Fianna Fáil, contrary to its avowed stance in the election of that year, in which it had attracted support from a volatile segment of middle-class voters. The collapse of the arrangement with Fianna Fáil in acrimonious circumstances at the end of 1994 had let in the Fine Gael-led government without removing the tarnish from Labour's image. Dick Spring, who had made a considerable international impact as Foreign Minister from 1992 to 1997, resigned as Labour Party leader in November and was succeeded by a former Finance Minister, Ruairi Quinn.

The new government was headed by Fianna Fáil's Bertie Ahern, a 46-year-old former accountant who had been an impressive Finance Minister in the early 1990s. His principal ministers included Mary Harney, the Progressive Democrat leader, as Tanaiste (Deputy Prime Minister) and Charlie McCreevy (FF) as Minister for Finance. No fundamental alteration in public policy followed the change of administration. In particular, policy on Northern Ireland continued as before despite a supposed preference by Sinn Féin for Mr Ahern over Mr Bruton, whom the republican extreme had thought too accommodating towards unionist sensitivities. In the event, the Ahern government cooperated as closely as its predecessor with British ministers in encouraging the cautious progress of the Northern peace talks (see I.10). Nobody suggested that the new IRA ceasefire on 20 July, which made possible the admission of Sinn Féin to the talks, was a consequence of the change of regime in Dublin. Opinion in the Republic was that a bigger factor towards such progress as could be discerned in the North was the election of a Labour government in Britain. The new UK Prime Minister, Tony Blair, and his Northern Ireland Secretary, Dr Mo Mowlam, were credited with a more realistic commitment towards solving the problems of the North than the preceding Conservative administration.

Such differences of emphasis as arose between Dublin and London were relatively minor. As in the previous year, the Irish government protested against the decision of the Ulster police to allow an Orange march through a Catholic area at Drumcree in July, while the British were said to be unhappy with the release of some IRA prisoners in the Republic before Christmas to encourage continuing Sinn Féin cooperation in the peace process. Both governments expressed the same anxiety over breakaway movements which emerged on the nationalist and loyalist extremes. With the talks making little progress, this anxiety was not lessened by the shooting dead of a loyalist paramilitary leader inside the high security Maze prison on 27 December, followed by retaliatory killings of people within the nationalist community.

The substance of the peace talks remained closely guarded in the Republic, although tentative hints emerged from time to time. Mr Ahern acknowledged that amendments to the controversial articles of the Irish constitution which incorporated a claim to Northern Ireland could be submitted to referendum as part of a general settlement. He also said that his Foreign Minister, David Andrews, had spoken only for himself when he claimed that proposed cross-border bodies might exercise quasi-governmental powers.

The President, Mary Robinson, resigned on 12 September, three months before the end of her seven-year term, to become United Nations Commissioner for Human Rights. Her successor, inaugurated on 11 November after election in a national poll on 30 October with 59 per cent of the second-count vote, was the government candidate, Mary McAleese, a Northern nationalist. Although a distinguished academic lawyer and pro-vice-chancellor of Queen's University, Belfast, Mrs McAleese was little known in the Republic. Her success was attributed partly to her own 'presidential' demeanour during the election campaign and partly to the counter-productive effect of attempts to represent her as a fellow-traveller of Sinn Féin because of her participation in peace-making efforts in the North.

Five candidates (four of them women) contested the presidential election but a mere 50 per cent of the electorate cast their votes. A correspondingly low poll of 60 per cent had been recorded at the general election. This apathy was thought to point to public alienation from the political system following the revelation at a tribunal of inquiry that a former FF Taoiseach, Charles Haughey, had accepted IR£1.3 million in gifts from a prominent businessman while in office. The tribunal also elicited details of arrangements between the same businessman's firm and Michael Lowry, a former Fine Gael minister. The tribunal found that both politicians had been involved in tax evasion stratagems and further criticized Mr Haughey for failure to cooperate fully with its investigations. The inquiry found no evidence that political favours had been granted in return for the various payments received, but public disquiet over the revelations could not be doubted. It was still tangible when Mr Ahern's first choice as Foreign Minister, Ray Burke, resigned in October under repeated pressure from the media and the opposition to explain how he came to be offered a substantial payment towards FF funds by persons in the construction industry. In this case, no question arose of any kind of wrongdoing but it did little to assuage public concern over links between business and politics. The government established two new tribunals in the autumn to look further into aspects of the various matters which had come to light in 1997.

2. DENMARK—ICELAND—NORWAY—SWEDEN—FINLAND—AUSTRIA—
SWITZERLAND—EUROPEAN MINI-STATES

i. DENMARK

CAPITAL: Copenhagen   AREA: 43,000 sq km   POPULATION: 5,260,000 ('96)
OFFICIAL LANGUAGE: Danish
POLITICAL SYSTEM: parliamentary democracy
HEAD OF STATE: Queen Margrethe II (since Jan '72)
RULING PARTIES: coalition of Social Democrats (SD) & Radical Liberals (RV)
HEAD OF GOVERNMENT: Poul Nyrup Rasmussen (SD), Prime Minister (since Jan '93)
MAIN IGO MEMBERSHIPS (non-UN): NATO, EU, NC, CBSS, AC, OSCE, CE, OECD
CURRENCY: krone (end-'97 £1=DKr11.27, US$1=DKr6.87)
GNP PER CAPITA: US$29,890 ('95) or US$21,230 ('95) by PPP calculation

POUL Nyrup Rasmussen's minority two-party coalition of Social Democrats and Radical Liberals was still in place at the end of the year, after repeated predictions of a snap election proved unfounded. A year of solid economic growth (estimated at 2.75–3 per cent of GDP) and falling unemployment (7.5 per cent by November) brought fears of overheating, with a sharp decline in the current account surplus and a projected rise in inflation. Fiscal prudence thus continued to be the order of the day: the 1998 budget—agreed with the left-wing Unity List and Socialist People's Party—provided for a surplus of DKr7,000 million as a first step towards the government's target of reducing the national debt from 67 to 40 per cent of GDP by 2005. The 1997 surplus, however, was only achieved by DKr15,000 million being obtained from a partial sell-off of the state's holding in the national telephone company Tele Danmark. The budget provided for only a slight reduction in the overall tax burden, whilst increased taxes on cars and air fares as announced by the government in May led its former coalition partner, the Centre Democrats, to withdraw their parliamentary support.

When the government in October announced further austerity measures, including budget cuts, the stage seemed set for early elections. In the final analysis, however, none of the opposition parties seemed to relish the prospect. November's local elections showed the government parties to be neck and neck with their two main rivals on the centre-right, with both blocs obtaining around 38 per cent of the vote. The extreme right People's Party obtained 6.8 per cent, as religious and political leaders denounced an apparent wave of anti-immigrant sentiment. Plans by the government to introduce tighter immigration laws had been behind the resignation of the Interior Minister, Birthe Weiss, who had given way to Torkil Simonsen in October. Earlier, the centre-right had experienced a serious setback in February, when Conservative leader Hans Engell—previously tipped as the next non-socialist Prime Minister—resigned after crashing his car under the influence of alcohol. He was succeeded as party leader by Per Stig Moller.

Considerable political controversy was occasioned by the EU's Amsterdam Treaty concluded in June (see XI.3; XV.1.ii). Whilst Denmark was able to maintain the majority of its opt-outs from the Maastricht Treaty obtained in

1993, the provisions of the new treaty relating to asylum and immigration led the government to call a referendum on the issue, to be held in May 1998. End-of-year polls indicated that public support for the Amsterdam agreement was rising. This was in spite of the negative stance adopted by the Socialist People's Party, whose support for the Maastricht revisions had proved pivotal in 1993.

Controversy over Europe was heightened by a court case brought against the government and Prime Minister by 11 anti-EU activists. The group, which claimed that Denmark's accession to the Maastricht Treaty was unconstitutional, scored a significant victory during November, when the High Court decreed that the plaintiffs should be allowed access to confidential government documents relevant to the case. Although a verdict was unlikely before the Amsterdam referendum, the Prime Minister insisted that the poll would go ahead as planned, despite fears that a victory by the activists would invalidate the result.

On 15 January Queen Margrethe II celebrated her Silver Jubilee. In July Bill Clinton became the first serving US head of state to visit Denmark, where he voiced America's continuing support for the three Baltic republics' NATO aspirations in the aftermath of the Madrid summit (see XII.1). The US President's choice of venue was regarded as highly symbolic, for Denmark had shown itself to be the Baltic states' most committed supporter within NATO.

On a more tragic note, the ongoing 'biker war' (see AR 1996, p. 62) claimed another two dead and nine injured in Denmark during 1997, prompting lawmakers to consider a total ban on motorcycle groups.

ii. ICELAND

CAPITAL: Reykjavík AREA: 103,000 sq km POPULATION: 270,000 ('96)
OFFICIAL LANGUAGE: Icelandic
POLITICAL SYSTEM: parliamentary democracy
HEAD OF STATE: President Ólafur Ragnar Grímsson (since Aug '96)
RULING PARTIES: Independence (IP) & Progressive (PP) parties
HEAD OF GOVERNMENT: Davíd Oddsson (IP), Prime Minister (since April '91)
MAIN IGO MEMBERSHIPS (non-UN): NATO, EFTA/EEA, NC, OSCE, CE, OECD
CURRENCY: króna (end-'97 £1=ISkr119.10, US1=Isk72.59)
GNP PER CAPITA: US$24,950 ('95) or US$20,460 ('95) by PPP calculation

ICELAND'S strong economic performance continued during 1997. Fish catches exceeded the previous year's record by 200,000 tonnes, while unemployment was down to 3.3 per cent by the end of October. Nevertheless, strong growth in traditional exports such as fish and aluminium were insufficient to prevent a further sharp deterioration in the trade balance, which was on course to register a deficit of ISkr17,500 million for the year. The shortfall—occasioned primarily by increased imports of cars and industrial equipment—fuelled fears of overheating following recent hikes in purchasing power and consumption.

In response, the centre-right government of Davíd Oddsson put the accent on tighter fiscal and monetary policy. Although Iceland was on course for a budget surplus approaching ISkr1,000 million in 1997, plans were unveiled for a further 2 per cent cut in public spending during 1998. On 24 March representatives of employers' organizations and five trade unions arrived at a comprehensive wages agreement covering the period up to February 2000. The deal, which included a commitment to increase the minimum monthly wage to ISkr70,000 (about US$965) from the start of 1998, provided for pay increases broadly in line with the forecast rate of inflation, yet was followed by a wave of industrial action. In April-June fish-processing workers struck for seven weeks over demands for a monthly minimum of ISkr100,000, until government arbitration brought about a compromise settlement.

A poll taken in late November showed support for the ruling parties holding steady at 62 per cent, with the Independence Party up seven points on its 37 per cent score in the 1995 elections. At the national congress of the opposition People's Alliance held in the same month, party chairman Margrét Frímannsdóttir received the go-ahead to conduct negotiations with the Social Democrats on the formation of a united slate for the next general elections.

In his annual report to parliament on 6 November, Foreign Minister Halldór Asgrímsson stressed that, although EU membership was not on the agenda at present, the government wished to leave the door open to possible entry in the future. Reiterating the goal of closer cooperation with the Union via membership of the European Economic Area (EEA) and the Schengen Agreement (see XI.3; XI.4.v), Mr Asgrímsson also pointed to the need for Iceland to participate actively in discussions on European security through NATO and other trans-Atlantic forums. By the end of November, however, Iceland looked set for confrontation with the EU over the renegotiation of Schengen, the government demanding full voting rights on any new agreement made by the Council of Ministers.

Ongoing Icelandic-Norwegian disputes over fisheries reached new depths of acrimony during June-September, after an Icelandic fishing vessel was seized by the Norwegian coastguard and fined for alleged infringement of territorial regulations. However, relations improved noticeably in November, when the two countries agreed to resume negotiations over fishing limits in the Barents Sea 'loophole' (see AR 1996, p. 65). Prior to this, on 11 November, representatives from Iceland, Denmark, Norway and Greenland had signed a demarcation treaty determining respective fishing boundaries, although the dispute with the Faroe Islands over the boundaries of Iceland's economic zone remained unsettled at the end of the year.

iii. NORWAY

CAPITAL: Oslo   AREA: 324,000 sq km   POPULATION: 4,380,000 ('96)
OFFICIAL LANGUAGE: Norwegian
POLITICAL SYSTEM: parliamentary democracy
HEAD OF STATE: King Harald V (since Jan '91)
RULING PARTIES: Christian People's Party (KrF) heads minority coalition with Centre and Liberal parties
HEAD OF GOVERNMENT: Kjell Magne Bondevik (KrF), Prime Minister (since Sept '97)
MAIN IGO MEMBERSHIPS (non-UN): NATO, EFTA/EEA, NC, CBSS, AC, OSCE, CE, OECD
CURRENCY: krone (end-'97 £1=NKr12.11, US$1=NKr7.38)
GNP PER CAPITA: US$31,250 ('95) or US$21,940 ('95) by PPP calculation

THE general election of 15 September heralded the end of 11 years of minority government by the Labour Party, which was replaced by a new minority centre-right coalition of Christian People's, Centre and Liberal parties headed by Kjell Magne Bondevik. Labour again obtained the largest number of seats in the 165-seat parliament, winning 65 compared with a combined total of 42 for the three parties making up the new government; but Prime Minister Thorbjørn Jagland had vowed to stand down if his party did not improve on its 1993 score of 36.9 per cent. In the event, Labour obtained only 35.1 per cent, its second-worst showing since 1930.

Despite presiding over a flourishing economy—unemployment was down to only only 2.5 per cent in November—Mr Jagland's administration never recovered from its shaky start in 1996, when it was dogged by allegations of corruption and a string of embarrassing ministerial resignations (see AR 1996, p. 67). On the question of Norway's NKr50,000 million oil fund, Labour was alone in advocating continued investment of surplus revenues as opposed to using them to fund tax cuts or higher welfare spending. The traditional non-socialist opposition, however, was far from united on the issue, with splits especially apparent between the Centre Party and the Conservatives.

These divisions greatly benefited the far-right Progress Party led by Carl Hagen, whose calls for higher expenditure on welfare were coupled with demands for tighter immigration laws. Labour chose to focus its campaign on the potential damage to Norway's international reputation should the Progress Party gain power, a tactic which the traditional opposition parties characterized as a smokescreen to divert attention from the government's own shortcomings. The Progress Party finally emerged as the joint second-largest grouping in parliament with 25 seats, slightly ahead of the Conservatives with 23. Of the centrist parties, the Christian Democrats registered strong gains, winning 25 seats, whereas Centre Party representation collapsed from 25 seats to 11. The full results were as follows (1993 figures in parentheses):

	Seats	% of vote
Norwegian Labour Party	65 (67)	35.1 (36.9)
Progress Party	25 (10)	15.3 (6.3)
Christian Democratic Party	25 (13)	13.7 (7.9)
Conservative Party	23 (28)	14.3 (17.0)
Centre Party	11 (32)	7.9 (16.8)
Socialist Left Party	9 (13)	6.0 (7.9)
Liberal Party	6 (1)	4.5 (3.6)
Coastal Party	1 (0)	0.4 (0.1)
Red Electoral Alliance	0 (1)	1.7 (1.1)
Others	0 (0)	1.1 (2.4)
Total	165 (165)	

Mr Jagland predicted a short life for the Bondevik government, fuelling speculation that Labour had contrived a tactical electoral defeat with the aim of emerging reinvigorated from a short period of opposition. Whilst the new government won the backing of the Conservatives and the Progress Party for budget amendments adding NKr6,000 million to pensions and child benefit, it was soon confronted with the perennial risk of overheating in the economy. The Bondevik coalition also faced the prospect of a rough ride in parliament over Centre Party proposals to limit fossil fuel emissions by slowing down oil and gas production and halting construction of two new gas-fired power plants.

In European affairs, Norway was involved in disputes with the European Union (EU) over two of its main commodity exports. In May alleged dumping of Norwegian salmon in EU markets led to a new agreement with the Brussels Commission regulating the volume and minimum sales price of exports for the next five years. Potentially more intractable were Norway's objections to a new gas directive intended to open up the European gas market to suppliers outside the European Economic Area (EEA), through which Norway was linked with the EU. Resultant price decreases, it was feared, could significantly reduce Norway's earnings from gas exports. Norway's lack of formal influence within EU institutions was also felt over the Schengen Treaty, which was incorporated into the EU structure following the Amsterdam summit in June (see XI.3). Moves by the Euro-sceptic Bondevik coalition to postpone full Norwegian participation in the Schengen agreement set it at odds with the pro-EU Conservative and Labour parliamentary contingents, which refused to support the government position.

iv. SWEDEN

CAPITAL: Stockholm   AREA: 450,000 sq km   POPULATION: 8,840,000 ('96)
OFFICIAL LANGUAGE: Swedish
POLITICAL SYSTEM: parliamentary democracy
HEAD OF STATE: King Carl XVI Gustav (since Sept '73)
RULING PARTY: Social Democratic Labour Party
HEAD OF GOVERNMENT: Göran Persson, Prime Minister (since March '96)
MAIN IGO MEMBERSHIPS (non-UN): EU, NC, CBSS, AC, PFP, OSCE, CE, OECD
CURRENCY: krona (end-'97 £1=SKr13.07, US$1=SKr7.97)
GNP PER CAPITA: US$23,750 ('95) or US$18,540 ('95) by PPP calculation

WITH the minority Social Democratic government's mandate set to expire in September 1998, the campaign for the next parliamentary elections began in earnest when the Moderate Party leader, Carl Bildt, returned to Sweden in June after a two-year stint as the European Union's peace envoy in Bosnia. This diplomatic interlude had clearly done much to enhance the standing of Mr Bildt, who was voted most popular Swede in an annual poll held in September. Polls taken during the same month indicated that the Moderates—enjoying a narrow lead over the ruling Social Democrats (SAP)—had gained steadily in support since the return of their leader.

For many observers, the Persson government's chances of re-election hinged upon its progress in reducing unemployment. The Prime Minister's upbeat assessment of the economy at the opening of the *Riksdag* (parliament) in September was partially borne out by data suggesting that a clear upswing was finally underway after several years of recession and weak growth. Surging exports and growing domestic demand fuelled solid growth in industrial production during the first half of the year. Inflation, running at less than 2 per cent, was the second-lowest in the European Union. Predicted annual GDP growth of 2.1 per cent, however, was still insufficient to spur strong job creation. Open unemployment stood at 8.3 per cent in April, a higher level than when Mr Persson became Prime Minister a year before, although it later fell to 6.5 per cent by November.

Further measures to combat joblessness formed the centre-piece of the 1998 budget unveiled in April. Finance Minister Erik Åsbrink announced that the predicted 1997 budget deficit of 2.1 per cent would disappear entirely in 1998 and be transformed into an annual 2 per cent surplus thereafter. The austerity of recent years, Mr Åsbrink argued, left room for a major four-year programme of public-sector investment and expansion of state-funded labour market schemes. The SKr66,000 million allocated in April was doubled in September, when the Prime Minister pledged extra funding to prevent further lay-offs in welfare services, health-care and education. Whilst these measures did much to answer the critics of austerity within the ruling SAP, the government was attacked by industry and the opposition for its failure to cut taxes or to implement structural reform. In particular, the later package of measures placed a further question-mark over the government's informal alliance with the Centre Party, which by October seemed to be distancing itself from the Social Democrats.

The prospect of an alliance between the Centre Party and the Moderates appeared unlikely, however, given the parties' divergent views on the vexed questions of the nuclear power industry, the proposed single European currency and Sweden's relationship with NATO. Pressure by the anti-nuclear Centre Party was seen as the determinant factor behind a government U-turn on the nuclear issue in February, when the Industry Minister, Anders Sundström, announced that the first of two reactors at the Barsebäck plant in southern Sweden was to be closed in early 1998. With his statement, the minister contradicted earlier government claims that decommissioning would not begin before 2001 (see AR 1996, p. 69). The decision elicited a predictable response from the right-wing opposition, industry and the trade unions, which claimed that the early shutdown would lead to higher energy costs, increased fossil fuel emissions, lower competitiveness and increased unemployment.

In June the government finally ended speculation by announcing that Sweden would not join the single European currency at its inception in 1999. The decision, approved by a large majority in parliament in early December, nevertheless left the door open to Swedish entry at a later date. Citing majority public opinion, the Prime Minister pledged to hold a special election or a referendum on the issue should the government decide to recommend membership in the future. Within the opposition, the deeply Euro-sceptic Centre Party declared itself satisfied with the decision, although it had hoped that the SAP government would rule out membership before 2002. The pro-European Moderates, on the other hand, expressed their disappointment.

Sweden, in common with other Nordic countries, was rocked by revelations in 1997 that in the four decades up to 1976 as many as 60,000 women might have been sterilized under a eugenics law passed in the 1930s. The Health Minister, Margot Wallström, pledged a full inquiry into these 'barbaric' revelations, which did considerable damage to Sweden's international reputation. The government also launched an inquiry into claims that Sweden's wartime exports to Nazi Germany had been paid for with gold stolen from Jewish victims of the Holocaust (see also II.2.vii). In the course of 1997, fresh evidence came to light in the 11-year investigation into the murder of Prime Minister Olof Palme. A number of new witness statements led police to consider a retrial of Christer Pettersson, who had been convicted of the murder in 1989, only to be acquitted on appeal (see AR 1989, p. 170).

The year was marked by a further intensification of the debate over Sweden's international position. Addressing parliament in February, Foreign Minister Lena Hjelm-Wallén reiterated Sweden's policy of non-alignment, yet expressed cautious support for the expansion of NATO to former Warsaw Pact countries. The government also took further steps to strengthen ties with the alliance, approving participation in joint Partnership for Peace exercises held in May. Mr Bildt's Moderates, on the other hand, openly endorsed Sweden's entry into the alliance, while conceding that Swedish NATO membership might further complicate relations between Russia and the Baltic states. Strong support for EU enlargement to all three Baltic republics was also a factor in Sweden's opposition to the proposed merger of the Western European Union with the EU. Such a step, it was feared, might lead Russia to oppose EU membership for the Baltic states.

v. FINLAND

CAPITAL: Helsinki   AREA: 338,000 sq km   POPULATION: 5,150,000 ('96)
OFFICIAL LANGUAGES: Finnish & Swedish
POLITICAL SYSTEM: presidential democracy
HEAD OF STATE: President Martti Ahtisaari (since Feb '94)
RULING PARTIES: Social Democratic Party (SSDP), National Coalition (KOK), Left-Wing Alliance (VAS), Swedish People's Party (SFP) & Green Union (VL)
HEAD OF GOVERNMENT: Paavo Lipponen (SSDP), Prime Minister (since April '95)
MAIN IGO MEMBERSHIPS (non-UN): EU, NC, CBSS, AC, PFP, OSCE, CE, OECD
CURRENCY: markka (end-'97 £1=Fmk8.96, US$1=Fmk5.46)
GNP PER CAPITA: US$20,580 ('95) or US$17,760 ('95) by PPP calculation

POLITICALLY, the year was dominated by the debate on Finland's entry into the EU's economic and monetary union (EMU) and the single European currency to be launched in 1999. Prime Minister Paavo Lipponen (Social Democrat), a long-standing advocate of immediate accession to a single currency in 1999, received the overwhelming backing of his party at its annual congress held in September. With the support of the National Coalition and Swedish People's Party within the five-party 'rainbow' coalition government already assured, Mr Lipponen received a further boost in November, when a majority of members of the Left Alliance (VAS) gave their MPs authority to vote 'yes' on EMU. The VAS poll marked a victory for party leader Claes Andersson, who announced his decision to step down in May 1998.

In his single-minded pursuit of EMU membership, the Prime Minister frequently appeared at odds with public opinion. A number of surveys during the year suggested growing popular opposition to immediate entry, a poll in November showing that 57 per cent of Finns were opposed. The government, however, drew comfort from a parallel poll in which over half indicated that Finland should join if a majority of EU member states did so in the first wave. Public scepticism towards EMU was fuelled by continued high levels of unemployment, which declined only slightly (to 13.1 per cent in October) despite another year of strong economic growth. Finance Minister Sauli Niinistö (KOK) indicated that tax cuts and structural reform of the economy would come second to the continued drive to prune the budget deficit in order to meet EMU criteria.

Sceptics within the SSDP and the trade unions were appeased by an agreement reached in November on so-called EMU 'buffer funds' designed to counterbalance possible fluctuations in the business cycle following accession to a single currency. Inadequate convergence with other EU economies was one of the themes alluded to by the opposition Centre Party, which came out against immediate EMU entry at an extraordinary congress in September. However, opposition proposals for a referendum on the issue were voted down in December, when the constitutional committee of the *Eduskunta* (parliament) decided that the final decision on EMU entry belonged to the legislature. A vote on the issue was scheduled for February 1998, with the government expected to obtain a comfortable majority in favour.

Accusations of arrogance levelled at the government over EMU intensified during September and October, when a political crisis developed concerning the activities of a former SSDP chairman, Ulf Sundqvist. In July Mr Sundqvist had been ordered to pay damages of Fmk11.4 million to the state property handling company Arsenal for his role in the collapse of the STS bank during the early 1990s (see AR 1993, p. 78). When details of the final settlement were made public, however, it emerged that Mr Sundqvist—the former head of STS—had been required to pay only Fmk1.2 million, leaving the taxpayer to foot the bill for the remainder.

The ensuing public outcry prompted the resignation of Arja Alho (SSDP), the Taxation Minister who had approved the settlement, even though she had received the full backing of the Prime Minister for her handling of the issue. Ms Alho denied that she had committed any juridical error—a contention later confirmed by the constitutional committee of the parliament. Most damaging for the government, however, was the sense that it had seriously underestimated the depth of public feeling over the episode. In addition to causing an immediate slump in SSDP support at the polls, the Sundqvist affair appeared to have the more serious effect of undermining public confidence in the political class as a whole.

The one institution seemingly untainted by the episode was the presidency, as polls revealed that incumbent Martti Ahtisaari had enjoyed a steady rise in popularity over the year. For his part, President Ahtisaari expressed misgivings over proposals by the Constitution 2000 committee headed by Paavo Nikula (Green Union) aiming to limit the current prerogatives enjoyed by the President in the spheres of foreign policy and in the appointment of the Prime Minister. For many commentators, however, the Nikula proposals did not mark a radical departure, but merely clarified the existing division of responsibilities under the constitution.

Helsinki played host in March to the historic Clinton-Yeltsin summit on the expansion of NATO, on the eve of which President Yeltsin declared his opposition to possible Finnish membership of the alliance. In response, the *Eduskunta* reasserted the line that Finland was free to come to its own decision on the issue, although in practice Finland's military and strategic stance remained essentially unchanged. Attempts to enhance the country's role as a gateway between West and East were again in evidence during October, when the Prime Minister unveiled a new initiative— christened 'the Northern Dimension'—seeking to enhance ties between the Nordic countries, the EU and Russia. Agreements on visa-free travel were signed with all three Baltic states during the year, although Finland's unflinching support for Estonia's EU ambitions at the expense of Latvia and Lithuania set it at odds with its Nordic neighbours during the run-up to the EU's Luxembourg summit in December.

vi. AUSTRIA

CAPITAL: Vienna   AREA: 84,000 sq km   POPULATION: 8,050,000 ('96)
OFFICIAL LANGUAGE: German
POLITICAL SYSTEM: federal parliamentary democracy
HEAD OF STATE: Federal President Thomas Klestil (since Aug '92)
RULING PARTIES: Social Democratic (SPÖ) & People's (ÖVP) parties
HEAD OF GOVERNMENT: Viktor Klima (SPÖ), Federal Chancellor (since Jan '97)
MAIN IGO MEMBERSHIPS (non-UN): EU, OSCE, CE, PFP, CEI, OECD
CURRENCY: schilling (end-'97 £1=Sch20.82, US$1=Sc2.69)
GNP PER CAPITA: US$26,890 ('95) or US$21,250 ('95) by PPP calculation

JANUARY brought two surprises. First, a resolution was found to the acrimonious coalition dispute over the proposed acquisition of the Creditanstalt bank by Bank Austria, controlled respectively by the People's Party (ÖVP) and the Social Democratic Party (SPÖ), with an agreement on 12 January that privatization of the public stake in the former would be matched by similar privatization in the latter. Second was the announcement on 18 January by Dr Franz Vranitzky that he was stepping down as Federal Chancellor and as party chairman of the SPÖ. He explained that his decision was personal—ten years in office being a limit which he had set himself long before—and proposed that the serving Finance Minister, Viktor Klima, should succeed him in both posts. On 28 January Herr Klima was sworn in as Chancellor, together with the new SPÖ ministers whom he had chosen to work with him in the 'grand coalition' with the ÖVP. He was subsequently elected SPÖ chairman at a party congress on 9 April. Meanwhile, Dr Vranitzky had accepted an appointment as the OSCE's special envoy for Albania in March.

Herr Klima's arrival gave the coalition fresh impetus, with the result that the year was less rewarding politically for Dr Jörg Haider and his right-wing Freedom Party (FPÖ) than 1996 had been (see AR 1996, p. 74). In the absence of federal elections, the FPÖ concentrated on drafting a new party programme and on establishing an FPÖ trade union. The latter failed to prosper, as did an attempt to exploit public disquiet at the proposed sacrifice of the Austrian schilling to EU economic and monetary union (EMU) and a single European currency. Seeking support in November for a referendum on the issue, the FPÖ attracted only 254,000 signatures, sufficient to get the matter debated in parliament but hardly evidence of overwhelming public concern. For the government, the episode suggested that the new 'euro information' campaign launched by the government on 29 August had had some effect.

The FPÖ continued to perform well in opinion polls, although it did not fare as well as expected in provincial assembly elections held in Carinthia on 9 March and in Upper Austria on 6 October. Even so, both coalition partners lost votes to Dr Haider's party—in the SPÖ's case 4–5 per cent on both occasions—as the FPÖ succeeded in pushing the ÖVP into third place in Carinthia (though it failed to achieve a similar outcome in Upper Austria). Local political loyalties played their part here, Carinthia being home territory for Dr Haider; but the ÖVP was not helped by the uneven national performance of Dr Wolfgang Schüssel, the ÖVP federal leader and Foreign Minister. His outspoken campaign for

NATO membership during the first six months of the year was criticized as counter-productive, and he attracted unwelcome international publicity in July by allegedly insulting the chairman of the German Bundesbank.

Progress made on some difficult issues also improved coalition morale during the year. Tough new laws on immigration and asylum were agreed in March, to come into force on 1 January 1998, while on 18 September the new Finance Minister, Rudolf Edlinger, presented an agreed 1998–99 budget to parliament. In line with the government's objective of budgetary consolidation, and with the targets set by the Maastricht criteria for membership of EMU, the projected federal deficit for 1998 showed a further reduction, to Sch68,000 million or 2.6 per cent of GDP. The arrest on 2 October of a man suspected of responsibility for letter-bomb attacks on foreigners by the self-styled Bavarian Liberation Army was greeted with general relief, but also with sour comments that he had had to blow himself up before the police could find him.

On 7 November, after five months of hard coalition bargaining, a major pension reform package was approved by parliament. Although the original proposals had been much watered down and the process of reform would not begin until 2003, important changes were agreed to bring the system of calculating public-service pensions into line with the private sector. With both the budget and the pension reform adopted, the government was given additional room for manoeuvre by the strong export-led economic upturn evident during the year. Estimated growth in GDP for 1997 was 1.6 per cent, with inflation holding steady at 1.4 per cent and unemployment at 4.5 per cent, respectively the lowest and second-lowest figures in the EU.

Improved economic performance perhaps also helped to lessen public disenchantment with EU membership, although it remained unpopular. In line with EU competition requirements, the government introduced a draft law in February to end the state broadcasting monopoly. It also welcomed the selection of Vienna in June as the site of a new EU body monitoring racism and xenophobia. On 1 July Austria took over the presidency of the Schengen Agreement, although disagreement with Germany on the effectiveness of Austrian border controls delayed full Austrian membership until 27 October. Austria began to apply its Schengen commitments on 1 December, passport controls being abolished for flights to and from other Schengen countries and at minor border crossings between Austria, Germany and Italy. One bone of contention with Brussels remained Austria's refusal to ban anonymous savings accounts for small savers. Athough new accounts could no longer be opened, those already in existence had been frozen rather than closed. In October the EU Commission took Austria to the European Court of Justice, on the grounds that such accounts violated an EU directive against money-laundering.

In foreign policy, the government continued to be much-preoccupied with Central Europe and with the debate on future security policy. The latter continued to divide the coalition, with the ÖVP (and FPÖ) pushing vigorously for early NATO membership and the SPÖ arguing for caution and supporting neutrality. Chancellor Klima said in February that he had an open mind on the subject, but pointed out that Austria's neutrality law precluded the stationing of foreign troops or nuclear weapons in the country. The coalition partners agreed that a report on future security policy setting out all the options would be prepared for presentation to parliament in March 1998.

Austrian involvement in NATO's Partnership for Peace (PFP) proved less controversial. Formal arrangements were completed with the signature of a Status of Forces Agreement on 16 January during an official visit to Vienna by Javier Solana (the first by a NATO secretary-general), and by parliamentary approval on 17 April of a Law on Troop Deployment making it easier for Austrian troops to participate in humanitarian missions abroad. Austria took part in a large number of individual PFP projects, as well as contributing troops to the NATO-led Stabilization Force (SFOR) in Bosnia and to the relief operation in Albania. Given all this activity, it was perhaps surprising that the Defence Minister, Dr Werner Fasslabend, should have announced in November a plan to restructure and reduce overall numbers in the armed forces over the next two years.

vii. SWITZERLAND

CAPITAL: Berne   AREA: 41,300 sq km   POPULATION: 7,070,400 ('96)
OFFICIAL LANGUAGES: German, French, Italian & Rhaeto-Romanic
POLITICAL SYSTEM: federal canton-based democracy
RULING PARTIES: Christian Democratic People's (CVP), Radical Democratic (FDP), Social Democratic (SPS) & Swiss People's (SVP) parties
HEAD OF GOVERNMENT: Arnold Koller (CVP), 1997 President of Federal Council and Justice Minister
MAIN IGO MEMBERSHIPS: OECD, OSCE, CE, EFTA, PFP
CURRENCY: Swiss franc (end-'97 £1=SwF2.41, US$1=SwF1.47)
GNP PER CAPITA: US$40,630 ('95) or US$25,860 ('95) by PPP calculation

THE dispute over Switzerland's neutral stance during World War II and its banks' policies thereafter, which had started in the second half of 1996 (see AR 1996, p. 76), dominated political debate at least in the first half of 1997. The accusations were brought forward mainly by Jewish organizations, parts of the US administration and the US and British media, but also by the political left in Switzerland. They concentrated on two issues: first, the handling of unclaimed accounts of victims of the Holocaust by private banks; and second, the role of the Swiss National Bank as a purchaser of gold from the German Reichsbank (and therefore as supplier of much of the foreign currency with which the Nazi government had bought raw materials for its arms industry from other neutral states). Since much of this gold had been stolen by the Germans from occupied nations, Switzerland and other neutral countries had been required to hand over part of it to the Allied authorities after the war. The present dispute centred on gold which had remained in Swiss hands, as well as on unclaimed individual bank accounts.

The controversy in Switzerland over these criticisms, and especially about how to react to them, was very emotional in the first half of the year. For the political left, it was a good opportunity to attack the conservative parties which had formed the government during the war. In addition, the dispute gave the left support for its longstanding contention that it had not been the Swiss army which had saved Switzerland from German occupation, but rather economic collaboration. The left was therefore strengthened in its aim of abolishing the Swiss armed forces, or at least reducing them to half of their present strength. On the other hand, many of the older generation who remembered the hardships of the war, such as food rationing and years of army service, felt very frustrated at the latest wave of assertions.

Not used to being challenged from abroad, the Swiss government began the year by behaving rather awkwardly. Reacting to a proposal by Jewish organizations that the dispute could be settled by payment of around $100 million, an upset federal minister, Jean-Pascal Delamuraz (Radical Democratic Party), accused them of blackmail. The Social Democrats promptly accused him of antisemitism and demanded his resignation, although in vain. In May a US Under-Secretary of State, Stuart Eizenstat, published a report on Swiss policy during World War II, confirming the already-known fact of Swiss economic and financial collaboration with Nazi Germany. No-one denied this in Switzerland, but a part of public opinion criticized the report for not taking into account that Switzerland had been totally enclosed by Germany and its allies during World War II and had therefore had no other choice than to trade with them. The government made an official protest to the US government, on the grounds that Mr Eizenstat, in his foreword to the report, had accused Switzerland of prolonging the war and therefore of indirect responsibility for the millions of war and Holocaust victims.

The controversy cooled somewhat in the second half of the year, for a number of reasons. First, attention was no longer focused almost exclusively on Switzerland and was instead also directed at the other neutral states and at the countries allied with or occupied by Germany. Second, the Swiss banking sector and some industrial companies set up a fund of SwF275 million intended to relieve survivors of the Holocaust (mainly in Eastern Europe) who had not so far obtained any compensation from Germany. This fund started to make payments in November (whereas debate continued in Switzerland on a proposal for a much larger state fund for general relief actions tabled in March by the President of the Federal Council, Arnold Koller). And third, the Swiss banks took unprecedented steps towards greater openness. Not only did they engage international auditors and name a committee headed by the former president of the US Federal Reserve, Paul Volcker, to supervise their search for unclaimed accounts; they even published lists with thousands of names of holders of unclaimed accounts opened prior to the summer of 1945. The total amount in these accounts was about SwF80 million. Most of them had been opened long before the war and had belonged to Swiss citizens or people living in Switzerland (one example being the SwF12 account of Vladimir Ilyich Lenin dating from 1917).

These actions supplemented the efforts of parliament and government to promote thorough research into Switzerland's past (see AR 1996, p. 76), as well as the activities of a government-appointed task force headed by Thomas Borer. However, although some progress was made in restoring the image of Switzerland and its banks, the accusations and the pressure hardly abated. The World Jewish Congress appeared to remain convinced that there must be billions deriving from Holocaust victims in unclaimed accounts hidden in Swiss banks. Moreover, a class action by a group of Holocaust survivors against the major Swiss banks, demanding compensation of US$20,000 million, was pending in a New York court at year's end. In the same US state, officials declared a boycott of one Swiss bank, while in California a similar boycott was temporarily suspended in December, when Switzerland won some plaudits for its new open policy at a London conference convened to examine the whole 'Nazi gold' question.

Switzerland's bilateral negotiations with the European Union (EU), in progress for three years, almost stalled in December over the issue of transport by land. In spite of criticism from environmentalist groups, the Federal Council had reduced its proposal for a transit tax on heavy trucks from SwF600 to SwF400. But this was still not low enough for the EU Transport Ministers. Only an intervention by the Luxembourg EU presidency prevented a breakdown of the negotiations, which both sides hoped to bring to a conclusion in 1998. Considering the difficulties of reaching a bilateral agreement with the EU, the new leader of the Social Democrats, Ursula Koch, demanded that the government should reactivate its application for full membership, which had been deposited in Brussels in May 1992. However, aware that there would be no popular majority for EU membership in the near future, the government did not comply with Ms Koch's request. On the other hand, there seemed to be no majority for a strictly isolationist policy either. In a referendum on 8 June, Swiss voters rejected a proposal from several small right-wing parties that the government should not even be allowed to open negotiations on EU membership without the prior consent of the citizens.

The economic situation did not greatly improve in 1997. Forecasts projected GNP growth of only 0.5 per cent in the year and only limited improvement in 1998. The number of registered unemployed fell slightly, from 192,171 at end-1996 (5.3 per cent of the workforce) to 180,549 in December 1997 (5.0 per cent), while inflation remained at a very low level (0.5 per cent). Mergers of Swiss corporations and accompanying restructuring measures (such as the December union of two Swiss banks to form the second-largest bank in the world) delighted the stock market, but nourished fears among employees that they would have to pay the price for such 'globalization'.

Loss of confidence in the economic order helped the trade unions and the Social Democrats to obtain another success in a popular referendum on 28 September, when the citizens rejected some small cuts in the unemployment insurance system. The liberalization and privatization of the post and telecommunications sectors went through parliament without difficulty, an effort by some trade union groups to challenge the reform in a referendum ending in failure. Nevertheless, the Social Democrats continued to profit from the general feeling of economic insecurity, winning additional seats in all cantonal elections held in 1997. In Geneva an alliance of Social Democrats, Communists and Greens secured the first left-wing majority in a cantonal parliament for more than 60 years.

Measures to improve the poor state of the public finances became a top government priority, although agreement on their content remained problematical. Neither left-wing remedies such as tax increases nor the welfare budget cuts proposed by the conservative parties appeared to command a majority of the popular vote. Even the conservative majority in parliament was not very consistent in its efforts to reduce expenditure. As a general measure, the government's scheme to reduce the deficit to zero within five years was accepted; but the legislators were very reluctant to undertake concrete steps in this direction. They opposed, for example, a left-wing proposal to cut back on farming subsidies and insisted on a plan to construct two new railway tunnels through the Alps instead of only one.

In a national referendum on 28 September, Swiss citizens supported the government's liberal approach to the drugs problem. By a 71 per cent majority, they rejected an initiative which would have put an end to the state-controlled distribution of hard drugs to heavily-addicted persons, as started by the Swiss authorities in 1993.

In December the federal Vice-President and Foreign Minister, Flavio Cotti (Christian Democrat), was elected to the annually-rotating post of President of the Federal Council for 1998.

viii. EUROPEAN MINI-STATES

Andorra
CAPITAL: Andorra la Vella   AREA: 460 sq km   POPULATION: 70,000 ('96)
OFFICIAL LANGUAGE: Catalan
POLITICAL SYSTEM: parliamentary democracy
HEADS OF STATE: President Jacques Chirac of France & Bishop Joan Martí Alanis of Urgel (co-princes)
HEAD OF GOVERNMENT: Marc Forné Molne, President of Executive Council (since Dec '94)
MAIN IGO MEMBERSHIPS (non-UN) CE
CURRENCY: French franc & Spanish peseta

Holy See (Vatican City State)
CAPITAL: Vatican City   AREA: 0.44 sq km   POPULATION: 860 ('96)
OFFICIAL LANGUAGES: Italian & Latin
POLITICALSYSTEM: theocracy
HEAD OF STATE: Pope John Paul II (since '78)
HEAD OF GOVERNMENT: Cardinal Angelo Sodano, Secretary of State (since Dec '90)
MAIN IGO MEMBERSHIPS: OSCE
CURRENCY: Vatican lira (at par to Italian lira)

Liechtenstein
CAPITAL: Vaduz   AREA: 160 sq km   POPULATION: 32,000 ('96)
OFFICIAL LANGUAGE: German
POLITICAL SYSTEM: parliamentary democracy
HEAD OF STATE: Prince Hans Adam II (since Nov '89)
RULING PARTY: Patriotic Union (VU)
HEAD OF GOVERNMENT: Mario Frick, Prime Minister (since Dec '93)
MAIN IGO MEMBERSHIPS (non-UN): EFTA/EEA, OSCE, CE
CURRENCY: Swiss franc
GNP PER CAPITA: US$37,180 ('94 est.)

Monaco
CAPITAL: Monaco-Ville　AREA: 1.95 sq km　POPULATION: 32,000 ('96)
OFFICIAL LANGUAGE: French
POLITICAL SYSTEM: constitutional monarchy
HEAD OF STATE: Prince Rainier III (since '49)
HEAD OF GOVERNMENT: Michel Lévêque, Minister of State (since Feb '97)
MAIN IGO MEMBERSHIPS (non-UN): OSCE
CURRENCY: French franc

San Marino
CAPITAL: San Marino　AREA: 60.5 sq km　POPULATION: 25,000 ('96)
OFFICIAL LANGUAGE: Italian
POLITICAL SYSTEM: parliamentary democracy
HEADS OF STATE & GOVERNMENT: Captains-Regent Luigi Mazza & Marino Zanotti (Oct '97–March '98)
RULING PARTIES: Christian Democratic & Socialist parties
MAIN IGO MEMBERSHIPS (non-UN): OSCE, CE
CURRENCY: Italian lira

IN ANDORRA, the ruling Liberal Union (UL), led by Marc Forné, the President of the Executive Council (Cabinet), won an overwhelming victory in the general election of 16 February, taking 18 of the 28-seat General Council of the Valleys (the principality's legislature). The centre-right party had campaigned on a platform of greater deregulation and openness to foreign investment. A total of 82 per cent of the 10,837-member electorate participated in the poll. Sr Forné had come to power in December 1994 (see AR 1994, p. 89) after the collapse of the coalition government formed following the 1993 general election, the first to have been held under the new constitution promulgated that year.

During 1997 MONACO celebrated the 700th anniversary of the founding of the Grimaldi dynasty. The celebrations began on 7 January with a grand ball and continued throughout the year. Rumours that Prince Rainier, who had undergone a heart by-pass operation, was preparing to stand down in favour of his son Prince Albert persisted, despite Rainier's full participation in the anniversary celebrations. Moreover, there was reported to be growing concern at court about the fact that Prince Albert was still a bachelor and had therefore not produced an heir. As in previous years, most press attention focused on Prince Albert's sisters, the Princesses Caroline and Stephanie, both divorced. Lingering conjecture about the state of Princess Caroline's health was dispelled early in the year when she appeared at official functions looking fit and well.

In SAN MARINO the coalition of the Christian Democratic and Socialist parties which had been re-elected in the May 1993 general election (see AR 1993, p. 86), continued in office. As usual, in April and in October two new Captains-Regent took office at the start of six-month terms as joint heads of state.

In LIECHTENSTEIN Prime Minister Mario Frick won a snap election held on 31 January and 2 February. The election, called nine months early, produced little change in the composition of the 25-member *Landtag*, in which Herr Frick's Patriotic Union (VU) again won 13 seats, while the Progressive Citizens' Party (FBP) lost one of its ten seats to the pro-ecology Free List, whose legislative strength was thus increased to two. Herr Frick immediately began negotiations to continue the coalition which had kept the VU and the FBP in power since 1938. However, the coalition effectively collapsed on 10 March when the FBP voted to withdraw. Norbert Seeger, the FBP leader, said that the decision, taken at a party congress, was intended to create an effective opposition and allow the party to establish a clearer profile. Observers noted that there had been no discernible policy differences between the former coalition partners and suggested that the move was related to personal tension between their leaders. A new five-member government composed entirely of members of the VU was formally named by Prince Hans Adam on 9 April. Herr Frick remained Prime Minister was well as Minister of Finance, while Dr Andrea Willi retained the foreign affairs portfolio.

During 1997 the continuing frailty of the ageing Pope John Paul II, head of state of the HOLY SEE (Vatican) as well as head of the Roman Catholic Church, meant that his overseas itinerary was again limited. Nevertheless, he made five important foreign visits during the year, beginning in April with a two-day visit to Sarajevo, the capital of Bosnia-Hercegovina. The visit had been frequently postponed because of security concerns, which indeed overshadowed the visit after police discovered landmines and a remote-controlled detonator wired under a bridge which the Pope was scheduled to cross. Later, in April, he paid a three-day visit to the Czech Republic, which was followed in May by a visit to Beirut (Lebanon). On 31 May the Pope arrived in Poland for the start of a ten-day visit to his homeland. In August he attended the World Youth Days Festival in Paris, the highlight of which was an open-air mass at the Longchamp racecourse which attracted a congregation of between 750,000 and 1,000,000 people, one-third from outside France.

Having just celebrated the beginning of the 20th year of his pontificate, in October the Pope visited Brazil for the Second World Meeting with Families. The visit was his 80th foreign trip and his last of 1997. However, he made clear that in spite of growing concerns about his health he intended to continue making overseas pastoral visits, including one in early 1998 to Cuba, the only Latin American country he had not visited. The visit, the arrangements for which had taken many months of careful negotiations with the Communist Cuban government, had been confirmed in January 1997.

During 1997 the Vatican established diplomatic relations with Libya (in March), Guyana (June) and Angola (July). There were also state visits from Vice-President Lien Chan of the Republic of China (January); Israeli Prime Minister Binyamin Netanyahu (February); President Fernando Henrique Cardoso, the first Brazilian head of state ever to visit the Holy See (February); President Mary Robinson of Ireland (March); President Alberto Keinya Fujimori of Peru (June); and President Saul Carlos Menem of Argentina (September). The Pope also met with UN Secretary General Kofi Annan in March. In December the Vatican joined over 125 other states at Ottawa, Canada, in signing the international treaty banning the use, stockpiling, manufacture and export of anti-personnel landmines (see XII.2; XIX.5).

Figures published in mid-year indicated that for the fifth consecutive year the Vatican would achieve a budget surplus in 1997. The 1998 budget, tabled in November, was also projected to produce a surplus.

3. SPAIN—GIBRALTAR—PORTUGAL—MALTA—GREECE—CYPRUS—TURKEY

i. SPAIN

CAPITAL: Madrid   AREA: 505,000 sq km   POPULATION: 39,270,000 ('96)
OFFICIAL LANGUAGE: Spanish POLITICAL SYSTEM: parliamentary democracy
HEAD OF STATE: King Juan Carlos (since Nov '75)
RULING PARTY: Popular Party (PP)
HEAD OF GOVERNMENT: José María Aznar López, Prime Minister (since May '96)
MAIN IGO MEMBERSHIPS (non-UN): NATO, EU, WEU, OSCE, CE, OECD
CURRENCY: peseta (end-'97 £1=Ptas250.60, US$1=Ptas152.74)
GNP PER CAPITA: US$13,580 ('95) or US$14,520 ('95) by PPP calculation

SPAIN's informal governing coalition held together during 1997, providing José María Aznar's administration with the parliamentary support that it needed in order to achieve economic progress and thereby fulfil its prime objective of first-wave participation in the projected European monetary union (EMU) and single currency.

Sr Aznar's Popular Party (PP) retained the support of the Catalan and Basque nationalist parties, both of which voted on 23 October in favour of the government's budget for 1998. However, centre-periphery tensions were in evidence on several occasions. The Basque Nationalist Party (PNV) was critical of government policy towards the separatist Basque Homeland and Liberty (ETA) organization, and defied the central government by introducing a lower corporate tax rate in the Basque Country. Although the Basque regional government was granted unique powers to collect excise duties on gasoline, tobacco and alcohol, the PNV withdrew its blanket support for Sr Aznar in September, while declaring its willingness to consider future support on a case by case basis. The Prime Minister's position was reinforced in October by a pact with the four Canary Islands Coalition deputies, who pledged parliamentary support in return for funding concessions.

The largest nationalist force, the Catalan Convergence and Union (CiU) coalition headed by Jordi Pujol, gave strong support to Spain's pursuit of European economic convergence objectives, while issuing warnings of fresh Catalan demands in the future. On 7 October Sr Pujol assured the Prime Minister that the CiU deputies would back the central government until early 1999, to secure EMU membership (although in November he indicated that this support was guaranteed only until the end of 1997). On 15 October Sr Pujol called for Catalonia to be granted the same range of tax privileges enjoyed by the Basque region, by 2001, and on 24 November the CiU spokesman in the Congress of Deputies, Joaquim Molins, called furthermore for 'shared sovereignty' in Catalonia.

For many observers, the royal wedding on 4 October of the Infanta Cristina de Borbón, the younger daughter of King Juan Carlos and Queen Sofía, symbolized the evolution of Spain away from centralist state traditions, for the bridegroom was a Basque, Iñaki Urdangarín, and the ceremony took place in Barcelona. Besides the government's partnership with the nationalist parties, political stability derived from consensual relations between government and trade unions. On 9 April the major unions and employers' associations agreed to a labour market reform under which longer-term employment contracts were to be encouraged by the use of tax incentives for employers and a reduction in the compensation costs of redundancies. Subsequent legislation received broad Congress of Deputies approval in early June. Communist Party (PCE) opposition to the measure provoked a rebellion by three 'New Left' deputies within the PC-led United Left (IU), who absented themselves from Congress rather than vote as instructed.

Sr Aznar's government proceeded very slowly with economic liberalization measures and postponed the tax cuts that had been promised to supporters during the 1996 election campaign. A liberalization plan affecting regional television, telephone cabins and the water law was approved on 21 February. In September the government ruled out any tax cuts in 1998.

On 23 April, a report issued by the European Commission envisaged Spain joining EMU in the first wave of entrants, with better prospects than Italy, one of the G-7 countries. Falls in inflation, unemployment and the budget deficit all indicated that the country was on course for the single European currency. Unemployment remained high by European standards, but in national terms fell to the lowest figure since 1981 by dropping below 13 per cent in June.

Within the opposition, the major event of the year was the resignation of Felipe González on 20 June as general secretary of the Spanish Socialist Workers' Party (PSOE), which he had led since 1974. His resignation, at the start of the PSOE's 34th congress, was followed by the election of a González supporter, Joaquín Almunia, as party leader. The deputy party leader, Alfonso Guerra, and his supporters saw their presence on the party executive virtually eliminated. Sr Almunia, a 49-year-old former minister, made an appeal at the congress for more constructive relations between the PSOE and the IU.

This initiative came to nothing, however, owing to divisions within the United Left and the manner of their resolution. The PCE leader, Julio Anguita, responded to dissenting groups within the IU by removing them from the alliance. The removal of 'New Left' representatives from the leadership in July was followed in September by the expulsion of the Democratic Party of the New Left (PDNI), a break in IU relations with its Catalan partner, Initiative for Catalonia (IC), and the exclusion of the alliance's Galician federation, which had decided to present a joint list with the PSOE in regional elections held on 19 October. (In these, the left declined from second to third place as Manuel Fraga of the PP was returned as regional president.) Sr Anguita was re-elected as general coordinator of the IU at its fifth assembly in December, having purged the alliance of those favouring better relations with the Socialists.

Meanwhile, there were major developments in response to the problem of

ETA terrorism. On 3 February two leaders of the United People (HB) coalition were arrested for refusing to appear before the Supreme Court on charges of collaboration with ETA. On 7 March a protest strike called by HB proved a failure. In early July the Civil Guard managed to liberate José Antonio Ortega after he had been held captive by ETA for 532 days, while the family of businessman Cosme Delclaux secured his release after 233 days by paying a $10 million ransom.

ETA's revenge for the loss of Sr Ortega came on 10 July with the kidnap of Miguel Angel Blanco, a young PP councillor in Ermua. He was shot dead two days later, after ETA had made impossible demands for imprisoned members to be transferred to Basque prisons within 48 hours. During this episode, there was an unprecedented, massive movement of protest in repudiation of ETA, with over one million people participating in over 1,500 demonstrations throughout Spain. The movement was genuinely spontaneous, with civil society acting independently of political parties.

The government's response was to close the road to dialogue with ETA; to strengthen anti-terrorist cooperation with France (where 50 ETA suspects were arrested between January and November); and to proceed with a court case against the HB leadership, for having used ETA propaganda during its 1996 general election campaign. On 1 December the Supreme Court sentenced 23 HB leaders to seven years' imprisonment and fines of $3,400. In retaliation, ETA on 11 December assassinated another PP councillor, José Luis Caso, an event that led the European Council the following day to issue its first-ever formal condemnation of ETA.

Within the EU, the Spanish government experienced a number of setbacks, notwithstanding the progress on EMU. Sr Aznar's proposal to abolish political asylum for EU nationals ran into difficulties in March-April. On 23 July the European Commission asked Spain to change its law on digital television because it violated Community law. On 21 November Spain found itself in the embarrassing situation of opting out of the new EU employment initiative, deemed 'too costly' by Sr Aznar (see also XI.3). And in December the European Commission rejected the government's Coal Plan for 1998–2002, criticizing Spain's failure to fulfil commitments on coal subsidies and mine closures.

A more successful note was struck on 2 December by Spanish entry into the military structure of a reorganized NATO (once the UK had decided not to use its threatened veto—see II.3.ii; XII.1), Spain being allocated a sub-regional command. Spanish representatives had lobbied for the area covered by this command to include the Canary Islands and the waters between the archipelago and the Straits of Gibraltar. While securing the first of these objectives, they had to settle for a formula based on Spanish-Portuguese coordination in the case of the second.

The year also saw some high-profile trials. Of those reaching a conclusion, the most politically significant (together with the HB trials) was the 'Filesa' case. This ended on 28 October with the imprisonment of Socialist politicians

Carlos Navarro and Josep Maria Sala for activities pertaining to the illicit funding of their party. The PSOE had received $6.8 million through Filesa, a fictitious company set up to circumvent legal restrictions on private donations to political parties.

ii. GIBRALTAR

CAPITAL: Gibraltar   AREA: 6.5 sq km   POPULATION: 32,500 ('96)
OFFICIAL LANGUAGE: English
POLITICAL STATUS: Crown Colony, parliamentary democracy
HEAD OF STATE: Queen Elizabeth II
GOVERNOR: Sir Richard Luce
RULING PARTY: Gibraltar Social Democrats (GSD)
HEAD OF GOVERNMENT: Peter Caruana, Chief Minister (since May '96)
CURRENCY: Gibraltar pound (at par with UK pound)

THE floating of new ideas by Chief Minister Peter Caruana on the future constitutional status of Gibraltar failed to influence the agenda of bilateral British-Spanish talks during 1997.

In a meeting with British Foreign Secretary Robin Cook on 7 July, Mr Caruana expressed his desire for Gibraltar to lose its colonial status through becoming a crown dependency of the United Kingdom, or failing that, through full integration with Great Britain. His ideas envisaged Gibraltar losing colonial features—such as the special legislative powers held by the UK-appointed Governor and the control over the civil service exercised by the Deputy Governor—and possibly acquiring a modified status within the European Union (EU). The Chief Minister's rather general proposals sought to avoid the decolonization scenario envisaged in the Treaty of Utrecht, under which sovereignty would revert to Spain if Britain decided to relinquish it. However, there was nothing in them for Madrid, and London warned that the 'Spanish dimension' could not be ignored.

Gibraltarian disgruntlement over heavy-handed Spanish border controls had been expressed in a demonstration by 5,000 people on 13 May. Animosity toward Spain had grown since January, when Madrid had threatened to cease recognizing passports issued in Gibraltar. On the commercial front, there was a more welcome development in June, when Britain granted Gibraltar full equivalence in insurance services, facilitating local plans to offer services throughout the EU.

The election of a Labour government in Britain encouraged optimism in London and Madrid concerning the possibility of progress on the issue of sovereignty, but this was quickly overshadowed by complications arising from the reorganization of NATO (see also XII.1). In January, despite Gibraltarian opposition, Spain had revived the idea of co-sovereignty with the UK, followed by a reversion of sovereignty after 50–75 years. The Spanish formula, originally proposed in the mid-1980s, offered Gibraltarians a choice of nationality, the retention of a special tax status within the EU and substantial political autonomy, while the lure for Britain was the prospect of a joint investment programme and improved relations with Spain overall. Discussed further at a December meeting between Mr

Cook and the Spanish Foreign Minister, Abel Matutes, the outcome was a British readiness to explore the proposal further. However, UK policy continued to be that any future changes would need to be approved by Gibraltar's population, as stipulated in the constitution of 1969.

Gibraltar became a critical issue in the run-up to the NATO reorganization, finally approved in December. For several months, the UK government threatened to block Spain's application for full military membership of NATO, demanding that Spain should first lift its restrictions on access to Gibraltar for NATO ships and planes. Spain proved inflexible over airspace restrictions, fearing that any concession might be construed as acceptance of British sovereignty over the isthmus on which the airport was built (and which was not ceded in the Treaty of Utrecht). In October Madrid's call for joint British-Spanish military control over the airport was rejected by London, mindful of Gibraltar's refusal to accept joint control of it for civil purposes following the Hispano-British airport agreement of 1987.

Britain dropped its threatened veto in early December, leaving the problem to be resolved bilaterally. Under the NATO reorganization, fourth-tier commands such as that previously based in Gibraltar were abolished, while Spain acquired a sub-regional command. However, the UK retained the potential to block appointments to the Spanish headquarters unless Madrid improved access to Gibraltar.

Other important events for Gibraltar included the appointment in February of its first civilian Governor, Sir Richard Luce, and the death on 1 July of its former longstanding political leader, Sir Joshua Hassan (see XX: Obituary).

iii. PORTUGAL

CAPITAL: Lisbon   AREA: 92,000 sq km   POPULATION: 9,902,000 ('94)
OFFICIAL LANGUAGE: Portuguese
POLITICAL SYSTEM: presidential/parliamentary democracy
HEAD OF STATE: President Jorge Sampaio (since March '96)
RULING PARTY: Socialist Party (PS)
HEAD OF GOVERNMENT: António Guterres, Prime Minister (since Oct '95)
MAIN IGO MEMBERSHIPS (non-UN): NATO, OECD, EU, WEU, OSCE, CE, CPLP
CURRENCY: escudo (end-'97 £1=Esc302.64, US$1=Esc184.46)
GNP PER CAPITA: US$9,740 ('95) or US$12,670 ('95) by PPP calculation

As if to confirm the aphorism that 'no news is good news', the remarkable developments achieved in Portugal over the past few years—which in 1997 again gave it the distinction of a national growth rate above the European Union (EU) average—continued to go largely unreported in the international media. Indeed, during the year the only Portuguese events that reached the foreign headlines were the unusually severe storms and floods in October and November in Lisbon, the Azores and the southern cork-producing province of Alentejo.

Portugal's continuing economic boom was due to a convergence of favourable conditions, in which successive governments of the Social Democrats (PSD) and the presently-ruling Socialist Party (PS) had made the best possible use of the benefits of EU membership. In addition to direct transfers from Brussels amounting to an average of 3 per cent of GNP a year, Portugal had received a major EU loan for specific development programmes as well as increased foreign investment in a wide range of manufacturing industries, while EU-inspired privatization of major public services was yielding substantial government income. These inflows had allowed a total investment of some $3,000 million to be made in a spectacular infrastructural scheme scheduled for completion in early 1998, making 1997 one of the most positive years in a period of remarkable modernization, visible in an array of major construction projects throughout the country. At the close of the year the Bolsa de Valores (Lisbon stock exchange) was formally recognized as having made the transition from an emerging to a developed market.

Portugal's modernizing trend was now an accepted fact for the economic analysts of EU capitals, and also for the Portuguese generation born into it. Those old enough to remember the times when little Portugal, despite its ancient far-flung overseas empire, was deservedly stereotyped as one of the most backward European agrarian countries, suitable only for tourism, were in a better position to understand the deeper significance of the accelerated process of change. Whereas in the past, with Portugal's back turned on Spain and Europe, most railways and motor roads ran vertically from north to south, the new motorways and bridges now led eastwards to Spain, promoting cross-border contacts and integrating the Portuguese road network with those of Spain and Western Europe as a whole.

The fact that most current infrastructural development was centred in or near Lisbon led to some criticism in rival Oporto and other cities which, with some justification, resented the traditional favouritism towards the ever-expanding capital. Other critics doubted the wisdom of concentrating such a big part of the overall investment, some $1,600 million, on the Expo'98 project intended to commemorate the 500th anniversary of Vasco da Gama's arrival in India in 1498. However, the details of the scheme revealed that behind the apparent festive extravagance was a valid and timely purpose, namely the need to reclaim the neglected Lisbon docklands on the northern bank of the Tagus. Moreover, the previous PSD government's success in engaging UNESCO and other institutions in the cultural themes of Expo'98 served to stimulate international interest, as was shown by the impressive number of countries and environmental organizations anxious to fill the 140 exhibition pavilions as soon as they were ready.

The main political events of 1997 were intertwined with the ramifications of the accelerating modernization process and the aim of qualifying for the forthcoming decisive stage of European integration, the single European currency. As early as 11 January the Expo'98 director, António Cardoso e Cunha (a former EU commissioner and the second consecutive PSD member to hold the post), was replaced by Torres Campos, another high-ranking technocrat more to the liking of the PS government. The reason for the replacement was said to be disagreement over the escalating costs of the mega-exhibition. In mid-July the Planning Minister, João Cravinho, confirmed that the basic budget for Expo'98 had shot up from Esc35,000 million to Esc85,000 million

Following press disclosures of alleged tax evasion on a property purchase, António Vitorino resigned as Defence Minister on 8 November. A consequential cabinet reshuffle on 23 November was notable for the re-emergence of the ageing Professor José Veiga Simão, who had been Education Minister at the time of the fall of the Caetano regime in 1974, as the new Minister of Defence. The bi-polarization of power and popularity between the ruling PS and the opposition PSD was confirmed by local council elections of 14 December, when the PS obtained 40.5 per cent and 128 seats, against 35.1 per cent and 127 seats for the PSD, while both the Communist-led United Democratic Coalition (CDU) and the right-wing Popular Party (PP) fell back, to 12.6 and 8 per cent respectively.

Following a pattern observable in other countries, Finance Minister António de Sousa Franco committed the PS government to 'more social spending without increased taxes', proposing a budget for 1998 in which the drive towards the single European currency took precedence over other criteria. Such was the degree of consensus on this aim that, in a situation where the government was four seats short of a majority, the opposition PSD leader, Marcelo Rebelo de Sousa, called on his party to abstain in the parliamentary voting on the budget.

Portugal's enthusiasm for EU integration inevitably impacted on its oldest bilateral relationship, namely the 600-year-old Anglo-Portuguese Alliance. Despite the continued cordiality of bilateral relations, Portugal found itself at divergence with its old ally on matters such as the single European currency and EU enlargement. While Britain was cautious, to say the least, about EU economic and monetary union, the Portuguese remained keen adherents. At the same time, Britain's enthusiasm for enlargement was not shared by the Portuguese, who feared that they might be losers in the future reallocation of assistance funds and saw little opportunity for increased trade in the Eastern European markets. Indeed, Portugal hinted that it might eventually use its veto on the enlargement issue unless its established benefits were safeguarded.

The other main (but for now less important) direction of Portugal's foreign policy, trade and investment continued to be the Portuguese-speaking world, whose six other states were now linked to the former colonial power within the Community of Portuguese-Speaking Countries (see XI.2.iii). Bilateral connections with Brazil deriving from a common language were further strengthened by joint membership of the Association of Ibero-American States. In Portuguese-speaking Africa, however, Portuguese influence faced competition from France in Guinea-Bissau, surrounded as it was by French-speaking countries, while in Mozambique and Angola the speed and scale of economic change were rapidly creating new geopolitical perspectives. The authorities in Mozambique, which had joined the (mainly English-speaking) Commonwealth in 1995, pointedly distanced themselves from the commemoration of the fifth centenary of the arrival of Vasco da Gama in 1497 on his way to India, as economic integration with South Africa gathered pace. As for Angola, close relations with Portugal and Brazil were seen by Luanda as a way of maintaining the country's cultural-national identity; nevertheless, it currently supplied the United States with some 7 per cent of its oil imports (three times as much as Kuwait at the time of the Iraqi invasion),

The dispute with Indonesia over East Timor remained unresolved in 1997, despite intercession by President Mandela of South Africa. Towards the end of the year, the Indonesian economic crisis (see IX.1.vi) left little hope of an early disentanglement of the dispute, one of two remaining postscripts to the old Portuguese empire. The other was Macao, where the British withdrawal from Hong Kong and the first months of Chinese administration (see IX.2.ii) were keenly followed in light of the formal reversion to China scheduled for December 1999.

iv. MALTA

CAPITAL: Valletta AREA: 316 sq km POPULATION: 370,000 ('96)
OFFICIAL LANGUAGES: Maltese & English
POLITICAL SYSTEM: parliamentary democracy
HEAD OF STATE: President Ugo Mifsud Bonnici (since April '94)
RULING PARTY: Malta Labour Party (MLP)
HEAD OF GOVERNMENT: Alfred Sant, Prime Minister (since Oct '96)
MAIN IGO MEMBERSHIPS (non-UN): NAM, CWTH, OSCE, CE
CURRENCY: lira (end-'97 £1=Lm0.65, $US1=Lm0.39)
GNP PER CAPITA: US$8,000 ('94)

A dull year of economic slowdown and party bickering suddenly erupted into life and fury when Dom Mintoff, the 81-year-old former Labour Prime Minister, launched a series of astonishing attacks in parliament on the present Labour government of Dr Alfred Sant. The occasion was the debate on the budget on 10–14 November, the danger for the government being that it had a majority of only one: 35 members to 34.

Mr Mintoff's campaign opened on 8 November when he threatened to withhold his vote for the budget if he were not given an hour of parliamentary time to speak. On 10 November, intervening repeatedly during debate on a budget procedural motion, he excoriated the Deputy Prime Minister and Foreign Minister, George Vella. He then broadened his targets to include the government's economic policy; the Nationalist opposition, which was being 'taken for a ride' by Europe; the European Union (EU) itself; the Catholic Church, which should 'fund its own schools and theology classes'; and the business class, accusing it of paying insufficient taxes.

There were farcical moments, as when the government majority was saved by Dr Francis Agius, a Nationalist MP who mistakenly voted with Labour. More serious was the fact that Mr Mintoff voted against the government, then stayed away from parliament. The result on one vote was a 34–34 tie, whereupon the Speaker, Miriam Spiteri Debono, cast her vote for the government. The Labour Party responded by convening an emergency conference of its members on 24 November, when the leadership was given a vote of confidence of over 90 per cent and Dr Sant stood firm in defence of the budget. Thereafter, as with the sudden violence and ensuing calm of a Mediterranean storm, political peace returned to the island.

Prior to the November drama, Dr Sant's government had remained precarious at a time when the economy lacked buoyancy. The governor of the Bank of Malta, Francis Vassallo, in a speech on 21 April marking the 30th anniversary of the bank's foundation, ruled out any danger of a recession. However, the first half of the year was spent devising ways of meeting a shortfall in state finances following the incoming Labour government's decision to abolish VAT (see AR 1996, p. 88). The government was handicapped by the resignation on 27 March of its Finance Minister, Lino Spiteri, who was succeeded by Leo Brincat. Nevertheless, VAT came to an end at the beginning of July and was replaced by a new tax system based on enhanced fiscal duties. The government then conducted a vigorous campaign against unnecessary price increases.

There were difficulties, too, at Malta Drydocks. An efficiency review by consultants Appledore International, commissioned in January, was submitted on 4 July. It concluded that there was need for a 'painful transition from the current position of huge and ongoing losses to a slimmed-down but commercially-viable ship repair operation', taking advantage of Malta's three key factors—'location, low costs and technical competence'. Meanwhile, unemployment remained low at 4.3 per cent.

The introduction of the new tax regime provoked an angry quarrel between government and opposition over the use of broadcasting time. The opposition leader, Dr Eddie Fenech Adami, complained that, whereas the government had spent a good deal of time explaining the new duties, the opposition's request for the right to reply had been ignored by the government-owned Public Broadcasting Services (PBS). After a court ruling that there had been imbalance, the Broadcasting Authority told the PBS to give time to the opposition party; but that too was ignored. When the Nationalists sought to raise the 'constitutional illegality' of the PBS in parliament, the Speaker refused to allow an adjournment debate.

The Central Office of Statistics issued figures in July showing that 2.4 per cent of the total number of married men and women could be classified as 'separated couples', the percentage rising to 6.7 in the age group 16 to 19. The figures were well below those given by the Maltese Divorce Movement (campaigning for an end to the existing ban on divorce).

By contrast with domestic politics, foreign policy was uneventful. The government more than once raised the issue of UN sanctions against Libya, the Prime Minister questioning their usefulness during a seminar at the Islamic World Studies Centre in Marsascala on 24 March. Speaking as Foreign Minister at a Non-Aligned Movement meeting in New Delhi early in April, Mr Vella said: 'While the Maltese government will continue to respect these sanctions, Malta is of the opinion that a decision by the Security Council to suspend the sanctions has long been overdue.' Libya was not represented, however, at the large 'Euro-Med' conference held in Malta 1–16 April. Meanwhile, the Labour government reaffirmed its decision not to apply for full EU membership.

v. GREECE

CAPITAL: Athens   AREA: 132,000 sq km   POPULATION: 10,500,000 ('96)
OFFICIAL LANGUAGE: Greek
POLITICAL SYSTEM: parliamentary democracy
HEAD OF STATE: President Kostas Stephanopoulos (since March '95)
RULING PARTY: Pan-Hellenic Socialist Movement (PASOK)
HEAD OF GOVERNMENT: Kostas Simitis, Prime Minister (since Jan '96)
MAIN IGO MEMBERSHIPS (non-UN): NATO, EU, WEU, OSCE, CE, BSEC, OECD
CURRENCY: drachma (end-'97 £1=Dr467.58, US$1=Dr284.99)
GNP PER CAPITA: US$8,210 ('95) or US$11,710 ('95) by PPP calculation

As so often in the past, questions of foreign relations, and in particular Greece's troubled relationship with Turkey, dominated the political scene in 1997.

Early in the year there were some hopeful indications of an improvement in bilateral relations with Turkey. The attendance of General Ismail Karadayi, the Chief of the Turkish General Staff, at the 25 March national day reception in the Greek embassy in Ankara was clearly intended as a goodwill gesture of some significance. At the European Union-Turkey Association Council meeting on 30 April both countries agreed to the appointment of committees of 'wise men' to help make suggestions for the resolution of the Aegean dispute. At the same time, Greece maintained its veto on EU financial aid to Turkey, while Ankara repeated it assertion that any move by Greece to extend its territorial waters from six to 12 miles would be regarded as a *casus belli*. Opposition to the establishment of the committees was expressed by 32 deputies of the ruling Pan-Hellenic Socialist Movement (PASOK). A declaration by President Demirel in the course of a May television interview, that the sovereignty of up to 130 islands in the Aegean was debatable, caused an angry reaction in Greece.

Following pressure from the US Secretary of State, Madeleine Albright, a 'convergence of views' agreement was signed by the Greek Prime Minister, Kostas Simitis, and the Turkish President at the NATO summit in Madrid in July. Both countries agreed to respect each other's sovereign rights in the Aegean and to renounce the use of force, affirming their commitment to 'peace, security and the continuous development of good-neighbourly relations'. In October, however, the Greek government declared the Madrid agreement void after a very serious escalation in tension between the two countries. This was precipitated by the participation, under the terms of the Greece-Cyprus common defence policy, of elements of the Greek armed forces in manoeuvres on Cyprus. Greece claimed that the aircraft carrying the Greek Defence Minister, Akis Tsokhatsopoulos, to and from the island had been intercepted by Turkish planes, which contrary to existing agreements were armed. Turkey counter-claimed that a Greek warship had tried to ram a Turkish submarine and that Greece was assisting Kurdish separatists. Nonetheless, despite this very serious escalation of tension, the Turkish Prime Minister, Mesut Yilmaz, agreed to attend the summit of Balkan leaders convened in Crete on 3–7 November with the aim of improving regional cooperation.

Relations between Greece and Turkey, however, worsened again as a consequence of the Luxembourg meeting of EU leaders in mid-December (see

XI.3). The decision to exclude Turkey from negotiations for the next round of EU enlargement, criticism of its human rights record, combined with the EU's willingness to open accession negotiations with Cyprus in advance of any settlement of the Cyprus problem provoked a very strong Turkish reaction (see also II.3.vi). This was not assuaged by a statement from Mr Simitis on 16 December that Greece did not wish to exclude Turkey from the EU and would welcome its accession provided that it played by the EU's rules.

Foreign Minister Theodoros Pangalos visited Macedonia in March, the first such visit by a senior Greek government figure since Macedonia had become an independent state. However, no agreement was reached on the contentious issue of the name of the independent Macedonian state during this visit, or at subsequent meetings held under the auspices of the United Nations in New York in June. During a visit by Mr Simitis to Albania in July, Greece undertook to make available a $72 million dollar loan (see also III.2.i).

On 21 March Costas Karamanlis was elected leader of the conservative New Democracy, the main opposition party. He easily defeated Miltiades Evert, who had been elected leader in 1993 and had led the party to defeat in the September 1996 elections (see AR 1996, p. 92), and Georgios Souflias, a former minister. At 41, Mr Karamanlis was the youngest-ever leader of a major political party in Greece, where there was a tradition of gerontocratic political leadership. Nonetheless, his accession to the leadership of the party founded by his uncle, former President Konstantinos Karamanlis, was in keeping with traditional Greek political mores whereby dynastic connections remained important.

The publication of the archive/memoirs of former President Karamanlis in May provoked controversy. He dismissed his arch-rival, the late Andreas Papandreou (see AR 1996, pp. 556–7), as not only 'a common cheat, a demagogue and a hypocrite' but also a danger to his country. Moreover, advanced old-age did not appear to have mellowed his longstanding feud with ex-King Constantine, whom he accused of involvement in a coup plot to regain his throne in 1975, as he (Mr Karamanlis) struggled to restore Greece to democratic rule after the collapse of the colonels' dictatorship. This sparked a counter-claim by the ex-king that Mr Karamanlis had himself advocated a coup in 1966. In June the Supreme Court upheld the legality of the government's nationalization of royal properties, this decision prompting suggestions that the former king might take his claim to the European Court of Human Rights.

The Deputy Foreign Minister, Georgios Papandreou, created a stir in May when he called for the decriminalization of soft drugs. The government declared that it had no plans for such a measure, while the leader of the Communist Party of Greece, Aleka Papariga, strongly criticized Mr Papandreou.

Strikes by public- and private-sector workers continued early in the year in protest against government austerity measures aimed at preparing Greece to join the single European currency within five years. Farmers set up blockades in pursuit of their demands for lower fuel prices, cuts in VAT, the rescheduling of debts and higher support prices for agricultural products. There was also a prolonged teachers' strike, while educational reforms announced in August by

Gerasimos Arsenis, the Minister of Education, provoked protests and sit-ins by university students. In May thousands of policeman demonstrated outside the Ministry of Public Order to demand better pay and conditions.

The terrorist group '17 November' continued to operate with impunity, claiming responsibility for the killing on 28 May of shipowner Costas Peratikos. In a bulletin sent to the newspaper *Eleftherotypia*, the group criticized what it termed the scandalous circumstances of the Peratikos group's acquisition of the previously state-owned Elefsina shipyards in 1992 and said that it had made two previous attempts to assassinate Mr Peratikos.

In December the first convention of the World Council of Hellenes was held in Thessaloniki, being an attempt to mobilize the resources of the Greek diaspora in the furtherance of Greece's national interests. Greeks of the diaspora were held to number 7 million in 141 countries. At one of the convention sessions, the Minister of Culture, Evangelos Venizelos, declared that, although a small country, Greece had all the characteristics of a 'cultural super-power'.

The International Olympic Committee's announcement in September that it had preferred Athens over Rome as host city for the 2004 Olympics was greeted with enormous enthusiasm, and a sharp rise in the Greek stock exchange. The decision helped to assuage the disappointment caused when Athens had been passed over for the centennial Olympics in 1996.

Throughout the year, the northern Greek city of Thessaloniki enjoyed the status of Cultural Capital of Europe. The most significant related event, attended by large numbers, was undoubtedly the magnificent 'Treasures of Mount Athos' exhibition, which brought together in the recently-established Byzantine Museum many priceless artefacts that had never previously been allowed to leave the Holy Mountain. On 23 November President Stephanopoulos unveiled a memorial to the city's once-substantial Jewish community, which had been almost completely wiped out by German deportations to extermination camps during World War II.

vi. CYPRUS

CAPITAL: Nicosia   AREA: 9,250 sq km   POPULATION: 848,587 ('96); 648,000
  Greek Cypriots in south (Planning Bureau est.)and 200,587 Turkish Cypriots, Turks and others in north ('96 census)
POLITICAL SYSTEM: separate presidential democracies in Greek area and in Turkish Republic of Northern Cyprus (recognized only by Turkey)
HEAD OF STATE & GOVERNMENT: President Glafkos Clerides (since Feb '93); Rauf Denktash has been President of Turkish area since Feb '75
MAIN IGO MEMBERSHIPS (non-UN): (Greek Cyprus) NAM, OSCE, CE, CWTH
CURRENCY: Cyprus pound (end-'97 C£1=£0.87, US$1=£0.53)
GNP PER CAPITA: Greek Cyprus US$13,298 ('95); TRNC US$4,087 ('95)

THE most elaborately prepared UN-sponsored peace talks since 1991 collapsed in August after the Turkish Cypriot leader, Rauf Denktash, insisted on recognition of the self-declared Turkish Republic of Northern Cyprus (TRNC) as a precondition for their continuation. In December the European Union (EU) confirmed that accession negotiations would begin with the government of the Republic in April 1998 and declined to include Turkey even in a B-list of candidates for enlargement. Ankara responded that it would no longer discuss political issues such as Cyprus with the EU and that unless Brussels changed its position by mid-1998 it would withdraw its application for membership. Mr Denktash asserted that as a consequence the inter-communal talks process was 'dead'.

The year had begun with relations still soured by the previous year's killings on the 'green' ceasefire line and with a new crisis developing over the Greek Cypriot decision to purchase Russian-made S-300 anti-aircraft missiles that could challenge Turkey's air superiority over the island (see AR 1996, p. 95). Encouraged by US and some European criticism of the Greek Cypriot initiative, the TRNC government described it as 'an act of aggression', while Turkey warned that it was prepared to use military force to prevent deployment of the missiles. Intensive US and other mediation succeeded in defusing the immediate crisis by mid-January, on the basis of a Greek Cypriot undertaking that the missiles would not be deployed until 1998 at the earliest. However, the episode served to confirm the total absence of trust between the two sides and to solidify further the existing negotiating deadlock.

During a visit to Ankara by Mr Denktash in January, he and President Demirel of Turkey issued a joint statement saying that Cyprus should accede to the EU only after a constitutional settlement and after Turkish admission. It also warned that, if the Greek Cypriots continued to develop air and naval facilities to support Greek warplanes and warships under the terms of their March 1994 joint defence agreement, then Turkey and the TRNC would develop a 'joint defence concept' involving the construction of air and naval bases on the island. Mr Denktash further threatened that if the S-300 missiles were deployed the Varosha district of Famagusta, once home to 30,000 Greek Cypriots and left derelict since the 1974 Turkish invasion, would be opened to settlement. During the visit, a new economic cooperation agreement was agreed by which the TRNC was to get $250 million in aid to ease an economic crisis that had seen the Turkish Cypriot administration unable to meet its financial obligations to public-sector workers and farmers.

In April the new UN Secretary General, Kofi Annan, appointed as his special representative to Cyprus Diego Córdovez, a former Ecuadorian Foreign Minister and the man who had negotiated the 1989 Russian withdrawal from Afghanistan. In June US President Bill Clinton appointed as his special Cyprus emissary Richard Holbrooke, the man who had brokered the 1995 Dayton accord which ended the civil war in Bosnia & Hercegovina

Intensive diplomatic contacts by, among others, special UK representative Sir David Hannay paved the way for the first formal negotiations between the community leaders since 1993. The first round was held at the resort of Troutbeck in up-state New York on 9–12 July and the second at Glion near Montreux, Switzerland, on 11–15 August. Moderated by Sr Córdovez, the sessions were closed, limited to President Glafkos Clerides, Mr Denktash and their advisers. Between these two formal sessions there were informal meetings between Mr Clerides and Mr Denktash in Nicosia. In the event, the Nicosia talks produced the only practical result of the whole exercise, namely an agreement to work towards resolving the emotionally-charged issue of missing persons.

The Troutbeck negotiations took place against the positive backdrop of a joint declaration by Greece and Turkey at the July NATO summit in Madrid to abide by international treaties, to resolve outstanding differences by arbitration and to abjure the use of force. A draft negotiating document produced by Sr Córdovez contained constitutional proposals which spoke of Cyprus as a federal state with a single sovereignty and a single citizenship which would emanate equally from both communities who would establish the federation. The federal constituents would administer their own communal affairs and there would be political, but not numerical, equality in federal institutions as well as safeguards to ensure that the federal government could not take actions inimical to the interests of either community. There were objections to the Córdovez document from both sides but, since neither wanted to be seen as responsible for a collapse of the talks, a second round was agreed for August.

In the interim, the European Commission published *Agenda 2000*, its blueprint for the EU for the period 2000–06. In the section on enlargement it reiterated that accession negotiations would begin with Cyprus in 1998—regardless of whether there was a constitutional settlement—and excluded Turkey from the list of potential candidates, citing low economic development, a poor human rights record, disputes with EU member Greece, and continuing failure to resolve the Cyprus issue. The new Turkish coalition government led by the Motherland Party responded by mounting a vigorous diplomatic campaign to secure inclusion, but was unable to make concessions over Cyprus because the coalition included the Democratic Left Party under Bülent Ecevit, who as Prime Minister in 1974 had ordered the Turkish invasion of Cyprus. Now Deputy Prime Minister, Mr Ecevit put Cyprus ahead of Europe on the Turkish foreign policy agenda and insisted on an adamantine line that unless the federal settlement was one of dual sovereignty Turkey would annex the northern territory.

Mr Denktash said that the EU's acceptance of the unilateral application of the Greek Cypriot government struck at the heart of the TRNC's efforts to be treated as an equal sovereign partner. On 6 August Turkey and the TRNC agreed to establish an Association Council wherein every step towards unilateral EU accession would be matched by corresponding measures of economic and political integration between the TRNC and the mainland. At the Glion round of negotiations, Mr Denktash demanded that he be afforded equal status with Mr Clerides, while the Greek Cypriot leader insisted that the negotiations should discuss issues such as property and residence rights and the expulsion of mainland settlers before dealing with constitutional matters. The talks were discontinued with no date set for a resumption.

In September the Turkish Prime Minister, Mesut Yilmaz, announced that he had instructed the military to take 'measures' to prevent deployment of the

S-300 missiles. A Cypriot-flagged vessel was stopped and searched in the Sea of Marmara, ostensibly to check if it was carrying weapons components. The Greek government declared that any military action against Cyprus would constitute a cause for war. Greek Cypriot military exercises in October featured the call-up of 9,000 reservists and manoeuvres involving a large arsenal of heavy weaponry with Greek air and naval support. There were a reported 150 incursions of Cypriot airspace by Turkish warplanes, which engaged in repeated mock dogfights with Greek jets. Turkish fighter planes even buzzed the aircraft of the Greek Defence Minister as he flew to Cyprus to observe the war games, and again on his return journey (see also II.3.v). Turkish military exercises on the island in November simulated repulsion of an attack from south Cyprus, while Turkish commandos destroyed mock missile installations. The US administration called for a moratorium on flights over the island by both Greece and Turkey for fear that an accident could spark hostilities.

The EU summit in Luxembourg on 12–13 December accepted the *Agenda 2000* recommendations, confirming that accession negotiations with Cyprus would commence in April 1998. Turkey would be invited to attend a European conference of prospective members but its name would not be added to the list of formal candidates until it improved its record on human rights and could demonstrate that it accepted other EU principles such as peaceful coexistence and good neighbourliness. Meeting with Mr Yilmaz days later in Washington, President Clinton said Turkey was a significant ally of the West and should not be isolated. However, when US Secretary of State Madeleine Albright criticized the EU's decision at a NATO meeting, she was brusquely rebuffed by her German counterpart, Klaus Kinkel.

On 23 December the UN Security Council passed its semi-annual resolution extending the mandate of the UN Force in Cyprus (UNFICYP), also calling for a resumption of peace talks in March once Greek Cypriot presidential elections were concluded. Mr Denktash described the resolution as 'not applicable' since it referred to the Greek Cypriots as the Cyprus government. He said he would in future only participate in talks between two sovereign states where he was recognized as the president of one of them.

On the domestic political scene, questions were raised early in the year about whether 78-year-old President Clerides would run for re-election in February 1998 after he was admitted to hospital suffering from chest pains. These proved not to be serious, and in the autumn Mr Clerides declared that he would run again, backed by the Democratic Rally (DISY). As the year closed, his main challenger among five other contenders was George Iakovou, a former Foreign Minister, standing as an independent but with the backing of both the Communist Party (AKEL) and the Democratic Party (DIKO). DIKO had been the junior coalition partner in Mr Clerides government until withdrawing on 5 November, its five ministers being replaced by non-party appointees.

In the TRNC, Dervis Eroglu's coalition government of his right-wing National Unity Party (UBP) and the conservative Democratic Party (DP) survived the year despite intense internal squabbling and defections from the DP. In September

Mr Eroglu underwent angiography in Turkey, while in October Mr Denktash, who had suffered a heart attack in 1996, was again under doctors' care for an irregular heartbeat.

vii. TURKEY

CAPITAL: Ankara   AREA: 779,000 sq km   POPULATION: 62,600,000 ('97)
OFFICIAL LANGUAGE: Turkish
POLITICAL SYSTEM: parliamentary democracy
HEAD OF STATE: President Süleyman Demirel (since May '93)
RULING PARTIES: Motherland Party (ANAP) heads minority coalition with Democratic Left (DSP) and Democratic Turkey (DTP) parties
HEAD OF GOVERNMENT: Mesut Yilmaz (ANAP), Prime Minister (since July '97)
MAIN IGO MEMBERSHIPS (non-UN): NATO, OSCE, OECD, CE, OIC, ECO, BSEC
CURRENCY: lira (end-'97 £1=LT341,249.24, US$1=LT207,990.00)
GNP PER CAPITA: US$2,780 ('95) or US$5,580 ('95) by PPP calculation

THE fall of the Islamist-led coalition government in June did not help Turkey realize its ambition of being officially named as a candidate for full membership of the European Union (EU) in the enlargement process inaugurated in Luxembourg in December. As the year ended, a minority secularist government in Ankara faced difficult economic choices at home and problems with the EU and its Muslim neighbours abroad. However, domestic discontent was held in check by the determination of civil society organizations and of the armed forces to keep secularist politicians in power, and Islamists out of it.

The coalition government formed in June 1996 by Necmettin Erbakan, leader of the Islamist Welfare Party (RP), with Tansu Çiller's centre-right True Path Party (DYP) as junior partner (see AR 1996, pp. 96–7), gradually fell apart in the first half of the year. Tension between secularists and Islamists rose during the Ramadan fast in January, when Mr Erbakan invited leaders of the theoretically-banned dervish fraternities to an official breakfast in the Prime Minister's residence. Then, on 1 February, the RP mayor of the Ankara suburb of Sincan invited the Iranian ambassador to address a protest rally against the Israeli occupation of Jerusalem. A woman television journalist trying to record his denunciation of cooperation with Israel—in which Turkey was involved—amid scenes of Islamic fervour was assaulted by the crowd. The civil authorities reacted by asking the ambassador to leave the country and by arresting the mayor of Sincan. On 4 February the military came out openly in support of the secularist opposition by sending an armoured column to the streets of the suburb.

On 28 February President Süleyman Demirel chaired a meeting of the National Security Council (NSC) at which the military commanders demanded determined action against 'religious reaction'. Prime Minister Erbakan signed the NSC recommendations, which involved a drastic reduction in the number and size of religious schools; but as he delayed implementation, Mrs Çiller came under pressure to leave the coalition. Threatened by defections from DYP ranks, Mrs Çiller persuaded Mr Erbakan to hand over the premiership to her in preparation for early elections. However, when Mr Erbakan resigned on 18 June, President Demirel called not on Mrs Çiller, but on Mesut Yilmaz, leader of the centre-right Motherland Party (ANAP), to form the new government.

Mr Yilmaz quickly succeeded in putting together a coalition with the Democratic Left Party (DSP), led by the veteran social democrat Bülent Ecevit, and the new Democratic Turkey Party (DTP), consisting of DYP defectors grouped round the former speaker of parliament, Hüsamettin Cindoruk. Although still short of a parliamentary majority, the new coalition was supported by the second centre-left party, the Republican People's Party (CHP), led by Deniz Baykal. The new government assumed office on 30 June, its programme being endorsed in parliament on 12 July by 281 votes to 256. On 18 August the legislature passed a law extending compulsory secular education to eight years. This entailed the closure of religious 'middle schools' (for 13- to 16-year-olds), stricter control of Koranic courses and enforcement of a vocational status on religious high schools, whose intake was limited to the staffing needs of mosques.

On 14–15 June, a few days before his resignation, Mr Erbakan chaired an Islamic meeting in Istanbul which gave birth to the 'Developing Eight' (D-8) organization of Islamic countries. The new government paid little attention to this initiative, concentrating instead on developing relations with the West. Believing that Mrs Çiller had endangered national interests by being too compliant in her campaign for EU membership, Mr Yilmaz, Mr Ecevit and the new Foreign Minister, Ismail Cem (a member of the DSP) toured European capitals insisting that Turkey had a right, under the 1963 treaty of association, to be treated as a candidate in the enlargement process, at least on a footing of equality with others. They refused to make any concessions to Greece or Greek Cypriots as the price of candidature, and warned that the opening of membership negotiations between the EU and the Greek Cypriot-controlled Republic of Cyprus would be met by the integration with Turkey of the Turkish Republic of Northern Cyprus (which Turkey was alone in recognizing). Joint Greek-Greek Cypriot military exercises were followed by Turkish exercises in the same area, and there were allegations of buzzing of aircraft and of violations of air space (see also II.3.v). In the circumstances, a meeting between Mr Yilmaz and the Greek Prime Minister in Crete in November, in the margins of a Balkan conference, proved fruitless.

The European policy of the Yilmaz government suffered a setback on 13 December, when an EU summit in Luxembourg did not name Turkey among candidates for enlargement, while confirming the promise to start membership negotiations with Cyprus early in 1998. The only concession to Turkey was an invitation to a standing European conference which would review conditions under which it could become a candidate. These included respect for human rights and minorities and progress in relations with Greece and in the solution of the Cyprus problem. The following day the Turkish government turned down the invitation to the European conference and suspended the political dialogue with the EU. It also accused the EU of failing to meet its obligations under the customs union which had come into force on 1 January 1996—although the union was not renounced by Ankara.

Turkey's difficulties in its relations with Muslim states had in the meantime been exposed when, on 11 December, President Demirel left the Tehran summit of the Organization of the Islamic Conference a day early (see XI.2.iv). Before departing, he had been obliged to listen to implicit criticism of his country for its cooperation with Israel, whose Defence Minister was at the time on an official visit to Turkey. President Demirel responded by criticizing countries which supported terrorism.

Other foreign policy developments were more positive. On 15 December the Russian Prime Minister, Viktor Chernomyrdin, paid a successful visit to Ankara, signing an agreement for the construction of a pipeline under the Black Sea capable of bringing 16,000 million cubic metres of Russian natural gas a year to Turkey. The following day the Turkish Prime Minister flew to Washington for talks with President Clinton. US mediation cooled Turkey's dispute with the EU, and Mr Yilmaz did not repeat his threat to withdraw his country's membership application if it was not named a candidate within six months.

The main emphasis of the Washington talks was on the Turkish economy, as the Yilmaz government sought the support of the IMF for its three-year programme to bring down inflation. The 1998 budget, which aimed to halve the growth rate to 3 per cent and reduce inflation from more than 90 to 50 per cent by the end of the year, was approved by parliament on 25 December by 301 votes to 217. As the year ended, the IMF was still pressing for quicker and more determined action. During the first nine months of the year, the economy grew by 6.2 per cent, while the Istanbul stock exchange rose by over 60 per cent in real terms by the end of November. The volume of foreign trade rose by 7 per cent in the first eight months of the year, with exports growing faster than imports. In the first nine months, the number of foreign visitors increased by 15 per cent to a record level of nearly 8 million.

Casualties mounted as the security forces continued their efforts to defeat the 13-year old insurgency of the Kurdistan Workers' Party (PKK). Turkish armed forces crossed repeatedly into the Kurdish areas of northern Iraq, where they were supported by the militia of Mustafa Barzani's Kurdistan Democratic Party (KDP), against both the PKK and Jallal Talibani's Patriotic Union of Kurdistan (PUK).

Provisional results of the census held in November showed that the growth rate of the population had dropped from 2.2 per cent in the five years to 1990 to an annual average of 1.5 per cent in the subsequent seven years, and that the country's population numbered 62,600,000.

III CENTRAL AND EASTERN EUROPE

1. POLAND—BALTIC REPUBLICS—CZECH REPUBLIC—SLOVAKIA—
HUNGARY—ROMANIA—BULGARIA

i. POLAND

CAPITAL: Warsaw   AREA: 313,000 sq km   POPULATION: 38,700,000 ('96)
OFFICIAL LANGUAGE: Polish
POLITICAL SYSTEM: presidential democracy
HEAD OF STATE: President Aleksander Kwasniewski (since Dec '95)
RULING PARTIES: Solidarity Electoral Alliance (AWS) & Freedom Union (UW)
HEAD OF GOVERNMENT: Jerzy Buzek (AWS), Prime Minister (since Oct '97)
MAIN IGO MEMBERSHIPS (non-UN): OSCE, CE, PFP, CEI, CEFTA, CBSS
CURRENCY: new zloty (end-'97 £1=Zl.5.79, US$1=Zl.3.53)
GNP PER CAPITA: US$2,790 ('95) or US$5,400 ('95) by PPP calculation

THE political landscape shifted rightwards. Following the victory of nationalist and Catholic parties in September parliamentary elections, a centre-right coalition government was formed. It promised greater emphasis on privatization and economic reform and reaffirmed a policy of rapid integration within NATO and the European Union (EU).

Regrouping of the numerous small parties on the right, all eliminated in the 1993 election, began with the formation of Conservative People's Party (SKL) on 12 January. A conservative political theorist, Aleksander Hall, often an isolated voice during the communist period, became chairman of its political council. This challenge did not go unnoticed by the ruling left coalition. Professor Marek Belka, a specialist in money and banking, was appointed Minister of Finance on 4 February. He announced a wide programme of structural reforms and privatization, starting with the Trade Bank, copper and precious metals mining, energy refining and telecommunications.

Most of this programme was accepted by the public. However, the final closure of the Gdansk Shipyard (see AR 1996, p. 100), the birthplace of Solidarity in 1980, led to anti-government protests in Gdansk itself and outside ministerial headquarters in Warsaw. To head them off, the government declared a partial reprieve under which 2,000 (of the 3,800) made redundant would be reinstated. They were to complete five new vessels for the state-owned shipping company, and thereafter act as ancillary workers to the more successful yard in Szczecin.

In April the Polish parliament finally agreed a new constitution to replace the interim 'little constitution' of December 1992. The new document strengthened parliament in relation to the presidency, the majority required to overturn a presidential veto being reduced from three-fifths to two-thirds. Presidential powers over appointments were reduced, though the right to choose the heads of defence, security and Supreme Court were retained.

Opposition to the new constitution had come mainly from trade unions, on the grounds that it did not make a sufficiently clear break with the communist past. It was also opposed by the Catholic Church for its failure to prohibit abortion. This was highlighted in May during an 11-day pilgrimage to his homeland by Pope John Paul II, whose homilies directly contradicted the stance of the President (and later parliament) on the abortion question. Nevertheless, the new constitution was approved by a national referendum on 25 May, with a 57 per cent vote in favour. The Confederation of Independent Poland (KPN) complained that the turnout (43 per cent) was below the 50 per cent required by the previous constitution, but this appeal was rejected by the Supreme Court on 15 July.

Meanwhile, a NATO summit in Madrid on 8–9 July had formally invited Poland, together with the Czech Republic and Hungary, to join the alliance as full members in April 1999. Because of his opposition to one of the preconditions for membership—civilian control of the military—the Chief of the General Staff, General Tadeusz Wilecki, had been dismissed in March. Among the general public, opinion continued to be overwhelmingly in favour of NATO accession.

During the summer the ruling coalition of the Democratic Left Alliance (SLD) and Polish Peasant Party (PSL) came close to collapse when the junior PSL tabled a vote of no confidence in the Prime Minister, Wlodzimierz Cimoszewicz. He survived by promising relief, through the advance purchase of grain, for farmers affected by heavy flooding in July. The Oder and Neisse rivers had overflowed and the historic city of Wroclaw, also badly damaged, was granted emergency government funding.

The centre-right regrouped to fight the general elections called for 21 September. Some three dozen populist and Catholic parties were assembled around the Solidarity trade union as a Solidarity Electoral Alliance (ASW). It headed the poll with 33.8 per cent of the vote and 201 of the 460 lower house seats. Second came the ruling SLD, which increased its share of the vote to 27.1 per cent and its lower house representation to 164 seats. But its PSL coalition partner collapsed to 7.3 per cent and 27 seats, which left the balance of power with the Freedom Union (UW) of intellectuals and former opponents of the communist government, which won 13.4 per cent and 60 seats. The pro-market Movement for Reconstruction of Poland took 5.6 per cent and six seats, while the two remaining lower house seats went to a German minority organization. The Labour Union (UP), with 4.7 per cent, and other groupings which polled under 5 per cent did not qualify for entry into the new parliament.

The ASW and the UW then held protracted negotiations on a coalition government, eventually agreeing to propose Jerzy Buzek (58), a Protestant and founder member of Solidarity in 1980, as Prime Minister. Sworn in on 31 October, the new government contained 17 ASW ministers (in addition to Mr Buzek) and six from the UW. The original architect of the economic shock therapy of 1989–91, Leszek Balcerowicz (UW), became Deputy Prime Minister and Finance Minister. Two more veterans of the Solidarity period, both now UW members, were given prominent posts: Bronislaw Geremek as Foreign Minister and Janusz Onyszkiewicz as Minister of Defence. Also noteworthy was the appointment of former Prime Minister Hanna Suchocka (UW) as Justice Minister. The ASW applied for official registration as a political party on 13 November.

Despite the change of personnel, the broad lines of established policy continued. The new government's parliamentary programme, presented on 10 November, reaffirmed the rights of private property, including land, and promised measures to foster Christianity and family values. External priorities were to promote entry into the EU and integrate Poland rapidly with NATO. Like all new governments, it promised to reduce bureaucracy.

As part of developing an even-handed foreign policy, President Kwasniewski had travelled to the Ukraine in late May to sign a declaration of reconciliation. This condemned both the murders of Poles by Nazi Ukrainian nationalists in 1943 and the deportation of up to 100,000 Ukrainians from communist Poland in 1947. But the main thrust of government policy was westwards. Preparations for NATO entry in April 1999 were accelerated by a 'Weimar Triangle' meeting (of Germany, France and Poland) on 3 November, when a three-year programme of joint military exercises was announced. The following month, at an EU summit in Luxembourg, Poland was formally included among the 'first wave' of six applicant countries with which accession negotiations would be opened in 1998 (see XI.3).

ii. ESTONIA—LATVIA—LITHUANIA

Estonia
CAPITAL: Tallinn   AREA: 45,000 sq km   POPULATION: 1,500,000 ('96)
OFFICIAL LANGUAGE: Estonian
POLITICAL SYSTEM: democratic republic
HEAD OF STATE: President Lennart Meri (since Oct '92)
RULING PARTIES: Estonian Coalition Party (EK) heads coalition
HEAD OF GOVERNMENT: Mart Siimann (EK), Prime Minister (since March '97)
MAIN IGO MEMBERSHIPS (non-UN): OSCE, CE, PFP, CBSS
CURRENCY: kroon (end-'97 £1=K23.66, US$1=K14.42)
GNP PER CAPITA: US$2,270 ('95) or US$3,370 ('95) by PPP calculation

Latvia
CAPITAL: Riga   AREA: 64,000 sq km   POPULATION: 2,600,000 ('96)
OFFICIAL LANGUAGE: Latvian
POLITICAL SYSTEM: democratic republic
HEAD OF STATE: President Guntis Ulmanis (since July '93)
RULING PARTIES: multi-party coalition including Saimnieks, Latvian Way & Union for Fatherland and Freedom (TUBS)
HEAD OF GOVERNMENT: Guntars Krasts (TUBS), Prime Minister (since July '97)
MAIN IGO MEMBERSHIPS (non-UN): OSCE, CE, PFP, CBSS
CURRENCY: lats (end-'97 £1=L0.97, US$1=L0.59)
GNP PER CAPITA: US$2,270 ('95) or US$3,370 ('95) by PPP calculation

Lithuania

CAPITAL: Vilnius   AREA: 65,000 sq km   POPULATION: 3,750,000 ('96)
OFFICIAL LANGUAGE: Lithuanian
POLITICAL SYSTEM: democratic republic
HEAD OF STATE: President Algirdas Brazauskas (since Nov '92)
PRESIDENT-ELECT: Valdas Adamkus
RULING PARTIES: Homeland Union (TS) & Lithuanian Christian Democratic Party (LKDP)
HEAD OF GOVERNMENT: Gediminas Vagnorius (TS), Prime Minister (since Dec '96)
MAIN IGO MEMBERSHIPS (non-UN): OSCE, CE, PFP, CBSS
CURRENCY: litas (end-'97 £1=L6.53, US$1=L4.00)
GNP PER CAPITA: US$1,900 ('95) or US$4,120 ('95) by PPP calculation

IF principled resignation in democracies indicated political maturity, then the Baltic states had claim to this virtue in 1997.

In ESTONIA, the combination of luck and political acumen which had seen Prime Minister Tiit Vähi through difficult patches in 1996 (see AR 1996, p. 134) came to an end in the New Year, when rumours circulated about his illegal role in privatizing apartments in Tallinn, including that of his own daughter. Mr Vähi, whose Coalition Party (EK) had close links with the Tallinn city council, narrowly survived a no-confidence vote early in February, but the pressure was enough to prompt his resignation on 25 February, ostensibly to devote time to clearing his own name. Mart Siimann, also of the EK, was sworn in as the new Prime Minister on 17 March. Little changed on the policy front, however. The continuing emphasis, above all, on preparing for European Union (EU) membership was duly rewarded later in the year (see below).

In LATVIA, the departure from office of Prime Minister Andris Skele was a more protracted affair. On 20 January he too resigned following criticism of his chosen nominee as Finance Minister—a post left vacant since the previous October. When Mr Skele was reappointed on 29 January, with 70 members of parliament for his government and only 17 against, little seemed to have changed. In local elections on 9 March, however, the combined parties of the left took some 22 per cent of the vote, being particularly successful in Riga and Daugavpils. Juris Bojars, leader of the opposition Social Democratic Party, argued that the results indicated dissatisfaction with the social policies of successive Latvian governments. Mr Skele responded by launching a vitriolic and ill-judged personal attack against the flamboyant Mr Bojars, the Prime Minister's reward being a very critical press.

By the summer Mr Skele's increasingly beleaguered cabinet was also suffering from newspaper attacks on ministers allegedly holding paid positions in the private sector, contrary to their own anti-corruption legislation. The first resignation in this affair was that of Rihards Piks, the Minister for Culture, in late June. The following month witnessed a heated denial by the Transport Minister, Vilis Kristopans, that he too had violated the law on corruption. The Prime Minister—who was regarded by opponents as too assertive and indifferent to opposing views—finally succumbed to the crisis of confidence and resigned on 28 July. The continuity of his general policy line was maintained by his successor, Guntars Krasts, who secured the parliamentary support of the four largest parties early in August.

Even in LITHUANIA, where in 1996 Prime Minister Adolfas Slezevicius had to be prised out of office (see AR 1996, p. 135), resignation caught on. The Finance Minister, Rolands Matliauskas, was the first to go in February, over allegations of misdealing for a private bank prior to entering government. Indeed, he resigned on the day of his arraignment for embezzlement charges. Clearly, the conservative government of Gediminas Vagnorius could not afford to endanger its much proclaimed 'clean hands' policy, which had helped it to oust the Lithuanian Democratic Labour Party from office in the first place. There were also signs of tension between the government and President Brazauskas. The latter was deprived by parliament of his right to nominate the prosecutor-general, after sharp disagreements over a candidate for the post.

President Brazauskas was also afflicted by his own political maturity. In his October announcement that he would not seek a second term of office, he cited as harmful to Lithuania's image abroad his differences with parliament, his age and his Communist past. After the opening round of presidential elections on 21 December, the outgoing President announced that he would support first-placed Arturas Palauskas against second-placed Valdas Adamkus in the run-off in January 1998.

The governments of all three Baltic states continued to push hard for entry to the EU and NATO, which EU officials increasingly, if disingenuously, stressed were separate processes. In the sphere of European enlargement, the emphasis was placed on practical preparation and its considerable costs. In a long-awaited recommendation in July, the European Commission recommended in its wisdom that Estonia, but not yet Latvia and Lithuania, should be invited to begin accession negotiations. President Meri of Estonia observed that such negotiations would finally consign the former Soviet Union to the dustbin of history. Latvian and Lithuanian leaders, in contrast, barely disguised their disappointment at being relegated to a later EU enlargement. Although trying hard to maintain a display of goodwill towards their Estonian counterparts, they continued at every opportunity to promote the idea of a common starting-line for all three states.

It was argued in Riga and Vilnius, with some justice, that there was little to separate the three countries economically. Lithuania pointed out that the European Commission's recommendations had been made on the basis of outdated statistics. The message was not entirely lost, as EU member states tried to soften the blow. In October the German Foreign Minister, Klaus Kinkel, reaffirmed Germany's closeness to all three Baltic countries, while Hans van den Broek, the European commissioner for foreign relations, reassured Lithuania and Latvia that 'differentiation in no way implies discrimination'. The EU Luxembourg summit in December duly extended a formal invitation to Estonia to begin accession negotiations in 1998 (see XI.3).

The three Baltic republics nonetheless continued slowly to consolidate relationships with each other during the year, beginning in January with the extension of the Baltic free trade agreement to cover agriculture. The irksome clash over sea borders between Latvia and Estonia was resolved by an agreement in July.

Much effort was devoted to improving the inter-operability of their forces in preparation for NATO membership. Plans were laid for Lithuania to be the monitoring centre for joint air space, for Latvia to assume the task of coordinating the proposed joint Baltic peacekeeping force (BALTBAT) and for Estonia to be the base for a joint naval squadron (BALTRON). President Meri rightly hailed as unprecedented the 'Baltic Challenge' peace-keeping exercise at Paldiski in late July, involving eight countries. All the more tragic was the drowning of 14 Estonian soldiers during an exercise in September in Kurkse Bay (also near Paldiski), where poor surveillance was found to be the main cause of the accident.

The mix of promise and frustration experienced by the Baltic states in the matter of EU enlargement was duplicated over NATO. Concerns about the West's preoccupation with Russia's viewpoint had not been allayed during the weeks following the signature of the NATO-Russian Founding Act in May (see XII.1; XIX.1), even though the agreement represented no change in the West's refusal to allow Russia any veto on NATO enlargement. As expected, the NATO summit held in Madrid in July confirmed that none of the three would be in the first round of NATO enlargement, although it was stressed that the door remained open for the Baltic states. For his part, President Yeltsin repeatedly warned that Russia would be forced to reconsider its agreement with NATO should the latter expand to the Baltic countries, whilst Prime Minister Chernomyrdin saw NATO's enlargement as the 'largest strategic mistake in the aftermath of the Cold War'.

The Latvian Foreign Minister, Valdis Birkavs, wryly noted that the Baltic countries, having escaped their past through independence, were now to be 'detained by geography'. Indeed, Russia's continuing drive to retain a controlling voice over its 'near abroad' was very evident, although the new NATO-Russian relationship appeared to be influencing the choice of Moscow's tactics. Given the importance of settled borders for any NATO (or EU) aspirant, it was not surprising that Russia refused to finalize details of border agreements with Latvia and Estonia, citing, in the face of all objective findings, the alleged abuse of the human rights of Russian minorities in the two small countries. On the other hand, Russia finally signed a border agreement with Lithuania in October— the first of its kind with any post-Soviet nation. For good measure, President Yeltsin offered Russian Federation security guarantees for the Baltic countries, in December proposing deep cuts in military forces on Russia's western frontier.

Although comparatively welcome, these developments were seen in Baltic capitals as means towards the old end—the prevention of NATO enlargement to the Baltic states. Following a meeting on 10 November, the three Baltic Presidents pointedly reaffirmed their commitment to Atlantic security structures by politely but firmly rejecting President Yeltsin's offer. Their reason was that 'unilateral security decrees do not correspond to the spirit of the new Europe'. The Baltic states now awaited the oft-postponed meeting with President Clinton, rescheduled for January 1998, and the signature of the US-Baltic Charter, described by the US ambassador to Latvia as a 'politically-binding statement in bilateral cooperation'. The US permanent representative to NATO,

Robert Hunter, asserted that the proposed pact would increase the interaction between the Baltic republics and the United States, allowing the latter to act as a facilitator between the Baltics and Russia, whilst also promoting reform and integration.

What the US-Baltic Charter would not do, when it was signed, was to offer any security guarantees, it being carefully stressed by officials that the accord was not a substitute for entry to NATO. Not all were convinced. The overall impression was that the West's response to the challenges of integrating the Baltic countries into Europe during 1997 left much to be desired in terms of coherence and vision.

iii. CZECH REPUBLIC

CAPITAL: Prague   AREA: 30,450 sq km   POPULATION: 10,350,000 ('96)
OFFICIAL LANGUAGE: Czech
POLITICAL SYSTEM: parliamentary democracy
HEAD OF STATE: President Václav Havel (since Jan '93)
RULING PARTIES: coalition of Civic Democratic Party (ODS), Christian Democratic Union-Czechoslovak People's Party (KDU-CSL) & Civic Democratic Alliance (ODA)
HEAD OF GOVERNMENT: Josef Tosovsky (non-party), Prime Minister (since Dec '97)
MAIN IGO MEMBERSHIPS (non-UN): OSCE, CE, PFP, CEI, CEFTA, OECD
CURRENCY: koruna (end-'97 £1=K57.32, US$1=K34.94)
GNP PER CAPITA: US$3,870 ('95) or US$9,770 ('95) by PPP calculation

THE year was the Czech Republic's most eventful in its short history as an independent state. It brought the downfall of the country's seemingly invincible Prime Minister, Vaclav Klaus, and an end to economic stability. These events overshadowed the country's significant foreign policy achievements of 1997: the eagerly-anticipated invitations to join NATO and to begin membership talks with the European Union (EU).

The political crisis began in the spring after a sudden economic crash. The cabinet's delay in drafting transparent financial market regulations, together with its failure to guarantee sufficient industrial restructuring, were seen as basic problems. Its procrastination in confronting regional reform, health care, education, housing, transportation and energy reform was also criticized, although some of these issues were at last addressed towards the end of the year. On 23 October, for example, parliament approved a long-awaited constitutional law dividing the country into 14 regions.

A package of austerity measures was approved on 16 April to alleviate the growing trade and budget deficits and to curb rising public-sector wages. By late May, however, the economic crisis had intensified. The Czech National Bank (CNB) was forced to raise interest rates and to spend some $3,000 million to defend the koruna, which was under continuing pressure from speculators. On 26 May the CNB abolished the 15 per cent band in which the exchange rate had been allowed to fluctuate. The following day the Czech currency lost 10 per cent of its value against the US dollar, this marking the end of seven years of currency stability.

Amidst the economic crisis the government was also criticized for its inadequate communication with the population and opposition. Public frustration had already been clear in the 1996 elections, in which the three ruling parties had won only 99 of 200 parliamentary seats. Mr Klaus had therefore been obliged to form a minority government (see AR 1996, pp. 101–2), consisting of his Civic Democratic Party (ODS) together with the Christian Democratic Union-Czech People's Party (KDU-CSL) and the Civic Democratic Alliance (ODA). Spring opinion polls showed a steady drop in public trust in the government, as President Vaclav Havel began to call for its resignation.

On 28 May the chairmen of the three ruling coalition parties announced a second package of austerity measures, while Mr Klaus for the first time admitted to economic policy mistakes. Also announced was a government reshuffle that included the replacement of two economic ministers. On 10 June the government narrowly survived a parliamentary vote of confidence, called for by the then Prime Minister. Two deputies who had been expelled from the opposition Social Democratic Party (CSSD) helped to give the government victory by 101 votes to 99. Meanwhile, the ODA was experiencing its own internal problems, replacing its party chairman twice in 1997.

The Prime Minister's position became more precarious on 23 October, when the Foreign Minister (and ODS deputy chairman), Josef Zieleniec, suddenly resigned from both positions, partly because he had not been informed about ODS party financing matters. On 8 November President Havel named Jaroslav Sedivy as Mr Zieleniec's replacement, also making new appointments to the interior portfolio as well as to that of labour and social affairs. On the same day some 60,000 workers organized an anti-government demonstration in Prague.

It became known in late November that the ODS had accepted two large donations in 1995 from the winner of a privatization tender, while rumours of other shady dealings also surfaced. Finance Minister Ivan Pilip and former Interior Minister Jan Ruml, both ODS, demanded that Mr Klaus should resign, while the KDU-CSL and ODA decided to leave the coalition. On 30 November the Prime Minister announced the cabinet's resignation, later urging ODS members to join the 'constructive opposition'. Although Mr Klaus was re-elected chairman at an extraordinary ODS congress on 14 December, internal tensions within the party continued to mount, culminating in the creation of a rival faction by Mr Ruml and Mr Pilip on 19 December. On 17 December President Havel designated the CNB governor, Josef Tosovsky, as the new Prime Minister and charged him with forming a government, on which negotiations were still in progress at year's end. Early parliamentary elections were expected in mid-1998, opinion polls showing that the CSSD would win the most votes.

The political crisis was accompanied by economic deterioration, including a rise in unemployment to 5.2 per cent and an annual inflation rate of 10 per cent. The budget deficit widened sharply to K15,700 million, while the trade deficit was expected to reach K140,000 million in December. The economy was also adversely affected in July by severe flooding, which caused 48 deaths and an estimated K60,000 million in damage.

In foreign affairs, a long-awaited Czech-German declaration aimed at reconciling past grievances was signed on 21 January by Mr Klaus and the German Chancellor, Helmut Kohl. Relations with Slovakia reached a low point, resulting in Slovakia's temporary recall of its ambassador to the Czech Republic on 9 April. However, the exchange of two villages and other border land on 25 July closed the issue of the common state border. In the same month a NATO summit in Madrid formally invited the Czech Republic (together with Hungary and Poland, but not Slovakia) to join the alliance in 1999, while in December the EU's Luxembourg summit included the Czech Republic among the 'first wave' of six applicant countries with which accession negotiations would be opened in 1998 (see XI.3).

Czech-Canadian ties were complicated when a Czech television report depicting Czech Gypsies (Roma) living well in Canada influenced some 1,000 Roma to request political refugee status in Canada by late September. Canada reimposed visas for Czechs in October, but hundreds of Czech (and Slovak) Roma continued to arrive in Britain in search of political asylum.

iv. SLOVAKIA

CAPITAL: Bratislava   AREA: 18,930 sq km   POPULATION: 5,400,000 ('96)
OFFICIAL LANGUAGE: Slovak
POLITICAL SYSTEM: parliamentary democracy
HEAD OF STATE: President Michal Kováč (since March '93)
RULING PARTIES: coalition of Movement for a Democratic Slovakia (HZDS), Workers' Association of Slovakia (ZRS) & Slovak National Party (SNS)
HEAD OF GOVERNMENT: Vladimir Meciar (HZDS), Prime Minister (since Dec '94)
MAIN IGO MEMBERSHIPS (non-UN): OSCE, CE, PFP, CEI, CEFTA
CURRENCY: koruna (end-'97 £1=K57.13, US$1=K34.82)
GNP PER CAPITA: US$2,950 ('95)

FOR Slovakia, 1997 brought fierce political conflict and growing international isolation. While the other Visegrad countries (Hungary, Poland and the Czech Republic) were invited to join NATO and to start membership talks with the European Union (EU), Slovakia was left behind because of its political problems.

Especially controversial was a referendum on 23–24 May which was supposed to ask three questions proposed by the ruling parties concerning NATO membership and a fourth question on direct presidential elections put forward by the opposition. Prime Minister Vladimir Meciar's Movement for a Democratic Slovakia (HZDS) rejected the idea of direct presidential elections and asked the Constitutional Court to decide whether the constitution could be changed through a referendum. The court ruled that, although such a referendum was legal, its results would not be binding on the parliament. Interior Minister Gustav Krajci then ordered that the ballots be distributed without the fourth question, with the result that over 90 per cent of eligible voters boycotted the referendum. Criticizing the government's intervention, Foreign Minister Pavol Hamzik tendered his resignation on 26 May and was replaced on 11 June by Zdenka Kramplova, the first woman to hold the post.

Another case in which the government disregarded the Constitutional Court involved Frantisek Gaulieder, who had been stripped of his mandate as a parliamentary deputy in December 1996 after quitting the HZDS parliamentary caucus (see AR 1996, p. 105). Although the court ruled on 24 July that the parliament had violated Mr Gaulieder's constitutional rights, the ruling parties on 30 September voted against reinstatement. Meanwhile, several cases of politically-related violence remained unresolved, including the August 1995 kidnapping of President Michal Kovác's son and the April 1996 death in a car explosion of a former policeman who had links to the Kovác case (see AR 1996, pp. 103–4). Believing that his son would not receive a fair trial in Slovakia in the controversial Technopol fraud case, President Kovác on 12 December used his prerogative to pardon his son and all the others accused in the case.

The ruling coalition squabbled over bank and TV privatization during 1997, and also over the 1998 state budget. The HZDS's junior partners—the Slovak National Party and the Workers' Association—occasionally sided with the opposition, preventing the passage of several controversial laws. Generally, opposition protests had little effect in parliament, although a five-party opposition electoral bloc—formed in June and called the Slovak Democratic Coalition (SDK)—immediately surpassed the HZDS in public support. An agreement between the SDK and the ethnic minority Hungarian Coalition, intended to form the basis for cooperation after the September 1998 parliamentary elections, was signed on 2 December. In contrast, the ex-communist Party of the Democratic Left preferred to remain an 'independent opposition party'. On 18 June the EU-Slovakia parliamentary committee challenged Slovakia to reform its political system by November if it wished to be included in the first round of EU entry negotiations. While the position of opposition deputies on key parliamentary committees did improve somewhat, the Slovak government ignored another EU recommendation by rejecting the idea of a minority language law on 4 November.

Although analysts had predicted an economic slow-down in 1997, annual GDP growth remained at a healthy 6 per cent in the third quarter, while the annual inflation rate was just 6.4 per cent in December. The state budget deficit was more problematic, reaching K36,999 million (US$1,100 million), Slovakia's highest since independence. Rapid growth in domestic consumption combined with the cabinet's cancellation of the import surcharge on 1 January contributed to a worrying trade deficit in the first half of the year. On 16 July the Finance Ministry announced the introduction of a new 7 per cent import surcharge on consumer goods and food. As a result, trade deficit growth began to slow in late 1997.

In addition to problems with NATO and the EU, Slovakia also experienced a cooling in relations with two neighbours. In Hungary there was a widespread belief that Slovakia was not fulfilling certain aspects of the 1995 bilateral state treaty, particularly concerning minority rights, while Slovakia's partial victory over Hungary in an International Court of Justice ruling of 25 September on the Gabcikovo-Nagymaros dam dispute (see XV.1.i) was accepted somewhat grudgingly in Budapest. Meanwhile, ties with the Czech Republic were complicated in April over the division of former Czechoslovakia's remaining common property, the Slovak government recalling its ambassador from Prague for 20 days to demonstrate its discontent. Mr Meciar and the then Czech Prime Minister, Vaclav Klaus, finally met on 10 October, but the collapse of the Czech government in November (see III.1.iii) served to stall further exchanges in 1997.

v. HUNGARY

CAPITAL: Budapest   AREA: 93,000 sq km   POPULATION: 10,250,000 ('96)
OFFICIAL LANGUAGE: Hungarian
POLITICAL SYSTEM: parliamentary democracy
HEAD OF STATE: President Arpád Göncz (since Aug '90)
RULING PARTIES: Hungarian Socialist Party (MSP) heads coalition with Alliance of Free Democrats (SDS)
HEAD OF GOVERNMENT: Gyula Horn (MSP), Prime Minister (since July '94)
MAIN IGO MEMBERSHIPS (non-UN): OSCE, CE, PFP, CEI, CEFTA
CURRENCY: forint (end-'97 £1=Ft335.86, US$1=Ft204.71)
GNP PER CAPITA: US$4,120 ('95) or US$6,410 ('95) by PPP calculation

THE year was one of the most successful in foreign policy terms that Hungary had ever experienced. The country was invited to join NATO in 1999 and to be among the 'first wave' states to be included in accession negotiations for membership of the European Union (EU). Given the political and economic development of Hungary since the end of communism, together with the country's geo-strategic importance as a stable state close to the conflict in former Yugoslavia, its inclusion in the first phase of NATO and EU eastward enlargement was in part predictable. It was a significant success nonetheless, especially in light of Hungary's 20th-century history of invariably ending up in a defeated foreign-policy position. The country's relations with its immediate neighbours were more varied, but once again the Budapest government was seen as having gone out of its way to build the best relationships possible in the circumstances. This was regarded as helpful in preparing the acceptance of Hungary, in the European security context, as a factor of stability rather than one of instability. The fact that Hungary had taken major steps in seeking to find stable arrangements with its neighbours where sizeable ethnic Hungarian communities lived was likewise important in strengthening Hungary's claim to be a responsible member of the international system.

As far as EU membership was concerned, the Hungarian government was clearly determined that the accession negotiations should be completed as rapidly as feasible, though the claim of Prime Minister Gyula Horn that these could be concluded by 2000 appeared optimistic. Speaking again on this topic in August, Mr Horn admitted that there were considerable obstacles to integration, not least that Hungary's GDP per capita was currently only 37 per cent of the EU average. Other observers voiced doubts concerning the country's legislative, juridical and administrative capacity to implement the EU's *acquis communautaire* in time, albeit that Hungary was not in a worse position than other 'first wave' candidates.

As regards NATO membership, the costs of accession were seen as a considerable obstacle. The Hungarian armed forces were under-equipped and various figures were circulated as to the expenditure necessary for modernization. In this connection, it was announced that Hungary would move towards a professional rather than a conscript army. After much political dispute on the questions to be put, a national referendum on 16 November yielded an 85.3 per cent 'yes' vote on the single issue of whether Hungary should join NATO. Anti-NATO groups claimed that the turnout of only 49 per cent had invalidated the referendum, but the electoral commission ruled that the result was valid because more than 25 per cent of the total electorate had voted in favour.

Hungary's relationship with Romania had undergone a major shift in a positive direction, two factors being significant in helping to bring this change about. The 1996 Hungarian-Romanian Basic Treaty (see AR 1996, pp. 108, 111) had laid the foundations, but it was the change of government in Romania in November 1996 that created a new attitude in Bucharest from which both sides profited. At the level of atmospherics, the change was palpable, with genuine goodwill being apparent on both sides. The Budapest government recognized that it was in Hungary's interest that Romania be integrated into the overall European security architecture as early as possible, both to ensure the stability of its eastern neighbour and to contribute to an easing of tensions over the status of Romania's ethnic Hungarian minority.

The shift in relations was certainly sufficiently well-founded to enable both governments to ignore the anti-Hungarian initiatives of Gheorghe Funar, the Romanian nationalist mayor of Cluj, who used various devices to try and block the opening of a Hungarian consulate in the Transylvanian capital (see also III.1.vi). On the other hand, attempts to improve relations with Slovakia were nothing like as successful. In essence, the Slovak government found itself incapable of responding to Hungarian overtures, aggravating rather than alleviating tensions. The explanation for this attitude had to be sought in the configuration of Slovak domestic politics. In the political arena, the ethnic Hungarian community in Slovakia became a football, as the leadership tried to mobilize support by relying on anti-Hungarian slogans.

Relations between Hungary and Slovakia were further bedevilled by the issue of the barrage on the River Danube between Gabcikovo and Nagymaros (see also III.1.iv). The Hungarians had earlier renounced the bilateral treaty governing the construction of the barrage, the entire matter being referred to the International Court of Justice at The Hague for adjudication. The verdict, delivered in September, largely accepted the Slovak position that Hungary was in breach of international law in suspending further work on the barrage (see XV.1.i). Subsequent discussions between the two states failed to produce any way forward, not least because Hungary was reluctant to resume construction work on the part of the barrage that it was supposed to build, for environmental and cost reasons.

In domestic affairs, the austerity package introduced in 1995 began to produce positive results. Slowly, the Hungarian economy showed signs of improvement as the growth rate rose, and with it the standard of living, though inflation remained uncomfortably high at close to 20 per cent. The government—or to be precise the dominant partner in the coalition, the Hungarian Socialist Party—seemed well set to reap the benefits in the 1998 general elections, helped by the continuing disarray of the opposition and, indeed, by the weakness of its coalition partner, the Free Democrats.

The opposition seemed quite unable to unite around any philosophy or ideal, not least because it was caught in the central dilemma of post-communist conservatism: what precisely did conservatism mean under post-communism, and what was a conservative to conserve? In the Hungarian case, as elsewhere, the temptation to rely on milder or harsher forms of nationalism was strong. The Hungarian Democratic Forum, which had dominated the 1990–94 coalition, was definitively split, with the nationalist wing in the ascendant. The Christian Democrats were fading under the twin burden of internal splits and lacklustre leadership. This left the Young Democrats with the task of providing serious opposition to the government, although the populist Smallholders' Party showed enduring strength, commanding anything up to a fifth of the electorate. In particular, the opposition seemed quite incapable of capitalizing on the persistent and far-reaching corruption that surrounded the ruling MSP. However frequently this issue was raised, there was no sign that dubious practices were diminishing. Public opinion appeared to be passive on such matters.

vi. ROMANIA

CAPITAL: Bucharest   AREA: 237,500 sq km   POPULATION: 22,700,000 ('96)
OFFICIAL LANGUAGE: Romanian
POLITICAL SYSTEM: presidential democracy
RULING PARTIES: multi-party coalition including Christian Democratic National Peasants' Party (PNTCD), Social Democratic Union (USD), Hungarian Democratic Union of Romania (UDMR), Democratic Party (PD), National Liberal Party (PNL) & Romanian Alternative Party (PAR)
HEAD OF STATE: President Emil Constantinescu (since Nov '96)
HEAD OF GOVERNMENT: Victor Ciorbea (PNTCD), Prime Minister (since Nov '96)
MAIN IGO MEMBERSHIPS (non-UN): OSCE, CE, CEI, PFP, BSEC
CURRENCY: leu (end-'97 £1=L13,240.47, US$1=8,070.00)
GNP PER CAPITA: US$1,480 ('95) or US$4,360 ('95) by PPP calculation

FOR many Romanians the first full year in office of the centrist government under Prime Minister Victor Ciorbea was marked by disappointed expectations. Romania failed to be included among the initial wave of formerly communist-ruled countries that were invited to join NATO or were offered membership negotiations with the European Union (EU). At home the promised free-market reforms, when introduced, resulted in more hardship than benefits—at least in the short term—for the majority of the population. Meanwhile, relations between the partners in the coalition government formed in November 1996 (see AR 1996, p. 110) came under severe strain even sooner than most observers had predicted.

The year began with tough talking and tough action that were designed to tackle some of the most widely-detested aspects of the legacy left behind by ex-President Ion Iliescu's eight-year post-communist administration. In January President Emil Constantinescu announced an anti-corruption campaign. As the campaign gathered pace, several senior figures in the state-owned and private banking sectors were either dismissed or charged with corruption. The authorities also initiated a crack-down on those in public service who had benefited from high-risk pyramid investment projects, such as the notorious Caritas scheme that had crashed in 1994. However, it was not until a few days before the end of the year that the government announced legislation to outlaw such schemes.

At the end of April Virgil Magureanu, the powerful director of the Romanian Intelligence Service (RSI), handed in his resignation following extensive criticism compiled by a special parliamentary commission. The report accused the RSI of involvement in illegal activities, including phone-tapping. Mr Magureanu was replaced by Costin Georgescu, who was regarded as a close associate of President Constantinescu.

For most Romanians, though, the hallmark of Mr Ciorbea's administration was its willingness to introduce unpopular economic measures. These began with the near doubling of petroleum and diesel prices in January, which was part of the government's policy of removing subsidies. A month later the Prime Minister announced a stabilization policy to eliminate the remaining price controls on energy and foodstuffs, to liberalize the foreign-exchange market, to establish a more transparent taxation system, and to speed up privatization.

Even before the official announcement of the freeing of foreign-exchange rates, the leu had begun a steep decline. Between the elections (in November 1996) and the first week of February its value had gone down from just under 3,500 lei to the US dollar to nearly 6,500 lei. The price increases, reduced public spending and the prospect of large-scale redundancies in loss-making companies led to a wave of industrial unrest in the spring, involving engineering workers, health-service staff and miners. These were followed by further disturbances in August after the government had proposed the closing-down of 17 major loss-making companies, including three of Romania's nine oil refineries. However, some of the expected labour troubles were avoided when the government offered relatively generous redundancy pay, averaging 6–12 months' wages, and early retirement on favourable terms.

The protests in the streets were clear proof that the Ciorbea administration's honeymoon period with a large section of the electorate was now over. The opposition was quick to try to exploit the apparent change of mood in the country. But the two parliamentary motions of no-confidence put foward in June by Mr Iliescu's Party of Social Democracy in Romania (PSDR) and by the two ultra-nationalist parties were easily defeated by the governing majority. The parliamentary challenge to the government was further weakened by the split in the ranks of the PSDR following a failed attempt in June by several reformers to replace Mr Iliescu as party leader by the former Foreign Minister, Teodor

Melescanu. In September their new party, the Alliance for Romania, was formally registered.

The splits within the opposition were matched by signs of a developing rift between the two main parties in the governing coalition, the Christian Democratic National Peasants' Party (PNTCD) and the Democratic Party (DP). The dispute came into the open in August over the new law on land restitution. The law allowed for the return of up to 50 hectares of agricultural land to the pre-communist era owners, whereas the DP favoured a limit of 10 hectares on the grounds that most of the former owners did not have sufficient capital to work larger plots of land profitably.

There were renewed problems within the coalition in December when the DP's two influential ministers in the government were replaced. Adrian Severin resigned as Foreign Minister, after making unsubstantiated allegations that several politicians and newspaper editors had been working for a foreign power, and was replaced by Andrei Plesu, a respected dissident intellectual of the communist era. Traian Basescu, the popular Minister of Transport, left because he felt the government was too slow in carrying through reforms.

At the same time, the DP was becoming increasingly concerned with Mr Ciorbea's leadership style, as cabinet meetings dragged on for 12 hours or more, often in an unproductive fashion. Despite some protestations to the contrary, by the end of the year there were signs that the DP-led grouping might be preparing to pull out of the ruling coalition government. Such a decision would leave the administration in the hands of the alliance headed by the PNTCD and the ethnic Magyars' Hungarian Democratic Union in Romania (HDUR).

Only a few months earlier it had looked as though the HDUR might leave the coalition after the Senate had insisted on amending a new education law to ensure that, even where Hungarian-language teaching was made available, history and geography would be taught in Romanian. Nevertheless, there was no doubt that the position of the Hungarian minority had greatly improved since the new government came into office. This was also reflected in warmer relations with Hungary (see III.1.v). The Hungarian President, Arpád Göncz, visited Romania in May and said that his country, a front-runner for both NATO and EU membership, was supporting Romania's integration into the Euro-Atlantic institutions.

However, Bucharest's foreign policy aspirations suffered a double blow in July when NATO decided not to include Romania in the first batch of new members for 1999 and the European Commission recommended that Romania should not be among the five ex-communist countries with which the EU was scheduled to open accession talks in 1998. The two negative responses followed more than six months of vigorous campaigning by the newly-installed government, which had even enlisted the help of the exiled former King Michael (whose citizenship was restored in February) to lobby on behalf of Romania. NATO's refusal to invite Romania to join the alliance came in spite of vigorous support by France and several Mediterranean countries. The eventual decision was the outcome of a cautious American policy that was determined to limit initial expansion to three members. Yet there were clear signs that, if Romania continued on the path being followed by the Ciorbea government, it would be among the first candidates for future NATO membership after 1999. Meanwhile, Bucharest had given renewed proof of its commitment to bringing security to the Balkans. In addition to continuing its contribution to the peace-keeping operation in Bosnia & Hercegovina, in April Romania despatched troops to Albania as part of the Italian-led 'Operation Alba' designed to help restore stability after an anti-government uprising (see III.2.i).

The European Commission's ruling that excluded Romania from membership negotiations with the EU was a disappointment, though it did not come as a surprise. There was little more Mr Ciorbea's government could have done to make up for the relatively slow progress under the Iliescu administration towards a functioning market economy. Romania was lagging behind the Central European candidates in a whole range of areas, including land property rights, the restructuring of the financial sector and public administration, and modernization of the judicial, police and penal systems.

Nearer home, though, improved relations with Hungary were matched by better links with Ukraine. In June Romania and Ukraine signed a cooperation treaty which confirmed the inviolability of their common border. The Romanian government thus, after years of reluctance to do so, finally accepted that Romanian territories annexed by the Soviet Union under the 1939 Molotov-Ribbentrop Pact would remain within Ukraine. The two countries also pledged to reach agreement within three years on the demarcation of the Black Sea shelf and on the status of Serpents' Island—or, in the absence of an accord, to refer the matter to the International Court of Justice.

vii. BULGARIA

CAPITAL: Sofia   AREA: 110,000 sq km   POPULATION: 8,400,000 ('96)
OFFICIAL LANGUAGE: Bulgarian
POLITICAL SYSTEM: parliamentary democracy
HEAD OF STATE: President Petar Stoyanov (since Jan '97)
RULING PARTIES: Union of Democratic Forces (UDF) & People's Union (PU), allied as United Democratic Parties
HEAD OF GOVERNMENT: Ivan Kostov (UDF), Prime Minister (since May '97)
MAIN IGO MEMBERSHIPS (non-UN): OSCE, CE, PFP, CEI, BSEC, Francophonie
CURRENCY: lev (end-'97 £1=L2,928.65, US$1=L1,785.00)
GNP PER CAPITA: US$1,330 ('95) or US$4,480 ('95) by PPP calculation

THE first weeks of 1997 saw Bulgaria come closer to economic and political breakdown than at any time since the end of communism.

The year opened with the governing Bulgarian Socialist Party (BSP) seeking to re-establish itself in power after the snap resignation of its previous leader and Prime Minister, Zhan Videnov, in December 1996 (see AR 1996, p. 112). Notwithstanding opposition demands for immediate elections and daily street demonstrations at the scarcity of bread and the collapse of the currency, the

BSP announced that the Interior Minister, Nikolay Dobrev, would establish a consensus government of radical reform. On 10 January, as the BSP sought to outmanoeuvre an opposition motion for elections, a crowd outside parliament rioted, stormed the building and set part of it on fire. Police counter-measures left over a hundred injured, including a former Prime Minister, Filip Dimitrov. The incident provoked a wave of revulsion against Mr Dobrev, who abandoned his attempts to find coalition partners in February.

By then the country was on the verge of anarchy, with hundreds of thousands on strike, anti-government protesters blockading roads and rampant inflation destroying public confidence in authority. Intervening on 4 February, the Supreme Consultative Council on National Security, a presidential body, decreed that elections would be held in April and empowered the President to appoint a caretaker cabinet.

Events conspired to give the opposition Union of Democratic Forces (UDF) a decisive advantage. Following his inauguration on 19 January, the UDF victor in the October 1996 presidential election, Petar Stoyanov, went onto the attack against the BSP, blaming it for the state of the country and praising the protesters. On 12 February the new President appointed the UDF mayor of Sofia, Stefan Sofiyanski, as head of a caretaker government. His objectives were to restore social stability and government authority and to negotiate a rescue package with international lenders.

On 25 February the UDF and the second-largest opposition grouping, the People's Union, agreed to form a coalition government after the elections; later they also agreed to stand on a common electoral platform as the United Democratic Parties (UDP). At first the ethnic-Turkish Movement for Rights and Freedoms (MRF) seemed set to become part of the alliance but on 5 March it withdrew. Later the MRF leadership formed an unprecedented axis with Liberals, Monarchists and breakaway Agrarians, called the Alliance for National Salvation (ANS). However, the MRF's branches across northern Bulgaria rebelled and entered into local understandings with the UDP. While the opposition came together, the BSP suffered its most damaging split since communism. On 22 February a group of centre-left deputies, many with backgrounds in the former Komsomol (Communist Youth), formed the Euro-Left, uniting with several earlier splinter groups.

The realignment contributed to an extraordinary result on 19 April. The UDP won 52.36 per cent of the vote and 137 of the 240 seats, while the BSP was reduced to 22.07 per cent and 58 seats. Of the smaller parties, the ANS took 19 seats, Euro-Left 14 and the Bulgarian Business Bloc 12. On 8 May the new parliament overwhelmingly backed the UDP's 'National Salvation Declaration', committing Bulgaria to eventual EU and NATO membership, radical economic reform and new measures of decommunization. The result paved the way for UDF leader Ivan Kostov to become Prime Minister and to present his cabinet on 19 May.

The Kostov government continued the policies of its predecessor and even retained several of his ministers, including Aleksandur Bozhkov (Deputy Premier and Industry Minister) and Bogomil Bonev (Interior Minister). By the end of the year, the continuing high public support for Mr Kostov and the UDP was testimony to what had been achieved. Emergency imports, the liberalization of prices, the encouragement of sowing and a crackdown on speculators had solved the grain crisis. Inflation had been cut back from the triple-digit excesses of January, so that the government could credibly set a 16 per cent target for 1998.

In addition, a campaign was started against organized crime, the key measure being a bill in July, based on Italy's anti-mafia laws, which set mandatory prison sentences for membership of mafia-style gangs, strengthened the penalties for drug-smuggling and tax evasion and imposed a tougher control of firearms. After replacing the top police chiefs and the head of the National Intelligence Service, the government enacted a law in November restructuring the security forces and making them more accountable. A similar effort was made to overcome the problems of under-funding, ill-discipline, demoralization and corruption in the armed forces, once the air-force chief, Lieut.-General Mikho Mikhov, had been appointed commander-in-chief in June.

Bulgaria's reorientation in foreign policy began in February with a firm commitment by the Sofiyanski government to seek NATO membership. In April Bulgaria participated in a 15-day NATO exercise and in July attended the alliance's Madrid summit. Mr Kostov's government reacted phlegmatically to the decisions of both NATO and the European Union (EU) not to include Bulgaria among the countries selected for fast-track accession. A declaration on EU membership passed by parliament on 23 July said Bulgaria would continue to bring its laws into line with European norms.

In October the government signed a European Minorities Convention in Strasbourg, undertaking to extend the rights of ethnic groups like Turks and Gypsies. Signature of the convention led to renewed polemics with Macedonia over the national identity of the population of Bulgaria's Pirin region. Subsequently, both Russia and Yugoslavia were offended by the decision not to invite them to a summit of South-East European Defence Ministers held in Sofia on 3 October, at which Italy and the United States were represented. On the same day the Presidents of Romania, Turkey and Bulgaria met in Varna to discuss cooperation over infrastructure projects, crime control and European integration.

The difficulties with Russia were highlighted by polemics over gas prices, the collapse of the joint Topenergy company and accusations that the Russian ambassador in Sofia had been spying. In November the Bulgarian Foreign Minister, Nadezhda Mihaylova, made a ground-breaking tour of Armenia, Azerbaijan, Kazakhstan, Uzbekistan and Turkmenistan to seek alternative energy sources and routes. A parliamentary debate on relations with Russia in October was followed by a trip to Moscow by Ms Mihaylova, but a planned visit by President Stoyanov was postponed.

The pro-Western stance of Mr Kostov's government, and important gestures like the scrapping of entry visas for EU nationals and the liberalization of the Foreign Investments Law, helped Bulgaria to secure some $1,2000 million in stand-by and development loans. The main source was the IMF, which insisted in return that Bulgaria set up a currency board, adopt a stabilization programme and reform its banking system. The currency board, established in June under Swiss-born Martin Zaimov, pegged the lev to the Deutsche Mark and helped the government push through a sharply deflationary budget, cutting central spending and lowering economic subsidies. An ambitious programme adopted in June, after Asen Dyulgerov had taken over as head of the Privatization Agency, envisaged that nearly 600 large disposals would be made by January 1998. Although its full implementation was frustrated by red tape, the Industry Ministry nevertheless reported the conclusion of 164 deals raising some $700 million, the largest being the sale of the copper-works in Pirdop to a Belgian company.

Ironically in a year that saw the 86-year-old one-time dictator, Todor Zhivkov, released from house arrest, the UDP put forward bills to outlaw the former communist regime and to open police files from 1923 to 1989 to the public. The Interior Ministry published a list of politicians alleged to have been state security agents under Mr Zhivkov, which included the MRF leader, Ahmed Dogan. Moves were made to prosecute members of the 1995–96 Videnov government over the grain export scandal, the former Prime Minister himself being rumoured to have attempted suicide.

2. ALBANIA—BOSNIA & HERCEGOVINIA—CROATIA— MACEDONIA—SLOVENIA—YUGOSLAVIA

i. ALBANIA

CAPITAL: Tirana   AREA: 29,000 sq km   POPULATION: 3,460,000 ('96)
OFFICIAL LANGUAGE: Albanian
POLITICAL SYSTEM: parliamentary democracy
HEAD OF STATE: President Rexhep Mejdani (since July '97)
RULING PARTIES: Socialist Party (PS) holds presidency and heads government coalition
HEAD OF GOVERNMENT: Fatos Nano (PS), Prime Minister (since July '97)
MAIN IGO MEMBERSHIPS (non-UN): OSCE, PFP, CE, CEI, BSEC, ICO
CURRENCY: lek (end-'97 £1=AL239.54, US$1=AL146.00)
GNP PER CAPITA: US$670 ('95)

In 1997 Albania descended into anarchy. The disorders caused around 2,000 deaths, mostly accidental, persuaded 15,000 Albanians to flee into exile, and witnessed widespread looting and destruction, even of archaeological treasures such as those at Butrint.

The problems began in January when it became clear that a number of pyramid investment schemes were collapsing. In Albania these schemes had provided an income for many whose state pensions or salaries were meagre; it was also widely believed that they provided the means by which corrupt elements could launder money. On 23 January the People's Assembly stepped in and froze the assets of two schemes; it then enacted that, in order to avoid inflation, future interest payments would be made gradually. Serious rioting broke out in Tirana immediately, as a result of which the Assembly granted President Sali Berisha special powers to restore and maintain order.

These powers were extensively but ineffectively deployed when even more serious rioting broke out in Tirana in February. Once again the cause of the disorder was financial. The largest private concern in the country, Vefa Holdings, had used deposit schemes to raise capital and it too was forced to cut and then suspend interest payments. It was in the south, however, that the disorders were the most serious. Again, the feared collapse of a pyramid investment scheme, this time Gjallica, was the spur. The company had its headquarters in the southern town of Vlore, where 30,000 protesters crowded into the city centre on 5 February. Here anger over the financial crisis quickly merged with resentment against the Democratic Party of Albania (PDS) government in general and at the actions of its police forces in particular, especially the National Information Service (SHIK) or secret police.

On 1–2 March crowds overran SHIK headquarters in Vlore; soon arms stores throughout the south were being captured or abandoned. Weapons of all varieties, from handguns to tanks and even fighter aircraft, were taken over by the protesters. The government declared a state of national emergency on 1 March, and on the same day President Berisha made his first concession to the protesters by ordering Prime Minister Alexander Meksi to resign. Having been re-elected by the Assembly for a second four-year term on 3 March, the President made further concessions on 9 March when he agreed to the formation of a government of national reconciliation and to the holding of elections in June. On 11 March an interim government was formed under Bashkim Fino of the opposition Socialist Party of Albania (PSS), whose cabinet included representatives from all the major parties but no member of the previous administration.

These concessions did little to pacify the south. By mid-March at least a third of the entire country was beyond government control and the disorder was spreading northwards and becoming more political. A National Committee for Public Salvation was established by the rebels, who demanded President Berisha's resignation and their own inclusion in any talks on the formation of a new government. A further indication of the collapse of civil authority was the emptying of the country's gaols, one beneficiary of which was the former Socialist Prime Minister, Fatos Nano, who walked out of prison on 13 March and was officially pardoned two days later.

Mr Fino's main priority was to restore order, one of his first acts as Prime Minister having been to ask for foreign help to do so. Neither NATO nor the European Union (EU) showed any collective enthusiasm for such a task, but a number of states, led by Italy, concluded that help should be given. At the end of March, with the approval of the EU and the endorsement of the UN Security Council, a force of 6,000 troops was organized, with Italy providing the largest contingent. Deployment of these troops in Albania, in what was called 'Operation Alba', began on 11 April and did much to restore calm, assisted by domestic reconciliation moves. At the end of March Mr Fino had begun negotiations with rebel leaders, while on 1 April the PSS had decided to return to parliament for the first time since the elections of 1996 (see AR 1996, pp. 122–4). Another important factor in reducing the political temperature was the Organization for Security and Cooperation in Europe (OSCE), whose special representative, former Austrian Chancellor Franz Vranitzky, made a number of journeys to Albania (see also XI.4.ii). By 9 May all ten main political parties had agreed that elections should be held before the end of June, and further mediation by Dr Vranitzky ironed out difficulties over a new electoral law. In an effort further to calm the electoral campaign, the PSS and the PDS signed a 'pact for the future' in Rome on 23 June.

The first round of voting was held on 29 June. In 32 constituencies where no candidate secured a majority a second round was held on 6 July, whilst two constituencies had to have a third round on 13 July. The new electoral law had increased the number of seats in the Assembly from 140 to 155, though the number chosen by proportional representation was unchanged at 40. The PSS won an overwhelming victory, taking 101 seats. Their nearest rivals, the PDS, won 29 seats, while the Social Democratic Party took eight and seven other parties obtained representation.

There was another vote on 29 June. On 13 April Leka Zogu, claimant to the Albanian throne, had returned from South Africa and had demanded a referendum on the restoration of the monarchy. Since none of the political parties objected, the consultation went ahead and produced a 66.74 per cent majority in favour of remaining a republic, with 33.26 per cent favouring a restoration of the monarchy. Leka returned to South Africa on 12 July.

President Berisha resigned on 23 July. The following day the Assembly elected Rexhep Mejdani of the PSS as his successor. On the same day a new government was formed under the leadership of Fatos Nano (PSS) and including a number of smaller parties, so that it easily commanded the two-thirds majority necessary to enact constitutional change. The programme of the new government committed it to the restoration of order, the elimination of corruption and crime, the reconstruction of the armed forces and the reform of the administration.

All these were necessary objectives, but government action was constrained by a number of factors. The first was lack of money. Although the anarchy of the spring had paralysed the economy, many government payments continued, producing inflation and a soaring budget deficit. When a donors' conference in Brussels in October agreed to a $600 million loan, there were stringent conditions: taxes had to be increased (the first step having already been taken on 1 October with a hike in VAT from 12.5 to 20 per cent); government expenditure was to be reduced; and the pyramid schemes were to be liquidated. Legislation to this last effect was enacted in mid-November, while in December Mr Nano announced the abolition of 15,000 government jobs.

A further constraint on the government was the continuing deep divide between the two major political groups. The disorders of the early months of the year had done nothing to foster a disposition to compromise and cooperate, both major parties being sharply criticized on this account by a Council of Europe delegation visiting Tirana in November. One particularly harmful effect of interparty hostility was that it severely complicated relations between the new PSS central authorities and local mayors, most of whom were Democrats.

The final constraint on government activities was that public violence was by no means entirely subdued, despite the lifting of the state of emergency on 24 July. In October it was estimated that no more than 10 per cent of the weapons stolen in the spring had been returned, and there was still widespread willingness to use them in pursuit of crime or in personal and political disputes. On 16 September a PDS deputy was shot and wounded by a Socialist opponent in the parliament building. During the turmoil of January-April armed crime had burgeoned. That it was still a major problem at the end of the year was shown when three policemen were killed in one week in December in a series of highway robberies. The Interior Ministry ordered that, in any future confrontations with masked robbers, policemen should shoot to kill without firing warning shots.

For the first half of the year Albania could devote little attention to foreign policy. After the formation of the Nano government, however, agreements were signed with Greece in August and in October under which the position of Albanian workers in Greece was further regularized, a Greek consulate was to be established in Korca and education in Greek in Albanian schools was to be expanded (see also II.3.v). Agreements with Italy in August and November went some way towards regulating the flow of migrants from Albania to that country. Both Greece and Italy promised help in the rebuilding of the Albanian armed forces. In November full diplomatic relations were established with Yugoslavia, while in December an agreement focusing on border security was signed with Macedonia.

ii. BOSNIA & HERCEGOVINA

CONSTITUENT ENTITIES: Federation of Bosnia & Hercegovina & Republika Srpska (Serb Republic)
CAPITAL: Sarajevo   AREA: 51,129 sq km   POPULATION: 4,500,000 ('91)
OFFICIAL LANGUAGE: Serbo-Croat
POLITICAL SYSTEM: federal republic
MAIN RULING PARTIES: Party of Democratic Action (SDA), Croatian Democratic Union (HDZ), Serb National Alliance (SNS)
HEADS OF STATE AND GOVERNMENT: Alija Izetbegović (President of Republic of Bosnia & Hercegovina); Vladimir Soljic (President of Muslim-Croat Federation); Biljana Plavšić (President of Republika Srpska)
PRIME MINISTERS: Haris Silajdzic & Boro Bošić (Republic of Bosnia & Hercegovina); Edhem Bicakčić (Muslim-Croat Federation); vacant (Republika Srpska)
MAIN IGO MEMBERSHIPS (non-UN): OSCE, CEI
CURRENCY: dinar
GNP PER CAPITA: US$3,590 ('90 est.)

THE difficulty of realizing the 1995 Dayton peace agreement provisions for free movement of persons and the return of refugees was underlined throughout the year. The 30,000-strong NATO-led Stabilization Force (SFOR), which had replaced the previous Implementation Force (IFOR) in December 1996 (see AR 1996, p. 122), succeeded in preventing any large-scale resumption of armed hostilities. But tensions and suspicions remained pervasive, erupting into violence from time to time and inhibiting efforts to implement the Dayton terms. Within the Republika Srpska (RS), a major confrontation developed between President Biljana Plavšić and the hardline supporters of her predecessor, Radovan Karadžić.

In February violence broke out between Croats and Muslims in Mostar, where an inter-communal administration was supposed to have been established in mid-1996 (see AR 1996, pp. 116–7). International intervention led to the suspension of the local chief of police and three officers, as the authorities endeavoured to reduce the influence of Mafia-type gangs. A bomb exploded in the city on 18 September, injuring 30 people.

The International Commission of Arbitration, set up under the terms of the Dayton agreements to rule on the future of the north-eastern Bosnian town of Brčko, announced on 14 February that it would defer its decision, because of the extreme sensitivity of the issues (see AR 1995, p. 127 map). Brčko would therefore remain under international control at least until March 1998. The head of the commission was replaced in March by US diplomat Robert W. Ferrand. On 20 June the UN high representative in Bosnia, Carl Bildt (Sweden), was replaced by a Spanish diplomat, Carlos Westendorp. Meanwhile, amidst extremely high security, Pope John Paul II had made a papal visit to Sarajevo on 12–13 April, meeting members of all three major ethnic groups in the city (see also II.2.viii; Pt XIII).

Although a wide spectrum of local and international opinion held that conditions were not suitable for the conduct of free and fair municipal elections (originally scheduled for September 1996), it was deemed to be important for sustaining the momentum of the Dayton process that these were not delayed further. Voters were permitted to register either in the municipality in which they had lived in 1991, or where they currently lived. The run-up to polling saw an intense and highly-politicized debate about the conditions of registration and voting, amid constant allegations on all sides of fraud and misconduct.

A conference of international aid donors, originally planned for December 1996 (see AR 1996, p. 121), eventually took place on 23–24 July in an attempt to exert leverage on the different ethnic factions to work more effectively together. The conference issued a direct warning to the Republika Srpska authorities that they should be more prepared to cooperate with the other Bosnian entity and with UN War Crimes Tribunal at The Hague. Meanwhile, on 1 July, the Bosnian government had reached an agreement with the London Club of private creditor banks under which its share of the collective debt of former Yugoslavia was set at 10.58 per cent. This left only Federal Yugoslavia without international agreement on its debt share.

The municipal elections were held on 13–14 September, under the scrutiny of the Organization for Security and Cooperation in Europe (OSCE). The provisions for absentee voting by refugees permitted predominantly Muslim parties to take control of the councils in Mostar and Srebrenica, although in several cities the elected bodies were only able to meet under the direct supervision of SFOR troops.

The principal political issue confronting Bosnia & Hercegovina throughout the year remained the difficulty of promoting integration at any level between the Muslim-Croat entity and the RS. The Bosnian Serbs' determination to press for greater integration with Serbia proper (one of the constituent republics of Yugoslavia—see III.2.vi) bore fruit in an accord signed on 28 February promoting 'special ties', especially in trade and economic cooperation.

However, the contradiction between these agreements and pressure from the international community to promote inter-entity cooperation brought to the surface the deepening political rift between Momčilo Krajisnik (the Serb member of Bosnia's collective presidency) and President Plavšić of the RS. On 28 June a full-scale crisis was precipitated when Mrs Plavšić suspended Dragan Kilać as RS Interior Minister, accusing him and other close supporters of Dr Karadžić of corruption. The following week, in an assertion of her authority and giving the lie to earlier claims that she was Dr Karadžić's proxy, she dissolved the RS Assembly elected in September 1996 (see AR 1996, p. 117) and called new elections for September.

Dr Karadžić's Serbian Democratic Party (SDS), which had an overall majority, not only continued to meet in the Assembly in defiance of her order but also, on 19 July, expelled her from the party. The result was a highly acrimonious split and the establishment by Mrs Plavšić and her faction of a new party, the Serb National Alliance (SNS). Throughout the summer she remained under SFOR guard, fearing an assault by forces loyal to Dr Karadžić. Gradually, however, and with some assistance from SFOR, her supporters gradually consolidated their hold over key institutions, particularly the security forces and the communications media. Her position was greatly strengthened in September by an open declaration of loyalty by General Pero Colić, the commander-in-chief of the RS Army.

The elections to the 83-member RS Assembly, held on 22–23 November, resulted in the SDS losing its overall majority and in gains for moderate formations. SDS representation was almost halved, to 24 seats, while the Muslim-led Coalition for a Single and Democratic Bosnia & Hercegovina won 16, the new SNS 15, the nationalist Serb Radical Party (SRS) 15, the Socialist Party 9, the Social Democratic Party 2 and the Independent Social Democrats 2. On 27 December President Plavšić nominated Mladen Ivanić (SNS) as the new RS Prime Minister, but as the year ended his efforts to form a coalition of politicians and technocats seemed certain to founder on the combined opposition of the SDS and SRS.

Progress in constructing the inter-entity institutions envisaged by the Dayton agreements was painfully slow in 1997, not least because of persistent Serb resistance. The formation of a central bank, which was to issue a common currency, was announced on 15 April, but there was no speedy fulfilment of its task of issuing a new currency, to be called the mark. Widespread problems were encountered by refugees attempting to return to their homes. One of the worst incidents occurred in late July and early August, when Croat residents in Jajce compelled more than 400 Muslim would-be returnees to abandon the attempt.

The International War Crimes Tribunal at The Hague (see AR 1996, p. 121) saw significant development of its work, having indicted a total of 74 persons (54 Serbs, 17 Croats and three Muslims). On 7 May the first war crimes verdict since the post-1945 Nuremberg and Tokyo trials was pronounced, when a Serb defendant, Dušan Tadić, was found guilty on 11 of the 31 charges against him. Separately from The Hague proceedings, the German authorities were pursuing charges against 50 people accused of war crimes in former Yugoslavia.

In a sensational interview with the Belgrade newspaper *Vecernje Novosti* of 26 May, Dr Karadžić hinted that, were he to be brought to face charges at The Hague, his evidence would directly incriminate the Yugoslav Serbian leadership. International pressure for Dr Karadžić to be brought to trial mounted from several directions, as when US mediator Richard Holbrooke, visiting Belgrade on 5 August, solicited the support of President Milošević for his arrest. However, both the former Bosnian Serb leader and his former military commander, General Ratko Mladić, remained at large at the end of the year. The publication in the weekly magazine *Dani* on 7 November of material said to incriminate figures close to the Bosnian federal leadership in the cover-up of war crimes committed by Bosnian government forces was received with indignation by the ruling Party of Democratic Action.

In an attempt to provide Bosnian citizens with sources of information not controlled by political extremists, SFOR troops on 1 October took control of four television transmitters controlled by groups loyal to Dr Karadžić. The action was specifically authorized by the UN Secretary-General, by Sr Westendorp and by the NATO command, after the stations had carried repeated allegations that The Hague tribunal was biased against Serbs.

International acknowledgement that the Dayton timetable for the withdrawal of UN troops was too optimistic was signalled by the announcement on 26 November, by Sr Westendorp, that an extension of the SFOR mandate would be necessary for 'two or three years' beyond the original mid-1998 target-date for withdrawal of the force.

iii. CROATIA

CAPITAL: Zagreb AREA: 56,538 sq km POPULATION: 4,777,000 ('94 est.)
OFFICIAL LANGUAGE: Croatian
POLITICAL SYSTEM: presidential republic
RULING PARTY: Croatian Democratic Union (HDZ)
HEAD OF STATE & GOVERNMENT: President Franjo Tudjman (since May '90)
PRIME MINISTER: Zlatko Matesa (since Nov '95)
MAIN IGO MEMBERSHIPS (non-UN): OSCE, CE, CEI
CURRENCY: kuna (end-'97 £1=K10.40, US$1=K6.34)
GNP PER CAPITA: US$3,250 ('95)

UPPER house, regional and local elections in April confirmed the political dominance of the Croatian Democratic Union (HDZ) headed by Franjo Tudjman (75), who secured easy re-election as President in June despite persistent reports that he was suffering from stomach cancer (see AR 1996, p. 118). The Croatian government's less-than-enthusiastic support for the Dayton peace process, together with its strongly nationalist orientation, resulted in increasing international isolation in 1997. Nevertheless, by year's end Croatia was on the verge of recovering full control within its international borders, as Serb-populated Eastern Slavonia prepared for transfer from temporary UN administration to the authority of Zagreb.

The government's desire to include Eastern Slavonia in the electoral process delayed polling for the Chamber of Districts (upper house) and for regional and local councils until 13 April. The HDZ increased its majority in the 68-member upper house, winning 42 of the 63 elective seats, although Dalmatia and Istria re-emerged as strongholds of opposition. Local elections in Eastern Slavonia passed off without serious incident. In spite of high participation by the Serb population of the region, swelled by many thousands of refugees, a well-organized postal vote among Croat refugees enabled Croat parties to take control of the city council of Vukovar. Although the result was broadly endorsed by observers of the Organization for Security and Cooperation in Europe (OSCE), there was criticism of the unequal access to the communications media permitted to the contending parties.

Similar OSCE criticism was voiced about the conduct of the presidential elections on 15 June, when President Tudjman was returned for a further term of office with 61.4 per cent of the vote. In a turnout of only 54.6 per cent, a Social Democratic candidate took 21 per cent and a Social Liberal contender 17.6 per cent. Following a series of conciliatory gestures to the Serb population, the region of Eastern Slavonia also participated in the elections, although dissatisfaction persisted because of the slowness of the return to their homes of both Serb and Croat refugees. International concern about the situation resulted in the renewal of the mandate of the UNTAES monitoring force in Eastern Slavonia to 15 January 1998.

Recognizing the progress made towards normalization in Croatia, the IMF in March approved a credit of US$486 million to support the government's economic reform programme. On 1 July, however, the World Bank postponed its decision on a $30 million loan following pressure from a US government concerned about Croatia's limited backing for the Dayton process. In spite of opposition from the US State Department, the IMF credit was confirmed in October, reportedly in response to the arrest in Croatia of several of those indicted by the International War Crimes Tribunal at The Hague.

Allegations persisted that the Croatian government was ambivalent in its support for the Dayton agreements, to which it reacted with some displeasure, pointing out that several individuals had been sent to appear before The Hague tribunal. After the publication of an interview in *Feral Tribune*, admitting his involvement in atrocities in the recent hostilities, Miro Bajramović was arrested on 1 September. His admission was embarrassing to the authorities, not only because he had not been arrested to that point but also because he implicated several high-ranking officials, including a former Interior Minister. Ten of the 17 indicted Croats surrendered to tribunal officials in Split on 6 October, including Dario Kordić, who was accused of leading the massacre at Ahmići in Bosnia in April 1993.

The contentious nature of The Hague proceedings in Croatia was underlined on 9 August, when Dobroslav Paraga, leader of the radical nationalist Party of Rights 1861 and head of the paramilitary Croatian Defence Association (HOS) during the recent hostilities, issued a formal request to the tribunal to indict President Tudjman, Defence Minister Gojko Susak and several other leading political figures, alleging that they bore responsibility for war crimes.

In the sphere of external relations, President Tudjman's inauguration speech on 5 August featured an impassioned rejection of the possibility of Croatia ever joining a union of Balkan states. A degree of countervailing pragmatism was apparent in the signature in Belgrade on 15 September of six agreements on economic cooperation with Federal Yugoslavia, while on 11 November the rail link between Croatia and Serbia was reopened after six years of closure. Nevertheless, constitutional changes adopted in November included a prohibition on any procedure which would lead to the incorporation of Croatia in any association of Balkan states. Also causing puzzlement and anger in some quarters (including neighbouring Slovenia) was the new constitutional definition of Croatia as 'the national state of the Croatian people and a state of members of ethnic minorities and others who are its citizens'. Taken together, the changes were seen as confirming the isolationist and nationalist proclivities of the Tudjman government, as demonstrated by Croatia's pointed absence from a summit of Balkan states held in Crete on 3–4 November.

One issue on which the Croatian authorities did not get their way was the struggle of the independent station Radio 101 against government attempts to close it down (see AR 1996, p. 118). Having in January secured a reversal of an earlier decision to give its frequency to a rival station, the Zagreb-based Radio 101 was finally awarded a new five-year licence on 4 November. Other running battles between the government and the independent media, notably the satirical weekly *Feral Tribune*, continued throughout the year. On 29 December the editor of *Karlovacki List* was badly beaten up and warned against continuing his outspoken criticism of the government.

iv. MACEDONIA

CAPITAL: Skopje AREA: 25,713 sq km POPULATION: 1,936,877 ('94)
OFFICIAL LANGUAGE: Macedonian
POLITICAL SYSTEM: presidential republic
RULING PARTIES: Social Democratic Alliance of Macedonia (SDSM), Party of Democratic Prosperity (PDP) and Socialist Party of Macedonia
HEAD OF STATE & GOVERNMENT: President Kiro Gligorov (since Dec '90)
PRIME MINISTER: Branko Crvenovski (since Sept '92)
MAIN IGO MEMBERSHIPS (non-UN): OSCE, CE
CURRENCY: denar (end-'97 £1=D90.09, US$1=D54.91)
GNP PER CAPITA: US$860 ('95)

THE normalization of Macedonia's situation took a further step forward on 19 March with a visit to Skopje by the Greek Foreign Minister, Theodoros Pangolos (see also II.3.v), although no progress was made during the year in negotiations on the name of the state, to which the Greek government had consistently pressed objections (see AR 1995, p. 122). Further improvement in Macedonian-Greek relations was indicated by a meeting between President Gligorov and Prime Minister Simitis during the Crete summit of Balkan states on 3–4 November, although the Macedonian leader said afterwards that Greece's refusal to recognize a state called Macedonia remained a major source of regional tension.

On 26 March agreement was reached with the London Club of private creditor banks on Macedonia's share of the collective debt of the former Yugoslavia, allocating 5.4 per cent of the principal to Macedonia (see AR 1996, p. 119). The following month the IMF approved a structural adjustment loan of US$75 million to support the economic reform programme. The IMF was also involved in advising the government on its plans to provide partial reimbursement for the estimated 30,000 people who had lost money in the collapse of the Bitola TAT pyramid investment scheme. In the aftermath of the collapse, three senior economic officials were arrested and the governor of the National Bank was dismissed.

Dissatisfaction with the government's handling of the TAT affair was fanned by the opposition IMRO party, which mounted a large demonstration in Skopje on 15 May calling for new elections. On 29 May an extensive reshuffle of the three-party coalition government (of the Social Democratic Alliance of Macedonia, the Socialist Party of Macedonia and the ethnic Albanian Party of Democratic Prosperity) brought in eight new ministers. According to Prime Minister Branko Crvenovski, the changes would strengthen the government in its struggle against current economic problems, as well as against crime and corruption.

The focal issue of Macedonian politics continued to be relations between the Slav Macedonian majority and the Albanian minority. Access to education and to the communications media continued to be contentious matters, to which was added the Albanian minority's claim to the right to fly their national flag. Contradictory opinions on this question were delivered by the Minister of Justice and the Constitutional Court in May and June respectively, while new legislation on 8 July failed to resolve the issue in practice. On 17 September the mayor of Gostivar was sentenced to 13 years' imprisonment for 'fanning national, racial and ethnic intolerance', his offence having been to fly the Albanian flag from the town hall. He was subsequently released without explanation.

In spite of these problems, Macedonia and Albania were able to act together to improve border security, following ministerial meetings in October focusing on arms smuggling in the wake of the breakdown of civil order in Albania (see III.2.i). In light of the acute instability in Albania, the the UN Security Council had voted on 9 April not to reduce the size of the 1,100-strong UN Preventive Deployment Force (UNPREDEP) stationed in Macedonia. .

v. SLOVENIA

CAPITAL: Ljubljana   AREA: 20,251 sq km   POPULATION: 1,989,000 ('94)
OFFICIAL LANGUAGE: Slovene
POLITICAL SYSTEM: presidential republic
RULING PARTIES: Liberal Democracy of Slovenia (LDS), Slovene People's Party (SLS) &
    Democratic Party of Pensioners (DeSUS)
HEAD OF STATE & GOVERNMENT: President Milan Kučan (since April '90)
PRIME MINISTER: Janez Drnovšek (since April '92)
MAIN IGO MEMBERSHIPS (non-UN): OSCE, CE, PFP, CEI
CURRENCY: tolar (end-'97 £1=T276.39, US$1=T168.46)
GNP PER CAPITA: US$8,200 ('95)

ON 9 January Janez Drnovšek was re-elected as Premier by the narrow margin of 46 votes to 44 in the Assembly, after his Liberal Democracy Party had negotiated a coalition with Marijan Podobnik's Slovene People's Party and the Democratic Party of Pensioners. The new government, formed following the defection of a member of the Christian Democrats, received a vote of confidence on 27 February.

On 31 July Goran Thaler was forced to resign as Foreign Minister, for the second time in just over a year (see AR 1996, p. 119), amid opposition criticism of his acceptance of European Union (EU) demands for changes to article 68 of Slovenia's constitution, as a condition of further progress in the country's entry negotiations. The required changes, which were intended to bring Slovenian rules on the foreign ownership of real estate into line with EU norms, raised fears among many Slovenes of a restoration of Italian and Austrian economic control. Mr Thaler was replaced by Boris Frlec.

In a presidential election on 23 November, incumbent Milan Kučan was re-elected outright in a single round of voting, winning 55.6 per cent of the vote. Although President Kučan remained popular, his victory was in part assured by the inability of the parties to cooperate, with the result that seven other candidates were on the ballot paper.

Slovenia's omission from the first wave of new members of an enlarged NATO put a dampener on the government's endeavours to distance the country from its former Balkan partners. More positively, Slovenia was elected to one of the non-permanent seats on the UN Security Council on 14 October, while in December an EU summit in Luxembourg formally included Slovenia among the six applicant countries with which substantive accession negotiations would be opened in 1998.

vi. FEDERAL REPUBLIC OF YUGOSLAVIA

CONSTITUENTS: Montenegro (13,812 sq km), Serbia (88,316 sq km)   CAPITAL: Belgrade
AREA: 102,128 sq km   POPULATION: 10,600,000 ('91)
OFFICIAL LANGUAGE: Serbo-Croat
POLITICAL SYSTEM: federal republic
RULING PARTIES: Socialist Party of Serbia heads coalition in Serbia; Democratic Party of Socialists of Montenegro heads coalition in Montenegro
HEAD OF STATE & GOVERNMENT: President Slobodan Milošević
PRESIDENTS OF CONSTITUENT REPUBLICS: Milan Milutinovic (Serbia) & Momir Bulatović (Montenegro)
PRESIDENT-ELECT: Milo Djukanović (Montenegro)
PRIME MINISTERS: Radoje Kontić (Yugoslavia); Mirko Marjanović (Serbia); Milo Djukanović (Montenegro)
MAIN IGO MEMBERSHIP (non-UN): OSCE
CURRENCY: new dinar (end-'97 £1=ND9.62, US$1=5.87)
GNP PER CAPITA: n.a.

A long series of student-led opposition rallies that began in late 1996 (see AR 1996, p. 120) continued in Belgrade throughout January. They focused mainly on official delay in recognizing victories by the opposition Zajedno coalition in the local government elections of November 1996, but were also fuelled by dissatisfaction with deteriorating economic conditions. Unusually, the Serbian Orthodox Church issued a statement supporting the demonstrations, which were broken up by the security forces on 2–4 February with considerable violence. Following intervention by the Organization for Security and Cooperation in Europe (OSCE) on 11 February, the Serbian Assembly legislated to reinstate the results, opposition majorities being installed in several city councils, including Belgrade and Nis. Student demonstrations continued throughout February directed primarily at educational grievances. The rector of Belgrade University was compelled to resign on 19 March.

In spite of the widespread discredit brought to the Milosevic regime by these events, disorder within the Zajedno coalition parties prevented them from making political headway. They were unable to nominate a common candidate for the federal presidency, so that by the end of June it was acknowledged that Zajedno no longer existed in any effective sense. In the parliamentary balloting on 15 July, Slobodan Milošević of the Socialist Party of Serbia (SPS) was elected unopposed by substantial majorities of each house of the Federal Assembly, being sworn in on 23 July. Mr Milošević had served as President of Serbia since 1989 and was constitutionally barred from seeking a third term when his current mandate expired later in 1997; hence his pre-emptive decision to switch to the federal presidency.

The SPS had a less easy passage in elections to the Serbian Assembly on 21 September and in simultaneous first-round polling for the Serbian presidency. The party contested the elections in a 'Joint List' alliance which also embraced the Yugoslav United Left (YUL)—headed by Mr Milošević's wife, Mirjana Marković—and New Democracy (ND). In the Assembly polling, the Joint List failed to obtain an overall majority, winning 110 of the 250 seats, while Vojislav Sešelj's ultra-nationalist Serbian Radical Party (SRS) made substantial gains to win 82 seats. The nationalist Serbian Renewal Movement (SPO) led by Vuk Drašković also polled well, as did various regional parties; but the constituents of the former Zajedno alliance were punished for their disunity.

In the presidential elections, the Joint List candidate, Zoran Lilić, headed the first-round polling with 35.7 per cent, against 27.3 per cent for Mr Seselj (SRS) and 20.6 per cent for Mr Drasković (SPO). The second round on 5 October produced a narrow victory for Mr Sešelj over Mr Lilić, but the outcome was declared invalid because the turnout was less than 50 per cent. A new contest was accordingly held on 7 and 21 December, in which Mr Lilić was replaced as the SPS candidate by Milan Milutinović, hitherto federal Foreign Minister. The outcome was a comfortable (59.2 per cent) second-round victory for Mr Milutinovic, amid much evidence of electoral fraud, especially in Kosovo, where the Albanian population boycotted the vote.

Freedom of the press remained a live political issue in the Yugoslav federation in 1997, new legislation being proposed in March envisaging restrictions on the activities of the private media. On 25 March, however, the Economic Court in Belgrade issued a ruling which enabled the controversial television station BK to extend its range, and in April the government yielded to pressure and withdrew its proposals.

Serbia's Deputy Minister of the Interior, Radovan Stojičić, was assassinated in Belgrade on 11 April, as was the YUL secretary-general, Zoran Todorović, on 24 October. Both were believed to have close links with President Milošević and his wife Mirjana, it being speculated that their murders were linked to others in the capital in which Mafia-style gangs were believed to be implicated. Such killings provided a dramatic reminder of the corruption into which management of the Serbian economy had descended. The economic probity of the government was also called into question by the conduct of the partial sell-off of the publicly-owned Telecom system.

The first open cracks began to appear in relations between the federation's constituent republics of Serbia and Montenegro in February, when the Montenegrin Prime Minister, Milo Djukanović, criticized Mr Milošević's handling of the crisis in Belgrade. The conflict quickly took the form of a struggle between Mr Djukanović and the Montenegrin President, Momir Bulatović (a Milošević loyalist), for control of the ruling Democratic Party of Socialists of Montenegro (DPSCG). A court adjudication in August failed to resolve the contested legitimacy of their respective presidential candidatures, with the result that both men remained candidates, representing rival DPSCG factions.

After an acrimonious campaign, Mr Bulatović narrowly headed the firstround polling on 5 October but was overtaken by Mr Djukanović in the second round a fortnight later, his winning margin being fewer than 6,000 votes. Despite accusations of electoral fraud, accompanied by violent demonstrations by supporters of Mr Bulatović, Mr Djukanović's election was confirmed by the Assembly on 29 December. His victory was widely interpreted as indicating a strengthened mood in Montenegro in favour of greater independence from Serbia and consequential changes in the structure of the Yugoslav federation.

The state of relations between Serbs and the ethnic Albanian majority in Kosovo fluctuated widely during the year. In early April informal contacts took place in New York between Serb officials and representatives of the Kosovo government-in-exile. Subsequently, however, relations between the two communities deteriorated, as the policy of non-violent resistance previously espoused by the Democratic League of Kosovo began to crumble. Several attacks on the Serbian security forces were believed to be the work of a 'Liberation Army of Kosovo', while large anti-Belgrade student demonstrations took place in Priština between October and December. Hopes of better Serb-Kosovar relations were raised when President Milošević met the new Albanian Prime Minister, Fatos Nano, at the Balkan summit in Crete on 3–4 November. However, the contact had yielded no obvious fruit as the year ended.

3. RUSSIA, EASTERN EUROPE AND THE CAUCASUS

i. RUSSIA

CAPITAL: Moscow   AREA: 17,075,000 sq km   POPULATION: 148,000,000 ('96)
OFFICIAL LANGUAGE: Russian
POLITICAL SYSTEM: federal republic
HEAD OF STATE & GOVERNMENT: President Boris Yeltsin (since June '91)
RULING PARTIES: Our Home is Russia (NDR) heads fluid coalition
PRIME MINISTER: Viktor Chernomyrdin (NDR), since Dec '92
MAIN IGO MEMBERSHIPS (non-UN): CIS, OSCE, G-8, CE, PFP, CBSS, BSEC, AC
CURRENCY: rouble (end-'97 £1=R9,844.20, US$1=R6,000.00)
GNP PER CAPITA: US$2,240 ('95) or US$4,480 ('95) by PPP calculation

RUSSIA was the largest of the countries that had begun the transition from Communist Party rule after 1989, and one in which the transition was particularly slow to yield positive results for its long-suffering population. Boris Yeltsin had won a convincing presidential victory in the summer of 1996, but his health difficulties had led to repeated absences from the Kremlin throughout the year and to a struggle for influence within his immediate circle (see AR 1996, pp. 127–30). Continuing into 1997, the struggle was conducted between the country's major financial-industrial groups, embracing the largest banks, key sectors of the economy and the newspapers and television stations in which they had acquired a controlling interest. The wider political situation was one of relative stability, apart from a far-reaching government reshuffle in the spring; but this was set against a background of continuing economic decline and widening social differences, accompanied by an increase in organized crime and corruption. Domestic changes were also reflected in an increasingly assertive foreign policy, featuring attempts to develop relations with China and eastern neighbours that would counterbalance the continuing advance of NATO and the European Union (EU) into what had formerly been a zone of undisputed Soviet influence.

President Yeltsin's continuing incapacity led to a formal attempt at impeachment in January, launched by Communist Party deputies, and to the cancellation of a planned visit to the Netherlands. The resignation call fell just short of the required majority (of half of the full membership of the State Duma), but the deputies agreed in February to ask for an official report on the state of the President's health. Mr Yeltsin reasserted his authority with a forceful state of the union address to the Federal Assembly in early March. He gave a bleak assessment of the current state of the Russian economy and declared himself 'dissatisfied with the government', drawing particular attention to public order and fiscal indiscipline. The speech was followed by two important government appointments. Anatolii Chubais, the President's chief of staff and former architect of the privatization programme, became First Deputy Prime Minister in charge of economic reform, while the youthful and reformist governor of Nizhnii Novgorod, Boris Nemtsov, was appointed to a second first deputy premiership with particular responsibility for housing and utilities. The Duma majority responded by attacking the appointment Mr Chubais in particular as a 'direct challenge to Russian public opinion'.

There was a further government change in May when President Yeltsin, 'indignant' over the state of the Russian armed forces, dismissed both the Defence Minister, General Igor Rodionov, and the Chief of the General Staff for their failure to implement necessary reforms. General Igor Sergeev, hitherto commander of the strategic missile troops, was appointed to succeed General Rodionov. In a series of decrees issued in July, the President himself ordered a cut of half a million in armed forces personnel by the end of 1998. The chairman of the Duma's defence committee (and a former Russian commander in 1994–96 Chechen conflict), General (retd.) Lev Rokhlin, had meanwhile accused the President of having 'doomed the armed forces to destruction' and of being personally responsible for the debacle in Chechenya. Subsequently, General Rokhlin's 'All-Russian Movement in support of the Army, Military Science and the Defence Industry' held its founding congress in September, with strong support from Communist and nationalist politicians.

Other ministers in difficulty during the year included Justice Minister Valentin Kovalev, who was obliged to resign in July when he was shown in a videotape in the company of several naked women in a sauna which was reputedly the haunt of a Russian criminal syndicate. In November it was the turn of Mr Chubais to suffer a blow to his reputation when he admitted receiving an implausibly large book advance from a company that had been involved in privatizing state firms. President Yeltsin refused Mr Chubais's offer of resignation and retained him as First Deputy Premier but stripped him of the additional title of Finance Minister.

There were no national elections during the year, but a series of contests for governorships in Russia's regions and republics extended from late 1996 into the early months of 1997. Incumbents, of whatever party, were generally successful, most of them supporters of Mr Yeltsin (who had been responsible for many of the original appointments). Where positions changed hands, the Popular-Patriotic Union of Russia, a Communist/nationalist alliance, provided most of the victors. In a February by-election, Alexander Korzhakov, who had been Mr Yeltsin's bodyguard and confidant until his dismissal in June 1996 after the first round of the presidential election (see AR 1996, p. 128), won a vacant seat in the State Duma. His memoirs, which claimed that Mr Yeltsin had several times attempted suicide, were published later in the year. The State Duma seat had been vacated by Alexander Lebed, the charismatic army general who had been a presidential candidate in 1996 and then, briefly, Secretary of the Security Council. Mr Lebed himself formed a Russian People's Republican Party during the year as part of a 'third force' that would provide a political alternative 'to both the Communists and the current democratic elite, since both are alien to the people'.

It was a year in which the economy stabilized after several years of contraction, but in which there few signs of real recovery. The annual rate of inflation for 1996 was reported as standing at 22 per cent, the lowest figure since 1990; the 1997 target was 12 per cent. However, there were continuing difficulties about tax collection, which were of especial concern to Russia's international creditors, and about the payment of wages, particularly to pensioners and state employees. A nationwide day of strike action was called on 27 March in protest over wage arrears; government sources suggested that two million people had taken part, whereas the trade unions claimed over 20 million. President Yeltsin, in an address to the federal upper house in September, promised that the state would play a greater role in the economy; there would be no return to the state planning of the Soviet period, but he admitted that 'the market in itself is not the panacea for all ills' and warned that 'the state will not tolerate any attempts to pressurize it by representatives of business and banks'.

The rouble came under pressure towards the end of the year, as the economic difficulties in East Asia (see XVIII.1) undermined the confidence of the financial markets, producing a sharp fall in the stock exchange. The currency itself was redenominated with effect from the start of 1998, 1,000 old roubles becoming one new rouble. The move led to fears of disguised inflation, but was intended by the Russian government to indicate that the instability of the recent past had come to an end.

One of the main concerns of ordinary Russians throughout the year was organized crime. The danger that it represented was underlined by a number of attacks on senior figures in government, including the Deputy Finance Minister (who was responsible for tax collection); he escaped alive, amid much disquiet at what was the first murder attempt on a senior government member. The editor of a business newspaper, Vadim Biryukov, was less fortunate; he was found murdered in his garage. And the deputy governor of St Petersburg (who was chairman of that city's property committee) was assassinated on 18 August. There was discouraging news on other fronts too, including a warning in June that only 54 per cent of Russian men over 16 were likely to reach the age of 60 and the announcement in November that Russia had topped the international corruption league table produced by a business risks consultancy. By the end of the year, in one of his regular radio addresses, Mr Yeltsin was warning that Russians were in danger of losing their spiritual values as they plunged into a new world of materialism. He called upon the widely-despised 'new rich' to play their part in a process of civic renewal and upon ordinary Russians to show more compassion for each other in the 'harsh struggle for their daily bread'.

The Chechen conflict had dominated domestic politics from December 1994 until the 1996 presidential elections, but the ceasefire concluded in August 1996 (see AR 1996, p. 130) led to the cessation of formal hostilities and to a continuing process of negotiation punctuated by minor incidents. Presidential elections took place in the republic in January, when Aslan Maskhadov, who had been prime minister in the acting government and who had negotiated the ceasefire with Alexander Lebed, won an easy first-round victory with 59 per cent of the vote. Mr Maskhadov was regarded as the most moderate of the candidates but he remained committed to the cause of full independence, appointing a commission to negotiate 'inter-state relations' with Russia on the basis of the August 1996 ceasefire. President Yeltsin and Mr Maskhadov signed a more formal peace treaty in Moscow on 12 May; it bound both parties to abjure the use of force and to establish relations based upon the 'generally accepted principles and standards of international law'. It did not of itself resolve the question of Chechenya's constitutional status, which was due to be resolved, in accordance with the August 1996 agreement, by the end of 2001. The relationship was also complicated by the kidnapping of Russian journalists in the republic and by the introduction of Islamic in place of Russian law, leading to the public execution of convicted murderers.

The central issue in Russian foreign policy throughout the year was the threatened expansion of NATO into what had been the Soviet sphere of influence in Central/Eastern Europe and possibly to the Baltic republics of the former USSR. In a representative statement of the Russian government's position, Mr Chubais warned in February that the expansion would 'inevitably lead to a new dividing-line across the whole of Europe' and that it would be the 'biggest mistake made in Western policy for 50 years'—one that would change the 'whole political landscape' and force Russia to 'rethink' its own external policy. The enlargement, he went on, would be tolerable only if a binding friendship treaty were concluded between Russia and the NATO states which would prohibit the stationing of nuclear weapons and the establishment of NATO bases on the territory of former Warsaw Pact countries.

Continued discussions led to the signature in Paris on 27 May of a Founding

Act on Mutual Relations, Cooperation and Security by President Yeltsin and NATO's 16 heads of government, allowing for the alliance's eastward expansion but also creating a permanent joint council to discuss issues of common security (see XII.1; XIX.1). Under the accord, Russia and NATO formally declared that they no longer regarded each other as adversaries and spoke of the beginning of a 'fundamentally new relationship'. For his part, President Yeltsin made it clear that Russia still had a 'negative attitude' to the alliance's eastward expansion; indeed, he had warned earlier in the month that NATO's expansionist plans represented the most serious dispute that had taken place between Russia and the United States since the 1962 Cuban missile crisis.

The NATO states, for their part, confirmed that they had 'no intention, plan or reason' to deploy nuclear weapons or establish nuclear storage sites on the territory of prospective new members, also assuring Russia that they would not station 'substantial' numbers of conventional forces in the region. There could, however, be no Russian veto on the alliance's decisions. Accordingly, the Madrid NATO summit in July duly invited three former Warsaw Treaty states (the Czech Republic, Hungary and Poland) to join the alliance as full members by 1999, also leaving an 'open door' for Slovenia, Romania and the three Baltic states to join at a later date. The Russian Foreign Minister, Yevgenii Primakov, declared the decision to be 'the biggest mistake in Europe since the end of World War II', later complaining in a December speech that the West was trying to force Moscow into a humiliating 'patron and client' relationship.

The groundwork for the Founding Act had been laid in a series of bilateral meetings earlier in the year. Mr Yeltsin was sufficiently recovered to hold a summit meeting with President Clinton in Helsinki on 20–21 March, their 12th such meeting since 1993. The main focus of the talks was the contentious issue of NATO enlargement, but they also discussed arms control and the prospects for economic partnership. Russia, it was agreed, would sign a document defining its relationship with NATO, despite its continuing opposition to enlargement; the relationship would be one that would provide for 'consultation, coordination and, to the maximum extent possible, joint decision-making and action on security issues of common concern'. Russia won a pledge that nuclear weapons would not be stationed on the territory of new member states, although President Yeltsin dropped the demand that the document should be legally binding; instead it was agreed that it would be 'an enduring commitment at the highest political level'. It was also agreed that the two countries would begin to negotiate a new strategic arms reduction treaty (START III) as soon as the Duma had ratified the 1993 START II treaty (see AR 1993, pp. 551–4). Russia was promised an enhanced role in the G-7 group of industrialized nations, it being agreed that the forthcoming G-7 summit in the United States would be called 'the summit of the eight' (see XVIII.1).

There were important dealings with other states during the year, including talks with the Chancellor Helmut Kohl of Germany in April, at the end of which Mr Yeltsin announced that he would sign a new security charter with NATO to formalize Russia's new role in European security. China's President Jiang Zemin visited Moscow in late April, signing a document which welcomed the 'positive trend towards a multi-polar world'; he addressed the State Duma in the course of his visit, taking the opportunity to stress the need for a strategic partnership between the two countries. President Yeltsin undertook a return visit to China in November, bringing a formal end to territorial disputes that dated from the seventeenth century and speaking of a 'constructive partnership'. Trade between the two countries nonetheless remained at a level which Boris Nemtsov, in the course of the visit, described as 'ridiculously low', and there was no agreement on the financing of an ambitious and long-discussed natural gas pipeline.

On his way to China, President Yeltsin held an informal summit with the Japanese Prime Minister at Krasnoyarsk (Siberia) on 1–2 November in which the two leaders committed themselves to signature of a formal peace treaty by 2000. However, it was unclear how they would resolve their major difference, namely the status of the southern Kurile islands held by Russia since 1945 but claimed by Japan. Symbolically, perhaps, a fishing trip on the Yenisei river by the two leaders yielded only a single and 'not very big' fish, hooked by the Japanese rather than the Russian leader.

A presidential visit to Sweden on 2–5 December was less successful, as Mr Yeltsin behaved erratically, publicly scolding other members of his party and appearing to believe that he was actually in Helsinki. His unscheduled announcement that Russia would 'unilaterally cut its number of nuclear warheads by another third' was later described as merely a 'proposal' by a Russian spokesman. Soon after returning to Moscow, President Yeltsin was admitted to a sanatorium until the end the year, suffering from 'an acute viral infection'.

ii. BELARUS—UKRAINE—MOLDOVA

Belarus
CAPITAL: Minsk   AREA: 208,000 sq km   POPULATION: 10,400,000 ('96)
OFFICIAL LANGUAGES: Belarusan & Russian
POLITICAL SYSTEM: presidential
HEAD OF STATE & GOVERNMENT: President Alyaksandr Lukashenka (since July '94)
RULING PARTY: Belarusan Patriotic Movement (BPR)
PRIME MINISTER: Syargey Ling, Prime Minister (since July '94)
MAIN IGO MEMBERSHIPS (non-UN): CIS, OSCE, PFP, CEI
CURRENCY: Belarusan rouble (end-'97 £1=BR67,842.94, US$1=BR41,350.00)
GNP PER CAPITA: US$2,070 ('95) or US$4,220 ('95) by PPP calculation

Ukraine
CAPITAL: Kyiv   AREA: 604,000 sq km   POPULATION: 51,800,000 ('96)
OFFICIAL LANGUAGE: Ukrainian
POLITICAL SYSTEM: democratic republic
HEAD OF STATE & GOVERNMENT: President Leonid Kuchma (since July '94)
RULING PARTY: Inter-Regional Reform Bloc (MBR) links ruling circle
PRIME MINISTER: Valery Pustovoytenko (since July '97)
MAIN IGO MEMBERSHIPS (non-UN): CIS, OSCE, CE, PFP, BSEC, CEI
CURRENCY: hryvna (end-'97 £1=K3.12, US$1=K1.90)
GNP PER CAPITA: US$1,630 ('95) or US$2,400 ('95) by PPP calculation

Moldova

CAPITAL: Chisinau (Kishinev)   AREA: 34,000 sq km   POPULATION: 4,380,000 ('96)
OFFICIAL LANGUAGE: Moldovan
POLITICAL SYSTEM: democratic republic
HEAD OF STATE & GOVERNMENT: President Petru Lucinschi (since Jan '97)
RULING PARTY: Agrarian Democratic Party of Moldova (PDAM)
PRIME MINISTER: Ion Ciubuc (since Jan '97)
MAIN IGO MEMBERSHIPS (non-UN): CIS, OSCE, CE, CEI, PFP, BSEC
CURRENCY: Moldovan leu (end-'97 £1=ML7.68, US$1=ML4.68)
GNP PER CAPITA: US$920 ('95)

IN BELARUS, the approval of a new constitution in controversial circumstances in November 1996 (see AR 1996, pp. 132–3) was followed in January by changes in the structure and composition of the government. Syargey Ling, acting Prime Minister since November, was confirmed in his post by parliamentary vote in February. Opposition politicians meanwhile formed a coalition 'shadow cabinet' to resist what they saw as increasingly authoritarian policies on the part of President Lukashenka; there were attacks on individual oppositionists, amid demonstrations by trade union and other bodies against the President's pro-Russian policies. The first secretary at the US embassy in Minsk was asked to leave the country in March, having been accused of participating in an anti-Lukashenka rally; the US government, in response, withdrew its ambassador and expelled a Belarusan diplomat from Washington. The Council of Europe's Parliamentary Assembly, responding to these developments, voted in January to suspend Belarus's observer status (see XI.4.i).

Relations with Russia were much more cordial, following the treaty of April 1996 establishing a Community of Sovereign Republics between the two states (see AR 1996, p. 131). In January President Yeltsin suggested the creation of joint currencies, taxation systems and energy supply, the two Presidents taking the same position in a joint statement after they had met in Moscow in March. In April a treaty was signed which committed the two countries to future integration; and in May a Charter of the Union was signed in Moscow, amplifying the union treaty and pledging 'voluntary unification' at some future date. It was envisaged that the agreement would be open to ratification by other states, in practice other former Soviet republics interested in restoring some of their previous associations. The first session of the new Russo-Belarusan Parliamentary Assembly, created under the terms of the treaty and charter, took place in mid-June. In a highly symbolic act it adopted the music of the former Soviet national anthem as the anthem of the new union, while its chairman, Russian State Duma speaker Gennadii Seleznev, described the December 1991 agreement to dissolve the USSR as the 'betrayal of the century'. In spite of these agreements, however, integration remained superficial, and there were many sources of tension, including the arrest in Belarus of Russian journalists accused of border violations but in practice 'guilty' of giving too much attention to the domestic opposition.

In neighbouring UKRAINE, President Kuchma announced changes to the cabinet in February in an apparent attempt to deal with corruption and to strengthen the country's financial stabilization programme. In his state of the union address in March Mr Kuchma made a sharply-worded attack on Prime Minister Pavlo Lazarenko and the Ukrainian government for 'corruption and inefficiency' and for the country's persisting 'financial chaos'. Following the speech it was announced that the government had established a Supervisory Council to deal with the economic crisis, headed by a Deputy Prime Minister, which would oversee tax reform and the problem of wage and pension arrears.

Mr Lazarenko eventually resigned from the premiership on 1 July, reportedly suffering from health problems but also facing accusations of delaying President Kuchma's economic reform programme and serious allegations of corruption. He was replaced on 11 July by Valery Pustovoytenko, a former mayor of Dnepropetrovsk who had headed Mr Kuchma's 1994 election campaign. The new Prime Minister, in a speech to the Supreme Council, promised to reform the government and improve its record of cooperation with the legislature; and he undertook personally to lead the effort to pay wage and welfare arrears. Appointments to the new cabinet followed in late July and early August. In September the Supreme Council adopted a law that altered the voting system for legislative elections to a mixed system of majority voting in single-member constituencies and proportional representation in a republic-wide competition of parties and political alliances, subject to a 4 per cent threshold. New parliamentary elections were due to be held on this basis in March 1998.

A security pact was signed with the NATO countries in July, giving Ukraine the right to call for 'consultations' if it felt threatened. Relations with Russia, meanwhile, remained difficult. In February the Ukrainian parliament voted to reject an agreement signed in 1994 between the Russian and Ukrainian Prime Ministers and covering the division of Soviet assets, new conditions being presented to Russia for ratification of the agreement. President Kuchma himself blamed Russia for the poor state of relations between the two countries, complaining in an interview in the Russian press of Russia's 'prejudiced attitude towards Ukraine'. On 30–31 May, however, President Yeltsin paid his first official visit to Ukraine since 1990, in the course of which a ten-year treaty of friendship, cooperation and partnership was signed. It followed a visit by Prime Minister Viktor Chernomyrdin during which agreement was reached on the berthing of the Black Sea fleet and other contentious issues.

IN MOLDOVA, Petru Lucinschi was formally inaugurated as the new President on 15 January, following his election victory over incumbent Mircea Snegur in December 1996 (see AR 1996, p. 133). His choice of Prime Minister was the chairman of the State Accounting Chamber, Ion Ciubuc, who formed a government dominated by the majority Agrarian Democratic Party. In February, however, a new political formation, the Movement for a Democratic and Prosperous Moldova, was launched to support the newly-elected President and his policies.

In April agreement was reached on a memorandum of understanding on the normalization of relations with the breakaway Dnestr region, it being agreed that Russia and Ukraine would act as 'guarantors'. The memorandum of understanding was formally signed in Moscow on 8 May and was hailed by some commentators as a breakthrough. However, it did not commit either side to more than further talks on the nature of their relations within 'the framework of a single state'. Nor did it clarify what status would eventually be given to the breakaway region.

iii. ARMENIA—GEORGIA—AZERBAIJAN

Armenia
CAPITAL: Yerevan   AREA: 30,000 sq km   POPULATION: 3,800,000 ('96)
OFFICIAL LANGUAGE: Armenian
POLITICAL SYSTEM: democratic republic
HEAD OF STATE & GOVERNMENT: President Levon Ter-Petrosyan (since Aug '90)
RULING PARTY: Pan-Armenian National Movement
PRIME MINISTER: Robert Kocharyan (since March '97)
MAIN IGO MEMBERSHIPS (non-UN): CIS, OSCE, PFP, BSEC
CURRENCY: dram (end-'97 £1=D820.14, US$1=D499.87)
GNP PER CAPITA: US$730 ('95) or US$2,260 ('95) by PPP calculation

Georgia
CAPITAL: Tbilisi   AREA: 70,000 sq km   POPULATION: 5,500,000 ('96)
OFFICIAL LANGUAGE: Georgian
POLITICAL SYSTEM: democratic republic
HEAD OF STATE & GOVERNMENT: President Eduard Shevardnadze (since Oct '92)
RULING PARTIES: Citizens' Union coordinates fluid coalition
MAIN IGO MEMBERSHIPS (non-UN): CIS, OSCE, PFP, BSEC
CURRENCY: lari
GNP PER CAPITA: US$440 ('95) or US$1,470 ('95) by PPP calculation

Azerbaijan
CAPITAL: Baku   AREA: 87,000 sq km   POPULATION: 7,575,000 ('96)
OFFICIAL LANGUAGE: Azeri
POLITICAL SYSTEM: democratic republic
HEAD OF STATE & GOVERNMENT: President Geidar Aliyev (since June '93)
RULING PARTY: New Azerbaijan Party (YAP)
PRIME MINISTER: Artur Rasizade (since July '96)
MAIN IGO MEMBERSHIPS (non-UN): CIS, OSCE, PFP, BSEC, OIC, ECO
CURRENCY: manat (end-'97 £1=M6,480.76, US$1=M3,950.00)
GNP PER CAPITA: US$480 ('95) or US$1,460 ('95) by PPP calculation

IN ARMENIA, there were changes in government early in the year, following President Levon Ter-Petrosyan's re-election in September 1996 (see AR 1996, p. 133). In March the President appointed Robert Kocharyan as Prime Minister in place of Armen Sarkissian, who had resigned for health reasons after just four months in office. Mr Kocharyan had previously been president of the self-proclaimed republic of Nagorno-Karabakh, the Armenian-speaking enclave within Azerbaijan. It was widely believed that President Ter-Petrosyan had hoped, by appointing Mr Kocharyan, to relieve the tension that had built up as a result of the controversial nature of his own re-election. Mr Kocharyan's appointment was described by the Azerbaijani government, for its part, as a 'provocation'.

President Ter-Petrosyan visited Russia in August for talks with President Yeltsin, in the course of which a treaty of 'friendship, cooperation and mutual understanding' was signed, renewing a similar protocol that had been in effect since 1991.

There were also governmental changes in neighbouring GEORGIA, after criticisms of the performance of ministers by President Shevardnadze. A new Finance Minister was appointed in May, together with a new Industry Minister. President Shevardnadze himself made his first official visit to Armenia the same month. The central issue in foreign and domestic policy was, however, the long-running dispute with the breakaway republic of Abkhazia. In August President Yeltsin made proposals for the peaceful resolution of the dispute, which were warmly welcomed by Mr Shevardnadze. The proposals envisaged substantial autonomy for Abkhazia, while at the same time insisting on the territorial integrity of Georgia as a whole. Not surprisingly, they were rejected by the Abkhazia president on the grounds that the region no longer formed part of Georgia. Both sides, however, accepted that the dispute should be resolved by peaceful means. In further discussions in September Abkhaz representatives indicated that they would be prepared to accept a 'union state' of Georgia and Abkhazia, under which key policy areas (such as defence and foreign affairs) would be jointly administered.

There was a greater emphasis on foreign affairs in AZERBAIJAN, featuring visits to Turkey and the United States by President Aliyev. During the Turkish visit in May the two sides signed a declaration envisaging a 'strategic partnership', while President Aliyev's Washington trip at end of July yielded the signature of an accord on military cooperation envisaging regular consultations. In a speech in September the President advocated closer relations with the United States in the political and economic spheres as well as a greater measure of military cooperation under the aegis of NATO's Partnership for Peace programme.

Sporadic fighting continued with Armenian forces throughout the year, in spite of the ceasefire concluded in July 1994 (see AR 1994, p. 151). Relations were further strained by the election of Arkadii Gukasyan as president of the self-declared Republic of Nagorno-Karabakh on 1 September with 90 per cent of the vote. As explained above, the position had become vacant because of Robert Kocharyan's departure to become Armenian Prime Minister. Mr Gukasyan was congratulated by the Armenian President on his success, but the election was declared illegal by the Azerbaijani government and seemed likely to prejudice ongoing negotiations between the contending parties under the auspices of the Minsk Group of the Organization for Security and Cooperation in Europe (see XI.4.ii).

IV THE AMERICAS AND THE CARIBBEAN

1. UNITED STATES OF AMERICA

CAPITAL: Washington, DC   AREA: 9,372,614 sq km   POPULATION: 269,000,000 ('97)
OFFICIAL LANGUAGE: English
POLITICAL SYSTEM: democratic federal republic
HEAD OF STATE & GOVERNMENT: President Bill Clinton, Democrat, since Jan '93 (*for full cabinet list see* XIX.8)
RULING PARTIES: the President is a Democrat; Congress is controlled by the Republicans
MAIN IGO MEMBERSHIPS (non-UN): NATO, OSCE, OECD, G-7, OAS, NAFTA, APEC, AC, CP, SPC, ANZUS
CURRENCY: dollar (end-'97 £1=US$1.64)
GNP PER CAPITA: US$26,980 ('95)

IN the year following the re-election of Bill Clinton (Democrat) to the presidency and the Republican Party's retention of control of Congress (see AR 1996, pp. 148–51), little appeared to have changed in American politics. However, there was a greater willingness to compromise on key issues such as the budget, after the protracted struggles of 1995–96 involving the closing-down of the government bureaucracy on two occasions. The President's personal popularity continued to run at high levels despite the sexual harassment suit brought against him by Paula Jones and ongoing investigations into contributions to Democratic Party election campaign finances. Above all, the President continued to benefit from a booming economy, which saw declining inflation and unemployment together with increased earnings.

Mr Clinton perhaps benefited too from further revelations concerning the Kennedy family, since he was often compared with President Kennedy. The Kennedys were in the news in August when Joseph Kennedy, son of Robert F. Kennedy, abandoned his campaign to become governor of Massachusetts, announcing that he no longer wished to subject the family to constant media attention. Mr Kennedy had been involved in a bitter divorce from his first wife and had been embarrassed by revelations that his brother Michael had had an affair with his children's teenage babysitter in 1995. In September John F. Kennedy Jnr. described his cousins Joseph and Michael as 'poster boys for bad behaviour' in an editorial in his magazine *George*. The publication in November of Seymour Hersh's critical study of John F. Kennedy, *The Dark Side of Camelot*, emphasized the dead President's sexual peccadilloes and links with the Mafia. Further tragedy hit the family when Michael Kennedy was killed in a skiing accident in Aspen, Colorado, on 31 December. He had once been regarded as a likely candidate to assume the family's political mantle, but his reputation had been seriously damaged by revelations of his affair.

Aviation safety continued to be a matter of national concern, as accidents and incidents continued to happen. A US Air Force A-10 jet plane on a routine training exercise from Tucson, Arizona, mysteriously disappeared without warning or apparent trace over Colorado on 2 April. The wreckage of the plane was not discovered until after the snows had thawed at the end of the month, but the cause of the accident remained unknown. On 7 August three crew men and a guard were killed when a DC-8 cargo plane owned by Fine Air Services crashed near a commercial centre shortly after take-off from Miami international airport. The following month 11 people died in a series of military aviation accidents.

Natural disasters also made the headlines when some of the worst storms in 30 years were experienced by the mid-west at the start of March. Torrential rain and tornadoes hit parts of Arkansas, Texas, Kentucky, Mississippi, Tennessee and Ohio, causing massive destruction, widespread flooding and the deaths of some 48 people. After visiting parts of his home state of Arkansas, President Clinton said that the storm had damaged 'places and people we know well' and that 'our hearts are with everyone who lost loved ones, homes and businesses'. He declared the affected region a disaster area and pledged additional federal funds to assist in the recovery. In April the 50,000 inhabitants of Grand Forks, North Dakota, were ordered to leave the city amid a combination of flooding and fires caused when the Red River broke its banks following the worst winter in memory. This too was declared a disaster area. On 27 May a series of tornadoes swept through Texas north of Austin, killing 27 people, most of them in the small town of Jarrell.

POLITICAL AFFAIRS. On the opening day of the new US Congress on 7 January, Newt Gingrich (Republican) narrowly secured re-election as Speaker of the House of Representatives. Author of the Republicans' 'Contract with America' (see AR 1995, p. 146; 1994, p. 168) and former scourge of the Clinton administration, Mr Gingrich had been found guilty of ethical lapses in 1996 (see AR 1996, p. 151). In defeating the Democratic candidate, Richard Gephardt, by 216 votes to 205, he became the first Republican for 68 years to serve two consecutive terms as Speaker. However, the decline in Mr Gingrich's standing was underlined on 21 January when the House ethics sub-committee recommended that he be given an official reprimand and fined $300,000 for breaches of normal congressional conduct. This was the most severe penalty ever imposed on a Speaker, but was short of a censure which would have forced his resignation.

Scandals involving the President resurfaced on 13 January when lawyers acting for Paula Jones asked the Supreme Court to require Mr Clinton to answer the charges of sexual harassment brought by their client, a former Arkansas state employee (see AR 1994, p. 162). The court had previously ruled that the suit should be postponed until after the November 1996 elections. Ms Jones alleged that in 1991, while Mr Clinton was governor of Arkansas, he had called her to a hotel room in Little Rock, exposed himself to her and requested oral sex. Ms Jones claimed that she could describe identifying features of the President's genitalia.

On 20 January Mr Clinton was sworn in for his second term. In his inaugural address the President looked back over America's past achievements and called upon the country to 'keep our democracy forever young'. Urging Americans to face the 21st century and 'to shape the forces of the information age and global society', he pointed to the nation's positive achievements in terms of economic growth, in getting people from welfare to work and in making the streets safer. He also suggested that the argument about government had been resolved, asserting: 'Government is not the problem and government is not the solution. We, the American people, are the solution'. Speaking on Martin Luther King's birthday, the President looked toward the millennium but warned that the country was still affected by 'the divide of race'. Referring to 'the dark impulses that lurk in the far regions of the soul everywhere', he declared: 'We shall overcome them'.

Mr Clinton also spoke of a 'new vision of government, a new sense of responsibility, a new spirit of community' in a land in which 'education will be every citizen's most prized possession', and where streets would be safe and drug free. He went on to suggest that, in returning a President of one party and a Congress dominated by another, the electorate had not intended 'to advance the politics of petty bickering and extreme partisanship'.

In the face of allegations about possible illegal fund-raising activities for the 1996 elections (the most expensive in history), President Clinton on 21 January announced new controls on Democratic Party funding. Among them were a ban on contributions from foreign citizens and corporations, an annual ceiling of $100,000 on individual donations and closer scrutiny of all donations of more than $5,000. During his first press conference on 28 January, the President admitted making mistakes in allowing White House and federal officials to participate in fund-raising 'coffee mornings' during the 1996 campaign. On 29 January the Director of the Federal Bureau of Investigation (FBI), Louis Freeh, informed Congress that he had appointed a team of investigators to examine the activities of an Asian fund-raiser for the Democratic Party, John Huang. Stories of 'red gold' centred on revelations that Mr Huang, a former senior official in the Commerce Department, had raised $4 million in campaign funds from Chinese contributors (much of it later returned as improper). FBI investigations into 'Chinagate' revealed that Mr Huang had been a frequent visitor to the Chinese embassy, raising fears that espionage might be involved as well as corruption.

President Clinton gave his fifth State of the Union message on 4 February. In his hour-long address to both houses of Congress he said that, after four years of continued economic growth, low unemployment, falling crime rates and declining welfare rolls, 'the state of our union is strong'. However, warning against inaction, he called upon America to prepare for the 21st century, asking that 'this Congress be the Congress that finally balances the budget' and for 'a bipartisan process to preserve social security and reform Medicare for the long run'. At the same time, Mr Clinton rejected proposals for a constitutional amendment requiring a balanced budget, on the grounds that it 'could cripple our country in time of crisis'.

On a more positive note, the President further suggested that a bill reforming campaign finance be enacted before 4 July; that an additional two million people be removed from welfare rolls by 2002; and that education should be the 'number one priority for the next four years'. In line with this last point, he outlined a 'call to action for American education' based on ten principles, central to which was the notion of national standards with national tests in key subjects. He also said that two years of college education, supported by tax credits and scholarships, should become universal in America by the 21st century and that all schools and libraries should have access to the Internet by 2000. The President also emphasized the need to 'give more families access to affordable, quality health-care', outlining measures to ensure that temporarily unemployed workers should not lose their health insurance. Targeting crime, Mr Clinton called for more community policing, 'an assault on juvenile crime' and an enlarged anti-drugs effort.

In the sphere of foreign policy, Mr Clinton called for the expansion of NATO, cooperation in the Asia-Pacific community, talks with North Korea and 'deeper dialogue' with China. He pointed to the need to expand US exports to Asia and Latin America in order to capitalize on growing markets. Reminding Americans of their country's role at the start of the Cold War, the President called upon the nation to 'do what it takes to remain the indispensable nation—to keep America strong, secure and prosperous for another 50 years'.

The President presented his budget for fiscal 1998 on 6 February, against a background of sustained economic growth, an inflation rate of less than 3 per cent, low interest rates and unemployment at 5.4 per cent. The $1,700,000 million budget offered tax cuts of $98,000 million spread over five years in the form of relief to enable poorer children to enter higher education and tax credits for the children of middle-income families. Expenditure on Medicare and on defence was to be cut, while spending on health-care provision for children and unemployed workers was to be increased, as was spending on education. The administration also called for a significant increase in the foreign affairs budget, including $1,570 million to pay arrears of dues owed to bodies such as the United Nations (see XI.1). Overall, the administration claimed that the budget would turn the current deficit into a surplus by 2002. The Republican response to the budget was generally positive, and attempts to pass an amendment to the constitution requiring balanced budgets, introduced at the end of January, foundered in the House because of uncertain support. In March the measure failed in the Senate, one vote short of the required two-thirds majority.

Allegations of illegal fund-raising activities in the Democratic Party continued to grow following a report in the *Washington Post* on 14 February, written by the famous investigative journalist Bob Woodward, that the Chinese embassy in Washington had been used to direct funds towards the election campaign. The scandal intensified on 21 February when John Huang refused to hand over documents requested by the House of Representatives' government reform and oversight committee, as did Webster Hubbell, a former associate US Attorney-General recently released from gaol for offences connected with the Whitewater affair (see AR 1994, 161, 168; 1995, pp. 150, 152; 1996, 141, 144–5).

Kenneth Starr, the independent prosecutor investigating the Whitewater affair, caused some confusion on 17 February when he announced his intention to resign in August to take up a university post. He subsequently said that his earlier decision had been 'unwise' and that he would stay on. Leaked extracts of his report into the events surrounding the death of Vincent Foster in July

1993 (see AR 1993, p. 156) confirmed that it was a suicide and that the White House had not been involved in a cover-up.

Further charges of sleaze in the Clinton administration erupted at the end of February as a result of documents released by Harold Ickes, a former deputy White House chief of staff who had resigned after being passed over for the top job. The documents showed that contributors to Democratic Party campaign funds had been rewarded with over-night accommodation in the Lincoln Room of the White House, seats on the presidential plane and photo opportunities at White House events; total proceeds from 938 people recorded as having stayed in the Lincoln Room had been $10 million. Such 'selling' of the White House appeared to involve not only President Clinton himself—a hand-written note by him itemizing charges for such activities emerged—but also the Vice-President, Al Gore, who until then had been untouched by any sleaze allegations. Responding to reports that he had been the administration's 'solicitor-in-chief' for the White House entertaining, Mr Gore admitted making fund-raising calls from his office but said he had charged them to the Democratic national committee (DNC). Although he argued that he had done nothing illegal or improper, the Vice-President said on 3 March that he would not repeat the practice.

Hillary Clinton also became involved in the fund-raising scandal on 4 March when Republican congressmen published a memorandum signed by her suggesting that a White House database, paid for from public funds, could be merged with a DNC database of potential donors. Mr Gingrich claimed that what was emerging represented 'the most systematic effort to get around the law that we have seen since Watergate'. The public appeared to remain largely indifferent to the affair, showing more interest in the 'Chinagate' scandal, which gathered impetus when it was admitted on 6 March that a payment of $50,000 had been received by Hillary Clinton's chief of staff, Margaret Williams, from Johnny Chung, a Chinese-American businessman and regular visitor to the White House. Although Ms Williams claimed that she had simply forwarded the cheque to the DNC as a donation, the story encouraged charges that federal campaign donations had been made on government property—an illegal act. Furthermore, there were suggestions that the payments had been made in return for preferential treatment. Later in March the scandal widened when it emerged that there had apparently been a plot to make contributions to some 30 Democratic congressional candidates. Six of those targeted had been warned by the FBI and two, Diane Feinstein and Richard Gephardt, announced that they were returning $12,000 and $22,000 respectively to various donors.

The President suffered another setback on 17 March when Anthony Lake, his first choice to head the Central Intelligence Agency (CIA) in succession to John M. Deutch, withdrew his nomination after three days of hearings before the Senate joint intelligence committee. Mr Lake had been questioned particularly about fund-raising activities, arms shipments from Iran to Bosnia and his management record as National Security Adviser. In his letter to the President, Mr

Lake asserted that Washington had 'gone haywire' and described the nomination process as 'a political football in a game with constantly moving posts'. Having unsuccessfully attempted to persuade Mr Lake to change his mind, Mr Clinton on 19 March nominated the deputy director of the CIA, George Tenet, to take over the directorship. Some days earlier the CIA had opened an investigation into allegations of improper contacts between the agency and the DNC following a story in the *Wall Street Journal* that Donald Fowler, DNC chairman in 1995, had contacted the CIA with a view to keeping Roger Tamraz, an important campaign contributor, on the White House guest list despite investigations into his possible involvement in international embezzlement.

One source of embarrassment for the President abated on 15 April when James McDougal, his original partner in the Whitewater property investment firm in Arkansas (see AR 1996, pp.141, 144–45), was sentenced to three years in prison on charges of fraud. The relatively light sentence was a result of Mr McDougal's cooperation with the independent prosecutor, Mr Starr. Meanwhile, Attorney-General Janet Reno refused to appoint an independent counsel to investigate Democratic Party fund-raising in the 1996 campaign on the grounds that there was not yet sufficient evidence of high-level wrongdoing. Nonetheless, evidence continued to surface of covert contributions by the Chinese government.

In April President Clinton nominated a former governor of Massachusetts, the liberal Republican William Weld, as ambassador to Mexico. However, the nomination was persistently blocked by the chairman of the Senate foreign relations committee, the arch-conservative Jesse Helms, who argued that Mr Weld was soft on drugs. Mr Clinton described Mr Helms as 'despotic' and vowed to fight on, but Mr Weld finally withdrew his nomination on 15 September. He said he intended to return to New England, 'where no-one has to approach the government on bended knee to ask it to do its duty'.

On the basis of an agreement between President Clinton and Republican congressional leaders, a bipartisan accord designed to balance the budget by 2002 was announced on 16 May. Both political parties claimed to have achieved their goals, the Democrats pointing to increased funding for education and health insurance for children, while the Republicans emphasized the tax-cutting elements. The agreement followed roughly the proposals submitted by President Clinton, including cuts in spending on Medicare and Medicaid, offset by expanded health-care cover for children of parents who could not afford health insurance. Tax cuts of $135,000 million were to be spread over five years. The process of implementing the budget began with the passage by both houses of tax-cutting legislation in June.

On 27 May the Supreme Court ruled that the President had no immunity in the courts for private acts and that the sexual harassment case brought against him by Paula Jones could go ahead. Ms Jones's lawyers said that they would seek a quick hearing and a deposition from President Clinton. They also suggested, however, that an out-of-court settlement might be possible if the President made 'some kind of admission . . . and something that could be interpreted as an apology'. Mr Clinton's lawyer responded that such a settlement was most unlikely because 'the President did nothing wrong'.

In line with his calls for inter-racial tolerance, President Clinton opened a year-long campaign against racism with a speech in San Diego on 14 June in support of affirmative action and against the 're-segregation' of higher education. He therefore implicitly rejected the decision of Californian voters in November 1996 to accept Proposition 209 banning consideration of race and gender in state hiring, contracting and education. The following month the President announced the establishment of an Advisory Board on Race under the chairmanship of Professor John Hope Franklin.

On 23 June the Supreme Court ruled in favour of a lower court decision that Hillary Clinton could not prevent the Arkansas federal jury investigating the Whitewater affair from having access to her private notes relating to conversations about the suicide of Mr Foster and invoice records from her Arkansas law firm. The ruling was seen as a possible breakthrough in the three-year-long inquiry which might lead to Mrs Clinton facing an indictment. On 8 July the Senate governmental affairs committee began its investigation into possible campaign funding irregularities. Its chairman, Fred Thompson (Republican), opened proceedings by announcing that the committee had firm evidence of covert Chinese contributions. It was also claimed that John Huang had agreed to testify in return for limited immunity, although this was opposed by Attorney-General Reno.

On 3 July, in papers filed in court in Little Rock, Arkansas, President Clinton made his first formal response to the Paula Jones allegations. He denied that he had sexually propositioned Ms Jones and asked that the case be dismissed or quickly scheduled for trial. At the end of the month Ms Jones's lawyers issued a subpoena on another woman requiring that she give testimony concerning alleged sexual advances made to her by Mr Clinton, indicating that they intended to show a pattern of sexual harassment. It was assumed that this step was intended to increase pressure for an out-of-court settlement. In August the judge in Little Rock refused to dismiss the case and set the trial date for 26 May 1998.

The spirit of bipartisan cooperation was celebrated on 5 August as President Clinton signed two bills which would cut taxes, raise spending on several social programmes and achieve a balanced budget by 2002. Signing the legislation, Mr Clinton said: 'We have fulfilled the responsibility of our generation to guarantee opportunity to the next generation.' Speaker Gingrich claimed that by passing the legislation 'we have proven that the American constitutional system works'. However, on 11 August the President used his line-item veto power for the first time since it had been granted to him in 1996 (see AR 1996, p. 143), removing three items from the bills (two from the tax side and one relating to expenditure).

Continuing its hearings on the campaign finance issue, the Senate government affairs committee on 4 September heard that Buddhist monks had destroyed papers relating to fund-raising after a visit by Vice-President Gore to their temple in 1996. Mr Gore had previously denied any knowledge of fund-raising dimensions to the visit, which had been arranged by John Huang. Later that week the

New York Times published a memo written by one of Mr Gore's aides for a fund-raising strategy meeting in 1996. The memo appeared to suggest that both Mr Gore and the President would be central in fund-raising activities in the White House, but Mr Gore's office claimed that it had not been tabled at the meeting. On 3 September Attorney-General Reno announced that she was initiating the procedures which could lead to the appointment of a special prosecutor should the evidence against Mr Gore warrant it. On 20 September, moreover, Ms Reno announced that she had opened a similar inquiry into whether President Clinton had illegally solicited campaign contributions by telephone from the White House during the 1996 election campaign.

In September Paula Jones's lawyers, Joseph Cammerata and Gilbert Davis, withdrew from the case after their client had apparently refused a settlement of $700,000 offered by the White House. Talk of a possible settlement had first been aired in June, but was complicated by the President's refusal to offer anything which might be construed as an apology, other than an acknowledgement that he had met Ms Jones. On 15 September the White House denied that it had played any part in initiating an Internal Revenue audit of Ms Jones's finances which had begun five days after she had rejected the settlement offered. At the end of September a Dallas lawyer, Donovan Campbell, took over the legal representation of Ms Jones, indicating that he would press for a trial rather than a settlement.

President Clinton on 16 September outlined proposals to obtain special powers to negotiate US trade deals without their being subject to subsequent congressional amendment—the so-called 'fast-track authority'. This authority had been withdrawn by Congress in 1994, and President Clinton had already made two earlier attempts to have it restored. As opposition in Congress continued, on 7 November the House of Representatives postponed a vote on the legislation at the President's request, to enable the administration to lobby for support. However, in view of Republican intransigence, the President finally withdrew the legislation from the congressional agenda on 10 November rather than face defeat.

Urging Congress to pass the bipartisan McCain-Feingold Bill aimed at limiting campaign expenditure, Mr Clinton asserted at a news conference on 7 October that 'a fund-raising arms race' had 'overwhelmed and consumed both parties and candidates all over our country'. He did not regret taking advantage of what was available under the existing system but was in favour of changing the system, calling upon Congress 'to strike a blow against politics as usual'. Despite his appeals, the McCain-Feingold Bill failed to secure adoption in the face of a determined Republican filibuster.

Meanwhile, Senator Thompson (chairman of the committee investigating the President's re-election campaign) had accused the White House of dragging its feet in releasing video-tapes of coffee-morning meetings between Mr Clinton and Democratic Party donors. When the 44 tapes were finally released, hopes that they would defuse the suspicion backfired when one of them turned out to lack a soundtrack. The meeting in question involved John Huang. The belated release of the tapes was due to an oversight, according to a White House spokesman, who said: 'We inadvertently did not realize that these tapes were in existence.'

In October lawyers acting for Paula Jones asked that the President provide them with records of any medical examinations which he had failed to make public and also to submit to independent examination to check for 'distinguishing characteristics' in his genital region. Mr Clinton's lawyers had earlier claimed that the President was 'a normal man' and that 'there are no blemishes, there are no moles, there are no growths'. As the pre-trial processes continued, lawyers on both sides began gathering evidence. While Mr Clinton's team interviewed relatives and male friends of Ms Jones, Ms Jones's lawyers collected statements from Dolly Browning, a Dallas lawyer who claimed to have had an affair with Mr Clinton, and also from Gennifer Flowers, who had made similar claims in 1992 (see AR 1992, p. 154).

On 10 October President Clinton issued a second veto on legislation which would have proscribed 'partial-birth', or late, abortions. The President said that he wanted the legislation—which he had previously vetoed in 1996 (see AR 1996 p. 143)—to include a proviso to allow such abortions in the event not just of a threat to the woman's life but also to her health. Reintroduced, the bill had been passed by the House in March with more than the two-thirds majority needed to over-ride the veto, but had been three votes short of such a majority in the Senate in May (so that the President was entitled to exercise his veto).

The Republican Party scored a number of successes in 'off-year' elections on 4 November. Their most significant victory was in Virginia, where James Gilmore defeated a strong Democratic challenge for the governorship previously held by George Allen (Republican). In New Jersey the incumbent Republican governor, Christine Whitman, just held off the challenge of James McGreevey, her near-defeat being attributed to her liberal stance on issues such as abortion. In New York City, Mayor Rudolph Giuliani became the first Republican since the 1930s to be elected for a second term. His success was largely due to falling crime rates and the city's improving economy.

At the beginning of December President Clinton again highlighted civil rights when he hosted town hall meetings on race and spoke in support of affirmative action. He also made clear that he would continue to support the appointment of Bill Lann Lee, a prominent civil rights lawyer, to a senior position in the Justice Department. Republicans in the Senate had blocked the appointment because of Mr Lee's support for affirmative action.

SOCIAL AND LEGAL AFFAIRS. Several major trials occurred during the year. In Santa Monica, California, the jury in the civil trial of the former football star and actor, O. J. Simpson, on 4 February found him liable for the deaths of his former wife, Nicole Simpson, and her friend Ronald Goldman, awarding the victims' families over $8 million in compensation. The unanimous verdict came after a four-month trial which effectively overturned the 'not guilty' verdict in the criminal trial of Mr Simpson in 1995 (see AR 1995, p. 158). In the civil trial the jury of ten whites, one Asian and one person of mixed race was clearly not convinced by Mr Simpson's testimony and was also presented with new evidence which linked him to the scene of the crime. On 10 February they awarded additional punitive damages of $25 million divided equally between the families of the deceased. The two verdicts left America as divided as it had been after the earlier acquittal, with 70 per cent of whites believing Simpson to be guilty of the murders, while 70 per cent of African-Americans believed him innocent.

The trial of Timothy McVeigh, the 29-year-old Gulf War veteran accused of the Oklahoma bombing in 1995 (see AR 1995, pp. 149–50), opened in Denver, Colorado, on 31 March, jury selection being completed by 22 April. The judge insisted that for their own protection the jury should remain hidden behind a screen, identified only by number, while television cameras and court artists were banned from the room.

A separate Justice Department inquiry into FBI forensic methods seriously threatened to discredit some of the evidence concerning explosives used in the bombing. Most of the evidence against McVeigh was circumstantial, depending on the testimony of friends and associates. A key witness was Michael Fortier, who had pleaded guilty to knowing about the plot. Giving evidence on 12 May, he claimed that McVeigh had wanted to 'bomb the building on the anniversary of Waco [see AR 1993, p. 159] to cause a general uprising in America'. He said that five months before the bombing McVeigh had shown him where he would plant the bomb. After four days of deliberation, the jury found McVeigh guilty on 2 June. President Clinton commented that 'this is a very important and long-overdue day for the survivors and families of those who died in Oklahoma City'. After the jury of seven women and five men had on 13 June given their recommendation in favour of the death penalty, McVeigh was formally sentenced to death by lethal injection on 14 August. The second trial in connection with the bombing opened in Denver on 29 September, when Terry Nichols faced charges identical to those against McVeigh (and also faced a possible death penalty).

The trial of Ramzi Ahmed Yousef, the alleged mastermind behind the bombing of the World Trade Center in February 1993 (see AR 1993, p. 158), began in New York on 5 August, together with that of his alleged accomplice, Eyad Ismail. Security during the trial, the third in connection with the bombing, was particularly tight because the police had discovered an apparent plot by two Palestinians to bomb the New York City underground a few days earlier. Two suspects were charged on 29 August. On 12 November Yousef and Ismail were both found guilty of murder and conspiracy to cause an explosion.

Louise Woodward, a British teenager employed as an au pair in Boston, became the centre of enormous media attention on both sides of the Atlantic following her arrest in February in connection with the death of nine-month-old Matthew Eappen, the child left in her care. On 5 March a grand jury agreed that there were grounds for her to face charges of first-degree murder after hearing that the baby had suffered brain damage after being violently shaken. Ms Woodward (19) strenuously denied the charges and refused to accept any plea bargaining on a lesser charge, so that her trial began on 7 October. Funded mainly by supporters in Britain, her defence team included Barry Scheck, who had previously been a member of O.J. Simpson's successful team. Together with Andrew Good, he attacked the prosecution's forensic evidence and suggested that the injury from which the baby died had been sustained earlier than the alleged incident involving Ms Woodward. The trial also raised the issue of working mothers and child-care and for a while focused on Mrs Deborah Eappen, the baby's mother. Ms Woodward's own appearance on the stand suggested that inexperience rather than any deliberate act of violence might have contributed to the baby's death.

Despite the weight of evidence supporting reasonable doubt of guilt, on 30 October the all-white jury of nine women and three men returned a verdict of guilty of second-degree murder, carrying an automatic sentence of life imprisonment. Under Massachusetts law, however, the judge, Hiller Zobel, had the right either to accept the verdict, or to allow an appeal or to reject the jury's conclusion. On 10 November Judge Zobel ruled that, given the absence of 'malice', to allow the conviction to stand would be a miscarriage of justice. He therefore imposed a reduced conviction of involuntary manslaughter and a gaol sentence of 279 days—the time Ms Woodward had already spent in jail during the trial. As a consequence, she was released from custody. While American public opinion had appeared to support the lesser charge, many were shocked by the apparent leniency of the sentence. The prosecution immediately lodged an appeal and Ms Woodward was forbidden to leave the state. A date for the appeal was subsequently set for March 1998.

There was also considerable public interest throughout the year in the murder on Boxing Day 1996 of a child beauty queen, six-year-old JonBenet Ramsay, in Boulder, Colorado. Hours after her mother had reported the girl's kidnapping, the body was discovered and moved from the basement of the family home by the girl's father, John Ramsay, during the police search. The failure of the police to make any arrests, and their apparent incompetence in investigating the murder scene, led to considerable criticism. The prime suspects appeared to be the girl's parents, who later left the area and began to conduct an investigation of their own.

Only days before the scheduled opening of his trial in Sacramento, California, in December, Theodore Kaczynski, the former mathematics professor charged with being the 'Unabomber' (see AR 1996 p. 153), persuaded his defence team not to plead mental insanity. Kaczynski had threatened to dismiss his lawyers if they persisted in producing psychiatric testimony that he suffered from paranoid schizophrenia. The government also confirmed that it had rejected Kaczynski's offer to plead guilty if the prosecution did not ask for the death penalty.

Conspiracy theories concerning a possible cover-up of the true causes of the TWA flight 800 disaster in July 1996 (see AR 1996, pp. 138–9) emerged again on 13 March when former Kennedy aide Pierre Salinger claimed to have evidence that the plane had been hit by 'friendly fire' in the form of a missile from a US Navy ship taking part in exercises. Mr Salinger claimed to have radar pictures showing the missile in flight just before it hit the plane. Federal investigators and navy spokesmen denied the charges. The FBI finally declared the case closed on 18 November, having found no evidence of either a bomb or a missile explosion and concluding that the likely cause had been a fuel tank explosion. Also on 18 November, the FBI announced that two bomb explosions in Atlanta in January—one outside a family planning clinic, the other at a lesbian nightclub—might be linked to the July 1996 bombing in Atlanta's Olympic Park, which had resulted in two deaths (see AR 1996, p. 139). Fragments of the bombs found at the scene seemed to be similar to the devices used in the later incidents.

The armed forces came under renewed scrutiny following reports on 14 January that two of four women enrolled at the Citadel military academy in Charleston, South Carolina, had withdrawn after alleging they had been subjected to severe sexual harassment. Four students were suspended and a total of 11 others were charged with disciplinary offences. It was also reported on 23 January that court martial proceedings had begun at West Point, the elite military academy, following an allegation of rape brought by a female cadet.

In June General Joseph Ralston of the US Air Force withdrew his nomination to replace General John Shalikashvili as Chairman of the Joint Chiefs of Staff when it became apparent that he would face an uphill struggle for confirmation because he had admitted to committing adultery ten years previously (while separated from his wife). On 11 September the US Army issued its findings on the sex scandals which had erupted in the Aberdeen training camp in Maryland in 1996 (see AR 1996, pp. 153–4). Admitting that there was 'widespread evidence of discrimination by male commanders against female troops', the report said that new training guidelines and increased supervision would be introduced to make the army 'a wholesome and safe place'. Major-General Robert Shadley, former commander at the Aberdeen base, was officially reprimanded.

In October the US Army announced that it had removed Gene McKinney from the post of sergeant-major after court martial proceedings had begun against him on 22 charges of indecent assault, adultery and obstruction of justice. Mr McKinney, who had served in the army for nearly 30 years and was the first African-American to become the 'top enlisted man', denied the charges, which he claimed were racially motivated.

The presidential advisory committee on Gulf War veterans' illnesses published a draft report in October, concluding that chemical exposure was an 'unlikely' cause of 'Gulf War syndrome'. The panel also recommended that the Defence Department should not lead any further investigation into the matter because it had lost the confidence of veterans' groups. According to press articles on 26 October, a separate report by the House committee on government reform seconded the latter conclusion, while concluding that toxic agents, chemical weapons and pesticides were the probable causes of the veterans' illnesses. Earlier in the year, the CIA had admitted on 9 April that up to 20,000 US personnel serving in the Gulf War might have been exposed to low doses of deadly nerve gas because of a failure to alert ground commanders to the presence of chemical weapons in a dump blown up at after the war. This admission ended three years of official denials that the CIA had known of the dangers.

Further evidence of the frailty of US intelligence services emerged on 6 October when the Justice Department announced that three people had been charged with spying for East Germany, the Soviet Union and South Africa during and after the Cold War. James Clark (a private investigator), Theresa Squillacote (a former senior employee at the Pentagon) and her husband, Kurt Stand, were arrested after they had passed documents to FBI agents posing as Russian and South African spies. The Justice Department claimed that the three had been passing secrets since the early 1970s. In June a former CIA agent, Harold Nicholson, had been gaoled for 23 years after he had admitted selling information to Russia. He was the highest-ranking CIA officer ever to be convicted for spying. Edwin Pitts, a former FBI officer also convicted of spying, was sentenced to 27 years in prison in June.

The Supreme Court handed down some significant decisions during the year (see also XV.3). On 26 June it ruled that the 1996 Communications Decency Act (see AR 1996, p. 152), designed to control pornography on the Internet, was contrary to the First Amendment guarantee of free speech. The following day it ruled that the requirement in the Gun Control Act that state officials should carry out background checks into prospective gun purchasers was a violation of separate state sovereignty. The Court also ruled on 26 June that terminally-ill but mentally competent individuals had no constitutional right to receive assistance in committing suicide. It did not, however, require states to legislate against such action.

The tobacco industry came under increasing pressure during 1997. In February a new law was implemented requiring identification for the purchase of cigarettes in order to stop sales to juveniles. On 20 June a settlement between the tobacco industry and 40 states which had sued for the cost of treating smoking-related illnesses was agreed. The companies agreed to pay $368,500 million in compensation, mainly for Medicare bills, over 25 years. In addition, they accepted reductions in cigarette advertising, a rise in the price of cigarettes by about 62 cents per pack and fines if youth smoking was not reduced to agreed levels. However, on 9 July President Clinton urged the tobacco companies to reconsider elements of the agreement which threatened to limit the government's regulatory powers, or he would 'walk away' from the deal. On 17 September he called upon Congress to pass tougher legislation to restrict youth access to cigarettes, to control advertising aimed at minors and raise cigarette prices if the industry failed to meet targets on curbing youth smoking. On 10 October the five main manufacturing companies agreed to a $300 million out-of-court settlement in an action brought in Florida on behalf of 60,000 non-smoking air-flight attendants who had claimed that passive smoking had damaged their health.

At the end of April members of a group known as the 'Republic of Texas Militia', wanted on charges of kidnapping, assault and other charges, were surrounded by police officers outside their compound in Fort Davis, West Texas. The siege ended on 3 May when four men surrendered in a military-style ceremony. Two other members of the group escaped, precipitating a large-scale search. Police found pipe bombs and gas tanks along with other weapons in the compound. Richard McLaren, the leader of the group, was sentenced to 99 years in prison on 4 November, and his associate, Robert Otto, to 50 years.

Gun control continued to be a major issue through the year. On 28 February bystanders in North Hollywood, Los Angeles, were horrified when two armour-clad robbers, foiled in their attack on a bank, fired assault rifles at police and civilians. Both suspects were killed and eight police officers and three civilians were wounded. Later in the year the Los Angeles police department announced that it had acquired 600 military-surplus M-16 rifles to boost its firepower, California's governor, Pete Wilson, declaring: 'Never ever again do I want to see officers from the LA police department outgunned.' Further fears of spreading gun violence in Los Angeles surfaced after another bank robbery ended in a shoot-out in a busy street on 16 September. One of the robbers was killed and another wounded. The Californian senator, Diane Feinstein, had earlier appealed to Prime Minister Binyamin Netanyahu of Israel not to allow the export of Uzi machine-guns to the United States. In the week of the latest shooting she called upon President Clinton to help stem imports of rifles which avoided exclusion by means of cosmetic changes to their specifications.

At the end of September Governor Wilson of California vetoed a bill banning the manufacture and sale of small, cheap handguns known as 'Saturday night specials'. Mr Wilson, whose father had himself been shot dead by a criminal, defended his action on the grounds that 'millions of law-abiding Californians ... have felt the need to own concealable weapons, not for sport but to protect themselves and their property'. In November President Clinton imposed a four-month ban on the importation of modified assault weapons in order to allow himself time to consider ways of restricting sales of such weapons permanently. Commenting on the ban, Mr Clinton remarked: 'You don't need an Uzi to go deer-hunting.'

Several other shooting incidents made the headlines in 1997. On 23 February one tourist was killed and several were wounded in a shooting on the observation deck on 86th floor of the Empire State Building in New York. The gunman, a 69-year-old Palestinian who shot and killed himself, left a note denouncing the United States, Britain and France for their support of Israel. On 1 October Luke Woodham (16) entered his high school in Pearl, Mississippi, and shot dead two girls, including his ex-girlfriend. He also wounded seven others and had apparently stabbed his mother. A letter written by Woodham, an overweight loner teased by fellow students, suggested that his action was in response to bullying.

Religious sects and organizations attracted attention, if for very different reasons. On 27 March 39 members of the Heaven's Gate cult, including their leader Marshall Applewhite, apparently committed mass suicide in a mansion near San Diego, California. The group were reported to believe that, after killing themselves, they would rendezvous with a space-craft following in the wake of the Hale-Bopp comet (see XIV.1). Meanwhile, an all-male religious organization, the 'Promise Keepers', had attracted public attention with a series of rallies across the country, culminating in a gathering of over 700,000 in Washington on 4 October. Launched in 1990 by a former football coach, Bill McCartney, the 'Promise Keepers' required men to accept the role of head of the family, to lead a pure ethical and sexual life and to uphold the Christian faith. Feminist and other groups were critical of the organization's emphasis on traditional male/female roles and general conservatism. American trade unions made news when workers of United Parcel Service (UPS) staged a nationwide strike on 4–19 August. UPS controlled 80 per cent of small parcel deliveries in the United States, so that the strike had a considerable negative impact on economic activity and was widely seen as the most significant for 20 years. The strikers were protesting against conditions of service for the part-time workers who made up 60 per cent of the company's workforce. A settlement was reached when the company agreed to increase basic pay for full- and part-time workers and to make a considerable number of part-time posts full-time over five years.

In November James Hoffa Jr., son of the notoriously corrupt former (and late) union boss Jimmy Hoffa, seemed set to take over the leadership of the Teamsters' Union after a judge ruled that the current president, Ron Carey, had laundered $735,000 of union funds for his re-election campaign in 1996. The court decision was seen as a blow for the union movement, given Mr Carey's previous reputation as an anti-corruption candidate who had reinvigorated the Teamsters and led them to victory in the UPS dispute. Within hours of his announcement that he would take a leave of absence at the end of November, the federally-appointed Independent Review Board filed charges against Mr Carey.

On racial matters, there was considerable public protest in August following the alleged torture of a Haitian, Abner Louima, in a New York police station. It was reported on 23 August that four officers had been charged with aggravated assault, torture and acting upon racial motivation. Mayor Giuliani responded by establishing a task force to investigate the allegations, while the federal government also launched a civil rights investigation into the New York police department.

The world's first surviving septuplets were born on 26 November to Bobbi McGaughey in Des Moines, Iowa. Mrs McGaughey had been treated with fertility drugs, and both she and her husband had rejected the option of selective abortion. The four baby boys and three girls were successfully delivered by caesarean section by a 40-strong medical team.

FOREIGN AFFAIRS. President Clinton arrived in Helsinki on 20 March for a summit meeting with President Yeltsin of Russia (see III.3.i). Although wheelchair-bound following an accident, Mr Clinton was able to take a full part in discussions on arms control, economic cooperation and the enlargement of NATO. On 27 May President Clinton welcomed the signing of the Russia-NATO Founding Act (see XII.1; XIX.1), declaring: 'We look forward toward a new century with a new Russia and a new NATO, working together in a new Europe of unlimited possibility.'

Continuing US attempts to secure peace in the Middle East included a round of shuttle diplomacy by special envoy Dennis Ross in March and May and a personal week-long visit by Secretary of State Madeleine Albright in September (see also V.1; V.2.i). After endorsing Israeli Prime Minister Netanyahu's 'security first' approach, Ms Albright also called upon the Israelis to take a 'time-out' in the construction of new settlements on Arab land. On 18 December she announced that President Clinton would invite Israeli and Palestinian leaders to Washington early in 1998 with the aim of reviving the peace process.

At the start of year President Clinton issued a unilateral ban on the export of anti-personnel land-mines and called for the beginning of negotiations on an international ban. However, the United States declined to sign the international treaty banning anti-personnel land-mines agreed in Oslo on 17 September (see XII.3; XIX.5), the government's objections focusing on the treaty's failure to exempt South Korea, where land-mines were seen as essential to the defence of that country and the 37,000 US troops stationed there. President Clinton said that 'no-one should expect our people to expose our armed forces to unacceptable risks', while subsequently ordering the Pentagon to develop alternative weapons to make land-mines obsolete by 2006.

From November the Clinton administration attempted to mobilize international opinion behind a tough response to Iraq's exclusion of UN weapons inspectors seeking to ensure compliance with UN Security Council resolutions banning Iraqi possession of weapons of mass destruction (see also V.2.vi; XI.1). Following a visit to Qatar on 16 November, when she claimed that the dispute was not between Iraq and the United States 'but between Iraq and the law', Secretary of State Albright went on to various Gulf states to seek backing for possible military action, but with little success. For his part, Mr Clinton appealed to the Russian and French Presidents to use their influence with Iraq to achieve a peaceful solution to the crisis.

Concerned about the possible knock-on effects of the Asian economic crisis on US markets (see XVIII.1), Mr Clinton used the opportunity of the annual gathering of the Asia-Pacific Economic Cooperation (APEC) forum held in Vancouver (Canada) on 24–25 November to discuss the latest developments with other leaders of the Pacific rim countries (see also XI.5.iii). Notwithstanding the rapidly-mounting evidence of deep-seated problems in the 'Asian tiger' economies, the US President declared: 'This is a time for confidence in Asia.'

2. CANADA

CAPITAL: Ottawa   AREA: 9,9970,610 sq km   POPULATION: 29,960,000 ('96)
OFFICIAL LANGUAGES: English & French
POLITICAL SYSTEM: federal parliamentary democracy
HEAD OF STATE: Queen Elizabeth II (since Feb'52)
GOVERNOR-GENERAL: Roméo LeBlanc (since Feb '95)
RULING PARTY: Liberal Party (since Oct '93)
HEAD OF GOVERNMENT: Jean Chrétien, Prime Minister (since Oct '93)
MAIN IGO MEMBERSHIPS (non-UN): NATO, OECD, OSCE, G-7, OAS, NAFTA, APEC, CP, CWTH, Francophonie
CURRENCY: Canadian dollar (end-'97 £1=Can$2.34,US$1=Can$1.43)
GNP PER CAPITA: US$19,380 ('95) or US$21,130 ('95) by PPP calculation

ALTHOUGH the threat of Quebec independence receded in 1997, Canada emerged from a general election held on 2 June with a political landscape more confused than ever before. The middle-of-the-road Liberal Party under Prime Minister Jean Chrétien, in power since November 1993, saw its parliamentary majority seriously reduced. Going into the election, the Liberals held 174 of the 295 seats in the House of Commons; after the voting their standing had been cut to 155 in an expanded 301-seat Commons.

M. Chrétien called the election on 27 April, six months short of the normal four-year term for Canadian governments. He emphasized the national government's careful management of Canada's federal system, by which shared jurisdictions had been transferred to the provinces where changes were requested and were appropriate. He dwelt on his government's success in reducing the federal deficit, from Can$45,000 million in 1993 when the Liberals took office, to Can$17,000 million for the fiscal year 1997–98. He pointed to a robust economy in 1997 and the virtual elimination of inflation. With conditions so propitious for the return of the government, most observers predicted an easy Liberal victory.

In the event, M. Chrétien gained his victory but not in the decisive fashion he desired. In the Atlantic region, plagued by high unemployment and where the Chrétien government had cut support for unemployment insurance, the Liberals lost 20 seats. In Quebec the government, riding the tide of an upsurge of support for federalism, gained seven seats over the 19 they had won in 1993. However, the separatist Bloc Québécois (BQ) retained the majority of the province's French-speaking ridings, holding 44 of the 75 Quebec seats. The BQ captured only 38 per cent of the popular vote in Quebec compared with 49 per cent won in the 1993 election. The Liberals' stronghold turned out to be the largest Canadian province, Ontario, which they had dominated in 1993 and did so again. They won 101 of the 103 Ontario seats, one of the remaining seats being taken by a Liberal who had been read out of the caucus. The sweeping Liberal victory derived from the fact that the conservative vote in many Ontario ridings was split between the Progressive Conservative Party (PCP) and the western regional Reform Party, which was attempting to break into the central Canadian province.

Moving westward, the three prairie provinces and British Columbia decisively rejected M. Chrétien and his Liberals. Here the Reform Party, only ten years old, captured the bulk of seats: 35 in the prairie provinces and 25 in British Columbia. Its 60 seats allowed it to displace the BQ as the official opposition in the House of Commons. Preston Manning from Alberta, the movement's founding and only leader, assumed the post of Leader of the Opposition and moved into the Ottawa residence attached to that position. Reform's appeal lay in its emphasis on a smaller role for governments, a tighter control over public expenditures and the promotion of law and order measures. But the core of its message was that the concerns of western Canada were not adequately understood nor dealt with by the traditional political parties. For too long their focus had been primarily on issues of concern to Ontario and Quebec.

Two smaller parties, the PCP and the New Democratic Party (NDP), made solid gains, the former emerging from the election with 20 seats, the latter with

21. The PCP's seats were won in Nova Scotia and New Brunswick, together with five in Quebec and two elsewhere. Its showing resulted largely from the energetic campaigning of its magnetic 38-year-old fluently bilingual leader from Quebec, Jean Charest, who was seen by Quebeckers as the most attractive of the federalist leaders. The NDP had long been the progressive voice in Canadian politics. In the 1997 election it was led by a new and vigorous political figure from Nova Scotia, Alexa McDonough, who strongly attacked the Chrétien government for its cuts to social programs and urged that more attention be given to job creation. The party won eight seats in Nova Scotia and New Brunswick (something that had never happened before), picked up nine more on the prairies and four in British Columbia and Yukon. It had held only nine seats in the previous parliament. The full results of the election were as follows (1993 figures shown in parentheses):

	Seats		% of vote	
Liberal Party	155	(177)	38.5	(41.6)
Reform Party	60	(52)	19.4	(18.1)
Bloc Québécois	44	(54)	10.7	(13.9)
Progressive Conservatives	20	(2)	18.8	(16.1)
New Democratic Party	21	(9)	11.0	(6.6)
Independent	1	(1)	0.3	(–)
Minor parties	0	(0)	1.3	(3.7)

The Liberals could proudly claim that under an earlier French-Canadian prime minister, Sir Wilfrid Laurier, they had led Canada into the twentieth century and that they were likely to be in power, again under a prime minister from Quebec, when the 21st century dawned. But their parliamentary majority in 1997 was smaller than Sir Wilfrid's's had been and less than M. Chrétien's four years before. Their standing as a national party was damaged as a consequence of the June election, which in fact had been won by regional forces. In the west, Reform represented the dominant voice; in French-speaking Quebec, the separatists held most of the seats; in the Atlantic provinces the Liberal ranks were thinned; only in Ontario was the party unchallenged. The result was a new pattern in Canadian politics whose consequences were difficult to predict. It was unlikely that the four smaller parties could ever find common ground against the governing Liberals; for, to varying extents, each represented sectional differences. In the past, differences between parts of Canada had been negotiated and reconciled within the structure of national parties; they were now brought out into the open. This would result in a fractious parliament which might well find it more challenging than before to deal with questions of national unity.

Prime Minister Chrétien and a new cabinet were sworn in on 11 June. There were 27 full ministers and eight secretaries of state (junior ministers), a slightly larger number than before. Eight members of the new administration were new appointees and eight were women. For the most part, the previous team was kept in place, although two ministers who had lost their seats in the Maritimes had to be replaced. The most important change was the promotion of Anne

McLellan, a former law teacher from Alberta, to the sensitive post of Minister of Justice. Paul Martin, whom most observers saw as M. Chrétien's heir apparent, continued as Finance Minister and Lloyd Axworthy as Minister of Foreign Affairs.

M. Chrétien had sought to avoid discussion of constitutional change during the election campaign, realizing that Canadians, after years of struggling with the question, preferred to concentrate on other issues. But he continued to involve his government in fashioning new administrative arrangements designed to meet the demands of the provinces. Partial control over immigration was handed to some provinces which desired to become more active in the area. Quebec was given responsibility for managing job-training intended to help unemployed workers re-enter the labour force. Four other provinces also entered into agreements on this subject. These arrangements, claimed the Prime Minister, showed that 'flexible federalism' could meet the needs of Quebeckers as well as other Canadians.

At the same time, Ottawa made it clear that it was prepared to set out a stronger line against Quebec separatism, preparing for a reference to the Supreme Court of Canada, as announced in 1996 (see AR, 1996, p. 159), on the legality of secession. Its legal argument, or *factum*, was filed in February and a date in February 1998 was tentatively set for the hearing of the reference. M. Chrétien's Minister for Intergovernmental Affairs, Stéphane Dion, a young professor of constitutional law from Montreal, spoke vigorously in bringing forward the dangerous consequences of secession. In two open letters to the Quebec government, released on 11 and 26 August, M. Dion emphasized that Quebec would invite anarchy if it attempted to leave Canada in a fashion outside the law. There being no provision for separation in Canada's constitution, it was obvious that such a momentous step could only be taken with the consent of all the parties to the compact. Division, the minister stressed, was one of the most 'consequence-laden choices' any society could make. Contrary to what the Quebec government claimed, international law provided no support for a unilateral declaration of independence by the province. Only if a 'substantial consensus' of the residents of Quebec, through a referendum posing a clear question, voted in favour of secession could the subject be even considered. Moreover, Quebec could not assume that its borders would remain inviolate if it seceded from Canada. M. Dion's words showed a firmer tone than the federal government had previously displayed and were clearly directed at moderate opinion in Quebec.

In September the premiers of all the provinces except Quebec entered the unity debate. Urged by Roy Romanow of Saskatchewan to show more leadership, they met in Calgary on 14 September to draft a message for Quebec. A statement resulting from 11 hours of discussion recognized Quebec's 'unique character' within a federation in which all provinces and all citizens enjoyed 'equality of status'. It was agreed that each province would institute a consultative process whose results could be distilled into resolutions for later approval by each provincial legislature. These messages could be used by the federalist side in a future election in Quebec.

The year saw a loss of support for the separatist cause within Quebec. Premier Lucien Bouchard, the charismatic leader of the governing Parti Québécois, found himself mired in difficulties with health-care workers, public service unions and the unemployed as he tried to bring the province's finances in order. His goal was to eliminate the province's Can$22,000 million deficit by the year 2000; he would not ask Quebeckers to vote on independence before the province's books were balanced. The contrast between a weak Quebec economy hampered by political uncertainty and a stronger economy elsewhere in Canada also worked against the appeal of separation. In May former premier Jacques Parizeau, who had been replaced by M. Bouchard after the defeat of the sovereignty referendum in 1995 (see AR 1995, pp. 162–4), dropped a bombshell. He admitted that he had devised a secret plan by which the Quebec national assembly would have passed a unilateral declaration of independence if a 'yes' vote had been expressed in the referendum. He had been persuaded to take this step, he said, by the former French President, Valéry Giscard d'Estaing, who regarded it as vital if Quebec was to gain the recognition of other countries. M. Parizeau's words contradicted the stated position of the secessionists during the referendum campaign: that there would be no immediate constitutional change following a 'yes' vote; instead, they had promised negotiations to work out a new partnership with the rest of Canada..

Embarrassed by M. Parizeau's revelation, which hurt the separatists' credibility with moderate Quebec opinion, M. Bouchard immediately dissociated himself from the former premier's remarks. Public opinion polls in December showed that 62 per cent of Quebeckers would vote 'no' to Quebec becoming an independent country separate from Canada. Committed separatists made up about 40 per cent of the Quebec electorate, almost the same proportion registered in the first sovereignty referendum in 1980. In the 1995 referendum, the 'yes' vote had climbed to almost 50 per cent but this was on a question calling for sovereignty combined with a partnership with the rest of Canada.

Economic growth was strong in Canada in 1997, the gross domestic product (GDP) being expected to increase by almost 4 per cent. Consumers showed more confidence in the future, their optimism bolstered by low interest rates and marginal increases in the consumer price index. Exports, especially to the United States, which now took 80 per cent of Canada's sales abroad, fuelled the expansion in the economy. Unemployment, hovering around 9 per cent of the labour force during the year, remained a worrying problem, however.

The Chrétien government took pride in its success in bringing the federal deficit under control. Finance Minister Paul Martin, in a budget brought down on 18 February, announced a deficit target of Can$17,000 million for the 1997–98 fiscal year. On 15 October he revealed that the actual deficit for the 1996–97 year had been only Can$8,900 million, the lowest in two decades. There was little doubt that the target for 1997–98 would be easily met and that a balanced budget would shortly follow.

The lucrative Pacific salmon fishery off the north-west coasts of Canada and the United States erupted as a contentious issue during the summer of 1997, arising from the fact that salmon moved through the coastal waters of one state to reach their spawning rivers in another. Thus, for instance, Alaska (US) fishermen customarily caught chinook and sockeye salmon swimming in from the Pacific to streams in British Columbia (Canada) in which they had been hatched. The fishery was supposed to be governed by principles of equity and conservation laid down in the Pacific Salmon Treaty of 1985, but this instrument had been inoperative for several years. In the United States the management of the ocean fishery was a function of the states; in Canada it was a federal responsibility. Moreover, negotiations over the sharing of the salmon stock had been frustrated by the demands of the 'stakeholders', i.e. commercial fishing interests and aboriginal groups, whose wishes were largely determining the bargaining position of the United States. Commercial fish farming, whose output had increased markedly in recent years, had led to over-fishing, as fishermen attempted to maintain their incomes.

Against this background, the summer of 1997 was a tense one for fishermen all along the 7,000 kilometres of coastline stretching from Washington and British Columbia to Alaska. Premier Glen Clark of British Columbia, hoping to put pressure on the United States, threatened to cancel an agreement allowing US naval vessels to use a submarine testing facility on the east coast of Vancouver Island. On 19 July a ferry travelling between Washington and Alaska was blockaded for three days at Prince Rupert, a British Columbia port, by almost 200 boats belonging to Canadian fishermen angry at what they termed over-fishing by their Alaskan neighbours. Prime Minister Chrétien and President Bill Clinton discussed the problem at the Denver 'summit of the eight' on 20–22 June, M. Chrétien urging that the complex dispute be referred to binding arbitration but getting a refusal from Mr Clinton. Eventually, the dispute was referred to two 'eminent persons', who were instructed to meet with 'stakeholders' to explore new approaches. Their recommendations had not been received by the end of the year.

Canada's principal diplomatic success in 1997 was its leadership of a group of like-minded nations in the drafting of an international treaty banning the production, export and use of anti-personnel landmines (see XII.2; XIX.5). Landmines represented one of the most tragic aftermaths of war, it being estimated that 110 million such weapons were buried in countries around the world, exacting a toll of about 25,000 people, mostly civilians, each year. Accordingly, at a meeting in Ottawa in October 1996, the Canadian government had challenged the international community to move to a decisive ban on landmines by the end of 1997. Intense lobbying occurred in many capitals, the diplomatic effort being accompanied by a vigorous campaign by humanitarian agencies helped by the involvement of Diana, Princess of Wales. A draft convention banning landmines was hammered out at a conference in Oslo, Norway, in early September. The United States asked for exceptions allowing it to maintain landmines to defend South Korea, but the 89 countries in Oslo refused to accept this amendment and approved the draft treaty. On 10 October the movement received an important boost with the award of the Nobel Peace Prize to Jody Williams of

Vermont (USA), coordinator of the International Campaign to Ban Landmines. At a formal signing ceremony in Ottawa on 2 December, representatives of 125 countries endorsed a treaty to outlaw the deadly weapon. The United States, China and Russia refused to sign, although the Russian government indicated that it hoped to give its support later.

3. LATIN AMERICA

ARGENTINA—BOLIVIA—BRAZIL—CHILE—COLOMBIA—ECUADOR—
PARAGUAY—PERU—URUGUAY—VENEZUELA—CUBA—DOMINICAN REPUBLIC
AND HAITI—CENTRAL AMERICA AND PANAMA—MEXICO

i. ARGENTINA

CAPITAL: Buenos Aires   AREA: 2,766,890 sq km   POPULATION: 35,220,000 ('96)
OFFICIAL LANGUAGE: Spanish   POLITICAL SYSTEM: federal presidential democracy
HEAD OF STATE & GOVERNMENT: President Carlos Saúl Menem (since July '89)
RULING PARTY: Justicialist (Peronist) Party (since Dec '89)
MAIN IGO MEMBERSHIPS: OAS, SELA, ALADI, Mercosur
CURRENCY: peso (end-'97 £1=AP1.64, US$1=AP1.00)
GNP PER CAPITA: US$8,030 ('95) or US$8,310 ('95) by PPP calculation

IN late January the Economy Minister, Roque Fernández, gave international investors a promise that there would be no devaluation of the currency for at least ten years. The country was enjoying a state of unaccustomed prosperity, but there were storm clouds on the horizon. The assassination the same month of José Luis Cabezas, a leading investigative reporter and photographer on assignment in Pinamar for *Noticias*, raised serious concern. Unrest at the privatization of the National Mortgage Bank (BHN) led to physical clashes between government and opposition deputies on the floor of Congress on 29 April and the suspension of the sitting.

There was continuing unrest in the provinces, partly modified by the announcement in May that a $600 million loan from the World Bank would be used for social welfare to offset the effects of continuing high unemployment, currently around 15 per cent. The threat of trade sanctions by the United States because of Argentina's alleged failure to protect intellectual property rights was bitterly resented, provoking legislators to threaten retaliation. Despite the announcement in August by Governor Eduardo Duhalde of a three-year social action plan for the province of Buenos Aires, a general strike on 14 August was widely supported outside the capital

With mid-term elections due in October, new alignments emerged. In April the former Economy Minister, Domingo Cavallo, formed his own party to seek the presidency in 1999. Subsequently, on 9 July, he and Gustavo Béliz (a former Interior Minister) jointly launched an alliance called Action for the Republic-New Democracy (AR-ND) with a stinging attack on alleged governmental corruption. Meanwhile, the Justice Minister since 1996, Elías Jassan, had been forced to resign on 26 June after press reports of his telephone conversations with a controversial local businessman had made it clear that links that he had publicly denied did in fact exist. On 3 August the two main opposition parties, the Radical Civic Union (UCR) and the Front for a People in Solidarity (Frepaso), agreed to run joint lists in the elections and to remain in alliance subsequently, holding open primaries for the 1999 presidential contest.

Official corruption was a major opposition theme in the mid-term elections held on 26 October. Although only half the seats were at stake, the (Peronist) Justicialist Party (PJ) lost its overall majority in the Chamber of Deputies, its representation being reduced to 118 seats (out of 257) against 110 for the UCR-Frepaso Alliance, the balance being held by small provincial parties. A notable casualty was Hilda Duhalde, wife of Eduardo, who was defeated by Gracela Fernández Mejide in the province of Buenos Aires, while in the federal capital the Alliance candidate, Carlos Alvarez, easily defeated both Daniel Scioli of the PJ and former Economy Minister Domingo Cavallo.

In a communiqué issued on 3 January to mark the 164th anniversary of Britain's establishment of sovereignty over the Falkland Islands (Islas Malvinas), President Menem reasserted both Argentina's claim to the islands and his policy of seeking a peaceful resolution to the dispute. To this end, the assistance of President Clinton of the United States was to be sought. On 12 June, following the change of government in Britain, the Argentinian President reiterated his commitment to 'peaceful means and dialogue' on the Falklands/Malvinas issue, on 4 November receiving in return an invitation to visit Britain in 1998. During an official visit on 15–19 October, President Clinton commended Argentina's role in recent UN peace-keeping operations and announced that he would seek 'non-NATO ally' status for it, so that Argentina could receive a wider range of US weapons. Brazil and Chile both reacted to the suggestion with concern.

On 25 March a Spanish judge issued an international arrest warrant against former President Leopoldo Galtieri for his alleged role in the death of three Spaniards and the disappearance of some 350 others during the military dictatorship of 1976–83. On 11 October, moreover, after a former Argentinian officer had given voluntary testimony about the so-called 'dirty war', the judge issued further warrants against Admiral (retd.) Emilio Massera and other former naval officers.

Enrique Gorriarán Merlo, a 56-year-old former guerrilla, was sentenced to life imprisonment by a federal court on 2 July for the attack on the La Tablada barracks in 1989 (see AR 1989, p. 64).

ii. BOLIVIA

CAPITAL: La Paz and Sucre   AREA: 1,099,000 sq km   POPULATION: 7,600,000 '96)
OFFICIAL LANGUAGES: Spanish, Quechua, Aymará
POLITICAL SYSTEM: presidential democracy
HEAD OF STATE & GOVERNMENT: President Hugo Banzer Suárez (since Aug '97)
RULING PARTIES: Democratic Nationalist Action (AND) heads coalition with Civic Solidarity Union (UCS), Conscience of the Fatherland (Codepa), New Republican Force (NFR) & Movement of the Revolutionary Left(MIR)
MAIN IGO MEMBERSHIPS (non-UN): NAM, OAS, ALADI, SELA, AG, CA
CURRENCY: boliviano (end-'97 £1=Bs8.83, US$1=Bs5.38)
GNP PER CAPITA: US$800 ('95) or US$2,540 ('95) by PPP calculation

IN presidential elections held on 1 June, only seven percentage points separated the first five candidates. Despite outspoken criticism of his human rights record while in power in 1971–78, the former dictator, General (retd.) Hugo Banzer Suárez, of the right-wing Democratic Nationalist Action (ADN), headed the poll with 22.3 per cent of the votes cast, while Juan Carlos Durán of the ruling National Revolutionary Movement (MNR) came second with 17.7 per cent. Four days later General Banzer announced a pact with the social-democratic Movement of the Revolutionary Left (MIR), Conscience of the Fatherland (Condepa) and the Civic Solidarity Union (UCS), thus securing the necessary 50 per cent of votes in the new Congress to clinch victory. At the same time he undertook to maintain existing government policies, including the US-backed campaign to eradicate illicit coca growing. Confirmed by Congress on 5 August with the support of 118 of the 157 deputies, he was inaugurated the next day, appointing Javier Murillo (ADN) as Minister of Foreign Affairs and an independent, Edgar Millares, as Minister of Finance.

A five-year action plan announced by President Banzer on 26 November envisaged raising general Bolivian living standards, alleviating poverty and eradicating corruption, as well as ending foreign interference in the country's affairs and removing Bolivia from the international drugs trade. Specific targets included a 3 per cent cut in government expenditure, 7 per cent annual economic growth, completion of the privatization programme (especially of poorly-exploited mining operations) and construction of some 1,850 kilometres of new roads to improve links with neighbouring countries.

iii. BRAZIL

CAPITAL: Brasília   AREA: 8,512,000 sq km   POPULATION: 158,500,000 ('96)
OFFICIAL LANGUAGE: Portuguese   POLITICALSYSTEM: federal presidential democracy
HEAD OF STATE & GOVERNMENT: President Fernando Henrique Cardoso (since Jan '95)
RULING PARTIES: Brazilian Social Democratic Party (PSDB) heads coalition with Brazilian Labour Party (PTB), Liberal Front Party (PFL), Brazilian Progressive Party (PPB), Popular Socialist Party (PPS) & Brazilian Democratic Movement Party (PMDB)
MAIN IGO MEMBERSHIPS (non-UN): OAS, ALADI, SELA, Mercosur, AP, CPLP
CURRENCY: real (end-'97 £1=R1.83, US$1=R1.12)
GNP PER CAPITA: US$3,640 ('95) or US$5,400 ('95) by PPP calculation

IN the early months of the year, a constitutional amendment passed both the Chamber of Deputies (on 28 January) and Senate (on 4 June) and was promulgated on 5 June, allowing the re-election of the President, state governors and mayors. With President Fernando Henrique Cardoso of the Brazilian Social Democratic Party (PSDB) doing well in the opinion polls, his leading position looked secure, especially after his most likely challenger in 1998, Paulo Maluf, was implicated in a financial scandal in São Paulo.

In other scandals, two deputies were forced to resign in May after the newspaper *Folha de São Paulo* had published transcripts of conversations showing that they had accepted bribes to pass the constitutional amendment. The Supreme Federal Tribunal, however, refused a request by the opposition to intervene. At the end of the year the mayor of São Paulo, Celso Pitta (of the Brazilian Progressive Party), was convicted of involvement in a multi-million dollar bond fraud and sentenced to loss of office and an eight-year suspension of his political rights. Pending appeal hearings, however, Sr Pitta remained in office.

In early June Luis Inácio da Silva ('Lula') was forced to resign as honorary president of the Workers' Party (PT) because of corruption allegations against a close associate; soon afterwards the charismatic Luiza Erundina, a former mayor of São Paulo, resigned from the PT and joined the Brazilian Socialist Party (PSB). Left-wing parties meeting on 2 October failed to agree on a single opposition presidential candidate when the PSB refused to endorse 'Lula', who was accordingly launched as candidate of the PT alone in December.

The defection of former Finance Minister Ciro Gomes from the PSDB in August proved to be the harbinger of further important resignations from the party, while the decision of another co-author of the 1994 real stabilization plan, former President Itamar Franco, to join the PMDB raised the possibility of a rival centrist candidate being presented in the 1998 presidential elections. However, the decision of both the PMDB on 9 October and the PTB on 23 October to back President Cardoso's candidacy placed his re-election virtually beyond doubt.

Though it had not reached its target of 2.5 per cent of GDP, the government was able to claim a substantial reduction in the fiscal deficit in 1996. Moreover, inflation in 1996 had fallen to 10.03 per cent—the lowest rate since 1950—and the real remained closely pegged to the US dollar. On 6 May a 41.7 per cent stake in the Rio Doce Valley Company (CVRD), currently the world's largest iron-ore producer, was sold to a consortium headed by Companhia Siderúrgica Nacional (CSN), for a sum eqivalent to US$3,081 million. Deputies also approved a constitutional amendment allowing certain public services to be put out to tender. On 10 June a government motion to allow lower salaries for state and municipal civil servants than the constitutional minimum for federal employees was defeated when it failed to attain the necessary three-fifths majority in the Chamber. It was finally carried on 19 November, however, following the President's announcement of a stringent austerity package designed to restore economic confidence. The 51 measures in the package included 33,000 civil service redundancies, federal and state budget cuts, an acceleration of the privatization programme, a 10 per cent increase in personal taxation rates, and higher petrol, alcohol and tobacco prices.

Amid continuing rural unrest, a massive demonstration by the Landless Workers' Movement (MST) took place in the capital on 17 April. In response the President offered to accelerate the distribution of land. After one of the MST leaders, José Rainha, had been sentenced on 11 June to 26 years' imprisonment for the murder of a landlord and a policeman in 1989, President Cardoso issued a decree discouraging further land invasions by prohibiting the land reform agency from distributing land which had been occupied. At the same time, as promised, the decree established speedier procedures in the event of government expropriation. Occupations nevertheless continued in São Paulo state, where 49 people were arrested and 20 injured on 8 August when police cleared illegally-occupied land outside Brasília.

In October flooding following heavy rains made thousands homeless in the southern states, especially Rio Grande do Sul.

iv. CHILE

CAPITAL: Santiago AREA: 756,000 sq km POPULATION: 13,994,000 ('94)
OFFICIAL LANGUAGE: Spanish POLITICAL SYSTEM: presidential democracy
HEAD OF STATE & GOVERNMENT: President Eduardo Frei (since March '94)
RULING PARTIES: Christian Democratic Party (PDC) heads Coalition for Democracy (CPD)
MAIN IGO MEMBERSHIPS (non-UN): OAS, ALADI, SELA, NAM, APEC
CURRENCY: peso (end–'97 £1=Ch$721.99, US$1=Ch$440.05)
GNP PER CAPITA: US$4,160 ('95) or US$9,520 ('95) by PPP calculation

ON 28 May a group of former members of the Christian Democratic Party (PDC), which was the largest component of the ruling Coalition for Democracy, formed a new party, the Popular Christian Party (PPC). With the aid of PPC votes, the Senate on 15 July rejected for the third time a government-sponsored constitutional amendment to abolish the eight 'designated' seats in the upper house. A fourth attempt was promised by the government, however, after the former dictator, General Augusto Pinochet Ugarte, announced his intention to retire as army commander-in-chief in March 1998 (as scheduled) and to take up a seat as senator-for-life. In a related move, right-wing deputies sought to impeach Servando Jordán, the president of the Supreme Court, which had the power to nominate three of the senators.

On 15 October the head of the Navy, Admiral Jorge Martínez Busch, took early retirement to take up another of the designated Senate seats, being succeeded by Vice-Admiral Horacio Patricio Arancibia. On 30 October Major-General Ricardo Izurieta was named as General Pinochet's successor. The Defence Minister later confirmed that General Pinochet's deputy, General Guillermo Marín, would retire with him and that the number of generals would fall from 45 to 40.

In legislative elections held on 11 December, the ruling Coalition for Democracy maintained its 70-seat majority in the 120-member Chamber of Deputies, although its share of the vote slipped five percentage points compared with 1993, to 50.5

per cent. The Coalition also won 11 of the 20 contested seats in the 47-member Senate. A feature of the poll was the strong showing of the right-wing Independent Democratic Union (UDI), which took 17 Chamber seats and 14.4 per cent of the vote within the Union for the Progress of Chile headed by National Renewal (RN), which itself won 23 lower house seats on a 16.8 per cent vote share.

In mid-October an earthquake centred some 225 kilometres north of Santiago and measuring 6.8 on the Richter scale killed eight people, injured 98 and left more than 15,000 homeless.

v. COLOMBIA

CAPITAL: Santa Fe de Bogotá   AREA: 1,141,750 sq km   POPULATION: 35,700,000 ('96)
OFFICIAL LANGUAGE: Spanish   POLITICAL SYSTEM: presidential democracy
HEAD OF STATE & GOVERNMENT: President Ernesto Samper Pizano (since Aug '94)
RULING PARTIES: Liberal Party (PL) heads coalition with Social Conservative Party (PSC) and Alliance for Colombia (AC)
MAIN IGO MEMBERSHIPS (non-UN): OAS, ALADI, SELA, AG, CA, ACS, NAM
CURRENCY: peso (end-'97 £1=Col$2,144.23, US$1=Col$1,306.90)
GNP PER CAPITA: US$1,910 ('95) or US$6,130 ('95) by PPP calculation

PRESIDENT Ernesto Samper Pizano proclaimed a state of economic emergency on 13 January, after a collapse of prices on the international coffee and banana markets in late 1996 had exacerbated Colombia's economic problems resulting from over-valuation of the peso. Austerity measures, including a further reduction in public spending, restrictions on pay increases in the public sector, the extension of the sales tax and further efforts to stamp out tax evasion, were strongly criticized by the unions.

There was criticism, too, of the leniency of the sentences passed on 17 January by a judge in Cali on Gilberto and Manuel Rodríguez Orejuela, alleged to have dominated the Cali drugs cartel for some 20 years, as they were believed also to have donated US$6 million to President Samper's election campaign. For the second year in succession, President Clinton refused (on 28 February) to 'certify' the government's efforts to combat the drugs trade. In response, the government suspended crop-eradication flights on 5 March. However, when Almabeatriz Rengifo López was appointed Justice Minister on 22 April (replacing Carlos Medellín Becerra, who had resigned to take part in the election campaign), she quickly presented a bill in Congress to establish the government's right to allow the extradition of Colombian nationals (the Constitutional Court having ruled that it did not have such authority). Congress was, inevitably, slow to take up the challenge, and on 25 November voted not to make the provision retroactive. Shortly beforehand, the government had confiscated the property of the late head of the Cali cartel, José Santacruz Londoño.

The President's appointment of Guillermo González Mosquera to the key post of Defence Minister on 4 February had meanwhile come under attack, on account of his alleged links with drugs interests. Criticism was resumed when

16 soldiers died in a clash with Revolutionary Armed Forces of Colombia (FARC) guerrillas on soon after the FARC had released photographs of the 60 soldiers they were still keeping hostage. After evidence had circulated that in 1989 Sr González had accepted a campaign contribution from a leading drugs trafficker, he resigned on 16 March. The new Defence Minister was Gilberto Echeverri Mejía, who openly advocated talks with guerrillas and paramilitaries to end a decade of violence.

Following mediation by the Catholic Church, the International Red Cross and former US President Jimmy Carter, President Samper in June ordered the evacuation of troops from a large part of the department of Caquetá for a month, with the result that the military hostages were released on 15 June. The affected area was reoccupied on 23 June after public expressions of discontent from senior military commanders, notably Generals Haroldo Bedoya Pizzaro and Manuel José Bonnet, after two soldiers and 18 guerrillas had died in a clash between the FARC and the army in Uraba on 17 June. General Bedoya was dismissed a week later (and replaced by General Bonnet), after President Samper, in his annual message to Congress on 20 July, had promised stricter controls on the armed forces. Though senior officers denounced the move and accused the President of truckling to US demands, the President then proposed a Peace Commission to negotiate terms with both the FARC and the National Liberation Army (ELN).

On 21 August the FARC command agreed to enter into talks, but the earlier assassination (on 8 August) of Senator Jorge Cristo of the ruling Liberal Party (PL) was attributed to the ELN, which had declared leading politicians to be legitimate targets. On 4 September General Bonnet launched a major offensive against the FARC, claiming the deaths of more than 600 guerrillas and effectively putting an end to the peace process, although President Samper, by again offering an amnesty to the FARC on 24 September, apparently wished to keep the process alive. On 16 October the government rejected a peace plan sponsored by a prospective PL presidential candidate, Juan Manuel Santos, and supported by other leading figures, since it would have required President Samper to step down.

The ELN released three hostages on 1 November in response to the government's announcement of a temporary ceasefire. However, hopes that this was a prelude to formal talks with both the ELN and the FARC receded when a 300-strong group of the latter ambushed a remote army camp in the south on 21 December, killing ten soldiers and taking 18 hostage.

On the domestic social front, public sector employees began an indefinite nationwide strike on 11 May, quickly bringing the country to a standstill. A week later the government conceded a 20 per cent pay rise and a major slowdown in the privatization programme. In the political sphere, the Interior Minister and close ally of the President, Horacio Serpa Uribe, resigned on 27 May to contest the 1998 presidential elections (and was replaced by Carlos Holmes Trujillo, former Peace Commissioner and negotiator with the guerrillas). The polls, however, strongly favoured Alfonso Valdiveso Sarmiento, who had resigned as Prosecutor-General on 8 May to run in the elections (and had been replaced by Alfonso Gómez Mendez).

In regional elections held on 26 October no voting took place in more than 150 towns for fear of violence, many candidates withdrawing because of death threats. The ruling Liberal Party took 19 of the 32 departmental governorships (and the opposition Social Conservatives only four) and also won control of 412 local councils. Enrique Peñalosa, an independent Liberal, was an easy winner in the contest for mayor of Bogotá, to succeed the dynamic and charismatic Antanas Mockus.

vi. ECUADOR

CAPITAL: Quito   AREA: 270,500 sq km   POPULATION: 11,700,000 ('96)
OFFICIAL LANGUAGE: Spanish   POLITICAL SYSTEM: presidential democracy
HEAD OF STATE & GOVERNMENT: President Fabián Alarcón Rivera (since Feb '97)
RULING PARTIES: Alfarist Radical Front (FRA) heads loose coalition
MAIN IGO MEMBERSHIPS (non-UN): OAS, ALADI, SELA, AG, CA, NAM
CURRENCY: sucre (end-'97 £1=S/.7,247.79,US$1=S/4,417.50)
GNP PER CAPITA: US$1,390 ('95) or US$4,220 ('95) by PPP calculation

THE brief rule of President Abdala Bucaram Ortiz, inaugurated in August 1996 (see AR 1996, p. 169), came to an abrupt end on 6 February, when Congress voted by 44 votes to 34 that he was 'mentally incapacitated'. Utility prices had been doubled and even trebled in January as part of a rigorous austerity package, but nationwide strikes and demonstrations at the President's populist interpretation of free-market policies had stirred Congress to revolt and to oust Sr Bucaram.

Sr Bucaram, who had cultivated both his eccentricities and his nickname of El Loco ('the madman'), responded to the Congress vote by refusing to hand over power to Vice-President Rosalia Arteaga, the 41-year-old former Education Minister, who claimed to be the constitutional successor. Although this claim was disputed by those who believed that the Speaker of Congress should succeed, on 8 February the deputies by a small majority chose Sra Arteaga as interim President, the first woman to hold Ecuador's highest office. Three days later Congress changed its mind, over two-thirds of the deputies voting for the Speaker, Fabián Alarcón Rivera, to become interim President for 18 months until fresh elections could be held. He was sworn in on 12 February and his appointment was ratified by referendum on 25 May. Having resigned as interim President shortly before the second Congress vote, Sra Arteaga subsequently resumed her post as Vice-President.

On 11 April a court ordered the arrest of ex-President Bucaram on criminal charges of embezzlement and nepotism, despite which he was granted political asylum in Panama shortly afterwards. On 10 July Congress dismissed all the members of the Supreme Court, claiming justification in the referendum decision in favour of the interim President and depoliticization of the judiciary.

However, widespread protests that Congress was delaying constitutional reform led the acting President to agree in August to convene a representative Constituent Assembly.

Elections to the Assembly held on 30 November resulted in the Social Christian Party winning 21 of the 70 seats, followed by Popular Democracy (10), the Ecuadorian Roldosista Party (7) and Alfarist Radical Front (7). Convening on 20 December, the Assembly elected former President Osvaldo Hurtado as its chairman.

Seven Ecuadorian soldiers, allegedly captured by Peruvian forces on 13 May while planting mines on land disputed by Peru, were repatriated two days later. A sixth round of talks, in Brasília on 24–28 November, brought some progress in the Ecuador-Peru dispute, both sides agreeing in principle to make peace and to seek agreement on the demarcation of their common land border.

vii. PARAGUAY

CAPITAL: Asunción   AREA: 406,752 sq km   POPULATION: 4,800,000 ('96)
OFFICIAL LANGUAGE: Spanish   POLITICAL SYSTEM: republic
HEAD OF STATE & GOVERNMENT: President Juan Carlos Wasmosy (since Aug '93)
RULING PARTY: Colorado Party (ANR-PC)
MAIN IGO MEMBERSHIPS (non-UN): OAS, ALADI, SELA, Mercosur
CURRENCY: guarani (end-'97 £1=G3,3,691.57,US$1=G2,250.00)
GNP PER CAPITA: US$1,690 ('95) or US$3,650 ('95) by PPP calculation

THE Ministers of Interior, Education and Integration resigned on 11–12 February following a split in the ruling Colorado Party (ANR-PC) over the succession to President Juan Carlos Wasmosy, who was not eligible for re-election in 1998. President Wasmosy's candidate, Finance Minister Carlos Facetti, was opposed by the President's bitter rival, Luís María Argaña, who as ANR-PC president had significant support within the party but had been defeated for the nomination in 1993 (see AR 1993, p. 179). Later, on 21 August, the ANR-PC executive voted to impeach the President, while the armed forces were reported to be concerned about the possible candidature of the former army commander-in-chief, General Lino César Oviedo Silva, who still faced charges arising from his insurrection in 1996 (see AR 1996, p. 170).

In the event, it was General Oviedo who won the ANR-PC nomination in a controversial primary election in September in which he obtained 36.75 per cent of the vote to 34.97 per cent for Sr Argaña. Domingo Laíno for the third time received the nomination of the opposition Authentic Radical Liberal Party (PLRA). General Oviedo lost no time in attacking President Wasmosy for alleged corruption, and continued to do so from hiding when the President ordered him to be put under 'disciplinary arrest'.

News of a major banking scandal in June was followed on 3 July by a cabinet reshuffle in which Ubaldo Scavone was replaced as Minister of Industry and Commerce by Atilio R. Fernández, whose interior portfolio went to Miguel

Angel Ramírez. Following General Oviedo's escape from arrest, Sebastián González Insfran, the Justice and Labour Minister, resigned on 3 November, while the army commander, General Oscar Rodrígo Díaz Delmas, was forced to retire on 24 November and replaced *ad interim* by General Evaristo González Maldonado.

After the Supreme Court had upheld the President's arrest order, General Oviedo gave himself up to military poice on 12 December. At the end of the month the electoral court rejected a petition seeking to nullify his victory in the ANC-PC primary elections in September.

viii. PERU

CAPITAL: Lima   AREA: 1,285,000 sq km   POPULATION: 23,750,000 ('96)
OFFICIAL LANGUAGES: Spanish, Quechua, Aymará
POLITICAL SYSTEM: presidential democracy
HEAD OF STATE & GOVERNMENT: President Alberto Keinya Fujimori (since July '90)
RULING PARTIES: New Majority-Change 90 heads government coalition
PRIME MINISTER: Alberto Pandolfi Arbulu (since April '96)
MAIN IGO MEMBERSHIPS (non-UN): NAM, OAS, ALADI, SELA, CA, AP
CURRENCY: new sol (end-'97 £1=NS4.47, US$1=NS2.72)
GNP PER CAPITA: US$2,310 ('95) or US$3,770 ('95) by PPP calculation

THE 126-day siege of the Japanese embassy in Lima (see AR 1996, pp. 171–2) ended abruptly on 22 April in a bloodbath after protracted efforts to reach a peaceful outcome had ended in stalemate.

On 31 January President Alberto Keinya Fujimori met the Japanese Prime Minister, Ryutaro Hashimoto, in Toronto, after some further negotiated releases had raised hopes of a peaceful resolution. However, during five rounds of talks with a government negotiator between 11 and 24 February, the leader of the 17-member Tupac Amaru Revolutionary Movement (MRTA) group, Néstor Cerpa Cartolini, continued to demand the release of some 400 imprisoned guerrillas and a safe passage out of the country. The talks were broken off on 7 March when the guerrillas detected tunnelling activity. Despite successful efforts by the Japanese government to find a country willing to accept the guerrillas, both they and the government refused to agree to a deal.

After both the Interior Minister and the national police chief had resigned on 19 March, their replacements, General César Saucedo Sánchez and General Fernando Diaderas, took the decision to launch the carefully-planned attack. Lulled into over-confidence, four of the guerrillas were killed outright when a mine was exploded under the basement where they were playing football. Commandos then burst into the building from all sides. Two soldiers died and one of the 72 hostages, Supreme Court judge Carlos Giusti, died shortly afterwards of a heart-attack. All the guerrillas were killed, including not only those who offered to surrender but also those who had been wounded. President Fujimori was triumphant, and it seemed unlikely that the MRTA would be able to carry out their threat of reprisal action. Five generals were among 19 people immediately charged by the military authorities in connection with the security lapse.

On 29 May Congress voted to dismiss three judges of the seven-member Constitutional Tribunal, after they had opposed as unconstitutional the 1996 law allowing President Fujimori to run for a third term. Amid large-scale street protests and criticism of the dismissals by the Archbishop of Lima, the resignation of the tribunal's president left it inquorate. The action was seen as one more of many abuses of power by the President, whose stock had fallen sharply by mid-June. Reports of the use of assassination and torture by the army intelligence service (SIE), and the wealth of its head, Vladimir Montesinos (the President's closest adviser), provided a focus for public anger. Antigovernment protests grew in July, fanned by the news that the government had been systematically tapping telephones not only of journalists but also of the former UN Secretary-General, Javier Pérez de Cuellar, whose Union for Peru (UPP) was in negotiation with other parties to present a combined opposition front.

A cabinet reshuffle on 16 July strengthened military influence within the government. Eduardo Ferrer Costa replaced Francisco Tudela as Foreign Minister, following the latter's resignation 'for reasons of conscience'; General César Saucedo Sanchez replaced General Tomás Castillo Meza as Defence Minister; and General José Villanueva Ruesta took over General Saucedo's previous post as Interior Minister. On 17 July senior military officers swore a public oath of loyalty to the President. However, a week later an opposition newspaper published documents suggesting strongly that the President had not, as he had always claimed, been born in Peru and thus was ineligible to hold office.

Meanwhile, there was evidence that the Maoist Sendero Luminoso (Shining Path) guerrillas were still active. A series of car bombings in mid-May were attributed to them, while on 15 August they threatened to kill oil workers of the French Elf-Aquitaine company in Satipo, halting operations and obtaining supplies of food and medicines.

Growing tension between the government and the military leadership approached open confrontation in December when President Fujimori disclosed that he was 'evaluating' whether to retain General Nicolás Hermoza Ríos as armed forces supremo. The latter responded by summoning all his regional commanders to Lima, receiving their pledges of unconditional support in a stage-managed ceremony on 20 December also attended by the chiefs of the navy, air force and police. Emergency cabinet meetings convened by the President produced an order to General Hermoza to send the regional commanders back to barracks. He complied, although underlying strains were again apparent when several of his supporters were passed over in an end-of-year military reshuffle.

In simultaneous cabinet changes, President Fujimori appointed a presidential aide, Daniel Hokama Tokashiki, to a second stint in the important portfolio of energy and mines (held since September 1996 by Prime Minister Alberto Pandolfi Arbulu) and also dismissed the Transport Minister, Elsa Carrera, hitherto regarded as one of his closest supporters.

ix. URUGUAY

CAPITAL: Montevideo   AREA: 176,200 sq km   POPULATION: 3,200,000 ('96)
OFFICIAL LANGUAGE: Spanish   POLITICAL SYSTEM: presidential democracy
HEAD OF STATE & GOVERNMENT: President Julio María Sanguinetti (since March '95)
RULING PARTIES: Colorado Party holds presidency and heads government including the Blanco and People's Government parties
MAIN IGO MEMBERSHIPS (non-UN): OAS, ALADI, SELA, Mercosur, NAM
CURRENCY: new peso (end-'97 £1=NUr$16.38, US$1=Nur9.99)
GNP PER CAPITA: US$5,170 ('95) or US$6,630 ('95) by PPP calculation

ON 13 January a constitutional amendment simplifying the electoral procedure for both national and local elections came into force, having been ratified by a referendum on 8 December 1996 by 1,015,828 votes to 930,288. A widely-observed strike on 29 May in Paysandú brought business and urban and rural labour together in protest at continuing unemployment. In April a petition by Senator Rafael Michelini seeking authority to investigate possible burial sites of 'disappeared' persons in military installations was accepted by a judge. However, the Appeals Court ruled on 14 June that any such crimes committed before 1 March 1985 were covered by the Full Stop Law (see AR 1987, pp. 79–80).

x. VENEZUELA

CAPITAL: Caracas   AREA: 912,000 sq km   POPULATION: 22,140,000 ('96)
OFFICIAL LANGUAGE: Spanish   POLITICAL SYSTEM: presidential democracy
HEAD OF STATE & GOVERNMENT: President Rafael Caldera Rodríguez (since Feb '94)
RULING PARTIES: 17–party National Convergence (CN) coalition
MAIN IGO MEMBERSHIPS (non-UN): OAS, ALADI, SELA, AG, CA, ACS, OPEC, NAM
CURRENCY: bolívar (end-'97 £1=Bs827.10, US$1=Bs504.12)
GNP PER CAPITA: US$3,020 ('95) or US$7,900 ('95) by PPP calculation

IN his annual report to Congress on 13 March, President Rafael Caldera Rodríguez defended his continuing programme of austerity. On the eve of the address, massive demonstrations had taken place in the streets of the capital, coupled with threats of strikes from several public sector unions. The latter were angered both at a fall in personal real incomes of some 30 per cent in 1996 and at concessions made to selected workers in February. However, with more than 18 per cent of the population unemployed, the economic situation of most Venezuelans was critical.

Cabinet changes on 21 March intensified speculation both that the 81-year-old President was ill and that a military coup was imminent. On 2 July Vice-Admiral Tito Manglio Rincón Bravo was sworn in as Defence Minister, in place of General Pedro Nicolas Valencia Vivas. At the end of July Lieut.-General (retd.) Hugo Chávez Frias, leader of the abortive military coup of 1992 (see AR 1992, p. 182), for which he had later been pardoned, launched a new political party, the Fifth Republican Movement, to support his candidature for the presidency in December 1998. Antonio Ledezma, the mayor of Caracas, was also expected to contest the election.

An attempt to impeach the Finance Minister, Luis Raúl Matos Azócar, over a controversial foreign debt transaction foundered on 11 November when opposition Democratic Action (AD) deputies in Congress failed to support the motion, thereby denying it the required two-thirds majority. Little more than a month later, however, Sr Matos Azócar bowed to political realities and resigned (on 19 December). He was replaced by Freddy Rojas Parra, hitherto Trade and Industry Minister.

On 9 July 59 people were reported killed and 320 injured when an earthquake measuring 6.9 on the Richter scale hit the region around the Caribbean coastal town of Cariaco, 470 kilometres east of the capital.

xi. CUBA

CAPITAL: Havana AREA: 115,000 sq km POPULATION: 11,140,000 ('96)
OFFICIAL LANGUAGE: Spanish POLITICAL SYSTEM: one-party republic
HEAD OF STATE & GOVERNMENT: President Fidel Castro Ruz (since Jan '59)
RULING PARTY: Cuban Communist Party (PCC)
MAIN IGO MEMBERSHIPS (non-UN): ACS, SELA, NAM
CURRENCY: peso (end-'97 £1=Cub$37.74, US$1=Cub$23.00)
GNP PER CAPITA: n.a.

ALTHOUGH there had been a substantial improvement in the economy over the previous two years, conditions remained very difficult in 1997. The 1996–97 sugar harvest brought in only 4.2 million tonnes, compared with 4.4 million tonnes the previous year. Anger continued at the pretensions of the United States, through the 1996 Helms-Burton Act (see AR 1996, pp. 155, 174), to impose its notion of 'democracy' on Cuba. On 29 January President Fidel Castro Ruz publicly rejected financial assistance offered by the US Agency for International Development (USAID). The Washington-based Association for World Health confirmed in March that the health of Cubans had been adversely affected by the blockade.

On 22–23 January the Canadian Foreign Minister, Lloyd Axworthy, visited Havana and signed an agreement for closer cooperation. Canadian legislation enabling Canadian companies subject to sanctions under the Helms-Burton Act to sue for damages in Canadian courts had come into effect on 1 January. Talks continued between representatives of the European Union and the United States to avert action by the former against the act, but relations between Cuba and Spain in particular were tense. An EU decision to suspend action for six months, the Cubans noted, did not solve the problem. A bilateral trade agreement was signed with South Africa on 16 April.

On 7 May the Cuban government publicly accused the United States of waging biological warfare against Cuba by distributing a potato pest, a complaint being lodged with the United Nations in Geneva in August. The US government claimed that a US crop-spraying aircraft which had overflown Cuba in October 1996 had made smoke simply to advertise its presence. On 6 June Cuba complained to the World Trade Organization (WTO) about the effect of US congressional moves further to tighten sanctions.

Bombs exploded in the lobbies of the Nacional and Capri hotels in Havana on 12 July, injuring three people and adversely affecting the tourist trade. On Moncada Day (26 July) Raúl Castro Ruz, the Minister of Defence, claimed that dissident groups had received financial aid from the US government, which it accused of 'open and unacceptable interference' in the country's internal affairs. Four further hotel bombs followed, one killing an Italian businessman. A 31-year-old Salvadorean, Raúl Ernesto Cruz León, was arrested and was said on 11 September to have given irrefutable evidence that his campaign had been funded by the US-based Cuban-American National Foundation (CANF)—whose founder, Jorge Mas Canosa, died in the United States on 23 November. The US State Department denied involvement and stressed that it did not condone the bombings. On 26 November a US citizen, Walter Van Der Veer, was sentenced to 15 years' imprisonment for conspiracy against the state.

More than a million people attended a May Day rally commemorating the life of Ernesto 'Che' Guevara, at which his wife and family were present. His body, rediscovered in Valle Grande, Bolivia, was subsequently returned to Cuba on 12 July, together with those of three other Cuban guerrillas, and placed in a specially-constructed mausoleum in the main square of Santa Clara. In a six-hour speech to the fifth congress of the Cuban Communist Party (PCC), held in Havana on 8–10 October, President Castro placed the blame for the recent bombings on the United States.

A decree issued by President Castro in December reinstated Christmas Day as a Cuban public holiday, after nearly 30 years in which the regime had deemed celebration of Christmas to be detrimental to the sugar harvest. The decision was seen as a goodwill gesture in advance of a scheduled visit to Cuba by Pope John Paul II in January 1998 (see also II.2.viii).

xii. DOMINICAN REPUBLIC AND HAITI

Dominican Republic
CAPITAL: Santo Domingo   AREA: 48,400 sq km   POPULATION: 8,000,000 ('96)
OFFICIAL LANGUAGE: Spanish   POLITICAL SYSTEM: presidential democracy
HEAD OF STATE & GOVERNMENT: President Leonel Fernández (since Aug '96)
RULING PARTY: Dominican Liberation Party (PLD)
MAIN IGO MEMBERSHIPS (non-UN): OAS, SELA, ACS, ACP
CURRENCY: peso (end-'97 £1=RD$24.20, US$1=RD$14.75)
GNP PER CAPITA: US$1,460 ('95) or US$3,870 ('95) by PPP calculation

Haiti
CAPITAL: Port-au-Prince   AREA: 27,750 sq km   POPULATION: 7,300,000 ('96)
OFFICIAL LANGUAGE: French   POLITICAL SYSTEM: presidential democracy
HEAD OF STATE & GOVERNMENT: President René Préval (since Feb '96)
RULING PARTY: Lavalas Political Organization
PRIME MINISTER: vacant
MAIN IGO MEMBERSHIPS (non-UN): OAS, SELA, ACS, ACP, Francophonie
CURRENCY: gourde (end-'97 £1=G27.82, US$1=G16.95)
GNP PER CAPITA: US$250 ('95), US$910 ('95) by PPP calculation

RELATIONS between the DOMINICAN REPUBLIC and Haiti deteriorated in January when the former began to deport Haitian immigrants and their children. More than 16,000 had been expelled by 25 February, when the government claimed that expulsions had ceased. José Francisco Peña Gómez, unsuccessful candidate in the June 1996 presidential elections (see AR 1996, p. 175), announced his retirement from politics on grounds of ill health.

In HAITI, President René Préval on 7 February presided over the distribution of some 1,000 hectares of land to families in the department of Artibonite. Critics of the IMF structural adjustment programme initiated a censure motion on the government of Prime Minister Rosny Smarth, but it was defeated on 27 March by 37 votes to 29. Municipal elections held on 6 April, as part of the effort to restore international confidence, were marred by a low turnout and accusations of ballot-rigging, following which further strikes and violent incidents finally forced M. Smarth to resign on 9 June. An economist, Eric Pierre, was named as his successor on 25 July, but his nomination was rejected by the Chamber of Deputies on 26 August by 43 votes to nine. Meanwhile, M. Smarth continued as Prime Minister in a caretaker capacity.

Further talks initiated by the President on 16 September failed to achieve agreement on the political crisis, with the result that on 20 October M. Smarth announced that he was leaving office. On 3 November the President nominated actor and former minister Hervé Denis in his place, but he too failed to secure parliamentary endorsement in December. In consequence, Haiti ended the year without a Prime Minister in post.

On 8 September at least 250 people (possibly many more) drowned when an overcrowded ferry, the *Fierte Gonavivence*, capsized in the port of Montrouis.

xiii. CENTRAL AMERICA AND PANAMA

Guatemala
CAPITAL: Guatemala City   AREA: 109,000 sq km   POPULATION: 10,800,000 ('96)
OFFICIAL LANGUAGE: Spanish   POLITICAL SYSTEM: presidential democracy
HEAD OF STATE & GOVERNMENT: President Alvaro Arzú Irigoyen (since Jan '96)
RULING PARTIES: National Advancement Party (PAN) heads coalition
MAIN IGO MEMBERSHIPS (non-UN): OAS, SELA, CACM, ACS, NAM
CURRENCY: quetzal (end-'97 £1=Q10.10, US$1=Q6.15)
GNP PER CAPITA: US$1,340 ('95) or US$3,340 ('95) by PPP calculation

El Salvador
CAPITAL: San Salvador   AREA: 21,400 sq km   POPULATION: 5,650,000 ('96)
OFFICIAL LANGUAGE: Spanish   POLITICAL SYSTEM: presidential democracy
HEAD OF STATE & GOVERNMENT: President Armando Calderón Sol (since June '94)
RULING PARTY: National Republican Alliance (Arena)
MAIN IGO MEMBERSHIPS (non-UN): OAS, SELA, CACM, ACS
CURRENCY: colón (end-'97 £1=C14.36, US$1=C8.75)
GNP PER CAPITA: US$1,610 ('95) or US$2,610 ('95) by PPP calculation

Honduras
CAPITAL: Tegucigalpa   AREA: 112,000 sq km   POPULATION: 5,750,000 ('96)
OFFICIAL LANGUAGE: Spanish   POLITICAL SYSTEM: presidential democracy
HEAD OF STATE & GOVERNMENT: President Carlos Roberto Reina Idiaquez (since Jan '94)
PRESIDENT-ELECT: Carlos Roberto Flores Facussé
RULING PARTY: Liberal Party of Honduras (PLH)
MAIN IGO MEMBERSHIPS (non-UN): OAS, SELA, CACM, ACS, NAM
CURRENCY: lempira (end-'97 £1=L21.66, US$1=L13.20)
GNP PER CAPITA: US$600 ('95) or US$1,900 ('95) by PPP calculation

Nicaragua
CAPITAL: Managua   AREA: 120,000 sq km   POPULATION: 4,700,000 ('96)
OFFICIAL LANGUAGE: Spanish   POLITICAL SYSTEM: presidential democracy
HEAD OF STATE & GOVERNMENT: President Arnaldo Alemán (since April '97)
RULING PARTY: Liberal Alliance (AL)
MAIN IGO MEMBERSHIPS (non-UN): OAS, SELA, CACM, ACS, NAM
CURRENCY: córdoba (end-'97 £1=C$16.41, US$1=C$10.00)
GNP PER CAPITA: US$380 ('95) or US$2,000 ('95) by PPP calculation

Costa Rica
CAPITAL: San José   AREA: 51,000 sq km   POPULATION: 3,400,000 ('96)
OFFICIAL LANGUAGE: Spanish   POLITICAL SYSTEM: presidential democracy
HEAD OF STATE & GOVERNMENT: President José María Figueres (since May '94)
RULING PARTY: National Liberation Party (PLN)
MAIN IGO MEMBERSHIPS (non-UN): OAS, SELA, CACM, ACS
CURRENCY: colón (end-'97 £1=C400.22, US$1=C243.94)
GNP PER CAPITA: US$2,610 ('95) or US$5,850 ('95) by PPP calculation

Panama
CAPITAL: Panama City   AREA: 77,000 sq km   POPULATION: 2,270,000 ('96)
OFFICIAL LANGUAGE: Spanish   POLITICAL SYSTEM: presidential
HEAD OF STATE & GOVERNMENT: President Ernesto Pérez Balladares (since Sept '94)
RULING PARTIES: Democratic Revolutionary Party (PRD) heads coalition
MAIN IGO MEMBERSHIPS (non-UN): OAS, SELA, NAM
CURRENCY: balboa (end-'97 £1=B1.64, US$1=B1.00)
GNP PER CAPITA: US$2,750 ('95) or US$5,980 ('95) by PPP calculation

ON 22 January a four-year plan was signed in Brussels to give international support to the peace agreement for GUATEMALA concluded in December 1996 (see AR 1996, p. 177). China, however, vetoed the proposal of the UN Security Council to send 155 observers to the country to verify the implementation of the accord. In February the membership of the Truth Commission appointed to investigate human rights violations during the 36-year civil war was announced. On 31 July the former Minister of Interior, Danilo Parrinello, his deputy and the former police chief, Salvador Figueroa, were sentenced to ten years' imprisonment for the murder of a student in 1994.

US Secretary of State Madeleine Albright, during a visit on 4 May, was asked by both government and opposition to provide more help to support the peace process. On 18 June former guerrillas elected a national committee under the presidency of Ricardo Ramírez ('Commandante Rolando Moran') to transform the Guatemalan National Revolutionary Unity (URNG) into an effective political party. However, President Alvaro Arzú Irigoyen's dismissal on 3 July of both the Defence Minister, General Julio Balconi, and the Chief of Staff, General Sergio Camargo, was seen as strengthening hard-line military influence. Their replacements were, respectively, General Héctor Barrios Zelada and General Marco Tulio Espinosa (who had previously served as head of the presidential guard). The new Defence Minister subsequently stated in September that neither he nor the army could frustrate the peace accords, following complaints from Sr Ramírez of army interference.

In EL SALVADOR, the ruling National Republican Alliance (ARENA) lost seats to the opposition Farabundo Martí National Liberation Front (FMLN) in legislative elections on 16 March, securing only 28 seats in the 84-member Assembly against 27 for the FMLN, formerly a guerrilla movement and now a legal social democratic party. The National Conciliation Party (PCN) won 11 of the remaining seats and the Christian Democrats seven, giving the centre-left a majority. The FMLN also won control of 100 municipalities and elected Héctor Silva as mayor of San Salvador on a programme of fiscal rectitude. On 19 May a new cabinet-rank post of Environment Minister was created, being entrusted to Miguel Araujo.

Arnoldo Alemán Lacayo of the right-wing Liberal Alliance (AL) was sworn in as President of NICARAGUA on 10 January following his election victory in October 1996 (see AR 1996, p. 177). In his inaugural address he referred specifically to two continuing problems: the contested nationalization of property by the former Sandinista government and the continuing violence in the north. Two days previously the Supreme Court had declared unconstitutional 80 laws passed by the outgoing National Assembly since 22 November 1996. In response, the Sandinistas, led by former President Daniel Ortega Saavedra, boycotted the opening of the new Assembly, thus handing all the key positions to the right-wing parties. Early strains in the government coalition were apparent on 12 May when the right-wing Nationalist Liberal Party (PLN) withdrew from the AL.

Demonstrations by students culminated on 23 July in violent clashes with police in Managua. Following talks between the government and the Sandinista National Liberation Front (FSLN), a draft bill to regularize land seizures under the Sandinista government and to provide compensation was presented to Congress. Nevertheless, the FSLN subsequently organized 'self-defence brigades' to protect 22 companies nationalized under the Sandinista government. On 6 November the government signed an agreement for the disarming of the Andrés Castro United Front (FUAC), the last active insurgent group.

Following the detention in May by Nicaraguan vessels of 17 Honduran fishing vessels in the Gulf of Fonseca, the government of HONDURAS reasserted its right to define its territorial waters in the region. On 21 August, with the sanction of Pope John Paul II, the Archbishop of Tegucigalpa, Oscar Andrés Rodríguez Maradiaga, was appointed interim head of the country's police force to oversee its transition from military to civilian control, while in September it was decided to merge the office of army commander-in-chief with that of Defence Minister with effect from January 1998. In presidential elections held on 30 November the president of the National

Assembly, Carlos Roberto Flores Facussé of the ruling Liberal Party (PLH) easily defeated Alba Nora Gunera de Melgar of the National Party (PNH), obtaining 52.7 per cent of the votes cast. In simultaneous legislative elections the PLH took 67 seats, the PNH 55 and three small parties 6. The PLH thus retained a majority in the 128-member National Congress (which in October had voted to reduce its size to 80 members subject to ratification by the incoming legislature).

There was growing concern in COSTA RICA about the loss of the nation's forest and the environmental impact of tourism. The government of President José Maria Figueres of the National Liberation Party (PLN) was unchanged in 1997, remaining securely in office despite the narrow PLN majority in the Legislative Assembly.

In July some 1,200 troops were dispatched to the Darien region of PANAMA to quell unrest stemming from the influx of refugees from Colombia. Tension continued to rise, however, and in November a number of serious clashes resulted in the death of one policeman and injuries to three others. A conference organized by President Ernesto Pérez Balladares to convince the world that the country was capable of managing the Panama Canal after 1999 was boycotted by China, and hence by all UN agencies and most foreign leaders, because of Taiwanese participation.

xiv. MEXICO

CAPITAL: Mexico City   AREA: 1,958,000 sq km   POPULATION: 97,000,000 ('96)
OFFICIAL LANGUAGE: Spanish   POLITICAL SYSTEM: federal presidential democracy
HEAD OF STATE & GOVERNMENT: President Ernesto Zedillo Ponce de León (since Dec '94)
RULING PARTY: Party of the Institutionalized Revolution (PRI), since 1929
MAIN IGO MEMBERSHIPS (non-UN): OAS, SELA, ALADI, ACS, APEC, NAFTA, OECD
CURRENCY: peso (end-'97 £1=Mex$13.22, US$1=Mex$8.06)
GNP PER CAPITA: US$3,320 ('95) or US$6,400 ('95) by PPP calculation

IN a demonstration of its confidence on 15 January, the government of President Ernesto Zedillo Ponce de León repaid, three years early, the last instalment of the emergency loan it had received from the United States to avert default following the 'tequila crisis' of December 1994 (see AR 1994, p, 202). A three-year national development plan announced by the government on 3 June was designed to prevent a repetition of the 1994 crisis. Growth overall in 1996 had been 5.1 per cent and the value of bilateral trade with the United States had amounted to US$140,000 million. In 1997 growth was expected to rise to 6.5 per cent and inflation slightly to exceed the government's 15 per cent target. The peso, however, continued to fall relative to the US dollar, and in November the Mexican stock market was badly shaken by developments in South-East Asia (see XVIII.1). The government responded by establishing a contingency loan fund of $2,500 million to support the peso.

Fresh US support was also forthcoming for the war against drugs. The arrest on 19 February of General Jesús Gutiérrez Rebolledo, the head of the National Institute for Combating Drugs (INCD), on charges of aiding and abetting the smuggling of cocaine was followed by the dismissal of 36 of his subordinates and the formation on 1 May of a new anti-drugs force. In March new measures to curb money-laundering were announced. Rumours circulated freely that other very senior politicians were implicated, including former President Carlos Salinas de Gortari, currently reported to be living in exile in Dublin. Though the US Congress was openly critical of the Mexican government's efforts, President Clinton in the end certified that Mexico was cooperating actively against drug-trafficking. Further, on a state visit on 6–7 May, he emphasized the closeness of bilateral cooperation between the United States and Mexico, before signing new agreements designed to enhance efforts against illegal immigration, drug-trafficking and money-laundering.

In July the notorious cocaine baron Amado Carrillo Fuentes died during an operation to change his appearance. The surgeon and two of his colleagues disappeared in October, their mutilated bodies being found on 3 November in oil drums on the road from Mexico City to Acapulco. On 13–14 November President Zedillo visited Washington in an effort to stress that progress had been made in Mexico's anti-drugs campaign. The Canadian ambassador, Marc Perron, had been withdrawn the previous month after publicly describing the campaign as 'a joke'.

The choice of candidates within the ruling Party of the Institutionalized Revolution (PRI) became increasingly acrimonious, an ominous development for the party being the defeat of its candidates in state and municipal elections in Morelos on 16 March. In February a new formation, the Party of the Democratic Centre (PCD), was launched by the former Foreign Minister, Manuel Camacho Solís, who had resigned from the PRI in 1995. This was, however, too late for the new party to contest the mid-term elections on 6 July, which brought the first signs of a substantial realignment in Mexican politics.

In the first-ever election for the mayoralty of the federal capital, Cuauhtemoc Cárdenas Solórzano of the opposition Party of the Democratic Revolution (PRD), with 48.1 per cent of the votes cast, decisively defeated both the PRI candidate and the nominee of the Party of National Action (PAN). As only 32 of the Senate's 128 seats were being filled, the PRI was able to retain control of the 128-member upper house, in which its post-election representation was 76 seats, against 33 for the PAN, 14 for the PRD and five others. In the elections to the Chamber of Deputies, however, the PRI lost its overall majority for the first time in its history. Winning only 31.9 of the votes cast nationally, the party held only 239 seats against 261 won by the opposition parties, among which the PRD obtained 125 seats and the PAN 121. The PRI also lost the governorships of both Nuevo León and Querétaro to the PAN. In subsequent state elections on 19 October, the PRI retained control of Tabasco but the PRD and PAN made important gains in Veracruz. In Jalisco on 9 November, moreover, the PAN won 20 of the seats in the 40-member state legislature, against the PRI's 17 and three for other parties.

Opposition parties on 21 August drew up a three-year 'democratic governability accord' and rejected the PRI's claim to control Congress, electing Porfirio Muñoz Ledo as Speaker of the Chamber of Deputies when it convened on 1 September. In his annual address, President Zedillo pointedly warned deputies to stay within government spending limits or risk financial instability. The new Speaker, in reply, pledged to curb excesses of presidential power. On 9 September Humberto Roque Villanueva resigned as president of the PRI and was succeeded by Mariano Palacios Alcocer, a federal deputy and former ambassador to Portugal. Talks between government and opposition parties, suspended in November 1996, were resumed on 3 November at the invitation of President Zedillo, the discussions focusing in the first instance on differences over the proposed 1998 budget.

Talks between the government and the insurgent Zapatista Army of National Liberation (EZLN) were resumed following conciliatory statements by the latter in January. Seven alleged guerrillas had been released on 3 January after a judge overturned their convictions for terrorism. Following a six-month lull, fresh clashes between Popular Revolutionary Army (ERP) guerrillas and security forces were reported from Guerrero in May, three soldiers being killed and 10 wounded in two attacks at Atoyac de Alvarez on 27 May. Subsequently, however, the guerrillas announced a unilateral truce for the period of the elections. In August troops were withdrawn from three areas of Chiapas state, while on 12 September unarmed Zapatista guerrillas participated in a public rally in the capital without incident. In contrast, the killing of Indians in Chiapas continued, at least 45 Tzotzil being massacred in a single attack by right-wing paramilitaries on 22 December at Acteal, near San Cristóbal de las Casas. The latest killings were widely seen as part of a general government strategy to crush insurgency in the state.

Widespread damage was caused in the south of Guerrero state by hurricane Pauline, which hit Acapulco on 9–10 October, killing 111 and making thousands homeless. Experts attributed the hurricane to the 'El Niño' phenomenon that was distorting weather patterns in many areas of the eastern Pacific (see XIV.3).

4. THE CARIBBEAN

JAMAICA—GUYANA—TRINIDAD & TOBAGO—BARBADOS—
BELIZE—GRENADA—THE BAHAMAS—WINDWARD AND LEEWARD ISLANDS—
UK DEPENDENCIES—SURINAME—NETHERLANDS ANTILLES AND ARUBA—
US DEPENDENCIES

i. JAMAICA

CAPITAL: Kingston   AREA: 11,000 sq km   POPULATION: 2,550,000 ('96)
OFFICIAL LANGUAGE: English   POLITICAL SYSTEM: parliamentary democracy
HEAD OF STATE: Queen Elizabeth II
GOVERNOR-GENERAL: Sir Howard Cooke
RULING PARTY: People's National Party (PNP)
HEAD OF GOVERNMENT: Percival J. Patterson, Prime Minister (since March '92)
MAIN IGO MEMBERSHIPS (non-UN): OAS, SELA, ACS, Caricom, ACP, CWTH, NAM
CURRENCY: Jamaican dollar (end-'97 £1=J$57.10, US$1=J$34.80)
GNP PER CAPITA: US$1,510 ('95) or US$3,540 ('95) by PPP calculation

IN parliamentary elections held on 18 December, P.J. Patterson led the People's National Party (PNP) to its third consecutive term, the longest time that a party had held continuous power in Jamaica. The PNP won 50 seats on a 56 per cent vote share, the opposition Jamaica Labour Party (JLP) securing 10 seats with 39 per cent. The breakaway National Democratic Movement (NDM), formed by JLP dissidents in 1995 (see AR 1995, p. 187), failed to win a seat, taking only 5 per cent of the vote.

A number of measures were introduced in an effort to curb Jamaica's violent political culture, including tighter election laws and the establishment of a private citizens' watchdog group. There was also a visit by a delegation from the US Carter Center (run by the former President) which included prominent black American 'role models', such as the boxer Evander Holyfield and General Colin Powell. However, there were three deaths on election day, a 'war' between rival supporters in August Town and gun battles in Tivoli Gardens. The dead included a former PNP parliamentary candidate, while the NDM general secretary was shot and injured. Embarrassingly for the PNP, the Minister of Tourism, John Junor, was forced to resign after engaging in a gun battle with a JLP supporter. Lost ballot papers, late electoral registers and missing names caused the Elections Advisory Commission to express dissatisfaction with the American firm contracted to provide the electoral facilities.

Crime had continued to be a problem throughout the year, a notable case being the murder of the Venezuelan ambassador on 6 November. To speed executions, the government placed a nine-month limit on death-penalty appeals to external institutions and pulled out of the International Convention on Civil and Political Rights.

Having secured assurances on its sovereignty, Jamaica signed a 'ship-rider' agreement with the United States in May allowing US anti-drugs enforcement agents, in cooperation with their Jamaican counterparts, to enter Jamaican airspace and territorial waters in pursuit of suspected drug-traffickers. Soon afterwards tension developed when local fishermen claimed that they had been searched by the US Coastguard in Jamaican waters, for which the Jamaican government demanded a US apology.

In the external policy sphere, Prime Minister Patterson visited Cuba on 28 May, receiving the Order of José Martí (the highest Cuban honour awarded to non-Cubans) and agreeing to extend diplomatic and economic ties between the two countries.

In the economic arena, at the end of January the government established the Financial Sector Adjustment Company (FINSAC), making over J$8,000 million available to help the ailing financial sector. At the end of the year the government was obliged to secure a $100 million 'bridging loan' from Citibank Jamaica to cover its fiscal deficit, which had been worsened by the crisis in the Asian and international capital markets (see XVIII.1). On a more positive note, an Australian-Canadian joint venture company began gold mining in December at the Main Ridge project in Clarendon, where 1.2 million grams of gold were 'proven in the prospect'.

Michael Manley, Prime Minster of Jamaica in 1972–80 and 1989–92, died from cancer on 6 March at the age of 72 (see XX: Obituary).

ii. GUYANA

CAPITAL: Georgetown AREA: 215,000 sq km POPULATION: 840,000 ('96)
OFFICIAL LANGUAGE: English
POLITICAL SYSTEM: cooperative presidential democracy
RULING PARTY: People's Progressive Party-Civic (PPP-C)
HEAD OF STATE & GOVERNMENT: President Janet Jagan (since Dec '97)
PRIME MINISTER: Sam Hinds (since Dec '97)
MAIN IGO MEMBERSHIPS (non-UN): OAS, SELA, AP, ACS, Caricom, ACP, CWTH, NAM
CURRENCY: Guyana dollar (end-'97 £1=G$233.80, US$1=G$142.50)
GNP PER CAPITA: US$590 ('95) or US$2,420 ('95) by PPP calculation

PRESIDENT Cheddi Jagan, founder and leader of the People's Progressive Party (PPP) and first Premier of what was then British Guiana in 1953, died of a heart attack on 6 March at the age of 78 (see XX: Obituary). An estimated 150,000 people from all of Guyana's communities—a fifth of the population—came to see his body before it was cremated in a state funeral. Also given a state funeral was the poet and freedom fighter, Martin Carter, who died on 13 December at the age of 70.

The Vice-President and Prime Minister, Sam Hinds, succeeded to the presidency *ad interim* on the death of Dr Jagan, whose American-born widow Janet (76), a co-founder of the PPP, succeeded Mr Hinds to become Guyana's first woman Prime Minister. On 2 April Donald Ramoutar was unanimously elected as the new general secretary of the ruling party—officially called the PPP-Civic.

General elections were held on 17 December for a new National Assembly and also for the presidency (the 1980 constitution specifying that the presidential candidate of the party with the most votes in the legislative elections became President). Mrs Jagan was named the PPP-Civic candidate, while the main opposition People's National Congress (PNC) nominated Desmond Hoyte, its leader and himself a former President. Four different international and local observer teams monitored the electoral process, which became fraught with controversy. The longstanding divide between the mainly Asian support of the PPC-Civic and the mainly African following of the PNC was again much in evidence, with the admixture of PNC attacks on Mrs Jagan because she was white.

During the ballot counting, the PNC accused the PPP-Civic of electoral fraud and objected to an early declaration that Mrs Jagan had won. It then tried to prevent Mrs Jagan's inauguration by legal action, as pro-PNC crowds gathered almost daily in the capital and clashed violently with the police. On 19 December, however, the elections commissioner declared the PPP-Civic to be the clear winner and Mrs Jagan took her presidential oath the same day, amid much drama. PNC protesters and a court official attempted to stop the swearing-in ceremony (which was attended by US, UK, Caricom and national officials), but a PNC-initiated court injunction was ignored by Mrs Jagan.

Announced on 30 December, the final results showed that the PPP had obtained 220,667 votes and the PNC 161,901, the two parties being allotted 34 and 26 seats respectively in the 65-member Assembly. Amid continuing violent protests by PNC supporters, the electoral commission proposed that the results should be audited by an international body, but the PNC countered that it would only accept fresh elections. Earlier in the year, the government had recommended constitutional changes to remove the right of the President to dissolve the National Assembly against its will and to delete constitutional references to socialism.

Guyana obtained significant benefit in 1997 from the 'highly-indebted poor countries initiative' of the Paris Club of creditor countries. Between them, Trinidad and Tobago (Guyana's largest bilateral creditor), the United States, Germany, the Netherlands, the United Kingdom, Norway and Sweden forgave Guyana around US$1,000 million of its outstanding foreign debt, representing about half the total.

In other developments, lawyers representing 23,000 people in Guyana set into motion a class-action suit against the Canadian gold-mining company responsible for the Omai cyanide spill in 1995 (see AR 1995, p. 187). The late Walter Rodney, the radical scholar and founder of the Working People's Alliance (WPA), was honoured by the University of Guyana, which dedicated a chair in history to his memory.

iii. TRINIDAD & TOBAGO

CAPITAL: Port of Spain   AREA: 5,128 sq km   POPULATION: 1,260,000 ('96)
OFFICIAL LANGUAGE: English   POLITICAL SYSTEM: parliamentary republic
RULING PARTIES: United National Congress (UNC) & National Alliance for Reconstruction (NAR)
HEAD OF STATE: President Arthur N.R. Robinson (NAR), since March '97
HEAD OF GOVERNMENT: Basdeo Panday (UNC), Prime Minister (since Nov '95)
MAIN IGO MEMBERSHIPS (non-UN): OAS, SELA, ACS, Caricom, ACP, CWTH, NAM
CURRENCY: Trinidad & Tobago dollar (end-'97 £1=TT$10.17, US$1=TT$6.20)
GNP PER CAPITA: US$3,770 ('95) or US$8,610 ('95) by PPP calculation

THE country's first contested election for the presidency on 14 February was won by A.N.R. Robinson, Prime Minister in 1986–91, the current Minister Extraordinaire for Tobago and outgoing leader of the National Alliance for Reconstruction (NAR), the junior member of the ruling coalition. Elected by the two houses of parliament jointly, all previous Presidents had been returned unopposed. In the February contest, Mr Robinson received 46 votes against 18 for Anthony Lucky, a High Court judge and candidate of the opposition People's National Movement (PNM).

The result suggested that four PNM members had voted against Judge Lucky. In separate defections the same month, two PNM MPs declared themselves independent and were promptly appointed to the cabinet dominated by the United National Congress (UNC). Both cited problems with the PNM leader, Patrick Manning, one describing the party as 'drifting rudderless because of a lack of leadership'. As a result, the PNM dropped from being on par with the UNC to holding only 15 lower house seats.

In a by-election in the new President's former Tobago constituency on 5 May, the controversial Morgan Job (a talk-show host and economist) won the seat comfortably for the NAR. In objection to Dr Job's candidacy, however, Pamela Nicholson MP resigned from the party (while remaining in the cabinet as an independent) and campaigned on behalf of a former NAR member standing as an independent. Moreover, Dr Job's subsequent appointment as Minister for Tobago Affairs caused a split between the Tobago and Trinidad arms of the NAR. Whereas the chairman of the NAR's Tobago steering committee supported the appointment, the party's newly-elected Trinidad-based leader, Nizam Mohammed (a former Speaker of the House but not presently an MP), claimed that it had not been sanctioned by the party and threatened to abandon the UNC-NAR coalition. Further problems were apparent in November, when a former NAR leader, Carson Charles, joined the UNC together with 30 supporters.

The Tourism and Industrial Development Corporation director resigned in April after being found guilty of corruption in the Piarco airport expansion. The chairman of the Airport Authority also resigned, whereas the Prime Minister refused the resignation of the Minister of Works. In July the government secured the passage of a bill—against PNM opposition—allowing the commissioner of police to stay past mandatory retirement age in order to finish overseeing the government's three-year campaign against crime. In December the PNM refused to debate the government's budget proposals, the first time an opposition party had done so.

In June the government reported a dispute with Venezuela to the Organization of American States. Between April and May three incidents involving Venezuelan coastguards interfering with Trinidadian citizens had provoked strongly-worded protests from Trinidad's Minister of Foreign Affairs. A meeting between Prime Minister Basdeo Panday and President Caldera of Venezuela in Caracas did little to ease the tension. Also in June, Trinidad and Tobago was listed by the UN Development Programme as having made most progress in poverty reduction among 78 developing countries.

One man was killed and 100 people were made homeless in a mud volcano eruption in February. George Chambers, who succeeded Eric Williams as Prime Minister in 1981, died on 4 November aged 69.

iv. BARBADOS

CAPITAL: Bridgetown   AREA: 430 sq km   POPULATION: 270,000 ('96)
OFFICIAL LANGUAGE: English   POLITICAL SYSTEM: parliamentary democracy
HEAD OF STATE: Queen Elizabeth II
GOVERNOR-GENERAL: Sir Clifford Husbands
RULING PARTY: Barbados Labour Party (BLP)
HEAD OF GOVERNMENT: Owen Arthur, Prime Minister (since Sept '94)
MAIN IGO MEMBERSHIPS (non-UN): OAS, SELA, ACS, Caricom, ACP, CWTH, NAM
CURRENCY: Barbados dollar (end-'97 £1=B$3.30,US$1=B$2.01)
GNP PER CAPITA: US$6,560 ('95) or US$10,620 ('95) by PPP calculation

IN May Barbados signed a 'ship-rider' agreement providing for anti-drugs cooperation with the United States on a similar basis to that provided for in the US-Jamaica accord concluded concurrently (see IV.1.1). The Barbadian government entered into the agreement after its concerns about infringement of sovereignty had been met by the banning of random patrols, the requirement of express prior permission, full US reciprocity covering the US Virgin Islands and Puerto Rico, and a specification that US nationals would have no immunity from any legal proceedings.

In an unusual development in April, an MP for the governing Barbados Labour Party (BLP) drew attention to what he claimed were growing links between the opposition Democratic Labour Party (DLP) and the government of Antigua and Barbuda. Relations had already been strained when Prime Minister Owen Arthur publicly criticized his Antiguan counterpart, Lester Bird, at the Caricom inter-sessional conference in February for suggesting the appointment of a DLP-associated candidate over a BLP nominee as the head of Caricom's regional negotiating machinery (RNM).

The budget introduced in March anticipated a 9.7 per cent increase in government expenditure in 1997/98. With foreign reserves at more than B$600 million, it was argued that the government could sustain a fiscal deficit of 3 per cent of GDP for increased spending on education, health and social security. In

January the DLP had refused to take part in parliamentary debate on the introduction of value-added tax, objecting that the measure had been rushed. In May new regulations concerning company takeover bids and plans for a new Securities Act were published. At the end of year the government announced that it planned to introduce a bill to curb money-laundering.

Sir John Dear, a member of the team that negotiated the independence of Barbados in 1966, died on 1 April.

v. BELIZE

CAPITAL: Belmopan   AREA: 23,000 sq km   POPULATION: 224,000 ('96)
OFFICIAL LANGUAGE: English   POLITICAL SYSTEM: parliamentary democracy
HEAD OF STATE: Queen Elizabeth II
GOVERNOR-GENERAL: Sir Colville Young
RULING PARTY: United Democratic Party (UDP)
HEAD OF GOVERNMENT: Manuel Esquivel, Prime Minister (since June '93)
MAIN IGO MEMBERSHIPS (non-UN): OAS, SELA, ACS, Caricom, ACP, CWTH, NAM
CURRENCY: Belize dollar (end-'97 £1=BZ$3.28, US$1=BZ$2.00)
GNP PER CAPITA: US$2,630 ('95) or US$5,400 ('95) by PPP calculation

IN local elections in March the opposition People's United Party (PUP) won all seven town councils for the first time in Belizean history. Prime Minister Manuel Esquivel of the United Democratic Party (UDP) responded by announcing major cabinet changes on 22 April, including the appointment of Alfredo Martínez as Trade and Industry Minister and of Rueben Campos to the newly-created Ministry of National Coordination and Mobilization. In July the government conducted a full re-registration of the electorate, under the supervision of observers of the Organization of American States.

On 28 February the US government 'decertified' Belize on the grounds that it was failing to take adequate measures against drug-trafficking. Belize was, however, granted a 'vital national interest' waiver from the resultant US sanctions. A White House statement declared that 'corruption at the highest levels of government continues to be a notable problem'. Earlier that month the US authorities had requested the extradition of a Belizean consul-general's husband who had returned to Belize after being arrested in Canada on drugs-related charges.

In May a former PUP chairman of the Social Security Board was tried on corruption charges related to the privatization of the Belize Electricity Company. Two months later 22 police officers, including an assistant superintendent, were suspended pending disciplinary or criminal proceedings for misconduct in drugs-related cases. In November a passport-forgery seizure implicated a senior official in the Ministry of Foreign Affairs in an immigration scandal, similar to one that had surfaced in 1995. After Belize's largest prison escape in April, comprehensive improvements in the prison system were implemented.

In talks in Miami in February Belize and Guatemala discussed possible approaches to a solution of their territorial dispute, although without making any progress on the substantive issues. On 1 August a group of Taiwanese fired on two Belizean fishing boats, giving rise to protests in Belize over the granting of lobster-farming licences to a number of Taiwanese companies.

A state of emergency was declared in Belize City in June after a fire had left 100 families homeless and destroyed or badly damaged over 20 buildings.

vi. GRENADA

CAPITAL: St George's   AREA: 344 sq km   POPULATION: 98,000 ('96)
OFFICIAL LANGUAGE: English   POLITICAL SYSTEM: parliamentary democracy
HEAD OF STATE: Queen Elizabeth II
GOVERNOR-GENERAL: Sir Daniel Williams
RULING PARTY: New National Party (NNP)
HEAD OF GOVERNMENT: Keith Mitchell, Prime Minister (since June '95)
MAIN IGO MEMBERSHIPS (non-UN): OAS, SELA, ACS, Caricom, OECS, ACP, CWTH, NAM
CURRENCY: East Caribbean dollar (end-'97 £1=EC$4.43, US$1=EC$2.70)
GNP PER CAPITA: US$2,980 ('95)

AFTER much public dispute, Grace Duncan was removed from her posts as Minister of Health, Housing and Environment and Deputy Prime Minister on 16 July. The government claimed that in an interview the previous day she had made 'vulgar' comments by referring to Prime Minister Keith Mitchell as 'a little boy'. Once a close ally of Dr Mitchell, Ms Duncan had earlier been publicly accused by the Prime Minister of leaking cabinet information. She was replaced in the departmental posts by Roger Radix, the position of Deputy Premier being abolished.

In February a request was rejected for the release from prison on humanitarian grounds of Phyllis Coard and Colville (Kamau) McBarnette, who were serving life sentences for the 1983 murder of the then Prime Minister, Maurice Bishop. In the same context, plans were announced to set up a national commission to investigate the record of the 1979–83 New Jewel government headed by Mr Bishop. Praise for Cuba's 'immense role' in assisting Grenada's development between 1979 and 1983 was voiced by Dr Mitchell during a five-day visit to Cuba in April. An economic cooperation agreement was signed during the visit, the first by a Grenadian Prime Minister to Cuba since 1983.

Plans to work together against the government on major national issues were announced in May by five opposition parties, namely the National Democratic Congress (NDC), the Grenada United Labour Party (GULP), the Democratic Labour Party (DLP), the National Party (NP) and the Maurice Bishop Patriotic Movement (MBPM). The following month saw the launch of Grenada's eighth party, the Grenada Progressive Party (GPP), which aimed to recruit women and young people.

In April more than half of Petit Martinique's population of 800 clashed with armed police as they demonstrated against plans for a coastguard building to assist the government's anti-narcotics campaign.

Sir Eric Gairy, independent Grenada's first Prime Minister in 1974–79, died on 23 August, having not recovered from his stroke in 1996 (see XX: Obituary). He was given a state funeral.

vii. THE BAHAMAS

CAPITAL: Nassau   AREA: 14,000 sq km   POPULATION: 276,000 ('96)
OFFICIAL LANGUAGE: English   POLITICAL SYSTEM: parliamentary democracy
HEAD OF STATE: Queen Elizabeth II
GOVERNOR-GENERAL: Sir Orville Turnquest
RULING PARTY: Free National Movement (FNM)
HEAD OF GOVERNMENT: Hubert Ingraham, Prime Minister (since Aug '92)
MAIN IGO MEMBERSHIPS (non-UN): OAS, ACS, Caricom, ACP, CWTH, NAM
CURRENCY: Bahamas dollar (end-'97 £1=B$1.64, US$1=B$1.00)
GNP PER CAPITA: US$11,940 ('95) or US$14,710 ('95) by PPP calculation

IN the Bahamas' first-ever early elections, called on 14 March, the incumbent Free National Movement (FNM) led by Hubert Ingraham won a sweeping victory, taking 34 Assembly (lower house) seats on a 57 per cent vote share, the other six going to the opposition Progressive Liberal Party (PLP) led by Sir Lynden Pindling. The new Assembly was reduced from 49 to 40 seats, the constituencies having been redesigned to achieve a less unequal distribution of voters. Announced on 18 March, Mr Ingraham's new government included three new ministers, most of the other responsibilities being reshuffled. On 9 April Italia Johnson (FNM) was elected as the first woman Speaker of the House of Assembly.

The PLP's further defeat followed a commission of inquiry's finding in February that Sir Lynden had acted improperly in accepting US$750,000 from property developers during his chairmanship of the Bahamas Hotel Corporation in 1992 (when he had also been Prime Minister). The commission also found the Pindling government guilty of 'gross mismanagement' resulting in losses of US$46 million, although it recommended that no further action be taken against the former Prime Minister. Following the elections, Sir Lynden resigned as PLP leader and on 7 July announced his retirement from politics.

Unprecedented flooding and a tornado in June prompted the establishment of a disaster relief fund of US$5 million, which in turn forced a reallocation of earlier budget priorities. In October the closure of the Gulf Union Bank affected 2,200 Bahamian depositors and motivated the establishment of a depositors' insurance fund. A revival of GDP growth in 1996 to 4 per cent (after rates of under 1 per cent in 1994 and 1995) was maintained in 1997, mainly because of a buoyant tourism industry. Up to 5,000 new hotel rooms were projected for the period 1998–2002, an increase of approximately a third.

Diplomatic relations were established with China, those with Taiwan being accordingly discontinued, although the government hoped to maintain relations with the island. A group of 110 Haitian illegal immigrants were repatriated in May, bringing the total sent back in 1997 to 414. A further 500 Haitians were detained during a five-week period in July-August.

viii. WINDWARD AND LEEWARD ISLANDS

Antigua & Barbuda
CAPITAL: St John's   AREA: 440 sq km   POPULATION: 65,000 ('96)
OFFICIAL LANGUAGE: English   POLITICAL SYSTEM: parliamentary democracy
HEAD OF STATE: Queen Elizabeth II
GOVERNOR-GENERAL: Sir James B. Carlisle
RULING PARTY: Antigua Labour Party (ALP)
HEAD OF GOVERNMENT: Lester Bird, Prime Minister (since March '94)
MAIN IGO MEMBERSHIPS (non-UN): OAS, ACS, OECS, Caricom, ACP, CWTH
CURRENCY: East Caribbean dollar (see above)
GNP PER CAPITA: US$6,970 ('94)

Dominica
CAPITAL: Roseau   AREA: 750 sq km   POPULATION: 71,000 ('96)
OFFICIAL LANGUAGE: English   POLITICAL SYSTEM: parliamentary republic
HEAD OF STATE: President Crispin Sorhaindo (since Oct '93)
RULING PARTY: United Workers' Party (UWP)
HEAD OF GOVERNMENT: Edison James, Prime Minister (since June '95)
MAIN IGO MEMBERSHIPS (non-UN): OAS, ACS, OECS, Caricom, ACP, CWTH, Francophonie
CURRENCY: East Caribbean dollar (end-'97 £1=EC$4.43, US$1=EC$2.70)
GNP PER CAPITA: US$2,990 ('95)

St Christopher (Kitts) & Nevis
CAPITAL: Basseterre   AREA: 260 sq km   POPULATION: 41,500 ('96)
OFFICIAL LANGUAGE: English   POLITICAL SYSTEM: parliamentary democracy
HEAD OF STATE: Queen Elizabeth II
GOVERNOR-GENERAL: Sir Cuthbert Sebastian
RULING PARTY: St Kitts-Nevis Labour Party (SKNLP)
HEAD OF GOVERNMENT: Denzil Douglas, Prime Minister (since July '95)
MAIN IGO MEMBERSHIPS (non-UN): OAS, ACS, Caricom, OECS, ACP, CWTH
CURRENCY: East Caribbean dollar (see above)
GNP PER CAPITA: US$5,170 ('95)

St Lucia
CAPITAL: Castries   AREA: 616 sq km   POPULATION: 160,000 ('96)
OFFICIAL LANGUAGE: English   POLITICAL SYSTEM: parliamentary democracy
HEAD OF STATE: Queen Elizabeth II
GOVERNOR-GENERAL: Perlette Louisy
RULING PARTY: St Lucia Labour Party (SLP)
HEAD OF GOVERNMENT: Kenny D. Anthony, Prime Minister (since May '97)
MAIN IGO MEMBERSHIPS (non-UN): OAS, ACS, OECS, Caricom, ACP, CWTH, NAM
CURRENCY: East Caribbean dollar (see above)
GNP PER CAPITA: US$3,370 ('95)

St Vincent & the Grenadines
CAPITAL: Kingstown   AREA: 390 sq km   POPULATION: 113,000 ('96)
OFFICIAL LANGUAGE: English   POLITICAL SYSTEM: parliamentary democracy
HEAD OF STATE: Queen Elizabeth II
GOVERNOR-GENERAL: Sir David Jack
RULING PARTY: New Democratic Party (NDP)
HEAD OF GOVERNMENT: Sir James F. Mitchell, Prime Minister (since July '84)
MAIN IGO MEMBERSHIPS (non-UN): OAS, ACS, OECS, Caricom, ACP, CWTH
CURRENCY: East Caribbean dollar (see above)
GNP PER CAPITA: US$2,280 ('95)

IN ANTIGUA & BARBUDA, the arrival of some 3,000 displaced Montserratians (see IV.4.ix) put the country's social facilities under considerable strain in 1997. In February the government was reported to have decided to close down five out of six Russian offshore banks suspected of money-laundering for the Russian mafia. The following month the opposition Barbuda People's Movement (BPM) won all nine seats in Barbuda council elections. The UK government confirmed that biological warfare tests were carried out off the coast of Antigua in 1948, agreeing to forward relevant files from the UK Ministry of Defence. The first permanent ambassador to Cuba was appointed in July.

In early December Molwyn Joseph was reappointed to the government as Minister of Planning and Implementation, some 14 months after his resignation as Finance and Social Security Minister in the wake of a car importation scandal (see AR 1996, p. 188). Later in the month, political opposition to a planned Malaysian-owned tourist island culminated in the Prime Minister's brother, Vere Bird Jr., being shot in the jaw during negotiations for the relocation of the island's sole resident couple. A former minister, Mr Bird had been barred from public office in 1990 because of his alleged involvement in illegal arms dealing.

In DOMINICA, the police commissioner, his deputy and five other officers were sent on leave in November following an investigation into corruption in the force. A constitutional report was commissioned for publication in 1998.

In ST KITTS & NEVIS, elections to the Nevis Assembly on 24 February resulted in the separatist Concerned Citizens' Movement (CCM) winning three of the five elective seats, against two for the Nevis Reformation Party (NRP), which also favoured secession. Despite regional diplomatic efforts to preserve the federation, on 13 October the Nevis Assembly voted unanimously in favour of secession and the holding of an independence referendum in 1998, in which a two-thirds majority of voters would be required. The island's Premier, Vance Amory (CCM), noted that Nevis provided two-fifths of the federation's tax revenue while receiving only one-fifth of public expenditure, and suggested that an independent Nevis could rely on tourism and offshore banking. In the United States, official concern was expressed that drug-cartel criminals had penetrated 'to the highest levels' in both Nevis and St Kitts.

Earlier, the establishment of a St Kitts-Nevis Defence Force was authorized, mainly to counter drug-trafficking. On 5 December the leader of the opposition People's Action Movement (PAM), Hugh Heyliger, was arrested and charged with contempt for failing to testify at an investigation of alleged official corruption during the 1980–1995 PAM administration.

In general elections in ST LUCIA on 23 May the opposition St Lucia Labour Party (SLP) led by Kenny Anthony won 16 of the 17 Assembly seats against only one for the United Workers' Party (UWP), which had governed almost continuously since 1964. The outgoing Prime Minister and UWP leader, Vaughan Lewis, failed to retain his own seat, announcing his retirement from politics in June. Dr Anthony immediately called for the resignation of all members of statutory corporations and made a number of novel non-political appointments, notably that of Perlette Louisy as St Lucia's first woman Governor-General. Sworn in on 26 May, his government included the former leader of the now defunct Progressive Labour Party, George Odlum, who became Minister of Foreign Affairs and International Trade. In November Dr Anthony introduced a supplementary budget to 'breathe new life into the economy' by the imposition of drastic cuts in government expenditure.

The founder of the SLP, Vincent Cato, who had led the country to full independence in 1979, died on 10 February aged 81.

The Prime Minister of ST VINCENT AND THE GRENADINES, Sir James Mitchell, lashed out at the US media early in the year after two programmes had accused the local authorities of corruption in a murder trial of two US citizens. In May Sir James took the opportunity to discuss the case (which was eventually dismissed) with President Clinton at the Caricom summit in Barbados (see also XI.5.iv). Later in the year a member of the opposition United Labour Party was dismissed as managing director of East Caribbean Flour Mills after 'serious potential improprieties' were reported by auditors.

ix. UK DEPENDENCIES

Anguilla
CAPITAL: The Valley   AREA: 96 sq km   POPULATION: 8,250 ('96)
OFFICIAL LANGUAGE: English   POLITICAL SYSTEM: representative democracy
GOVERNOR: Alan Poole
RULING PARTIES: Anguilla United (AUP) & Anguilla Democratic (ADP) parties
HEAD OF GOVERNMENT: Hubert Hughes (AUP), Chief Minister (since March '94)
MAIN IGO MEMBERSHIPS: OECS, Caricom (obs.)
CURRENCY: East Caribbean dollar (end-'97 £1=EC$4.43, US$1=EC$2.70)

Bermuda
CAPITAL: Hamilton   AREA: 53 sq km   POPULATION: 64,000 ('96)
OFFICIAL LANGUAGE: English   POLITICAL SYSTEM: representative democracy
GOVERNOR: Thorold Masefield
RULING PARTY: United Bermuda Party (UBP)
HEAD OF GOVERNMENT: Pamela Gordon, Prime Minister (since March '97)
MAIN IGO MEMBERSHIPS: Caricom (obs.)
CURRENCY: East Caribbean dollar (see above)

British Virgin Islands
CAPITAL: Road Town   AREA: 153 sq km   POPULATION: 18,000 ('96)
OFFICIAL LANGUAGE: English   POLITICAL SYSTEM: representative democracy
GOVERNOR: David MacKilligin
RULING PARTY: Virgin Islands Party (VIP)
HEAD OF GOVERNMENT: Ralph O'Neal, Chief Minister (since May '95)
MAIN IGO MEMBERSHIPS: OECS (assoc.), Caricom (assoc.)
CURRENCY: East Caribbean dollar (see above)

Cayman Islands
CAPITAL: George Town, Grand Cayman   AREA: 259 sq km   POPULATION: 32,000 ('96)
OFFICIAL LANGUAGE: English   POLITICAL SYSTEM: representative democracy
GOVERNOR: John Owen
MAIN IGO MEMBERSHIPS: Caricom (obs.)
CURRENCY: East Caribbean dollar (see above)

Montserrat

CAPITAL: Plymouth   AREA: 102 sq km   POPULATION: 4,000 ('96)
OFFICIAL LANGUAGE: English   POLITICAL SYSTEM: representative democracy
GOVERNOR: Frank J.Savage
HEAD OF GOVERNMENT: David Brandt, Chief Minister (since Aug '97)
MAIN IGO MEMBERSHIPS: OECS, Caricom, ACS
CURRENCY: East Caribbean dollar (see above)

Turks & Caicos Islands

CAPITAL: Cockburn Town   AREA: 430 sq km   POPULATION: 14,500 ('96)
OFFICIAL LANGUAGE: English   POLITICAL SYSTEM: representative democracy
GOVERNOR: John Kelly
RULING PARTY: People's Democratic Movement (PDM)
HEAD OF GOVERNMENT: Derek H. Taylor, Chief Minister (since Jan '95)
MAIN IGO MEMBERSHIPS: Caricom (assoc.)
CURRENCY: East Caribbean dollar (see above)

THE decision of the UK government in January to invoke its 'reserve powers' in an effort to bring the financial laws of all of its dependencies into line with domestic anti-money-laundering legislation provoked a generally negative reaction in Caribbean administrations which had not adopted such legislation. The then UK Foreign and Commonwealth Secretary, Malcolm Rifkind, explained that the government was prepared to use the reserve powers to enable governors to enact appropriate legislation if the local legislature failed to do so and if such legislation was necessary in the interests of 'public order, public faith or good government'. However, the Chief Minister of ANGUILLA, Hubert Hughes, accused London of 'blackmail' and of offering 'only one option [sic], either independence or serfdom'.

In BERMUDA, David Saul of the United Bermuda Party (UBP) was replaced as Prime Minister on 27 March by Pamela Gordon (hitherto Minister of Environment, Planning and National Resources), who became the colony's first woman head of government and also, at 41, the youngest. Three months later Lord Waddington retired as Governor, being succeeded by Thorold Masefield. Subsequently, the UK government agreed to undertake a one-year clean-up of oil pollution in caves which the Royal Navy had used as a dump for 50 years. In July foreign fast-food chains were banned from Bermuda, in the interests of maintaining the island's attractiveness to tourists. An MP of the opposition Progressive Labour Party resigned from the party after being convicted in October of sexual assault, remaining in the House of Assembly as an independent.

In the BRITISH VIRGIN ISLANDS, a minister was dismissed soon after speaking out against the UK government's 'reserve powers' policy announced in January (see above). A new criminal code was passed in April and a new prison was opened on 16 May. Willard Wheatley, who had been Chief Minister in 1971–79, died on 2 January aged 81.

In the CAYMAN ISLANDS, some 1,000 people staged the dependency's biggest-ever demonstration in March in protest against new taxes, fees and levies introduced to cover the record 25.4 per cent increase in expenditure in the 1997 budget. The government immediately announced the formation of an Economic Council in conjunction with the private sector to seek alternative revenue measures.

The Minister of Community Development, McKeeva Bush, was dismissed on 24 October after it was found that US$11 million had been fraudulently loaned by the recently-closed First Cayman Bank, where he was a salaried director.

Conditions on MONTSERRAT deteriorated dramatically in late June when another major eruption of the Soufrière Hills volcano (see AR 1995, p. 197; 1996, p. 191), followed by one from the Chance's Peak volcano, killed 19 people, destroying surrounding villages and causing damage estimated at US$33 million. The southern two-thirds of the island, including the capital, became uninhabitable, necessitating the evacuation of some 5,000 people, while many businesses and banks closed their Montserrat branches. By November the remaining population was estimated to number only some 4,000, less than half the figure of June 1995.

As conditions worsened, protests and demonstrations gathered strength in the remaining third of the island, focused on both the Montserrat authorities and on what was regarded as the inadequate response of the UK government to the crisis. On 21 August Bertrand Osborne resigned as Chief Minister and was replaced by David Brandt (an independent). There ensued a vitriolic public dispute over the aid and relief effort, in which the UK International Development Secretary, Clare Short, came in for particular criticism in Montserrat for what appeared to be her unsympathetic attitude. At one stage Mr Brandt declared: 'Effectively we are at war with the British government.' On 1–2 September, however, a visit by George Foulkes, the UK Under-Secretary for International Development, during which he pledged £48.5 million for a five-year sustainable development plan and £6.5 million in emergency housing aid, eased local anger somewhat. A Montserrat government report in December described conditions on the island as still 'appalling' and efforts to remedy them as totally inadequate, just stopping short of recommending total evacuation.

In the TURKS AND CAICOS ISLANDS, the dependency's rice mill was closed as a result of newly-introduced European Union (EU) rice import quotas designed to protect EU producers. A group of long-term prisoners was transferred from Montserrat to the Turks and Caicos in November.

x. SURINAME

CAPITAL: Paramaribo   AREA: 163,000 sq km   POPULATION: 428,000 ('96)
OFFICIAL LANGUAGE: Dutch   POLITICAL SYSTEM: republic
HEAD OF STATE: President Jules Wijdenbosch (since Sept '96)
RULING PARTIES: National Democratic Party (NDP) heads coalition
HEAD OF GOVERNMENT: Vice-President Pretaapnarain Radhakishum (BVD), since Sept '96
MAIN IGO MEMBERSHIPS (non-UN): OAS, SELA, AP, ACS, Caricom, ACP, NAM
CURRENCY: Suriname guilder (end-'97 £1=Sf657.92, US$1=Sf401.00)
GNP PER CAPITA: US$880 ('95) or US$2,250 ('95) by PPP calculation

THE Central Bank of Suriname warned on 19 March that two unregulated 'pyramid' savings schemes run by local trading companies, which had attracted millions of dollars from thousands of investors by offering monthly interest payments of 10 per cent, faced inevitable collapse in a situation described by one observer as a 'monetary time-bomb'. Three months later an announcement by one company that it could no longer pay interest sparked violent protest demonstrations and the looting of the supermarket owned by the company's head. The government called for an investigation in August.

On 25 August President Jules Wijdenbosch dismissed the Finance Minister, Motilal Mungra of the (Hindu) Movement for Renewal and Democracy (BVP), claiming that he had told lies about government policy, particularly presidential expenditures. His dismissal impelled the BVP and another small party to withdraw from the ruling coalition headed by the President's National Democratic Party (NDP), which was thereby reduced to minority status in the National Assembly. However, it subsequently rebuilt a working majority with smaller parties, while Tjan Gobardhan was appointed to the finance portfolio.

Politically-motivated violence continued to be a major problem. On 11 April the wife of the BVD vice-chairman was seriously injured by a parcel bomb, the first such incident in Suriname. After an hour-long gun battle in October, 17 people, including some military personnel, were arrested in connection with a suspected plot to overthrow the government. The armed forces commander attributed the incident to poor service conditions, lack of equipment and boredom.

On 19 March President Wijdenbosch announced that Suriname would join forces with neighbouring countries to set up a multilateral organization to track down and prosecute drug-traffickers. A week earlier the government had cooperated with the Dutch authorities to introduce tighter drugs surveillance for flights from Suriname to the Netherlands. The Dutch government subsequently filed a formal request for the extradition of the former military dictator of Suriname, Desi Bouterse, on charges of smuggling drugs into the Netherlands. Col. (retd.) Bouterse was currently 'Councillor of State' in the Wijdenbosch administration.

Negotiations with the Caribbean Development Bank were completed in September under which Suriname became the first borrowing member outside the Commonwealth Caribbean. At the Caricom summit in June (see also XI.5.iv) Suriname signed an economic and technical cooperation agreement with Jamaica. President Wijdenbosch visited Indonesia in October, signing agreements on cooperation in agriculture, fisheries and other economic sectors.

xi. NETHERLANDS ANTILLES AND ARUBA

Netherlands Antilles
CAPITAL: Willemstad (Curaçao)   AREA: 800 sq km   POPULATION: 200,000 ('96)
OFFICIAL LANGUAGES: Dutch, Papiamento, English
POLITICAL SYSTEM: parliamentary, under Dutch Crown
GOVERNOR: Jaime M. Saleh
RULING PARTIES: Antillean Reconstruction Party (PAR) heads coalition
HEAD OF GOVERNMENT: Miguel Pourier (PAR), Prime Minister (since March '94)
CURRENCY: Neth. Antilles guilder (end-'97 £1=Naf2.94, US$1=NAfl.79)
GNP PER CAPITA: n/a

Aruba
CAPITAL: Oranjestad   AREA: 193 sq km   POPULATION: 70,000 ('96)
OFFICIAL LANGUAGE: Dutch
POLITICAL SYSTEM: parliamentary, under Dutch Crown
GOVERNOR: Olindo Koolman
RULING PARTIES: Aruban People's Party (AVP) & Aruban Liberal Organization (OLA)
HEAD OF GOVERNMENT: Jan Hendrick (Henny) Eman (AVP), Prime Minister (since July '94)
CURRENCY: Aruba guilder (end-'96 £1=Af2.94, US$1=Afl.79)
GNP PER CAPITA: n/a

IN the NETHERLANDS ANTILLES, the rice industry was threatened in January by a newly-introduced European Union (EU) quota on the importation of duty-free rice from the overseas countries and territories (OCTs) linked to the EU under the Lomé Convention. The Dutch government, current holder of the EU presidency, was criticized for not using its veto to block the decision and for not consulting the Netherlands Antilles, whose Prime Minister, Miguel Pourier, officially registered dissatisfaction with The Hague. The employees of the state-controlled airline ALM initiated strike action in April, prompting the government to suspend operations and to implement a restructuring plan. A devastating fire at the end of July occurred in the Curaçao oil refinery operated by Petroleos de Venezuela, one of the plant's two towers being damaged beyond repair.

Legislative elections in ARUBA on 12 December produced no change in the *Staten*, the Aruban People's Party (AVP) again winning 10 seats, the People's Electoral Movement (MEP) 9 and the Aruban Liberal Organization (OLA) 2. The AVP-OLA coalition, whose collapse in October had precipitated the elections, was not thought likely to be re-established because of the AVP's support for US extradition applications against the powerful Mansur family—who were prominent OLA supporters—on drug-trafficking and money-laundering charges.

In April the Tourism Minister told a conference in the Bahamas that tourism accounted for 35 per cent of total employment in Aruba. Since the launch of the country's tourism plan in 1986, unemployment had been reduced from 40 per cent to zero by 1990, since when full employment had been maintained.

xii. US DEPENDENCIES

Puerto Rico
CAPITAL: San Juan   AREA: 9,103 sq km   POPULATION: 3,700,000 ('96)
OFFICIAL LANGUAGES: Spanish & English
POLITICAL SYSTEM: democratic commonwealth
GOVERNOR: Pedro Rossello
RULING PARTY: New Progressive Party (PNP)
CURRENCY: US dollar (end-'97 £1=$1.64)

US Virgin Islands
CAPITAL: Charlotte Amalie   AREA: 342 sq km   POPULATION: 105,000 ('96)
OFFICIAL LANGUAGE: English POLITICAL SYSTEM: democratic dependency
GOVERNOR: Roy Schneider (independent)
CURRENCY: US dollar (see above)

THE US House resources committee on 21 May approved the Status Plebiscite Bill providing for another referendum in the Commonwealth of PUERTO RICO on the island's status. In the last referendum in 1993, the Commonwealth option had won 48.4 per cent of the vote, statehood 46.2 per cent and independence 4.4 per cent. Local reaction to the bill included criticism of a clause enjoining that if statehood were chosen the island's only official language would be English. In May Puerto Rican teachers rejected a proposal from the Education Department to replace Spanish with English as the medium of instruction in state schools. In November a landmark Supreme Court ruling recognized Puerto Rican citizenship as distinct from US citizenship.

Governor Pedro Rossello was sworn in for a second four-year term on 2 January, following his re-election in November 1996 (see AR 1996, p. 195). The February budget projected a 3.1 per cent increase in expenditure, although more than half the 145 government agencies were to have their budgets cut. A bill authorizing the privatization of the Puerto Rico Telephone Company provoked a one-day strike by 100,000 government employees on 10 October. The government also declared that it would sell its health centres in 11 areas. In July an additional $170 million was allocated for improving the police services.

In San Juan, the capital, nearly half a million people were affected by water-rationing in June and July. In June lack of water in fire hydrants resulted in a fire destroying almost 30 houses.

In the US VIRGIN ISLANDS, 25 people including a US customs inspector were arrested or indicted in late October in an operation against a ring trafficking in drugs, weapons and currency. Alcoa World Alumina & Chemical announced that it would reopen its operations in St Croix, which had been closed in 1994.

V MIDDLE EAST AND NORTH AFRICA

1. ISRAEL

CAPITAL: Jerusalem   AREA: 22,000 sq km   POPULATION: 5,650,000 ('96)
OFFICIAL LANGUAGE: Hebrew   POLITICAL SYSTEM: parliamentary democracy
HEAD OF STATE: President Ezer Weizman (since March '93)
RULING PARTIES: Likud-Gesher-Tsomet alliance heads coalition with Shas, National Religious Party, Yisrael Ba-Aliya, Third Way & United Torah Judaism
HEAD OF GOVERNMENT: Binyamin Netanyahu (Likud), Prime Minister (since June '96)
CURRENCY: new shekel (end-'97 £1=NSh5.82, US$1=NSh3.55)
GNP PER CAPITA: US$15,920 ('95) or US$16,490 ('95) by PPP calculation

THE year was a difficult one for Israel. The peace process with the Palestinians effectively ground to a halt (see also V.2.i). Relations with Jordan, which had been marked by the warm personal ties between King Husain and Israel's late Prime Minister, Yitzhak Rabin, turned decidedly frosty (see also V.2.iii). The death toll of Israeli soldiers in southern Lebanon continued to mount (see also V.2.v). On the domestic front, moreover, the government staggered from one crisis to the next, with many ministers in the ruling coalition openly expressing their lack of confidence in the leadership of Binyamin Netanyahu. Even the celebrations marking the opening of the 15th Maccabiah Games in July were marked by tragedy when a pedestrian bridge in the Ramat Gan stadium collapsed, resulting in the deaths of four Australian athletes.

The year started on a seemingly positive note for the peace process between Israel and the Palestinians. After several months of protracted negotiations during the latter part of the previous year (see AR 1996, pp. 200–1, 204–5), Israel and the Palestinians finally signed an agreement on 15 January which provided for the redeployment of Israeli troops in the West Bank town of Hebron. Whilst this redeployment had been stipulated in the 'Oslo II' accords signed by the previous Israeli government, the Hebron agreement held a particular symbolic significance since it marked the first agreement signed between the new Likud-led government of Mr Netanyahu and the Palestinian Authority. There was widespread optimism that this agreement would serve as a catalyst and put the stalled peace process back on track. Indeed, the agreement did not focus exclusively on the modalities of Israeli redeployment in Hebron but also laid out a timetable for further pullbacks of Israeli troops from the West Bank in addition to a series of further confidence-building measures, such as the opening of a safe passage between the West Bank and Gaza and the opening of air and sea ports in Gaza. The aim was to move the peace process forward on the basis of a commitment to resume 'final-status' negotiations within two months of the completion of the Hebron withdrawal.

Such optimism proved to be ill-founded and short-lived. Before the ink had time to dry on the Hebron agreement, the peace process soon suffered a blow from which it failed to recover throughout the remainder of the year. Mr Netanyahu succeeded by only the narrow margin of 11 votes to seven in getting the

Israeli cabinet to approve the Hebron deal. Indeed, Benny Begin, the son of former Israeli Prime Minister Menachem Begin, immediately resigned as Minister of Science in protest. In order to keep his fragile coalition together, the Prime Minister needed to make a gesture to appease its more right-wing elements. In a highly controversial move, the Israeli government announced at the end of February that it would start building a new Jewish settlement at Har Homa/ Jabal Abu Ghneim in Arab East Jerusalem. Although the construction of Jewish housing in Jerusalem was not strictly forbidden under the terms of the Oslo agreements, such a move was seen as undermining the spirit of those agreements, in that the two sides had agreed that the status of Jerusalem would be determined by the final-status talks. By unilaterally embarking on the construction of a new Jewish settlement, the Israeli government was therefore widely perceived as trying to create 'new facts' on the ground and thereby pre-empting the outcome of any negotiations over the future of the city.

In spite of widespread criticism from the Palestinians and the Arab world, and the near universal condemnation of the international community, the Israeli government would not be deflected from its decision. The start of the building at Har Homa in early March brought an effective halt to talks between Israel and the Palestinians and led to a further deterioration in Israel's relations with the Arab world. The Egyptian President, Husni Mubarak, declared that the new construction heralded the beginning of a new era of violence in the region, whilst Jordan's King Husain wrote to Mr Netanyahu declaring that his actions were destroying the peace process and that he was rapidly losing confidence in his leadership.

The King's letter to Mr Netanyahu reflected growing discontent within Jordan with the peace process and a distinct cooling in relations between the two countries. The disclosure of the letter and the public rift between the two leaders was quickly overshadowed by an unprovoked attack by a Jordanian soldier on 12 March on a group of Israeli teenage schoolgirls, seven of whom were killed and six wounded. The shooting took place at Nayarayim, a small enclave between Israel and Jordan on the banks on the river Jordan which had been leased to Jordan by Israel as part of the Israel-Jordan peace treaty. Two days later, in a moving act of public contrition, King Husain visited Israel to pay his personal condolences to the families of the bereaved.

King Husain's gesture won him widespread admiration in Israel, reinforcing the high personal esteem in which he was held by the Israeli population. But the shooting of the schoolgirls did not bring an end to the emerging rift in relations between the two countries. At the beginning of May a planned meeting between Mr Netanyahu and Crown Prince Hasan of Jordan at the site of the shooting in Nayarayim was cancelled by Jordan because of an absence of agreement over the allocation of fresh water to be supplied to Jordan by Israel—a dispute settled only after a secret meeting between King Husain and Mr Netanyahu. Relations deteriorated further on 22 September, when gunmen opened fire and wounded two Israeli embassy security guards in Amman. But worse was to follow. On 25 September Israeli Mossad agents were arrested in Amman following a bungled assassination attempt on the life of Khalid Masha'al, the head of the Hamas political bureau in Jordan. The failed attack in broad daylight on Jordanian soil caused outrage and brought relations between the two countries to crisis point. King Husain publicly vented his anger with Israel and threatened to break off diplomatic relations. The crisis was only defused by the release from gaol in Israel of the founder and spiritual leader of Hamas, Shaikh Ahmad Yasin, together with a number of Palestinian and Jordanian political prisoners, who were flown to Amman on 1 October and made a triumphant return to Gaza one week later.

Suicide terrorist attacks by Islamic extremists against civilian targets in Tel Aviv and Jerusalem featured again in 1997. In March a bomb exploded at the Apropos café in Tel Aviv on the Jewish festival of Purim, killing three young women. At the end of July two suicide bombers exploded devices in the Mahane Yehuda market in Jerusalem, killing 14 Israelis and leaving over 150 injured from the blast. At the beginning of September a similar double suicide attack took place in Jerusalem in the crowded downtown Ben Yehuda pedestrian mall, killing four Israelis and injuring nearly 200 people. The response of the Israeli government to the two latter attacks was swift and punitive, the Palestinian Authority being held responsible for failing to prevent them. Demanding that the Authority take effective action against Hamas and other Islamic rejectionist groups, the Israeli government announced the immediate suspension of any contacts and the postponement of all talks with Palestinian officials. These measures were matched by an internal and external closure of the Palestinian self-rule areas, preventing Palestinians from travelling between the towns of the West Bank and also from working in Israel. The Israeli government also decided to suspend the transfer of tax revenues owed to the Palestinian Authority until it was satisfied that effective measures were being taken to curb terrorist activities against Israeli civilian targets. The measures were amongst the harshest to have been imposed against the Palestinians in the aftermath of terrorist attacks and drew widespread criticism from the international community for the economic hardship they caused for the Palestinian population in the West Bank and Gaza.

Israel's ongoing conflict with Hizbullah guerrillas in southern Lebanon continued to take its toll of Israeli lives (see also V.2.v). In February two military helicopters ferrying troops and ammunition under cover of darkness to the Israeli security zone collided and crashed just before they crossed the Lebanese border, all 73 personnel on board being killed. The accident, the worst recorded in Israeli military history, left the country reeling in shock. In September an Israeli military operation involving an elite naval commando unit ended in disaster when it was ambushed: 12 soldiers died, the highest casualty toll sustained by Israel in any single operation in Lebanon since 1985. This failed operation followed a similar incident at the end of August, when four soldiers of the elite Golani infantry brigade had burned to death after they, too, had been ambushed whilst on patrol in southern Lebanon.

The increasing death toll of Israeli soldiers led to growing disquiet amongst the Israeli public over the military presence in southern Lebanon and increasing public debate about policy on Lebanon. In November the Movement for Peaceful Withdrawal from Lebanon, comprising many prominent political figures, was launched with the aim of pressuring the government to abandon its policy of maintaining a security zone in southern Lebanon and unilaterally to pull Israeli troops back to the international border.

On the domestic front, it was a difficult year for Mr Netanyahu. His problems stemmed from the fact that he presided over a coalition comprising eight parties, each with its own agenda and set of concerns. They were compounded by the lack of confidence of several of his coalition partners, as well as many within his own Likud party, in his leadership qualities. Following Benny Begin's departure from the government in January over the Hebron agreement, other ministers regularly threatened to resign, and some did so. In August Dan Meridor resigned as Finance Minister, announcing that he had lost all confidence in the Prime Minister, while Foreign Minister David Levy was close to leaving the government in the summer because of what he claimed was the absence of any meaningful consultation by Mr Netanyahu and the stagnation in the peace process. Mr Levy repeated his threat at the end of the year during the discussions surrounding the government budget for the forthcoming financial year.

Mr Netanyahu's severest challenge came at the start of the year when the country was rocked by allegations of improprieties in the appointment on 10 January of Roni Baron, a little-known lawyer and a member of Likud's central committee, as the country's new Attorney-General. Mr Baron resigned within 12 hours, after his appointment had been greeted with astonishment by the legal profession amid claims about his unworthiness for the post. Twelve days later Israeli television news alleged that Mr Baron had been appointed to ensure that Shas (the largest ultra-orthodox party in the ruling coalition) would support the Hebron agreement, in return for a promise that Aryeh Deri, the Shas leader and former Minister of Interior, who was on trial for charges of bribery and fraud, would be offered an attractive plea bargain by the new Attorney-General. These allegations resulted in a two-month investigation by the police, who made the unprecedented recommendation that Mr Netanyahu should be indicted for 'breach of trust' over the Baron affair, together with Tzachi Hanegbi, the Minister of Justice, and Avigdor Lieberman, the director-general of the Prime Minister's office and one of his closest aides. Notwithstanding the police recommendations, however, Mr Baron's successor as Attorney-General, Elyakim Rubinstein, announced on 20 April that no charges would be filed on the grounds that there was insufficient evidence of criminal wrongdoing. At the same time, the report issued by Mr Rubinstein was highly critical of the government's decision-making procedures, describing Mr Netanyahu's behaviour over the appointment of Mr Baron as 'puzzling and bewildering'.

The year also witnessed a changing of the guard in the leadership of the opposition Labour Party. Following his defeat at the polls in May 1996, Shimon Peres finally stood down as Labour leader, his decision marking the end of a long and distinguished political career. In internal party elections on 3 June,

Ehud Barak, a former army chief of staff, won a clear victory in the first round of voting over the three other candidates—namely Yossi Beilin (one of the key architects of the 1993 Oslo peace accords), Shlomo Ben Ami (Israel's first ambassador to Spain) and Ephraim Sneh (a former Minister of Heath)—securing just over 50 per cent of the total votes cast.

On 17 April Israel's sixth President and former head of military intelligence, Chaim Herzog, passed away aged 78 (see XX: Obituary).

2. ARAB WORLD AND PALESTINIANS—
EGYPT—JORDAN—SYRIA—LEBANON—IRAQ

i. THE ARAB WORLD AND THE PALESTINIANS

THE future of the Israeli-occupied territories (OT) dominated attention. Israel continued to undermine the 1993 Oslo framework agreement by deepening Jewish colonization. The Palestinian National Authority (PNA), under the ageing Yassir Arafat, had simultaneously to face hard-line Israelis and Arab rejectionists. No solution or compromise on Jerusalem was in sight.

Israeli and Palestinian representatives met on 15 January to consider Hebron, an Arab city with biblical appeal. Assisted by King Husain of Jordan, they decided that Palestinian police should largely replace Israeli forces and that a planned Israeli withdrawal from the West Bank should be advanced from May 1999 to mid-1998. Under US encouragement, the two sides agreed to continue the peace process: Israel undertook to deploy further out of the West Bank, release some Palestinian prisoners and resume negotiations (on Gaza port and airport, for example), while the Palestinians said that they would revise their National Charter—but did not in 1997—and promised to counter Palestinian violence.

Mr Arafat was soon forecasting the declaration of an independent Palestine by mid-1998. Israel's Prime Minister, Binyamin Netanyahu, responded by issuing the first of many threats to reoccupy all the West Bank. The Palestinian leader hurriedly denied any intention of declaring Palestinian statehood before a permanent settlement had been reached.

Israeli-Palestinian agreement on Jerusalem had always looked remote. Now the Israelis, in contravention of the Oslo provision that the status of the city should be left to the very last, launched another large settlement in east Jerusalem. President Clinton voiced his disapproval of the Jerusalem building, but on 7 March the US representative at the UN Security Council vetoed a resolution opposing it. Condemned by the UN General Assembly, Israel's action provoked Mr Arafat, unmollified by simultaneous Israeli permission for Arab building, to break off negotiations. The US mobile negotiator, Dennis Ross, could not break the deadlock. The Palestinians rejected Israeli compromise proposals— whereby, for example, negotiations on the final status of the OT would be advanced from 1999 to 1997—and declined Israeli offers to withdraw more rapidly if the Palestinians would reduce their presence in Jerusalem or do more to combat the increasing violence.

In March a Tel Aviv bomb killed three Israeli women. The following month violence and killings arose mainly from Palestinian indignation over the new Jewish buildings in Jerusalem. After Mr Clinton had urged Mr Netanyahu to revive the peace process, Mr Arafat on 8 April authorized a temporary renewal of contact to discuss security. Meanwhile, Arab Foreign Ministers meeting in Cairo in late March had proclaimed the severance of all contact with Israel except by Egypt and Jordan.

In mid-April Mr Arafat met David Levy, then still Israel's Foreign Minister, in the first high-level Israeli-Palestinian contact for some weeks. US participation in negotiations, said the Palestinian leader, was now essential. On 10 June Mr Netanyahu refused to delay Jewish building in Jerusalem and faced growing resistance to compromise from extremist colleagues. Meanwhile, violence resumed in Hebron and continued until mid-July, when the Palestinians agreed to deploy more police to keep order and the Israelis ended their siege and removed road blocks.

Neither Israel nor the PNA could prevent indiscriminate violence by suicidal rejectionists: in attacks on 30 July in Jerusalem and on 4 September in Tel Aviv a total of 22 people were killed by suicide bombers. The second incident neutralized any benefits from measures taken to restore confidence after the first. Many militants were arrested by Palestine police and all terrorism was emphatically condemned when Mr Arafat, King Husain and President Mubarak of Egypt met in Cairo.

Israeli repression suited the rejectionists: the immediate border closures, by putting thousands of Palestinians out of work, intensified resentment of Israeli occupation. However, on 25 September Israeli agents were—humiliatingly for the Israelis, providentially for the Palestinians— caught after attempting an assassination in Amman (see V.2.iii). As a result, Israel was forced by King Husain into various acts of clemency towards Palestinians.

On 8 October Mr Arafat and Mr Netanyahu had their first meeting for seven months, agreeing to meet regularly thereafter. 'Not a moment too soon', commented President Clinton, who received Mr Arafat and Shimon Peres (now in the Israeli opposition), while deferring a further meeting with Mr Netanyahu. The US Secretary of State, Madeleine Albright, publicly criticized Israel for building new settlements and witholding money due to the PNA.

Despite US pressure, new rounds of talks were unfruitful. Mr Netanyahu personally disliked the peace process and was hampered by disunity inside his cabinet and party (see V.1). Infrastructure Minister Ariel Sharon, in particular, was planning permanent Israeli 'security zones' in the OT which amounted to radical departures from the Oslo principles: the Palestinians would have no continuous area to administer, their towns and villages being separated from each other, surrounded by Jewish settlements and cut off from Jordan. Mr Netanyahu was reported in December as saying that 'Judaea and Samaria' (the West Bank) were 'part of Israel proper'.

Israeli-Palestinian discussions towards the end of the year centred on how far and how fast the OT should pass to the Palestinians. Mr Netanyahu pushed for a slower territorial hand-over than provided for under the Oslo framework, while promising in return to slow down settlement-building. The Oslo agreements, he contended, did not exclude more building in established Jewish settlements. He rejected the idea of a Palestinian state and repeatedly threatened, as before, to re-occupy all the OT if the Palestinians declared one. In December the Israeli Prime Minister told Mrs Albright that his cabinet needed more time to consider further Israeli withdrawals. After also meeting Mr Arafat, the US Secretary of State announced that further talks would take place in 1998.

The Palestinians maintained their claim to Jerusalem, where they attempted their own census of the estimated 180,000 Arab inhabitants, while Israel hurriedly legislated to make the exercise illegal. They also declared independence to be their ultimate intention and rejected Mr Netanyahu's scheme for proceeding at once to the last stage of the peace process.

Despite improvement in the Palestinians' standing abroad (highlighted in December when Mr Arafat received red-carpet treatment at the Tehran Islamic summit—see XI.2.iv), the credit of their administration at home was eroding. Regular brutality, extending to torture and murder, was perpetrated by Palestinian policemen, particularly on those suspected of collaboration—by selling land to Jews, for example. Nor did the Palestinian system provide, like the Israeli, checks on abuses of power. Some Palestinian policemen were accused of attacking Israeli settlements.

A committee set up to investigate the misuse of $326 million of government funds found corruption endemic in all ministries and recommended the PNA's dissolution and replacement by professionals. The legislature then called by 51 votes to four for the executive's dissolution. Sixteen ministers offered their resignations, which Mr Arafat would not accept.

At the beginning of the year Israel owed the PNA an estimated $12 million net. After the summer's major terrorist attacks the Israelis stopped payment and pressed European governments, unsuccessfully, to follow suit. Repayment was again halted by the second big terrorist attack in September (although it resumed later). Most seriously on that occasion, the Israeli authorities prevented Palestinian workers from travelling to their jobs in Israel. Although the PNA received regular subventions from Europe, the Gulf states (especially Saudi Arabia) fell behind with their promised payments. Even before Israel's restrictions on migrant labour, unemployment in the OT had doubled and per caput income had fallen sharply.

Mr Arafat continued to travel incessantly but showed signs of wear. He was reported to have blacked out during more than one meeting, ascribing this to the after-effects of his serious air accident in Libya in 1992 (see AR 1992, p. 209). Born in 1929, he had been the Palestinian leader since 1969.

ii. EGYPT

CAPITAL: Cairo   AREA: 1,000,000 sq km   POPULATION: 61,500,000 ('97)
OFFICIAL LANGUAGE: Arabic   POLITICAL SYSTEM: presidential democracy
HEAD OF STATE & GOVERNMENT: President Mohammed Husni Mubarak (since '81)
RULING PARTY: National Democratic Party (NDP)
PRIME MINISTER: Kamal Ahmad Ganzuri (since Jan '96)
MAIN IGO MEMBERSHIPS (non-UN): AL, OAPEC, OAU, OIC, NAM
CURRENCY: Egyptian pound (end-'97 £1=E£5.57, US$1=E£3.39)
GNP PER CAPITA: US$790 ('95) or US$3,820 ('95) by PPP calculation

APPARENTLY brighter prospects were disastrously clouded in November when Islamic terrorists killed over 60 foreign sightseers in one day, shattering Egypt's vital tourist trade. Abroad, Israeli intransigence undermined President Husni Mubarak's efforts to promote the Arab-Israeli peace process. These developments overshadowed economic progress and a new scheme to bring fresh areas under cultivation. The government remained inflexible when faced with opposition.

Fundamentalist terrorism was not abating. An armed attack on the President in early February might have been an isolated criminal enterprise: but only days later one of the recurrent attacks on Copts in upper Egypt killed nine of them. It was soon claimed by the Jama'at al Islamiyya, whose 1996 ceasefire offer had been rejected (see AR 1996, p. 206). The Ministry of Awqaf (Religious Endowments) promised a five-year anti-Jama'at campaign to bring all mosques and preachers under its control.

Terrorist attacks occurred throughout the year, mostly in upper Egypt. On 18 September, in Cairo, nine Germans were shot, having apparently been mistaken for Israelis. The Jama'at leadership rejected an appeal by Jama'at prisoners that the movement should cease opposing the government and killing Copts. The troubles culminated on 17 November in slaughter at Luxor. Over 60 foreign tourists (mostly Swiss and Japanese but including some Britons) and four Egyptians were shot by a Jama'at group. President Mubarak rushed down with the Interior Minister, General Mohammed al Alfi, whom he immediately and humiliatingly replaced. The Jama'at later attributed the killing to younger members acting independently, pledging that it would not attack tourists again. Meanwhile, tourism dried up: the Economics Minister forecast that Egypt would have lost $500 million by mid-1998.

Six days later President Mubarak attacked Britain for its tolerance of Islamic groups who used London as a base for subversion in the Arab world. Over £2 million had, allegedly, been sent from London to the Jama'at; sermons in British mosques had advocated the assassination of Arab leaders; and Britain had refused to extradite those responsible. In response, the British ambassador in Cairo explained that Britain was examining ways of controlling the London activities of Middle Eastern exiles.

Faced with such terrorist fanatics, the Egyptian government mainly targeted its overt opponents, particularly the Muslim Brotherhood, hundreds of whose members were arrested, and the opposition press. It went for professional associations (particularly journalists and lawyers) under Brotherhood influence, trying to prevent their meetings. On 17 May the Interior Minister warned against Brotherhood infiltration, and the government seemed resolved on purging Egyptian society of political Islam. In February the National Assembly had renewed legislation allowing detention without trial for another three years. Egypt's human rights association alleged that 16,700 political prisoners, mainly Islamists, were in prison, many without trial. The public prosecutor, Rija'a al Arabi, was given special powers over the press.

Kamal Ahmad Ganzuri remained Prime Minister throughout the year. In July he reshuffled his cabinet, concentrating more power in his own hands, dropping the woman Economics Minister (who was allegedly too closely connected with business) and replacing her with an experienced Copt, Yusuf Boutros-Ghali. Ten new provincial governors were appointed, notably in Alexandria and Minya. In local elections in April the government party won on a low poll.

President Mubarak concentrated his activity abroad, working hard, but with little success, on the intractable problem of Israel's continued occupation of Arab territory (see V.2.i). He was often on the move between North America, Europe and the Middle East; but it was still unclear how far Washington's Middle Eastern policy could free itself from pro-Israeli congressional influence. The Egyptian leader denounced the expansion of Jewish settlements and snubbed US attempts to bring Arabs and Israelis together at a November economic conference in Qatar. He still declined to follow US ostracism of Libya, which he visited in June; there were plans for a pipeline to carry Libyan crude oil to Egypt

The economy showed striking improvements and innovations. The drive to free the state from involvement in industry accelerated, although government retained a majority share in many privatized enterprises, particularly in the loss-making textile sector. By mid-1997 public-sector companies were showing profits 20 per cent higher than in 1996, much of the proceeds being earmarked for the early retirement of surplus labour. Private capital could now enter the aviation sector and operate without paying sales tax or customs duties.

There were two projects to extend cultivation beyond the overcrowded Nile valley and Delta. One, inaugurated by President Mubarak in January and costing an estimated $800 million, would eventually take Nile water, through a 420-kilometre canal, to a new agricultural area in the south-west. Another, partly financed by Kuwait, opened a canal under the Suez Canal to irrigate over 500,000 acres in Sinai and provide land for up to a million Egyptians.

Meanwhile, in the Delta and Nile valley, traditional land tenure was changed immediately and radically. Instead of the Nasser-era system of low fixed rents, landlords could now legally charge an economic rent or alternatively evict tenants and farm the land themselves, growing crops such as fruit that were more capital-intensive and lucrative than cotton. A government fund to help the peasants buy their own land appeared insufficient. The Brotherhood and the Islamist groups sided with the government, the left-wing Tajammu movement and the Nasserists with the peasants. People died in landlord-tenant clashes. The government strove to keep the peace and violence subsided.

Egypt's population had now reached 61.5 million but was growing at only 2.1 per cent annually. Illiteracy had fallen from 49.6 to 38 per cent. Urban population was now increasing 13 per cent faster than in the country, suggesting that townward migration was slowing. Inflation was only 5 per cent in 1997, economic growth being forecast at 5.5 per cent. External debt was only 50 per cent of GNP; but the lowish figure for average annual income per caput of $1,250 concealed a much lower figure—less than $600 for well over half the population.

iii. JORDAN

CAPITAL: Amman AREA: 97,000 sq km POPULATION: 5,200,000 ('96)
OFFICIAL LANGUAGE: Arabic POLITICAL SYSTEM: monarchy
HEAD OF STATE & GOVERNMENT: King Husain ibn Talal (since Aug '52)
PRIME MINISTER: Abdul Salam Majali (since March '97)
MAIN IGO MEMBERSHIPS (non-UN): AL, OIC, NAM
CURRENCY: dinar (end-'97 £1=JD1.63, US$1=JD0.71)
GNP PER CAPITA: US$1,510 ('95) or US$4,060 ('95) by PPP calculation

KING Husain faced familiar difficulties. The 1991 Gulf War had deprived Jordan of financial support from abroad. The population was divided between Palestinian townsmen and 'Transjordanian' peasants and Bedouin, the latter groups holding disproportionate power. Wanting an Arab nationalist policy which the country could not afford and irked by the government's rigidity, the Palestinians boycotted the November elections. Successful and attempted killings involving Israelis intensified anti-Israeli feeling.

Of Jordan's neighbours, Israel now had an intransigent right-wing government, while Syria disliked King Husain's pro-Western policy. Trade with Kuwait resumed but not diplomatic relations or migration. In January Lebanon released Iraqi diplomats accused of murdering a Jordanian and in December Iraq executed four Jordanian smugglers, whereupon Jordan recalled its chargé in Baghdad and demanded reductions in Iraq's Amman embassy.

King Husain did much to secure the Hebron agreement (see V.2.i) but failed to prevent Israel's planned expansion into Arab Jerusalem. On 12 March a Jordanian soldier on the frontier killed seven visiting Israeli children. King Husain hurried to Israel from Spain to tender his regrets, the soldier being later imprisoned for life.

A week later, on 19 March, King Husain unceremoniously replaced his Prime Minister, Abdul Karim Kabariti, with one of the latter's predecessors, Abdul Salam Majali (see AR 1995, p. 210). With unusual animus, the King accused the outgoing Prime Minister of weakness and immoderate ambition. Mr Kabariti, a Palestinian, reportedly thought that the King had gone too far in his expressions of sympathy over the Israeli schoolgirls' death.

Anti-Israeli feeling increased, and with it opposition to King Husain's policy. Some schoolboys were arrested for distributing anti-Israeli leaflets and a few days later the head of the businessmen's professional association urged Arabs to stop trading with Israel. The King himself regularly criticized Israeli behaviour in the occupied territories. He met President Clinton and Binyamin Netanyahu (Israel's Prime Minister) when in America in April for prostate surgery, but without result for the peace process. In June he attacked Mr Netanyahu for stalling and encouraged European intervention.

Israel's abstraction of more than its agreed share of Jordan water provoked strong protests from Prince Hasan in early May. A few days later, on 8 May, Mr Netanyahu agreed to supply Jordan with more water (25 million cubic metres per annum) and soon began to pump it.

The Israelis gave King Husain a weighty propaganda advantage on 25 September when their agents attempted to murder the Hamas representative in Amman, Khalid Masha'al. Possessing forged Canadian passports, the Israeli agents were arrested after a street attack on Mr Masha'al during which they injected him with poison. The Israelis' involvement was initially denied but a publicly indignant King Husain forced them to provide an antidote to the poison, with the result that Mr Masha'al survived. Under a bargain reached between Prince Hasan and Mr Netanyahu, the Israeli agents responsible were expelled in return for the release by Israel of 70 Palestinian prisoners, including the old, blind but influential Hamas founder, Shaikh Ahmad Yasin. The King did not meet the Israeli Prime Minister again for two months.

There was much popular resentment against Israel and disapproval of Jordan's links with it. In January thousands demonstrated against an Israeli trade fair, the local press association demanding a boycott. In May the press law was invoked to forbid abuse of the royal family and to ban opposition weeklies. Amid protests by journalists and trade unions, the government threatened to close professional associations, saying that their campaign against normalization with Israel was 'outside their proper sphere'. Shopkeepers were arrested for displaying anti-Israel posters.

In July the Muslim Brotherhood, Jordan's largest political organization, called a boycott of the November elections. The King dissolved parliament on 29 August. After he had personally met the Brotherhood leader on 24 July, it was announced that international observers would monitor the polling. But the boycott soon looked complete, with two former Prime Ministers joining it. The opposition denounced the peace treaty with Israel, besides attacking the electoral advantage given to rural over urban constituencies and the new law restricting press freedom.

The boycott cleared the ground for the government's mainly tribal supporters, who on 4 November won 62 of the 80 seats in the House of Representatives, the remaining 18 going to nationalist and left-wing candidates and to independent Islamists. Voting was heavier in the countryside than in the towns but average turnout was only 54 per cent, the lowest since 1989. The one woman in the outgoing House lost her seat. On 22 November the King appointed the new 40-seat Senate, which included ex-Prime Minister Kabariti but excluded

the two other former Prime Ministers who had campaigned against the elections.
Unemployment had become a serious difficulty since the mass return of Jordanians from Kuwait. In August measures were taken to reduce drastically the half-million foreign workers (mostly Egyptians). Proceeds from privatizations would now go to relieve poverty, and restrictions on foreign ownership of companies were to be eased. Foreign exchange reserves reportedly rose to three months' import bill cover, while government revenues were up by 40 per cent on 1996. On 24 November the government approved the 1998 budget, which allowed for a small deficit, to be covered by foreign aid.
Jordan found trade and financial relations with Iraq to be inescapable, the level of its trade with Israel having proved disappointing. An agreement in January provided for Jordanian imports of cheap Iraqi oil, while exports to Iraq under the UN's 'oil-for-food' deals (see V.2.vi) allowed some repayment of Iraq's debts. This trade also increased revenues at Aqaba, where port dues were halved in July.
As always, Jordan had to rely heavily on funds from abroad, to meet its current deficit and outstanding debts. In June the United States lent Jordan $100 million and found another $100 million for Jordan's social security and water supply by an equivalent cut in payments to Israel and Egypt. The IMF increased Jordan's credit facility in February by over 10 per cent, to $330.5 million, its vice-president praising Jordan's economic policies. The World Bank lent $30 million to improve camps for refugees from Kuwait, and the Paris Club of creditor countries wrote off another $63.4 million of Jordan's foreign debt.

iv. SYRIA

CAPITAL: Damascus   AREA: 185,000 sq km   POPULATION: 13,850,000 ('96)
OFFICIAL LANGUAGE: Arabic   POLITICAL SYSTEM: presidential
HEAD OF STATE & GOVERNMENT: President Hafiz al-Asad (since March '71)
RULING PARTY: Baath Arab Socialist Party
PRIME MINISTER: Mahmud Zuabi, Prime Minister (since Nov '87)
MAIN IGO MEMBERSHIPS (non-UN): AL, OAPEC, OIC, NAM
CURRENCY: Syrian pound (end-'97 £1=S£68.66, US$1=S£41.85)
GNP PER CAPITA: US$1,120 ('95)or US$5,320 ('95) by PPP calculation

PRESIDENT Hafiz al-Asad remained in control but was reported to be in declining health. His personal priorities—pan-Arab over domestic and economic affairs—still prevailed, strengthened by the new Israeli hard line and by increasing friction with Turkey. Both factors induced a rapprochement with Iraq and improved relations with Jordan. At home, criticism had only a moderate effect on the longstanding dirigiste economic policy which still discouraged potential foreign investors. Efforts were made to tackle Syria's large foreign debts.
Although the Israeli government repeatedly urged peace talks without prior conditions, Syria held fast to its position that Israel should honour its previous

readiness to discuss the return of the Golan (see AR 1995, p. 212). In February more Golan settlements were announced by the Israelis, who in July said that withdrawal was conditional on parliamentary approval by a (clearly unobtainable) two-thirds majority. In August President Asad told an Israeli Arab delegation that he thought a withdrawal unlikely while Binyamin Netanyahu remained Israel's Prime Minister. Meanwhile, the government regularly blamed Israel for anti-Syrian violence, including a bomb attack on a Damascus bus on 31 December in which 11 people died. In April Israel warned that Syria was acquiring gas warfare techniques.

Since hope of softening Israel's new hard line rested on US influence, Damascus was again ready for extensive discussions with Washington, mostly through its roving envoy, Dennis Ross. When Syria wanted to buy tank guns from South Africa, the Israelis raised the alarm and South Africa withdrew the offer under US pressure. In November, however, President Clinton's decision to remove Syria from the US list of countries deemed to be soft on drug-traffickers was seen by the Syrian press as a possible prelude to the removal of Syria from the list of countries with state complicity in terrorism.

Faced with growing tension with Israel and Turkey, Syria and its neighbours continued their rapprochement (see AR 1996, p. 210). In May a Syrian business delegation, seeking to profit by the partial lifting of the UN embargo on Iraq, visited Baghdad and signed preliminary agreements. On 2 June the Syrian-Iraqi frontier was opened for the first time for 18 years, enabling Iraqi businessmen to visit Damascus. The Foreign Minister, Abdul Khaliq Khaddam, argued that, although it was too soon to renew full relations, neighbouring states must help the Iraqi people. Syria was also keen to reopen the former IPC pipeline from Iraq, closed since 1982. Reconciliation influenced propaganda: Damascus and Baghdad stopped their reciprocal radio attacks and a similar arrangement was made with Amman. In another initiative, Syria invited Foreign Ministers from Egypt and the Gulf Cooperation Council (GCC) states to meet in Latakiyya on 26 June to study the formation of a common market.

At home, the President's health continued to be uncertain: his prostate had been operated on, but reports of grave illness were belied by his later activity. The death of his son Basil (see AR 1994, p. 230) had removed the most suitable successor but public praise by the Damascus Mufti of another son, Bashir al-Asad, confirmed him as a probable successor. Efforts were made to discourage other members of the family from exploiting their influence.

Financial anxieties continued, Syria being heavily indebted abroad. The president of the World Bank (IBRD) came in June to discuss Syrian debts of over $400 million. The government agreed to settle over five years, the first instalment being paid on 1 September. Saudi Arabia, which helped in negotiations with the IBRD, was reportedly arranging a settlement of $300 million owed to the Saudi-based Islamic Development Bank. In November the German government sent a delegation to discuss large debts, mostly to the former East German regime; the Syrians wanted to treat the East German debts separately but Bonn refused. Other debtors were not so fortunate; a Bulgarian firm was obliged to take payment in sorghum to settle a debt of $14 million. Businessmen were now freer to speak their minds and often did so. They criticized the government's failure to attract foreign investment, claiming that it was being discouraged by temporizing and by unreasonable refusals. Delay was also allegedly obstructing large projects put forward by the Arab Fund for Economic and Social Development and other bodies. Central bank figures showed that Syria's visible deficit was rising, as imports increased and exports remained almost stationary.

Oil companies had, like other potential investors, suffered from Syrian demands which made operations uneconomic. Nevertheless, the French oil company ELF signed an exploration and production agreement with Syria in February.

v. LEBANON

CAPITAL: Beirut   AREA: 10,000 sq km   POPULATION: 3,000,000 ('96)
OFFICIAL LANGUAGE: Arabic   POLITICAL SYSTEM: presidential, power-sharing
HEAD OF STATE & GOVERNMENT: President Elias Hrawi (since Nov '89)
RULING PARTIES: government of national unity
PRIME MINISTER: Rafiq Hariri, Prime Minister (since Oct '92)
MAIN IGO MEMBERSHIPS (non-UN): AL, OIC, NAM, Francophonie
CURRENCY: Lebanese pound (end-'97 £1=L£2,505.35, US$1=L£1,527.00)
GNP PER CAPITA: US$2,660 ('95)

THERE were no major changes affecting Lebanon in 1997. Syria retained its veto and Rafiq Hariri the premiership: a brush with between him and President Elias Hrawi was resolved. The government rejected Israel's persistent suggestions of a separate peace and for action against the Hizbullah movement, but Israel clung to its security zone (SZ) in southern Lebanon. Continuous fighting in the south cost lives on both sides. Lebanese Shias, including Hizbullah members, openly entered politics, while an unofficial Shia leader fanned discontent. The public deficit grew, the government being readier to cut expenditure than to raise taxes. Teachers struck again for more pay.

A total of 73 Israeli military personnel were killed on 4 February when two helicopters collided during a bungled raid in southern Lebanon. Desultory shooting continued in the south between the Iranian-supported Hizbullah and their Israel-supported opponents, the South Lebanese Army (SLA), Hizbullah attacks producing Israeli retaliation which killed civilians as well as guerrillas.

Violence increased in August with tit-for-tat attacks. On 18 August the SLA—acting, the Israelis claimed, without their knowledge—shelled Sidon, following which Hizbullah fighters fired ineffective rockets into Israel, which responded with heavier attacks. At one of its periodical meetings the international monitoring group (see AR 1996, p. 212) blamed Israel for attacking civilians and Hizbullah for bombarding Israel. On 5 September 12 Israelis died in an ambush. By year's end over 100 Israeli soldiers and Lebanese guerrillas, together with up to 50 civilians, had been killed since January. Irish soldiers of the UN Interim Force in Lebanon (UNIFIL) were wounded in June by Israeli-laid mines.

Some Israelis wanted to bargain an Israeli withdrawal from the SZ against an amnesty for the SLA, but no compromise seemed attainable with Binyamin Netanyahu as Prime Minister. The SLA's General Lahud offered to withdraw from Jezzine, a Maronite town north of the SZ, if the Lebanese army would garrison it, thus protecting the inhabitants from Hizbullah. But he opposed an Israeli withdrawal from the SZ: his men had worked with Israel for 20 years, he said, 600 having been killed. The Beirut government's position remained that, while Israel continued to occupy the SZ, it would not use troops to prevent Hizbullah fighters crossing the frontier (and they would not stop doing so of their own accord).

In January the government released Iraqi diplomats accused of murdering an anti-Iraqi Jordanian, causing indignation in Amman. Despite Japanese requests for their extradition, a batch of seasoned Japanese terrorists, arrested in the Beqa'a Valley, were freed in July. This was reportedly a Syrian decision rather than a Lebanese one, Syrian-controlled Beqa'a being a haven for such extremists.

The Pope visited Lebanon on 10–11 May, being met on arrival by the President and Prime Minister, and celebrated Mass for a huge congregation. He called for Christian-Muslim reconciliation and Lebanon's complete independence, regretting the presence of non-Lebanese forces on Lebanese territory, without mentioning Syria or Israel.

On 29 July the United States removed the 1987 ban on its citizens visiting Lebanon. In September Madeleine Albright, the new US Secretary of State, included Lebanon in her first Middle Eastern tour. Lebanon, she said, must recover sovereignty over all its territory, and she pledged US help towards economic reconstruction. She also urged the government to hold elections and free the press.

In the Beqa'a, a former leader of Hizbullah called for non-payment of taxes and denounced the ban on opium cultivation, for which promised compensation remained unpaid; the government, he alleged, was spending on infrastructure what was due to the poor. When he declared the Beqa'a closed to ministers, the army threatened to prosecute. In December he called off his blockade.

The government postponed till 1998 the municipal elections which had been repeatedly put off for political and security reasons. This fresh but limited postponement was to avoid friction between President and Prime Minister, the latter fearing that elections would engender conflict and thus alarm potential investors. In mid-October it was also agreed, on the insistence of Nabih Berri (Speaker of the National Assembly), and after the usual visits to Damascus, to prolong the existing parliament.

Following the 1996 attack on Syrian troops (see AR 1996, p. 212), an army court in March passed gaol sentences on militant followers of the exiled Maronite leader, Michel Aun, whose own death sentence was later commuted to life imprisonment. In April police arrested the trade union leader, Abu Rizq. The government's favoured substitute, though endorsed by the courts, could not control the situation. The ILO accused the government of undue interference and unlawful arrest. In September the government again attacked unlicensed broadcasting stations (see AR 1996, p. 213) and troops forcibly closed another station operated in Tripoli by a Sunni group: two men were killed. In October Amnesty International attacked Lebanon for human rights violations, which could no longer all be blamed on Syria.

Budget forecasts of rising revenue and falling expenditure proved optimistic: by July the domestic deficit was already an unacceptably large percentage of GDP and external debt had quadrupled since 1993. Every proposal to increase taxation was opposed by one powerful interest or another. Bankers protested at increased government borrowing, but in June the World Bank agreed to lend Lebanon $420 million. Mr Hariri's proposal to borrow $1,000 million abroad would have significantly raised public debt as a percentage of GDP and was rejected by the cabinet in September. However, Mr Berri's proposal to borrow $1,600 million abroad and $400 million from Lebanese banks was approved on 4 December. The balance of payments was kept positive, despite a rising visible deficit, by inward investment, but little reached industry and agriculture, so that there was a steady slowdown of the economy. Profits in the vast Solidaire project to rebuild Beirut (see AR 1994, p. 232) fell heavily from their 1996 level because of the delay between erecting buildings and getting rent for them.

vi. IRAQ

CAPITAL: Baghdad   AREA: 438,000 sq km   POPULATION: 20,000,000 ('96)
OFFICIAL LANGUAGE: Arabic   POLITICAL SYSTEM: presidential
HEAD OF STATE & GOVERNMENT: President Saddam Husain (since July '79), also Prime Minister
    & Chairman of Revolutionary Command Council
RULING PARTY: Baath Arab Socialist Party
MAIN IGO MEMBERSHIPS (non-UN): AL, OPEC, OAPEC, OIC, NAM
CURRENCY: dinar (end-'97 £1=ID1,968.84, US$1=ID1,200.00)
GNP PER CAPITA: n/a

PRESIDENT Saddam Husain again successfully defied Anglo-Saxon governments who wished, not always privately, for his overthrow. Others, less preoccupied with the Iraqi leader's alleged threat to peace, were increasingly unwilling to follow. Some of Saddam's neighbours—though more exposed to him— were also reluctant to toe the US-UK line. His ruthless regime was strengthened by continuing divisions among the Kurds, some of whom accepted his help in combating others. Despite hardships, the Iraqi people seemed unlikely by themselves to overthrow the regime.

The UN Security Council ruled that President Saddam must obey the UN resolutions of 1990–91 on disarmament before the boycott of Iraq's oil exports, relaxed in December 1996 (see AR 1996, p. 215), could be lifted. Iraq failed to satisfy the UN that it had genuinely abandoned all its unusual and proscribed weapons. Revelations made in Amman in 1996 by the brothers Kamil (see AR

1996, p. 214) to Rolf Ekeus, then the UN's man in Iraq, had opened his and other eyes, despite Baghdad's contrary assurances. The UN Special Commission on Iraq (UNSCOM) was thus not satisfied when in late April the Iraqi Foreign Minister, Tariq Aziz, told the Security Council that no banned weapons, or materials to make them, were now left. Meanwhile, limited oil exports continued haltingly.

The US government was loath to make peace with President Saddam or to resign itself to others' doing so, suggesting only that it would improve ties with a new government in Baghdad. In the Security Council, Washington could count on unqualified support only from Britain among the other permanent members. The Council declined to condemn Iraq for flying pilgrims to and from Jeddah, notwithstanding the embargo on Iraqi international flights. In early June the Iraqis themselves halted the flow of oil until August, being anxious to demonstrate their freedom of action and to exploit worldwide sympathy for the Iraqi people.

In October Richard Butler, who had succeeded Mr Ekeus at UNSCOM, accused Iraq of not accounting for its biological weapons and of impeding his officials. At the Security Council on 23 October, however, the United States and Britain accepted a compromise on anti-Iraq action. The Baghdad government then threatened to freeze relations with UNSCOM pending an end to the embargo unless all ten American members in the 40-member UN inspection team were removed, subsequently beginning to refuse entry to US members of the team. Lakhdar Brahimi of the UN failed to persuade the Iraqis to revoke the expulsions, and on 14 November the whole team left. Thus firmly challenged, Iraq retreated. On 20 November it rescinded its ban on the Americans, and the whole team promptly returned. President Saddam then insisted that his many palaces should be exempt from search but invited representatives of Security Council powers to visit them.

Other tensions concerned Iraqis making trips abroad, such as pilgrimages to Saudi Arabia. The US government, supported only by Britain, demanded anti-Iraq restrictions, but failed to carry others with them. France and Russia, owed billions by Iraq for arms purchases, were increasingly unwilling to follow. America's Middle Eastern friends and allies, such as Saudi Arabia, Turkey and even Kuwait, also hesitated to follow the US line.

In Kurdistan division between the Kurdish Democratic Party (KDP) and the Patriotic Union of Kurdistan (PUK) enabled Baghdad to play one off against the other. Outside powers, mainly the United States and Britain but also Egypt, repeatedly but vainly pressed the Kurds to unite. Meanwhile, the Turks reportedly secured Iraqi Kurdish complicity in fighting the Turkish Kurds. Turkish units twice occupied Iraqi territory in force. The Iranian-supported Islamic Movement in Iraqi Kurdistan (IMIK) also entered the fray, but with Baghdad's help the KDP was now dominant.

In common hostility to the United States and Turkey, Iraq and Syria now came together. The Syrian-Iraqi frontier was reopened on 2 June (see also V.2.iv) and both governments halted broadcasts hostile to each other, as did Iraq and

Jordan following their resumption of relations in May (see V.2.iii). The Iraq-Syrian rapprochement increased in opposition to Turkish plans for another dam, against which Iraq's Foreign Minister protested to the Arab League.

Iraq's differences with Turkey underlay a surprise reconciliation with Tehran. Though Iran had earlier been blamed for attacks on Iranian exiles in Iraq, in September Iraq opened the Iranian frontier for pilgrims to Kerbela, while Iran released Iraqi prisoners of war. At December's Tehran conference of the Organization of the Islamic Conference (see XI.2.iv) the Iranian Prime Minister offered reconciliation to Iraq.

Internally, little seemed changed. There was a routine cabinet reshuffle on 24 August and the usual unverifiable stories from exiles of executions of President Saddam's opponents. One exiled opposition leader admitted that the Iraqi leader was now stronger than before. The President's wayward son, Uday Husain, had by the summer somewhat recovered from being shot in December 1996 (see AR 1996, p. 214). Reported to have amassed a personal fortune of $5,000 million, Saddam erected a statue to his son-in-law, Husain Kamil, who had been murdered in February 1996 (no doubt with the President's approval).

Oil importers were systematically preparing to resume large-scale purchasing in the post-sanctions future, causing vehement protests by Iraqi exiles against what was seen as tacit acceptance of an outlaw regime. Russia, whose assured sources of oil were reduced as a result of the Central Asian republics' independence, had the necessary technology and led this group. Senior Russian figures visited Baghdad in March, explaining that they had to pursue Russia's own interests and recover Iraq's debts by helping develop the large new Rumayla and Qurna fields in the south. The former was expected to produce 600,000 barrels per day (bpd). Contracts were signed and ratified in the spring, it being understood that oil could not flow while sanctions lasted. A similar provisional contract was signed with China. Shipment of, and payment for, these exports was naturally delayed. It was doubtful whether the Turks would wait so long: in May they signed a contract for the supply of Iraqi natural gas.

Although food prices fell substantially in the first part of the year, and food rations increased, UNICEF reported in June that 27 per cent of Iraq's three million children were still undernourished.

A former Prime Minister, Mohammed Fadhil Jamali, died in Tunis on 24 May aged 81 (see XX: Obituary).

3. SAUDI ARABIA—YEMEN—ARAB STATES OF THE GULF

i. SAUDI ARABIA

CAPITAL: Riyadh   AREA: c.2,000,000 sq km   POPULATION: 18,000,000 ('96)
OFFICIAL LANGUAGE: Arabic   POLITICAL SYSTEM: monarchy
HEAD OF STATE & GOVERNMENT: King Fahd ibn Abdul Aziz (since June '82), also Prime Minister
HEIR APPARENT: Crown Prince Abdullah ibn Abdul Aziz (since June '82), also First Deputy Prime Minister
MAIN IGO MEMBERSHIPS (non-UN): AL, OPEC, OAPEC, GCC, OIC, NAM
CURRENCY: riyal (end-'97 £1=SRls6.15, US$1=SRls3.75)
GNP PER CAPITA: US$7,040 ('95)

MYSTERY continued to shroud the June 1996 al-Khobar car bomb in which 19 American servicemen died (see AR 1996, pp. 216–7). A Saudi national, Hani Abd al-Rahim al-Sayegh, who had been arrested in Canada and extradited to the United States in June for the offence, had all charges against him dropped when he refused to testify on 8 September. Saudi Arabia applied for his extradition the following day. Difficulties were expected with the request because of American anger at the start of the year over Saudi secrecy in connection with investigations into the al-Khobar affair. Janet Reno, the US Attorney-General, pointed out in January that American investigators had been denied access to 40 persons, mainly Shias with links to Iran who had been held by the Saudi authorities.

Despite hints that Iran might have been involved in the al-Khobar incident, Saudi Arabia's relations with Tehran continued to improve throughout the year, especially after the election of Ayatollah Khatami as Iran's new President in May (see VIII.1.i). The Saudi Minister of State, Abdulaziz bin Abdullah al-Khuwaiter, took messages from King Fahd and the Crown Prince to the new President in July, thus strengthening the improvement in relations which had been fostered by Syria six months before. The reconciliation with Iran, like that with Syria, had been hastened by the stagnating Arab-Israeli peace process and by Turkey's rapprochement with Israel, as well as by common concerns over OPEC oil production levels. Problems still remained over the question of Iranian claims to the Abu Musa-Tunbs group of islands in the Persian Gulf, regarded by the Saudis as belonging to the United Arab Emirates. Nonetheless, this did not prevent the Crown Prince from attending the summit of the Organization of the Islamic Conference held in Tehran in mid-December (see XI.2.iv)—an indication both of the waning power of the pro-American lobby around the ailing King Fahd in Riyadh and of Saudi disillusion with American policy in the Middle East.

One of the most difficult issues in foreign relations for Saudi Arabia was the trial of two British nurses accused of the murder of an Australian colleague, Yvonne Gifford, in December 1996. Their trial, which concluded at the end of September, resulted in Lucille McLauchlan being sentenced to 500 lashes and eight years in prison for her role in the murder. The expected death sentence on her alleged accomplice, Deborah Parry, was delayed while the opinion of the victim's family was sought, since under Saudi law they had the right to insist on or waive the death penalty. Frank Gifford, the brother of the victim, at first demanded the death penalty but in October was eventually persuaded to accept A$1.7 million instead, his decision being accepted by the Saudi High Sharia Court on 11 November. The money was provided by a trust fund, created by British companies with interests in Saudi Arabia, including British Aerospace, Rolls Royce, GEC, Glaxo and Tate & Lyle. The initial sentence on Ms McLauchlan raised a storm of protest in Britain and a protest from the Foreign Secretary, Robin Cook, which was rejected by Ghazi al-Ghosaibi, the Saudi ambassador in London. Mr Cook later discussed the matter with the Saudi Foreign Minister, Prince Saud al-Faisal, in New York, following which the tensions subsided. Nonetheless, in late October Amnesty International attacked the Saudi justice system, accusing it of unfairness, tolerating the use of torture and espousing the death sentence—to considerable official anger.

In domestic terms, the year was dominated by an appalling accident on 15 April during the annual Haj (Muslim pilgrimage), when fire swept through a tented camp on the plain of Mena in Mecca, containing pilgrims from the Indian sub-continent. At least 217 persons died and a further 1,290 were injured. The incident recalled the tragedy during the pilgrimage in 1994, when 270 people died in a stampede after a walkway collapsed (see AR 1994, p. 237). In September the Saudi authorities warned that migrant workers without the proper documentation would be expelled when an amnesty expired on 16 October. By the due date, over 100,000 illegal migrants had left the kingdom, although hundreds of thousands of others were believed to have remained behind. In August, as the first four-year term of the kingdom's Consultative Council (*Majlis*) came to an end and half the existing 60 members were replaced by new appointees, King Fahd announced that it would be expanded to 90 members in future.

Saudi Arabia also dealt with a series of regional issues during the year. At the end of 1997 border negotiations were undertaken with Kuwait and Yemen, the Yemeni border having been the scene of armed clashes in late June (see V.3.ii). At an OPEC meeting in Jakarta on 28 November, Saudi representatives were able to push through a general increase in OPEC quotas, increasing aggregate production by 10 per cent to 27.5 million barrels per day (b/d) and the Saudi quota by 12 per cent to 8.76 million b/d. Used to justify the OPEC decision, buoyant oil prices during the year were expected to result in Saudi oil revenues rising by 7 per cent. According to official sources, increased revenues would be used to pay off arrears owing to farmers ($853 million) and to finance the Saudi loan of $4,300 million for 61 new aircraft contracted in November (and guaranteed by the government) as well as the proposed $2,000 million Shuaiba power plant.

The confidence expressed in this move reflected the strength of oil markets in 1996 and 1997. The 1997 budget, presented on 30 December 1996, reflected a $12,000 million windfall increase in oil revenues in 1996, to SRls177,000 million compared with an original budget forecast of SRls131,000 million. Other positive factors included strong GDP growth of 8.6 per cent in 1996, together with the first current-account surplus since 1982, of SRls700 million compared with a deficit the previous year of SRls19,900 million. Revenues in 1997 were conservatively forecast at SRls164,000 million (on the basis of an average oil price of $16 per barrel) and expenditure projected at SRls181,000 million, representing a 20 per cent increase on 1996. The latter increase included a 50 per cent rise in spending on education, to SRls41,700 million, and an 11 per cent rise in security costs, to SRls50,000 million.

The year also saw the beginnings of significant economic reform in Saudi Arabia, featuring plans to privatize the Saudia national airline. Pressure for reform came from the IMF, although the latter body recognized that GDP growth was still too slow for major change and that the policies of privatization of the public sector and 'Saudization' of the labour force ran counter to each other. The kingdom also sought World Trade Organization membership in April, although the negotiations on the Saudi request were expected to be protracted. A move to support the private sector was made in October when the regulations for listing on the bourse were published. This followed the launching in July of a new investment fund allowing non-Saudis to invest in the kingdom's private sector for the first time.

The public sector still dominated growth in the oil industry in 1997. In February the state company Aramco took over BP's and Shell's lifting rights under the al-Yamamah contract, while in October news emerged of a proposed $3,500 million development plan for the expected 500,000 b/d Shaybah field and the Ras Tanura and Rabigh refinery upgrades. On the joint venture front, Yanpet (a consortium of Sabu and Mobil) obtained a $2,320 million loan for a doubling of its petrochemical output, and Sasref (Aramco and Shell) obtained $200 million for a thermal cracker upgrade. Abroad, Saudi Aramco took a 35 per cent stake in Petrogal, Portugal's state oil company, the price being $1,300 million, representing the company's largest European investment to date.

ii. YEMEN

CAPITAL: Sana'a AREA: 540,000 sq km POPULATION: 13,400,000 ('96)
OFFICIAL LANGUAGE: Arabic POLITICAL SYSTEM: presidential
HEAD OF STATE & GOVERNMENT: President (Gen.) Ali Abdullah Saleh (since May '90)
RULING PARTY: General People's Congress (GPC)
PRIME MINISTER: Faraj Said bin Ghanem (since May '97)
MAIN IGO MEMBERSHIPS (non-UN): AL, OIC, NAM
CURRENCY: Yemeni rial (end-'97 £1=YRls203.45, US$1=YRls124.00)
GNP PER CAPITA: US$260 ('95)

ON 27 April Yemen held its first legislative elections since the civil war in 1994. According to the official results announced on 5 May, the ruling General People's Congress (GPC) led by President Ali Abdullah Saleh won an outright victory, capturing 187 of the 301 seats in the Assembly—64 more than in the previous elections in 1993. The Yemeni Alliance for Reform (Islah), the GPC's erstwhile coalition partner, saw its representation fall, from 62 to 53 seats in all. At the same time, the party leader, Shaikh Abdullah bin Hussain al-Ahmar, was re-elected as Speaker of the Assembly and the elections also ensured that the moderate wing of his party forced out the radicals from parliamentary representation. In the results, independent candidates won 54 seats (compared with 47 in 1993), the remaining seven going to Baathists and Nasserists. The Yemen Socialist Party (YSP), the former sole ruling party in South Yemen, boycotted the elections because of irregularities in the electoral arrangements. Although 11 people died during the campaign, observers concurred that the electoral process had been generally fair. Announced on 15 May, the new government, under the premiership of Faraj Said bin Ghanem, contained 14 new ministers.

Violence continued to mark the domestic scene, particularly in former South Yemen. Bombs exploded in Aden on 28 July and 50 persons were arrested, mainly members of the YSP and the League of the Sons of Yemen. The League's exiled leader, Abd ul-Rahman Ali al-Jifri, claimed (through his organization in Britain) that the bombs had been planted by the Yemeni government in an attempt to discredit the opposition. Eight car bombs exploded in Aden at the end of October, followed by a further car bomb on 16 November, although no casualties were reported. According to the Interior Minister, Brigadier Hussain Muhammad Arab, four groups were arrested. Two days later a trial of 31 persons accused of attacking and robbing military posts opened in Sana'a, where it was claimed that 'foreign agents' had also been involved.

Tribal tensions also continued to be high, with regular reports of foreigners being captured and held for ransom. In October northern tribes blocked the main Sana'a-Ta'izz road in protest at IMF-inspired increases in fuel prices, while at Dhamar on 20 October three persons died in clashes with the security forces. The Deputy Premier, Abd al-Karim Iriani, claimed that Saudi agents had been behind the unrest. Indeed, tensions with Saudi Arabia continued to be high throughout the year, border clashes being reported in late June. The tensions were dissipated by American intercession but rose again after the Saudi-owned television station in London, Middle East Broadcasting Corporation, transmitted an interview with Mohammed al-Bid, the former South Yemen leader held responsible in Sana'a for the 1994 civil war, who was on trial *in absentia* in Yemen.

In addition to the strains with Saudi Arabia, Yemen's quest to join the Gulf Cooperation Council remained blocked in 1997, while tensions with Eritrea over the Humaish archipelago continued. At the same time, Yemen was able to record several successes in the foreign policy field. In mid-November the President made his first official visit to Britain—indeed, the first visit by a Yemeni head of state since 1967, when Britain had evacuated Aden. Shortly before, on 31 October, Yemen was accorded IMF aid of SDR 370.6 million towards its 1997–2000 development plan. Earlier in the year, on 16–18 June, a donor conference in Brussels organized by the World Bank and the Commission of the European Union raised $1,800 million in economic aid for Yemen.

In return for this generosity, of course, Yemen had to agree to undergo economic reform, involving liberalization of the domestic economy and removal of consumer subsidies. In mid-year the World Bank registered its pleasure with the progress made to date, noting that inflation had fallen from 70 per cent in 1995 to 11 per cent the following year and that the budget deficit had been cut to 2.5 per cent of GDP. The Bank pointed out, however, that still deeper cuts were needed in consumer subsidies, suggesting that the $500 million subsidy on grains should be removed.

The tensions caused by these developments had been highlighted in January 1997, however, when the Islah party boycotted the budget debate in protest both at the lack of discussion of the budget bill and at the proposed cuts in religious and education funding. The subsequent budget, placed before the Assembly on 28 December, appeared to reflect these concerns; for it provided for a 12 per cent increase in the budget deficit, with expenditure set at $2,822 million and revenues (61 per cent coming from oil and gas sales) projected to reach $2,709 million. Both figures were 12 per cent higher than in the previous budget. The new budget was passed by 165 votes to 5.

iii. ARAB STATES OF THE GULF

United Arab Emirates
CONSTITUENTS: Abu Dhabi, Dubai, Sharjah, Rasal-Khaimah, Fujairah, Umm al-Qaiwin, Ajman
FEDERAL CAPITAL: Abu Dhabi   AREA: 77,000 sq km   POPULATION: 1,865,000 ('96)
OFFICIAL LANGUAGE: Arabic   POLITICAL SYSTEM: federation of monarchies
HEAD OF STATE: Shaikh Zayad bin Sultan al-Nahayyan (Ruler of Abu Dhabi), President of UAE (since Dec '71)
HEAD OF GOVERNMENT: Shaikh Maktoum bin Rashid al-Maktoum (Ruler of Dubai), Vice-President and Prime Minister of UAE (since Nov '90)
MAIN IGO MEMBERSHIPS (non-UN): AL, OPEC, OAPEC, GCC, OIC, NAM
CURRENCY: dirham (end-'97 £1=Dh6.03, US$1=Dh3.67)
GNP PER CAPITA: US$17,400 ('95) or US$16,470 ('95) by PPP calculation

Kuwait
CAPITAL: Kuwait   AREA: 18,000 sq km   POPULATION: 2,000,000 ('96)
OFFICIAL LANGUAGE: Arabic   POLITICAL SYSTEM: monarchy
HEAD OF STATE: Shaikh Jabir al-Ahmad al-Jabir al-Sabah (since Dec '77)
HEAD OF GOVERNMENT: Crown Prince Shaikh Saad al-Abdullah as-Salim as-Sabah, Prime Minister (since Feb '78)
MAIN IGO MEMBERSHIPS (non-UN): AL, OPEC, OAPEC, GCC, OIC, NAM
CURRENCY: dinar (end-'97 £1=KD0.50, US$1=KD0.31)
GNP PER CAPITA: US$17,390 ('95) or US$23,790 ('95) by PPP calculation

Oman
CAPITAL: Muscat   AREA: 300,000 sq km   POPULATION: 2,200,000 ('96)
OFFICIAL LANGUAGE: Arabic   POLITICAL SYSTEM: monarchy
HEAD OF STATE & GOVERNMENT: Shaikh Qaboos bin Said (since July '70)
MAIN IGO MEMBERSHIPS (NON-UN): AL, GCC, OIC, NAM
CURRENCY: rial (end-'97 £1=OR0.63, US$1=OR0.39)
GNP PER CAPITA: US$4,820 ('95) or US$8,140 ('95) by PPP calculation

Qatar

CAPITAL: Doha   AREA: 11,400 sq km   POPULATION: 600,000 ('96)
OFFICIAL LANGUAGE: Arabic   POLITICAL SYSTEM: monarchy
HEAD OF STATE & GOVERNMENT: Shaikh Hamad bin Khalifa al-Thani (since June '95)
MAIN IGO MEMBERSHIPS (non-UN): AL, OPEC, OAPEC, GCC, OIC, NAM
CURRENCY: riyal (end-'97 £1=QR6.10, US$1=QR3.64)
GNP PER CAPITA: US$11,600 ('95) or US$17,690 ('95) by PPP calculation

Bahrain

CAPITAL: Manama   AREA: 685 sq km   POPULATION: 575,000 ('96)
OFFICIAL LANGUAGE: Arabic
HEAD OF STATE: Shaikh Isa bin Sulman al-Khalifah (since Dec '61)
HEAD OF GOVERNMENT: Shaikh Khalifa bin Sulman al-Khalifa, Prime Minister (since Jan '70)
MAIN IGO MEMBERSHIPS (non-UN): AL, OAPEC, GCC, OIC, NAM
CURRENCY: dinar (end-'96 £1=BD0.62, US$1=BD0.38)
GNP PER CAPITA: US$7,840 ('95) or US$13,400 ('95) by PPP calculation

THE major problems facing the Arab states of the Gulf during 1997 differed little from those of the previous year (see AR 1996, pp. 220–5). Iraqi non-compliance with United Nations sanctions, continued unrest in Bahrain and Qatari truculence towards Saudi Arabia and Bahrain formed part of this continuum. Yet there were new factors as well. The Amir of Qatar and his father patched up their quarrel; the Doha Middle East and North Africa Economic Summit was effectively torpedoed by the stagnation in the Arab-Israeli peace process; and Qatar and Egypt engaged in a violent war of words. In the United Arab Emirates difficulties over revenues forced Dubai to abandon its attempt to maintain an independent defence force and to opt, instead, for participation in the federal security structure. In addition, all of the Gulf states had to come to terms with the election victory of Mohammed Khatami in Iran in May, which had major implications for Gulf security, particularly after the successful conference of the Organization of the Islamic Conference in Tehran in December (see XI.2.iv).

The year opened in QATAR with the Amir, Shaikh Hamad bin Khalifa al-Thani, being reconciled with his father, Shaikh Khalifa. The two had been at daggers drawn since the latter's deposition by his son in June 1995 (see AR 1995, p. 224). The negotiations took place in Paris and it was anticipated that Shaikh Khalifa would eventually return to Qatar as the 'father of the nation'. The major outstanding issue between them—Shaikh Khalifa's attempt to sequestrate Qatari revenues—had been settled in an out-of-court settlement in October 1996, despite an attempted coup against his son from within the Qatari armed forces in February 1996 (see AR 1996, p. 223). The 110 arrested ringleaders of the coup attempt were put on trial in Doha on 26 November, but the proceedings were immediately adjourned until February 1998. Saudi Arabia was embarrassed by a Qatari decision to allow Amnesty International observers into the coup leaders' trial. Further irritation was caused by Qatari suggestions that Egypt had been behind the coup plot.

Other outstanding Qatari business was tidied up in early March when the Amirate agreed to renew diplomatic ties with Bahrain during a visit to Manama by the Qatari Foreign Minister, Shaikh Hamid bin Jassim bin Jabr al-Thani, to his Bahraini counterpart, Shaikh Muhammad bin Mubarak al-Khalifa. Relations had degenerated in late 1996 when Bahrain, because of its ongoing maritime dispute with Qatar over the Huwwar islands, refused to attend the annual Gulf Cooperation Council (GCC) summit in Doha. Indeed, as suggested above, Qatari tensions with Saudi Arabia did not ease during the year, not least because of Qatar's decision to allow the creation of Al-Jazira Television—an unregulated satellite television service for the Arab world that was deliberately too outspoken for Saudi comfort. Nor did the Saudi rulers appreciate the Amir's comments on American policy in the Gulf during his visit to the United States in June, when he criticized the policy of dual containment and called for a re-think over United Nations sanctions on the grounds that the Iraqi people had suffered enough.

The problems came to a head in mid-November over the issue of the fourth annual Middle East and North Africa Economic Summit, which was held in Doha, the Qatari capital. In view of the crisis over the Middle East peace process (see V.2.i), only seven Arab delegations—from Djibouti, Jordan, Kuwait, Mauritania, Oman, Tunisia and Yemen—actually attended the summit, despite considerable American pressure and the presence of the US Secretary of State, Madeleine Albright. In diplomatic terms, no advance was made beyond Mrs Albright's public criticism of Israeli intransigence over the peace process. Jordan and Israel signed agreements for joint ventures in the Irbid region, while Qatar itself was able to firm up gas-sector contracts worth $2,000 million, involving Mobil financing for the North Field, Phillips funding for a new petrochemical complex and Canadian-Norwegian participation in a new aluminium complex. The Qatari Foreign Minister's attacks on Saudi Arabia and Egypt for their absence from the meeting did nothing to improve relations with either state.

In BAHRAIN, the major emphasis during the year continued to be on the issue of internal security. On 26 March the State Security Court sentenced 15 Shias to terms of imprisonment of between three and 15 years for plotting to overthrow the government of the Amirate. They formed part of an 81-member group—called Hizbullah-Bahrain and claimed by the government to be Iranian-backed—which had been uncovered in June 1996. Eleven persons were acquitted and sentences on 55 others were to be announced later. A further eight persons, accused of being ring-leaders in the plot, were sentenced *in absentia* in late November to prison terms of between five and 15 years for the same offence.

Despite these measures, however, unrest continued throughout the year, with riots in mid-year in Shia villages outside the capital, Manama, even though 110 persons had been arrested in mid-June. The riots were sparked off by reports of deaths in custody and underlined the continuing tensions between government and the predominantly Shia population. The government promised to create 20,000 jobs to ease Shia resentments, but these were not expected to be assuaged while Shia leaders were kept in prison or under house arrest.

Elsewhere in the Gulf region, relative domestic calm was maintained, apart from a mysterious attack, on 6 June, on the leader of the Arab nationalist

Democratic Forum in KUWAIT, Abdullah an-Nibari, who was left severely injured. Although his colleagues suspected governmental figures of responsibility for the attack, which had come in the wake of Forum accusations of official corruption, the government quickly arrested three Kuwaitis and two Iranians, who were charged four days later with attempted murder.

Otherwise, the primary focus was on governmental and constitutional change, including the emergence on 20 May of a new political organization in Kuwait, called the National Democratic Rally and led by the former GCC secretary-general, Abdullah Bishara. In the UAE there was a cabinet reshuffle in March, involving eight ministerial changes, and new federal Oil and Finance Ministers were appointed in May. The Qatari Justice Minister, Najib Mohamed an-Nuaimi, resigned in June, and the Kuwaiti Health Minister, Anwar Abdullah an-Nuri, bowed out in October.

In October the Kuwaiti National Assembly rejected government calls for the introduction of personal taxation unless the issue of official corruption was tackled first. In Oman Sultan Qaboos authorized elections on 16 October to a candidate body for a new *Majlis ash-Shura*—a consultative institution originally created in January 1992—by an electoral college of 51,000 persons, 10 per cent of them women. Of the 164 elected members of the candidate body (from 736 candidates, including 27 women), 64 were later selected as members of the new *Majlis,* which replaced the 23-member body selected in 1994. The selection was accompanied by a ministerial reshuffle in December.

Defence concerns also played an important part in Gulf affairs, particularly in view of the crisis between the UN inspection team and the Iraqi regime which erupted in November (see V.2.vi). In October Kuwait purchased Sea Skua missiles from British Aerospace for $100 million, to install on French patrol boats which had cost $500 million. A further order for 16 Apache helicopters and associated missiles worth $800 million was placed in the United States. Despite these commitments, a subsequent $200 million Kuwaiti order for Chinese 155-mm howitzers (against competing bids from South Africa, Britain and America) caused consternation in the United States. American anxiety was assuaged, however, by the UAE's preference, in September, for 50 Lockheed-Martin F-16 fighters worth $6,000 million, against European competition.

The general buoyancy in oil prices eased the economic situation in the Arab states of the Gulf during 1997, although the financial crisis in Asia led to a reassessment in the later part of the year. In Qatar, increased importance was placed on oil as a source of revenue. In September output was set to rise to 600,000 b/d by the end of the year—well above the OPEC quota—so that GDP growth would be as high as 15.5 per cent for the year. The current-account deficit, however, was expected to reach 36 per cent of GDP, alongside a chronically high budget deficit, while external debt was expected to total 108 per cent of GDP, as a result of the development of Qatar's oil and gas potential. The bad news had begun in March when Israel announced that it would pull out of the degasification plant project at Aqaba, which was to be based on liquid natural gas from Qatar. For its part, Oman had to face a Thai withdrawal from a liquid natural-gas deal which would have meant exports of 1 million tonnes per year in 2000 rising to 2.2 million tonnes per year five years later. Similar anxieties surrounded gas deals with South Korea and Japan, with the result that Oman began reconsidering the potential of the Indian market instead.

The UAE federal budget in February was based on more optimistic expectations. Expenditure was increased by 8.8 per cent to $5,470 million and revenues were projected to rise by 8.4 per cent to $5,130 million, leaving a 16 per cent increase in the deficit to $258 million. The Kuwaiti budget, published in September, anticipated expenditure of $15,500 million, against revenues of $10,300 million, with a resultant deficit (before commitments for the Fund for Future Generations) of $4,200 million. Surprisingly, in view of the massive proposed deficit, the National Assembly endorsed a government promise that the deficit would be eliminated by the year 2000.

The Kuwaiti Assembly was less welcoming to a proposal, made at the end of the year, to open the upstream oil sector to foreign participation, except for limited periods, as permitted under the constitution. The issue, nonetheless, could not be ignored, for Kuwait's oil plan to raise production from 2.1 million b/d in 1997 to 2.5 million b/d by the year 2000, and to 3 million b/d five years later, would need foreign expertise and would cost an estimated $5,190 million. There had been similar National Assembly objections to proposals at the start of the year to privatize the public sector; although 12 state companies were targeted by the World Bank for privatization, including telecommunications, water transport and ports. In addition, plans were discussed at the end of the year to open the Kuwait bourse to foreign investors—a sure sign of the changing times in the Gulf region.

4. SUDAN—LIBYA—TUNISIA—ALGERIA—MOROCCO—WESTERN SAHARA

i. SUDAN

CAPITAL: Khartoum   AREA: 2,500,000 sq km   POPULATION: 29,000,000 ('96)
OFFICIAL LANGUAGE: Arabic   POLITICAL SYSTEM: Islamist/military regime
HEAD OF STATE & GOVERNMENT: President (Gen.) Omar Hasan Ahmed al-Bashir (since Oct '93), previously Chairman of Revolutionary Command Council (since June '89)
MAIN IGO MEMBERSHIPS (non-UN): AL, OAU, COMESA, OIC, ACP, NAM
CURRENCY: dinar (end '97 £1=D264.63, US$1=D161.29)
GNP PER CAPITA: n/a

THE military successes of the Sudan People's Liberation Army (SPLA) and the forces of the National Democratic Alliance (NDA) in January demonstrated the weakness of Sudan's Islamic fundamentalist regime, which sought to enlist the support of sympathetic African, Arab and Muslim countries. The SPLA captured the towns of Kurmuk, Geissan and Shali near the Ethiopian border and threatened to take Damazin, a town on the site of a hydroelectric power plant supplying most of Khartoum's electricity. In north-eastern Sudan the government barracks at Gadamyeeb (north-east of Kassala town) fell to Sudan Alliance Forces (the military wing of the NDA). These military defeats prompted President al-Bashir to declare a 'holy war' and general mobilization of the armed forces, while SPLA positions in the captured areas were bombed by government planes and government reinforcements were sent to the disputed areas.

Further military encounters took place in March when the SPLA attacked Kaya, a garrison near the Ugandan border, and captured government soldiers and ammunitions. The towns of Yei and Kajo Kaji, as well as Yirol in Bahr Al-Ghazal state, fell to the SPLA, which threatened the regional capital, Juba. Later in the year SPLA forces shot down a government MiG-21 fighter plane over the town of Aswa in eastern Equatoria. To counteract SPLA successes, the government signed a peace agreement with five SPLA splinter factions in April. Significant among these groups was the Southern Sudan Independence Movement (SSIM) headed by Riak Machar, who was appointed head of the Southern States Coordination Council formed to govern southern Sudan. The agreement had little effect, however, since the majority of the SPLA remained in opposition. The NDA held its fourth meeting in Asmara, Eritrea, in June under the chairmanship of its president, Sayyid Muhammed Osman al-Mirghani, and recommended the intensification of military operations against the Sudanese regime.

The internal conflict and related tensions with Uganda (which was accused by Sudan of supporting the SPLA) were the themes of talks between President al-Bashir and President Museveni of Uganda held in South Africa in August at the invitation of President Mandela and also attended by President Mugabe of Zimbabwe. However, Colonel John Garang, leader of the SPLA, did not attend. In the same month the Sudanese President visited Malawi, Mozambique, Tanzania and Zambia seeking to enlist their good offices in bringing about a peaceful solution to the conflict in southern Sudan. In October-November government and SPLA representatives attended peace negotiations in Nairobi sponsored by the Inter-Governmental Authority on Development (IGAD) and chaired by Kenya. However, disagreement between the two sides resulted in the talks being adjourned until April 1998. Whereas the government offered autonomy for the south, the SPLA wanted a confederation of northern and southern states as an interim step, leading within two years to a referendum in southern Sudan on secession from the confederation. Colonel Garang subsequently met President Mubarak of Egypt in Cairo to discuss the outcome of the Nairobi negotiations. Urged not to intensify the conflict in the south, Colonel Garang assured the Egyptian President that the unity of Sudan was important and that 'the SPLA is neither against Islam nor against the Arabs'.

Not only Uganda but also Eritrea and Ethiopia were accused by Sudan of providing personnel and equipment for the SPLA and the forces of the NDA, with resultant strains in relations. In response, Sudan was accused by these countries of supporting militant opposition groups in each, notably the Christian fundamentalists in Uganda. In April Uganda admitted that its troops had entered southern Sudan, killing 60 Sudanese soldiers and 68 Ugandan rebels and taking 114 Sudanese soldiers prisoner. Sudan, on the other hand, claimed that 300 Ugandan soldiers were killed in the operation. The Sudanese government denied claims by Eritrea that it had plotted to assassinate the Eritrean President, Issaias Afewerki.

Iraq, Syria, Qatar, Yemen and Libya pledged or sent military help to Sudan to stem the advances of the opposition. However, efforts by Vice-President Al-Zubair Mohammed Salih during talks in Cairo to enlist the support of Egypt were unsuccessful, the Egyptian government stating that it would not provide military or financial assistance to Sudan. An offer to mediate in the Sudanese conflict by Shaikh Zayad, President of the United Arab Emirates, produced no positive outcome. In another initiative, Sudan sent its Minister of State for Foreign Affairs to Kuwait to resume the diplomatic relations severed as a result of Sudan's support for Iraq during the Gulf War. He apologized for Sudan's mistakes towards Kuwait and its people.

Iran, Sudan's main ally, was reported in February to have supplied six Russian MiG-21 warplanes and other equipment to assist Sudan in its military confrontation with the SPLA. The secretary-general of the Sudanese National Congress called in July for partnership with Iran to lead the Islamic world in a united front against the West. The embargo by the US State Department on the sale of arms and transfer of capital to Sudan was followed in November by an order, signed by President Clinton, prohibiting US trade and bank loans to Sudan and freezing Sudan's assets in the United States. Madeleine Albright, the US Secretary of State, stated that these measures were in response to Sudan's 'continued sponsorship of international terrorism, its efforts to destabilize neighbouring countries and its abysmal record on human rights'.

Anti-government demonstrations took place in January in Khartoum, it being reported that many people were arrested, including doctors, lawyers and other professionals. To counteract what it called 'external support for the SPLA', the government in June, and again in October, carried out the unpopular policy of conscripting school-leavers into the Popular Defence Force (PDF). No school-leaver was allowed to join a university or to repeat an academic year, or to leave the country or obtain employment, unless he or she first did service in a PDF camp.

The International Monetary Fund (IMF) revised its assessment of Sudan's economic performance due to a fall in the inflation rate, improved growth, increased taxation and improved tax collection. The suspended monthly payment to the IMF in lieu of debt was resumed when Malaysia undertook to contribute US$7 million towards the payment. However, the World Bank suspended operations in Sudan, on the grounds that its funds did not benefit the ordinary people.

The future of Sudan's economic recovery continued to be seen in terms of the exploitation of its oil resources. Canada's International Petroleum Corporation (IPC), Petronas of Malaysia and ÖMV of Austria were given concessions for oil exploration and production. Canada's Arakis Energy Corporation stated that its Sudan subsidiary had completed the Al-Nar 72(a) discovery well in southern Sudan, which was estimated to be capable of producing more than 2,600 barrels a day. A contract worth US$300 million was awarded to the China

Petroleum Technology and Development Corporation and Germany's Mannesmann Handel for the supply of oil pipeline to link the Muglad basin in the south to an export terminal on the Red Sea. Sudan was allocated loans and aid worth US$105 million by the Islamic Development Bank and various Arab and UN agencies, this sum being earmarked for heightening the Roseires Dam, road construction, improved agricultural seeds, health centres, multi-purpose agricultural schemes, veterinary centres and nutrition projects.

ii. LIBYA

CAPITAL: Tripoli   AREA: 1,760,000 sq km   POPULATION: 4,899,000 ('94)
OFFICIAL LANGUAGE: Arabic   POLITICAL SYSTEM: socialist 'state of the masses'
HEAD OF STATE: Col. Muammar Qadafi, 'Leader of the Revolution' (since '69)
HEAD OF GOVERNMENT: Mohammed Ahmed al-Manqoush, Secretary-General of General People's Committee (since Dec '97)
MAIN IGO MEMBERSHIPS (non-UN): AL, OPEC, OAPEC, AMU, OAU, OIC, NAM
CURRENCY: dinar (end-'97 £1=LD0.63, US$1=LD0.38)
GNP PER CAPITA: n/a

UN sanctions against Libya were renewed unchanged throughout the year. But the Qadafi regime could take some satisfaction from the growing support for their removal on the basis of Tripoli's proposal that the two Libyan suspects in the 1988 Lockerbie airliner bombing should be put on trial not in the United Kingdom or the United States but in a neutral third country (see also XI.5.i). Both the Arab League and the Organization of African Unity stepped up their campaign for the removal of UN sanctions, and two permanent members of the Security Council, Russia and China, urged acceptance of Libya's compromise offer. There was also support from the Vatican, which established diplomatic relations wih Tripoli in March, while in October the South African President, Nelson Mandela, raised the issue at the Commonwealth conference in Edinburgh, calling on the Scottish authorities to allow a trial in a neutral location to ensure that justice was seen to be done. President Mandela visited Libya for talks with Colonel Qadafi before and after the conference.

Also in October, hearings began at the International Court of Justice at The Hague to determine whether the Court, the preferred neutral location, could be a legally acceptable venue for the trial. The United States and Britain, however, remained firmly opposed to Libya's compromise proposal, ensuring that sanctions would probably remain in force for the foreseeable future. For his part Colonel Qadafi continued openly to flout the air embargo, and in July Tripoli's permanent representative at the UN announced that Libya would behave as if sanctions did not exist.

In the United States, Senator Alfonse D'Amato, the architect of the controversial 1996 Iran and Libya Sanctions Act (see AR 1996, p. 228), campaigned for an international ban on Libyan oil sales. However, growing criticism was voiced, especially from the American business community, at the US government's use of unilateral economic sanctions for political ends. Further evidence of sanctions-busting trade with Libya by certain European companies seemed likely to aggravate the already strained relations between the United States and its NATO allies. Early in the year the German authorities announced that they had conclusive evidence of the Libyan government's direct involvement in the bomb attack on a Berlin discotheque in 1986 which became the pretext for US air raids against Libya some days later. In France, investigations into the 1989 bombing of a French airliner over the Sahara ended with demands for the trial of six Libyans, including a brother-in-law of Colonel Qadafi.

Libya remained excluded from participating in cooperation between the European Union (EU) and southern Mediterranean states, which had begun in Barcelona in 1995, and was not invited to the conference of Foreign Ministers held in Malta in April 1997. Relations with Turkey, badly strained in 1996 (see AR 1996, p. 229), deteriorated even further when Colonel Qadafi denounced Ankara's military alliance with Israel and its military incursions into northern Iraq. In contrast, the Libyan leader made efforts to improve relations with the Palestinians by allowing those Palestinians stranded for months at the Egyptian border after being expelled from Libya to return to their homes and jobs. Libya and Tunisia were united in calling for efforts to revive the Arab Maghreb Union and diplomatic efforts were made to improve Tripoli's relations with its sub-Saharan neighbours.

In January six senior army officers and two civilians, all from the powerful Warfallah tribe, were executed after being convicted of spying for the United States and trying to overthrow the regime. The executions went ahead against the wishes of the leaders of the Warfallah tribe. Fighting between militant Islamist groups and the security forces continued, and in July the Militant Islamic Group claimed responsibility for an unsuccessful attempt on the life of Musa Kusa, a leading figure in the regime. The opposition remained deeply divided, however, and there were rumours that the latest opposition group to emerge, the Libyan Patriots Movement, might be government-backed. There were also reports of secret meetings between government officials and members of exiled opposition groups. At its annual meeting at Sirte, the General People's Congress approved new legislation, the so-called 'Charter of Honour', imposing collective punishment on families or tribal clans of Libyans convicted of certain crimes, but clearly directed principally against opponents of the regime. The charter was strongly criticized by London-based Amnesty International in its report on gross human rights violations in Libya.

During the year Major Abdel Salam Jalloud, for many years Colonel Qadafi's second-in-command but placed under house arrest after the 1993 abortive army coup, was brought back into the regime. In rare changes to the General People's Committee (cabinet) at the end of December, Mohammed Ahmed al-Manqoush was appointed Secretary (broadly equivalent to Prime Minister). His predecessor, Abd al-Majid al-Qaud, became Secretary for the Great Man-made River Project.

iii. TUNISIA

CAPITAL: Tunis AREA: 164,000 sq km POPULATION: 9,150,000 ('96)
OFFICIAL LANGUAGE: Arabic POLITICAL SYSTEM: presidential
HEAD OF STATE & GOVERNMENT: President (Gen.) Zayn al-Abdin Ben Ali (since Nov '87)
RULING PARTY: Constitutional Democratic Rally (RCD)
PRIME MINISTER: Hamid Qarwi (since Sept '89)
MAIN IGO MEMBERSHIPS (non-UN): AL, AMU, ICO, OAU, OIC, NAM, Francophonie
CURRENCY: dinar (end-'97 £1=D1.89, US$1=D1.15)
GNP PER CAPITA: US$1,820 ('95) or US$5,000 ('95) by PPP calculation

IN November President Ben Ali celebrated the tenth anniversary of his takeover of power from former head of state Habib Bourguiba. During the year his cabinet debated a range of political reforms, which the President claimed would strengthen pluralism, and he sought to invigorate the ruling Rassemblement Constitutionnel Démocratique (RCD) by attracting more young people and women. Addressing foreign critics, he insisted that Tunisia was a state of law and a country of human rights. But his government remained intolerant of all opposition. In February a decree was issued giving the Interior Ministry greater powers of surveillance over political gatherings. Later in the year it was announced that the law was to be strengthened to restrict the activities of Tunisian critics who spread false information to 'foreign parties', a move directed at Tunisian activists with links to international human rights organizations.

In April, when several trade unionists called for greater democracy and criticized the leadership of the Union Générale des Travailleurs Tunisiens (UGTT) for collaborating with the government, a number were promptly arrested. Mohamed Mouada, the former leader of the opposition Mouvement des Démocrates Socialistes (MDS), who had been released from gaol at the end of 1996, remained under police surveillance and was arrested again in late December charged with an attempted coup d'état and links with foreign organizations. After being interrogated by police, M. Mouada was allowed to return home but his telephone line was cut. His arrest followed a visit to Europe, where he had talks with officials at the Quai d'Orsay in Paris and at the British Foreign Office. The split in the MDS between the faction led by Ismail Boulahya, who was recognized as party leader by the government, and that led by Mohammed Ali Khalfallah, which was opposed to collaboration with the regime, deepened and virtually paralysed the party.

In a new report on Tunisia, London-based Amnesty International stated that, while the government expressed its commitment to human rights, it was guilty of a 'widening circle of repression' reaching out to the families and associates of political opponents, and that large-scale human rights abuses continued to take place. Amnesty International later joined several other international organizations in calling on the regime to stop its 'campaign of intimidation' against human rights activists. In the European Parliament an announcement by a group of MEPs that they planned another resolution condemning Tunisia for human rights abuses suggested that this issue would continue to cast a shadow over Tunisia's relations with the European Union (EU). Ironically, Tunisia was unanimously elected to the UN Human Rights Commission in May. Soon afterwards the government tried to improve its relations with the Ligue Tunisienne pour la Défense des Droits de l'Homme (LTDH), describing the organization as a 'national asset' but calling on it to prove its 'patriotism and sense of responsibility'.

In January Prime Minister Hamid Qarwi went to Madrid for the first annual meeting agreed under the 1995 treaty of friendship with Spain. Although the meeting dealt mainly with economic cooperation, the Spanish Prime Minister, José María Aznar, raised his concerns over Tunisia's human rights record. During a state visit to Rome in May, President Ben Ali sought increased Italian economic aid, and the two countries agreed to cooperate in preventing illegal immigration from Tunisia. But later in the year relations became strained when Tunisia seized several Italian boats which it claimed were fishing illegally in Tunisian waters. On his first visit to Tunis in August, the new French Foreign Minister, Hubert Vedrine, stated that relations between the two countries remained close and that a new partnership agreement would be signed during President Ben Ali's state visit to France, although no date was set for the visit, which had originally been scheduled for September 1996. Cooperation on joint projects with Libya continued to progress, and a state visit to Tunis by the Amir of Qatar in June illustrated the gradual improvement in relations with the Gulf states since the 1990–91 Gulf crisis. In contrast, relations with Israel were frozen in response to Israeli intransigence towards the Middle East peace process (although Israel's liaison office in Tunis remained open).

In June the cabinet approved the ninth development plan (1997–2001), covering a period when the Tunisian economy would become more closely integrated with that of the EU. The plan envisaged greater economic liberalization, financial and fiscal reforms and the modernization of some 2,000 companies.

iv. ALGERIA

CAPITAL: Algiers   AREA: 2,382,000 sq km   POPULATION: 28,500,000 ('96)
OFFICIAL LANGUAGE: Arabic   POLITICAL SYSTEM: quasi-military regime
HEAD OF STATE & GOVERNMENT: President (Brig.-Gen.) Liamine Zéroual (since Jan '94)
RULING PARTIES: National Democratic Rally (RND) heads coalition
PRIME MINISTER: Ahmed Ouyahia (since Jan '96)
MAIN IGO MEMBERSHIPS (non-UN): AL, OPEC, OAPEC, AMU, OAU, OIC, NAM
CURRENCY: dinar (end-'97 £1=DA96.20, US$1=DA58.63)
GNP PER CAPITA: US$1,600 ('95) or US$5,300 ('95) by PPP calculation

EARLY in the year a new political party, the Rassemblement Nationale Démocratique (RND), was created under the leadership of Abdelkader Bensalah, the president of the National Council of Transition (CNT). The launching of the RND was delayed as a result of the assassination in late January of Abdelhak Benhamouda, the secretary-general of the powerful Union Générale des Travailleurs Algériens (UGTA), who had been the first choice to lead the new party. The RND was immediately dubbed 'the President's party', although M. Bensalah denied this and maintained that it was a centre party with support throughout the country. The party announced that it would field candidates in all constituencies, its lists including Prime Minister Ouyahia and many ministers. All political parties were given until May to restructure their organizations to take account of new legislation or be dissolved. In order to comply with the ban on the use of religious symbolism, the 'moderate' Islamist Hamas party reluctantly agreed to change its name to Harakat Moushtama Issilm (HMI), meaning 'Movement of Society for Peace'. Most of the legalized political parties indicated that they would participate in the forthcoming elections, but a few groups, such as the Mouvement pour la Démocratie en Algérie (MDA), refused to take part and the banned Front Islamique du Salut (FIS) called for a boycott. In early March the CNT adopted a new electoral law providing for voting by proportional representation, completing the President's package of political reforms. Meeting in Madrid in April, representatives of the main opposition parties, including the FIS, called for the opening of a dialogue for peace. Although divided over whether or not to participate in legislative elections, the signatories of the 1995 Rome pact (see AR 1995, pp. 233–4) reaffirmed their belief that only a political solution would bring the country's continuing chronic violence to an end.

In the June elections, which took place amidst massive security precautions, the RND emerged as the biggest party in the lower house of the new bicameral parliament, winning 155 of the 380 seats contested. The HMI (ex-Hamas) came second with 69 seats, followed by the former sole ruling party, the Front de Libération Nationale (FLN), which performed better than expected by winning 64 seats. Ennahda, the other legalized Islamist party, also did well, taking 34 seats. In contrast, the centre-left parties, especially the Front des Forces Socialistes (FFS), won fewer seats than in the previous election. According to the government, the turnout was 65.5 per cent, the highest rates of abstention being recorded in Kabylia and in the capital, Algiers. Most parties complained of irregularities, and opposition leaders insisted that the turnout had been lower than the official figures indicated. Many of the international observers monitoring the elections expressed some reservations about the fairness of the electoral process.

President Zéroual claimed that the elections represented 'a new and important victory' in the struggle against the militant Islamist opposition. But critics condemned them as a facade and insisted that they had been held to give the regime, in which real power remained with the generals, a veneer of legitimacy in the eyes of Western governments. Ahmed Ouyahia was reappointed Prime Minister, and on 25 June a new coalition government was announced consisting of 30 ministers and ministers-delegate, the FLN and the HMI each being allocated seven portfolios and the RND the rest.

The RND won a sweeping victory in local elections for provincial and municipal councils held on 23 October. All major political parties complained of widespread electoral fraud, the opposition parties organizing massive street demonstrations on a scale not seen for many years. President Zéroual refused to annul the elections, and street protests continued with some violent clashes between demonstrators and the police. Elections by indirect suffrage for two-thirds of seats in the new 144-member upper house of parliament, the Conseil de la Nation, took place on 25 December, the President appointing the remaining 48 members two days later. The RND commanded an overall majority in the new chamber.

On 5 July President Zéroual ended the state of emergency in force for five years. Some days later, following secret negotiations, Abassi Madani, the leader of the FIS, together with the party's number three, Abdelkader Hachani, were released from detention. It was reported that a deal had been struck between the presidency and the FIS under which the party would be restored to legality, but under a new name, and in return would renounce all forms of political violence, dissolve its armed wing, the Armée Islamique du Salut (AIS), and end its armed struggle against the regime. These negotiations were rumoured to have led to a power struggle among the military chiefs pitting President Zéroual and his faction against that of the leading '*éradicateur*' (hardliner) and the regime's number two, General Mohamed Lamari. According to one source, the President was very nearly ousted in a coup d'état and owed his survival to strong American backing. In the end, however, the generals closed ranks. Negotiations with the FIS came to nothing, Abassi Madani was once again placed under house arrest and at the end of October President Zéroual declared that the file on the FIS was 'closed permanently'. A unilateral ceasefire announced by the AIS from 1 October appeared to hold, although some claimed that the military wing of the FIS was already a spent force.

The cycle of violence continued throughout the year and intensified in the late summer and autumn when a series of horrific massacres took place in villages south of Algiers, an area increasingly referred to as the 'triangle of death'. In some cases virtually entire communities of several hundred people were slaughtered, no-one being spared, not even babies. Some of the victims had their throats cut or were burnt alive and many were horribly mutilated. Some of the attacks took place near army barracks but the security forces did not intervene to stop the slaughter. The extremist Groupe Islamique Armée (GIA) was widely held responsible for the massacres but some claimed that most of the GIA factions had been infiltrated and were controlled by military intelligence. There were even claims that some of the killings were carried out by army units disguised as Islamist guerrillas. In France, human rights organizations held 'a day for Algeria' on 10 November and called for the creation of an international commission to investigate the atrocities. Further horrific massacres occurred in late December, claiming even more lives.

v. MOROCCO

CAPITAL: Rabat   AREA: 460,000 sq km   POPULATION: 27,500,000 ('96)
OFFICIAL LANGUAGE: Arabic   POLITICAL SYSTEM: monarchy
HEAD OF STATE & GOVERNMENT: King Hassan II (since '61)
RULING PARTIES: National Entente members participate in cabinet
PRIME MINISTER: Abdellatif Filali, Prime Minister (since May '94)
MAIN IGO MEMBERSHIPS (non-UN): AL, AMU, OIC, NAM
CURRENCY: dirham (end-'97 £1=DH16.01, US$1=DH9.76)
GNP PER CAPITA: US$1,110 ('95) or US$3,340 ('95) by PPP calculation

ON 28 February 11 political parties, including five from the opposition, signed a political pact with the Interior Minister, Driss Basri, aimed at 'strengthening the democratic regime based on the monarchy'. All the signatories agreed to abide by the law. The authorities agreed to treat all political parties equally, and to ban illegal practices. For their part the political parties promised to mobilize their supporters in 'a positive spirit' and not to contest, *a priori*, the integrity of future voting. To ensure that the forthcoming local and national elections were fair, the authorities and the opposition parties agreed, after long negotiations, that new electoral lists would be drawn up and a national commission established to oversee the elections.

The scale of irregularities in previous elections was revealed when the Moroccan press published figures which indicated that 4.5 million voter registrations out of an electorate of some 13 million were unreliable. An opposition spokesman claimed that after 40 years of independence no-one could claim to know the real political map of the country. The authorities appeared to have entered the February pact because they calculated that the successful integration of Morocco into the world economy required political reforms, if only to satisfy key international organization such as the World Bank and IMF. The main opposition parties, which had previously resisted King Hassan's attempt to persuade them to enter the government, probably concluded that, having secured a lower house directly elected by the people, they were unlikely to win further concessions from the palace in the short term.

The political pact was put to the test first in local elections held in June. Despite some complaints of irregularities, the elections for 24,253 seats on municipal councils and communes were judged to have been relatively fair, with a turnout officially estimated at 75 per cent. The Koutla opposition front—comprised of Istiqlal, the Union Socialiste des Forces Populaires (USFP), the Parti du Progrès et du Socialisme (PSS) and the Organisation pour l'Action Démocratique et Populaire (OADP)—achieved a better result than in the 1992 elections, winning almost 32 per cent of the seats. However, the right-wing Wifaq coalition, of the Union Constitutionnelle (UC), the Mouvement Populaire (MP) and the Parti National Démocratique, with 30 per cent, and the centre-right grouping led by the Rassemblement National des Indépendants (RNI), with 26 per cent, retained overall control. During the election campaign the Koutla for the first time outlined its moderate economic programme in an attempt to reassure the business community.

In August, in the run-up to legislative elections in November, King Hassan, as was customary, appointed a non-partisan government, replacing ministers affiliated to political parties with technocrats. Significantly, Driss Basri, the long-serving and powerful Interior Minister, retained his post. The King again called for elections free of irregularities and repeated that his goal was to see members of opposition parties enter the government. Elections for 16 new regional councils with considerable financial powers were held in October, following the passage in March of a bill granting greater autonomy to the regions.

Voting for the wholly-elected 325-member Chamber of Representatives in the new bicameral parliament took place on 14 November, and was considered to have been fairer than previous elections despite some complaints. A total of 16 of the country's 18 legalized parties participated, but voter turnout was officially put at only 58.3 per cent. The opposition Koutla bloc, which had been widely predicted to dominate the new chamber, won only 102 seats, 57 of which went to the USFP, while Istiqlal secured a disappointing 32. The bloc therefore hardly improved on the number of seats it had gained by direct voting in the 1993 elections and won fewer seats overall, whereas right-wing and centre-right parties performed much better. The right-wing Wifaq took 100 seats, half of which were won by the UC, and the centre-right parties 97 seats, of which 46 went to the RNI. The Mouvement Populaire Démocratique et Constitutionnel (MPD-C),which had merged with the Islamist Al-Islah wal-Tajdid in January, won nine seats. King Hassan was expected to form a coalition government early in 1998.

Indirect elections for the new 270-seat upper house, the Chamber of Councillors, were held on 5 December, with local councils nominating candidates for almost two-thirds of the seats, the remainder being filled by professional bodies and trade unions. The results placed the right-wing and centre-right parties in a dominant position, with a total of 166 seats, whereas the Koutla front took only 44. The upper house was vested with the power to require the dismissal of the government in the event of successful motion of no confidence.

Despite the 1996 fisheries accord with the European Union (EU), a new dispute erupted over Spanish fishing vessels operating in Moroccan territorial waters. King Hassan criticized Israel's policies in the occupied territories and refused all contact with Prime Minister Netanyahu's administration, although he did not close down Morocco's liaison office in Tel Aviv. In September Morocco reached a compromise agreement with Polisario over the long-delayed UN referendum on the future of the disputed Western Sahara (see V.4.vi). Visits to Rabat by the French Foreign Minister, Hubert Vedrine, in July and by Prime Minister Lionel Jospin in December indicated that the new administration in Paris was eager to show that Morocco remained a key partner in France's Mediterranean strategy.

vi. WESTERN SAHARA

CAPITAL: Al Aaiún   AREA: 252,000 sq km   POPULATION: 164,000 ('82)
STATUS: regarded by Morocco as under its sovereignty, whereas independent Sahrawi Arab Democratic Republic (SADR) was declared by Polisario Front in 1976

DURING the year some progress was made on removing the obstacles that had prevented the organization of the long-delayed UN referendum on the future of the disputed territory (see AR 1996, pp. 235–6). In March the new UN Secretary-General, Kofi Annan, appointed James Baker, a former US Secretary of State, as his special envoy for the Western Sahara, while the UN Security Council renewed the mandate of the UN Mission (MINURSO) to the end of September. The United States threatened to withdraw its support for the mission unless progress was made by that time.

Between June and September Mr Baker chaired a series of face-to-face talks between the Moroccan government and representatives of Polisario in Lisbon, London and Houston. Despite admitted difficulties, in mid-September a compromise agreement was reached on the highly contentious issue of who would be eligible to vote in the long-delayed referendum, now scheduled for December 1998. The special envoy appeared to have persuaded the Moroccans to accept a lower figure for the number of eligible voters than they had originally demanded. Agreement was also reached on the quartering of military forces of the two sides in the disputed territory, the repatriation of refugees and the release of detainees. After the agreement, the Moroccan Prime Minister, Abdellatif Filali, declared that the referendum would merely reaffirm Moroccan sovereignty over the Western Sahara, which he insisted would always remain an integral part of the Moroccan kingdom.

Morocco continued its campaign to weaken support for Polisario in the Organization of African Unity. By September ten states had withdrawn recognition from the self-proclaimed Saharan Arab Democratic Republic in return for financial assistance from Morocco. Some observers predicted that, if Polisario failed to win the referendum, the movement would split and that much of its leadership would defect to Morocco.

VI EQUATORIAL AFRICA

1. HORN OF AFRICA—KENYA—TANZANIA—UGANDA

i. ETHIOPIA—ERITREA—SOMALIA—DJIBOUTI

Ethiopia
CAPITAL: Addis Ababa   AREA: 1,128,000 sq km   POPULATION: 57,500,000 ('96)
OFFICIAL LANGUAGE: Amharic   POLITICAL SYSTEM: presidential
HEAD OF STATE: President Negaso Gidada (since Aug '95)
RULING PARTIES: Ethiopian Peoples' Revolutionary Democratic Front (EPRDF) heads coalition
HEAD OF GOVERNMENT: Meles Zenawi, Prime Minister (since Aug '95)
MAIN IGO MEMBERSHIPS (non-UN): OAU, COMESA, ACP, NAM
CURRENCY: birr (end-'97 £1=Br10.99, US$1=Br6.69)
GNP PER CAPITA: US$100 ('95) or US$450 ('95) by PPP calculation

Eritrea
CAPITAL: Asmara   AREA: 94,000 sq km   POPULATION: 3,500,000 ('96)
OFFICIAL LANGUAGES: Arabic & Tigrinya   POLITICAL SYSTEM: presidential
HEAD OF STATE & GOVERNMENT: President Issaias Afewerki (since May '93)
RULING PARTY: People's Front for Democracy and Justice (PFDJ)
MAIN IGO MEMBERSHIPS (non-UN): OAU, COMESA, ACP, NAM
CURRENCY: nakfa, at par with Ethiopian birr (see above)
GNP PER CAPITA: n/a

Somalia
CAPITAL: Mogadishu   AREA: 638,000 sq km   POPULATION: 9,250,000 ('96)
OFFICIAL LANGUAGES: Somali & Arabic   POLITICAL SYSTEM: transitional
HEAD OF STATE & GOVERNMENT: disputed
MAIN IGO MEMBERSHIPS (non-UN): AL, OAU, ACP, OIC, NAM
CURRENCY: shilling (end-'97 £1=SSh4,298.63, US$1=SSh2,620.00)
GNP PER CAPITA: n/a

Djibouti
CAPITAL: Djibouti   AREA: 23,000 sq km   POPULATION: 600,000 ('96)
OFFICIAL LANGUAGES: Arabic & French   POLITICAL SYSTEM: presidential
HEAD OF STATE & GOVERNMENT: President Hassan Gouled Aptidon (since June '77)
RULING PARTY: Popular Rally for Progress (RPP)
PRIME MINISTER: Barkat Gourad Hamadou (since Sept '78)
MAIN IGO MEMBERSHIPS (non-UN): AL, OAU, ACP, OIC, NAM, Francophonie
CURRENCY: Djibouti franc (end-'97 £1=DF291.59, US$1=DF177.72)
GNP PER CAPITA: US$780 ('93)

ETHIOPIA. Human rights abuses by the Ethiopian Peoples' Revolutionary Democratic Front (EPRDF) government attracted increasing international attention. British aid was suspended after vehicles supplied as part of an aid programme were used in the assassination of the president of the Ethiopian Teachers' Association by uniformed police in Addis Ababa in May. Human rights' monitoring organizations also reported the forcible repatriation of Ethiopian dissidents seeking refuge in Djibouti and Somaliland, and the extensive harassment, imprisonment and occasionally death of suspected regime opponents, especially in the Oromo, Somali, Southern and Beni-Shangul regions. Peace negotiations with the opposition Oromo Liberation Front collapsed in October, prompting a further clampdown on Oromo activists. A large number of journalists were gaoled. Several terrorist attacks occurred, especially in eastern Ethiopia, and in April grenades were thrown in hotels and restaurants in Addis Ababa.

Charges were formally filed in February against former dictator Mengistu Haile-Mariam, who was still living in Zimbabwe, and 5,197 members of his regime, for offences including genocide, war crimes, homicide and wilful injury. Only 2,246 of the accused were currently being held in detention, the remainder being charged *in absentia*. Trials of just over 200 defendants started in March. The former EPRDF Prime Minister, Tamrat Layne, and eight others were also charged in March with abuse of power.

The economy continued to grow, though unevenly, with 7 per cent real GDP growth for the year to June 1997. Despite the excellent 1996 harvest, however, the Disaster Prevention and Preparedness Committee (DPPC) stated in March that about three million people continued to need relief food, while a drought in the Somali-inhabited Ogaden region affected 600,000 people. A late start to the main rains in August left a further half a million people needing relief in the Oromo region. Late in the year, moreover, very heavy unseasonal rains associated with the El Niño phenomenon affected the harvest in much of the country, leaving prospects for 1998 uncertain. The DPPC announced in December that five million people were at risk of famine. The government pressed ahead with the privatization of state assets, the country's only operating gold mine at Legadembi being sold to the National Mining Company, owned by Saudi-Ethiopian businessman Mohammed al Amoudi. New banknotes were introduced at the end of the year.

In January the Sudanese government accused Ethiopia of attacking Kurmuk in eastern Sudan, after Sudanese People's Liberation Army (SPLA) forces took the town, and relations remained poor throughout the year. Ethiopian forces attacked bases in Somalia operated by the Islamist movement Al-Itahad al-Islami in June, withdrawing late in the year. Various Islamic opposition movements based in Somalia announced a new grouping, the Oromo, Somali and Afar Liberation Alliance, in September. The Ethiopian government actively sought a favourable outcome to the conflicts in Somalia, sending arms to the groups which it supported. In April over 50 Kenyans, including 16 security officers, were killed by a cattle-raiding gang which had crossed the border from Ethiopia. Relations with Egypt were affected both by different approaches to the Somali problem and by tensions over the use of water from the Blue Nile. Construction of the Tis Abbay II hydroelectric project on the Blue Nile got under way, and four further projects were also formulated, including one for another Nile tributary, the Takazze.

The US Secretary of State, Madeleine Albright, visited Addis Ababa in December, confirming continuing US support for the government. A visit by President Scalfaro of Italy in November, during which he apologized for the Italian invasion of Ethiopia in 1935, was the first by an Italian head of state since 1941.

Former Crown Prince Asfa Wossen, eldest son of the late Emperor Haile

Selassie, died in the United States on 17 January aged 80 (see XX: Obituary); he had long been in poor health and was buried in Addis Ababa.

ERITREA. The constitutional assembly voted unanimously in May to adopt the new national constitution, with only slight changes from the draft proposed by the constitutional commission. Elections took place for regional assemblies earlier in the year, from which members would be indirectly elected to a new National Assembly. The economy continued to grow at a healthy rate, as post-war reconstruction proceeded, and a new national currency, the nakfa, was introduced at par with the Ethiopian birr, which had previously been used. Its name was taken from the town in northern Eritrea which had symbolized resistance during the long war for independence. The trade deficit remained massive, with 1996 exports at $71 million and imports at $442 million. The government of President Issaias Afewerki was increasingly eager to attract foreign investment, licences being awarded to US and South African companies for oil and gold exploration. There were also close ties with South Korea, especially for construction projects, and a World Bank loan for port development was announced in December.

Relations with Sudan remained extremely bad, as Sudanese National Democratic Alliance (NDA) rebels based in Eritrea threatened the critical road link between Khartoum and Port Sudan in January (see also V.4.i). The former Sudanese Prime Minister, Sadiq al-Mahdi, signalled his support for the NDA by taking refuge in Eritrea. In June the Sudanese government alleged that an Eritrean invasion was imminent, while Eritrea accused Sudan of plotting to assassinate President Issaias. In May foreign employees of the United Nations High Commission for Refugees (UNHCR) were ordered out of the country for 'activities incompatible with their responsibilities', an action apparently resulting from differences between the government and UNHCR over the repatriation of Muslim refugees from Sudan.

SOMALIA. The country continued to lack any effective government, remaining divided between a large number of armed factions, which in turn were largely based on historic clan divisions. One group of 26 factions, led by Osman Ali Ato's United Somali Congress (USC) and Ali Mahdi Mohammed's Somali Salvation Alliance (SNA), met in Ethiopia in January, establishing the National Salvation Council. However, this was boycotted by a rival group, led by Hussein Aydid's Somali National Alliance (SNA), which was in turn associated with Kenya. Mr Aydid, who referred to himself as 'President of the Somali Republic', introduced new banknotes in October, but neither these nor his presidency were recognized by rival factions. Leaders of both groups met in Cairo in November and December, agreeing on the establishment of a transitional national government; although many such agreements had collapsed in the past, the year ended on a note of optimism.

Sporadic factional fighting was reported, notably in Mogadishu in September and in Baidoa in October, but open conflict generally remained at a low level.

In some parts of the country, such as Bossasso in the north-east, a flourishing export trade resumed. On the other hand, the major areas of agricultural production in the Juba and Wabe Shebelle valleys were devastated by unseasonal floods in October and November, displacing at least a quarter of a million people and leading to outbreaks of cholera. Lawlessness in the area obstructed relief operations, and several aid agencies withdrew relief workers in November, after kidnappings for ransom in Mogadishu.

In the breakaway Somaliland Republic (the former British or Northern Somaliland), Mohammed Ibrahim Egal was re-elected president in February, with the support of 223 members of the 315-member National Communities Conference. His unexpected resignation in December, ostensibly for health reasons, was refused by the Conference. Djibouti became the first country officially to recognize Somaliland in November. A visit to Hargeisa by a US delegation in December, in connection with Secretary of State Albright's visit to Ethiopia, further enhanced Somaliland's diplomatic profile.

DJIBOUTI. The security situation remained relatively quiet, despite the killing of 11 soldiers in September by a breakaway faction of the Afar-based Front for the Restoration of Unity and Democracy (FRUD) led by Ahmed Dini, who had refused to accept the 1996 peace agreement under which FRUD was legalized. Eight Ethiopian Afar militants were arrested in October and handed over to the Ethiopian authorities, an action which helped to prompt a European Parliament resolution in December expressing alarm over the human rights situation in the country.

The pro-government faction of FRUD was registered as a political party in April and contested legislative elections held on 19 December in an alliance with the ruling Popular Rally for Progress, the alliance winning all 65 seats. The opposition National Democratic Party and Party of Democratic Renewal alleged that the poll was flawed by irregularities. President Hassan Gouled Aptidon appointed a new government after the election, including several FRUD ministers; Barkat Gourad Hamadou, Prime Minister since 1978, retained his post.

The French Minister of Defence announced in December that the French garrison in Djibouti, the largest in Africa, would be reduced from 3,200 to 2,600 men. Although this decision formed part of a general review of French military commitments, it also reflected a declining level of French aid to Djibouti.

ii. KENYA

CAPITAL: Nairobi   AREA: 580,000 sq km   POPULATION: 33,000,000 ('96)
OFFICIAL LANGUAGES: Kiswahili & English   POLITICAL SYSTEM: presidential
HEAD OF STATE & GOVERNMENT: President Daniel Arap Moi (since Aug '78)
RULING PARTY: Kenya African National Union (KANU)
MAIN IGO MEMBERSHIPS (non-UN): OAU, COMESA, ACP, CWTH, NAM
CURRENCY: shilling (end-'97 £1=Ksh103.61, US$1=Ksh63.15)
GNP PER CAPITA: US$280 ('95) or US$1,380 ('95) by PPP calculation

PRESIDENTIAL and parliamentary elections on 29 December returned Daniel Arap Moi as President and gave the Kenya African National Union (KANU), the ruling party, a working majority in the National Assembly, although not the two-thirds majority required for major constitutional change. The polling was marred by intimidation, vote-rigging and major defects in organization, a problem compounded by flooding in the coastal and north-eastern provinces. However, even if the elections—in which ethnic considerations were paramount—had been 'free and fair', the opposition was too disunited to have a realistic prospect of winning. Mwai Kibaki, the Democratic Party leader and former national Vice-President, emerged as President Moi's strongest challenger, the results giving him 31.1 per cent of the vote against the incumbent's winning share of 40.1 per cent, while three other opposition candidates recorded an aggregate of some 28 per cent. President Moi met the constitutional requirement of obtaining 25 per cent support in five provinces, his share of the total vote being an improvement on the 36.8 per cent which he secured in 1992. In the simultaneous parliamentary elections, KANU won 107 of the 210 elective seats as against 102 obtained by nine opposition parties. Out of 25 KANU cabinet ministers who stood, 12 were defeated.

During the campaign, party manifestos were replete with promises and platitudes. Serious issues were ignored, including a six-week nurses' strike, which paralysed a health service characterized by corruption, low wages and low morale. Violent incidents resulting in many deaths occurred in Nairobi, Kitui, Mombasa and several other areas where the security forces intervened, often brutally, to suppress demonstrations and rallies at which opposition politicians, students, clergymen and members of other civil groups called for democratic constitutional reforms to precede the elections. Faced with the prospect of further mass action, President Moi on 17 July conceded the need to establish a constitutional review commission and to talk with the opposition parties. The latter were divided over the strategy to adopt. Some favoured discussions with the government; among them were the faction of FORD-Kenya (the Forum for the Restoration of Democracy-Kenya) led by Michael Wamalwa, the party's leader and presidential candidate, and FORD-Asili, led by Kenneth Matiba (who subsequently boycotted the elections). Others, however, held out for more far-reaching changes, to be obtained—they believed—by further mass protest. The disunity of the opposition resulted in a low turnout for a general strike on 8 August.

Discussions between opposition and KANU MPs began on 28 August and led to agreement on a series of constitutional and electoral reforms. In October ten parties were registered, though the registration of three others was refused and opposition rallies were broken up by the police. As 15 foreign missions in Nairobi called jointly for the reforms to be implemented, a 12-day teachers' strike was settled, while on 22 October the President ordered the police not to disrupt peaceful opposition rallies. On 3 November the National Assembly passed constitutional amendments giving all political parties and presidential candidates equal access to the state-owned media, also allotting the opposition ten places on the expanded (21-member) electoral commission. Parliament was dissolved on 10 November.

The reform legislation came too late for some of the opposition parties to organize their campaigns. Safina, founded in 1995 by the palaeontologist Richard Leakey and not registered until 26 November, failed to achieve its main objective of persuading all the opposition parties to unite behind a single candidate for the presidency. As it was, the anti-Moi vote was divided between the four main challengers, namely Mwai Kibaki, Michael Wamalwa, Raila Odinga (leader of the National Democratic Party) and Charity Ngilu. A businesswoman and an opposition MP since 1992, Mrs Ngilu campaigned on a feminist platform, receiving fewer votes than any of the other three candidates.

Accordingly, an opposition movement hopelessly divided by personal ambitions and ethnic considerations prolonged the life of a discredited regime facing major problems of political instability and economic and social decline. Widespread corruption, and the government's failure to prosecute the 'big men' involved in it, was one of the main reasons for the IMF's suspension of its structural adjustment loan to Kenya in July. The return to the cabinet in January of Nicholas Biwott, who had been dismissed as Minister of Energy because of Western donor pressure in 1990, did not inspire international confidence. Foreign companies were finding Nairobi too run-down and, because of the soaring crime rate, too dangerous a place in which to work. In an economic survey released in May, Professor George Saitoti, the Planning and National Development Minister and also Vice-President, admitted that some 45 per cent of the country's population lived in abject poverty, unable to meet their basic food and other needs.

In these difficult circumstances, Finance Minister Musalia Mudavadi continued to pursue a reforming programme. In his June budget, he announced that both corporate and personal taxes were to be reduced to cushion low-income earners against inflation and to encourage investment, savings and job creation. Revenue collection procedures would be streamlined, making tax evasion more difficult, and emphasis was to be placed on completing existing projects that were viable rather than on initiating new ones. Priority would be given to improving and maintaining infrastructure, social services, primary education, basic and preventive health care, and rural water supply. The efficiency of the state-owned telecommunications and railway companies would be improved by opening them to private sector participation.

iii. TANZANIA

CAPITAL: Dar es Salaam/Dodoma   AREA: 945,000 sq km   POPULATION: 31,000,000 ('96)
OFFICIAL LANGUAGES: Kiswahili & English   POLITICAL SYSTEM: presidential
HEAD OF STATE & GOVERNMENT: President Benjamin Mkapa (since Nov '95)
PRESIDENT OF ZANZIBAR: Salmin Amour (since Oct '90)
RULING PARTY: Chama cha Mapinduzi (CCM)
PRIME MINISTER: Frederick Sumaye (since Nov '95)
MAIN IGO MEMBERSHIPS (non-UN): OAU, COMESA, SADC, ACP, CWTH, NAM
CURRENCY: shilling (end-'97 £1=Tsh1,014.94, US$1=Tsh618.60)
GNP PER CAPITA: US$120 ('95) or US$640 ('95) by PPP calculation

DESPITE the introduction of multi-partyism, Chama cha Mapinduzi (CCM), the ruling party, tightened its grip on power. President Benjamin Mkapa was elected chairman by acclamation at a party congress in November, but failed to secure the election of Frederick Sumaye, the Prime Minister, as his deputy. The post of CCM vice-chairman went to John Malecela, a former Prime Minister on the socialist wing of the party, whom Mr Mkapa had relegated to the backbenches.

The opposition parties were not only badly organized but also weakened by personal rivalries. The Civic United Front (CUF) was recognized as the official parliamentary opposition; all of its 24 MPs represented Zanzibar/Pemba constituencies. It was allied with the United Democratic Party (UDP), whose four MPs held constituencies in the Lake Victoria area. One of these seats (Magu, near Mwanza) was won for the party during the year by its leader, John Cheyo, at the expense of the CCM and the National Convention for Construction and Reform (NCCR). As deputy leader of the parliamentary opposition, Mr Cheyo proved to be an effective government critic. The NCCR was weakened by a split into rival factions.

In Zanzibar, the CUF won a December by-election for the Mkunazini constituency (Stone Town) with a sharply-reduced majority over the CCM; the arrest of 12 CUF leaders on sedition charges immediately before the election might have affected the result. The CUF's persistent refusal to recognize Salmin Amour (CCM) as the islands' rightful president and its boycott of the Zanzibari House of Representatives were considered mistaken by the mainland party and resulted in a damaging split between the two party wings.

The country remained politically stable despite the grim socio-economic conditions which its government faced. There was growing inequality, high unemployment, increasing crime, a weak infrastructure and run-down social services. For the President, the solution was a market-economy strategy which stressed privatization (recognized to be behind schedule), foreign investment and tourism, and entailed reducing the number of civil servants. With the backing of the Corruption Commission under Judge Joseph Warioba, a former Prime Minister, he continued to fight corruption, though with only mixed success according to some critics. Western donors pressed for action to be taken against those identified as corrupt by the commission. Over 20 newspapers were now available to expose flaws in government policy and performance: it was argued, for example, that nascent domestic industries producing such goods as textiles and construction materials had been hard hit by the abolition of protective import tariffs.

In February the Paris Club of creditor countries relieved Tanzania of US$1,000 million of its $7,800 million debt. However, the stark facts—as revealed by Daniel Yona, the Minister of Finance—were that only 20 per cent of tax revenues went on running the government and rebuilding infrastructure; of the remainder, 40 per cent went on debt-servicing and another 40 per cent on state sector wages and salaries. According to the IMF, the earliest that Tanzania could expect relief under its new 'heavily indebted poor countries' scheme was 2002.

In his June budget, Mr Yona introduced new taxation measures designed to promote the private sector and encourage investment. The aim was to achieve a growth rate of 5.5 per cent, bring down inflation to 10 per cent, reduce the current-account deficit and improve government self-reliance. Approximately 68 per cent of revenue (predicted at TSh975,600 million, or about $1,560 million) would be allocated to recurrent expenditure and 32 per cent to a reduced number of development projects. High priority was to be given to run-down social services and to improving infrastructure. The mining and petroleum sectors were to receive preferential treatment, but—perhaps surprisingly—no significant measures were introduced to boost agriculture. Civil servants were given a modest pay rise. In Zanzibar's separate budget, approximately 77 per cent of total expenditure (estimated at TSh55,500 million, or about $90 million) would be recurrent and 23 per cent developmental.

The Burundi government accused Tanzania of harbouring Hutu rebels who used their camps as a base from which to attack Burundi, insisting that disarming these rebels was a precondition of its taking part in regional peace talks (see also VII.1.ii). Further efforts were made to facilitate the movement of human and financial resources between Kenya, Tanzania and Uganda. Severe drought and food shortages over much of the country in September were followed in the next two months by flooding in the coastal regions, causing widespread loss of life and property.

iv. UGANDA

CAPITAL: Kampala   AREA: 240,000 sq km   POPULATION: 20,500,000 ('96)
OFFICIAL LANGUAGE: English   POLITICAL SYSTEM: presidential
HEAD OF STATE & GOVERNMENT: President Yoweri Museveni (since Jan '86)
RULING PARTY: National Resistance Movement (NRM) heads broad-based coalition
PRIME MINISTER: Kintu Musoke (since Nov '94)
MAIN IGO MEMBERSHIPS (non-UN): OAU, COMESA, ACP, CWTH, OIC, NAM
CURRENCY: shilling (end-'97 £1=Ush1,863.84, US$1=Ush1,136.00)
GNP PER CAPITA: US$240 ('95) or US$1,470 ('95) by PPP calculation

PRESIDENT Yoweri Museveni won recognition for his relatively efficient administration and capitalist-type policies when Uganda became the first country in Africa to benefit from the debt reduction plan of the World Bank and the IMF. Oxfam, one of the country's many non-governmental organizations, championed its case but was disappointed at the amount of relief awarded. The extent of government decentralization was impressive, though district and sub-county councils, especially, continued to face serious problems of staffing, finance and the quality of councillors. In February President Museveni persuaded MPs to lower the minimum academic qualifications for councillors which, in his view, had been set unrealistically high in the draft 1996 Local Government Bill.

In his budget speech on 12 June, Finance Minister Mayanja Nkangi said that his principal objectives were to revamp the Uganda Revenue Authority and to simplify, modernize and consolidate the taxation system, thus promoting trade liberalization and international competitiveness, and also relieving poverty in accordance with the government's Poverty Eradication Action Plan. State subsidies to parastatals would be reduced and privatization would continue, with the focus shifted to larger enterprises such as Uganda Posts and Telecommunications and the collapsed Uganda Commercial Bank. Since the minister anticipated a shortfall of USh43,000 million (approximately US$39 million) in revenue for the year projected at USh776,000 million ($698 million) as a result of tax evasion and smuggling, belt-tightening was necessary; accordingly, government expenditure was cut by 23 per cent. Positive measures included reducing import duties from 30 to 20 per cent and corporate tax from 35 to 30 per cent. Expenditure on education was increased in order to provide free primary education for four children in each family. Encouragement was given to tourism, a fast-growing sector of the economy. The monopoly of the Cotton Development Organization was ended, enabling farmers to buy cotton seed from private suppliers.

Continued rebel activity, and poor roads, seriously hampered development in the north. A divided and discontented army, alleged to be involved in smuggling and other corrupt practices, was incapable of preventing the (nominally Christian fundamentalist) Lord's Resistance Army (LRA) ravaging the Gulu and Kitgum districts before retreating to its bases in Sudan (see also V.4.i). The policy of placing civilians from the war-torn districts in protection centres was not working well; relief food sometimes did not reach them and in April famine threatened. President Museveni and other East African leaders pursued a regional initiative to end the 14-year old war in the Sudan, whose government gave refuge to the LRA in retaliation for Uganda's alleged support of the Sudan People's Liberation Army. The Museveni government also played a part in establishing Laurent Kabila in power in the Congo (see VII.1.i), though disparate rebel groups backed by soldiers of the ex-Zaïrean and Rwandan armies launched periodic raids along Uganda's southern and western borders.

Women caring for Uganda's 1.5 million orphans—mostly the victims of war and AIDS—were organized into groups and received support from the Uganda Women's Effort to Save Orphans (UWESO); on average, each woman looked after seven orphans. President Museveni's autobiography, *Saving the Mustard Seed* (sub-titled 'The Struggle for Freedom and Democracy in Uganda'), was published during the year.

2. GHANA—NIGERIA—SIERRA LEONE—THE GAMBIA—LIBERIA

i. GHANA

CAPITAL: Accra   AREA: 240,000 sq km   POPULATION: 18,000,000 ('96)
OFFICIAL LANGUAGE: English POLITICAL SYSTEM: presidential
HEAD OF STATE & GOVERNMENT: President Jerry Rawlings (since Nov '92), previously Chairman of Provisional National Defence Council (since '81)
RULING PARTIES: National Democratic Congress (NDC) heads coalition
MAIN IGO MEMBERSHIPS (non-UN): OAU, ECOWAS, ACP, CWTH, NAM
CURRENCY: cedi (end-'97 £1=C3,707.99, US$1=C2,260.00)
GNP PER CAPITA: US$390 ('95) or US$1,990 ('95) by PPP calculation

THE shadow of the millennium fell across the new year when on 7 January Jerry Rawlings was sworn in as President for his second and final four-year term. Observers were already wondering who would stand in the elections due in the year 2000. The ruling National Democratic Congress (NDC) argued that the constitution should be amended to allow a third term, Vincent Assiseh (the party's press secretary) suggesting a three-year extension. President Rawlings was reticent, but told the state opening of parliament that the 1992 constitution was a 'living document' which could be adapted to changing conditions.

The debate continued throughout the year, enlivened by the suggestion that the President's wife, Nana Konadu Agyemen-Rawlings, should stand. When asked, the lady would not say 'yes', but also declined to say 'no'. The argument took a further turn in June when the opposition New Patriotic Party (NPP) won a by-election in the Ashanti constituency of Afigya-Sekere, depriving the government of the two-thirds majority in parliament required to change the constitution.

Uncertainty marked the new government of 72 ministers and deputies, many of whom could not be sworn in until later in the year because of a wrangle over the vetting procedure by a parliamentary appointments committee. The opposition insisted that ministers who continued in office from the previous administration should be vetted along with the new appointments. The President, who had the option of appointing non-parliamentarians as ministers, refused. In May the leader of the NPP, J.H. Mensah, filed a suit in the High Court, challenging the appointment of Kwame Pepreh as Finance Minister, who was thus unable to present the budget on time. After the court had delivered an ambiguous judgment in June, the opposition parties staged a series of walkouts from parliament, as the government continued in disarray. There were no legally-appointed ministers in a number of posts, until the President resorted to the subterfuge of appointing ministers without designating their office. That parliament continued to meet and debate was due in large measure to the influence of the Speaker, Justice D.F. Annan.

The government was handicapped by the loss of the former Minister of Finance, Kwesi Botchwey, who had accepted an academic appointment at the Massachusetts Institute of Technology. The effect could be seen in the other major theme of the year—corruption and financial irregularities. President Rawlings inveighed against corruption as 'economic murder' and stressed the need for 'probity and accountability'. However, when the Commission on Human Rights and Administration of Justice (CHRAJ), chaired by Justice Emile Short, found three ministers guilty of malfeasance, the government issued a White Paper exonerating them on 15 April.

In September the Attorney-General and Justice Minister, Obed Asamoah, had to explain how millions of cedis belonging to the NDC came to be stolen from his house by two policemen sent to guard him. Other scandals involved the mishandling of funds by an investment company, whose collapse cost investors some C20,000 million. In July the governor and deputy governor of the Bank of Ghana, G.K. Agama and Theresa Owusu, were not reappointed when their contracts expired, after the bank had admitted that it could not account for C60,000 million of public monies transferred for government use. In the same month, after a popular outcry, the President had to postpone a price increase of 180 per cent introduced in June by the Volta River Authority for the supply of power to the Electricity Corporation of Ghana. Meanwhile, the government began to campaign once again for the reintroduction of value-added tax (VAT), despite the serious anti-VAT riots of May 1995 (see AR 1995, p. 248).

In general terms the economy moved forward, GDP growth being estimated at 5.2 per cent. New deposits of high-grade iron ore were found at Adum Banso in the Western region and were expected to contribute substantially to foreign-exchange earnings. Inflation was still high at over 30 per cent, but the target figure of 15 per cent was believed to be within reach.

The government did not neglect its external obligations, being represented at the Commonwealth heads of government meeting in Edinburgh in October (see XI.2.i) and at UNIDO, OAU, ECOWAS and other gatherings. An interesting light was shone on Ghana's external relations in August when it was revealed that the Libyan government had authorized the transfer of over £300,000 to the bank account of the deputy foreign editor of *The Guardian* newspaper in London. According to the disclosures, the money had been used to help fund the unsuccessful libel suit brought in 1993 by Kojo Tsikata, former head of Ghana's security service, against *The Independent* newspaper (see AR 1994, p. 270). *The Guardian* journalist concerned, a personal friend of Mr Tsikata, admitted receiving the money but said that she had not known of its Libyan provenance.

ii. NIGERIA

CAPITAL: Abuja   AREA: 924,000 sq km   POPULATION: 120,000,000 ('96)
OFFICIAL LANGUAGE: English   POLITICAL SYSTEM: military rule
HEAD OF STATE & GOVERNMENT: General Sani Abacha, Chairman of Provisional Ruling
    Council and of Federal Executive Council (since Nov '93)
MAIN IGO MEMBERSHIPS (non-UN): OAU, ECOWAS, OPEC, ACP, NAM
CURRENCY: naira (end-'97 £1=N124.15, US$1=N75.67)
GNP PER CAPITA: US$260 ('95) or US$1,220 ('95) by PPP calculation

NIGERIA's quarrel with the international community about its lack of democracy and poor human rights record continued through 1997, although its efforts to restore democracy in neighbouring Sierra Leone following the coup in that country received some praise (see VI.2.iii). Despite deep suspicions as to their real worth, further steps were taken towards a return to civilian rule in 1998, while the economy benefited from a rise in oil prices.

In the 1997 budget presented in January, the Finance Minister, Anthony Ani, doubled spending on the rural areas, 32 per cent of total expenditure of N146,000 million being set aside for infrastructure, agriculture, water resources and rural development. Expenditure on health and education was also increased, while defence spending, at N17,500 million, represented 12 per cent of the total as opposed to 10.9 per cent in 1996. The increased budgetary expenditure was made possible by a rise in the price of oil from US$16 to $17 a barrel, Mr Ani reporting that as a result foreign exchange reserves had risen from $1,440 million to $4,090 million. Oil production for 1997 was expected to run at the level of 2.04 million barrels per day (b/d) and to produce revenue of $11,000 million, up 13.5 per cent over 1996.

Following two bombings in December 1996 (apparently targeting the military administrator, Colonel Muhammad Marwa), two soldiers were killed and 29 wounded by a bomb in Lagos on 7 January. No-one claimed responsibility. Another bomb in the capital in mid-February injured five soldiers and three civilians, while an attack on an army barracks in Yaba suburb of Lagos on 7 May wounded five soldiers; a second explosion nearby caused a general panic and four suspects were arrested. On 12 May a bomb explosion in Ibadan, the capital of Oyo state, wounded soldiers and police travelling on a truck; two more bombs at Onitsha killed four civilians and wounded others.

Following the May bombings, the assistant police commissioner, Zachary Bin, who chaired the presidential task force on terrorism, claimed that the bombs were the work of the opposition National Democratic Coalition (NADECO), which was led by the exiled Wole Soyinka. Earlier in the year, on 12 March, Mr Soyinka and three others living abroad had been among 15 people charged with treason for causing explosions and waging war on General Sani Abacha (the regime's leader). Carrying the death penalty, the charges followed an interview by Mr Soyinka in the *Washington Post* threatening legal action against General Abacha for describing him as a terrorist.

In another interview carried by the *Washington Post* on 5 February, General Abacha said that he might stand as a presidential candidate in the elections scheduled for 1998, claiming that his programme to restore civilian rule was on schedule and that his efforts to achieve economic stability were succeeding. He attacked foreign criticisms of his human rights record as unjustified and blamed the delay in holding local elections—which he had postponed from the previous December to mid-March—on the bomb attacks in Lagos.

On 10 February registration of voters, seen as the first stage in the return to civilian rule, began at over 100,000 centres. The postponed local elections were held on 15 March and turnout was described as massive, with more than 90 per cent of the electorate taking part in some regions. They were the first elections to be held since the army takeover in November 1993. In two outbreaks of violence, students at the University of Ile calling for the release of Chief M.K.O. Abiola (see AR 1996, p. 249) stormed a polling booth, while at Onitsha police used tear gas to disperse a crowd of 2,000 demonstrators who accused electoral officials of fraud.

Strained relations with the Commonwealth were a feature of the year, following the suspension of Nigeria's membership in 1995 (see AR 1995, pp. 251, 381). In February the Commonwealth Ministerial Action Group (CMAG) met in London and called for further evidence concerning alleged human rights violations in Nigeria (see also XI.2.i). At a further meeting in London in July, the CMAG heard new evidence from opponents of the Abacha regime, who appealed for the imposition of comprehensive sanctions against Nigeria on the grounds that the existing sanctions were having no effect. Canada, the most outspoken Commonwealth critic of Nigeria, subsequently suspended diplomatic relations with the Abacha government. The Commonwealth heads of government meeting in Edinburgh in October maintained its suspension of Nigeria and warned that it could face oil sanctions if it failed to restore democracy in 1998. Nigeria was not permitted to take part in the meeting.

Outbreaks of communal fighting occurred near Warri in Delta state during April between members of the rival Ijaw and Itsekiri communities, apparently because of a decision by the local government to move its municipal offices from an Ijaw to an Itsekiri area. A number of people were reported to have been killed, although precise figures were not available. The unrest involved Anglo-Dutch Shell, 100 of whose employees were taken hostage by some of the rival combatants. As a result, Shell decided to close down 11 wells, six of them in Delta state, thus reducing the company's oil output by 210,000 b/d. On 9 April Shell announced that six wells would remain closed, while three others (which had been vandalized) would be reopened as soon as possible. The violence continued, so that on 23 April the government sent troops to the region to restore order. The disruptions caused a loss of production totalling 1.5 million barrels. Lagos was affected by oil shortages during April: troops were posted at petrol stations to keep order and other economic activities had to be curtailed. Shell claimed that the shortages resulted from technical and distribution factors rather than the communal fighting at Warri.

Nigeria's huge project to market its natural gas ran into trouble in June when the Minister of Petroleum Resources, Dan Etete, dismissed the board of the Nigeria Liquefied Natural Gas Company (NLNG), apparently because he disliked the contractual terms which gave Royal Dutch Shell (with a shareholding of 25.6 per cent) the right to nominate the managing director. The foreign partners—Shell, Agip and Elf—urgently sought clarification. Costed at US$4,000 million, the project was the largest in sub-Saharan Africa. Construction work had finally begun in 1996, 30 years after the project was first mooted, with the aim of marketing the first gas in 1999. Fearing political interference, the foreign participants were prepared to go ahead only if the Nigerian government had a minority stake in the NLNG.

On 2 July the government announced the election timetable that would lead to the restoration of civilian government on 1 October 1998. It was seen as a calculated snub to external demands for an earlier return to civilian rule. Elections to state assemblies were set for December, with polling for the national parliament to follow on 25 April 1998. Gubernatorial and presidential elections would be held in two rounds on 1 and 15 August 1998. Governors would be sworn in on 21 September and the new President and National Assembly would be inaugurated on 1 October 1998. The state assembly elections took place as scheduled on 6 December, the 989 seats being contested by five registered parties. According to official results, the United Nigeria Congress Party won 500 seats and the Democratic Party of Nigeria 151.

Meanwhile, in a speech delivered on 17 November (the fourth anniversary of his coup), General Abacha had announced the dissolution of the Federal Executive Council (cabinet). A new ministerial team was installed on 15 December, those dropped including Major-General Abdulkarim Adisa and Major-General Tajudeen Olarenwaju, while new appointments included Major-General Patrick Azika as Minister of Communications. Less than a week later, on 21 December, the regime announced that it had foiled a coup plot and that several military leaders had been arrested, including Major-General Adisa and Major-General Olarenwaju, as well as the Chief of General Staff, Lieut.-General Oladipo Diya. Observers noted that those arrested were from the Yoruba ethnic group of southwestern Nigeria, a centre of opposition to the Abacha regime.

The opposition NADECO claimed on 26 December that the government had invented the coup plot as a pretext for a political purge and to divert attention from the death in prison on 9 December of former Vice-President Shehu Musa Yar'Adua (aged 54). Shortly after the 1993 coup, General Yar'Adua had orchestrated a motion in the constituent assembly that General Abacha should relinquish power immediately. With other leading opponents of the new regime, he had been arrested, tried in secret by a military tribunal and condemned to death, although an international outcry had resulted in his sentence being commuted to 25 years in prison. The regime declined to give details of the cause of his death.

iii. SIERRA LEONE

CAPITAL: Freetown   AREA: 72,000 sq km   POPULATION: 4,450,000 ('96)
OFFICIAL LANGUAGE: English   POLITICAL SYSTEM: presidential
HEAD OF STATE & GOVERNMENT: Lt.-Col. Johnny Paul Koroma seized power in May 1997 from
   Alhaji Ahmed Tejan Kabba (in office since March '96)
MAIN IGO MEMBERSHIPS (non-UN): OAU, ECOWAS, OIC, ACP, CWTH, NAM
CURRENCY: leone (end-'97 £1=Le1,476.63, US$1=Le900.00)
GNP PER CAPITA: US$180 ('95) or US$580 ('95) by PPP calculation

HOPES for a continuation of democratic government and economic reconstruction were dashed by a new military coup on 25 May. Styling itself the Armed Forces Revolutionary Council (AFRC), the army junta chose at its leader Major

Johnny Koroma, in detention at the time of the coup for seeking to overthrow the government the previous September. The AFRC gave as their reasons for overthrowing President Ahmed Tejan Kabba, and the Sierra Leone People's Party government, fear of the country's disintegration into renewed factional conflicts owing to ineffective national leadership. Also cited were the government's failure to deal with growing corruption, alleged erosion of democratic rule, a neglect of the needs of the armed forces and a favouring of the popular militia, the Kamajors, over the regular army.

The AFRC also took a more sympathetic position towards the Revolutionary United Front (RUF), which had still to be incorporated into the government after the signing of the Abidjan peace accord in 1996 (see AR 1996, p. 251). The RUF leader, Foday Sankoh, though detained in Nigeria, supported the coup, and his forces made common cause with the AFRC when ECOMOG peacekeeping forces of the Economic Community of West African States based in Sierra Leone sought to enforce regional and international sanctions against the military junta.

Despite the international isolation and condemnation of the AFRC and amid fighting between the AFRC/RUF and ECOMOG/Kamajor forces, the military junta remained in control of the country at the end of the year. On the diplomatic front, negotiations continued to bring about a restoration of the Kabba government by peaceful means.

iv. THE GAMBIA

CAPITAL: Banjul   AREA: 11,300 sq km   POPULATION: 1,150,000 ('96)
OFFICIAL LANGUAGE: English   POLITICAL SYSTEM: military/presidential
HEAD OF STATE & GOVERNMENT: President (Col.) Yahya Jammeh (since Sept '96), previously Chairman of Armed Forces Provisional Ruling Council
RULING PARTY: Alliance for Patriotic Reorientation and Reconstruction
MAIN IGO MEMBERSHIPS (non-UN): OAU, ECOWAS, ACP, CWTH, OIC, NAM
CURRENCY: dalasi (end-'97 £1=D16.52, US$1=D10.07)
GNP PER CAPITA: US$320 ('95) or US$930 ('95) by PPP calculation

FRESH from his personal victory in the presidential election of September 1996 (see AR 1996, pp. 251–2), the former army leader and now President, Yahya Jammeh, went on to achieve similar success in the parliamentary elections held on 2 January. His Alliance for Patriotic Reorientation and Reconstruction (APRC) swept the polls, winning 33 of the 45 directly-elected seats in the enlarged and renamed National Assembly. In view of the banning of the former ruling People's Progressive Party (PPP) and the two leading opposition formations (the National Convention Party and Gambia People's Party) and their leaders, opposition groups were forced to reconstruct themselves under new organizations and leaders. Headed by Oussainou Darboe, a lawyer, the United Democratic Party came second with seven seats, while the National Reconciliation Party led by Hamat Bah, a hotelier, took two seats. The previously unsuccessful People's Democratic Organization for Independence and Socialism won one seat and there were two successful independent candidates.

While the new constitution undoubtedly favoured the APRC, and there was evidence of electoral malpractice favouring the government, the APRC victory also owed much to its superior organization and judicious use of public patronage, and to the continuing, if diminishing, personal reputation of President Jammeh as a reforming leader. Secure in his ascendancy at home, the President spent much of the year seeking to promote his administration's reputation abroad, having previously been ostracized by the international community for seizing power by force from an elected government. Growing acceptance of his position was reflected in the renewal of aid programmes, the return of large numbers of foreign tourists, his presence at the Commonwealth heads of government meeting held in Edinburgh in October (see XI.2.i) and at other international gatherings. The Gambia also secured election to a non-permanent seat on the UN Security Council.

v. LIBERIA

CAPITAL: Monrovia AREA: 97,750 sq km POPULATION: 2,800,000 ('96)
OFFICIAL LANGUAGE: English POLITICAL SYSTEM: republic
HEAD OF STATE & GOVERNMENT: President Charles Taylor (since July '97)
RULING PARTY: National Patriotic Party of Liberia (NPPL)
MAIN IGO MEMBERSHIPS (non-UN): OAU,ECOWAS, ACP, NAM
CURRENCY: Liberian dollar (end-'97 £1=L$1.64,US$1=L$1.00)
GNP PER CAPITA: n/a

AFTER several false dawns, seven years of civil war finally came to an end in 1997 with the disarming and disbanding of the armed factions contesting control of the state and the return of an elected civilian government. Despite lingering doubts about the intentions of rival warlords, preparations for a return to competitive party politics took place in the spring with the conversion of armed factions into political parties in February and the holding of presidential and parliamentary elections, under international scrutiny, on 19 July.

Owing to the enormous displacement of the population, of which an estimated 40 per cent had been forced to flee to neighbouring countries, seats were awarded on the basis of the parties' share of the national vote. Charles Ghankay Taylor, previously a much-vilified warlord, and his reconstituted organization now called the National Patriotic Party of Liberia (NPPL), won an overwhelming 82 per cent of the vote, defeating eight other presidential candidates as well as other civilianized military factions and several political parties set up by former politicians. Requiring a minimum of 2 per cent of the national vote for seats in the House of Representatives and 4 per cent for the Senate, only three parties qualified for seats in both chambers. The NPPL gained 64 seats in the House and 21 in the Senate, while both the Unity Party and Alhaji Kromah's All-Liberian Coalition (ALCOM, previously the ULIMO-K military faction) won two Senate seats and three in the House. Three other parties won seats in the House, namely the Alliance of Political Parties, the United People's Party (two each) and the Liberia People's Party (one).

Mr Taylor's victory was attributed to several factors: the fragmentation of the opposition; his undoubted superior organization and financial resources; his deliberate cultivation of a statesmanlike image, stressing remorse and reconciliation; and a general feeling among the populace that he was the person most likely to return the country to normality. Following his inauguration on 2 August, the new President consciously adopted a policy of reconciliation and national integration. Despite his overwhelming strength in Congress, he appointed leaders of rival parties and technocrats to his cabinet and initiated a programme of economic rehabilitation designed to benefit the country as a whole. However, with an empty treasury, a $US3,000 million external debt and continuing widespread corruption, the new government had first to generate the necessary resources. Its economic policy gave priority to fiscal probity and revenue generation, while at the same time encouraging domestic and overseas private investors.

The new government's foreign policy sought to restore national sovereignty after years of anarchy and external intervention. This policy led to some friction with the ECOMOG peace-keeping force of the Economic Community of West African States and with Nigeria, the dominant ECOMOG participant. President Taylor was critical of the ECOMOG/Nigerian role in Sierra Leone (see VI.2.iii) and several thousand Nigerians were deported. By December the ECOMOG presence in Liberia had been substantially reduced, its much-criticized mission having been successfully accomplished.

3. WEST AFRICAN FRANCOPHONE STATES—CENTRAL AFRICAN FRANC ZONE

i. SENEGAL—MAURITANIA—MALI—GUINEA— CÔTE D'IVOIRE—BURKINA FASO—TOGO—BENIN—NIGER

Senegal
CAPITAL: Dakar AREA: 196,000 sq km POPULATION: 8,500,000 ('96)
OFFICIAL LANGUAGE: French POLITICAL SYSTEM: presidential democracy
HEAD OF STATE & GOVERNMENT: President Abdou Diouf, since Jan '81
RULING PARTIES: Socialist Party (PS) heads coalition
PRIME MINISTER: Habib Thiam (PS), since April '91
MAIN IGO MEMBERSHIPS (non-UN): OAU, ECOWAS, UEMOA, ACP, OIC, NAM, Francophonie
CURRENCY: CFA franc (end-'97 £1=CFAF990.25, US$1=CFAF603.55)
GNP PER CAPITA: US$600 ('95) or US$1,780 ('95) by PPP calculation

Mauritania
CAPITAL: Nouakchott AREA: 1,000,000 sq km POPULATION: 2,235,000 ('96)
OFFICIAL LANGUAGES: French & Arabic POLITICALSYSTEM: presidential
HEAD OF STATE & GOVERNMENT: President (Col.) Maaouiya Ould Sidi Mohammed Taya (since Jan '92); previously Chairman of Military Council of National Salvation (from Dec '84)
RULING PARTY: Democratic and Social Republican Party (PRDS)
PRIME MINISTER: Mohammed Lemine Ould Guig (since Dec '97)
MAIN IGO MEMBERSHIPS (non-UN): OAU, ECOWAS, UEMOA, AMU, AL, OIC, ACP, NAM, Francophonie
CURRENCY: ouguiya (end-'97 £1=OM273.09, US$1=OM166.45)
GNP PER CAPITA: US$460 ('95) or US$1,540 ('95) by PPP calculation

VI.3.i. WEST AFRICAN FRANCOPHONE STATES

Mali
CAPITAL: Bamako AREA: 1,240,000 sq km POPULATION: 10,500,000 ('96)
OFFICIAL LANGUAGE: French POLITICAL SYSTEM: presidential
HEAD OF STATE & GOVERNMENT: President Alpha Oumar Konaré (since April '92)
RULING PARTY: Alliance for Democracy in Mali (ADEMA)
PRIME MINISTER: Ibrahim Boubakar Keita (since April '92)
MAIN IGO MEMBERSHIPS (non-UN): OAU, ECOWAS, UEMOA, AL, OIC, ACP, NAM, Francophonie
CURRENCY: CFA franc (see above)
GNP PER CAPITA: US$250 ('95) or US$550 ('95) by PPP calculation

Guinea
CAPITAL: Conakry AREA: 246,000 sq km POPULATION: 6,500,000 ('96)
OFFICIAL LANGUAGE: French POLITICAL SYSTEM: presidential
HEAD OF STATE & GOVERNMENT: President (Gen.)Lansana Conté (since Dec '93); previously Chairman of Military Committee for National Recovery (from April '84)
RULING PARTY: Party of Unity and Progress (PUP)
PRIME MINISTER: Sidya Touré (since July '96)
MAIN IGO MEMBERSHIPS (non-UN): OAU, ECOWAS, OIC, ACP, ACP, NAM, Francophonie
CURRENCY: Guinean franc (end-'97 £1=GF1,863.84, US$1=GF1,136.00)
GNP PER CAPITA: US$550 ('95)

Côte d'Ivoire
CAPITAL: Abidjan AREA: 322,000 sq km POPULATION: 14,500,000 ('96)
OFFICIAL LANGUAGE: French POLITICAL SYSTEM: presidential
HEAD OF STATE & GOVERNMENT: President Henri Konan Bédié (since Dec '93)
RULING PARTY: Democratic Party of Côte d'Ivoire (PDCI)
PRIME MINISTER: Daniel Kablan Duncan (since Dec '93)
MAIN IGO MEMBERSHIPS (non-UN): OAU, ECOWAS, UEMOA, ACP, NAM, Francophonie
CURRENCY: CFA franc (see above)
GNP PER CAPITA: US$660 ('95) or US$1,580 ('95) by PPP calculation

Burkina Faso
CAPITAL: Ouagadougou AREA: 275,000 sq km POPULATION: 10,250,000 ('96)
OFFICIAL LANGUAGE: French POLITICAL SYSTEM: presidential
HEAD OF STATE & GOVERNMENT: President (Capt.) Blaise Compaoré (since Dec '91); previously Chairman of Popular Front (from Oct '87)
RULING PARTY: Organization for Popular Democracy-Labour Movement (ODP-MT)
PRIME MINISTER: Kadre Desiré Ouédraogo (since Feb '96)
MAIN IGO MEMBERSHIPS (non-UN): OAU, ECOWAS, UEMOA, OIC, ACP, NAM, Francophonie
CURRENCY: CFA franc (see above)
GNP PER CAPITA: US$230 ('95) or US$780 ('95) by PPP calculation

Togo
CAPITAL: Lomé AREA: 57,000 sq km POPULATION: 4,000,000 ('96)
OFFICIAL LANGUAGES: French, Kabiye & Ewe POLITICAL SYSTEM: presidential
HEAD OF STATE: President (Gen.) Gnassingbé Eyadema (since '67)
RULING PARTY: Rally for the Togolese People (RPT)
PRIME MINISTER: Kouassi Klutse (since Aug '96)
MAIN IGO MEMBERSHIPS (non-UN): OAU, ECOWAS, UEMOA, ACP, NAM, Francophonie
CURRENCY: CFA franc (see above)
GNP PER CAPITA: US$310 ('95) or US$1,130 ('95) by PPP calculation

Benin
CAPITAL: Porto Novo AREA: 113,000 sq km POPULATION: 5,750,000 ('96)
OFFICIAL LANGUAGE: French POLITICAL SYSTEM: presidential
HEAD OF STATE & GOVERNMENT: President Mathieu Kérékou (since March '96)
MAIN IGO MEMBERSHIPS (non-UN): OAU, ECOWAS, UEMOA, ACP, NAM, Francophonie
CURRENCY: CFA franc (see above)
GNP PER CAPITA: US$370 ('95) or US$1,760 ('95) by PPP calculation

Niger

CAPITAL: Niamey   AREA: 1,267,000 sq km   POPULATION: 8,850,000 ('96)
OFFICIAL LANGUAGE: French   POLITICAL SYSTEM: republic
HEAD OF STATE & GOVERNMENT: President (Brig.-Gen.) Ibrahim Barre Mainassara (since Jan '96)
RULING PARTY: National Union of Independents for Democratic Renewal
PRIME MINISTER: Ibrahim Assane Maiyaki (since Dec '97)
MAIN IGO MEMBERSHIPS (non-UN): OAU, ECOWAS, UEMOA, ACP, OIC, NAM, Francophonie
CURRENCY: CFA franc (see above)
GNP PER CAPITA: US$220 ('95) or US$750 ('95) by PPP calculation

SENEGAL. It was a quieter year politically in Senegal, between the controversial municipal and regional elections of November 1996 (see AR 1996, p. 255) and the parliamentary elections due in May 1998. Skirmishing in the run-up to the latter prompted the formation of a dissident tendency within the ruling Parti Socialiste (PS). Led by Djibo Ka, a former senior minister, the new grouping was known as Renouveau Démocratique (RD) and attracted a segment of supporters from within the PS, on a platform of reconciliation, respect for differences and pluralism. On 11 November M. Ka and ten other leading members of his tendency were suspended from the PS for three months. If reconciliation proved impossible, it was expected that RD candidates would run on a separate ticket in the 1998 polls. Their main opponent appeared to be the powerful PS secretary-general, Ousmane Tanor Dieng, who enjoyed the support of President Abdou Diouf.

The split in the PS was of potential benefit to the 20 opposition parties, which were still smarting after the victory of the PS steam-roller in the municipal elections. The main opposition leader, Maître Abdoulaye Wade of the Parti Démocratique Sénégalais (PDS), remained in the government as Minister of State, but joined in the campaign early in the year for the setting-up of an independent electoral commission. When President Diouf conceded, as a half-way house, the creation of an 'election observatory', Me Wade's response was ambivalent. At the end of the year he was still resisting pressure from party militants to leave the government, insisting that he was 'in opposition to the PS, not to the government'.

The political game in Dakar seemed far removed from the worsening crisis in Casamance, Senegal's southern-most region, where a separatist movement had been operating since 1982. A series of truces and ceasefires in the past five years had never worked, because splits in the Mouvement des Forces Démocratiques de la Casamance (MFDC) had prevented peace talks from taking place. In July a delegation from the MFDC external wing based in France returned to Ziguinchor, the regional capital, to try and coordinate a platform for talks; but the visit was accompanied by a guerrilla attack in Ziguinchor by a faction opposed to talks. This led to an escalation of incidents between dissidents and Senegalese troops, resulting in a high death toll on both sides. In December the situation was aggravated by evidence that for the first time the dissidents were using landmines, easily obtained over the Guinea-Bissau border.

Against this background, there was increasing recognition in the Senegalese government that some form of international mediation, either by France or by neighbouring West African countries, was permissible. It was also acknowledged that the tough line pursued by the armed forces chief of staff, General Lamine Cissé, needed to be accompanied by greater flexibility in discussion with the separatists, as long as they acknowledged Senegal's unity and territorial integrity. General Cissé retired at the end of the year.

MAURITANIA. In presidential elections in December, the incumbent Maaouiya Ould Taya of the ruling Parti Républicain Démocratique et Social (PRDS) was re-elected with more than 90 per cent of votes in the first round. This caused little surprise, since most of the opposition parties boycotted the poll because of dissatisfaction with the electoral arrangements. The President was officially credited with having obtained 801,190 votes, against 61,869 for his nearest rival, former Planning Minister Ould Cheikh Malainine. Following the elections, a new Prime Minister was appointed in the person of Mohammed Lemine Ould Guig, a former director of higher education. He replaced Ould Mohammed Khouna, who had resigned before the results of the election were announced.

Although criticized by human rights organizations for harassing the opposition and censoring the press, the Ould Taya regime earned praise from the IMF and World Bank for putting new order into the country's finances. A growth rate of nearly 5 per cent in both 1996 and 1997, annual inflation of only 5 per cent and a reduction of the proportion of the population under the poverty threshold from 57 to 50 per cent were considered a laudable record for one of Africa's poorest countries, surviving in mainly desert conditions.

MALI. The reputation which Mali had been establishing for itself as one of the 'new model' African states, where functioning democracy went hand in hand with economic reform, took a knock in April when parliamentary elections were so bungled that they had to be cancelled and called again in July. Although there were opposition charges of rigging, it appeared that poor organization and over-dependence on computers caused most of the confusion. This did not prevent opposition parties from boycotting the presidential election in May, although it was almost certain that President Alpha Oumar Konaré was going to be re-elected in any case. A further irony was that Mali was one African country with an independent electoral commission, which bore a heavy responsibility for the fiasco.

In the presidential election President Konaré was re-elected outright in the first round on 11 May with 96 per cent of the valid vote, although only 28.4 per cent of registered voters actually went to the polls (a figure not too different from the 1992 turnout) and nearly a third of those returned blank or invalid ballots. The opposition parties refused to recognize the results, a stance which led to the detention of their leaders for about ten days during the President's inauguration.

The boycott continued during the rescheduled parliamentary elections, which were held in two rounds on 20 July and 3 August. The final results gave the ruling Alliance pour la Démocratie au Mali (ADEMA) 129 of the 147 seats in the Assembly. A week after the second round, ten of the most significant leaders of what was called the 'radical opposition', were arrested and charged with murder in connection with the lynching of a policeman at a protest rally. They were still in detention at the end of the year. A new coalition government under the continued premiership of Ibrahim Boubakar Keita was formed in September.

Political problems did not prevent President Konaré from being warmly received in the United States in November, when he met President Clinton and told the Council on Foreign Relations that 'democracy is a process that takes time and patience'. Mali continued to find favour in Washington, with both the US government and the financial institutions, for having put its economic house in order, achieving encouraging growth and low inflation.

GUINEA. Even though Guinea appeared to have digested the dramatic events of the previous year, when an army mutiny had nearly shattered the regime (see AR 1996, p. 256), the political situation remained fragile. The opposition parties, although legal and functioning in parliament, complained of repression and expressed concern at the government's determination that President Lansana Conté should be re-elected in 1998 as candidate of the ruling Parti de l'Unité et le Progrès (PUP). An opposition campaign for an independent electoral commission was turned down by the government in September.

There was uncertainty as to the fate of the 56 soldiers, both officers and other ranks, arrested after the 1996 mutiny. In November they smuggled out a letter to the National Assembly complaining at their poor conditions and at the fact that, although the whole army had taken part in the mutiny, only they had been arrested.

CÔTE D'IVOIRE. In the middle of President Konan Bédié's five-year term, the emphasis was very much on the economy, even though prolonged student agitation led to the university's academic year being a virtual write-off. Statistically, the economy appeared to be performing better and better, due in part to a continued boom in the two key export commodities, cocoa and coffee. Annual GDP growth had risen from 0.4 per cent in 1993 to 7 per cent in the 1995–97 period, so that the President and his economy-oriented Prime Minister, Daniel Kablan Duncan, began to talk of growth in double figures by the year 2000, making Côte d'Ivoire an 'African elephant' to match the 'Asian tigers'.

There were those who felt that this scenario was too optimistic, because the economy was still too dependent on aid and commodity markets and was still not attracting enough private investment, in spite of systematic efforts to that end. Moreover, the IMF was discontented with the government's slow progress on economic reforms, especially its reluctance to restructure the agricultural marketing system—not least because it provided a 'slush fund' for the ruling Parti Démocratique de la Côte d'Ivoire (PDCI). At the end of the year the IMF and World Bank had not approved funding for the country's 1997–2000 structural adjustment programme.

BURKINA FASO. President Blaise Compaoré continued to carry all before him politically. Parliamentary elections held on 11 May (after a two-month postponement for logistical reasons) resulted in a convincing victory for the ruling Congrès pour la Démocratie et le Progrès (CDP), which won 101 of the 111 seats in the National Assembly. With two seats going to an associated party, the presidential majority amounted to 103 seats, while two opposition parties took eight seats. Four constituencies in which polling had been cancelled voted again before the end of May to produce this final result, which was validated by the Supreme Court. The Prime Minister, Kadre Desiré Ouédraogo, presented his resignation and was reappointed on 11 June with a reshuffled cabinet.

That the elections were free of violence and found by observers to be generally 'free and fair' gave rise to speculation that the country had simply tired of political controversy. In October the tenth anniversary of the assassination of former President Thomas Sankara—in which President Compaoré was generally thought to have been implicated—passed almost unobserved. Even the late President's close political friend, President Rawlings of Ghana, finally overcame his distaste and undertook a working visit to Ouagadougou in December, his first in the ten years since Captain Sankara's assassination.

TOGO. Little by little, Togo's 'dinosaur' leader, President Gnassingbé Eyadema, who marked his 30 years in continuous power in January, was clawing back the political initiative, while making only absolutely necessary concessions to democratic practice. Having installed Kouassi Klutse as a 'tame' Prime Minister in 1996 (see AR 1996, p. 258), he continued to use the slender majority of his Rassemblement du Peuple Togolais (RPT) in the National Assembly to pass a tight electoral code in a session boycotted in protest by opposition MPs (now numbering only 37 out of 81). In August there was an attack on the home of former Premier Edem Kodjo, this being followed in November by an attack on the leader of the main opposition party, Yaovi Agboyigbo, while he was visiting northern Togo.

At the same time, there were signs that the economy, in recession since the political troubles of the early 1990s, was beginning a partial recovery. The World Bank and the IMF gave the government's reform programme their blessing and resumed aid, although the German government remained unconvinced and maintained its suspension of aid. The German stance resulted in the blocking of European Union aid programmes, even though the joint assembly of the European Parliament and the Lomé Convention states held a meeting in Togo in October.

BENIN. Now regarded as one of Africa's model democracies, Benin had an uneventful year, although controversies over continuing austerity triggered a series of protests and strikes. Despite official attempts at improvement, relations with Nigeria were subject to occasional border tensions because of support given in southern Benin to clandestine operations in Nigeria and the occasional facilitating of exits for political refugees.

NIGER. In spite of his victory in what some described as the 'shotgun election' of July 1996 (see AR 1996, p. 259), President Ibrahim Barre Mainassara continued to experience difficulties from a discontented political class, still angry at the January 1996 coup. In addition, a continuing disastrous economic and financial situation led to sporadic industrial action by unpaid civil servants. There was also a series of clashes with dissident Touareg movements, compounded by a problem with Toubou rebels in the east, the latter possibly a spill-over from conflict in Chad (see VI.3.ii). A joint operation with the Chad government in July appeared to contain the Toubou insurgents, at least for the time being.

Difficulties in implementing a harsh economic reform programme led to an impasse with donors, although France continued to give support. The situation was so critical by November that President Mainassara dissolved the government installed the previous December under Amadou Boubacar Cissé, who was replaced as Prime Minister by Ibrahim Assane Maiyaki, a former Minister of Foreign Affairs. The new government included the Touareg leader, Rhissa Ag Boula (president of the Front for the Liberation of Air and Azawak), but there was no opposition figure in the team.

At the beginning of the year there had been a violent confrontation between security forces and opposition demonstrators, following which three opposition leaders—former President Ousmane Mahamane, Mamadou Tandja and Mamadou Issoufou—were detained for several weeks. Tensions continued through the year, at the end of which another opposition leader, former Prime Minister Amadou Hama, was linked to an alleged plot to assassinate President Mainassara. M. Hama's party called the plot a fabrication by an 'authoritarian and unpopular leadership'.

ii. CHAD—CAMEROON—GABON—CONGO-BRAZZAVILLE— CENTRAL AFRICAN REPUBLIC—EQUATORIAL GUINEA

Chad
CAPITAL: Ndjaména   AREA: 1,284,000 sq km   POPULATION: 6,500,000 ('96)
OFFICIAL LANGUAGES: French & Arabic   POLITICAL SYSTEM: presidential
HEAD OF STATE & GOVERNMENT: President (Col.) Idriss Déby (since Dec '90)
RULING PARTIES: Patriotic Salvation Movement (MPS) & Union for Democracy and the Republic (UDR) head fluid coalition
PRIME MINISTER: Nassour Owaido Guelendouksia (since May '97)
MAIN IGO MEMBERSHIPS (non-UN): OAU, CEEAC, OIC, ACP, Francophonie, NAM
CURRENCY: CFA franc (end-'97 £1=CFAF990.25, US$1=CFAF603.55)
GNP PER CAPITA: US$180 ('95) or US$700 ('95) by PPP calculation

Cameroon
CAPITAL: Yaoundé   AREA: 475,000 sq km   POPULATION: 13,600,000 ('96)
OFFICIAL LANGUAGES: French & English   POLITICAL SYSTEM: presidential
HEAD OF STATE & GOVERNMENT: President Paul Biya (since Nov '82)
RULING PARTY: Democratic Rally of the Cameroon People (RDPC)
PRIME MINISTER: Peter Mafany Musonge (since Sept '96)
MAIN IGO MEMBERSHIPS (non-UN): OAU, CEEAC, OIC, ACP, Francophonie, NAM
CURRENCY: CFA franc (see above)
GNP PER CAPITA: US$650 ('95) or US$2,110 ('95) by PPP calculation

Gabon

CAPITAL: Libreville   AREA: 268,000 sq km   POPULATION: 1,300,000 ('96)
OFFICIAL LANGUAGE: French   POLITICAL SYSTEM: presidential
HEAD OF STATE & GOVERNMENT: President Omar Bongo (since March '67)
RULING PARTY: Gabonese Democratic Party (PDG)
PRIME MINISTER: Paulin Obame-Nguema (since Oct '94)
MAIN IGO MEMBERSHIPS (non-UN): OAU, CEEAC, OPEC, OIC, ACP, Francophonie, NAM
CURRENCY: CFA franc (see above)
GNP PER CAPITA: US$3,490 ('95)

Congo-Brazzaville

CAPITAL: Brazzaville   AREA: 342,000 sq km   POPULATION: 2,700,000 ('96)
OFFICIAL LANGUAGE: French   POLITICAL SYSTEM: presidential
HEAD OF STATE & GOVERNMENT: President Denis Sassou-Nguesso (since Oct '97)
RULING PARTIES: Congolese Movement for Democracy and Integral Development (MCDDI) is included in ruling coalition
MAIN IGO MEMBERSHIPS (non-UN): OAU, CEEAC, ACP, Francophonie, NAM
CURRENCY: CFA franc (see above)
GNP PER CAPITA: US$680 ('95) or US$2,050 ('95) by PPP calculation

Central African Republic

CAPITAL: Bangui   AREA: 623,000 sq km   POPULATION: 3,400,000 ('96)
OFFICIAL LANGUAGE: French   POLITICAL SYSTEM: presidential
HEAD OF STATE & GOVERNMENT: President Ange-Félix Patassé (since Sept '92)
RULING PARTY: Central African People's Liberation Party (MPLC)
PRIME MINISTER: Michel Gbezera-Bria (since Jan '97)
MAIN IGO MEMBERSHIPS (non-UN): OAU, CEEAC, OPEC, OIC, ACP, Francophonie, NAM
CURRENCY: CFA franc (see above)
GNP PER CAPITA: US$340 ('95) or US$1,070 ('95) by PPP calculation

Equatorial Guinea

CAPITAL: Malabo   AREA: 28,000 sq km   POPULATION: 410,000 ('96)
OFFICIAL LANGUAGES: Spanish & French   POLITICAL SYSTEM: presidential
HEAD OF STATE & GOVERNMENT: President (Brig.-Gen.) Teodoro Obiang Nguema Mbasogo (since Aug '79)
RULING PARTY: Democratic Party of Equatorial Guinea (PDGE)
PRIME MINISTER: Angel Serafin Seriche Dugan (since March '96)
MAIN IGO MEMBERSHIPS (non-UN): OAU, CEEAC, ACP, Francophonie, NAM
CURRENCY: CFA FRANC (SEE ABOVE)
GNP PER CAPITA: US$380 ('95)

CHAD. The long transition process in Chad was completed early in the year with the holding of parliamentary elections in two rounds on 5 January and 23 February. The results announced on 3 March gave the ruling Mouvement Patriotique du Salut (MPS) of President Idriss Déby 55 seats out of 125. There were eight seats still undeclared, which the Supreme Court on 21 March announced had been allocated to the MPS, which therefore commanded a narrow overall majority of 63 seats. Thirty-one seats were won by the Union pour la Renouveau et la Démocratie (URD) led by Abdelkader Wadal Kamougue, the remaining seats going to smaller parties. Opposition parties' protests about electoral malpractice were muted, and several from their ranks took positions in a new broad-based administration, notably Saleh Kebzabo, who had been a major critic of the regime until becoming Foreign Minister in August 1996. Lieut.-Colonel Kamougue, like M. Kebzabo a southerner, became the president of the National Assembly.

The completion of the transition was accompanied by further conciliation with dissident groups, notably the Front d'Action pour une République Fédérale (FARF). This was important, as the FARF was based in the far south, near the site of the oil reserves expected to transform Chad's finances from the year 2000. The euphoria was short-lived, however, because in October the reconciliation fell apart with a punitive attack by government troops on FARF elements in the town of Moundou. The leadership went on the run and resumed random attacks in the area.

CAMEROON. It had been predicted that 1997 would be a difficult year for Cameroon politically, because both parliamentary and presidential elections were scheduled. The parliamentary elections were originally set for March, but a presidential decree postponed them to 17 and 31 May. Prior to the postponement, tension had been raised by an outbreak of unrest in Northwest province, one of the two anglophone provinces and main fief of the opposition Social Democratic Front (SDF). A wave of arrests followed a series of attacks on police stations and gendarmeries, an indefinite curfew being imposed in the province. The government ascribed the attacks, in which ten people were killed, including three gendarmes, to the radical anglophone Southern Cameroons National Council. The SDF suggested that they had been engineered by the authorities to disrupt the elections.

Nonetheless, the parliamentary poll went ahead with all parties taking part, including the SDF, which had boycotted the previous such poll in 1992. There were heavy security measures in place, and no serious violence was reported. Observers such as those from the Commonwealth found a number of shortcomings in the organization of the elections, especially in the compiling of voters' lists, and in the absence of an independent electoral commission. The results were more favourable than predicted for the ruling Rassemblement Démocratique du Peuple Camerounais (RDPC), which obtained an overall majority of 109 seats out of 180. The SDF took 43 seats and the Union Nationale pour la Démocratie et le Progrès (UNDP) of Bello Bouba Maigari only 13, the rest going to smaller parties. The Supreme Court confirmed the result, throwing out petitions by the opposition parties for annulment on the grounds of alleged fraud.

The presidential election on 12 October was boycotted by the main opposition leaders (Fru Ndi of the SDP and M. Maigari) in support of their campaign to have the polling postponed, although there were nine other candidates apart from the incumbent, Paul Biya. Unsurprisingly, the latter was re-elected with 92.6 per cent of the vote, his nearest rival scoring only 2.8 per cent. More surprising was the claim that over 70 per cent of voters participated, when the opposition 'ghost towns' campaign in the main cities was reportedly quite effective. After the poll there was an atmosphere of resignation among the opposition parties, some of which entered into negotiations on joining the government. In December M. Maigari took a ministerial job, but the SDF was still holding out as the year ended.

GABON. Parliamentary elections held in December 1996, with repolling for nine seats in January, produced an overall majority of 82 seats in the new 120-member National Assembly for the ruling Parti Démocratique Gabonais (PDG). The PDG also obtained a large majority in Gabon's first-ever elections to the 91-member Senate held in January-February.

President Omar Bongo was heavily, if unsuccessfully, involved between June and October in mediating in the conflict which had broken out in the neighbouring (Republic of) Congo-Brazzaville (see below). He also seemed to become increasingly disillusioned with the French, in part because a Paris magistrate tried to connect him with scandals in the recently-privatized Elf oil company of France.

CONGO-BRAZZAVILLE. With Zaïre's name change to the Democratic Republic of the Congo in May (see VII.1.i), most commentators resumed referring to the Republic of the Congo as Congo-Brazzaville. This change came shortly before the outbreak on 5 June of a horrendous four-month civil war centred on the capital, which was left in a shattered state.

The conflict was the culmination of a prolonged power struggle between the incumbent President, Pascal Lissouba, and his predecessor, Denis Sassou-Nguesso, who had lost the presidential election of August 1992 (see AR 1992, pp. 274–5). An earlier conflict in 1993–94 had led both men to set up militias to defend themselves, President Lissouba's being known as the 'Zulus' and the ex-President's the 'Cobras'. The third main political leader, Bernard Kolelas (mayor of Brazzaville), also formed his own militia, called the 'Ninjas', although the latter initially remained neutral when the fighting broke out.

The immediate cause of the dispute was the impending presidential election, which had been scheduled for 27 July. Both leaders were manoeuvring for position in the run-up to the poll and each accused the other of importing arms and planning to use violence to secure victory. Accusing M. Sassou-Nguesso of plotting a coup d'état on 5 June, President Lissouba ordered an assault on his residence in the Mpila district of the capital, triggering hostilities in which both sides moved to control certain *quartiers*. In the ensuing deadlock, parts of the capital were looted. President Bongo of Gabon was brought in to mediate, while the French (having evacuated their nationals and then pulled out their troops) called for a UN intervention force. The Security Council was most reluctant to become involved, however, certainly while there was no prospect of a lasting ceasefire.

After 40 days of hostilities, President Bongo's mediation briefly paid off when a ceasefire was signed by the two sides on 13 July, but it lasted only four days. The outline agreement proposed by the Gabonese President provided for a short extension of President Lissouba's mandate and a government of national union. Some African countries expressed willingness to take part in a peace force, but the inability of the two protagonists to accept a reconciliation proved to be a crucial stumbling-block. President Lissouba's supporters were suspicious of the Gabonese President because he was married to M. Sassou-Nguesso's daughter; they also suggested that he had succumbed to French pressure because of oil politics. A mediation offer by President Kabila of the Democratic

Republic of Congo was not taken up, since he was believed to support President Lissouba. There were rumours of mercenaries being recruited by both sides.

By late August it was reported that over 4,000 people had been killed, while thousands of refugees had fled to neighbouring countries. The fighting also began to spread outside the capital, to M. Sassou-Nguesso's home area in the north, where he was trying to consolidate a territorial base. At that stage the President's forces retained control of the vital oil port of Pointe Noire, the main access point for his arms supplies. The balance appeared to tilt against M. Sassou-Nguesso in September when Bernard Kolelas came off his neutral perch by accepting President Lissouba's offer of the premiership in a government of national union. In fact, the move proved to be a grave miscalculation, since M. Sassou-Nguesso was about to administer the *coup de grâce*, playing the trump card of his friendship with the Angolan government of President dos Santos.

Although President Lissouba's forces recaptured some areas of Brazzaville in early October, on 12 October Angolan troops from Cabinda moved in to take control of Pointe Noire on behalf of M. Sassou-Nguesso. At the same time, the Cobras began to reclaim areas of Brazzaville, even as M. Lissouba was in Kinshasa seeking military assistance from President Kabila. Within three days M. Lissouba's troops were in full flight, the President himself fleeing to West Africa (and M. Kolelas to Kinshasa). On 23 October M. Sassou-Nguesso entered Brazzaville and was sworn in as President, in one of the few buildings left standing in the capital. A government of national union was formed and elections were promised within two years, as residual guerrilla opposition was swiftly crushed.

The overthrow of the Lissouba government was seen as a severe blow to democratic rule in Africa. It was also regarded as a triumph for *realpolitik* engineered by an alliance of French and US oil companies anxious to see the internal conflict ended so that they could exploit major new offshore finds.

CENTRAL AFRICAN REPUBLIC. The year began badly with the killing of two French soldiers in Bangui by army mutineers, who had begun their third action in November 1996 (see AR 1996, p. 263). This incident provoked immediate heavy reprisals by French forces on the mutineers' positions, in which several were killed. The French justified the brutality of the riposte on the grounds that their soldiers had been shot in the back, adding that they would be sending 300 more troops to reinforce the 2,000 already stationed in the country.

This was in fact the last throw of the French, since agreements in place since December 1996 provided for their forces to be phased out and replaced by African troops of the Inter-African Mission to Monitor the Bangui Accords (MISAB), which was mandated to gather and disarm the mutineers. MISAB was set up with French logistical support and included 500 troops from Senegal, Chad, Gabon, Togo and Burkina Faso, commanded by General Amadou Toumani Touré of Mali. With two significant setbacks in May and June, when violence flared between MISAB and the rump of the mutineers, the process was completed in July when the vast majority of the mutineers had gone back to barracks.

There was a parallel political reconciliation, featuring the setting-up of a 'government of action for the defence of democracy' in February (to coincide with the MISAB takeover), headed by Michel Gbezera-Bria. This followed the 24 January ceasefire, which also involved a new political accord, since the recurrence of the mutiny had led to new demands for the removal of President Ange-Félix Patassé. The new government included 11 opposition members and 12 from the presidential tendency. In May the opposition ministers walked out of the government because of the killing of three former mutineers, at a period when violence was once more on the increase. However, after the crisis had been resolved in July, the ministers returned to their vacant posts in August.

MISAB completed the disarmament process by the end of September, remaining in the CAR for a further period to supervise the reconciliation process, with the blessing of the UN Security Council. Meanwhile, the French had announced in August that they would be closing their two bases in Bangui and Bouar in 1998, and withdrawing all troops.

EQUATORIAL GUINEA. In August the leader of the opposition in exile, Severo Moto, was sentenced *in absentia* to 101 years' imprisonment for 'high treason to the fatherland, attacking the government and illegal possession of arms and explosives'. Twelve others (including four Spaniards) were also sentenced *in absentia*. At the same time, the court approved the banning of Sr Moto's Progress Party (PP). The plot was said to have been discovered in the Angolan enclave of Cabinda when an arms cache was found on a boat heading to Equatorial Guinea. Sr Moto had returned to exile in Spain after his unsuccessful attempt to stand for the presidency in 1996 (see AR 1996, p. 263).

At a meeting held in Kinshasa in October the PP joined with several other opposition parties to form a new political 'platform' called Colina (the National Liberation Council). It aimed at bringing about a change of government 'at all costs' because of the persistent dictatorship in the country.

The government in Malabo declared a freeze in diplomatic relations with Spain in September, in protest at the Spanish decision to maintain Sr Moto's status as a political refugee. It also announced that French would become the country's second official language after Spanish.

VII CENTRAL AND SOUTHERN AFRICA

1. CONGO-KINSHASA—BURUNDI AND RWANDA—GUINEA-BISSAU AND CAPE VERDE—SÃO TOMÉ & PRÍNCIPE—MOZAMBIQUE—ANGOLA

i. DEMOCRATIC REPUBLIC OF THE CONGO (EX-ZAÏRE)

CAPITAL: Kinshasa   AREA: 2,345,000 sq km   POPULATION: 42,700,000 ('96)
OFFICIAL LANGUAGE: French   POLITICAL SYSTEM: presidential
HEAD OF STATE & GOVERNMENT: President Laurent Kabila (since May '97)
RULING PARTIES: Alliance of Democratic Forces for the Liberation of the Congo (AFDL) heads coalition with Union for Democracy and Social Progress (UDPS) & Patriotic Front (FP)
MAIN IGO MEMBERSHIPS (non-UN): OAU, CEEAC, ACP, Francophonie, NAM
CURRENCY: zaïre (end-'97 £1=Z225,596.23, US$1=Z137,500.00)
GNP PER CAPITA: US$120 ('95) or US$490 ('95) by PPP calculation

ON 16 May President Mobutu Sese Seko, head of state for 32 years, abandoned his capital, Kinshasa, and left the country, seeking asylum first in Togo, then in Morocco, where he died of cancer on 7 September (see XX: Obituary). The next day troops of the rebel movement, the Alliance of Democratic Forces for the Liberation of Congo-Zaïre (AFDL), entered the city, being given as warm a welcome as they had received in other towns they had occupied. Their leader, Laurent Kabila, promptly proclaimed himself President and announced that the country's name would be the Democratic Republic of the Congo, as it had been from 1964 to 1971, when President Mobutu, as part of his policy of 'authenticity', had changed it to Zaïre.

The rebellion had developed with astonishing speed. It had begun with the revolt of the Banyamulenge, a Tutsi group living in South Kivu, whom the Zaïrean authorities had attempted in September 1996 to drive out of the country (see AR 1996, p. 265). Within weeks the revolt had spread through both North and South Kivu, the Tutsi rebels joining forces with other opponents of President Mobutu under the leadership of Laurent Kabila, who had been fighting the government for over 30 years. Thus was born the AFDL. The rebels were clearly receiving support from the armies of Rwanda and Uganda, although the extent of this backing was not revealed until the war was over (see also VI.1.iv; VII.1.ii).

By 15 March the rebels were in control of Kisangani, the country's third largest city, in whose feeble defence the Zaïrean army (FAZ) had received support from foreign mercenaries, some of Serb origin. By 9 April Lubumbashi, the capital of Katanga (the name Shaba was now dropped), was in rebel hands, followed quickly by the Kasai provinces. Only to the east of Kinshasa was there some heavy fighting, the FAZ being joined by troops from the rebel Angolan UNITA movement and by soldiers of the old Rwandan army (ex-FAR), while the rebels received some assistance from Angolan government forces. The soldiers of the FAZ, ill-equipped, ill-disciplined and erratically paid, were

notorious looters but showed little stomach for a fight. None of President Mobutu's one-time allies—France, Belgium and Morocco, which had given him vital military aid in the late 1970s—were now prepared to try and prop him up.
The international community was particularly concerned over the plight of the refugees from Rwanda. Of the 1.1 million who had fled to Zaïre in 1994, at least 600,000 had returned to Rwanda. But this still left many thousands unaccounted for, and there were disturbing stories of refugees retreating with the FAZ being abandoned and massacred. There was no agreement on how the refugees could be helped, and so nothing effective was done for them.

The international community proved equally impotent in its efforts to achieve a negotiated settlement. The South African government, which enjoyed strong US backing, succeeded in bringing M. Kabila and President Mobutu face to face at a meeting held on 3 May on board a South African warship moored off the coast of the Republic of Congo, President Mandela himself acting as mediator. By this time, however, M. Kabila was in a strong enough position to reject out of hand President Mobutu's offer to hand over power to the Speaker of the Zaïrean parliament, who would then appoint a prime minister to organize elections.

As the new government of the Democratic Republic of the Congo, the AFDL started off with certain obvious disadvantages. It had been in existence for only a few months and was basically a military movement with only a thin political veneer. Some of its most senior members had been in exile for years and were out of touch with local realities. It had as yet no members from the western half of the country, and the easterners were divided between 'Rwandans' (mainly Tutsi like the Banyamulenge, who spoke Kinyarwanda) and the Katangese. Finally, there was uncertainty about the leader himself. M. Kabila had been a follower of Patrice Lumumba, for whose murder in 1961 he held the United Nations largely responsible. Of his time as an almost unknown resistance fighter, there were contradictory versions. Some spoke of him as a popular guerrilla leader who had created a 'socialist mini-state with collective farms and revolutionary schools'; others dismissed him as a self-aggrandizing minor warlord. What was already clear was that by temperament he was an authoritarian.

One of the new government's first acts was to suspend all political parties. In the first ministerial appointments, four posts went to members of the old opposition parties and nine to the AFDL. Etienne Tshisekedi, the leader of the Union for Democracy and Social Progress (UDPS) and the country's best-known opposition politician, who enjoyed massive support both in Kinshasa and in his home province Western Kasai, was given no niche in the new order. Nor did the government, at least in Kinshasa, show much interest in cultivating those supporters of 'civil society' (such as members of trades unions, community associations and human rights groups) which had formed the grassroots opposition to the Mobutu regime. In the provinces there were reports of local governors being chosen at mass meetings from opposition politicians or leaders of important ethnic groups, but these civilians found that they had little real power. Decision-making was in the hands of the local military commanders.

Nevertheless, President Kabila's first speeches held out hopes to those favouring full democratization: a constitutional assembly was to be elected; a referendum would be held on a new constitution; and presidential and legislative elections would take place by April 1999. Meanwhile, the AFDL would form a transitional government with the task of 'restoring things to working order', with special stress on road construction, the mechanization of agriculture and electrification.

Statistics provided by international agencies revealed the country's economic and social plight. In 1996 GDP was just over half what it had been in 1988. Between 1991 and 1994 the incidence of malnutrition among children in Kinshasa doubled, cholera epidemics were of frequent occurrence and bubonic plague had reappeared. The plantation economy, once vital, was collapsing: palm oil production had fallen from 95,000 tonnes in 1988 to 18,000 tonnes in 1996. The breakdown of internal communications meant that food-deficit provinces like Katanga or Kasai could no longer obtain produce from food-surplus Kivu, most of whose surplus was now exported to Rwanda and Uganda. Copper production dropped from 506,000 tonnes in 1988 to 38,000 in 1996. Total exports of copper, worth US$1,300 million in 1988, fell to only $176 million in 1996. Since 1990 the external debt had doubled to $14,000 million.

The new government's relations with the country's major aid donors were severely strained by uncertainty over the fate of the Rwandan refugees. There was little doubt that some massacres had taken place, but when the United Nations attempted to set up a commission to investigate it was faced with Congolese obstruction. The personnel of the commission was changed in August to meet Congolese objections, but the new commissioners found their work constantly being blocked.

In October Human Rights Watch/Africa, a non-governmental organization based in New York, published a 40-page report with the challenging title 'What Kabila is Hiding'. The report spelt out its conclusions in its first sentence: 'The Rwandan Patriotic Army and the AFDL carried out massive killings of civilian refugees and other violations of basic principles of international humanitarian law during attacks on refugee camps in the former Zaïre that began in late 1996 and in the ensuing seven months as war spread across the country.' One section contained the findings of a study of an 80-kilometre stretch of road along which the armies and the refugees had passed: abundant human remains and the testimony of eye-witnesses provided irrefutable evidence of wanton killing. There were also clear indications, said the report, that the Congolese government was now trying to remove all physical traces of any massacres and intimidating eye-witnesses into silence.

In early December a meeting of the 'Friends of Congo' was held in Brussels. Coordinated by the World Bank, it brought together the Western powers (including France, whose relations with the new government were exceptionally strained), Japan, multinational agencies, South Africa and Uganda. The Congo delegation presented an elaborate reconstruction programme drawn up with the assistance of an American corporation: its total cost was put at $1,630 million, only a third of which could be raised internally. With donor countries taking the line that aid should be conditional on respect for democratic principles and human rights, not much concrete assistance was forthcoming. The European Union agreed to unblock funds frozen since 1992 to the value of $75 million, while the US and Belgian governments offered smaller amounts. A committee was set up to investigate the situation with regard to foreign debt.

Private business, the Congolese hoped, would be more sympathetic: another meeting was held in Brussels attended by representatives of Belgian and US companies. The big mining corporations, it was clear, were again becoming interested in Congo's abundant mineral resources. As the year ended, however, it was apparent that the AFDL government had not yet succeeded in winning the trust either of the mass of the Congolese people, who talked of a 'successor dictatorship', or of the major donor countries.

ii. BURUNDI AND RWANDA

Burundi
CAPITAL: Bujumbura   AREA: 28,000 sq km   POPULATION: 6,500,000 ('96)
OFFICIAL LANGUAGE: French & Kirundi   POLITICAL SYSTEM: transitional
HEAD OF STATE & GOVERNMENT: Maj. Pierre Buyoya (since July '96)
PRIME MINISTER: Pascal-Firmin Ndimira (since July '96)
MAIN IGO MEMBERSHIPS (NON-UN) OAU, CEEAC, ACP, Francophonie, NAM
CURRENCY: Burundi franc (end-'97 £1=Fbu663.86, US$1=Fbu404.62)
GNP PER CAPITA: US$160 ('95) or US$630 ('93) by PPP calculation

Rwanda
CAPITAL: Kigali   AREA: 26,300 sq km   POPULATION: 7,750,000 ('96)
OFFICIAL LANGUAGES: French, Kinyarwanda & English   POLITICAL SYSTEM: presidential
HEAD OF STATE & GOVERNMENT: President Pasteur Bizimungu (since July '94)
RULING PARTIES: Rwandan Patriotic Front (FPR) & Republican Democratic Movement (MDR) head coalition
PRIME MINISTER: Pierre-Célestin Rwigyema (MDR), since Aug '95
MAIN IGO MEMBERSHIPS (non-UN): OAU, CEEAC, ACP, Francophonie, NAM
CURRENCY: Rwanda franc (end-'97 £1=RF571.77, US$1=RF348.49)
GNP PER CAPITA: US$180 ('95) or US$540 ('95) by PPP calculation

In BURUNDI, there was no let-up in the civil war between the Tutsi-dominated army and Hutu guerrillas (see AR 1996, pp. 267–8). The fighting was sometimes described as 'heavy' or 'fierce' and not infrequently accompanied by brief accounts of massacres of civilians with the death toll often in the hundreds. President Buyoya's strategy appeared to be to inflict a crushing military defeat on the guerrillas. Defence expenditure for the year was 70 per cent higher than in 1996 and there was talk of raising a 100,000-strong army. At the same time, the government resorted to the classic tactic of forcing the peasantry to move into 're-groupment camps' where they could be prevented from maintaining contact with the guerrillas. Within the camps reports spoke of disturbing conditions, with much malnutrition and a constant risk of epidemics.

The President's all-out war for Tutsi survival did not commend itself to all

Tutsi. The leader of the monarchist Party of the People's Reconciliation (PRP), at one time regarded as an anti-Hutu extremist, described Major Buyoya's policy as 'madness', adding: 'He forces the people to mass together instead of creating conditions which could reduce tension.' Former President Jean-Baptiste Bagaza, whom Major Buyoya had ousted in a coup in 1987, founded the Party for National Renewal (Parena), which appeared to have some contacts with Hutu militants in the Forces for Defence of Democracy (FDD). M. Bagaza was put under house arrest in January. Two months later several army officers and senior officials of Parena were also arrested, accused of laying anti-tank mines in the capital, Bujumbura, as part of a plot to overthrow the President. In April over 40 army officers accused of complicity in the assassination of President Melchior Ndadaye and six ministers in 1993 were placed on trial. In May *Africa Confidential* reported that 'more and more Burundi Tutsis want Bagaza to take over the government, negotiate with the guerrillas and encourage the neighbouring states to relax the embargo'.

A report published in February by the Watson Institute at Brown University (USA) on 'The Humanitarian Impact of Economic Sanctions on Burundi' reckoned that the effect on the civilian population had been 'serious and substantial', creating shortages of fuel, retail goods, medicines, agricultural fertilizers and other commodities. Extensive smuggling relieved shortages but led to high prices and created 'hyper-inflation'. In Bujumbura the effect was particularly severe, leading to the closure of the port and of many factories, thus causing serious unemployment. The Food and Agriculture Organization (FAO) reported that there were virtually no fertilizers in the country at the time of planting, while health and education services were also seriously affected. The regime could thus present sanctions as being a direct attack on the people, not just the government of Burundi. The collapse of the Mobutu regime provided the Tutsi government with a potentially friendly neighbour on its western frontier (see VII.1.i), but relations with Tanzania to the east were increasingly strained by periodic border clashes.

During the year the government of RWANDA became deeply involved in the political situation in neighbouring Zaïre, renamed the Democratic Republic of the Congo (ibid.). In the last weeks of 1996 there had been reports that soldiers of the Rwandan Patriotic Army (RPA) had been giving aid to the rebels in North and South Kivu, but it was not clear whether they were there as individual volunteers or had been sent in greater strength by the government in Kigali. Such reports persisted until the war ended in May, but the Rwandan role still remained unclear, in part because Western journalists were denied access to forward areas.

After the fighting had ended, however, the Rwandan Defence Minister, General Paul Kaganne, gave two remarkably frank interviews, the first to the *Washington Post* (7 July) and the second to the *Mail and Guardian* of South Africa (8–14 August). General Kaganne expressed his government's profound exasperation with 'the international community' for its total failure, in spite of many warnings, to intervene in 1994 to prevent genocide. He also criticized the failure to separate ex-FAR soldiers and Interahamwe militiamen from ordinary civilians in the refugee camps in Zaïre and so to prevent the Hutu diehards from using the camps as bases from which to launch raids into Rwanda. In these circumstances, said General Kaganne, the Rwandan government had had no alternative but to act on its own, though with some covert American backing, to dismantle the refugee camps, to 'destroy the structure' of the Hutu army and militia, and finally to overthrow President Mobutu, the Hutus' main supporter. As for the killing of refugees, he claimed that this had been 'by individuals not organizations'.

Events were soon to show that the victory of the Rwandan Tutsi was less complete than their spectacular success had at first suggested. Among the 600,000 refugees who returned to Rwanda in 1996 were many Hutu militants. Other militants succeeded in holding out in North Kivu, where they formed alliances with local anti-Tutsi groups. Consequently, there were numerous incidents within Rwandan territory, creating in the north-west a state of civil war: Hutu attacked government posts and Tutsi communities, and the army retaliated, often with great violence. Both sides were guilty of atrocities.

Another consequence of the 1994 genocide was the large number of detainees—rising to some 120,000 during the year—accused of complicity in the killings and held in prisons and detention centres, often in appalling conditions. The first trials were held at the beginning of the year and resulted in some death sentences, but the legal process was very slow and few further trials took place. As for the UN International Criminal Tribunal for Rwanda based in Arusha (Tanzania), it proved even less effective in bringing prominent Hutu suspected of genocide to justice and was publicly criticized for its inefficiency (see also XV.1.i).

In so stressful a situation it was not difficult for critics of the Rwandan government to find evidence of human rights abuses, as did Mary Robinson, the newly-appointed UN High Commissioner for Human Rights, on a three-day visit in December. However, by and large the Rwandan government continued to enjoy the support of the international community and with it a generous amount of financial aid.

iii. GUINEA-BISSAU AND CAPE VERDE

Guinea-Bissau
CAPITAL: Bissau   AREA: 36,000 sq km   POPULATION: 1,100,000 ('96)
OFFICIAL LANGUAGE: Portuguese   POLITICAL SYSTEM: presidential
HEAD OF STATE & GOVERNMENT: President (Brig.-Gen.)João Bernardo Vieira (since Nov '80)
RULING PARTY: African Party for the Independence of Guinea and Cape Verde (PAIGC)
PRIME MINISTER: Carlos Correia (since June '97)
MAIN IGO MEMBERSHIPS (non-UN): OAU, ECOWAS, ACP, OIC, NAM, CPLP
CURRENCY: CFA franc (end-'97 £1=PG990.25, US$1=PG603.55)
GNP PER CAPITA: US$250 ('95) or US$790 ('95) by PPP calculation

Cape Verde

CAPITAL: Praia   AREA: 4,000 sq km   POPULATION: 400,000 ('96)
OFFICIAL LANGUAGE: Portuguese   POLITICAL SYSTEM: presidential
HEAD OF STATE & GOVERNMENT: President Antonio Mascarenhas Monteiro (since March '91)
RULING PARTY: Movement for Democracy (MPD)
PRIME MINISTER: Carlos Veiga (since Jan '91)
MAIN IGO MEMBERSHIPS (non-UN): OAU, ECOWAS, ACP, NAM, CPLP
CURRENCY: Cape Verde escudo (end-'97 £1=CVEsc156.38, US$1=CVEsc95.31)
GNP PER CAPITA: US$960 ('95) or US$1,870 ('95) by PPP calculation

THE political scene in GUINEA-BISSAU was dominated by a constitutional crisis. In June President Vieira appointed Carlos Correia as Prime Minister without consulting members of the National Assembly. They retaliated by effectively blocking all government business. The matter was taken to the Supreme Court and a solution was found. On 12 October the President dismissed the Prime Minister but reappointed him the next day after consultation with the 15-member Council of State and party leaders.

In CAPE VERDE the year was uneventful, the government of President Antonio Mascarenhas Monteiro remaining securely in office. The economy continued to provide Cape Verdians with a better standard of living than that obtaining in most other sub-Saharan states.

iv. SÃO TOMÉ & PRÍNCIPE

CAPITAL: São Tomé   AREA: 965 sq km   POPULATION: 130,000 ('96)
OFFICIAL LANGUAGE: Portuguese   POLITICAL SYSTEM: presidential
HEAD OF STATE & GOVERNMENT: President Miguel Trovoada (since March '91)
RULING PARTY: Movement for the Liberation of São Tomé and Príncipe-Social Democratic Party (MLSTP-PSD)
PRIME MINISTER: Raul Bragança Neto (since Nov '96)
MAIN IGO MEMBERSHIPS (non-UN): OAU, CEEAC, ACP, NAM, CPLP
CURRENCY: dobra (end-'97 £1=Db3,921.27, US$1=Db2,390.00)
GNP PER CAPITA: US$350 ('95)

THE year was largely uneventful in domestic politics. In the foreign policy sphere, it was revealed in May that São Tomé & Príncipe had agreed to establish diplomatic relations with Taiwan, on the basis of an offer of generous aid by the latter. It was reported that the move was favoured by President Trovoada, against the opposition of much of his government.

v. MOZAMBIQUE

CAPITAL: Maputo   AREA: 800,000 sq km   POPULATION: 18,000,000 ('96)
OFFICIAL LANGUAGE: Portuguese   POLITICALSYSTEM: presidential
HEAD OF STATE & GOVERNMENT: President Joaquim Alberto Chissano (since Nov '86)
RULING PARTY: Front for the Liberation of Mozambique (Frelimo)
PRIME MINISTER: Pascoal Mocumbi (since Dec '94)
MAIN IGO MEMBERSHIPS (non-UN): OAU, COMESA, SADC, ACP, CWTH, OIC, NAM, CPLP
CURRENCY: metical (end-'97 £1=Mt18,859.84, US$1=Mt11,495.00)
GNP PER CAPITA: US$80 ('95) or US$810 ('95) by PPP calculation

MOZAMBIQUE retained its reputation of being 'the darling of the donor countries', with 160 foreign aid agencies working in the country and aid contributing about

60 per cent of the budget. However, as the London *Economist* pointed out on 11 October in an article headed 'Neo-colonialism', 'One, largely unmentioned, reason why Mozambique is getting plenty of foreign aid is that much of the country is not run by Mozambicans. In theory this is a transitional measure until Mozambicans are trained and gain experience. In the meantime, however, foreigners are having a huge impact.' Thus the customs service was now being run by a Briton, who was given the target of increasing customs revenue by 50 per cent in the first year. A Danish agency was overhauling the legal system and other foreigners were running sections of the education and health services.

Investors responded very favourably to the new situation and a sizeable part of the economy was now in foreign hands. Two concessions aroused particular comment. The government agreed to hand over an area reckoned to be as large as Israel in the extreme south of the country to a Texan billionaire, James Ulysses Blanchard III, for development into a tourist complex with hotel and casino, beach houses, game parks and a steam train for game watching. The second concession was in Niasa, the largest and least populated of Mozambique's ten provinces, with only 200,000 of its 12 million hectares of arable land under cultivation. An agreement with the South African Chamber for Development of Agriculture in Africa provided land for Afrikaner farmers who wanted to leave South Africa. By mid-1997 14 South African families had settled in Niasa. In a manner seen as typical of the Frelimo government's centralizing 'top-to-bottom' approach, both concessions had been made without consulting local people.

vi. ANGOLA

CAPITAL: Luanda   AREA: 1,247,000 sq km   POPULATION: 11,800,000 ('96)
OFFICIAL LANGUAGE: Portuguese   POLITICAL SYSTEM: presidential
HEAD OF STATE & GOVERNMENT: President José Eduardo dos Santos (since Sept '79)
RULING PARTY: Popular Movement for the Liberation of Angola-Workers' Party (MPLA-PT) heads nominal coalition
PRIME MINISTER: Fernando José da França Dias van Dunem (since June '96)
MAIN IGO MEMBERSHIPS (non-UN): OAU, COMESA, SADC, ACP, NAM, CPLP
CURRENCY: kwanza (end-'97 £1=Kw421,869.87, US$1=Kw257,128.00)
GNP PER CAPITA: US$410 ('95) or US$1,310 ('95) by PPP calculation

EVER since the signing of the 1994 peace agreement, known as the Lusaka protocol, between the MPLA and Unita (see AR 1994, p. 298), the country had been in a state described by local observers as an 'armed truce'. Most commentators saw the main obstacle to a genuinely stable peace as being presented by the undiminished ambition of the Unita leader, Dr Jonas Savimbi, to become Angola's President and undisputed ruler. Failing that, he demanded a 'special status' as 'principal adviser' to the President, with executive powers for himself. Given his constant prevarications, it seemed likely that arguments about his exact status were simply ploys to allow time for further developments.

Dr Savimbi retained two powerful assets. He had at his disposal an armed force of well-trained, battle-hardened men estimated to number at least 15,000. Some of these men had been moved across the frontier into Zaïre (latterly the Democratic Republic of the Congo), where he was able to count on the support of President Mobutu until the collapse of the Mobutu regime in May (see VII.1.i). Other men had been through the demobilization process but had then rejoined their leader. Such forces, together with other supporters, enabled Unita to maintain a significant presence in at least two-thirds of the country, although 80 per cent of the population was estimated to be living in government-controlled territory. His second vital asset was that Unita maintained a tight grip on the country's two richest diamond-producing provinces, North and South Luanda: diamond production to an estimated value of $500 million a year enabled him to equip and maintain his armed force.

The Unita leader was, however, prepared to accept some sections of the Lusaka protocol. It was agreed that 70 Unita nominees should take up the National Assembly seats won by the party in the 1992 election and that Unita members should also fill the ministerial and other appointments allocated to the party by the protocol. In the new national army, the Angolan Armed Forces (FAA), Unita was to provide 26,000 men; only 6,000 had come forward by March and another 5,000 by July.

Although little progress had been made with the handing-over of Unita territory to state administration, it was decided to go ahead with the formal installation of a 'government of unity and national reconciliation' in which Unita received four of the 28 ministerial posts. On 11 April an elaborate installation ceremony was held in Luanda, attended by 30 heads of state. The most notable absentee, however, was Dr Savimbi, who remained at his stronghold at Bailundo. He had been allowed the title of 'president of the largest opposition party' but sent a message saying that it was too dangerous for him to travel to Luanda.

The MPLA government took advantage of the rebellion in Zaïre, providing Laurent Kabila and his AFDL rebels with direct aid by airlifting to Bukavu members of the ex-Katangese gendarmerie. The latter had been settled in Angola since the 1970s, when they had launched two unsuccessful invasions of Shaba province. Later, when the fighting came closer to Angola, the Angolan army provided a certain amount of direct assistance. In October, morever, an Angolan force helped ex-President Denis Sassou-Nguesso to bring about the overthrow of the Lissouba government in the Congo Republic (see VI.3.ii). Both President Lissouba and the far more important President Mobutu had been friendly to Dr Savimbi, the Mobutu regime having indeed been his staunchest ally for 20 years, allowing a steady stream of aid to reach Unita from Zaïre. Towards the end of the year the government in Luanda began putting pressure on the Zambian authorities, alleging that aid was still being flown to Dr Savimbi from bases in Zambia.

In May and June there were reports of heavy fighting between government forces and Unita, as the government attempted to gain control of the frontier with Congo and of some of the diamond fields. Later in the year came reports of military activity by Unita in the central and southern provinces, leading to fears of a full-scale resumption of the civil war.

The mandate for the UN Angola Verification Mission (UNAVEM III) expired on 30 June. It was replaced by a much smaller UN Observer Mission in Angola (UNOMA). On 23 August the UN Security Council passed a resolution for the imposition of further sanctions on Unita for failing to observe the Lusaka protocol. Imposed on 31 October, the sanctions required all member-states to close down Unita offices in their territories and to ban entry by Unita officials. As with other sanctions against Unita, however, it was uncertain how effectively these new measures could be implemented.

One ray of hope in a gloomy situation was provided by reports of the enthusiasm with which Unita members who had come to Luanda to take up executive and legislative positions were now participating in the work of central government. Clearly, there were growing divisions between the moderates now in Luanda and the hard-liners who surrounded Dr Savimbi in Bailundo.

Diana, Princess of Wales, spent three days in Angola in January (see also I.1). Her visit, arranged by the British Red Cross to take in war-shattered areas, was highly effective in publicizing the impact of landmines on the civilian population. It therefore added strength to the mounting campaign for the banning of such weapons culminating in the signature of an international treaty in December (see XII.1; XIX.5).

Oil exploration during the year, especially by the French company Elf-Aquitaine, revealed new and exceptionally rich offshore oil deposits within Angolan waters.

2. ZAMBIA—MALAWI—ZIMBABWE—BLNS STATES

i. ZAMBIA

CAPITAL: Lusaka   AREA: 750,000 sq km   POPULATION: 9,200,000 ('96)
OFFICIAL LANGUAGE: English   POLITICAL SYSTEM: presidential
HEAD OF STATE & GOVERNMENT: President Frederick Chiluba (since Nov '91)
RULING PARTY: Movement for Multi-Party Democracy (MMD)
MAIN IGO MEMBERSHIPS (non-UN): OAU, COMESA, SADC, ACP, CWTH, NAM
CURRENCY: kwacha (end-'97 £1=K2,366.71, US$1=K1,442.50)
GNP PER CAPITA: US$400 ('95) or US$930 ('95) by PPP calculation

THE London publication *Africa Confidential* reported on 4 December that 'at home and abroad there is disillusionment with Chiluba's isolated and insecure government', in painful contrast to the enthusiasm and goodwill with which the President and his Movement for Multi-Party Democracy had been greeted in 1991 after their decisive victory in one of contemporary Africa's few genuinely democratic elections. The disillusionment had many causes, nor was it a recent development. Already in 1995 there had been clear signs of the government's loss of popularity (see AR 1995, p. 274). In 1996 its tampering with the constitution had led most of the opposition parties to boycott that year's general election, while aid donors expressed their displeasure at the President's undemocratic stance by halting all aid payments, thus greatly increasing the country's economic difficulties (see AR 1996, p. 272).

In spite of its difficulties over aid, the government stuck rigidly to the fiscal and monetary policies laid down by the IMF. This had the effect of reducing inflation to 19.9 per cent, the lowest level in ten years; but cuts in public expenditure meant the closing of some schools, while civil servants had to face delays in receiving their pay. The government stuck equally firmly to its privatization policy, and in so doing threw 80,000 parastatal employees out of work. At the same time, some ministers and their cronies were doing very well out of the new arrangements, thus fuelling public resentment.

A significant stage in the denationalization of the copper mines was marked when the government reached an agreement with a South African-Canadian consortium giving the three companies concerned exclusive rights to develop the country's richest copper mine. Concurrently, the agricultural sector was reported to be particularly severely affected by lack of government support, many commercial farmers being on the verge of bankruptcy.

The country's economic situation therefore seemed to many people to be worsening, as the government was growing increasingly authoritarian. The opposition accused the President of 'lumping too many dictator's powers on his plate', while a popular song heard in the streets of Lusaka contained the line 'Chiluba stole the seat [a reference to the unsatisfactory 1996 election] and should be caged'. Such signs of popular discontent drew an angry response from the Home Affairs Minister, Chitalu Sampa, who told parliament that 'people cannot be allowed to talk any-how against the state'.

Workers for local organizations concerned with democracy and human rights found themselves being subjected to increasing surveillance, while independent-minded journalists felt themselves to be under threat. The weak political opposition was now made up of no less than 12 parties, some of them very small, linked together in a loose and not very effective coalition. In August former President Kenneth Kaunda was slightly wounded when police used live ammunition to disperse a rally of his supporters. He accused the government of attempting to assassinate him.

On 28 October a group of junior army officers led by Captain Steven Lungu (alias 'Captain Solo') made an extremely amateurish attempt at a coup. They began by attempting to arrest the army commander, General Nobby Simbeye. He escaped but the plotters found his house well-stocked with Windhoek beer and were reported to have been drunk when they took over the national radio station in Lusaka. Broadcasting to the nation, 'Captain Solo' delivered a four-hour oration in which he claimed to have been inspired by an angel to overthrow the government in the name of a previously-unknown National Redemption Council. Loyal troops stormed the radio station, where 'Captain Solo' was found hiding in a rubbish bin. One soldier was killed.

The government immediately proclaimed a state of emergency, under which 90 people were arrested, 84 of them army officers but including one prominent politician, Dean Mungomba, leader of the Zambia Democratic Congress. Ex-President Kaunda was out of the country at the time of the coup attempt, but on 25 December, shortly after his return, he too was taken into custody on suspicion of complicity in the plot. The arrest of so respected an elder statesman provoked international protests, leading to his partial release a few days later, although he remained under house arrest. Members of the opposition suspected that the attempted coup had been stage-managed by the government to discredit its opponents. Some government supporters alleged that the plotters were in close touch with the government of Angola, which regarded President Chiluba as being too friendly with the Unita leader, Jonas Savimbi, and would therefore have welcomed his removal (see also VII.1.vi).

ii. MALAWI

CAPITAL: Lilongwe   AREA: 118,500 sq km   POPULATION: 10,200,000 ('96)
OFFICIAL LANGUAGE: English   POLITICAL SYSTEM: presidential
HEAD OF STATE & GOVERNMENT: President Bakili Muluzi (since May '94)
RULING PARTIES: United Democratic Front (UDF) heads coalition with Malawi National
   Democratic Party (MNDP) & United Front for Multi-Party Democracy (UFMD)
MAIN IGO MEMBERSHIPS (non-UN): OAU, COMESA, SADC, ACP, CWTH, NAM
CURRENCY: kwacha (end-'97 £1=MK35.45, US$1=MK21.60)
GNP PER CAPITA: US$170 ('95) or US$750 ('95) by PPP calculation

ON 25 November former President Dr Hastings Kamuzu Banda died in a clinic in Johannesburg (see XX: Obituary). Officially his year of birth was given as 1906, but it was widely believed that he was very close to being a centenarian. The government announced that, 'notwithstanding his record of brutality', he should be given a state funeral.

The Malawi Congress Party (MCP), the main opposition party, announced on 3 April that it was ending its ten-month-long boycott of parliament. The Roman Catholic Church had acted as mediator in helping the MCP to reach a settlement with President Bakili Muluzi, both sides agreeing that the dispute had been caused by 'constitutional flaws'. In July the President thoroughly reorganized his government, abolishing some ministries and merging others. He retained as ministers the four rebels from the Alliance for Democracy (AFORD) who had stayed in their posts when the party decided to end its coalition with the dominant United Democratic Front (see AR 1996, p. 275).

The UK charity Christian Aid published disturbing figures about AIDS in Malawi: in a population of some 10 million, 330,000 people were known to be suffering from the disease, one in three pregnant women were HIV-positive and there were 600,000 orphans resulting from AIDS-related deaths.

iii. ZIMBABWE

CAPITAL: Harare   AREA: 390,000 sq km   POPULATION: 11,900,000 ('96)
OFFICIAL LANGUAGE: English POLITICAL SYSTEM: presidential
HEAD OF STATE & GOVERNMENT: President Robert Mugabe (since Dec '87); previously Prime Minister (from April '80)
RULING PARTY: Zimbabwe African National Union-Patriotic Front (ZANU-PF)
MAIN IGO MEMBERSHIPS (non-UN): OAU, COMESA, SADC, ACP, CWTH, NAM
CURRENCY: Zimbabwe dollar (end-'97 £1=Z$30.52, US$1=Z$18.60)
GNP PER CAPITA: US$540 ('95) or US$2,030 ('95) by PPP calculation

THE year seemed likely to be remembered as the one in which, after 17 years of unfettered rule, President Robert Mugabe and his ZANU-PF government finally lost both its grasp on affairs and the trust of the Zimbabwean people. From January onwards the administration was repeatedly and publicly confronted—by demonstrations involving students, war veterans and trade unions, by censure in the press and, unprecedentedly, by rebellion amongst its own members. At the ruling party's annual congress in December, rank-and-file criticism forced the sudden reversal of a major piece of tax legislation. By the end of the year the government had all but ceded control of macroeconomic policy to the International Monetary Fund (IMF) and the World Bank.

The personal reputation of the President—who had been re-elected unopposed in March 1996, though with a distinct lack of enthusiasm (see AR 1996, pp. 275–6)—was progressively dented by a series of embarrassing scandals. In February a contract for the construction of a new terminal at Harare airport was unexpectedly awarded to a company associated with Mr Mugabe's nephew. Later a licence for a cellular telephone network was similarly granted to 'insider interests'. During April it emerged than a payment of Z$800,000 had been made, under the War Victims' Compensation Fund, to the President's brother-in-law, Reward Marufu. The Fund, established to compensate those who had served in the country's war of liberation, according to their level of disability, paid out Z$400 million during the year, a conspicuous proportion going to cabinet ministers and ZANU-PF MPs. The government later admitted that there had been fraudulent looting of the fund, as well as abuses of the National Housing Guarantee Fund, set up to underwrite the cost of homes for VIPs.

Agricultural productivity was, as always, determined by rainfall. This year, unusually, the problem was excessive rain in the early months, with farms reported water-logged, dams spilling and crops rotting in the fields. Reduced acreages, following a punitive tobacco levy the previous year, damaged the country's most profitable export. More widely, the economy as a whole remained depressed. Investor confidence was hit by rising interest rates and by increased costs of energy, transport and labour, the latter a reflection of effective militancy by trade unions. Export earnings were down, mining in particular suffering from the lowest world prices in a decade for gold, nickel and copper, while the manufacturing sector encountered sluggish demand as a result of regular price hikes. On the other hand, revenue from tourism rose by 7.5 per cent, contributing a full 5 per cent of GDP.

The government claimed significant advances in steps towards 'indigenous empowerment' during the year, Z$42 million being spent on the construction of wells and small dams in rural areas, Z$70 million on schools and training colleges, and Z$30 million on the upgrading of housing. This level of expenditure seemed trivial, however, when compared with the Z$570 million allocated to the state secret service arm, the Central Intelligence Organization, or with the sums generated in a sequence of privatizations of parastatals and other state enterprises begun during the year. One such sale, of government shares in the Delta Corporation, Zimbabwe's largest company, realised Z$1,400 million.

The most significant privatization of all, the much-anticipated Land Redistribution Bill, took effect in mid-November with the listing of 1,503 white-owned farms designated for compulsory and uncompensated reallocation to 'the landless people of Zimbabwe'. Among those gazetted for appropriation were some of the largest and most profitable farms in the country, including one described as the single most productive tobacco farm in the world. Anxious farmers threatened an immediate reduction in agricultural productivity likely to reduce production by as much as 25 per cent, worth Z$6,000 million, over the next three seasons.

The already fragile economy moved decisively into crisis in July and August when, after 17 years of avoidance, the government was finally forced to bow to demands for compensation from an increasingly vociferous lobby of ex-combatants. The promise of a one-off tax-free gratuity of Z$50,000, and a pension of Z$2,000 a month for life for up to 70,000 veterans of the country's liberation struggle, called for the expenditure of Z$3,600 million beyond even the Z$15,000 million deficit already projected in the budget of 24 July. The World Bank immediately suspended balance-of-payments support, while the IMF announced plans to withhold provision for the country's structural adjustment programme (see AR 1996, p. 276), which was already running well behind schedule.

By early November the looming consequences of this unscheduled debt of 5 per cent of the government's total annual expenditure had produced a collapse in investor confidence and a reluctance to trade in the country's currency. Rumours of a critical shortage of foreign exchange and talk of a breakdown in relations between the government and the IMF led to panic in the money markets. On 14 November, subsequently designated 'Black Friday', the Zimbabwe dollar crashed, falling to a rate of 46 to the pound sterling, although it later recovered some ground to settle at a level equivalent to a 75 per cent depreciation within a single day. In an attempt to revive its fiscal credibility, the government announced sweeping cuts in capital expenditure. On 22 December the Minister of Finance, Dr Herbert Murerwa, travelled to Washington to seek to persuade the World Bank to release the Z$1,000 million of structural credit it had earlier suspended.

For the man in the street the dollar's collapse led to immediate rises in fuel, transport, electricity and postal charges as well as in the prices of food and basic commodities, compounded in December by a 2.5 per cent increase in sales tax. That month a proposal to fund the war veterans' payments through a 5 per cent levy on all taxpayers provoked open hostility among the government's own MPs. The Zimbabwe Congress of Trade Unions responded by calling a one-day general strike, which led to violent demonstrations on the streets of Harare. However, only when faced with a massed rebellion of his own party members at the ZANU-PF annual congress in Mutare did the President back down. A government which had begun the year confident of a buoyant economy and fiscal consolidation now faced the most sustained crisis of its existence.

iv. BOTSWANA—LESOTHO—NAMIBIA—SWAZILAND

Botswana
CAPITAL: Gaborone   AREA: 580,000 sq km   POPULATION: 1,500,000 ('96)
OFFICIAL LANGUAGE: English   POLITICAL SYSTEM: presidential democracy
HEAD OF STATE & GOVERNMENT: President Sir Quett Ketumile Masire (since '80)
RULING PARTY: Botswana Democratic Party (BDP)
MAIN IGO MEMBERSHIPS (non-UN): OAU, SADC, SACU, ACP, CWTH, NAM
CURRENCY: pula (end-'97 £1=P6.20, US$1=P3.78)
GNP PER CAPITA: US$3,020 ('95) or US$5,580 ('95) by PPP calculation

Lesotho
CAPITAL: Maseru   AREA: 30,000 sq km   POPULATION: 2,300,000 ('96)
OFFICIAL LANGUAGES: English & Sesotho   POLITICAL SYSTEM: monarchy
HEAD OF STATE: King Letsie III (since Jan '96)
RULING PARTY: Basotho Congress Party (BCP)
HEAD OF GOVERNMENT: Ntsu Mokhehle, Prime Minister (since April '93)
MAIN IGO MEMBERSHIPS (non-UN): OAU, COMESA, SADC, SACU, ACP, CWTH, NAM
CURRENCY: loti/maloti (end-'97 £1=M8.01, US$1=M4.88)
GNP PER CAPITA: US$770 ('95 or US$1,780 ('95) by PPP calculation

Namibia
CAPITAL: Windhoek   AREA: 824,000 sq km   POPULATION: 1,600,000 ('96)
OFFICIAL LANGUAGES: Afrikaans & English   POLITICAL SYSTEM: presidential democracy
HEAD OF STATE: President Sam Nujoma (since March '90)
RULING PARTY: South West Africa People's Organization (SWAPO)
HEAD OF GOVERNMENT: Hage Geingob, Prime Minister (since March '90)
MAIN IGO MEMBERSHIPS (non-UN): OAU, SADC, SACU, ACP, CWTH, NAM
CURRENCY: Namibian dollar/SA rand (end-'97 £1=N$8.01, US$1=N$4.88)
GNP PER CAPITA: US$2,000 ('95) or US$4,150 ('95) by PPP calculation

Swaziland
CAPITAL: Mbabane   AREA: 17,350 sq km   POPULATION: 940,000 ('96)
OFFICIAL LANGUAGES: English & Siswati   POLITICAL SYSTEM: monarchy
HEAD OF STATE: King Mswati III (since '86)
HEAD OF GOVERNMENT Sibusiso Barnabas Dlamini, Prime Minister (since July '96)
MAIN IGO MEMBERSHIPS (non-UN): OAU, COMESA, SADC, SACU, ACP, CWTH, NAM
CURRENCY: lilangeni/emalangeni (end-'97 £1=E8.01, US$1=E4.88)
GNP PER CAPITA: US$1,170 ('95) or US$2,880 ('95) by PPP calculation

THE annual summit of the heads of government of the Southern African Development Community (SADC) in Blantyre, Malawi, in September was notable in that a number of institutional issues were finally brought to a head (see also XI.5.ii). First, the moratorium on new members was scrapped, with the inclusion of the Seychelles and the Democratic Republic of the Congo (DRC), formerly Zaïre. Second, a long-brewing difference of opinion over the structure of the

SADC's Organ on Politics, Defence and Security (OPDS) reportedly led to President Mandela threatening to quit as SADC chairman, a post which he was not due to relinquish until 1999.

The admission of the two new member-states would, in the short term at least, undermine SADC's programme of action, while at the same time benefiting regional political solidarity. Even before the enlargement, the SADC's programme of so-called development integration remained little more than a theoretical ambition, its secretariat's managerial capacity being already overstretched in dealing with a complex and diverse region fraught with social, political and economic sensitivities and challenges. This problem was compounded by the organizational difficulty created by the disbursement of responsibility for the various SADC sectors, including water, energy, trade, transport and tourism, among its member-states. In this context, inter-state communication and application to regional rather than national programmes remained slack at best.

The former Zaïre's inclusion in the SADC illustrated perfectly the mismatch between bureaucratic capacity and political ideals. While both President Mandela and his deputy, Thabo Mbeki, were reportedly very keen to admit the DRC, this sentiment was not shared by South African officials, who feared the loss of institutional focus that could result. It was of course ironic that President Mandela's stance towards the DRC did not rest easily with his public pronouncements on the need for democracy in the region.

The SADC had hardly been blessed with the cocktail of capacity and commitment necessary for success measured in terms of regional economic growth and prosperity as well as political stability. Noble goals had suffered the consequences. Following the signing of the SADC free trade protocol in August 1996, members were supposed to have ratified the agreement and drawn up a schedule for tariff dismantling within six months. By the 1997 annual summit, however, only two countries had ratified the protocol and little progress had been made on the tariff schedule. Member-states were also supposed to have submitted lists of sensitive products by the end of October as part of efforts to free trade exchanges, but this deadline was also missed. Such tardiness had immediate (and potentially expensive) implications. For example, South Africa was held up in its talks with the European Union (EU) over a free trade agreement, because its neighbours had been slow in providing Pretoria with a list of sensitive products critical to the negotiations. Moreover, although the SADC was throughout the year embroiled in a review and rationalization of its own bureaucratic structures, it remained unclear how this process would be affected by the new need to take on the huge development backlog of Laurent Kabila's DRC.

If the effects of the membership expansion were a long-term issue for the SADC, the construction and role of the OPDS as a committee responsible for regional conflict resolution and democratic practice was far more pressing. The most intractable and contentious disagreement was whether the OPDS should report to the regular SADC summit (the South African and Botswanan position) or whether there should be a separate summit and NATO-style bureaucracy for the OPDS (as favoured by Zimbabwe, Namibia and Zambia). If the OPDS was to operate with separate summit status, there was of course the danger that it would be used as a personal political tool. Its current chairman was President Mugabe of Zimbabwe, who was seen as wanting to reduce President Mandela's infuence and to use the OPDS to counter the regional trend to liberalization and resultant creation of centres of domestic power outside his control (see also VII.2.iii). On the other hand, some in the region argued that a powerful OPDS would help to counter South Africa's overwhelming strength and influence; indeed, the impasse illustrated how few regional allies South Africa really possessed.

The clash of views on the summit question led to a suspension of the OPDS until a solution could be reached. Following the Blantyre meeting, the South African Deputy Foreign Minister, Aziz Pahad, announced that a special summit would be held on the issue in Luanda on 30 September. However, this meeting was later cancelled in view of President Mugabe's refusal to attend.

The renegotiation of the tariff-sharing formula of the Southern African Customs Union (SACU) member-states (South Africa, Namibia, Botswana, Lesotho and Swaziland), which had commenced in 1995, dragged on through 1997. Failure to reach agreement on the new formula was principally the result of South Africa's ongoing negotiations with the EU to establish a free trade area (FTA) within 12 years, which cast doubts on the future viability of SACU. There were concerns about the fiscal impact of the FTA on SACU member-states, their potential loss of revenue being estimated at between 5 and 15 per cent. At the same time, it was stressed by South Africa that these were fiscal rather than economic costs, which could be offset through alternative means of taxation such as value-added tax (VAT) and would be experienced anyway as South African tariffs came down under the rules of the World Trade Organization (WTO).

BOTSWANA. The announcement in November that President Masire would retire in March 1998 was remarkable in the context of the African continent, where leaders were commonly removed only by death or deposition. His rule had been noteworthy for its stability, engendered by diamond-based prosperity, which, though perhaps fortuitous, owed much to careful financial management and the will to resist grandiose schemes. The President's successor until the 1999 elections was expected to be the incumbent Vice-President and Minister of Finance and Development Planning, Festus Mogae, a trained economist of long standing with a strong leadership record in the Botswana Democratic Party (BDP). A bill passed by parliament in October virtually assured the Vice-President of the succession, although challenges to his election in 1999 were expected to come from two other party stalwarts: the present chairman, Ponatshego Kedikilwe, and the Minister of Works, Daniel Kwelagobe.

A new potential challenge to the ruling party came from the United Action Party (UAM), founded in September under the leadership of a former BDP member and director of the Botswana National Productivity Sector, Ephraim

Setshwaelo, who was dissatisfied with the lack of action to combat unemployment and other problems of the young. The new party could be said to straddle the gap between the conservatism of the BDP and the radicalism of the Botswana National Front (BNF).

An additional potential threat to the BDP was the reduction in the voting age to 18 years as a result of a referendum on constitutional reform held on 4 October. The resultant enfranchisement was expected to increase the voting roll by some 37,000, the majority being urban voters and including large numbers of disenchanted youth.

On 10 December the journalists Caitlin Davies and Letswetswe Phaladi appeared in the Maun magistrates court accused of spreading alarm under section 59 of Botswana's penal code. Many Batswana saw the trial as reflecting a hardening of the government's attitude towards civil rights activism.

GDP growth for 1997 was projected to exceed 7 per cent, up slightly from 1996 and fuelled by settlement of the protracted international dispute in the diamond markets. Diamonds continued to account for half of government revenue and 70 per cent of exports by value, the anticipated completion of the Orapa 2000 mine being expected to boost diamond output further. Annual inflation was down only marginally in 1997, but fell below the psychologically significant 10 per cent level. Unemployment continued to be high at around 20 per cent, despite strenuous efforts to broaden the manufacturing base. The eighth national development plan, launched in April and due to run until 2003, concentrated heavily on the reduction of poverty and unemployment, in particular by improved infrastructure such as roads, water, schools and training institutions. Education in Botswana already boasted the highest teacher/pupil ratio in Africa.

In the manufacturing sector, the Hyundai vehicle assembly plant was due to come into production early in 1998, with an estimated production capacity of 30,000 vehicles a year for the southern African market. Agriculture, still struggling with earlier drought problems, now accounted for less than 4 per cent of GDP. Wildlife continued to be hemmed in ever more closely to make room for ever more cattle (mainly to take advantage of EU access), despite the fact that wildlife tourism had become the third-largest earner of foreign exchange. Other problems arose from the ghettoizing of the surviving San bushmen, on similar grounds. The signing of the UN Convention on Trade in Endangered Species (CITES) in June allowed Botswana (along with Nambia and Zimbabwe) to export ivory with effect from 1999.

Much-discussed 'wild cards' for the future included evidence that up to 30 per cent the population was infected with HIV; unexplained high expenditure on sophisticated military weaponry, including tanks and jet-fighters; and the dispute with Namibia (now before the International Court of Justice) over future water abstraction from the Kunene river and its possible effects on the Okavango swamps. The two latter developments seemed likely to be interrelated.

LESOTHO. As an isolated and small African country, Lesotho in 1997 could be said to represent in microcosm the woes of the continent. An abortive police rebellion in February was extinguished by the army in March with tacit South African approval. In June, to a background of several months of chicanery and infighting, the ruling Basutoland Congress Party (BCP) imploded, following a deft political masterstroke by its ageing and ailing leader, the 78-year-old Prime Minister, Ntsu Mokhehle. Mr Mokhehle resigned from the BCP, simultaneously creating a new party called the Lesotho Congress for Democracy (LCD), taking with him all the cabinet ministers and two-thirds of the MPs. With the acquiescence of the Assembly's Speaker, he remained in office, forcing the rump BCP into the role of official opposition.

Without allies the dominant LCD faced a stern test in the elections expected in late April or May 1998, particularly as the BCP and the former ruling Basotho National Party (BNP) moved closer together in opposition to Mr Mokhehle's coup. The BCP deputy leader and national executive secretary, Molapo Qhobela, was confirmed as leader of the party in June after a court-ordered election, with former leader Tseliso Makhakhe staying on as national chairman. On 13 October the Senate passed a motion to suspend discussion on bills coming from the National Assembly, effectively blocking government legislation, although its appeals to King Letsie III that he should dissolve parliament were unsuccessful.

Mr Mokhehle's introduction of improved parliamentary oversight of the military paid dividends in maintaining public order in potentially delicate circumstances. A further unifying factor lay in the general acceptance of King Letsie III's enthronement in October. By the end of the year it was clear that Mr Mokhehle would hand over the premiership after the 1998 elections, the favourites to succeed him being the Deputy Prime Minister, Pakalitha Mosisili, and the Foreign Minister, Kelebone Maope.

Following five years of real annual GDP growth of over 10 per cent (rising to an estimated 14 per cent in 1996), the 1997 figure seemed unlikely to exceed 7 per cent. The country had adhered fairly successfully to IMF guidelines and had succeeded in obtaining further investment from the Far East for manufactures, mainly in textiles. The Lesotho National Development Corporation worked energetically in this area, as well as moving ahead with privatization. A new airline, Air Lesotho, was formed out of the sale of Lesotho Airways Corporation in September. A further plus for the economy was the high proportion of manufactured goods (72 per cent) in Lesotho's total exports. Adverse factors, apart from the rapidly-growing number of those seeking work, included the threat of massive redundancies in South Africa's gold mines, employing a large proportion of Basotho workers, in the wake of the collapse in gold prices. It was feared that up to two-thirds of the estimated 93,000 migrant miners might lose their jobs as a result. Miners' remittances effectively accounted for 40 per cent of Lesotho's GNP.

Some additional revenue would accrue to Lesotho during 1998 with the coming on stream of the first phase of the joint South African- Lesotho Highlands Water

Scheme at the beginning of the year, producing a reliable monthly income as well as the prospect of inexpensive electricity later in the year.

NAMIBIA. Politically, a major issue in Namibia was the question of a third five-year term for President Nujoma in 1999. Obtaining the required two-thirds parliamentary majority presented little difficulty, given the overwhelming SWAPO majority, but the question was expected to resurface at the SWAPO congress due in mid-1998. Local government elections scheduled for December 1997 were postponed on technical grounds until February 1998, when the opposition Democratic Turnhalle Alliance (DTA) was expected to pick up some support as a result of low voter turnout combined with the weakness of some SWAPO branches. However, the fact that its main ethnic support base, the Ovambos, constituted over half the population meant that SWAPO was highly unlikely to lose political control. Minorities could therefore continue to feel ignored, although whites continued to be cushioned by their dominant role in commerce.

Other events of political moment revolved around the government's determination to restrict public—in particular the media's—access to information in the public domain, using the Powers, Privileges and Immunities of Parliament Act of 1996, with the objective of hindering investigation into suspected official corruption. Of lesser moment, but a pointer nevertheless, was President Nujoma's agreement to rescind a package of outrageous ministerial perks engineered by Prime Minister Hage Geingob earlier in the year. As a result of this affair, Mr Geingob appeared to have lost support in his quest to succeed to the presidency, for which the Trade and Industry Minister, Hidipo Hamutenya, was now seen as a strong contender. The long-awaited White Paper on land reform emerged in September as a damp squib, devoid of concrete recommendations while acknowledging the need for productive agriculture.

Signals were mixed in the economic sphere. The start of a new offshore diamond recovery operation and increased quotas for fishing were positive factors. However, continuing semi-drought conditions, caused in part by the El Niño weather distortion effect (see XIV.3), rendered agriculture generally an unknown quantity. Public debt increased by 31 per cent over the 1996 figure, amid growing uncertainty as to how it would be financed. Whilst government moves to rein in expenditure were taken seriously, taxation was already running at 40 per cent of GDP (against an average of 14 per cent for developing countries generally), so that it seemed that resort would have to be made to overseas funding.

At the same time, the government pressed ahead with raising funds for major infrastructural projects, including the controversial US$2,500 million Epupa Falls dam and a power station at Oranjemund. Other projects included a desalination plant at Walvis Bay and a major electricity power connection to the South African grid to ensure adequate supplies. Only the first two schemes would be self-funded, although financing the others was not thought to be a serious problem, given the current low level of external debt of only US$200 million. Work also continued on the expansion of the Walvis Bay harbour, anticipating completion of the trans-Kalahari road link.

SWAZILAND. The year came and went with no discernible progress at all towards resolution of the country's constitutional problems, despite the appointment of the much-heralded Constitutional Review Commission in July 1996 (see AR 1996, p. 281). The process effectively lost momentum and credibility following the withdrawal of the People's United Democratic Movement (PUDEMO), trade union representatives and other reputable public figures. Despite the protestations of sincerity at the outset, for the participants it became increasingly obvious that the government had no serious intention of embarking on any reform that would imperil the status quo so far as the royal house and its supporters were concerned. Fatherly advice from President Mandela was ignored, and his oblique reference at the SADC Malawi meeting to the imposition of sanctions on undemocratic regimes was also understandably brushed aside.

Little change could therefore be expected in the coming year, particularly as the opposition itself seemed to be disintegrating and union activity less than united. Although the Swaziland Federation of Trade Unions (SFTU) continued to pressure the government to redraft the controversial Industrial Relations Act of 1996, work stoppages called in October were poorly planned and had to be called off after just two days. The government's response to increased political opposition was, *inter alia*, to publish the Media Control Bill, ostensibly to 'encourage responsible standards of journalism'. In reality, however, the bill was seen as little more than a crude attempt to muzzle the country's free press, especially the outspoken *Times of Swaziland*.

Reflecting these wider political uncertainties, the Swazi economy continued to limp along in 1997, albeit with a small GDP increase of 0.5 per cent (compared with 2.5 per cent in 1996). The 1996/97 Central Bank of Swaziland report highlighted sluggish activity, leading to increased trade and current-account deficits. High interest rates continued to deter investment and expansion, but government expenditure as a proportion of GDP maintained its rise. Although international trade as a whole remained in surplus, there was a growing trade deficit with South Africa, even though exports to that country grew substantially, particularly in manufactured goods.

On the credit side, an Investment Promotion Act was passed and some major expansion occurred. New enterprises included a vehicle-assembly plant with 1,000 new jobs, aiming to supply other member-countries of the Common Market for Eastern and Southern Africa (COMESA), formerly the Preferential Trade Area.

3. SOUTH AFRICA

CAPITAL: Pretoria   AREA: 1,220,000 sq km   POPULATION: 41,900,000 ('95 est)
OFFICIAL LANGUAGES: Afrikaans, English & nine African languages
POLITICAL SYSTEM: transitional multi-racial democracy
HEAD OF STATE & GOVERNMENT: President Nelson Mandela (since May '94)
RULING PARTIES: African National Congress (ANC) & Inkatha Freedom Party (IFP)
MAIN IGO MEMBERSHIPS (non-UN): OAU, SADC, SACU, CWTH, NAM
CURRENCY: rand (end-'97 £1=R8.01, US$1=R4.88)
GNP PER CAPITA: US$3,060 ('95) or US$5,030 ('95) by PPP calculation

THE South African scene in 1997 could be described at best as fluid. Abortive attempts at forming party alliances in advance of the 1999 elections characterized the early part of the year. On a positive note, the new constitution came into force on the 4 February.

President Mandela formally retired as chairman of the African National Congress (ANC) in December, to be succeeded by Deputy President Thabo Mbeki, whose position as deputy chairman went to Natal ANC leader Jacob Zuma, after a failed challenge by Winnie Madikizela-Mandela, divorced wife of the President. Mr Mbeki was now well-placed to take over from Mr Mandela as President after the 1999 elections.

The official opposition National Party (NP) experienced an upheaval in August, when former State President F.W. de Klerk also resigned as leader, making way for the youthful but relatively low-profile Marthinus van Schalkwyk. The latter was faced with the challenge of remodelling the party into a contemporary organization. Even its principal base in the Western Cape appeared to be fading, although the ANC was also believed to have lost strength nationally, from 63 per cent support in the 1994 election to 56 per cent in current opinion polls. Such shifts were, of course, commonplace between elections, but clearly reflected dissatisfaction among the electorate over the pace of the government's delivery on pre-1994 promises.

Surveys showed that South Africa remained a racially-fractured society three years after the ANC had been swept to power. Support for the ANC, President Mandela and perceptions of the government's record were all skewed along racial lines. Nearly 80 per cent of blacks intended to vote for the ANC, as against just 3 per cent of whites. Half of black families expected to be better off in 1998 than in 1997, against less than one-fifth of whites. Overall, while 80 per cent of blacks and 70 per cent of whites had believed that the country was heading in the right direction in June 1994, three years later the corresponding figures had dropped to 65 and 20 per cent.

Other interesting developments included the formation of a new party in September: the United Democratic Movement (UDM), an alliance between unlikely bedfellows Roelf Meyer, a former NP cabinet member, and Bantu Holomisa, the former Transkei military leader and prominent ANC member. However, representing an attempt to break the quasi-racial straitjacket still dominating South African politics, the UDM seemed unlikely to make a strong impact. The numerically small but vociferous opponent of the government in parliament, the Democratic Party (DP), had been historically and substantially 'English' in support; but the defection to the DP in December of several major NP figures, including long-time Eastern Cape leader Tertius Delport, signalled a long-anticipated shift in alignments. The right wing, represented by such disparate figures as the anachronistic Eugene Terreblanche on the one hand and the pragmatic Afrikaner homeland promoter, General (retd.) Constand Viljoen of the Freedom Front on the other, was increasingly seen as a spent force, although the latter engaged during 1997 in inconclusive discussions over the establishment of an Afrikaner *Volkstaat*.

The Truth and Reconciliation Commission (TRC) continued to function, with the focus shifted, by the end of 1997, to amnesty applications and the victims reparations process. Having received some 7,000 applications for amnesty, it had an enormous backlog of cases to work through. According to the TRC chairman, Desmond Tutu, clearing the backlog could take years, and certainly past the intended deadline of 30 June 1998. Highlights of the year included the appearance of Winnie Madikizela-Mandela before the commission in November. The evidence against her and of the activities of her Mandela United Football Team during the 1980s appeared inconclusive. The other prominent figure requested to appear was the former State President, P.W. Botha. His rejection of the call resulted in a court summons for contempt, scheduled to be heard January 1998, at which he agreed to appear.

In the foreign realm, close ties with the United States came under particular strain twice during the year, first over a mooted arms deal with Syria in March, but subsequently abandoned, and later over the visit by President Mandela to Libya prior to his attendance at the Commonwealth heads of government meeting in Edinburgh (see V.4.ii). In April South Africa's role in attempting to mediate a solution to the Zaïrean conflict from a naval vessel anchored off the coast of Congo-Brazzaville (see VII.1.i) was heralded as the start of a new period of South African diplomatic engagement with the continent. The Zaïrean episode was characterized by Deputy President Mbeki, in a speech in the United States in April, as the signal event in an 'African renaissance'. During 1997, however, President Mandela's mediation attempts in Sudan and Zaïre, and in trying to bring about democratic reforms in Swaziland (see VII.2.iv), met with little success. The same could be said for his efforts to break the deadlocks over East Timor and the Lockerbie bombing case.

South Africa's switch in diplomatic relations from Taiwan to the People's Republic of China took place painlessly on 31 December, the embassy of the former being downgraded to a cultural/trade centre and the latter's office being upgraded to embassy status. Little impact on trade relations with Taiwan was anticipated, given that almost all of its trade worldwide was conducted on the basis of official non-recognition.

Talks between South Africa and the European Union (EU), on the establishment of a free trade area (FTA) as part of a comprehensive bilateral agreement, ground on during the year. Many in Pretoria had initially favoured full membership of the Lomé Convention allowing preferential access for some 70 African, Caribbean and Pacific (ACP) states to EU markets, in line with an apparent belief that South Africa 'deserved' to be accorded the status of a developing rather than developed state. In March 1996, however, a dual track (Lomé and FTA) solution had been offered by Brussels. Under this scenario, South Africa was invited to join the Lomé Convention as a qualified member, able to participate in Lomé institutions, to benefit from rules of origin applicable to ACP products and to have access to European Development Fund (EDF) funding; but it would not be eligible for Lomé trade preferences, since the EU believed that, as an 'advanced developing' nation, South Africa could not morally expect to receive them. This offer of membership was endorsed by the EU Commission in March 1997.

The second track involved the establishment of an FTA (after a transitional period), along with sectoral agreements on fisheries, wine and spirits, as well as cooperation on broader trade-related economic and political matters such as competition policy, investment promotion and protection, and on judicial-criminal issues. However, the talks were problematic throughout 1997, reportedly because of the length of the EU's list of sensitive products to be excluded from the FTA. The list amounted to some 39 per cent of South African agricultural exports to the EU, but represented only around 4 per cent of total EU imports from South Africa. Even though the EU made it clear that the list of agricultural exclusions was subject to negotiation, Pretoria effectively used its objections to delay the talks until it was ready with its own mandate. Hence the process during 1997 was big on rhetoric and low on progress.

The future of the talks was also complicated by a number of short- and longer-term factors, including the scheduled 1998 renegotiation of the Lomé Convention (of which all the other member-states in the Southern African Development Community were full members), the negotiation of a new formula for the Southern African Customs Union and the SADC's 1996 agreement to establish a free trade area by the year 2004 (see VII.2.iv). Nevertheless, by the end of 1997 there seemed a real prospect that a conclusion to the talks would be achieved by mid-1998, South Africa anticipating a more sympathetic hearing under the British EU presidency in the first half of the year.

Nearer to home, the success of the Maputo Corridor development scheme with Mozambique was a major boost, helped considerably by private South African and World Bank investment. The development was already having subsidiary benefits in Kwa-Zulu Natal and Swaziland, in the shape of planned upgrading of transport routes linking to the corridor.

The South African economy continued to grow modestly at an annual rate of about 2 per cent, although below the pace of population growth. Projections for 1998 showed little change. With so-called 'jobless growth' the norm and official unemployment at around 30 per cent, it was not surprising that the Growth, Employment and Redistribution (GEAR) strategy—the government's liberal macro-economic policy—received a hostile reception from organized labour. Matters were not helped by the collapsing gold price (from US$350 per ounce to a low of $280 over the year) and the disastrous East Asian economic crisis in the second half of 1997 (see XVIII.1). The latter was expected to place a dual strain on South Africa's exports, for which there would be fewer customers in the Far East, while competition from that region would be greater because of local currency depreciation.

Inflation remained under control in 1997 at just under 8 per cent, a fractional reduction being forecast for 1998. The South African rand held up well, emerging as the third strongest in a basket of currencies against the US dollar (after its sharp depreciation in earlier years). Credit was undoubtedly due in part to the measured but progressive relaxation of controls over foreign exchange and foreign investment, in compliance with international and particularly IMF norms.

In the defence sector, the scaling-down of military strength (specifically in relation to ground forces) continued to be a major preoccupation, the aim being a reduction in overall numbers from 95,545 (including 21,119 civilians) to 70,000 (including a civilian component of about 25 per cent) by the year 2001. The grossly under-funded naval vote at last seemed set for redress, over R10,000 million being allocated on paper for new vessels (including submarines and corvettes), ancilliary equipment and re-equipment. Expenditure would be spread over a number of years, it being envisaged that counter-trade and local content would be important elements. Several major Western powers had bids on the table, decisions being expected early in 1998. The future of South Africa's armaments industry looked decidedly more shaky during 1997, as the government implemented strict sales criteria through its National Conventional Arms Control Committee (NCACC), chaired by the Water and Forestry Minister, Professor Kader Asmal.

South Africa's crime rates remained among the highest in the world, despite the appointment of a prominent businessman, Meyer Khan, as head of the South African Police Services (SAPS) charged with producing a strategy for more effective policing. The rate of murder per 100,000 of the population dropped from 49.8 in the first nine months of 1994 to 41 in the corresponding period in 1997, armed robbery falling from 156.1 to 116.1 over the same period. While the official figures for many categories of crime (excluding common robbery, rape, indecent assault, burglary and assault) came down in 1997, victim studies showed that 66 per cent of those mugged and 75 per cent of those assaulted did not report the crime to the police. Only crimes with insurance implications were invariably reported. Arguably, the perception that crime was spiralling out of control had more to do with the state of the criminal justice system than with the incidence of crime. There had been a steady decline in the rates of conviction for crime in South Africa since 1988, while the prison system was in disarray. Whereas South Africa's prisons had an official capacity of 100,000 prisoners, the annual daily average during 1997 was 141,000. Political violence dropped, however, from a peak of 4,406 deaths in 1993 to 1,057 in 1996.

For the poor, there was progress on the upgrading of services such as water, electrification and housing, but still far short of the government's election promises. In the spheres of education and health, achievement fell woefully short, amid endless argument as to whether mismanagement or inadequate funding was to blame.

VIII SOUTH ASIA AND INDIAN OCEAN

1. IRAN—AFGHANISTAN—CENTRAL ASIAN REPUBLICS

i. IRAN

CAPITAL: Tehran   AREA: 1,650,000 sq km   POPULATION: 63,200,000 ('96)
NATIONAL LANGUAGE: Farsi (Persian)   POLITICAL SYSTEM: Islamic republic
SPIRITUAL GUIDE: Ayatollah Seyed Ali Khamenei (since June '89)
HEAD OF STATE & GOVERNMENT: President Mohammed Khatami (since Aug '97)
MAIN IGO MEMBERSHIPS (non-UN): OPEC, ECO, CP, OIC, NAM
CURRENCY: rial (end-'97 £1=Rls4,922.01, US$1=Rls3,000.00)
GNP PER CAPITA: US$4,650 ('94) by PPP calculation

THE gradual evolution of the Islamic Republic of Iran from its revolutionary roots was confirmed on 23 May, when Mohammed Khatami was elected President in a landslide victory against his hardline opponents, winning 69 per cent of the votes cast in a heavy turnout, officially given as 88.1 per cent of those eligible. The new President ran on a platform of respect for human and political rights, with an emphasis on freedom and cultural liberalism. He also endorsed policies of economic growth and development of the modern sectors, which was a direct challenge to the conservative and isolationist views of the Islamic traditionalists. The large majority achieved by Mohammed Khatami clearly indicated the desire for change among the population at large and opened the way for a further surge in the continuing process of secularization and modernization of government.

A new 22-member cabinet was introduced to the *Majlis* (parliament) on 13 August. The previous First Vice-President, Dr Hassan Habibi, was reappointed for an initial period of six months to assist in a smooth transition from old to new administrations. The important post of Minister of the Interior went to Abdullah Nouri, a comparative liberal with experience at this ministry in 1989–92, while the culture and Islamic guidance portfolio was taken by Dr Ataollah Mohajerani, another advocate of a more open society and freer press. Dr Hossein Namazi was appointed Minister of Finance and Economic Affairs, a sign of a more active role for this ministry.

Similarly, the new Minister of Oil, Bijan Namdar-Zanganeh, was a technocrat of known administrative abilities in the other departments of state closely concerned with economic welfare. Some ministries remained with their incumbents from the last government, the most significant including agriculture, labour and construction. A positive policy towards the outside world was ensured in the allocation of the foreign affairs portfolio to Dr Kamal Kharrazi, an experienced representative at the United Nations, who had been amongst the first to suggest that Iran wanted to adhere to international diplomatic norms. The new cabinet retained an anchor of conservative figures, such as Dorri Najafabadi (intelligence), Hossein Mozaffar (education), and Esmail

Shustari (justice), who could be expected to slow down the process of change, despite the liberal and youthful bent of the rest of the cabinet. However, given the dismissal of so many hardliners from positions of power, the motivation for reform at cabinet level appeared strong.

The election of Mohammed Khatami gave a fillip to constitutional reform. The new President began to implement the rule of civil law to protect personal rights, seemingly at the expense of religious practice. Following the presidential election, a challenge also came from Ayatollah Montazeri and the senior clerics in the holy city of Qom to the very legitimacy of the personal status of the sitting spiritual leader of Iran, Ayatollah Seyed Ali Khamenei, and to the religious justification for his constitutional role. A possible separation of the political from the religious leadership of the country, amounting to a major alteration in the constitution, was presaged by the subsequent intellectual and street conflicts which affected Iran in late 1997 on the issue of *velatyat-e faqih*, or spiritual rule.

Following the May election, the retiring President, Hashemi Rafsanjani, retained his important post as chairman of the Expediency Council (the powers of which had been greatly augmented in March) and continued to play an influential part in the management of the regime. In October former Prime Minister Hossein Moussavi was appointed as the new President's senior adviser, bringing some vision but a left-wing Islamic tinge to the otherwise reformist government apparatus. In a change which effectively de-politicized the armed forces, Mohsen Rezai, an outspoken Islamic conservative, resigned as head of the Revolutionary Guards in September, making way for a commander uninvolved in political life.

Despite the atmosphere of enlightenment that followed the presidential election, the leader of the progressive Freedom Movement of Iran, Ibrahim Yazdi, was arrested in December and released only after strong representations by followers of President Khatami. Attacks on cinemas and cinema-goers by fundamentalists remained a problem for the authorities in the second half of the year, as *hizbullahi* mobs sought to demonstrate that the old Islamic ideas still ruled.

In foreign affairs, the change of leadership gave opportunities for a new initiative to restore relations with the United States. The Iranian Foreign Minister, supported by the new President, made it clear after the election that Iran would pursue its national interests rather than ideology in dealing with Washington. Importantly, President Khatami declared shortly after the election that the Iranian revolution was no longer for export. The US State Department responded in a positive manner, offering in December to take part in a dialogue with Iran. Meanwhile, US sanctions on Iran remained in place, including the Iran-Libya Sanctions Act (ILSA) of 1996, and there was no lessening in US congressional concern with Iran's build-up of missile and atomic technology, or with Iran's opposition to the Middle East peace process and its involvement in international terrorism.

Iran's desired orientation towards Europe suffered a setback on 10 April when a German court ruled that the then Iranian political leadership had been directly involved in the 1992 attack on the Mykonos restaurant in Berlin in which four Iranian-Kurdish dissidents had been killed. As a result of the German court's verdict, four Iranian diplomats were expelled from Germany and all European Union (EU) members temporarily withdrew their heads of mission from Iran, returning them only on 14 November. Iran was also the source of EU-US friction as a result of its award of a contract to Total of France, Gazprom of Russia and Petronas of Malaysia for development of the South Pars gas field in the Persian Gulf. The US government threatened to implement ILSA sanctions against Total, which prompted strong reactions in France and the possibility of EU counter-sanctions against the United States. For the United Kingdom, the Salman Rushdie affair diminished in political significance as the Iranians made it amply clear that the *fatweh* against the author had effectively lapsed.

Tehran drew closer diplomatically to Russia and China, whose supply of advanced armaments to Iran caused US and Israeli dismay. The main thrust of Iranian foreign policy, however, was towards fellow Islamic states, especially those of the Persian Gulf region. This policy was sealed by Iran's successful hosting of a summit of the Organization of the Islamic Conference (OIC) on 9–11 December (see XI.2.iv). The meeting was used by Iran to demonstrate that it now lived by acceptable diplomatic norms, was internally self-confident and keen to co-exist with its neighbours in a positive way.

The economy remained marginally buoyant, modestly stimulated by the higher oil revenues of recent years. Government budgetary allocations in 1997/98 totalled the equivalent of US$62,900 million (at the floating exchange rate of the day), up 37 per cent on the preceding Iranian year, with the bulk of funds allotted to state entities to cover their recurrent costs. New investments in petroleum and industry were restrained by a shortage of funds in the state coffers, where priorities were for defence and debt repayment, there being a parallel lack of confidence in the private sector. The presidential election result gave some optimism that more positive expansion of the economy might now be possible. It was clear, however, that the problems of a deteriorating currency (which fell to an unofficial rate of Rls4,800 to the US dollar at end-December), annual inflation hardening at 25 per cent and chronic unemployment would not be solved overnight. There was also a fall in oil prices in late-1997, which cast a shadow over the future performance of the domestic economy.

ii. AFGHANISTAN

CAPITAL: Kabul   AREA: 650,000 sq km   POPULATION: 19,000,000 ('96)
OFFICIAL LANGUAGES: Pushtu, Dari (Persian)   POLITICAL SYSTEM: transitional
LEADERSHIP: Mohammad Omar, Leader of the Taleban (in power since Sept '96), Mohammad Rabbani, Chairman of Interim Council (since Sept '96)
MAIN IGO MEMBERSHIPS (non-UN): ECO, CP, OIC, NAM
CURRENCY: afghani (end-'97 £1=Af7,793.32,US$1=Af4,750.00)
GNP PER CAPITA: n/a

THE civil war in Afghanistan dragged on throughout 1997 with neither the Taleban regime nor their opponents able to achieve a decisive victory. The Taleban maintained control over large areas of the country, including Kabul, and continued to impose strict Islamic fundamentalist rule upon those within their jurisdiction. Nevertheless, as a year of almost continuous fighting came to an end, little military progress had been made by either side in the increasingly attritional struggle.

The year began well for the Taleban. In January they captured the strategically important airbase at Baghram before moving north to the Salang Pass, the main route linking southern and northern Afghanistan. They then swung west in order to outflank the strong defensive positions established by forces under the command of the ethnic Uzbek leader, General Abdul Rashid Dostam. By the end of February the Taleban had captured the Shibar Pass, thereby opening a route northwards to General Dostam's headquarters in Mazar-i-Sharif, Afghanistan's second-largest city. The other element of the anti-Taleban alliance—that commanded by former Afghan Defence Minister Ahmed Shah Masud—attempted to relieve the pressure on General Dostam. His forces made a series of limited attacks near the Panjsher valley in April, and in early May inflicted heavy casualties on the Taleban during an offensive against the city of Jabul-us-Siraj.

The military situation was transformed on 17 May when General Malik Pahlawan, General Dostram's commander in the western province of Fariab, defected to the Taleban. His treachery opened the western approach to Mazar-i-Sharif, which on 24 May was captured by his forces, accompanied by several detachments of Taleban militiamen. The fall of Mazar-i-Sharif and its surrounding provinces briefly appeared to herald the end of the war; for it left the Taleban in control of around 90 per cent of the country and forced General Dostam to take refuge in Uzbekistan. However, in a further dramatic development, on 27 May General Pahlawan's forces turned on their lightly-armed Taleban allies, killing many and capturing others. This second betrayal coincided with an offensive by General Masud's forces against Taleban positions north of Kabul which succeeded in recapturing much of the ground lost earlier in the year. Although the Taleban remained in control of 20 of the country's 29 provinces, they were estimated to have lost more than 2,000 experienced fighters in the rout at Mazar-i-Sharif.

A new alliance, the United Islamic Front for the Salvation of Afghanistan (UIFSA), was established in June under General Masud's overall command. Amidst heavy fighting in July, UIFSA forces made further territorial gains. The Taleban adopted a 'scorched earth' policy in retreat, poisoning wells, destroying food stocks and laying landmines. However, in August the fighting reached a stalemate with both sides occupying heavily fortified positions. The UIFSA controlled a salient which ran south from the southern escarpment of the Hindu Kush mountain range, along the so-called old road across the Shamwali plain, to a point some 20 kilometres north of Kabul. Along the second major route which crossed the plain (the so-called new road), General Masud's forces were held at the Hotki Pass, some 30 kilometres from Kabul. Although the UIFSA continued to press Taleban positions, no further progress was achieved as the campaigning season drew to a close.

In contrast to their military successes, anti-Taleban forces suffered a major political setback on 21 August when Abdorrahim Ghafurzai, the former Foreign Minister who had served as Prime Minister in the self-declared government of the anti-Taleban alliance, was killed in an air crash. Several other senior alliance leaders were also amongst the 15 people who died in the accident. Mr Ghafurzai was a widely respected liberal and a civilian figure capable of attracting widespread support to the struggle against the Taleban. Significantly, he was also one of the few ethnic Pushtuns who had chosen to fight the Pushtun-dominated Taleban in an alliance formed mainly of ethnic Uzbek and Tajik Shias.

There was a further realignment of the anti-Taleban forces in October when a UIFSA meeting in Pol-e-Khomri chose General Dostam (who had returned to Afghanistan in September) as Vice-President of the movement and overall military commander. A month later General Dostam's forces seized General Pahlawan's headquarters in northern Fariab province and forced the commander to flee into Turkmenistan.

The Taleban's military successes in the first half of the year militated against the likelihood of a negotiated settlement to the war by appearing to offer the chance of outright victory. The apparently decisive breakthrough in May encouraged Saudi Arabia to join Pakistan in extending diplomatic recognition to the Taleban regime, but caused alarm in Russia and Iran, both of which pledged support for the Central Asian republics if the Taleban were to advance beyond Afghanistan's borders. However, as the fighting descended into stalemate there were tentative signs that the two sides were edging towards negotiations. In early November the UIFSA unilaterally released more than 200 Taleban prisoners and called for ceasefire talks. The Taleban responded by accepting a prisoner exchange, negotiated by UN officials, and the UIFSA released further Taleban prisoners in December.

However, with both sides in the conflict continuing to receive support from beyond Afghanistan's borders, the possibility of meaningful peace negotiations remained dependent on international diplomacy. In December a series of three UN-brokered meetings in New York brought together representatives from Afghanistan's neighbours, together with a US delegation, in a move designed to staunch the flow of arms to the warring factions. The negotiations were instigated by UN trouble-shooter Lakhdar Brahimi and also involved the US Assistant Secretary of State for South Asian Affairs, Karl Inderfurth, and ambassadors from Iran, China, Pakistan, Russia, Tajikistan, Turkmenistan and Uzbekistan. Although no immediate progress was made, the involvement of the United States was significant and remained the most likely conduit through which pressure could be applied to persuade Pakistan to cut its supplies of arms and fuel to the Taleban. Such a step would contribute to the military stalemate and thereby increase the likelihood of the emergence of a negotiated settlement to the conflict.

iii. KAZAKHSTAN—TURKMENISTAN—UZBEKISTAN— KYRGYZSTAN—TAJIKISTAN

Kazakhstan
CAPITAL: Akmola   AREA: 2,717,300 sq km   POPULATION: 17,000,000 ('96)
OFFICIAL LANGUAGES: Kazakh & Russian   POLITICAL SYSTEM: presidential
HEAD OF STATE & GOVERNMENT: President Nursultan Nazarbayev (since Feb '90)
RULING PARTY: Party of People's Unity of Kazakhstan (PNEK)
PRIME MINISTER: Nurlan Balgimbayev (since Oct '97)
MAIN IGO MEMBERSHIPS (non-UN): CIS, PFP, OSCE, ECO, OIC
CURRENCY: tenge (end-'97 £1=T125.50, US$1=T76.49)
GNP PER CAPITA: US$1,330 ('95) or US$3,010 ('95) by PPP calculation

Kyrgyzstan
CAPITAL: Bishkek   AREA: 198,500 sq km   POPULATION: 4,500,000 ('96)
OFFICIAL LANGUAGES: Kyrgyz & Russian   POLITICAL SYSTEM: presidential
HEAD OF STATE & GOVERNMENT: President Askar Akayev (since Oct '90)
RULING PARTIES: Social Democratic Party & Democratic Movement
PRIME MINISTER: Apas Jumagulov (since Dec '93)
MAIN IGO MEMBERSHIPS (non-UN): CIS, PFP, OSCE, ECO, OIC
CURRENCY: som
GNP PER CAPITA: US$700 ('95) or US$1,800 ('95) by PPP calculation

Tajikistan
CAPITAL: Dushanbe   AREA: 143,100 sq km   POPULATION: 6,000,000 ('95)
OFFICIAL LANGUAGE: Tajik
POLITICAL SYSTEM: presidential
HEAD OF STATE & GOVERNMENT: President Imamali Rakhmanov (since Nov '92)
RULING PARTY: Communist Party & People's Party of Tajikistan
PRIME MINISTER: Yahya Azimov (since Feb '96)
MAIN IGO MEMBERSHIPS (non-UN): CIS, PFP, OSCE, ECO, OIC
CURRENCY: Tajik rouble
GNP PER CAPITA: US$340 ('95) or US$920 ('95) by PPP calculation

Turkmenistan
CAPITAL: Ashgabat   AREA: 448,100 sq km   POPULATION: 4,010,000 ('94)
OFFICIAL LANGUAGE: Turkmen   POLITICAL SYSTEM: presidential
HEAD OF STATE & GOVERNMENT: President (Gen.) Saparmurad Niyazov (since Jan '90)
RULING PARTY: Democratic Party of Turkmenistan (DPT)
MAIN IGO MEMBERSHIPS (non-UN): CIS, PFP, OSCE, ECO, OIC, NAM
CURRENCY: manat
GNP PER CAPITA: US$920 ('95)

Uzbekistan
CAPITAL: Tashkent   AREA: 447,400 sq km   POPULATION: 22,633,000 ('94)
OFFICIAL LANGUAGE: Uzbek   POLITICAL SYSTEM: presidential
HEAD OF STATE & GOVERNMENT: President Islam Karimov (since March '90)
RULING PARTY: People's Democratic Party (PDP)
PRIME MINISTER: Otkir Sultonov (since Dec '95)
MAIN IGO MEMBERSHIPS (non-UN): CIS, PFP, OSCE, ECO, OIC, NAM
CURRENCY: sum
GNP PER CAPITA: US$970 ('95) or US$2,370 ('95) by PPP calculation

THE unresolved conflict in Tajikistan remained a matter of grave concern. At the end of 1996 there had seemed to be real grounds for hope that the government and the United Opposition (UTO) might be reconciled (see AR 1996, p. 292). Within weeks, however, tensions had resurfaced. In January, and again in August, there were insurrections within an elite brigade of the government forces. On 30 April the Tajik President survived an assassination attempt. Incidents such as these highlighted ongoing rivalries and regional disaffection.

It was largely thanks to the unremitting efforts of Russia, Iran and the United Nations that the peace process continued, albeit haltingly, and that a further agreement was reached on 18 May, this time regarding the legalization of the three main opposition parties (Islamic Rebirth, Lali Badakhshan and the Democratic Party) and the opposition media. On 27 June a 'final' peace agreement and 'protocol of mutual understanding' was signed in Moscow by President Rakhmanov and the UTO leader, Said Abdullo Nuri, in the presence of President Yeltsin of Russia, UN envoy Gerd-Dietrich Merrem and senior officials from Iran and other countries. In July a further 'pact on mutual forgiveness' was signed and endorsed by the newly-formed Commission for National Reconciliation.

Said Abdullo Nuri returned to Dushanbe on 11 September, after five years' absence. In discussions on a timetable for implementing the peace agreement, it was agreed that a coalition government should be formed in which the UTO would hold 30 per cent of the posts. Parliamentary elections, with the participation of all political parties, were scheduled for 1998. Said Abdullo Nuri urged UTO field commanders to cooperate with government troops to crush illegal independent formations, many of which were involved in drug-smuggling, hostage-taking and other criminal activities. Unwelcome proof of this was given in mid-November, when a French couple were kidnapped by guerrillas. The wife was fatally wounded during a rescue attempt by the security forces. Most of the guerrillas, including their leader, were killed. By the end of December the fragile truce between the government and the UTO was beginning to disintegrate.

In Kazakhstan, President Nazarbayev embarked on a major restructuring of the government apparatus in late February. The number of ministries and state agencies was drastically reduced (from 20 to 14 and 13 to six respectively) and the Ministry of Oil and Gas was replaced by a new national oil and gas company, KazakhOil. The reason for the cutbacks was partly financial. However, there was also a political motive, since the campaign was clearly aimed at reducing the power of the government and increasing the President's direct control over the running of the country. The reforms were introduced while the Prime Minister, Akezhan Kazhageldin, was abroad, and it seemed as though he personally was under threat of dismissal. In fact, he remained at his post for several months longer, finally resigning on 10 October, apparently on grounds of ill-health. The chairman of KazakhOil, Nurlan Balgimbayev, took over the premiership, while departmental reforms resulted in a further streamlining of the bureaucracy.

Another milestone in Kazakh political life was the transfer of the capital from Almaty (in the south-east) to Akmola (north-central region). After several postponements the official inauguration finally took place on 13 December in a ceremony attended by the Kyrgyz and Uzbek Presidents. The reasons for the move were far from clear. One of many explanations was that Akmola would be equally accessible from all parts of the country. Many Kazakhs, however, were concerned that the cost of the move, estimated at US$10–14,000 million, was an unjustifiable expense in a time of economic hardship. Also, the harsh climate (including winter temperatures often at -40 degrees centigrade), the lack of basic facilities and the shortage of accommodation discouraged people from migrating en masse to the new capital. Almaty seemed set to remain the financial and cultural centre of the country for some time to come.

In the other Central Asia states there were no major political changes in 1997. Throughout the region a certain degree of economic stabilization appeared to be taking place, though the pace of reforms tended to be slow and halting. Official government statistics often varied markedly from assessments made by foreign specialists. Hence it was difficult to gain an accurate picture. There was, perhaps, greatest openness on such questions in Kyrgyzstan. In March President Akayev outlined his economic policy for the year, highlighting privatization as a key issue. Some 500 mostly small and medium-sized enterprises were earmarked for privatization, either by means of auctioning for cash or by setting up special privatization projects for large businesses. However, the President pointed to poor management of enterprises and financial institutions, as well as delays and non-payment of taxes, as major obstacles to growth.

In Uzbekistan privatization appeared to be proceeding smoothly. Private investors could buy shares in privatization investment funds at special 'stock shops', up to a limit of 100 shares per family member per fund. The take-up rate of shares was good. On 12 February the European Bank for Reconstruction and Development (EBRD) announced its second medium-term credit line facility (of ECU 96 million) to support the Uzbek private sector. The first credit line (worth half this amount), made available in 1993, had been fully lent on to small and medium-sized enterprises. The EBRD's first vice-president, Ron Freeman, expressed satisfaction at the successful use of these funds, seeing it as an indication of the rising level of good investment projects being generated in the country.

There was a dramatic increase of activity in the hydrocarbons sector, especially in Kazakhstan, which stressed its resolve to become the sixth-largest oil producer in the world by 2010. Plans for pipelines proliferated (see map on p. 301). Early in the year it was announced that the Japanese Mitsubishi group had formed a consortium with US Exxon and the Chinese National Petroleum Company to develop a pilot project for the Trans-Asia gas pipeline to connect gas fields in Uzbekistan and Turkmenistan with China's Pacific coast via Kazakhstan and mainland China (to an estimated length of 6,130 kilometres and at a projected cost of US$9,500 million); three possible routes were under consideration by Japanese experts. More problematic were the proposed projects for oil and gas pipelines from Turkmenistan to Pakistan via Afghanistan (estimated length 1,043 kilometres, projected cost US$1,900 million). Nevertheless, President Niyazov of Turkmenistan remained optimistic. The US oil company Unocal and its strategic partner Saudi Arabian Delta Nimir, with whom the Turkmen government signed a memorandum of agreement in May, also seemed confident of success. The rival Argentinian oil company Bridas likewise continued to make preliminary preparations in the hope of participating in the project. A senior Pakistan official indicated that the line would be operational within five years.

VIII.1.iii. CENTRAL ASIAN REPUBLICS

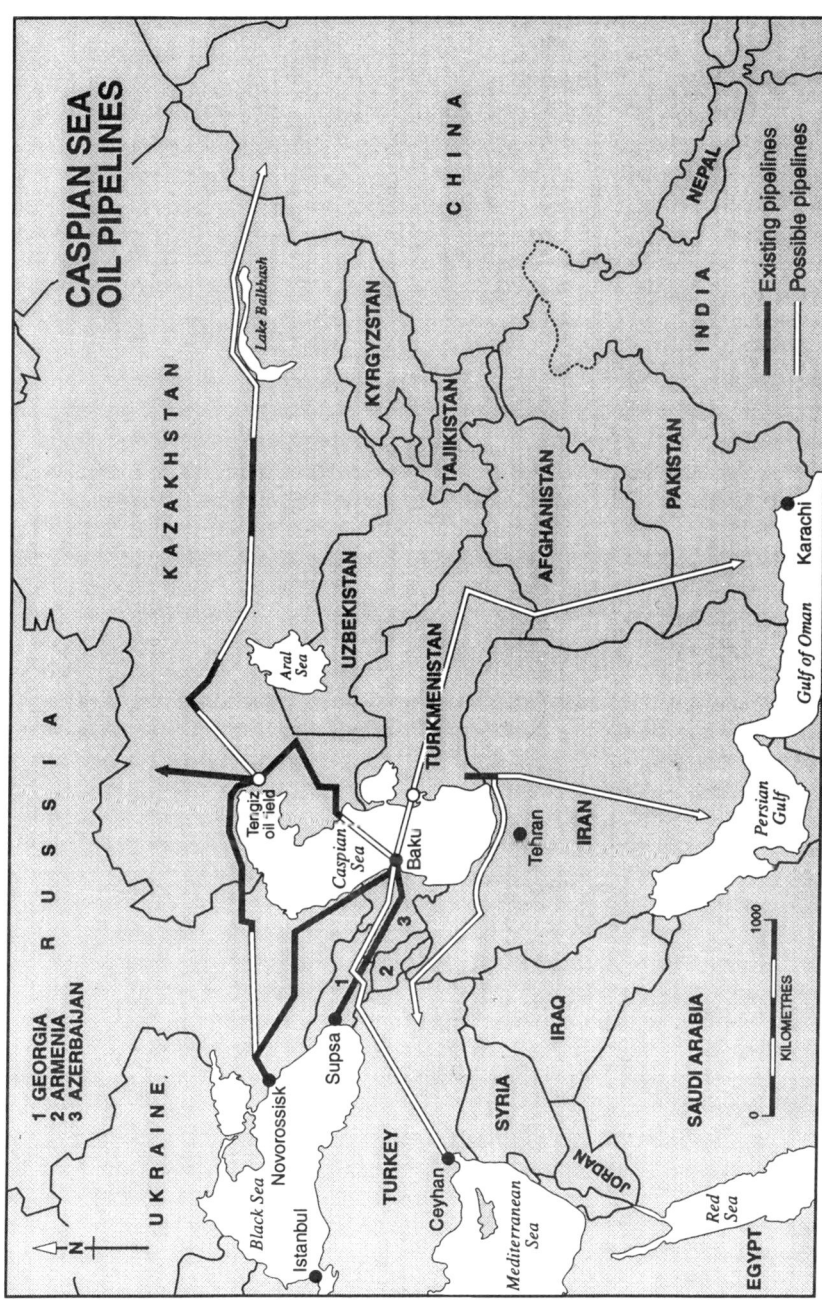

However, though little mention was made of the unstable situation in Afghanistan (see VIII.1.ii), it was likely that the project would depend on reaching an accommodation with the Taleban regime in Kabul.

The long-running saga of the Caspian Pipeline Consortium (CPC) continued. This, the most advanced of the Central Asian pipeline projects, aimed to construct an oil pipeline from the Kazakh Tengiz field to the Russian Black Sea port of Novorossisk. Agreement on the revised share structure (proposed in December 1996) was finally reached in mid-May, with Russia acquiring a 24 per cent stake, Kazakhstan 19 per cent and various other interests the other 57 per cent. However, in early autumn the CPC suddenly suspended construction work because of unresolved financial and legal disputes with Russian local authorities. Furthermore, the Central Bank of Russia had failed to grant the CPC permission to open an offshore bank account as specified in the contract. In mid-November shareholders rejected the CPC's draft budget for 1998, requesting a revision. By the end of the year, in the light of these problems, it was widely accepted that the pipeline would probably not be completed on schedule in 1999.

The difficulties with pipeline routes did not prevent the export of Kazakh oil. The first regular shipments of crude oil from the Tengiz field began at the end of July, delivering between 100,000 and 150,000 barrels per day to Black Sea terminals at Novorossisk (Russia) and Batumi (Georgia) for onward shipment through the Bosphorus Straits to world markets. Test shipments had previously (1996) been sent to Azerbaijan, where crude was processed for local use; an equivalent swap of Azerbaijani oil was sent by rail to Batumi for onward shipment. Overall, these alternative routes were found to be successful, and it was decided to use them until such time as the CPC pipeline could be completed.

Other interim export facilities for Kazakh oil included a 1996 swap deal with Iran, implementation of which began in mid-1997. The agreement allowed Kazakhstan to ship across the Caspian an initial 2 million tonnes per year (increasing eventually to 6 million tonnes) for refining and distribution in northern Iran; in exchange, Iran would assign an equivalent amount of crude to Kazakhstan at a terminal in the Gulf or at one of its European storage facilities. To the east, moreover, Kazakhstan began transporting crude oil by rail to China, the first shipment (1,400 tonnes) arriving in Xinjiang on 21 October. It was anticipated that up to 200,000 tonnes would be sent to China by this route before the end of 1997, the volume to be significantly increased in 1998–99. In the autumn, Canadian Hurricane Hydrocarbons registered a joint venture with a Kazakh company to complete construction of a rail trans-shipment terminal on the Kazakh-Chinese border.

Existing pipelines, meanwhile, continued to be used. In all, the Soviet-era network still handled some 95 per cent of Kazakh crude oil production. The main western pipeline, capable of transporting 10–11 million tonnes per year, ran 3,000 kilometres from Uzen to Samara in the Volga region, while the 400-kilometre Kenkyuk-Omsk pipeline carried oil from the Aktyubinsk fields to a Siberian refinery. Similarly, all existing Turkmen pipelines also ran through Russia.

Among new projects already in hand was the gas pipeline from Korpedzhe in western Turkmenistan to Kord Kuy in north-western Iran. Under construction since 1996, it was completed in autumn 1997 and officially opened on 29 December. The US government, initially opposed to an extension of this pipeline to Turkey and Europe because of Iranian involvement, dropped its objection in mid-1997. The project aroused considerable international interest, as companies such as Royal Dutch Shell and Sofregaz of France submitted bids for the construction contract, on which work was scheduled to commence in early 1998. Another project, the building of a gas pipeline linking Uzbekistan, Kyrgyzstan and Kazakhstan, encountered some financial problems, but the Kazakh section and about 70 per cent of the Kyrgyz section had been completed by the autumn.

In 1996 most of the debates concerning the Caspian Sea had focused on its legal status, which had not previously been defined in international law. Efforts to resolve this question continued in 1997, mainly through the Special Working Group on the Caspian, consisting of official representatives from the five littoral states. However, a new issue arose that greatly complicated the situation. At the end of January Turkmenistan laid claim to offshore oilfields which were already being developed on Azerbaijan's behalf by an international consortium. Both states insisted that the oilfields lay within their sovereign waters, even though the whole question of 'sovereign waters' was still open to dispute since no legal regime had as yet been agreed for the Caspian.

Turkmenistan's position was not supported by either Russia or Iran. Russia did try to act as a mediator, but its role was somewhat compromised when, in July, the Russian companies Rosneft and LUKoil concluded an agreement with the Azerbaijani state oil company to develop one of the disputed fields. The Russian companies later withdrew from the deal. Azerbaijan, especially after President Aliyev's successful visit to Washington at the end of July (see III.3.iii), seemed to be gaining the upper hand. Subsequently, though, a number of large investors began to rally behind Turkmenistan, eager to exploit the country's rich land and offshore resources. In the autumn the Turkmen government held important showcase presentations of 11 large oil and gas fields (including one of the disputed fields) in London, Vienna and Houston. A tender for development rights from 1 September to 28 November attracted a response from several major corporations, including Shell, Mobil and Amoco. By the end of the year the dispute with Azerbaijan had still not been resolved. Meanwhile, in October, a dispute over offshore oil fields claimed by both Kazakhstan and Russia emerged. Thus the legal problems of the Caspian, far from decreasing in 1997, looked set to become yet more complicated in the future.

Apart from hydrocarbons, Central Asian gold deposits attracted substantial international attention in 1997. Occupying ninth position in the world in terms of confirmed gold reserves, Kazakhstan was hoping to develop this resource to help revitalize the country's economy, but numerous problems were encountered. The government, having finally rejected the revised bid made by the Canadian Teck Corporation and US First Dynasty Mines for the concession to develop the massive Vasilkovskoye field, continued to seek a better offer. Financing of the troubled Bakyrchik field was taken over in mid-1997 by US Gerald Metals and Indochina Goldfields; despite encouraging geological reports, the performance of this project had been poor, resulting in mounting losses for the operating companies in 1995–96. There were also problems in the Stepnogorsk fields, where production had fallen sharply; in August the Kazakh government rescinded the contract granted to the Canadian firm Gold Pool for managing the mine.

In Uzbekistan (ranked fourth in the world in terms of estimated gold deposits), the situation was more stable. Zarafshan Gold, a joint venture of the Uzbek government and Newmount Gold of the United States, was expected to increase production to over eight tonnes of gold by the end of 1997, while several exploration projects were in progress. Kyrgyzstan's Kumtor mine, managed and partly owned by Canadian Cameo, also performed well, having contributed 19 per cent of the country's GDP in 1996. Production rose significantly in 1997, and the mine seemed set to achieve an annual output of 16.5 tonnes from 1998 onwards. Though its reserves were smaller than those of Uzbekistan and Kazakhstan, Kyrgyzstan succeeded in attracting more investment in the gold-mining sector than either in 1997.

High-level foreign contacts in 1997 gave some indication of the emerging trends in the foreign-policy priorities of the Central Asian states. These included, for Kazakhstan, official visits by President Scalfaro of Italy in May, Chinese Premier Li Peng in September, Spanish Prime Minister José María Aznar in October and President Shevardnadze of Georgia in November. In the other direction, President Nazarbayev visited Turkey in August, Kuwait, Abu Dhabi, Bahrain and Oman in late August-early September, and Germany and the United States in November. The itinerary of Kyrgyzstan's President Akayev's included visits to Armenia, Georgia and Azerbaijan in April and to South Korea in June. Among notable visitors to Bishkek were President Demirel of Turkey in July, the German Economics Minister in August, Malaysian Prime Minister Mahathir Mohamad in September, Russian Premier Chernomyrdin in October and Hillary Clinton in November.

President Rakhmanov of Tajikistan made two important visits abroad in 1997, to Saudi Arabia in July and to the United States in October. As regards Turkmenistan, President Niyazov's schedule was somewhat restricted by his heart condition, which in September required major surgery (carried out in Munich). He visited Iran in February, and again in December for the summit of the Organization of Islamic Conference (see XI.2.iv), and also went to Moscow in August. In May he hosted the summit of the Economic Cooperation Organization (ECO), which was attended by leaders of the ten member states and by senior representatives of international financial and developmental institutions. President Karimov of Uzbekistan hosted visits by President Scalfaro of Italy in May, by the Italian Prime Minister in September and by President Arpád Göncz of Hungary in October. In November he had talks with President Demirel of Turkey in Ankara.

2. INDIA—PAKISTAN—BANGLADESH—NEPAL—BHUTAN—SRI LANKA

i. INDIA

CAPITAL: New Delhi   AREA: 3,287,000 sq km   POPULATION: 980,000,000 ('96)
OFFICIAL LANGUAGES: Hindi & English   POLITICAL SYSTEM: parliamentary democracy
HEAD OF STATE: President Kocheril Raman Narayanan (since July '97)
RULING PARTIES: United Front coalition
HEAD OF GOVERNMENT: Inder Kumar Gujral (Janata Dal), Prime Minister (since April '97)
MAIN IGO MEMBERSHIPS (non-UN): SAARC, CP, CWTH, NAM
CURRENCY: rupee (end-'97 £1=Rs64.50, US$1=Rs39.31)
GNP PER CAPITA: US$340 ('95) or US$1,400 ('95) by PPP calculation

IN August India celebrated the 50th anniversary of its independence. Throughout the year its foreign policy sounded well-intentioned but was tentative and at best incremental in practice, while relations with Pakistan remained mostly acrimonious and combative, despite attempts to restart a constructive dialogue. A fundamentally weak and certainly heterogeneous United Front (UF) coalition at the centre managed to cling to office throughout the year, but only by changing Prime Ministers in April. Even so, the President dissolved the 545-member *Lok Sabha* (lower house of the bicameral legislature) on 4 December and called for an early general election in 1998. National self-criticism and doubt were more evident than self-confidence during most of the year.

Kocheril Raman Narayanan (76), the incumbent Vice-President, was chosen by the electoral college in July as President, becoming the first Harijan (or Untouchable) to hold the post. He polled an unprecedented 956,290 votes against his rival's 50,000, succeeding a Brahmin, Shankar Dayal Sharma. The new Vice-President was Krishan Kant (70), former governor of Andhra Pradesh. One of the new President's early discretionary acts was to ask the Union cabinet to reconsider a recommendation that he should dissolve the recently-elected government of the Hindu-nationalist Bharatiya Janata Party (BJP) in Uttar Pradesh (India's most populous state and a major political prize) and impose federal rule, following a brawl in the state assembly. In effect, the President successfully overruled the Union Prime Minister on this issue.

During the year two of India's most faction-ridden and turbulent states, Punjab and Kashmir, inched back to relative peace and normalcy after state elections were held in both. Many commentators claimed that the crises of recent years in these two states had derived directly from excessive interference by successive Congress governments at the centre. However, the two states that attracted most notoriety in 1997 were Uttar Pradesh and Bihar, two of the poorest, most populous and therefore electorally crucial states, where nakedly opportunistic politics seemed to be rampant.

The travails and decline of the 112-year-old Congress party appeared to continue, its lack of organization and general disarray being patent. The once-impressive Congress legacy was tarnished by corruption charges against many of its top leaders, including former Prime Minister P.V. Narasinha Rao, who was succeeded as parliamentary leader on 3 January by Sitaram Kesri, hitherto Congress president. Soon after the announcement that there would be an early general election from mid-February to early March 1998, Sonia Gandhi (Italian-born widow of former Prime Minister Rajiv Gandhi) declared that she would, for the first time, campaign actively for Congress. Accordingly, from early December the 'Sonia factor' became a matter to conjure with in relation to the forthcoming polling. At the year ended pundits were predicting another hung parliament at the centre.

H.D. Deve Gowda's government fell after a dramatic parliamentary session which ended a little before midnight on 11 April. Ten days of hectic negotiations ensued, during which Congress and UF leaders eventually agreed to rescue their tenuous alliance and to reinstate a United Front government with a new leader acceptable to Congress and Mr Kesri. Congress withdrew its semi-detached acceptance of Mr Deve Gowda as Prime Minister because he was too zealous in pursuing corruption cases against Congress leaders, and perhaps because Mr Kesri aspired to the prime ministership himself. In the event, Congress and the UF coalition reconstituted their precarious alliance for two main reasons: they were not ready to face a fresh election and they feared that, if they continued to disagree, the BJP was likely to take advantage of the situation.

The political manoeuvring and uncertainty lasted until 22 April, the deadline set by the President for any party, or grouping, to prove that it commanded a majority in parliament. Accordingly, on 22 April the incumbent Foreign Minister, Inder Kumar Gujral (78), was sworn in as India's 12th Prime Minister. The quietly-spoken Mr Gujral was a product of partition, his family having migrated from Lahore to Delhi in 1947. His first decision was to retain all but one of the previous government's ministers, in the interests of continuity.

The first serious challenge to the Gujral government came from within, barely a week after its formation. Laloo Prasad Yadav, the maverick chief minister of Bihar and widely regarded as one of the political chieftains who had ensured Mr Gujral's elevation, threatened to bring down the UF government at the centre if his state government in Patna was dismissed. Mr Yadav, along with 55 other bureaucrats and politicians, had been charged by the Central Bureau of Investigation (CBI) of involvement in a $270 million 'fodder' corruption scandal, involving the diversion of public money to buy fodder for herds of cattle that did not exist.

Mr Gujral, who had promised to make a campaign against corruption one of the hallmarks of his premiership, seemed irresolute in the face of these threats, doing nothing other than feebly repeating that the law would be allowed to take its course. Having split the UF in Bihar by forming his own Rashtriya Janata Dal (RJD) party, Mr Yadav was arrested in August, but installed his wife, Rabri Devi Yadav (a housewife with little education), to govern the state in his place.

On 26 August the Speaker of the *Lok Sabha*, Purno A. Sangma, addressed the House under rule 360 of the constitution, which gave him the right to do this on his own initiative, although it had never previously been exercised. Thus on the 50th anniversary of independence he opened a four-day debate on the state of the nation by praising the survival of democracy in India. At the same time, he also dwelt much on failures—such as India's 460 million illiterates and its share of only 1 per cent share of the world's exports. He also laid stress on the importance of wealth generation, saying that 'even China has come to accept this'.

After Mr Gujral became Prime Minister in April, he retained the foreign affairs portfolio which he had held in the previous government. This gave a further lease to the so-called 'Gujral doctrine', which envisaged improving relations with India's immediate neighbours, who were traditionally wary of its dominant size, population and economic and military weight. Mr Gujral advocated that India should renegotiate its ties with its six South Asian neighbours—fellow members of the South Asian Association for Regional Cooperation (SAARC)— and make concessions without insisting on reciprocity.

The India-Bangladesh treaty signed in December 1996, on sharing water from the Ganges river flowing through both countries, had considerably improved bilateral relations. In March New Delhi and Dhaka agreed to establish a transit route through Bangladesh, linking West Bengal with Tripura in India's far northeast. The direct link would reduce the distance between the two Indian states from 2,200 kilometres to only 350. Bangladesh was expected to earn some 30,000 million rupees annually from freight charges on the transit route.

Similarly, relations with Nepal improved with the signing of the Mahakali agreement to generate hydro-electric power and with the inauguration of a direct transit route between Nepal and Bangladesh through India. Nepal subsequently sought to test India's goodwill further by renegotiating the 1950 India-Nepal Treaty of Peace and Friendship on terms which would make it more favourable to Kathmandu.

Again citing the 'Gujral doctrine' as its rationale, the Indian government made it clear that it was now firmly committed to a policy of non-intervention in the internal affairs of Sri Lanka. The Sri Lankan government stressed the need for 'fast-track' trade with India and pressed for the removal of tariff and non-tariff barriers to boost commercial relations.

In contrast, relations with Pakistan continued to be generally troubled, not to say turbulent, over the future of the disputed territory of Kashmir (see also VIII.2.ii). In the last quarter of 1997 each country blamed the other for frequent gunfire across the line of control between their armies. Yet the year had started well, as the two governments ended three years of deadlock and resumed diplomatic negotiations in March. Much publicity was given to the fact that both Mr Gujral and his Pakistani counterpart, Nawaz Sharif, came originally from Punjab and spoke the same language. A hot-line was established between the two leaders, although it proved to be of little use when firing across the border assumed disturbing proportions later in the year. In April, before he was sworn in as Prime Minister, Mr Gujral signed an agreement with Pakistan's Foreign Minister, Gohar Ayub Khan, to release several hundred detained fishermen who had inadvertently strayed into each other's waters. However, other disputes, such as the Siachen glacier, the Sea Creek maritime boundary and the Wutar barrage, remained unresolved and continued to be overshadowed by the Kashmir dispute.

Repeated clashes along the line of control in Kashmir well nigh nullified the effects of an agreement signed on 23 June to resolve longstanding disputes through dialogue. A third round of bilateral talks between the two foreign secretaries (the senior ministry officials) ended inconclusively in September. Pakistan continued to insist that, unless there was a substantial dialogue on Kashmir, other bilateral issues would remain unresolved. Though India agreed to set up a mechanism, including a working group on Kashmir, it continued to insist that Kashmir was legitimately an integral part of India. India also continued to accuse Pakistan of fomenting terrorism in the Kashmir valley. During the year the US government branded the Pakistan-trained Harkal-ul-Ansar movement as a terrorist gang. In July 1995 the group had abducted and later killed four Western tourists in Kashmir. The Indian government construed the American judgment as vindication of its claims that Pakistan had been funding and training separatist terrorist groups on India's territory.

India's relations with each of the world's major powers—the United States, China and Russia—improved marginally in 1997. India and Russia strengthened their trade and diplomatic ties, which had deteriorated somewhat in the immediate post-Cold War years. Mr Deve Gowda made a high-profile visit to Moscow in March, his last diplomatic visit abroad as Prime Minister, confirming an accord under which Russia was to build two nuclear reactors in Tamil Nadu. The project, worth $4,000 million, was expected to produce two million kilowatts of power.

US-Indian relations also improved somewhat during 1997. The US government temporarily set aside its concern about India's refusal to sign the Nuclear Test-Ban Treaty, to concentrate instead on improving trade between the two countries. At a meeting with Mr Gujral in New York on 22 September, President Clinton avoided all mention of the controversial Kashmir issue. Indians had earlier resented US criticisms of their human rights record whilst no open criticism was made of Pakistan's alleged role in terrorist activity in Kashmir. A series of high-level visits in 1997, including one by Secretary of State Madeleine Albright in November, laid the ground for a visit by the US President planned for 1998.

In June India revealed one of its hitherto best-guarded defence secrets when it declared its stockpile of chemical weapons, and its production and storage facilities, to the Organization for the Prohibition of Chemical Weapons at The Hague. States signatory to the 1993 Chemical Weapons Convention had until 2007 to destroy their chemical stockpiles.

India remained wary of China, as it had been since the 1962 Sino-Indian war, but relations between the two countries improved somewhat following the state visit by China's President, Jiang Zemin, in November 1996 (see AR 1996, p. 300). Discussions continued over their disputed border regions, work continuing on a series of 'confidence-building measures', such as the withdrawal of some troops from the border region and pledges not to fight again over the area.

The Indian government expressed keenness to become a permanent member of the UN Security Council when the United Nations began an official review of the issue (see XI.1). Under one set of proposals, permanent seats would be allocated not only to Germany and Japan but also to the developing countries of Asia, Africa and Latin America (operating as three blocs). However, most foreign commentators felt that it would not be easy for India to obtain a permanent seat by this route, not only because it had refused to sign the Test-Ban and Non-Proliferation treaties but also because of Pakistani and other opposition or indifference to India's candidature.

India's overall economic performance remained buoyant, despite political uncertainties about the durability of the Union government in the first quarter of 1997 and attendant doubts about the reform process begun in 1991. For the third consecutive year India's GDP was officially estimated to have grown by about 7 per cent in the fiscal year ending on 31 March 1997, putting the country among the world's best-performing economies, according to the World Bank.

Despite being a rather weak politically, the Gujral administration pledged to continue the country's economic liberalization. However, some independent analysts warned that the government was too weak to implement thoroughly the tough measures required in the country's sixth year of restructuring. These included the need to increase the prices of oil and petroleum products, to cut government spending and to reduce subsidies. A modest rise in oil and petroleum prices was eventually enacted in September, but most foreign experts said that at least one more was required before the end of the year—and this did not happen. The government's avowed good intentions were often rendered inoperative in practice, because of the variable cross-currents of the coalition partners and because populism took precedence over fiscal and economic good sense.

The 1997–98 budget, unveiled on 28 February, reduced corporate and personal taxation, cut import tariffs and raised the ceiling on aggregate holdings for foreign institutional investors in Indian companies from 24 to 30 per cent. The budget elicited praise for Finance Minister Palaniappan Chidambaram from taxpayers and industrialists alike. The World Bank characterized his proposals as 'a creative but fiscally-risky supply-side initiative', which sought to reactivate private investment and to widen the tax net by lowering taxes. The budget envisaged an increase of almost 17 per cent in revenue collections, while trimming the fiscal deficit to 4.5 per cent of GDP in 1997–98 from 5 per cent in 1996–97.

The government took several measures during the year to strengthen the country's banking system, to increase the day-to-day autonomy of banks and to improve the functioning of financial markets. Virtually all interest rates became bank-determined, and the cash-reserve ratio requirement was reduced from 14 to 10 per cent in January. The government's credit policy, announced in April, freed the bank rate, further opened up foreign-exchange markets and made the credit-delivery system more flexible and transparent.

The biggest immunization campaign in world history reached its half-way mark in India in 1997. The aim was to immunize 125 million children against polio so that India could be declared polio-free by the World Health Organization by 2005. In 1995 India had 60 per cent of the world's polio cases; by the end of 1997 this figure had halved.

ii. PAKISTAN

CAPITAL: Islamabad   AREA: 804,000 sq km   POPULATION: 134,000,000 ('96)
OFFICIAL LANGUAGE: Urdu   POLITICAL SYSTEM: parliamentary democracy
HEAD OF STATE: President Mohammed RafiqTarar (since Dec '97)
RULING PARTY: Pakistan Muslim League (PML)
HEAD OF GOVERNMENT: Nawaz Sharif,Prime Minister (since Feb '97)
MAIN IGO MEMBERSHIPS (non-UN): OIC, SAARC, ECO, CP, CWTH, NAM
CURRENCY: Pakistan rupee (end-'97 £1=PRs72.20, US$1=PRs44.01)
GNP PER CAPITA: US$460 ('95) or US$2,230 ('95) by PPP calculation

HIGH drama, not to say melodrama, characterized Pakistani politics for much of 1997. The constitution was tested to its limits by conflicts between Prime Minister Nawaz Sharif, the President and the judiciary. Although at the end of the year Nawaz Sharif was the unchallenged master of the field, many observers considered that the battles had done permanent damage to the country's institutions. Political priorities meant that little attention was given to the economy. After a false dawn in the middle of the year, the impasse with India remained unaltered.

The year opened with the caretaker government of Meraj Khalid still in place. Elections both to the National Assembly and to the provincial assemblies were held on 3 February and were seen as meeting basic democratic norms by outside monitoring teams. Although there was considerable voter apathy, the Pakistan Muslim League (PML), led by Nawaz Sharif, won a massive majority of 134 out of 204 contested seats in the National Assembly. The Pakistan People's Party (PPP), demoralized by the failure of its previous spell in office, which had ended in humiliation in November 1996 (see AR 1996, pp. 301-3), gained a paltry 18. The renamed Muttahida Qaumi Movement (MQM, previously Mohajir Qaumi Movement) retained its firm hold on Karachi, winning 12 seats. In the provincial elections, the PML, regarded as pre-eminently a Punjabi party, swept the board in the Punjab, but was also able to play the leading role in subsequent coalition governments in Sindh (with the MQM) and North-West Frontier Province (with the Awami National Party).

Nawaz Sharif very soon demonstrated that he was willing to use his majority to amend the constitution. On 1 April the National Assembly repealed key sections of the 8th amendment, imposed by General Zia in 1985, which gave the President the power to dismiss the Prime Minister—power which had been used in 1988, 1990, 1993 (although overturned by the Supreme Court) and 1996. This step was publicly welcomed by most sections of Pakistan society, although there were some reservations that it might give the Prime Minister too unfettered a position. Later in the year another constitutional amendment, the 14th, was passed which effectively restricted the rights of members of the National and provincial assemblies to challenge their leaders. At the same time, Nawaz Sharif decided not to abolish the Council for Defence and National Security, which had been established in January and was regarded by many as giving undue power to both the President and the army chief. Instead, he chose to ignore the Council.

The 14th amendment, together with an ongoing tussle between judiciary and Prime Minister over who had the final say in the appointment of judges to the higher courts, sparked off a series of confrontations between the various institutions of the state. The initial issue over the appointment of judges appeared to have been resolved when Nawaz Sharif conceded defeat at the end of October, but the Supreme Court under Chief Justice Sajjad Ali Shah then raised the stakes by summoning the Prime Minister to answer contempt of court charges arising from the previous conflict. Mr Sharif duly appeared in court on 18 November but refused to tender an apology. Reportedly under advice from the army chief, General Jahangir Karamat, the case was postponed until 28 November, but on that day PML supporters, with the connivance of senior party leaders, stormed the court building.

Having already begun a parliamentary counter-offensive, the Prime Minister then succeeded in splitting the judiciary, persuading a 'rebel' bench of Supreme Court judges to issue an order suspending the Chief Justice on the grounds of alleged irregularities in his initial appointment. The Chief Justice, aided by President Farooq Leghari, who had earlier shown some unhappiness at the turn of events, hit back by suspending the 14th amendment and by threatening to restore the President's power to dismiss the government. For a couple of days it seemed possible that the army would be forced to intervene to break the deadlock in some way, but in the end the President gave way and resigned on 2 December, while the Chief Justice made way for an acting appointee. The army's role was seen as crucial, precisely because it did not appear ready to intervene. A PML senator and retired judge, Mohammed Rafiq Tarar, who was little-known except for his rigidly orthodox Islamic views, was elected as President on 31 December, winning 642 of the 766 electoral college votes cast by members of the central and provincial legislatures. The year ended, therefore, with Nawaz Sharif in full control of the country, but having lost much of the goodwill that he had earlier enjoyed.

One of the issues that had brought down the PPP government in 1996 was that of corruption, and the government used it to maintain the pressure on the Bhutto family and its supporters. In addition, Benazir Bhutto's husband, Asif Ali Zardari, remained imprisoned the whole year on charges arising out of the murder of Murtaza Bhutto (see AR 1996, p. 302). Corruption reached into the armed forces as well, and in April the navy chief, Admiral Mansoorul Haq, was dismissed on charges that also affected the Bhutto family. The opposition countered that the process of accountability was one-sided and did not cover the previous period when Mr Sharif had been in office. It was also claimed that policy on grain-trading was changed in such a way as to favour merchants who supported the PML.

Relations with the MQM remained a tricky political area for the Prime Minister. He depended on the party as an essential part of the PML-led government in Sindh, but the two parties remained deeply suspicious of each other. The level of violence in Karachi rose sharply during the year, with victims on all sides. Sunni-Shia conflict also erupted into violence on numerous occasions during the year, especially in the Punjab. Public attention focused on the role of madrassahs, or religious schools, as training grounds for young militants. Attacks on the small Christian minority were also linked to this upsurge in violence. In August the government responded by passing an Anti-Terrorism Act, which gave the police and judiciary sweeping powers in areas declared to be terrorist-affected. There was, however, sharp criticism from many quarters, worried about the effect on civil rights.

The economic situation inherited by the new government was extremely weak, no target being met for the financial year ending in June 1997. Manufacturing had grown by less than 2 per cent and GDP by only 3 per cent, and in March the IMF suspended its standby loan. To shore up the country's reserves, overseas Pakistanis were invited to deposit money at home, and $200 million was loaned by the Chinese. Nevertheless, partly to gain political mileage from standing up to the IMF and partly out of genuine conviction, Mr Sharif announced that he was rejecting the strict macro-economic targets prescribed by the IMF as part of its earlier package, and instead was pursuing a supply-side strategy designed to encourage industrial investment and growth. The strategy was launched initially at the end of March, when many taxes were slashed. The budget introduced on 13 June by the Finance Minister, Sartaj Aziz, levied no new taxes and reduced some excise duties in the hope that the very large fiscal deficit could be reduced thereafter once the economy began to grow faster. It was announced that there would be substantial cuts in government expenditure, including defence. Even so, defence and debt-servicing continued to take the major share, with little left over for development activities. At the end of the year the Lahore-Islamabad motorway, the first in South Asia, was opened, although critics described it as a white elephant.

In August the government managed to reach agreement with the IMF for a medium-term 'enhanced structural adjustment facility' worth a total of $1,600 million, despite the earlier difficulties. By the end of the year, however, the country was again in serious financial difficulty. In October there was an official devaluation of the rupee against the US dollar by more than 8 per cent, with further pressure on the rate thereafter. Foreign-exchange reserves shrank, while exports fell well short of the planned target. Domestically, revenue collections were substantially below the budget targets, and a poor cotton crop served to depress the rest of the economy. Foreign companies, especially in the power sector, were reluctant to proceed with major projects. This reluctance proceeded especially from a perception that big projects were being treated as political footballs. The cancellation of a large power project in Sindh, which had been negotiated with CEPA of Hong Kong under the PPP government, was seen as particularly problematic.

For a brief moment during the year there seemed a chance of a breakthrough in relations with India. Mr Sharif responded quickly to an initiative from the new Indian Prime Minister, I. K. Gujral, and a series of meetings, the first for several years, got under way at official and political level (see also VIII.2.i). The first was held in Delhi in March, the Foreign Ministers met in April, and there was a prime ministerial meeting during the course of the SAARC summit in the Maldives in May (see XI.5.iii). The most important development was an agreement in Islamabad, at a meeting between officials on 23 June, to divide the outstanding issues into 'baskets', each of which could be discussed separately. From Pakistan's point of view, the most important aspect of this was that Kashmir was included as an issue that was open for discussion at an early stage. However, the initial breakthrough could not be consolidated, and in September the initiative was abandoned. From August onwards there were several major incidents of firing along the line of control in Kashmir, military and civilian casualties being sustained on both sides. While diplomatic relations improved somewhat, military developments showed how carefully both sides had to tread. In early June there were US reports that India had moved some of its short-range Prithvi missiles closer to the Pakistan border, while on 2 July it was reported that Pakistan had tested its Hatf 3 missile (based on Chinese technology), whose 600-kilometre range would threaten Delhi.

The US Secretary of State, Madeleine Albright, visited Pakistan in November, although no significant progress was made on outstanding bilateral issues or on the deadlock with India. Earlier in the year Pakistan had allowed US officials to seize Aimal Kansi, who was wanted in connection with the murder of CIA staff in the United States, and remove him without going through the regular extradition process. The British monarch visited Pakistan in October to mark the 50th anniversary of independence in August 1947. On the sidelines of the visit there were attempts to persuade the British government to revise its stance on Kashmir, and some comments in Islamabad by the British Foreign Secretary, Robin Cook, were seen by India, where the Queen went after Pakistan, as leaning towards the Pakistan position.

The Pakistan connection with the Taleban regime in Afghanistan became more apparent during the year (see also VIII.1.ii). When the Taleban made an apparent military breakthrough in May, by capturing the main northern city of Mazar-i-Sharif, Pakistan was quick to accord the regime diplomatic recognition, although other countries still held back. Subsequent Taleban setbacks were then an embarrassment to Pakistan.

iii. BANGLADESH

CAPITAL: Dhaka   AREA: 144,000 sq km   POPULATION: 118,000,000 ('96)
OFFICIAL LANGUAGE: Bengali   POLITICAL SYSTEM: parliamentary democracy
HEAD OF STATE: President Shahabuddin Ahmed (since July '96)
RULING PARTIES: Awami League heads coalition
HEAD OF GOVERNMENT: Sheikh Hasina Wajed, Prime Minister (since June '96)
MAIN IGO MEMBERSHIPS (non-UN): SAARC, CP, OIC, CWTH, NAM
CURRENCY: taka (end-'97 £1=Tk74.57, US$1=Tk45.45)
GNP PER CAPITA: US$240 ('95) or US$1,380 ('95) by PPP calculation

THIS was another year which demonstrated the venomous nature of Bangladeshi national politics, the deep distrust and personal animosities affecting relations between top leaders, and the ways in which political competition and its accompanying uncertainties and instabilities, together with periodic climatic hazards, could adversely affect the economic life of much of the population.

Former President Mohammed Ershad, gaoled for 23 years for corruption and murder in 1991, was released on bail in January. He was allowed to leave the country twice, ostensibly for medical check-ups and to visit friends. The secretary-general of General Ershad's Jatiya Party (JP), Anwar Hossain, a minister in Sheikh Hasina's 'consensus government', was asked by his party to resign his cabinet post to enable the JP to join the opposition. He did not comply, but the party's prospects looked gloomy anyway. It suffered a split in July, when some party stalwarts left to form a separate party, the JP (Zafar-Moazem), while several prominent leaders crossed over to the ruling Awami League (AL). A large number of rural JP leaders joined the opposition Bangladesh National Party (BNP).

From 30 August the BNP, with 113 seats in the 330-member parliament, boycotted its sessions, ostensibly in order to press a number of demands. It accused the AL of curbing the opposition's right to speak in parliament and of filing 'false cases' against BNP leaders and activists. The AL denied these charges, the Prime Minister urging the BNP to return to parliament as being the best forum in which to settle political issues. In December the BNP also demanded the cancellation of the peace accord on the Chittagong Hill Tracts (see below).

Sheikh Hasina continued to travel abroad extensively, for which she was criticized by the opposition and some of the media. As in recent years, Bangladesh was active at the United Nations as well as in many other international agencies, whilst also trying to improve bilateral ties with a number of countries. Its success in extending small lines of credit to the 'unbankable' poor was why the Prime Minister was offered and accepted the co-chair at the first 'Microcredit Summit' held in New York in January, alongside Hillary Clinton, wife of the US President. In early March Sheikh Hasina attended the Inter-Parliamentary Union's meeting on women in New Delhi, and later that month she had talks in Islamabad with Pakistan's Prime Minister, Nawaz Sharif.

In May Sheikh Hasina attended the ninth summit of the South Asian Association for Regional Cooperation (SAARC) in Malé (Maldives), where she also had talks with SAARC's other six heads of state or government (see XI.5.iii). A subsequent six-day visit to Japan enabled her to have discussions with the host Prime Minister and other Japanese leaders. In August she attended a UN agency meeting in Germany and then took three weeks' leave of absence in Florida to be with her daughter, who was pregnant. There being no provision for the head of government to take such leave, she set up a small office in Florida to maintain close contact with Dhaka during her time away.

After returning home in early September, the Prime Minister soon left again on official visits to Indonesia and the Philippines. She also attended the Commonwealth heads of government meeting (CHOGM) in Edinburgh in late October (see also XI.2.i). During the CHOGM, Sheikh Hasina inaugurated a Jute Museum in Dundee and received an honorary doctorate from the University of Dundee. On 1 December it was announced that M.A. Wajed Miah, the scientist husband of the Prime Minister, had taken over as chairman of the Bangladesh Atomic Energy Commission.

Despite a marked improvement in relations between Dhaka and New Delhi, the trade imbalance between the two countries sharply increased in India's favour. A government spokesman in Dhaka had said in 1996 that India was planning to give concessions to Bangladesh, allowing its goods widespread access to the Indian market. Nothing of this plan had materialized by the end of 1997.

Agriculture, accounting for about a third of the country's GDP, continued to dominate the economy. Favourable weather resulted in bumper food-grain production, as well as a high raw jute crop, but continuing sluggishness in the economy meant that farmers were denied a good price for their surplus rice and raw jute. The low price for these two most important crops in rural areas, according to one estimate, would mean a loss of up to Tk20,000 million for farmers. This income would normally have gone towards the purchase of consumer goods, its absence being one of the major reasons behind the continuing sluggishness of the economy and low inflation.

On 1 December, amid tight security, polling began in month-long staggered local council elections, after weeks of campaigning had left up to 15 dead and many hundreds injured. A total of 4,298 councils—many consisting of clusters of villages and representing the lowest tier of government—were contested by nearly 150,000 candidates, while some 36,000 women vied for another 12,741 seats reserved for women. Analysts commented that the elections—the first since Sheikh Hasina took office in June 1996—were a big political test for her government's ability to organize free and fair polling. The BNP leader, Begum Khaleda Zia, warned that her party would launch a campaign to oust the government if it believed the elections were rigged.

The 22-year-long insurgency in the south-eastern Chittagong Hill Tracts, in which over 10,000 people had been killed since 1975, appeared to be brought to an end by the signature on 2 December of a peace treaty granting the mainly Buddhist Chittagong tribesmen a substantial measure of local autonomy. Signed by the government and the political wing of the Shanti Bahini insurgents, the treaty also provided for a general amnesty and the surrender of arms within 45 days. It was accompanied by the start of the repatriation of some 50,000 Chittagong tribesmen from camps in India's Tripura state, where they had taken refuge as the conflict had intensified.

Claiming that the treaty posed a threat to the country's territorial sovereignty, the BNP and its opposition allies called nationwide protest strikes on 7 and 10 December, accompanied by outbreaks of serious violence in the Chittagong region. The year therefore ended with growing political unrest, the return of general strikes and a deterioration in law and order, while attacks by politically-backed trade unionists on successful manufacturing industries meant that the overall prospects for investment, both foreign and local, appeared bleak.

iv. NEPAL

CAPITAL: Kathmandu   AREA: 147,000 sq km   POPULATION: 21,000,000 ('96)
OFFICIAL LANGUAGE: Nepali   POLITICAL SYSTEM: parliamentary democracy
HEAD OF STATE: King Birendra Bir Bikram Shah Deva (since '72)
RULING PARTIES: National Democratic Party (RPP) heads coalition with Nepal Congress Party (NCP) & Nepal Goodwill Party (NSP)
HEAD OF GOVERNMENT: Surya Bahadur Thapa (RPP), Prime Minister (since Oct '97)
MAIN IGO MEMBERSHIPS (non-UN): SAARC, CP, NAM
CURRENCY: Nepal rupee (end-'97 £1=NRs96.44, US$1=NRs58.78)
GNP PER CAPITA: US$200 ('95) or US$1,170 ('95) by PPP calculation

HAVING embraced multi-party democracy as recently as 1990 (before which the King had been virtually an absolute ruler), Nepal had been governed since then by a series of sprawling and largely inefficient coalition governments. Each had been burdened with huge cabinets of almost 50 ministers, most appointed to accommodate the diverse political interests and with little attention given to their ministerial capacity or potential. These factors, making for governmental uncertainty and unwieldiness, persisted during 1997—if anything in aggravated form.

In March Prime Minister Sher Bahardur Deuba of the Nepal Congress Party (NCP) was forced to resign after his government lost a vote of confidence in the House of Representatives. He was replaced by Lokendra Bahadur Chand, leader of the National Democratic Party (RPP), who formed a new coalition including the dominant Communist Party of Nepal-United Marxist-Leninist (CPN-UML) and the pro-India Nepal Sadbhavana (or Goodwill) Party (NSP) Party.

In two-phase local council elections in May, the CPN-UML won over 56 per cent of the seats, the NCP nearly 30 per cent, the RPP 10 per cent and the NSP a little over 1 per cent. The remaining seats went to other pro-leftist and pro-democracy independents. Allegations of electoral irregularities came from various quarters, most notably from the Foreign Minister, Dr Prakash Chandra Lohani, who resigned in protest on 11 June, also citing other differences with his government colleagues.

Dr Lohani (the RPP general secretary) said in his resignation letter to the Prime Minister that he could not condone the government decision to change at will top leaders heading important organizations of national security, or the use of the state machinery by 'leftists' to win the local elections. 'Our coalition partners', asserted Dr Lohani with reference to the CPN-UML, 'unleashed an orgy of violence and hooliganism against our workers with the tacit support and approval of the administration'.

Mr Chand survived as Prime Minister until 4 October, when he too was obliged to resign after losing a vote of confidence in parliament. The defeat followed a series of ministerial resignations and an open split in his own RPP, whose president (and former Prime Minister), Surya Bahadur Thapa, had backed the no-confidence motion tabled by the NCP. Two days later Mr Thapa was named to head a new government, which as formed later in the month included representatives of his faction of the RPP as well as the NCP and the NSP. The CPN-UML, now in opposition, abstained in the vote approving the new government on 9 October.

On 3 December Mr Thapa expanded his cabinet from 23 to 47 members, but the volatilities of Nepali politics were evident in the resignation the same day of former Prime Minister Krishna Prasad Bhattarai from the NCP's central working committee. Party sources surmised that Mr Bhattarai would try to form an alliance between other disgruntled members of the NCP and the main opposition CPN-UML. Nepali officials said on 8 December that the partners of the ruling coalition had agreed on a common agenda, although there was no word on a proposed power-sharing accord which might give much-needed political stability to the kingdom.

According to the 1997 human development report for South Asia published by a Pakistan-based organization, two-thirds of Nepal's labour force was female but their total earned income was less than half that of men. Nepal was one of the only two countries in the world where males had a longer life expectancy than females. Similarly, its adult literacy level for women was recorded as only 13 per cent, whereas male adult literacy was 39 per cent. Human development levels varied very greatly in different parts of Nepal, however. In the capital, Kathmandu, average life expectancy was as high as in Singapore and the literacy rate of 70 per cent was ahead of the average for the developing world. On the other hand, human distress overall in Nepal remained high. More than 50 per cent of the population did not have access to safe water or sanitation and the under-five mortality rate was very high, two-thirds of the deaths being associated with malnutrition.

v. BHUTAN

CAPITAL: Thimphu   AREA: 46,500 sq km   POPULATION: 695,000 ('95)
OFFICIAL LANGUAGES: Dzongkha, Lhotsan,English   POLITICAL SYSTEM: monarchy
HEAD OF STATE & GOVERNMENT: Dragon King Jigme Singye Wangchuk (since '72)
MAIN IGO MEMBERSHIPS (non-UN): SAARC, CP, NAM
CURRENCY: ngultrum (end-'97 £1=N64.50, US$1=N39.31)
GNP PER CAPITA: US$420 ('95) or US$1,260 ('95) by PPP calculation

BHUTAN's political and economic agenda for 1997 and the years ahead was laid down by the King, Jigme Singye Wangchuk, in an address broadcast on National Day, 17 December 1996. The emphasis during the 1997–2002 plan period would be on health and education, constructing more roads in the countryside and donating land to landless peasants. Bhutan's development record in recent years, he claimed, had been impressive: education was free and primary health cover had reached 95 per cent of the population, while telephone services were now available even in remote parts of the rugged Himalayan kingdom. The King also admitted, however, that 'constant security threats'—especially in the southern districts bordering India, where much of the population was ethnic Nepalese—had made it difficult 'successfully to implement all the planned development projects'. Moreover, although the economy remained predominantly agricultural, urbanization in recent years had led to new troubles such as juvenile delinquency and drug abuse.

In a controversial move in July, Bhutan's National Assembly decided that all relatives of anti-government activists in refugee camps in Nepal would be retired from government service. The suspicion of the Bhutanese authorities was that such ethnic Nepalese supported their relatives in Nepal and passed on 'sensitive information' to them.

Bhutan remained effectively under the personal rule of the King, although he was nominally answerable to the National Assembly and took advice from a special body of personal advisers. Demands for more political pluralism from educated Bhutanese were not rejected out of hand by the King, but he continued to insist that change must come gradually. His stated concern was not to unhinge Bhutan's difficult transition from the medieval society it was only a few decades ago into a modern nation-state. Even so, the country remained heavily dependent on assistance from UN agencies and bilateral donors. At their sixth roundtable meeting in Geneva in late January, 32 donor agencies (representing 11 governments, 17 multilateral bodies and four non-governmental organizations) pledged $450 million in new assistance to Bhutan.

vi. SRI LANKA

CAPITAL: Colombo   AREA: 64,500 sq km   POPULATION: 18,500,000 ('97)
OFFICIAL LANGUAGES: Sinhala, Tamil, English   POLITICAL SYSTEM: presidential democracy
HEAD OF STATE & GOVERNMENT: President Chandrika Bandaranaike Kumaratunga (since Nov '94)
RULING PARTIES: Sri Lanka Freedom Party (SLFP) heads People's Alliance coalition
PRIME MINISTER: Sirimavo Bandaranaike (since Nov '94)
MAIN IGO MEMBERSHIPS (non-UN): SAARC, CP, CWTH, NAM
CURRENCY: rupee (end-'97 £1=SLRs101.45, US$1=SLRs61.84)
GNP PER CAPITA: US$700 ('95) or US$3,250 ('95) by PPP calculation

THE government of President Chandrika Bandaranaike Kumaratunga continued throughout 1997 to put pressure on the Liberation Tigers of Tamil Eelam (LTTE), who were fighting for a separate state in the country's north and east for Sri Lankan Tamils, an eighth of the 18.5 million population. In 1996 the government had regained control over the northern Jaffna peninsula, pushing the LTTE into the forested Vanni region south of the town of Kilinochchi (see AR 1996, pp. 310–11). Changing strategy, government forces abandoned further southward movement to push from the south to gain road access to Jaffna. An operation confidently named 'Sure of Victory' was launched in May to capture the 76-kilometre highway between Vavuniya (220 kilometres north of Colombo) and Kilinochchi.

Control of this road would, besides further restricting the LTTE and bisecting its area of control, also make it easier to rehabilitate Jaffna and meet the needs of the 500,000 Tamils who had been persuaded to leave LTTE-controlled areas and return to their homes there. While the Tigers controlled the road, people and supplies could be moved only by air or sea—modes of transport both expensive and hazardous, being open to terrorist interdiction.

By the year's end, government forces had advanced more than two-thirds of the way, their progress slowed by heavy rain and four major LTTE counterattacks. Intense fighting resulted in heavy casualties: by mid-December 900 soldiers and 2,700 rebels had been killed in 1997, according to official figures, which were predictably contested by the LTTE.

The Tigers made sporadic raids in the eastern province, which they claimed to be part of the 'traditional homeland' of the Tamils despite the fact that it was peopled also by Muslims and Sinhalese. Their victims included, besides sundry soldiers, policemen and civilians, two MPs—one a Tamil of the mainstream Tamil United Liberation Front (TULF), the other a Muslim member of the opposition United National Party (UNP). They were killed in separate incidents in July, with several other civilians. In the same month the LTTE set fire to a ship used to ferry Tamils returning to their homes in Jaffna; it also captured a vessel chartered to carry food to Jaffna, shooting a North Korean crew member, reportedly to scare others into submission. In September a Chinese ship leaving an eastern port with ilmenite for the United States was set ablaze.

A bomb blast in Colombo on 15 October damaged the World Trade Centre (the capital's plushest building, housing the stock exchange) and two adjacent hotels; 20 people died and over 100, some of them foreigners, were injured. Casualties would have been higher had it not been a public holiday. Speculation linked the attack to the presence in one hotel of an American military team and Washington's action the previous week in naming the LTTE as one of 30 terrorist organizations under the US Anti-Terrorism Act of 1996. The US action was a big blow to the LTTE: its designation as a terrorist organization meant that it was a crime to give it funds or arms, that its members were barred from the United States and that its funds were liable to be blocked. Expatriate Tamils in North America, mainly middle-class professionals, had long been suspected of funding the LTTE, voluntarily or under pressure.

The Colombo government, which had been urging Western countries to block fund-raising for the LTTE, hailed the US decision. It was also cheered by a Canadian court's decision to deport a leading Tamil activist as a potential terrorist threat to Canada's security, after a lengthy hearing which rejected arguments that the LTTE was a 'liberation' organization. In some countries in Europe too, the LTTE encountered a less hospitable attitude than in the past.

While pursuing military action against the LTTE, President Kumaratunga also moved ahead with her plans to devolve a large measure of autonomy to the provinces, including the north and east. She was able to win the backing of Tamil political groups other than the LTTE, including some former militant combatants for a separate state; but the UNP, whose support was required for parliamentary approval, continued to stand aloof. It was reported that the UNP might suggest needs-based, asymmetric devolution, rather than the uniform, across-the-board devolution proposed by the government. Mrs Kumaratunga said that she would take the proposals to the people in a non-binding referendum in early 1998 if she failed to secure UNP support. There was some intensification of anti-devolution campaigning within the majority Sinhalese community, as well as calls for negotiation with the LTTE; neither was powerful enough to deflect the President.

The government suffered a few embarrassments, as when a medal-winning woman athlete complained loudly about unconventional overtures from the Sports Ministry, whose handpicked anti-bribery official had to be moved. Such local difficulties were ridden out, however. In June Mrs Kumaratunga reshuffled her cabinet, dropping the Transport and Highways Minister, Srimani Athulathmudali (leader of the Democratic United National Lalith Front), who had been less than enthusiastic about some government policies.

Despite the costly war, the economy made a robust showing in 1997. GDP growth reached an estimated 6 per cent, after a five-year low of 3.8 per cent in drought-hit 1996. Interest rates and inflation fell, while foreign reserves rose. The budget deficit was clipped to an estimated 7 per cent of GDP, the lowest for several years. The year ended, however, with concern about possible repercussions of the economic and financial turmoil engulfing several East Asian countries (see XVIII.1). Even if Sri Lanka was spared similar trauma, their heavy devaluations threatened to make Sri Lankan exports, notably garments, less competitive.

Political uncertainties notwithstanding, foreign investors showed confidence. In August Japan's Nippon Telegraph and Telephone, a world leader in telecommunications, paid $225 million for a 35 per cent share in Sri Lanka Telecom—and helped the government to retire a further slice of national debt. The next month international fund managers snapped up shares in a development bank, investing $73 million. Unilever, long established in Sri Lanka, enlarged its stake with an expensively-financed entry into the ice cream market.

Ken Balendra, a Sri Lankan businessman who headed John Keels, one of Colombo's largest conglomerates, was named as chairman of the $200 million South Asia Investment Fund launched at the Commonwealth summit held in Edinburgh in October (see also XI.2.i).

3. INDIAN OCEAN STATES

i. MAURITIUS

CAPITAL: Port Louis AREA: 2,040 sq km POPULATION: 1,140,000 ('96)
OFFICIAL LANGUAGE: English POLITICAL SYSTEM: parliamentary democracy
HEAD OF STATE: President Cassam Uteem (since June '92)
RULING PARTY: Mauritius Labour Party (MLP)
HEAD OF GOVERNMENT: Navin Ramgoolam (MLP), Prime Minister (since Dec '95)
MAIN IGO MEMBERSHIPS (non-UN): OAU, COMESA, SADC, IOC, ACP, CWTH, Francophonie, NAM
CURRENCY: rupee (end-'97 £1=MRs36.34, US$1=MRs22.15)
GNP PER CAPITA: US$3,380 ('95) or US$13,210 ('95) by PPP calculation

INCREASINGLY open disagreements within the government coalition came to a head on 21 June when Prime Minister Navin Ramgoolam dismissed Paul Bérenger, the Deputy Prime Minister and Minister of Foreign Affairs. All but one of the ministers from M. Bérenger's Mauritian Militant Movement (MMM) then resigned, bringing to an end the coalition with the Labour Party which had been in office since the December 1995 election (see AR 1995, p. 315). M. Bérenger was critical of what he described as the Prime Minister's immobility on major economic and social issues, in particular on the long-term measures needed to sustain the country's economic boom, such as further diversification and restructuring to cope with trade liberalization and competition from low-wage countries.

On 2 July Mr Ramgoolam announced a major reshuffle to fill the ministerial vacancies. Rajkeswur Purryag was appointed Deputy Prime Minister and Minister of Foreign Affairs and International Trade; he had previously been Minister for Economic Planning, Information and Telecommunications. The Prime Minister retained the defence, home affairs and several other portfolios. Rundheersing Bheenick, a former Finance Minister, returned to the cabinet as Minister of Economic Development and Regional Cooperation. The MMM minister who had refused to follow his colleagues out of the government, Rashid Beebeejaun, subsequently joined the Labour Party and retained his post as Minister of Land, Transport, Shipping and Public Safety.

Earlier, on 28 June, the National Assembly had unanimously reelected President Uteem for a second five-year term. Angidi Chettiar was elected Vice-President, replacing Rabindranath Ghurburrun.

According to official figures, GDP expanded by 5.0 per cent in 1997; exports from the Export Processing Zones (primarily textiles and clothing) were up by 10 per cent in nominal terms and 6 per cent in real terms; sugar production was up by 5.5 per cent in volume terms and 3.7 per cent in revenue terms; and tourist arrivals rose by 10.1 per cent to a record 536,000. The budget deficit was expected to narrow from 4.6 to 3.6 per cent in the 1997/98 financial year.

Reflecting concern about the longer-term economic outlook and political uncertainty, the rupee lost 12 per cent of its value against the US dollar in 1997, far more than in previous years, when the currency had been allowed to depreciate gently. Inflation also rose from 5.7 to 6.6 per cent over the year.

On 24 May Finance Minister Vasant Bunwaree announced that the sales tax on goods would be replaced by value-added tax (VAT) on goods and services in the 1997/98 financial year. The new tax was expected to improve tax buoyancy and promote investment activity.

In March Mauritius hosted the founding conference of the Indian Ocean Rim Association for Regional Cooperation (see XI.5.iii). The government offered to host the secretariat of the new organization, but no decision was taken on the issue.

ii. SEYCHELLES, COMOROS AND MALDIVES

Seychelles
CAPITAL: Victoria   AREA: 454 sq km   POPULATION: 75,000 ('96)
OFFICIAL LANGUAGES: Seychellois, English & French   POLITICAL SYSTEM: presidential
HEAD OF STATE & GOVERNMENT: President France-Albert René (since June '77)
RULING PARTY: Seychelles People's Progressive Front (SPPF)
MAIN IGO MEMBERSHIPS (non-UN): OAU, COMESA, IOC, ACP, CWTH, Francophonie, NAM
CURRENCY: rupee (end-'97 £1=SR8.42, US$1=SR5.13)
GNP PER CAPITA: US$6,620 ('95)

Comoros
CAPITAL: Moroni   AREA: 1,860 sq km   POPULATION: 650,000 ('96)
OFFICIAL LANGUAGES: Arabic & French   POLITICAL SYSTEM: presidential
HEAD OF STATE & GOVERNMENT: President Mohammed Taki Abdoulkarim (since March '96)
RULING PARTY: National Rally for Development (RND)
PRIME MINISTER: Nourdine Bourhane (since Dec '97)
MAIN IGO MEMBERSHIPS (non-UN): OAU, COMESA, IOC, ACP, CWTH, Francophonie, AL, OIC, NAM
CURRENCY: Comoros franc (end-'97 £1=FC742.10, US$=FC452.31)
GNP PER CAPITA: US$470 ('95) or US$1,320 ('95) by PPP calculation

Maldives
CAPITAL: Malé   AREA: 300 sq km   POPULATION: 250,000 ('96)
OFFICIAL LANGUAGE: Divehi   POLITICAL SYSTEM: presidential
HEAD OF STATE & GOVERNMENT: President Maumoun Abdul Gayoom (since Nov '78)
MAIN IGO MEMBERSHIPS (non-UN): SAARC, CP, CWTH, OIC, NAM, SADC
CURRENCY: ruffiya (end-'97 £1=R19.31, US$1=R11.77)
GNP PER CAPITA: US$990 ('95) or US$3,080 ('95) by PPP calculation

IN the SEYCHELLES, the economy steadied in 1997, after several years of depressed earnings from tourism and fishing. The government announced further measures to liberalize the tourism sector, including the privatization of four hotels. Fishing and fish processing expanded significantly, with plans to create up to 2,000 jobs in the coming years and fish exports expected to overtake tourism as the country's major foreign-currency earner in 1999. Efforts to develop offshore financial activities, launched in 1995 and seen as potentially the third pillar of the economy, were beginning to bear fruit. By the year end around 2,500 companies had been registered at the offshore centre, and the Seychelles was said to have 1 per cent of the global offshore market.

Despite the pressures on the balance of payments and the rupee in recent years, the government continued its policy of gradual economic liberalization while protecting people's living standards. As in previous years, most of the 1997 budget was devoted to maintaining the islands' welfare system, which—most unusually for Africa—provided free health care and education, old-age pensions and unemployment benefit.

The prospects of President René and the Seychelles People's Progressive Front (SPPF) in the 1998 elections were boosted in November, when the two main opposition parties, the Democratic Party (DP) and the United Opposition (UO), failed to agree an election pact. This had been suggested by the UO, but rejected by the DP, which had proposed instead that UO candidates should run on the DP ticket.

Joseph Belmont, hitherto Minister of Administration and Manpower, was appointed Minister of Foreign Affairs, Planning and Environment after the death on 11 April of Danielle de Saint Jorre. Born in 1941, Ms Jorre had taught and studied in Britain until the early 1970s, first becoming a government minister in 1977 and later the Seychelles high commissioner in London (1983–89). A champion of Seychelles culture, she had been the inspiration behind the annual Festival Kreol, which brought together artists and performers from French-Creole-speaking countries, and had compiled the first Seychellois-French dictionary.

The Seychelles was admitted to the Southern African Development Community (SADC) on 8 September. The government also expressed an interest in joining the newly-formed Indian Ocean Rim Association for Regional Cooperation (see XI.5.iii).

As part of its efforts to boost the country's tourism industry and global profile, the government sponsored the Miss World pageant on 22 November. In the three weeks leading up to the event, the 86 contestants took part in fashion shows and photographic shoots and helped out in charity events and environmental programmes.

In the COMOROS, a general strike on the island of Anjouan (Nzwani) in March turned into an open rebellion, in which the airport was stormed and several people killed, before an army clampdown and mass arrests restored order. This was a precursor of a much more dramatic development on the island at the beginning of August, after several months of deteriorating relations between the island and the capital, Moroni, on Grand Comoro (Njazidja).

On 3 August separatists on Anjouan declared the island's independence from the Federal Republic of the Comoros. The declaration was signed by the movement's head, Abdallah Ibrahim, who led a demonstration to the former government palace and raised the French flag and that of the sultans who had ruled Anjouan before colonization. The separatists were seeking to be recolonized by France and called on the French to 'hear the cries of distress of the people of Anjouan'. On 5 August they elected M. Ibrahim as president, shortly after which the neighbouring island of Mohéli (Mwali) also proclaimed its secession from the Comoros.

The French reacted by reiterating their commitment to the 'territorial integrity' of the Comoros and showed no sign of wanting to reimpose their authority. The government in Moroni tried sending troops to retake Anjouan, but they were rebuffed: many were killed or captured. The government of President Mohammed Taki Abdoulkarim sought intercession from the Organization of African Unity (OAU), which sent an envoy, Pierre Yeré, who set up talks in Addis Ababa in September, though these were subsequently delayed until December. Meanwhile, President Taki had sacked several of his advisers and the government of Prime Minister Ahmed Abdou, which was replaced by a 'state transition commission' including three Anjouanais.

The new authorities on Anjouan proceeded to organize their own referendum on 26 October, when 99 per cent of the electorate voted for independence. After the referendum, they formed a 'government' of six ministers and seven secretaries of state, and sent out two ambassadors, one of whom, former Premier Abdou Madi, defected after he left the island.

An eight-member OAU observation force arrived on Anjouan in November and the OAU international conference on the Comoros was finally held in Addis Ababa on 10–13 December. Although the OAU had also proclaimed its support for the Comoros' territorial integrity, the conference agreed only to hold an 'inter-island conference' in the near future to define a new institutional framework 'which will meet the legitimate aspirations of the Comoran people'.

In a move towards national reconciliation, President Taki on 7 December appointed a new government headed by Nourdine Bourhane, a former Health Minister and secretary-general in the President's office, who had links with Anjouan. Nevertheless, as the year ended, the Federal Republic of the Comoros was effectively a disintegrated state.

In the MALDIVES, the economy, based on tourism and fishing, performed well in 1997 and the outlook gave cause for optimism, but this was tempered by growing concern over the archipelago's long-term future in the face of environmental threats. In May the Maldives hosted a summit meeting of the South Asian Association for Regional Cooperation (see XI.5.iii).

Along with several island states in the Pacific region, the Maldives was in a unique position in that the projected raising of sea levels in the 21st century caused by global warming could well submerge many if not all of the low-lying archipelago's 1,192 islands and atolls. According to respected estimates, on current trends sea levels would rise between 30–60 centimetres over the next century. Some 80 per cent of the Maldives' land area lay below 1 metre, and the highest point was only 2.4 metres.

Speaking at the Earth Summit review conference in New York in June (see XIV.3), President Gayoom said that 'the threat to my country remains as alarming and as urgent as ever', continuing: 'Today I leave here with the fear that, unless we all act now and with a renewed commitment, my country and many countries like us would neither have a voice nor a seat at a future [summit].' Along with other members of the Association of Small Island States (AOSIS), the Maldives continued to argue for a 20 per cent reduction in emissions of carbon dioxide, the main 'greenhouse' gas, by the year 2005.

Provisional figures showed that GDP had expanded by around 6 per cent in 1997, fractionally down on the 1996 figure of 6.5 per cent. Reduced public spending and a tight monetary policy kept inflation subdued at around 3 per cent, and the current-account balance was in surplus for the second year running on the back of a record number of tourist arrivals (365,000, up from 338,000 in the previous year) and two years of record fish catches.

On 28 May the government announced that it would ask international oil companies to resume searching for oil in Maldives waters. Prospectors would be required to submit detailed schedules outlining measures to protect the environment. Preliminary searches for oil by Shell in the late 1980s and early 1990s had produced no favourable results.

In June the Maldives football team conceded 59 goals and scored none in six qualifying matches for the 1998 World Cup (including a record 17–0 loss to Iran), prompting speculation in the international media that it might be the worst national team in the world. The team's success in reaching the final of the South Asia Gold Cup (after draws with Bangladesh and India and a 2–1 victory over Sri Lanka) in Nepal in September received less coverage. India defeated the Maldives in the final by 5–1.

iii. MADAGASCAR

CAPITAL: Antananarivo   AREA: 587,000 sq km   POPULATION: 14,000,000 ('96)
OFFICIAL LANGUAGES: Malagasy & French   POLITICAL SYSTEM: presidential
HEAD OF STATE & GOVERNMENT: President Didier Ratsiraka (since Jan '97)
HEAD OF GOVERNMENT: Pascal Rakotomavo (since Feb '97)
MAIN IGO MEMBERSHIPS (non-UN): OAU, COMESA, IOC, ACP, Francophonie, NAM
CURRENCY: Malagasy franc (end-'97 £1=FMG8,203.50, US$1=FMG5,000.00)
GNP PER CAPITA: US$230 ('95) or US$640 ('95) by PPP calculation

IN an unusual twist to events at the end of 1996, Madagascar had narrowly voted its former marxist military dictator, Didier Ratsiraka, back into office as President (see AR 1996, p. 316). Inaugurated on 31 January, President Ratsiraka appointed Pascal Rakotomavo as Prime Minister, who formed a government at the end of February. That it was opened to several different political tendencies accounted for its unwieldy size, there being three deputy prime ministers, 26 ministers and two secretaries of state.

In March President Ratsiraka went on a tour of Europe and the United States to reassure donors that he was a reformed character, disposed to cooperate with international institutions and to pursue liberal economic policies. This led to some improvement in relations with the IMF and the World Bank, but the country's economy and finances were still in difficulties.

Parliamentary elections which were due to have been held in June were postponed for ten months to give more time to prepare voters' lists.

IX SOUTH-EAST AND EAST ASIA

1. MYANMAR (BURMA)—THAILAND—MALAYSIA—BRUNEI—
SINGAPORE—INDONESIA—PHILIPPINES—VIETNAM—
CAMBODIA—LAOS

i. MYANMAR (BURMA)

CAPITAL: Yangon (Rangoon)   AREA: 676,500 sq km   POPULATION: 50,000,000 ('96)
OFFICIAL LANGUAGE: Burmese   POLITICAL SYSTEM: military regime
HEAD OF STATE & GOVERNMENT: Gen. Than Shwe,Chairman of State Peace and Development Council and Prime Minister (since April '92)
MAIN IGO MEMBERSHIPS (non-UN): ASEAN, CP, NAM
CURRENCY: kyat (end-'97 £1=K10.26, US$1=K6.25)
GNP PER CAPITA: n/a

ON 15 November Myanmar's ruling State Law and Order Restoration Council (SLORC) dissolved itself before re-emerging under a new label—the State Peace and Development Council (SPDC). This was widely interpreted as an attempt to improve Myanmar's international image by drawing on Indonesia's *dwifungsi* system, giving the military a 'dual function' in matters of both security and government. Analysts noted that in late September the still-influential former military ruler, Ne Win, had paid a visit to Indonesia (his first public appearance since 1989), returning a visit to Myanmar by Indonesia's President Suharto in February. The SLORC's 21-member council was replaced by a 19-member military grouping, its members largely younger regional commanders but with Myanmar's four senior generals in prominent positions. Only the Chairman, General Than Shwe, also held a post in the new cabinet, which drew its membership mainly from the Union Solidarity and Development Association. Outgoing SLORC members were assigned to a new, apparently relatively powerless, advisory committee. The changes were viewed as having strengthened the position of Lieut.-General Khin Nyunt, Myanmar's intelligence chief and the presumed protégé of Ne Win.

On 4 June the SLORC released 300 opposition National League for Democracy (NLD) members whom it had earlier detained, apparently in an attempt to prevent a gathering at the home of the NLD leader, Aung San Suu Kyi. The NLD was permitted to hold a congress there on 27–28 September, attended by 700 delegates. Ms Suu Kyi noted that the SLORC had 'tried to be cooperative'. On 8 June U Tin Shwe, a founder-member of the NLD, died in prison in Yangon, aged 87. U Kyaw Din, another NLD member, died while serving a two-year sentence on 20 October, apparently of natural causes.

Myanmar, along with Laos, was formally admitted to the Association of South-East Asian Nations (ASEAN) on 23 July, at a meeting of ASEAN Foreign Ministers in Kuala Lumpur. The admission had been approved at an earlier meeting in May. The prospect of the country's accession to ASEAN had drawn criticism from the US government and the European Union (EU), which highlighted Myanmar's poor human rights record.

After the collapse of peace talks on 31 January, the SLORC mounted an assault against forces of the Karen National Union (KNU). Around 20,000 Karen refugees were said to have fled across the border to Thailand and there were reports that the KNU's headquarters at Htiker Pler had been abandoned. On 6 April a bomb exploded at the home of SLORC member Lieut.-General Tin Oo, killing his eldest daughter. The SLORC blamed the attack on exiled opposition groups in Japan, while opposition spokesmen suggested that it was the result of a power struggle within the SLORC.

In late January PepsiCo announced its complete withdrawal from Myanmar, having come under intense pressure from human rights groups. On 22 April the US Secretary of State, Madeleine Albright, announced the imposition of economic sanctions against Myanmar, outlawing new US investments in the country.

A confidential IMF report predicted that economic growth in Myanmar would falter and recommended a devaluation of the kyat. Economic growth in fiscal year 1996–97 was 6.1 per cent, down from an average of 8.25 per cent over the previous four years. Myanmar's economic prospects had darkened still further by the end of the year with a loss of foreign confidence and slackening investment, rising inflation (estimated at 40 per cent by late October), a depreciating currency and serious flooding in the main rice-growing region.

ii. THAILAND

CAPITAL: Bangkok AREA: 513,000 sq km POPULATION: 61,000,000 ('96)
OFFICIAL LANGUAGE: Thai POLITICAL SYSTEM: constitutional monarchy
HEAD OF STATE: King Bhumibol Adulyadej (Rama IX) (since June '64)
RULING PARTIES: Democrat Party (DP) heads eight-party coalition
HEAD OF GOVERNMENT: Chuan Leekpai, Prime Minister (since Nov '97)
MAIN IGO MEMBERSHIPS (non-UN): ASEAN, CP, APEC, NAM
CURRENCY: baht (end-'97 £1=B78.99, US$1=B48.15)
GNP PER CAPITA: US$2,740 ('95) or US$7,540 ('95) by PPP calculation

THE year was one of economic crisis for Thailand. The signs became evident when Finance Minister Amnuay Virawan suspended trading in bank and financial sector stocks at the beginning of March in an effort to prevent a number of finance companies from collapsing under the weight of their bad debts. In mid-May the baht came under intense speculative pressure, causing the Bank of Thailand (BoT) to spend US$10,000 million defending the currency. A series of government measures to stem the crisis proved ineffective. On 19 June Mr Amnuay resigned as Finance Minister in apparent frustration at having to work with Chatichai Choonhaven, who had earlier been appointed as economic policy coordinator. The new Finance Minister was Thanong Bidaya.

The crisis came to a head at the end of June. Further speculative attacks, which the BoT initially attempted to resist, forced the baht off its US dollar peg and on 2 July it was allowed to float. The baht immediately depreciated from 25=US$1 to 29.50=US$1 as a wave of speculative attacks and depreciations hit other currencies in the region. The stock market fell in tandem. On 25 July the governor of the Bank of Thailand, Rerngchai Marakanond, resigned. Mr Thanong turned to the IMF for assistance. At the beginning of August a series of economic reforms were announced. Foremost among them was the decision to suspend 42 finance companies, bringing the total suspended since July to 58. On the basis of the announced reforms the IMF on 20 August agreed a loan package worth US$17,200 million. Major donors, along with the IMF, included Japan, Australia, China, Hong Kong, Malaysia and Singapore, as well as the World Bank and Asian Development Bank.

The failure to rebuild confidence led Mr Thanong to announce a further package of reforms on 14 October, including raising taxes and tightening controls on banks and finance companies. However, a delay in their introduction, and in some cases their watering-down following intense lobbying, led to a further slump in confidence. The impression was that the Thai government was not serious about radical change. Mr Thanong resigned on 19 October, to be replaced as Finance Minister by Kosit Panpiamrat.

The political fall-out from the economic crisis continued through the year, as Prime Minister Chaovalit Yongchaiyut and his government came in for intense criticism. Two cabinet reshuffles during August did little to help and there was talk of military intervention. On 24–26 September General Chaovalit used his promised support for a vote on a new constitution to defeat a no-confidence motion. The main elements of the new constitution included a directly-elected upper house, a minimum educational level for MPs of a university degree, guaranteed freedom of the press, an independent election commission to monitor elections, centralized vote-counting, a House of Representatives consisting of 400 single-constituency seats and 100 seats drawn from party lists, the provision that cabinet ministers would relinquish their seats, and compulsory voting.

There was further speculation about impending military intervention in late October as General Chaovalit's cabinet met in emergency session. However, it seemed that both the army and the King rejected any such moves and on 25 October a new cabinet was sworn in. This lasted less than a fortnight: on 7 November General Chaovalit resigned as Prime Minister after less than a year in power. Former Prime Minister Chuan Leekpai, leader of the Democrat Party (DP), stitched together a new eight-party coalition of the DP, Chart Thai, the Social Action Party, Ekkaparb, Seritham, Palang Dharma, the Thai Party and most of Prachakorn Thai, commanding the support of 208 of the 393 members of the House of Representatives. His new government was sworn in on 14 November.

Local analysts applauded the peaceful change of government but wondered whether Mr Chuan would be able to solve Thailand's dire economic situation, given the mixed make-up of his coalition. Tarrin Nimmanahaeminda was appointed as the year's fourth Finance Minister and managed to negotiate a

slight loosening of the terms of the IMF's rescue package. On 8 December all but two of the 58 suspended finance companies were allowed to fail, and the IMF welcomed the steps that the new Thai government had taken to restructure the financial sector.
At year's end there was little sign of an end to the economic crisis. On 31 December the baht was trading at over 48 to the US dollar, compared with 25 a year earlier, while the stock market index stood at 366, against 832 a year earlier. GDP growth in 1997 was expected to be a dismal 0.6 per cent, against an estimate of 6.6 per cent at the beginning of the year.

iii. MALAYSIA

CAPITAL: Kuala Lumpur   AREA: 132,000 sq km   POPULATION: 20,500,000 ('96)
OFFICIAL LANGUAGE: Bahasa Malaysia   POLITICAL SYSTEM: federal democracy
HEAD OF STATE: Ja'afar ibni Abdul Rahman, Sultan of Selangor (since April '94)
RULING PARTY: National Front coalition
HEAD OF GOVERNMENT: Dr Mahathir Mohamad, Prime Minister (since July '81)
MAIN IGO MEMBERSHIPS (non-UN): ASEAN, APEC, CP, OIC, CWTH, NAM
CURRENCY: ringitt (end-'97 £1=M$6.51, US$1=M$3.97)
GNP PER CAPITA: US$3,890 ('95) or US$9,020 ('95) by PPP calculation

MALAYSIA experienced a major economic reverse during the second half of the year, which was effectively confronted only in December when the Finance Minister and Deputy Prime Minister, Anwar Ibrahim, announced a series of austerity measures aiming to restore a measure of investor confidence. The process of reverse had been precipitated in early July by Thailand's decision to float the baht (see IX.1.ii). This had a devastating effect on the value of the ringitt, which fell by 35 per cent against the US dollar, and also on the Kuala Lumpur stock exchange, where share prices fell by 40 per cent. Malaysia's economic difficulties were aggravated by the public rhetoric of the Prime Minister, Dr Mahathir Mohamad, who blamed them on 'rogue speculators', and also by his abortive attempt to control foreign-exchange trading. In October, his public suggestion that there might have been a Jewish agenda behind the fall in value of the ringitt provoked a deterioration in relations with the United States (see below).

Speculation continued about the relationship between the Prime Minister and his deputy, despite Dr Mahathir's endorsement of Anwar Ibrahim as his chosen successor at the annual general assembly of the United Malays National Organization (UMNO) in September. That assembly was marked by resistance to Dr Mahathir's call for moderation in applying Islamic values. Islam had continued to register in Malaysian politics. In January an important by-election for the state legislature in Kelantan was won narrowly by the ruling Parti Islam (PAS), in spite of the dissolution of the Semangat 46 party in 1996 and the return of its members to the UMNO fold (see AR 1996, p. 320). In July three young Muslim women were fined by the Selangor *sharia* high court after pleading guilty to dressing indecently by taking part in a beauty contest. In November two university professors were arrested under the Internal Security Act for propagating the teachings of the Shia version of Islam. They were released under a legal technicality in December and then immediately rearrested.

Muhammad Muhammad Taib resigned in April as chief minister of the state of Selangor following the decision by Australian authorities to charge him with making a false currency declaration at Brisbane airport the previous December (see AR 1996, p. 321). He was succeeded in May by Abu Hassan Omar, the federal Minister for Domestic Trade and Consumer Affairs, but only took leave of absence as one of UMNO's vice-presidents.

A marked deterioration in relations with Singapore occurred in March in response to disparaging comments by Senior Minister Lee Kuan Yew about the state of law and order in the cross-causeway state of Johor, made in a written affidavit published during court proceedings against an opposition politician (see IX.1.v). Tension also arose in the relationship with Indonesia because of the heavy pollution of Malaysia's atmosphere during August to October caused by forest fires in Sumatra and Borneo, in the main set, deliberately to burn off land for commercial agriculture (see IX.1.vi; XIV.3).

Dr Mahathir used the occasion of the 30th meeting of ASEAN Foreign Ministers in Kuala Lumpur in July to launch a bitter attack on the thrust of American policies in East Asia. His call for renegotiation of the United Nations Declaration on Human Rights was resisted strongly by the US Secretary of State, Madeleine Albright. Relations deteriorated further in November after a draft resolution had been tabled in the US House of Representatives calling on Dr Mahathir either to apologize or to resign for his remarks about a Jewish agenda being behind Malaysia's economic crisis. This was countered by a vote of confidence in the Prime Minister in Malaysia's lower house. Threatening telephone calls were received by the US embassy in Kuala Lumpur. At the end of the year, US ambassador John Malott reported an easing of tensions as Malaysia came to terms with the real sources of its economic adversity and how best to overcome it.

iv. BRUNEI

CAPITAL: Bandar Seri Bagawan   AREA: 5,765 sq km   POPULATION: 300,000 ('96)
OFFICIAL LANGUAGES: Malay & English   POLITICAL SYSTEM: monarchy
HEAD OF STATE & GOVERNMENT: Sultan Sir Hassanal Bolkiah (since '67)
MAIN IGO MEMBERSHIPS (non-UN): ASEAN, APEC, OIC, CWTH, NAM
CURRENCY: Brunei dollar (end-'97 £1=B$2.78, US$1=B$1.70)
GNP PER CAPITA: US$14,240 ('94)

SULTAN Hassanal Bolkiah assumed the office of Finance Minister in February following the resignation of his brother, Prince Jafi Jefri Bolkiah. In August, in Los Angeles, a US district court judge ruled that the Sultan, as a head of state, could not be sued by a former Miss USA who claimed that she had been held captive in his palace for use as a sex slave. He deferred his decision in the case of Prince Jefri, who was joined in the case.

During a visit to the sultanate in May by Germany's Chancellor Helmut Kohl, an agreement was signed to develop a US$1,200 million oil refinery to enable Brunei to export petroleum products in addition to crude oil. In July Brunei signed a memorandum of understanding with Taiwanese and Japanese companies to build a US$1,000 million refinery and petrochemicals complex as the first step towards developing a petrochemicals industry.

v. SINGAPORE

CAPITAL: Singapore   AREA: 620 sq km   POPULATION: 3,000,000 ('96)
OFFICIAL LANGUAGES: Malay, Chinese, Tamil, English   POLITICAL SYSTEM: parliamentary
HEAD OF STATE: President Ong Teng Cheong (since Aug '93)
RULING PARTY: People's Action Party (PAP)
HEAD OF GOVERNMENT: Goh Chok Tong, Prime Minister (since Nov '90)
MAIN IGO MEMBERSHIPS (non-UN): ASEAN, APEC, CP, CWTH, NAM
CURRENCY: Singapore dollar (end-'97 £1=S$2.78, US$1=S$1.70)
GNP PER CAPITA: US$26,730 ('95) or US$22,770 ('95) by PPP calculation

GENERAL elections were held on 2 January with only 36 seats contested in an enlarged legislature of 83. The ruling People's Action Party (PAP), led by Prime Minister Goh Chok Tong, which had been returned to office on nomination day, secured an overwhelming victory, winning 34 of the elective seats as well as holding the remaining uncontested 47. It recovered two seats lost in 1991 and also reversed an adverse electoral trend by attracting 65 per cent of the valid vote. Prime Minister Goh claimed afterwards that his party's victory demonstrated that Singapore's voters had rejected Western-style liberal democracy. Opposition seats were won respectively by the Workers' Party and the Singapore People's Party. The latter was successfully represented by Chiam See Tong, previously of the Singapore Democratic Party, which lost all three seats won in 1991.

The elections were bitterly fought, the PAP advising electors that constituencies voting against the ruling party would enjoy a low priority in the upgrading of public housing. The multi-member Cheng San constituency attracted most attention, the Workers' Party candidate, Tang Liang Hong, being described by the PAP as an anti-Christian Chinese chauvinist. Prime Minister Goh made the electoral outcome in Cheng San a test of his political standing, campaigning extensively there; his own constituency was uncontested. In the event, the PAP secured victory with 54.8 per cent of the vote. Subsequent cabinet changes involved changes of responsibilities and not of personnel.

After the elections, Tang Liang Hong fled to Malaysia, claiming to be in fear of his life. He had lodged a police complaint during the campaign concerning the allegations made against him by PAP leaders, including Lee Kuan Yew and Goh Chok Tong, who in turn filed 11 law suits against Mr Tang for defamation, in particular for his claim that they were liars. In March Singapore's High Court found Mr Tang guilty of libelling the Prime Minister and other leading members of the PAP. In May he was ordered to pay record damages of S$8.08 million, although this sum was reduced on appeal to S$4.53 million in November.

In August a second defamation trial began involving J.B Jeyaretnam, secretary-general of the Workers' Party, who had stood with Tang Liang Hong in Cheng San. The basis for the suit against him was that during an election rally he had announced that Mr Tang had filed reports to the police on his complaints against the Prime Minister and other PAP leaders. Mr Jeyaretnam had assumed the third opposition seat in the parliament as a non-constituency member in fulfilment of the constitutional requirement that a minimum of three seats be held by the opposition. In September a High Court judge found against Mr Jeyaretnam, awarding damages of S$20,000, which was only one tenth of what Prime Minister Goh's lawyers had sought.

In March Lee Kuan Yew apologized unreservedly for remarks made about the Malaysian state of Johor which had caused a marked deterioration in bilateral relations. In an affidavit seeking to discredit Tang Liang Hong's claim that he had fled there out of fear for his life, Lee Kuan Yew had described Johor as 'notorious for shootings, muggings and car-jackings'. Malaysia's Foreign Minister, Abdullah Ahmad Badawi, in accepting the apology, said that restoring the previous level of relationship would take time.

Although its stock market suffered and its currency experienced a marginal depreciation, Singapore did not share the acute economic adversity of its closest regional neighbours during the second half of the year (see XVIII.1). Moreover, Singapore pledged US$1,000 million to Thailand and US$10,000 million to Indonesia in stand-by funds under separate rescue packages sanctioned by the International Monetary Fund.

In December a Deputy Prime Minister, Lee Hsien Loong, was appointed chairman of the Monetary Authority of Singapore in succession to Finance Minister Richard Hu.

vi. INDONESIA

CAPITAL: Jakarta   AREA: 1,905,000 sq km   POPULATION: 198,000,000 ('96)
OFFICIAL LANGUAGE: Bahasa Indonesia   POLITICAL SYSTEM: presidential
HEAD OF STATE & GOVERNMENT: President (Gen. rtd.) Suharto (since March '66)
RULING PARTY: Joint Secretariat of Functional Groups (Golkar)
MAIN IGO MEMBERSHIPS (non-UN): ASEAN, APEC, CP, OIC, OPEC, NAM
CURRENCY: rupiah (end-'97 £1=Rp9,844.25, US$1=Rp6,000.00)
GNP PER CAPITA: US$980 ('95) or US$3,800 ('95) by PPP calculation

IN 1997 a range of unprecedented difficulties descended on Indonesia's political and economic elite. The year began with a major outbreak of inter-ethnic conflict, continued in political instability and ended with the national economy in perhaps its most parlous state for three decades.

In early January widespread violence broke out in Kalimantan province (Indonesia's portion of the island of Borneo). At the root of the problem was the resentment of the indigenous Dayak population against settlers from other parts of Indonesia, in particular Madura. The violence continued sporadically throughout the first half of the year, some reports suggesting several hundred deaths among the settlers. The crisis fuelled the continuing debate about the state's 'transmigration' programme, which had already contributed to major difficulties elsewhere in the archipelago, most notably in Irian Jaya (New Guinea).

Ethnic/separatist conflict also continued in East Timor, where tension increased around the national elections at the end of May. The death in Indonesian hands of resistance leader David Alex in June brought renewed foreign attention to the problem. Congressional criticism of human rights abuses in the territory had caused President Suharto to withdraw from planned joint military exercises with the United States and to cancel an order for F-16 fighters. Alternative aircraft would instead be purchased from Russia. A more cautious response followed Nelson Mandela's visit in July, when the South African President met the East Timorese leader, José Gusmão, who was in prison in Jakarta, and called for his release. In the new diplomacy of the post-Cold War era Washington had clearly become more 'offendable' than Pretoria. There was, though, no obvious sign that Jakarta would modify its approach in the territory. In November troops attacked the campus of Dili University during a vigil to commemorate the sixth anniversary of the 'cemetery massacre' of 1991 (see AR 1991, p. 337).

The weeks prior to the legislative elections of 29 May were marked by considerable state repression and public disorder. At the beginning of March Sri Bintang Pamungkas, leader of the 'unapproved' opposition Indonesian United Democratic Party (PUDI), was arrested and charged with subversion after calling for a boycott of the poll. Similarly, at the end of April Budiman Sudjatmiko of the small leftist People's Democratic Party (PRD) was sentenced to 13 years in prison for his alleged part in the Jakarta riots of the previous July. At the same time clashes were taking place between the two factions of the 'official' opposition group, the Indonesian Democratic Party (PDI). The origins of the conflict lay in the government-orchestrated purge of its leader, Megawati Sukarnoputri, daughter of Indonesia's first President, General Sukarno, who had been overthrown by General Suharto three decades previously (see AR 1996, p. 324).

The PDI faction loyal to the old leadership disputed the right of what they saw as government infiltrators to stand as the party's representatives in the elections. More serious trouble came, however, from the supporters of the leading 'official' opposition grouping, the Muslim-based United Development Party (PPP), who felt themselves to be victims of a government 'dirty tricks' campaign in several parts of the country. PPP supporters rioted in Jakarta in May, while in Madura alleged anti-PPP irregularities and attendant violence caused the poll there to be re-run in June.

In the event, the governing Golkar movement won the elections easily, taking 325 of the 425 elective seats in the People's Representation Council with 74 per cent of the vote (up from 68 per cent in 1992). Of the 'legal' opposition parties, the PPP won 89 seats with 23 per cent (17 per cent in 1992) and the PDI, clearly disabled by its internal convulsions, only 11 with 3 per cent (down from 15 per cent). An additional 75 members of the lower house were nominated by the President.

Close on the heels of the political instability of the election period came a major economic crisis. In July and August the rupiah, in common with neighbouring currencies, fell victim to international currency speculators. After a vain attempt to shore it up, the government abandoned its fixed exchange rate and allowed the rupiah to float. Inevitably it went into a fall, which continued until the end of the year. Hand-in-hand with the currency crisis came a collapse in the value of shares on the Jakarta stock market. While the crisis was one which afflicted all the so-called 'tiger' economies of the region (see XVIII.1), the underlying problems of Indonesia seemed particularly serious. This at any rate was the conclusion of the IMF, which, as a condition of its intervention, required far-reaching structural reform. A weak banking system, regulatory rigidities and protected monopolies all had to be tackled. Initially, President Suharto appeared to balk at these conditions, in part, perhaps, because of his own family's notorious involvement in the country's 'crony capitalism'. Hopes that bilateral arrangements with Singapore and Japan might provide an alternative route out of the crisis were soon disappointed. There remained some doubt at the end of the year, however, about the government's commitment to full implementation of the reforms required by the IMF.

These structural economic woes were made worse by the disastrous climatic and environmental conditions of 1997. The El Niño weather phenomenon, which periodically raised temperatures and brought drought to the South-East Asia and South Pacific regions, combined with illegal agricultural burning practices to trigger disastrous and uncontrollable forest fires in September and October (see also XIV.3). Worst affected were Kalimantan, Sumatra and Sulawesi, but the entire country—and neighbouring Singapore and Malaysia—suffered grievously from the resulting smog. One probable consequence was Indonesia's worst-ever air disaster on 26 September, when an A-300 Airbus crashed on approach to Medan in Sumatra, killing all 234 on board. Less immediately, the drought, fires and smog badly affected food production, with a consequent rise in prices. This, of course, came at a time of greatly increased unemployment in the wake of the broader economic crisis.

The year ended in deep and inter-related economic and political uncertainty. At the drastically reduced exchange rate of the rupiah, Indonesia's external debts were higher than its annual GDP and there were few signs of improvement on the horizon. The situation was further complicated by growing questions about the health of 76-year-old President Suharto and his capacity to continue in office. In October he had been nominated as Golkar's candidate for a seventh term and it was assumed that his adoption by the 1,000-strong People's Consultative Assembly would be automatic. By December, however, his evident infirmity (in particular his failure to attend scheduled overseas summits) gave rise to widespread comment on his future. On the positive side, the unprecedented frankness and openness of this speculation was itself a comment on the extent of recent change in Indonesia's social and political climate. More worryingly, however, the regime had no tried and tested machinery to manage any succession.

vii. PHILIPPINES

CAPITAL: Manila   AREA: 300,000 sq km   POPULATION: 70,000,000 ('96)
OFFICIAL LANGUAGE: Filipino   POLITICAL SYSTEM: presidential democracy
HEAD OF STATE & GOVERNMENT: President Fidel Ramos (since May '92)
RULING PARTIES: Lakas ng Edsa/National Union of Christian Democrats heads coalition
MAIN IGO MEMBERSHIPS (non-UN): ASEAN, APEC, CP, NAM
CURRENCY: peso (end-'97 £1=P67.51, US$1=P41.15)
GNP PER CAPITA: US$1,050 ('95) or US$2,850 ('95) by PPP calculation

THE year in the Philippines was one of political gamesmanship, economic confusion and faltering but discernible progress on the problems of separatist violence. The presidential elections, scheduled for 1998, saw Manila politics dominated by what became known locally as 'cha-cha' or 'charter change'. The change in question related to the legal bar to second presidential terms. The constitution of 1987, drawn up in the wake of the Marcos dictatorship, permitted only one six-year term per incumbent. Throughout 1997, however, President Fidel Ramos was ambiguous in his pronouncements about his future and permitted a supposed 'grass roots' movement (the 'people's initiative') to campaign for a referendum for a constitutional amendment which would have permitted him to run again in 1998.

The 'cha-cha' campaign was blocked by the courts and opposed by an influential coalition from within the political class. A Supreme Court ruling in June against change should have marked a definitive end to the matter, but the issue was kept alive by the President's continued opacity. In September, on the 25th anniversary of President Marcos's declaration of martial law, more than half-a-million people demonstrated in central Manila against any change. They were addressed by the elite of the anti-Marcos revolution, including his successor, Corazon Aquino, and the Archbishop of Manila, Cardinal Jaime Sin. The cardinal was quoted by *The Economist* as warning that a second presidential term would 'lead us back into the dark ages of pre-martial law political dynasties, war-lordism, corruption, sham democracy and debilitating poverty'.

The continuing uncertainty was fuelled by the refusal of President Ramos to indicate a favoured successor in the expected Filipino way. The absence of an 'anointed' candidate hobbled the early stages of the governing party's campaign. When, in June, the Secretary of Defence, General Renato de Villa, joined the ruling party, it was assumed to be a preparation for his nomination. However, by then resigned to stepping down, the President caused considerable surprise in December by naming the Speaker of the House of Representatives, José de

Venecia, as his favoured successor. An angry General de Villa immediately announced his intention to run on his own account. At the end of the year, therefore, the contest seemed wide open. The front-runners appeared to be Vice-President Joseph Estrada, a former B-movie star with a colourful personal life and a powerful populist appeal, and the glamorous, politically well-connected Senator Gloria Macapagal Arroyo.

The wrangles over 'cha-cha' took place against a steadily-deteriorating economic situation. The currency crises afflicting the region as a whole reached the Philippines in July (see also XVIII.1). The peso was left to float and dropped sharply against the US dollar. IMF intervention followed, but there was considerable popular reaction against the consequences of the crisis. At the beginning of October Manila was brought to a standstill by a strike in protest against oil-price rises caused by the devaluation of the peso. Much to the concern of local and foreign business interests, the Supreme Court ordered a 30-day freeze on further price increases. Concern deepened the following month when the court ruled that the deregulation of the oil industry, a centre-piece of the government's economic reform programme introduced in February, was unconstitutional. This, along with the introduction in November of indigenous land rights laws, which could affect mineral exploration, somewhat undermined the government's commitment to full-scale economic liberalization.

Some progress was made during 1997 on the issue of Muslim separatism on Mindanao—though the process was punctuated by various setbacks. In January peace talks opened with the Moro Islamic Liberation Front (MILF), which had not endorsed the 1996 agreement with the Moro National Liberation Front (MNLF) (see AR 1996, pp. 325–6). A ceasefire was agreed, but the peace process stalled in June following an outbreak of fighting between government troops and MILF guerrillas. Talks resumed the following month after Manila had enlisted the mediation of Nur Misuari, former leader of the MNLF and now, after the 1996 agreement, governor of the autonomous region of Mindanao. While there appeared to be a genuine determination on both sides to reach agreement, further fighting took place in October. A new ceasefire, more detailed in its terms, was agreed in mid-November.

In the foreign policy field, the Philippines' relations with Singapore improved after a visit by Prime Minister Goh Chok Tong in June. This provided the opportunity for a rapprochement after a period of difficulty following the hanging of a Filipina maid by Singapore in 1995 (see AR 1995, p. 329). The year saw further tension with Beijing over the disputed Spratly Islands, with Manila claiming unacceptable Chinese naval and fishery incursions in April and May. However, an inter-governmental agreement in June, to give prior warning of naval movements in the area, eased the situation.

viii. VIETNAM

CAPITAL: Hanoi   AREA: 330,000 sq km   POPULATION: 75,000,000 ('96)
OFFICIAL LANGUAGE: Vietnamese   POLITICAL SYSTEM: socialist republic
RULING PARTY: Communist Party of Vietnam (CPV)
HEAD OF STATE: President Tran Duc Luong (since Sept '97)
PARTY LEADER: General Le Kha Phieu, CPV general secretary (since Dec '97)
HEAD OF GOVERNMENT: Phan Van Khai, Prime Minister (since Sept '97)
MAIN IGO MEMBERSHIPS (non-UN): ASEAN, NAM, Francophonie
CURRENCY: dong (end-'97 £1=D20,167.48, US$1=D12,292.00)
GNP PER CAPITA: US$240 ('95)

THE 10th National Assembly was elected on 20 July. It was reported that over 99 per cent of eligible voters, some 43 million people, had cast their votes for 663 candidates standing for 450 seats. All candidates had been vetted by the authorities. Nonetheless, 112 of the 450 successful candidates were not members of the Communist Party of Vietnam (CPV). The first session of the Assembly was held on 20–29 September and a new leadership team was elected. Notable appointments included Tran Duc Luong as President (in place of General Le Duc Anh) and Phan Van Khai as Prime Minister (replacing Vo Van Kiet). The new Prime Minister was characterized as a leading reformist (in October he stressed the need to reform the ailing state-owned enterprise sector), and the new President as a conservative technocrat.

Do Muoi remained general secretary of the CPV until the end of the year, when he was replaced by 66-year-old General Le Kha Phieu, the army's political commissar. Like his predecessor, the new party leader was characterized as a conservative, although he stated on his appointment that he would continue the process of economic restructuring. The CPV central committee also announced the retirement of Do Muoi, Le Duc Anh and Vo Van Kiet from the politburo.

There were bouts of rural unrest in the northern province of Thai Binh and in the southern province of Dong Nai. Economic difficulties, high taxes and corrupt local officials were identified as the main causes. At the end of January the CPV adopted new ethical guidelines to stem the spread of corruption in the party, the military and the government bureaucracy.

In March China and Vietnam clashed verbally over a disputed maritime area believed to be rich in oil and gas. A Chinese rig which had begun drilling was withdrawn on 11 April after talks in Beijing. On 19 November the Vietnamese embassy in Beijing lodged an official protest when China awarded a contract for gas exploration in the area to Atlantic Richfield Corporation.

US Secretary of State Madeleine Albright visited Vietnam on 26–28 June, the first such visit since the end of the Vietnam war. In mid-November President Jacques Chirac of France visited Hanoi, holding talks with President Tran Duc Luong and Prime Minister Phan Van Khai before attending a francophone summit (see XI.2.ii). At the end of the month the Russian Prime Minister, Viktor Chernomyrdin, had talks in Hanoi with his Vietnamese counterpart.

During the latter months of 1997 the State Bank of Vietnam tightened currency controls to thwart unwelcome speculative pressure on the dong. However, the regional currency crisis forced the central bank to widen the trading band of the dong from 5 to 10 per cent on 14 October, causing an immediate 4.7 per cent fall in its value against the US dollar. Progress on privatization of state-owned enterprises was slow: by late 1997 only 14 small firms, out of a stock of 6,000, had been 'equitized'. GDP growth in 1997 was expected to slow to 8 per cent from 9.3 per cent in 1996, and foreign investment was generally depressed. While inflation stood at 4 per cent, the current-account deficit for the year was forecast to reach over US$3,000 million, or 12 per cent of GDP. There were also suggestions in October that bad debt held by local banks might be higher than official figures indicated. Oil exploration in Vietnam's South China Sea waters also tailed off.

Douglas 'Pete' Peterson, a former prisoner-of-war, arrived in Hanoi on 9 May as the first 'post-war' US ambassador to Vietnam, declaring that this marked the full normalization of diplomatic relations between the two countries. Vietnam's ambassador to Washington, Bang Van Le, took up his post on 14 May.

On 31 July Bao Dai, the last Emperor of Vietnam, died in France aged 83. He had ascended to the throne in 1925 and abdicated in 1945, after Ho Chi Minh had declared the creation of the Republic of Vietnam (see XX: Obituary).

ix. CAMBODIA

CAPITAL: Phnom Penh   AREA: 181,000 sq km   POPULATION: 10,000,000 ('96)
OFFICIAL LANGUAGE: Khmer   POLITICAL SYSTEM: monarchy
HEAD OF STATE: King Norodom Sihanouk (elected Sept '93)
RULING PARTIES: United National Front for an Independent, Neutral, Peaceful and Cooperative Cambodia (FUNCINPEC) & Cambodian People's Party (CPP) head coalition
HEADS OF GOVERNMENT: Ung Huot, First Prime Minister (since Aug '97); Hun Sen, Second Prime Minister (since Oct '93)
MAIN IGO MEMBERSHIPS (non-UN): CP, Francophonie, NAM
CURRENCY: riel (end-'97 £1=R5,593.15, US$1=R3,409.00)
GNP PER CAPITA: US$270 ('95)

ON 4 July Second Prime Minister Hun Sen, leader of the Cambodian People's Party (CPP), mounted a coup d'état, ousting First Prime Minister Norodom Ranariddh and his FUNCINPEC party from the government. Fighting between the rival groups continued in Phnom Penh for three days before Hun Sen established control of the capital. Prince Ranariddh fled to Thailand and from there to France. Fighting between forces loyal to Prince Ranariddh and Hun Sen continued through August and September, the former gradually losing ground. The UN Centre for Human Rights released a report on 4 September claiming that 41 senior military officers and Ranariddh loyalists had been hunted down, tortured and executed. On 10 July the Association of South-East Asian Nations (ASEAN) decided to defer Cambodia's accession to the organization (which had been scheduled for 23 July) and offered to mediate. The coup was widely condemned, but otherwise the international response was muted. On 17 September the United Nations decided to keep Cambodia's seat vacant during the 52nd UN General Assembly (see XI.1).

On 16 July Hun Sen announced that the Minister of Foreign Affairs and International Relations, Ung Huot, would replace Prince Ranariddh as First Prime Minister. The appointment was confirmed on 6 August by the National Assembly, which also voted to withdraw Prince Ranariddh's immunity from prosecution. Hun Sen turned down a request from King Norodom Sihanouk to negotiate with Prince Ranariddh. A meeting of the National Assembly on 16 September surprisingly rejected a cabinet reshuffle which would have further extended Hun Sen's power. The CPP held its 23rd congress on 25–27 October and laid plans for general elections later scheduled for July 1998. As the congress opened, King Sihanouk left Cambodia for medical treatment in China. Before departing, he said that he despaired over recent events in Cambodia and that he would withdraw from government affairs.

Relations between Prince Ranariddh and Hun Sen had deteriorated sharply in the months leading up to the coup, fighting between their respective forces having erupted in Battambang in February. On 19 April Hun Sen announced that 12 FUNCINPEC legislators were defecting to the CPP. Although two days later eight of the 12 pledged their continued support for Prince Ranariddh, the four who switched allegiance were sufficient to overturn FUNCINPEC's small majority. This became known as the 'soft coup'. Through March and April virtually no government business was conducted. On 16 June fighting broke out between bodyguards of the two Prime Ministers (leaving three dead), following which each party accused the other of trying to assassinate its leader.

A grenade attack on a demonstration led by opposition leader Sam Rangsi of the Khmer Nation Party (KNP) outside the National Assembly in Phnom Penh on 30 March caused 16 deaths and injured around 150. Sam Rangsi escaped with minor injuries and blamed Hun Sen for the attack. It was reported on 1 August that Sam Rangsi had been replaced as leader of the KNP By Kong Muni.

In early June there was speculation that Khieu Samphan, the nominal leader of the Khmers Rouges (KR), was on the verge of brokering an agreement with FUNCINPEC in which former KR leader Pol Pot, along with two other key KR members (Son Sen and Ta Mok), would agree to go into exile in exchange for immunity from prosecution. This would allow Khieu Samphan to re-enter mainstream Cambodian politics and perhaps ally himself with FUNCINPEC and the KNP—a scenario which some observers saw as having provoked the Hun Sen coup of July. It seemed that Pol Pot then reneged on the deal and had Son Sen killed. On 19 June Ta Mok captured Pol Pot as he attempted to flee Anlong Veng, a KR stronghold, and had him tried by a 'people's' court, which sentenced him to life imprisonment for the murder of Son Sen. In mid-October Nate Thayer became the first journalist to interview Pol Pot since 1979, finding the former leader to be 'very ill and perhaps close to death'. In the interview, Pol Pot denied that the Cambodian genocide of 1975–79 had ever occurred. Ta Mok, in contrast, in an apparent attempt to distance the KR from the past, admitted that the Pol Pot regime had committed crimes against humanity.

On 3 September a Vietnam Airlines Tupolev-134 crashed while landing at Phnom Penh's Pochentong's airport, killing 63 passengers and crew.

x. LAOS

CAPITAL: Vientiane AREA: 237,000 sq km POPULATION: 5,000,000 ('96)
OFFICIAL LANGUAGE: Laotian POLITICAL SYSTEM: people's republic
RULING PARTY: Lao People's Revolutionary Party (LPRP)
HEAD OF STATE: President Nouhak Phoumsavan (since Nov '92)
HEAD OF GOVERNMENT: Gen. Khamtay Siphandon, LPRP chairman (since Nov '92) and Prime Minister (since Aug '91)
MAIN IGO MEMBERSHIPS (non-UN): ASEAN, CP, Francophonie, NAM
CURRENCY: new kip (end-'97 £1=KN1,867.12, US$1=KN1,138.00)
GNP PER CAPITA: US$350 ('95)

ON 23 July Laos, along with Myanmar, was formally admitted to the Association of South-East Asian Nations (ASEAN) at a meeting of ASEAN Foreign Ministers in Kuala Lumpur. The admission had been approved at an earlier meeting in May.

On 21 December elections were held for the 99-seat National Assembly, the turnout being officially given as 99.4 per cent of eligible voters. All candidates were approved by the Lao Front for National Construction, the mass organization dominated by the ruling Lao People's Revolutionary Party (LPRP); of the 159 standing, 41 were members of the outgoing Assembly. Commentators observed that many of the candidates were party members and identified a shift away from reformist technocrats towards old-style communists. They also noted an increase in the number of candidates from minority ethnic groups. These changes were, in turn, linked to the economic fallout of the financial crisis in Thailand (see IX.1.ii) and to worries over ethnic tensions. Broader issues connected with the spread of corruption and the rise of certain social 'ills' were also thought to have played a role. Of four 'independent' businessmen permitted to stand, only one was successful, whereas the three LPRP politburo and ten central committee members who stood were all elected.

The third National Assembly held its 10th session over 16 days ending on 12 April. Legislation approved included a new land law which authorized the transfer of land titles to relatives and their use as collateral in obtaining bank loans.

The Lao economy suffered from the Thai financial crsis and its regional fallout (see IX.1.ii; XVIII.1). The Lao kip lost value as the Thai baht depreciated, falling from US$1=978 kip in December 1996 to $1=1,780 in November, before recovering to $1=1,138 by year's end. Efforts by the government to control currency transactions were viewed as harmful in the medium term and some analysts worried that the economic crisis might encourage hardliners to reverse the economic reform programme. Inflation during the year rose from around 11 per cent in January to 27 per cent by September. In November it seemed likely that the US$1,400 million Nam Theun 2 hydropower project would go ahead—despite the opposition of international environmental groups.

On 9–10 November US Deputy Secretary of State Strobe Talbott led a high-level delegation to Laos. He promised US support for removing unexploded ordnance remaining from the war in Indochina and also stated that the United States was working towards granting Laos most-favoured-nation trading status.

2. CHINA—HONG KONG—TAIWAN—JAPAN—SOUTH KOREA—
NORTH KOREA—MONGOLIA

i. PEOPLE'S REPUBLIC OF CHINA

CAPITAL: Beijing   AREA: 9,600,000 sq km   POPULATION: 1,223,890,000 ('96)
OFFICIAL LANGUAGE: Chinese   POLITICAL SYSTEM: people's republic
HEAD OF STATE: President Jiang Zemin (since March '93)
RULING PARTY: Chinese Communist Party (CCP)
PARTY LEADER: Jiang Zemin, CCP general secretary (since June '89)
CCP POLITBURO STANDING COMMITTEE: Jiang Zemin, Li Peng, Zhu Rongji, Li Ruihuan, Hu Jintao, Wei Jianxing, Li Lanqing
CCP CENTRAL COMMITTEE SECRETARIAT: Hu Jintao, Ding Guangen, Wei Jianxing, Wen Jiabao, Zhang Wannian, Luo Gan, Zeng Qinghong
CENTRAL MILITARY COMMISSION: Jiang Zemin, chairman (since Nov '89)
PRIME MINISTER: Li Peng (since Nov '87)
MAIN IGO MEMBERSHIPS (non-UN): APEC
CURRENCY: renminbi (RMB) denominated in yuan (end-'97 £1=Y13.58, US$1=Y8.28)
GNP PER CAPITA: US$620 ('95) or US$2,920 ('95) by PPP calculation

UNUSUALLY in recent years, developments outside the economic sphere were to the fore in 1997. A watershed, whose ultimate auguries had yet to be divined, was the death of Deng Xiaoping on 19 February at the age of 93 (see XX: Obituary). Although he had held supreme power for fewer years than Mao Zedong, Deng's impact on China was no less profound than that of his predecessor. His most lasting legacy was the remarkable economic growth and structural change which characterized China's development in the Dengist era. On the other hand, his refusal to sanction political reform alongside economic modernization, and the bloody suppression of demonstrations in Tiananmen Square to which it led in June 1989, were a permanent stain on his reputation.

The aftermath of Deng Xiaoping's death was still evident in September, when the Chinese Communist Party (CCP) convened its 15th national congress. Its central theme, set out in a keynote speech by Jiang Zemin (party leader as well as head of state), was the enshrinement in the party constitution, alongside 'Marxism-Leninism-Mao Zedong Thought', of Deng's 'theory of building socialism with Chinese characteristics'. Jiang also addressed economic issues and his comments on China's ailing state-owned enterprises (SOEs) attracted widespread attention. His call for accelerated state enterprise reform, mistakenly interpreted by some as a call for privatization of SOEs, presaged a more flexible approach to existing problems. Meanwhile, important changes in the composition of senior party bodies also emerged from the 15th congress. The most significant was the removal of Qiao Shi, hitherto regarded as a prime ministerial candidate, from the CCP central committee, its politburo and associated standing committee.

Another historical watershed was China's recovery, at midnight on 30 June, of sovereignty over Hong Kong and the transformation of the former British colony into a Special Administrative Region (SAR) of the Chinese People's Republic (see IX.2.ii). International anxieties about the erosion of democratic rights and freedoms in the wake of the handover proved unfounded and the promised autonomy of the SAR seemed to have been preserved in the first six months of its existence. The most striking evidence of this was perhaps the hands-off attitude maintained by Beijing in the face of the economic difficulties affecting Hong Kong at the end of the year.

China's foreign relations in 1997 were dominated by summit meetings between Chinese leaders and their counterparts in Russia, Japan and the United States. China sought to use these encounters to enhance its role as a global diplomatic, as well as economic, actor. Efforts to establish long-run 'strategic' and 'cooperative' partnerships were rewarded by further improvements in bilateral relations with all three countries, although the full potential of cooperation remained constrained by differences on important issues, such as those affecting Taiwan and human rights. Meanwhile, notwithstanding halting progress in multilateral negotiations on accession to the World Trade Organization (WTO), China's participation in a wide variety of multilateral bodies reflected international recognition of the critical political and economic role it had to play in the global community.

A major theme that emerged in the wake of Deng's death was the imperative of maintaining the continuity of the Dengist reformist strategy, encapsulated in his theory of 'building socialism with Chinese characteristics'. To this end, economic construction, supported by systemic reforms and the open-door policy, would remain at the heart of the domestic agenda. No less important was the need to preserve party unity under the leadership of Jiang Zemin and the central committee.

On 25 February—the day after Deng's funeral—Jiang Zemin delivered a eulogy at a memorial meeting in the presence of 10,000 people. His speech highlighted Deng's achievement as the 'core of the party's second generation of central collective leadership'. It noted his repudiation of the errors of the Cultural Revolution and reaffirmed the significance of his theory of 'building socialism with Chinese characteristics'.

In the wake of Deng's death, there was no evidence of unrest in Beijing, nor of widespread overt grief of the kind that had surrounded the deaths of Zhou Enlai (1976) and Hu Yaobang (1989). However, unconfirmed reports from Hong Kong suggested that fears of instability within the army had caused division-level units of the People's Liberation Army (PLA) to be transferred to the Chinese capital and that armed forces were on maximum alert.

Government leaders throughout the world recognized the significance of Deng

Xiaoping's passing and rehearsed his major contribution to China's recent development. Hong Kong sources drew attention to his role in formulating the idea of 'one country, two systems'—the guiding principle governing the retrocession to China of sovereignty over the British crown colony. President Clinton praised Deng's contribution to the normalization of bilateral relations—sentiments echoed in a message from the Russian President, Boris Yeltsin. In general, Deng's contributions to Chinese domestic and foreign policies were acknowledged in messages from government leaders throughout the world.

Two other senior members of China's gerontocracy died in 1997. On 2 February the death was announced of Qin Jiwei (82), a veteran of the Long March, whose military career had culminated in his appointment as Minister of Defence. On 26 April the death was reported of Peng Zhen, at the age of 95. After being removed from office in the Cultural Revolution, Peng had been readmitted to the CCP central committee and its politburo, retiring in 1988.

The enshrinement of Deng Xiaoping's 'theory of building socialism with Chinese characteristics' was the central theme of the 15th party congress, held in Beijing in September. In his keynote speech as party general secretary, Jiang Zemin called on all CCP members and Chinese citizens to 'hold high the great banner of Deng Xiaoping Theory and push forward the cause of building socialism with Chinese characteristics to the 21st century in all spheres'. He ranked Deng Xiaoping's theoretical contribution alongside that of Mao Zedong and proposed that the CCP should explicitly stipulate in its constitution that Deng Xiaoping Theory be included as part of its 'guiding ideology.' Jiang spoke of the challenges and opportunities inherent in the wide economic, scientific and technological gaps that existed between China and developed countries. He emphasized the debt which China's economic success since the 14th national party congress (in 1992) owed to accelerated reforms, undertaken in the wake of Deng's 1992 tour of southern China. During this period, annual GDP growth had averaged 12.1 per cent, benefiting in varying degrees urban and rural populations, all the major economic sectors, and all regions of the country. With reforms under way across a wide range of sectors, the market had become a major arbiter of resource allocation, while China's involvement and integration in the global economy had also expanded significantly.

Jiang Zemin's economic message was explicitly up-beat, although he also acknowledged the persistence of structural economic imbalances and warned of the threat which population growth and environmental pressures posed to the sustainability of China's development momentum. Central to China's successful modernization was the need to adjust the ownership structure of economic assets and Jiang's explicit call for accelerated enterprise reform were widely, if mistakenly, interpreted as sanctioning privatization of SOEs.

THE ECONOMY. A modest slowing of GDP growth was again a feature of China's economic performance in 1996 and 1997, indicating the government's efforts to restrain inflationary pressures. In 1996 the rate of economic growth fell by half a point to 9.7 per cent, the rate of retail price inflation meanwhile dropping sharply from 14.8 to 6.1 per cent. Such evidence in favour of an economic 'soft landing' was reinforced by official results for 1997, suggesting that GDP growth of 8.8 per cent had been accompanied by retail price inflation of a mere 0.8 per cent. In both years all three major sectors benefited from the buoyant GDP growth performance. As in the recent past, however, industrial growth (up by 12.3 and 11.1 per cent in the respective years) was again significantly higher than that of agriculture (5.1 and 3.5 per cent) and services (8 and 8.2 per cent). Living standards meanwhile continued to improve for both urban and rural residents. In 1996 and 1997 real average per capita income in the countryside rose by 9 and 4.6 per cent, compared with increases of only 3.3 and 3.4 per cent in cities.

The erratic trend of China's recent merchandise trade performance was repeated in 1996 and 1997. Overall, the growth of such trade slowed dramatically in 1996 (from 18.6 to 3.2 per cent); with import growth outstripping that of exports, the trade surplus fell from US$16,700 million to 12,300 million. This pattern was, however, reversed in 1997, when a sharp increase in exports (by 20.9 per cent), alongside modest import growth (by 2.5 per cent), generated a rise in the merchandise surplus to US$40,340 million. China's attraction as a destination for foreign investment meanwhile remained undiminished, utilized inflows of overseas capital rising by 14.2 and 15.7 per cent in 1996 and 1997 respectively.

Premier Li Peng's report to the eighth National People's Congress (NPC) on behalf of the State Council in March afforded an opportunity to review the strengths and weaknesses of government economic policy. He cited the simultaneous maintenance of economic growth and control of inflationary pressures as evidence of government's improved macroeconomic control. He also spoke of progress in reducing indebtedness and liability rates and increasing profit and tax remittances in some large-scale enterprises. At the same time, however, Premier Li acknowledged the existence of serious difficulties and contradictions in China's economic and social development. Chief amongst these were the weakness of the macroeconomic base, the persistence of structural imbalance in the economy, agricultural deficiencies, poor quality and low productivity in many areas of economic activity (including SOEs), and the severity of demographic and employment pressures. Despite efforts to improve government accountability, there was also evidence of more widespread corruption—'bureaucratism, formalism and boasting'—by government officials.

Looking ahead, the Chinese Premier outlined the main tasks for 1997. As regards rural areas, he called for an integrated policy package that would strengthen agriculture and facilitate the establishment of more township and village enterprises (TVEs), especially in central and western regions. The interior was also expected to benefit from a rise in fixed investment, directed towards agriculture, irrigation and infrastructural construction, as well as the development of basic and 'pillar' industries.

Li Peng reaffirmed that the central thrust of economic reform remained the resolution of the severe problems faced by China's state enterprises. The heaviest burden of losses was carried by SOEs in textile, coal-mining, machine-building and ordnance industries, their problems being attributed to poor management, a lack of market competitiveness and the weight of the social burdens which they carried.

Environmental issues attracted domestic and international concern. The severity of China's water crisis was highlighted by the failure of the Yellow River on nine separate occasions during 1997 to reach its outflow into the Bohai Gulf. The grave consequences were manifested in terms of increased sedimentation, damage to the surrounding region's ecology, and the implications for fulfilment of the Yellow River's role as a supplier of water to some 140 million people, 16 million hectares of arable land and more than 50 large and medium-sized cities in north and north-west China. Further progress towards continued implementation of the 'Three Gorges Project' was evidenced during November in the blocking of the main stream of the Yangtze River—China's most important river artery. This event signalled the beginning of the construction of two parallel earth-and-stone coffer dams, to be completed over a six-year period.

POLITICAL AND SOCIAL AFFAIRS. Li Peng's report stressed that social and political stability, as well as economic development was essential to China's successful modernization. Despite some success in combating crime through the recent 'strike hard' campaign, he conceded that social order was far from stable. In particular, greater effort was needed to counter violent and drug-related crime, economic offences, and the criminal activities of secret societies. In the face of widespread corruption at all levels of government, the central discipline inspection commission issued regulations designed to enhance organizational and ideological control by the central authorities, strengthen discipline and combat corruption.

Preservation of national unity was another imperative in the face of serious unrest in Muslim regions of north-west China. In February, outbreaks of looting were reported from Yining (Xinjiang), while several bomb explosions in Urumqi were said to have killed and injured many people. After two bomb explosions occurred in Beijing in March, there were unconfirmed reports that troops in Beijing, Lanzhou, Xinjiang and Tibet had been placed on a state of high alert and, subsequently, that five PLA and armed police divisions had been dispatched to Xinjiang in order to suppress separatists. The gravity of the situation was made clear in references to the activities of ethnic separatists, who allegedly sought to use terrorism and sabotage to replace rule from Beijing with an independent Islamic state in north-west China.

In the face of widespread criticism of China's human rights record, Chinese officials rehearsed the familiar position that the most important of human rights were those of subsistence and development. They pointed out that since 1978 the number of people living in poverty in China had fallen from 250 to 58 million—a reduction whose global significance was evidenced by the fact that the proportion of poverty-stricken people living in China had fallen from 25 to under 5 per cent. A more direct consequence of Western pressure on China was the release on parole, in November, of the prominent political dissident, Wei Jingsheng (see AR 1996, p. 331). The official explanation for his release was that Wei was ill and needed treatment overseas, although, coming so soon after Jiang Zemin's visit to Washington (see below), it seemed more likely that Wei's release and departure to the United States were the direct consequences of Jiang's summit meeting with President Clinton.

An unconfirmed report from Hong Kong suggested that targets for structural reform of government administration, set in 1993, had almost been fulfilled. The number of ministries, commissions and other organs directly under the State Council had been reduced from 68 to 59, and almost two million officials throughout the country had been removed from party and government administrative organs. It was also revealed that membership of the CCP currently stood at 58 million—9.92 million more than at the time of the 14th national party congress in 1992.

An important administrative development was the decision to make the city of Chongqing a provincial-level municipality under central government authority. With a surface area of some 80,000 square kilometres and a total population of over 30 million, Chongqing (in Sichuan) would not only become the economic and transport hub of south-west China and the Upper Yangzi region but also overtake Shanghai to become China's largest city.

EXTERNAL RELATIONS. A familiar tenet of foreign policy statements was that, despite lowered international tension and a move towards multi-polarization in global relations, 'hegemonism and power politics' remained a potent threat to peace. Premier Li Peng described the growing gap between rich and poor as a principal source of increased tension in the world and spoke of China's desire to enhance its role in the peace-keeping, diplomatic activities of the United Nations and other regional organizations in order to resolve such tension. President Jiang Zemin drew particular attention to the threat which ethnic, religious and territorial conflicts posed to regional peace and spoke of the Chinese government's commitment to the pursuit of an independent foreign policy, designed to create a 'just and rational new international political and economic order', based on the five principles of peaceful coexistence.

A brief visit to Beijing in February by the US Secretary of State, Madeleine Albright, set an optimistic tone which came increasingly to characterize Sino-US relations during 1997. Ms Albright met Jiang Zemin and Li Peng, and held substantive talks with the Chinese Foreign Minister, Qian Qichen, in which both sides reaffirmed their common wish to establish closer bilateral ties. Such hopes were echoed when, at the end of April, Qian Qichen made a reciprocal visit to Washington and held further talks with Ms Albright, as well as consulting with President Clinton about preparations for Jiang Zemin's forthcoming state visit.

Also in Washington, in an address to a joint meeting of representatives of the US Council on Foreign Relations, the US-China Business Council and the National

Committee on US-China Relations, Foreign Minister Qian spoke of some of the issues on which China and United States continued to differ. In a reference to the 'China threat' theory, he insisted that China's foreign policy concealed no expansionist designs. As regards the bilateral trade imbalance, he pointed out that China was primarily an exporter of low-value, high-volume goods— activities which posed no threat to American workers' jobs. He also reaffirmed his government's commitment to upholding human rights and insisted that the change of administration in Hong Kong would pose no threat to democracy in the territory.

On 26 October Jiang Zemin left Beijing to undertake the first visit to the United States by a Chinese head of state for 12 years. Following talks in the White House, President Jiang and President Clinton issued a joint statement, covering a wide range of bilateral and international issues. It conceded differences of view in some areas (for example, human rights), but expressed a determination to look beyond the short term in the interests of enhancing cooperation and creating a long-run 'constructive strategic partnership'. In response to Chinese concern about American relations with Taiwan, the US side reaffirmed its commitment to a 'one China' policy and the principles enshrined in the previous three Sino-US joint communiques.

Jiang Zemin and President Clinton agreed on the desirability of regular, reciprocal presidential visits and other high-level exchanges. They also undertook to establish a presidential communications link between Beijing and Washington. In the economic sphere, Jiang gave a commitment to implement further 'substantial' tariff reductions in order to help secure China's membership of the WTO. An important bilateral trade initiative was the signing of an agreement for the purchase by China of 50 Boeing aircraft worth US$3,000 million.

Both leaders lent their support to the Universal Declaration of Human Rights and reaffirmed their governments' shared commitment to safeguarding and furthering such rights and other basic freedoms. Differences in this area, they insisted, should be resolved through inter-governmental and non-governmental dialogue, pursued in the spirit of 'equality and mutual respect'. There was also talk of possible cooperation in combating international organized crime.

In recent years China's relationship with Russia had progressed more smoothly than that with the United States, and a further strengthening of Sino-Russian ties was in evidence in 1997 (see also III.3.i). In April Jiang Zemin travelled to Moscow, where he held a summit meeting with President Boris Yeltsin and signed an agreement celebrating the establishment of a 'strategic partnership' between the two countries. Jiang insisted that the creation of such a partnership was no mere expedient, but reflected a long-run, strategic goal. Mr Yeltsin referred to an identity of views on many international issues and spoke of his expectation that remaining problems of border demarcation would soon be resolved.

Even before President Yeltsin began his third state visit to China, there were hints that significant progress had been made towards the resolution of the demarcation of the eastern sector of the Sino-Russian border. On 10 November, following talks between the Russian and Chinese Presidents, a joint declaration was signed. It stated not only that all questions relating to the eastern border sector had been settled, but also that both sides were ready to implement demarcation work relating to the western sector. Meanwhile, Li Peng expressed confidence that the target of raising the value of bilateral trade to US$20,000 million by the year 2000 would be fulfilled on time.

High-level contacts also took place in 1997 between China and other former Soviet republics. The single most important was Li Peng's visit to Kazakhstan, where he and Premier Nursultan Nazarbayev witnessed the signing of three energy-related agreements, worth US$9,500 million (see also VIII.1.iii). One of these provided for the construction of a 3,000 kilometre pipeline from Kazakhstan to western China (see map on page 301). Earlier, it had been announced that China and Russia would also cooperate in developing a gas field in the Irkutsk region and building a gas pipeline from Russia to South Korea, via Mongolia and China.

Sino-Japanese relations were dominated by reciprocal prime ministerial visits. In September Ryutaro Hashimoto arrived in Beijing on his first visit to China as Japanese Prime Minister (see also IX.2.iv). In response to Li Peng's plea for a proper regard for the historical lessons of Japan's war record, Mr Hashimoto acknowledged the losses and suffering caused as a result of Japanese aggression in Asia. He added that his forthcoming visit to north-east China (the region occupied by Japan between 1931 and 1945) was intended to demonstrate his wish to use history in order to guide the future.

In a reference to ongoing defence cooperation talks between Japan and the United States, Li Peng warned Mr Hashimoto that China would not tolerate the scope of such cooperation embracing the Taiwan Strait. The Japanese Premier responded by reaffirming his government's commitment to earlier Sino-Japanese declarations acknowledging Taiwan as an integral part of China. (Despite such reassuring messages, the Chinese government continued for many months afterwards to voice concern about the supposed ambiguity of Japan-US defence guidelines and associated evidence of a shift from the previous emphasis on mere defence considerations.)

Many of the sentiments expressed by Li Peng were echoed in Jiang Zemin's discussions with Mr Hashimoto. In particular, Jiang hailed the decision to institute annual summit meetings between Chinese and Japanese leaders as an important means of eliminating misunderstandings between the two sides and strengthening bilateral ties. It was also revealed during Mr Hashimoto's visit that Japan had agreed to provide yen loans worth US$2,000 million in order to fund 14 projects in China during 1997. This decision marked the resumption of Japan's aid programme to China, most of which had been suspended in August 1995 following the continued implementation of the Chinese nuclear test programme (see AR 1995, pp. 341, 427).

Li Peng held further discussions with Mr Hashimoto in Tokyo in November. In an echo of earlier summit meetings with Russian and American leaders, he emphasized the need for China and Japan to view the development of bilateral relations from 'a long-term and strategic perspective'. Through Premier Hashimoto, Li Pen extended an invitation to the Japanese Crown Prince to visit China in 1998. Both sides hailed the recent signing of a new fisheries agreement and the Chinese Premier also expressed satisfaction with the agreement on merchandise trade, as well as with progress in ongoing negotiations on market access. He insisted that, if outstanding problems were properly handled, the potential for further trade and economic cooperation was enormous. An agreement on environmental cooperation was also signed.

The persistence of Chinese concerns about Japan's wartime record was underlined following the 60th anniversary of the 'Marco Polo Bridge Incident' (on 7 July 1937)—an occasion which offered an opportunity to reflect on the legacy of the events of that period. The message which one official Chinese source sought to convey was unequivocal: 'To adopt a correct view of history is the political basis for developing Sino-Japanese relations, . . . the starting-point for establishing mutual trust . . . and an essential pre-condition to friendship'.

Following the discovery in 1996 of some 1,000 chemical weapon shells at a construction site in Heilongjiang and a subsequent agreement to arrange for the disposal of chemical weapons left in China, a Japanese investigation team travelled to Shenyang in late September to begin preparatory work. It was estimated that some 700,000 chemical munitions had been left in China at the end of the war—90 per cent of them in Jilin province.

The most senior West European leader to visit China in 1997 was Jacques Chirac, who in May became the first French President to undertake a state visit for 14 years. Following talks with Jiang Zemin on bilateral and international issues, the two sides issued a joint declaration—later described by M. Chirac as the most important document in bilateral relations to have emerged since 1964—which spoke of a broad identity of views on a range of issues, including the need for closer bilateral ties and cooperation, and the establishment of a 'comprehensive partnership'. British relations with China were dominated by implications of the retrocession of sovereignty over Hong Kong (see IX.2.ii). Meanwhile, other high-level European visitors to China included the Presidents of Portugal and Finland and the Italian Prime Minister.

Relations between Taiwan and the mainland were generally at a low ebb throughout the year (see IX.2.iii), although mutual political manoeuvrings seemed not to have seriously impeded the continued expansion of economic ties. Typical was an article in *People's Daily* (of 30 January), which celebrated the second anniversary of Jiang Zemin's eight-point proposal on the Taiwan issue. It coupled praise for Jiang's policy initiative of 1995 with an attack on Taiwan's alleged advocacy of the establishment of 'two equal political entities' and encouragement to 'split the country and rule under separate regimes'. Predictable, too, was the condemnation which the Dalai Lama's visit to Taiwan in March attracted in China, one report accusing President Lee Teng-hui of scheming with the Tibetan leader to 'divide the mainland'. Mainland sources described Taiwan's 'pragmatic diplomacy' as the main reason for strained relations across the Taiwan

Strait. It drew particular attention to alleged attempts by the Taiwan authorities to create 'two Chinas' or 'one China, one Taiwan', but noted that Taipei had suffered recent setbacks as a result of the severance of its diplomatic relations with South Africa and the Bahamas.

Throughout 1997, a constant stream of visits by senior officials from countries around the world attested to the importance which China had come to attach to raising its diplomatic profile. A similar rationale informed its active participation in a wide variety of multilateral activities, including four-party talks on the situation on the Korean peninsula (see IX.2.v).

ii. HONG KONG SPECIAL ADMINISTRATIVE REGION

CAPITAL: Victoria   AREA: 1,073 sq km   POPULATION: 6,100,000 ('95)
STATUS: Special Administrative Region of the People's Republic of China (from 1 July 1997
CHIEF EXECUTIVE: Tung Chee-hwa (from July '97)
ADMINISTRATIVE SECRETARY: Anson Chan (since July '97), previously Chief Secretary (since Sept '93)
MAIN IGO MEMBERSHIPS: APEC
CURRENCY: Hong Kong dollar (end-'97 £1=HK$12.72, US$1=HK$7.75)
GDP PER CAPITA: US$24,639 ('96 est.)

DEVELOPMENTS in Hong Kong were dominated by the retrocession to China, at midnight on 30 June, of sovereignty over the last surviving major British colony. The handover was the climax of a process that had been under way since the signing of the 1984 Sino-British Joint Declaration (see AR 1984, pp. 515–24) and marked the end of a period of history which had begun with the ceding to Britain of Hong Kong island under the Treaty of Nanking in 1842.

The coolness of relations between the authorities in Beijing and the last governor of Hong Kong, Chris Patten, persisted until the very end of British rule. The handover ceremony itself was, however, characterized by the punctilious courtesy to be expected of such a formal occasion, during which senior British and Chinese government representatives expressed a shared hope that the beginning of a new era in Hong Kong's history might also mark the start of a more positive phase in bilateral relations. Fears of encroachment on Hong Kong's traditional freedoms in the wake of the return of the colony to China were not realized. By the end of the year there was a widespread feeling that the first six months of Chinese rule had proceeded more smoothly and comfortably than might have been expected.

The members of the first Executive Council of the Hong Kong Special Administrative Region (HKSAR), unveiled by Chief Executive Tung Chee-hwa in January, were mainly political and business leaders enjoying strong links with the mainland. In the same month Rita Fan was elected as Speaker of the Provisional Legislative Council (PLC), a pro-China body established at the end of 1996 to replace the Hong Kong Legislative Council (Legco). The legality of the HKSAR PLC was to remain unrecognized by the British and US governments. Its members met in plenary session several times before the handover, to review existing Hong Kong legislation, one of its motions stating that from 1 July 1997 any demonstrations in the HKSAR would require advance police permission. The same proposal provided for the disbandment of organizations which had political ties overseas. Meanwhile, in Beijing, standing committee members of the National People's Congress (NPC) had adopted a ruling on existing legislation in Hong Kong. Its message was that most laws would be retained, although a few that were considered to be in opposition to the Basic Law would be revised or rescinded.

Despite Beijing's insistence that Hong Kong's stability and prosperity would be preserved, such initiatives fuelled anxieties about the possible impact of a more draconian style of government after 30 June. The ambiguity inherent in the principle 'one country, two systems' again surfaced when a pledge that Hong Kong's press freedom would be fully guaranteed was qualified by the assertion that 'any freedom is relative and limited; there is no absolute freedom or freedom without limits in the world'.

A motion on the Hong Kong budget for 1997–98 was placed before PLC members in May. Estimated expenditure and revenue were HK$203,000 million and HK$234,700 million respectively, generating a surplus of HK$31,700 million. It was anticipated that as of 1 April 1998 fiscal reserves available to the HKSAR government (including the Land Fund) would total HK$359,000 million.

In the run-up to the handover, meetings of the Sino-British Joint Liaison Group (JLG) and its subsidiary bodies addressed various administrative, military and financial issues, including the transfer of official archives and government assets, arrangements for Hong Kong's defence and security, and preparations for the handover ceremony. The talks, although sometimes halting, secured some important agreements, including one that three advance parties of the future People's Liberation Army (PLA) garrison of the HKSAR would arrive shortly before the handover. It transpired that some 509 officers and men would be allowed to enter the territory at 21.00 hours on 30 June. The official response to fears about the stationing of PLA troops in Hong Kong was that their presence, in numbers smaller than that of the former British garrison, was mainly intended to signal the resumption of Chinese sovereignty over the region.

A senior official of the People's Bank of China insisted that the independent currency-issue mechanism of the Hong Kong Monetary Authority would be retained from 1 July 1997. The monetary systems of China and the HKSAR would reflect a 'mutually independent relationship' and support would be given to maintaining a fixed exchange-rate link between the Hong Kong and US dollars. Elsewhere, it was noted that some 214 international treaties would still apply to Hong Kong after 30 June (including 87 to which China was not yet a party) and that the HKSAR would continue to participate in the activities of 34 international organizations.

The days leading up to the handover saw the performance of various rites of passage, such as the signing by Chinese and British representatives of a minute providing for the transfer of the assets and liabilities of the Hong Kong government. The final meetings of Hong Kong's Legislative and Executive Councils also afforded a last opportunity for the Chinese to reiterate their official rejection of the constitutional status of these bodies, as well as of the responsibility which they allegedly bore for derailing the hoped-for 'through train' arrangement.

The Prince of Wales arrived in Hong Kong on 28 June to fulfil his role as representative of the Queen at the handover ceremony. The next day saw the arrival of the Chinese Foreign Minister, Qian Qichen, followed on 30 June by President Jiang Zemin and Premier Li Peng as well as the British government delegation, headed by Prime Minister Tony Blair (see also I.7). In talks with Jiang Zemin and Li Peng, Mr Blair expressed the hope that Hong Kong would become a bridge in the development of a new cooperative relationship between China and Britain. Discussions also took place between both countries' Foreign Ministers and between Qian Qichen and Madeleine Albright, the US Secretary of State, who was quoted as saying that Washington, like London, was determined to monitor closely China's promise to hold elections to the HKSAR's new legislature within a year.

At 16.30 hours on 30 June the governor's standard was lowered and the last British governor left Government House for the last time. At the handover ceremony itself, President Jiang noted the historic significance of the occasion and hailed Deng Xiaoping's pivotal role as the architect of the idea of 'one country, two systems'. He thanked all those in China and Britain who had contributed to the settlement and reaffirmed his government's determination to pursue policies designed to facilitate a 'high degree of autonomy' in Hong Kong's legal and socio-economic system. Despite the Chinese government's assumption of responsibility for Hong Kong's foreign relations and defence, the status of the region as a free port, as well as an international financial, trading and shipping centre, would be preserved. The Chinese leader added that the HKSAR 'shall gradually develop a democratic system that suits Hong Kong's reality'. Tung Chee-hwa echoed such sentiments and spoke of his determination to strengthen Hong Kong's economic vitality.

Although neither Mr Blair nor Ms Albright were present in person, the British and US authorities sent representatives to the subsequent swearing-in ceremony for members of the new Legislative Council, who included Tung Chee-hwa, 60 PLC members, 14 members of the HKSAR Executive Council, 34 judges and 23 principal officials. A number of demonstrations occurred in the wake of the handover ceremony, notably one outside the Legislative Council offices in central Hong Kong organized by members of the Democratic Party led by Martin Lee. Another, instigated by members of the Hong Kong Alliance in Support of the Patriotic Movement in China, demanded a review of events surrounding the recent political upheavals in China and the release of pro-democracy activists, calling for the end of one-party dictatorship and the establishment of a democratic system.

On 8 October Tung Chee-hwa delivered his first policy address as Chief Executive. His remarks focused on economic and social issues and included calls for housing and land use reforms, as well as the announcement of the creation of a commission to oversee Hong Kong's strategic development. He spoke of the government's intention to undertake a major expansion of housing construction in both public and private sectors. The statement won praise from many quarters, but also fierce criticism from those who deplored his failure to address human rights issues and accused him of seeking to depoliticize local culture in favour of the creation of a 'purely economically-driven' Hong Kong.

Speaking later the same month, Chief Executive Tung interpreted recent sharp falls in the Hang Seng share index as a reaction to economic crisis unfolding elsewhere in the region (see XVIII.1). In the face of such difficulties, there was a notable absence of interference with the working of the Hong Kong stock market, although the HKSAR government displayed a willingness to use foreign currency reserves in support of its determination to defend the status of the Hong Kong dollar and maintain its peg to the US dollar.

On 2–3 December the 41st meeting of the JLG was held in Beijing, the first such meeting since the handover. The Chinese side reaffirmed its commitment to abide by the spirit of the 1984 Sino-British Joint Declaration and to work with Britain to fulfil the JLG's programme during the coming two years. Although the two sides remained divided on a number of issues, it was authoritatively reported that the JLG discussions had not been acrimonious.

iii. TAIWAN

CAPITAL: Taipei   AREA: 35,981 sq km   POPULATION: 21,357,000 ('95)
OFFICIAL LANGUAGE: Chinese   POLITICAL SYSTEM: presidential
HEAD OF STATE & GOVERNMENT: President Lee Teng-hui (since Jan '88, popularly elected March '96)
RULING PARTY: Kuomintang (KMT)
PRIME MINISTER: Vincent Siew (since Sept '97)
MAIN IGO MEMBERSHIPS : APEC
CURRENCY: new Taiwan dollar (end-'97 £1=NT$53.60, US$1=NT$32.67)
GDP PER CAPITA: US$12,872 ('96 est.)

THE shaping influence of mainland China on Taiwan's domestic development and foreign relations had long been apparent and was so again during 1997. Continuing economic and cultural exchanges across the Taiwan Strait concealed the reality of slow progress towards genuine rapprochement, despite appeals from both sides for the resumption of dialogue, suspended by Beijing in June 1995 following President Lee Teng-hui's visit to the United States (see AR 1995, p. 344). Towards the end of the year, however, there were indications of a thawing of relations.

Official Taiwan sources expressed condolence in the wake of Deng Xiaoping's death in February (see IX.2.i) and spoke of the impact of Dengist reforms in mobilizing Taiwanese funds, labour and technology in support of economic development and improved living standards in mainland China. The chairman of the Mainland Affairs Council insisted, however, that Deng's passing would have no effect on Taiwan's policy towards the mainland.

The caution which had consistently characterized Taiwan's attitude towards political talks with Beijing was reflected in official reaction to the recovery of sovereignty over Hong Kong. Widespread satisfaction at the event was qualified by concern for the region's future. Vice-President Lien Chan (then also Prime Minister) was dismissive of the idea of 'one country, two systems', describing it as a 'makeshift formula devised . . . because the communist system cannot be imposed on the former British colony'. He was unequivocal in insisting that the same arrangement could not be applied to Taiwan—an 'independent country with its own 86-year history'. President Lee likewise welcomed the end of colonial rule in Hong Kong, but insisted that Beijing's formula for reunification with Taiwan was simply 'wishful thinking', not least against the background of recent progress towards democratization in Taiwan.

In January, following private talks in Hong Kong by unofficial representatives from China and Taiwan, initial agreement was reached to restore limited cross-strait sea links. It was expected that the beneficiaries of the agreement, which provided for trans-shipment links between Kaohsiung (Taiwan) and Xiamen and Fuzhou (Zhejiang province), would be foreign-registered ships previously routed through Hong Kong. Following the resumption of a direct shipping link in April, it was revealed that approval had been given to four Chinese and six Taiwanese companies to establish cross-strait shipping services.

There was a suggestion that such agreements might serve as a model for the restoration of direct air links between China and Taiwan. However, government officials in Taipei gave a cautious response to calls from the mainland that comprehensive cross-strait links should be opened, including postal delivery services, even though local firms and businesses were more receptive to the idea. The Taiwan authorities took the view that such overtures were rooted in the political strategies of the People's Republic. The official line was that discussion of such matters remained premature and had to be considered in relation to national security, given Beijing's denial of the reality of separate rule on the two sides of the Taiwan Strait and its refusal to renounce the use of force in the interests of reunification.

The mainland government's efforts to isolate Taiwan internationally were also regarded as a major impediment to the establishment of direct links. In this context, Lee Teng-hui cited Beijing's political ambitions *vis-à-vis* Taiwan as a further reason for moving cautiously in the development of bilateral economic and trade ties. The background to his warning lay in the rapid recent growth of cross-strait trade and investment. Between 1992 and 1996 the value of two-way trade grew, on average, by 27 per cent per annum to reach US$18,980 million in 1996, while the cumulative value of utilized Taiwan investment in the mainland was US$31,900 million. In the face of such spectacular expansion—but also worried by mainland efforts to eliminate Taiwan as a diplomatic force in the world community—Taipei had, in 1996, instituted a 'no haste, be patient' policy towards investment in mainland China. Its impact was reflected in a 54 per cent year-on-year decline in such investment in January-September 1997, although Taiwan remained the third largest source of overseas capital to the mainland after Hong Kong and Japan. Meanwhile, in a further effort to control capital flows to China, the Ministry of Economic Affairs confirmed the implementation of new regulations, banning investments of over US$50 million in the mainland.

The most notable recent success in Beijing's strategy of seeking to enforce Taiwan's diplomatic isolation was the decision of the South African government to sever its ties with Taiwan in favour of establishing full diplomatic relations with mainland China, to take effect on 1 January 1998 (see AR 1996, pp. 341-2.). Despite further setbacks, Taiwan sought to maintain a high diplomatic profile in the international community through the dispatch of high-ranking government officials to Central America, the Eastern Caribbean, Iceland, Malaysia and Singapore.

In Taiwan itself, there were signs of the further erosion of the authority of the ruling Kuomintang (KMT) party. In April and May social and public order unrest precipitated the resignations of two ministers and eventually forced President Lee to institute a cabinet reshuffle in which Vincent Siew took over the premiership from Lien Chan (who remained Vice-President). The most significant domestic development was, however, the outcome of local government elections in November, which resulted in a major victory for the pro-independence Democratic Progressive Party (DPP), which won 12 of the 23 contested seats. By contrast, the KMT lost seven of the 15 seats it had previously held, leaving independent candidates in control of the three remaining seats. For the first time in Taiwan's history, the DPP secured a higher share of the popular vote than the KMT (43 per cent against 42 per cent), leading some to argue that the DPP would replace the KMT as the ruling party. In the wake of the subsequent resignation of Wu Poh-hsiung, Vice-Premier Chang Hsiao-yen was confirmed as KMT secretary-general.

Earlier in the year, the 15th KMT congress had re-elected Lee Teng-hui unopposed as party chairman. A possible precursor of future developments was the emergence of James Soong as recipient of the highest number of votes cast in the election of candidates to the new KMT central committee. Mr Soong, a former KMT secretary-general and governor of Taiwan in 1993–97, was widely perceived as a rival to Lee Teng-hui and a future candidate for Taiwan's presidency.

Taiwan emerged at the end of year relatively unscathed by the financial and economic crises affecting other countries of South-East and East Asia (see XVIII.1). In October, however, the central bank was forced to intervene in an effort to stem recent falls in share prices and to support the Taiwan dollar. In an attempt to restore confidence, the overall ceilings on foreign investment in domestic shares, as well as on overseas holdings in any single stock, were raised by five percentage points. Meanwhile, officials of the Ministry of Finance expressed great concern about the possible impact of a continuing fall in the

Hong Kong dollar on Taiwan's competitiveness in international markets and on its exports to Hong Kong.

iv. JAPAN

CAPITAL: Tokyo   AREA: 378,000 sq km   POPULATION: 125,760,000 ('96)
OFFICIAL LANGUAGE: Japanese   POLITICAL SYSTEM: parliamentary democracy
HEAD OF STATE: Emperor Tsugu no Miya Akihito (since Jan '89)
RULING PARTY: Liberal-Democratic Party (LDP)
HEAD OF GOVERNMENT: Ryutaro Hashimoto, Prime Minister (since Jan '96)
MAIN IGO MEMBERSHIPS (non-UN): APEC, CP, OECD, G-7
CURRENCY: yen (end-'97 £1=Y217.11, US$1=Y132.33)
GNP PER CAPITA: US$34,640 ('95) or US$22,110 ('95) by PPP calculation

FOR the Japanese government, 1997 was something of an *annus horribilis*, as the authorities proved unable or unwilling to tackle deep-seated financial weaknesses that were greatly aggravated by the burgeoning crisis of neighbouring 'Asian tiger' economies (see XVIII.1). The country was administered throughout the year by the Liberal-Democratic Party (LDP) government led by Ryutaro Hashimoto since January 1996 (see AR 1996, pp. 345–6), in loose alliance with the Social Democratic Party of Japan (SDPJ) and the small Sakigake party.

In his New Year message to the Diet, the Prime Minister stressed the need for overhaul of the economy, including a reduction of the budget deficit, and made administrative reform a major plank of his programme, setting up five studies on fiscal, monetary, economic, social and educational policy. The financial reforms subsequently announced were intended to prepare the nation for deregulation in advance of the 'big bang'—an important step which entailed enhancing the powers of the Bank of Japan, while weakening those of the much-criticized Ministry of Finance. The programme for financial deregulation by the start of 2000 was announced in June.

An increase in consumption tax from 3 to 5 per cent, which had been announced in 1996, was introduced on 1 April. Though the increase was necessary to improve government revenues, the new imposition was unpopular. Its effect was to destabilize the economy; and the yen fell against the dollar. Confidence began to evaporate and the contagion spread widely in East Asia (see below).

The financial scandals of previous years continued to haunt the government and were compounded in March by the trouble which engulfed Nomura Securities, one of the largest stock-broking companies, which had given favourable treatment to organized crime syndicates. Police raided the headquarters of Nomura, and other security houses were also under examination throughout the year.

The government was also embarrassed by the sensitive issue of accidents at nuclear power plants. A fire and explosion occurred at Tokaimura nuclear reprocessing plant in March, resulting in the slight exposure of workers to radioactivity and the plant's long-term closure. The nuclear management appeared to issue a misleading version of the incident, which led to severe criticism by the Prime Minister. An advanced thermal reactor in Fukui prefecture was closed on 16 April following the leak of radioactive titium.

Externally, the Prime Minister started the year by making a tour of South-East Asian countries as part of the regular summit meetings between Japanese and ASEAN leaders. He enunciated the 'Hashimoto doctrine' of greater consultation between these countries and called on them to help China to become a 'constructive partner'. In April he was able to report that the 126-day siege of the Japanese ambassador's residence in Lima, Peru, had been ended with the release of hostages, though the episode raised many problems about the security of Japanese diplomatic premises abroad (see IV.3.viii).

At the end of April Mr Hashimoto visited the United States to confer with President Clinton. High on the agenda was the question of Okinawa, whose economy had for some years been a matter of concern for the Tokyo government. Several plans for the economic revival of the prefecture had recently been studied, including the creation of a free-trade zone for the region. Such proposals were complicated, however, by the delicate issue of the large US military presence, which was currently fundamental to the economy of the islands. The Tokyo government had earlier taken powers to arrange for the leasing of private land in Okinawa to the United States for military purposes under the US-Japan security treaty, but strong opposition had come from some landowners and islanders who wanted to reduce the presence of US forces (see AR 1996, p. 347). Mr Hashimoto had then obtained cross-party agreement for legislation to be pushed through the Diet, enabling the government compulsorily to acquire the land needed.

During the Washington talks President Clinton drew attention to the renewed upward movement in Japan's trade surplus with the United States, asking for measures to be taken to stimulate domestic demand. The subject recurred when they again met at the G-7 summit in Denver in June, when the President called for greater deregulation in Japan in order to improve the prospects for increasing US exports. His call heralded a new round of American-Japanese trade tensions.

The two leaders also promised to cooperate in the security field, especially in light of current tensions on the Korean peninsula. The question surfaced on 7 June with the leaking of amended guidelines on US-Japan defence cooperation (finally officially released on 23 September). These drew Japan into a more proactive role under which it would provide the United States with facilities and services (such as mine-sweeping) in areas around Japan. What worried some in Japan, and led to protests throughout East Asia (see below), was the unspecified nature of Japan's military commitment under the new arrangement.

One serious US-Japanese commercial dispute persisted throughout the year. In protest at the discriminatory treatment of US vessels in Japanese ports, the Federal Maritime Commission (FMC), a body independent of the administration, threatened in February to impose surcharges on vessels of Japan's major shipping companies entering US ports. These warnings led to an unprecedented 24-hour strike of port labour throughout Japan. The surcharges were postponed but were ultimately enforced in September. When the shipping companies, with the approval of the Japanese government, refused to pay, the FMC threatened to impound vessels seeking entry to US ports. After delicate negotiations, the FMC, at the request of the President, agreed to hold the ruling in abeyance. Modified arrangements were announced, coming into force on 1 December.

Following the sarin gas attack on the Tokyo underground in March 1995 (see AR 1995, p. 348), the Japanese government had revoked Aum Shinrikyo's status as a religious corporation, but the public security commission did not outlaw the cult. The sect therefore continued to recruit new adherents, though its membership had dropped from 10,000 to about 1,000. While it was forced into bankruptcy, and much of its land and other assets were lost, it was once again operating profitable businesses. The members appeared to be faithful to Shoko Asahara, the sect's guru and spiritual leader, even though he was in prison awaiting sentence.

An important judicial decision was taken over school textbooks in August. The Supreme Court ruled that the Ministry of Education had acted illegally by censoring and omitting references in school textbooks to Unit 731, the germ warfare unit operated by the Imperial Japanese Army mainly in Manchuria, and recommended that textbooks should be censored as little as possible. Professor Saburo Ienaga, an experienced campaigner for veracity in history taught to schoolchildren, who had previously lost several law-suits, was on this occasion vindicated and awarded compensation.

To mark the 25th anniversary of the restoration of Sino-Japanese diplomatic relations, Mr Hashimoto visited China early in September, for the first time as Prime Minister (see also IX.2.i). In the summer he had come through a dispute with China over the Senkaku Islands, a small group of uninhabited islands to the north-east of Taiwan. Parties of Japanese activists had landed on these islands (to which China had some claim) and planted the Japanese flag there. There were widespread protests in China, Taiwan and Hong Kong against these unofficial actions. Fortunately, both governments reacted in a restrained manner and a serious crisis was averted.

In Beijing the Prime Minister ran into strong opposition over the implications of the new US-Japan defence guidelines. The Chinese Premier, Li Peng, had earlier stated that their extension to cover Japan's support of the United States in an emergency in the Taiwan Strait was unacceptable. Mr Hashimoto gave assurances and confirmed that Japan was committed to a 'one China' policy, but there was vagueness in the undertaking. Accordingly, Premier Li returned to the issue when he paid a return visit to Japan in November. In spite of the disagreement over Taiwan, however, the two sides had much in common in their views of the security threat posed by North Korea and promised to hold regular top-level meetings in future.

The Prime Minister travelled to Krasnoyarsk (Siberia) early in November for talks with President Yeltsin, the meeting signalling an improvement in Russo-Japanese relations (see also III.3.i). As a token of the improved climate, the *Admiral Vinogradov* had visited Tokyo at the end of June, becoming the first Russian navy ship to do so since 1905. The two leaders reached a many-sided agreement on cooperation in the economic, energy, educational and defence spheres, most of them of economic advantage to Russia. In return, the Japanese side received confirmation that the two governments would try to resolve the long-standing Northern Territories dispute with the aim of achieving signature of a peace treaty by 2000.

Mr Hashimoto was re-elected LDP president for a second term in September and consequently continued to serve as Prime Minister, using the occasion to reshuffle his cabinet. In order to balance portfolios among the various LDP factions, he initially allocated the cabinet-level post of Director-General of the Management and Coordination Agency to Koko Sato, who had served a prison term because of his involvement in the Lockheed scandal in the 1970s. In response to an outburst of public indignation, Mr Sato quickly resigned, and Mr Hashimoto offered a public apology for his misjudgment.

The planned changes in the structure of government, announced at the beginning of the year, had been passed for study to the Administrative Reform Council, which had published its recommendations in August. Stung by opposition from within his own party and the bureaucracy, Mr Hashimoto had to tone down proposals for reorganizing the central government in the final report, which was approved by the cabinet at the end of November. In particular, decisions on revised functions for the Ministry of Finance were deferred until 1998, while the more radical proposals by the banks for the privatization of the government's commercial services (such as posts and communications) were watered down. The insurance business operated by the post office was likely to be privatized by 2001, but nothing was decided about postal savings.

In the event, the reform plans paled into insignificance amid the financial crisis which overwhelmed the country in the last two months of the year, as the turmoil in the economies of South Korea and South-East Asia exposed weaknesses in all parts of the financial sector and the lack of transparency in its approach. In November the Hokkaido Takushoku Bank—the tenth-largest in the hierarchy of 'city banks'—announced its closure. The bank had been in difficulties over bad loans for some years and even the Finance Ministry's efforts to prevent its collapse had failed. The situation worsened when Yamaichi Securities, the oldest and fourth-largest stock-broking firm in Japan, also filed for closure, this being the largest financial collapse of its kind since the end of World War II. Many subsidiary bankruptcies took place lower down the spectrum.

Mr Hashimoto, who had been praised for his efforts to reduce government spending, adopted a fiscal reform programme on 28 November which would reduce the budget deficit from 7 per cent of GDP to less than 3 per cent by 2003. He also proposed a tight budget for the next fiscal year, involving cuts in the foreign aid budget (on which Japan had long prided itself) and in defence and public works expenditure. However, faced with the many-sided financial crisis, the government decided to make its first priority the economic and financial recovery of the country. With some reluctance, the cabinet authorized the use of public funds to support the banking system. In a supplementary budget for 1997, it introduced temporary income tax cuts worth ¥2,000,000 million and allocated ¥10,000,000 million of funds for disaster protection and public works in order to stabilize the financial sector and to drive the economy out of stagnation. These complex and contradictory measures were designed as a pump-priming package.

Though there was much criticism of the government's handling of the economy, the political situation of the government at the end of the year was mixed. On the one hand, the LDP regained its majority in the lower house of the Diet by the defection of members from other parties. At the end of the year, moreover, the New Frontier Party (Shinshinto), which had formed the largest opposition grouping in the Diet for the past four years, broke up into six separate parties. It seemed likely that centre-left groups would coordinate their policies, while the right wing, under Ichiro Ozawa, would woo disaffected groups within the LDP. The political arithmetic, therefore, left the LDP stronger. On the other hand, the government's handling of the financial crisis not only gave rise to much dissent within LDP ranks but also deprived it of much popular appeal.

v. SOUTH KOREA

CAPITAL: Seoul   AREA: 99,392 sq km   POPULATION: 44,545,000 ('96 est.)
OFFICIAL LANGUAGE: Korean   POLITICAL SYSTEM: presidential democracy
HEAD OF STATE & GOVERNMENT: President Kim Young Sam (since Feb '93)
RULING PARTY: New Korea Party (NKP)
PRIME MINISTER: Koh Kon (since March '97)
MAIN IGO MEMBERSHIPS (non-UN): APEC, CP, OECD
CURRENCY: won (end-'97 £1=SKW2,780.99, US$1=SKW1,695.00)
GNP PER CAPITA: US$9,700 ('95) or US$11,450 ('95) by PPP calculation

OPPOSITION leader Kim Dae Jung won the presidential elections in December, when the country's finances were in a parlous state despite the underlying strength of the economy.

In January bankruptcy proceedings against the Hanbo steel and construction industry *chaebol* (conglomerate) marked the biggest corporate collapse in a decade. Hanbo's founder, Chung Tai Soo, and the presidents of the Korea First and Cho Hung banks, which had issued loans to Hanbo, were arrested on fraud charges. Mr Chung was found guilty and sentenced to 15 years' imprisonment for bribing bankers and politicians to arrange loans to Hanbo.

In a television broadcast in February, President Kim Young Sam apologized to the nation for the Hanbo scandal, mentioning that one of his sons was implicated. The son, Kim Hyun Chul, was convicted in October of accepting the equivalent of US$3.6 million in bribes and laundering $3.8 million in cash from businessmen seeking government contracts. He was sentenced to three years' imprisonment and a fine of SKW1,440 million. His conviction was seen as a serious blow to President Kim's election chances.

Meanwhile, on 3 March, President Kim had appointed the sixth Prime Minister of his presidency, Lee Soo Sung being replaced by Koh Kun, a former mayor of Seoul. A substantial cabinet reshuffle followed immediately, featuring the appointment of Kang Kyung Shik, a close ally of the President who had held the finance portfolio in the early 1980s, as Deputy Prime Minister and Minister of Finance and Economy.

In July another *chaebol*, the car-making Kia Group, defaulted on loans amounting to SKW2,770 million. Its main creditor, the Korea First Bank, which had lent SKW3,400,000 million to insolvent companies against its equity capital of SKW1,900,000 million, sought help from the Korea Asset Management Corporation, a government body buying up bad bank loans at a discount and selling them on. In October Kang Kyung Shik proposed the nationalization of a major part of the Kia Group to prevent a chain of bankruptcies and instability in the financial market. The Kia Group's management rejected the plan.

As corporate failures mounted, the won began to fall. In October South Korea's central bank, the Bank of Korea, announced that it would lend the equivalent of $1,000 million to 19 investment banks whose bad loans exceeded 50 per cent of their capital. Concurrently, the Finance Ministry announced a package of measures to boost the Seoul stock exchange, but shares and the won slumped further after the US credit agency Standard & Poor reduced South Korea's long-term foreign currency debt-rating. Bank of Korea intervention in support of the won increased fears that the government would lack foreign currency reserves to service the foreign debt.

Kang Kyung Shik was an early ministerial casualty of the crisis, being replaced on 19 November by Lim Chang Yul, hitherto Minister of Trade, Industry and Energy. Mr Lim immediately announced an economic stabilization package, but the US and Japanese governments withheld financial support until the package had been agreed with the IMF. The President's announcement on 21 November that the government was seeking $20,000 million in standby loans from the IMF to avoid defaulting was greeted with shock in the South Korean media. The won and shares rose briefly, then plunged again as opinion spread that $20,000 million would not be enough. Banks were calling in their loans, as patriotic Koreans queued up to donate their gold jewellery to the nation's reserves. The won hit a new low of SKW1,836 to the dollar, having lost more than half of its value at the start of the year.

After protracted negotiations, IMF officials on 3 December agreed a $57,000 million loan guarantee package, of which $10,000 million was to be in the form of 'accelerated aid'. About $15,000 million of the country's $100,000 million short-term debt was due for repayment by the end of the year and another $15,000 million in January 1998. The gross foreign debt amounted to $156,900 million as of the end of November. The IMF deal obliged the government to keep interest rates high, end restrictions on foreign investment in South Korea, bail out leading banks and toughen labour market reform.

Amidst the financial turmoil, presidential elections on 18 December were won by Kim Dae Jung of the National Congress for New Politics (NCNP), with 10.32 million votes (40.3 per cent of the ballot), against 9.93 million (38.7 per cent) received by the candidate of the ruling New Korea Party (NKP), Lee

Hoi Chang. The President-elect and the outgoing President quickly signed a six-point cooperation agreement for the transition period up to the presidential inauguration scheduled for 25 February 1998. With the former's agreement, presidential pardons were granted to ex-Presidents Chun Doo Hwan and Roh Tae Woo, who had been imprisoned in 1996 for amassing 'slush funds' while in office (see AR 1996, pp. 349–50).

As proposed by Presidents Clinton and Kim in April 1996, preparations for four-party talks between South and North Korea, the United States and China, to establish a permanent peace mechanism on the Korean pensinsula in place of the 1953 armistice agreement, finally got under way with a series of meetings in New York in March. This was the first time in three years that North and South Korean officials had met. Several subsequent meetings became bogged down in North Korean demands for the withdrawal of US troops from South Korea or for food aid as a condition of attendance. It was only in November that all parties agreed to attend the first round of formal talks in Geneva on 9 December. Conducted by the South Korean ambassador to France, a North Korean Deputy Foreign Minister, a US Assistant Secretary of State and a Chinese Deputy Foreign Minister, the session was described as 'cordial and productive'. The next round was due to be held in Geneva in March 1988.

vi. NORTH KOREA

CAPITAL: Pyongyang   AREA: 123,370 sq km   POPULATION: 23,486,000 ('95 est.)
OFFICIAL LANGUAGE: Korean   POLITICAL SYSTEM: people's republic
RULING PARTY: Korean Workers' Party (KWP)
PARTY LEADER: Kim Jong Il, KWP general secretary (since Oct '97)
HEAD OF STATE: vacant since death of Kim Il Sung in July 1994
PRIME MINISTER: Kim Yong Nam (acting since Feb '97)
MAIN IGO MEMBERSHIPS (NON-UN): NAM
CURRENCY: won (end-'97 £1=NKW3.61, US$1=NKW2.20)
GNP PER CAPITA: US$920 ('94 est.)

KIM Jong Il became the official party leader in October in succession to his late father, Kim Il Sung, as severe food shortages encouraged the country to adopt a more cooperative approach in foreign relations. (For the four-party talks on a Korean settlement launched in 1997, see IX.2.v.)

A statement in the name of the Korean Workers' Party (KWP) central committee and central military commission on 8 October solemnly declared that the 'great leader' Kim Jong Il had been 'officially elected' secretary-general of the ruling party. The statement followed a short campaign of nomination by military and provincial party organizations, but lacked the formality of a central meeting.

Contrary to expectations, Kim Jong Il did not become President of the Democratic People's Republic of Korea (DPRK) on the third anniversary of Kim Il Sung's death in July. Kim Yong Nam, Deputy Premier and Foreign Minister, gave the memorial address marking the end of official mourning. A joint resolution by the party, government and military, exalting Kim Il Sung's life and exploits, proclaimed changes to the North Korean calendar which turned 1912, the year of Kim Il Sung's birth, into 'Chuche 1' and his birthday, 15 April, into the 'Festival of the Sun'.

Hwang Chang Yop, secretary of the KWP central committee, defected to the South Korean embassy in Beijing in February on his way home from a visit to Japan. He was taken to Manila for debriefing and arrived in Seoul in April. The North Korean ambassador to Egypt, Chang Sung Kil, defected to the United States in August, with his wife and elder brother, a trade official in France. The ex-ambassador was thought to be better informed than Mr Hwang about Pyongyang's affairs.

Catherine Bertini, executive director of the UN World Food Programme (WFP), announced in March, after a visit to North Korea, that the country was running out of food. Centrally-distributed food rations had fallen to 350 calories a day; people were trying to augment their rations with roots and dried leaves; children were stunted by malnutrition. The WFP launched an appeal for $126 million worth of food and medicine for North Korea and began distributing 250 grams of food per day to children under six.

US congressman Tony Hall visited North Korea in October, accompanying a US government survey team looking into the food shortages. There was no famine at the time of the visit, food distribution having been restored after its breakdown February-May. The North Koreans said that they would need 1.5 to 2 million tonnes of extra food in the spring of 1998, but the WFP and US Department of Agriculture estimate was that 2.5 to 3 million tonnes would be required. North Korean officials blamed the food shortage on natural disasters, but the US team said that the country's economic system was also to blame.

Meeting for the first time in five years, North and South Korean Red Cross officials agreed in Beijing in May that South Korea would deliver 50,000 tonnes of flour to the North under South Korean Red Cross supervision. Another food delivery of 50,000 tonnes was agreed in July. A third meeting in Beijing in December discussed a new South Korean offer—its economic crisis permitting (see IX.2.v)—to send another 100,000 tonnes in 1998, but the North rejected South Korean Red Cross supervision of distribution.

The Korean Energy Development Organization consortium supplying two light-water reactors to North Korea held the ground-breaking ceremony at Kumho near Shimpo in August. Some 5,000 South Korean engineers were eventually expected to work on the project. A by-product was the opening of the first telephone link between North and South Korea. After talks in Bangkok, North Korea signed an agreement with South Korea in October permitting foreign commercial flights through North Korean air space.

At talks in New York in June US representatives tried to persuade North Korea to halt development and export of Nodong-1 missiles to Syria and Iran. US-North Korean talks in Beijing in September dealt with the defection of the two North Korean diplomats, which had prompted North Korea's suspension of the missile talks. US concerns about the missiles were raised with a North Korean delegation at the State Department in November. Establishment of liaison offices in Washington and Pyongyang and the search in North Korea for US Korean War personnel 'missing in action' (MIAs) were also discussed.

Against the usual background of anti-American rhetoric, punctuated by occasional shooting incidents in the demilitarized zone (DMZ), the year had been remarkable for efforts to mend various international fences. On the sixth anniversary in December of Kim Jong Il's being 'elected' Supreme Commander of the Korean People's Army, Pyongyang radio reported him as saying: 'We do not intend to consider the USA to be our sworn enemy and hope that DPRK-US relations will be normalized'.

In Moscow in June North Korean and Russian Deputy Foreign Ministers discussed a new treaty emphasizing economic cooperation, to replace the 1961 USSR-DPRK friendship treaty. North Korean and Japanese officials, meeting in Beijing in August, agreed to reopen the normalization talks which had broken down in 1992. The Japanese and North Korean Red Cross agreed in Beijing in September to allow Japanese wives of North Koreans to pay short visits to Japan.

vii. MONGOLIA

CAPITAL: Ulan Bator   AREA: 1,566,500 sq km   POPULATION: 2,353,300 ('96)
PRINCIPAL LANGUAGE: Halh (Khalkha) Mongolian   POLITICAL SYSTEM: republic
HEAD OF STATE: President Natsagiyn Bagabandi (since June '97)
RULING PARTIES: Democratic Alliance (of Mongolian National Democratic & Social
   Democratic parties) dominates People's Great Hural
PRIME MINISTER: Mendsayhany Enhsayhan (since July '96)
MAIN IGO MEMBERSHIPS (non-UN): NAM
CURRENCY: tögrög (end-'97 £1=T1,287.56, US$1=T784.76)
GNP PER CAPITA: US$310 ('95) or US$1,950 ('95) by PPP calculation

MONGOLIA's presidential elections on 18 May were won by Natsagiyn Bagabandi, candidate of the opposition Mongolian People's Revolutionary Party (MPRP), with 60.8 per cent of the ballot. He defeated the incumbent President Punsalmaagiyn Ochirbat, representing the ruling Democratic Alliance (DA) coalition parties, who received 29.8 per cent. Jambyn Gombojav, a member of the People's Great Hural (parliament), who had resigned from the MPRP and was standing for the Mongolian United Heritage (conservative) Party (MUHcP), obtained 6.6 per cent of the vote.

Mr Bagabandi, the MPRP parliamentary leader, had been adopted as the party's presidential candidate after his election to the new post of party chairman at the MPRP's 22nd congress in February. After the presidential elections, general secretary Nambaryn Enhbayar replaced Mr Bagabandi as chairman of the MPRP and then won the by-election for Mr Bagabandi's Great Hural seat. The former MPRP general secretary, Büdragchaagiyn Dash-Yondon, who had led the party to defeat in the 1996 legislative elections and had been replaced by Mr Enhbayar (see AR 1996, p. 354), became the new President's political adviser. The MUHcP's only elected member in the Great Hural, Ochirbatyn Dashbalbar, was elected party leader in June.

One of President Bagabandi's early moves was to decree the return of awards to the late Yumjaagiyn Tsedenbal, the 'Mongolian Brezhnev'. Mr Tsedenbal had been MPRP leader for 44 years, Prime Minister in 1952–74 and then head of state until being ousted by his MPRP colleagues in 1984. He had been deprived of his awards by Mongolia's first democratically-elected government and had died in Moscow in 1991 (see AR 1991, pp. 365, 581).

Nambaryn Enhbayar's first act on taking the oath as a Great Hural member was to launch a censure motion against the DA government, although it was rejected 17 days later by the government majority. Meanwhile, the MPRP was refusing to hand over the country's archives for 1921–90 on the pretence that they were 'party' rather than 'state' archives. MPRP members of the Great Hural demanded the deletion of references to their party's role in the Stalinist purges from draft legislation on the rehabilitation of victims.

Natsagiyn Bagabandi's election victory was attributable in part to the MPRP's manifesto commitment to social support for the poor. The DA coalition had failed to halt the growth of poverty, which affected 20 per cent of households. Privatization of urban housing free of charge was launched in March, but made slow progress. Auctions of small shops and businesses continued. Mongol Bank (the central bank) ordered the closure of the People's Bank and the Insurance Bank in February, as they approached bankruptcy, and refloated them as the Preservation Bank and the Restoration Bank respectively.

The exchange rate of the tögrög against the US dollar depreciated by over 20 per cent to a six-month low of US$1=T847 in March; it picked up to T778 in May but then fell back again and stabilized at around T800 in September. Foreign currency reserves at the end of December amounted to $157.11 million, the figure for net reserves being $107.1 million. Annual inflation fell to 17.5 per cent (from 53.2 per cent for 1996), while industrial production went up by 4.3 per cent and GDP rose 3.3 per cent year-on-year. Sales of gold to Mongol Bank by mining enterprises in 1997 amounted to a record 8,902.3 kilograms, almost three tonnes more than the 1996 figure. The foreign trade deficit, at $25.4 million, was slightly smaller than the year before.

Grain production in 1997 amounted to 239,295 tonnes, more than in 1996 but still insufficient to meet annual demand. The annual livestock census in December recorded a new high of nearly 31.3 million head, the main growth being in goats. However, President Bagabandi had pointed out in September that quality and productivity were as important as numbers. It was reported that 395,400 people (17 per cent of the population) were engaged in herding, but only 16 per cent of the 170,100 herding households had the minimum 250 head needed to make a living.

Incursions into Mongolian territory at Lake Buir by Chinese fish poachers in September led to the killing of one intruder and the hospitalization of a Mongolian border guard in Hailar. Cross-border smuggling and cattle-rustling continued between Mongolia's north-western provinces and Tuva (Russian Federation), despite the installation of extra border markers. Two Russian priests arrived in March to re-establish an Orthodox presence in Mongolia at a service attended by local Russians, the first to be held since the Holy Trinity church in Ulan Bator was closed in 1928. Long-hoped-for visits by President Yeltsin and Premier Viktor Chernomyrdin did not materialize. The longstanding rouble debt issue remained unsettled.

Defence Minister Dambiyn Dorligjav met US military leaders in Hawaii and the commander of US forces in the Pacific visited Mongolia. MPRP spokesmen expressed concern about the USA's growing role as Mongolia's 'third neighbour'. Britain's Duke of Edinburgh spent a few days in Mongolia in March in his role as honorary president of the World Wide Fund for Nature. The Malaysian Prime Minister, Dr Mahathir Mohamad, visiting Mongolia in September, offered student training, palm oil, an air agreement and duty-free shops. Malaysia also expressed interest in aiding the Egiyn Gol hydroelectric station project (although Mongolia later showed more interest in a firmer Czech offer).

Mongolia joined the World Trade Organization (WTO) in January. Customs tariffs on all imports, except tobacco and spirits, were abolished in May. To protect garment manufacturers, a tariff of T4,000 per kilogram was imposed on unprocessed cashmere exports. The Mongolian Assistance Group (aid donors), meeting in Tokyo in October, pledged $256.09 million in aid for 1998—the Asian Development Bank and Japan offering around $60 million each and South Korea $21 million.

Mongolia was concerned that the financial crises in other Asian countries (see XVIII.1), including Malaysia, Japan and South Korea, might reduce their capacity for aid and investment. The decline in international copper and gold prices was adversely affecting the balance of payments, and Mongolia was pinning its hopes on its uncertain oil reserves.

X AUSTRALASIA AND THE PACIFIC

i. AUSTRALIA

CAPITAL: Canberra   AREA: 7,687,000 sq km   POPULATION: 18,260,000 ('96)
OFFICIAL LANGUAGE: English   POLITICAL SYSTEM: federal parliamentary democracy
HEAD OF STATE: Queen Elizabeth II   GOVERNOR-GENERAL: Sir William Deane
RULING PARTIES: Liberal-National coalition
HEAD OF GOVERNMENT: John Howard, Prime Minister (since March '96)
MAIN IGO MEMBERSHIPS (non-UN): APEC, SPC, SPF, CP, ANZUS, OECD, CWTH
CURRENCY: Australian dollar (end-'97 £1=A$2.52, US$1=A$1.54)
GNP PER CAPITA: US$18,720 ('95) or US$19,940 ('95) by PPP calculation

THERE were no changes of government in Australia during the year, but opinion polls recorded a steady, and then accelerating, decline in the popularity of the Liberal-National Party coalition both at the national level and in Victoria and South Australia. The economy was said by Treasurer Peter Costello to be in good shape, but the Australian dollar sank to a four-year low, unemployment remained above 8 per cent and by the end of the year there was growing concern about the impact of Asian financial crises on Australia. Inflation and interest rates remained low and share prices high. The sale of one-third of the telecommunications public utility Telstra was launched on 17 November, realizing $A8,570 million for the government and making one-quarter of all adults private-sector shareholders. A slowly growing number of workplace agreements were signed under the Workplace Relations Act, as trade union membership continued to decline (see AR 1996, p. 359).

Economic issues were, for once, less important to the media and public opinion than ethnic and specifically Aboriginal problems. The enthusiasm generated by the election of Pauline Hanson to parliament in March 1996 (see AR 1996, p. 358) evaporated by mid-year in a welter of mutual recrimination within the far right and through media boredom. Her 'Pauline Hanson One Nation Party' was launched on 11 April but did not contest any elections during the year. Its meetings were attacked by demonstrators and its opinion-poll support had dropped to 3 per cent by the end of the year. Attempting to capture public attention, Ms Hanson recorded a television message to be broadcast 'after her assassination'. While this did not happen, excerpts were broadcast nevertheless, further detracting from her credibility. Thirty years after the last execution in Australia, she urged a referendum on the death penalty in December. By the end of the year the issue of Asian immigration was well buried, to the relief of government and business, who feared its impact on trade, tourism, student recruitment and investment.

In contrast, the issue of Aboriginal land rights was kept very much alive, to the increasing embarrassment of the national coalition government. The High Court decision in the Wik case (see AR 1996, p. 359) prompted the government to develop a ten-point plan to protect pastoral lease-holders and otherwise clarify the situation. Prime Minister John Howard launched the plan symbolically at the remote Queensland pastoral town of Longreach in May. A Native Title Bill was introduced to amend that of the previous government, but was itself severely amended in the Senate. This prompted Mr Howard to threaten an election for both houses of parliament if this was repeated—the only procedure left for resolving further deadlocks.

The major churches took up Aboriginal issues, a notable contribution being a report from the Human Rights and Equal Opportunity Commission on the 'stolen generations' of Aboriginal children removed from their parents between the 1880s and the 1960s. The refusal of the Prime Minister to issue a collective apology to the Aboriginal people was widely condemned. Instead, the government offered monetary compensation to assist those seeking relatives or having suffered under the previous policies. The government sought to change the leadership of the Aboriginal and Torres Strait Islander Commission and the Council for Reconciliation, but their chosen replacements were little more sympathetic than their predecessors.

The basic issues in the land rights controversy were whether pastoral leases on Crown land expunged Aboriginal land rights and whether consultation with Aborigines was needed over changes to land use under such leases, especially for mining, cash crops and tourist development. The state governments of Queensland and Western Australia were especially anxious to resolve the problem, as were mining and pastoral interests. Having unexpectedly won the Wik decision, Aboriginal interests were determined to defend the new legal situation. The only elections to be directly affected were held on 30 August in the Northern Territory, where Aborigines formed nearly one-quarter of the population. The Country Liberal Party (CLP) under Shane Stone increased its representation in the legislative assembly to 18 seats, against seven for the territorial Australian Labor Party (ALP). There was a slight swing towards the CLP, which took a strong stand against the Wik decision, but Labor had never won a Northern Territory election.

The Northern Territory government was frustrated in its plan to legalize euthanasia by the passage of a prohibiting bill through the Commonwealth parliament (see AR 1995, p. 362; 1996, p. 360). The legislation stopped the Australian Capital Territory (ACT) from approving a similar policy. The ACT was also prevented from introducing a controlled trial for heroin users by Commonwealth opposition. In its place, the Commonwealth in November announced a $A87.5 million campaign to 'get tough on drugs'.

The resistance of the government coalition to Aboriginal claims was its most publicized problem, but not necessarily its most important one. A poorly-explained attempt to increase nursing home fees for the elderly lost it much support among part of its natural constituency. In September scandals surrounding the travel expenses of parliamentarians forced the resignation of three ministers and the Prime Minister's most important staff member. A report handed down by the Auditor-General on 22 December exonerated the ministers from criminality but criticized their administration. Another government MP, Michael Cobb, was less fortunate and faced criminal charges. The scandal arose from attacks on a Labor defector, Senator Mal Colston, who also faced charges, as did a Liberal MP. It had an impact on the Labor deputy leader in the Senate, Nick Sherry, who attempted suicide on being investigated but eventually returned to the backbenches at the end of the year. One response by the government was the abolition of the responsible Department of Administrative Services altogether. The scandals increased public scepticism about politicians, which was also manifest in support for minor independents in elections and opinion polling.

The Prime Minister took an ambivalent line on the republican issue raised by his Labor predecessor, Paul Keating. Although a monarchist, Mr Howard pledged himself, as a member of the constitutional convention charged with recommending any change, to canvass public opinion on the question. The convention, which was due to convene in February 1998, was constructed in equal parts of 76 official nominees and 76 elected members. Republicans claimed that there was a monarchist bias among the nominees but secured a clear majority among the elected. In a departure from normal practice, voting was postal and voluntary under a complex system of proportional representation, producing a response of only 46 per cent. Political parties did not contest and there were several different republican and monarchist slates, as well as many independent candidates. Final results, declared on 22 December, gave republicans 45 seats, monarchists 27 and unknown 4. Republicans led monarchists in all states and territories except South Australia (4 to 4) and Tasmania (2 to 3). There was a considerable variation in voter response, which was highest in Victoria and the ACT and lowest in Queensland, New South Wales and the Northern Territory. National support for republican candidates was 56.4 per cent and a majority of state Liberal leaders declared their support for a republic, which was also the official policy of the Labor opposition. Any change to the constitution recommended by the convention required approval in a compulsory referendum.

In state politics, the Liberal-National coalition government of Jeff Kennett in Victoria suffered two by-election defeats at provincial Gippsland West on 1 February and suburban Mitcham on 13 December, both with huge swings. These results were interpreted as showing discontent with the style of the premier and, in the second case, with his downgrading of the functions of the state auditor-general, who had criticized his government. Victoria faced a potential crisis with the news in December that the Crown Casino, a major source of public revenue, was making substantial losses due to a run of luck by overseas gamblers.

In South Australia, the Liberal government led by John Olsen came close to defeat on 11 October, winning only 23 seats in the 47-member house of assembly, against Labor's 21, two independent Liberals elected from rural areas and one for the National Party. The government also failed to win control of the upper legislative council, where the Australian Democrats increased their representation to three, having won 16 per cent of the vote. The South Australian Liberals continued to be rent by factional disputes, as were the Liberals in Western Australia,

New South Wales and Queensland. Most of the disputes centred on the selection of candidates, but there was also an ideological element involving moderates in South Australia and right-wing factions in the other states (see AR 1996, p. 360). The ALP remained fairly undisturbed, except for the resignation from the party of New South Wales legislative council member Franca Arena, who campaigned on the basis of revelations of paedophile activity from the Royal Commission investigating the New South Wales police force (see AR 1995, p. 360).

The most serious blow to the coalition was the defection to Labor in October of the popular leader of the Australian Democrats, Senator Cheryl Kernot, who was promptly nominated for a marginal Queensland seat for the next election. Government support in the opinion polls dropped to 37.5 per cent against 46 per cent for Labor, remaining behind until showing a modest recovery in mid-December, although 54 per cent were still 'dissatisfied' with Mr Howard. In part, this reflected the persistent criticism of the Prime Minister by most of the national print media during the year.

Australia continued to seek close relations with Asia and pledged financial assistance to Thailand, South Korea and Indonesia following their financial crises in the second half of the year (see XVIII.1). Aid with food distribution was also extended to Papua New Guinea, peace-keeping offices being extended in the Bougainville conflict involving the provision of unarmed troops to a peace-monitoring group on the island (see X.1.ii). Relations with Indonesia remained good despite popular agitation against its activities in East Timor (see IX.1.vi). In April Australia declined to co-sponsor the annual resolution on human rights observance in China at the UN Commission on Human Rights, an improvement in relations with China having been confirmed by an official visit to Beijing by Mr Howard in March. Australia found itself isolated at the Kyoto conference on climate change in December, but secured a compromise allowing it to increase its 'greenhouse' gas emissions by 8 per cent (see XIV.3; XIX.6). The outcome was hailed as a victory by Mr Howard, but did nothing to improve the government's relations with the conservation movement. The immigration intake continued to be tightened and reduced. Australia was condemned by the UN Commission on Human Rights for its detention of Cambodian asylum-seekers for up to four years. The Dutch Prime Minister, Wim Kok, visited Australia on 11 November.

Among those who died during the year were the former Chief Justice, Sir Garfield Barwick (see XX: Obituary), and the distinguished public servant Herbert Cole ('Nugget') Coombs, who was given a state funeral. Others who died included INXS lead singer Michael Hutchence, found dead in a Sydney hotel, and the last of the original ANZAC soldiers to land at Gallipoli in April 1915, Ted Mathews, aged 101, who was also given a state funeral. Eighteen people died in a landslide in the Snowy Mountains ski resort of Thredbo on 31 July and four Australians died in the collapse of a bridge at the Maccabiah sports meeting in Israel on 4 July (see also V.1).

The most important development in sport was the agreement between the

Australian Rugby League and the Super-League for a joint competition, though some details remained to be resolved (see AR 1995, p. 361). The dispute between the two bodies had been accompanied by declining match attendances and considerable disaffection among supporters.

ii. PAPUA NEW GUINEA

CAPITAL: Port Moresby   AREA: 463,000 sq km   POPULATION: 4,100,000 ('96)
OFFICIAL LANGUAGES: Pidgin, Motu, English   POLITICAL SYSTEM: parliamentary democracy
HEAD OF STATE: Queen Elizabeth II GOVERNOR-GENERAL: Wiwa Korowi
RULING PARTIES: People's National Congress (PNC) heads coalition with People's Progress Party (PPP) & Pangu Pati (PP)
HEAD OF GOVERNMENT: Bill Skate (PNC), Prime Minister (since July '97)
MAIN IGO MEMBERSHIPS (non-UN): APEC, CP, SPC, SPF, ACP, CWTH, NAM
CURRENCY: kina (end-'97 £1=K2.87, US$1=K1.75)
GNP PER CAPITA: US$1,160 ('95) or US$2,420 ('95) by PPP calculation

THE year was perhaps the most difficult in Papua New Guinea's 22 years of independence. Military, political and environmental crises all afflicted a country already beset with major social and economic problems.

Difficulties began at the end of February when Prime Minister Sir Julius Chan admitted—following Australian press reports—that the government was employing foreign mercenaries in the fight against the secessionist rebellion on Bougainville. The contract was with a London company, which had subcontracted to one based in South Africa. The mercenaries' function, according to the government, was merely to provide training. Subsequent accounts, however, indicated a much more direct role. In mid-March the crisis deepened when the commander of the Papua New Guinea Defence Force (PNGDF), Brigadier-General Jerry Singherok, implicitly threatening a military coup, demanded that the Prime Minister should resign. He was immediately dismissed by a furious Sir Julius, who revealed Gen. Singherok's own involvement in contracting the mercenaries.

Despite easily surviving a parliamentary vote of confidence, the Prime Minister was faced with mounting disorder on the streets and agreed to step down pending an inquiry into the affair. The mercenary leader, 'Lieut.-Colonel' Tim Spicer, had been arrested but was allowed to leave the country after giving evidence to the inquiry. On 2 June Sir Julius announced that he was resuming the premiership, since the inquiry's report—which he then leaked—had effectively cleared him of wrong-doing. As leader of the People's Progress Party (PPP), his insistence on returning to office was dictated by the impending general election, which was to take place over a two-week period from 14 June. As in the past, the outcome was unpredictable. Parties abounded, but allegiance to them by both candidates and voters was weak—and there was an average of some 22 hopefuls contesting each of the 109 seats.

Released on 15 July, the results showed a familiar multiplicity of representation, the PPP's 16 seats being the highest tally, followed by Pangu Pati, the other main ruling party, with 15. Seven other parties won between two and nine seats each, while six 'others' and 38 independents were also elected. Defeated candidates included Sir Julius Chan and several cabinet ministers. After the customary Machiavellian wrangling, Port Moresby mayor Bill Skate, whose People's National Congress (PNC) had won only five seats, became the new Prime Minister, in coalition with the PPP, Pangu and various independents.

Mr Skate's honeymoon, if such it was, proved to be short-lived. By November he was fighting to remain in power after being filmed boasting of his connections with Port Moresby's notorious criminal gangs and of arranging the murder of a rival. He reacted by dismissing Deputy Prime Minister Chris Haiveta (the Pangu leader) and Agriculture Minister Andrew Baing (the new PPP leader), accusing them of orchestrating a smear campaign against him. The turmoil intensified in early December when Pangu and PPP first announced that they were joining the opposition and then decided, for the most part, to stay in the government. Mr Skate carried out a major government reshuffle on 15 December, elevating supportive Pangu and PPP members and dismissing those who had opposed him.

Whatever the impact of the mercenaries on the politics of the central government, they seemed to have done little to change the military situation on Bougainville, which remained stalemated. In July ten days of talks took place in Christchurch, New Zealand, between the Port Moresby government and the various island factions, including the Bougainville Revolutionary Army (BRA). However, Francis Ona, the BRA leader, followed his usual practice of absenting himself from the negotiations, thus weakening the ceasefire agreement which emerged. A second round of talks was held in October, but again Mr Ona failed to appear. At the end of 1997, therefore, after a decade of guerrilla war, the Bougainville crisis seemed no closer to resolution.

Natural as well as man-made horrors afflicted Papua New Guinea during 1997. The El Niño phenomenon, which disrupted the climate of the entire Pacific region during the year (see XIV.3), brought unprecedented drought and consequent famine, particularly to the remote subsistence farming regions of the highlands. By the end of the year about one million people were threatened by serious food shortage.

In the foreign policy field, relations with Australia were damaged by the revelation of the mercenary affair, Canberra reiterating its longstanding position that a settlement in Bougainville could be reached only through negotiation. The crisis also affected relations with neighbouring Solomon Islands, although in July, following tensions over PNGDF incursions (see AR 1996, p. 362), a further border agreement was signed in the Solomons capital, Honiara, reiterating mutual respect for territorial integrity.

2. NEW ZEALAND—PACIFIC ISLAND STATES

i. NEW ZEALAND

CAPITAL: Wellington   AREA: 270,000 sq km   POPULATION: 3,570,000 ('96)
OFFICIAL LANGUAGE: English   POLITICAL SYSTEM: parliamentary democracy
HEAD OF STATE: Queen Elizabeth II GOVERNOR-GENERAL: Sir Michael Hardie Boys
RULING PARTIES: National Party (NP) & New Zealand First
HEAD OF GOVERNMENT: Jim Bolger (NP), since Oct '90
MAIN IGO MEMBERSHIPS (non-UN): ANZUS (suspended), APEC, SPC, SPF, CP, OECD, CWTH
CURRENCY: New Zealand dollar (end-'97 £1=NZ$2.84, US$1=NZ$1.73)
GNP PER CAPITA: US$14,340 ('95) or US$16,360 ('95) by PPP calculation

NEW Zealand acquired its first woman Prime Minister when Jenny Shipley (45), a National Party (NP) cabinet minister since 1990, assumed office on 8 December. Her predecessor, Jim Bolger, had been the party's leader since 1986 and had become Prime Minister following the 1990 general election. Mr Bolger agreed to resign in early November when he was advised that a substantial majority of NP members of parliament preferred Ms Shipley, his resignation averting certain defeat in a formal leadership vote of the NP parliamentary caucus. He was given a further month in office, leaving Ms Shipley as Prime Minister-in-waiting and allowing him to represent New Zealand at an APEC meeting in Vancouver. On formally taking office on 8 December, Ms Shipley carried out a substantial reshuffle of the government, in which Mr Bolger was included as Minister of State with special responsibility for APEC affairs.

First elected to parliament in 1987, Ms Shipley was more firmly committed than Mr Bolger to privatization and free-market economics and was regarded by her colleagues as a more tough-minded leader. She had held two high-spending portfolios, social welfare and health, in each area attracting criticism from those unhappy with her cost-conscious policies. Her capture of the party leadership could be characterized as a cool and competent coup, consummated on Mr Bolger's return from what had been a successful appearance representing New Zealand at the Commonwealth heads of government meeting in Edinburgh (see XI.2.i), followed by a fence-mending official visit to Paris.

The change of leadership reflected the steep decline in the popularity of both Mr Bolger and the coalition government of the NP and the New Zealand First (NZF) party, despite the fulfilment of some popular promises, including the removal of doctors' fees for children aged six and under. In May the leader of the opposition Labour Party, Helen Clark, moved past Mr Bolger in the opinion polls as the public's preferred Prime Minister, her lead widening in subsequent months. Ironically, the departure of Mr Bolger owed a great deal to the particular erosion of support for NZF, which had waged a strong campaign against both the Prime Minister and the NP in the 1996 election campaign, before agreeing to enter into a coalition partnership which kept them in power (see AR 1996, pp. 363–5). Although only four of the 17 New Zealand First MPs had parliamentary experience, the coalition agreement had awarded cabinet posts to five of the 17 (and non-cabinet ministerial posts to a further four), with the result that several incumbent NP ministers had not been reappointed. Concerns about the policy compromises made by the two parties in their coalition negotiations were therefore complemented by criticism focusing on the competence and conduct of some members of the NZF caucus. In August 1997 one NZF cabinet minister had been dismissed, for attacking the government's health policies. A month later the NP side of the coalition suffered a loss when Christine Fletcher, the only other woman MP on the NP executive apart from Ms Shipley, resigned her junior ministerial post over the government's policy-making style. She was soon calling for a change of leadership (but was not, as it turned out, included in Ms Shipley's reshuffled administration in December).

One source of irritation with Mr Bolger among MPs of his own party was his close association with the NFF leader, Deputy Prime Minister Winston Peters, the first Maori to be appointed to the position. Mr Peters had been dismissed from Mr Bolger's first government in 1991 and had formed the populist NFZ in 1993 after being excluded from the NP parliamentary caucus. By September 1997 opinion polls were showing that support for NZF had fallen below the 5 per cent level needed to win party-list seats in parliament under New Zealand's system of proportional representation. While this requirement did not apply to parties winning at least one constituency seat, the polls also suggested that Mr Peters, once the country's most popular politician, might lose his own constituency at the next election.

In a referendum in September New Zealanders voted by an overwhelming margin (92 per cent) to reject a new compulsory superannuation retirement programme. The proposal had been an NZF initiative and the result was interpreted, inevitably, as a verdict on the Bolger-Peters coalition government. National Party MPs had been at liberty to campaign for or against the programme. Mr Bolger had been associated with the proposal, while Ms Shipley was prominent in the opposition to it.

The Bolger government won praise within New Zealand and around the Pacific for its sponsorship of two rounds of peace talks involving representatives of the combatants in the long-running conflict on the Papua New Guinea island of Bougainville (see XI.1.ii). The talks led to an agreement for the dispatch of a multinational unarmed peace-monitoring mission to the island, with New Zealand service personnel among those taking part. The rare plaudits from all parties in the House for the Minister of Foreign Affairs, Don McKinnon, included suggestions of a possible Nobel Peace Prize nomination (although this did not save him from losing the NP deputy leadership after Ms Shipley became Prime Minister). The New Zealand government (as well as many individual New Zealanders) took a vigorous part in the international campaign against antipersonnel landmines, the government signing the resultant international agreement in Ottawa in early December (see XII.2; XIX.5). The government also participated in the Kyoto conference on global warming, where it called upon developing, as well as industrialized, nations to accept the need for limitations on the emission of greenhouse gases (see XIV.3; XIX.6).

Within the country there were some unusual ecological issues to resolve. In a rare act of rural civil disobedience, farmers escalated their war against the country's rabbits (an introduced species) by importing and releasing a virus in defiance of a government ban. Their 'germ warfare', against what had become an enormous rabbit population, began in South Island and was legalized retrospectively when the government concluded that it would be unable to stop the virus from spreading to North Island as well. Another incident arising out of environmental imbalance ended differently when public protests against a programme to cull a breed of wild horses led to many of the animals being saved.

New Zealand's race relations remained a sensitive subject which emerged in a variety of settings. Some of the strongest criticism of New Zealand's many new MPs, elected in the first proportional representation election in 1996, focused on the aggressive stance of some of the more prominent among the record number (15) of Maori MPs. In June the most prominent among them, Deputy Prime Minister Peters, was formally rebuked by a parliamentary committee for assaulting another MP, while Alamein Kopu, a Maori MP elected on the Alliance list, attracted widespread criticism when she resigned from her party but refused to resign from parliament. There were also some unusual incidents outside parliament involving Maoris. The America's Cup yachting trophy, the oldest in any sport and on display in Auckland after it had been won by a New Zealand crew in 1995, was smashed with a sledgehammer by a Maori activist viewing it as a symbol of oppression. In another episode, a photographer was clubbed by a Maori taking part as a 'warrior' during an otherwise stately procession to the new national museum in Wellington.

Responses to perceived Maori radicalism were varied and wide-ranging. The government expressed reservations about a draft UN declaration on the rights of indigenous peoples lest it encourage Maori claims to sovereignty and rights of self-determination. Maori groups were advised by Mr Peters that the government would review their funding if they did not control radical elements who had disrupted commemorations of the signing of the Treaty of Waitangi in the past (see AR 1995, p. 367; 1996, p. 365). Concern about the strength of the country's gangs, which were predominantly Maori, led to legislation giving the police greater powers to enter and disarm their heavily-fortified headquarters. The organizational activity of small groups of skinheads and neo-Nazi extremists was deplored by the country's independent race relations conciliator following several attacks on non-white immigrants.

At the same time, however, further progress was made on the settlement of longstanding Maori land claims. Agreement was reached with the South Island's Ngai Tahu tribe, which received a formal apology from the government, over NZ$170 million in compensation and the renaming of a large number of sites precious to the tribe. Among these was the country's highest mountain, which became known by the twin name of Aoraki/Mount Cook. The government also enacted legislation giving Maori owners of land leased in perpetuity by farmers greater control over their property.

Remarkably, these moves towards reconciliation and the resolution of Treaty of Waitangi grievances were led by Prime Minister Bolger, a North Island farmer whose government had been condemned by Maori spokesmen several years earlier over its decision to impose a non-negotiable cap of NZ$1,000 million for the settlement of all remaining Maori land claims. On his last day in parliament as New Zealand's Prime Minister, however, Mr Bolger became the recipient of thanks from Maoris for his leadership, in a speech which so moved him that he was unable to complete his reply to it.

ii. PACIFIC ISLAND STATES

Fiji
CAPITAL: Suva   AREA: 18,375 sq km   POPULATION: 785,000 ('96)
OFFICIAL LANGUAGES: Fijian, Hindi & English   POLITICAL SYSTEM: republic
HEAD OF STATE: President Ratu Sir Kamisese Mara (since Nov '93)
RULING PARTY: Fijian Political Party (SVT)
HEAD OF GOVERNMENT: Maj.-Gen. Sitiveni Rabuka (SVT), Prime Minister (since May '92)
MAIN IGO MEMBERSHIPS (non-UN): SPC, SPF, CP, ACP, CWTH
CURRENCY: Fiji dollar (end-'97 £1=F$2.54, US$1=F$1.55)
GNP PER CAPITA: US$2,440 ('95) or US$5,780 ('95) by PPP calculation

Kiribati
CAPITAL: Tarawa   AREA: 1,000 sq km   POPULATION: 80,000 ('96)
OFFICIAL LANGUAGES: English & Kiribati   POLITICAL SYSTEM: republic
HEAD OF STATE & GOVERNMENT: President Teburoro Tito (since Sept '94)
RULING PARTY: Christian Democratic Unity Party (CDUP)
MAIN IGO MEMBERSHIPS: SPC, SPF, ACP, CWTH
CURRENCY: Australian dollar (end-'97 £1=A$2.52, US$1=A$1.54)
GNP PER CAPITA: US$920 ('95)

Marshall Islands
CAPITAL: Dalap-Uliga-Darrit   AREA: 200 sq km   POPULATION: 58,000 ('96)
OFFICIAL LANGUAGES: English & Marshallese
POLITICAL SYSTEM: republic
HEAD OF STATE & GOVERNMENT: President Imata Kabua (since Jan '97)
MAIN IGO MEMBERSHIPS (non-UN): PC, SPF
CURRENCY: US dollar
GNP PER CAPITA: US$1,680 ('94)

Federated States of Micronesia
CAPITAL: Palikir (Pohnpei)   AREA: 701 sq km   POPULATION: 118,000 ('96)
OFFICIAL LANGUAGES: English
POLITICAL SYSTEM: republic
HEAD OF STATE & GOVERNMENT: President Jacob Nena (since May '97)
MAIN IGO MEMBERSHIPS (non-UN): SPC, SPF
CURRENCY: US dollar
GNP PER CAPITA: n/a

Nauru
CAPITAL: Domaneab   AREA: 21.4 sq km   POPULATION: 11,000 ('96)
OFFICIAL LANGUAGES: Nauruan & English   POLITICAL SYSTEM: republic
HEAD OF STATE & GOVERNMENT: President Kinza Clodumar (since Feb '97)
MAIN IGO MEMBERSHIPS: PC, SPF
CURRENCY: Australian dollar (end-'97 £1=A$2.52, US$1=A$1.54)
GNP PER CAPITA: US$20,000 ('89)

Samoa
CAPITAL: Apia   AREA: 2,842 sq km   POPULATION: 166,000 ('96)
OFFICIAL LANGUAGES: English & Samoan   POLITICAL SYSTEM: constitutional monarchy
HEAD OF STATE: Susuga Malietoa Tanumafili II (since Jan '62)
RULING PARTY: Human Rights Protection Party
HEAD OF GOVERNMENT: Tofilau Eti Alesana, Prime Minister (since April '88)
MAIN IGO MEMBERSHIPS (non-UN): SPC, SPF, ACP, CWTH
CURRENCY: tala (end-'97 £1=T4.52, US$1=T2.76)
GNP PER CAPITA: US$1,120 ('95) or US$2,030 ('95) by PPP calculation

Solomon Islands
CAPITAL: Honiara   AREA: 28,000 sq km   POPULATION: 385,000 ('96)
OFFICIAL LANGUAGE: English   POLITICAL SYSTEM: parliamentary democracy
HEAD OF STATE: Queen Elizabeth II GOVERNOR-GENERAL: Moses Puibangara Pitakaka
RULING PARTY: Liberal Party (LP) heads Alliance for Change coalition
HEAD OF GOVERNMENT: Bartholomew Ulufa'alu (LP), Prime Minister (since Aug '97)
MAIN IGO MEMBERSHIPS (non-UN): SPC, SPF, ACP, CWTH
CURRENCY: Solomon Islands dollar (end-'97 £1=SI$7.71, S$1=SI$4.70)
GNP PER CAPITA: US$910 ('95) or US$2,190 ('95) by PPP calculation

Tonga
CAPITAL: Nuku'alofa   AREA: 750 sq km   POPULATION: 99,000 ('96)
OFFICIAL LANGUAGES: Tongan & English   POLITICAL SYSTEM: monarchy
HEAD OF STATE: King Taufa'ahua Tupou IV (since Dec '65)
HEAD OF GOVERNMENT: Baron Vaea, Prime Minister (since Aug '91)
MAIN IGO MEMBERSHIPS: SPC, SPF, ACP, CWTH
CURRENCY: pa'anga (end-'97 £1=T$2.52, US$1=T$1.54)
GNP PER CAPITA: US$1,630 ('95)

Tuvalu
CAPITAL: Fongafle   AREA: 26 sq km   POPULATION: 9,750 ('96)
OFFICIAL LANGUAGE: English   POLITICAL SYSTEM: constitutional monarchy
HEAD OF STATE: Queen Elizabeth II GOVERNOR-GENERAL: Sir Tulaga Manuella
HEAD OF GOVERNMENT: Bikenibeu Paeniu, Prime Minister (since Dec '96)
MAIN IGO MEMBERSHIPS: SPC, SPF, ACP
CURRENCY: Australian dollar (end-'97 £1=A$2.52, US$1=A$1.54)
GNP PER CAPITA: n/a

Vanuatu
CAPITAL: Port Vila   AREA: 12,000 sq km   POPULATION: 167,000 ('96)
OFFICIAL LANGUAGES: English, French & Bislama   POLITICAL SYSTEM: republic
HEAD OF STATE: President Jean-Marie Leye Lenelgau (since March '94)
RULING PARTIES: Union of Moderate Parties (UMP) & Melanesian Progressive Party (PPP)
HEAD OF GOVERNMENT: Serge Vohor (UMP), Prime Minister (since Dec '95)
MAIN IGO MEMBERSHIPS (non-UN): SPC, SPF, ACP, CWTH, Francophonie
CURRENCY: vatu (end-'97 £1=VT203.20, US$1=VT123.85)
GNP PER CAPITA: US$1,150 ('94) or US$2,640 ('94) by PPP calculation

PACIFIC Island leaders raised the issue of global warming on a number of occasions, pointing out that even a relatively modest rise in sea levels could make some low-lying coral atolls uninhabitable (see also XIV.3). There were suggestions that changes in weather patterns might already be taking place, as a succession of tropical storms battered several island states. Cyclone Hina caused considerable damage to Tonga in March, hundreds of families losing their homes. Tuvalu suffered from Cyclone Keli in June, when many buildings were destroyed. In the Cook Islands, Cyclone Martin wiped out two tiny atolls in November, causing 19 deaths, before moving on to French Polynesia, where another nine people were killed. Cyclone Pam struck the Cook Islands a month later, devastating most of the export fruit crops on the main island of Rarotonga.

Moves towards reconciliation on the Papua New Guinea island of Bougainville (see X.1.ii) were welcomed by Pacific island states. The five-nation observer group sent to the island to monitor compliance with the truce agreement included participants from Fiji, Tonga and Vanuatu, the only island states with personnel able to assist.

The US island of Guam was the scene of an airline tragedy on 5 August when a Korean Air flight crashed and 226 passengers and crew were killed. The airline subsequently discontinued all service to Guam and to Saipan (in the neighbouring Northern Marianas).

There were several changes of government in the region in 1997. Provisions in the constitution of the Federated States of MICRONESIA stipulating that the Vice-President should take over in the event of presidential disability were used for the first time when President Bailey Olter suffered a stroke and was declared incapacitated. As a result, Vice-President Jacob Nena formally assumed the presidency in May, becoming the first to hold the office from the federation's smallest state, Kosrae.

The MARSHALL ISLANDS also obtained a new President following the death in office of Amata Kabua in December 1996 (see AR 1996, p. 367). On 14 January the Nitijela (parliament) elected the late President's cousin, Imata Kabua, who announced that all members of the previous cabinet would be reappointed in the interests of continuity. A powerful traditional chief from Kwajalein atoll, the new President was reputed to be one of the richest people in the Marshall Islands, as a result of US rental payments for a missile test site on the atoll.

Despite concerns expressed by other Pacific island states, the government of the Marshall Islands continued to explore the possibility of a nuclear-waste disposal facility being established on one of its many coral atolls. Meanwhile, islanders from Enewetak atoll, the site of US atmospheric nuclear tests in 1948–58, persisted in their efforts to obtain hundreds of millions of dollars in compensation for loss of land and health damage.

In the Commonwealth of the NORTHERN MARIANA ISLANDS (a US dependency), former governor Pedro P. Tenorio, a Republican, regained office in the November elections, defeating incumbent governor Friolan C. Tenorio, a Democrat.

A political deadlock on NAURU, which had seen a succession of Presidents, was broken following an early general election in February. The new parliament elected Kinza Clodumar as the island's President.

Parliamentary elections in the SOLOMON ISLANDS in August also produced a change of government. The leader of the Liberal Party, Bartholomew Ulufa'alu, was elected Prime Minister, at the head of a coalition of small parties and independents known as the Alliance for Change.

In VANUATU, the Prime Minister, Serge Vohor, reorganized his government in May, dropping the Vanuaaku Party of the then Deputy Prime Minister, Donald

Kalpokas, from his coalition and bringing in the Melanesian Progressive Party of Barak Sope. Mr Vohor also reinstated his predecessor as Prime Minister, Maxime Carlot Korman, appointing him as Minister of Foreign Affairs.

The elections scheduled in FIJI for 1999 were to be held under a new constitution finally approved in June—one less discriminatory towards citizens of Indian descent. The new text retained protection for communal land held by indigenous Fijians, but removed provisions prohibiting Indo-Fijians from high political office. Approval of the new constitution made it possible for Fiji to be readmitted to the Commonwealth and for Prime Minister Sitiveni Rabuka to attend the Commonwealth heads of government meeting in Edinburgh in October (see XI.2.i). Mr Rabuka also made a formal apology to Queen Elizabeth II at Windsor Castle for her removal as Fiji's head of state following his 1987 military coup (although Fiji remained a republic under its new constitution).

In TONGA, pressure continued to be placed on journalists and legislators critical of the government and the country's constitution. The country's only independent newspaper, *The Times of Tonga*, was advised that its licence to publish would be reviewed.

A desire for improved communication led to the installation of a direct-dial telephone and fax service in the New Zealand dependency of TOKELAU, the last territory in the world to introduce a telephone service. The dependency had previously relied on short-wave radio links to Samoa. The service, made possible by aid from New Zealand, the UN Development Programme and the International Telecommunication Union, was expected to contribute to greater unity among the people of its three widely-separated atolls.

The sense of unity among Samoans was somewhat strained when the government of Western SAMOA acted to remove 'Western' from the country's name, 35 years after it became the first Pacific island territory under colonial rule to regain its independence. Initiated by Prime Minister Tofilau Eti Alesana, the move sparked complaints among law-makers in American Samoa, who argued that the change implied that residents of the US territory were less 'Samoan' than their neighbours to the west. In the Samoan capital, Apia, there were protests, too, as 6,000 people retraced the route of a famous march against New Zealand rule nearly 70 years earlier. Led by traditional leaders, the protests were directed at the government's alleged economic mismanagement, as well as at reported corruption in connection with the sale of Samoan passports.

In a potentially more far-reaching development, Samoa celebrated the establishment of its first university, the National University of Samoa, made possible largely through aid from the United States and Japan.

XI INTERNATIONAL ORGANIZATIONS

1. UNITED NATIONS AND ITS AGENCIES

DATE OF FOUNDATION: 1945   HEADQUARTERS: New York, USA
OBJECTIVES: To promote international peace, security and cooperation on the basis of the equality of member-states, the right of self-determination of peoples and respect for human rights
MEMBERSHIP (END-'97): 185 sovereign states; those not in membership of the UN itself at end-1997 were the Holy See (Vatican), Kiribati, Nauru, Switzerland, Tonga and Tuvalu, although all were members of one or more UN specialized agency
SECRETARY-GENERAL: Kofi Annan (Ghana)

ALTHOUGH reform of the United Nations seemed to dominate the year, other important developments also deserved to be noticed. The General Assembly established new assessment scales and used the Uniting for Peace Procedure for the first time in 15 years, while the 2nd Assembly committee in New York used new technology to conduct a joint meeting with UNCTAD in Geneva. The Security Council held what was only its third meeting at full ministerial level and was briefed for the first time by non-governmental organizations. It also held a number of special debates; authorized a multinational protection force and a monitoring mission; imposed three new sanctions regimes; created five new peace-keeping missions and enlarged the size and mandate of one other; and authorized new rules of engagement for a special police protection unit in Haiti.

52ND GENERAL ASSEMBLY. Hennadiy Udovenko (Ukraine) was elected president of the 52nd General Assembly session, to which 18 heads of state, one crown prince, 14 prime ministers, 16 deputy prime ministers, 111 foreign ministers, four other ministers and 12 heads of delegation made statements during the 12-day general debate held in September. On 14 October the Assembly elected Bahrain, Brazil, Gabon, The Gambia and Slovenia as the new non-permanent members of the Security Council for two years from 1 January 1998 to replace Chile, Egypt, Guinea-Bissau, South Korea and Poland. The other five non-permanent members serving in 1997 were Costa Rica, Japan, Kenya, Portugal and Sweden.

Those addressing the Assembly included Robin Cook, the new UK Foreign and Commonwealth Secretary, who stated that Britain's recently-elected Labour government was firmly committed to the United Nations. While maintaining his predecessor's view that Britain should retain its permanent membership status, Mr Cook favoured a modernized, legitimate Security Council that included Japan and Germany in an expanded permanent membership with a balance between developed and developing countries. He also said that Britain wanted sound UN finances and expected every country, however large or small, to pay UN dues in full and on time. Mr Cook welcomed the UN's policy of putting 'gender perspective' into all areas of its work.

XI.1. UNITED NATIONS AND ITS AGENCIES

UN REFORM. Secretary-General Kofi Annan presented his report on reform of the United Nations to a special meeting of the 51st General Assembly on 16 July, claiming that his proposals amounted to a 'quiet revolution' in that they envisaged the most extensive and far-reaching reform in the history of the organization. Their purpose was to strengthen the organization and to prepare it to meet the challenges of the future, in particular to create a 'development dividend' by shifting resources from administration to economic and social activities. Potential savings on the regular UN budget were estimated at $200 million by 2002.

In a resolution adopted by consensus on 12 November, the 52nd General Assembly endorsed the Secretary-General's proposals which did not have direct budgetary implications for member-states. These included the appointment of a senior management group in the UN secretariat that would function like a cabinet and the creation of a strategic planning unit in the Secretary-General's office to identify and analyse emerging global issues and trends. Also agreed was a restructuring of the secretariat's work programme around five core areas (peace and security, economic and social affairs, development cooperation, humanitarian affairs and human rights), accompanied by a reduction in its size, administrative costs and production of documentation. All the major UN groups had reservations about some aspects of the proposals, so that the Secretary-General was requested to report back on their implementation to the 53rd Assembly session.

The reform proposals with budgetary implications were the subject of a wide-ranging resolution adopted by the General Assembly on 19 December, also without a vote. First, the Assembly agreed to the appointment of a Deputy Secretary-General, who would assist the Secretary-General in leading and managing the operations of the secretariat and would act for him in his absences. The Assembly noted that the Secretary-General would appoint the Deputy Secretary-General following consultations with member-states and that his or her term of office would not exceed that of the Secretary-General.

The second set of reforms covered specific areas of UN policy formulation. The Assembly endorsed Mr Annan's recommendations that the UN Disarmament Commission and the 1st Assembly committee (on disarmament and international security) should attempt to rationalize their work. It also invited the UN Economic and Social Council to consider the Secretary-General's proposals for reform of its organization and work, endorsing his recommendation that the High-Level Advisory Board on Sustainable Development should be discontinued. In the sphere of development cooperation, the Assembly gave qualified approval to the establishment of a new system of 'core resources', requesting closer integration of the UN Development Programme, the UN Population Fund and the United Nations Children's Fund. It also accepted the Secretary-General's proposal that the UN emergency relief coordinator should be renamed the humanitarian assistance coordinator, while retaining responsibility for natural disaster relief.

The most controversial of Mr Annan's proposals was for the creation of a 'revolving credit fund' of up to $1,000 million, financed by voluntary contributions, from which debtor governments would be able to borrow in order to pay UN arrears. The Assembly declined to approve this proposal on 19 December, instead asking the Secretary-General to submit further details by the end of March 1998. There were also mixed results for Mr Annan in the management section of the resolution. The Assembly established, in the programme for 1998/99, a development account to be funded from possible reductions in administration and other overhead costs but insisted that this should not affect full implementation of mandated programmes and activities. Again the Secretary-General was asked to provide a detailed report by March 1998, also covering his proposal for 'results-based' budgeting. The Assembly noted that the Secretary-General had submitted a draft code of conduct (to govern the performance of international civil servants) and agreed to expedite its consideration.

A final section of the 19 December resolution on longer-term changes asked the Secretary-General to present further details (again by the end of March 1998) on his proposals for a new concept of trusteeship; for a 'Millennium Assembly' and a related 'People's Millennium Forum for Representatives of Civil Society'; for a special ministerial commission to examine the constitutional relationship between the UN and the autonomous specialized agencies; and for the adoption of specific time-limits on General Assembly mandates, which would then require explicit review and renewal.

SECURITY COUNCIL ENLARGEMENT. Intensive debate continued in UN and other diplomatic circles on the possible enlargement of the permanent membership of the Security Council, without substantive result in 1997. Various scenarios were advanced by competing regional and sub-regional groups anxious to secure a permanent seat for their favoured candidate or candidates, some involving modification of the right of veto currently exercised by each permanent member. The five existing permanent members (China, France, Russia, the United States and the United Kingdom), while accepting the principle of Security Council enlargement, showed little inclination to expedite change (which required amendment of the Charter). Each made it clear that it would not support any plan which involved the disappearance of its own seat or which limited its veto.

BUDGET AND ASSESSMENT SCALES. On 22 December the General Assembly, with little time for debate, approved the UN budget for the 1998–99 biennium as well as new assessment scales, reaffirming the fundamental principle that the expenses of the organization should be apportioned among the member-states broadly according to their capacity to pay. Whereas the Secretary-General had proposed a no-growth budget of $2,583 million, which he described as negative growth in real terms, the Assembly appropriated only $2,532 million.

Agreement on new assessment scales was always likely to be difficult, not only because there would inevitably be winners and losers but also because of the added complication that the United States was demanding that its assessment be gradually reduced over the next three years. The major questions were how to measure each state's share of world income and over what period of time; what level of adjustment should be made for low per capita income and for debt burden; and to what degree should there be qualifications to the principle of capacity to pay.

In the new scales, gross national product was used for the first time; the statistical period was reduced from 7.5 to 6 years; the discount for low per capita income was reduced from 85 to 80 per cent of the world standard income (and the discount for debt burden was lowered for 1998 only); the maximum level of assessment remained at 25 per cent (which meant that the United States would continue to pay less than its proportionate share of world income); the minimum contribution was reduced from 0.01 to 0.001 per cent (which meant that the poorest states would continue to pay more than their share of world income); and the 'scheme of limits', limiting year-on-year variations in assessments, would be phased out over three years.

The United States failed to obtain an assessment reduction from 25 to 22 per cent by 1998 and to 20 per cent by the year 2000. There was fierce resistance to this proposal for several reasons. Other members resented US threats to leave the organization if its demands were not met and were dismayed by the failure of the US House of Representatives in November to act on draft legislation for payment of part of the US arrears. Richer members, particularly the European Union states, believed that the existing ceiling was already a significant exception to the principle of capacity to pay and that an even-lower ceiling would be unreasonable and contrary to the principle of equity.

The scales eventually agreed meant that 80 per cent of the UN budget would be contributed by ten states (the United States, Japan, Germany, France, Italy, the United Kingdom, the Russian Federation, Canada, Spain and the Netherlands) and that 30 states would pay the new minimum of 0.001 per cent.

FINANCIAL SITUATION. UN finances continued to be in a perilous state in 1997. At the end of December the combined regular budget and peace-keeping accounts had a positive balance of $669 million; but the peace-keeping current account showed a surplus of $791 million, so that the regular budget had a deficit of $122 million. A reduced deficit compared with 1996 was due to an underspend of $54 million in the 1996–97 biennium budget and unexpected contributions in December, notably from the United States. Without these unusual factors, the deficit would have been $74 million higher, at about $195 million. Total unpaid assessments at 31 December 1997 were some $2,000 million, of which about $426 million were regular budget arrears (79 per cent owed by the United States) and $1,574 million unpaid peace-keeping assessments (60 per cent owed by the United States). The total US debt was about $1,300 million.

The United Nations' total end-of-year debt to member-states for peace-keeping troops and equipment was $884 million, owed to more than 70 states. France was owed the largest amount ($127 million), while five states were owed more than $40 million, namely the United Kingdom, the Netherlands, Pakistan, Belgium and India. It was clear, therefore, that to support its regular budget activities the United Nations was borrowing from a fund that was already inadequate to pay its debts to states that had undertaken peace-keeping on its behalf.

On a brighter financial note, Ted Turner, the founder of the CNN news media network, announced on 19 September that he would donate $1,000 million to the United Nations to support its humanitarian work. The donation would be made in the form of Time Warner stock in ten annual instalments of $100 million.

10TH EMERGENCY SPECIAL SESSION. On 7 and 21 March US vetoes prevented the Security Council from adopting draft resolutions expressing deep concern about a newly-announced Israeli building project at Har Homa/Jabal Abu Ghneim in Arab East Jerusalem (see V.1; V.2.i)) and calling upon Israel to refrain from such settlement activities. On 13 March, after the first veto, the resumed 51st regular session of the General Assembly passed a similar resolution, which was ignored by the Israelis. After construction had started on 18 March and the second US veto on 21 March, the Arab and Non-Aligned states requested an emergency special session of the General Assembly under the Uniting for Peace Procedure, which had not been used for 15 years.

The 10th emergency special session convened on 25 April, and reconvened in July and November. It passed three resolutions, all by overwhelming majorities, condemning Israel's construction of the new settlement and all other illegal actions in the occupied territories, and demanding that Israel should accept the applicability to the occupied territories of the Geneva Convention on the Protection of Civilian Persons in Time of War.

19TH SPECIAL SESSION. The General Assembly held its 19th special session on 23–28 June, to review progress on the decisions of the 1992 'Earth Summit' in Rio de Janeiro (see AR 1992, pp. 458–60, 546–52). Addressed by 198 speakers, including 22 heads of state and 20 heads of government, the session acted by consensus to adopt a programme of further implementation which reaffirmed all the principles contained in the Rio Declaration on Environment and Development and in the accompanying Forest Principles. The Assembly's president, Razali Ismail of Malaysia, said that, although it was disappointing that the session had been unable to adopt a political statement, it had made an honest attempt at an appraisal of developments since the Rio conference, with nothing swept under the carpet (see also XIV.3).

INTERNATIONAL TREATIES. On 3 December a Convention on the Prohibition of the Use, Stockpiling, Production and Transfer of Anti-personnel Mines and their Destruction was opened for signature in Ottawa, having been adopted in Oslo in September (see XII.2; XIX.5). The treaty acknowledged the United Nations' role as a primary forum for continued efforts towards universal application, the Secretary-General being assigned depository, mediatory, diplomatic, investigative, facilitative and administrative functions in regard to the convention.

OTHER IMPORTANT DECISIONS. The 52nd General Assembly approved the launching of a draft International Convention for the Suppression of Terrorist Bombing and voted for the convening of a diplomatic conference of plenipotentiaries in Rome in June-July 1998 to finalize and adopt a convention to create the world's first permanent international criminal court. It also decided that the third UN Conference on the Exploration of Outer Space would take place in 1999 as a special session of the Outer Space Committee and that special sessions of the Assembly would be held on illicit drugs (in 1998), population and development (in 1999), social development (in 2000) and human settlements (2001).

SECURITY COUNCIL MINISTERIAL MEETING. On 25 September the Security Council held a ministerial-level meeting, its third in the 52-year history of the United Nations. In a presidential statement, the Council expressed grave concern at the number and the intensity of armed conflicts in Africa, which threatened regional peace, caused massive human dislocation and suffering, perpetuated instability and diverted resources from long-term development. The Secretary-General was requested to submit a report to the Council by February 1998 providing concrete recommendations on ways to prevent and address such conflicts, and suggesting how to lay the foundations for durable peace and economic growth following their resolution. The Council would then review promptly the recommendations of the Secretary-General and take steps consistent with its responsibilities under the UN Charter.

NON-GOVERNMENTAL ORGANIZATIONS. On 12 February three non-governmental organizations—Oxfam, Care and Médecins Sans Frontières—briefed members of the Security Council (acting informally), the officers of the Economic and Social Council and the General Assembly's second and third committees on the crisis in the Great Lakes region of Africa. Organized by Juan Somavia (the Chilean ambassador), the occasion was the first time that the Security Council had consulted with NGOs. Following this precedent, on 15 September the secretary-general of Amnesty International briefed members of the Security Council, officials from the specialized agencies and the UN secretariat on the human rights dimensions of preventing and managing conflict and rebuilding societies. The September meeting was arranged by Antonio Monteiro, the UN ambassador of Portugal.

SECURITY COUNCIL TRANSPARENCY. In a further attempt to meet the demand for greater transparency in its work, the Security Council decided on 21 June that each monthly presidency would produce a report on the work of the Council for that month, to be attached to the Council's annual report to the General Assembly. On 22 December the ten non-permanent members presented a memorandum on transparency calling for a more responsive, active and open decision-making process in the Council. Their demands included a re-examination of the Council's rules of procedure (last amended in 1982), the registration of the various types of informal consultations, written records of all formal meetings whether public or private, and greater participation by non-members in the formal meetings of the Council

IRAQ: 'OIL FOR FOOD'. UN-authorized oil exports from Iraq, the proceeds of which would be used partly to purchase humanitarian assistance for the people of Iraq, had commenced on 10 December 1996 for an initial period of 180 days (see AR 1996, p. 374). Acting under chapter 7, the Security Council on 4 June unanimously adopted resolution 1111 authorizing a second period of 180 days beginning on 8 June. The Council was subsequently informed by the Secretary-General that the target of $1,000 million from oil sales every 90 days would not be met in the third 90-day period because the Iraqi government had suspended sales from 8 June to 13 August. Acting again under chapter 7, the Council decided in resolution 1129 of 12 September, adopted by a vote of 14 to 0 with Russia abstaining, that the first 90-day period of the second 180-day period could be extended by 30 days, and that during the remaining 60 days not more than $1,000 million of oil could be sold. On December 4 the Council, by resolution 1143, approved a third 180-day period from 5 December.

IRAQ AND UNSCOM. Between June and December, in the face of persistent attempts by Iraq to restrict the activities of inspectors of the UN Special Commission (UNSCOM) and the expulsion of US members of the team (see V.2.vi), the Security Council insisted that Iraq was responsible for the safety and the security of UNSCOM personnel and equipment and that the United Nations alone determined the composition of the inspection teams. It also reiterated that the inspection teams must have immediate, unconditional and unrestricted access to any and all areas, facilities, equipment, records and means of transport which they wished to inspect, as well as to officials and other persons under the authority of the Iraqi government whom the inspectors wished to interview.

Iraq was condemned for repeated violation of its obligations. In resolution 1137 of 12 November, which was adopted unanimously, the Council acted under chapter 7 to impose travel restrictions on Iraqi officials who had not cooperated with UNSCOM. The sanctions would be lifted one day after the UNSCOM executive chairman reported to the Council that the Iraqi government and its officials were cooperating fully and unconditionally with the Special Commission.

LIBYA. In January, April and May the Security Council expressed concern about illegal international flights by Libyan aircraft in violation of the sanctions imposed in 1992 (see also V.4.ii).

CENTRAL AFRICAN REPUBLIC. In resolution 1125 the Security Council on 6 August determined that the situation in the Central African Republic (see VI.3.ii) continued to constitute a threat to international peace and the security of the region. It approved the continued operations of the Inter-African Mission to Monitor the

Bangui Accords (MISAB), including the supervision of the surrender of the arms of former mutineers, militias and all other persons unlawfully bearing arms. Acting under chapter 7 of the UN Charter, it authorized the participating states and those providing logistical support to ensure the security and freedom of movement of their personnel. In resolution 1136 of 6 November the Security Council extended the MISAB mandate for a further three months and requested the Secretary-General to establish a trust fund to assist with the costs of the mission.

ANGOLA. Having allowed two grace periods, the Security Council on 29 October (in resolution 1135) imposed sanctions on the National Union for the Total Independence of Angola (Unita) for failing to complete all of its obligations under the 1994 Lusaka Protocol and relevant Security Council resolutions (see VII.1.vi). The sanctions consisted of travel restrictions on senior officials and adult members of their families, the closure of all Unita offices abroad, and the prevention of flights by or for Unita.

The mandate of the UN Angola Verification Mission (UNAVEM) was progressively extended until 30 June. On 1 July the Council established the UN Observer Mission in Angola (UNOMA), which was to assist the parties in consolidating peace and reconciliation. The mandate was renewed on 31 October until the expected completion of its work on 1 February 1998.

SIERRA LEONE. In presidential statements on 27 May, 11 July and 6 August, the Security Council condemned the overthrow of the democratically-elected government of Sierra Leone (see VI.2.iii) and called for the immediate and unconditional restoration of constitutional order. The Council warned that, if the military regime did not renounce its declared intention to remain in power and resume negotiations with ECOWAS representatives without delay, appropriate measures would be taken to restore the democratically-elected government. On 8 October, by resolution 1132 and acting under chapter 7 of the Charter, the Council decided that travel restrictions should be imposed on members of the junta and adult members of their families and that a petroleum and arms embargo should be imposed against Sierra Leone. The resolution authorized ECOWAS, where necessary, to halt inward maritime shipping in order to inspect and verify their cargoes and destinations.

The Council welcomed the agreement of 23 October between ECOWAS and the junta by which the democratic government would be reinstated within six months; but a presidential statement of 14 November reminded states of their obligation to maintain the sanctions in the interim.

LIBERIA. On 30 September the UN Mission in Liberia, which had been in that state since 1993, successfully completed its mandate, a key element of which had been the holding of the presidential and legislative elections on 19 July (see VI.2.v).

WESTERN SAHARA. Following his appointment in March as the Secretary-General's personal envoy for Western Sahara, former US Secretary of State James Baker held talks in London, Lisbon and Houston in which the differences between the parties over the holding of a self-determination referendum in the territory were resolved (see V.4.vi). On 20 October, in resolution 1133, the Security Council decided to extend the mandate of the UN Mission for the Referendum in Western Sahara (MINURSO) until 20 April 1998. The holding of the referendum was provisionally scheduled for December 1998.

GUATEMALA. The Security Council on 20 January unanimously adopted resolution 1094 authorizing for a three-month period the attachment to the UN Mission for the Verification of Human Rights in Guatemala (MINUGUA) of 155 military observers and medical personnel to verify the implementation of the ceasefire agreement signed by the government and the Guatemalan National Revolutionary Unity (URNG) on 29 December 1996 (see AR 1996, p. 177). China had vetoed the original draft on 10 January because the Guatemalan government had invited the Taiwan authorities to the peace agreement signing ceremony. On 22 May the Council welcomed the successful implementation of the military observers' mission.

HAITI. Following the expiry of the mandate of the UN Mission in Haiti (UNMIH) on 31 July, the Security Council created two new missions. Established on 30 July by resolution 1123, the UN Transition Mission in Haiti was limited to a four-month mandate until 30 November. The second, created on 28 November by resolution 1141, was the UN Civilian Police Mission in Haiti, with a one-year mandate until 30 November 1998. Taking on part of the UNMIH mandate, both new missions were charged with assisting the government in the professionalization of the national police. Both included civilian police officers, who carried personal weapons and were protected by special units authorized to use force in self-defence under the same rules of engagement as had applied to the military missions.

ALBANIA. On 28 March the Security Council, by a vote of 14 to 0 (with China abstaining), adopted resolution 1101 asserting that the crisis in Albania (see IV.2.i) constituted a threat to international peace and security. It welcomed the offer by Italy to organize and command a temporary and limited multinational protection force which, acting in a neutral and impartial manner, was to safeguard the delivery of humanitarian assistance and to help create a secure environment for international organizations in Albania. It authorized the member-states to ensure the security and freedom of movement of the personnel of the force; limited the operation to three months; and decided that the cost of the operation would be borne by the participating states.

Following a 45-day extension, on 14 August the Council noted with appreciation that the mandate of the force had been successfully fulfilled.

GEORGIA. The Security Council on 30 January (resolution 1076) and 31 July (resolution 1124) approved six-month extensions of the mandate of the UN Observer Mission in Georgia (UNOMIG). On both occasions it expressed disappointment at the lack of progress in the implementation of the 1994 Moscow agreement on the status of Abkhazia (see AR 1994, p. 152) and encouraged the Secretary-General to continue his efforts to assist with resolving the dispute.

TAJIKISTAN. Having extended the mandate of the UN Mission of Observers in Tajikistan (UNMOT) in June and September, the Security Council on 14 November, under resolution 1138, expanded the size of the mission to enable it to assist in the implementation of the internal peace agreement concluded in June-July (see VIII.1.iii). The UNMOT mandate was extended until 15 May 1998.

FORMER YUGOSLAVIA. Charged with contributing to implementation of the civilian aspects of the 1995 Dayton Accords, the UN Mission in Bosnia & Herzegovina (UNMIBH) continued to consist of the International Police Task Force (IPTF), civil affairs and human rights officers, and the UN Mine Action Centre. By resolutions 1103 and 1107, the Security Council decided to increase the authorized strength of the IPTF from 1,721 to 2,027 to enable it to carry out additional tasks arising from the Brcko arbitration award (see III.2.ii) and the human rights monitoring assigned by the Peace Implementation Council's London conference held in December 1996. After an incident in Mostar on 10 February involving an violent assault on a group of civilians attempting to visit a graveyard in the presence of the IPTF, in which one person died and others were wounded, the Security Council demanded on 11 March that the responsible authorities should suspend all relevant police officers and institute prosecutions without further delay. On 19 December, by resolution 1144, the Council extended the UNMIBH mandate until 21 June 1998.

The UN Transitional Administration for Eastern Slavonia, Baranja and Western Sirmium (UNTAES) continued its efforts to assist with the peaceful reintegration of this ethnically-mixed region into Croatia (see III.2.iii). In January, March and October the Council expressed concern about the extent to which the government of Croatia was honouring its commitments to the Croatian Serbs—in particular about the slow pace of the return of displaced persons and refugees to their homes. It urged the Croatian government to accelerate its efforts to improve conditions of personal and economic security, to remove bureaucratic obstacles to the rapid issuance of documentation to all Serb families and to resolve promptly property issues. It also called upon Croatia to resolve uncertainty about the interpretation of the amnesty law and to put an end to arbitrary arrests, particularly of Serbs returning to Croatia. On 14 July, in resolution 1120, the Council extended the UNTAES mandate until 15 January 1998. It also endorsed a plan for a gradual devolution of executive responsibility for civil administration in the region, together with a restructuring of UNTAES and a gradual reduction of its military component.

On 19 December the Security Council unanimously adopted resolution 1145 in which it established a support group of 180 civilian police to monitor the performance of the Croatian police in the Danube region and the return of displaced persons. The support group's nine-month term was scheduled to begin on 16 January 1998.

The mandate of the UN Preventive Deployment Force (UNPREDEP) in Macedonia was extended three times in 1997 (see also III.2.iv). On 9 April, because of the civil turmoil in Albania (see III.2.i), the Council adopted resolution 1105 in which it suspended a planned reduction of the UNPREDEP military component. On 28 May, by resolution 1110, the UNPREDEP mandate was renewed for another six months, with the proviso that from 1 October, if conditions were suitable, there would be a two-month phased reduction of the military component by 300 all ranks. On 28 November, by resolution 1140, the Council decided that UNPREDEP would be terminated on 31 October 1998 and its military component withdrawn immediately afterwards. The Secretary-General was requested to submit a recommendation on the type of international presence that would be the most suitable after that date.

The mandate of the UN Mission of Observers in Prevlaka (UNMOP), charged with monitoring the demilitarization of the Prevlaka peninsula between Croatia and Yugoslavia, was twice extended for six months by the Security Council, on 14 January (resolution 1093) and 14 July (resolution 1119).

OTHER PEACE-KEEPING FORCES. The Security Council approved successive six-month extensions of the mandates of the UN Force in Cyprus (UNFICYP), until 30 June 1998; the UN Interim Force in Lebanon (UNIFIL), until 31 January 1998; and the UN Disengagement Observer Force (UNDOF) on the Golan Heights, until 31 May 1998.

DAG HAMMARSKJÖLD MEDAL. On the 22 July the Security Council unanimously adopted resolution 1121 by which it established the Dag Hammarskjöld Medal as a tribute to the more than 1,500 persons from 85 states who had lost their lives while serving in UN peace-keeping operations. The Secretary-General was requested to establish criteria and procedures for awarding and administering the medal.

2. OTHER WORLD ORGANIZATIONS
i. THE COMMONWEALTH

DATE OF FOUNDATION: 1931   HEADQUARTERS: London, UK
OBJECTIVES: To maintain political, cultural and social links between (mainly English-speaking) countries of the former British Empire and others subscribing to Commonwealth democratic principles and aims
MEMBERSHIP (END-'97): Antigua & Barbuda, Australia, Bahamas, Bangladesh, Barbados, Belize, Botswana, Britain, Brunei, Cameroon, Canada, Cyprus, Dominica, Fiji, The Gambia, Ghana, Grenada, Guyana, India, Jamaica, Kenya, Kiribati, Lesotho, Malawi, Malaysia, Maldives, Malta, Mauritius, Mozambique, Namibia, Nauru, New Zealand, Nigeria (*suspended*), Pakistan, Papua New Guinea, St Kitts & Nevis, St Lucia, St Vincent & the Grenadines, Samoa, Seychelles, Sierra Leone, Singapore, Solomon Islands, South Africa, Sri Lanka, Swaziland, Tanzania, Tonga, Trinidad & Tobago, Tuvalu, Uganda, Vanuatu, Zambia, Zimbabwe (*total 54*)
SECRETARY-GENERAL: Chief E. Chukwuemeka Anyaoku (Nigeria)

FOR the first time in 20 years the Commonwealth heads of government meeting (CHOGM) was held in Britain—in Edinburgh, Scotland, on 24–27 October. It came at a period when the Commonwealth was gaining international prestige, with more countries trying to join and Britain giving it higher foreign-policy priority than for many years and designating 1997 as UK Year of the Commonwealth. The new Prime Minister, Tony Blair, was host and 51 countries were represented, 43 by heads of state or prime ministers, which was a record number.

Fiji had just been readmitted to the Commonwealth (1 October). Prime Minister Sitiveni Rabuka, whose coup had caused membership to lapse in 1987, attended the CHOGM, as did Ahmed Tejan Kabba, who had been removed as President of Sierra Leone by military coup five months earlier (see VI.2.iii). That he was the first ousted leader to attend a CHOGM confirmed that the Commonwealth recognized him, not coup leader Johnny Koroma, as the elected head of state.

Novel features marked the 1997 CHOGM. It was preceded by a Commonwealth business forum in London (22–23 October). Top businessmen and seven heads of government attended. The forum report provided input for a CHOGM economic declaration entitled *Promoting Shared Prosperity* (see XIX.3). In addition, Queen Elizabeth for the first time attended and spoke at the CHOGM opening session, accompanied by Prince Philip and the Prince of Wales. The tradition that the Queen remained in the wings of the CHOGM, wherever held, was thereby broken. Another innovation was a Commonwealth centre, providing a shop window for 80 non-governmental organizations (NGOs). It was visited by 25,000 people, the interest manifesting the increasingly important role of what was now dubbed the 'people's Commonwealth'. A Commonwealth youth forum was held in parallel with the CHOGM, its 230 delegates representing every member country.

The economic declaration dealt with cooperation between the public and private sectors and problems of globalization, in particular those facing smaller and weaker states. It proposed a new trade and investment access facility to help developing countries adjust, training centres to enhance export management, a business council to increase private-sector involvement in trade and investment promotion, and a Commonwealth code of good practice for national policies to attract private capital flows. The business forum was to become a regular feature of the CHOGM. The council would be created under Lord Cairns of Britain and Cyril Ramaphosa of South Africa.

Nigeria, being suspended, was not represented in Edinburgh. The leaders discussed the report of the first two years of the eight-member Commonwealth ministerial action group (CMAG), set up in Auckland in 1995 to monitor human rights and good governance (see AR 1995, pp. 381–2). They accepted its recommendation to continue Nigeria's suspension pending the promised handover to civilian rule on 1 October 1998 (see VI.2.ii). Some human rights NGOs wanted Nigeria expelled immediately and voiced dissatisfaction with the decision. The CMAG was authorized 'to examine instances of serious and persistent violation of the political values set out in the Harare Declaration', this being seen as extending its remit to monitor any errant member if required. The composition of the CMAG was changed, Botswana replacing South Africa and Barbados replacing Jamaica.

The CHOGM also endorsed a report of the intergovernmental group on criteria for Commonwealth membership (see XIX.3) which laid down that an applicant country should 'as a rule, have had a constitutional association with an existing Commonwealth member' and referred to 'acknowledgment of the role of the British monarch . . . as Head of the Commonwealth'. This appeared to suggest publicly for the first time that the headship would pass to the Prince of Wales and his heirs. Hitherto, it was seen as vested in the person of the Queen, not the British monarch.

At the customary retreat for leaders (which was cut to one day in St Andrew's), the summit discussed membership applications from Rwanda, Yemen and Palestine. All three were put on hold. Rwanda was supported mainly by Uganda. Palestine had several backers, but was ruled out until it became a sovereign state.

Two more regional Commonwealth private investment initiative funds were set up in 1997. A South Asia fund was launched during the CHOGM with a $200 million target. Earlier, the Kula fund for the Pacific joined the Africa fund, launched in 1996.

The small states were vocal at the Edinburgh CHOGM. At a meeting of the Commonwealth ministerial group on small states on 24 October they sought more attention for their political, economic and environmental vulnerability and their difficulties in the globalized economy. A new version of the 1985 advisory group report on small island vulnerability, entitled *A Future for Small States*, with recommendations to governments, was tabled. At the full CHOGM, Commonwealth governments pledged new funding—notably for the Commonwealth Fund for Technical Cooperation and the Commonwealth of Learning, as well as for human rights and media training.

During 1997 Commonwealth teams observed elections in Pakistan, Cameroon, Papua New Guinea and Guyana. The findings on the Cameroon parliamentary elections (see VI.3.ii)) were particularly critical. In Pakistan a

group led by former Australian Prime Minister Malcolm Fraser made recommendations believed to have led to constitutional changes under which the President lost the power to dismiss a government (see VIII.2.ii).
  In February African Commonwealth heads of government met in Kasane, Botswana, to discuss democracy and good governance. A 'round-table' held beforehand in Gaborone brought together, uniquely, 41 representatives of both government and opposition parties. Proposals for strengthening democracy in Africa were passed to the heads.
  The Commonwealth secretary-general, Chief Emeka Anyaoku, pursuing his good offices role, mediated in Papua New Guinea in the March government crisis over the hiring of military mercenaries to fight in Bougainville (see X.1.ii). His intervention led Sir Julius Chan to step aside as Prime Minister pending an inquiry and new elections.
  Commonwealth Education Ministers met in Gaborone (28 July–1 August). Their main theme concerned the exploitation of new technology in education in the 21st century. When Commonwealth Finance Ministers met in Port Louis, Mauritius (15–17 September), the British Chancellor of the Exchequer, Gordon Brown, launched proposals known as the 'Mauritius mandate', by which it was hoped all 'heavily-indebted poor countries' (HIPCs) would by 2000 be involved in a process to end their debt problems. An expert group was to be set up to address, *inter alia,* corruption.
  The secretary-general attended the handover ceremony in Hong Kong (see IX.2.ii). In talks with the Chinese, it was agreed that Hong Kong NGOs could continue their links with Commonwealth NGOs.

ii. FRANCOPHONE AND PORTUGUESE-SPEAKING COMMUNITIES

Francophone Community (Francophonie)
DATE OF FOUNDATION: 1997   HEADQUARTERS: Paris, France
OBJECTIVES: To promote cooperation and exchange between countries wholly or party
   French-speaking and to defend usage of the French language
MEMBERSHIP (END-'97): Belgium, Benin, Bulgaria, Burkina Faso, Burundi, Cambodia,
   Cameroon, Canada, Cape Verde, Central African Republic, Chad, Comoros,
   Democratic Republic of Congo, Republic of Congo, Côte d'Ivoire, Djibouti, Dominica,
   Egypt, Equatorial Guinea, France, Gabon, Guinea, Guinea-Bissau, Haiti, Laos,
   Lebanon, Luxembourg, Madagascar, Mali, Mauritania, Mauritius, Moldova, Monaco,
   Morocco, New Brunswick (Canada), Niger, Quebec (Canada), Romania, Rwanda, St
   Lucia, Senegal, Seychelles, Switzerland, Togo, Tunisia, Vanuatu, Vietnam (*total 47*)
SECRETARY-GENERAL: Boutros Boutros-Ghali (Egypt)

Community of Portuguese-Speaking Countries (CPLP)
DATE OF FOUNDATION: 1996   HEADQUARTERS: Lisbon, Portugal
OBJECTIVES: To promote political, diplomatic, economic, social and cultural cooperation
   between member-states and to enhance the status of the Portuguese language
MEMBERSHIP (END-'97): Angola, Brazil, Cape Verde, Guinea-Bissau, Mozambique, Portugal,
   São Tomé & Príncipe (*total 7*)
EXECUTIVE SECRETARY: Marcolino Moco (Angola)

  FRANCOPHONE COMMUNITY. A major development in the evolution of the Francophone Community— known by the collective appellation 'La Francophonie'—

came at the seventh biennial francophone summit, held in Hanoi, Vietnam, on 14–16 November, which agreed to the formal establishment of a permanent secretariat and the nomination of a secretary-general. The decisions were generally seen as taking the movement closer to the institutional structure of the Commonwealth (see XI.2.i), although the latter grouping placed less emphasis on the linguistic base of its operations (in spite of the fact that English was undoubtedly its working language).

The Hanoi summit was attended by representatives from 49 states, regions and overseas departments/territories, out of an estimated 55 eligible to attend. Some of those present only had French-speaking minorities, including Canada (Quebec and New Brunswick), Mauritius and Seychelles, as well as the Caribbean states of St Lucia and Dominica (where French patois was spoken). Also present were observer delegations from non-francophone Albania, Macedonia and Poland, which declared support for the preservation of cultural and linguistic diversity against English-language domination. Absent from Hanoi was the Democratic Republic of the Congo (ex-Zaïre), Africa's largest French-speaking country, whose new President, Laurent Kabila, denounced the Francophone Community as 'an extension of neo-colonialism', although apparently without actually withdrawing.

Another significant aspect of the summit was the venue. It was the first francophone summit to be held in Asia since the series was inaugurated with the Versailles summit of 1986. Subsequent summits had been in Quebec (1987), Senegal (1989), Paris (1991), Mauritius (1993) and Benin (1995). The declaration issued by the Hanoi gathering (see XIX.4) stated that the heads of state, governments and delegations greeted 'the holding for the first time of a francophone summit in Asia, which therefore underlines the universal dimension of the Francophone Community and its presence in a region known for its dynamism'.

For France, the holding of the summit in Vietnam had a particular resonance, because of the bitter legacy of colonial history and the memories of France's eviction from Indochina in 1954 as a result of the nationalist/communist rebellion of Ho Chi Minh. The breakthrough in reconciliation had been achieved by the visit of the late President Mitterrand in 1993 (see AR 1993, p. 344), but the summit, and the official visit of President Chirac which preceded it, was an important development. Less than one per cent of Vietnamese now spoke French, and if Vietnam was belatedly to become an 'Asian tiger' it was unlikely to do so through any francophone connections. Nevertheless, the Vietnamese felt that participation would give them a particular window to the world that was an alternative to Americanizing 'globalization'.

This trend was, indeed, the great bogey of Francophonie. The Hanoi declaration began with a recognition of 'challenges tied to accelerated globalization and the necessity to make the best of it in order to avoid the risks of increasing uniformization, dependence and marginalization, which particularly hurt the most disinherited'. This was a thrust which had been seen at previous francophone summits of the 1990s: in Mauritius in 1993, for example, all states present had been mobilized behind France's struggle for a 'cultural exemption' on free trade in commodities such as films (see AR 1993, p. 327). The declaration also indicated movement in the direction of a stronger economic agenda. In the past it had tended to concentrate on language-related problems, including support for French-speaking minorities and the difficulties of the French language in English-dominated information technology. This was one reason why President Mitterrand had been keen to see the movement strengthened by the establishment of a proper secretariat. Accordingly, the theme of the Hanoi summit was 'strengthening francophone cooperation and solidarity for peace and economic and social development'. Declaring that they were conscious of the need to reinforce 'the economic dimension', the delegates agreed to work towards cooperation for sustainable development, with special stress on 'new technologies of information and communication'. The declaration also had a South-South dimension, speaking of the 'traditional spirit of francophone solidarity' and 'mutual aid', and containing an article on human resources in the service of development, notably 'education and training'.

The partial parallel with the Commonwealth was taken further with the introduction of a more openly political dimension, which previous summits had tended to avoid, except perhaps in corridor discussions. The Hanoi declaration spoke of a 'commitment to bring an active contribution to the prevention and peaceful settlement of conflicts', with special mention for 'regional mechanisms' and the preventive diplomacy of the UN. There was even some open disagreement, evidenced at the closing session, on the advisability of Commonwealth-style sanctions on human rights or democracy issues. Canadian Premier Jean Chrétien expressed support for such a step, but President Chirac insisted that sanctions did not belong to 'the tradition of the francophone area', adding: 'Our slogan is rather to convince than to constrain.' The latter point of view, unsurprisingly, had the strong support of the Vietnamese.

A feeling on the part of African states that the new 'global' approach of Francophonie somehow downgraded their position led to an astonishing rearguard action against the nomination of Boutros Boutros-Ghali of Egypt (the former UN Secretary-General) as the secretary-general of the new Francophone Community. He was supported by President Chirac, but several African countries, feeling that Dr Boutros-Ghali was being foisted upon them, put up Emile Derlin Zinsou (a former President of Benin). It took serious arm-twisting to persuade them to withdraw his candidacy, following which Dr Boutros-Ghali was elected unopposed for a four-year term. Dr Zinsou was given the job of heading a francophone election observatory.

On the other hand, the Africans supported the successful candidacy of Roger Dehaybe (Belgium) to head a new Francophone Agency, against French opposition. The new body was to replace the Agency for Cultural and Technical Cooperation (ACCT), which had provided the main institutional framework for francophone cooperation since its creation in 1970.

COMMUNITY OF PORTUGUESE-SPEAKING COUNTRIES. The first 18 months from the formal institutionalization of the Community of Portuguese-Speaking Countries (CPLP) in July 1996 (see AR 1996, pp. 86, 537–9) were mainly devoted to the installation of a permanent secretariat in an old and elegant aristocratic mansion in central Lisbon, acquired, re-equipped and donated by the Portuguese as their contribution to the new association, which linked seven states with a combined population of over 200 million people. The secretariat was inaugurated on 10 July to act as the coordinator of CPLP inter-governmental meetings and cultural cooperation, under an executive secretary, Marcolino Moco (a former Prime Minister of Angola), assisted by a deputy executive secretary, Rafael Branco (a former São Tomé & Príncipe cabinet minister). They had been elected for the first term of exercise, it being envisaged that the posts would be filled on a rotation basis among the member countries.

The CPLP was modelled more on the Commonwealth than on the Francophone Community (see above), insofar as it was intended to be less metropolitan-centred and had as a key role the strengthening of bilateral relations between the members. It was noted, for example, that Angola and Brazil had great potential for expanded cooperation, being nearer to each other across the Atlantic than either was to Portugal. The Commonwealth model was also apparent in matters of procedure. Meetings of the CPLP Council of Ministers would alternate with a biannual summit of heads of state, the next summit being scheduled to take place in 1998 in Praia, capital of Cape Verde, at a precise date to be announced.

Given the numerical preponderance of African countries and the ethnic demography of Brazil, it was hardly surprising that African concerns were prominent in the deliberations of the CPLP Council of Ministers at their 1997 meeting in Salvador da Bahia, Brazil, on 17–18 July. Diplomatic questions discussed included the current reform of the United Nations structure (see XI.1), on which the CPLP expressed support for Brazil's quest for a permanent seat on the Security Council. Also considered was the situation in East Timor (annexed by Indonesia in 1976 but still recognized as a Portuguese dependency by the United Nations), on which it urged self-determination for the East Timorese people (see also IX.1.vii).

A session of CPLP Agriculture Ministers took place in Rome on 10 November during the 29th conference of the Food and Agriculture Organization (FAO). For practical reasons, it was envisaged that the opportunity provided by such wider international conferences would be used to facilitate future CPLP interministerial meetings where possible.

The first year of CPLP secretariat activities in Lisbon was heavily occupied with preparations for Expo'98 (see II.3.iii). In particular, the secretariat was involved in organizing the participation of the CPLP in a joint pavilion designed to introduce the newest international association to the eight million foreign visitors expected to converge on the Portuguese capital between May and October 1998.

iii. NON-ALIGNED MOVEMENT AND DEVELOPING COUNTRIES

Non-Aligned Movement (NAM)
DATE OF FIRST SUMMIT: 1961   HEADQUARTERS: rotating with chair every three years
OBJECTIVES: Originally to promote cooperation between states not aligned with either the Western industrialized world or the Communist bloc; following the demise of the latter, to provide an international forum for less-powerful states, particularly in the UN framework
MEMBERSHIP (END-'97): 113 countries (*see AR 1995, p. 386, for list*)
CHAIRMAN: President Ernesto Samper Pizano of Colombia

Group of 77 (G-77)
DATE OF FOUNDATION: 1964   HEADQUARTERS: United Nations centres
OBJECTIVES: To act as an international lobbying group for the countries of the South on development questions
MEMBERSHIP (END-'97): 132 developing countries (*those listed in AR 1996, p. 385, minus South Korea, plus China & Eritrea*)

AT the start of the year Costa Rica, the outgoing coordinator of the Group of 77, hosted a South-South Conference on Trade, Investment and Finance on 13–15 January. This was the first major conference aimed at updating the 1981 Caracas Programme of Action for Economic Cooperation among Developing Countries. Instead of the former radical emphasis on collective self-reliance, the G-77 called for the benefits that some countries had gained from globalization and liberalization to be extended by integration of all countries into the global economy. There was a new focus on networking in the private sector and proposals for a business seminar and a G-77 trade fair.

The language adopted at San José implied that the successful countries of South-East Asia should take the lead in promoting trade, investment, technological cooperation and joint ventures. There were many sound ideas to overcome the practical barriers to cooperation, but not a single time-bound proposal for specific action. The 15 suggestions for follow-up were addressed more to the UN system than to action by the developing countries themselves, and they were mainly in the form of general aspirations for change. It was ironic that, after repeated calls from the G-77 for better collaboration between the United Nations and the Bretton Woods institutions, the ministers found it necessary to request greater interaction between the G-77 in New York and the Group of 24, representing developing countries at the World Bank and the IMF in Washington. The weakness of the institutional structures and in 'the political will' of the G-77 was recognized in the call for a South summit, but by the end of the year (during which the G-77 coordinator was Tanzania) the idea had made no progress.

The '12th' Ministerial Conference—actually the ninth in the triennial series—of the Non-Aligned Movement (NAM) took place in New Delhi on 7–8 April. Priority was given to the process of reforming the United Nations, which was seen as both a threat, with the danger of development activity being cut, and an opportunity, in light of the possibility that procedures would be changed to loosen Western domination (see also XI.1). The ministers were agreed that the Security Council should be expanded from 15 to at least 26 members to accommodate a higher proportion of seats for the Non-Aligned, although no position could be agreed on any proposals for new permanent members. On Security Council procedure, the New Delhi consensus was that the veto should be curtailed and that, as a first step, it should be restricted to the application of sanctions, peace enforcement and other actions under Chapter VII of the UN Charter. The Council should be more responsible to the wider UN membership and improve its reporting to the General Assembly.

While the NAM ministers endorsed the usual strong positions against weapons of mass destruction, they again deferred to Indian opposition to the Comprehensive Nuclear Test-Ban Treaty (see AR 1996, pp. 300, 423–4, 542–3). They also failed to support a ban on anti-personnel landmines (see XII.2; XIX.5), instead demanding access to new technology 'to perform the legitimate defensive role of landmines'. Worries about keeping the International Criminal Tribunal at The Hague free from political control by the Security Council carried over to an illogical position that the global court should be compatible with state sovereignty. On Libya's dispute with the United Nations over the 1988 Lockerbie airliner bombing, the Movement endorsed joint proposals by the OAU and the Arab League that a trial of the Libyan suspects should be held at The Hague or in some neutral country (see V.4.ii).

The chapter on economic issues from the NAM conference was generally similar in tone to the declaration from the G-77 San José meeting. The current orthodoxy was turned against its authors in a call for 'the developed countries to undertake necessary structural adjustments and refrain from protectionist tendencies'. There was also criticism of the poor implementation of the Uruguay Round measures of interest to developing countries, particularly in agriculture and textiles. Even before the financial crises in South-East Asia (see XVIII.1), the Non-Aligned called for the World Bank and the IMF to make a major contribution towards international financial stabilization and to develop new financial instruments to mitigate risks from unstable capital flows. The move away from the positive approach to environmental concerns of the early 1990s continued, because of disillusionment with the failure to gain new financial resources and technology transfer, as had been agreed at the Rio Earth Summit of June 1992. The extent of the change was evident in the assertion that 'an over-emphasis on environmental protection has undermined development'.

Throughout the year there was a high level of disappointment with the failure of the Middle East peace process, which was brought to crisis-point by the Israeli decision to commence building a new settlement on the outskirts of occupied East Jerusalem (see V.1; V.2.ii). After a US veto on condemnation of Israel by the Security Council on 7 March, the UN General Assembly on 13 March appealed to Israel not to go ahead, but construction started five days later. A second veto on 21 March led Qatar, on behalf of the Arab League and with the support of Colombia on behalf of the Non-Aligned, to request the UN Secretary-General to convene an emergency special session of the General Assembly. The New Delhi ministerial conference was important in giving momentum to this procedure. By 22 April the necessary 93 endorsements had been submitted for the tenth emergency special session to take place on 24–25

April. The resolution passed by the Assembly was comprehensive in its condemnation of all Israeli settlement activity since 1967, receiving 134 votes in favour and being opposed only by Micronesia, the United States and Israel.

Having been adjourned rather than closed, the General Assembly was resumed for one day on 15 July to receive a report on the Israeli response to its resolution. This time an even stronger resolution was passed by the same overwhelming majority. The wording moved towards economic sanctions and the possibility of the suspension of Israel from UN membership. At the request of the Arab League and the Non-Aligned, another resumption of the special session occurred on 13 November, the Assembly going on to recommend that Switzerland should convene a conference of the parties to the Geneva Conventions to consider measures to enforce a halt to the settlements.

Other NAM meetings during the year included a meeting of experts on science and technology in March, a conference of ministers of culture in September and the annual meetings of both the Non-Aligned and the G-77 in New York in September. It was decided in New Delhi that the 12th summit of the NAM would be held in South Africa.

Despite extensive consultations on the applications for NAM membership from Bosnia & Hercegovina and Costa Rica, no decision was made on them in 1997, so that membership did not change (see AR 1995, p. 386). The G-77 admitted Eritrea (hitherto the only African non-member since its independence in 1993), while South Korea left the group (having joined the OECD in 1996), although it reserved the right to attend meetings. The San José conference marked the first time that the People's Republic of China had participated in G-77 activities outside the UN system, the session being described as a meeting of 'the Group of 77 and China'. In September China was officially listed as a full member rather than an associate of the G-77, whose total membership therefore stood at 132.

iv. ORGANIZATION OF THE ISLAMIC CONFERENCE (OIC)

DATE OF FOUNDATION: 1970   HEADQUARTERS: Jeddah, Saudi Arabia
OBJECTIVES: To further cooperation among Islamic countries in the political, economic, social, cultural and scientific spheres
MEMBERSHIP (END-'97): Afghanistan, Albania, Algeria, Azerbaijan, Bahrain, Bangladesh, Benin, Brunei, Burkina Faso, Cameroon, Chad, Comoros, Djibouti, Egypt, Gabon, The Gambia, Guinea, Guinea-Bissau, Indonesia, Iran, Iraq, Jordan, Kazakhstan, Kuwait, Kyrgyzstan, Lebanon, Libya, Malaysia, Maldives, Mali, Mauritania, Morocco, Mozambique, Niger, Nigeria, Oman, Pakistan, Palestine, Qatar, Saudi Arabia, Senegal, Sierra Leone, Somalia, Sudan, Suriname, Syria, Tajikistan, Togo, Tunisia, Turkey, Turkmenistan, Uganda, United Arab Emirates, Yemen, Zanzibar (total 55)
SECRETARY-GENERAL: Azeddine Laraki (Morocco)

IN March the heads of state and government of the then 54 members of the Organization of the Islamic Conference (OIC) attended an extraordinary summit in Islamabad, Pakistan, held to celebrate the forthcoming 50th anniversary of

Pakistan's independence. Delegates lauded Pakistan's contribution to 'all just Islamic causes'; urged Israel to withdraw from all occupied territories and to cooperate in the Middle East peace process; called for the preservation of the sovereignty, independence and territorial integrity of both Bosnia & Hercegovina and Albania; opposed aggression against Azerbaijan; and reaffirmed solidarity with the self-declared Turkish Republic of Northern Cyprus (TRNC). They also called for an early political solution in Afghanistan, emphasizing the principles of non-intervention and non-interference. Although the leaders declined to allow the Taleban regime to occupy Afghanistan's seat in the organization, a Taleban delegation was present at the summit. The Taleban interpreted this as an important diplomatic victory, suggesting that full OIC recognition would be granted soon.

At its annual meeting in New York in early October, the coordinating committee of OIC Foreign Ministers unanimously approved the admission of Togo as the organization's 55th member. Two months later, on 9–11 December, the OIC held its eighth summit meeting in Tehran, Iran (the seventh summit having been held in Casablanca, Morocco, in December 1994—see AR 1995, pp. 387–90). Those attending included three kings and 27 presidents, as well as Crown Prince Abdullah ibn Abdul Aziz of Saudi Arabia, Vice-President Taha Yassin Ramadan of Iraq and Yassir Arafat, President of the Palestine National Authority. Prince Abdullah and Vice-President Ramadan were respectively the most senior Saudi and Iraqi representatives to visit Iran since the 1979 Islamic revolution.

The timing of the summit—some four months after Mohammed Khatami's election as President of Iran (see VIII.1.i)—and the diplomatic kudos gained from playing host to the Islamic world's leadership went some way towards reasserting Iran's stature in the international community in the face of US attempts to isolate it. The summit also served to highlight the intensity of the internal debate within the Iranian leadership over future foreign policy. In particular, attention was drawn to the contrasting opening speeches delivered by President Khatami and by the Iranian spiritual leader, Ayatollah Ali Khamenei. While the latter used the occasion to attack Western materialism and warn of the danger posed by Western culture, President Khatami stressed the need for increased dialogue between the Muslim world and the West.

The new Iranian President held a series of high-level bilateral meetings on the fringe of the summit. Particular emphasis was laid on improving relations with the Gulf Cooperation Council (GCC) states, President Khatami signalling a renewed willingness to address longstanding grievances between Iran and some of the GCC states, particularly the United Arab Emirates and Bahrain (see also XI.5.i). During a round of talks with President Khatami, Crown Prince Abdullah reportedly proposed that Saudi Arabia should broker a dialogue between Iran and the United States. In his talks with the Iraqi Vice-President, President Khatami was reported to have said that it was time to turn over a 'new leaf' in Iran-Iraq relations. For his part, Mr Ramadan announced on his arrival in Iran that he was bearing a message from the Iraqi President, Saddam Husain, although no details were disclosed.

Also on the fringe of the Tehran summit, the heads of state and government of the recently-formed 'Developing Eight' (D-8) group held an informal meeting. Launched in Istanbul in June on the initiative of the then Turkish Prime Minister, Necmettin Erbakan, the D-8 consisted of Bangladesh, Egypt, Indonesia, Iran, Malaysia, Nigeria, Pakistan and Turkey. Although its precise objectives remained largely undefined, the new group was seen as aiming to provide a specifically Islamic voice on international economic issues.

While Iran used the Tehran summit to seek to consolidate its own international position, some other delegations made efforts to focus attention on the deepening military alliance between Turkey and Israel. However, resolutions proposed by Iraq and Syria that were openly critical of Turkey were toned down to avoid straining relations with Ankara. Nevertheless, President Süleyman Demirel of Turkey responded to the criticism by leaving the summit before its final day.

The communiqué issued at the end of the gathering, dubbed the 'Tehran declaration', condemned the continued Israeli occupation of Palestinian and other Arab lands (such as the Golan Heights) as being in contravention of all relevant international agreements and conventions. The summit participants called for the restoration of the legitimate rights of the people of Palestine to facilitate their return to their homeland, the establishment of a Palestinian state with Jerusalem as its capital, and freedom of movement for Palestinians. It also urged the eradication of all weapons of mass destruction in the Middle East and demanded that Israel should sign the Nuclear Non-Proliferation Treaty.

The participants expressed 'regret' at the continuation of clashes and violence in Afghanistan (see VIII.1.ii) and announced their total support for negotiations between rival Afghan factions and for the establishment of a broad-based government in that country. They also encouraged regional and international efforts aimed at stopping bloodshed and establishing permanent peace in Afghanistan. On other current issues, the summit reaffirmed the OIC's solidarity with the Muslim people of Bosnia & Hercegovina; called on Armenia to withdraw all of its forces from Azerbaijani territories; expressed support for the people of Jammu and Kashmir, stressing that they should be allowed self-determination based on UN resolutions; called on the UN to remove sanctions against the Libyan people and to act according to the initiatives offered by regional organizations; and announced its full support for the Muslim Turkish community of Cyprus.

The summit condemned terrorism in all forms and methods, stressing that the killing of innocent people was forbidden in Islam. It called for the campaign against international terrorism to continue and, in a veiled reference to West European countries (the UK in particular), called for the practice of granting asylum to terrorists to be stopped. Participants also expressed their concern over the perceived growing tendency in the West to depict Islam as a new threat to the world. In this context, they demanded that realistic and practical steps should be taken to combat negative propaganda and misunderstandings and to present a true image of Islam, as 'the religion of peace, freedom and salvation'. They agreed to utilize 'modern innovations in the fields of communication and information' to present the principles of Islam to the world.

In the economic sphere, the summit invited OIC member countries to undertake collective and tangible efforts to increase trade and investment in the Islamic world, urging them to increase their cooperation and involvement in the global system of economic decision-making. They also stressed the importance of cooperation among Islamic countries on various environmental issues at regional and international levels.

Reference was made in the communiqué to the need for increased cooperation between the United Nations and the OIC, and for the active involvement of Secretary-General Kofi Annan. With regard to the UN structural reform currently in progress (see XI.1), Mr Annan was asked to seek to ensure maximum democratization of the decision-making process within the United Nations. Towards that end, the participants called for the allocation of a more effective role to OIC members in the UN Security Council as well as in some other forums of the organization.

Côte d'Ivoire was admitted as an observer member of the OIC at the Tehran meeting. It was agreed that the next OIC summit would be held in Doha, Qatar, in 2000.

3. EUROPEAN UNION

DATE OF FOUNDATION: 1952   HEADQUARTERS: Brussels, Belgium
OBJECTIVES: To seek ever-closer union of member states
MEMBERSHIP (END-'97): Austria, Belgium, Denmark, Finland, France, Germany, Greece, Ireland, Italy, Luxembourg, Netherlands, Portugal, Spain, Sweden, United Kingdom (*total 15*)
PRESIDENT OF EUROPEAN COMMISSION: Jacques Santer (Luxembourg)
EUROPEAN CURRENCY UNIT: £1=ECU1.50, US$1=ECU0.91 (end-'97)

THE year was one of consolidation and preparation in the European Union (EU). The Inter-Governmental Conference (IGC) for modifying the treaties was concluded in Amsterdam in June, introducing modest but important changes in the way the EU would function in future. Member-states struggled to adapt their policies and to prepare their economies for the launch of economic and monetary union (EMU), involving in particular a single European currency. The Union institutions looked forward to the negotiations on enlargement with certain countries of Central/Eastern Europe.

The change of government in Britain in May (see I.4) improved the atmosphere of EU business, facilitating the reaching of agreement in Amsterdam, while an unexpected Socialist victory in France the following month (see II.1.ii) threatened a change in French policy and major negotiating difficulties for the EU. These dangers quickly passed, however, and Prime Minister Lionel Jospin was soon following the traditional French line in European policy, with some extra emphasis on employment and the need for more political control of monetary policy.

The level of unemployment continued to haunt the big continental economies. Even as economic growth picked up, there seemed to be little new job-creation. Efforts were made to identify solutions at the European level, leading to an employment summit in November; but the disciplines required for EMU made it impossible to boost jobs through increased public spending, so that all the emphasis was on creating more private-sector employment.

CHANGING THE TREATIES. The deadline for completing negotiations to change the EU treaties was the end of June, at the conclusion of the Dutch presidency. Launched in the previous year to negotiate the new texts, the IGC had made slow progress. The British Conservative government was hostile to several modifications which other member-countries found essential; since unanimity was required, it was therefore generally accepted that the most sensitive issues could not be resolved until the British general election had taken place. Furthermore, the traditional alliances seemed to be working less effectively in driving the pace of negotiation, there being little evidence of effective Franco-German cooperation.

Almost no progress was achieved in the first three months of 1997. Once the UK election date had been fixed for 1 May, however, the Dutch presidency announced that there would be a European summit at Nordwijk on 23 May to prepare for the June European Council which was to conclude the IGC negotiations. The Nordwijk gathering turned out to be on the eve of the French polls unexpectedly called by President Chirac, so was little more than an occasion for the new British Prime Minister, Tony Blair, to meet his EU colleagues. Mr Blair indicated a more constructive British approach to European business and made it clear that his government's priorities would be job creation, competitiveness, the environment and human rights, while insisting on a British model of flexible labour markets.

After France's elections on 25 May and 1 June, attention shifted to the new French Prime Minister. Although M. Jospin had not questioned the previous government's approach to the IGC, as Socialist leader he had laid down certain conditions concerning French membership of EMU. His demands lent a sense of crisis to the final days of the IGC process, threatening the Dutch schedule, but were dealt with in the final package.

The Treaty of Amsterdam negotiations were concluded at the European Council on 16–17 June. A key aim of the new treaty was to set the scene for enlargement, but the Amsterdam participants failed to agree the necessary institutional changes, such as the number of members in a future European Commission, the extent of majority voting and the weighting of votes in the Council of Ministers in an enlarged EU. Conflicting interests between smaller and larger member states could not be resolved.

For this reason press coverage of Amsterdam was largely negative, but the new treaty did succeed in targeting weaknesses in EU mechanisms evident after the 1991 Maastricht negotiations (see AR 1991, pp. 561–6). It streamlined EU policy-making, strengthened the common foreign and security policy, put justice and home affairs on a stronger EU basis and introduced a new treaty section on employment. It also extended the scope of the European Parliament's powers in areas such as environmental policy and transport, reduced and simplified EU procedures and gave the Parliament a stronger role in the appointment of the European Commission. In addition, it incorporated the Schengen open-frontiers agreement into the EU treaty framework, so introducing freedom of movement for all citizens to travel passport-free throughout the 13 countries of the Schengen area. Britain and Ireland—not Schengen signatories—would be free to join when they chose.

One of the most significant developments was the commitment to create a 'single European area of freedom, security and justice' within five years, covering external border controls, asylum and immigration, and measures to combat crime. These policy areas were largely brought into the full EU decision-making system with qualified majority voting, although Chancellor Kohl of Germany, long an advocate of a federal European system but under pressure from the *Länder* (German states) not to surrender the veto, decided that unanimity would be preferable on immigration and other issues. This marked an important turning-point in German policy. Also noteworthy was a new treaty commitment concerning respect for certain fundamental principles, such as liberty, democracy, respect for human rights, fundamental freedoms and the rule of law. The ancillary provision for suspension of voting rights if a member-state breached the principles was important in the context of new countries joining the Union.

The new treaty also strengthened the as yet ineffective European common foreign and security policy (CFSP), which had been largely discredited during the crisis of former Yugoslavia. A Franco-German proposal to integrate the Western European Union (WEU) defence organization into the EU was successfully resisted by Britain (supported by Denmark, Finland, Ireland and Sweden); instead, the relationship between the WEU and the EU was more clearly defined, the 'Petersberg tasks' of humanitarian, peace-keeping and peace-making missions being brought within the scope of EU defence policy. The European Council would be able to decide on common strategies to be implemented by the EU in areas where the member-states shared important interests, subject to a right of veto 'for important and stated reasons of national policy'. A policy-planning and early-warning unit would be set up in the Council of Ministers to assist the presidency and the secretary-general, who would be more actively involved in the CFSP.

A longstanding French demand, particularly important to M. Jospin, was for a new chapter on employment to be incorporated into the treaty, but Germany and the outgoing British government had been opposed. The compromise found at Amsterdam effectively allowed the employment provisions of the Social Chapter agreed by 14 member states at Maastricht in 1991 to be brought fully into the new text (see also below). Whereas Britain had opted out in 1991, the new Labour government acceded to the Social Chapter, although both Britain and Germany remained reluctant to give job-creation a greater role in EU affairs.

The Amsterdam Treaty was formally signed on 2 October in Luxembourg, initiating the process of ratification by the European Parliament and 15 national parliaments.

ECONOMIC AND MONETARY UNION. At the beginning of 1997 there were doubts over whether EMU would be launched on schedule on 1 January 1999, and many more doubts as to which countries would qualify. The British Conservative government was increasingly hostile to the whole idea and made it quite clear that Britain would not be part of it. Confidence quickly spread, however. The European Commission forecast in the spring that all EU countries except Italy and Greece would have budget deficits low enough to allow them to qualify for EMU by 1999. The IMF was more sceptical, suggesting that both France and Germany would fail to meet the targets, but still predicting that EMU would begin on time. By October the Commission was giving Italy the all-clear as well (see XVIII.2: Table 44).

The determination of most European governments to participate in a single currency from the start, and to take the tough budgetary measures needed, convinced the financial markets that even countries like Finland, Italy and Spain could become founder members. Interest rates fell in the peripheral countries—triggering a virtuous circle of lower borrowing costs and reduced deficits—and currency values settled down, as the markets accepted that membership from 1999 was a real prospect for up to 11 EU countries. By the end of the year there was widespread confidence that all except four would join from the start. Britain, Denmark and Sweden had their political reservations, and Greece still had to make up ground in reducing its budget deficit. There were, however, a few doubts about the timetable, notably from Bundesbank president Hans Tietmeyer, who said that postponement would cause no great problem.

The politics of EMU continued to dog the project. The German government insisted in April that the criteria would be rigorously applied, Finance Minister Theo Waigel expressing confidence that the target for the budget deficit would be met by Germany. 'We must achieve the 3 per cent; 3 per cent remains 3 per cent', he wrote in *Bild am Sonntag*, adding: 'Anything less would damage the credibility and acceptability of the euro.' A month later the German government proposed a revaluation of gold held by the Bundesbank, its intention being to reduce the budget deficit figures. This caused a big outcry among other EMU partners and German commentators, including the Bundesbank, which saw it as unacceptable creative accounting. The gold revaluation idea was quickly modified, but its appearance made it much more difficult for the German government to oppose Italian participation in the launch of EMU, which was also likely to require some creative accounting.

The election of a new French government posed a bigger problem: before the Amsterdam summit the French Socialists had laid down four conditions which in their view would have to be met before France could join EMU. All were calculated to diminish German control of the project and especially to weaken the Bundesbank model for the European Central Bank (ECB). Prime

Minister Jospin said that the participation of Italy and Spain was 'necessary and possible'; that monetary union must include a pledge to create jobs; that the power of the ECB must be balanced by political control of economic policy; and that the euro must not be overvalued against the dollar and the yen—in other words that the euro's international exchange rate should be managed.

These French demands were modified by events. Admission of Italy and Spain looked increasingly likely as the year progressed, although Italy's public-sector debt was still well above the Maastricht criterion. A pledge on job-creation was expressed through the Employment Chapter in the Amsterdam Treaty (see above) and a commitment to hold an 'employment summit' in the autumn (see below). Most contentious was France's longstanding demand for political control over economic policy. This aim, and the idea of establishing an Economic Council to determine economic policy at EU level, had been around since the conception of EMU and was actively discussed when the text of a Stability and Growth Pact was negotiated at the end of 1996. The pact, designed to guarantee budgetary stability in the member-countries, was formally agreed in Amsterdam, but the French demand could be acknowledged only through a compromise Resolution on Growth and Employment and nothing more concrete. This was enough for M. Jospin to defend his acceptance of the Amsterdam package back home, but was not the end of the story.

In the last months of the year the French increased their pressure for the establishment of a 'Euro-X' Council—'X' representing the number of countries fully participating in EMU—to consider budget, tax and exchange-rate policies. Since the British would not be part of this group, they were strongly opposed to its creation and fought hard at the Luxembourg summit in December to limit its powers, while gaining access to its deliberations where possible. Meanwhile, France's relations with its neighbours over EMU had not been improved when President Chirac and M. Jospin announced early in November that a Frenchman should run the ECB. Their preference was for Jean-Claude Trichet, governor of the Bank of France, whose candidacy undermined the widespread assumption that Dutchman Wim Duisenberg, head of the ECB's precursor, the European Monetary Institute (EMI), would get the job. Mr Duisenberg was the favoured candidate of most member-states.

The British position on EMU was transformed by the change of government on 1 May, when Conservative hostility to UK involvement gave way to a generally-welcoming tone from Labour. The incoming Chancellor of the Exchequer, Gordon Brown, showed particular enthusiasm for early British membership, setting the newly-independent role for the Bank of England (see I.5) partly in the context of monetary union, although Prime Minister Blair indicated at the Nordwijk meeting in May that Britain was unlikely to join in the first wave. The increasing market confidence that up to 11 countries could launch EMU increased the pressure on Britain. This widening of the EMU base would leave those countries outside much more vulnerable to currency movements, having to bear the brunt of any speculative pressures, while the economic consequences of being a lone outsider were potentially considerable, both in terms of inward investment and business dealings with European partners. Furthermore, many fundamental and practical decisions would have to be taken by the EU in the first half of 1998 (when Britain would hold the EU presidency), including confirmation of those countries deemed fit to join and nomination of the six-member ECB board on which Britain badly wanted a seat. Any standing-back would leave British ministers outside the negotiating game. Emergence of the idea of an informal 'Euro-X' Council of the EMU countries was therefore a further blow, exclusion being seen as potentially damaging for Britain.

A suggestion that the British might go for an early referendum and sign up quickly for EMU appeared in a *Financial Times* article during the summer parliamentary recess. The article moved the markets, but then began to create political confusion, leading to Mr Brown's statement on EMU to the House of Commons on 27 October. The Chancellor gave an unequivocal British government commitment to British membership—but not yet. Various tests of convergence would need to be met, although preparations should now begin. The statement got a bad press, not so much because of the substance of the Chancellor's remarks, but because they followed a period of confusion over government policy. In fact, the agenda was now clear: British membership would be a reality by 2002 or thereabouts, subject to the return of a Labour government at the next general election and endorsement of EMU by voters in a referendum.

The timetable for the launch of EMU was confirmed by EU Finance Ministers in April. The EMI and the European Commission would put forward their recommendations on which countries met the Maastricht criteria in March 1998, to allow a decision by the European Council at the beginning of May, and the ECB would be created immediately after this decision. Ministers subsequently decided that bilateral exchange rates between participating currencies should be set at the same time, to diminish the possibility of large fluctuations in the lead-up to 1 January 1999, when all these currencies would be irrevocably linked as units of the euro. Agreement was also reached on the design of euro coins to be minted for use from the beginning of 2002, while the design of euro notes was finalized in November.

EMPLOYMENT. Faced with an average level of unemployment of nearly 11 per cent in the EU and the fact that the disciplines for EMU were limiting governments' ability to produce new jobs in the public sector, the June European Council in Amsterdam agreed to hold a summit devoted to job-creation. This took place in Luxembourg on 21 November. No short-term solutions were identified, but it was decided that annual national plans should be drawn up for getting people into work, with guidelines at a European level. The plans would be presented at the June 1998 European Council in Cardiff.

It was also agreed that 10,000 million ECU in additional funding should be provided from the European Investment Bank for small and medium-sized businesses, plus 450 million ECU from the EU budget over three years. The EU leaders established common guidelines for job-creation and helping the young and long-term unemployed for incorporation into the national plans, including a general commitment that every unemployed young person should be offered a new start before they had been unemployed for six months, in the form of training, retraining, work experience or a job. There was a commitment to simplify rules on small businesses and to encourage the development of self-employment.

The British Labour government saw its mission as persuading European partners that the most effective way to create new jobs was through flexible labour markets. This message was delivered to European Socialist Party leaders by Chancellor Brown in May and was re-emphasized at all subsequent EU meetings on employment. The word 'entrepreneurship' entered the European employment policy language for the first time.

ENLARGEMENT. In July the European Commission launched Agenda 2000, a package to prepare the way for the opening of accession negotiations with the countries of Central/Eastern Europe which had applied to join the EU. The Commission analysed the state of the ten candidates and recommended that negotiations should begin with the Czech Republic, Estonia, Hungary, Poland and Slovenia (see map on page 409). It also set out a strategy for the future policy evolution of the Union, covering the financial framework, the common agricultural policy and funds for economic development.

The Commission's opinions on the membership applications were based on the criteria laid down in Copenhagen in 1993, including democracy, human rights, the rule of law and protection of minorities, as well as economic factors and the ability of the countries concerned to adjust to EU membership. Enlargement could bring considerable political and economic advantages, said the Commission, but would also demand sectoral and regional adjustments to deal with the wider diversity. All applicant countries would be expected to apply key elements of the single market, to resolve outstanding border disputes and to implement the body of EU law. A total of 21,000 million ECU would be available to support the candidate countries before accession, particularly to strengthen their administrations and institutions and to boost investment in business and infrastructure.

Agenda 2000 formed the basis for the decisions of the Luxembourg Council in December, when EU leaders decided that negotiations should begin on 30 March 1998 with the Czech Republic, Estonia, Hungary, Poland and Slovenia. Cyprus would also be included. Preparations for negotiations with Bulgaria, Latvia, Lithuania, Romania and Slovakia would be speeded up. The Turks were furious that they had not been included in either list. They presented the most immediate political problem, since they regarded this new phase in the EU's development as a crucial test of European attitudes to their country's future, whereas the Greeks fiercely opposed any commitment to Turkish membership. While Turkey's eligibility for membership was confirmed in Luxembourg, the Council communiqué stated that its political and economic conditions were not satisfactory. The Council tried to offer some consolation in the form a standing European conference, including Turkey, which would have its first meeting in

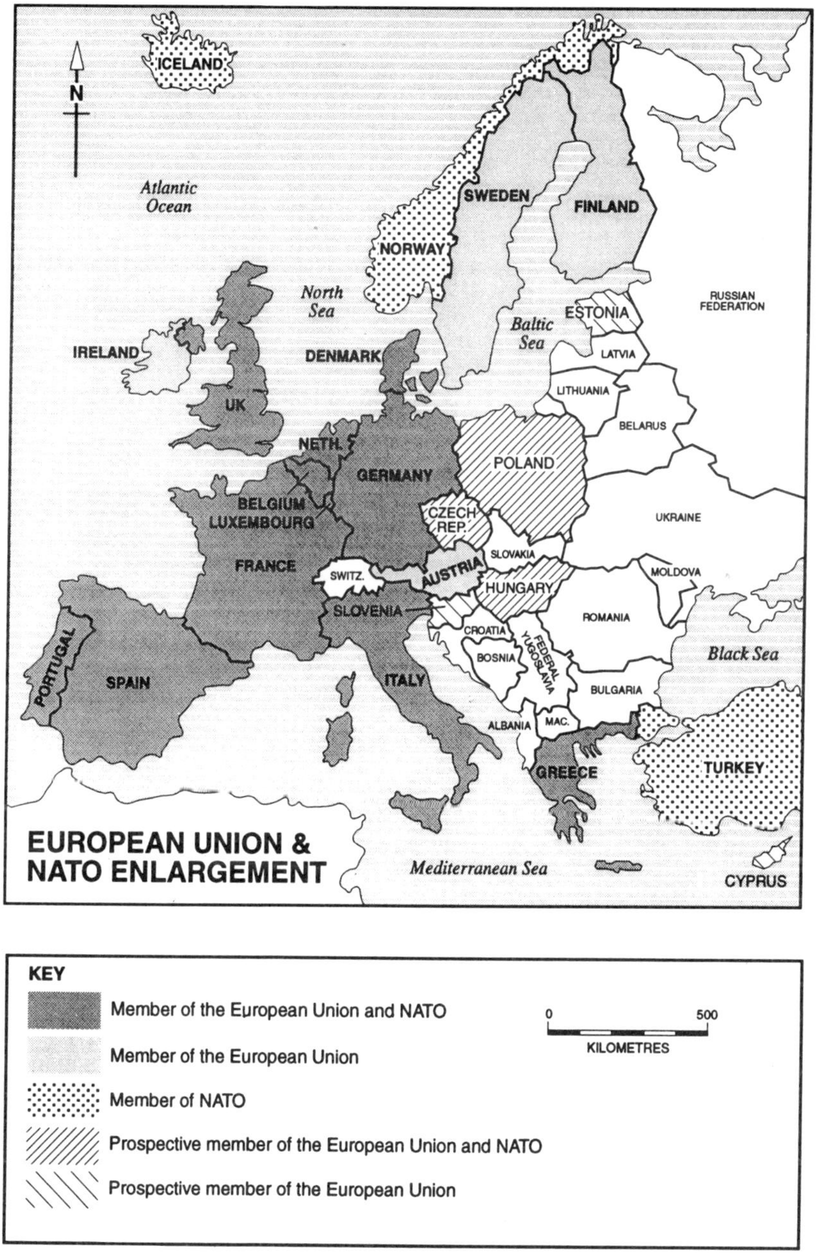

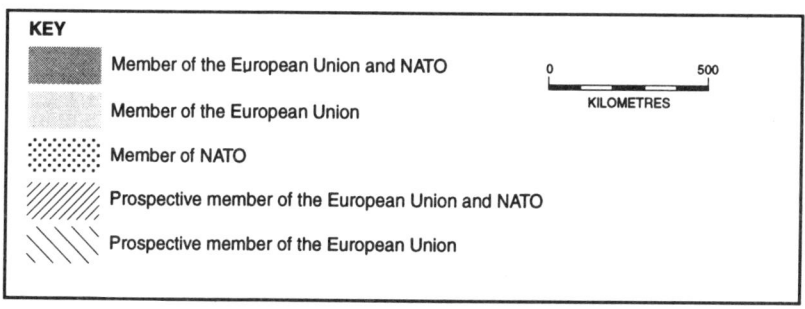

EUROPEAN UNION &
NATO ENLARGEMENT
N
ICELAND
Atlantic Ocean
NORWAY
SWEDEN
FINLAND
North Sea
Baltic Sea
ESTONIA
RUSSIAN FEDERATION
LATVIA
LITHUANIA
BELARUS
IRELAND
UK
DENMARK
NETH.
GERMANY
POLAND
BELGIUM
LUXEMBOURG
CZECH REP.
UKRAINE
SLOVAKIA
FRANCE
SWITZ.
AUSTRIA
HUNGARY
MOLDOVA
SLOVENIA
ROMANIA
CROATIA
BOSNIA
FEDERAL YUGOSLAVIA
Black Sea
PORTUGAL
SPAIN
ITALY
BULGARIA
ALBANIA
MAC.
GREECE
TURKEY
Mediterranean Sea
CYPRUS
KEY
Member of the European Union and NATO
Member of the European Union
Member of NATO
Prospective member of the European Union and NATO
Prospective member of the European Union
0
500
KILOMETRES

March 1998 under the UK presidency before the enlargement talks began. This initiative did nothing to calm the Turks, however (see III.3.vii).

Enlargement would imply far-reaching changes within the existing European Union. In its analysis of budgetary needs, the Commission argued that the present budget contribution ceiling should be adequate for an enlarged EU until 2006, at 1.27 per cent of member-states' GNP. The common agricultural policy should continue to shift from price support to direct payments. Market support for agricultural products would be reduced, but milk quotas would be extended to 2006. A coherent rural policy would be developed. The scale of the structural funds for economic development should be retained at current levels of 0.46 per cent of GNP, amounting to a total of 275,000 million ECU from 2000 to 2006, of which 45,000 million ECU would be devoted to enlargement.

TRADE RELATIONS. There was a good start to the year in EU-US trade relations, as World Trade Organization (WTO) agreements were reached on information technology and telecommunications; but then strains began to show. Several issues built up the tension, often in the context of the new WTO disputes settlement procedure.

The most political issue, causing the EU to consider using the WTO disputes mechanism, was US sanctions legislation (the Helms-Burton and D'Amato Acts) targeting companies trading with Cuba, Iran and Libya. Tension rose following investment activities in Cuba by the Italian telecoms operator STET, while Total announced plans to invest $2,000 million in Iran's oil industry. President Clinton refrained from applying sanctions, but the threat remained.

Other issues of contention followed rulings on banana imports and hormones in beef. Responding to a US complaint, the WTO found that the EU's system of banana import quotas, designed to protect the economies of the banana producers in the Caribbean and African ex-colonies, conflicted with international trade law. A US complaint against the EU ban on imports of beef containing growth hormones was also upheld, but subject to appeal. These cases led the EU agriculture commissioner, Franz Fischler, to question the WTO's democratic mandate, drawing a sharp response from his trade relations colleague, Sir Leon Brittan.

MAD COW DISEASE. The crisis over 'mad cow disease' or BSE (see AR 1996, pp. 17, 392–3) precipitated a marked shift of institutional power in the EU extending well beyond the particular issue. Members of the European Parliament were able to exploit the European Commission's failure to handle the crisis effectively, issuing a committee report in February which included the threat to use parliament's powers to dismiss the college of commissioners if their response did not match up to parliament's demands. The Commission president, Jacques Santer, responded by promising everything that parliament wanted: to implement major changes in Commission organization and to propose new initiatives to the Council of Ministers in light of the parliament's report. The consumer protection activities of the Commission under Emma Bonino were strengthened and a series of scientific committees reformed and brought together under a single organization.

The European response to BSE continued to sour relations with Britain while the Conservative government remained in office, but the incoming Labour team was able to take a more detached view. The EU ban on the export of cattle and beef from Britain was maintained throughout the year. Further trade problems loomed as planned EU health controls on gelatine threatened supplies of many foodstuffs and pharmaceuticals from the United States.

ALBANIA. The crisis in Albania (see III.2.i) led to the provision of EU emergency aid and technical assistance in a joint initiative with the IMF and the World Bank, particularly to limit the damage caused by the collapse of pyramid finance schemes. A high-level mission was dispatched by the EU presidency in March, including representatives from Greece, Italy and the Organization for Security and Cooperation in Europe, to establish what action was necessary to protect any advisory mission which might be sent for civil police or military operations. The WEU structure was involved in the provision of help for the evacuation of expatriates and in establishing policing capabilities.

SINGLE MARKET. A major milestone in the process of completing the European single market was the end-of-year deadline for the liberalization of telecommunications infrastructure and services in Europe. Industrial restructuring continued apace and expanded in sectors such as the media, financial services and telecommunications. European regulatory activity increased. A total of 150 major mergers, each representing global turnover of at least 5,000 million ECU, were notified to the Commission's merger task force during 1997, a 15 per cent increase over the previous year. These included the Boeing takeover of McDonnell Douglas, which was authorized by the Commission after the company had agreed to undertakings demanded by the Commission.

4. EUROPEAN ORGANIZATIONS

i. COUNCIL OF EUROPE

DATE OF FOUNDATION: 1949 HEADQUARTERS: Strasbourg, France
OBJECTIVES: To strengthen pluralist democracy, the rule of law and the maintenance of human rights in Europe and to further political, social and cultural cooperation between member-states
MEMBERSHIP (END-'97): Albania, Andorra, Austria, Belgium, Bulgaria, Croatia, Cyprus, Czech Republic, Denmark, Estonia, Finland, France, Germany, Greece, Hungary, Iceland, Ireland, Italy, Latvia, Liechtenstein, Lithuania, Luxembourg, Macedonia, Malta, Moldova, Netherlands, Norway, Poland, Portugal, Romania, Russia, San Marino, Slovakia, Slovenia, Spain, Sweden, Switzerland, Turkey, Ukraine, United Kingdom (*total 40*)
SECRETARY-GENERAL: Daniel Tarschys (Sweden)

THE Council of Europe's role in setting standards in the field of human rights and developing international law and its potential to promote democracy, cohesion and stability throughout Europe were both demonstrated and enhanced in

1997, most notably at the second summit in the organization's history. It was held on 10–11 October in Strasbourg, the 40 current member-states and the four candidate countries all being represented by heads of state or government. This was the first year since 1987 in which no new member-state was admitted to the Council of Europe. Consideration of the application for membership from Belarus was frozen in January following the disputed constitutional referendum of the previous November (see AR 1996, p. 133). At the same time, programmes of assistance continued for Bosnia & Hercegovina and the three Transcaucasian states (Armenia, Georgia and Azerbaijan), to facilitate their eventual membership.

At the Strasbourg summit, governments resolved to ensure that commitments accepted by member-states were effectively honoured, principally on the basis of the confidential procedures previously adopted by the Committee of Ministers. To complement these, the Parliamentary Assembly established a new permanent committee in April, charged with giving greater focus and coherence to its monitoring activities. The Assembly was also active in encouraging the political agreement of 9 May in Albania, which formed the basis for the parliamentary elections held in early July (see III.2.i). The Assembly subsequently joined with the Organization for Security and Cooperation in Europe (OSCE) in judging them to be 'acceptable, given the prevailing circumstances' (see also XI.4.ii).

A process lasting over six years reached fruition in Spain on 4 April when the European Convention on Human Rights and Biomedicine was opened for signature and signed by over 20 member-states. The convention set out principles for the protection of human rights and the dignity of the human being with regard to the application of biology and medicine, covering areas such as genetic testing and intervention, scientific research and organ removal. Its value as a framework was demonstrated when, in response to concern generated by the successful cloning of a sheep in Scotland (see XIV.1), an additional protocol banning the cloning of human beings was agreed with unprecedented rapidity for adoption in November and signature in January 1998.

The Strasbourg summit was preceded by increased efforts to implement agreements entered into at the first Council of Europe summit held in Vienna in 1993 (see AR 1993, pp. 420–1). During 1997 the Framework Convention for the Protection of National Minorities obtained sufficient ratifications to enter into force, while the 11th Protocol to the Human Rights Convention, providing for the creation of a single court, was finally ratified by all member-states. The latter completion enabled the heads of state and government to instruct the Committee of Ministers to establish the new court on 1 November 1998—a process set to begin with the election of judges by the Parliamentary Assembly in early 1998. It was also agreed at the summit to study the implementation of a Finnish proposal for a commissioner for human rights to promote respect for human rights in member-states.

In addition to these developments regarding human rights and the reaffirmation of the Council of Europe's fundamental principles, the declaration and action plan of the summit covered three main areas: social cohesion, security of citizens, and democratic values and cultural diversity (see XIX.2 for text). With regard to the first, the establishment of a specialized unit for monitoring, comparing and handling issues linked to social cohesion was agreed. In relation to the second, new impetus was given to work to establish principles and legal standards concerning the fight against terrorism, corruption, organized crime and drug abuse. In the third domain, the summit agreed to the launch of a 'European heritage campaign' in 1999 and the development of a European policy for the application of new information technologies. The action plan was marked by a particular concern for the interests of children, supporting a new programme to promote their interests and undertaking to review national legislation with the aim of ensuring common standards for the protection of children.

The summit's outcome did not match some of the expectations previously voiced in the Parliamentary Assembly, notably in that the action plan was less ambitious than the declaration. The summit instructed the Committee of Ministers to carry out the structural reforms needed to adapt the organization to its new tasks and its enlarged membership, and to improve its decision-making process; the Committee of Ministers established a 'committee of wise persons' to give advice in these areas. Although the summit made no new budgetary commitments, the high-level political endorsement of the Council of Europe implicit in the summit and the wide-ranging programme agreed there was likely to prove invaluable in the future as the Council of Europe sought to reinforce its unique role in Europe's political and security architecture.

ii. ORGANIZATION FOR SECURITY AND COOPERATION IN EUROPE (OSCE)

DATE OF FOUNDATION: 1975   HEADQUARTERS: Vienna, Austria
OBJECTIVES: To promote security and cooperation among member states, particularly in respect of the resolution of internal and external conflicts
MEMBERSHIP (END-'97): Albania, Armenia, Austria,Azerbaijan, Belorussia (Belarus), Belgium, Bosnia & Hercegovina, Bulgaria, Canada, Croatia, Cyprus, Czech Republic, Denmark, Estonia, Finland, France, Georgia, Germany, Greece, Holy See (Vatican), Hungary, Iceland, Ireland, Italy, Kazakhstan, Kyrgyzstan, Latvia, Liechtenstein, Lithuania, Luxembourg, Macedonia, Malta, Moldova, Monaco, Netherlands, Norway, Poland, Portugal, Romania, Russia, San Marino, Slovakia, Slovenia, Spain, Sweden, Switzerland, Tajikistan, Turkey, Turkmenistan, Ukraine, United Kingdom, United States, Uzbekistan, Yugoslavia (*total 54*)
SECRETARY-GENERAL: Giancarlo Aragona (Italy)

ON 1 January Switzerland handed over the chairmanship of the Organization for Security and Cooperation in Europe (OSCE) to Denmark. The new chairman-in-office was the Danish Foreign Minister, Niels Helveg Petersen, on whose shoulders fell the main responsibility for representing the public face of the OSCE over the following 12 months.

An indication of the key concerns which dominated the OSCE agenda in

1997 could be gleaned from the meeting of the ministerial 'troika' in Vienna on 18 June. The troika consisted of the past, present and future chairmen of the OSCE (in 1997 Switzerland, Denmark and Poland respectively) and usually met twice a year with the OSCE secretary-general to discuss the current agenda. The Vienna meeting began by considering matters arising from the Lisbon OSCE summit in December 1996 (see AR 1996, p. 401), in particular the mandates for the new posts of representative on media freedom and coordinator of OSCE economic and environmental activities. The troika then considered a special report on the OSCE Security Model (see below), which had also been agreed in outline at Lisbon. This was followed by an assessment of the OSCE's major international responsibilities in Albania, Belarus, Bosnia & Hercegovina and Croatia, along with progress reports on developments in Nagorno-Karabakh, the former Yugoslav Republic of Macedonia, Chechenya and the Federal Republic of Yugoslavia.

The role of the OSCE was to provide a means of pan-European diplomacy on a comprehensive range of issues, from human rights and press freedom to economic development and European security. The OSCE's specific contribution to these issues was through 'norm-setting' (on human rights standards and the peaceful settlement of disputes), preventive diplomacy and post-conflict rehabilitation. Much of the work of the OSCE was geographically focused on the post-communist lands of Central/Eastern Europe—particularly the former Soviet Union and former Yugoslavia, where a number of vicious nationalist conflicts had erupted. This geographical focus was apparent from the location of the ten OSCE missions, all of which were situated in the former USSR and the Balkans.

An issue of major concern for Mr Petersen from early on in the year was the rapid disintegration of legitimate political authority in Albania, following the collapse of the pyramid-savings schemes (see IV.2.i). The chairman-in-office appointed the former Austrian Chancellor, Franz Vranitzky, to act as his personal representative to Albania, his role being to act as the OSCE's 'trouble-shooter', mediating between different political groups and coordinating international activities. Dr Vranitzky set about his new responsibilities with considerable energy and imagination, and quickly proposed that a multinational 'coalition of the willing' should be formed to protect the civilian humanitarian relief effort. This was established under Italian leadership (see also II.1.iii). Subsequently, the role of Herr Vranitzky and the OSCE in Albania was two-fold: to coordinate the international relief effort and to provide practical assistance in rebuilding democratic political institutions, in close cooperation with the Council of Europe. To this end, an OSCE presence was established in April, consisting of a main office in Tirana and two regional offices.

The mid-year Albanian elections were described as 'adequate and acceptable' by the OSCE, which subsequently concentrated on providing advice and assistance in democratic development. Its role was a practical example of the 'OSCE first' principle, by which regional crises in Europe would first be referred to the OSCE, and only later to the United Nations if and when OSCE efforts were unsuccessful. Dr Vranitzky's considerable achievements were formally recognized by both the Albanian Prime Minister, Fatos Nano, who presented him with an award, and by the OSCE itself, which awarded him the organization's first-ever 'distinguished service' medal.

Throughout the year, OSCE efforts were also engaged elsewhere in the Balkans. In Bosnia, energies were focused on the September municipal elections, which were widely regarded as central to the success of the peace process and a vital part of the OSCE mandate (see III.2.ii). In launching an OSCE 'democratization programme' in February, the OSCE head of mission, Robert Frowick, described the elections as 'among the mission's highest priorities'. The elections themselves involved 2,400 polling supervisors and approximately 250 international observers drawn from 27 OSCE countries. In the end, the elections went ahead relatively smoothly, leading NATO secretary-general Javier Solana to commend the OSCE for 'its steadfastness in overcoming many obstacles'.

Another growing OSCE responsibility in 1997 was Croatia. Following the reintegration of Eastern Slavonia into Croatia, and the planned withdrawal of the UN peace-keeping mission (UNTAES) by early 1998, the OSCE would be the only international mediating organization left in Croatia. The mandate of the existing OSCE mission was therefore expanded to cover Eastern Slavonia, particularly as regards the return of refugees and displaced persons, and the protection of minority rights. There was a steady build-up of OSCE personnel in Croatia to about 250, making the mission one of the OSCE's largest, on a par with that in Bosnia. Meanwhile, in the neighbouring Federal Republic of Yugoslavia, the OSCE sought to organize proximity talks between the government and opposition, and was successful in getting President Milošević to recognize the results of the 1996 local elections, 'as found by the OSCE mission'.

A further OSCE success in the Balkans was achieved in June when a subregional arms control agreement was signed between five former warring parties, involving reductions in the level of conventional armaments in six crucial categories. Progress in implementing the agreement was initially slow, but by 31 October, over 6,000 weapon systems had been destroyed. The agreement was backed up by an intrusive inspection regime to ensure compliance.

The success of the OSCE sub-regional arms control agreement in the wartorn Balkans illustrated another of the organization's main responsibilities—reducing military tensions in Europe through arms limitations and confidence-building measures. The main concern in 1997 was the renegotiation of the 1990 Treaty on Conventional Forces in Europe (CFE). The first stage was concluded on 23 July when it was agreed to replace the outmoded bloc-to-bloc structure of the treaty by 30 national ceilings and to create a system of territorial ceilings replacing the old zonal arrangement. New national ceilings were to be set for tanks, armoured personnel carriers, artillery, warplanes and attack helicopters, and all states agreed to reduce their CFE holdings below current levels (see also XII.2). The second phase of the negotiations began in September and was expected to last a year.

A major task for the Danish chairman-in-office in 1997 was overseeing work on the OSCE Security Model for the 21st Century. The agenda was set out in the Lisbon declaration, elaboration continuing thereafter in an *ad hoc* Vienna committee established to draft a politically-binding Charter for European Security. This document was expected to outline a framework for cooperation between the various international organizations and institutions involved in European security, and would include a Platform for Cooperative Security as one of its elements. Mr Petersen suggested that the international effort in Albania was a good example of such cooperative security in practice, while the security role of the OSCE was underlined in the NATO-Russia Founding Act signed in Paris on 27 May (see XIX.1). Both parties committed themselves to strengthening the OSCE, 'including developing further its role as a primary instrument in preventive diplomacy, conflict prevention, crisis management, post-conflict rehabilitation and regional security cooperation'.

For the OSCE, the year effectively ended with the ministerial council in Copenhagen on 18–19 December, when Mr Petersen asserted that the organization had 'confirmed its ability as a ready, workable and reliable instrument to deal with crises'. The OSCE had notched up a number of successes, notably in Albania and Bosnia & Hercegovina. In Estonia and Latvia the work of the OSCE high commissioner for national minorities, Max van der Stoel, had also brought steady progress. On the other hand, OSCE efforts had not borne fruit in places like Nagorno-Karabakh, Moldova, Belarus or Kosovo.

The Copenhagen council addressed one of the organization's perennial problems, namely money. A financial restructuring package was discussed, the OSCE budget for 1998 being set at US$49.3 million. Many saw this as a modest sum indeed, given the OSCE's critical role in furthering security and cooperation in Europe.

iii. EUROPEAN BANK FOR RECONSTRUCTION AND DEVELOPMENT (EBRD)

DATE OF FOUNDATION: 1991   HEADQUARTERS: London, UK
OBJECTIVES: To promote the economic reconstruction of former Communist-ruled countries on the basis of the free-market system and pluralism
MEMBERSHIP (END-'97): Albania, Armenia, Australia, Austria, Azerbaijan, Belarus, Belgium, Bosnia & Hercegovina, Bulgaria, Canada, Croatia, Cyprus, Czech Republic, Denmark, Egypt, Estonia, European Investment Bank, European Union, Finland, France, Georgia, Germany, Greece, Hungary, Iceland, Ireland, Israel, Italy, Japan, Kazakhstan, Kyrgyzstan, South Korea, Latvia, Liechtenstein, Lithuania, Luxembourg, Macedonia, Malta, Mexico, Moldova, Morocco, Netherlands, New Zealand, Norway, Poland, Portugal, Romania, Russia, Slovakia, Slovenia, Spain, Sweden, Switzerland, Tajikistan, Turkey, Turkmenistan, Ukraine, United Kingdom, United States, Uzbekistan (*total 60*)
PRESIDENT: Jacques de Larosière (France)

THE outgoing president of the EBRD, opening its annual general meeting held in London on 14–15 April, announced that the doubling of the bank's capital, agreed the year before at the Sofia meeting (see AR 1996, pp. 402–3), had become legally effective by the taking-up by more than half the members of two-thirds of the additional shares. The increase in the capital base to the full 20,000 million ECU was completed by the end of the year.

As foreseen, the bank would soon commit all of its initial 10,000 million ECU capital—10,256 million ECU from foundation in 1991 to end-1997—and in principle could not undertake more without recapitalization. In practice, that danger was not imminent, because gross disbursements to September 1997 totalled only 5,100 million ECU, of which 1,100 million ECU had already been repaid. Moreover, the bank was now able to plough back a regular and substantial annual profit—a net 16 million ECU in 1997 (against 5 million ECU in 1996); banking operations, including dividends from its now substantial equity holdings in the post-communist economies, contributed half of overall income, tight cost control continued and there were no major non-performers in the portfolio.

Satisfactory as the financial out-turn was, however, there was criticism both within and outside the bank that lending had become too conservative, particularly by a preference for taking shares in industrial enterprises only where a Western strategic investor also had equity. The bank insisted on some co-finance because its purpose was not only to back businesses and infrastructure development in 26 transitional economies, but also to attract other foreign investors to its region. Nevertheless, as the bank's annual Transition Report showed for late 1997, 19 of the 26 countries had securities exchanges and a framework for securities trading, and nine already had modern company laws, notably for shareholders' rights.

The critique was that, flush as it was with loanable funds, the bank could be more adventurous in going further beyond a radius of safe countries or projects. It was mixed with concern that an earlier dynamism had been dissipated by the loss of top management. The president, Jacques de Larosière (France), announced at the annual meeting that he would not be a candidate when his four-year term expired on 30 September. As an interim measure, he agreed to stay on until the end of January 1998, but no successor had been named by the end of the year, mainly because the French government was seeking for its nationals both the presidency of the bank and the governorship of the prospective European Central Bank (an appointment also unsettled by the year's end—see XI.3).

The bank's leadership was also impaired by the departure of the first vice-president, Ron Freeman (United States), and the vice-president for finance, Bart le Blanc (France); their replacements were respectively Charles Frank (United States) and Steven Kaempfer (Netherlands). Among a number of other senior staff who left during the year was the deputy vice-president, Guy de Selliers (Belgium), who had served with the bank since 1990 (before its formal foundation).

iv. NORDIC, BALTIC AND ARCTIC ORGANIZATIONS

Nordic Council
DATE OF FOUNDATION: 1952   HEADQUARTERS: Stockholm, Sweden
OBJECTIVES: To facilitate legislative and governmental cooperation between member states, with particular reference to proposals of the Nordic Council of Ministers
MEMBERSHIP (END-'97): Denmark, Finland, Iceland, Norway, Sweden (*total 5*)
SECRETARY-GENERAL: Anders Wenström (Sweden)

Baltic Council
DATE OF FOUNDATION: 1992   HEADQUARTERS: rotating
OBJECTIVES: To promote political, economic and social cooperation between the three Baltic republics
MEMBERSHIP (END-'97): Estonia, Latvia, Lithuania (*total 3*)

Council of the Baltic Sea States (CBSS)
DATE OF FOUNDATION: 1992   HEADQUARTERS: rotating
OBJECTIVES: To promote political, economic and other cooperation between Baltic littoral and adjacent states
MEMBERSHIP (END-'97): Denmark, Estonia, Finland, Germany, Latvia, Lithuania, Norway, Poland, Russia, Sweden (*total 10*)

Arctic Council (AC)
DATE OF FOUNDATION: 1996   HEADQUARTERS: Ottawa, Canada
OBJECTIVES: To promote cooperation between Arctic states (involving indigenous communities) on environmental issues and on the social and economic development of the region
MEMBERSHIP (END-'97): Canada, Denmark, Finland, Iceland, Norway, Russia, Sweden, United States (*total 8*)

THE network of organizations uniting the states of the Nordic, Baltic and Arctic regions continued to flourish during the year. This was despite considerable differences between the partners on a number of issues, most notably those pertaining to the future deepening and widening of the European Union (EU).

The year was marked by a further stage in the development of the Council of Baltic Sea States (CBSS), building on the 1996 Visby declaration (see AR 1996, p. 405). At the sixth CBSS ministerial session, held in Riga on 2–3 July, the Foreign Ministers of the 11 member states agreed that a permanent secretariat for the organization should be established in the near future. To this end, the committee of senior officials was instructed to prepare recommendations on the mandate, financing and location of the body. Whilst noting encouraging progress in the implementation of the EU Commission's Baltic Sea region initiative, the meeting highlighted the considerable challenges which lay ahead in the spheres of infrastructure, energy, differing legal frameworks, crime and the environment.

Environmental issues also provided the main focus for the activities of the Arctic Council, which integrated the existing programmes of the Arctic Environmental Protection Strategy into its activities during a meeting of Environment Ministers in Alta, Norway on 13 June.

Division was more apparent than unity at the 49th session of the Nordic Council held in Helsinki on 10–13 November, when the goal of policy alignment on EU issues (see AR 1996, pp. 404–5) again proved elusive. On the question of EU enlargement, Finland alone was in favour of the selective '5 + 1' model advocated by the Commission (and adopted by the European Council in December), under which formal accession negotiations would started with Estonia, the Czech Republic, Hungary, Poland and Slovenia plus Cyprus (see XI.3). Finland's partners argued, unsuccessfully as it turned out, for a 'regatta' approach of starting negotiations with all applicants simultaneously.

On EU economic and monetary union (EMU), Finnish Prime Minister Paavo Lipponen caused ripples with his assertion that Finland alone amongst the Nordic countries had taken the 'European way'—a comment not entirely borne out by surveys of Finnish public opinion published during the same week. The list of recommendations adopted at the session included calls for greater coordination in the spheres of asylum policy and environmental taxation, but the participants failed to reach agreement on a common strategy to reduce unemployment.

On a more positive note, the new-found emphasis on security issues (see AR 1996, p. 405) was further underlined during the year. For the first time in the history of the Council, the 49th session included addresses by the Nordic Defence Ministers, whilst a final recommendation upheld the view that every country had a right to decide its own security policy as a step towards the creation of a generalized European security framework. This statement was most likely adopted in response to Russia's offer of unilateral security guarantees to the Baltic states announced in October.

Continued impetus to Nordic-Baltic cooperation was confirmed with the signing of a new agreement between the Nordic Council and the Baltic Council on 26 September. The document, which provided for a strengthening of inter-parliamentary cooperation, superseded a previous cooperation agreement going back to 1992. The Prime Ministers of Estonia, Latvia and Lithuania attended the 49th session of the Nordic Council, where Guntars Krasts (Latvia) voiced the fear that inviting only Estonia to begin accession negotiations with the EU might upset cooperation between the three Baltic states.

By contrast, the 11th session of the inter-parliamentary Baltic Assembly—held in Vilnius on 7–8 November—was notable for its downplaying of national rivalries over EU entry. A resolution on EU integration welcomed the Commission opinion on the start of negotiations with Estonia, and stated merely that similar negotiations with Latvia and Lithuania should begin 'as soon as possible'. The deepening of inter-Baltic cooperation, meanwhile, was hailed as 'important and complementary to the processes of EU enlargement and trans-Atlantic integration', while other resolutions called for enhanced cross-border cooperation along the lines of Norden and Benelux groupings.

The Benelux experience had also been alluded to at the tenth session of the Baltic Assembly, held in the Estonian town of Pärnu on 25–26 April, when the three Baltic Premiers reaffirmed their intention to dismantle remaining barriers to free trade between their countries over the course of the year. Whilst adopting a resolution on political and economic support for Chechenya, the meeting stopped short of discussing the recognition of Chechen independence or the political situation in Belarus. Russia's offer of security guarantees to the three states met with a polite refusal from the 11th session, which declared that guarantees of Baltic security were best sought within the framework of the all-European security system and accession to the EU and NATO.

v. OTHER EUROPEAN ORGANIZATIONS

European Free Trade Association (EFTA)
DATE OF FOUNDATION: 1960   HEADQUARTERS: Geneva, Switzerland
OBJECTIVES: To eliminate barriers to non-agricultural trade between members
MEMBERSHIP (END-'97): Iceland, Liechtenstein, Norway, Switzerland (*total 4*)
SECRETARY-GENERAL: Kjartan Jóhannsson (Iceland)

Central European Free Trade Association (CEFTA)
DATE OF FOUNDATION: 1992   HEADQUARTERS: rotating
OBJECTIVES: Reducing trade barriers between members with a view to their eventual membership of the European Union
MEMBERSHIP (END-'97): Czech Republic, Hungary, Poland, Romania, Slovakia, Slovenia (*total 6*)

Central European Initiative (CEI)
DATE OF FOUNDATION: 1992   HEADQUARTERS: rotating
OBJECTIVES: To promote the harmonization of economic and other policies of member states
MEMBERSHIP (END-'97): Albania, Austria, Belarus, Bosnia & Hercegovina, Bulgaria, Croatia, Czech Republic, Hungary, Italy, Macedonia, Moldova, Poland, Romania, Slovakia, Slovenia, Ukraine (*total 16*)

Black Sea Economic Cooperation Council (BSEC)
DATE OF FOUNDATION: 1992   HEADQUARTERS: Istanbul, Turkey
OBJECTIVES: To promote economic cooperation between member states
MEMBERSHIP (END-'97): Albania, Armenia, Azerbaijan, Bulgaria, Georgia, Greece, Moldova, Romania, Russia, Turkey, Ukraine (*total 11*)
DIRECTOR: Eugeny Kutuvoy (Turkey)

THE European Free Trade Association (EFTA) was more visible in 1997 than in previous years. At a meeting in Geneva on 19 June, the Foreign Ministers of the four member states signed a free-trade agreement with Morocco and declarations on cooperation with Jordan and Lebanon, bringing the number of free-trade agreements between EFTA and countries in the Mediterranean region and Central/Eastern Europe to 13, and the number of cooperation declarations to seven. Talks on a free-trade agreement with Tunisia continued to progress, while negotiations with Cyprus were expected to open soon. The Foreign Ministers declared their satisfaction with EFTA's external relations and said that the final aim was the creation of a comprehensive Euro-Mediterranean free trade area.

Since three of its four members (Iceland, Liechtenstein and Norway) participated in the European Economic Area (EEA) along with the 15 European Union (EU) member states, relations with the EU remained of paramount importance for EFTA. Iceland, Liechtenstein and Norway stepped up their participation in EU programmes, and also intensified their involvement in the preparation of EU draft law. Also in 1997, the EEA decided to extend liberalization of the telecommunications market to the three EFTA countries. EFTA continued to be particularly interested in EU moves to liberalize the natural gas market, since Norway was a major supplier of the EU market and wanted to be heard on this issue.

Membership of the Central European Free Trade Association (CEFTA) went up to six when Romania signed the membership documents on 12 April and formally joined CEFTA on 1 July. The annual CEFTA summit, held in Portoroz, Slovenia, on 12–13 September, was attended by the Prime Ministers of the six member states, while the Premiers of Bulgaria, Croatia, Lithuania, Macedonia and Ukraine, as well as the Latvian Foreign Minister, attended parts of the proceedings. At the summit, the six member states decided that tariff and other barriers on intra-CEFTA agricultural trade would gradually be eliminated. Bulgaria was invited to open membership talks, which according to officials were expected to be concluded within a year. A meeting of the CEFTA Economy and Foreign Trade Ministers in Warsaw in December signed a protocol governing agricultural quotas. The ministers also reviewed CEFTA's past work and endorsed a plan for the future work of CEFTA's expert group aimed at reducing the differences between member states' agricultural systems, supporting exports of food products, and protecting the farming sector.

The loosely-organized Central European Initiative (CEI), with 16 member states, continued to be the biggest grouping in Central/Eastern Europe. In 1997 the CEI presidency was held by Bosnia & Hercegovina, its 'troika' for the year also including Austria (which had been acting president in 1996) and next-in-line Croatia. The CEI's annual summit took place in Sarajevo on 28–29 November, drawing around 200 ministerial and other official participants from the 16 member states. The summit adopted three documents—a Sarajevo Declaration, a Final Document and an Action Plan for 1998–99—calling *inter alia* for better communication among member states and stressing the need to protect minority rights.

Prior to the Sarajevo summit, a number of other CEI meetings had taken place. On 23–24 January the national coordinators of 14 of the 16 members met in Sarajevo to draw up the CEI's agenda for the year and to discuss several joint projects. On 7 June Sarajevo hosted a Foreign Ministers' plenary meeting, while on 25 October the Speakers of the CEI members states' national parliaments met in the Italian city of Trieste to discuss the position of national parliaments *vis-à-vis* international and regional institutions and the contribution of parliaments in the fight against organized crime. Italian Deputy Foreign Minister Piero Fassino said at the Trieste meeting that the CEI could help to prevent new divisions in Europe and was important as a means of holding together those countries aspiring to European Union and NATO membership but still some way off from achieving these goals.

The Presidents of eight states of Central/Eastern Europe (Austria, Czech

Republic, Germany, Hungary, Italy, Poland, Slovenia and Slovakia) met on 7 June for their annual sub-regional summit, this year in the Slovenian town of Portoroz. The Presidents called for the swift integration of ex-communist states into the EU and NATO, although President Milan Kucan of Slovenia warned that peoples must not lose their identity in the rush for European unity. The summit agreed not to enlarge the number of eight participating Presidents but decided that the host could invite guests with the consent of the other heads of state.

The Black Sea Economic Cooperation (BSEC) group held a summit conference in Istanbul on 28–30 April, attended not only by the 11 member states but also by several hundred ministerial and business representatives from some two dozen other countries. Earlier in the month government officials from BSEC countries and representatives of the International Monetary Fund (IMF) and the European Bank for Reconstruction and Development (EBRD) had participated in a conference in Tbilisi, Georgia, on reviving the historic Silk Road trading route between Asia and Europe. As part of such a revival, the so-called TRASECA project foresaw the expansion of existing road, rail and telecommunications links as well as ferry services across the Caspian and Black Seas.

On 9–11 December the Moldovan capital Chisinau hosted the 10th session of the BSEC parliamentary assembly. President Petru Lucinschi called on member countries to coordinate economic and commercial legislation and to transform the organization into one with a 'well-defined judicial status', since this would facilitate relations with other regional, European and international organizations, as well as with international financial institutions. The Moldovan President also called on member states to set up a free-trade zone and said that they could play a major role in the exploitation and transportation of Caspian Sea oil (see VIII.1.iii and map on page 301). The assembly elected Romanian Senate chairman Petru Roman as its chairman for 1998, in succession to Moldova's Dumitru Motpan.

The Turkish banker Ersoy Vulkan was officially named as head of the Black Sea Trade and Development Bank based in the Greek city of Thessaloniki. However, the bank's opening, which had been scheduled for May, was delayed as some shareholder countries apparently failed to pay their share of the equity capital.

5. ARAB, AFRICAN, ASIA-PACIFIC AND AMERICAN ORGANIZATIONS

i. ARAB ORGANIZATIONS

League of Arab States
DATE OF FOUNDATION: 1945   HEADQUARTERS: Cairo, Egypt
OBJECTIVES: To coordinate political, economic, social and cultural cooperation between member-states and to mediate in disputes between them
MEMBERSHIP (END-'97): Algeria, Bahrain, Comoros, Djibouti, Egypt, Iraq, Jordan, Kuwait, Lebanon, Libya, Mauritania, Morocco, Oman, Palestine, Qatar, Saudi Arabia, Somalia, Sudan, Syria, Tunisia, United Arab Emirates, Yemen (*total 22*)
SECRETARY-GENERAL: Ahmad Esmat Abdel Meguid (Egypt)

Gulf Cooperation Council (GCC)
DATE OF FOUNDATION: 1981   HEADQUARTERS: Riyadh, Saudi Arabia
OBJECTIVES: To promote cooperation between member states in all fields with a view to achieving unity
MEMBERSHIP (END '97): Bahrain, Kuwait, Oman, Qatar, Saudi Arabia, United Arab Emirates (*total 6*)
SECRETARY-GENERAL: Jameel al-Hujilan (Saudi Arabia)

Arab Maghreb Union (AMU)
DATE OF FOUNDATION: 1989   HEADQUARTERS: Casablanca, Morocco
OBJECTIVES: To strengthen 'the bonds of brotherhood' between member-states, particularly in the area of economic development
MEMBERSHIP (END-'97): Algeria, Libya, Mauritania, Morocco, Tunisia (*total 5*)
SECRETARY-GENERAL: Mohammed Amamou (Tunisia)

THE League of Arab States was seized of two issues during 1997: the deadlock in the Middle East peace process and the continuing crisis over Western accusations of Libyan involvement in the Lockerbie affair (the destruction of an American airliner by a bomb over the Scottish town of Lockerbie in December 1988 with the loss of 259 lives).

At their meeting in Cairo in September, Arab League Foreign Ministers called once again for an easing of the United Nations sanctions on Libya and, for the first time, called for an end to the air embargo on travel to and from Libya (see also V.4.ii). The League's communiqué called for flights to be permitted for 'humanitarian purposes', foreign national travel and religious purposes. The League's intervention allegedly infuriated the UN Secretary-General, Kofi Annan, because of the implicit threat to the sanctions regime. The League's communiqué was not, however, limited to Libya. Given the blockage in the Middle East peace process caused by the intransigence of the Netanyahu government (see V.1; V.2.i), the Foreign Ministers reiterated their support for a continued suspension of Arab participation in the multilateral round of the peace negotiations and of direct Arab negotiations with Israel until a lasting and comprehensive peace agreement had been achieved.

Several representative meetings of the Gulf Cooperation Council (GCC) took place during the year. GCC Foreign Ministers met in Riyadh at the end of May and registered their concern over Turkish incursions into northern Iraq and over the stagnation in the Middle East peace process. They also expressed hopes for positive developments in regional relations with Iran in the wake of the election of Mohammed Khatami as President earlier in the month (see VIII.1.i) and called on Iraq to cooperate with the UN Special Commission (UNSCOM) investigating its armaments. The Foreign Ministers met again at Abha (Saudi Arabia) on 15 July and called on Iraq to comply with the UN sanctions regime fully as the only way in which the regime itself could eventually be ended. They also reiterated their support for the United Arab Emirates (UAE) in its territorial dispute with Iran over Abu Musa and the Tunb Islands.

In a further meeting in Kuwait on 25–26 November, the Foreign Ministers adopted recommendations for the forthcoming 18th GCC summit, while the GCC Finance Ministers drew up proposals on financial issues designed to complete the economic integration of GCC states. At the 18th annual GCC summit held in Kuwait on 20–22 December the GCC leaders welcomed the improvement in relations with Iran, although they continued to support the UAE's claim to the disputed Gulf islands. They criticized Europe for its willingness to harbour terrorists masquerading as political refugees and renewed their calls on Iraq to acknowledge its guilt over the invasion of Kuwait, also demanding that it should fulfil its obligations towards the United Nations.

The Kuwait summit also decided to plan for a GCC-wide consultative assembly and approved measures agreed earlier by GCC Finance Ministers to integrate their economies. These involved tariff unification, integration of power grids and arrangements to encourage foreign and intra-GCC investment. In the security field, the leaders agreed to create an early-warning defence system for the GCC region over the next two years, involving a $88 million radar network and a $70 million communications system.

The Damascus Declaration Group, involving the GCC states together with Egypt and Syria, continued in its virtually moribund state throughout the year. The Foreign Ministers of the states concerned met in Damascus on 25–26 June to discuss plans to create a free-trade area between them. The move was largely dictated by Arab disappointment at the lack of progress in the Middle East peace process and observers expected little to come of the initiative. At the meeting, the Foreign Ministers also expressed their concern at the growing closeness between Israel and Turkey, particularly in the military field.

ii. AFRICAN ORGANIZATIONS AND CONFERENCES

Organization of African Unity (OAU)
DATE OF FOUNDATION: 1963   HEADQUARTERS: Addis Ababa, Ethiopia
OBJECTIVES: To promote the unity, solidarity and cooperation of African states, to defend their sovereignty and to eradicate remaining traces of colonialism
MEMBERSHIP (END-'97): Algeria, Angola, Benin, Botswana, Burkina Faso, Burundi, Cameroon, Cape Verde, Central African Republic, Chad, Comoros, Democratic Republic of the Congo, Republic of Congo, Côte d'Ivoire, Djibouti, Egypt, Equatorial Guinea, Eritrea, Ethiopia, Gabon, Gambia, Ghana, Guinea, Guinea-Bissau, Kenya, Lesotho, Liberia, Libya, Madagascar, Malawi, Mali, Mauritania, Mauritius, Mozambique, Namibia, Niger, Nigeria, Rwanda, Sahrawi Arab Democratic Republic, São Tomé & Príncipe, Senegal, Seychelles, Sierra Leone, Somalia, South Africa, Sudan, Swaziland, Tanzania, Togo, Tunisia, Uganda, Zambia, Zimbabwe (*total 53*)
SECRETARY-GENERAL: Salim Ahmed Salim (Tanzania)

Economic Community of West African States (ECOWAS)
DATE OF FOUNDATION: 1975   HEADQUARTERS: Abuja, Nigeria
OBJECTIVES: To seek the creation of an economic union of member states
MEMBERSHIP (END-'97): Benin, Burkina Faso, Cape Verde, Côte d'Ivoire, Gambia, Ghana, Guinea, Guinea-Bissau, Liberia, Mali, Mauritania, Niger, Nigeria, Senegal, Sierra Leone, Togo (*total 16*)
EXECUTIVE SECRETARY: Lansana Kouyate (Guinea)

West African Economic and Monetary Union (UEMOA)
DATE OF FOUNDATION: 1994   HEADQUARTERS: Ouagadougou, Burkina Faso
OBJECTIVES: To promote the economic and monetary union of member states
MEMBERSHIP (END-'97): Benin, Burkina Faso, Côte d'Ivoire, Guinea-Bissau, Mali, Niger, Senegal, Togo (*total 8*)

Southern African Development Community (SADC)
DATE OF FOUNDATION: 1992   HEADQUARTERS: Gaborone, Botswana
OBJECTIVES: To work towards the creation of a regional common market
MEMBERSHIP (END-'97): Angola, Botswana, Democratic Republic of the Congo, Lesotho, Malawi, Mauritius, Mozambique, Namibia, Seychelles, South Africa, Swaziland, Tanzania, Zambia, Zimbabwe (*total 14*)
EXECUTIVE SECRETARY: Kaire Mbuende (Namibia)

Common Market for Eastern and Southern Africa (COMESA)
DATE OF FOUNDATION: 1993 (succeeding Preferential Trade Area)
HEADQUARTERS: Lusaka, Zambia
OBJECTIVES: To establish a full free-trade area
MEMBERSHIP (END-'97): Angola, Burundi, Comoros, Democratic Republic of the Congo, Eritrea, Ethiopia, Kenya, Lesotho, Madagascar, Malawi, Mauritius, Namibia, Rwanda, Sudan, Swaziland, Tanzania, Uganda, Zambia, Zimbabwe (*total 19*)
SECRETARY-GENERAL: Bingo wa Mutharika (suspended)

Economic Community of Central African States (CEEAC)
DATE OF FOUNDATION: 1983   HEADQUARTERS: Libreville, Gabon
OBJECTIVES: To establish a full free-trade area
MEMBERSHIP (END-'97): Burundi, Cameroon, Central African Republic, Chad, Democratic Republic of the Congo, Republic of the Congo, Equatorial Guinea, Gabon, Rwanda, São Tomé & Príncipe (*total 10*)
SECRETARY-GENERAL: Kasasa Mutati Chinyata

East African Commission (EAC)
DATE OF FOUNDATION: 1996 (reviving former East African Community)
HEADQUARTERS: Nairobi, Kenya
OBJECTIVES: To promote economic integration between member states
MEMBERSHIP (END-'97): Kenya, Tanzania, Uganda (*total 3*)

THE annual summit of the Organization of African Unity (OAU) took place, as not infrequently in the past, in the shadow of a suddenly-erupting crisis, in this case that of Sierra Leone (see VI.ii.3). The 33rd summit was held on 2–4 June, in the Zimbabwean capital, Harare, while the coup in Freetown overthrowing the civilian government of President Ahmed Tejan Kabba took place on 25 May, even as African ministers were converging on Harare.

The fact that the Sierra Leone coup actually took place on Africa Day, marking the anniversary of the founding of the OAU in 1963, was an additional affront to the organization, in which many member-states already had strong reservations about military governments. This was particularly strongly articulated by President Mugabe of Zimbabwe, who took on the chairmanship of the OAU for the first time. It was the first time, also, that Harare had ever hosted the summit. In his welcoming speech he expressed grave concern at events in Sierra Leone, saying that the OAU would not rest until a democratically-elected government was restored in that country, telling a press conference later: 'There is now a definite attitude to coups and illegitimate governments. We are getting tougher and tougher each time as we move into the future.' One result of the timing was that the summit passed a unanimous resolution giving the green light for the ECOMOG monitoring group of the Economic Community of West African States (ECOWAS) to intervene in Sierra Leone with the aim of restoring President Kabba to power (see VI.2.iii).

The summit witnessed a difference of opinion between President Mugabe and the UN Secretary-General, Kofi Annan of Ghana, in their respective speeches at the opening session. Mr Mugabe said that democracy had to be 'judiciously pursued', but criticized Western governments for demanding instant democracy in Africa: 'There is need to avoid the danger of being compelled by self-appointed mentors to go through the motions of democracy without enthroning the substance.' Mr Annan's emphasis was distinctly different. Noting that criticisms of human rights violations were viewed by some African leaders as 'an imposition, if not a plot, by the industrialized West', the UN Secretary-General continued: 'I find these thoughts truly demeaning—demeaning of the yearning for human dignity that resides in every African heart.'

The Harare summit unanimously re-elected the organization's secretary-general, Salim Ahmed Salim (Tanzania), for a third four-year term. A move by Côte d'Ivoire's Foreign Minister, Amara Essy, to float his own candidacy prior to the summit foundered from lack of support. This was the first time that any OAU secretary-general had served more than two terms, Mr Salim's re-election being a measure of his prestige in Africa and internationally, deriving in part from the acknowledged increased efficiency of the secretariat. He was also praised for the cautious but useful involvement of the OAU in trying to build up, with support from Britain, France and the United States, an African intervention capacity.

Now known as the African Crisis Response Initiative, this capacity involved the training and equipping of selected troops from individual African armies, although it was not yet anticipated that anything as ambitious as an African High Command would be created. The project was still regarded with suspicion by some countries, notably Nigeria, which, in spite of its substantial peacekeeping experience, had not yet become involved in the exercise.

Other subjects of resolutions at Harare included Liberia, Burundi and the continuing vexed question of Libya's alleged involvement in the 1988 Lockerbie airliner bombing, on which the summit repeated earlier OAU resolutions that the accused Libyans should be tried by courts other than those of Britain and the United States. The summit also called for the democratization of the United Nations and for two African states to be allocated permanent seats on the Security Council (see also XI.1).

On economic matters, the summit adopted a strategy for the African Economic Community (AEC) planned to be inaugurated in 2025, after a process of uniting the continent's existing regional groupings. These were listed as the Southern African Development Community (SADC), ECOWAS, the Common Market for Eastern and Southern Africa (COMESA), the East African Commission (EAC), the Arab Maghreb Union (AMU) and the Economic Community of Central African States (CEEAC). The current chairmen of the SADC and COMESA, respectively Presidents Chissano of Mozambique and Chiluba of Zambia, both endorsed the strategy, but the current chairman of ECOWAS, President Abacha of Nigeria, was notably absent. To accompany the strategy, the OAU set in motion the Alliance for Africa's Industrialization (AAI) sponsored by the UN Industrial Development Organization (UNIDO). The summit resolution recognized that 'without sustainable industrial development, African economies will be condemned to persistent economic crises'.

Observers noted that the six groupings mentioned in the AEC strategy had reached different stages of development. The SADC, for example, was widely commended for the progress it had made in different areas of regional integration, whereas the larger and much more diffuse COMESA grouping, stretching from Namibia to the Horn of Africa, was barely off the drawing-board. The CEEAC and the AMU also had little substance as yet, while the EAC—an attempt to revive the old East African Community—had been set up as recently as 1996. Founded in 1975 (and the oldest of the groupings), ECOWAS had been much more successful on the level of politics and security than on economic integration: its trade liberalization measures had made extremely slow progress and plans for a monetary union none at all.

One of the reasons for ECOWAS's lack of progress on monetary union was that some of its 16 members were also part of the West African Monetary and Economic Union (Union Économique et Monétaire Ouest Africain, UEMOA) set up in 1994 as a merger of the old West African Monetary Union and the West African Economic Community (Communauté Économique Ouest Africaine, CEAO). Although the merger had been pushed strongly by both the French and the European Union (and in May was boosted by the accession of Guinea-Bissau, which entered the franc zone at the same time), it still experienced difficulties. At a ministerial meeting in November, it was decided to delay the start of a common external tariff (leading to a customs union) from 1 January

1998 to 1 January 2000. Instead, a programme of more gradual tariff reductions over the next two years was introduced. At the same time, a UEMOA Stock Exchange (Bourse Regionale des Valeurs, BRV) was established in Abidjan (for formal opening on 1 January), into which was absorbed the Côte d'Ivoire Stock Exchange.

A measure of the SADC's success was likewise its continuing expansion, the Democratic Republic of the Congo (formerly Zaïre), a potential economic giant, and the Seychelles being admitted as new members. The accessions took place at the SADR summit, held in Malawi in September, which was also notable for a proposal from President Mandela for sanctions against those members which did not practise democratic values. Behind this was a row with President Mugabe of Zimbabwe over control of the newly-created SADC Organ for Politics, Defence and Security (see also VII.2.iv).

In personnel decisions in 1997, ECOWAS appointed another Guinean, Lansana Kouyate, to replace the ailing Edouard Benjamin as executive secretary, while COMESA suspended Bingu wa Mutharika as secretary-general pending a commission of inquiry into the organization's finances.

iii. ASIA-PACIFIC ORGANIZATIONS

Association of South-East Asian Nations (ASEAN)
DATE OF FOUNDATION: 1967   HEADQUARTERS: Jakarta, Indonesia
OBJECTIVES: To accelerate economic growth, social progress and cultural development in the region
MEMBERSHIP (END-'97): Brunei, Indonesia, Laos, Malaysia, Myanmar, Philippines, Singapore, Thailand, Vietnam (*total 9*)
SECRETARY-GENERAL: Rodolfo C. Severino (Philippines)

Asia-Pacific Economic Cooperation (APEC)
DATE OF FOUNDATION: 1989   HEADQUARTERS: Singapore
OBJECTIVES: To promote market-oriented economic development and cooperation in the Pacific Rim countries
MEMBERSHIP (END-'97): Australia, Brunei, Canada, Chile, China, Hong Kong, Indonesia, Japan, South Korea, Malaysia, Mexico, New Zealand, Papua New Guinea, Philippines, Singapore, Taiwan, Thailand, United States (*total 18*)
EXECUTIVE DIRECTOR: Jack A. Whittleton (Canada)

Pacific Community (SPC)
DATE OF FOUNDATION: 1947 (as South Pacific Commission)
HEADQUARTERS: Nouméa, New Caledonia
OBJECTIVES: To facilitate political and other cooperation between member states and territories
MEMBERSHIP (END-'97): American Samoa, Australia, Cook Islands, Fiji, France, French Polynesia, Guam, Kiribati, Marshall Islands, Federated States of Micronesia, Nauru, New Caledonia, New Zealand, Niue, Northern Mariana Islands, Palau, Papua New Guinea, Pitcairn Islands, Samoa, Solomon Islands, Tokelau, Tonga, Tuvalu, United States, Vanuatu, Wallis & Futuna Islands (*total 26; the UK, which had withdrawn in 1996, was due to rejoin in January 1998*)
DIRECTOR-GENERAL: Bob Dun (Australia)

South Pacific Forum (SPF)
DATE OF FOUNDATION: 1971   HEADQUARTERS: Suva, Fiji
OBJECTIVES: To enhance the economic and social well-being of the people of the South Pacific, in support of the efforts of the members' governments
MEMBERSHIP (END-'97): Australia, Palau, Cook Islands, Fiji, Kiribati, Marshall Islands, Federated States of Micronesia, Nauru, New Zealand, Niue, Papua New Guinea, Samoa, Solomon Islands, Tonga, Tuvalu, Vanuatu (*total 16*)
SECRETARY-GENERAL: Noel Levi (Papua New Guinea)

South Asian Association for Regional Cooperation (SAARC)
DATE OF FOUNDATION: 1985   HEADQUARTERS: Kathmandu, Nepal
OBJECTIVES: To promote collaboration and mutual assistance in the economic, social, cultural and technical fields
MEMBERSHIP (END-'97): Bangladesh, Bhutan, India, Maldives, Nepal, Pakistan, Sri Lanka (*total 7*)
SECRETARY-GENERAL: Nacem ul-Hasan (Pakistan)

Indian Ocean Rim Association for Regional Cooperation (IORARC)
DATE OF FOUNDATION: 1997
OBJECTIVES: To promote cooperation in trade, investment, infrastructure, tourism, science, technology and human-resource development in the Indian Ocean region
MEMBERSHIP (END-'97): Australia, India, Indonesia, Kenya, Madagascar, Malaysia, Mauritius, Mozambique, Oman, Singapore, South Africa, Sri Lanka, Tanzania, Yemen (*total 14*)

DURING the second half of the year, meetings of the major Asian regional organizations were dominated by the financial crisis which swept across much of Asia following the devaluation of the Thai currency in July (see XVIII.1).

The crisis was the main topic on the agenda of an informal summit meeting of the heads of state and government of the Association of South-East Asian Nations (ASEAN) held in the Malaysian capital, Kuala Lumpur, in mid-December. The gathering was also attended by President Jiang Zemin of China, Prime Minister Ryutaro Hashimoto of Japan and Prime Minister Koh Kun of South Korea. The talks were marked by a sense of growing dissatisfaction with the IMF's emergency assistance programmes to the troubled Asian economies (the IMF having in recent months arranged rescue packages worth a total of more than US$80,000 million for Thailand, Indonesia and South Korea). A statement issued by the ASEAN leaders at the end of the meeting called for global efforts to help combat the fall in value of the region's currencies. The leaders also agreed to accelerate the reduction of regional tariffs to help combat the crisis.

The heads of state and government and the economic ministers of the 18 member countries of the Asia-Pacific Economic Cooperation (APEC) forum held their fifth annual meeting in late November in Vancouver, Canada. Inevitably, the summit was dominated by the financial crisis. Whilst some countries reportedly pressed for the creation of a regional assistance programme for ailing Asian economies, others (notably the United States) voiced concerns over the potential undermining of the IMF's authority through such a move. Despite such disagreements, it was widely acknowledged that the summit had been more topical and dynamic than previous meetings and that the United States had played a central role in redefining APEC's scope and direction, by placing it much more firmly in the context of the global economy.

The deliberations in Vancouver resulted in the APEC leaders expressing support for a plan to liberalize trade in nine sectors, including fish and fish products, forestry products, energy, chemicals and telecommunications. The details of the plan were to be finalized by June 1998 and implemented in 1999. The final communiqué of the summit also agreed to work towards a successful conclusion of World Trade Organization (WTO) negotiations on financial services liberalization by the 12 December deadline (see also XVIII.1). Agreement was also reached on admitting Vietnam, Peru and Russia as new APEC members in 1998, after which there would be a ten-year moratorium on further expansion.

Aside from the Asian financial crisis, the other major theme which dominated ASEAN affairs during 1997 was the decision to accord membership to Myanmar (Burma). When ASEAN Foreign Ministers met their European Union (EU) counterparts in Singapore in February, differences over human rights issues in Myanmar and the Indonesian-annexed province of East Timor prevented any agreement on an 'action plan' to replace the expired EU-ASEAN agreement of 1980, which had laid the foundations for cooperation on trade issues. The Myanmar military government had been widely criticized in Europe for its continued suppression of the pro-democracy movement led by Nobel laureate Aung San Suu Kyi.

Despite intense European opposition, a meeting of ASEAN Foreign Ministers in Kuala Lumpur in May agreed to admit Myanmar, Cambodia and Laos into the regional organization in July. In an apparent attempt to limit the potential for disputes with Western states, Malaysia's Foreign Minister, Abdullah Ahmad Badawi, said that the new members would not attend meetings with ASEAN 'dialogue partners' (a group which included the United States and the EU) at the organization's annual Foreign Ministers' meeting in July. The US government reacted cautiously to the prospective accession of Myanmar, having imposed economic sanctions against that country in April and having lobbied other ASEAN states to delay or refuse the admission. After the decision had been taken, however, US officials stressed that ASEAN and the United States shared the same approach of 'constructive engagement' towards the Myanmar junta.

The 30th annual session of ASEAN Foreign Ministers duly took place in late July in Kuala Lumpur. Immediately prior to the meeting, Myanmar and Laos had been formally admitted as members, thereby increasing ASEAN's total membership to nine. In early July it had been announced that Cambodian membership had been delayed pending a settlement of the internal conflict which had erupted in the country in early July (see IX.1.ix). A joint communiqué issued at the close of the meeting expressed 'regret' that Cambodia could not be admitted and confirmed that its observer status remained unchanged. The ministers expressed hope that a peaceful solution could be found to the current conflict, so that Cambodia would soon be able to join the organization and thereby 'fulfil the vision of an ASEAN community of ten'. The ministers also approved the appointment of Rodolfo C. Severino of the Philippines as secretary-general of ASEAN from 1 January 1998 for a five-year term.

The fourth ASEAN Regional Forum (ARF) was held in Subang Jaya, Malaysia, in late July. Delegates from 21 countries attended the meeting, which was dominated by events in Cambodia. It was also reported that the US Secretary of State, Madeleine Albright, had used the meeting as an opportunity to denounce the Myanmar junta, which was represented at the meeting by Foreign Minister U Ohn Gyaw.

The 29th meeting of ASEAN Economic Ministers (AEM) was held in Kuala Lumpur in mid-October. Malaysian Prime Minister Mahathir Mohamad addressed the opening session and advocated sound economic policies as the best defence against the currency speculation which had precipitated the regional currency crisis. Dr Mahathir said that, in order to achieve long-term ASEAN prosperity, member countries should cooperate in formulating a macroeconomic policy to ensure the achievement of a stable, sustainable economic base. (For Dr Mahathir's citation, in other speeches in October, of 'rogue speculators' and an international Jewish conspiracy as causes of the Asian financial crisis, see IX.1.iii.)

Finance Ministers from the 25 Asian and European countries which had been represented at the inaugural Asia-Europe Meeting (ASEM) in Thailand in March 1996 met in Japan in late September. Attended by the 15 EU member states plus Brunei, China, Indonesia, Japan, South Korea, Malaysia, the Philippines, Singapore, Thailand and Vietnam, the meeting sought to establish principles and common policy tasks, being part of the preparation for the second ASEM summit scheduled for April 1998. During the meeting the ministers agreed on five principles for enhanced economic cooperation between Asia and Europe, namely transparency, consistency, non-discriminatory liberalization, open regionalism and compliance with international rules. They also established three policy goals: greater economic interaction; sustained and stable economic growth; and improvement of the business environment towards increased trade and investment.

A meeting of the Melanesian Spearhead group (consisting of Fiji, Papua New Guinea, the Solomon Islands, Vanuatu and the Kanak population of the French overseas territory of New Caledonia) took place in Fiji in May. During the course of the meeting it was agreed that Papua New Guinea and the Solomon Islands would cooperate in an attempt to resolve the Bougainville secessionist conflict in Papua New Guinea (see also X.1.ii). The conflict had been a continuing source of tension between the two countries, in that the Solomon Islands (the population of which was culturally and ethnically close to the inhabitants of Bougainville) had frequently been accused by Papua New Guinea of providing tacit support for the rebellion.

The 26 member states of the South Pacific Commission, meeting in Nouméa, New Caledonia, in late May, agreed to rename the organization the Pacific Community, which was seen as more accurately representing its geographical extent. The established SPC abbreviation was preserved by unofficially adding 'Secretariat of the' to the official title. The meeting also agreed a new contributions structure and established a new Small Islands States Fund to provide money for technical advice and training for 12 small Pacific states and territories. At an SPC conference in Australia in October, the United

Kingdom announced that it would rejoin the organization in 1998 (having withdrawn in 1996 citing a lack of clear direction and the proportion of funds spent on administration).

The heads of government of the 16-member South Pacific Forum (SPF) held their 28th annual summit in the New Zealand dependency of the Cook Islands in mid-September. Proceedings were dominated by discussions on greenhouse gas emissions and measures to cope with global warming, Australia refusing to sign any communiqué which called for legally-binding targets for the cutting of greenhouse emissions (see also X.1.i). The Australian position was criticised by most of the smaller countries, which had been anxious to set such targets. At the meeting, Noel Levi of Papua New Guinea was unanimously elected secretary-general of the SPF, replacing Ieremia Tabai of Kiribati.

The ninth summit of the South Asian Association for Regional Cooperation (SAARC) was held in the Maldives in May, bringing together the heads of state or government of Bangladesh, Bhutan, India, the Maldives, Nepal, Pakistan and Sri Lanka. The leaders pledged to speed up the dismantling of tariffs and bureaucratic obstacles to trade, and to bring forward the date for the establishment of a regional free-trade zone from 2005 to 2001.

The Indian Ocean Rim Association for Regional Cooperation (IORARC) was set up at a meeting of Foreign Ministers from 14 countries in Mauritius on 5–7 March. The new organization's charter stressed the development of regional trade as a top objective, to be achieved in particular by removing impediments to trade and lowering tariff barriers. The work programme adopted by the ministers focused on promoting trade, investment and technology transfers. Opening the meeting, Prime Minister Navin Ramgoolam of Mauritius pointed out that in 1994 trade among the Indian Ocean Rim countries had accounted for only 22 per cent of their total trade, adding: 'There is huge scope for us to do better. The opportunities are immense, and our association is long overdue.' A number of countries, including Iran, Pakistan, Seychelles and Thailand, subsequently expressed interest in joining the new organization.

iv. AMERICAN ORGANIZATIONS

Organization of American States (OAS)
DATE OF FOUNDATION: 1951   HEADQUARTERS: Washington DC, USA
OBJECTIVES: To facilitate political, economic and other cooperation between member states and to defend their territorial integrity and independence
MEMBERSHIP (END-'97): Antigua & Barbuda, Argentina, Bahamas, Barbados, Belize, Bolivia, Brazil, Canada, Chile, Colombia, Costa Rica, Cuba (*currently excluded*), Dominica, Dominican Republic, Ecuador, El Salvador, Grenada, Guatemala, Guyana, Haiti, Honduras, Jamaica, Mexico, Nicaragua, Panama, Paraguay, Peru, St Kitts & Nevis, St Lucia, St Vincent & the Grenadines, Suriname, Trinidad & Tobago, United States, Uruguay, Venezuela (*total 35*)
SECRETARY-GENERAL: César Gaviria Trujillo (Colombia)

Rio Group
DATE OF FOUNDATION: 1987   HEADQUARTERS: rotating
OBJECTIVES: To provide a regional mechanism for joint political action
MEMBERSHIP (END-'97): Argentina, Bolivia, Brazil, Chile, Colombia, Ecuador, Guatemala, Mexico, Panama, Paraguay, Peru, Trinidad & Tobago, Uruguay, Venezuela (*total 11*)

Southern Common Market (Mercosur)
DATE OF FOUNDATION: 1991   HEADQUARTERS: Montevideo, Uruguay
OBJECTIVES: To build a genuine common market between member states
MEMBERSHIP (END-'97): Argentina, Brazil, Paraguay, Uruguay (*total 4*)
ADMINISTRATIVE SECRETARY: Manuel Olarreaga (Uruguay)

Andean Community (CA)
DATE OF FOUNDATION: 1969   HEADQUARTERS: Lima, Peru
OBJECTIVES: To promote the economic development and integration of member states
MEMBERSHIP (END-'97): Bolivia, Colombia, Ecuador, Venezuela (*total 4*)
SECRETARY-GENERAL: José Antonio García Belaunde (Peru)

Caribbean Community and Common Market (Caricom)
DATE OF FOUNDATION: 1973   HEADQUARTERS: Georgetown, Guyana
OBJECTIVES: To facilitate economic, political and other cooperation between member states and to operate certain regional services
MEMBERSHIP (END-'97): Antigua & Barbuda, Bahamas, Barbados, Belize, Dominica, Grenada, Guyana, Haiti, Jamaica, Montserrat, St Kitts & Nevis, St Lucia, St Vincent & the Grenadines, Suriname, Trinidad & Tobago (*total 15*)
SECRETARY-GENERAL: Edward Carrington (Trinidad & Tobago)

Association of Caribbean States (ACS)
DATE OF FOUNDATION: 1994   HEADQUARTERS: Port of Spain, Trinidad
OBJECTIVES: To foster economic, social and political cooperation with a view to building a distinctive bloc of Caribbean littoral states
MEMBERSHIP (END-'97): Caricom members (*see above*) plus Colombia, Costa Rica, Cuba, Dominican Republic, El Salvador, Guatemala, Haiti, Honduras, Mexico, Nicaragua, Venezuela (*total 25*)
SECRETARY-GENERAL: Simón Molina Duarte (Venezuela)

Organization of Eastern Caribbean States (OECS)
DATE OF FOUNDATION: 1981   HEADQUARTERS: Castries, St Lucia
OBJECTIVES: To coordinate the external, defence, trade and monetary policies of member states
MEMBERSHIP (END-'97): Antigua & Barbuda, Dominica, Grenada, Montserrat, St Lucia, St Kitts & Nevis, St Vincent & the Grenadines (*total 7*)
DIRECTOR-GENERAL: Swinburne Lestrade (Dominica)

THE 27th general assembly of the Organization of American States (OAS) was held in Lima, Peru, on 1–5 June. A total of 35 resolutions were approved, of which the most important were those dealing with the maintenance of an international peace-keeping presence in Haiti, action against drug-trafficking and the eradication of landmines.

A meeting of Trade Ministers from 34 countries took place in Belo Horizonte, Brazil, on 14–16 May. They agreed that formal negotiations to create a Free Trade Area of the Americas (FTAA) (see AR 1994, p. 450) should begin at a second 'Summit of the Americas' to be held at Santiago de Chile in March 1998, expressing the tentative view that the FTAA would be compatible with existing sub-regional groupings. No agreement on the order of negotiations was reached, however, and the issue was deferred to a further meeting of Trade Ministers in Costa Rica in February 1998.

The US President, Bill Clinton, attended a Central American summit in San José on 8 May, at which he expressed his hope for closer collaboration. The Central American delegates hoped for access to the North American Free Trade Agreement (NAFTA) on equal terms. However, President Clinton offered only to ask the US Congress to review President Reagan's Caribbean Basin Initiative (CBI) to allow selective duty-free access for certain products within the context of the future FTAA. On 2 September the Presidents of the Central American republics, meeting in Managua, Nicaragua, signed a declaration, committing themselves to create a regional political union on the model of the European Union (EU).

The 11th summit of heads of state and government of the Rio Group, which met on 21–23 August at Asuncion, Paraguay, condemned the principle of the unilateral application of national laws by one state against another as a violation of sovereignty, also condemning the US Helms-Burton Act in particular. The leaders agreed to cooperate to secure free trade between member states and to work towards the creation of the FTAA, while also endorsing the objective of sustainable growth. Proposals for the reform of the UN Charter to enhance the region's representation on the Security Council were also agreed, though comments by President Carlos Menem of Argentina criticizing Brazil's bid for a permanent seat were badly received in Brasilia (see also XI.1).

The Finance Ministers of the Southern Common Market (Mercosur), together with the Chilean Finance Minister, met in Asuncion on 23 April, failing to resolve a dispute between Brazil and the other three Mercosur members over Brazil's imposition in March of restrictions on the financing of imports. At the 12th Mercosur summit, held in Asuncion on 12 June, the six participating Presidents (of the four full members and associates Chile and Bolivia) agreed to support the creation of the FTAA, to strengthen relations with the EU and to accelerate the integration of their economies by improving government competitiveness. During an official visit to Brazil on 13–15 October, President Clinton stated categorically that previous US criticisms could be ignored and that Mercosur did not conflict with the goal of achieving the FTAA.

In mid-April the Peruvian government announced its intention to withdraw from the Andean Community, formerly the Andean Pact (*Acuerdo de Cartagena*), which it had rejoined in 1994. It failed to be represented at the summit meeting held in Sucre, Ecuador, on 23 April. At the seventh Ibero-American summit, held on 8–9 November on the Venezuelan Isla de Margarita, and attended by 23 heads of state and government, representatives of the Andean Community and Mercosur agreed in principle to form a single trading bloc.

CARIBBEAN ORGANIZATIONS. Following the Central American summit (see above), President Clinton attended a meeting of heads of government of the Caribbean Community and Common Market (Caricom), held on 10 May at Bridgetown, Barbados, at which the President of Haiti was also present. Again he made encouraging noises about revising the CBI but made no concessions either on NAFTA parity or on the thorny 'dollar bananas' question, where US action in the World Trade Organization (WTO) to protect its banana importers (see also XI.3) threatened to bankrupt several Caribbean states overnight. At the same time, the US leader pledged assistance for Caribbean economic diversification and promised to introduce a bill to widen the range of products eligible for duty-free access to the US market.

At the 18th summit of CARICOM heads of state, held at Montego Bay, Jamaica, on 2–6 July, Haiti was formally admitted as the organization's 15th member. A decision was deferred, however, on Cuba's application to negotiate a free trade treaty with the Community, which reaffirmed its aim of achieving a single market by 1999 and a common currency soon thereafter. The targets of universal secondary education in Caricom states by 2005, together with a doubling of college and university students, were also endorsed. The summit decided to establish a 'Caricom village' in volcano-devastated Montserrat and expressed the hope that British aid for the territory would be more forthcoming (see IV.4.ix).

The Montego Bay summit also decided to create a 'regional negotiating machinery', based in Barbados and headed by Sir Shridath Ramphal (the former Commonwealth secretary-general), who would represent Caricom members in external trade negotiations. His first priority would be the negotiation of the fifth Lomé Convention between the EU and the African, Caribbean and Pacific (ACP) states scheduled to take place in 1998.

In late July a meeting between Caricom and Dominican Republic representatives within the Cariforum framework established guidelines for a free-trade agreement covering goods, services and investment. A similar agreement was planned with Colombia, as were closer ties with Cuba and the Mercosur grouping.

Meeting in May, the board of governors of the Caribbean Development Bank (CDB) approved an application from the People's Republic of China to become a non-borrowing member. In a joint presentation, five dependent territories appealed to the CDB to change its lending criteria (based on GDP per capita), claiming that they took no account of the problems of small islands in providing basic services and amenities.

On 13 November the secretaries-general of CARICOM and the Association of Caribbean States (ACS) signed an agreement providing for regular consultation and collaboration, together with exchanges of information to avoid duplication of work.

The Organization of Eastern Caribbean States (OECS) was allocated US$165 million by the EU to assist the diversification efforts of the banana-producing countries and to establish 'core groups of efficient banana growers'. The Florida-Caribbean Cruise Association in November voiced strong objections to a decision by the OECS to impose an environmental levy of US$1.50 per person on all visitors, effective 1 December. The levy was expected to produce annual revenue of some US$2.7 million.

XII DEFENCE, DISARMAMENT AND SECURITY

THE transfer of emphasis from defence towards security was again evident in 1997, in that military threats to world peace continued to diminish while non-military threats acquired greater momentum. The non-military threats involved criminal activities of one type or another which imperilled the security of individuals by destruction of the environment, by corruption of youth through drugs, or by destabilization of national economies through laundering of the financial proceeds of crime or through electronic fraud or theft.

Arms control negotiations showed promise of continued reductions in holdings of strategic warheads and the vehicles for their delivery, provided that the START II Treaty obtained ratification from the Russian parliament (which was not forthcoming in 1997) and that START III could be got under way. US-Russian negotiations continued on the differentiation of 'theatre missile defences' from 'strategic defences', resulting in the signing of an understanding on the 1972 Anti-Ballistic Missile Treaty.

Tactical nuclear weapons were one class of nuclear armaments not yet subject to limitation by treaty. These short-range weapons had so far not featured in disarmament negotiations, in which the priority had been the control of strategic weapons. However, the proposed enlargement of NATO was likely to change this situation, as Russia saw that tactical nuclear systems were the ones most likely to be deployed by NATO in the territories of its new members (if grounds and a legal basis existed for nuclear deployment).

Defence procurement remained at a level of cost which tended to cause concern to the lay person. At least part of the reason appeared to be that governments were locked into procurement contracts which they could not break without paying substantial penalties and/or accepting serious levels of unemployment in strategic industries. Justification for levels of procurement was not always obvious, but it remained important to acquire major items at levels permitting a proportion of any front-line equipment to be withdrawn as necessary for upgrading, since threats could change in nature and scale, the strength of the force being maintained from reserve stocks. In addition, military equipment, although usually designed to withstand damage, tended to receive firm handling, and so often had a shorter life than might have been expected.

1. NATO AND EUROPEAN SECURITY

North Atlantic Treaty Organization (NATO)
DATE OF FOUNDATION: 1949   HEADQUARTERS: Brussels, Belgium
OBJECTIVES: To ensure the collective security of member states
MEMBERSHIP (END-'97): Belgium, Canada, Denmark, France, Germany, Greece, Iceland, Italy, Luxembourg, Netherlands, Norway, Portugal, Spain, Turkey, United Kingdom, United States (*total 16*)
SECRETARY-GENERAL: Javier Solana (Spain)

XII.1. NATO AND EUROPEAN SECURITY

Partnership for Peace (PFP)
DATE OF FOUNDATION: 1994   HEADQUARTERS: Brussels, Belgium
OBJECTIVES: To provide a framework for cooperation between NATO and the former communist and neutral states of Europe and ex-Soviet Central Asia
MEMBERSHIP (END-'97): Albania, Armenia, Austria, Azerbaijan, Belarus, Bulgaria, Czech Republic, Estonia, Finland, Georgia, Hungary, Kazakhstan, Kyrgyzstan, Latvia, Lithuania, Macedonia, Malta, Moldova, Poland, Romania, Russia, Slovakia, Slovenia, Sweden, Switzerland, Turkmenistan, Ukraine, Uzbekistan (*total 28*)

Western European Union (WEU)
DATE OF FOUNDATION: 1952   HEADQUARTERS: Brussels, Belgium
OBJECTIVES: To provide a framework for defence and security cooperation between European states
MEMBERSHIP (END-'97): Belgium, France, Germany, Greece, Italy, Luxembourg, Netherlands, Portugal, Spain, United Kingdom (*total 10*)
SECRETARY-GENERAL: José Cutileiro (Portugal)

THE beginning of the process of NATO's expansion to include Central/East European states which had formerly been members of the Warsaw Pact stimulated active discussion and disagreement at various levels, both in the existing NATO members and in the former Warsaw Pact states, especially Russia. The process had a dimension that was rarely commented upon in the Western media, namely that acceptance into the alliance offered the Central/East European states protection against any aggression by the United States and the existing NATO partners. However, their principal motivation was clearly to secure themselves against any resurrection of Russian aggression. In the latter context, it was understandable that states which were once involuntarily co-opted into the Warsaw Pact—in a quasi-colonial relationship with the USSR—should seek reassurance that that experience would not be repeated. That the USSR no longer existed did nothing to mitigate the feeling in the former Soviet republics, some of them sharing a boundary with the Russian Federation, that the combination of strategic paranoia and imperialist ambition which drove the expansion of the Imperial Russian Empire in the nineteenth century, and of the Soviet sphere of influence in the twentieth, might be merely in abeyance pending a return to more favourable economic conditions.

It was clear that Russia would take time to come to any degree of acceptance of its diminished role and would continue to see itself as a shaper of world history. Indeed, Russia remained a great power, retaining sufficient military strength (in nuclear weaponry) to be a formidable opponent, even though post-Soviet events had diminished both the size and the effectiveness of the Russian armed forces. In consequence, Western negotiators understood that Russia had to be treated as a great power, not a country to be dictated to or over-ridden in decisions affecting its status and influence.

It was therefore necessary for the decision to prepare for an expansion of NATO's ambit to be accompanied by reassurance that the process represented no imaginable threat to the security or prestige of the Russian Federation. At the same time, however, many experts accepted that it would be difficult to persuade the Russian people that states which had formerly been unwilling (and junior) partners of the USSR had not joined NATO in order to share in humiliating what remained of the former Soviet empire. That such feeling existed had to be reckoned with in the West's dealings with the Russian Federation, and with other major components of the former USSR, such as Ukraine, which were not candidates for NATO membership.

NATO ENLARGEMENT. The first formal steps towards the incorporation of certain Central/East European states into the alliance were taken at a NATO summit held in Madrid on 8–9 July. It was decided that preparations should commence for the accession of the Czech Republic, Hungary and Poland on a time-scale which would enable those states to achieve membership by NATO's 50th anniversary in April 1999 (see map on page 409). The first step in the process was the signing of protocols of accession, which had to be ratified both by the applicants and by each of the existing member-states before the prospective new members could proceed to the next stage of the process of joining.

Two things were certain concerning the enlargement of NATO: first, standardization of procedures was a necessity in an alliance built on the concept of tight integration; second, standardization of equipment had to be achieved in order to eliminate the problems of supplying multinational forces. Although a particular state's armed forces might prefer to use the equipment with which they were familiar, the alliance could not realistically accept the difficulties of having to supply stores (ammunition, for example) to mixed forces, some of which were equipped to NATO standard while others used ex-Soviet equipment.

The costs of NATO enlargement were sure to be substantial, but remained to be defined with clarity. A report prepared by the US Congressional Budget Office, which had assumed that Slovakia as well as the other three 'Visegrad' states would join NATO, estimated the total cost to existing members at $54,000 million and the average cost to each new member at $51,900 million for the period 1996–2010, covering the development of an initial capability to defend the territory of the enlarged alliance by the year 2001 and progressing to full capability by 2009. The estimates were based on anticipated average costs of $3,600 million per annum for each of the existing 16 members and $3,460 million per year for each new member. In sharp contrast, a study prepared by NATO itself of the costs of adding two new members (one large state and one small) assessed total costs for the putative 18 states at $5,000 million over a ten-year period ($27.7 million per member per annum).

The fact that these two studies were predicated on different assumptions made it extremely difficult to compare them. The difficulty was compounded by the fact that the US study attempted to assess the costs to be expected in upgrading the national forces of all members, old and new, to the enhanced operational capability which would allow for deployment and reinforcement into the territories of the new members. Moreover, to add to the uncertainty about costs, another US study (also assuming the accession of all four Visegrad states) produced projections ranging from $10,000 million to $110,000 million over a ten- to 15–year period. These figures were the calculated costs for the whole enlarged alliance, so the cost per member averaged over the 20 nations (16 existing members plus four new ones) would be between $500 million and $5,500 million over the stated period. It was clear that a truly authoritative estimate of costs would be forthcoming only when general agreement had been reached on the parameters within which the assessment was carried out. Until such research was carried out within an agreed set of parameters, results such as those quoted above remained merely interesting and of little practical use.

EURO-ATLANTIC PARTNERSHIP COUNCIL (EAPC). The formation of the EAPC was agreed by NATO Foreign Ministers in conference in May. The aims of the new body were to provide an expanded political dimension for the Partnership for Peace (PFP); to develop an operational role for the PFP; and to bring the PFP partners into the NATO decision-making and planning processes. More specifically, the PFP partners would be involved in the political direction of NATO-led operations in which they took part and a new political-military structure for PFP operations would be set up, including a steering committee in which all partners could be represented.

Active measures envisaged to develop an operational role for the PFP partners included the participation of PFP forces in joint exercises with NATO covering the whole range of NATO activities; the involvement of PFP personnel in the planning and control of joint exercises and operations; and the establishment of PFP staff personnel in NATO headquarters.

NATO-RUSSIA FOUNDING ACT. The Founding Act on Mutual Relations, Cooperation and Security between NATO and the Russian Federation was signed in Paris on 27 May, as part of the preparation for the Madrid summit meeting (see XIX.1 for text). The aim of the accord was to foster consultation and cooperation between NATO and Russia, with a view to rendering the enlargement of NATO more easily acceptable to the latter (see also III.3.i).

NATO-UKRAINE CHARTER. The Charter on a Distinctive Partnership between NATO and Ukraine was signed in Madrid on 9 June in the context of the NATO summit. It established a NATO-Ukraine Commission with a remit to meet not less than twice per year and gave the former Soviet republic the right to call for 'consultations' with NATO if it felt threatened. The accord bound the signatories to promote the full development of the EAPC and the enhanced PFP (of which Ukraine was a member), envisaging Ukrainian involvement in operations such as UN and OSCE peace-keeping activities, as well as in Combined Joint Task Forces (CJTF) when the North Atlantic Council agreed to such participation for specific operations.

CONVENTIONAL FORCES IN EUROPE (CFE) TREATY. Under the Founding Act, NATO and Russia agreed to work towards rapid adaptation of the CFE Treaty in the light of the very different security conditions of 1997 compared with those prevailing when the treaty was signed in November 1990 (see AR 1990, pp. 432–7). On the basis of an agreement reached in Vienna on 24 July between NATO, Russia and the 13 other signatories, detailed negotiations started in the Austrian capital in September with the aim of producing a revised text of the treaty incorporating reduced levels of 'treaty-limited equipment' (TLE) by the end of 1998.

The main points of the outline agreement covered the abolition of the bloc-versus-bloc format of the treaty, substituting limitations on national holdings for limitations on bloc holdings; reductions in national quotas; continuation of the stationing and temporary deployment of forces; definition of regional limitations to eliminate the possibility of any destabilizing build-up of forces; maintenance of the transparency provisions of the treaty; and maintaining an open option for other European states to accede to the treaty.

2. ARMS CONTROL

STRATEGIC ARMS REDUCTION TREATIES (START II & II). Implementation of the 1991 START I Treaty (see AR 1991, pp. 555–7) continued in 1997. At the beginning of the year the United States possessed 755 inter-continental ballistic missiles (ICBMs) as against 762 in Russia plus 115 ICBMs without warheads retained in Ukraine. The United States also had 480 submarine-launched ballistic missiles (SLBMs), against Russia's 664, and 329 strategic bomber aircraft against Russia's 79 and 44 in Ukraine.

In declarations following their summit meeting in Helsinki on 20–21 March, Presidents Yeltsin and Clinton set out US-Russian understandings on the START II Treaty signed in 1993 (but not yet ratified by Russia) and on a START III Treaty. As regards START II, they agreed that the reduction to fewer than 3,500 warheads on each side (which had been due to be completed by 2003) would be phased over a longer period and completed by 2007, which would be the target date for START III. Negotiations on START III would begin when Russia had ratified START II, the target levels for strategic warheads being 2,000 to 2,500 on each side. The Presidents also agreed that all warheads on strategic delivery vehicles, due to be eliminated by the new date set for START II, should be removed or deactivated by agreed means by 31 December 2003.

Fitting together the dates for START II and START III would allow Russia to maintain parity with the United States when only the single-warhead ICBMs required by START II remained. Observers were agreed that to expand its SS-27 missile force to a level of 3,000–3,500 warheads, as previously envisaged under START II, would probably exceed Russia's capacity, assuming that there was a desire to aim for this level of armament.

COMPREHENSIVE TEST-BAN TREATY (CTBT). In March the preparatory commission CTBT Organization (CTBTO) agreed on a structure for a provisional technical secretariat and made the first six appointments to the secretariat. By 10 July 144 states had signed the treaty—which had been opened for signature in September 1996 (see AR 1996, pp. 423–4, 542–3)—and four had ratified it. Of the 44 specified states whose ratification was required for the treaty to enter into force, India, Pakistan and North Korea had not signed it as at the end of 1997. Indian objections to the treaty were reiterated by successive governments in New Delhi, and Pakistan could not be expected to sign if Indian did not.

TREATY ON THE NON-PROLIFERATION OF NUCLEAR WEAPONS (NPT). Brazil acceded to the NPT in June, becoming the 186th full treaty member.

INTERNATIONAL ATOMIC ENERGY AGENCY (IAEA). The IAEA board of governors, having approved (in 1995) Part I of a plan to strengthen the agency's verification system, reached agreement on Part II on 15 May. Among its main provisions, Part II enjoined the provision of data on activities related to the nuclear fuel cycle, even when those activities did not specifically involve actual nuclear materials. This category embraced research and development activity, and any other non-nuclear activity which supported in any sense the nuclear fuel cycle. Also covered was a requirement that access should be given to any place on the site of a nuclear facility. This requirement was to include access to decommissioned facilities, to any other place where nuclear material was to be found, and to nuclear-related locations identified by the IAEA, whether manufacturing facilities or not. Also covered in Part II was the use at such locations of environmental sampling as well as other techniques and measures.

It was noted by expert observers that the additional elements of the IAEA safeguards regime provided for under Part II provided no guarantee that covert nuclear-weapons programmes would be detected.

ANTI-BALLISTIC MISSILE TREATY (ABMT). The joint US-Russian statement issued at the Helsinki summit in March included an understanding on the 1996 ABMT as a basis for concluding negotiations on distinguishing strategic weapons from theatre missile defences (TMD). Both Presidents reaffirmed their commitment to the ABMT and set out their understanding on a supplementary agreement as follows: target missiles used in TMD testing should be speed-limited to 5 kilometres a second; target missiles should be range-limited to 3,500 kilometres; undertakings should be given not to develop, test or deploy any space-based TMD interceptor, or component based on alternative technology which might take the place of such an interceptor; provisions for transparency should be included to foster mutual confidence.

The two Presidents stated that neither state had plans to introduce TMD interceptors capable of speeds in excess of 5.5 kilometres a second (in the case of land-based and air-based missiles) and of 4.5 kilometres a second (sea-based missiles). It was further stated that neither side planned to carry out tests against target missiles with MIRV (multiple independently-targeted re-entry vehicles), or against strategic ballistic-missile re-entry vehicles. It was also confirmed that neither state had plans to carry out flight-testing of any higher-velocity TMD system against a ballistic-missile target before April 1999.

The joint Helsinki statement also focused on potential development of TMD systems, calling for consultation to be required in the event of the arrival of new technologies. Such consultations would be entered into to avoid violation or circumvention of the ABM Treaty, and not to give either side a veto over the research and development programmes of the other.

CHEMICAL AND BIOLOGICAL WEAPONS. The UN Convention on the Prohibition of the Development, Production, Stockpiling and Use of Chemicals and their Destruction signed in January 1993 (see AR 1993, pp. 436, 555–7) came fully into force on 29 April. The United States ratified the convention on 25 April, in time to preserve the right to appoint members to the Organization for the Prohibition of Chemical Weapons (OPCW). By the end of 1997, 105 of the 165 signatories had ratified the convention (the non-ratifiers including Russia).

Progress in drafting a verification protocol for the Biological and Toxin Weapons Convention (BTWC) was slow. Despite an extension of the time allotted for the drafting of the protocol, the group of governmental experts responsible for the task continued to encounter difficulty in a number of areas. As regards the definition of terms, there was uncertainty as to whether a list of bacteriological agents and toxins should be agreed. The difficulty in this matter arose from the possibility that the process of alteration of a formally-agreed list to incorporate new discoveries in the field of biotechnology might be too slow to allow effective action to be taken against the development of weapons based on such newly-discovered agents. Also problematical was the defining of equipment and activities which were to be subject to verification. This difficulty reflected the central problem of control of all chemical and bacteriological weapons—that the agents on which such weapons were based were produced in facilities which were difficult to distinguish from ordinary chemical and biotechnological production or research installations.

UN REGISTER OF CONVENTIONAL ARMS. The number of states providing details of their transactions in conventional weapons to the UN Register had reached almost 100 by mid-1997. The Register classified weapons and weapons systems under seven categories: main battle tanks; armoured combat vehicles; artillery of 100-millimetre calibre and greater; combat aircraft; and attack helicopters (armed helicopters with built-in fire-control systems).

UN LANDMINES CONVENTION. A UN Convention on the Prohibition of the Use, Stockpiling, Production and Transfer of Anti-personnel Mines and on their Destruction was formally opened for signature at a ceremony held in Ottawa (Canada) on 3–4 December (see XIX.5). The convention was immediately signed by 125 countries, at least 40 ratifications being required for it to enter into force. As expected, it was not signed by the United States, Russia, China (the world's largest producer of landmines), India, Pakistan, Israel and most other Middle

East states, all of which had reservations of various kinds about it terms. Nevertheless, the inauguration of the convention represented a significant diplomatic success for Canada (see also IV.2), which had launched its own initiative for a global ban on landmines following the limited outcome of UN deliberations on the issue in 1996 (see AR 1996, p. 425).

The text of the convention had been adopted by some 90 states at a conference held in Oslo (Norway) on 1–17 September. Under its terms, signatories would be obliged to destroy all stockpiles of anti-personnel mines by 2005 as well as all mines deployed on their territory. The US refusal to endorse the draft was justified by President Clinton on the grounds that it failed to take account of the United States' 'special responsibilities as the world's only superpower'. In particular, the US government had demanded a nine-year grace period before the convention would be enforced in Korea, claiming that landmines were an essential part of the defence of South Korea and the 37,000 US troops stationed there. It had also sought inclusion of a clause that would enable a country to suspend its adherence to the convention if it became the victim of aggression.

NOBEL PEACE PRIZE. The 1997 Nobel Peace Prize was awarded jointly to the International Campaign to Ban Landmines (ICBL) and the ICBL coordinator, Jody Williams (USA), for their work in furtherance of the banning and clearance of anti-personnel devices. The Nobel committee of the Norwegian parliament, making the award, paid tribute to the ICBL and Ms Williams for having 'in the space of a few years changed a ban on anti-personnel mines from a vision to a feasible reality'. The UN convention agreed in Oslo in September and opened for signature in Ottawa in December (see above) was seen by the committee as 'to a considerable extent the result of their important work'. Founded in 1991 as a joint initiative of US and German peace activists, the ICBL linked over 1,000 affiliated organizations and groups at the time of the award. Its international profile had been greatly enhanced by the active support given by Diana, Princess of Wales, prior to her death on 31 August.

3. DEFENCE EXPENDITURE AND PROCUREMENT

A major characteristic of the procurement cycle in countries with their own military production industries was long lead-time. The separate processes of formulation of requirement, design, testing and development, construction and testing of prototypes, and production added up to an interval of seven to ten years for modern weapons to come into service. The cost of modern combat aircraft, in particular, had increased to a level beyond the financial capacity of a single manufacturer. Even the US aviation industry, by far the world's largest, had seen its biggest companies succumb first to the need for state assistance in the development of military programmes, and secondly to the need to amalgamate with former rival companies. The time was gone when single aircraft manufacturers designed and built aircraft to a government specification, and then sought to win government contracts against competitors' designs.

In Europe, this pattern had been visible for a longer time. European manufacturers had been amalgamating since the 1960s, and intra-national amalgamation of companies had been succeeded by the setting-up of international consortia to produce both civil transport and military combat aircraft. The effect of adding an international dimension to the procurement process was that project lead-times became even longer than in the era of national production. For example, whereas the Tornado multi-role combat aircraft had come into service with the air forces of Germany, Italy and the UK from 1982, some 13 years after the formation of its Panavia design consortium in 1969, the European fighter aircraft project for Germany, Italy, Spain and the UK, which began with the formation of the Eurofighter consortium in 1986, was not expected to put aircraft into service until the early 21st century.

Statistics for the defence spending of the nations of the world in 1996 indicated that states could be divided into three main categories: those committed to procurement plans instituted during the period of super-power confrontation; those engaged in maintenance procurement (buying to replace wastage and obsolescent equipment); and those which were enhancing the equipment of their armed forces against a perceived threat or vulnerability, present or future. Broadly speaking, countries in the third category allocated a greater proportion of national resources to defence than those in the other two, so that the statistics for expenditure as a percentage of gross domestic product (GDP) by geographical area were a pointer to the areas in which countries had the greatest perception of potential military threat.

As shown in the table on page 445, the states of the Middle East and North Africa region, at 6.8 per cent, recorded the highest average expenditure on defence as a percentage of GDP in 1996 (mainly because Israel, Kuwait, Oman, Qatar and Saudi Arabia had defence spending levels ranging from just over 10 per cent of GDP up to nearly 16 per cent). In second and third places respectively came the Central and South Asia region (5.3 per cent) and East Asia and Australasia (4.6 per cent), while Central and Latin America had the lowest proportion (1.8 per cent). As also shown in the table, the corresponding figure for Russia as a single country was 6.5 per cent, nearly double the 3.6 per cent recorded by the United States (with a total GDP some 20 times bigger than Russia's), while the global average was 4.3 per cent.

DEFENCE SPENDING BY REGION (1996)[1]
(global average: 4.3%)

regions
Mid-East/North Africa 6.8
Central/South Asia 5.3
East Asia/Australasia 4.6
Non-NATO Europe 3.8
Sub-Saharan Africa 3.0
NATO Europe 2.3
Central/Latin America .... 1.8[2]

single countries
Russian Federation 6.5
United States 3.6

[1]Country-by-country average GDP percentage by region.
[2]Includes Caribbean countries.
(*Data from IISS, London*)

4. NON-TRADITIONAL THREATS

THE end of the Cold War had resulted in the emergence of new or different threats to the security of societies. In fact, some had been in existence for quite long periods of time, but had tended to be masked by the confrontation between nuclear-armed powers.

Genuinely new non-traditional threats were mostly related to new technologies and new approaches to commerce. Crimes such as computer-assisted fraud rode on the back of the electronic funds-transfer systems which had come into increasing use since the mid-1960s. They were sometimes seen as being victimless, in that money stolen by falsification of transactions involving interbank communications was made good by insurance companies. However, although such activities did not seem to affect the individual citizen, they did have potentially serious consequences for national economies because of the scale on which they were often carried out.

From a Western perspective, it had seemed that there was relatively little crime in the erstwhile Soviet Union. It was more likely, however, that the firm hand of Soviet repression had merely forced criminal organizations to go underground and perhaps even to become better organized. The breakdown in law and order which followed the collapse of the Soviet Union and Soviet-era economic structures enabled criminal groups in Russia, and similar groups originating from other parts of the ex-USSR, to become highly active and to found large-scale enterprises, in particular in the marketing and export of drugs.

These criminal groups quickly spread their ambit beyond the bounds of the ex-USSR, to many countries of Europe and to North America, where their operations in the United States were taken very seriously by the federal authorities. Apparently ready to do business with anyone, Russian criminals were believed to have established close collaboration with the drugs gangs of Colombia and elsewhere.

A particular matter for official concern was the apparent ability of the Russian gangs to procure ex-military weapons in large quantities, including sophisticated heavy-duty equipment. In one celebrated episode, Russian criminals were reported to have attempted to sell two ex-Soviet submarines to Colombian drug-dealers. This deal did not come to fruition, but commentators noted that a submarine would be a near-perfect vehicle for clandestine transport and delivery of goods in bulk.

The more serious threat posed by criminals' access to national weapons stores arose from the possibility of their gaining control of nuclear weapons, which would give them the ability to blackmail governments themselves or to sell such material to rogue governments or organizations.

A number of proposals were made in 1997 as to how groups of states might set about updating procedures for dealing with international crime or instituting new procedures where none currently existed. In the Pacific Rim region, members of parliament from some 20 of the Pacific Rim countries took part in a conference in January at which enhanced regional cooperation to combat terrorism was one of the topics. In Europe, the Russian Minister of the Interior, Anatoliy Kulikov, and the then UK Home Secretary, Michael Howard, held talks in Moscow on 28 January, the main subject being cooperation against organized international crime. The ministers agreed on the development of interaction between security agencies in the campaign against economic crime in particular.

In October the new UK Prime Minister Tony Blair, travelled to Moscow for talks with President Yeltsin. In the course of the visit Mr Blair signed an accord with the Russian Prime Minister, Viktor Chernomyrdin, on fighting international organized crime. The accord recognized the need for closer cooperation between national security services to offset the expansion of the influence of mafia groups generally, and especially the Russian 'Mafiya' organizations.

At the end of the year, the director of the Russian Interpol bureau disclosed that in 1997 his bureau had received over 30,000 inquiries and reports from its partners in other countries; and that more than 300 criminals wanted in a variety of other countries had been detained in Russia in the course of the year.

By late 1997 the Russian Interpol bureau had set up procedures for the interchange of information with all the other member forces of Interpol, and had established close cooperation with security forces in France, Germany, Italy, Austria, Switzerland and Belgium. The director, speaking of measures to counter international crime, stated that the Russian parliament was in the process of discussing measures against money-laundering and illegal cross-border transfers of funds, taking into consideration the deliberations and recommendations of the Council of Europe and the United Nations. Legislation passed in the United States, France and Italy was being studied as part of the process of amending Russian law.

The director of the US Federal Bureau of Investigation visited Moscow in November, for talks with senior officials on progress in combating international crime. The particular aim of the visit was to discuss cooperation between the FBI on the one hand and the Russian Ministry of the Interior and the Federal Security Service on the other.

XIII RELIGION

IMPLICIT RELIGION. The death of Diana, Princess of Wales, on 31 August (see I.1; XX: Obituary) provoked an outpouring of grief and devotion, especially in Britain but also across the world, that astonished observers. On the west coast of America, for example, street banners carried the words 'May the spirit that was in Diana live in you'. Yet the churches, which had long been praying for religious revival, seemed taken aback by devotions and sacrifices which touched on areas which they had neglected—death and life after death. Diana was a royal figure, an icon, passing from a fairy-tale wedding and family, to divorce and final tragedy. The 'humbling, astonishing' response, as the Archbishop of Canterbury called it, to the 'people's princess' revealed the need for ritual and sacrifice in what theologians termed 'implicit religion' or 'contemporary spirituality'. The death of Mother Teresa of Calcutta in the same week (see below) added an aura to Princess Diana, who had visited her Missionaries of Charity in India.

Leaving flowers at the scene of an accident or death had become a custom in recent years, notably after the murder of 16 children at Dunblane in March 1996 (see AR 1996, p. 34). The practice reached a peak for Diana, for whom fields of flowers, most of them in paper or cellophane wrapping and soon giving off a smell of decay, were laid at St James's, Kensington and Buckingham palaces in London and at the site of her death in Paris. Flowers were accompanied by cards, letters or poems, the most common words used being 'angel', 'soul', 'heaven', 'paradise', 'love', 'grace' and 'peace'. Many letters addressed to Diana and her lover, Dodi Fayed (a Muslim), prayed that they would have peace and happiness in heaven, 'free from earthly troubles'. There were also posters, paintings, photographs, rosaries and huge numbers of teddy-bears, as well as innumerable candles like votive offerings, some so large that they must have come from church shops. Willing sacrifice was evident in the long queues of people waiting seven or eight hours, day and night, often in the rain, to sign the books of condolence. They included many young couples, parents with children, businessmen in dark suits, white and non-white people—perhaps a majority of women, but only just. The original six books of condolence at St James's Palace had to be increased to 43, in which people poured out their affection and faith. The burial place of Diana, at Althorp Park in Northamptonshire, looked set to become a religious shrine. The churches, slowly, opened for private prayer or held special services, and 3,000 people attended a Requiem Mass in Westminster Cathedral (Britain's premier Roman Catholic church). The funeral service itself, held in Westminster Abbey on 6 September, was conducted with gravity combined with a modern touch, showing the Church of England at its compelling best.

While the Diana phenomenon revealed widespread belief in life after death, a new UK Christian handbook called *Religious Trends* cited opinion polls as showing that 71 per cent of British people had some sort of belief in God. Just over 50 per cent of British children were baptized in a church, 47 per cent of people married there, and 95 per cent had a Christian funeral. There were large increases in the number of religious books, up from 2,600 in 1993 to 4,300 in 1996, and in religious bookshops, up from 314 to 550. In July, however, a proposed Christian television station in Britain, evangelical but modern, was closed before it began broadcasting because it ran out of money (see AR 1996, p. 435). A similar enterprise in Canada, Vision TV, had been successful for ten years, partly through being open to people of all faiths, from Anglicans to Zoroastrians.

Church congregations in Britain continued to decline in 1997, the main churches experiencing an estimated drop of 1.6 per cent. A handful offering 'charismatic' services attracted crowds—Holy Trinity, Brompton, in central London, claiming thousands every Sunday—but this style of worship was criticized as 'a church within the Church', attracting the young but repelling some of the old. Greek Orthodox churches experienced revival, small in numbers but appealing to some who decried the staleness or vagueness of the establishment. In general, private religion rather than communal organization seemed to express the mood of the time. Other social organizations, including political parties, trade unions, scouts and girl guides, reported similar difficulty with social membership. Of the other major faiths in Britain, Jews shared in the Christian decrease, but Muslims, Hindus, Sikhs and Buddhists benefited from strong communal ties and the appeal of the unknown.

On 27 June the 1,400th anniversary of the arrival of St Augustine's Roman Church mission to England was celebrated, especially in Kent. Some pilgrims followed the missionary's route from Rome, held a service where he landed, near Ramsgate, and proceeded to the ruins of St Augustine's Abbey. In Canterbury Cathedral a long procession, chiefly of Anglicans and Roman Catholics, sang in English and Latin, being welcomed by Archbishop George Carey and hearing a sermon from Cardinal Basil Hume. The first blessings were given separately by the two leaders and the final part by the two together.

The churches began, somewhat belatedly, to prepare for the millennium, with *Millennium News,* published by the united Churches Together in England, advising local congregations to make their own projects and also to take part in general community plans. The government was reminded that the millennium took its very name and time from the approximate date of the birth of Jesus Christ, and gave assurances that this Christian aspect would be celebrated. Pope John Paul II was more forward in his thinking, calling synods of church leaders and preparing a jubilee year in 2000, with Rome as the centre of pilgrimage.

VATICAN RULE. On 2 January the Congregation for the Doctrine of the Faith in Rome issued a 'notification', signed by Cardinal Joseph Ratzinger and approved by Pope John Paul II, declaring that Fr Tissa Balasuriya of Sri Lanka had 'deviated from the truth of the Catholic faith', could not be 'considered a Catholic theologian', and had 'incurred excommunication' (see AR 1996, p. 434). Fr Balasuriya had been sent a list of alleged errors, to which he replied at length, stating that his position had been misrepresented on 58 points. Then he was told to sign a 'profession of faith' which declared 'infallibly' that the Church had no authority to ordain women to the priesthood. He proposed instead a more comprehensive profession, the 'Credo of Pope Paul VI', in the context of 'theological development and church practice since Vatican II'. This was rejected and excommunication followed.

There was widespread protest against the Vatican action, the Roman Catholic weekly *The Tablet* calling it 'An Alarming Excommunication' and asking: 'What sort of justice is this, which finds a man guilty before he has had the chance to prove his innocence, and denies him his freedom and rights? Where is the due process of law? Without that process, there is tyranny.' Swiss theologian Hans Küng pointed out that Fr Balasuriya had not simply been silenced but also excommunicated, commenting: 'This is really a new step. It means he cannot even participate in the Eucharist as a lay person. It is just horrible.' *The Tablet* opened a 'Balasuriya File', which throughout the year printed statements from many eminent Catholics, nearly all supporting Fr Balasuriya.

In December, after years of controversy (see AR 1996, p. 433), the Vatican transferred Bishop Wolfgang Haas from Chur in Switzerland to a newly-formed archdiocese of Vaduz in Liechtenstein. The whole of that country had belonged to the Chur diocese of 680,000 people, but the 'promotion' was to a new archdiocese of only 25,000. There had been constant protests both against the appointment of Bishop Haas to Chur, overriding the right of the cathedral chapter to elect the bishop, and against his authoritarian style, which had earned him the nickname of 'oilskin bishop' because arguments ran off him like water. Repeated requests for his resignation or removal, finally supported by the Swiss government, resulted in the move to Vaduz though there were noisy demonstrations at his consecration.

Pope John Paul II visited Bosnia in April, going ahead despite the discovery of mines beneath a bridge he was to cross (see also II.2.viii; III.2.ii), pleading for forgiveness and reconciliation between Catholic and Orthodox after the recent conflict, and for brotherhood and 'sincere dialogue' with Muslims. In August the Pope met a million young people in Paris at a world youth day, celebrating an open air Mass on the anniversary of the St Bartholomew Massacre of Protestants in France in the sixteenth century and deploring such acts 'condemned by the Gospel'. In November the Pope insisted that the Church must repent of hostility to the Jews before observing the millennium. At the end of September French Roman Catholic bishops, at the site of a World War II deportation camp at Drancy, near Paris, made a public declaration of 'repentance' for complicity and silence when 75,000 Jews had been deported from France to Nazi death camps.

A proposed meeting between the Pope and Patriarch Alexis II of Moscow at Vienna in June was cancelled at the last moment by the Russian Holy Synod. Cold relationships between the two churches were attributed to 'false missionaries' from the West in Russia since the collapse of communism, and the revival of Catholic churches among Orthodox people. In June the Russian Duma passed a bill limiting religious freedom by creating a category of 'religious groups', with strict limitations on worship, pilgrimage, publications, finance and property. In July it seemed that President Yeltsin had amended this bill, but in September a new form was passed that was even more severe, forbidding or limiting religions oppressed during the communist era and giving special legitimacy to the Russian Orthodox Church.

The death in Calcutta on 5 September of Mother Teresa (see XX: Obituary), 87-year-old founder of the Missionaries of Charity, brought tributes from all over the world. The Pope hailed her as 'mother of the poor' and 'a shining example of love', though he was not well enough to attend her funeral. Mother Teresa had long been ill, and this year accepted as her successor the Indian Sister Nirmala, but she was active to the end. Mother Teresa was given an Indian state funeral in Calcutta, the body carried on the gun carriage used for the funeral of Mahatma Gandhi in 1948, accompanied by Indian soldiers, bishops, priests, women missionaries and vast crowds. The Presidents of India and Italy, the Queens of Spain and Jordan, and 400 other dignitaries gathered for a service in a sports stadium. After a Mass there were offerings of lights, flowers, water, wine and bread, hymns in English, and prayers and chants by Hindus, Muslims, Sikhs, Buddhists and Parsis. The burial was in the mother house of the mission and a bugle played the Last Post.

INDIAN CHURCH PROGRESS. On 27 September the Church of South India (CSI) celebrated its first 50 years, following Indian political independence by a month. The original four uniting churches—Anglican, Methodist, Presbyterian and Congregationalist—had given an example to the West by joining together episcopal and non-episcopal churches. There was further union with the Calvinist-Lutheran Basle Mission in 1968, but negotiations with Baptists had been unsuccessful. The CSI model had inspired other churches in the sub-continent, where the Church of North India, with similar uniting churches, had been born in 1970. Since autonomy and union the CSI had increased the number of its dioceses from 14 to 21; current membership was around 2.8 million, in 10,114 congregations, and there were 2,244 pastors. Women's ordination began in 1976, though there were still hesitations over the employment of female ministers. The Church had an extensive social network, including 1,930 schools, 38 colleges, 51 polytechnics, 104 hospitals and clinics, and 512 hostels for poor children. About three-quarters of CSI members were Dalits ('broken' or 'oppressed', the traditional 'Untouchables'), who received specialized and higher education; but there were tensions between traditional Dalits and others categorized as backward classes. Attempts to increase the use of indigenous Indian religious practices—songs, lamps, flowers and incense—had not been successful, as fundamentalist groups repudiated them, while the number of ashrams (retreat houses) declined. Although the CSI was no longer seen as an agent of foreign culture, it was conservative and was faced with growing Hindu and Muslim missions in education and community development.

THE RABBINATE. Dr Jonathan Sacks, Britain's Chief Rabbi (himself an Orthodox Jew), came under continuing pressure (see AR 1996, p. 435). By attending a memorial meeting for the revered late Reform leader, Rabbi Hugo Gryn, Dr Sacks offended the ultra-Orthodox. However, in a leaked private letter in March to one of their leaders, he wrote of his distress at having to praise Rabbi Gryn, whom he described as 'a person who was amongst those who destroy the faith'. This brought a storm of protest from Reform and Liberal Jews, who questioned the very title Chief Rabbi and demanded separate representation from the Orthodox in public affairs.

Deeper tensions existed in Israel, where Orthodoxy dominated religious life, with its monopoly of marriages, divorces and funerals, and also conversion to Judaism, which was recognized only if it was done according to Orthodox law. When Reform Jews petitioned the Israeli Supreme Court to achieve parity, the Orthodox countered with a Conversion Bill designed to entrench their position. The issue was complicated by the position of American Jewry, whose largest communities were overwhelmingly Conservative or Reform (i.e. not Orthodox) and which numbered about 200,000 converts. To the age-old question 'Who is a Jew?' (see AR 1986, p. 391), the traditional answer was that a Jew was the child of a Jewish mother, or one converted according to Orthodox law; but American reformers also recognized 'patri-lineal' validity, covering the children of Jewish fathers who had married non-Jews.

In November Israel and the Vatican signed an agreement to legalize Catholic institutions in all areas of Israel—said to be the first time they had received such recognition for 500 years. But the Latin Patriarch of Jerusalem said that a visit to Israel by the Pope was not yet feasible, since Arab Christians from Bethlehem were not allowed to travel to Jerusalem. In London in February Queen Elizabeth II and the President of Israel unveiled a monument to Raoul Wallenberg, the Swedish diplomat who had saved thousands of Jews from the Nazis in Budapest during World War II by giving them Swedish passports and shelter under his country's flag.

ISLAMOPHOBIA. This term was coined by Muslims living in the West to describe negative images of Islam in the Western media, which were claimed to go back through Zionism to the Inquisition and the Crusades. In November a Muslim Council of Britain was launched to represent over 250 Islamic organizations and to seek to influence public opinion. However, the image of Islam was not improved by the continued vicious attacks and massacres of innocent civilians in Algeria by the Islamic Salvation Front (see V.4.iv)), and there were violent actions by religious fanatics elsewhere. In February churches and houses of Christians were destroyed in the Punjab province of Pakistan, while Egyptian Muslim militants not only committed further atrocities against Coptic Christians but also, in November, slaughtered some 70 Western tourists at Luxor, in the worst single attack on foreigners since the fundamentalist campaign began in 1992 (see V.2.ii).

Nevertheless, a Christian-Muslim conference in Vienna on 13–16 May urged the need for peace and understanding, and Dr Zaki Badawi, principal of the Muslim College in London, spoke of his 'sadness and alarm' at the atrocities in Pakistan and Algeria. Dr Badawi was also a leader in the campaign against female circumcision. After an American cable television programme on this ancient custom had been shown in Egypt, the rector of Al-Azhar University declared the practice to be contrary to Islamic law. A ban subsequently announced by the Minister of Health was upheld after an appeal against it. Female circumcision was not practised in most Muslim countries, but it prevailed in Egypt, Sudan, and parts of east and central Africa. Defenders of the practice contended that it preserved female chastity and was an African custom threatened by Western liberalism (the Mau Mau rebellion in Kenya in the 1950s having been triggered by a government ban on girls being circumcised). Dr Badawi insisted that this 'savage practice' should be banned, pointing out that the major Islamic schools of law said nothing about it and that it was only permitted by the Shafi'i school dominant in north Africa.

CHINESE RELIGION. An official government White Paper gave an optimistic picture of the state of religion in the People's Republic of China, especially Protestant Christianity. Whereas church estimates had modestly reckoned numbers of all Chinese Christians to be between three and nine million, this official document claimed that there were more than ten million Protestants in China, with 12,000 churches and 15,000 clergy. Catholics were stated to have four million Chinese members, with 4,000 churches, but these were under the control of the state-approved Catholic Patriotic Association, which for 40 years had appointed its own bishops independently of the Pope (see AR 1958, p. 367; 1965, p. 376). An 'underground' Roman Catholic Church, loyal to the Pope, with its own separate conferences, was thought to have a more numerous active membership. There were also numbers of Protestants who preferred to remain outside the control of the China Christian Council, and many millions of Chinese who practised traditional folk religions.

The White Paper also recorded that there were 18 million Muslims in China, mostly in the north-west, with 30,000 mosques served by 40,000 imams. Daoist religion was credited with 25,000 priests and nuns, and Buddhism with 200,000 monks and nuns and 13,000 temples. Of Tibet, it was boldly claimed that 'citizens' rights to freedom of religion have been thoroughly carried out' and that there were 1,700 'places for Buddhist activity', with 46,000 resident monks and nuns. Commentators recalled, however, that a survey of Tibet in the 1950s had referred to 2,700 monasteries with some 100,000 monks. In October the biography of a 64-year-old Tibetan monk, Palden Gyatso, entitled *Fire under the Snow*, told of the monk's 33 years in prisons and 'reform through labour' camps, while all his fellow monks had been killed or driven to suicide. The Dalai Lama, who was still at odds with the Chinese government over the appointment of a new Panchen Lama (see AR 1996, p. 436), had urged publication of this book as revealing the travails of Tibetan Buddhists.

BOOKS OF THE YEAR. 'Midsummer madness' described the sale of 110,000 copies in a fortnight in the United States of Michael Drosnin's *The Bible Code*, which claimed to reveal secret clues in the Hebrew Bible foretelling events thousands of years later, such as the Holocaust and the Kennedy assassination. *The Oxford Dictionary of World Religions*, edited by John Bowker, had 80 contributors on the faiths of humanity, while *Religion in the Modern World* by Steve Bruce discussed variations 'from cathedrals to cults', and Paul Heelas in *The New Age Movement* described a modern phenomenon. In *Does Christianity Cause War?*, David Martin discussed religion and politics. Marc Ellis, in *Unholy Alliance*, examined religion and atrocity, while Terry Lovell, in *The Financial Downfall of the Church of England*, researched its mishaps and recovery. In *Goodbye to Catholic Ireland* Mary Kenny interpreted its culture, and in *Mother Teresa: Beyond the Image* Anne Sebba gave a critical assessment of her life and work. *Teaching Religion* by Terence Copley described 50 years of religious education. In *African Christianity*, Paul Gifford gave valuable information, while in *Christianity in China* Daniel Bays and his team described progress from the eighteenth century. Nicholas de Lange and eight historians narrated *The Illustrated History of the Jewish People*, and in *The Turkish Labyrinth; Atatürk and the New Islam* James Pettifer sketched political Islam. Kate Zebiri in *Muslims and Christians Face to Face* provided popular and academic material from Islam and Christianity in what was perhaps the religious book of the year.

XIV THE SCIENCES

1. SCIENTIFIC, MEDICAL AND INDUSTRIAL RESEARCH

SPACE, ASTRONOMY AND PHYSICAL SCIENCES. The highlight of the year in space was the landing, on 4 July, of the US *Mars Pathfinder*. This low-cost mission was a test for new technologies in Martian exploration. It landed using a combination of heat-shield, parachutes and inflatable balloons to slow its entry through the atmosphere and to protect it as it bounced to a standstill. After a tense few minutes at mission control, cheers went up when the first signals for 21 years were received from the Martian surface. The three petal-shaped sides of the lander opened up to reveal scientific instruments and a little six-wheeled Mars rover called *Sojourner*, which set off on the Martian surface and began analysing the rocks. The first rock it looked at, nicknamed 'Barnacle Bill', changed geologists' opinions about Mars. It was a volcanic rock containing quartz, more like a terrestrial volcanic rock than those found on the Moon and expected on Mars. Both lander and rover continued to function for 83 days, much longer than their planned 30-day lifetime, before batteries ran flat in the cold air and transmissions ceased. Meanwhile, a second craft, *Mars Global Surveyor*, had entered into orbit around the red planet, using the atmosphere to slow it into a low orbit from which to survey the surface. The spacecraft detected a weak magnetic field on Mars for the first time.

A much larger US spacecraft, *Cassini*, was launched on 15 October on a long route round Venus, the Earth and Jupiter, to arrive at Saturn in the year 2004. Then a European probe, called *Huygens*, was due to separate, enter the atmosphere of the moon Titan and attempt to land on its surface. Titan was expected to have seas of liquid methane beneath its orange smog of hydrocarbons. Meanwhile, *Cassini* itself was due to go into orbit around Saturn and to survey that planet, its rings and moons. The *Galileo* probe continued its successful mission in orbit around Jupiter, detecting a magnetic field on the moon Ganymede and finding evidence that the ice on Europa might be thin enough for liquid oceans to exist. In December, *Galileo* reached the end of its two-year primary mission but continued to function, despite minor communications problems, and began an extended mission to study Europa and the volcanic moon Io. The *Pioneer 10* spaceprobe celebrated 25 years in space since its launch in 1972 but, with only one instrument still working, it was decided to switch it off and stop tracking it.

The European space programme recovered from the previous year's disastrous maiden flight of the *Ariane V* rocket (see AR 1996, p. 439) by launching its second *Ariane V* successfully from Kourou in French Guiana on 30 October. The hope was that this big rocket would capture up to half the market for launching major satellites into geostationary orbit. A full replacement mission for the four *Cluster* spacecraft destroyed by the explosion of the first *Ariane V* was approved by the European Space Agency. In China a *Long March 3B* rocket took off successfully for the first time after a crash the previous year. Japan launched a new rocket, named the *Mu-5*, carrying a scientific satellite called *MUSES-B*, which unfurled an eight-metre radio antenna to extend radio astronomy into space, making a telescope effectively 30,000 kilometres across.

There was an ongoing drama in space centred on the ageing Russian *Mir* space station. There were successful dockings with the US space shuttle and a succession of visiting astronauts, but *Mir* suffered faults with its airconditioning and with oxygen generators. As a result, cosmonauts had to burn oxygen-releasing candles and a fault in one of these led to a potentially serious fire in February. On 29 April the American astronaut Jerry Linenger became the first American to join a Russian on a space walk. However, on 25 June, during a practice docking manoeuvre, an unmanned *Progress* supply craft struck a solar panel on the *Spektr* module, causing an air leak. In a tense few minutes, the cosmonauts sealed off the damaged module, cutting power cables that trailed through the hatch in the process. *Mir*'s power ran low, it started to tumble slowly in space and was plunged into darkness. For a while it looked as if *Mir* would have to be abandoned, but slowly it was brought under control and some power returned. Later, however, the drama continued with further power losses and computer failures. Repairs were postponed after the commander, Vasily Tsibilyev, developed an irregular heartbeat. A replacement crew arrived in August and cosmonauts entered the damaged module, where they successfully reconnected power leads, but occasional computer failures and other problems continued on *Mir*. In February the space shuttle *Discovery* performed the second refurbishment mission to the Hubble space telescope, fitting it with a new infra-red camera and other instruments.

The most spectacular sky sight from Earth proved to be comet Hale-Bopp, which became bright in the evening sky around March for more than a month and kindled widespread interest in the night sky. Although distant from Earth, it appeared to have a very large nucleus and left a long bright tail of dust. Professional astronomers used the Hubble space telescope to study the birth of stars in radiation-filled tornadoes of dust in the lagoon nebula 5,000 light-years away. Britain's James Clarke Maxwell telescope in Hawaii looked into the heart of the tornado at the wavelength given off by carbon monoxide gas. That revealed a knot of gas 30 times the mass of the Sun, believed to be contracting to form a new star. Observations of flickering X-rays from the disc of gas surrounding a probable black hole gave evidence for an effect called 'frame-dragging', predicted by Einstein, in which the very fabric of space and time becomes distorted and twisted by the gravity of the spinning object.

The Compton Gamma Ray Observatory detected radiation produced by a 3,000-light-year fountain of anti-matter above the centre of the Milky Way galaxy. By following up observations by the Italian *BeppoSAX* satellite with optical telescopes on Earth, the sources of bursts of gamma rays were finally pinned down. They turned out to be at cosmological distances. The only explanation that astronomers could think of was that the bursts were caused by neutron stars or even black holes merging with a tremendous explosion. The final catalogue of results from the European satellite *Hipparcos* were published in 1997. That satellite measured star positions and sometimes distances with great accuracy. By refining distance estimates of so-called Cepheid variable stars in our own galaxy, it was possible to use such stars in more distant galaxies to re-estimate the scale of the universe. The result meant that the universe must be 10 per cent bigger than previously thought and therefore that it was 10 per cent older. Astronomers were thus spared from the embarrassment of having to explain how there could be stars that were older than the age of the universe.

The science fiction concept of 'tele-portation' came a small step nearer with the successful transfer of photons carrying all the information needed to describe a proton. The scientists had yet to add a proton to the system, but in principle a single particle of matter could be reproduced from the information at a remote site. There were hints from work at Germany's HERA accelerator, near Hamburg, that a new form of matter had been observed. It appeared to be a meson—a hybrid particle carrying some of the properties of quarks and some of leptons. If the discovery was confirmed, it would provide a bridge between two very different sorts of matter and might explain how matter came out of the Big Bang that began the universe.

Scientists working at the Massachusetts Institute of Technology made a rudimentary atom laser. Just as a normal laser created a special form of pure light, so an atom laser could generate a pure beam of matter. Such devices might be used to make atomic-scale electronic circuits. A new and non-polluting engine was announced by American engineers. Instead of simply burning petrol, the engine broke it down to produce hydrogen gas which was combined with oxygen in a fuel cell, generating electricity directly. In theory, it was potentially more efficient than a petrol engine, producing only carbon dioxide and water as waste. A new pressurized-drilling technique was used to drill into Blake Ridge, located in the western Atlantic at a depth of nearly 3,000 metres, to sample deposits of what were known as gas hydrates. It was estimated that the deposits could contain more than 35 million million tons of carbon in the form of solid methane. A new technique was developed at Imperial College, London, for using ultra-sound to spot corrosion in pipes in chemical plants and oil refineries without removing insulation and lagging. There were more than 20 million kilometres of such pipes around the world.

In the United States, a research team at Harvard University developed ways of making molecules with water-repellent surfaces that could be made to huddle together into clumps of particular shapes. The team suggested that the technique might be used for making microscopic electronic circuits that assembled themselves, and even for making paints that could change colour at a flick of a switch. Japanese scientists developed a way of coating glass with a thin crystalline film of titanium oxide. Ultraviolet light in sunlight would alter the coating so that any water or grease would spread evenly and instantly over the surface, producing in effect self-cleaning windows.

Intel, the microchip manufacturer, developed a way of doubling the amount of information held in silicon memory chips, by holding two bits of information in each transistor. Australian scientists developed a microscopic form of bio-sensor, which could be incorporated into electronic chips to detect trace quantities of substances such as sugars or hormones. In Britain, an electricity company solved some of the difficulties of using the supply grid to provide online Internet information, opening up the prospect that personal computers would be able to communicate with the Internet through their electrical supply leads rather than via telephone lines.

BIOLOGICAL AND MEDICAL SCIENCES. The most stunning biological achievement of 1997 came from a barn near Edinburgh, capital of Scotland. Researchers at the Roslin Institute had taken the nucleus from an udder cell of a six-year-old adult sheep and placed it in the empty egg cell of another sheep. The lamb that resulted was a clone. Named Dolly, she was born in late February and became a media sensation. Whilst clones had been produced before, they had only been possible from embryonic cells. Later in the year the same team announced the production of two more cloned sheep, named Polly and Molly. Made from embryo cells, they had been genetically-engineered to produce the human blood-clotting factor IX in their milk. The immediate intention was that clones could establish herds quickly for the production of human pharmaceuticals in sheep milk; but the technique also raised the possibility that clones of adult humans might also become possible, prompting some people to call for a ban on their production. The debate was particularly intense in the United States, where monkey embryo cells had been cloned into whole monkeys. Cloning also raised the possibility that cells might be grown in laboratory culture for use in transplants. Amid fears that animal organs might harbour unknown deadly viruses, the British government in January announced a moratorium on the transplantation of organs from animals into humans.

In Britain, the year began with a sense of uncertainty about a new form of Creutzfeld-Jacob (CJD) disease. Studies clearly linked the new human form with 'mad cow disease', or bovine spongiform encephalopathy (BSE), but no-one was sure whether 14 reported human cases were the beginning of a major epidemic or whether the cases would remain isolated. It seemed that, although CJD could be caught from eating infected beef, the mutant form of the prion protein that caused the disease did not infect easily. Research in Zürich showed that the prion protein was first taken up into the blood and thus into white blood cells; from there it probably infected the brain via nerve cells. The Zürich-based biotechnology company Prionics was working on a test for the mutant protein in blood, while other research suggested that small samples of cells from the tonsils might provide a way of diagnosing the disease without having to sample brain tissue. It was suggested that it might be possible to engineer cattle genetically so that they became resistant to BSE, and that drugs to prevent CJD developing in humans might one day be possible. Meanwhile, calls by leading scientists for an inquiry into the BSE outbreak met with a positive response from Britain's new Labour government.

The number of people infected by the AIDS virus, HIV, rose to 30 million worldwide in 1997, and was increasing at the rate of about 16,000 new infections each day, according to the UN AIDS Programme. Despite the best efforts of scientists and doctors, the only useful drugs were still far too expensive for the countries most in need. However, treatment with three anti-viral drugs in combination, though expensive, was producing such good results that some scientists predicted that the treatment might help to repair the body's immune system and rid it of HIV altogether. Attempts to produce an effective vaccine continued, with promising tests in chimpanzees of a vaccine made of viral DNA. Although no vaccine had yet proved effective in humans, evidence was mounting that a live attenuated vaccine might be the answer. The risks of such a vaccine were unknown, but this did not prevent a group of doctors and health activists from volunteering to be the first humans to be injected with the live vaccine.

Although 1997 marked the centenary of the discovery in India by Ronald Ross that malaria was spread by mosquitoes, the problem still seemed to be as bad as ever: three million people died from the disease every year, and resistance to the common anti-malarial drugs was still spreading. Nevertheless, there were several promising lines of research, including the discovery of how some sorts of mosquito resisted malaria and the development of a potential vaccine that would not only prevent the parasite from infecting the human liver but also stop it developing within mosquitoes. One vaccine had its first tests in a small number of humans, the results showing that six out of seven volunteers were protected. A heat-treated vaccine against the cholera bacterium showed promising results in a trial on nearly 70,000 people in Vietnam. Although there were cholera vaccines already, this one was cheap and not prone to damage if stored in the heat.

A US team developed a DNA vaccine able to protect against the deadly Ebola virus (see AR 1995, pp. 266, 447). The World Health Organization (WHO) announced that, despite the availability of effective drug treatments, tuberculosis (TB) was still the world's leading infectious killer of young people and adults. There was particularly worrying evidence of drug-resistant TB from Russia, Latvia, Argentina, Côte d'Ivoire and India. However, US scientists were developing a new generation of drugs targeted on enzymes that the TB bacterium used to build a protective wall around itself. There was also evidence that the rising rate of asthma in developed countries was linked to the falling number of chest infections such as TB. This led Japanese and British doctors to suggest that a vaccine based on the TB bacterium might reduce susceptibility to asthma.

The WHO also suggested that food-poisoning might be 300 times more frequent than had previously been recognized, particularly in Africa, where there was little surveillance. A limited, but serious, outbreak of food-poisoning, caused by a variety of the E-coli bacterium, led to a number of deaths in Scotland. It was suggested that antibiotic-resistant bacteria might be spread from chickens that had been fed antibiotics. A new and particularly virulent strain of influenza was identified in Hong Kong and linked to a form of influenza in birds. The authorities responded by ordering the slaughter of all chickens in the territory, this drastic action appearing to bring the 'chicken flu' outbreak under control by the end of the year.

The WHO called on politicians to join the fight against what it described as a 'global tobacco epidemic'. While tobacco use was in decline among men in developed countries, the WHO said that the 'epidemic' was now spreading to men in developing countries and to women everywhere. Research suggested that non-smokers who lived with a smoker increased their risk of developing lung cancer and heart disease by about 25 per cent. China was chosen as the venue for the year's world anti-tobacco conference, since the Chinese were smoking one in every three of all the cigarettes smoked in world.

Smoking notwithstanding, there was good news about many aspects of health, including life expectancy. Statistics showed that between 1985 and 1995 global average life expectancy had increased by more than three years, to 65, and that the gap in life expectancy between industrialized and developing countries had narrowed to just over 13 years since 1955. On the downside, the WHO warned that increased life expectancy, combined with changes in life-style, would lead to global epidemics of cancer and degenerative diseases in the next 20 years.

One development in the battle against cancer came from the first tests of what was called anti-sense therapy, in which DNA that was the mirror-image of defective cancer genes was used to block their action. It proved useful against cases of lymphoma. On the other hand, scientists reported that gene therapy—the introduction of new genes into cells of patients to treat disease—had turned out to be more difficult than expected, although new ways of introducing the genes were under development. The discovery of master genes controlling development led to the creation of headless frog embryos. One bizarre suggestion was that headless human embryos might be grown so that their organs could be used for transplantation.

There were several developments in the understanding of human origins. A team of American and Ugandan scientists found remains of a large ape-like creature that lived in Uganda 20 million years ago. It was suggested that the creature, named Morotipithecus, might represent the root of the family tree of apes. There was more genetic evidence that modern humans evolved in Africa, while thousands of stone tools, two-and-a-half million years old, were discovered in northern Ethiopia. Some remarkably well-made spears were unearthed in Germany and dated as being 400,000 years old, suggesting that sophisticated tool-making emerged long before the so-called cultural revolution of 40,000 years ago. Controversial dating of rock art at Jinmium, in northern Australia, suggested that Aboriginal people might have been there as long as 120,000 years ago. Spanish scientists discovered fossil remains of the earliest-known humans in Europe, dating back 800,000 years. It seemed that they might have been victims of cannibalism. Evidence from genetic material isolated from a Neanderthal bone suggested that Neanderthals were not closely related to modern humans and did not inter-breed with our immediate ancestors.

Advances in forensic science included research in Australia showing that enough genetic material was left in human finger-prints for scientists to conduct DNA 'finger-printing' (i.e. genetic profiling), while British scientists reported that they were able to obtain a genetic profile from a single cell left behind at the scene of a crime. The significance of genetic 'finger-printing' was demonstrated when it was used to secure the conviction of a suspect whose victim's blood was found on a coat which also held hairs from the white cat that had lived with the suspect.

Finally, the year saw the disclosure of evidence from damaged bones suggesting that the giant carnivorous dinosaur Tyrannosaurus was susceptible to gout.

NOBEL PRIZES The 1997 Nobel Prize for Physiology or Medicine was awarded to Stanley Prusiner of the United States, for his proposal that prion proteins were the infectious agents in diseases such as CJD and its animal versions. The Nobel Prize for Physics went jointly to Steven Chu, Claude Cohen Tinnoudji and William Phillips, for their theories and experiments on cooling atoms to record low temperatures using laser beams. Half of the Chemistry Prize was awarded to Paul Bayer and John Walker, for their work on how the molecule ATP transferred energy within the body; the other half went to the Danish scientist Jen Skou, for his research on how cells in the human body maintained their chemical balance.

2. INFORMATION TECHNOLOGY

HUMAN intellect was laid low by computer power in May, when Garry Kasparov, the world chess champion, was defeated for the first time by Deep Blue, a parallel processing supercomputer constructed by International Business Machines (IBM). The human's defeat was perceived by some to have had a sensational, even sinister, element—and Kasparov himself was reported to be extremely downhearted; but most commentators saw it as an inevitable development, stressing the positive aspect, namely that ever-more powerful machines capable of following complex rules would be invaluable tools in numerous application areas. At much the same time, the UK experienced its first 'wired' general election, following the example of the US presidential election of the previous year. Whilst perhaps only 5 per cent of the electorate had the means of access, all of the major parties as well as independent bodies and pressure groups placed material on the World Wide Web (WWW) in order to stimulate discussion.

ELECTRONIC COMMERCE. Initiatives in the realm of 'e-commerce', where entrepreneurs continued to perceive new opportunities, showed how established practices and structures which had appeared at one time unassailable were nevertheless vulnerable in a networked environment.

Tangible evidence of how a traditional market-place could be shaken by a new entrant taking advantage of Internet technology was afforded by the flotation of Amazon.com. This company, an Internet book retailer which launched on the US stock market in May, saw its share price rise by more than 30 per cent on the first day of trading. Not having the overheads of bookshop premises, and enjoying the benefits of a geographically much wider customer base than traditional mail-order businesses, Amazon.com demonstrated that a new economic model facilitated by the Internet could have an impact on the businesses of even market leaders like Barnes & Noble, which saw its prices undercut on hundreds of best-selling titles.

On the eastern side of the Atlantic, the success of online bookshops like Amazon.com brought US editions into the European market via mail order in higher volumes than before. Consequently, a number of the more traditional book retailers sought to mobilize their resources in this direction. Some players, including The Internet Bookshop—the UK's largest online bookseller—contemplated the possibility of offering US editions in the UK themselves. However, these moves encountered stern warnings from the UK Publishers' Association, with the result that, at least in the short term, The Internet Bookshop removed from its catalogues the US editions of titles available in UK editions.

Another area where the Internet facilitated new start-ups was, perhaps surprisingly, the food retail sector. New York-based NetGrocer took an approach similar to Amazon.com's, but in relation to non-perishable foodstuffs, and was able to cater for special dietary needs. In the same sector, Peapod chose to adopt a more localized solution, using employees to carry out customers' shopping and to deliver the goods.

Interestingly, awareness of the opportunities and threats represented by the Internet could even bring together traditional competitors in order to forestall potential new rivals. For example, in the UK, the ADHunter consortium was set up to compete against other media by offering nationally an enhanced classified advertising service on the Web. Formed initially by a small number of the largest regional newspaper groups, the consortium extended its services on a subscription basis to all local newspaper publishers. AutoHunter was the first service to go live during the year, followed by JobHunter, with PropertyHunter in preparation.

PAYMENTS AND SECURITY. A definitive version of the SET (Secure Electronic Transactions) standard was published in 1997, after a year or so of testing following its initial launch by Microsoft working in association with MasterCard, Visa, American Express and other relevant organizations (see AR 1996, pp. 446–7). Encryption and digital signature techniques were at the centre of the SET initiative, but in general such technologies continued to be viewed with caution by officialdom. Despite some slackening of its position, the US government still placed encryption in the same category as weapons technology. Nevertheless, in the course of the year a number of specific licences were granted for the export from the USA of software using 128-bit encryption, the beneficiaries including, for example, Netscape Communications. The French government was also reported to have relaxed regulations relating to encryption technology.

A related field in which useful developments were achieved was that of 'micropayments' technology, intended to facilitate the secure recording and execution of large numbers of small payments, such as might be needed by an electronic newspaper wishing to charge for access to news on the basis of a variable price per article. One such product announced during the year was Digital Equipment's MilliCent system.

GROWING PAINS. Internet businesses were not, however, without difficulties or even downright failure. Fast growth brought its own problems, with, for example, both America Online (AOL) and Microsoft being caught by surprise by sheer volume of traffic. AOL ended the year triumphant, having taken over the online service subscribers of rival CompuServe; but it had a difficult beginning to the year. Its switch from a time-related pricing structure to a flat monthly fee in December 1996 placed its networks under extreme pressure early in 1997, such that users trying to log on found that they frequently encountered the engaged tone. After threats of legal action, AOL ended up offering refunds to frustrated customers. Later in the year, Microsoft also had a severe crisis, being forced temporarily to shut down its e-mail service one day in April when the volume of transmissions exceeded the available capacity of the Microsoft Network (MSN).

A different sort of volume-related problem, affecting users, was the focus of increasing attention, namely the burgeoning quantities of unsolicited e-mail messages being received by subscribers to Internet services. This practice, known in the USA as 'spamming', was even the subject of bills introduced into both chambers of the US Congress, although a solution to the problem was more likely to result from software designed to vet the provenance of e-mail messages and to permit users to say whether they wished to view them or not.

One large-scale experiment brought to a conclusion during the year, without a particularly successful outcome, was Time Warner's 'full service network', which had been launched in Orlando, Florida, in 1994 to offer interactive television services, including home-shopping, games and information, as well as movies on demand (see AR 1994, p. 479). Based upon dedicated set-top boxes linked to cable delivery, the service had been introduced before Internet-based services began to take off and lost out to cheaper ways of delivering interactive services to television screens. Much more serious was the fate of Industry.Net, one of the pioneers of e-commerce, which went out of business after failing to establish an ambitious electronic marketplace on the WWW.

PIRACY. Unauthorized replication and sale of copyright material continued to be a serious problem despite vigorous actions to combat these practices. In August Singapore police raided the CD-ROM replication plant of SM Summit Holdings, a listed Singaporean company, taking away materials alleged to have been used in manufacturing counterfeit software. Later the same month Egyptian police seized over 2,000 unauthorized CDs. In an interesting approach to the suppression of piracy, it emerged that the Egyptian authorities had concluded an agreement with Microsoft whereby the manufacture of its software for the Arab market would be contracted to Egyptian companies. Comparable problems were also manifesting themselves on the WWW, although enforcement in a networked environment was obviously more difficult. In June, however, the Recording Industry Association of America (RIAA) took legal action against Web sites located in California, New York and Texas, alleging that the sites had permitted unauthorized downloading of copyright music by users. Action was also taken in the UK by the management company representing the rock music group Oasis against unofficial Web sites for fans which provided access to a variety of songs, music and related merchandise.

OPTICAL DISCS. Problems over standards again beset the high-density storage medium correctly designated as digital versatile disc (DVD), although often referred to as digital video disc in view of its first major application. Standards for the medium, which offered a storage capacity of between 4.7Gb and 17Gb (1Gb=1,000Mb) compared with the 650Mb of a standard CD-ROM (1Mb=1,000,000 bytes), had been agreed for the sub-species used for film distribution and for computer read-only applications (see AR 1996, pp. 447–8). Commercial rivalries, however, led to the possibility of two erasable/rewritable versions coming to market, namely DVD-RW, supported by the Japanese company Sony and the Dutch company Philips, and DVD-RAM, supported by other manufacturers. Industry negotiations over a standard for use in audio distribution also failed to result in a consensus.

CHIP TECHNOLOGY. In the market-place, the US company, Intel, the world's largest manufacturer of semiconductors, launched the Pentium II to succeed the Pentium (which had first appeared in 1993—see AR 1993, pp.461–2) and Pentium Pro processor chips. In the research sector, however, it was being recognized that the limits of existing chip technology were being approached. Accordingly, nanotechnologists were focusing on possible sub-atomic solutions involving single-electron technology or quantum physics.

GOVERNMENT INITIATIVES. In July both the Clinton administration in the USA and the European Commission produced important statements of policy relating to issues surrounding e-commerce. Perhaps intending to upstage the European initiative, the US government issued *A Framework for Global Electronic Commerce* on 1 July, a week before the issue, on 8 July, of a major prepared communiqué at the end of a 29-nation ministerial conference in Bonn (Germany) with the theme 'Global Information Networks: Realizing the Potential'. The 69-point communiqué—the Bonn declaration—covered a wide range of issues, including data security and cryptography; privacy and data protection; electronic commerce and fiscal issues; democratization of information technology; content providers (including the responsibility of carriers) and users; intellectual property rights; the role of the private sector; and the role of the public sector. Although both documents were clear as to principles, it was evident that implementing the policies would require sustained and protracted effort.

In many respects, including the principle of minimum fiscal interference in e-commerce, the US and European documents were in broad agreement. Two areas of significant disagreement did emerge, however. Firstly, European ministers considered the availability of strong encryption technology as critical for the development of electronic commerce, whilst the USA rehearsed the 'national security' argument. Secondly, European ministers favoured legal safeguards relating to personal data, whilst the USA expressed a preference for the 'private efforts of industry working in cooperation with consumer groups'.

LEGAL AND REGULATORY ISSUES. Two long-running cases continued into 1997. In the USA, the Supreme Court upheld the decision of a lower court (see AR 1996, p. 445) that parts of the Communications Decency Act were unconstitutional since they conflicted with the right of free speech embodied in the First Amendment of the US constitution. Meanwhile, pursuant to police raids carried out in late 1995 (see AR 1995, p. 452), the managing director of CompuServe in Germany was indicted by the Bavarian authorities in April on the grounds that the service had facilitated access to pornographic and racist material banned in Bavaria. The latter case highlighted the difficult question of the responsibility of carriers for material transmitted over networks—an issue subsequently clearly identified by both the Clinton and the EU policy documents (see above).

Another recurrent wrangle, concerning the practices of Microsoft, the giant US software company, erupted again in 1997. In October the US Justice Department took action against Microsoft on the grounds that it was in breach of the terms of a consent decree recorded in 1995 in relation to Microsoft's licensing practices for personal computer operating systems (see AR 1995, p. 455). Specifically, the contention of the Justice Department was that Microsoft was putting undue pressure on distributors to accept its Internet browser software, Internet-Explorer, by 'bundling' it with its Windows 95 operating system—whereas, according to the Justice Department, the browser should have been offered as a separate product which distributors would then have been free to accept or not. An interim judgment forced Microsoft to offer Windows 95 without the browser software, but the full case was not scheduled to be heard until 1998.

3. THE ENVIRONMENT

IF international conferences solved environmental problems, then 1997 would have gone down in history as a year when much was achieved, containing as it did two highly-publicized environmental gatherings—the 'Earth Summit + 5' and the Kyoto Climate Conference. In the event, both were widely perceived by environmentalists as failures. The year also saw the launch of a controversial plan to renew commercial whaling, the completion of the first stage in the building of the world's biggest dam and a growth in the smuggling of chlorofluorocarbons (CFCs). In terms of issues, climate dominated the year, not only at the two summits. Much of South-East Asia was covered with a dense smog for several months; and a potentially severe El Niño event affected Asia, Africa and large parts of the Americas. In Britain, 1997 was the warmest year on record.

The 'Earth Summit + 5' (officially the second UN Conference on Environment and Development) was held in New York on 23–27 June. Marking five years since the original Earth Summit in Rio de Janeiro (see AR 1992, pp. 458–9), the conference was convened to review progress since then. It came immediately after a meeting of the G-7 group of industrialized nations in Denver, Colorado, at which US President Bill Clinton spoke against cutting emissions of greenhouse gases (see also XVIII.1). Earlier, the European Union (EU) had proposed that developed nations should adopt a target for the year 2010 of reducing emissions to 15 per cent below their level in 1990. Amid intense speculation about what he would say, President Clinton came to address the New York summit on its penultimate day. What he did say was that the United States would not cut its own emissions but would spend $1,000 million helping less developed nations to cut theirs. This idea of 'emissions trading' was to surface again in Kyoto.

Meanwhile, the signs were that industrialized nations were not even going to meet the modest goal, to which they had signed up in Rio, of holding emissions in 2000 to 1990 levels. Data from the International Energy Agency, which monitored energy-related emissions, indicated a rise of as much as 14 per cent above 1990 levels by 2000. Several new signs of global warming were noted through the year. Russian scientists found that spring in the northern hemisphere now arrived a week earlier than it did ten years previously. The Siberian city of Yakutsk declared a state of emergency mid-way through the summer because the permafrost on which it was built was melting, causing buildings to collapse. In the southern hemisphere, whaling records showed that the ice surrounding Antarctica during summer had shrunk by 25 per cent over the last 40 years.

Discussion on the other two Rio conventions—on bio-diversity and desertification—was almost entirely lacking at the New York follow-up conference. Informally, observers were in broad agreement that, as with climate change, little was being done to implement these two conventions. This view was partially confirmed later in the year when the EU announced that it was taking ten of its member states to court for failing to implement measures to protect bio-diversity.

On the other hand, there was plenty of discussion on forests. In the run-up to the Earth Summit + 5, the Worldwide Fund for Nature (WWF) had promoted its 'Forests for Life' campaign, which aimed to get every nation to protect at least 10 per cent of its existing trees (and to which 20 states had so far signed up). This campaign received a significant boost at the conference itself, where the World Bank president, James Wolfensohn, vowed to take a country's forest-protection record into account when allocating financial assistance. However, many non-governmental organizations (NGOs) left New York as disappointed on forests as they were on climate change. There had been talk of a new forestry convention, but that did not materialize. Campaigners were also depressed by the refusal of producers and consumers of forestry products to sign up to proposals which would legally bind them to implement existing international agreements.

More positively, forestry campaigners succeeded during the year in setting up two new 'buyers groups'—of companies which agreed to abide by standards on sustainable forest management laid down by the Forest Stewardship Council (FSC), an international coalition of NGOs. The new groups were established in Germany and the United States. Also encouraging were the announcements by Niger and Burkina Faso of plans to plant a total of 12 million trees in an attempt to restrain the spread of the Sahara Desert.

Immediately following the Earth Summit + 5, governments and NGOs began preparing their negotiating positions for the UN Climate Change Conference subsequently held in Kyoto (Japan) on 1–11 December. The gathering was thought by many observers to be the most important environmental conference ever held, as projections showed a doubling in atmospheric carbon dioxide by the middle of the next century, sea level rises of as much as a metre, the creation of millions of refugees and new epidemics of disease. Scientists also said that, in order to keep the present global temperature stable, greenhouse gas emissions would have to be cut immediately by around 60 per cent.

This magnitude of cut was, however, not on the table in Kyoto. The EU held firm to its '15 per cent by 2010' proposal; Japan suggested a target of 5 per cent by 2012; Australia said it should be allowed an 18 per cent increase. Politicians from developing nations—especially the Alliance of Small Island States, which were particularly at risk from sea-level rise—routinely urged the adoption of stringent targets. Attention inevitably focused on the line that the United States would take.

An opinion poll in September showed that around 70 per cent of Americans believed global warming to be a real and potentially damaging phenomenon, and that over half wanted President Clinton to make it a priority issue. Despite these figures, and a speech by President Clinton acknowledging that US energy consumption was inequitably high, the administration was hamstrung by the knowledge that whatever agreement it reached in Kyoto would have to be ratified by Congress. Leaders of both houses had indicated they would veto any document containing significant cuts, and the Senate had passed a resolution saying that developing nations must sign up to curbs if America did, contradicting one of the central tenets of the Rio accord. Leaders of the US oil and automobile industries campaigned vigorously against emissions cuts.

The eventual US position was that emissions in 2010 should be no higher than 1990 levels—in other words, no more than the Rio target and ten years later. US negotiators also demanded that the Kyoto accord should contain provisions for 'emissions trading', whereby, rather than cutting its own emissions, a rich nation could pay another country to reduce. This concept was not supported by the developing-world lobby, which feared that the USA would pay countries of the former Soviet bloc to keep their emissions down. In fact, these countries already emitted far less than they did in 1990 as a consequence of their economic regression.

After a conference characterized by posturing and brinkmanship on all sides, a compromise was eventually reached on 10 December on a new protocol (see XIX.6). A total of 38 developed countries agreed on a range of individual national targets for cuts in emissions of between 5 and 8 per cent by 2008–2012, and there was some provision for emissions trading. Many important details remained undecided, however. Although conference chairman Raul Estrada suggested that the final day of the conference would be remembered as 'the day of the atmosphere', environmental campaigners and many delegates from developing nations were far less satisfied. Not the least of the problems remaining was that the US Congress might well not ratify the agreement (which provided for a 7 per cent reduction in US emissions).

During the latter part of the year, large tracts of South-East Asia were covered by a thick smog. In Kuala Lumpur and other parts of Malaysia, many people took to wearing masks when going outside. Brunei, Singapore and parts of Indonesia were also severely affected—Thailand and the Philippines less so. The principal cause was forest fires in some of the large, sparsely-inhabited Indonesian territories, in particular Sumatra and Kalimantan (the Indonesian part of Borneo). Blame for the fires fell mainly on large land-owners, private and corporate, who used fire as a cheap method of felling trees and extending their plots, often illegally. 'Slash-and-burn' subsistence farmers were also held responsible.

The catastrophe caused a political uproar within ASEAN, the Malaysian Prime Minister, Dr Mahathir Mohamad, demanding action from the Indonesian government and assistance from the West. Several developed nations sent firefighters, as did Malaysia itself; but the scale of the fires, combined with unusual climatic conditions, meant that their efforts were largely abortive. The effects of the smog were felt in many areas of life. Airports were shut for long periods, hundreds of thousands of people were admitted to hospital with respiratory ailments, sea voyages were cancelled and schools closed. Estimates of the economic consequences ran into many millions of dollars. At least 200,000 hectares of forest were destroyed. The Indonesian government revoked the licences of over 30 companies operating in the fire zones.

The smog came to an end in November with the arrival of monsoon rains delayed by El Niño effects (see below). Nevertheless, the vast scale of the fires and the weakness of the rains meant that underground peat and coal deposits were probably still smouldering, making fresh fires likely when dry weather resumed. The year ended with a warning from the International Centre for Research in Agroforestry that fires—and therefore smogs—would become progressively more severe each year unless governments of the region, including Indonesia, tackled the behaviour of the companies responsible.

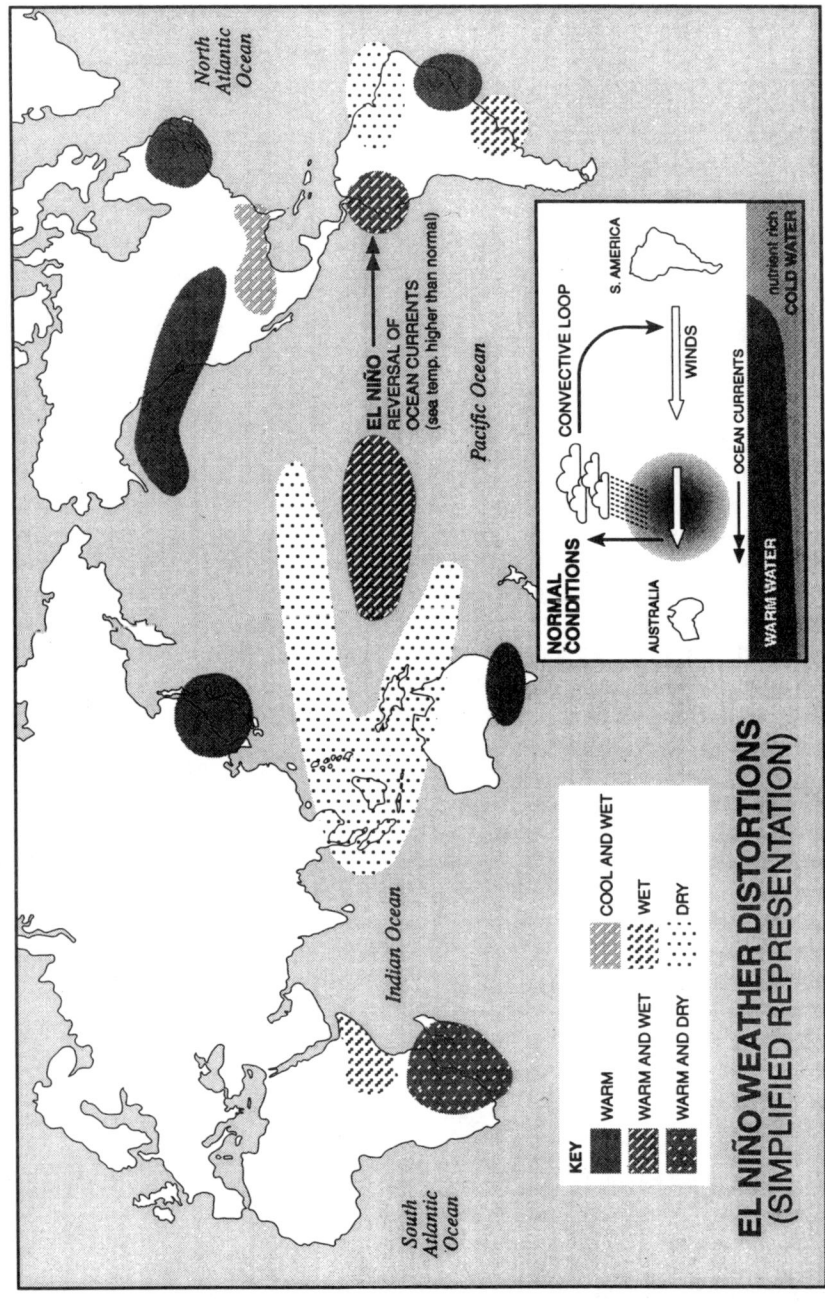

EL NIÑO WEATHER DISTORTIONS
(SIMPLIFIED REPRESENTATION)

Burning trees, smog and health alerts were not confined to South-East Asia. Brazil and Australia also endured unusually strong and long-lasting forest fires, again exacerbated by El Niño (see map on facing page). Early indications were that the 1997 El Niño phenomenon was one of the most severe on record, sea temperatures in the eastern Pacific being roughly 3°C above the seasonal average. Rains came late to East Asia and Australia. The east coast of South America was drier than usual, and the west coast warmer and wetter—an effect that continued northwards into Californian waters, where several tropical fish species were spotted, drawn by the warm sea. Economic effects in Africa included the loss of around a quarter of Kenya's tea crop and the destruction of cocoa plantations in Côte d'Ivoire, while in Latin America the government of Costa Rica declared a state of emergency because of El Niño's impact on the rice, bean, coffee and fishing industries. As the year ended, the full economic picture was only just beginning to emerge.

Important conferences on wildlife in 1997 included one to review the Convention on the International Trade in Endangered Species (CITES), held in Harare on 9–20 June, and the annual session of the International Whaling Commission (IWC), held in Monaco on 20–24 October. Both witnessed angrier scenes than usual. Immediately before the CITES conference started, the WWF released a list of what it said were the ten most endangered species on the planet. The Beluga sturgeon, broad-leaf mahogany and the medicinal herb goldenseal were on the list, alongside tigers, turtles and the black rhino. The CITES session itself, however, was dominated by the elephant, as Botswana, Namibia and Zimbabwe wanted a limited lifting of the ban on trading in ivory. This proposal was opposed by Western countries, while blocs of developing nations retaliated by preventing the adoption of some US proposals. South Africa lobbied similarly for a lifting of the embargo on white rhinoceros products. Eventually, the ivory ban was partially lifted, the three nations being allowed to sell 60 tonnes of stockpiled tusks to designated Japanese firms. Environmental groups were to be involved in a monitoring process to check that no newly-hunted ivory entered the chain.

The IWC meeting considered a controversial proposal from the Irish Republic for a complete restructuring of the way whaling was regulated. The plan envisaged the rescinding of the IWC's blanket worldwide ban on commercial whaling (which was being circumvented by Japan and Norway in any case); instead, the oceans would be declared a sanctuary but every country would be allowed to hunt in its own coastal waters. The idea was presented as a compromise to prevent the IWC falling apart, but was opposed by environmentalists, who feared that more states would start whaling. The meeting ended with an agreement to study the proposal and discuss it again in 1998.

Perhaps the most threatened group of species on the planet, however, were man's closest relatives, the primates. Reports in April by the WWF and in August by the Worldwatch Institute showed that half of the great apes faced extinction in the near future. The main problem was habitat loss: the WWF study noted that in Indonesia, for example, only 2 per cent of the orang-utan's original forest remained.

This news was given added urgency later in the year by reports that villagers in Sumatra were killing orang-utans fleeing from the forest fires (see above).

Another anniversary marked in 1997 was the completion of ten years of ozone-layer protection. In September delegates gathered in Montreal to toast the success of the 1987 Montreal Protocol (see AR 1987, pp. 436–7), as a result of which levels of ozone-damaging gases such as CFCs in the atmosphere had started to decline. Celebrations were tempered, however, by research showing a growing black-market in CFCs now that their production was banned in the industrialized world.

The major controversy at the Montreal meeting was over a US proposal that methyl bromide, a cheap and widely-used pesticide, should be phased out by developed countries by 2005. Other delegates, including some from EU states, responded that available substitutes were no less harmful and that the Americans were merely pursuing their own national interests, having already legislated for a national ban on methyl bromide. The US view prevailed and the proposal was adopted, developing countries being given an extra ten years' grace before they too had to phase out the pesticide.

Dams and their consequences formed a recurring theme over the year. In November Chinese engineers completed the coffer dam portion of the Three Gorges Dam on the River Yangtse, which would be the world's biggest (see also IX.2.i). Earlier, work had begun on diverting the Yellow River in preparation for a dam intended to prevent the disastrous floods which regularly devastated the area. The Bakun Dam in Malaysia was put on hold indefinitely, a casualty first of wrangles between contracted companies and then of East Asia's currency crisis. A scientific survey, published in March, found that the Iron Gates Dam on the Danube between Yugoslavia and Romania had resulted in an increase in poisonous algae and a decrease in fish stocks in the Black Sea, 1,000 kilometres downstream.

In Chile a group of indigenous Indians vowed to 'shed their blood' to prevent the building of the Ralco Dam. An independent review of the Pangue Dam, also in Chile, heavily criticized the World Bank for ignoring its own guidelines on environmental-impact assessment and on compensation for indigenous peoples. The chief author of the report claimed that elements within the World Bank had tampered with it before publication. In an attempt to meet the growth of such adverse comment, the World Bank, together with the International Union for the Conservation of Nature (IUCN), convened an international workshop on dam-building in Geneva in April. It brought together delegates from governments, NGOs, companies and funding agencies. The result was a joint working group which would draw up a set of international standards.

An agreement on sharing water resources between countries was concluded at the United Nations in May. It set out the rights of upstream and downstream states, should disputes arise. The need for such an agreement was demonstrated in April when Turkey announced the construction of two new dams on the Tigris, which encountered strong criticism from downstream Iraq. Meanwhile, environmentalists warned of the devastating effects on wildlife if an international plan went ahead to dam and dredge the Pantanal region of South America, one of the most bio-diverse areas on the planet. In March, on World Water Day, the UN warned that 80 countries were currently short of water, and that it would become an increasingly scarce resource in the coming years. The UN estimated that within a few decades around two-thirds of the world's population would suffer from 'moderate to severe water stress'.

Another factor behind water shortages was pollution. A survey by Azerbaijan's state ecology committee found that half the country's factories were polluting lakes and rivers—a situation which was believed to pertain in most other former Soviet republics as well. A Greenpeace study found that in Dzerzhinsk, a chemical-manufacturing town 300 kilometres from Moscow, the concentration of dioxins in ground-water was 50 million times above the international standard.

The Chinese government launched a crackdown on pollution which involved the closure of thousands of factories, the establishment of an environmental police force in Shanghai and the first steps towards a national ban on leaded petrol. The Indian authorities also got tough, making drivers put their vehicles through emissions tests before allowing them to buy fuel, and banning the import for processing of toxic and hazardous waste. However, some campaigners claimed that corruption allowed many offenders to slip through the net. Urban smogs caused health alerts in many places—Mexico City, Paris and Athens being among the worst-affected. Researchers in Pakistan demonstrated that urban pollution could adversely affect crops growing 50 kilometres away; and in the United States scientists linked pollutants, such as lead and manganese, to violent behaviour and an anti-social personality.

Research published in Finland in January and in the United States in November produced new evidence of a decline in male fertility linked to chemicals such as DDT and PCB (polychlorinated biphenyl) in the environment. At Chernobyl in Ukraine, scientists uncovered evidence that the nuclear accident in 1986 (see AR 1986, pp. 100–1, 395–6, 406–8) had caused permanent genetic damage to birds in the area.

Finally, in 1997 the world was told the monetary worth of nature. An American scientist, Robert Costanza, led a team which added up all the different services which the natural world provided to human beings—waste-recycling, provision of clean water, pollination, soil formation, etc.—and concluded that nature's monetary value to the human race was $33,000,000 million a year. The researchers suggested that this figure should be taken into account by governments when formulating policy. As the year ended, however, there was little to indicate that politicians were taking this advice on board.

XV THE LAW

1. INTERNATIONAL LAW—EUROPEAN COMMUNITY LAW

i. INTERNATIONAL LAW

THE International Court of Justice had eight cases before it but gave judgment on the merits in only one, the Hungary/Slovakia case concerning the Gabcikovo-Nagymaros project (see also III.1.iv/v). The dispute arose over the construction and operation of a series of dams on the River Danube. In 1977 Hungary and Czechoslovakia had concluded a treaty for the building of dams to produce hydro-electricity, control floods, and improve navigation on the Danube between Bratislava and Budapest. In 1989 Hungary unilaterally suspended performance of the treaty, claiming that the project threatened its environment and the water supply of Budapest. It subsequently purported to terminate the treaty. Slovakia, as the successor to Czechoslovakia, demanded that Hungary carry out its treaty obligations; it planned, and put into operation, a variant of the original project on its own territory.

The Court found that both Hungary and Slovakia had breached their obligations under the 1977 treaty. By 14 votes to 1 it rejected Hungary's argument that in 1989 a state of necessity had permitted it to suspend its obligations under the treaty. The doctrine of necessity could be accepted only exceptionally: an essential interest of the state had to be threatened by a grave and imminent peril; the action had to be the only means of safeguarding that interest; and the state taking action must not have contributed to the occurrence of the state of necessity.

The Court also rejected Slovakia's argument that Hungary's suspension of performance in 1989 had made it impossible to carry out the project as originally provided for and that therefore Czechoslovakia had been entitled to proceed with a solution as close to the original project as possible. The Court found (10–5) that the Czechoslovak project had not come within the limits of the 1977 treaty and had violated certain express provisions.

At the same time, the Court held (11–4) that Hungary had not been entitled to terminate the treaty in May 1992. Hungary put forward five arguments from the law of treaties to justify its action. The Court had to examine crucial questions of the law of treaties and of state responsibility. First, Hungary again invoked the doctrine of necessity. The Court held that this was not a ground for termination of a treaty; a treaty could be terminated only in accordance with the grounds in the Vienna Convention on the Law of Treaties. Second, Hungary claimed that performance of the treaty was impossible; and third, that there had been a fundamental change of circumstances. Fourth, it contended that Czechoslovakia had, in its planning and operation of a variant of the original treaty, committed a material breach. Finally, Hungary argued that international environmental law had changed so much that it overrode the 1977 treaty. The Court rejected all these arguments, stressing the stability of treaty relations and taking a restrictive view of the right of states to terminate treaties.

On 6 February Judge Stephen Schwebel (USA) was elected president of the International Court of Justice, while Christopher Weeramantry (Sri Lanka) was elected vice-president.

Important developments occurred in the international criminal tribunals for the former Yugoslavia and Rwanda. At the start of the year the Rwanda tribunal was investigated by the United Nations because of concerns over its management; the report, published in February, found serious mismanagement and violations of UN rules and regulations. As a result, the registrar and the deputy prosecutor resigned on 26 February. During the year problems continued with the safety of witnesses and their attendance, delays, inadequate structures and resources. Nevertheless, some progress was made. Hearings on the merits were held in several trials and by the end of the year two cases were nearing completion: Jean-Paul Akayesu, a former local government officer, and Georges Rutaganda, former vice-president of the Interahamwe militia, were both prosecuted for genocide and crimes against humanity. Over 20 suspects were held in custody in Arusha (Tanzania).

The president and vice-president of the tribunal, Laity Kama (Senegal) and Yacov Ostrovsky (Russia), were re-elected for two years on 3 June. Judge Antonio Cassese resigned after four years as president of the appeal chamber common to the Yugoslav and the Rwandan tribunals (and of the tribunal for the former Yugoslavia); he was replaced by Judge Gabrielle Kirk McDonald (USA).

The Yugoslavia tribunal gave judgment on the merits in one case, the *Tadić* case, which was the first full international war crimes trial since the post-World War II trials at Nuremberg and Tokyo (see also III.2.ii). On 7 May Dushan Tadić was convicted; he was found guilty on 11 of the 31 counts arising from his actions during the armed takeover and ethnic cleansing of Muslim and Croat areas by the Bosnian Serbs, and also from his acts in the camps run by the Republika Srpska. He was found guilty on a general charge of persecution as a crime against humanity and also of ten acts involving beatings of prisoners. The lengthy judgment was important for its documenting of the Bosnian Serb policy and tactics of ethnic cleansing and also for its discussion of the law on the grave breaches regime of the 1949 Geneva Conventions, of international humanitarian law in non-international armed conflict, and of crimes against humanity.

Tadić was acquitted on nine charges because of lack of evidence, while 11 charges were held to be inapplicable. By a majority, the trial chamber found that charges of 'grave breaches' of the Geneva Convention relative to the Protection of Civilian Persons in Time of War were not available. These offences could only be committed in an international armed conflict and if the victims were in the hands of an occupying power of which they were not nationals. According to the chamber, the prosecution had not shown that the Bosnian

Serbs were agents of Serbia and Montenegro (i.e. rump Yugoslavia) at the time the crimes were committed. They had acted in coordination but Serbia and Montenegro did not exercise command and control over the Bosnian Serbs. Tadić was sentenced to 20 years' imprisonment, following which both the defence and the prosecution appealed.

The first trial involving alleged offences by Muslims and Croats against Bosnian Serbs started on 10 March. The case against Zejnil Delalić, Hazim Delić, Zdravko Mucio and Esad Landzo arose out of murder and torture at the Celebici camp in Bosnia in 1992. On 24 June the trial began of Tihomir Blaskić, the Bosnian-Croat general accused of the ethnic purging of Muslims in central Bosnia in 1992–93. However, most of the 78 indicted, including the Bosnian Serb leaders, Radovan Karadžić and Ratko Mladić, were still not in the tribunal's custody.

The Arbitral Tribunal for the Dispute over the Inter-Entity Boundary in the Brcko area made its award in the dispute between the Republika Srpska and the Federation of Bosnia & Hercegovina on 14 February. The three-member tribunal had been established under the 1995 General Framework Agreement for Peace in Bosnia & Hercegovina (the Dayton accords). The tribunal said that, although legal doctrine precluded the acquisition of territory by force, it did not automatically follow that the Federation was entitled to the Brcko area. The Bosnian Serb campaign to wrest sovereignty had been conducted against the Republic of Bosnia & Hercegovina, not against the Federation, which was not then in existence. The Republic of Bosnia & Hercegovina now had legal sovereignty over the whole of its territory, so the injury had already been remedied in terms of international law. Moreover, the application of the principles of the historical, demographic, cultural and political ties to the area did not give a clear answer to the dispute. In the light of the demographic diversity before the war, it was not clear that either entity had sufficiently dominant ties to justify the award of exclusive control. The tribunal must be concerned with the Dayton principles, the return of refugees, restoration of property, compensation, and free movement. It would have to fashion a solution consistent with these principles to ensure long-term stability.

Accordingly, the tribunal found that, although equitable principles required it to take account of the welfare of the past and present Brcko community, legal principles did not require the award of the area to one party. Therefore, it was inappropriate to make a final choice as to which party should get control of the town, in a situation where the Federation and the Republika Srpska were less stable now than had been expected when the Dayton agreement was made. However, the tribunal recognized that it had a duty to make a choice and held that, after an interim period of international supervision, either party could return to the tribunal and request further action.

As regards multilateral treaties, the *Convention on the Prohibition of the Development, Production, Stockpiling and Use of Chemical Weapons and on their Destruction* (see AR 1993, p. 436) entered into force on 29 April. This was a landmark, being a multilateral disarmament treaty to eliminate an entire category of weapons. Four of the five permanent members of the UN Security

Council were parties (the exception being Russia—see XII.2). The UN *Convention on the Prohibition of the Use, Stockpiling, Production and Transfer of Anti-Personnel Mines and on their Destruction* was opened for signature in Ottawa on 3 December (see XIX.5). However, some of the largest manufacturers of mines, notably the USA, China, Russia, India and Pakistan, did not sign.

After more than 20 years of negotiation in the International Law Commission, the 1993 *Convention on the Law of the Non-Navigational Uses of International Watercourses* was adopted by the UN General Assembly and opened for signature on 21 May. The most difficult issue was the balance between the rights of upstream and downstream states, consensus in this area having proved impossible. Accordingly, the convention simply established general principles for the use and management of international watercourses and to assist in the settlement of disputes. It encouraged states to enter into specific agreements concerning watercourses they shared.

The Kyoto Protocol to the *1992 Climate Change Convention* was concluded on 11 December to deal with global warming (see XIV.3; XIX.6). The final text was disappointing to many environmentalists and vulnerable island states because the obligation to reduce emissions of climate-changing pollution was limited to developed states and the targets were to cut emissions by only an average 5.2 per cent by 2012. Detailed provisions on implementation were left for a later conference.

The Council of Europe concluded two treaties on human rights. The *Convention on Human Rights and Biomedicine* was concluded on 4 April (see also XI.4.i). This created common standards for the protection of the human person in the context of the development of the biomedical sciences; it was relevant to organ transplants, the use of substances of human origin and medical research on human beings. The *Convention on Nationality* was opened for signature on 7 November, the first international text to try to update international law on this topic. It was partly a response to the problems of nationality in the context of state succession, arising out of the break-up of the former USSR and the former Yugoslavia. It regulated the situation of persons in danger of being left stateless. It also aimed to facilitate the acquisition of a new nationality and the recovery of a former nationality, to ensure that nationality could not be arbitrarily withdrawn, and to guarantee that procedures governing applications for nationality were fair and open to appeal.

The European Court of Human Rights heard about 80 cases, mostly on the right to a fair trial, but also about subjects such as freedom of speech, expropriation of property and pre-trial detention. Six of the most important cases went to the grand chamber for judgment. Of these, three were against Turkey. In *Aydin v. Turkey*, the rape and abuse of the applicant by a state official was held to have been an especially grave form of ill-treatment: the accumulation of acts of physical and mental violence amounted to torture in violation of the Convention. The other two cases against Turkey related to the government's treatment of the Kurds. In *Zana*, Turkey was partly vindicated; the imposition of a prison sentence on a former mayor of Diyarbakir, who had supported the Kurdistan

Workers' Party (PKK) in an interview with a journalist, was held to have been justified. The Court ruled that at the time of the interview the PKK had been involved in terrorist activities against civilians in south-east Turkey, so that the restriction on freedom of expression answered a pressing social need. In the same ruling, however, the Court found that the conduct of the former mayor's trial did not live up to the standards of the Convention. In *Mentes* the Court held that the burning of houses in south-east Turkey by the security forces was a breach of the right to family life and that Turkey offered no effective domestic remedy against such actions.

The International Tribunal for the Law of the Sea gave its first judgment on 4 December in the case of *The Saiga*, between St Vincent & the Grenadines and Guinea. The case arose out of the seizure by Guinea of a vessel supplying oil to fishing vessels off its coast. St Vincent demanded the release of its ship. The judgment of the tribunal was complex and covered a wide range of issues under the Law of the Sea Convention, including the scope of coastal state jurisdiction in the exclusive economic zone and the contiguous zone, and the doctrine of hot pursuit.

ii. EUROPEAN COMMUNITY LAW

THE highlight of 1997 was undoubtedly the signing of the Treaty of Amsterdam on 2 October (see XI.3; XIX.2); but in other respects also it was a year of massive legal consolidation and change. For instance, the Dublin Convention on Asylum at last received all its ratifications, its coming into force on 1 September being immediately followed by two decisions implementing the convention and laying down its rules of procedure.

The Amsterdam Treaty itself was a strange document, unlike either the 1986 Single European Act (see AR 1986, pp. 344–5, 415–6) or the 1991 Maastricht Treaty (see AR 1991, pp. 465–7; 561–7). The former had established a framework for foreign policy coordination and the latter had created a new organism (the European Union) and the 'pillar' structure to fit inside it, not to mention the framework for the forthcoming monetary union. In contrast, the Amsterdam Treaty was purely an amending treaty, introducing its innovations by incorporating them, through amendment, into the existing basic treaties, especially the EC Treaty and the Union Treaty. Indeed, perhaps its most far-reaching contribution to development of the Union was its radical tidying-up of those two treaties. This was no simple technical exercise: some of the changes represented major political developments, and the result was a drastically-altered treaty structure which would require much effort from lawyers in order to master it.

The easiest of these major changes followed from the change of government in the United Kingdom and its consequent acceptance of the Community's new ambitious programme to develop employment and social rights. The UK's adamant opt-out from this programme had led to the inclusion of the 'Social Chapter' in the Maastricht Treaty as a separate protocol adhered to by only 14 of the 15 member states. When the new UK government reversed the policy and wished to opt in, there was no longer any need for the constitutionally very peculiar arrangements in the Social Chapter protocol. Consequently, the protocol was deleted at Amsterdam and its substantive content was inserted in its natural place in the EC Treaty (at Art. 117 *et seq.*), which now constituted a powerful series of provisions giving the EC/EU wide powers to legislate and to develop an extensive employment and social policy. This was reinforced by a new Title VIII on Employment, which was to operate in tandem with the social policy provisions.

Second, agreement was at last reached on removing the by now extensive legislation on immigration and asylum from inter-governmental control. These matters were therefore deleted from the third pillar of the Union Treaty (Title VI on Justice and Home Affairs, which was renamed 'Provisions on Police and Judicial Cooperation in Criminal Matters') and brought into the EC Treaty as a new Title IV on 'Visas, Asylum, Immigration and Other Policies related to Free Movement of Persons'. This had two major (and intended) consequences. First, legislation on these matters would follow the normal Community processes, involving the Commission, the Council and the European Parliament and would be subjected to proper political scrutiny—instead of the previous process which was secret and controlled by member states' government officials meeting together in the K.4 Committee. Second, Art. L of the Union Treaty ceased to apply to these matters, with the result that the European Court would now have jurisdiction. However, the United Kingdom, Ireland and Denmark, maintaining their hostility to surrender of control over their borders as regards non-Community aliens, obtained an opt-out expressed not only in special protocols to that effect but also in Art. 73q of Title IV itself.

Third, the Schengen Agreement, which was concluded and developed outside the Union context by a limited number of member states, was 'patriated' into the Union Treaty in the form of a protocol to both the EU and the EC Treaties which provided for the integration into those treaties of the 'Schengen *acquis*', i.e. all the existing texts which had already been issued under the 1985 Schengen Agreement. Interestingly, although the protocol made the 'Schengen *acquis*' part of the EU Treaty, no-one knew precisely what the *acquis* consisted of, since most of the texts were secret. No list was appended to the protocol, nor was specific provision made for their publication.

An important constitutional innovation was made, resulting partly from continental frustration at the persistently negative attitude of the former UK government, by the addition to the Union Treaty of a new Title on 'Closer Cooperation'. This would allow groups of member-states to pursue closer integration among themselves on particular matters (as happened with Schengen) but to use the Community institutions in doing so (unlike Schengen). This carefully-controlled acceptance of a multi-speed Europe was hedged with powerful safeguards.

The extensive addition of new groups of provisions and shifting of blocks of text from one part of the EC/EU treaty system to another revealed the chaotic state of the treaties' structure, which had already been stretched almost to breaking-point by the Single European Act and the Maastricht Treaty. The Commission took the opportunity, while polishing and finalizing the text for signature at Amsterdam in October (after it had been agreed by the member-states at the European Council meeting in June), to clean up the chaos by renumbering all the treaty articles in a simple single sequence. The renumbering was incorporated into a table of concordance, which formed part of the Treaty of Amsterdam and so would come into effect when that Treaty entered into force after obtaining its 15 ratifications.

The renumbering, which was completely unexpected and not even hinted at during the European Council meeting in June, was first revealed (without any press announcement) on the EC Council's Internet web site in late July. It caused consternation among judges and lawyers, all of whom would have to learn a completely new set of numbers to replace old favourites such as Art. 85, Art. 30 or Art. 177. An unexpected benefit from the renumbering process, however, was the decision by the Commission to remove from the EC Treaty the large number of out-dated articles. For instance, Art. 241, providing that 'the Council shall meet within one month of the entry into force of this [EEC] Treaty', lost its purpose when the Council did meet for the first time—in 1957!—but remained a part of the treaty, as did a large number of other spent articles and paragraphs. All of these were removed during the renumbering process, so that the Amsterdam Treaty, when it came into force, would provide interested parties with clean, pristine-looking texts of the EC and Union Treaties.

Apart from the Amsterdam Treaty, a number of very significant other developments took place in 1997. Among these was the replacement in December of the EC's free trade agreements with the three Baltic states by full-blown 'Europe Agreements'. As a result, those three states became closely integrated into the EC legal system, since the Europe Agreements required that the main body of Community law should be introduced into their own domestic systems even before negotiations on future accession to the EU could make any substantive progress. The same applied to Turkey, in spite of the European Union's clear message in December that Turkey would not be considered for membership in the foreseeable future. Within the context of the EC-Turkey customs union, the Commission issued a long list of Community harmonizing legislation which Turkey was required to adopt as part of its internal law. At the same time, relations with Europe's 'far east' (the former Soviet Union) began to take on legal significance with the signature with Ukraine of the first of the long-awaited 'partnership agreements' (less extensive than association or Europe Agreements, but nevertheless requiring some form of legal alignment).

Of particular concern to lawyers was the adoption in December of a directive allowing lawyers from one member-state to practise in another member-state on a permanent basis, whether they described themselves by their home-state title or wished to use a host-state title (and thus appear to the public to be part of the host-state legal profession). This directive came after a long period of disagreement between the legal professions of the different member-states.

Equally technical but less controversial was the adoption of a convention on the service of legal documents between member-states, an important feature in the free flow of cross-border litigation. Also on cross-border legal proceedings, the San Sebastian version of the EC Judgments Convention finally came fully into force for all member-states on 1 October. In December a related convention on jurisdiction in divorce and maintenance cases was adopted.

2. LAW IN THE UNITED KINGDOM

THE first steps were taken to bring about a substantial measure of devolution of powers from the Westminster parliament to Scotland and Wales (see also I.6; I.8; I.9). Referendums were held in September, as a result of which bills were introduced into parliament to enable the setting-up of separate legislative assemblies.[1] A second constitutional shift was initiated by the introduction into parliament of a bill to incorporate the European Convention on Human Rights into English Law.[2] The courts followed the traditional doctrine of the separation of powers, holding that the Parliamentary Commissioner for Standards operated under the auspices of parliament, and hence his decisions could not be reviewed by the courts.[3] After a history of important litigation fixing the relationship between English law and European Community law, the Divisional Court held that the failure to incorporate a Community Directive in English Law gave a right to compensation but not not to exemplary damages[4] (see also XV.1.ii).

In the wake of the handover of Hong Kong to China (see IX.2.ii), the *British Nationality (Hong Kong) Act* provided for certain citizens of Hong Kong to be given British nationality. The House of Lords held that there was no reason to suppose that there was a serious risk of injustice or oppression by the Chinese government if a person was extradited to Hong Kong.[5]

Overturning the Court of Appeal, the House of Lords held that a local authority responsible for the provisions of social services was allowed to take into account the cost of providing some service in determining whether there was a need for it.[6] The Court of Appeal adopted a similar approach in determining what constituted 'suitable' education;[7] but financial considerations did not justify a health authority's policy of ignoring a Department of Health circular and not prescribing a drug.[8] The High Court upheld the surcharge of £27 million imposed on the former leader and deputy leader of the Westminster City Council.[9]

The Court of Appeal allowed a widow to export the sperm of her deceased husband to Belgium in order to receive artificial insemination there, notwithstanding that the retention of the sperm after the husband's death had been an offence under English law.[10] The High Court held that it had a power at common law to cause a minor to be detained to undergo medical treatment;[11] but the Court of Appeal held that there was no power to force an adult woman of sound mind to have a caesarian operation,[12] nor to detain an autistic adult for assessment and treatment without using the compulsory powers contained in the *Mental Health*

Act 1983.[13] An important ambiguity in the law was cleared up by the decision of the Court of Appeal that the father of an illegitimate child might make an application relating to the surname of the child who was living with its mother, though stressing that such an application should not be lightly granted.[14] In another case, a non-custodial mother failed in an application that the children should be forced to keep her maiden name.[15]

Substantial increases in the costs of litigation were brought into effect in January.[16] Two months later the Divisional Court held that the Lord Chancellor had acted unlawfully in not making provision for the fees to be reduced in cases of hardship.[17] Further changes designed to speed up legal process and to make it more accessible and less costly were heralded by an announcement by the new Lord Chancellor, Lord Irvine of Lairg.[18] The *Civil Procedure Act* introduced a new system for making procedural rules and provided for the setting-up of a Civil Justice Council to oversee the operation of the civil justice system. The administrative arrangements for magistrates' courts were streamlined by the *Justices of the Peace Act*. In the courts, the House of Lords refused to overturn the assignment of a cause of action by the liquidator of a company to an individual entitled to legal aid: apparent abuses of the system of legal aid should be dealt with by the rule-making powers of the Lord Chancellor rather than on an *ad hoc* basis.[19]

Minor changes to the powers of the police were contained in the *Criminal Evidence (Amendment) Act*. The House of Lords held that the Home Secretary had acted wrongly in refusing to take into account post-conviction factors in fixing the term of youth custody to be served by juveniles convicted of murder;[20] their lordships also stressed that, once a tariff had been fixed by the Home Secretary, it was not open to him subsequently to increase it.[21] The *Crime (Sentences) Act* reversed the effect of these decisions.[22] In addition, aiming to stiffen the penalties imposed on those convicted of serious offences, the act introduced significant changes to the rules relating to long-term imprisonment; in particular, it provided for substantial minimum periods of imprisonment to be imposed for second or third convictions of a range of serious offences. New guidelines for sentencing in magistrates' courts were introduced[23].

Three men who had spent 18 years in prison after being convicted for murder were released after new evidence was brought to light.[24] The Criminal Cases Review Commission took over responsibility for the overseeing of alleged miscarriages of justice from the Home Office; by the end of the year it had referred six cases to the Court of Appeal.[25] The Court of Appeal decided that the Home Secretary had power to refuse to allow prisoners to be visited by journalists unless the latter gave undertakings that they would not use any information so obtained for professional purposes.[26]

Several measures were taken to deal with problems of public order. The *Confiscation of Alcohol (Young Persons) Act* gave powers to police constables to confiscate alcohol from minors in public places; the *Firearms (Amendment) Act* brought in substantial restrictions on the types of weapon which individuals might be allowed to have in their possession; and the *Knives Act* introduced new criminal offences relating to the sale or possession of knives. The interests of victims and potential victims of sexual offences were given additional protection by the *Sexual Offences (Protected Material) Act* and the *Sex Offenders Act*. The latter statute provided that individuals who had served terms of imprisonment for sexual offences should be under a duty to notify the police of their places of residence, as well as allowing for the prosecution in England of those who committed sexual offences abroad. The Divisional Court ruled that it might be lawful for the police to disclose to local residents that a released paedophile was living in their area,[27] and guidelines as to the appropriate circumstances in which this should be done were subsequently introduced.[28] Further restrictions on released sexual offenders and those guilty of anti-social behaviour were heralded by the *Crime and Disorder Bill*. The *Police Act* provided for the setting up of a National Criminal Intelligence Service to support the law-enforcement functions of the police; and several statutes dealt with aspects of the administration of the police force.[29]

It was held by the House of Lords that the making of harassing telephone calls which seriously affected the health of the victim might constitute an assault causing grievous bodily harm.[30] A more general solution was provided by the *Protection from Harassment Act*, introducing a criminal offence of harassment. In addition, the Act provided victims of harassment with a civil remedy for damages, incidentally enabling the House of Lords to remove such cases from the scope of the tort of nuisance and restore this tort to its traditional scope in remedying interferences with an occupier's enjoyment of land.[31] It was later emphasized that the Act was not so broad in its scope that it could be used against those exercising a right to protest about a matter of public interest,[32] though the Divisional Court held that there was no right to demonstrate on the highway, even where the defendants' acts were peaceable and non-obstructive.[33]

In other developments in criminal law, the House of Lords held that where a man stabbed a woman causing her child to be born prematurely, as a result of which the child died, he could be guilty of manslaughter but not of murder.[34] Their Lordships again considered the circumstances in which a participant in a joint enterprise should be convicted of aiding and abetting a murder committed by another participant, holding that it was sufficient that he had envisaged that his partner might have killed unless the partner's means of killing was fundamentally different from what had been envisaged.[35]

The House of Lords consolidated the division between private law and public law in refusing to allow an action in tort at the suit of a person refused interim accommodation by a Local Housing Authority,[36] though the Court of Appeal made it clear that in appropriate circumstances a person might be able to choose between seeking judicial review and bringing an action for damages.[37] The boundaries here remained uncertain. May J refused to impose liability in tort on coastguards;[38] similarly, the Court of Appeal held that a fire brigade was not liable in tort for failing properly to put out a fire, but that liability would arise if it negligently made the fire worse;[39] and it was held that liability might arise after an educational psychologist failed to diagnose a child as suffering from dyslexia.[40] The Court of Appeal allowed the issue of an injunction to restrain an espionage agent from receiving profits from a book which he had written; the court held that the circumstances were such that it was appropriate to allow the use of such a remedy to uphold the criminal law; in addition, in a potentially very wide-reaching holding, it stated that restitutionary damages might be available in actions for breach of contract.[41]

In the first case of its kind in the High Court, Ian Kennedy J awarded damages to a professional footballer injured in a tackle.[42] It was established that the police might be liable for the tort of misfeasance in public office;[43] the Court of Appeal laid down guidelines for the award of damages in actions brought against the police for improper conduct,[44] and held that the police might be liable when a sane person in their custody committed suicide.[45] A woman recovered damages against her former husband who had raped her,[46] and damages of £74,000 were awarded to a woman who had been raped by her former superior;[47] in neither case had there been a criminal prosecution.

After a libel trial lasting over 300 days, McDonald's Restaurants were awarded damages of £60,000 against two environmental campaigners.[48] A former government minister, Jonathan Aitken, was held entitled to have his libel action against a national newspaper heard without a jury;[49] the action was subsequently abandoned and the plaintiff resigned from the Privy Council.[50]

The House of Lords refused to grant a mandatory injunction against a company which had contracted to keep open a store; only in exceptional circumstances would the other contracting party be entitled to a remedy other than the award of damages.[51] It was held by the House of Lords that former employees of a company which had been run dishonestly might recover damages in respect of their diminished prospects of future employment.[52]

The House of Lords held that the occupant of a chalet bungalow which had become so firmly embedded in the ground as to be treated as annexed to the land was entitled to the protection of the Rent Acts.[53] The House of Lords, following an earlier decision, reiterated that notice to determine a joint tenancy might effectively be given by one of two joint tenants.[54] Their Lordships held that a letter giving notice to determine a lease had to be given the interpretation which would be made by a reasonable recipient,[55] although in another case they ruled that a letter from the Home Office requiring a person to leave the country had to be unequivocal.[56]

1. *Government of Wales Bill*; *Scotland Bill*
2. Human Rights Bill
3. R v. *Parliamentary Commissioner for Standards, ex parte al-Fayed, The Times* 13 November (Court of Appeal)
4. R v. *Secretary of State for Transport, ex parte Factortame (No 5), The Times* 11 September
5. R v. *Secretary of State for the Home Department, ex parte Launder* [1997] 1 WLR 839
6. R v. *Gloucestershire County Council, ex parte Barry* [1997] 2 WLR 459
7. R v. *East Sussex County Council, ex parte Tandy* [1997] 3 WLR 884; see too *F v. Harrow London Borough Council, The Times* 29 December (Moses J)
8. R v. *North Derbyshire Health Authority, ex parte Fisher, The Times* 2 September

9. *The Times* 20 December
10. *R* v. *Human Fertilization and Embryology Authority, ex parte Blood* [1997] 2 WLR 806
11. *In re C (a Minor) (Medical Treatment: Court's Jurisdiction), The Times* 21 March
12. *In re M B (Caesarian Section), The Times* 18 April
13. *L* v. *Bournewood Community and Mental Health NHS Trust, The Times* 8 December
14. *Dawson* v. *Wearmouth, The Times* 22 August
15. *In re C (Minors) (Change of Surname), The Times* 8 December
16. *The Times* 14 January
17. *R* v. *Lord Chancellor, ex parte Witham, The Times* 13 March
18. *Sunday Times* 19 October
19. *Norglen Ltd* v. *Reeds Rains Prudential Ltd* [1997] 3 WLR 1177
20. *R* v. *Secretary of State for the Home Department, ex parte Venables* [1997] 3 WLR 23
21. *R* v. *Secretary of State for the Home Department, ex parte Pierson* [1997] 3 WLR 492
22. *R* v. *Secretary of State for the Home Department, ex parte Stafford, The Times* 28 November (Court of Appeal); *R* v. *Secretary of State for the Home Department, ex parte Hindley, The Times* 19 December (Divisional Court)
23. *The Times* 7 April
24. *The Times* 22 February
25. CCRC 020/97, 023/97, 028/97, 030/97
26. *R* v. *Secretary of State for the Home Department, ex parte Simms, The Times* 9 December
27. *R* v. *Chief Constable of North Wales Police, ex parte AB* [1997] 3 WLR 724
28. *The Times* 11 November
29. *Police and Firemen's Pensions Act*; *Police (Health and Safety) Act*; *Police (Insurance of Voluntary Assistants) Act*; *Police (Property) Act*
30. *R* v. *Ireland* [1997] 3 WLR 534
31. *Hunter* v. *Canary Wharf Ltd* [1997] 2 WLR 684
32. *Huntingdon Life Sciences Ltd* v. *Curtin, The Times* 11 December
33. *Director of Public Prosecutions* v. *Jones* [1997] 2 WLR 578
34. *Attorney-General's Reference* (No. 3 of 1994) [1997] 3 WLR 421
35. *R* v. *Powell* [1997] 3 WLR 959
36. *O'Rourke* v. *Camden London Borough Council* [1997] 3 WLR 86
37. *Trustees of the Dennis Rye Pension Fund* v. *Sheffield City Council* [1997] 4 All ER 747
38. *OLL Ltd* v. *Secretary of State for the Home Department, The Times* 22 July
39. *Nelson Holdings Ltd* v. *British Gas plc, The Times* 7 March; *Capital and Counties plc* v. *Hampshire County Council* [1997] 3 WLR 331
40. *Phelps* v. *Hillingdon London Borough Council, The Times* 10 October
41. *Attorney-General* v. *Blake, The Times* 22 December
42. *McCord* v. *Swansea City AFC Ltd, The Times* 11 February
43. *Bennett* v. *Commissioner of Police of the Metropolis, The Times* 24 October
44. *Thompson* v. *Commissioner of Police of the Metropolis* [1997] 3 WLR 403
45. *Reeves* v. *Commissioner of Police of the Metropolis, The Times* 20 November
46. *The Times* 10 September
47. *The Times* 5 November
48. *The Times* 20 June
49. *Aitken* v. *Preston, The Times* 21 May
50. *The Times* 21 June, 25 June
51. *Co-operative Insurance Society Ltd* v. *Argyll Stores (Holdings) Ltd* [1997] 2 WLR 898
52. *Mahmud* v. *Bank of Credit and Commerce International SA (in liquidation)* [1997] 3 WLR 95
53. *Elitestone Ltd* v. *Morris* [1997] 1 WLR 687
54. *Harrow London Borough Council* v. *Johnstone* [1997] 1 WLR 459, following *Hammersmith and Fulham London Borough Council* v. *Monk* [1992] 1 AC 478
55. *Mannai Investment Co Ltd* v. *Eagle Star Life Assurance Co Ltd* [1997] 2 WLR 495
56. *Chief Adjudication Officer* v. *Wolke* [1997] 1 WLR 1640

3. UNITED STATES LAW

THE US Supreme Court, in *Printz* v. *United States*, made its most significant decision since 1992 on the respective rights of the state and federal governments under the Tenth Amendment of the US constitution, which reserved to the states those powers not expressly granted by the constitution to the federal government. In *Printz*, the Court held unconstitutional, as an interference with the sovereignty reserved to the states, a federal law which required that state and local law enforcement officials should conduct background inquiries about a person who proposed to purchase a handgun. The decision prompted two federal court judges to hold unconstitutional, for similar reasons, a federal law which prohibited state motor-vehicle records from being disclosed to direct-marketing companies. Those decisions were expected to be reviewed on appeal to the federal Court of Appeals.

The Supreme Court also reached important decisions about human rights. In *Vacco* v. *Quill* and *Washington* v. *Glucksberg*, it held that state laws in New York and Washington which made it a crime to assist a terminally-ill person to commit suicide were valid because a person did not have a general right to commit suicide. In *Reno* v. *American Civil Liberties Union*, it ruled that a federal law which prohibited transmission of indecent material on the Internet was invalid because it imposed too broad a restriction on freedom of expression (see also IV.1). In *Schenck* v. *Pro Choice Network*, the Court held invalid an injunction against aggressive abortion demonstrations on the pavements near women's health clinics in two New York cities. A federal court in North Carolina ruled that the American Broadcasting Company was liable for $5.5 million in punitive damages for fraud and trespass when its journalists, in the course of an investigation of a supermarket chain, falsified resumés to obtain jobs with that chain; freedom of the press did not permit these violations of private rights. An appeal was lodged against the judgment.

The Ninth US Circuit Court of Appeal held valid Proposition 209, a law enacted by referendum in California in 1996 which prohibited the granting of preferences based on race by state and local government agencies (see AR 1996, p. 466). The Fifth US Circuit Court of Appeal held that an admission criterion used by a college or university based on race was permissible only to correct specific instances of past discrimination at that institution and not to achieve a more diverse student body or to remedy the effects of discrimination generally in society. Initiatives similar to Proposition 209 were proposed in three other states.

In *Amchem Products Inc.* v. *Windsor*, the Supreme Court fixed a limit on the trend in product liability cases, epitomized in the asbestos cases, whereby all claims were consolidated into a single case by all existing and possible claimants. A total of 20 defendants in a huge asbestos class action agreed to pay $1,300 million to tens of thousands of possible claimants in a settlement approved by a federal court in Philadelphia and upheld by the Third US Court of Appeals.

The court, however, held that the potential claimants had different interests from those who already suffered from the effects of asbestos, and so could not be combined into a single case.

The tobacco companies, the attorney-generals of 40 states which had initiated suits against those companies and attorneys who acted for individuals in several hundred cases reached agreement to propose a settlement of all existing and future tort claims against the tobacco companies: the tobacco companies would pay $368,500 million over 25 years to settle all class actions against them; future class actions would be prohibited; punitive damages awarded in all individual cases during each year in the future would be limited to $5,000 million; the Food and Drug Administration would be granted authority to regulate tobacco products but would not be permitted to ban nicotine before 2009; tobacco companies would endeavour to reduce smoking by teenagers by 67 per cent over the next 20 years; internal documents of the tobacco companies, protected as attorney-client records, would be released by them; and tobacco companies would give notice that nicotine was addictive and that smoking caused cancer and other diseases.

A bill was introduced in Congress to enact the laws necessary to implement the proposal, but it had not been passed by year's end. In California, the court of appeal upheld awards against a tobacco company of $1.3 million in compensatory damages and $700,000 in punitive damages to a smoker for injuries to him caused by smoking cigarettes sold by that company. The punitive damages were the first to be awarded against a tobacco company. An Alabama judge approved a far-reaching settlement of a class action against the Liggett Group for injuries caused by smoking its cigarettes: present and future claimants would have to claim from the $500,000 to $600,000 that would be paid annually under the settlement. The tobacco companies also agreed to pay over 25 years, in their settlements of claims with the state attorney-generals of Florida and Mississippi, $11,300 million and $3,600 million respectively.

A New York court awarded $5.9 million to three plaintiffs against Digital Equipment Corporation for repetitive stress injuries suffered from use of computer keyboards made by the defendant; the verdict was based on the defendant's failure to warn users of the potential for such injuries. A woman whose husband divorced her and married another woman obtained from a North Carolina court a judgment for $1 million against the latter woman for alienation of affection. No such case had been recorded before.

A total of 74 prisoners were executed in the United States in 1997, the most since 1955, when 76 were executed. In Texas, a state law which expedited appeals was ruled valid, after a challenge in 1996; 37 executions resulted in that state. The Louisiana Supreme Court upheld the death penalty for the rape of a child, the first case since 1977 in which capital punishment had been imposed for a crime other than homicide. The case was expected to be the subject of an appeal to the US Supreme Court.

The California Supreme Court held valid an injunction obtained against a gang by the city of San José with the aim of prohibiting a wide range of gang actions, such as use of gang hand-signals and beepers in public. Following the decision, 15 more cities in California applied for similar injunctions, while other cities outside California began to study how they might also use injunctions against gangs.

XVI THE ARTS

1. OPERA—MUSIC—BALLET & DANCE—THEATRE—CINEMA—
TELEVISION & RADIO

i. OPERA

IN a flurry of activity between January and July, the Royal Opera revived ten of its best productions of recent years, and staged for the first time Pfitzner's *Palestrina*, an extremely lengthy, musically second-rate and dramatically arid work enlivened only by a number of fine cameo performances from distinguished singers such as Nicolai Gedda, Sergei Leiferkus and Ekkehard Wlaschiha. The company's annual Verdi Festival produced both the 1857 and 1881 versions of *Simon Boccanegra*; but a new production of *Macbeth*, having been rehearsed for weeks, was cancelled a few days before the opening night. Because of a series of management blunders, not enough time had been allowed for technical rehearsals, there was a shortage of stagehands because of redundancies, and the storeroom where the set was to be kept had already been demolished. Nicholas Payne, the director of the Royal Opera, admitted that he had been at fault and offered to resign, but was persuaded by the board to remain. The Royal Opera House closed after a lack-lustre gala farewell concert in July, and was expected to reopen, enlarged and renovated, in the year 2000.

After its summer break, the company returned to perform in several other London venues. Excellent new productions of Handel's *Giulio Cesare*, Rameau's *Platée* and Britten's *The Turn of the Screw* were mounted in the Barbican Theatre, Verdi's *Otello* was unsatisfactorily staged at the Royal Albert Hall, and quite dreadful productions of Lehar's *The Merry Widow* and Rossini's *Il Barbiere di Siviglia* were unveiled at the Shaftesbury Theatre to almost universal disapprobation on the part of critics and public. In Graham Vick's staging, *The Merry Widow* was stripped of all its verve and gaiety, while the decor, credited to Richard Hudson, was to all intents and purposes non-existent. Nigel Lowery's *Barbiere* was a childish comic-strip joke at the expense of that elegant masterpiece of *opera buffa*.

Chris Smith, the Secretary of State for Culture, Media and Sport in Britain's new Labour government, made the suggestion that the Royal Opera, the Royal Ballet, and English National Opera should all be made to share the Royal Opera House when it reopened. To halt accusations that he had already decided upon this course of action, he commissioned Richard Eyre, former director of the National Theatre, to head an inquiry into the future of opera in London. Eyre's committee was expected to report in May 1998. Meanwhile, a House of Commons select committee reported in December, recommending that, in view of its incompetence, the board of the Royal Opera House be dissolved, and criticizing in the strongest possible terms not only the board but also the company's management structures. Within days, the chairman, Lord Chadlington, and all the members of the board had offered their resignations.

At the London Coliseum, English National Opera presented three new productions. The earliest and most ebullient of Rossini's great comic operas, *The Italian Girl in Algiers*, was directed by Howard Davies who was fortunately content to be faithful to the spirit and style of the piece. Della Jones was a somewhat matronly Isabella, but her grasp of Rossinian style was impressive, and Charles Workman was an engaging Lindoro. Janacek's harrowing *From the House of the Dead*, given a not very convincing production by Tim Albery in unhelpful and unatmospheric decor by Stewart Laing, was conducted persuasively by Paul Daniel. Matthew Warchus's staging of Verdi's *Falstaff*, first performed earlier in the year by Opera North in Leeds, did not transfer well to the large stage of the Coliseum, but Alan Opie's portrayal of the lecherous old knight was convincing on all levels.

Opera North also offered an inept production of Wagner's *Tannhäuser* by David Fielding, about which the authoritative magazine *Opera* wrote: 'For a blind man this was a highly acceptable evening'. The company's other new productions were Mozart's *Cosi Fan Tutte*, limply directed by Tim Albery in minimal sets, and a sensitive staging by David Pountney of a twentieth-century masterpiece, Martinu's *Julietta*. Scottish Opera presented an intelligent production of Johann Strauss's ever-popular *Die Fledermaus* by Giles Havergal; Saint-Saëns's *Samson et Dalila*, directed and designed by Anthony MacDonald, with Mark Lundberg an expressive Samson and Carolyn Sebron a Dalila who was vocally more steely than seductive; and Verdi's *Rigoletto* in a production which most critics agreed was calamitous. Welsh National Opera's four new offerings were Bizet's *Carmen* and Beethoven's *Fidelio*, both invigoratingly directed by Patrice Caurier and Moshe Leiser, David Pountney's acceptable *Simon Boccanegra*, and Mozart's *La Clemenza di Tito*, unobtrusively staged by Yannis Kokkos and brilliantly conducted by Sir Charles Mackerras.

The summer season at Glyndebourne began with *Manon Lescaut*, Puccini's not entirely satisfactory answer to Massenet's *Manon*. Graham Vick's production robbed the work of its individuality and, as the lovers Manon and Des Grieux, Adina Nitescu and Patrick Denniston were by no means ideal casting. Much more enjoyable was Rossini's relatively unfamiliar *Le Comte Ory*, an engaging comedy about a licentious Count and his followers at the time of the crusades. If there was not much delicacy in Jerome Savary's staging, there was plenty of wit, and the principal singers, most of them making their British debuts, were all first-rate, especially Marc Laho, an energetic Ory who dispatched his fiendishly high notes with ease. Andrew Davis was the spirited conductor.

At the Brighton Festival, New Sussex Opera mounted the first British performance of Gottfried von Einem's *Danton's Death*. The staging was unsatisfactory, but the cast, headed by Andrew Slater as Danton, sang and acted well. Also new to Britain was Lorenzo Ferrero's delightful opera for children, *The Sorcerer's Daughter*. The Buxton Festival offered Haydn's *Il Mondo della Luna*, performed by the Dublin Opera Company, and a delightful triple bill consisting of Cimarosa's *Il Maestro di Capella*, Menotti's *The Telephone*, and Wolf-Ferrari's *Susanna's Secret*.

Among singers who died in 1997 were Charles Craig, one of the finest British lyric-dramatic tenors to have emerged in the post-war years; Karl Ridderbusch, a leading German bass of the 1960s and '70s, particularly noted for his Wagner roles; Kenneth Neate, the Australian tenor who was a leading singer with the Royal Opera in the early post-war years; and Elisabeth Hoengen, the Austrian mezzo-soprano who sang with the Vienna State Opera from 1943 until her retirement in 1970. Sir Georg Solti, the distinguished conductor of Strauss and Wagner operas, also died during the year (see XX: Obituary).

ii. MUSIC

CHANGE and uncertainty continued in 1997. Increasing contact between different world cultures and the development of multi-ethnic societies led composers to seek new forms of musical expression and a greater universality of musical language. Pluralism could only lead to radical cultural changes. It seemed, however, that the pace of change had outrun the popular understanding; there was no accepted standard of aesthetic judgement. What could be detected was a general swing away from the extremes of the *avant-garde* styles of the 1950s and 1960s in favour of a new conservatism; a sense that the new radicalism should not break with the established musical language of past traditions; a sense that the listener mattered.

Classical music worldwide faced a seriously contracting market in 1997. Audiences were lower, CD sales plummeted, state subsidies were slashed. All this happened against a background of an ever-advancing pop music industry. Indeed the mass popular market consisted of pop music, becoming commercialized and trivialized in the process. Whereas Elton John's re-written version of *Candle in the Wind*, which was sung at the funeral of Diana, Princess of Wales, could sell 30 million copies in 37 days, the financial situation facing the classical record industry was very different. Companies retracted, dropping many top artists, while orchestra and concert managers were forced to economize with fewer rehearsals, less expensive soloists and conductors. The financial difficulties of opera houses particularly caught the headlines, and the quote of the year was made, with unconscious irony, by Gerald Kaufman, chairman of the House of Commons culture committee, when he said that parliament would prefer Covent Garden to be run by a philistine rather than by ballet and opera lovers who were incompetent.

If the established repertoire naturally made up the greater part of the classical season, it was the new, innovative performances that provided the leaven. Exploratory work was the first to suffer in times of cutback and financial stringency; but different countries had differing priorities in meeting the challenge. In Germany music, particularly new music, flourished. The year began with the Munich Biennale, with different events in different months. Hans Werner Henze, the retiring director, had put the city at the heart of German operatic life, and January saw four new operas—three by German composers. Chief among them were Henze's own one-act neo-classical *Venus and Adonis*, his 13th opera, in which he sought to revitalize old traditions; also a new opera by Helmut Lachenmann, *Das Mälchen mit den Schwefelhölzern*, which received its premiere. Based partly on Hans Andersen's *The Little Match Girl*, it also juxtaposed the new with the traditional, but its aesthetic basis was more radical than Henze's, and presented more of an intellectual challenge. The orchestra, which included electronics, was spaced round the auditorium in a 'total sonic environment', and the music was the source of every aspect of the opera, whether visual or to do with movement and gesture. Lachenmann's work, complex, subtle, sophisticated, was the far-reaching result of 30 years' experience. The other two operas were by younger, more overtly experimental composers. Michael Obst, in his opera *Solaris*, was successful in his use of electronics, particularly the spatial techniques developed at IRCAM, but less successful in writing for voices. Hanna Kulenty, a Polish composer, in her opera *The Mother of Black Winged Dreams*, used minimalist techniques, derived from Louis Andriessen, to portray female psychological problems.

The next instalment of the Munich Biennale, in April, introduced two new Music Theatre works. The first, Roderick Watkins's *The Juniper Tree*, was comparatively straightforward and unremarkable; the second, Moritz Eggert's *Helle Nächte*, was more challenging, though, perversely, less convincing in performance, attempting as it did a fusion of Western and Eastern cultures, and embodying electronics. A straight orchestral premiere, Sylvano Bussotti's *Souvenir d'Italie*, was more successful. 'Musica Viva', also in Munich, included less radical twentieth-century works for orchestra, as well as some for smaller ensembles, reflecting the more conservative 1990s. Louis Andriessen's *Hout* was jazz-influenced, while John Adams's *Shaker Loops* derived from Aaron Copland. It fell to György Ligeti's *Mysteries of the Macabre*, with virtuoso trumpet playing, to provide, literally, a show-stopping finale.

Other concert series in Germany were based on various periods and trends of the twentieth century. The Musik-Biennale in Berlin reprised the 1970s in their *avant-garde* and Webernist aspects, but avoiding simplistic compositions. Such works as Boulez's *Rituel in Memoriam Bruno Maderna*, Mathias Spahlinger's *Morendo*, Harrison Birtwistle's *The Triumph of Time*, set the benchmark. A strong impression was made by Richter de Vroe's new piece *Éraflurer* for violin and orchestra, as well as the more established Helmut Lachenmann's *Kontrakadenz*, and Luigi Nono's political protest of 1971, *Como una ola de fuerza y luz*. In Cologne the Musik-Triennale offered its audiences those German and other composers particularly associated with the Cologne School of *avant-garde* and electronic music of the 1950s and 1960s. Mauricio Kagel was well represented, and Karlheinz Stockhausen, with *Freitag aus Licht, Gruppen,* etc. These were offset by Louis Andriessen's *Trilogie des Letaten Tager*, and York Holler's sumptuously-romantic *Aura,* given its European premiere by the Chicago Symphony Orchestra under Daniel Barenboim.

Music for smaller ensembles was provided in nearby Witten. The 1997 Wittener Tage featured German and Italian composers of the 1960s and 1990s. Franco Evangelisti's *Die Schachtel* (1962) was a concert suite taken from a theatre work, representing 1960s radicalism, while Klaus Huber's *Lamentationes sacrae et profanae ad responsoria Gesualdo* (1997) was a re-working of Gesualdo's original in microtonal harmonic language. Electronics featured in *Live,* 18 short songs for ensemble and electronics by Iris ter Schiphorst and Helmut Ochring, and in *Sirene/Gespenster* (1997), which resulted from the assimilation by its composer, Luca Francesconi, of the electronic technology of IRCAM. These concerts were brought to a conclusion by Helmut Lachenmann's *Zwei Gefühle,* with recitation by the composer.

The music of Germany, showing a strong priority for German composers and German music, was in marked contrast to the musical situation in other countries. In Britain, for instance, priority was given first to performers, second to the somewhat vague goal of a 'balanced musical culture', which tended to downgrade, if not to marginalize, the British composer. The year began in London with a Lutoslawski festival in the Barbican, promoted by the BBC. This series was the precursor of a large number of performances worldwide of Lutoslawski's music. The Cello Concerto was toured with Lynn Harrell and the City of Birmingham Symphony Orchestra under Sir Simon Rattle; the Concerto for Orchestra was toured by the Chicago Symphony Orchestra under Daniel Barenboim; *Dance Preludes* was played extensively in America by the University of Wisconsin New Music Ensemble; *Grave* was toured in Australia by the Australian Chamber Orchestra. There were several others. It was a good year for Lutoslawski, who had died in 1994 (see AR 1994, p. 596).

There followed a double Stravinsky festival, of concert works in London and elsewhere, and of stage works in Paris. Two of the leading new music festivals of 1997, Bath and Huddersfield, gave prominence to the Greek composer Iannis Xenakis and the French composer Pascal Dusapin respectively, losing their nerve when it came to British composers. Of the two, Xenakis received far the fuller treatment. He celebrated his 75th birthday in 1997, and the occasion was marked by his receiving an honorary degree from Bath University and by the performance of 13 of his works at the city's festival. His computer-based method of sound synthesis, based on the laws of physics, led to complexities, harsh and abrasive textures, and a calculated sonic maelstrom. It lacked a compensating lyricism and a structural balance. However powerful they proved in performance, his works remained experimental; he did not discover a new musical language because he did not set out to find one.

One of the most interesting and significant premieres of the year, promoted jointly by the BBC and RTE, took place in St Patrick's Cathedral, Dublin—not of a new twentieth-century work, but of a piece by the eighteenth-century English composer Samuel Wesley, *Missa de Spiritu Sancto*, rediscovered after 213 years. The 90-minute work, composed in 1784 when the composer was just 18, made for a festive and joyous occasion in 1997. The Mass, by the most important composer of the classical period in England—notable enough in itself—was written when its performance in London was impossible, and was first performed over two centuries later as a symbol of unity, against the background of a divided culture, a divided church, and a divided country. It rewrote English musical history. Those who had maintained over the years that the two centuries of English music between Purcell and Elgar were a musical wasteland were mistaken. The year also saw another notable Wesley performance, namely the recording by the Bochmann Quartet of the String Quartet in E flat (1810).

From the considerable number of new performances in 1997, whether in concert or on CD, some stood out. Greater prominence was given than in previous years to Magnus Lindberg, John Corigliano and John Tavener. Two Chinese composers were active. After a busy year in 1996, Tan Dun had several performances in 1997, including *Symphony 1997* (Heaven Earth Mankind) in which he conducted the Asian Youth Orchestra, playing traditional Chinese instruments, with cellist Yo-Yo Ma, in a concert in Hong Kong, to mark the reunification of Hong Kong with China. The other Chinese composer, Bright Sheng, was prominent in America; first in New York, later on tour with the National Traditional Orchestra of China, and Yo-Yo Ma, in *Spring Dances*; next at the Santa Fe Chamber Music Festival, in *The Silver River*.

American composers whose works received distinctive performances in 1997 were, on CD, Milton Babbitt, Wallingford Riegger, Morton Feldman, and the trio of minimalists Philip Glass, Steve Reich and John Adams; and in concert Elliott Carter, whose *Clarinet Concerto* was heard in Paris with Alain Damiens, and Boulez conducting the Ensemble Inter Contemporain. British music distinctively performed included, on CD, the complete String Quartets of Alan Rawsthorne, played by the Flesch Quartet, and in concert Sir Peter Maxwell Davies's new oratorio *Job*, heard at the Barbican in London.

Among those who died in 1997 were the conductors Sir Georg Solti, Hans-Hubert Schonzeler, and Albert Rosen; the Russian pianist Svyatoslav Richter; the British composers Wilfred Josephs and Robert Simpson; the recorder player and early music specialist Carl Dolmetsch; the harpsichordist George Malcolm. (For Solti, Rosen, Dolmetsch and Richter, see XX: Obituary.)

BOOKS OF THE YEAR. The year was richer than usual in books of importance. Studies in depth of individual composers: *Arvo Pärt*, by Paul Hillier; *Gorecki*, by Adrian Thomas; *Vincent d'Indy and His World*, by Andrew Thomson; *Ruth Crawford Seeger: American Composer*, by Judith Tick; *Pfitzner's Palestrina*, by Owen Toller; *Conversations with Iannis Xenakis*, by Bálint Andras Varga. Studies of musical trends in the late twentieth century: *When the Music Stops*, by Norman Lebrecht; *Broadway Babies Say Goodnight: Musicals Then and Now*, by Mark Steyn. Studies in the aesthetics of music, history and musicology: *Analytical Strategies and Musical Interpretation*, ed. Craig Ayrey and Mark Everist; *Constructive Dissonance: Arnold Schoenberg and the Transformations of 20th Century Culture*, ed. Juliana Brand and Christopher Hailey; *Rationalizing Culture: IRCAM, Boulez and the Institutionalization of the Musical Avant Garde*, by Georgina Born; *Bach and the Patterns of Invention*, by Laurence Dreyfus; *L'impressionisme et la musique*, by Michel Fleury; *Stravinsky and the Russian Tradition: a Biography of the Works through Mavra*, by Richard Taruskin.

iii. BALLET & DANCE

GREAT performances rather than exciting productions dominated dance in 1997. Altynai Asylmuratova danced with Roland Petit's Ballet de Marseilles in *Coppélia* and *The Leopard*; in English National Ballet's mammoth *Swan Lake*; and with the Kirov as Kitri in *Don Quixote* and Zobeide in *Schéhérazade;* appearing witty, elusive, tragic and sensual as the roles required. Peter Boal showed effortless style and virtuosity in George Balanchine's masterpiece *La Source* and other works for New York City Ballet. At the Paris Opéra Elisabeth Platel and Nicolas Le Riche were stunning in Pierre Lacotte's *La Sylphide*, while Roland Petit's *L'Arlésienne* became a mesmerising drama as enacted by Isabelle Guérin and Manuel Legris. Also in Paris, Mikhail Baryshnikov, at 49, gave his first solo recitals. Although the only new work seen by the present author was a disappointing 'work in progress', which he performed to the throbbing of his own magnified heartbeat, no-one could have left the theatre disappointed by his dancing. For all such artistry, one was grateful.

The Edinburgh Festival became a rich showcase for dance. Unfortunately *Tharp!*—Twyla Tharp's latest collection of choreography for an essentially new company, was disappointing, diminishing in excitement as the evening progressed, but San Francisco Ballet showed that they were a likeable company who maintained a mixed repertory. They were at their best in Mark Morris' *Drink to me only* and ballets by George Balanchine; *Stravinsky Violin Concerto* had just the required dynamic, and their performances of *Symphony in C* were stronger than those by either the Kirov or the Royal Ballet, who had both just presented it in London. As an artistic director Helgi Tomasson showed an ability to programme interesting productions but his own works were the weakest in their repertory. Australian dance was represented by the world premiere of Bangarra Dance Theatre's *Fish*. However well-meaning this polemical dance was, its monotonous choreography, which married native elements with contemporary dance, did not convey its concerns for Aboriginal culture. Exposure on this level seemed premature and only Djakapuura Munyarrun appeared a majestic presence on stage. Meanwhile the difficulties that companies from the former Soviet Union faced was emphasized by the Tbilisi Ballet, a reputable company, performing on the Fringe in old-fashioned costumes and to taped music which did no justice to the dancers. Within the festival *Végétal*, by Ballet Atlantique Régine Chopinot, proved mesmerising, with dancers constructing and destroying sculptures, designed by Andy Goldsworthy, of stones, branches and leaves. This work, however, divided audiences, many becoming restless, considering that the dance lacked action.

Mark Morris was back in Edinburgh; his dancers contributed to life in a New York bar and then in an aquarium, with entertaining collaboration with the Royal Opera, *Platée*. Earlier in the year the company had celebrated Morris' on-going collaboration with the 80-year old composer, Lou Harrison, with the creation of *Rhymes With Silver* which had the added bonus of designs by Howard Hodgkin. Another master choreographer, Jerome Robbins, created *Brandenburg*, a little heavy on the juvenile jollity, but made memorable by a *pas de deux* in which the protagonists Nikolaj Hübbe and Lourdez Lopez barely touched one another.

The year revealed novice choreographers worth watching. New York City Ballet presented its third Diamond Project of new classical choreography in which Christopher Wheeldon's *Slavonic Dances*, fusing folk and ballet vocabularies, proved most satisfying. Earlier in February he had created a new full-evening production, *A Midsummer Night's Dream*, for Colorado Ballet. In Britain Christopher Hampson showed promise and a facility for fluent arrangement of steps in *Perpetuum Mobile* for English National Ballet, bringing to attention young dancers, Tamara Rojo and Nathan Coppen.

In 1997 the fashion for reworking 'classics' continued. *Cinderella*, to Serge Prokofiev's score, received revisionist treatment (without fairies) in both Australia and Britain. Australian Ballet performed Stanton Welch's version in which *Cinderella* (Miranda Coney), feisty and independent, retaliated at her step-sisters' unkindness and fell in love with Dandini (Damien Welch) instead of the conceited prince. In London Matthew Bourne's *Cinderella*, set in the London Blitz, was strong on imagery but weak on choreography. Sarah Wildor (on loan from the Royal Ballet) played the mousy heroine with Adam Cooper as the wounded pilot she falls for. Both productions benefited from the presence of a former ballerina. In Melbourne Marilyn Jones was the ghost of Cinderella's mother and in London Lynn Seymour played Cinderella's particularly nasty stepmother. Other revisionist productions included Britain's Northern Ballet who set their *Giselle* in a mid-twentieth century ghetto; City of London Ballet and Cullberg Ballet of Sweden both presented *The Sleeping Beauty*. For Cullberg (whose production by Mats Ek celebrated the company's 30th anniversary) Aurora, a drug-addict, fell asleep as a result of an overdose. While other companies tampered with the classics, English National Ballet presented new traditional readings of *Swan Lake* (in the oval arena of the Royal Albert Hall, London, with a cast of 60 swans making impressive patterns) and *The Nutcracker*, updated so that the party was chic and contemporary, the dolls and sweets were today's favourites, but the narrative was little changed.

John Neumeier created a stylish *Sylvia* in poster-paint colours for the Paris Opéra ballet using their brilliant dancers and large stage to great effect, but some critics were upset by the cuts and rearrangement of Leo Delibes' charming score. Without any doubt the Paris Opéra Ballet was the most interesting company of 1997, with an incredibly wide repertory. Mixed bills included Pina Bauch's *Rite of Spring*; Antony Tudor's tragic *Dark Elegies*, Leo Staats' charming *Soir de Fête* and an unfortunately misguided revival of Léonide Massine's *Symphonie Fantastique*.

In St Petersburg Valery Gergiev, responsible for the ballet as well as the opera, did his best to revitalize the Kirov and himself conducted a programme to music by Igor Stravinsky, including new, but not very satisfactory, choreography for *Les Noces*, staged by 23-year-old Alexei Miroshnicho, and *The Rite of Spring*. Nevertheless for overseas tours the company played safe with full-evening productions and well-known ballets. After a disastrous start to the year, with a tired *Nutcracker* at the London Coliseum, they returned in July with their old *Don Quixote*, new to British audiences, which was praised for its high spirits and exciting opening cast although the production was considerably cut down for touring.

Neither the acquisition of Twyla Tharp's *Push comes to Shove* nor the creation of Glen Tetley's sextet *Amores* enhanced the reputation of the Royal Ballet, and the closure of the Royal Opera House for rebuilding left it homeless, presenting popular ballets in less than ideal venues. Scottish Ballet's future was uncertain following the resignation of its artistic director, Galina Samsova, after funding from the Scottish Arts Council had been withheld. However, for their Christmas seasons in Edinburgh and Glasgow they mounted Frederick Ashton's *La Fille mal gardée* (a ballet also staged in New Zealand and Rome) thanks to the loan of sets and costumes from Birmingham Royal Ballet. Birmingham Royal Ballet, itself flourished with its individual repertory, under David Bintley's, direction including his own *Edward II*, Balanchine's *Orpheus* and a mixed bill to jazz.

Full-evening productions remained popular. Kim Brandstrup created a successful new *Cupid and Psyche* for the Royal Danish Ballet. Ronald Hynd found himself in demand to revive his *Nutcracker* for Nice Ballet, his *Rosalinda* for Berlin Ballet and his *The Merry Widow* for Vienna and American Ballet Theatre. In the latter, Nina Ananiashvili and Susan Jaffe were stylish as the eponymous Hanna, the former passionately partnered by Guillaume Graffin. Also for American ballet, Theater Lar Lubovitch created his *Othello*, poor in conception and derivative in its score by Elliot Goldenthal, and, regrettably, with the former Alvin Ailey dancer, Desmond Richardson, under-used in the title-role. Ben Stevenson created a new *Dracula*, co-produced by Houston Ballet and Pittsburgh Ballet Theatre, while Boston Ballet chose to invite Natalya Dudinskaya to mount Konstantin Sergeyev's Bolshoi production of *The Pirate* (*Le Corsaire*), its first staging for an American company.

Back in St Petersburg in October, Dudinskaya was fêted for her life-long contribution to dance. Meanwhile, Canadian ballerina Karen Kain danced her farewell season before retirement, and in Stuttgart the memory of choreographer John Cranko was honoured by a season of his ballets to mark the seventieth anniversary of his birth. Reid Anderson's new, strong, Stuttgart Ballet paid homage to the previous generation of dancers—many of them Anderson's own contemporaries. For Schwetzingen the German State Opera Ballet commissioned three ballets from Hans Werner Henze. There was a dated feel to the works (partly recycled from earlier compositions) but Mark Baldwin's choreography for *Labyrinth*, fusing classic and contemporary techniques, was entertaining, using the corps de ballet as the patterning of the maze. Nevertheless Lyons Opera Ballet's all-Mozart programme, with creations from Hervé Robbe and Bill T. Jones and a revival of Jiri Kylian's *Petit Mort*, seemed more up-to-date.

iv. THEATRE

IN the United Kingdom, finance dominated the thinking of all those concerned with the state of contemporary theatre. This focus was not so much on the astounding advance and daily takings recorded for the two blockbuster musicals, *Chicago* and *Beauty and the Beast*, the first a revitalized revival of the John Kander/ Fred Ebb show from 1975, with its cynical but now all-too-credible premise that the criminal justice system in the United States was a branch of show business, and the second a lavish staging of the Disney cartoon feature. The money generated by these two musicals was indeed phenomenal, but what concerned practitioners in the publicly-funded sector was the diminishing stream of subsidy. Many had hoped that better times were on their way with the arrival of a new government not only popularly-supposed to favour the arts but on record for stressing its importance to a vital society. However, far from experiencing a year of increased financial support, most theatres suffered further cutbacks from funding bodies, to the point where three significant London theatres were threatened with insolvency and/or closure.

Ironically, the crisis developed concurrently with the lavish distribution of money drawn from the National Lottery. Regrettably, this cornucopia's still unreformed remit allowed it to provide money only for structural rebuilding or for such ventures as community education and outreach, none for staffing nor for the production of plays within the glamorous new buildings. An article by Tim Supple, artistic director of the Young Vic, drew attention to the dilemma facing so many theatres: 'Soon London may have at least 10 new or radically-improved theatres thanks to the Lottery, at a total cost of at least £180 million. This is a splendid project and in some cases badly needed. Yet at the Young Vic we still cannot afford to create more than three new productions a year, rehearse for more than five weeks or pay our actors more than £260 a week.'

One of the theatres due to close early in 1998 was Greenwich Theatre, stripped of its £210,000 funding, while a dome of uncertain significance rising on a patch of toxic ground in the same borough was estimated to be costing the country something over £700 million. It began to seem that if a theatre took the decision to employ an ingenious feasibility consultant to produce a proposal containing enough buzz-words—'multi-ethnic', 'multi-disciplinary', 'local participation'—then the money would arrive in the next post. In the London borough of Islington a hitherto unknown group received £175,000 to stage a Bangladeshi community musical at the Barbican while the Almeida and King's Head theatres, long-established and valuable establishments in the same borough, lost funding.

At the end of the year Cameron Macintosh, the multi-millionaire producer of *Cats, Miss Saigon* and other eternity-running musicals, provided money for the King's Head and the Gate (one of the most imaginative of London's fringe theatres) to haul themselves back from the brink of insolvency. Generous private and corporate funders had been helping many theatres survive from month to month, and sponsorship of single productions at the National and the Royal Shakespeare Company(RSC) had long been regular practice. But the general picture remained perilous and profoundly short-sighted.

The RSC's new pattern of touring, in which productions from Stratford played a season in Plymouth as well as in Newcastle, was held to be a success, but a continuing problem for the company continued to be the difficulty of fitting the productions from its three theatres at Stratford into the two theatres at its London base in the Barbican. An imaginative scheme to rebuild Collins Music Hall, Islington Green, gutted by fire 40 years ago, to accomodate transfers from the Swan had to be postponed, but once again the company was able to use the Young Vic as its third London theatre. *The Comedy of Errors*, an excellent production and so alert to the play's darker content as to become almost a 'Tragicomedy of Errors', ended its lengthy national and international tour here in the autumn.

All the RSC's major productions made, or were due to make, the roundabout journey from Stratford to London in the course of the year. An imaginative pairing coupled *Hamlet* with the revenge drama that influenced it, Thomas Kyd's *The Spanish Tragedy*, a play so seldom revived that few members of its audience knew of it save by repute. Blistering performances by Siobhan Redmond and Robert Glenister in Michael Boyd's production gave life to the tragedy of old Hieronimo, a victim of injustice who bites out his tongue rather than explain his conduct.

Matthew Warchus's ruthlessly-cut *Hamlet*, left with no Fortinbras, no battlements and many a great line missing, marooned Alex Jennings, sardonic and febrile, in a barren Elsinore. Moreover, Michael Boyd came unstuck with his heavy-handed *Much Ado About Nothing* (Redmond and an urbane Jennings again), awkwardly bulging with 'comic' business. Some Shakespeares had been done so often that directors sweated blood to dream up their own fancy version. By contrast, *Cymbeline* was seldom revived more than once in a decade, and though Adrian Noble infused its Roman and ancient British scenes with the spirit of the orient, in both costume and design, his direction brought a unifying power to a play that could be piercingly beautiful but unwieldy.

As well as playing Imogen, the sorely-tried heroine in *Cymbeline*, Joanne Pearce (Mrs Noble) gave a performance of strikingly corroded passion in *Little Eyolf*. Playing opposite a powerfully overwrought Robert Glenister as Allmers, she and Noble's first-rate cast brought Ibsen's drama of remorse to life as seldom before. Two other Shakespeares, conceived as touring productions, exemplified the sometimes wayward nature of RSC achievement: the always interesting Michael Sheen starred in a 20th century *Henry V* (director Ron Daniels) that bizarrely pitted a French army mounted on silver horses against English soldiers armed with rifles; yet Michael Attenborough's staging of *Romeo and Juliet*, first seen in the intimacy of the Barbican Centre's Pit, showed how successfully the company could work in small auditoria. Ray Fearon and Zoë Waites, both heartbreakingly young, played the star-cross'd lovers.

Other RSC productions of the season included Antony Sher in Rostand's *Cyrano de Bergerac*, which later transferred to the West End, and a pageant-like *Henry VIII*, both directed by Gregory Doran, who subsequently directed a vividly-moving Philip Voss as Shylock in *The Merchant of Venice*. One of the country's finest verse-speakers, Voss also played Malvolio in Noble's production of *Twelfth Night*. Katie Mitchell directed a well-acted but utterly muddled *The Mysteries*, billed as 'a medieval play event' but a mish-mash of the medieval text, excerpts from modern novels and weird innovations from her co-writer Edward Kemp. Laurence Boswell, director of Ben Elton's *Popcorn*, still running in the West End, staged a deliriously carnival-like *Bartholomew Fair*, set somewhere like a modern day Notting Hill but otherwise remarkably faithful to the tone of the original Ben Jonson.

The RSC continued its custom of including in its season a new play by a living dramatist, making virtual house dramatists of Peter Whelan and the American Richard Nelson, but it had been the National Theatre's achievement to show a broader commitment to contemporary authors. In the vast Olivier auditorium Roger Michell revived Harold Pinter's 1965 classic *The Homecoming*, with Michael Sheen as the spivvish Lenny outmanoeuvred by Lindsay Duncan's Ruth; in the kinder Lyttelton, Arnold Wesker's *Chips With Everything*, with added swearwords (forbidden by the censor in 1962) was performed with meticulous efficiency by Howard Davies's cast, but the verbosity and creaking turns of plot were very evident.

David Hare's *Amy's View* (Lyttelton, director, Richard Eyre) gave meaty roles to Dame Judi Dench and Samantha Bond as mother and daughter in a largely backstage play spanning the social ups and downs of the past 20 years. Bearing some similarities in argument to *Skylight*, the production followed his earlier play to the West End. Tom Stoppard, erudite as ever and as dazzlingly witty, wrote *The Invention of Love* (Cottesloe and then Lyttelton; director, Richard Eyre again) in which John Wood's A.E. Housman, at the point of death, meets his younger self (Paul Rhys), and darts in and out of classical scholarship, overlapping with several eminent Victorians including Oscar Wilde. Stoppard's most prominent theme contrasted the disastrous climax to Wilde's life with Housman's snail-like concern for textual studies and a lifelong obsession with a heterosexual athlete. Meeting one another after death on the shores of the Styx, the still ebullient Wilde calls out: 'Better a fallen rocket than never a burst of light'. The distinguished cast, moving through time on Anthony Ward's atmospheric set, made the evening an occasion to cherish, though audiences were required to work hard to keep up with the glittering cascade of lines.

Frank McGuinness's *Mutabilitie* (Cottesloe) was also packed with ideas and set in a partly mythical past, in this case Ireland in 1598, but the result was unfortunately a turgid and bewildering evening, presenting an argument for Anglo-Irish compromise through an encounter (non-historical) between the poet Edmund Spenser, in Ireland on Queen Elizabeth I's service, and a secretly Catholic Shakespeare. Trevor Nunn unhelpfully directed. Early 20th century Ireland, or rather Oireland, was the setting for another play by the prolific young Martin McDonagh, *The Cripple of Inishmaan* (Cottesloe). Set on a remote island in 1934, where Robert Flaherty is directing his documentary film *Man of Aran*, the ceaseless flow of cute Oirish sentences, though frequently hilarious, could not disguise an unattractive hardness at the play's heart. (For a month in the summer the Royal Court devoted a season to three other McDonagh plays: *The Beauty Queen of Leenane*, first produced there the previous year, *A Skull in Connemara* and *The Lonesome West*.)

A more successful play, truly contemporary both in its content and in its fondness for plunging into a scene without the clutter of preliminaries, proved that Patrick Marber, author of *Dealer's Choice* and now *Closer* (Cottesloe), was no single-play man. A bleak view of modern ways of loving and betrayal, *Closer* was directed with stylised realism by the author, whose quartet of players (Liza Walker an enigmatic stripper, Sally Dexter a photographer, Ciaran Hinds a doctor, Clive Owen an obituarist) helped his play to win several awards.

In his last year as artistic director of the National before handing over to Trevor Nunn, Richard Eyre directed the most moving and absorbing *King Lear* (Cottesloe) to have been seen in recent memory. Ian Holm, for many years so tormented by stage fright that he dared not work in the theatre, gave a deeply-felt, intelligently-thought performance in this most taxing of roles, again and again making the lines sound newly-minted in the cauldron of his brain. Nunn's production of Ibsen's *An Enemy of the People* (Olivier), a heavy-handed play at the best of times, was hampered by a cluttered stage and an unusually melodramatic performance by Sir Ian McKellen.

For an *Othello* notable for Simon Russell Beale's supremely evil, envious, rancorous, toad-like Iago, the Olivier stage was transformed by Sam Mendes and his designer Anthony Ward into an enclosed courtyard ominously shadowed in the manner of *film noir*. But this was not style for the sake of it: the warning shadows were the outward expression of inward states. Claire Skinner, innocent and candid, played Desdemona and David Harewood did well to avoid being entirely out-acted by Russell Beale.

In the West End, and four years after its triumphant debut, Sir Peter Hall's star-studded production of *An Ideal Husband*, alert to the nuances of the Wildean subtext, appeared for what was billed as its 'final return season', first at the Haymarket and then at the Gielgud. More recent political events were recalled in *Tom and Clem* (Aldwych), a fairly competent first play by

Stephen Churchett, set in 1945 Potsdam where Labour Prime Minister Clement Attlee (Alec McCowen), prim and pragmatic, was shown crossing swords with Michael Gambon's Tom Driberg, the maverick MP and full-throated homosexual. In *A Letter of Resignation* (Comedy), by the more experienced Hugh Whitemore, Tory Prime Minister Harold Macmillan (Edward Fox) suffered the double blow of learning about the Profumo scandal and remembering how his own wife (a jolly Clare Higgins) betrayed him with a fellow MP. The feckless Windsors hit the stage twice, in a 'romantic royal musical' *Always*, which did not last long at the Victoria Palace, and in Snoo Wilson's *HRH*, concentrating on the Duke of Windsor's unsavoury admiration for Hitler and lasting somewhat longer at the Playhouse.

Two American imports did poorly: Terrence NcNally's perhaps unintentionally camp *Master Class* (Queen's) in which Patti LuPone flounced and bitched in a manner intended to resemble Maria Callas; and the winsome musical based by Neil Simon on his play *The Goodbye Girl* (Albery). The first London revival since 1966 of Edward Albee's *A Delicate Balance* (Haymarket) lasted longer and proved that the play itself, a mysterious dark comedy, holds up well. The performances of Dame Maggie Smith and Eileen Atkins were characteristically eye-catching and masterfully precise respectively.

For most of the year the Royal Court, still exiled to the West End, offered short viewings of new playwrights, notably Conor McPherson's *The Weir*, set in an Irish pub peopled with story-tellers, and due to return for a longer run in 1998. This warm and touching play was directed by Ian Rickson, soon to take over from Stephen Daldry as the Royal Court's artistic director. But the year's most hopeful event, cruelly halted after only nine months, was the residency of the newly-formed Peter Hall Company in the Old Vic. A repertory company of prestigious actors from several generations was engaged to play seven nights a week in a season made up of seven 'classics' under Hall's immediate supervision, and five new plays selected by Dominic Dromgoole, the former artistic director of the Bush. Carol Churchill's *Cloud Nine*, David Rabe's fast-talking *Hurlyburly* and a revival of Harley Granville Barker's *Waste* opened the season, which continued with the exquisitely poignant *Prayers of Sherkin* by Sebastian Barry, author of *The Steward of Christendom*, where Catherine Cusack wonderfully played a girl torn between love for a man and love for the religion of her father. Sir Peter Hall himself directed *Waiting for Godot*, which he had introduced to London 42 years earlier in almost his first professional work for the theatre. With Alan Howard and Ben Kingsley as Vladimir and Estragon, this finely-wrought production was due to transfer to Broadway. It played to capacity business, and though not all the productions did this well the sudden announcement by the Mirvishes, the Old Vic's Canadian owners who had restored it to its former elegance, that the season was to end in December and the theatre sold came as a shocking blow, not only to Sir Peter Hall, Dominic Dromgoole and their talented company, but to all lovers of quality drama.

v. CINEMA

LOOKED at from the financial point of view, 1997 was a year in which the cinema triumphed. Hollywood gathered up its highest American gross in a decade, total domestic box-office receipts rising 8.3 per cent to $6,240 million and some 12 films grossing the magic $100 million. That benchmark was exceeded by 17 films internationally, even though Hollywood was not as successful abroad as it was at home. Attendances rose significantly in many other parts of the world.

However, if it was a good year for the world's most populist and popular film-making centre, it was not one to remember with much affection as far as quality was concerned. Among the top grossers, only two or three could possibly be labelled either ambitious or imaginative, except in the realm of state-of-the-art special effects. The top three films in America, for instance, were *Men in Black*, an amusing but lightweight romp through the clichés of science fiction; *The Lost World*, Steven Spielberg's undistinguished successor to *Jurassic Park*; and *Liar Liar*, a frenetic, but hardly witty, comedy starring Jim Carey.

The only US movies that could be called notable in the top dozen were John Woo's *Face/Off*, easily this Hong Kong director's best American picture, which had Nicolas Cage and John Travolta exchanging faces (but not minds) amid a plethora of balletic action sequences, and Robert Zemeckis' *Contact*, a long and sometimes tedious, but at least intelligent, attempt to suggest that outer space might not be just a playground for movie-makers.

The lack of quality, in favour of quantity and expense—most of the successful movies cost well over $50 million to make—led to an extraordinary 1997 Oscar ceremony, at which the Academy members consistently rejected their own products and gave a shoal of awards to British director Anthony Minghella's *The English Patient*, culled from impeccable literary sources and refused finance by all the major studios. Minghella's film, which starred Ralph Fiennes and Kristin Scott Thomas (for whose role Hollywood had suggested Demi Moore), was stopped and started twice for lack of finance but finally carried all before it at the world box-office. Perhaps the Academy realized that it was the sort of grand romance that Hollywood used to make but dare not make now. Added to that, even the nominations rejected almost all the mainstream product. It was therefore no real surprise that Richard Rush, the leading actor of the Australian *Shine*, about pianist David Helfgott, who fought a brave battle against breakdown, won the 'best actor' accolade, and that Frances McDormand was made 'best actress' for the Coen brothers' British-produced *Fargo*.

Most of the 1997 Oscar nominations were, of course, for films which opened in 1996; but had the awards been later in the year the same unorthodox results would have been probable. Paul Schrader, one of America's better writer-directors, stated that it was no longer possible to make a serious film in Hollywood. Irony, as in *Fargo*, was possible, but nothing deeper. It looked as if he was right, although the release of a slew of better pictures at the turn of the year suggested that the 1998 Oscars might give Hollywood's film-makers more credit.

Curtis Hanson's *LA Confidential*, based on the James Elroy novel about corruption in 1950s Los Angeles, proved to be the most intelligent commercial film of the year, as well as one of the most entertaining. James Cameron's epic *Titanic* opened at Christmas and immediately established itself as another favourite for the 1998 'best picture' Oscar.

Most of the best American pictures came from the independent sector where such films as *Swingers, Bound, Grosse Point Blank* and *Private Parts* made their mark. But, on the whole, it was left to the British to convince discerning Americans that the cinema was not just a bolt-hole for teenagers and those who wanted easy and preferably spectacular entertainment. If *The English Patient* proved that big, romantic movies could still be made, Peter Cattaneo's *The Full Monty*, about a posse of unemployed Sheffield steelworkers turning to stripping to get off welfare, showed that a small-budget film about a non-American society could appeal to the whole world. The film not only made a record amount of money in Britain, comfortably beating every American super-production, but seemed to please audiences everywhere. So too did the rather less charming and less skilful *Bean*, starring Rowan Atkinson.

Other substantially British films to succeed were *Mrs Brown*, about Queen Victoria and John Brown, her Scots ghillie, and Iain Softley's adaptation of the Henry James novel *The Wings of a Dove*, with Dame Judi Dench starring in the former and Helena Bonham-Carter in the latter, both getting high praise. Mike Leigh's *Career Girls* was not as successful as his previous *Secrets and Lies*, but still received much praise, as did Gary Oldman's powerfully dramatic *Nil by Mouth*, the star actor's first venture into direction. Kenneth Branagh's formidably ambitious four-hour-long and star-studded *Hamlet* was his most notable achievement yet as actor-director.

The new Labour government in Britain gave the British film industry grounds for hope that the revival would continue, with the introduction of some of the tax incentives available elsewhere in Europe, while National Lottery money was also available to assist the making of more British films. There were two caveats; first, much of the profit from successful British films went to their American and other foreign backers; second, more would not necessarily mean better.

In continental Europe, there were signs that, though Hollywood's domination was hardly broken, national film-makers could still make a mark. As usual, this was most true of France, whose government insisted that French-language films should continue receive considerable state aid, for both production and distribution. The French film industry's most heady triumph was actually in English with a substantially non-French cast—Luc Besson's *The Fifth Element*, a science-fiction fantasy which more than repaid its large cost. In Germany, national films, mostly comedies, now earned over 25 per cent of overall box-office takings, while in other European countries a similar trend seemed to be slowly developing. In Italy, for instance, only four of the top ten films of the year were American rather than Italian or other European. In northern Europe, the prestige gathered by Lars von Trier's *Breaking the Waves* helped the Scandinavian cinema to regain some confidence.

The success of *Kolya*, the Czech film awarded the 1997 'best foreign film' Oscar, was a stimulus to those Central/East European countries whose once-burgeoning film culture had been dealt a near-mortal blow by the wholesale move from state subsidy to private enterprise. Russia's film industry still floundered, however, largely because of lack of funds and because cinemas were unwilling to display anything but Hollywood pictures. Nevertheless, *The Thief*, a wartime story presented in competition at Venice, went on to achieve much praise, while Aleksandr Sokurov, the poet of the Russian cinema and a former disciple of Andrei Tarkovsky, made a superb art film called *Mother and Son*.

Neither Latin America nor Africa could claim a much better fate than Russia. In both continents, television held sway over cinematic ventures. It was left to India, Japan and the Chinese-speaking territories to prove that American domination was not yet total. In each of these countries, home-grown product managed to vie with American fare in 1997. India, in particular, had a good year, not with quality productions but with commercial fare which, having proved popular in India, travelled well in the Middle East, Northern Africa and in most territories where Indian immigration was substantial. Consequently, many of the 'Bollywood' epics were at least partly made outside India—Australia's Sydney Bridge being a popular new location for song-and-dance numbers. In Australia, a good box-office year was not paralleled by any revival of Australian film-making after the success of *Shine*, largely because the economic situation led the government to review and decrease funding. Australian film-makers, like some British, preferred to make their way in Hollywood, where Buz Luhrmann's lively, updated *Romeo and Juliet* won both critical and popular success.

Despite some successes, there were still considerable fears that national cinema industries all over the world would eventually fall prey to the all-embracing culture of Hollywood with its relatively huge finances for production and publicity and its ability to make movies which suited popular taste everywhere. 1997 was a year of renewed hope for a few countries like Britain, but many small nations, though they continued to make films, found it more and more difficult to get the money to do so and the theatre space in which to show them.

The death, within 48 hours of one another, of James Stewart and Robert Mitchum, and later of Japan's Toshiro Mifune, best known in the West for his roles in Kurosawa films, further depleted the ranks of the great actor-stars of the cinema's golden era. Among the film-makers who died were Sam Fuller, American master of 'tabloid cinema' and the 103-year-old Carlo Bragaglia, doyen of the Italian cinema. (For Stewart and Mitchum, see XX: Obituary.)

vi. TELEVISION & RADIO

IN television, 1997 was the year of the 'docu-soap' a popular form of the fly-on-the-wall documentary. The genre had a distinguished history through programmes such as *Police*, a profile of the Thames Valley Police, which changed the rules on the treatment of rape victims, and *The House*, the all-revealing series on bungling and malice behind the scenes at the Royal Opera House Covent Garden.

The rash of docu-soaps, which stimulated renewed charges of the 'dumbing-down' of television, was led by *Driving School* and *Hotel*, with many others such as *Cruise* and *Pleasure Beach* already in the schedules. *Driving School* in particular, although it won both awards and large audiences, caused worries among serious documentary makers. To what extent was choreography involved and did it cross over the fine line between a documentary observing life into the realms of light entertainment? More traditional documentary makers also worried that the success of the 'docu-soap' would mean fewer slots in the schedule available for their work. Television executives loved docu-soaps, however. They were cheap to make, often less than half the cost of a drama, and they could easily bring in an audience of 10 million or more.

Christmas also turned out to be a worry for broadcasters. The BBC won in the ratings war, as it always did at Christmas. The problem was that millions of viewers simply went missing. In 1996 the three-part farewell series of *Only Fools and Horses* was seen by 24.35 million (see AR 1996, p. 483); this time the top BBC programme was *Men Behaving Badly*, with a mere 16.34 million, and audiences were down all over the Christmas period. No-one could discover where they went: there was no large rise in viewing figures for cable and satellite. The explanation might have been a combination of programmes that were not good enough and a waning of the public's long-lasting love affair with television. Certainly Will Wyatt, chief executive of BBC Television, was sufficiently concerned to set up an internal inquiry to compare the 1997 performance with that of Christmases past.

One cause could be ruled out. It was not the year's new television station, Channel 5, launched on 30 March by The Spice Girls, which made the difference. After nine months on air, the channel, which by the end of the year could be received by around 70 per cent of the UK audience, took a 3.2 per cent share of actual viewers. This was in line with the modest aspirations for the channel, which promised to be modern, mainstream and 'stripped and stranded', a reference to the fact that it showed the same kind of programmes at the same time every day. Showing a film every night at 9pm proved to be a modest success with audiences, and the more informal Channel 5 News, with no desks and a strong presenter in Kirsty Young, caused other television news organizations to re-examine what they were doing.

Above all else, it was a year of musical chairs at the top of British broadcasting. The process began in January when Michael Grade, the chief executive of

Channel 4, unexpectedly announced his resignation to become executive chairman of First Leisure, the bingo night-club and entertainment group (and Grade family company). The vacancy at Channel 4 was eventually filled by the BBC's Michael Jackson, who had started his career as an independent producer making programmes for the channel. Mr Jackson's departure led to a reshuffle at the Corporation which brought more power for Alan Yentob, who became director of television with overall responsibility for the BBC's new digital ventures.

At ITV the top job of chief executive of the ITV Network Centre, responsible for commissioning all of ITV's nationally-shown programmes, went to Richard Eyre, group chief executive of Capital Radio. He took over in September and promised to produce a plan designed to reverse ITV's five-year decline in the ratings, particularly among younger viewers. It was also the end of an era at British Sky Broadcasting, the immensely profitable satellite channel. Sam Chisholm, who had become chief executive of the recently-merged BSkyB Television venture in 1990 (when it had been losing £14 million a week), announced in June that he was stepping down. In the previous 12 months BSkyB had pretax profits of £257 million on a turnover of £1,000 million. The 57-year-old Mr Chisholm attributed his departure to poor health, which was true, but there had also been, behind the scenes, a deterioration of his relationship with Rupert Murdoch, chairman of The News Corporation, which owned 40 per cent of BSkyB. Mr Chisholm was replaced by Mark Booth, a 40-year-old American who, more than a decade previously, had launched the satellite music television channel GMTV in Europe.

The biggest thing that did not happen in 1997 was the launch of up to 200 channels of digital satellite television. The launch was supposed to take place in the autumn but was eventually postponed. By the end of the year it was already clear that the full commercial launch of the venture would not take place until the autumn of 1998. The largest cable company, Cable & Wireless Communications, decided to throw in its lot with Sky and to mount a simultaneous digital cable launch of its 200 channels—whenever that turned out to be.

The other arm of the digital television revolution—digital terrestrial, which did not require a satellite dish or cable link—also took important strides forward, having been almost written off by many observers. In January digital terrestrial came to life when it was revealed that three powerful groups—the two largest ITV companies (Carlton Communications and Granada) and BSkyB—had created a joint venture, British Digital Broadcasting (BDB), to bid for the largest block of commercial frequencies. They were opposed by NTL the large cable and broadcasting services company. In July the Independent Television Commission (ITC) chose BDB, but not until weeks of secret negotiations over the structure of the BDB venture. The ITC decided that BSkyB's presence as a partner involved too much concentration of power and insisted that the satellite group should leave the venture, although it would supply, under contract, its vital programming, namely Sky Sports and Sky Movies.

The BBC played the digital game enthusiastically. In one week in November the Corporation launched new channels for cable and satellite in a joint venture with the Flextech programming company, vastly expanded its Internet site and launched News 24, its domestic 24-hour news service. News 24 had been intended for digital television but, when that was delayed, the BBC decided to go ahead anyway, the new channel being carried on cable networks and shown on conventional television in the middle of the night. The BBC said in July that overall it would invest around 9 per cent of its £2,000-million-a-year licence fee revenues on digital services over the next five years—a sum that could easily reach £1,000 million when the capital equipment costs of digital were included.

As the digital plans were trundled out, to complaints that too much was being spent on the future and not enough on current programmes, a very traditional BBC row broke out in September about the managerial structures of news. The plan was to put all the BBC's news output—radio and television—in the hands of five executive editors. The aim was to save money and reduce duplications across the Corporation, but the plan was widely seen as reducing the autonomy of editors of individual programmes such as *Newsnight* and *Today*. Sir Christopher Bland, the BBC chairman, intervened in the face of revolts by famous presenters such as Jeremy Paxman and John Humphreys and the BBC decided that it had all been a misunderstanding: individual programme editors held onto most of their autonomy. There was also controversy in the making when the new controller of Radio 4, James Boyle, announced a raft of changes to be implemented in April 1998. The world waited to see how that most conservative of audiences took to dozens of scheduling changes and the dropping of a number of long-running programmes such as the arts magazine *Kaleidoscope*, the satirical *Weekending*, *Does He Take Sugar?* (for the disabled) and *Sport on Four*.

In commercial radio, the big story involved some of the country's most famous names. It began in May when Richard Branson decided to merge his Virgin Radio station with Capital to create by far the largest commercial radio group in Britain. While the matter was under consideration by the competition authorities Mr Branson did a secret deal with controversial radio and television presenter Chris Evans and his Ginger Productions company, under which Evans was to be the new group's main presenter and owner.

The ITV network, apart from trying to reverse declining audiences, continued the process of consolidation. Granada paid £710 million for Yorkshire-Tyne Tees Television, while Scottish Media (the renamed Scottish Television) bought its neighbour Grampian for £105 million. Scottish also signalled its intentions on Ulster by taking a stake in the Belfast-based ITV company. ITV was also finally told by the government that the Channel 4 funding formula—originally designed as a safety net for Channel 4—would be phased out over two years. The decision meant that Channel 4 would be able to keep around £90 million a year of its own money, rather than having to hand it over to ITV. The government said that the channel's licence would have to be redrawn to make sure that the extra money was used to make more original British programming and to reduce the number of American imports.

Abroad, some of the grand designs for world domination of satellite broadcasting came to nothing. Rupert Murdoch's plans to launch his own ASkyB satellite television venture in the USA fell apart, and he was forced to concentrate his satellite hopes on PrimeStar, an existing service operated by a group of large cable companies. A very depressed Mr Murdoch commented that it was a matter of discretion over valour. In Europe digital television projects received a mixed reception. In Germany and Italy the progress was slow but in France, where two competing companies (Canal Satellite and TPS) had so far signed up a total of 1.2 million subscribers, satellite television was considered *très chic*.

Behind the usual battles and tantrums of the broadcasting world there was growing worry over the increasing power of the computer companies, Microsoft and Bill Gates in particular (see also XIV.2). Mr Gates seemed to be moving into the 'content' business and indeed bought a large chunk of a US cable operator. In a difficult year this was another worry for Mr Murdoch. 'We don't want Gates to get control of our picture—that's the real thing—but it may be possible to work out a deal', he said in an interview in June. Certainly the computer companies were pushing ahead with the production of new machines that were also television sets. The strategy was obvious. Computers were in perhaps 30–40 per cent of homes in the developed world but television sets were in 99 per cent of homes.

Such future battles over who would control the supply of images to the home were overshadowed by the biggest television programme of the year probably in the history of television—the death and subsequent funeral of Diana, Princess of Wales (see I.1). On the Sunday of her death more than 20 million people in Britain watched the television coverage at some time during the day. For Diana's funeral the number rose to more than 30 million—a very high proportion of those available to watch. It proved that the 'missing millions' were not really missing at all and demonstrated once again the key role still played by national network television, however many channels there might be, in uniting the nation.

2. VISUAL ARTS—ARCHITECTURE

i. VISUAL ARTS

FROM the point of view of the conservation of the past, 1997 could lay equal claim in the memory of art lovers as an *annus mirabilis,* in which two major new museums were unveiled to world attention, or an *annus horribilis* of destruction for loved monuments.

Italy took the brunt of woe. On the night of 11 April Turin Cathedral succumbed to a blaze which completely destroyed the chapel of the Holy Shroud, a baroque masterpiece by the seventeenth-century architect Guarino Guarini. The legendary shroud, believed by some to bear the imprint of Christ's face, was by good fortune being stored in an unaffected portion of the church, as the altar where it was usually housed had just been restored at a cost of over £1 million. Ironically, the scaffold used in this restoration was blamed for intensifying the conflagration.

The tragedy in Turin was but a portend, however, for the earthquake which struck central Italy on 26 September, damaging an estimated 80 per cent of monuments in Umbria and the Marches. Extensive damage to the Franciscan convent in Assisi claimed highly important murals in the upper basilica by Cimabue, although the seminal frescoes by Giotto in the lower basilica were undamaged. A complicated and audacious crane operation saved the tympanum of the church from crushing murals by Ambrogio Lorenzetti below.

Italy was saved from another potential assault on its artistic heritage when plans to extract natural gas from the Adriatic were vetoed because of claims that the process would sink Venice by 12 inches. No such cultural compunction seemed to inhibit the plans of the Chinese government in its bid to create the ecologically and economically questionable Three Gorges Dam on the Yangtse river, which would inundate a vast tract of central China currently occupied by 2 million people in several cities and hundreds of towns (see IX.2.i; XIV.3). Money that had been set aside to preserve, or at least document, a host of cultural treasures seemed likely to have to be diverted to pacifying compulsorily-relocated inhabitants.

While acts of vandalism continued to occur in 1997—including the threat of Islamic militants to blow up the colossal carved Buddha in Afghanistan's Bamiyan Valley and the assault on a Casimir Malevich painting in Amsterdam by a self-styled 'destruction artist'—the completion of two major museum projects to designs by leading American architects of the day were the more positive legacy of the year. The new headquarters of the Getty Center in Los Angeles, California, perched on an acropolis in Malibu, was the culmination of 13 years of planning and construction, at a cost of around $1,000 million. The Getty's archaeological holdings remained at its old museum down the road (housed in a reconstruction of a Roman villa), while the new centre housed various departments, educational facilities and a conservation institute with an ambitious and far-reaching global remit. The campus was designed by Richard Meier, employing the purist modernist idiom which distinguished his design, although uncharacteristically using stone as well as his usual gleaming white surfaces.

Media attention tended to be diverted from this major achievement by the more glamorous design by Meier's peer, Frank Gehry, for the new Guggenheim Museum in the Basque capital of Bilbao, Spain. Built in the former shipyards of the port, Gehry's cavernous galleries were crowned by a irregular swathe of metallic roofs, dominating the skyline of the city. The audacious originality of the design was compared by critics to Frank Lloyd Wright's legendary design of the 'mother' museum in New York. It had long been the plan of the New York museum's director, Thomas Krens, to open European outposts in order to make his institution the first truly multinational art museum. Another branch was projected for Berlin.

In Britain, a change of government introduced a new spirit of optimism in relation to arts policy. The name of the Department of National Heritage was changed to Culture, Media and Sport, signalling a fresh and modern approach, as did a re-hang of paintings at 10 Downing Street in which priority was given to living artists. However, old dilemmas concerning such issues as museum charges remained on the agenda. Initially, Labour had been against museum charges, even advocating that the National Lottery should favour applications from institutions which did not charge over those which did. Later in the year the new government signalled its approval of institutions such as the National Museums and Galleries on Merseyside, which had introduced an annual pass to all its venues priced at £3. The year ended with uncertainty as to the government's position on this important issue.

On the broader question of arts funding, the incoming Labour government immediately aroused indignation by deciding that National Lottery money should be allocated to health and education projects, thus undermining the basic principle that the scheme should benefit 'five good causes' separate from mainstream Treasury concerns. The banning of tobacco sponsorship also had implications for arts funding, as it had for sports (see Pt XVII).

A five-year legal battle to overturn a clause in the will of Sir William Burrell, the tycoon who had bequeathed his massive art collection to the city of Glasgow, was won by the city. Sir William had stipulated that works should not be loaned abroad, but the director of the City Galleries, Julian Spalding, argued that improvements in the quality of air shipping had changed the situation. Five Scots peers heard the case and found largely in favour of the plaintiffs. The result was welcomed by Neil MacGregor, the director of the National Gallery, but Sir Denis Mahon, the collector and scholar who had promised many important works to national collections, felt strongly that the decision would inhibit future donations.

By coincidence, several major international exhibitions which normally took place at differing yearly intervals all occurred in 1997: the Venice Biennale, the Whitney Biennial in New York, the five-yearly Documenta in the German town of Kassel and the ten-yearly sculpture survey in nearby Münster. The European events took place in the summer, alongside the annual art fair in Basle (Switzerland) and a newly-introduced biennial in Lyon (France), making for a concentrated festival of contemporary art. It was impossible, however, to detect a consistent aesthetic in the range of work on view.

The Venice Biennale was curated by the New York-based Italian critic Germano Celant. The choice of an Italian was significant. The previous incumbent, in charge of the centennial Biennale in 1995 (see AR 1995, pp. 495–6), had been the French curator Jean Clair, the first non-Italian to hold the post, but he had fallen out with the authorities. Celant's chosen theme was 'Past-Present-Future', a nebulous title which, in contrast to the strident approach of his predecessor, had little intellectual thrust. In addition to the established national pavilions in the Biennale Gardens at the far end of the city, many countries staged exhibitions scattered across Venice. To showcase younger artists, Celant restored the

Aperto, the abolition of which by Clair had been a bone of contention with the authorities.

The tenth Documenta in Kassel was curated by Catherine David of France, the first woman to do so in the exhibition's history. The purpose of Documenta had originally been to reintroduce Germans to modern art following the collapse of the Third Reich, Kassel being chosen as the venue partly because it was then on the border with East Germany. German reunification in 1990 had, however, taken that edge off subsequent exhibitions. Catherine David tended to select political and cerebral artists for the 1997 showings, which were spread across the town in a variety of venues. Although there were record attendances, the exhibition was greeted by many critics as a dry and visually-unstimulating event.

The sculptor Rachel Whiteread, whose work largely consisted of plaster or resin casts of the negative space around familiar objects, represented Britain at the Venice Biennale, and was also a presence at Münster. The previous year she had been selected to undertake the Holocaust memorial in the Judenplatz in Vienna (see AR 1996, p. 488), but it became clear in 1997 that the project was to be shelved. This disappointment followed the demolition of her temporary work *House* by local planners in East London only weeks after its completion—to widespread indignation in the arts community. However, these setbacks did not appear to impede her growing international reputation. One public commission obtained by her in 1997 was to cast the space around a water-tank on top of a building in New York City's SoHo district. Although a temporarily-sited piece, it was constructed in such a way as to enable reconstruction afterwards, thus avoiding the tribulations of *House*.

Whiteread was also included in the most controversial and media-attended London exhibition of the year, 'Sensation: Young British Artists from the Saatchi Collection', which was staged at the Royal Academy of Arts. Charles Saatchi, the advertising agent, had amassed an extensive collection of contemporary art, one area of specialization being the work of the generation of neo-conceptual artists to emerge in the late 1980s, the leading lights being Whiteread and Damien Hirst. Hirst, indeed, had become a household name, his trademark idiom—tanks in which animals or fish were preserved in formaldehyde—becoming as talked about and lampooned as Henry Moore's pierced figures once were.

The controversial centre-piece of 'Sensation', however, was by a lesser-known artist, Marcus Harvey, who made a very large painted image of the face of Moors murderer Myra Hindley, based on her police arrest photograph of the early 1960s, with the paint stamped onto the canvas with the cast of a child's hand. After the work had been condemned by the director of a children's charity, the mother of one of Hindley's victims appealed to the Academy to withdraw the piece from the exhibition, which had yet to open. The decision to keep it in infuriated several academicians, three of whom—Craigie Aitchison, Gillian Ayers and Michael Sandle—resigned from the institution. Such gestures only excited further press attention, as did ink attacks upon *Myra*, and the exhibition attracted huge crowds, the earnings helping to offset the RA's enormous deficit.

Another much talked-about exhibit in the 'Sensation' show was a tent by Tracy Emin, in which the artist stitched the names of all the people she had ever slept with (leaving it ambiguous as to whether 'slept with' was to be taken literally or as the familiar euphemism for 'had sex with'). Emin was the subject of a lively exhibition of drawings, appliqué work and video-recorded lectures at the South London Gallery, as well as the subject of an extensive interview with the rock musician David Bowie in a special edition of the magazine *Modern Painters* devoted to the 'Young British Artists', as the neo-conceptualists collected by Saatchi were then known. This in turn raised many eyebrows, since the magazine had previously championed a traditionalist approach and had been opposed to what it had deemed to be 'institutionalized avant-gardism'. Its shift towards a more fashionable position was seen by some as due to the influence of Bowie, who had joined the editorial board.

Other significant shows of 1997 in London included an exhibition focusing on the late work of the French painter Georges Braque at the Royal Academy; a retrospective of the American abstract painter Ellsworth Kelly at the Tate Gallery; shows of recent sculpture by Tony Cragg and Cathy de Monchaux at the Whitechapel Gallery; a survey of the modern still-life organized by the Museum of Modern Art in New York and staged at the Hayward Gallery; Coptic funerary portraits mounted at the British Museum; recent paintings by the realist figure-painter Euan Uglow shown at his dealers, Browse & Darby, significant because of the marked bravura and confidence of the artist's tight observational approach; and a selection of works by Piet Mondrian, many of them early works pre-dating his adoption of his familiar, paired-down abstraction. The last was selected by the British painter Bridget Riley from the Gemeenthaus Museum in The Hague, which lent the works while its building was being renovated.

One foreign show deemed to be highly significant was the survey 'The Twentieth Century', staged in Berlin and co-curated by the Royal Academy's exhibitions secretary, Norman Rosenthal. This exhibition had originally been intended for London venues, but apparently the necessary funds could not be raised (one consequence being that the gap in the Royal Academy's schedule was filled at short notice by the 'Sensation' exhibition). In New York the Guggenheim staged a retrospective of Robert Rauschenberg (whose 'neo-dada' work of the 1950s had anticipated the Pop movement), not only at its uptown and SoHo galleries but also at a commodious commercial gallery space, so that it earned the dubious honour of being the year's largest exhibition devoted to a living artist. Widely believed to be of superior aesthetic merit, however, was the exhibition reassembling the private collection of Edgar Degas, including works by him that he had held or bought back, masterpieces by Ingres and Eugène Delacroix (some purchased following his death by the National Gallery in London) and paintings by contemporaries such as Edouard Manet and Paul Gauguin. This exhibition, which had its sole showing at the Metropolitan Museum, was a much-expanded version of a display first put together by the

National Gallery in London to complement the 'Late Degas' exhibition held there the previous year.

The Henry Moore Foundation sent a retrospective of Moore's work on tour to five Latin American cities. Surprisingly, the first venue was Havana, anticipating the Pope's visit to Communist Cuba scheduled for January 1998. Like the Pope, Moore had tended to be exploited as a cultural icon of democracy and freedom. An exhibition of his work sent to Russia some years earlier had coincided with the failed hard-line coup of August 1991 and subsequent final collapse of communism in that country.

The year also witnessed increasing international attention for Chinese art. The return of Hong Kong to Chinese rule at the end of June (see IX.2.ii) precipitated some movement of art treasures out of the territory while it remained a British colony; but of more significance was the presence for the first time of the People's Republic of China at the Venice Biennale. One of the artists representing China there, the American-based realist Chen Yifei, was the subject of a solo exhibition at London's Marlborough Gallery. There was also great buoyancy in the Asian art market, for both antiques and contemporary art, although the crash of the 'Asian tiger' economies towards the end of the year (see XVIII.1) was expected to curtail this trend. Meanwhile, at end-of-year contemporary sales in London, work by the Chinese artist Zao Wou Ki sold for quadruple the initial estimates, suggesting that interest in current Asian art was not limited to local markets.

Notables of the world visual arts scene who died in 1997 included the following: Roy Lichtenstein, the American Pop artist; Willem de Kooning, leading post-war painter and doyen of the New York School; Theodor Stamos, abstract expressionist painter; Victor Vasarely, the pioneer of Op Art; Douglas Huebler, a pioneer of conceptual art; Dora Maar, photographer, painter and mistress of Picasso; William S. Burroughs, the writer also acclaimed as an artist late in his career; James Lee Byars, performance artist; Masuo Ikeda, Japanese printmaker; German artist Martin Kippenberger; and Robert Mallary, a pioneer of computer art. Deaths in Britain included those of Raymond Coxon, mural painter (in his 101st year); William Gear, Scottish abstract painter; Nicolette Gray, collector; Malcolm Hughes, constructivist painter; Michael Joffe, art historian and former keeper of the Fitzwilliam Museum, Cambridge; Janet Leach, potter; Kim Lim, sculptor; Tim Mara, professor of print-making at the Royal College of Art; Myfanwy Piper, distinguished writer on art and widow of John Piper; Kenneth Rowntree, landscape painter; and Carel Weight, figure painter and teacher, at the Royal College, of Hockney, Kitaj *et al.* (For Burroughs, de Kooning and Lichtenstein, see XX: Obituary.)

ii. ARCHITECTURE

MUCH of the year in the UK was spent with an anxious eye on the millennium, and particularly the £758 million 'Dome' building project designed to celebrate the advent of the 21st century on a peninsular site in the London Borough of

Greenwich. This building—technically a cable-stayed gridshell structure—would cost about £40 million and would house the Millennium Experience, an event which grabbed headlines consistently all year, due in part to its latter-day champion, Peter Mandelson, Minister without Portfolio in the incoming Labour government. Problems included the choice of materials used for the roof: initially a contract went to a German firm for PVC, then to an American one for Teflon after howls of protest from conservation groups.

The Millennium building, designed by the Richard Rogers Partnership with engineer Buro Happold, also had its detractors and critics on both sides of the House of Commons, largely because of the total cost of the Dome plus exhibition, estimated at £758 million, some £400 million of which would come from the National Lottery. Other criticisms focused on the intention that the Dome would be a 'temporary' building, with an undecided afterlife, and on the fact that nobody quite knew what was going to be inside it. As the year came to a close, design adviser Stephen Bayley, appointed to take charge of plans for the interior, announced his resignation, precipitating calls for Mr Mandelson to follow suit. At this critical moment, however, Prime Minister Tony Blair decided to press on with the plans which former Tory Deputy Prime Minister Michael Heseltine had put in train. The 'Euan factor'—the influence of Mr Blair's young son—and the fact that Sir Richard Rogers was made a life peer and informal architectural adviser to the government, could have helped.

Another *cause célèbre* building project—this time from Lord Rogers's onetime partner, Sir Norman Foster—failed to materialize, after a similarly high-profile debate in the media and pressure from the planners. This was the £400 million London Millennium Tower, which Sir Norman had proposed to build on the site of the City of London's former Baltic Exchange, bombed by the IRA in 1993. At 385 metres, it would have been the tallest building in Europe—and taller even than the Empire State Building in New York. After a glittering public relations launch, however, the tower drew attacks from bodies such as English Heritage, the London Planning Advisory Committee and the Royal Fine Art Commission. What emerged was that the planning system did not really have a mechanism to handle such extravagantly-tall buildings. Although the project was later abandoned when the owners (Trafalgar House/Kvaerner) sold the site, the debate continued.

Sir Norman Foster had a happier time with other projects, including the completion of the actual tallest building in Europe, the Commerzbank in Frankfurt. His half-domed Duxford Museum for the Imperial War Museum to house World War II US airplanes, which was funded by lottery money, opened to rave reviews. Back in London, his practice was triumphant in a major competition organized by Westminster City Council called 'World Squares for All'. Sir Norman's plan, subject to permission from myriad consultees, was to open up Whitehall by making it less of a traffic highway and more of a pedestrian-friendly environment, focusing on reworking Trafalgar and Parliament Squares, again with the aid of lottery money. North of the border, Sir Norman scored again with the opening of his Scottish Conference Centre in Glasgow, nicknamed the 'armadillo' because of its shell-like appearance. On a personal level, Sir Norman completed another phenomenal year with the award of the Order of Merit, the only architect currently to hold the honour.

The year was also, in line with the *fin de siècle* spirit, one in which major building projects were basically completed, not least of them Colin St John Wilson's new British Library in St Pancras, London. Deep initial scepticism emanated from the broadsheet newspapers, and Wilson revealed that the pillorying had forced the closure of his practice. Opinions soon changed once the critics were allowed inside, however. The building partially opened in November, after two decades of construction, and was vastly over budget; but it was safe to say it would secure Wilson's name in history. He was awarded a knighthood in the New Year Honours.

Another long-runnning London saga, the design of Paternoster Square, beside St Paul's Cathedral, also looked like reaching a final solution, when a long-awaited master-plan by Whitfield & Partners for its client, Mitsubishi Estates, finally saw the light of day. A planning application was submitted with building designs by MacCormac Jamieson Prichard, Michael Hopkins & Partners, Allies & Morrison and John Simpson & Partners, and with a new square as the centrepiece. Famously, the Prince of Wales had rejected all eight entries in a competition to redevelop the site in 1987 (see AR 1987, p. 484). It looked as if the Prince's influence on all things architectural was also drawing to a close. His Institute of Architecture decided to stop running a formal school of architecture.

Projects abroad caught the imagination more than those on home soil. Frank Gehry's new Guggenheim Museum in Bilbao was the sensation of the year—a sculpted, monumental, zinc-clad triumph in the Basque Country (see also XVI.2.i), which some believed could bring him the 1998 Gold Medal of the Royal Institute of British Architects (RIBA). In 1997 the award went to the self-taught Japanese architect (and former boxer), Tadao Ando, while the American Institute of Architects handed their version to Richard Meier, whose Getty Centre opened to gasps of delight in Los Angeles.

The RIBA swore in a new president, David Rock, who immediately began campaigning for better pay and treatment of his membership as well as looking to important debates outside the institute, such as those centring on demands for 4.4 million new homes in the UK within the next decade. Also of immediate concern was the state of disrepair of the RIBA's drawings collections and the possible need to find a new home for them, following the rejection of a Sir Michael Hopkins scheme to move them to the Round House in Camden, north London. Instead, the former railway turning shed held its own competition and chose John McAslan to turn it into a new arts venue.

One of the more controversial of the RIBA's actions was its decision to award the Stirling Prize, its biggest award, to Michael Wilford, the former partner of the late Jim Stirling, after whom the award was named. Mr Wilford won for his music school in Stuttgart, while in the City of London the same practice's No 1 Poultry Building was nearing completion. It too had been worked on by the Stirling Partnership.

'Pontomania' continued to be prevalent, a series of bridge commissions being awarded, many of them scooped by the architect Chris Wilkinson, who had a highly successful year. Most eye-catching was the Tyne Bridge scheme, designed by his practice, with engineers Gifford & Partners. To be built adjacent to the Baltic Flour Mills—also the subject of a lottery-funded competition, this time won by Ellis Williams—the bridge tilted to let ships pass, in an action similar to the blinking of an eye.

Not all bridge schemes spanned untroubled waters, however. Lifschutz Davidson, a practice which had done much to regenerate the South Bank area of London, became embroiled in the scandal of the year when Westminster City Council tried to exclude the architects from carrying out the execution of its Hungerford Bridge proposal. The architects had won a competition to design the project, which had been handed millions of pounds of lottery money; but Westminster tried to drop the architects in favour of an 'adopt and build' scheme, until the combined ranks of the construction institutes—and considerable media exposure—came to the rescue.

Following the general election, Labour's Deputy Prime Minister, John Prescott, was appointed to preside over a new 'super-ministry' covering the environment, transport and the regions, integrating what for decades had been the separate environment and transport departments in a new headquarters building designed by epr (*sic*) in Victoria. Marsham Street, however, the reviled former home of both departments which the previous government had tried to knock down, was still standing as the year ended. This was despite a government-run competition to redevelop, which was won with a classical scheme by the Italian firm Tagliaventi & Associates. Meanwhile, the new Department of Culture, Media and Sport—the renamed former Heritage Department—found coping with architectural politics difficult in its first six months under Secretary of State Chris Smith, with junior minister Mark Fisher taking on the architecture duties. More was hoped of it by the architectural profession.

Stylistically, deconstruction had a mixed time of it. Daniel Libeskind's ambitious tower project at the Victoria & Albert Museum's Boilerhouse failed to attract millennium lottery funding, on the grounds, ludicrously, that it was not distinctive enough. But the same architect did get the go-ahead at the Imperial War Museum's northern outpost in Salford, not far from where a Wilford-designed museum devoted to the work of L.S. Lowry would stand. Again, the Salford project was courtesy of lottery funds and stood as one of 14 'landmark' millennium projects chosen for their magnitude, design quality and regional spread by the Millennium Commission, the lottery distributing body. The others were all confirmed during the year and ranged from the Eden project, a Nicholas Grimshaw-designed mammoth series of 'biomes' in a former Cornish claypit, to a reworked Cardiff Arms Park, by the increasingly-successful Lobb Partnership. Lobb continued to reap the benefits of an increased interest in sports stadiums, even winning the job to design Sydney's Olympic Stadium and completing a number of UK Premier League club homes.

Among those who died in 1997 were David Allford, former chairman of YRM, the first publicly-quoted UK architect; former RIBA president Gordon Graham; and the highly influential Italian rationalist Aldo Rossi (see XX: Obituary).

3. LITERATURE

THE Italian dramatist Daniel Fo was an unexpected but imaginative choice for the 1997 Nobel Prize for Literature. His selection said a great deal for where literature was heading in the closing years of the twentieth century. A popular playwright, whose work, often created through improvization or with the cooperation of his actress wife Franca Rame, linked him with ancient forms of street theatre and *commedia dell'arte*, Fo cocked a snook at all forms of mainstream writing and at the bastions of middle-class society. Vulgar, brash, opposed to authority, irreligious, fantastical, Fo was the epitome of 'alternative' culture, but was increasingly being taken up by the very elite he sought to condemn. The Nobel Prize was seen by many as the net which had finally scooped him up into respectability.

In Britain the David Cohen British Literature Prize, awarded every second year to honour a British author for a lifetime's work, went to Dame Muriel Spark. Her lethal, elegant prose, rooted in a Catholic sensibility, might be seen as the antithesis of Fo's kind of writing, but Spark was subtly irreverent and she endeared herself to the public by promising, at her advanced age, to spend the prize money—the largest of any literary award in the country—on a new fast car, though she also ensured that her old school in Edinburgh, upon which she had based the setting of her most famous book, *The Prime of Miss Jean Brodie*, benefited from her success.

The Booker Prize was given to Arundhati Roy for *The God of Small Things*. This novel, the author's first, was the publishing sensation of the year, being dramatically snapped up by a London-based literary agent, David Godwin, whose faith in his newly-discovered writer was rewarded not only with excellent sales but with some of the highest accolades. Inevitably, there was also comment to the effect that the book's success was a triumph of marketing rather than talent.

Prizes undoubtedly sold books. They could not, however, forge a mass readership if they lacked popular appeal. In a survey of the ten most widely-borrowed novels from British public libraries in 1997, no fewer than nine were by the veteran northern writer Catherine Cookson, who had never won a serious prize. Even in a year which confirmed a continuing decline in the overall number of loans from public libraries, this was an astonishing achievement by a writer admired for her straightforward, warm-hearted story-telling.

It was not a year for much adventurousness in literary forms. Saul Bellow, a past Nobel laureate, was praised for the purism of his novella *The Actual*. After a long absence from fiction, Simon Gray, a well-regarded playwright, returned to novel-writing, where he had begun, with *Breaking Hearts*. Ian McEwan, Caryl Phillips, Bernice Rubens and Rose Tremain all added to their reputations. Martin Amis and Jeanette Winterson did not: both attempted to write in a style new to them and were reviled by the critics for their experimentation. This did not make them any the less attractive to the media, which continued to bestow anecdotal celebrity on them. The literary columns of the so-called quality newspapers in both Britain and the United States became more obsessed than ever with the trivia of authors' lives, personality profiles increasingly replacing literary evaluation.

It was an encouraging year for young black writers, the new names emerging including Ifeona Fulani, Courttia Newland and the mysteriously-named Q. Fred D'Aguiar and Ferdinand Dennis extended their art and there were many plaudits for Pauline Melville's *The Ventriloquist's Tale*. Among more senior black writers, Derek Walcott confirmed his talent with a collection called *The Bounty*, his first since winning the Nobel Prize for Literature in 1992 (see AR 1992, p. 507). Sadly there was no alleviation to the plight of Salman Rushdie, under an Iranian death threat since 1989, who continued to need a high level of protection. Moreover, another Nobel laureate, Wole Soyinka, was also obliged to go into hiding for large parts of the year after threats from the Nigerian government (see also VI.2.ii).

Several poets produced outstanding collections of their work, among them Charles Causley, John Fuller and Anne Stevenson. Most rewarding was the obvious extension of talent in new work by Andrew Motion (who also published a brilliant new life of John Keats), Don Paterson, confirming the energy of new Scottish writing, and Ted Hughes (the Poet Laureate), whose *Tales from Ovid* were far more than acts of homage or skilful translation but imaginative reinterpretations of the highest order.

Biography was the subject of a colloquium in Paris which brought together many of the leading practitioners of the art in Britain and France for a unique exchange over several days in November. Among the outstanding examples of the genre published in the year was the first volume of R.F.Foster's life of W.B.Yeats. Mikhail Gorbachev's *Memoirs* was by far the most important political reminiscence of the year. There were no fewer than three major biographies of Jane Austen; yet among the many lives of female writers which came out in the year, Jenni Calder's life of Naomi Mitchison, the Scottish writer who celebrated her 100th birthday in 1997, was the most affecting and original achievement. There was the usual demand for show-business writings, among which Mia Farrow's autobiography had the most gruesome self-absorption. Following her death in August, a revised version of Andrew Morton's notorious biography of Diana, Princess of Wales, was rushed out, part of a torrent of tributes, assessments and souvenir volumes which dominated book-shop stock throughout the world for the remainder of the year.

No death in 1997 made the international impact of Diana's (see I.1). Nevertheless, it was a year when several veterans of the literary scene died, some whose obituaries were brief or even non-existent having made contributions which might one day be recognized by literary historians as among the greatest of their age. Amos Tutuola, for example, was the father of modern African literature, a Yoruba-speaking Nigerian who broke all the rules of conventional prosody but had such vividness of imagination that he inspired a whole generation of story-tellers in Africa; his *The Palm-Wine Drinkard* became the first classic text of that continent. Other internationally-admired authors who died included Andrei Sinyavsky, a notable dissident in the former Soviet Union, and Allen Ginsberg, the guru not only of the 1960s 'beat' generation of Americans but also of countless young people all over the world, preaching a freer morality and spirituality than they had ever heard before (see XX: Obituary). Ginsberg was still capable of filling vast halls for his poetry readings only months before his death.

Four distinguished English prose writers died during the year. The doyen among them was V.S. Pritchett, undoubtedly one of the greatest writers of short stories not only in Britain but anywhere. He was deeply unfashionable at the time of his death in 1997, but critics were united in placing him among the most significant literary names of the century. Laurie Lee's future reputation seemed less secure, though there were many people prepared to argue that, even if *Cider with Rosie* and Lee's other country-scented books were perhaps not great literature, they were among the most loved English writings of modern times. P.H.Newby was the third major loss to contemporary English prose, and at the time of his death was probably the most neglected. Newby had won the first Booker Prize for Fiction in 1969 with *The Picnic at Sakkara*. When it began this prize had received little attention, and so Newby remained little-known except to dedicated admirers. As for Elspeth Huxley, who also died in 1997, she was still a well-regarded travel writer, particularly for her writings about East Africa, but she had become out of tune with modern approaches to her chosen genre and was seen by many readers to be very much part of a colonial cast of mind. (For Lee, Pritchett and Sinyavsky, see XX: Obituary.)

Naomi Mitchison was not the only writer to celebrate her centenary during the year. The Indian essayist Nirad C.Chaudhuri, author of *The Autobiography of an Unknown Indian*, was honoured on his 100th birthday by a university luncheon in Oxford at which he claimed to be the oldest author ever to have published a new book. In the year of India's 50th anniversary as an independent nation, it was remarkable that the four architects of modern Indian writing in English—Chaudhuri, Mulk Raj Anand, R.K.Narayan and Raja Rao—were all actively engaged in new work though all in extreme old-age.

Perhaps the greatest event for the literary world in the United Kingdom was the opening of the new British Library. Long, though unjustly, reviled as an expensive white elephant, the library almost immediately endeared itself to critics and users alike when it opened its doors (see XVI.2.ii). Tributes galore were made to the old Reading Room at the British Museum, in which Karl Marx and many others had worked, but the whiffs of resentful nostalgia surrounding its decommissioning were quickly dispelled as appreciation gathered for Colin St

John Wilson's brilliant reader-friendly design of the new premises, the largest civic building project in Britain this century. Serious publishing on the Internet was evident throughout the year, and increasingly books were marketed by putting specimen chapters on the World Wide Web so that people might be tempted to buy them. It was a moot point as to whether this development posed a fundamental threat to conventional publishing and book-selling, though there could be little doubt that they were affected by it. A libel case against the Poetry Society in Britain, for publishing a defamatory article on the Internet, was settled out of court; but the case underlined the new power of this form of global communication, and the attendant risks. Prophets continued to anticipate the death of literature and the end of reading as a consequence of the new technology. However, the fact that in Britain alone the number of newly-published books in one year leapt for the first time over the 100,000 mark suggested that the end of the literate world might not yet be nigh.

Among the leading titles published in 1997 were the following:

FICTION. Amis, Martin, *Night Train* (Cape); Atkinson, Kate, *Human Croquet*, (Doubleday); Baldeosingh, Kevin, *Virgin's Triangle* (Heinemann); Banks, Iain, *A Song of Stone* (Abacus); Banville, John, *The Untouchable* (Picador); Bawden, Nina, *A Nice Change* (Virago); Bellow, Saul, *The Actual: A Novella* (Viking); Bolger, Dermot, *Father's Music* (Flamingo);Brookner, Anita, *Visitors* (Cape); Brownjohn, Alan, *The Longest Shadows* (Dewi Lewis); Carey, Peter, *Jack Maggs* (Faber); Chamoiseau, Patrick (translated by Rejouis, Rose-Myriam and Vinokurow, Val), *Texaco* (Granta); Chandra, Vikram, *Love and Longing in Bombay* (Faber); Clarke, Arthur C., *3001: The Final Odyssey* (HarperCollins); Coe, Jonathan, *The House of Sleep* (Viking); Cusk, Rachel, *The Country Life* (Picador); D'Aguiar, Fred, *Feeding the Ghosts* (Chatto & Windus); Dennis, Ferdinand, *The Last Blues Dance* (HarperCollins); Donleavy, J.P., *The Lady who Liked Clean Rest Rooms* (Abacus); Dunmore, Helen, *Love of Fat Men* (Viking); Fischer, Tibor, *The Collector Collector* (Secker & Warburg); Freud, Esther, *Gaglow* (Hamish Hamilton); Fulani, Ifeona, *Seasons of Dust* (Harlem River Press); Gray, Simon, *Breaking Hearts* (Faber); Heath, Roy, *The Ministry of Hope* (Marion Boyars); Hill, Tobias, *Skin* (Faber); Hope, Christopher, *Me, the Moon and Elvis Presley* (Macmillan); James, P.D., *A Certain Justice* (Faber); Jolley, Elizabeth, *Lovesong* (Viking); Kennedy, A.L., *Original Bliss* (Cape); Kureishi, Hanif, *Love in a Blue Time* (Faber); MacLaverty, Bernard, *Grace Notes* (Cape); McEwan, Ian, *Enduring Love* (Cape); Massie, Allan, *Shadows of Empire* (Sinclair-Stevenson); Melville, Pauline, *The Ventriloquist's Tale* (Bloomsbury); Middleton, Stanley, *Brief Hours* (Hutchinson); Moggach, Deborah, *Close Relations* (Heinemann); Moore, Brian, *The Magician's Wife* (Bloomsbury); Newland, Courttia, *The Scholar* (Abacus); Nooteboom, Cees (translated by Rilke, Ina), *Roads to Santiago* (Harvill); O'Brian, Patrick, *The Yellow Admiral* (HarperCollins); Palmer, William, *The Pardon of Saint Anne* (Cape); Phillips, Caryl, *The Nature of Blood* (Faber); Pynchon, Thomas, *Mason and Dixon* (Cape); Q., *Deadmeat* (Sceptre); Ransmayr, Christoph (translated by Woods, John E.), *The Dog King* (Chatto); Read, Piers Paul, *Knights of the Cross* (Weidenfeld & Nicolson); Richler, Mordecai, *Barney's Vision* (Chatto and Windus); Roberts, Michele, *Impossible Saints* (Little, Brown); Roth, Philip, *American Pastoral* (Cape); Roy, Arundhati, *The God of Small Things* (Flamingo); Rubens, Bernice, *The Waiting Game* (Abacus); Saramago, José (translated by Rabassa, Gregory), *Blindness* (Harvill); Self, Will, *Great Apes* (Bloomsbury); Shields, Carol, *Larry's Party* (Fourth Estate); Sillitoe, Alan, *Alligator Playground* (Flamingo); Sivanandan, A., *When Memory Dies* (Arcadia); Taylor, Elisabeth Russell, *Present Fears* (Arcadia); Toibin, Colm, *Finbar's Hotel* (Picador); Tremain, Rose, *The Way I Found Her* (Sinclair-Stevenson); Vakil, Ardashir, *Beach Boy* (Hamish Hamilton); Vonnegut, Kurt, *Timequake* (Cape); Weldon, Fay, *Big Women* (Flamingo); White, Edmund, *The Farewell Symphony* (Chatto); Winterson, Jeanette, *Gut Symmetries* (Granta).

POETRY. Adcock, Fleur, *Looking Back* (OUP); Agard, John, *From the Devil's Pulpit* (Bloodaxe); Armitage, Simon, *Cloudcuckooland* (Faber); Breeze, Jean Binta, *On the Edge of an Island* (Bloodaxe); Burnside, John, *A Normal Skin* (Cape); Carver, Raymond, *All of Us: The Collected Poems* (Harvill); Causley, Charles, *Collected Poems 1951–1997* (Macmillan); Curnow, Allen, *Early Days Yet: New and collected poems 1941–1997* (Carcanet); Davie, Donald, *Poems and Melodramas* (Carcanet); Davies, Hilary *In a Valley of This Restless Mind* (Enitharmon); Dunmore, Helen, *Bestiary* Bloodaxe); Fainlight, Ruth, *Sugar Paper Blue* (Bloodaxe); Fuller, John, *Collected Poems* (Chatto); Hamburger, Michael, *Late* (Anvil); Harpur, James, *The Monk's Dream* (Anvil); Heaney, Seamus and Hughes, Ted (eds.), *The School Bag* (Faber); Higgins, Rita Ann, *Sunny Side Plucked* (Bloodaxe); Hill, Selima, *Violet* (Bloodaxe); Hughes, Ted, *Tales from Ovid* (Faber); Jennings, Elizabeth, *In the Meantime* (Carcanet); Johnson, Linton Kwesi, *Things and Times* (Bloodaxe); Joseph, Jenny, *Extended Smiles* (Bloodaxe); Kramer, Lottie, *Selected and New Poems* (Rockingham); Levi, Peter, *Reed Music* (Anvil); MacSweeney, Barry, *The Book of Demons* (Bloodaxe); Maguire, Sarah, *The Invisible Mender* (Cape); McKendrick, Jamie, *The Marble Fly* (OUP); Mitchell, Adrian, *Heart on the Left* (Bloodaxe); Motion, Andrew, *Salt Water* (Faber); O'Driscoll, Dennis, *Quality Time* (Anvil); Paterson, Don, *God's Gift to Women* (Faber); Porter, Peter, *Dragons in their Pleasant Palaces* (OUP); Reading, Peter, *Work in Regress* (Bloodaxe); Robertson, Robin, *A Painted Field* (Picador); Schmidt, Michael, *Selected Poems 1972–1997* (Smith/Doorstop); Smith, Iain Crichton, *The Human Face* (Carcanet); Stevenson, Anne, *The Collected Poems 1955–1995* (OUP); Tate, James, *Selected Poems* (Carcanet); Thwaite, Anthony, *Selected Poems 1956–1996* (Enitharmon); Walcott, Derek, *The Bounty* (Faber); Wicks, Susan, *The Clever Daughter* (Faber);Williams, C.K., *The Vigil* (Bloodaxe); Wright, Glyn, *Shindig* (Bloodaxe); Zephaniah, Benjamin, *Propa Propaganda* (Bloodaxe).

BIOGRAPHY/AUTOBIOGRAPHY. Anderson, Jon Lee, *Che Guevara: A revolutionary life* (Bantam); Aronson, Theo, *Princess Margaret: a Biography* (O'Mara); Bergreen, Laurence, *Louis Armstrong: An Extravagant Life* (HarperCollins); Brown, Colin, *Fighting Talk: The Biography of John Prescott* (Simon & Schuster); Brown, George Mackay, *For the Islands I Sing: an Autobiography* (John Murray); Calder, Jenni, *The Nine Lives of Naomi Mitchison* (Virago); Chambers, Colin, *Peggy: The Life of Peggy Ramsay, Play-Agent* (Nick Hern); Clapp, Susannah, *With Chatwin: Portrait of a Writer* (Cape); Cline, Sally, *Radclyffe Hall: A Woman Called John* (John Murray); Coetzee, J.M., *Boyhood:Scenes from Provincial Life* (Secker and Warburg); Connon, Bryan, *Somerset Maugham and the Maugham Dynasty* (Sinclair-Stevenson); Crick, Michael, *Michael Heseltine: A Life* (Hamish Hamilton); Diski, Jenny, *Skating to Antarctica* (Granta); Easton, Carol, *No Intermissions: the Life of Agnes de Mille* (Little, Brown); Farrow, Mia, *What Falls Away: A Memoir* (Doubleday); Forbes, Grania, *My Darling Buffy: the Early Life of the Queen Mother* (Richard Cohen); Foster, R.F., *W.B.Yeats: a Life–1: the Apprentice Mage 1865–1914* (OUP); Frank, Anne (ed. Frank, Otto H. and Pressler, Mirjam), *The Diary of a Young Girl* (Viking); Fryer, Jonathan, *André and Oscar and the Gay Art of Living* (Constable); Gorbachev, Mikhail (translated by Peronansky, Georges and Varsavsky, Tatiana), *Memoirs* (Doubleday); Graham, Katherine, *Personal History* (Weidenfeld & Nicolson); Hamilton, James, *Turner: a Life* (Hodder); Hibbert, Christopher, *Wellington: A Personal History* (HarperCollins); Hiney, Tom, *Raymond Chandler: A Biography* (Chatto); Johnson, Paul, *A History of the American People* (Weidenfeld & Nicolson); Kelly, Linda, *Richard Brinsley Sheridan: a Life* (Sinclair-Stevenson); Kenny, Anthony, *A Life in Oxford* ((John Murray); Kershaw, Alex, *Jack London: A Life* (HarperCollins); Lessing, Doris, *Walking in the Shade: Volume Two of my autobiography* (HarperCollins); Lewis, Geoffrey, *Lord Hailsham: a Life* (Cape); Lewis, Jeremy, *Cyril Connolly: A Life* (Cape); Makower, Frances, *Elizabeth Longford, the Authorised Biography* (Hodder); Mitchell, L.G., *Lord Melbourne 1779–1848* (OUP); Morgan, Kenneth O., *Callaghan: a Life* (OUP); Motion, Andrew, *Keats* (Faber); Myer, Valerie Grosvenor, *Obstinate Heart: Jane Austen-a Biography* (O'Mara); Nicholson, Nigel, *Long Life* (Weidenfeld & Nicolson); O'Connor, *The Secret Woman: A Life of Peggy Ashcroft* (Weidenfeld & Nicolson); O'Toole, Fintan, *A Traitor's Kiss: the Life of Richard Brinsley Sheridan* (Granta); Rayfield, Donald, *Anton Chekhov: a Life* (HarperCollins); Saul, Nigel, *Richard II* (Yale University Press); Schickel, Richard, *Clint Eastwood* (Cape); Sebba, Anne, *Mother Teresa:Beyond the Image* (Weidenfeld & Nicolson); Seldon, Anthony, with Baston, Lewis, *Major:*

A Political Life (Weidenfeld & Nicolson); Solzhenitsyn, Alexander, Invisible Allies (Harvill); Soyinka, Wole, The Open Sore of a Continent: A personal narrative of the Nigerian crisis (OUP); Spalding, Frances, Duncan Grant (Chatto); Thomas, R.S., Autobiographies (Dent); Uglow, Jenny, Hogarth: A Life and a World (Faber); Weintraub, Stanley, Albert: Uncrowned King (John Murray); West, Richard, The Life and Srange Surprising Adventures of Daniel Defoe (HarperCollins); Wilson, A.N., Paul: The Mind of the Apostle (Sinclair-Stevenson); Wolpert, Stanley, Nehru, A Tryst with Destiny (OUP).

OTHER. Amis, Kingsley, The King's English: a Guide to Modern Usage (HarperCollins); Blackburn, Robin, The Making of New World Slavery: from the baroque to the modern, 1492–1800 (Verso); de Botton, Alain, How Proust Can Change Your Life (Picador); Carter, Angela, Shaking a Leg: collected journalism and writing (Chatto & Windus); David, Hugh, On Queer Street: A Social History of Homosexuality 1895–1995 (HarperCollins); Dimbleby, Jonathan, The Last Governor: Chris Patten and the Handover of Hong Kong (Little, Brown); Dyer, Geoff, Out of Sheer Rage: In the Shadow of D.H.Lawrence (Little, Brown); Ferro, Marc, Colonization: A Global History (Routledge); French, Patrick, Liberty or Death: India's Journey to Independence and Division (HarperCollins); Greenfield, Susan, The Human Brain: A Guided Tour (Weidenfeld & Nicolson); Hattersley, Roy, Fifty Years On: A Prejudiced History of Britain since the War (Little, Brown); Hiro, Dilip, Sharing the Promised Land: An interwoven tale of Israelis and Palestinians (Hodder & Stoughton); Hobsbawm, Eric, On History (Weidenfeld & Nicolson); Hutton, Will, The State to Come (Vintage); John Paul II, Pope, Gift and Mystery: On the Fiftieth Anniversary of My Priestly Ordination (Doubleday); Keay, John, Last Post: The End of Empire in the East (John Murray); Marquez, Gabriel Garcia (translated by Grossman, Edith), News of a Kidnapping (Cape); Morrison, Blake, As If (Granta); Murdoch, Iris (ed. Conradi, Peter), Existentialists and Mystics: Writings on Philosophy and Literature (Chatto & Windus); Okri, Ben, A Way of Being Free (Phoenix House); Puttnam, David, The Undeclared War: The Struggle for Control of the World's Film Industry (HarperCollins); Ritchie, Harvey, The Last Pink Bits (Hodder & Stoughton); Sampson, Anthony, The Scholar Gypsy: The Quest for a Family Secret (John Murray); Sinclair, Iain, Lights Out for the Territory: Nine excursions in the secret history of London (Granta); Tsang, Steve Yui-sang Hong Kong: An Appointment with China (I.B.Taurus).

XVII SPORT

POLITICS AND SPORT. Horse-racing suffered as one of the targets of the IRA campaign to cause the maximum disruption with the minimum effort. False-alarm coded warnings were given which had to be taken seriously, as they were interspersed with the occasional real explosion. Shortly before the start time of the Grand National at Aintree, two coded warnings were received, so that the course had to be evacuated and racing abandoned for the day. There was major disruption for the thousands of spectators, though no bomb had in fact been planted.

The UK government's decision to ban sports' sponsorship by tobacco companies excluded Formula One motor-racing until into the 21st century, to the fury of other sports with international events. One of the excuses was that the venues would merely shift from Europe to countries which permitted such advertising. Another was that such motor sponsorship did not encourage more smoking—an assertion that common sense indicated was nonsense, as a well-timed report confirmed. Prime Minister Tony Blair was further embarrassed when it was revealed in November that the original decision in favour of a blanket ban had been reversed after a visit to 10 Downing Street by Formula One executive Bernie Ecclestone and that the latter had contributed £1 million to Labour Party funds. Mr Blair publicly apologized for the government's poor handling of the affair, adding that the donation would be repaid, although Formula One retained its temporary exemption from the tobacco sponsorship ban.

The concept of a sports 'centre of excellence' for Britain, originally proposed by the previous Prime Minister, John Major, was endorsed by the new government, but with the change that it was to be principally devoted to Olympic sports. Sheffield was the chosen site, it being stated that other sports centres would be embraced in the overall plan.

ATHLETICS. As usual, the United States was the lead country in the sixth World Athletics Championship staged in Athens, making an immediate impact when Maurice Greene defeated the holder, Canada's Donovan Bailey, in the prestigious 100-metres sprint. Bailey still got a gold medal, however, as Canada's relay team won the 4 × 100-metres again, after the Americans dropped the baton in the opening round. Marion Jones made it a double for the United States when she won the women's 100 metres. So close was the finish that Ukraine's Zana Pintussevich started on a celebration lap, believing she had won. Her distress changed to exultation when she did indeed win the 200 metres.

Among Germany's notable successes were Lars Riedl's fourth win in the discus and the victory of its women's 4 × 400-metre team, which came through to beat the US team into second place. America's men were given a hard race in this event, but held on for victory over Britain's promising quartet. Cuba dominated the jumping events, taking third place in the overall medals table. Jan Sotomeyor won the high-jump and Ivan Pedrosa the long-jump, while Yeolvis Quesada was ahead of Britain's Jonathan Edwards in the triple-jump. Kenya came a worthy fourth in the overall table because of its strength in long-distance running events, which were dominated by Africans generally. The Kenyans' most outstanding success was in filling the first three places in the steeplechase, with Wilson Boit Kipketer narrowly depriving Moses Kiptanui of a third successive gold medal. Another Kenyan-born runner, now competing for Denmark, Wilson Kipketer, led throughout the 800-metre race. He had recently equalled Sebastian Coe's long-standing world record and was soon to beat it. Another outstanding run came from Ethiopian Haile Gebrselassie, winner of the 10,000 metres. No world records were broken in the Athens championships, but the two Kipketers and Haile Gebrselassie were soon to do so.

Morocco was another country to do well: Hicham El Guerrouj won the 1,500 metres and Nezhe Bidouane stormed home in the women's 400-metre hurdles. The men's 400-metre hurdles was again won by American Allen Jones, despite a close challenge from Britain's Colin Jackson. The outstanding performance of the games was Ukrainian Sergey Bubka's sixth successive pole-vault win. The strong-man of the championships was Tomas Dvorak of the Czech Republic, who won the decathlon and might have set a new world record had he not eased up in the final event, the tiring 1,500 metres.

Given that the championships were being held in the Greek capital, there was high national symbolism in the route of the two longest events. Both the ladies' and the men's marathons started from Marathon and the course passed the tomb of the soldiers of Marathon. In the men's event, Spain filled the first two places, Abel Anton taking the gold medal. In the women's marathon, Japan's Hirami Sujuki was a comfortable winner, followed home by Portugal's defending title-holder, Manuela Machado.

The United States' winning overall tally was 18 medals, seven of them gold. Germany came second with ten medals (including five golds), followed by Russia with eight, although it was listed ninth in the official table, which only acknowledged gold. Britain had the eighth highest collection of medals (five silvers and a bronze), but was listed 26th because it failed to win gold. Jamaica, also with no golds, was listed 27th, despite winning seven medals overall. The official table followed the Olympic precedent, which also only recognized gold medals as of importance, despite the claim that taking-part was more important than winning.

ASSOCIATION FOOTBALL. Qualifying for the World Cup in France in 1998 was the principal target for all footballing countries. England's team started well under their new manager, Glenn Hoddle, and early in the year won a 'friendly' four-nations tournament in France, defeating the host country and the Italians and ending ahead of Brazil on points. In the World Cup qualifiers, however, defeat at Wembley by Italy put England's participation in the finals in jeopardy. Italy then obtained two away draws, while a series of comfortable wins left England a point ahead before the two again met in the final match of the group, this time in Rome. On the pitch a hard-fought game resulted in a 0–0 draw, which was enough for England to qualify for the World Cup finals. On the terraces there was a more one-sided confrontation. The English Football Association subsequently lodged a formal complaint about the provocative conduct of the Italian authorities against English supporters, many of whom sustained injuries in an indiscriminate assault by baton-wielding policemen.

Scotland also qualified for the World Cup finals, despite coming second in their group, which was won by Austria. Scotland had the highest points score of any runner-up, and so were assured of a place in France. The other eight European runners-up then drew lots to decide their opponents in two-leg play-offs for the final four places allotted to Europe. Italy were drawn against Russia and went through after bravely holding them to a 1–1 draw in freezing conditions in Moscow. The Republic of Ireland had also qualified for the play-offs, but were beaten by Belgium. In the Asian group, Hoddle's predecessor, Terry Venables, was now in charge of Australia, whose crucial match was against Iran. Australia were poised to qualify when leading 2–0 at home after a 1–1 draw away; but Iran equalized late in the game and won on the away-goals rule to enter the finals for the first time. The United States, which had staged the previous World Cup in 1994 (see AR 1994, pp. 541–2), also qualified for France, as did Jamaica, in the latter case for the first time.

In addition to automatic qualifiers Brazil (the holders) and host-nation France, 30 other nations were to compete in the 1998 World Cup finals. The all-important draw to establish eight groups of four teams, from which the top two would qualify for the final stages of the competition, resulted as follows:

Brazil	Italy	France	Spain	Holland
Scotland	Chile	Denmark	Nigeria	Belgium
Morocco	Cameroon	Saudi Arabia	Paraguay	South Korea
Norway	Austria	South Africa	Bulgaria	Mexico
	Germany	Romania	Argentina	
	USA	Colombia	Japan	
	Jugoslavia	England	Jamaica	
	Iran	Tunisia	Croatia	

Manchester United continued to dominate the English domestic game, manager Alex Ferguson guiding the team to its fourth Premier League title in five years. In Europe his team reached the semi-final of the Champions' League, only to lose to Borussia Dortmund of Germany, who went on to beat Juventus in the final. An Englishman did record a win in one European competition, when manager Bobby Robson (another ex-England manager) piloted Barcelona of Spain to victory in the European Cup Winners' Cup.

The English FA Cup Final featured a Chelsea team managed by Dutchman Ruud Gullit and full of overseas stars such as Gianfranco Zola of Italy, who was voted 'player of the year' in England. Opponents Middlesbrough had just suffered the blow of relegation from the Premiership and had lost to Leicester in the Coca Cola (League) Cup Final after a re-play. In the FA Cup Final, manager

Brian Robson's team had to endure another defeat: Chelsea's Roberto Di Mateo scored after only 45 seconds and Eddie Newton added a decisive second goal in the second half.

In Scotland, Walter Smith took Glasgow Rangers to a ninth successive Premiership title to equal Glasgow Celtic's record. Kilmarnock won the Scottish FA Cup and Celtic the Coca Cola Cup.

BOXING. The most publicized event of the year brought shame on the sport. In a heavyweight re-match between the once-invincible Mike Tyson and Evander Holyfield, the latter won again despite having half an ear bitten off. Tyson was fined $3 million and had his licence revoked, although only temporarily. The other notable heavyweight boxer was Britain's Lennox Lewis. His WBC title win over Oliver McCall was so devastating that the American stopped fighting, burst into tears and conceded defeat. Much more importantly for his reputation, Lewis demolished Andrzej Golota in America, knocking him out in the second round. With Holyfield beating American Michael Morer to add the IBF title to his WBA version, there were hopes that a fight between Lewis and Holyfield could be staged to determine an overall champion.

Another Briton to prove himself a true world-class champion was the flamboyant 'Prince' Naseem Hamed. Fighting in Britain, he added the IBF featherweight title to his WBO version by knocking out American Tom Johnson in the eighth round, then despatched Billy Hardy in the first round. He had a much harder defence in America, being floored himself three times before knocking out Kevin Kelley in the fourth.

CRICKET. An Ashes series between England and Australia always took pride of place in Test cricket. In an enthralling contest in the 1997 summer series in England, Australia emerged the 3–2 victors, one match being drawn. That was a much closer result than had been generally forecast, a leading Australian player having asserted his country could field three teams, all of which could easily beat England. Australian confidence had been bolstered by a string of Test victories, the last against South Africa and the one before that over the West Indies, to leave them the undisputed world leaders. However, that confidence was badly shaken when England won the pre-Test one-day series 3–0, all three victories by a comfortable six wickets. To add to Australian worries, captain Mark Taylor was struggling as opening batsman and their two match-winning bowlers, Glen McGrath and Shane Warne, were not at their best.

England turned the screw on the opening day of the first Test, as an inspired Darren Gough led an attack which took eight wickets before lunch. A brave innings by Shane Warne brought some relief for Australia, as did the fall of early English wickets, until a double century by Nasser Hussein, and a fine century by England's man of the series, Graham Thorpe, set up a commanding lead. Mark Taylor then rediscovered his best form in Australia's second innings, in which Greg Blewett also scored a century. But Australian hopes of saving the match were dashed when the England bowlers regained their fire, mopping up in good time for a convincing win.

The Australians were sufficiently shaken to send for a bowling reinforcement, in the person of Reiffel. With his backing, and with McGrath soon bowling well enough to be their man of the series, Australia reasserted themselves. As so often, McGrath's speed, lift and accuracy, coupled with Warne's exceptional wrist spin, proved a deadly combination. The Lord's Test was drawn, loss of time because of rain helping England to avoid probable defeat, after McGrath had taken 8 for 38 in their first innings. The next three Tests were won by Australia comfortably. The final Test at the Oval seemed to be following the same pattern as England made a paltry 180 on the opening day. That sparked renewed calls for the resignation of Mike Atherton, who had captained England for a record number of Tests. However, on a difficult pitch, fine left-arm spin bowling by the previously-overlooked Phil Tufnell confined Australia to a lead of 40 runs. A battling innings of 62 by Thorpe rescued England's second innings, although Australia were still favourites to win. However, Tufnell and Andy Caddick then ran through the Australian second innings to give England a welcome 19-run victory, these two between them taking 19 wickets in the match.

England had been fortified for the summer series by a 2–0 win in New Zealand, Australia by a more closely-contested 2–1 victory in South Africa. Australia then went on to overwhelm New Zealand, whose Test confidence had been briefly restored by a 2–0 win over Sri Lanka. Sri Lanka, however, continued to merit their title of world one-day champions with a series of wins in this form of the game. In a drawn Test series with India, moreover, they set a record Test innings score of 952, beating England's 902 for 7 against Australia in 1938.

At the year's end Pakistan confirmed their status as one of the top three countries, with Australia and South Africa, by beating the West Indies 3–0 in the Caribbean. That was encouragement for England, soon due to tour there. Further encouragement came as England defeated the West Indies twice, as well as Pakistan and India, in winning a one-day championship in Sharjah under the captaincy of Adam Holyoake (although Atherton was to retain the England leadership for the West Indies tour).

GOLF. The 32nd Ryder Cup match, on Spain's Valderrama course, was the highlight of the golfing year. Europe retained the trophy, beating the United States by a single point, with the scores 14½ to 13½ at the end of three days of fluctuating fortune. Europe won as a result of superior play in the four-ball and foursome matches, which left them leading 10½ to 5½. After receiving pep talks from captain Tom Kite and former US President George Bush, the Americans stormed back in the final day's singles. Such was their recovery that the result was still in the balance at the last hole of the final match, when Scotland's Colin Montgomerie made sure of a half to level with Scott Hoch, generously conceding a long putt to the American, since the match was already won.

Unusually for Valderrama, storms of torrential rain had delayed play on each of the first two days. Despite the resultant difficult conditions, the golf was of the highest standard throughout. For the Europeans, Montgomerie was outstanding with 3½ points from five matches, which might well have been four had that last putt not been conceded in the euphoria of overall victory. Germany's Bernhard Langer and Italy's Constantino Rocca also made major contributions (each recording three wins from four starts), as did Sweden's Per-Ulrik Johansson (with two from two). Particularly pleasing for the team was the fact that all 12 members scored at least one point. There was also vindication for captain Severiano Ballesteros (Spain) in the form of two wins for Britain's Nick Faldo, whose 'wild card' inclusion in place of an automatic qualifier, the Spaniard Angel Martin, had caused controversy. Injury had prevented Martin from playing for several weeks and he refused to undergo a preliminary fitness test. He was therefore not selected by Ballesteros, despite threatening to sue if he was omitted.

Scott Hoch was the most successful of the Americans with 2½ points from three starts (including the questionable half with Montgomerie). Lee Janzen and Jeff Maggert were the only others above average, each with two from three. The big US disappointments were the two players most publicized in advance: Tiger Woods scored only 1½ points from five starts, while Davis Love III ended with nil from four, the only one of the 24 competitors without a win.

Ballesteros was everywhere during the Valderrama event, giving advice that was inspirational for some, disturbing for others. His selections and his enthusiasm unquestionably played a part in Europe's win. For him it was a great honour to captain the team to a win in his home country. He also became the first man to have played in, and captained, winning Ryder Cup teams. Another record came from his controversial selection of Faldo, who increased his overall total of Ryder Cup wins to 28, beating American Billy Casper's previous record and justifying his choice. For Ballesteros, once as captain was enough. After the match he announced that for the next Ryder Cup he would seek to qualify for inclusion as a player once again.

The Americans had some consolation in the Alfred Dunhill Nations' Cup at St Andrew's, Scotland, by beating England 3–0 in the early stages. However, Europe again came off best when Sweden beat the US team 2–1 in the semi-final. The crucial victory came from Joachim Haeggman, whose world-record-equalling 27 for the first nine holes left him nine strokes ahead of British Open champion Justin Leonard, an impregnable lead despite a slump to 41 over the back nine. The final was a reverse of 1991, as South Africa won the event for the first time with a 2–1 victory over Sweden. Haeggman again figured in the decisive match, but this time as loser to South Africa's captain, Ernie Els. The South African star, however, was the lesser-known Retief Goosen, who won all of his five matches through the event.

Colin Montgomerie further enhanced his reputation by becoming Europe's leading golfer for a record fifth successive time. Yet a victory in the majors still eluded him. In the US Masters at Augusta the youthful phenomenon of the golf world, Tiger Woods, won with a record score of 270, further increasing his popularity and vast bank balance. Woods ended the season as America's top money-winner and second in the world ratings.

In the British Open, Justin Leonard beat off the close challenge of Jesper Parnevik (Sweden) and Darren Clarke (Ireland). Els won the US Open for the second time and also the World Match Play championship for the third successive year. The leading lady golfer was Britain's Alison Nicholas, who topped the European order of merit and won the US Open. Only five-feet tall, Alison was the smallest player on any professional tour.

MOTOR SPORT. Jacques Villeneuve (Canada) became world champion in only his second year in Formula One racing, following a remarkable record as American Indy Car champion and winner of the notorious Indianapolis 500. Before the final Formula One race, at Jérez in Spain, Germany's Michael Schumacher was one point ahead, after fluctuating fortunes in the previous 15 races. In a similar situation three years before, Britain's Damon Hill had been the chaser: under pressure from Hill, Schumacher had crashed his car and then spun across the track to take out Hill and thus to win the title (see AR 1994, pp. 545–6). On that occasion he had claimed that his damaged car was out of control. But when a similar collision occurred in 1997, as Villeneuve raced past Schumacher, the on-board television showed that the German had deliberately turned in to hit him, although this time his rival was not stopped.

Despite the German driver's protestations that he had simply made a rare error, one comment summed up the general view: 'Schumacher was left with his car in the gravel and his reputation in the gutter.' The Formula One governing body imposed only the meaningless penalty of disqualifying Schumacher from being runner-up, Villeneuve having nursed his battered car to third place and the title. His Williams-Renault was the outstanding car of the season and a comfortable winner of the constructors' championship. Only Schumacher's earlier brilliant driving had kept Ferrari in contention for part of the season. The McLaren team finished third, with the Scot David Coulthard winning twice and being deprived of a third win only by orders to let his Finnish team-mate, Mikka Hakkinen, pass him near the end of the Jérez race.

For Williams' boss Frank Williams, satisfaction at the continued dominance of his cars was overshadowed by the worry of a pending trial in Italy on charges of responsibility for the death of Ayrton Senna (Brazil) three years earlier, when the steering column of his Williams car had snapped (see AR 1994, p. 546). Happily, Williams, other members of his staff and race officials were exonerated in the brief judgment statement.

Fast as Formula One cars travelled, none came near *Thrust II*, which was built in Britain to challenge for the world land-speed record. Piloted by Andy Green, it reached a record 763 m.p.h. in Utah (USA), breaking the sound-barrier on land exactly 50 years after it had been broken in the air. The previous record-holder, Richard Noble, organized the team which broke his own record so comprehensively.

TENNIS. For the fifth year in succession America's Pete Sampras was number one in men's tennis. In the first of the four majors, he cruised to the final of the Australian Open, in which he crushed Spain's Carlos Moya by three sets to love to win his ninth Grand Slam title. Clay was not a good surface for his power game, however, and in the French Open Sampras was one of the early casualties, only two seeds surviving until the quarter-finals. The French final was also decided in straight sets, Brazil's Gustavo Kuerten defeating Sergei Briguera of Spain.

Sampras was at his best on Wimbledon's grass and duly recorded his fourth win in the British tournament. In the semi-finals he crushed Tod Woodbridge, who later won the doubles for the fifth successive year with Mark Woodforde. In the other semi-final Frenchman Cedric Pioline beat Germany's Michael Stich (who was playing his last tourament) to reach the final, in which Sampras again won in straight sets. During the tournament, Sampras lost only two of his 118 service games. Final confirmation of his top status came when he beat Patrick Rafter (Australia) in straight sets to win the Grand Slam Cup in Germany. In the Davis Cup finals, however, an injury forced Sampras to retire in the middle of his first match, his withdrawal setting up Sweden for a 5–0 win.

Unusually, two British nationals reached the Wimbledon quarter-finals, namely Tim Henman and Greg Rusedski, who also did well in minor tournaments. Rusedski overtook Henman in the rankings and later reached the final of the US Open, only to lose to Rafter.

In ladies' tennis, Switzerland's Martina Hingis was even more dominant. She won in Australia aged just 16 years and 3 months, the youngest winner for over a century. She also won at Wimbledon, defeating the Czech Republic's Jana Novotna in a close three-set final. Since she won the US Open as well, only a rare failure in the French Open deprived her of a clean sweep. Before playing in Paris, Hingis had injured herself while riding; even so, she reached the final, where the young Croatian, Eva Majoli, won in straight sets.

THE TURF. Following the bomb-scare on the Saturday (see p. 522), the Grand National steeplechase was successfully re-staged two days later, to the relief of the jockeys who had spent the weekend in their racing colours. The runaway winner was Lord Gyllene, ridden by Tony Dobin, with the grey Sunny Bay a distant second. Half the field of 36 finished the testing course, on the 50th and last time that the BBC commentary was provided by Peter O'Sullevan. His great contribution to racing was recognized by a knighthood and a memorial bust unveiled on the course. His last broadcast of all was at Newbury, where Sunny Bay won the Hennessy Gold Cup (and one of his own horses was also a winner).

Tony McCoy was champion jockey with 190 winners, including a Cheltenham double on the champion hurdler, Make a Stand, and the Gold Cup winner, Mr Mulligan. McCoy's new season began even more remarkably with over 150 winners by Christmas (and more than half the season yet to come). Martin Pipe was winning trainer in the 1996–97 season, accumulating over 200 successes.

On the flat, Kieran Fallon was champion jockey, Frankie Dettori's challenge fading when he suffered several suspensions. Fallon's tally of 202 winners included two Classic successes: on Sleepytime in the 1,000 Guineas and on Reams of Verse in the Oaks. Bosra Sham was another outstanding horse for Fallon and trainer Henry Cecil, but the winning trainer by a distance was Michael Stoute. His most successful horse was the ever-consistent Pilsudski, winner of £1.6 million in prize money. Pilsudski was second in the Prix de l'Arc de Triomphe, which was won for the second successive year by French jockey Olivier Peslier, this time on Peinture Célèbre.

The Derby was won by Benny the Dip (ridden by Willie Ryan, after Dettori had declined the ride), which beat Silver Patriarch by a short head. Silver Patriarch then won the St Leger, to give Pat Eddery the 4,000th winner of his long career. Singspiel was another big winner for Stoute, notably in the Dubai World Cup.

RUGBY UNION. The southern hemisphere's domination of rugby was briefly shattered by the British Lions on their tour of South Africa, the reigning world champions. Captained by England's player of the year, Martin Johnson, and managed by Fran Cotton, they soon combined into a formidable team. In the first Test in Cape Town, South Africa took an early lead, only for Matt Dawson, a replacement for injured scrum half Rob Howley, to inspire a surge to victory. In the second Test in Durban, South Africa again went ahead with three tries, only for Neil Jenkins' immaculate kicking to level the scores with five penalties. Jeremy Guscott then snatched the decisive score with a late dropped goal. The South Africans came back to win the final Test, but a series win was a satisfying triumph for the Lions.

The illusion that Britain had closed the gap in class with South Africa, New Zealand and Australia was rudely shattered at the end of the season. All three countries toured Britain, each of them overwhelming Scotland, Ireland and Wales. England alone provided resistance, obtaining creditable draws with Australia and New Zealand and providing challenging opposition in the matches which they lost against all three southern hemisphere sides.

In the Five Nations tournament, France dominated the season with a convincing Grand Slam win. They crushed Scotland and Ireland, but won a hard-fought match with Wales in Paris only narrowly. The deciding game was with England at Twickenham. Down 20–6, the French stormed back to win 23–20. That was a rare lapse by England, who were the outstanding 'home' team, defeating Ireland, Scotland and Wales by decisive scores and thus winning the Triple Crown for the 20th time. England's tally of 141 points was 15 higher than France's.

In club football, the French were also the stars of the European Heineken Cup. Although Leicester defeated Toulouse in one semi-final, they were overrun 28–9 in the final by Brive (who had disposed of Cardiff in the other semi-final). Wasps won the Courage League, while Leicester had the consolation of a Pilkington Cup success. In Scotland, Melrose achieved a rare League and Cup double.

RUGBY LEAGUE. In the Test series, Australia again proved too good for England. In the first game they cruised to a comfortable win. In the second at Old Trafford, England's captain, Andy Farrell, inspired his team to level the series. In the decider, however, it took the Australians just 45 seconds to score a try and to set themselves on the way to a 36–20 victory.

At club level, Australia also dominated the world championship, in which no British team reached the semi-final. Brisbane Broncos were the comfortable winners of the event. In England, St Helens again beat the Bradford Bulls in the Challenge Cup final, this time by 32–22. However, Bradford Bulls won the Super League after starting with 20 straight wins. As usual, the Premiership was dominated by Wigan, who were also the only British side to have more than one win in the world club competition.

AMERICAN ASPECTS. The Green Bay Packers won the Super Bowl American football final, defeating the New England Patriots in New Orleans by 35–21. There was nothing unexpected in the result, since the Packers were the season's best team; it was also the 13th successive win by the NFC champions over their AFC equivalents. The trophy was renamed the Lombardy Super Bowl, after Vincent Lombardy, the renowned Packers' coach who had led them to victory in the first two Super Bowls in the 1960s. Since then there had been no success for the Packers, who were the only team in either league which was owned by the community rather than by a rich owner.

In the match itself, the young Patriots team gave the Packers a hard fight and were leading 14–10 at the end of the first quarter. That aggregate score was a record for the first period in any Super Bowl, other records broken in the game including an 81-yard touchdown pass by Packers' quarter-back Brett Fabre. Most decisive of all was Desmond Howard's 99-yard kick return in the third quarter. This feat helped to make him the first specialist player in Super Bowl history to win the coveted 'most valuable player' award.

The Chicago Bulls were again the outstanding basket ball team. Their key player, Michael Jordan, was also America's richest and most popular sportsman. In World Series baseball, the final was between Florida Marlins and the Cleveland Indians, the Marlins becoming the champions.

XVIII ECONOMIC AND SOCIAL AFFAIRS

1. THE INTERNATIONAL ECONOMY

Organization for Economic Cooperation and Development (OECD)
DATE OF FOUNDATION: 1960   HEADQUARTERS: Paris, France
OBJECTIVES: To promote economic growth in member states and the sound development of the world economy
MEMBERSHIP (END-'97): Australia, Austria, Belgium, Canada, Czech Republic, Denmark, Finland, France, Germany, Greece, Hungary, Iceland, Ireland, Italy, Japan, South Korea, Luxembourg, Mexico, Netherlands, New Zealand, Norway, Poland, Portugal, Spain, Sweden, Switzerland, Turkey, United Kingdom, United States (*total 29*)
SECRETARY-GENERAL: Donald Johnston (Canada)

International Monetary Fund (IMF)
DATE OF FOUNDATION: 1944   HEADQUARTERS: Washington DC, USA
OBJECTIVES: To promote international monetary cooperation and to assist member states in establishing sound budgetary and trading policies
MEMBERSHIP (END-'97): 178 UN members plus Kiribati, Switzerland & Tonga (*total 181*)
MANAGING DIRECTOR: Michel Camdessus (France)

International Bank for Reconstruction and Development (IBRD/World Bank)
DATE OF FOUNDATION: 1944   HEADQUARTERS: Washington DC, Washington
OBJECTIVES: To make loans on reasonable terms to developing countries with the aim of increasing their productive capacity
MEMBERSHIP (END-'97): 176 UN members plus Kiribati, Switzerland & Tonga (*total 179*)
PRESIDENT: James D. Wolfensohn (United States)

World Trade Organization (WTO)
DATE OF INAUGURATION: 1996 (successor to General Agreement on Tariffs and Trade, GATT)
HEADQUARTERS: Geneva, Switzerland
OBJECTIVES: To eliminate tariff and other barriers to international trade and the facilitate international financial settlements
MEMBERSHIP (END-'97): 132 contracting parties
DIRECTOR-GENERAL: Renato Ruggiero (Italy)

THE world's economy expanded by about 4 per cent in 1997, according to estimates prepared by the International Monetary Fund (IMF). This was slightly higher than the growth recorded in 1996 (see AR 1996, pp. 510–11), despite the shock to the world economy from the crisis in East Asia (see below), the main effects of which were expected to be felt in 1998. World growth was accompanied by a slow-down in inflationary pressures. The rate of increase in consumer prices dropped from 2.4 to 2.2 per cent in advanced economies and from 13.2 to 10 per cent in developing economies. Countries in transition, which a few years previously had been experiencing hyper-inflation, slowed down from 40 to 32 per cent.

A notable feature of the year was the continued recovery of the former communist countries of Central/Eastern Europe, which together expanded by 2.1 per cent compared with 1.5 per cent the previous year. Russia's economy, which had contracted sharply every year since the demise of the USSR at the end of 1991, stabilized in 1997 amid predictions that in 1998 it would record its first positive growth since embracing capitalism. Developing countries expanded by over 6 per cent for the third year running, though Africa's growth fell back to 3.7 per cent after 5.2 per cent expansion in 1996.

However, if a prize had been awarded for 1997, it would probably have gone to the United States. Despite its already-huge size (accounting for 35 per cent of all OECD output), the US economy grew by 3.8 per cent without any visible signs of overheating. This marked the sixth successive year of positive economic growth, fuelled by a strong revival of US prowess in the area of information technology, as the Internet continued its rapid growth. Once again, the progress of the US economy owed much to the deft handling of monetary policy by the Federal Reserve under Alan Greenspan. For most of the year he resisted repeated pressure to increase interest rates, taking the view that there was a small risk of deflation to be balanced against the usual danger of inflation and, in any case, believing that the official figures over-stated the prevailing rate of inflation.

The normally-reserved OECD described the US performance as 'exceptional'. Unemployment in the United States shrank from 5.3 per cent a year earlier to only 4.7 per cent at end-1997—the lowest level for 25 years—while the trade deficit also came down, helped by exports expanding at 10 per cent (against a 9 per cent increase in the value of imports). To top everything, elimination of the budget deficit—an aim which had eluded the previous Republican administration—looked near to being achieved by the Democrats, who were traditionally associated with spending. Achievement of the balanced budget envisaged by President Clinton was helped not only by Mr Greenspan's monetary management but also by the fact that the Republicans controlling Congress kept a tight rein on any inclination of the Clinton administration to spend more money.

The economy of the European Union (EU) grew by 2.6 per cent in 1997—an improvement on the 1.7 per cent recorded for 1996. The stronger growth was welcomed as a sign that the EU might be starting to escape from a long recession even as its member-states took the necessary medicine to bring their budget deficits down to the level (3 per cent of GDP) required under the Maastricht Treaty for impending economic and monetary union (EMU). On the other hand, growth did little to alleviate aggregate EU unemployment, which remained stubbornly high at 19 million, provoking riots in France and Germany. Within the EU there were markedly different economic performances. Ireland continued its stunning performances of recent years with growth of 10.5 per cent (while easily qualifying for monetary union), whereas most other member-states recorded less than 3 per cent. The biggest surprise among EU countries was the way in which the economies regarded as 'fringe' candidates for monetary union the previous year (like Spain and Italy) improved dramatically, making it more likely that monetary union would start on time in 1999 with 11 founding members.

Britain set the pace among the larger EU economies with 3.4 per cent expansion compared with 2.4 per cent in Germany and 2.3 per cent in France (and only 1.3 per cent in Italy). Britain's economy marked its fifth successive year of expansion. Unemployment dropped from 6.6 per cent a year earlier to only 5 per cent, without any serious signs of inflation. The Bank of England raised interest rates five times—in steps of 0.25 per cent—after it was declared operationally independent in May by the incoming Labour government (see I.5). The rise in interest rates contributed to an increase in the effective exchange rate of sterling by nearly 20 per cent at one stage, leaving monetary conditions at the end of the year very tight and manufacturing companies complaining about being uncompetitive. The new Labour government announced that it would stick to the outgoing Conservatives' tight spending plans for two years. The only exception of any note was its 'welfare-to-work' programme, designed to get young people, single mothers and the long-term unemployed back to work—to be funded by a 'windfall tax' on privatized utilities expected to raise £35,000 million over five years. The government's plan was to engineer a 'soft' landing for the economy over the next year or two, during which growth would merely decelerate instead of sinking into a full recession, as had happened twice under the previous Conservative administration.

Among the three Central/East European countries which had joined the OECD in 1996, Poland was easily the star performer. Its economy grew by 6.7 per cent in 1997 against a forecast of 5.5 per cent, as price rises slowed from 18 to 13 per cent. This suggested that Poland had at last turned the corner as far as its economy was concerned and was now preparing itself for full membership of the EU (see also III.1.i; XI.3). Of the other ex-communist OECD members, Hungary also appeared to have turned a corner, achieving growth of 3 per cent compared with between 1 and 1.5 per cent in the two previous years. The Czech Republic, however, suffered a setback as the 4.4 per cent growth of the previous year collapsed to under 1 per cent and the authorities abandoned a fixed exchange-rate regime in the face of a rapid rise in imports fuelled by increased household consumption. Elsewhere in ex-communist Europe, Slovenia and the Slovak Republic continued to grow steadily, but Romania and Bulgaria contracted by 4 and 6 per cent respectively.

As regards the Russian economy, there were signs of significant improvement. Its long depression since the start of shock therapy in 1992, as it shed uneconomic communist-era industries and slowly adapted to free markets, seemed to have bottomed out in 1997, when inflation dropped to 12 per cent. The OECD pencilled in a projection of positive growth of 3 per cent for 1998 and 5 per cent the following year. Moreover, some economists believed that the Russian economy was growing in 1997 much more strongly than was suggested by the official statistics, which did not take account of activities not reported to the authorities for tax-avoidance reasons.

Elsewhere in the world, the Latin American region accelerated its revival with growth of just over 5 per cent, led by Mexico (7.2 per cent), Chile (6.2 per cent) and Argentina (7.3 per cent) and accompanied by average inflation down to 11.2 per cent in 1997 from 21.4 per cent the previous year. Brazil, by far the biggest regional economy, managed to expand by 3.5 per cent, despite a tough $18,000 million austerity programme imposed in October to counter a speculative assault on the currency (see IV.3.iii). During the year inflation was brought down from from 10 per cent in 1996 (and 23.2 per cent in 1995) to only 4.7 per cent—an impressive outcome for a country that had lived with hyper-inflation for a quarter of a century.

Among traditional developing economies, India's promising recovery continued with recorded growth of 4.7 per cent in 1997 (compared with 6.1 per cent in 1996) and inflation of only 5.5 per cent. Africa grew by only 3.7 per cent, against 5.2 per cent in 1996, but this might have been a deviation from an improving trend as more African countries set about restructuring their economies. Growth in Africa appeared to be more broadly-based than in the past, in that 35 out of 47 countries recorded expansion of 3 per cent or more, as against only 17 in 1992. A notable exception to the trend was South Africa, which was hit by a collapse in the world price of gold, on top of its restructuring problems (see VII.3). Growth nearly halved, to 1.7 per cent in 1997, while inflation edged up from 7.4 per cent to 8.6 per cent. However, this performance looked like success compared with that of Zimbabwe, where growth slumped from 8 to 2 per cent and inflation climbed from 21.7 to 25 per cent (see also VII.2.iii).

ECONOMIC CRISIS IN EAST ASIA. The single most important global economic event in 1997 was the near-collapse of a number of East Asian economies, including those of Thailand, South Korea, Malaysia, the Philippines and Indonesia. The crisis was all the more serious because virtually no-one had predicted it. The 'Asian miracle' had long been held up to others as a model of development, under which strong economic growth had been coupled with egalitarian policies that had reduced the proportion of Asians living on less than $1 a day from 60 per cent in 1975 to only 20 per cent in 1997. Few, if any, advanced industrial nations in the West could claim such relative success in relieving poverty (although poverty thresholds in the West were of course far above those of Asia).

If there was one date on which the Asian crisis could be said to have started, it was 2 July. On the previous day Hong Kong had reverted from British rule to the sovereignty of China (see IX.2.ii), an historic occasion which passed uneventfully for the Hong Kong dollar, which remained tied to the US dollar. On 2 July, however, the Bank of Thailand suddenly announced that it would no longer defend the beleaguered baht, which speculators had long regarded as overvalued (see IX.1.ii). That decision started a domino collapse of regional currencies in the following days and weeks, as speculators used their windfall gains from sinking one currency in order to sink another one. The Philippines, Indonesia, South Korea and Malaysia were all badly damaged, even Singapore being affected, although it weathered the storms better than most. Only a few months earlier, the IMF had welcomed South Korea's continued impressive macroeconomic performance and had praised the authorities for their 'enviable fiscal record'. Thailand had been similarly lauded for its 'remarkable economic performance and the authorities' consistent record of sound economic policies'.

The crisis was quite unlike previous economic collapses, because most East Asian countries sported budget surpluses or minimal deficits, high savings rates and low inflation. With the benefit of hindsight, commentators traced the causes to a loss of confidence within a system which, though relatively stable, depended on a high proportion of short-term foreign (private sector) loans which could be quickly withdrawn. Wrong-headed government policies also played a part, including lax financial regulation, misguided government guarantees and the maintenance of overvalued exchange rates linked to the dollar. The accumulation of short-term unhedged debt turned quickly into capital outflows when confidence collapsed. That in turn led to a vicious circle in which depreciating currencies pulled down asset values, so that private-sector balance sheets deteriorated even further and depression became almost self-fulfilling.

Some commentators, notably Professor Martin Feldstein of Harvard University in the United States, blamed Japan's Ministry of Finance for most of the woes of the Asian 'tiger' economies. He argued that, if Japan had reduced taxes in its 1997 budget instead of increasing them (see IX.2.iv), the subsequent Japanese recession, triggering competitive devaluations of 25 to 50 per cent throughout East Asia, would not have happened, neither would the crisis itself. Japan was by far the most powerful economy in Asia, so that other countries in the region were quickly affected by a fall in the value of the yen. Other influential American economists such as Professor Jeffrey Sachs, also of Harvard, contended that the rescue methods adopted by the IMF only made the crisis worse. He argued that Asia was reeling not from a crisis of fundamentals but from a self-fulfilling withdrawal of short-term loans—made worse by each investor's recognition that other investors were withdrawing their funds. He criticized the IMF for imposing a macroeconomic contraction on these economies on top of the panic they were already experiencing. For its part, the IMF argued that in its negotiations with the countries affected it was demanding no more fiscal tightening than was necessary to cover the costs of a restructuring of the financial sector and to promote the restoration of a sustainable balance of payments. It also argued that it had been obliged to recommend higher interest rates in order to attract international capital back to the affected countries, to rebuild their reserves and to bring their currencies out of the depths to which they had plummeted.

At one stage it had looked as though even Japan might be vulnerable, because the downward spiral of share and land prices (governing the bulk of the capital of the Japanese banks) had exposed the precarious state of the country's financial sector (itself heavily exposed to other Asian countries). The truth was that many of Japan's banks were technically bankrupt by Western accounting standards. The Japanese government decided on the unprecedented policy of allowing some of the worst banks to fall, in order to preserve the rest. On 17 November Hokkaido Takushoka, the country's tenth largest bank, went out of business—the first collapse of any of the top 20 Japanese banks since World War II (see IX.2.iv). The failure was confirmed not long after government figures had shown that, in the third quarter of 1997, the whole economy was contracting at an annual rate of 11 per cent. At the same time, Japan played a leading role with the IMF in supplying liquidity for its troubled Asian trading partners. It did so out of enlightened self-interest, in the belief that the region would emerge from the crisis intact only if the vicious downward spiral of the second half of the year could be turned into a virtuous one in which confidence gradually increased, foreign money returned and exchange rates and markets recovered to more realistic levels. By the turn of the year there were tentative signs of future recovery in the region.

The curious thing was that, for all the evidence of a real crisis, most of the

East Asian economies recorded impressive (by Western standards) growth rates for 1997 (apart from Japan's 1.9 per cent) and that all except Indonesia were expecting respectable positive growth rates in 1998. China continued to be the best-performing economy in the region, recording growth of around 9 per cent in 1997. China had managed to survive the duration of the Asian crisis without devaluing its currency, which could have propelled the region into another downward spiral. Tight monetary policies and a good harvest kept inflation low (at 3 per cent), although high interest rates curbed domestic demand and export prospects were reduced by the drop in economic activity throughout the region. As regards the immediate future, China prepared for strong rather than exceptional growth in 1998.

ANNUAL G-7 SUMMIT. The annual summit of the Group of 7 main industrialized countries (now increased to eight by the inclusion of Russia as an associate member) took place in Denver, Colorado, on 20–22 June. It continued the downbeat tone of recent such summits, at which very little of any importance had been agreed. The Denver summiteers agreed that democracy and the rule of law should be respected after Hong Kong had been handed back to China and that African countries should be helped to integrate into the world economy, especially if they promoted democracy and good governance. They also urged the revival of the Middle East peace process. The only major area of contention was US resistance to European pressure to reduce emissions of greenhouse gases in accordance with international agreements (see XIV.3). The unspoken sub-text of the conference was the startling success of the US economy compared with those of other participating countries.

WORLD TRADE ORGANIZATION. Three years of negotiations ended in Geneva on 15 February when 68 countries agreed a pact to liberalize telecommunications markets in a deal expected to boost sales and investment and to cut costs for consumers. It was predicted that the cost of international telephone calls could fall by more than 80 per cent. Charlene Barshefsky, acting US Trade Representative, described the accord as 'one of the most important trade agreements for the 21st century'.

Under the pact, the 68 participating countries, accounting for more than 90 per cent of world telecommunications revenues, pledged to open their markets to foreign competition, to allow overseas companies to buy stakes in domestic operators, and to be governed by common rules on fair competition in the sector, including voice telephony, data and fax transmissions, and satellite and radio communications. Sir Leon Brittan, EU trade commissioner, said that the accord would act as a catalyst for the European economy and was 'a major step in the creation of the information society'. At the end of 1997 the US Federal Communications Commission approved the measures agreed, making the United States the first country to implement fully the WTO accord to open domestic telecommunications to international competition.

INTERNATIONAL MONETARY FUND AND WORLD BANK. The year was likely to be remembered mainly for the IMF's controversial involvement in the rescue programmes for a number of East Asian economies (see above). These included a $16,700 million rescue package for Thailand, a $10,140 million stand-by credit for Indonesia, a $57,000 million rescue plan for South Korea (including a balanced budget, bank closures, opening firms to more foreign capital) and involvement in Malaysia's 'market-driven' measures. The IMF was widely criticized for not anticipating the crisis and for attaching draconian conditions to the programmes it negotiated. The IMF itself pointed out that, far from being caught unprepared, its managing director, Michel Camdessus, had made four visits to Thailand (where the crisis started) between July 1996 and July 1997 with the express purpose of warning the Thai authorities that they were on course for disaster. M. Camdessus argued that IMF insistence on balanced budgets did not imply a squeeze on the economy and that higher interest rates were absolutely necessary in the short-term to bolster confidence and attract money back into these countries in order to support their exchange rates. The US government was happy to cooperate with the IMF in trying to stabilize the Asian crisis, but as the year ended it had not overcome congressional resistance to the payment of increased US contributions in order to stabilize the IMF's own resources.

On the technical side, the agenda for strengthening the IMF's resources finally cleared the remaining hurdles at the annual meeting of the IMF and the World Bank (IBRD) in Hong Kong on 20–25 September. The 11th quota review yielded a 45 per cent increase in quotas (to $285,000 million), the equity allocation of special drawing rights being approved by the IMF Interim Committee. The new Arrangements to Borrow Group (which included Thailand) had its first formal session on the fringes of the plenary sessions of the IMF meeting. The funding for the IMF's enhanced structural adjustment facility still remained a problem, complicated by the 'heavily-indebted poor countries' (HIPC) debt relief initiative. Efforts by the UK delegation to establish a faster timetable to write down the debts of the HIPC countries drew a rebuke from World Bank president James Wolfensohn and a rebuff from the Germans, who feared that conditionality would be weakened and continued to oppose gold sales to close the funding gap.

Mr Wolfensohn made an impassioned speech to the Hong Kong meeting, promising to put poverty reduction and development at the heart of the World Bank's agenda for the new century. He wanted it to become a 'knowledge bank', affording clients all over the world full access to the bank's information base. He also pledged new emphasis on anti-corruption programmes. Mr Wolfensohn proved to be a strong advocate for the poor, although his abrasive manner caused him problems with shareholders, bank staff and officials, and also with the media. However, being unpopular was perhaps the fate of the man whom many observers regarded as the most effective and active World Bank president since Robert McNamara.

INTERNATIONAL DEVELOPMENT ASSOCIATION. The failure of the US Congress to approve full US funding of the IDA, despite the pleading of the US Treasury, remained a source of concern for developing countries as well as for the USA's G-7 partners. Even though arrangements for the 11th replenishment of IDA resources (IDA-11) were barely completed, meetings of the G-24 and the IMF Development Committee in Hong Kong in September began the first exploratory talks on IDA-12. The concern was that, with so much focus on private-sector flows to developing countries, the moral imperative behind the IDA had weakened. However, the World Bank pointed out that a large proportion of the private-sector flows went to only a small group of successful emerging market economies. Developing countries were urging that IDA-12 (which was due to start in June 1999 for a three-year period) should be replenished to the same level as IDA-10 in real terms—to about $20,000 million over three years. They wanted to see IDA funds more focused on initiatives to build capacity in Africa, and less in the larger Asian economies able to obtain private finance.

NOBEL PRIZE FOR ECONOMICS. The 1997 prize of $1 million went to Robert Merton of Harvard University and Myron Scholes of Stanford University for their work on a piece of algebra behind the valuation of stock options, by which billions of dollars were traded every day on the derivatives markets. Their technique—enabling an investor to buy or sell at a fixed price—had strong practical implications for traders and soon evolved into more complex financial instruments such as stock-index options. It was the second year running in which the Nobel Prize, usually associated with obscure economic theories, was related to work that many people could identify with, even if they could not understand it (see AR 1996, pp. 515–6).

2. ECONOMIC AND SOCIAL DATA

The statistical data on the following pages record developments from 1992 to the latest year, usually 1997, for which reasonably stable figures were available at the time of going to press. Year headings 1992 to 1997 are printed only at the head of each page and are not repeated over individual tables unless the sequence is broken by extending series of figures over a longer period than elsewhere on the page.

Pages to which the point is relevant include a comparative price index, allowing the current-price figures to be adjusted in accordance with changing values of money.

Unless figures are stated as indicating the position at the *end* of year, they should be taken as annual *totals* or *averages*, according to context.

Tables 2, 3, 4 and 5. Statistics which are normally reported or collected separately in the three UK home jurisdictions (England and Wales, Scotland, and Northern Ireland) have been consolidated into UK series only to show general trends. As the component returns were made at varying times of year and in accordance with differing definitions and regulatory requirements, the series thus consolidated may therefore be subject to error, may not be strictly comparable from year to year, and may be less reliable than the remainder of the data.

Symbols: — = nil or not applicable; .. = not available at time of compilation.

SOURCES

A. UNITED KINGDOM
GOVERNMENT SOURCES
Annual Abstract of Statistics: Tables 1, 2, 3, 4, 5.
Monthly Digest of Statistics: Tables 1, 11, 17, 18, 23, 24, 25.
Financial Statistics: Tables 9, 11, 12, 13, 14, 15, 16, 26.
Economic Trends: Tables 6, 7, 8, 9, 11, 26.
Social Trends: Tables 2, 3, 4, 5.
Department of Employment Gazette: Tables 19, 20, 21, 22.
Housing and Construction Statistics: Table 5.
UK National Accounts: Tables 8, 10.
ADDITIONAL SOURCES
National Institute of Economic and Social Research, *National Institute Economic Review*: Tables 6, 7, 8.
United Nations, *Monthly Bulletin of Statistics*: Table 1.
Financial Times: Tables 13, 15.

B. UNITED STATES
GOVERNMENT AND OTHER PUBLIC SOURCES
Department of Commerce, *Survey of Current Business*: Tables 27, 28, 29, 30, 31, 32, 37, 38, 40.
Department of Commerce, Bureau of the Census, *US Industrial Outlook*: Table 40.
Council of Economic Advisers, Joint Economic Committee, *Economic Indicators*: Tables 30, 36.
Federal Reserve Bulletin: Tables 33, 34, 35.
ADDITIONAL SOURCES
A. M. Best Co.: Table 35.
Insurance Information Institute, New York: Table 35.
Monthly Labor Review: Tables 38, 39.
Bureau of Economic Statistics, *Basic Economic Statistics*: Table 39.

C. INTERNATIONAL COMPARISONS
EU Commission, *Eurostat*: Table 44.
UN, *Monthly Bulletin of Statistics*: Tables 41, 42.
World Bank, *World Development Report*: Table 41.
IMF, *International Financial Statistics*: Tables 41, 43, 45, 46, 47, 48, 49.
OECD, *Main Economic Indicators*: Table 42.
US Arms Control & Disarmament Agency, *World Military Expenditures and Arms Transfers*: Table 50.
OECD, *Labour Force Statistics*: Table 51.

ECONOMIC AND SOCIAL DATA
2A. UNITED KINGDOM

SOCIAL

1. Population	1992	1993	1994	1995	1996	1997
Population, mid-year est. ('000)	58,006	58,191	58,395	58,606	58,801	..
Crude birth rate (per 1,000 pop.)	13·5	13·1	12·8	12·5	12·5	..
Crude death rate (per 1,000 pop.)	11·0	11·3	10·7	10·9	10·9	..
Net migration ('000)	−11	−2	+54	..	..	..
2. Health						
Hospitals(1):						
Available in-patient beds ('000)	232	219	212	206	..	..
Waiting list, end-March ('000)	918	995	1,065	1,044	1,048	..
Day care admissions ('000)	1,808	2,106	2,474	2,845	..	..
Family health services(1):						
Number of patients per doctor	1,922	1,902	1,900	1,887	1,885	..
Certifications of death ('000)(2) by:						
ischaemic heart disease	145·9	146·3	135·4	133·0	129·7	..
malignant neoplasm, lungs and bronchus	33·7	32·6	32·1	31·5	31·0	..
road fatality	4·1	3·4	3·3	3·2	3·2	..
accidents at work (number)(3)	368	339	296	272	258	..

(1) NHS, England
(2) England and Wales
(3) UK

3. Education						
Schools ('000)	34·3	34·1	33·8	33·6	33·4	..
Pupils enrolled ('000) in schools	9,368	9,513	9,571	9,714	9,813	..
Primary	4,849	4,923	4,998	5,065	5,142	..
Secondary	3,534	3,606	3,588	3,656	3,676	..
Pupils per teacher	17·1	17·3	17·5	17·8	17·9	..
Universities(1)	48	48	88	89	89	..
University students ('000)(2)	402	436	471	1,076	1,107	..
Full-time academic staff (3)	31,861	32,638	33,447	63,006	66,907	..
First degrees awarded(2)	79,637	84,893	89,107	211,841	226,626	..

(1) including former polytechnics from 1994
(2) including former polytechnics from 1994
(3) including former polytechnics from 1994, teaching and senior research staff only

4. Law and Order						
Police ('000)						
Full-time strength(1)	140·9	139·7	139·6	141·3	139·6	..
Ulster, full-time strength	8·2	8·5	8·5	8·4	8·4	..
Serious offences known to police ('000)(2)	6,041·0	5,926·3	5,627·3	5,457·7	5,488·6	..
Persons convicted, all offences ('000)(3)	1,547	1,460	1,442	1,388	1,438	..
Burglary or robbery(3)	50·7	46·7	44·0	44·8	39·1	..
Handling stolen goods/receiving, theft	131·1	124·8	123·0	116·7	117·3	..
Violence against person	45·2	40·6	39·1	30·8	31·6	..
Traffic offences	755	697	672	673	677	..
All summary offences	1,220	1,143	1,119	1,077	1,142	..
Prisons: average population ('000)	52·8	52·1	56·3	58·4	62·6	..

(1) Police full-time strength: Great Britain only. (2) Because of differences in juridical and penal systems in the three UK jurisdictions, totals of offences are not strictly comparable from year to year: they should be read only as indicating broad trends. (3) Specific offences: England, Wales and N. Ireland.

Overall price index (1990=100)	111·1	114·9	116·4	118·8	122·4	125·2

5. Housing

	1992	1993	1994	1995	1996	1997
Dwellings completed ('000)						
Total	172	179	185	189	179	178
by and for public sector(1)	31	38	38	40	30	..
by private sector	141	141	147	149	149	..
Homeless households ('000)(2)	161	167	154	144	..	..
Housing land, private sector, weighted average price (£/hect.)	408,341	334,675	366,276	391,544	..	..
Dwelling prices, average (£)	61,336	61,223	63,077	63,167	70,600	..

(1) Including government departments (police houses, military married quarters, etc.) and approved housing associations and trusts Great Britain. (2) Accepted by local authorities as in priority need. (3) Of properties newly mortgaged by building societies.

PRICES, INCOME AND EXPENDITURE

6. National Income and Expenditure
(£ million, 1990 prices)

	1992	1993	1994	1995	1996	1997
GDP at factor cost	466,456	476,800	498,231	511,935	525,051	541,995
GDP at market prices(1)	598,916	631,003	669,069	704,156	741,751	787,868
Volume index (1990 =100)	97·4	99·6	104·0	106·4	109·6	113·2
Components of gross domestic product:						
Consumers' expenditure	339,652	348,164	357,845	364,046	377,166	393,294
General government consumption	115,732	115,521	118,080	119,578	121,932	..
Gross fixed investment	95,973	96,586	100,778	102,249	104,121	..
Total final expenditure	680,703	703,430	735,682	758,194	785,456	..
Stockbuilding	–1,699	312	2,890	4,119	2,676	..
Adjustment to factor cost	70,992	71,822	74,070	75,977	76,496	..

(1) Current prices, £ '000 million: 'money GDP'

7. Fixed Investment
(£ million, 1990 prices, seasonally adjusted)

	1992	1993	1994	1995	1996	1997
Total, all fixed investment	95,973	96,586	100,778	102,249	104,121	..
Dwellings	18,335	19,661	20,371	20,322	20,106	..
Private sector	77,225	77,268	81,201	84·085	89,388	..
manufacturing	11,828	11,230	11,997	13,181	12,442	..
other	65,397	66,038	69,204	70,904	76,946	..
Government and public corporations	18,748	19,318	19,577	18,164	14,733	..

8. Personal Income and Expenditure
(£ million, seasonally adjusted, current prices unless otherwise stated)

	1992	1993	1994	1995	1996	1997
Wages, salaries and forces' pay	301,449	307,975	318,709	333,558	349,742	..
Current grants	80,052	88,537	92,630	96,168	98,212	..
Other personal income(1)	125,553	132,875	141,248	158,721	170,076	..
Personal disposable income	435,546	459,225	477,231	505,401	534,361	..
Real personal disposable income(2)	385,757	393,256	399,572	412,376	425,335	..
Consumers' expenditure	383,490	406,569	427,394	446,169	473,845	505,488
Personal savings ratio(3)	12·0	11·5	10·4	11·7	11·3	11·1

(1) From rent, self-employment (before depreciation and stock appreciation provisions), dividend and interest receipts and charitable receipts from companies. (2) At 1990 prices. (3) Personal savings as % of personal disposable income.

	1992	1993	1994	1995	1996	1997
Overall price index (1990=100)	111·1	114·9	116·4	118·8	122·4	125·3

XVIII ECONOMIC AND SOCIAL AFFAIRS

	1992	1993	1994	1995	1996	1997
9. Government Finance(1)						
(£ million)						
Revenue(2)	225,523	222,408	230,999	251,615	270,798	284,834
taxes on income	75,963	72,246	73,850	83,778	92,084	97,535
corporation tax	18,263	15,783	14,887	19,390	23,569	27,788
taxes on expenditure	87,977	87,850	91,082	98,041	105,355	110,394
value added tax	35,626	37,206	39,211	41,722	43,054	46,664
taxes on capital(3)	3,067	2,462	2,312	2,647	2,819	3,665
Expenditure(4)	244,174	267,074	281,205	293,319	306,448	313,993
net lending(5)	-7,983	-6,876	-3,893	-5,469	-2,265	-5,254
Deficit(-) or surplus	-18,473	-45,208	-49,980	-42,320	-35,650	-29,159

(1) Financial years ended 5 April of year indicated. (2) Total current receipts, taxes on capital and other capital receipts. (3) Capital gains, capital transfer tax, estate duty. (4) Total government expenditure, gross domestic capital formation and grants. (5) To private sector, public corporations, and overseas.

	1992	1993	1994	1995	1996	1997
10. Public Expenditure						
(£ '000 million, current prices)						
Health	34·9	36·8	38·7	40·9	43·2	..
Social Security	84·7	93·7	98·7	103·6	107·0	..
Education	31·9	33·9	35·7	37·4	39·1	..
Housing	6·1	6·6	5·9	5·7	4·9	..
Defence	24·4	24·6	24·0	22·9	23·0	..
Law and order	13·8	14·4	14·8	15·2	15·5	..
11. Prices and Costs (index 1990=100)						
Total UK costs per unit of output(1)	111·1	114·9	116·4	118·8	122·4	125·3
Labour costs per unit of output	110·5	110·9	110·5	112·1	114·4	..
Mfg. wages/salaries per unit of output	105·5	105·0	104·5	108·4	114·1	117·7
Import unit values	102·1	112·3	116·1	127·7	128·4	..
Wholesale prices, manufactures	109·1	113·1	115·8	120·6	123·8	125·2
Consumer prices	109·8	111·6	114·3	118·2	121·1	124·9

(1) Used as 'Overall price index' on all pages of UK statistics.

FINANCIAL

	1992	1993	1994	1995	1996	1997
12. Monetary Sector(1)						
(£ million, amounts outstanding at end of period)						
Notes and coins in circulation	16,770	17,795	18,749	20,007	20,856	21,995
M₀(2) (average)	19,380	20,507	21,957	23,198	24,816	25,676
M₂(3)	373,243	394,510	409,723	436,568	460,011	481,774
M₄(4)	517,251	543,449	565,724	622,189	682,660	720,722
Deposits						
domestic	397,213	422,680	441,795	528,643	606,119	747,355
overseas	678,208	702,556	752,480	852,956	831,568	1,045,471
Domestic lending						
private sector	483,252	501,725	520,610	603,589	683,496	883,996
public sector	19,481	23,736	28,062	37,249	33,480	33,261
Overseas lending	648,602	683,450	737,254	841,204	831,805	1,033,993

(1) Institutions recognized as banks or licensed deposit-takers, plus Bank of England banking dept. and other institutions adhering to monetary control arrangements. (2) M_0=Notes and coins in circulation plus banks' till money plus bankers' balance with Bank of England. (3) M_2=Notes and coin plus sterling retail deposits with banks and building societies. From 1992, retail deposits and cash in M_4. (4) M_4= Notes and coin plus all sterling deposits held with UK banks and building societies.

Overall price index (1990=100)	111·1	114·9	116·4	118·8	122·4	125·3

13. Interest Rates and Security Yields(1)
(% per annum, end of year)

	1992	1993	1994	1995	1996	1997
Treasury bill yield	6.44	4.95	6.00	6.31	6.26	7.13
Selected retail banks base rate	7.00	5.50	6.25	6.50	6.00	7.25
3 1/2% War Loan, gross flat yield(2)	9.18	7.97	8.03	8.22	8.10	7.12
10-year government securities(2)	8.90	7.53	8.10	8.15	7.85	6.99
Ordinary shares, dividend yield(2)	4.85	3.90	3.76	3.96	3.80	3.46
Interbank 3-month deposits	7.00	5.38	6.63	6.50	6.44	7.63
Instant access acounts medium balance	4.92	3.63	3.92	3.87	2.87	4.46

(1) Gross redemption yields, unless stated otherwise. For building societies see Table 16.
(2) Average during year.

14. Companies
(£ million unless stated)

	1992	1993	1994	1995	1996	1997
Total income	114,429	124,426	144,196	158,311	172,387	..
Gross trading profit in UK	77,560	86,768	100,688	107,976	119,284	..
Total overseas income	14,492	16,237	20.253	22,411	24,202	..
Dividends	28,519	29,377	32,488	42,034	46,835	..
Net profit	42,373	55,909	68,964	65,408	69,618	..
Companies taken over (number)	432	526	674	505	584	482
Total take-over consideration	5,941	7,063	8,268	32,600	30,742	25,141
Company insolvencies (number)(1)	24,424	20,708	16,728	14,536	13,461	12,610
Individual insolvencies (number)(1)	36,794	36,703	30,739	26,319	26,271	24,441

(1) England and Wales.

15. The Stock Market
(£ million unless stated)

	1992	1993	1994	1995	1996	1997
Turnover (£ '000 million)	2,089.0	2,830.1	2,951.9	2,344.2	2,814.5	1,539.3
ordinary shares (£000 mn.)(4)	433.9	564.0	606.0	646.3	748.4	1,012.5
New issues, less redemptions (value)						
Government securities	21,373	51,854	22,612	20,591	31,337	..
Local authority issues(1)	–19	+70	+545	+429	+846	..
UK companies	8,346	16,680	13,496	16,069	13,659	14,765
FT ordinary share index (1935=100)(2)	1,951.9	2,287.9	2,445.2	2,510.4	2,784.1	3,047.6
FT-Actuaries index All-share(3)	1,224.2	1,457.3	1,574.5	1,647.07	1,894.7	2,235.8
FTSE-Actuaries Indices(5)						
Gen. Industrial	1,490.9	1,808.4	2,004.6	1,917.7	2,049.7	2,001.2
Financial	1,429.0	2,065.8	2,253.0	2,448.0	3,038.0	4,300.9

(1) Includes public corporation issues.
(2) Average during year.
(3) 1962=100
(4) From 1990, UK and Irish only
(5) Dec 31 1985=1000.

16. Building Societies

	1992	1993	1994	1995	1996	1997
Interest rates (%): end year:						
Paid on shares, ave. actual	4.72	3.99	4.20	3.93	4.49	6.05
Mortgages, ave. charged	8.98	7.94	7.84	7.48	6.51	7.58
Basic rate	8.98	7.99	8.14	7.98	7.00	8.16
Shares and deposits, net acq. (£ min.)	11,696	10,243	8,499	14,378	11,050	17,601
Net advances, (£ min.)	14,748	11,162	14,372	16,041	17,208	15,031

Overall price index(1990=100)	111.1	114.9	116.4	118.8	122.4	125.3

XVIII ECONOMIC AND SOCIAL AFFAIRS

	1992	1993	1994	1995	1996	1997
17. Industrial Production						
(Index, average 1990=100, seasonally adjusted)						
All industries	96·2	98·3	103·2	105·9	107·9	109·4
Electricity, gas and water	107·4	111·8	113·1	116·7	123·7	126·3
Manufacturing industries	94·0	95·8	99·3	101·5	102·8	104·4
Food, drink and tobacco	100·0	100·1	104·4	106·0	107·3	109·2
Chemicals	105·1	107·7	112·3	117·5	119·4	118·6
Metal manufacture	86·0	84·8	86·7	89·0	89·0	91·1
Engineering and allied	91·2	92·4	98·6	101·3	104·4	108·4
Textiles	89·4	89·4	90·5	89·6	89·2	87·0
Intermediate goods	98·8	101·7	107·5	110·6	111·8	113·0
Consumer durables	89·0	90·5	97·8	101·1	106·0	109·2
Consumer non-durables	97·4	98·6	101·4	103·8	105·5	105·2
Investment goods	90·4	91·6	95·9	99.2	101·1	105·0
Construction, gross output	89·5	87·8	90·6	89·8	90·8	..
Man-made fibres	105·1	108·9	98·5	109·4	112·5	96·8
Crude steel (million tonnes)	16·2	16·6	17·3	17·6	18·0	..
Cars ('000)	1,292	1,375	1,466	1,532	1,686	1,698
Commercial vehicles ('000)	248	193	228	233	238	238

(1) Including imported chassis.

	1992	1993	1994	1995	1996	1997
18. Energy						
Coal, production (mn. tonnes)	84·5	68·2	49·0	53·0	50·2	48·5
Power station consumption (mn. tonnes)	78·5	66·2	62·4	59·6	54·9	47·0
Electricity generated ('000 mn. kwh.)	300·2	300·5	309·1	314·7	327·5	326·1
by nuclear plant ('000 mn. kwh.)	66·3	76·8	76·4	77·6	82·9	86·7
Natural gas production (GWh)	597,854	703,884	750,860	822,724	980,064	1,000,978
Crude oil output ('000 tonnes)(1)	94,200	100,100	119,000	121,800	121,800	120,100
Oil refinery output (mn. tonnes)(2)	75·5	75·8	75·0	73·7	75·4	72·4

(1) Including natural gas liquids.
(2) All fuels and other petroleum products.

LABOUR

	1992	1993	1994	1995	1996	1997
19. Employment						
(millions of persons, in June each year)						
Workforce(1)	28·43	28·28	28·16	28·11	28·18	28·11
Workforce in employment(2)	25·75	25·36	25·52	25·80	26·03	26·51
Employees: production industries	4·42	4·20	4·19	4·26	4·30	4·36
Manufacturing	4·08	3·91	3·92	4·02	4·06	4·11
Transport, storage and communications	1·35	1·32	1·31	1·29	1·28	1·31
Wholesale and retail trades	3·58	3·56	3·63	3·62	3·68	3·84
Education, health and social work	4·29	4·28	4·31	4·22	4·25	4·29
Financial intermediation	1·01	0·98	0·96	0·98	0·96	1·01
Public administration	1·46	1·43	1·38	1·35	1·33	1·30
Total employees	21·36	21·04	21·10	21·41	21·76	22·21
of whom, females	10·41	10·37	10·44	10·58	10·85	10·99

(1) Including claimant unemployed and employed workforce.
(2) Comprises employees in employment, the self-employed, the armed forces and those on work-related government training schemes.

	1992	1993	1994	1995	1996	1997
Overall price index (1990=100)	111·1	114·9	116·4	118·8	122·4	125·3

XVIII.2A. UNITED KINGDOM STATISTICS

	1992	1993	1994	1995	1996	1997
20. Demand for Labour						
Average weekly hours worked, manufacturing industry, April	41·5	41·3	41·7	42·2	41·9	42·0
Manufacturing employees:						
Total overtime hours worked ('000)(1)	9,630	9,460	8,420	8,480	..	..
Short time, total hours lost ('000)(1)	800	597	235	216	..	..
Unemployment, claimants over 18 (monthly ave. '000)(2)	2,765·0	2,900·6	2,619·4	2,308·2	2,104·2	1,582·8
Percentage of workforce	9·7	10·3	9·4	8·2	7·5	5·6
Unfilled vacancies, average ('000)	117·1	126·6	155·4	181·2	225·1	283·0
Work-related training programmes ('000)	325	311	302	225	181	167

(1) Great Britain. (2) Seasonally adjusted.

	1992	1993	1994	1995	1996	1997
21. Industrial Disputes						
Stoppages (number)(1)(2)	240	203	203	231	..	..
Workers involved ('000)(3)	142	383	107	170	353	129
Work days lost ('000), all inds., services	528	649	279	415	1303	230

(1) Excluding protest action of a political nature, and stoppages involving fewer than 10 workers and/or lasting less than one day except where the working days lost exceeded 100.
(2) Stoppages beginning in year stated.
(3) Directly and indirectly, where stoppages occurred; lay-offs elsewhere in consequence are excluded.

	1992	1993	1994	1995	1996	1997
22. Wages and Earnings						
Average earnings index (1990=100)						
Whole economy	114·8	118·5	123·2	127·4	132·3	138·1
Manufacturing	115·3	120·5	126·2	131·9	137·8	143·8
Average weekly earnings(1)(2)						
Men						
Manual	250·7	256·4	280·7	291·3	301·3	314·3
Non-manual	353·4	365·9	428·2	443·3	464·5	483·5
All occupations	295·9	304·6	362·1	374·6	391·6	408·7
Women						
Manual	156·6	162·2	181·9	188·1	195·2	201·1
Non-manual	227·6	238·4	278·4	288·1	302·4	317·8
All occupations	211·3	221·6	261·5	269·8	283·0	297·2
Average hours(3)	39·9	39·8	40·1	40·3	40·2	40·3

(1) In all industries and services, full time, GB.
(2) April.
(3) All industries and services, all occupations, men and women over 18 years.

	1992	1993	1994	1995	1996	1997
23. Productivity						
(Index of output per head 1990=100)						
All production industries(1)	111·8	119·3	127·1	129·4	129·9	131·5
Manufacturing	109·4	114·9	120·8	121·8	120·7	122·2
Food, drink and tobacco	107·1	110·1	116·4	118·6	121·4	123·8
Metal manufacture	102·0	106·8	109·4	110·1	107·4	109·3
Engineering	109·4	120·8	133·2	133·3	132·0	136·5
Textiles	108·6	109·8	110·4	109·8	109·5	105·9
Chemicals	120·2	128·1	142·4	149·2	156·5	160·5

(1) Excluding extraction of mineral oil and natural gas.

	1992	1993	1994	1995	1996	1997
Overall price index (1990=100)	111·1	114·9	116·4	118·8	122·4	125·3

TRADE

24. Trade by Areas and Main Trading Partners

(£ million; exports fob; imports cif)	1992	1993	1994	1995	1996	1997
All countries: *exports*	107,407	120,862	135,180	153,050	166,921	170,145
All countries: *imports*	124,998	138,369	149,896	167,243	179,578	183,124
European Union: *exports*	60,703	63,830	77,090	88,348	97,442	94,532
European Union: *imports*	65,609	68,913	83,492	92,104	101,846	99,595
Other Western Europe: *exports*	8,547	10,224	5,691	6,399	7,382	7,993
Other Western Europe: *imports*	14,512	16,296	9,548	10,686	11,828	11,342
North America: *exports*	13,971	17,384	19,437	20,574	22,437	23,948
North America: *imports*	15,718	18,297	19,891	23,048	25,745	28,067
Other OECD countries: *exports*(1)	3,991	4,699	5,454	6,456	10,922	10,770
Other OECD countries: *imports*(1)	8,970	10,064	10,591	11,428	14,355	15,171
Oil exporting countries: *exports*	6,014	6,526	5,660	6,330	8,095	9,786
Oil exporting countries: *imports*	3,078	3,801	3,196	3,252	3,750	3,971
Other countries: *exports*	12,477	15,875	18,724	20,686	22,662	23,896
Other countries: *imports*	15,465	18,710	19,946	22,974	28,212	29,016
E. Eur. & former USSR: *exports*(1)	1,704	2,324	2,823	3,759	2,275	2,679
E. Eur. & former USSR: *imports*(1)	1,646	2,288	2,831	3,377	2,535	2,776
Balance of trade in manufactures	–7,089	–8,183	–7,804	–8,020	–8,088	–8,220

(1) Revised definition: from 1996, Poland and Czech Republic in OECD.

25. Terms of Trade
(Index 1990=100)

	1992	1993	1994	1995	1996	1997
Volume of exports(1)	103·7	106·9	118·5	126·7	136·8	147·7
manufactures	104·0	107·0	117·0	127·0	139·0	151·0
Volume of imports(1)	100·9	104·8	109·2	113·8	124·5	135·6
Unit value of exports(1)	103·5	116·2	118·6	126·4	128·4	122·2
manufactures	104·0	117·0	120·0	129·0	129·0	123·0
Unit value of imports(1)	102·1	112·3	116·1	127·7	128·4	120·4
Terms of trade(2)	101·4	103·5	102·2	99·0	100·0	101·5

(1) Volume: seasonally adjusted; value: unadjusted. Balance of Payments basis.
(2) Export unit value index as percentage of import value index, expressed as an index on the same base.

26. Balance of Payments
(£ million: current transactions seasonally adjusted; remaining data unadjusted)

	1992	1993	1994	1995	1996	1997
Exports (f.o.b.)	107,343	121,409	134,666	153,077	166,921	170,145
Imports (f.o.b.)	120,447	134,787	145,497	164,659	179,578	183,124
Visible balance	–13,104	–13,460	–10,831	–11,628	–12,657	–12,979
Invisible balance	+4,950	+5,516	+4,747	+6,877	+6,970	+9,480
Current balance	–10,133	–10,756	–2,419	–3,872	–1,866	..
Direct investment overseas	–10,850	–17,737	–21,982	–27,927	–28,560	..
Portfolio investment overseas	–27,346	–84,144	+18,448	–38,115	–60,691	..
Bank lending abroad	–26,833	+3,187	–48,179	–26,871	–63,326	..
Direct investment in UK	+9,184	+10,298	+6,087	+14,325	+20,758	..
Portfolio investment in UK	+24,616	+45,542	+32,928	+19,453	+27,701	..
UK overseas bank borrowing	21,208	+23,110	+47,383	+36,546	+74,725	..
Net change in assets/liabilities	+4,986	+11,827	–3,374	+1,680	–2,198	..
Balancing item	+5,157	–1,532	+5,029	+1,992	+2,633	..
Official reserves, end of year	27,494	29,043	28,059	31,361	27,329	22,849
Overall price index (1990=100)	111·1	114·9	116·4	118·8	122·4	125·3

2B. UNITED STATES

27. Population	1992	1993	1994	1995	1996	1997
Population, mid-year est. (mn)	255·4	258·1	260·6	262·8	267·6	268·9
Crude birth rate (per 1,000 pop.)	15·9	15·6	15·0	14·8	14·8	..
Crude death rate (per 1,000 pop.)	8·5	8·8	8·8	8·8	8·7	..

28. Gross Domestic Product
($000 million current)

	1992	1993	1994	1995	1996	1997
Gross domestic product	6,038	6,343	6,931	7,254	7,636	8,081
Personal consumption	4,140	4,391	4,699	4,925	5,208	5,488
Gross private domestic investment	796	882	1,014	1,065	1,116	1,241
Net exports, goods and services	−30	−65	−96	−95	−95	−101
Government purchases	1,132	1,148	1,315	1,358	1,407	1,453

29. Government Finance
($000 million, seasonally adjusted)

	1992	1993	1994	1995	1996	1997
Federal government receipts	1,198	1,275	1,377	1,463	1,588	..
from personal taxes(1)	486	518	566	606	687	..
Federal government expenditure	1,479	1,530	1,567	1,638	1,698	..
Defence purchases	319	315	311	323	318	..
Grants to state/local govts.	168	180	196	212	218	..
Federal surplus or (−) deficit	−281	−255	−190	−174	−110	..
State and local govt. receipts	844	897	946	999	1,043	..
from indirect business tax(1)	424	452	480	489	509	..

(1) Includes related non-tax receipts on national income account.

30. Balance of Payments
($ million)

	1992	1993	1994	1995	1996	1997
Merchandise trade balance	−74,068	−96,097	−132,575	−173,424	−191,170	−198,934
Balance on current account(1)	−6,952	−67,886	−103,896	−148,154	−148,184	−166,446
Change in US private assets abroad(2)	63,759	146,213	130,875	307,856	358,422	426,105
Change in foreign private assets in US(2)	105,646	159,017	251,956	424,462	425,201	672,340

(1) Includes balance on services and remittances and US government grants other than military.
(2) Includes reinvested earnings of incorporated affiliates.

31. Merchandise Trade by Main Areas
($ million)

	1992	1993	1994	1995	1996	1997
All countries: *exports* (f.o.b.)	440,138	456,866	502,48 5	575,900	612,069	678,348
All countries: *imports* (f.o.b.)	536,276	589,441	668,58 4	749,347	803,239	877,282
Western Europe: *exports*	114,454	111,257	115,362	134,764	141,543	155,416
Western Europe: *imports*	111,287	120,947	132,925	145,409	157,601	172,916
Canada: *exports*	91,146	101,194	114,869	126,962	134,210	151,451
Canada: *imports*	100,871	113,310	131,115	145,119	155,893	168,051
Latin America						
exports	75,379	78,198	92,031	99,385	109,391	134,412
imports	69,179	75,173	88,526	106,238	123,844	139,496
Japan: *exports*	46,874	46,684	51,817	64,298	67,607	65,673
Japan: *imports*	97,387	107,228	119,135	123,577	115,187	121,359

| *Dollar purchasing power (1982–84=100)* | 71·3 | 69·2 | 67·5 | 65·6 | 63·7 | 62·3 |

XVIII ECONOMIC AND SOCIAL AFFAIRS

32. Merchandise Trade by Main Commodity Groups

($ million)	1992	1993	1994	1995	1996	1997
Exports:						
Food, feed and beverages	40,300	40,700	41,949	50,476	55,534	51,372
Industrial supplies, inc. energy	109,600	111,900	121,403	146,104	146,652	158,025
Capital goods	176,100	182,200	205,184	233,034	252,895	294,117
Automotive	47,000	52,400	57,614	60,555	65,021	73,390
Consumer goods	51,400	54,700	59,981	64,459	70,138	77,418
Imports:						
Food, feed and beverages	27,600	27,900	30,958	33,179	35,710	39,704
Industrial supplies, inc. energy	140,600	157,400	162,031	180,753	204,482	213,788
Capital goods	134,300	152,400	184,424	221,603	229,050	254,168
Automotive	91,800	102,400	118,271	124,484	128,938	140,720
Consumer goods	122,900	134,000	146,300	160,004	171,007	192,946

33. Interest Rates
(per cent per annum, annual averages, unless otherwise stated)

Federal Funds rate(1)		3·52	3·02	4·21	5·83	5·30	5·30
Treasury bill rate		3·43	3·02	4·25	5·51	5·02	5·07
Government bond yields: 3–5 years		5·30	4·44	6·27	6·25	5·99	6·10
Long-term (10 years or more)		7·52	6·45	7·41	6·93	6·80	6·67
Banks' prime lending rate(2)		6·25	6·00	7·15	8·83	8·27	8·44

(1) Effective rate.
(2) Predominant rate charged by commercial banks on short-term loans to large business borrowers with the highest credit rating.

34. Banking, money and credit
($000 million, outstanding at end of year, seasonally adjusted)

Money supply M1(1)	1,024·4	1,129·9	1,150·7	1,128·7	1,082·8	1,076·0
Money supply M2(2)	3,434·7	3,487·5	3,503·0	3,651·2	3,826·1	4,040·2
Money supply M3(3)	4,193·5	4,258·9	4,333·6	4,595·6	4,935·5	5,375·7
Currency	292·9	322·4	354·3	372·4	394·9	425·4
Demand deposits of commercial banks	339·1	384·0	384·3	391·0	403·6	397·1
Consumer credit	779·9	838·6	959·8	1,094·2	1,179·9	1,234·6
Motor vehicle contracts	262·7	288·0	328·9	364·2	392·4	415·3
Mortgage debt	4,094	4,269	4,462	4,692	5,022	..

(1) Currency plus demand deposits, travellers cheques, other checkable deposits.
(2) M1 plus overnight repurchase agreements, eurodollars, money market mutual fund shares, savings and small time deposits.
(3) M2 plus large time deposits and term repurchase agreements.

35. Insurance
($ billion, unless otherwise stated)

Property-liability, net premiums written	223·0	227·5	241·6	250·6	268·6	277·3
Automobile(1)	82·8	88·4	109·7	113·5	..	..
Underwriting gain/loss(2)	−19·4	−35·9	−17·8	−22·2	−16·7	−5·7
Net investment income(3)	34·2	33·7	32·6	33·7	38·0	41·3
Combined net income(3)	+14·8	−2·2	+14·8	+11·5	+21·3	+35·6
Rate of return, %(3)(4)	8·9	4·4	10·6	5·6	9·5	11·7
Life insurance, total assets, end-year	1,408·2	1,551·2	1,664·5	1,789·3	1,914·6	–

(1) Physical damage and liability, private and commercial. (2) After stockholder and policy-holder dividends and premium rebates. (3) Property, casualty. (4) Net income after taxes, divided by year-end policyholders' surplus.

Dollar purchasing power (1982–84=100)	71·3	69·2	67·5	65·6	63·7	62·3

36. Companies ($000 million)	1992	1993	1994	1995	1996	1997
Corporate profits(1)	428·0	492·8	570·5	650·0	735·9	..
Dividends	169·5	195·8	216·2	264·4	304·8	..

(1)With inventory valuation and capital consumption adjustments. adjustment.

37. The Stock Market
($ million, unless otherwise stated)

	1992	1993	1994	1995	1996	1997
Volume of trading in shares ('000)						
New York Stock Exchange	202,558	263,374	290,652	345,729	409,740	..
American Stock Exchange	14,171	18,188	17,951	20,387	22,567	..
Stock prices (end-year):						
Combined index (500 stocks)(1)	435·71	466·45	459·27	615·93	753·85	962·37
Industrials (30 stocks)(2)	3,301·11	3,754·09	3,834·44	5,117·12	6,549·37	7,909·82

(1) Standard and Poor Composite 1941–43=10. (2) Dow-Jones Industrial (Oct. 1928=100).

38. Employment
('000 persons)

	1992	1993	1994	1995	1996	1997
Civilian labour force(1)	126,982	128,040	131,056	132,304	133,943	136,297
in non-agricultural industry	114,391	116,232	119,651	121,460	123,264	126,159
in manufacturing industry	18,040	18,075	18,303	18,468	18,457	18,537
in agriculture	3,207	3,074	3,409	3,440	3,443	3,399
unemployed	9,384	8,734	7,996	7,404	7,236	6,739
Industrial stoppages(2) (number)	40	35	35	31	37	..
Workers involved ('000)	392	364	182	192	273	..

(1) Aged 16 years and over. (2) Beginning in the year & involving 1,000 workers or more.

39. Earnings and Prices

	1992	1993	1994	1995	1996	1997
Average weekly earnings per worker						
(current dollars): mining	638·31	646·78	666·628	683·91	707·13	732·30
contract construction	537·70	553·63	573·00	587·00	602·94	622·40
manufacturing	469·86	486·04	506·94	514·59	531·65	553·14
Average weekly hours per worker						
in manufacturing	41·0	41·4	42·0	41·6	41·6	42·0
Farm prices received (1990–92=100)	98·0	101·0	100·0	102·0	112·0	107·0
Wholesale prices (1982=100)	123·2	124·7	125·5	127·9	131·3	131·8
Fuels	84·0	87·1	82·4	72·1	92·6	100·4
Consumer prices (1982–4=100)	140·3	144·5	148·2	152·4	156·9	160·5
Food	137·9	140·9	144·3	148·4	153·3	157·3
Dollar purchasing power (1982–84=100)(1)	71·3	69·2	67·5	65·6	63·7	62·3

(1) Based on changes in retail price indexes.

40. Production

	1992	1993	1994	1995	1996	1997
Farm production (1992=100)	100·0	94·0	105·0	..	..	..
Industrial production (1992=100)	100·0	103·6	109·2	114·5	118·5	124·5
Manufacturing	100·0	103·8	110·0	116·0	120·2	127·0
Output of main products and manufacturers						
Coal (million tons)	1,015·0	992·4	1,033·5	1,032·9	1,063·9	1,094·8
Oil, indigenous (000 barrels/day)	7,199	6,870	6,662	6,560	6,465	6,411
Oil refinery throughput (000 barrels/day)	15,230	15,150	15,670	15,770	15,929	16,754
Natural gas ('000 mn. cu. ft.)	17,780	18,410	18,747	18,599	18,793	19,030
Electricity generated ('000 mn. kwh)	2,757	2,865	2,920	2,994	3,077	2,858
Steel, crude (million tons)	92·9	97·9	100·6	104·9	105·3	..
Aluminium ('000 tonnes)	4,121	4,042	3,700	3,750	3,577	..
Textile mill products (1992=100)	100·0	105·2	110·6	109·9	106·7	109·8
Chemicals (1992=100)	100·0	101·4	104·7	107·5	110·5	115.1
Motor vehicles and parts (1992=100)	100·0	113·6	129·8	131·0	130·2	136·9

2C. INTERNATIONAL COMPARISONS

41. Population and GDP, Selected countries	Area '000 sq. km.	Population (millions) mid-year estimate 1995	1996	Gross Domestic Product(1) US $ millions(2) 1995	1996
Argentina	2,767	34·77	35·22	279,522	297,460
Australia(3)	7,687	18·05	18·26	348,779	391,098
Belgium	31	10·14	..	269,199	268,249
Canada	9,976	29·61	29·96	565,651	601,628
China	9,561	1,221·5	..	697,620	..
Denmark	43	5·23	5·26	173,290	182,859
France	552	58·03	58·37	1,538,856	1,539,322
Germany(4)	357	81·64	81·91	2,414,067	2,352,472
India (incl. India-admin. Kashmir)	3,287	935·7	..	338,786	..
Irish Republic	70	3·58	..	61,932	67,392
Israel (excl. occupied areas)	22	5·54	..	86,711	..
Italy	301	57·19	57·40	1,087,237	1,214,272
Japan	378	125·50	125·76	5,006,173	4,599,706
Kuwait(5)	18	1·69	..	26,646	30,985
Netherlands	34	15·45	15·52	378,900	392,550
New Zealand(5)	270	3·54	3·57	59,762	65,883
Norway	324	4·36	4·38	146,147	157,802
Portugal	92	9·90	..	103,176	107,132
Saudi Arabia	2,200	17·88	..	125,266	..
South Africa	1,220	41·24	..	133,650	126,238
Spain	505	39·19	39·27	559,620	580,862
Sweden	450	8·83	8·84	229,179	250,223
Switzerland	41	7·04	7·07	303,932	294,336
Turkey	781	61·64	62·69	172,887	175,911
UK	244	58·60	58·80	1,101,662	1,159,250
USA	9,372	262·80	267·60	7,253,800	7,636,000

(1) Expenditure basis. (2) Converted from national currencies at average exchange rates. (3) Years beginning 1 July. (4) Combines East and West Germany. (5) Years beginning 1 April.

42. World Production (Index 1980=100)	1992	1993	1994	1995	1996	1997
Food(1)	126·5	128·8	129·0	132·3	137·7	..
Industrial production(2)	123·0	123·5	130·0	135·3	139·8	
Crude petroleum, nat. gas	95·9	99·5	103·8	105·4	107·8	
Manufacturing	125·9	125·8	133·1	139.1	143·8	
Chemicals	136·6	138·0	145·2	150·4	155·1	
Paper, printing, publishing	137·5	140·4	144·8	147·0	149·9	
Textiles	100·0	99·0	101·4	100·2	98·9	
Developed countries(3)	119·9	119·1	125·7	130·7	134·6	..
European Union	112·8	109·2	114·8	118·4	120·6	..
Developing market economies(4)	166·2	173·7	182·6	192·8	203·4	..
Caribbean, C. & S. America	113·9	116·6	122·9	121·8	123·5	..
Asia(5)	252·9	268·7	282·2	310·4	334·7	..
France(6)	97·6	93·9	97·4	99·0	99·8	..
Germany	101·8	95·6	99·7	101·3	101·0	..
Italy	98·9	96·5	101·5	107·0	105·2	..
UK	96·2	98·3	103·2	105·9	107·9	109·4
Japan	98·6	91·2	91·8	94·9	97·7	..
Sweden	93·4	94·4	104·2	113·7	116·6	..

(1) Excluding China. (2) Excluding former USSR and Yugoslavia. (3) N. America, Europe (excluding former Czechoslovakia and the European countries of former USSR), Australia, Israel, Japan, N. Zealand and S. Africa. (4) Manufacturing. (5) Excluding Japan and Israel. (6) Individual industrial countries 1990=100.

43. World Trade

($million. Exports f.o.b., imports c.i.f.)

	1992	1993	1994	1995	1996	1997
World(1): exports	3,755,000	3,743,000	4,230,000	5,033,000	5,264,300	..
World(1): imports	3,875,000	3,848,000	4,349,000	5,170,000	5,351,800	..
Western Europe: exports	1,718,495	1,593,170	1,803,070	2,190,700	2,221,260	..
Western Europe: imports	1,789,425	1,608,795	1,799,400	2,185,860	2,107,812	..
USA: exports	448,164	464,773	512,521	583,862	625,073	..
USA: imports	553,923	603,438	689,215	771,272	822,025	..
Germany: exports	422,271	380,154	427,100	508,508	288,468	..
Germany: imports	402,441	348,631	381,589	443,224	277,673	..
Japan: exports	339,885	362,244	397,005	443,125	410,901	..
Japan: imports	233,246	241,624	275,235	335,975	349,152	..
France: exports	235,871	210,319	234,781	286,168	288,468	..
France: imports	239,638	203,272	228,759	274,473	277,673	..
UK: exports	190,003	181,645	205,021	242,067	260,746	..
UK: imports	221,551	206,380	227,229	265,275	285,997	..
European Union: exports	1,538,650	1,468,144	1,664,023	2,027,528	2,094,209	..
European Union: imports	1,653,503	1,477,554	1,661,418	2,012,275	1,995,653	..
Australia, NZ, S. Afr: exports	76,071	77,521	85,084	94,526	104,231	..
Australia, NZ, S. Afr: imports	72,770	75,230	88,725	105,799	110,278	..
Central and E. Europe, CIS: exports	138,740	141,360	181,590	232,630	246,660	..
Central and E.Europe, CIS: imports	151,960	163,850	189,130	249,770	284,620	..
Latin America: exports	129,660	134,570	155,340	191,410	213,510	..
Latin America: imports	157,810	170,030	198,430	220,300	244,270	..
Middle East: exports	145,760	137,940	139,120	156,360	..	..
Middle East: imports	136,930	129,650	128,860	146,060	153,930	..
Asia: exports	585,540	646,290	768,110	931,860	972,600	..
Asia: imports	609,930	685,640	802,720	986,470	1,035,410	..
Africa: exports	84,630	86,020	88,930	102,920	..	..
Africa: imports	83,540	79,840	84,290	102,920	100,310	..

(1) IMF members.

	1992	1993	1994	1995	1996	1997
Unit value index of world exports (US$) (1990=100)	101·2	97·2	99·4	107·5	106·0	100·5

44. European Union Members' Performance on Maastricht EMU Criteria

	Budget deficit(1) % of GDP (3% ceiling)					Government Debt % of GDP (60% ceiling)				
	1993	1994	1995	1996	1997	1993	1994	1995	1996	1997
Belgium	7·5	5·1	4·1	3·3	2·1	137·0	135·0	133·7	130·6	122·2
Germany	3·5	2·4	3·5	4·0	2·7	48·2	50·4	58·1	60·8	65·1
Greece	14·2	12·1	9·1	7·9	4·0	11·8	110·4	111·8	110·6	61·3
Spain	6·8	6·3	6·6	4·4	2·6	60·5	63·1	65·7	67·8	108·7
France	5·6	5·6	4·8	4·0	3·0	45·6	48·4	52·8	56·4	68·8
Ireland	2·4	1·7	2·0	1·6	−0·9	94·5	87·9	81·6	74·7	58·0
Italy	9·6	9·0	7·1	6·6	2·7	119·3	125·5	124·9	123·4	66·3
Luxembourg	−1·7	−2·6	−1·5	−0·9	−1·7	6·2	5·7	6·0	7·8	121·6
Netherlands	3·2	3·4	4·0	2·6	1·4	80·8	77·4	79·7	78·7	6·7
Austria	4·2	4·4	5·9	4·3	2·5	62·8	65·1	69·0	71·7	72·1
Portugal	6·9	5·8	5·1	4·0	2·5	68·2	69·6	71·7	71·1	66·1
Finland	8·0	6·2	5·2	3·3	0·9	57·3	59·5	59·2	61·3	62·0
Sweden	12·3	10·8	8·1	3·9	0·8	76·0	79·3	78·7	78·1	55·8
Denmark	3·9	3·5	1·6	1·4	−0·7	80·1	76·0	71·9	70·2	76·6
UK	7·8	6·8	5·8	4·6	1·9	48·5	50·4	54·1	56·3	53·4

(1) Minus sign indicates budget surplus.

XVIII ECONOMIC AND SOCIAL AFFAIRS

45. Prices of Selected Commodities (Index 1990=100)	1992	1993	1994	1995	1996	1997
Aluminium, All origins (London)	76.6	69.5	90.0	110.1	91.9	97.5
Beef, Australia-N Z	95.8	102.1	91.0	74.4	69.6	72.4
Copper (London)	85.9	72.0	86.6	110.2	86.2	85.5
Cotton, Egyptian (L'pool)	70.2	70.3	96.6	119.1	97.6	96.0
Gold (London)	89.5	93.8	100.2	100.2	101.1	86.3
Newsprint (New York)	91.8	93.7	97.4	135.4	133.4	112.1
Rice, Thai (Bangkok)	98.0	87.7	99.6	118.5	124.9	111.8
Rubber, Malay (Singapore)	99.6	96.1	130.2	182.8	162.1	117.7
Soya Beans, US (R'dam)	95.4	103.4	102.5	105.1	123.4	119.7
Sugar, fob (Caribbean)	72.5	80.1	96.8	106.1	95.6	91.1
Tin, spot (London)	100.3	84.9	89.7	101.8	101.2	92.7
Wheat (US Gulf Ports)	111.5	103.5	110.5	130.6	152.8	117.8
Wool, greasy (Sydney)	67.7	53.8	72.4	88.8	72.9	..

46. Consumer Prices, Selected Countries (Index 1990=100)	1992	1993	1994	1995	1996	1997
Argentina	339	375	391	404	405	..
Australia	104.2	106.1	108.1	113.1	..	..
France	105.7	107.9	109.7	111.7	113.9	115.1
Germany	108.9	113.7	116.8	119.0	120.7	122.9
India	127.0	136.4	150.8	164.9	..	..
Japan	105.1	106.4	107.2	107.1	107.2	109.0
South Africa	131.3	146.0	157.0	170.5	183.2	..
Sweden	112.0	117.0	120.0	123.0	123.0	123.6
UK	109.8	111.6	114.3	118.2	121.1	124.4
US	107.4	110.6	113.4	116.6	120.0	122.4
Unit value index of world exports (US$) (1990=100)	101.2	97.2	99.4	107.5	106.0	100.5

47. Industrial Ordinary Share Prices (Index 1990=100) average	1992	1993	1994	1995	1996	1997
Amsterdam	107.0	125.4	152.1	162.1	204.1	..
Australia, all exchanges	105.0	120.9	138.1	136.2	152.0	170.7
Canada, all exchanges	99.5	114.1	125.2	129.6	153.9	,,
Germany, all exchanges	87.3	93.6	106.1	103.3	117.9	161.5
Hong Kong (31 July 1968=100)(1)	5,512	11,888	8,191	10,073	13,481	10,723.
Johannesburg	149.0	162.0	224.3	244.3	283.2	..
New York	125.5	132.3	138.0	164.1	203.1	261.5
Paris	102.3	112.6	112.5	102.5	115.9	152.7
Tokyo	62.6	69.9	73.3	63.3	73.6	63.9
UK	114.7	131.7	141.5	147.3	166.9	196.9

(1) Hang Seng index for Hong Kong Stock Exchange only: last trading day of year.

48. Central Bank Discount Rates (per cent per annum, end of year)	1992	1993	1994	1995	1996	1997
Canada	7.36	4.11	7.43	5.79	3.25	4.50
France	9.56	7.60	5.44	4.96	3.18	..
Germany	8.25	5.75	4.50	3.00	2.50	2.50
Italy	12.00	8.00	7.50	9.00	7.50	..
Japan	3.25	1.75	1.75	0.50	0.50	0.50
Sweden	10.00	5.00	7.00	7.00	3.50	..
Switzerland	6.00	4.00	3.50	1.50	1.00	1.00
UK	7.00	5.50	6.25	6.50	6.00	7.25
USA	3.00	3.00	4.75	5.25	5.00	5.00

49. Exchange Rates
(Middle rates at end of year)

	Currency units per US dollar (US$)					per £ (£)	
	1993	1994	1995	1996	1997	1996	1997
Australia (Australian dollar)	1·4733	1·2892	1·3443	1·2554	1·5321	2·1317	2·5338
Belgium-Luxembourg (franc)	38·15	31·83	29·43	32·01	36·92	54·34	61·06
Canada (Canadian dollar)	1·3239	1·4026	1·3639	1·3696	1·9282	2·3256	3·1888
China (yuan)	5·8000	8·4462	8·5812	8·2982	8·2798	14·0903	13·6931
France (franc)	5·9044	5·3367	4·8905	5·2450	5·9881	8·8725	9·9031
Germany (Deutschmark)	1·7365	1·5500	1·4313	1·5552	1·7921	2·6308	2·9638
Italy (lire)	1,712·0	1,622·3	1,586·4	1,529·8	1,759	2,587·8	2,909
Japan (yen)	111·61	99·77	103·16	115·43	129·95	195·26	214·91
Netherlands (guilder)	1·9422	1·7353	1·6031	1·7453	2·0172	2·9524	3·3360
Portugal (escudo)	176·7	159·20	149·39	156·57	183.33	264·85	303·2
South Africa (rand)	3·3977	3·5442	3·6455	4·6775	4·8675	7·9125	8·0499
Spain (peseta)	142·93	131·63	121·32	131·02	151·70	221·63	250·8
Sweden (krona)	8·3352	7·4340	6.6274	6·8615	7·8770	11·6069	13·027
Switzerland (franc)	1·4850	1·3086	1·1507	1·3489	1·4553	2·2818	2·4068
UK (£)(1)	1·4795	1·5645	1·5526	1·6916	1·6538	—	—
SDR	1·3736	1·4599	1·4865	1·4380	1·3493	1·1808	1·2257
ECU	1·1200	1·2300	1·3142	1·2530	1·1042	1·3564	1·5011

US$ per £.

50. Defence Expenditure

Military Expenditure (US$m)

	1992	1993	1994	1995	$ per(1) capita 1995	% of GDP 1995
France	46,760	47,390	48,960	47,770	826	3·1
Germany	45,800	42,750	41,020	41,160	496	1·9
Greece	4,539	4,621	4,811	5,056	482	5·5
Iran	5,029	6,041	5,449	4,191	65	2·6
Israel	7,735	7,452	8,171	8,734	1,646	9·8
Japan	46,030	47,760	49,300	50,240	401	1·0
Russia	159,200	125,000	93,000	76,000	513	11·4
Saudi Arabia	35,010	20,480	17,200	17,210	919	13·5
South Africa	3,281	3,537	3,015	2,895	71	2·2
Sweden	5,207	5,673	5,832	6,042	683	2·8
Turkey	5,437	6,111	6,168	6,606	108	4·0
UK	36,580	36,050	35,440	33,400	572	3·0
USA	305,100	297,600	288,100	277,800	1,056	3·8

51. Employment and Unemployment

Civilian Employment ('000)	1992	1993	1994	1995	1996	1997
USA	117,598	119,806	123,060	124,900	126,708	..
Japan	64,340	64,500	64,530	64,566	64,859	..
Germany(1)	26,694	36,026	35,885	35,777	35,360	..
France	22,008	21,777	21,734	21,936	21,925	..
UK	25,405	25,384	25,835	26,031	26,526	..
Unemployment (%)						
OECD	7·4	7·8	7·9	7·5	7·6	7·1
European Union	9·1	10·6	11·6	11·4	11·1	10·8
USA	7·5	6·9	6·1	5·6	5·4	5·0
Japan	2·2	2·5	2·9	3·1	3·3	3·4
UK	10·1	10·5	9·6	8·2	7·5	5·7

(1)From 1993, united Germany.

XIX DOCUMENTS AND REFERENCE

1. NATO-RUSSIA FOUNDING ACT

Printed below is the substantive text of the Founding Act on Mutual Relations, Cooperation and Security between the North Atlantic Treaty Organization and the Russian Federation, signed in Paris on 27 May 1997. (Text supplied by NATO Secretariat, Brussels.)

I. PRINCIPLES

Proceeding from the principle that the security of all states in the Euro-Atlantic community is indivisible, Russia and NATO will work together to contribute to the establishment in Europe of common and comprehensive security based on the allegiance to shared values, commitments and norms of behavior in the interests of all states.

Russia and NATO will help to strengthen the OSCE, including developing further its role as a primary instrument in preventive diplomacy, conflict prevention, crisis management, post-conflict rehabilitation and regional security cooperation, as well as in enhancing its operational capabilities to carry out these tasks. The OSCE, as the only pan-European security organization, has a key role in European peace and stability. In strengthening the OSCE, Russia and NATO will cooperate to prevent any possibility of returning to a Europe of division and confrontation, or the isolation of any state.

Consistent with the OSCE's work on a Common and Comprehensive Security Model for Europe for the 21st Century, and taking into account the decisions of the Lisbon summit concerning a charter on European security, Russia and NATO will seek the widest possible cooperation among participating states of the OSCE with the aim of creating in Europe a common space of security and stability, without dividing lines and spheres of influence limiting the sovereignty of any state.

Russia and NATO start from the premise that the shared objective of strengthening security and stability in the Euro-Atlantic area for the benefit of all countries requires a response to new risks and challenges, such as aggressive nationalism, proliferation of nuclear, biological and chemical weapons, terrorism, persistent abuse of human rights and of the rights of persons belonging to national minorities and unresolved territorial disputes, which pose a threat to common peace, prosperity and stability.

This Act does not affect, and cannot be regarded as affecting, the primary responsibility of the UN Security Council for maintaining international peace and security, or the role of the OSCE as the inclusive and comprehensive organization for consultation, decision-making and cooperation in its area and as a regional arrangement under Chapter VIII of the UN Charter.

In implementing the provisions in this Act, Russia and NATO will observe in good faith their obligations under international law and international instruments, including the obligations of the UN Charter and the provisions of the Universal Declaration on Human Rights as well as their commitments under the Helsinki Final Act and subsequent OSCE documents, including the Charter of Paris and the documents adopted at the Lisbon OSCE summit.

To achieve the aims of this Act, Russia and NATO will base their relations on a shared commitment to the following principles:

development, on the basis of transparency, of a strong, stable, enduring and equal partnership and of cooperation to strengthen security and stability in the Euro-Atlantic area;

acknowledgment of the vital role that democracy, political pluralism, the rule of law, and respect for human rights and civil liberties and the development of free market economies play in the development of common prosperity and comprehensive security;

refraining from the threat or use of force against each other as well as against any other state, its sovereignty, territorial integrity or political independence in any manner inconsistent with the UN Charter and with the Declaration of Principles Guiding Relations Between Participating States contained in the Helsinki Final Act;

respect for sovereignty, independence and territorial integrity of all states and their inherent right to choose the means to ensure their own security, the inviolability of borders and peoples' right of self-determination as enshrined in the Helsinki Final Act and other OSCE documents;

mutual transparency in creating and implementing defense policy and military doctrines;

prevention of conflicts and settlement of disputes by peaceful means in accordance with UN and OSCE principles;

support, on a case-by-case basis, of peacekeeping operations carried out under the authority of the UN Security Council or the responsibility of the OSCE.

II. MECHANISM FOR CONSULTATION AND COOPERATION: THE RUSSIA-NATO PERMANENT JOINT COUNCIL

To carry out the activities and aims provided for by this Act and to develop common approaches to European security and to political problems, Russia and NATO will create the Russia-NATO Permanent Joint Council. The central objective of this Permanent Joint Council will be to build increasing levels of trust, unity of purpose and habits of consultation and cooperation between Russia and NATO, in order to enhance each other's security and that of all nations in the Euro-Atlantic area and diminish the security of none. If disagreements arise, Russia and NATO will endeavor to settle them on the basis of goodwill and mutual respect within the framework of political consultations.

The Permanent Joint Council will provide a mechanism for consultations, coordination and, to the maximum extent possible, where appropriate, for joint decisions and joint action with respect to security issues of common concern. The consultations will not extend to internal matters of either Russia, NATO or NATO member-states.

The shared objective of Russia and NATO is to identify and pursue as many opportunities for joint action as possible. As the relationship develops, they expect that additional opportunities for joint action will emerge.

The Permanent Joint Council will be the principle venue of consultation between Russia and NATO in times of crisis or for any other situation affecting peace and stability. Extraordinary meetings of the Council will take place in addition to its regular meetings to allow for prompt consultations in case of emergencies. In this context, Russia and NATO will promptly consult, within the Permanent Joint Council in case one of the Council members perceives a threat to its territorial integrity, political independence or security.

The activities of the Permanent Joint Council will be built upon the principles of reciprocity and transparency. In the course of their consultations and cooperation, Russia and NATO will inform each other regarding the respective security-related challenges they face and measures that each intends to take to address them.

Provisions of this Act do not provide Russia or NATO, in any way, with a right of veto over the actions of the other nor do they infringe upon or restrict the rights of Russia or NATO to independent decision-making and action. They cannot be used as a means to disadvantage the interests of other states.

The Permanent Joint Council will meet at various levels and in different forms, according to the subject matter and the wishes of Russia and NATO. The Permanent Joint Council will meet at the level of Foreign Ministers and at the level of Defense Ministers twice annually, and also monthly at the level of ambassadors/permanent representatives to the North Atlantic Council.

The Permanent Joint Council may also meet, as appropriate, at the level of heads of state and government.

The Permanent Joint Council may establish committees or working groups for individual subjects or areas of cooperation on an ad hoc or permanent basis, as appropriate.

Under the auspices of the Permanent Joint Council, military representatives and Chiefs of Staff will also meet; meetings of Chiefs of Staff will take place no less than twice a year and also monthly at military representatives level. Meetings of military experts may be convened, as appropriate.

The Permanent Joint Council will be chaired jointly by a representative of Russia, the secretary-general of NATO and, on a rotation basis, a representative of one of the NATO member-states.

To support the work of the Permanent Joint Council, Russia and NATO will establish the necessary administrative structures.

Russia will establish a mission to NATO headed by a representative at the rank of ambassador. A senior military representative and his staff will be part of this mission for the purposes of the military cooperation. NATO retains the possibility of establishing an appropriate presence in Moscow, the modalities of which remain to be determined.

The agenda for regular sessions will be established jointly. Organizational arrangements and rules of procedure for the Permanent Joint Council will be worked out. These arrangements will be in place for the inaugural meeting of the Permanent Joint Council, which will be held no later than four months after the signature of this Act. The Permanent Joint Council will engage in three distinct activities:

consulting on the topics in Section III of this Act and on any other political or security issue determined by mutual consent;

on the basis of these consultations, developing joint initiatives on which Russia and NATO would agree to speak or act in parallel;

once consensus has been reached in the course of consultation, making joint decisions and taking joint action on a case-by-case basis, including participation, on an equitable basis, in the planning and preparation of joint operations, including peacekeeping operations under the authority of the UN Security Council or the responsibility of the OSCE.

Any actions undertaken by Russia or NATO, together or separately, must be consistent with the UN Charter and the OSCE's governing principles.

XIX.1. NATO-RUSSIA FOUNDING ACT

Recognizing the importance of deepening contacts between the legislative bodies of the participating states to this Act, Russia and NATO will also encourage expanded dialogue and cooperation between the Federal Assembly of the Russian Federation and the North Atlantic Assembly.

III. AREAS FOR CONSULTATION AND COOPERATION

In building their relationship, Russia and NATO will focus on specific areas of mutual interest. They will consult and strive to cooperate to the broadest possible degree in the following areas:

issues of common interest related to security and stability in the Euro-Atlantic or to concrete crises, including the contribution of Russia and NATO to security and stability in this area;

conflict prevention, including preventive diplomacy, crisis management and conflict resolution taking into account the role and responsibility of the UN and the OSCE and the work of these organizations in these fields;

joint operations, including peace-keeping operations, on a case-by-case basis, under the authority of the UN Security Council or the responsibility of the OSCE, and if combined joint task forces (CJTFs) are used in such cases, participation in them at an early stage;

participation of Russia in the Euro-Atlantic Partnership Council and the Partnership for Peace;

exchange of information and consultation on strategy, defense policy, the military doctrines of Russia and NATO, and budgets and infrastructure development programs;

arms control issues;

nuclear safety issues, across their full spectrum;

preventing the proliferation of nuclear, biological and chemical weapons, and their delivery means, combating nuclear trafficking and strengthening cooperation in specific arms control areas, including political and defense aspects of proliferation;

possible cooperation in theatre missile defence;

enhanced regional air-traffic safety, increased air-traffic capacity and reciprocal exchanges, as appropriate, to promote confidence through increased measures of transparency and exchanges of information in relation to air defense and related aspects of airspace management/control. This will include exploring possible cooperation on appropriate air defense related matters;

increasing transparency, predictability and mutual confidence regarding the size and roles of the conventional forces of Russia and member-states of NATO;

reciprocal exchanges, as appropriate, on nuclear weapons issues, including doctrines and strategy of Russia and NATO;

coordinating a program of expanded cooperation between respective military establishments, as further detailed below;

pursuing possible armaments-related cooperation through association with Russia with NATO's Conference of National Armaments Directors;

conversion of defense industries;

developing mutually agreed cooperative projects in defence-related economic, environmental and scientific fields;

conducting joint initiatives and exercises in civil emergency preparedness and disaster relief;

combating terrorism and drug trafficking;

improving public understanding of evolving relations between Russia and NATO, including the establishment of a NATO documentation center or information office in Moscow.

Other areas can be added by mutual agreement.

IV. POLITICAL-MILITARY MATTERS

Russia and NATO affirm their shared desire to achieve greater stability and security in the Euro-Atlantic area.

The member-states of NATO reiterate that they have no intention, no plan and no reason to deploy nuclear weapons on the territory of new members, nor any need to change any aspect of NATO's nuclear posture or nuclear policy—and do not foresee any future need to do so. This subsumes the fact that NATO has decided that it has no intention, no plan and no reason to establish nuclear weapon storage sites on the territory of those members, whether through the construction of new nuclear storage facilities or the adaptation of old nuclear storage facilities. Nuclear storage sites are understood to be facilities specifically designed for the stationing of nuclear weapons, and include all types of hardened above or below ground facilities (storage bunkers or vaults) designed for storing nuclear weapons.

Recognizing the importance of the adaptation of the Treaty on Conventional Armed Forces in Europe (CFE) for the broader context of security in the OSCE area and the work on a Common and Comprehensive Security Model for Europe for the 21st Century, Russia and the member-states of NATO will work together in Vienna with the other states parties to adapt the CFE Treaty to enhance its viability and effectiveness, taking into account Europe's changing security environment and the legitimate security interests of all OSCE participating states. They share the objective of concluding an adaptation agreement as expeditiously as possible and, as a first step in this process, they will, together with other states parties to the CFE Treaty, seek to conclude as soon as possible a framework agreement setting forth the basic elements of an adapted CFE Treaty, consistent with the objectives and principles of the Document on Scope and Parameters agreed at Lisbon in December 1996.

Russia and NATO believe that an important goal of CFE Treaty adaptation should be a significant lowering in the total amount of treaty-limited equipment permitted in the treaty's area of application compatible with the legitimate defense requirements of each state party. Russia and NATO encourage all states parties to the CFE Treaty to consider reductions in their CFE equipment entitlements as part of an overall effort to achieve lower equipment levels that are consistent with the transformation of Europe's security environment.

Russia and the member-states of NATO commit themselves to exercise restraint during the period of negotiations, as foreseen in the Document on Scope and Parameters, in relation to the current postures and capabilities of their conventional armed forces—in particular with respect to their levels of forces and deployments—in the treaty's area of application, in order to avoid developments in the security situation in Europe diminishing the security of any state party. This commitment is without prejudice to possible voluntary decisions by the individual states parties to reduce their force levels or deployments, or to their legitimate security interests.

Russia and the member-states of NATO proceed on the basis that adaptation of the CFE Treaty should help to ensure equal security for all states parties irrespective of their membership of a politico-military alliance, both to preserve and strengthen stability and continue to prevent any destabilizing increase of forces in various regions of Europe and in Europe as a whole. An adapted CFE Treaty should also further enhance military transparency by extended information exchange and verification and permit the possible accession by new states parties.

Russia and the member-states of NATO propose to other CFE states parties to carry out such adaptation of the CFE Treaty so as to enable states parties to reach, through a transparent and cooperative process, conclusions regarding reductions they might be prepared to take and resulting national treaty-limited equipment ceilings. These will then be codified as binding limits in the adapted treaty to be agreed by consensus of all states parties, and reviewed in 2001 and at five-year intervals thereafter. In doing so, the states parties will take into account all the levels of treaty-limited equipment established for the Atlantic-to-the-Urals area by the original CFE Treaty, the substantial reductions that have been carried out since then, the changes to the situation in Europe and the need to ensure that the security of no state is diminished.

Russia and the member-states of NATO reaffirm that states parties to the CFE Treaty should maintain only such military capabilities individually or in conjunction with others, as are commensurate with individual or collective legitimate security needs, taking into account their international obligations, including the CFE Treaty.

Each state party will base its agreement to the provisions of the adapted treaty on all national ceilings of the states parties, on its projections of the current and future security situation in Europe.

In addition, in the negotiations on the adaptation of the CFE Treaty, Russia and the member-states of NATO will, together with other states parties, seek to strengthen stability by further developing measures to prevent any potentially threatening build-up of conventional forces in agreed regions of Europe, to include Central and Eastern Europe.

Russia and NATO have clarified their intentions with regard to their conventional force postures in Europe's new security environment and are prepared to consult on the evolution of these postures in the framework of the Permanent Joint Council.

NATO reiterates that in the current and foreseeable security environment, the Alliance will carry out its collective defense and other missions by ensuring the necessary interoperability, integration, and capability for reinforcement rather than by additional permanent stationing of substantial combat forces. Accordingly, it will have to rely on adequate infrastructure commensurate with the above tasks. In this context, reinforcement may take place, when necessary, in the event of defense against a threat of aggression and missions in support of peace consistent with the UN Charter and the OSCE governing principles, as well as for exercises consistent with the adapted CFE Treaty, the provisions of the Vienna Document 1994 and mutually agreed transparency measures. Russia will exercise similar restraint in its conventional force deployments in Europe.

Russia and the member-states of NATO will strive for greater transparency, predictability and mutual confidence with regard to their armed forces. They will comply fully with their obligations under the Vienna Document 1994 and develop cooperation with the other OSCE participating states, including negotiations in the appropriate format, *inter alia*, within the OSCE to promote confidence and security.

Russia and the member-states of NATO will use and improve existing arms control regimes and confidence-building measures to create security relations based on peaceful cooperation.

Russia and NATO, in order to develop cooperation between their military establishments, will expand political-military consultations and cooperation through the Permanent Joint Council with an enhanced dialogue between the senior military authorities of Russia and of NATO and its member-states. They will implement a program of significantly expanded military activities and practical cooperation between Russia and NATO at all levels. Consistent with the tenets of the Permanent Joint Council, this enhanced military-to-military dialogue will be built upon the principle that neither party views the other as a threat nor seeks to the disadvantage the other's security. This enhanced military-to-military dialogue will include regularly-scheduled reciprocal briefings on Russian and NATO military doctrine, strategy and resultant force posture and will include the broad possibilities for joint exercises and training.

To support this enhanced dialogue and the military components of the Permanent Joint Council, Russia and NATO will establish military liaison missions at various levels on the basis of reciprocity and further mutual arrangements.

To enhance their partnership and ensure that this partnership is grounded to the greatest extent possible in practical activities and direct cooperation, Russia's and NATO's respective military authorities will explore the further development of a concept for joint Russia-NATO peace-keeping operations. This initiative should build upon the positive experience of working together in Bosnia & Hercegovina and the lessons learned there will be used in the establishment of CJTFs.

The present Act takes effect upon the date of its signature.

Russia and NATO will take the proper steps to ensure its implementation in accordance with their procedures.

The present Act is established in two originals in the Russian, French and English language.

The Government of the Russian Federation and the secretary-general of NATO will provide the Secretary-General of the United Nations and the secretary-general of the OSCE with the text of this Act with the request to circulate it to all members of the organizations.

2. COUNCIL OF EUROPE ACTION PLAN

The following is the text of an Action Plan adopted by the heads of state and government of the member-states of the Council of Europe at their second summit conference held in Strasbourg (France) on 10–11 October 1997. (Text supplied by Council of Europe, Strasbourg.)

The heads of state and government, meeting in Strasbourg on 10 and 11 October 1997, have outlined an Action Plan to strengthen democratic stability in the member-states, and have accordingly defined four main areas where there is scope for immediate advances and practical measures, together with a fifth field concerning structural reforms.

I. DEMOCRACY AND HUMAN RIGHTS

1. *Single Court of Human Rights.* The heads of state and government welcome the ratification of Protocol No 11 to the European Convention on Human Rights by all contracting parties, making it possible to establish the new single Court of Human Rights, and instruct the Committee of Ministers to take the necessary steps to set it up on 1 November 1998.

2. *Commissioner for Human Rights.* The heads of state and government welcome the proposal to create an office of Commissioner for Human Rights to promote respect for human rights in the member-states, and instruct the Committee of Ministers to study arrangements for its implementation, while respecting the competences of the Single Court.

3. *Compliance with member-states' commitments.* The heads of state and government resolve to ensure that the commitments accepted by the member-states are effectively honoured, on the basis of a confidential, constructive, non-discriminatory dialogue carried on within the Committee of Ministers and taking into account the monitoring procedures of the Parliamentary Assembly; they reiterate their determination to work together to solve the problems faced by member-states and consider that this monitoring process must be supported, where necessary, by practical assistance from the Council of Europe.

4. *Prohibition of the cloning of human beings.* The heads of state and government undertake to prohibit all use of cloning techniques aimed at creating genetically identical human beings and instruct to this end the Committee of Ministers to adopt an additional protocol to the Oviedo Convention on Human Rights and Biomedicine as soon as possible.

5. *Combating racism, xenophobia, antisemitism and intolerance.* The heads of state and government welcome the action taken in this field by the Council of Europe since the Vienna summit and resolve to intensify, for this purpose, the activities of the European Commission against Racism and Intolerance, while stressing the importance of close cooperation with the European Union.

6. *Protection of national minorities.* The heads of state and government, taking into account the imminent entry into force of the Framework Convention for the Protection of National Minorities, resolve to complement the Council of Europe's standard-setting achievements in this field through practical initiatives, such as confidence-building measures and enhanced cooperation, involving both governments and civil society.

II. SOCIAL COHESION

1. *Promotion of social rights.* The heads of state and government undertake to promote social standards as embodied in the Social Charter and in other Council of Europe instruments, and call for the widest possible adherence to these instruments; they resolve to improve the exchange of good practice and information between member-states and to intensify their cooperation in this field.

2. *New strategy for social cohesion.* The heads of state and government instruct the Committee of Ministers to define a social strategy to respond to the challenges in society and to carry out the appropriate structural reforms within the Council of Europe, including the setting up of a specialised unit for monitoring, comparing and handling issues linked to social cohesion.

3. *Programme for children.* The heads of state and government encourage the adoption of a programme to promote the interests of children, in partnership with the international and non-governmental organizations concerned.

4. *Social Development Fund.* The heads of state and government decide to reinforce the activities of the Social Development Fund, invite it to participate actively in the Council of Europe's action for social cohesion, and urge it to increase its investment effort in the social field and in job creation.

III. SECURITY OF CITIZENS

1. *Combating terrorism.* The heads of state and government call for the adoption of further measures to prevent terrorism and to strengthen international cooperation in combating terrorism, in accordance with the relevant provisions of international law, including international standards on human rights, and in the light of the recommendations adopted at the ministerial conference on terrorism held in Paris on 30 July 1996 [see AR 1996, pp. 539–41]; they note with interest the forthcoming holding of a parliamentary conference to study the phenomenon of terrorism in democratic society.

2. *Fighting corruption and organized crime.* In order to promote cooperation between member-states in the fight against corruption, including its links with organized crime and money-laundering, the heads of state and government instruct the Committee of Ministers:

to adopt, before the end of the year, guiding principles which are to be applied in the development of domestic legislation and practice;

to secure the rapid completion of international legal instruments pursuant to the Council of Europe's Programme of Action against Corruption;

to establish without delay an appropriate and efficient mechanism for monitoring observance of the guiding principles and implementation of the said international legal instruments.

They call on all states to ratify the Convention on Laundering, Search, Seizure and Confiscation of the Proceeds from Crime.

3. *Prevention of drug abuse.* The heads of state and government decide to strengthen their cooperation, through the Pompidou Group, with a view to tackling the problems relating to the use and trafficking of illicit drugs; they note with approval the new work programme of the group and welcome in particular those activities designed to prevent drug abuse among young people and to facilitate the reintegration of drug addicts and users into society.

4. *Protection of children.* The heads of state and government decide to review national legislation with the aim of ensuring common standards for the protection of children suffering from or at risk of inhuman treatment; they agree to extend their cooperation, within the Council of Europe, with a view to preventing all forms of exploitation of children, including through the production, sale, marketing and possession of pornographic material involving children.

IV. DEMOCRATIC VALUES AND CULTURAL DIVERSITY

1. *Education for democratic citizenship.* The heads of state and government decide to launch an initiative for education for democratic citizenship with a view to promoting citizens' awareness of their rights and responsibilities in a democratic society, activating existing networks, and including a new youth exchange programme.

2. *Enhancement of the European heritage.* The heads of state and government decide to launch a campaign in 1999 on the theme 'Europe, a Common Heritage', respecting cultural diversity, based on existing or prospective partnerships between government, educational and cultural institutions, and industry.
3. *New information technologies.* The heads of state and government resolve to develop a European policy for the application of the new information technologies, with a view to ensuring respect for human rights and cultural diversity, fostering freedom of expression and information and maximizing the educational and cultural potential of these technologies; they invite the Council of Europe to seek, in this respect, suitable partnership arrangements.

V. STRUCTURES AND WORKING METHODS

1. *Structural reform.* The heads of state and government, looking ahead to the 50th anniversary of the Council of Europe in 1999, instruct the Committee of Ministers to carry out the structural reforms needed to adapt the organization to its new tasks and its enlarged membership and to improve its decision-making process.
2. *Implementation of the Action Plan.* The heads of state and government instruct the Committee of Ministers to take the appropriate steps to ensure that this Action Plan is speedily implemented by the various Council of Europe bodies, in cooperation with European and other international organizations.

3. COMMONWEALTH SUMMIT DECLARATIONS

Below is the bulk of a declaration entitled 'Promoting Shared Prosperity' adopted by the 31st Commonwealth heads of government meeting (CHOGM) held in Edinburgh (Scotland) on 24–27 October. Also published is the 'Report of the Inter-governmental Group on Criteria for Commonwealth Membership' adopted by the same meeting. (Texts supplied by Commonwealth Secretariat, London.)

PROMOTING SHARED PROSPERITY

1. Today's globalized world poses both opportunities and challenges. Expanding trade and investment flows, driven by new technologies and the spread of market forces, have emerged as engines of growth. At the same time, not all countries have benefited equally from the globalization of the world economy, and a significant number are threatened with marginalisation. Globalization therefore needs to be carefully managed to meet the risks inherent in the process.
2. We believe that world peace, security and social stability cannot be achieved in conditions of deep poverty and growing inequality. Special measures are needed to correct this, and in particular to help the integration of countries, especially small states and the least-developed countries, in the global economy and address the uneven development that threatens many countries. To redress these problems, we believe the following broad principled approaches should be pursued:
   the world economy should be geared towards promoting universal growth and prosperity for all;
   there must be effective participation by all countries in economic decision-making in key international forums;
   the removal of obstacles that prevent developing countries playing their full part in shaping the evolution of the global economy; and
   international regimes affecting economic relations among nations should provide symmetrical benefits for all.
3. We also believe that commitment to market principles, openness to international trade and investment, the development of human and physical resources, gender equality, and good governance and political stability remain major components of economic and social progress; and that wealth creation requires partnerships between governments and the private sector. The Commonwealth, with its shared traditions and global reach, is uniquely placed to play a key role in promoting shared prosperity amongst its members.

Trade

4. We welcome the progress made in recent years in dismantling trade barriers and establishing a rule-based international trading system. However, significant barriers to trade in goods and services remain, and the benefits of the expansion of world trade are still unevenly shared. We have therefore resolved to:
   support expansion of duty-free market access with flexible rules of origin for the exports of the least-devloped countries; work for a successor arrangement to the Lomé Convention which, without prejudice

to the outcome, gives the ACP countries, particularly small states, adequate transitional arrangements; and in particular, encourage the European Union (EU) and World Trade Organization (WTO) members to accommodate the legitimate interests of the ACP banana producers and facilitate the diversification of their economies;

strengthen the multilateral trading system within the framework of the WTO, in order to prevent regional arrangements from becoming exclusive trading blocs and provide for the greatest flow of international trade on the basis of agreed rules which are fair and equitable; and support the full implementation of the Uruguay Round agreements;

oppose the introduction of new non-tariff barriers and the use of unilateral actions and bilateral pressures which run counter to the spirit of the WTO;

maintain the momentum towards freer trade through multilateral negotiations, as outlined in the built-in agenda and other issues under discussion in the WTO, including progress on agriculture and financial and other services, taking into account the interests of all countries at different stages of development; and

continue to support regional arrangements, consistent with multilateral liberalization under the WTO, which promote the economic growth of their members. Specifically we have decided to:

establish a Trade and Investment Access Facility under the Commonwealth umbrella to assist developing countries with the process of adjusting to, and taking advantage of, the opportunities of globalization. The new Facility will provide technical assistance to help countries identify and manage the potential economic and social impacts of trade in goods and services and investment liberalisation; identify new sources of revenue and market opportunities; and help countries fulfil WTO requirements. The Facility will be coordinated with the proposed WTO/UNCTAD/International Trade Centre (ITC) integrated framework for trade-related technical assistance;

explore the scope for deepening trade relationships among Commonwealth members, and therefore request the secretariat to report to us, before the 1999 CHOGM, on the scope and possible systems and mechanisms for improving trade among members of the Commonwealth, in ways which are consistent with the provisions of the WTO and regional trading arrangements;

launch a Commonwealth action programme to remove administrative obstacles to trade by simplifying and harmonising customs procedures, disseminating information, and eliminating bureaucratic and technical hurdles;

examine the growing importance of 'electronic commerce' in trade and the developmental implications of the use of cyberspace for commercial and financial transactions; and

promote Commonwealth Export Training Centres for management training in exporting and other trade-related skills.

5. We welcome the recommendations of the first ever Commonwealth Business Forum held in London on 22–23 October 1997. We believe that the Forum can be an important link between the private and public sectors and foster vibrant private sector business links. It should continue to meet every two years. We are also arranging to set up a Business Council, under Lord Cairns and Cyril Ramaphosa, made up of a small group of major private-sector leaders from different regions of the Commonwealth, as well as other mechanisms, in consultation with the Commonwealth secretary-general, to encourage greater private sector involvement in the promotion of trade and investment. In this context, we also agree to support and strengthen the work of the Commonwealth Partnership for Technology Management.

Investment

6. We believe that investment flows can bring substantial benefits, and that sound macro-economic policies and financial systems, strong regulatory and supervisory frameworks and political stability are essential in encouraging inward flows. At the same time, we recognize that volatility in such flows can greatly complicate economic management. They also remain concentrated in a few regions and countries. We agree to:

encourage investment flows by establishing an open and transparent investment regimes for business activity, and by simplifying bureaucratic procedures and regulations;

encourage capital exporting countries, where it is prudent, to consider relaxing restrictions on institutional investors to enable them to take advantage of portfolio diversification opportunities in emerging and new markets;

support the development of regional and multilateral arrangements and infrastructure that take into account the realities of developing countries, and that can help to facilitate private capital flows;

study the lessons to be learned from recent developments in currency markets and in particular on how countries can be protected from the destabilising effects of market volatility, including those resulting from speculative activities, and how the effectiveness of existing early warning systems can be improved; and

support strengthening of global and regional mechanisms to help countries handle capital market volatility. Specifically we have decided to:

XIX.3. COMMONWEALTH SUMMIT DECLARATIONS

endorse the recommendations of the Commonwealth working group on the role of national and international policies in promoting private capital flows, and call for the rapid finalization of a Commonwealth code of good practice for national policies that attract and sustain private capital flows;

welcome the launch of the Africa Fund, the Kula Fund for the Pacific and the South Asia Regional Fund under the aegis of the Commonwealth Private Investment Initiative (CPII); and call for the extension of CPII to embrace additional regions and sectors;

launch a Commonwealth investment promotion programme which will: help establish enabling environments for attracting private investment flows; encourage the creation of new mechanisms for risk insurance and guarantees; provide assistance for strengthening supervisory and regulatory frameworks; and improve the flow of information on investment opportunities; and

encourage 'smart partnerships' involving the private and public sectors.

Development

7. We welcome the improving growth prospects in many parts of the developing world, including evidence of recovery in sub-Saharan Africa. At the same time, we remain concerned at the persistence of extreme poverty in many countries and the lack of capacity to reduce it. We have therefore agreed to:

work to halve the proportion of people living in extreme poverty by the year 2015;

seek to reverse the decline in official development assistance (ODA) flows, recognizing the role of ODA as an essential instrument of partnership for development and poverty-reduction in developing countries, particularly the least-developed countries and small states, and for helping to create the conditions for increased trade and investment, including skills and infrastructure development;

work towards a comprehensive solution of the debt problem, and pursue vigorously the rapid implementation of the highly-indebted poor countries (HIPC) initiative, in line with the Mauritius Mandate, which has the aim of enabling HIPC countries to have embarked by the year 2000 on securing a sustainable exit from their debt burden; as well as consider extending such relief to other developing countries, including small states, in similar circumstances; and

promote the role of micro-credit schemes in reducing poverty through increased assistance from the international community.

8. We welcome the report of the chairman of the Commonwealth Ministerial Group on Small States and its recommendations for action based on the Commonwealth report, 'A Future for Small States: Overcoming Vulnerability'. In particular, we encourage international financial institutions to review their graduation policies, consider broader criteria covering the special vulnerabilities of their smaller members, and establish a task force to address the concerns of small states. We endorse the recommendation to set up a small ministerial group to discuss small states' concerns with major multilateral agencies and to report to governments on the outcome as soon as possible.

9. We underscore the importance of good governance, including increased openness in economic decision-making and the elimination of corruption through greater transparency, accountability and the application of the rule of law in economic, financial and other spheres of activity. We endorse the request by our Finance Ministers to the Commonwealth secretary-general to establish an expert group to work on these issues . . .

Conclusion

11. In pursuance of these commitments, we agree to enhance the Commonwealth's role in building consensus on global economic issues and on an equitable structuring of international economic relations.

12. We also agree to sustain and where possible increase bilateral assistance among our members; and to ensure the flow of resources to the secretariat and its various funds, especially the Commonwealth Fund for Technical Cooperation (CFTC); and to the Commonwealth Foundation, Commonwealth of Learning (COL) and the Commonwealth Partnership for Technology Management (CPTM).

13. We believe the Commonwealth can play a dynamic role in promoting trade and investment so as to enhance prosperity, accelerate economic growth and development and advance the eradication of poverty in the 21st century. We plan to pursue this with vigour.

CRITERIA FOR COMMONWEALTH MEMBERSHIP

Conventions

1. The Commonwealth is a voluntary association of sovereign, independent states. Unlike other international organizations, such as the United Nations, the Commonwealth has no charter or comparable instrument which makes express provision for the admission of new members. Any consideration of Commonwealth

membership should take into account the procedure which has evolved over time and become the established practice of the Commonwealth.[1]

2. New members of the Commonwealth, with one exception, have had a past association with another Commonwealth country, as colonies or protectorates or trust territories. This has become the established understanding governing admission to the Commonwealth.

Procedures for Applications

3. When a country wishes to apply for membership, the following procedures have generally been pursued:

a request for membership can be made before a country gains its independence, either from Britain or, as has happened in some instances, another Commonwealth country;

it has been the practice, especially in dependent territories, that a request for membership commands broad-based support in the country concerned. Evidence thereof has taken the form of a resolution by the local legislature expressing a desire to belong to the Commonwealth. There have been instances where, for one reason or another, such a resolution has not been introduced. However, a parliamentary resolution in support of Commonwealth membership from the country concerned is considered desirable;

a country applying for membership approaches the secretary-general directly. On receipt of the application, the secretary-general consults all existing members by correspondence or at a Commonwealth heads of government meeting if convenient;

once consultations have been completed, the decision on whether to admit a country into membership is reached on the basis of consensus by Commonwealth heads of government.

Precedents for Admission to the Commonwealth

4. Hitherto, all countries seeking admission to the Commonwealth have experienced either direct or indirect British rule, or have been linked administratively to some other Commonwealth country, as in the examples of Singapore, Papua New Guinea and most recently Namibia. Heads of government at Auckland in November 1995 decided, as an exceptional case and without creating a precedent, to accept the application by Mozambique for membership in recognition of its unique historical relationship with the Commonwealth.

5. While the majority of countries have sought Commonwealth membership prior to gaining independence and have supported this by legislative resolutions, there are examples of Commonwealth countries which have not followed this practice. Tonga was already independent when it sought membership in 1971 and supported its application by a resolution from the Legislative Assembly. In 1992 the Republic of Cameroon presented a formal instrument of acceptance of the Harare Declaration and a unanimously-adopted parliamentary resolution supporting the government's application for Commonwealth membership. There is no record, however, of any legislative process accompanying Western Samoa's application for full membership in 1970, some eight years after achieving independence. Maldives gained independence in 1965 yet did not consider applying for Commonwealth membership until 1980. Nor did Bangladesh, Zimbabwe or Mozambique, precede their applications for full membership with any legislative process.

6. The precedent of bilingualism and biculturalism, as well as of belonging to both the Commonwealth and La Francophonie (an international cultural community united through its use of the French language—see XIX.5), has already been set by Canada and is also followed by other Commonwealth countries, such as Mauritius, Seychelles, Dominica, St Lucia, Vanuatu and Cameroon.

Attributes of Commonwealth Membership

7. In order to become a member of the Commonwealth, an applicant country:

(*a*) should as a rule have had a constitutional association with an existing Commonwealth member; and

(*b*) should comply with Commonwealth values, principles and priorities as set out in the Harare Declaration. This declaration, as developed from time to time, is of the utmost importance in framing the Commonwealth's ethos to which members are committed.-

---

[1] A voluntary category of special members has been created for very small countries such as Nauru and Tuvalu which do not send representatives to heads of government meetings, but are entitled to attend ministerial meetings. They are not assessed for subscriptions but contribute voluntarily to the secretariat budget and to the budgets of the voluntary funds and programmes. Only independent states can become members or special members of the Commonwealth. However, some territories linked with Commonwealth member-states both contribute to and benefit from Commonwealth voluntary funds and programmes. Representatives of such territories do from time to time attend ministerial meetings as part of the delegation of the member government with which they are linked.-

XIX.4. HANOI DECLARATION OF FRANCOPHONE COMMUNITY   565

8. Commonwealth membership entails acceptance of Commonwealth practices and conventions, including the use of the English language as the medium of inter-Commonwealth relations, as well as acknowledgment of the role of the British monarch as a symbol of the free association and as such Head of the Commonwealth. Members should also accept the Commonwealth style of informality, intimacy and consensus. They should be willing and able to take part in Commonwealth consultations and to contribute, both financially and in other ways, to practical programmes of cooperation under the auspices of the Commonwealth, such as the Commonwealth Fund for Technical Cooperation (CFTC).

9. The unofficial, non-governmental Commonwealth is also an important part of the association. Here too the common language and background facilitates contact and understanding. Ability and willingness to contribute to the non-governmental Commonwealth may be relevant to an application for membership.

4. HANOI DECLARATION OF FRANCOPHONE COMMUNITY

Printed below is an English translation of the declaration of the Francophone Community adopted by the seventh summit of French-speaking states held in Hanoi, Vietnam, on 14–16 November 1997. (Translation, slightly amended, from Vietnam News Agency.)

1. We, chiefs of state, governments and delegations of countries sharing the French language, meeting from 14 to 16 November 1997 in Hanoi, Socialist Republic of Vietnam, have declared that:

2. Faced with challenges tied to accelerated globalization and the necessity to make the best of it in order to avoid the risks of increasing uniformization, dependence and marginalization which particularly hurt the most disinherited.

3. Conscious of the necessity to strengthen the economic dimension of the Francophone Community so that, together with its cultural and political dimensions, it can assure the perpetuity of the Francophone Community in the world of today and tomorrow, and recognizing the urgency of meeting the need of development of our peoples, as is indicated in the theme of the Hanoi summit: 'Strengthening Francophone cooperation and solidarity for peace and economic and social development';

4. Challenged by the persistence of crises and conflicts in all forms, foreign occupation of the territories of some member-countries, by poverty and under-development, which affect more particularly women and children;

5. Conscious, however, that, rich from the patrimony of diverse values and expressions, respectful of the identities of each partner, and considering culture as the foundation of development, the Francophone Community is affirming itself as an open, plural place of dialogue and exchanges;

6. Employing dialogue to facilitate the rapprochement of the people and their access to modernity, thanks to the links that the common usage of the French language has created, in the respect of partner cultures and languages and in cooperation with other linguistic spaces;

7. Reiterating our faith in the democratic values founded in respect for human rights and fundamental freedoms, and also in respect for the rights of peoples and respect for the rights of minority peoples;

8. Underlining the indissoluble ties between peace, democracy and development, between education and training, between economic growth, social progress and sustainable development which underscore our cooperation and our efforts in the pursuit of our ultimate goal: the well-being of our populations in independence, freedom and solidarity;

9. Considering that peace and development are better served by the pooling of resources and energies and that Francophone Community is conceived as a privileged space of multilateral consultation and action;

10. Considering the role played by the Francophone Agency in the anchorage of the intergovernmental Francophone Community on the international scene;

11. Greet the holding for the first time of a Francophone summit in Asia, which therefore underlines the universal dimension of the Francophone Community and its presence in a region known for its dynamism;

12. Take the commitment to bring an active contribution to the prevention and peaceful settlement of conflicts, when necessary in liaison with international organizations and by fully utilizing the competent regional mechanisms in the spirit of solidarity and conciliation, and to contribute to the strengthening of preventive diplomacy advocated by the United Nations, particularly in Africa and the Middle East;

13. Work toward the intensification of our activities of coordination, information and training in order to make our cooperation more dynamic and support the efforts of our countries for a sustainable development by basing ourselves on the exploitation and the sharing of scientific and technical gains, and particularly on the putting into practice the Montreal Plan of Action devoted to the new technologies of information and communication;

14. Decide to intensify our commitment to promote cultural exchange within the Francophone Community in all its forms, to facilitate the circulation of creative talents and their training, to assure the

exchange of their works and their access to aid and the artistic and cultural institutions in all our countries—by giving our support to the principle of a new governing convention among our states and governments. We ask the ministerial conference of the Francophone community to approve the contents of this convention as soon as possible;

15. Favour, in the traditional spirit of Francophone solidarity, mutual aid and the broadening of cooperation between developed countries and less-advanced countries as well as among the southern countries themselves;

16. Call upon all countries, organizations and participants in the Francophone family to exploit the rich potential offered by our multilateral cooperation in the domain of human resources in service of development, particularly by giving priority to education and training, and to integrate fully in this process the civil society, notably the youth and women;

17. Decide to bring the necessary financial, technical and human resources to multilateral cooperation, for the putting into effect of the plan of action which we adopt today;

18. Express our gratitude to the secretary-general of the Francophone Agency, for the eminent service he has rendered to the Francophone community over the past eight years;

19. Decide to turn the Hanoi summit into an important stage in the evolution of the institutions of the Francophone Community, through the putting into action of the revised Charter and the election of the secretary-general of the Francophone Community, which strengthen the international structure of our organization;

20. We welcome the election of the first secretary-general of the Francophone Community, Dr Boutros Boutros-Ghali, to whom we pledge our full support in the exercise of his high functions.

5. UN LANDMINES CONVENTION

Printed below are key extracts from the UN Convention on the Prohibition of the Use, Stockpiling, Production and Transfer of Anti-personnel Mines and on their Destruction, which was opened for signature at Ottawa, Canada, on 3–4 December 1997. (Text from United Nations, New York.)

Art. 1: General Obligations

1. Each state party undertakes never under any circumstances
(a) To use anti-personnel mines;
(b) To develop, produce, otherwise acquire, stockpile, retain or transfer to anyone, directly or indirectly, anti-personnel mines;
(c) To assist, encourage or induce, in any way, anyone to engage in any activity prohibited to a State party under this convention.

2. Each state party undertakes to destroy or ensure the destruction of all anti-personnel mines in accordance with the provisions of this convention.

Art. 2: Definitions

1. 'Anti-personnel mine' means a mine designed to be exploded by the presence, proximity or contact of a person and that will incapacitate, injure or kill one or more persons. Mines designed to be detonated by the presence, proximity or contact of a vehicle as opposed to a person, that are equipped with anti-handling devices, are not considered anti-personnel mines as a result of being so equipped.

2. 'Mine' means a munition designed to be placed under, on or near the ground or other surface area and to be exploded by the presence, proximity or contact of a person or a vehicle.

3. 'Anti-handling device' means a device intended to protect a mine and which is part of, linked to, attached to or placed under the mine and which activates when an attempt is made to tamper with or otherwise intentionally disturb the mine.

4. 'Transfer' involves, in addition to the physical movement of anti-personnel mines into or from national territory, the transfer of title to and control over the mines, but does not involve the transfer of territory containing emplaced anti-personnel mines.

5. 'Mined area' means an area which is dangerous due to the presence or suspected presence of mines.

Art. 3: Exceptions

1. Notwithstanding the general obligations under Article 1, the retention or transfer of a number of anti-personnel mines for the development of and training in mine detection, mine clearance, or mine

XIX.5. UN LANDMINES CONVENTION

destruction techniques is permitted. The amount of such mines shall not exceed the minimum number absolutely necessary for the above-mentioned purposes.

2. The transfer of anti-personnel mines for the purpose of destruction is permitted.

Art. 4: Destruction of Stockpiled Anti-personnel Mines

Except as provided for in Article 3, each state party undertakes to destroy or ensure the destruction of all stockpiled anti-personnel mines it owns or possesses, or that are under its jurisdiction or control, as soon as possible but not later than four years after the entry into force of this convention for that state party.

Art. 5: Destruction of Anti-personnel Mines in Mined Areas

1. Each state party undertakes to destroy or ensure the destruction of all anti-personnel mines in mined areas under its jurisdiction or control, as soon as possible but not later than ten years after the entry into force of this convention for that state party.

2. Each state party shall make every effort to identify all areas under its jurisdiction or control in which anti-personnel mines are known or suspected to be emplaced and shall ensure as soon as possible that all anti-personnel mines in mined areas under its jurisdiction or control are perimeter-marked, monitored and protected by fencing or other means, to ensure the effective exclusion of civilians, until all anti-personnel mines contained therein have been destroyed. The marking shall at least be to the standards set out in the Protocol on Prohibitions or Restrictions on the Use of Mines, Booby-Traps and Other Devices, as amended on 3 May 1996, annexed to the Convention on Prohibitions or Restrictions on the Use of Certain Conventional Weapons Which May Be Deemed to Be Excessively Injurious or to Have Indiscriminate Effects.

3. If a state party believes that it will be unable to destroy or ensure the destruction of all anti-personnel mines referred to in paragraph 1 within that time period, it may submit a request to a Meeting of the States Parties or a Review Conference for an extension of the deadline for completing the destruction of such anti-personnel mines, for a period of up to ten years.

4. Each request shall contain:
(a) The duration of the proposed extension;
(b) A detailed explanation of the reasons for the proposed extension, including: (i) the preparation and status of work conducted under national de-mining programs; (ii) the financial and technical means available to the state party for the destruction of all the anti-personnel mines; and (iii) circumstances which impede the ability of the state party to destroy all the anti-personnel mines in mined areas;
(c) The humanitarian, social, economic, and environmental implications of the extension; and
(d) Any other information relevant to the request for the proposed extension.

5. The Meeting of the States Parties or the Review Conference shall, taking into consideration the factors contained in paragraph 4, assess the request and decide by a majority of votes of states parties present and voting whether to grant the request for an extension period.

6. Such an extension may be renewed upon the submission of a new request in accordance with paragraphs 3, 4 and 5 of this article. In requesting a further extension period a state party shall submit relevant additional information on what has been undertaken in the previous extension period pursuant to this article . . . .

Art. 9: National Implementation Measures

Each state party shall take all appropriate legal, administrative and other measures, including the imposition of penal sanctions, to prevent and suppress any activity prohibited to a state party under this convention undertaken by persons or on territory under its jurisdiction or control.

Art. 10: Settlement of Disputes

1. The states parties shall consult and cooperate with each other to settle any dispute that may arise with regard to the application or the interpretation of this convention. Each state party may bring any such dispute before the Meeting of the States Parties.

2. The Meeting of the States Parties may contribute to the settlement of the dispute by whatever means it deems appropriate, including offering its good offices, calling upon the states parties to a dispute to start the settlement procedure of their choice and recommending a time-limit for any agreed procedure 3. This article is without prejudice to the provisions of this convention on facilitation and clarification of compliance . . .

Art. 17: Entry into Force

1. This convention shall enter into force on the first day of the sixth month after the month in which the 40th instrument of ratification, acceptance, approval or accession has been deposited.
2. For any state which deposits its instrument of ratification, acceptance, approval or accession after the date of the deposit of the 40th instrument of ratification, acceptance, approval or accession, this convention shall enter into force on the first day of the sixth month after the date on which that state has deposited its instrument of ratification, acceptance, approval or accession.

Art. 20: Duration and Withdrawal

1. This convention shall be of unlimited duration.
2. Each state party shall, in exercising its national sovereignty, have the right to withdraw from this convention. It shall give notice of such withdrawal to all other states parties, to the Depositary [the UN Secretary-General] and to the UN Security Council. Such instrument of withdrawal shall include a full explanation of the reasons motivating this withdrawal.
3. Such withdrawal shall only take effect six months after the receipt of the instrument of withdrawal by the Depositary. If, however, on the expiry of that six-month period, the withdrawing state party is engaged in an armed conflict, the withdrawal shall not take effect before the end of the armed conflict.
4. The withdrawal of a state party from this convention shall not in any way affect the duty of states to continue fulfilling the obligations assumed under any relevant rules of international law.

6. KYOTO CLIMATE CHANGE PROTOCOL

Printed below are extracts from the Protocol to the 1992 UN Framework Convention on Climate Change adopted on the final day of the third conference of states parties held in Kyoto, Japan, on 1–11 December 1997. (Text from United Nations, New York.)

Article 2

1. Each party included in Annex I, in achieving its quantified emission limitation and reduction commitments under Article 3, in order to promote sustainable development, shall:
   (*a*) Implement and/or further elaborate policies and measures in accordance with its national circumstances, such as: (*i*) enhancement of energy efficiency in relevant sectors of the national economy; (*ii*) protection and enhancement of sinks and reservoirs of greenhouse gases not controlled by the [1987] Montreal Protocol, taking into account its commitments under relevant international environmental agreements; promotion of sustainable forest management practices, afforestation and reforestation; (*iii*) promotion of sustainable forms of agriculture in light of climate change considerations; (*iv*) promotion, research, development and increased use of new and renewable forms of energy, of carbon dioxide sequestration technologies and of advanced and innovative environmentally-sound technologies; (*v*) progressive reduction or phasing-out of market imperfections, fiscal incentives, tax and duty exemptions and subsidies in all greenhouse-gas-emitting sectors that run counter to the objective of the Convention and apply market instruments; (*vi*) encouragement of appropriate reforms in relevant sectors aimed at promoting policies and measures which limit or reduce emissions of greenhouse gases not controlled by the Montreal Protocol; (*vii*) measures to limit and/or reduce emissions of greenhouse gases not controlled by the Montreal Protocol in the transport sector; (*viii*) limitation and/or reduction of methane through recovery and use in waste management, as well as in the production, transport and distribution of energy; &133;.
2. The parties included in Annex I shall pursue limitation or reduction of emissions of greenhouse gases not controlled by the Montreal Protocol from aviation and marine bunker fuels, working through the International Civil Aviation Organization and the International Maritime Organization, respectively. . .

Article 3

1. The parties included in Annex I shall, individually or jointly, ensure that their aggregate anthropogenic carbon dioxide equivalent emissions of the greenhouse gases listed in Annex IA do not exceed their assigned amounts, calculated pursuant to their quantified emission limitation and reduction commitments inscribed in Annex IB and in accordance with the provisions of this article, with a view to reducing their overall emissions of such gases by at least 5 per cent below 1990 levels in the commitment period 2008 to 2012.

XIX.6. KYOTO CLIMATE CHANGE PROTOCOL 569

2. Each party included in Annex I shall, by 2005, have made demonstrable progress in achieving its commitments under this Protocol.

3. The net changes in greenhouse gas emissions from sources and removals by sinks resulting from direct human-induced land-use change and forestry activities, limited to afforestation, reforestation, and deforestation since 1990, measured as verifiable changes in stocks in each commitment period, shall be used to meet the commitments in this article of each party included in Annex I. The greenhouse gas emissions from sources and removals by sinks associated with those activities shall be reported in a transparent and verifiable manner and reviewed in accordance with Articles 7 and 8.

4. Prior to the first session of the Conference of the Parties serving as the meeting of the parties to this Protocol, each party included in Annex I shall provide for consideration by the Subsidiary Body for Scientific and Technological Advice data to establish its level of carbon stocks in 1990 and to enable an estimate to be made of its changes in carbon stocks in subsequent years. The Conference of the Parties serving as the meeting of the parties to this Protocol shall, at its first session or as soon as practicable thereafter, decide upon modalities, rules and guidelines as to how and which additional human-induced activities related to changes in greenhouse gas emissions and removals by sinks in the agricultural soil and land-use change and forestry categories, shall be added to, or subtracted from, the assigned amount for parties included in Annex I, taking into account uncertainties, transparency in reporting, verifiability, the methodological work of the Inter-governmental Panel on Climate Change, the advice provided by the Subsidiary Body for Scientific and Technological Advice in accordance with Article 5 and the decisions of the Conference of the Parties. Such a decision shall apply in the second and subsequent commitment periods. A party may choose to apply such a decision on these additional human-induced activities for its first commitment period, provided that these activities have taken place since 1990.

5. The parties included in Annex I undergoing the process of transition to a market economy, whose base-year or period was established pursuant to decision 9/CP.2 of the Conference of the Parties at its second session, shall use that base year or period for the implementation of their commitments under this article. Any other party included in Annex I undergoing the process of transition to a market economy which has not yet submitted its first national communication under Article 12 of the convention may also notify the Conference of the Parties serving as the meeting of the parties to this Protocol that it intends to use a historical base year or period other than 1990 for the implementation of its commitments under this article. The Conference of the Parties serving as the meeting of the parties to this Protocol shall decide on the acceptance of such notification.

6. Taking into account Article 4, paragraph 6, of the Convention, in the implementation of their commitments under this Protocol other than those in this article, a certain degree of flexibility shall be allowed by the Conference of the Parties &133; to the parties included in Annex I undergoing the process of transition to a market economy.

7. In the first quantified emission limitation and reduction commitment period, from 2008 to 2012, the assigned amount for each party included in Annex I shall be equal to the percentage inscribed for it in Annex IB of its aggregate anthropogenic carbon-dioxide equivalent emissions of the greenhouse gases listed in Annex A in 1990, or the base year or period determined in accordance with paragraph 5 above, multiplied by five. Those parties included in Annex I for whom land-use change and forestry constituted a net source of greenhouse gas emissions in 1990 shall include in their 1990 emissions base-year or period the aggregate anthropogenic carbon dioxide equivalent emissions minus removals in 1990 from land-use change for the purposes of calculating their assigned amount.

Any party included in Annex I may use 1995 as its base year for hydrofluorocarbons, perfluorocarbons and sulphur hexafluoride, for the purposes of the calculation referred to above.

9. Commitments for subsequent periods for parties included in Annex I shall be established in amendments to Annex IB to this Protocol, which shall be adopted in accordance with the provisions of Article 21, paragraph 7. The Conference of the Parties serving as the meeting of the parties to this Protocol shall initiate the consideration of such commitments at least seven years before the end of the first commitment period mentioned in paragraph 7 above.

10. Any emission reduction units, or any part of an assigned amount which a party acquires from another party in accordance with the provisions of Article 6 and of Article 17, shall be added to the assigned amount for that party.

11. Any emission reduction units, or any part of an assigned amount, which a party transfers to another party in accordance with the provisions of Article 6 and of Article 17 shall be subtracted from the assigned amount for that party.

12. Any certified emission reductions which a party acquires from another party in accordance with the provisions of Article 12 shall be added to the assigned amount for that party.

13. If the emissions of a party included in Annex I during a commitment period are less than its assigned amount under this article, this difference shall, on request of that party, be added to the assigned amount for that party for subsequent commitment periods.

14. Each party included in Annex I shall strive to implement the commitments mentioned in paragraph 1 above in such a way as to minimize adverse social, environmental and economic impacts on developing country parties, particularly those identified in Article 4, paragraphs 8 and 9, of the Convention. In line with relevant decisions of the Conference of the Parties on the implementation of those paragraphs, the Conference of the Parties serving as the meeting of the parties to this Protocol shall, at its first session, consider what actions are necessary to minimize the adverse effects of climate change and/or the impacts of response measures on parties referred to in those paragraphs. Among the issues to be considered shall be the establishment of funding, insurance and transfer of technology.

Article 4

1. Any parties included in Annex I that have agreed to jointly fulfil their commitments under Article 3 shall be deemed to have met those commitments provided that their total combined aggregate anthropogenic carbon dioxide equivalent emissions of the greenhouse gases listed in Annex A do not exceed their assigned amounts calculated pursuant to their quantified emission limitation and reduction commitments inscribed in Annex B and in accordance with the provisions of Article 3. The respective emission level allocated to each of the parties to the agreement shall be set out in that agreement. . .

Article 5

1. Each party included in Annex I shall have in place, no later than one year prior to the start of the first commitment period, a national system for the estimation of anthropogenic emissions by sources and removals by sinks of all greenhouse gases not controlled by the Montreal Protocol. Guidelines for such national systems, which shall incorporate the methodologies specified in paragraph 2 below, shall be decided upon by the Conference of the Parties serving as the meeting of the parties to this Protocol at its first session.

2. Methodologies for estimating anthropogenic emissions by sources and removals by sinks of all greenhouse gases not controlled by the Montreal Protocol shall be those accepted by the Inter-governmental Panel on Climate Change and agreed upon by the Conference of the Parties at its third session. Where such methodologies are not used, appropriate adjustments shall be applied according to methodologies agreed upon by the Conference of the Parties serving as the meeting of the parties to this Protocol at its first session. Based on the work of, *inter alia*, the Inter-governmental Panel on Climate Change and advice provided by the Subsidiary Body for Scientific and Technological Advice, the Conference of the Parties serving as the meeting of the parties to this Protocol shall regularly review and, as appropriate, revise such methodologies and adjustments, taking fully into account any relevant decisions by the Conference of the Parties. Any revision to methodologies or adjustments shall be used only for the purposes of ascertaining compliance with commitments under Article 3 in respect of any commitment period adopted subsequent to that revision.

3. The global warming potentials used to calculate the carbon dioxide equivalence of anthropogenic emissions by sources and removals by sinks of greenhouse gases not controlled by the Montreal Protocol listed in Annex A shall be those accepted by the Inter-governmental Panel on Climate Change and agreed upon by the Conference of the Parties at its third session. Based on the work of, *inter alia*, the Inter-governmental Panel on Climate Change and advice provided by the Subsidiary Body for Scientific and Technological Advice, the Conference of the Parties serving as the meeting of the parties to this Protocol shall regularly review and, as appropriate, revise the global warming potential of each such greenhouse gas, taking fully into account any relevant decisions by the Conference of the Parties. Any revision to a global warming potential shall apply only to those commitments under Article 3 in respect of any commitment period adopted subsequent to that revision.

Article 6

1. For the purpose of meeting its commitments under Article 3, any party included in Annex I may transfer to, or acquire from, any other such party emission reduction units resulting from projects aimed at reducing anthropogenic emissions by sources or enhancing anthropogenic removals by sinks of greenhouse gases in any sector of the economy, provided that:

(*a*) Any such project has the approval of the parties involved;

(*b*) Any such project provides a reduction in emissions by sources, or an enhancement of removals by sinks, that is additional to any that would otherwise occur;

(*c*) It does not acquire any emission reduction units if it is not in compliance with its obligations under Articles 5 and 7;

(*d*) The acquisition of emission reduction units shall be supplemental to domestic actions for the purposes of meeting commitments under Article 3.

XIX.6. KYOTO CLIMATE CHANGE PROTOCOL

2. The Conference of the Parties serving as the meeting of the parties to this Protocol may, at its first session or as soon as practicable thereafter, further elaborate guidelines for the implementation of this article, including for verification and reporting.

3. A party included in Annex I may authorize legal entities to participate, under its responsibility, in actions leading to the generation, transfer or acquisition under this article of emission reduction units. ...

Article 10

All parties, taking into account their common but differentiated responsibilities and their specific national and regional development priorities, objectives and circumstances, without introducing any new commitments for parties not included in Annex I, but reaffirming existing commitments in Article 4, paragraph 1, of the Convention, and continuing to advance the implementation of these commitments in order to achieve sustainable development, taking into account Article 4, paragraphs 3, 5 and 7, of the Convention, shall:

(a) Formulate, where relevant and to the extent possible, cost-effective national, and where appropriate regional programmes to improve the quality of local emission factors, activity data and/or models which reflect the socio-economic conditions of each party for the preparation and periodic updating of national inventories of anthropogenic emissions by sources and removals by sinks of all greenhouse gases not controlled by the Montreal Protocol, using comparable methodologies to be agreed upon by the Conference of the Parties, and consistent with the guidelines for national communications adopted by the Conference of the Parties;

(b) Formulate, implement, publish and regularly update national and, where appropriate, regional programmes containing measures to mitigate climate change and measures to facilitate adequate adaptation to climate change.

Article 17

The Conference of Parties shall define the relevant principles, modalities, rules and guidelines, in particular for verification, reporting and accountability for emissions trading. The parties included in Annex B may participate in emissions trading for the purposes of fulfilling their commitments under Article 3. Any such trading shall be supplemental to domestic actions for the purpose of meeting quantified emission limitation and reduction commitments under that article.

Article 18

The Conference of the Parties serving as the meeting of the parties to this Protocol shall, at its first session, approve appropriate and effective procedures and mechanisms to determine and to address cases of non-compliance with the provisions of this Protocol, including through the development of an indicative list of consequences, taking into account the cause, type, degree and frequency of non-compliance. Any procedure and mechanism under this article entailing binding consequences shall be adopted by means of an amendment to this Protocol. . . .

Article 24

1. This Protocol shall be open for signature and subject to ratification, acceptance or approval by states and regional economic integration organizations which are parties to the Convention. It shall be open for signature at UN Headquarters in New York from 16 March 1998 to 15 March 1999. The Protocol shall be open for accession from the day after the date on which it is closed for signature. Instruments of ratification, acceptance, approval or accession shall be deposited with the Depositary [the UN Secretary-General]. . . .

Article 25

1. This Protocol shall enter into force on the 90th day after the date on which not less than 55 parties to the Convention, incoporating parties included in Annex I which accounted in total for at least 55 per cent of the total carbon dioxide emissions for 1990 of the parties included in Annex I, have deposited their instruments of ratification, acceptance, approval or accession. . .

Annex I

A. *Greenhouse gases*: carbon dioxide; methane; nitrous oxide; hydrofluorocarbons; perfluorocarbons; sulphur hexafluoride.

B. *Party-quantified emission limitation or reduction commitment (percentage of base year or period)*:
Australia 108; Austria 92; Belgium 92; Bulgaria* 92; Canada 94; Croatia* 95; Czech Republic* 92; Denmark 92; Estonia* 92; European Community 92; Finland 92; France 92; Germany 92; Greece 92; Hungary* 94; Iceland 110; Ireland 92; Italy 92; Japan 94; Latvia* 92; Liechtenstein 92; Lithuania* 92; Luxembourg 92; Monaco 92; Netherlands 92; New Zealand 100; Norway 101; Poland* 94; Portugal 92; Romania* 92; Russian Federation* 100; Slovakia* 92; Slovenia* 92; Spain 92; Sweden 92; Switzerland 92; Ukraine* 100; United Kingdom 92; United States 93. (*Countries that are undergoing the process of transition to a market economy.)

7. UNITED KINGDOM LABOUR CABINET

(as at 31 December 1997)

Prime Minister, First Lord of the Treasury and Minister for the Civil Service	Rt. Hon. Tony Blair, MP
Deputy Prime Minister and Secretary of State for the Environment, Transport and the Regions	Rt. Hon. John Prescott, MP
Lord Chancellor	Rt. Hon. The Lord Irvine of Lairg
Chancellor of the Exchequer	Rt. Hon. Gordon Brown, MP
Secretary of State for the Home Department	Rt. Hon. Jack Straw, MP
Secretary of State for Foreign and Commonwealth Affairs	Rt. Hon. Robin Cook, MP
President of the Board of Trade and Secretary of State for Trade and Industry	Rt. Hon. Margaret Beckett, MP
President of the Council and Leader of the House of Commons	Rt. Hon. Ann Taylor, MP
Secretary of State for Social Security and Minister for Women	Rt. Hon. Harriet Harman, MP
Chief Secretary to the Treasury	Rt. Hon. Alistair Darling, MP
Secretary of State for Northern Ireland	Rt. Hon. Marjorie (Mo) Mowlam, MP
Secretary of State for Culture, Media and Sport	Rt. Hon. Chris Smith, MP
Secretary of State for Education and Employment	Rt. Hon. David Blunkett, MP
Secretary of State for Defence	Rt. Hon. George Robertson, MP
Secretary of State for Health	Rt. Hon. Frank Dobson, MP
Lord Privy Seal and Leader of the House of Lords	Lord Richard of Ammanford
Secretary of State for Scotland	Rt. Hon. Donald Dewar, MP
Chancellor of the Duchy of Lancaster (Minister of Public Service)	Rt. Hon. David Clark, MP
Secretary of State for Wales	Rt. Hon. Ron Davies, MP
Secretary of State for International Development	Rt. Hon. Clare Short, MP
Minister of Transport	Rt. Hon. Gavin Strang, MP
Minister of Agriculture, Fisheries and Food	Rt. Hon. Jack Cunningham, MP

8. UNITED STATES DEMOCRATIC ADMINISTRATION
(as at 31 December 1997)

Members of the Cabinet:

President	Bill Clinton
Vice-President	Al Gore
Secretary of State	Madeleine K. Albright
Secretary of the Treasury	Robert E. Rubin
Secretary of Defence	William S. Cohen
Secretary of the Interior	Bruce Babbitt
Secretary of Agriculture	Dan Glickman
Secretary of Commerce	William M. Daley
Secretary of Housing & Urban Development	Andrew M. Cuomo
Secretary of Transportation	Rodney E. Slater
Secretary of Health & Human Services	Donna E. Shalala
Attorney-General	Janet Reno
Secretary of Labour	Alexis M. Herman
Secretary of Energy	Federico Pena
Secretary of Education	Richard W. Riley
Secretary of Veterans' Affairs	Jesse Brown

Other Leading Executive Branch Officials:

White House Chief of Staff	Erskine Bowles
Director of Office of Management & Budget	Franklin D. Raines
Chairman of Council of Economic Advisers	Janet L. Yellin
National Security Adviser	Samuel D. Berger
Head of Environmental Protection Agency	Carol Browner
Director of Central Intelligence Agency	George Tenet
Representative for Trade Negotiations	Charlene Barshefsky
Ambassador to United Nations	Bill Richardson
Director of National Economic Council	Gene Sperling
Director of Small Business Administration	Aida Alvarez
Director of US Information Agency	Joseph Duffey

XX OBITUARY

Asfa-Wossen, Crown Prince (b. 1916), was the son and heir of the Emperor of Ethiopia, Haile Selassie (Ras Tafari), and accompanied his father into exile in England when Mussolini's Italy conquered their homeland. His father was restored to the throne after World War II but was deposed by a military coup in 1974 and died the following year. The Crown Prince assumed the imperial title but declined to return to Ethiopia on the conditions demanded by the army dictatorship. The royal family moved in 1960 to the USA, where the Crown Prince died 17 January.

Awdry, Rev Wilbert Vere, OBE (b. 1911), British clergyman, achieved fame far beyond his home country for his books for children with speaking railway engines as their characters. Always a railway enthusiast, he wrote such stories for his son, but found a publisher in 1944 when *The Three Railway Engines* appeared, followed by *Thomas the Tank Engine*, which became a classic. After resigning his last charge of a parish in 1965 he devoted himself to writing, and besides his popular stories for children wrote or collaborated in works on industrial archaeology and railway history. Died 21 March

Banda, Hastings (b. 1906?), President of Malawi from 1966 and Life President from 1971, led one of the most conservative and stable regimes in Central Africa. After attending a missionary school, still a young boy he set off on foot for South Africa, where, while working as a hospital cleaner, he decided to become a doctor. Having saved enough to get to the USA, he worked his way to a degree at the University of Chicago. After studying medicine at a black university, he took his LRCP at Edinburgh in 1941, and practised as a doctor in England for 17 years. Persuaded by two fervent young nationalists, he returned to what was then called Nyasaland, to head the Malawi Congress Party which won overwhelming victory in 1961 against the proposed Central African Federation. In 1964 he became Prime Minister of independent Malawi, in 1966 President and in 1971 Life President. In office he pursued a very different policy from other Central African states, maintaining close links with South Africa and spurning the Organization of African Unity. He encouraged business ambitions, often corrupt. Regular elections were held, but Malawi was a one-party state, often sustained by violence. In 1993 a referendum, held under pressure from Western aid donors, showed a large majority in favour of multi-party democracy, and elections in the following year defeated Banda's party. Charged with murder of opponents, he was acquitted, but he admitted that atrocities had been committed in his regime. He retired from politics shortly before he died, 25 November

Bao Dai (b. 1913), was the last Emperor of Vietnam, succeeding to an ancient throne in 1926, and taking power in 1932, after completing his education in France. He abdicated in 1945, but returned in 1949 as head of state under French colonial rule. In 1954 he was deposed by an American-backed referendum, and thereafter lived in luxury in France, indulging his tastes for gambling and motor racing. Died 31 July

Barco Vargas, Virgilio (b. 1921), President of Colombia 1986–90, born to a rich Conservative family, turned Liberal after education at Boston University and the Massachusetts Institute of Technology. Inter-party violence in his constituency led to his temporary exile, but returning in 1954 he joined in negotiating peace. As a national senator he went on to hold ministerial posts between 1956 and 1964 and the London embassy in 1961–62, to which he was to return in 1990–92. In 1966 he became mayor of Bogotá, in 1969–74 a director of the World Bank, and in 1977 ambassador to Washington. Overwhelmingly victorious in the presidential election of 1986, he applied liberal reforms to the economy and fought Colombia's drug barons without conspicuous success. Died 20 May

Barwick, Sir Garfield, AK, GCMG (b. 1903)), Chief Justice of Australia 1964–81, was at the heart of a constitutional crisis in 1975, when he advised the governor-general, Sir John Kerr, that he had power to dismiss the Prime Minister, Gough Whitlam, after the Senate had blocked essential financial business. Of modest descent, Barwick had won a scholarship to study law, was called to the bar in 1926 and was made KC in 1941. Constitutional law became his speciality, and he appeared before the Privy Council in London as well as the state and federal courts. Prime Minister Menzies lured him into politics in 1958, naming him as Attorney-General and then, in 1961, Minister for External Affairs; but he was no great success as a politician and was happy to return to the exposition rather than expansion of the law. Died 13 July

Berlin, Sir Isaiah, OM, FBA (b. 1909), British philosopher, son of a Jewish timber merchant, was born at Riga, Latvia, then part of the Russian empire. Aged eight, he watched the Bolsheviks seize power in Petrograd; his family fled from their regime to London. He won a scholarship from St Paul's School to Corpus Christi College, Oxford, where he did brilliantly—a double first, fellowships at All Souls and New College, a professorship of social and political theory, and the headship of a house; he was the first president of Wolfson College, which he helped to found. He dissociated himself from the logical positivists, and settled instead to work on the history of political ideas. He was a stimulating lecturer, for those who could follow his extremely rapid speech, and a perpetual fount of anecdote in private. During World War II he wrote weekly dispatches to London from Washington, surveying the American political scene, and spent six months in Moscow, also as a diplomat, in 1945. There he met Anna Akhmatova and Boris Pasternak, both of whom he admired. He was also a warm, though distant, supporter of the new state of Israel. His books include a life of Karl Marx, *The Hedgehog and the Fox* and *Against the Current*; he also wrote a mass of essays, most of them propounding a liberal and pluralistic view of society. He was president of the British Academy 1974–77 and received 23 honorary degrees as well as his knighthood in 1957 and membership of the Order of Merit in 1971. Died 6 November

Bing, Sir Rudolf (b. in Vienna, 1902), British musical impresario, was general manager of the Metropolitan Opera, New York 1950–72. Earlier in life he had been a friend of Carl Ebert, who gave him his first job in Darmstadt, but Ebert was anti-Nazi and Bing was a Jew, and both fled Germany. Ebert summoned Bing to become assistant producer at Glyndebourne. After the war, he returned to Glyndebourne as general manager of the Opera, until his appointment to the Metropolitan Opera. He returned to Britain, to receive his knighthood in 1971 and after his retirement. His mental powers were failing, and back in New York in 1987 he spent the last part of his life in a Hebrew home for the aged in the Bronx. Died 2 September

Brennan, Justice William (b. 1906), was a member of the US Supreme Court for 32 years 1958–90, during which his judgments were a monument of constitutional resistance to the executive power and of the defence of individual rights. He had been a successful lawyer—mainly in labour cases—in New Jersey and from 1949 a state judge when President Eisenhower picked him for the Supreme Court. His liberalism flourished with the Court appointments by Presidents Kennedy and Johnson. Among his most famous rulings were *Baker v. Carr* (1962), which thwarted certain manipulations of the electoral system, *New York Times v. Sullivan* (1964), which enhanced the freedom of the press by ruling that a public official could not recover damages for a defamatory statement unless it had been made in malice, and *Times Inc. v. Hill* (1967), which applied the same test to defamatory statements about others prominent in the news. Appointments to the Supreme Court by later conservative Presidents hampered Justice Brennan's previously dominating influence, but it was not stilled until his retirement in 1990. Died 24 July

Burroughs, William (b. 1914), American writer, was most famed for his scatological book *The Naked Lunch* (1959), which distilled his own experiences as a former drug addict. The son of a successful industrialist, he was educated at Harvard and the University of Vienna, but then rejected bourgeois academia for the *demimonde* and the fringe of crime. His later works included *The Soft Machine* (1961 and 1968), *The Yage Letters* (1963), *The Job* (1970) and *The Wild Boys* (1972). Died 2 August

Calvin, Professor Melvin (b. 1911), American scientist, was awarded the Nobel Prize for Chemistry in 1941 for his pioneer work on chemical photosynthesis. After graduating from Michigan College of Science and the University of Minnesota he had spent two years at Manchester University before being recruited in 1937 to the chemistry faculty of the University of California at Berkeley, his workplace for the rest of his life. Before long he was concentrating on problems of photochemistry, working in a well-funded laboratory which, in 1963, when rebuilt, was named after him. Beyond photosynthesis, his interests spread to such speculative questions as the origin of life. Died 8 January

Compton, Denis, CBE (b. 1918), English cricketer, became an idol of the public, almost as much for his engaging personality as for his mastery of the game. He played for his county, Middlesex, at Lord's when he was 17, and for England a year later, scoring a century against Australia in 1939. After military service in World War II, he returned to brilliant form, hitting four successive centuries in Test matches in Australia 1946–47, and following this by scoring a total of 3,816 runs—averaging over 90 per innings—in the 1947 English season. In Test matches and the county game his splendid feats continued, despite painful trouble in his right knee, which hastened his retirement from first-class cricket in 1957. In his whole career he had scored nearly 15,000 runs and hit 60 centuries. His style at the wicket was far from classical, but he had a wonderful eye and inimitable footwork skill. He was also a very good footballer, playing for Arsenal until his knee gave way. Died 23 April

Cousteau, Jacques-Yves (b. 1910), French under-sea explorer and innovator, captured the imagination of millions all over the world when, in 1955, his film *The Silent World*, depicting the submarine scenes he had photographed, was released. He had entered the French Navy in 1930, and during World War II won the Légion d'Honneur for counter-intelligence during the Resistance. He was already working on under-water technique, and in 1943 he and Emile Gagnan invented an air-breathing apparatus which eventually became SCUBA and has since been used worldwide. He had already been experimenting with under-water photography and film. In 1952, on leave from the Navy to conduct scientific research, he converted a former British minesweeper into the diving research vessel *Calypso*. In 1956 he became director of the Monaco oceanographic research institute, which he vigorously revived, developing the world market for the aqualung and associated products and inventing submarine living-spaces for working divers. Cousteau never claimed to be a scientist, only an engineer and inventor who made things happen, and he had a gift for publicity in an environmental cause. Died 25 June

Dahanayake, Wijayananda (b. 1902), was Prime Minister of Sri Lanka 1959–60. Entering politics in 1935 and becoming mayor of Galle, he won a parliamentary seat in 1947 and was made Minister of Education in 1956. In that office he replaced English as the medium of instruction by Sinhala and Tamil. After the assassination of Prime Minister Bandaranaike in 1959 he became Prime Minister, but broke with his party, the Sri Lanka Freedom Party, and lost his seat at the general election which he promptly called. Retiring from politics in 1989, he died 6 May

Danilova, Alexandra (b. 1903), Russian ballerina, joined the imperial ballet school in St Petersburg at the age of eight, and graduated to the Kirov Ballet in 1920. After a tour in Germany with George Balanchine, in 1924 she was enlisted by Serge

Diaghilev in his Ballets Russes and became a star solo dancer. After Diaghilev's death she joined de Basil's Ballet Russe Company, in which she won international fame in such ballets as *Swan Lake*, *Petrushka* and *La Boutique Fantasque*. In 1938 she shared the status of prima ballerina in Massine's Ballet Russe de Monte Carlo, and for the next 14 years she was a world-admired star of ballet, beloved for her beauty, grace and technique. With Frederick Ashton she made a triumphant return to Covent Garden, London, in 1949. Balanchine, who had composed many new dances for her in this period, when she retired from the ballet stage in 1957 invited her to teach in his School of American Ballet. Still beautiful, she went on dancing until near the end of her life. Died 13 July

de Kooning, Willem (b. in Holland, 1904), American painter, was a leading figure in the modernist art movement called Abstract Impressionism. He had been apprenticed to a Rotterdam firm of commercial artists, who enabled him to acquire an academic art training at night school, and he went on to study at art schools in Brussels and Antwerp. In 1926 he arrived in the USA as a stowaway, and took a variety of jobs which led him to become a 'Sunday painter', mixing with other modernist artists like Arshile Gorky. From 1935 he gave his whole time to art; his first one-man exhibition was at the Egan gallery in New York in 1948. His painting *Woman 1* (1950–53) was included in the exhibition *The New American Painting* which was shown at the Tate Gallery in 1959. Distorted and macabre, his abstract paintings never lost touch with the human form. After the 1950s, his power declined, but his earlier works rose phenomenally in value, his *Interchange* (1950) selling for over $20 million. He gave up painting in 1990, and died 19 March

Deng Xiaoping (b. 1904), China's paramount leader, took power in 1978, winning a majority in the Communist Party's central committee, to which he had been restored after two years of disgrace for his opposition to Mao Zedong's Cultural Revolution; this was the second time he had been stripped of office for a similar reason. He had joined the party in 1924 and was a political commissar during the Long March of 1934–36. In Mao's People's Republic he became a Vice-Premier and Finance Minister in Zhou Enlai's cabinet, and in 1956 was elected to the standing committee of the politburo. He had won international attention for his tough negotiation with the Soviet Union in 1954–62. After Mao's death and his reinstatement in office he soon became master of the politburo and the arbiter of China's policy, in effect supreme leader of the country. He modernized the economy and the army, and presented a more agreeable face to the world, while stiffening party discipline and dealing ruthlessly with dissidents. As to Hong Kong, he coined the phrase 'One Country, Two Systems', but obdurately refused to countenance any system of open political democracy after the island's return to China. Died 19 February

Diana, Princess of Wales (b. 1961), was the third daughter of Viscount Althorp, who succeeded his father as Earl Spencer in 1975, whereupon she became Lady Diana Spencer. Her parents had separated in 1969. Lady Diana's schooling was followed by various jobs which exercised her talents for dancing and the care of young children. When her name was linked with that of the Prince of Wales she became the object of intense media interest, which never ceased thereafter. She and Prince Charles became engaged in February 1981 and were married in St Paul's Cathedral in July of that year. Two sons were born: Prince William in 1982, Prince Harry in 1984.

With her husband, the Princess of Wales took part in overseas tours, which brought them, in 1985, to stay with President Reagan at the White House. She also became patron of numerous charities, mostly concerned with the sick and the homeless. In 1992, however, a Sunday newspaper serialized a book giving evidence of strain in the marriage. The Prince of Wales was known to be intimate with another woman. At the end of 1992 the Prince and Princess decided to separate, and in 1996 they were divorced.

The Princess was well provided for, enabling her to live a life of her own, private and public. She had already shown concern with the problem of AIDS/HIV, which became a focus of her charitable work and of her gift for comforting, with many a personal gesture, the sick, the young and the disadvantaged of all races. She was also prominent in the campaign for ending the production and use of landmines. On her own, in Britain and abroad she became an idol especially for a younger generation. The penalty was being constantly surrounded by media operators whose intrusions would stop at nothing. The last and happiest of her affairs was with Dodi Fayed, who shared her tragic end in a high-speed car accident in Paris. Died 31 August

Dolmetsch, Carl (b. in France 1911), British musician, was the second son of Arnold Dolmetsch, famous for his study of early music and his revival of the recorder. The family had fled to London in 1914. His father had acquired a country retreat at Haslemere, Surrey, which became a focus of worship for the devotees of early music, and the scene of the Haslemere Festival. Much influenced by his father, Carl became a virtuoso recorder player, earning a BBC radio performance at the age of 14. In 1938 he became the first musical director of the Society of Recorder Players. In the course of his musical career he toured the USA and Europe, commissioned works by modern composers, reset Renaissance music, ran the Haslemere Festival for 50 years, and invented a plastic recorder which became the first musical instrument for millions of children all over the world. Died 11 July

Eysenck, Hans J. (b. in Germany, 1916), was professor of psychology, University of London, Institute of Psychiatry, 1955–83, and director of the psychological department, Maudsley Hospital 1946–83, during which time he published many books and learned papers which influenced psychological studies far and near. Though impeccably Aryan in descent, he had been called at school a 'White Jew' for his intense hostility to Nazism, and in 1934 he left Germany to continue his education in Britain. During World War II, as an 'enemy alien', he found employment at the emergency psychology hospital at Mill Hill. His subsequent work on genetic and environmental influences on psychological personality caused him to be attacked as a racist, a charge which he countered in his book *Race, Intelligence and Education* (1971). Died 4 September

Fleischman, Lawrence (b. 1923), American art collector and philanthropist, was inspired by a visit to the British Museum while on leave from the US Army in 1945. Born of immigrant Jewish parents, he married Barbara Greenberg in 1945, and together they formed a collection of American art, which was given an official tour of South America and exhibitions in Europe and Israel. In 1966 the Fleischmans bought a half-share in a New York gallery which specialized in American art, and in 1969 they founded the *American Art Journal*. In 1971, at the invitation of Pope Paul VI, Fleischman helped to create a collection of modern religious art, to be shown in the Vatican Museum. The Fleischmans' taste and expertise also embraced antiquities from Greece and Rome: their classical collection they donated in 1996 to the Getty Museum in Malibu. They gave bountifully to the Metropolitan Museum of Art in New York and to the British Museum, for which Fleischman agreed to lead fundraising in America. Died 31 January

Gairy, Sir Eric (b. 1922), was Prime Minister of Grenada 1974–79. His first job had been as an elementary school teacher, but he soon found his role as a trade union organizer, starting a powerful general union in 1950 and then the Grenada United Labour Party. He was Minister of Trade and Production 1956–57. After a spell out of office he became Chief Minister of Grenada 1961–63, and again in 1967, to lead an administration renowned for corruption, violent tactics and personal extravagance. In 1979 he was overthrown in an armed coup by the New Jewel Movement. He spent four years in the USA, then returned to Grenada, striving without success to regain power. Died 23 August

Ginsberg, Allen (b. 1926), American poet, was, in the 1950s, one of the original self-styled 'beats', rebels against conventional prosody and literary taste. In 1956 his long poem *Howl* survived an unsuccessful prosecution for obscenity to become almost a standard text for the disenchanted young of America. Homosexual, unconstrained by conscience or code, he published around a dozen books and much else, gave poetry readings in universities and preached the superiority of yoga over the narcotics in which he had himself indulged. Died 5 April

Grappelli, Stephane (b. in Paris, 1908), French jazz violinist, played with the gypsy guitarist Django Reinhart from 1934 until the latter's death in 1953. In the 1970s and '80s he made many recordings with the great violinist Yehudi Menuhin. Died 1 December

Hackett, General Sir John, GCB, DSO, MC (b. in Australia, 1910), British soldier-scholar, was C.-in-C. British Army of the Rhine 1966–68. Educated at Geelong School and New College, Oxford, he joined the Army in 1931. Already multilingual, he added Arabic after being posted to the Trans-Jordan Frontier Force in 1937. In World War II he served in the Syrian campaign and the Western Desert before raising and commanding the 4th Parachute Brigade. It fought in Italy and at Arnhem, where he was seriously wounded and taken prisoner. His escape and shelter by a Dutch family are narrated in his book *I Was a Stranger* (1977). After leading the British withdrawal from Palestine and attending the Imperial Defence College in 1951, he commanded first a brigade and then a division of the British Army of the Rhine. He was appointed GOC Northern Ireland in 1961 and Deputy Chief of the General Staff in 1963. His fluency in German was a valuable asset when he took command of the Army of the Rhine. Retiring from the Army in 1968, he became Principal of King's College, University of London, for the next seven years. His book *The Third World War* was published in 1978 and a sequel in 1981. He was president of the Classical Association in 1971. Died 7 September

Hahn, Emily (b. 1905), American author and traveller, was for 68 years an admired regular contributor to *The New Yorker* magazine, besides writing numerous books. Her first travel book, *Congo, Solo* (1933), was based on her two-year experiences in the Belgian Congo. In 1935 she bolted to the Far East, where she became the mistress of a Chinese poet and then fell in love with a British army officer, Major Charles Boxer, whom she married after his release from a Japanese prison camp at the end of World War II. Feminist, adventurous, heedless of convention, she maintained to the end a constant output of books and articles on exotic places and animals. Died 18 February

Harriman, Pamela (b. 1920), US ambassador to France, was described by a *Times* obituarist as one of the great courtesans of her age, which was odd for a woman of English noble birth (her father was Lord Digby, 11th Baron) who ended life as diplomatic representative of one great republic to another. She was, however, married three times, first to Randolph Churchill, secondly to Leland Hayward, the Broadway musical producer (1960–71), and thirdly to Averell Harriman (1971–86), with whom she had already had an affair in the 1940s. She had also had amorous liaisons with other men, notably Edward Murrow, the influential London correspondent of CBS during World War II. As the widow of a successful international statesman, having taken American nationality, she was an appropriate choice for the Paris embassy, where she died 5 February

Hassan, Sir Joshua, GBE, KCMG, LVO, QC (b. 1915), Chief Minister of Gibraltar 1964–69 and 1972–87, fought for the independence of Gibraltar under the British Crown against Spanish ambition and Whitehall colonialism. A successful barrister before World War II, in which he served as a gunner in the Gibraltar Regiment, he then entered politics, forming his own party and becoming mayor of the colony and its Chief Minister under a new self-governing constitution. Defying the coercion of General Franco, who closed the frontier, he nailed his colours to the mast of unqualified British sovereignty. He retired in 1987, replete with honours from the Crown. Died 1 July

Hershey, Alfred (b. 1908), shared with Max Delbrück and Salvador Luria the

Nobel Prize for Medicine in 1969 for their ground-breaking study of the genetic structure of viruses. The findings of their research were essential to scientific understanding of many diseases and conditions and their control by drugs. Hershey had studied at the University of Michigan (PhD, 1934), had taught at the University of Washington, St Louis, and had worked at the Cold Spring Harbor laboratory, where he was director of genetical research 1962–74. Died 22 May

Herzog, Chaim (b. in Ireland 1918), President of Israel 1983–93, had served in the British army 1939–47 after qualifying as a barrister, and retained his affection for Britain. His father was successively Chief Rabbi of Ireland and of Israel. In the turbulent early years of the Israeli state, when it fought for survival, then for enlargement, he alternated between a military career and his law practice and business interests. From 1975 to 1978 he was Israel's ambassador to the United Nations. In 1981 he was elected to the Knesset as a member of the Labour Party, which in 1983 decided to make him its candidate for the presidency, against Menachem Begin's Likud nominee, whom he narrowly defeated. Retiring after two terms of office, he died 17 April

Hogan, Ben (b. 1912), American golfer, was four times winner of the US Open championship. His golf career had started as a caddie at the age of 15; in 1929 he became a professional player, rising quickly to the top circuits. In 1949, after his first win in the US Open, he was seriously injured in a car crash, but the dedication that he gave to everything in golf brought him recovery to the pinnacle of success. In 1953 he won five major tournaments, including the US Masters (by five strokes), the US Open (by six), and the British Open (by four). Died 25 July

Hughes, Pat (b. 1902), British tennis player, won the Italian Open singles title in 1933, but it was in doubles that he excelled. In partnership with Fred Perry he won the doubles title at the French Open in 1933 and at the Australian Open in 1934, and reached the final at Wimbledon in 1932. Partnered by Raymond Tuckey he won the Wimbledon title in 1936. Retiring after World War II, in which he served in the RAF, he had a successful career, developing Dunlop's tennis equipment business and editing their *Lawn Tennis Almanac* 1939–58. Died 8 May

Ibuka, Masaru (b. 1907), Japanese electronic engineer, founded the Sony Corporation of Japan for the manufacture and marketing of transistor radios and other more complex products. With a likeminded partner, Akio Morita, whom he had met in the navy in World War II, together they founded a company called Tokyo Telecommunications Engineering, which they soon renamed Sony. Borrowing technology begun in the USA, Sony produced the first cheap pocket radio in 1957, the first transistor television in 1959, and the first solid-state video recorder in 1961. Later, the company expanded into more sophisticated electronic products, such as the Walkman portable cassette player. Retiring in 1976 from the Sony chairmanship, Ibuka launched the Sony Fund for Education to promote the teaching of science in schools. Died 19 December

Jacobs, Helen (b. 1908), American tennis player, won the Wimbledon championship in 1936, having taken the US national title four years running 1932–35. The misfortune of her tennis career was its overlap with that of Helen Wills Moody, a still stronger player, who won the US title seven times between 1923 and 1931. Their most famous encounter was in 1933 at Forest Hills, when Moody retired with unspecified injury when three games down in the final set. In World War II, Helen Jacobs joined the US Navy, and after 11 years' service held the rank of commander. She retired from competitive tennis in 1947, pursued a successful career in sports business and farming, and was also a prolific author. Died 2 June

Jagan, Cheddi (b. 1918), President of Guyana from 1992, was by profession a US-trained dentist before entering politics and, in 1950, founding the People's Progressive Party (PPP), with his American-Jewish wife Janet. As PPP leader, he headed pre-independence governments from 1957, drawing most support from ethnic Asian rural workers, but lost office in 1964, two years before independence. As a committed marxist, he conducted fierce opposition to governments of Forbes Burnham, a conservative backed by African Guyanese who died in 1985 after nearly 20 years as Prime Minister. Elected President in 1992, Jagan was obliged to preside over the country's economic revival under conventional policies, but he never forsook his socialist faith (and was succeeded in the presidency by his equally committed wife). Died 6 March

Jamali, Mohammed Fadhil (b. 1903), was the last surviving signatory of the Charter of the United Nations as Foreign Secretary of Iraq, a post he held for 15 years with a brief interlude as Prime Minister. He brought to Iraqi politics a profound ecumenical faith. When the royal regime was murderously overthrown he was sentenced to death, and was saved only by the intercessiion of world figures, including Pope John XXIII, and other Arab leaders. In exile he was made professor of the philosophy of education at the University of Tunisia, where he continued to promote the gospel of reconciliation and peace between nations and religions under the banner of 'moral rearmament'. Died 24 May

Jones, Professor R.V., CH, CB, FRS (b. 1911), was the brain behind Britain's defence against the German Luftwaffe in World War II. In June 1940, as scientific intelligence adviser in the Air Ministry, after giving the War Cabinet an account of the Luftwaffe's capability of precisely pinpointing its bomber targets he was promised all the resources needed to counter the menace. His string of successes, including defensive cover for the D-day landings, were chronicled in a television series and later his book *Most Secret War* (1978). In analysing intelligence he was a genius. Besides his British honours he was awarded the US Medals for Merit and Freedom.

Jones was educated at Alleyn's School and Wadham College, Oxford. After a two-year senior studentship at Balliol College he joined the Air Ministry in 1936, rising to director of intelligence ten years later.

In 1946 he accepted the chair of natural philosophy at the University of Aberdeen. There he pursued fundamental research, notably in the measurement of very small angles and motion. Among his many public services was the chairmanship of the British Committee for the History of Science. Died 17 December

Kelley, Clarence (b. 1911), was director of the US Federal Bureau of Investigation 1973–77. He had joined the staff of the FBI soon after taking a law degree in 1940, and served it for 20 years, with a break of two years in the Navy in World War II. Appointed chief of police in Kansas City in 1961, he tackled the force's notorious corruption and, less successfully, its alienation from the black community, and pioneered the computerization of police records. President Nixon chose him to head the FBI in 1973. There he applied both his cleansing and modernizing efforts to a system fossilized by his dictatorial predecessor, J. Edgar Hoover, but not without failures and criticism. In 1973 he retired, when President Carter made clear that his term would not be extended. Died 5 August

Kendrew, Sir John, FRS (b. 1917), shared with Max Perutz the 1962 Nobel Prize for Chemistry, for their research on the molecular structure of biological proteins, Perutz on haemoglobin, Kendrew on myoglobin. After graduating from Trinity College, Cambridge, in 1939, Kendrew joined the scientific staff of the Air Ministry for the duration of World War II, then returned to Cambridge, where he linked with Perutz. Together they formed the Medical Research Council for Molecular Biology. Kendrew became a Fellow of Peterhouse in 1954 and Fellow of the Royal Society in 1960. He was founder and editor-in-chief of the *Journal of Molecular Biology* until 1987, and founder and long-serving secretary-general of the European Institute of Molecular Biology. He was President of St John's College, Oxford, 1981–87. Died 23 August

Lee, Laurie (b. 1914), British author and poet, won instant fame and fortune with his semi-autobiographical novel *Cider With Rosie* (1959), celebrating the joys of country life in the Cotswold valley of Slad, where he spent his childhood and to which he returned after an adventurous earlier life. At the age of 14 he set off for London, which he fled for a wandering life in Spain, playing the violin for a living. When civil war broke out he was rescued, but he soon returned with the International Brigade, to endure many hardships and dangers as he renewed his wandering role. Back in England when World War II began, he worked as a scriptwriter for official film units until 1946, and then for other filmmakers, drifting into an impoverished bohemian circle. *Cider With Rosie* changed all that. It was followed by *As I Walked Out One Midsummer Morning* (1969) and *A Moment of War* (1991) recalling his experiences in Spain. Died 13 May

Lewenstein, Oscar (b. 1917), British film and stage producer, as general manager of the Royal Court Theatre and one of the founders of the English Stage Company presided over a new era or stage drama whose key work was John Osborne's *Look Back in Anger.* His leadership was crucial to the production of Brecht's *Mother Courage* and such plays as *A Taste of Honey* or *The Loneliness of the Long-Distance Runner.* He did much to give British drama a new image. Died 23 February

Lichtenstein, Roy (b. 1923), American artist, turned Pop Art—of which he was one of the fathers—into high art. He studied at the School of Fine Arts at Ohio State University 1940–43 and, after a break for war service, 1946–49. His first one-man show was in 1949 in Cleveland, Ohio. After working for a time as an engineering draughtsman he got a minor post at Rutgers University in New Jersey, and became one of a circle of experimental artists in New York. His first show, at the gallery of Leo Castelli in 1962, with the characteristic sharp outlines and flat high-coloured surfaces of what became familiar as Pop Art, was an outstanding success. His fame had begun. He exhibited at the Venice Biennale in 1966, at the Tate Gallery in London in 1968, and at the Guggenheim Museum in 1969. Wealth followed celebrity: in 1990 a picture by Lichtenstein sold for $6 million. Died 29 September

Listowel, Earl of, PC, GCMG (b. 1906), was Secretary of State for India at the time of its independence in 1947 and governor-general of Ghana 1957–60. A convinced socialist from his schooldays at Eton, he survived higher education at Balliol College, Oxford, and Magdalene College, Cambridge, with his faith intact, despite parental hostility. His father disinherited him, but could not prevent his succession to the earldom in 1931. His elevation to the House of Lords redirected his career from academic pursuits to politics. He was serving in army intelligence when, in 1941, he was made Chief Whip of the then few Labour members of the Upper House. Thereafter he served in various ministerial posts, notably as Secretary of State for the Colonies 1948–50, until Clement Atlee's successor as Prime Minister, Harold Macmillan, sent him to Ghana at the request of Kwame Nkrumah. After his return he served the House of Lords as chairman of committees 1965–76, a post well suited to his character and breeding. Died 12 March

Lorant, Stefan (b. 1901), Hungarian-born journalist, changed the style of photographic reporting from the stiff and formal to the intimate and revealing. In early life, quitting Hungary after World War I, he worked in Berlin and Vienna until in 1931 he became editor of the *Münchener Illustrierte Presse.* A Jew, he was imprisoned by the Nazi regime, but was released and reached England in 1934. While free-lancing he wrote a well-received *I Was Hitler's Prisoner.* A pocket-sized magazine, *Lilliput,* lost money but gained prestige for its originality. It was sold to the Hulton Press, for whom Lorant began to plan a new pictorial weekly. First published in 1938, *Picture Post* soon had an unprecedented sale of over a million. Lorant, however, having failed to gain British nationality, resigned the editorship in 1940 and moved to the USA. There he pursued the career of an author and scholar with a unique pictorial eye, exemplified in his *Lincoln: the Picture Story of His Life*. Died 14 November

Macapagal, Diosdado (b. 1910), President of the Philippines 1961–65, a lawyer by profession, had entered politics in 1949 as a Liberal member of the House of Representatives. Elected Vice-President in 1957, he favoured the agricultural poor from whom he had sprung. His presidency was calm, but his reforms were ineffectual, and after a single term he was defeated by Ferdinand Marcos. In 1971 he chaired a constitutional convention and he remained an active national figure into the 1980s. Died 21 April

Manley, Michael, PC (b. 1924), popularly known as 'Joshua', Prime Minister of Jamaica 1972–80 and 1989–92, was the son of Norman W. Manley, Jamaica's Prime Minister before independence. After graduating from the London School of Economics he became a journalist and trade union organizer in Jamaica and in 1969 succeeded his father as president of the People's National Party. In office from 1972 he pursued a socialist policy and fostered relations with Fidel Castro's Cuba, but when, after eight years in opposition, he again became Prime Minister he followed a moderate, even conservative line until retiring when afflicted by cancer. Died 7 March

Michener, James (b. 1907), American author, won the Pulitzer Prize in 1947 for his first novel, *Tales of the South Pacific*, which was the basis of the highly popular musical *South Pacific* and of a spectacular film. Thereafter he wrote many books, both fictional and non-fictional, of which *Hawaii* (1959), a massive historical novel, overladen with factual research, was typical. An orphan, he was adopted by a Quaker couple and well educated, with degrees at Swarthmore College and the University of Northern Colorado, where he went on to teach. Joining the US Navy as a reservist in World War II, he was posted to the South Pacific. After the success of his first book he wrote on many subjects, including Japanese prints, sport and archaeology. He was 90 when he published his last work, *A Century of Sonnets*. Died 16 October

Mitchum, Robert (b. 1917), American film actor, proved to be one of the best actors that Hollywood produced in his generation, though his first nomination for an Oscar—for his leading part in *The Story of G.I. Joe* (1945)—proved to be also his last. Born to a shattered family in Connecticut, he spent his early years as a vagabond, taking whatever manual work was on offer, until in 1937 he joined a theatre company in California, doing odd jobs. In 1943 he began film-acting, and there followed a string of nearly 80 films exploiting his peculiar talents and ironic personality, including *Holiday Affair* (1949), *The Sundowners* (1960), *Ryan's Daughter* (1971) and *Farewell, My Lovely* (1975). Died 1 July

Mobutu Sese Seko, (b. 1930), was President of Zaïre for 32 years from 1965, during which his mismanagement impoverished a naturally rich country while he himself amassed a huge fortune. The son of a cook in a Roman Catholic mission, he was conscripted into the army as a clerk 1950–57. He then turned to journalism and so to politics. His backing for Patrice Lumumba, who became Prime Minister of an independent Congo in 1960, was rewarded by appointment as chief of staff of the army. Mobutu built up a personal following in the army and took advantage of a political crisis to seize absolute power. He broke diplomatic relations with the Soviet Union, a move which gained him support from the West as an African ally in the Cold War, despite his evil actions at home. In 1967 he was elected chairman of the OAU.

As his country approached economic collapse, however, he came under pressure of demands for reform by the IMF and the World Bank. The end of the Cold War exposed the consequences of his misrule. An unpaid army was mutinous, and Mobutu was forced to accept an outward form of electoral democracy for an undetermined 'transitional period'. Zaïre's involvement in the mass movements following the Rwanda-Burundi breach did not help Mobutu's position. In October 1996 the Alliance of Democratic Forces for the Liberation of Congo-Zaïre launched an offensive led by Laurent Kabila. Mobutu, in Switzerland for treatment of prostate cancer, returned only to be forcibly defeated. He fled to Morocco, where he died 7 September,

Mosbacher, Emil (Bus) (b. 1922), American yachtsman, twice successfully defended the America's Cup against Australian challenges in 1962 and 1967. A multi-millionaire by inheritance, he was a small-boat sailor from early boyhood, and won a national championship at the age of 16. After World War II he returned to sailing, winning the International One Design class championships for eight years in succession. After his America's Cup victories he organized a number of spectacular events for tall ships *en masse*. Among his public services was that of chief of protocol in the Nixon presidency 1969–72. Died 13 August

Mother Teresa, *see* Teresa, Mother

Pritchett, Sir Victor, CH (b. 1900), British author and critic, as V.S. Pritchett ranked as an eminent 'man of letters', though he had no formal education beyond 15, when he went to work in a Bermondsey tannery. He soaked in life with its hazards, fun and tragedy from the streets of London. Then, as correspondent for the *Christian Science Monitor* in the Irish troubles in the 1920s, and the Spanish civil war, he published his first book in 1929 and his first collection of short stories, *The Spanish Virgin*, in 1930. He began reviewing books for *The New Statesman* magazine in 1928 and continued to do so for 50 years. Meanwhile he wrote countless short stories, a massive collection of which was published in 1990. They were his real métier: his few novels fell short of genius, while his sound biographies of Flaubert, Balzac and Turgenev demonstrated his literary taste as much as his scholarship. He drew scenes and characters for his plots mostly from the lower-middle-class scene in which he had been raised. Knighted in 1975, he became a Companion of Honour in 1993. Died 20 March

Purcell, Edward (b. 1912), American scientist, shared the 1952 Nobel Prize for Physics with Felix Bloch for their separate research into nuclear magnetism. His discovery of nuclear magnetic resonance he regarded as opening a new way of looking at the universe: it certainly was the key to many important advances in medicine, astronomy and other branches of science. Educated at Purdue University, he gained his doctorate at Harvard in 1938. During the latter years of World War II he worked at the radiation laboratory at MIT, then returned to Harvard where he gained a full professorship in physics in 1949, and held it until his retirement in 1960. Died 7 March

Richter, Svyatoslav (b. in Ukraine 1915), Russian pianist, was initially best known for his rendering of the music of Prokofiev, but his repertoire became widely inclusive. He made his debut at the age of 19 at a Chopin recital in Odessa, where he had been born of musicianly parents of Polish descent. From 1937 on he studied under Heinrich Neuhaus at the Moscow Conservatoire. In 1937 he gave the first performance of Prokofiev's 6th Sonata, followed by premieres of the 7th and 8th. He won the USSR music competition in 1945 and the Stalin Prize in 1949: high Soviet honours rewarded his distinction in 1965 and 1975. Not until 1960 did he travel to the West, two years after touring Russia with the Philadelphia Orchestra. In 1964 he attended to the Aldeburgh Festival, to play, *inter alia*, a piano duet with Benjamin Britten. His most memorable visit to London came in 1989, by which time he had been recognized as one of the most brilliant pianists of the century. Died 1 August

Rippon of Hexham, Lord, PC, QC (b. 1924), as Geoffrey Rippon, MP, Chancellor of the Duchy of Lancaster, was a right-hand man to Prime Minister Edward Heath in the approach to membership of the European Community (later the EU) in 1970–72, as negotiator in Brussels and as its champion in a suspicious House of Commons. He had been an MP since 1955, a member of the cabinet since 1963, and leader of the Conservative Party delegation to the Council of Europe and WEU 1967–70. In 1987 he was raised to the peerage and entered a prosperous business career, but he continued to play a part in politics as an elder statesman loyal to Heath. Died 28 January

Rodriguez, General Andres (b. 1924), was President of Paraguay 1989–93. Formerly a protégé of the dictatorial President Alfredo Stroessner, he led a military coup as commander of the 1st Army Corps, promising a return to democracy. A quick election confirmed his provisional presidency, and he set about a number of fundamental reforms. After the election of his successor he retired from politics. Died 21 April

Rosen, Albert (b. 1924), was principal conductor of the Radio Eireann (now the Irish National) Symphony Orchestra from 1968 to 1981, when he became its principal guest conductor, and in 1994 conductor laureate to Radio Telefis Eireann. Born in Vienna, he moved to Prague, where he became director of the Smetana Opera in 1965. His association with Ireland began thereafter. He conducted many times at the Wexford Festival, and often for the Dublin Grand Opera Soceity (now Irish Opera). His international credits included engagements in San Francisco, Paris and London, and notably too in Australia where he became principal conductor of the Australian Broadcasting Corporation in Adelaide. Died 23 May

Rossi, Aldo (b. 1931), Italian architect, designed a number of admired buildings in Italy and elsewhere, including the reconstructed opera house in Genoa and the Palace Hotel in Fukuoka, Japan. His book *L'Architectura della Citta* (1966, in English 1982) was a key text in advocacy of giving a poetic face to international Modernism. Died 4 September

Rowse, Alfred Leslie (A.L.), CH, FBA (b. 1903), British historian and author, would have been more widely admired by his academic peers for his brilliance in research and his many excellent books, were it not for his sharp-tongued disdain for criticism. The son of a Cornish china-clay miner, from a local grammar school he won a scholarship to Christ Church, Oxford, in 1922 and a fellowship of All Souls College in 1925. In 1954 he was appointed a senior fellow of the Huntingdon Library and for the next 20 years divided his time between California and Cornwall. His most notable coup was identification of Shakespeare's Dark Lady of the Sonnets, though it was challenged by many other historians. Among his many books were a group on aspects of Elizabethan England (1940–55), biographies of notables of the period, his controversial *Shakespeare's Sonnets* (1973), personal reminiscences (especially *A Cornish Childhood*, 1942) and poetry (*A Life: Collected Poems*, 1980). He was made a Companion of Honour in the year before he died, on 3 October.

Sinyavsky, Andrei (b. 1925), Russian writer, was one of the heroes, or victims, of a scandalously-biased Soviet trial of himself and Yuli Daniel in 1966, the basis of a BBC documentary *The First Freedom* (1967). Graduating from Moscow University, he soon made his mark as a literary critic, having Boris Pasternak of *Dr Zhivago* fame as his friend and mentor. His critical essays and a novel, *The Makepeace Experiment*, were published not in Russia but in the West, and were the gravamen of the Soviet challenges against him. After he had served his term in labour camps he moved to Paris and became professor of Russian literature at the Sorbonne, continuing to write books of literary criticism. Died 25 February

Solti, Sir Georg (b. in Hungary, 1912), British conductor, was music director of Covent Garden Opera 1961–71, and of the Chicago Symphony Orchestra 1969–91. After study at the Liszt Academy in Budapest, he began his conducting career as a répétiteur in the Hungarian State Opera, for whom he conducted *Figaro* in 1937, on the day when the Nazi German army marched into Austria. A Jew, he promptly left for Switzerland, where he lived by teaching music until the end of World War II, when he returned to conducting, with engagements in Munich, Salzburg, San Francisco and elsewhere, including Covent Garden Opera, of which he became music director in 1961. Though his demanding standards and his energetic style made him controversial, his brilliance, not least in Wagnerian operas, won him international fame. He took British citizenship in 1971 and was knighted in the same year. His music directorship of the Chicago Symphony Orchestra for over 20 years did not break his British connection, and he continued to conduct occasionally at Covent Garden, among other European opera houses, and to make many recordings for Decca, including a new cycle of Mozart opera. Died 5 September

Stewart, James (b. 1908), American film actor, had one of the longest and most successful careers in Hollywood. Born into a well-to-do family in Indiana, he studied architecture at Princeton University, but was caught up in amateur dramatics, joining the University Players, a company that included his life-long friend Henry Fonda. His professional career began in 1932 on the New York stage, whence he was soon recruited to Hollywood by MGM. His first star part was in *Born to Dance* in 1936. Soon he had established himself as the innocent but obdurate small-town boy, as in *Mr Smith Goes to Washington* (1939). The classic Western films which became his métier began with *Destry Rides Again* (1939), with Marlene Dietrich, and he won an Oscar for his acting in *The Philadelphia Story* (1940). In World War II he rose from private to colonel in the US Army Air Force, winning the Distinguished Flying Cross. Back in Hollywood, his film roles were more varied, and in Westerns more mature, than in his more youthful years, but his charm and acting skill remained. His versatility was shown by his parts in Hitchcock's *Rope* (1949), in *Harvey* (1950) and in his last film, *The Magic of Lassie* 1978. In 1984 Stewart was honoured with a special Academy Award for 50 years of achievement. Died 2 July

Stokes, Professor Donald (b. 1927), American political scientist, was co-author of two seminal books on electoral analysis, *The American Voter* (1960) and *Political Change in Britain* (with David Butler, 1969). A Quaker, a brilliant student, he took degrees at Princeton and Yale universities before moving to Michigan. In 1963 he joined Nuffield College, Oxford, to research the British electoral scene. In 1972 he left Michigan for Princeton, to become Dean of the Woodrow Wilson School of Public and International Affairs, where he worked with great success for 20 years, leaving for posthumous publication a work on *Basic Science and Technological Innovation.* Died 25 January

Syse, Jan (b. 1930), Norwegian politician, first elected to the Storting for the Conservative Party in 1973, was Prime Minister of a short-lived centre-right minority government 1989–90. Died 17 September

Taylor of Gosforth, Lord (b. 1930), Lord Chief Justice of England 1992–96, had been counsel in a number of notorious criminal cases before reaching the headship of the judiciary. Called to the bar in 1954 and taking silk in 1967, he rose quickly to the peak of the advocate's profession, becoming chairman of the Bar Council in 1979. In 1980 he was made a judge of the High Court and in 1988 a Lord Justice of Appeal. As LCJ he reversed several miscarriages of justice, criticizing both trial judges and the police, and helping to restore public confidence in the judicial system. He fought for the independence of the judiciary, and was a sharp critic of the Conservative Home Secretary's proposal of imposing minimum sentences upon judges' discretion. Died 28 April

Teresa, Mother (b. in Albania, 1910), Roman Catholic missionary, was awarded the Nobel Peace Prize in 1979 for her devoted service to the poor, the homeless and the dying in Calcutta, India; she declined its monetary award in favour of support for her causes. Born Agnes Bojaxhiu, in 1931 she made her first vows and took the name of Teresa. After learning English in Ireland she entered the congregation of Loreto nuns, who worked in India, and for 17 years she taught English and history at their St Mary's High School, in the well-to-do part of Calcutta, of which she became Principal. There, in 1946, she heard a call from God to work with the poorest of the poor; leave to forsake her post was granted two years later. She exchanged her nun's habit for the simple white sari with a blue border which became familiar to millions all over the world as her saintly reputation grew. In Calcutta she shared the daily hardships of the destitute for whom she worked. In 1950 she founded the Missionaries of Charity, which grew to establish more than 50 schools, orphanages and homes for the poor, in India and elsewhere. In 1952 she opened the Nirmal Hriday home for dying destitutes. Her international honours included the Pope John XXIII Peace Prize (1971), the Templeton Foundation Prize (1980), honorary membership of the Order of Merit (1983) and an honorary DD from Cambridge University (1977). Died 5 September

Tikhonov, Nikolai (b. in Ukraine 1905), Chairman of the Council of Ministers (Prime Minister) of the Soviet Union 1980–85, owed much of his political advancement to his long-standing friendship with Leonid Brezhnev. An engineer by training and profession, he had been a factory manager when, having joined the Communist Party in 1940, he moved into the political arena ten years later. His early advancement in office utilized his industrial experience, but in 1965 he became a deputy chairman of the Council of Ministers and in 1976 its First Deputy Chairman, succeeding Aleksei Kosygin as Chairman in 1980. When Gorbachev became the Soviet leader he was pressed into retirement in 1985 at the age of 80. Died 1 June

Todd, Lord, OM (b. 1907), British scientist, was awarded the Nobel Prize for Chemistry in 1957 for his work on the synthesis of nucleotides, the buildingblocks of DNA. Educated at the universities of Glasgow and Frankfurt, he held posts in Edinburgh, London and Oxford before becoming professor of chemistry at Cambridge in 1944. In 1965 he was elected Master of Christ's College, Cambridge. He was president of the British Association for the Advancement of Science 1969–70 and of the Royal Society 1975–80. In the course of his academic career he received honorary degrees from a score of British, American and other universities. He was a forceful chairman and administrator: among the bodies that he chaired were the Advisory Council on Scientific Policy (1952–64) and the Royal Commission on Medical Education (reported 1968). Knighted in 1954, Todd was raised to the peerage in 1962 and to the Order of Merit in 1977, six years after his nominal retirement. Died 10 January

Tonypandy, Viscount (b. 1909), as George Thomas, MP, was Speaker of the British House of Commons 1976–83. The son of a Rhondda miner, he was educated at a state school and University College, Southampton. In 1950 he was elected MP for Cardiff West, a seat he held for 33 years. He was Secretary of State for Wales 1968–70 and Deputy Speaker 1974–76, after holding junior office in the Home, Welsh and Commonwealth departments. A Methodist lay preacher, he became vicepresident of the Methodist Conference in 1960. Died 22 September

Versace, Gianni (b. 1946), Italian dress designer, was in the very top rank of grandees in the world of international *haute couture*. Born to a modest family in Reggio Calabria, he learnt the essentials of his craft from his mother, a dressmaker, for whom he worked for a time before moving to Milan, the fashion capital, serving as a designer of ready-to-wear clothes for several firms before launching on his own. His first signed collection in 1978 was warmly acclaimed, and in 1983 he won the L'Occhio d'Oro award for the best fashion designer of the autumn winter season. Designs for ballet and opera productions reinforced his fame. Soon he became a denizen of the international world of the rich and famous, with homes in Miami and New York and showrooms in Paris, London and Berlin, and with all the financial benefits of a magical name. His style was unique—-innovative, daring but always essentially elegant and feminine. Died in Miami by a murderer's hand 15 July

Villoresi, Luigi (b. 1909), Italian racing driver, began his career in 1931, but it was interrupted by internment as a prisoner-ofwar in World War II. Driving Maseratis, he won Grand Prix races in Europe and Argentina, in the 1940s, including the first Grand Prix at Silverstone in 1948. He continued driving both Formula One and sports cars until 1955, coming back to win the 1958 Acropolis rally in a Lancia. Died 24 August

Wales, Princess of, see Diana, Princess of Wales

Wedgwood, Dame Veronica, OM, DBE (b. 1910), British author and historian, made Britain (and nearer Europe) of the 16th and early 17th centuries her own historical territory. A brilliant student at Oxford, her first book was *Stafford* (1935), which she later revised as *Thomas Wentworth* (1961). There followed a stream of books on the period: *The Thirty Years' War* (1938), *The King's Peace* (1955), *The King's War* (1959), *The Trial of Charles the First* (1964, revised 1980) and biographical studies of leading figures of the age, Cromwell, Richelieu, Montrose among others. She also wrote a life of her uncle, Josiah Wedgwood, MP, *The Last of the Radicals* (1951). Though she was not an academic historian, her books brought the past to life for a wide public and she received honorary degrees from many British and American universities. Her honours, headed by the Order of Merit, were given less for her literary output than for her public service, including the presidency (1951–57) of the English branch of international PEN. Died 9 March

Wethered, Joyce (b. 1901) (Lady Heathcoat Amory), British golfer, reached international fame in 1929, when four years after 'retiring' from competitive golf she beat the American champion, Glenna Collett, in the final of the Ladies' Open at St Andrews. An exemplary stylist, she had learned the game mainly by careful imitation of top-class players at courses in Cornwall and the Highlands while on holiday. She was English Ladies' Champion 1920–24 and winner of the British Ladies' Open in 1922, 1924, 1925 and 1929. Three times she captained the British team in Curtis Cup contests. In 1937 she married Sir John Heathcoat Amory, Bt, owner of a Victorian house in Devon famous for its pictures and its gardens. He died in 1972, and the house was given to the National Trust. Died 18 November

Wiles, Professor Peter, FBA (b. 1919), pioneered the study of the Soviet economy throughout the Cold War, exposing its weaknesses when others vaunted its dynamism or feared its military strength. Entering New College, Oxford, as Senior Scholar from Winchester in 1938, his war service included breakthroughs in signals intelligence in the Western desert and Bletchley. Academic for the rest of his life (Oxford and the London School of Economics, with interludes in Sweden and the USA), his seminal work was comparative, analysing how the operation of the Soviet enterprise, government or foreign trade differed in method and outcomes from mechanisms under a market system. Of his many books, *Economic Institutions Compared* (1977) was his most notable work in political economy. Died 14 July

Zinnemann, Fred (b. in Austria 1907), was the most distinguished and innovative Hollywood film director of his time. He had abandoned his law studies in Vienna for a career in films, and in 1929 moved to America. He directed his first full-length feature film in 1942, but he reached the pinnacle of his trade with *High Noon* (1951), which turned a stock Western story into a masterpiece. He won the award of best director for *From Here to Eternity* (1953) and thereafter the titles of his films were a Hollywood roll of honour: *Oklahoma* (1955), *A Man For All Seasons* (1966), *Julia* (1977). In 1963, disillusioned with American values, he moved to England, where he lived for the rest of his life. Died 14 March

CHRONICLE OF PRINCIPAL EVENTS IN 1997

JANUARY

1 Lone Israeli gunman opened fire in West Bank town of Hebron injuring six Arabs as Israeli troops prepared to withdraw from town.
  Kofi Annan (Ghana) took office as UN's seventh Secretary-General, in succession to Boutros Boutros-Ghali.
2 In Libya, six senior officers and two civilians executed for alleged spying after being publicly paraded on television.
  At Singapore's general election, ruling People's Action Party gained 81 seats in 83-member parliament.
  In The Gambia, legislative elections, marking return to civilian rule, resulted in decisive victory for President Jammeh's Patriotic Alliance for Reorientation and Construction; a new government was appointed on 7 March.
5 In Yugoslavia/Serbia, Belgrade paralysed by cavalcade of cars and demonstration by more than 100,000 anti-government protesters; more than 400,000 took part in another demonstration on 13 Jan.
6 Representatives of 26 Somali factions met near Addis Ababa to form National Salvation Council as prelude to formation of government of national unity.
10 British PM John Major began five-day visit to India and Pakistan.
  Arnoldo Alemán Lacayo sworn in as President of Nicaragua.
15 Israeli and Palestinian cabinets approved new peace deal over disputed West Bank town of Hebron, 80 per cent of which was to be handed over to Palestinian Authority.
  In Bulgaria, ruling Socialists agreed to hold early elections in aftermath of violent opposition demonstrations in Sofia (see 19 April).
17 Under terms of peace deal, Israel withdrew its troops from most of Hebron.
19 Franz Vranitzky resigned as Chancellor of Austria after 11 years in office; he was succeeded by Viktor Klima, who named new cabinet on 24 Jan.
  PLO leader Yassir Arafat given hero's welcome on his return to Hebron after 32 years.
20 In USA, President Clinton inaugurated for second term; he was first Democrat since Franklin Roosevelt, 60 years previously, to be sworn in for second term.
22 In Bulgaria, Petar Stoyanov took office as President in succession to Zhelyu Zhelev, following Nov. 1996 election.
23 Following nation-wide anti-government riots, Albanian parliament banned pyramid investment schemes in which thousands had lost life savings.
27 Chechenya held presidential and parliamentary elections following end of two-year war; Chechen military commander Aslan Maskhadov gained decisive victory and was sworn in as President on 12 Feb.
29 Pakistan Supreme Court upheld President Leghari's decision to dismiss Benazir Bhutto as PM in Nov. 1996 for corruption and incompetence.
31 In Madagascar, former military dictator Didier Ratsiraka proclaimed President following victory over Albert Zafy in Dec. 1996 election.

FEBRUARY

3 Pakistan Muslim League, led by Mian Nawaz Sharif, gained landslide victory in general election in which fewer than 20 per cent voted; he was sworn in as PM on 17 Feb.
4 73 Israeli servicemen died when two helicopters crashed near border with southern Lebanon: it was worst tragedy in Israeli military history.

590　　CHRONICAL OF PRINCIPAL EVENTS IN 1997

In USA, President Clinton delivered State of Union address, offering 10-point plan to improve education and indicating that 1998 budget would aim to bring government spending in line with income by 2002.

5　In USA, in civil case brought by relatives of victims, former footballer O.J. Simpson, acquitted of murder in 1995 (see AR 1995, p. 158), found liable for deaths of his former wife Nicole Brown and Ronald Goldman.

Swiss government approved establishment of a fund by Swiss banks to compensate victims of the Holocaust and their heirs.

7　In Ecuador, state of emergency declared following congressional vote to remove President Abdala Bucaram on grounds of 'mental incapacity'; Speaker of Congress, Fabián Alarcón, appointed interim President.

8　In New Zealand, six dead, five seriously injured, when lone gunman went on rampage at ski resort of Raurimu, near Mt Ruapehu.

11　In Serbia, Socialist government of President Milosević passed emergency legislation recognizing opposition victories in Serbian local elections in Nov. 1996: opposition groups had staged weeks of street protests in Belgrade over alleged rigging of results.

12　An Iran-based foundation increased bounty for payable for killing author Salman Rushdie to $2.5 million; Rushdie had been under threat since issuing of *fatweh* in 1989 (see AR 1989, pp. 428–9, 493–4).

18　At meeting in Moscow with Russian Foreign Minister, US Secretary of State Madeleine Albright proposed formation of joint NATO-Russian peace-keeping and crisis-management unit.

19　Deng Xiaoping, paramount leader of China for 20 years and architect of economic reform, died aged 92 (see XX: Obituary).

20　In Indonesia, hundreds reported dead after three weeks of ethnic violence in province of West Kalintan.

23　In UK, geneticists at Roslin Institute in Edinburgh announced first successful cloning of an adult sheep ('Dolly') without need for sperm.

25　President Ezer Weizman of Israel on three-day state visit to UK.

In UK, Transport Secretary announced plans for privatization of London Underground.

27　In UK, Labour overturned Tory majority in by-election at Wirrall South by 7,888 votes on 17.2 per cent swing.

MARCH

2　In Albania, President Berisha declared state of emergency in response to mounting anti-government demonstrations; PM Alexander Meksi dismissed.

3　Israel's Defence Minister approved new plans for construction of thousands of Jewish homes on occupied Arab land (see 21, 30 March).

4　In UK, Social Security Secretary announced plans for biggest overhaul of state pensions for 50 years.

Koh Kun appointed PM of S. Korea, replacing Lee Soo Sung.

5　Albanian government rejected all offers of foreign mediation as country descended into state of anarchy.

6　In Poland, Gdansk shipyard, birthplace of Solidarity union, closed with loss of 3,800 jobs.

Samuel Hinds sworn in as interim President of Guyana following death of President Cheddi Jagan (see XX: Obituary); his widow, Janet Jagan, was appointed country's first woman PM on 17 March.

Sher Bahadur Deuba resigned as PM of Nepal; a new coalition government, led by Lokendra Bahadur Chand, was formed on 12 March.

11　In Russia, President Yeltsin dismissed most of his cabinet, asking PM Viktor Chernomyrdin and First Deputy PM Anatoly Chubais to draw up new list of ministers.

12　In Albania, President Berisha approved broad-based interim government led by Bashkim Fino (see 29 June); new government appealed for foreign intervention to restore order.

CHRONICLE OF PRINCIPAL EVENTS IN 1997

13 A Jordanian soldier shot dead seven Israeli schoolgirls on an outing to Hill of Peace in Jordan Valley.
   Nigeria filed charges of treason against Nobel laureate Wole Soyinka and 14 others.
14 A new government, led by Mart Siimann, took office in Estonia.
17 In UK, PM John Major announced a general election for 1 May.
19 Italy declared state of emergency until 30 June because of influx of more than 10,000 Albanian refugees.
   King Husain of Jordan appointed new government led by Abdul-Salam-al-Majali.
21 President Clinton and President Yeltsin held summit talks in Helsinki: they discussed arms control and economic cooperation but disagreed over expansion of NATO.
   In Israel, four dead, 46 wounded, when Islamic suicide bomb blew up coffee shop in Tel Aviv.
25 Pamela Gordon named first woman PM of Bermuda following resignation of David Saul.
26 Sir Julius Chan resigned as PM of Papua New Guinea following 10 days of political turmoil; John Gilheno named caretaker PM; Chan resumed office on 2 June (see 22 July).
   In USA, 39 found dead in mansion near San Diego, California; they were members of Heaven's Gate sect and had committed mass suicide.
28 UN Security Council approved Italian plan for multinational force to protect delivery of humanitarian aid in Albania (see 15 April).
29 In UK, Cambridge defeated Oxford by 2 lengths in University Boat Race.
30 At least 50 Arabs and two Israelis injured in fighting in West Bank: several days of fighting had followed Israeli decision to build 32,000 Jewish homes in east Jerusalem.
31 In Spain, 26 died in country's worst train crash in province of Navarre.

APRIL

2 President Yeltsin of Russia and President Lukashenka of Belarus signed agreement on creation of union between the two countries, a basis for closer economic, political and military links.
3 In UK, two IRA bombs found under M6 motorway near Birmingham caused widespread traffic chaos; there were further security alerts in London and the south-east on 21 April.
5 In UK, Grand National steeplechase abandoned because of IRA bomb scare; 60,000 race-goers evacuated from course; race was eventually run on 7 April and won by Lord Gyllene at 14–1.
7 Israeli PM Binyamin Netanyahu in Washington for talks with President Clinton.
11 In India, 10-month coalition government led by H.D. Deve Gowda resigned after defeat in vote of confidence in Lok Sabha; Inder Kumar Gujral formed new coalition on 21 April (see 29 Nov.).
   In Angola, Unity and National Reconciliation Government inaugurated under PM Fernando José da Franca van Dunem.
12 Pope John Paul II began historic two-day visit to Sarajevo; security forces foiled assassination plot shortly before his arrival.
12 Croatia held first post-war municipal elections as prerequisite to withdrawal of UN troops safeguarding Serb population in Eastern Slavonia.
15 Troops from France, Italy and Spain arrived in Albania to begin Operation Alba (Sunrise), Italian-led peace-keeping mission.
   In Saudi Arabia, more than 340 died in fires in pilgrim camps near Mecca during annual *Haj*.
17 President Yeltsin and Chancellor Kohl of Germany held summit talks in Baden-Baden but failed to end impasse over eastward enlargement of NATO.
19 In Bulgaria, centre-right United Democratic Forces gained decisive victory in general election; Ivan Kostov formed new government on 21 May.
22 Peruvian troops stormed residence of Japanese ambassador in Lima rescuing 71 hostages who had been held for 126 days by Tupac Amarú Revolutionary Movement guerrillas, all of whom died in assault.
   President Jiang Zemin of China began five-day visit to Russia for talks with President Yeltsin on bilateral and international issues.
30 UNHCR began airlift of Rwandan refugees from Kisangani, Zaïre, to Rwanda.

MAY

1 In UK general election, Labour gained landslide victory with majority of 179 seats; Conservatives failed to win any seats in Scotland or Wales in their worst election performance since 1832.
2 Tony Blair (43) appointed Britain's youngest PM since 1812; outgoing PM John Major announced intention to resign Tory leadership (see 19 June).
5 President Clinton on official visit to Mexico, first by a US President for 20 years; measures to combat corruption and drug-trafficking were high on his agenda.
6 Britain's new Chancellor of Exchequer, Gordon Brown, announced a quarter per cent rise in interest rates and that henceforth control of interest rates would rest with Bank of England rather than the government.
  India's former PM P.V. Narasimha Rao indicted on bribery charges.
7 US government report accused Switzerland of prolonging World War II by accepting gold looted by Nazis from occupied countries; report's contentions were rejected by Swiss Foreign Minister.
10 In Iran, more than 1,600 people died in earthquake near Afghan border.
  Pope John Paul II on two-day visit to Lebanon, his first to Middle East.
14 In UK, state opening of parliament; Queen's Speech foreshadowed 22 bills including measures on health, education, crime, constitutional change in Scotland, Wales and London and first Bill of Rights since 1689.
  NATO secretary-general Javier Solana and Russia's Foreign Minister Primakov reached historic agreement for expansion of NATO, allowing Poland, Czech Republic and Hungary to join Alliance (see 27 May).
15 President Chirac of France on three-day official visit to China.
16 British PM Blair, on first official visit to N. Ireland, offered exploratory talks with government officials to Sinn Féin before IRA ceasefire.
17 In Zaïre, President Mobutu (see XX: Obituary) fled to Morocco; his 32 years of autocratic rule ended with fall of Kinshasa to rebel troops of Laurent Kabila, who immediately proclaimed himself head of state and re-named country Democratic Republic of Congo.
18 At presidential elections in Mongolia, President Ochirbat decisively defeated by former communist Natsagiin Bagabandi, who was sworn in on 20 June.
20 In UK, Chancellor of Exchequer announced major reforms to City regulation, ending supervisory role of Bank of England.
22 In Russia, President Yeltsin dismissed Defence Minister Igor Rodionov and armed forces chief-of-staff for failure to implement military reform.
23 In Moscow, President Yeltsin and President Lukashenka of Belarus signed charter of union between the two countries, setting out terms of greater cooperation.
  EU leaders held one-day summit at Noordvijk, Netherlands; PM Blair announced that UK would accede to EU's Social Chapter.
25 In Iran, Mohammed Khatami gained landslide victory in presidential election; he was confirmed in office on 3 Aug.
  In Sierra Leone, government of President Kabba overthrown in military coup; Major Johnny Paul Koroma declared himself head of state (see 24 Oct.).
  In referendum in Poland, 56.8 per cent of those voting approved new constitution.
27 President Yeltsin attended NATO summit in Paris for signing of the Founding Act on Mutual Relations, Cooperation and Security (see XIX.1).
  President Mubarak of Egypt and Israeli PM Binyamin Netanyahu held talks at Sharm el-Sheikh in effort to resolve deadlock in peace process.
29 At legislative elections in Indonesia, ruling Golkar Party gained landslide victory amid allegations of ballot-rigging.
  President Clinton visited London for first talks with PM Blair.
30 400 Westerners evacuated from Sierra Leone as Nigeria poured troops into country in support of ousted government as nation-wide fighting intensified.

President Yeltsin on two-day visit to Ukraine where he and President Kuchma signed treaty of cooperation and friendship between Russia and Ukraine.
31 Pope John Paul II began 11-day visit to his native Poland.

JUNE

1 In second round of elections for French national assembly, combined left-wing parties gained 319 of 577 seats, ending rule of centre-right coalition; with Communist Party support, Socialist leader Lionel Jospin installed as PM on 3 June.
2 At general election in Canada, ruling Liberal Party led by PM Jean Chrétien gained narrow victory.
  In USA, Timothy McVeigh convicted of killing 168 people in 1995 Oklahoma bombing, America's worst act of terrorism (see AR 1995, pp. 149–50).
3 Ehud Barak replaced Shimon Peres as leader of Israel's opposition Labour Party.
5 In Algeria, multi-party legislative elections resulted in decisive victory for National Democratic Rally of President Zéroual, amid allegations of ballot-rigging; Ahmed Ouyahia reappointed PM.
6 In Irish general election, Fianna Fáil gained largest number of seats in Dáil; its leader, Bertie Ahern, formed coalition with Progressive Democrats on 26 June.
  British PM Blair in Bonn for talks with Chancellor Kohl on future of Europe; he held talks in Paris with President Chirac on 11 June.
13 President Chirac and PM Jospin of France held summit talks with Chancellor Kohl at Poitiers on differences over European monetary union.
15 In Croatia, President Franjo Tudjman returned to office for second term; international observers reported a flawed poll.
17 EU leaders concluded two-day summit in Amsterdam; they agreed reforms to prepare for admission of up to a dozen new members and adopted Treaty of Amsterdam revising various EU treaties; EU ministers formally signed the treaty on 2 Oct.
19 In UK, William Hague (36) defeated Kenneth Clarke in final ballot for Tory leadership to become youngest Tory leader since Pitt the Younger in 1783.
  G-7 summit of world's leading industrial nations opened in Denver, Colorado; Russia's President Yeltsin attended 'G-8' sessions on economic questions as equal partner.
20 In Turkey, President Demirel invited opposition leader Mesut Yilmaz to form government, following collapse of first pro-Islamic government led by Necmettin Erbakan.
  In UK, former Chief Secretary to Treasury Jonathan Aitken abandoned his libel action against *The Guardian* and Granada TV following disclosure of new evidence that he had lied.
  Former Spanish Foreign Minister Carlos Westendorp succeeded Carl Bildt as high representative of Bosnian Peace Implementation Council.
23 'Earth Summit II' at UN, New York, began five-day review of 1992 Rio summit on environmental issues; 85 heads of state or government attended.
26 Madeleine Albright on visit to Vietnam, first US Secretary of State to go there since end of Vietnam War in 1975.
29 Albania held elections for People's Assembly; results, declared in late July, gave opposition Socialist Party (PSS) easy victory over Democratic Party (PDS) (see 24 July).
30 At midnight, Hong Kong returned to Chinese sovereignty after 156 years as a British colony.

JULY

1 Tung Chee-Hwa sworn in as Chief Executive of Hong Kong.
2 In UK, Chancellor Brown delivered first Labour budget for 18 years: he announced £5,000 million windfall tax on privatized utilities and ending of tax relief on dividend income to pension funds.

In Thailand, amid intense speculative pressure, fixed exchange rates were abandoned and the baht was allowed to float; its steep fall in value helped to trigger similar crises in other states of the region.

4 US *Mars Pathfinder* spacecraft landed on Mars after 309-million-mile journey; its remote-control rover buggy *Sojourner* carried out experiments on surface of planet and sent pictures back to Earth for four months.

6 In Mexico, ruling Party of the Institutionalized Revolution suffered severe setbacks in first fully free multi-party elections for 68 years, as Party of Democratic Revolution made substantial gains.

In Cambodia, Prince Norodom Ranariddh removed from office as country's First PM in coup by Second PM, former Communist Party leader Hun Sen (see 6 Aug.).

Republican violence erupted throughout N. Ireland following parade by loyalist Orangemen in Catholic area of Drumcree.

7 In UK, government published White Paper outlining five-year plan to improve school standards.

In Kenya, seven died when riot police broke up anti-government demonstrations in Nairobi's Anglican cathedral and elsewhere.

8 NATO summit opened in Madrid; conference agreed to invite Poland, Hungary and Czech Republic to join alliance in time for 50th anniversary in 1999.

10 In Bosnia, SAS soldiers shot dead an indicted war criminal and arrested another in first such operation by 35,000-strong Stabilization Force.

In UK, 100,000 demonstrators gathered in London's Hyde Park to protest against proposed legislation to ban fox hunting and other blood sports.

11 The Philippines' peso was allowed to float, quickly falling to a four-year low against US dollar.

13 Violence erupted in northern Spain following murder of a young Basque town councillor by ETA separatist movement.

15 Serbian leader Slobodan Milošević elected unopposed as President of Federal Republic of Yugoslavia for four-year term.

In USA, renowned Italian fashion designer Gianni Versace shot dead at his Miami home (see XX: Obituary).

16 EU Commission president Jacques Santer presented Agenda 2000 plan for an expanded 21-member EU to include five former communist states plus Cyprus.

19 More than 100 people reported dead in Poland and Czech Republic after torrential rain had caused worst flooding in Eastern Europe this century.

In Liberia, presidential and legislative elections, held in accordance with Abuja peace agreement of 1996, resulted in overwhelming victory for former warlord Charles Taylor and his National Patriotic Party; he was sworn in as President on 3 Aug.

20 IRA announced restoration of 1994 ceasefire (broken in Feb. 1996), paving way for participation in all-party talks on future of N. Ireland (see 16 Sept.).

22 Papua New Guinea's parliament elected Bill Skate as PM following June legislative elections.

23 In UK, report of Sir Ron Dearing's inquiry on higher education recommended ending of free tuition for full-time students and an increase to 45 per cent of numbers entering further education.

In UK, government published White Paper outlining proposals for Scottish home rule (see 11 Sept.).

Albania's new parliament ended five-month state of emergency; Rexhep Mejdani elected President in succession to Sali Berisha, who had resigned; Socialist Party leader Fatos Nano named PM.

25 Kocheril Raman Narayanan sworn in as President of India, country's first 'untouchable' (outcaste) head of state.

South Korea's Kia Group, the eighth-largest conglomerate, defaulted on huge debts, exposing deep weaknesses in the banking and financial sectors.

In Cambodia, a Khmer Rouge 'people's tribunal' sentenced guerrilla leader Pol Pot (69) to life imprisonment; his government's policies in 1970s had led to death of two million Cambodians.

CHRONICLE OF PRINCIPAL EVENTS IN 1997

29 In UK, government published Green Paper outlining proposals for a directly-elected mayor for London.
30 Israel called off peace talks with Palestinians after two suicide bombers killed 13 in central Jerusalem.
   In Australia, 18 died when two ski lodges collapsed in landslide at ski resort in New South Wales.

AUGUST

5 In Thailand, faced with deepening economic crisis, the government approved a drastic reform package to ensure IMF support; IMF loans totalling $16,700 million were authorized on 16 Aug.
   Bolivia's Congress confirmed Gen. Hugo Bánzer Suárez as President; he would form coalition following close-run elections in June.
   Korean Air Boeing-747 crashed on US Pacific protectorate of Guam with loss of 220 lives.
   Ung Huot elected PM of Cambodia following overthrow of Prince Norodom Ranariddh in July.
   In UK, Conservatives held seat in Uxbridge by-election; majority up on general election.
   In UK, announcement of closure of South Crofty mine marked end of 3,000 years of tin mining in Cornwall.
14 India and Pakistan held celebrations to mark 50th anniversary of independence from Britain
   Indonesia abandoned fixed exchange rates, allowing the ruppiah to float.
18 Emergency talks were held in London as Britain stepped up plans for voluntary evacuation of remaining residents of Caribbean dependency Montserrat, devastated by volcanic eruptions; on 22 Aug. Montserrat's leaders rejected British compensation package.
21 Pope John Paul II began four-day visit to France; one million attended Mass at Longchamp racecourse on 24 Aug.
25 East Germany's last communist leader, Egon Krenz, gaoled for 6½ years for his government role in shooting of three defectors seeking to cross to the West.
26 South Africa's former President and National Party leader F.W. de Klerk announced his retirement from politics.
29 In Algeria, 300 died in massacre in three villages in Blida region; more than 1,500 believed to have died in Islamic attacks or army counter-insurgency operations since 5 June elections.
31 Diana, Princess of Wales, died in a car crash in Paris (see XX: Obituary); the following week saw an unprecedented outpouring of public grief throughout Britain; huge crowds attended her funeral procession in London on 6 September, which was seen by an estimated two billion television viewers worldwide.

SEPTEMBER

1 A three-week international conference on banning of anti-personnel landmines opened in Oslo; a draft treaty for a global ban was agreed by 89 nations, excluding USA, on 17 Sept. (see 10 Oct., 4 Dec.).
   In N. Ireland, David Trimble, leader of Ulster Unionist Party, held unprecedented talks with Archbishop Sean Brady, head of Catholic Church in Ireland.
3 300 government soldiers landed on breakaway Comoros island of Anjouan to quell month-long separatist movement; they were routed by the separatists.
4 Three Hamas suicide bombers attacked busy street in central Jerusalem, killing eight and injuring 200.
5 Moscow began celebrations to mark its 850th anniversary; the city's rebuilt Cathedral of Christ the Saviour had opened two days earlier.
12 Israeli servicemen died in clashes with guerrillas in southern Lebanon.

Athens was selected as venue for Olympic Games in 2004.
8 Hundreds died when overloaded ferry sank off Haiti.
10 US Secretary of State Madeleine Albright began her first tour of Middle East in attempt to resolve six-month break in Israeli-Palestinian peace talks.
11 In Scottish referendum, 74.3 per cent of voters endorsed proposal for Scottish Assembly; 63.5 per cent approved tax-raising powers for the new legislature.
12 Mary Robinson ended seven-year term as President of Irish Republic to become UN High Commissioner for Human Rights (see 31 Oct.).
13 World dignitaries attended the state funeral in Calcutta of Mother Teresa, who had died on 5 Sept. (see XX: Obituary).
15 At general election in Norway, no single party won outright majority in 165-seat Storting; a non-socialist coalition was formed by Kjell Magne Bondevik, leader of Christian People's Party, on 13 Oct.
16 All-party talks (including Sinn Féin representatives) on future of N. Ireland opened at Stormont.
18 In referendum on devolution for Wales, government plans for a Welsh Assembly were approved by a margin of 0.6 per cent on a 50 per cent poll.
In Egypt, 10 died in attack by Islamic terrorist militants on tourist bus in Cairo.
19 In UK, seven died, 170 injured when Inter City express crashed into freight train in west London.
Malaysia declared state of emergency in Sarawak: smoke pollution from forest fires in Indonesia had reached danger levels and produced dense haze.
21 At general election in Poland, Solidarity Electoral Alliance headed the poll with 33.8 per cent of vote; Jerzy Burek formed a new coalition government on 17 Oct.
23 US and Japan agreed new defence pact enabling Japanese troops to provide support for US forces in any regional conflict.
24 In Algeria, at least 85 reported dead in massacre by fundamentalist rebels in Algiers suburb; 45 had been murdered earlier in week in Medea province.
25 British jet-powered car *Thrust SSC*, driven across Nevada desert by Squadron-Leader Andy Green, set new world land-speed record of 714 mph; on 17 Oct. he improved on record, becoming first person to break sound barrier on land, reaching 764.18 mph.
26 In Italy, thirteenth-century Basilica of St Francis in Assisi suffered serious damage to its structure and works of art in earthquake which killed 11, left thousands homeless and did much other damage.
In Indonesia, all 234 died when Garuda Indonesian Airlines plane crashed in thick smog in Sumatra.

OCTOBER

1 Israel released ailing Shaikh Ahmad Yasin (61), founder of Islamic resistance movement Hamas, gaoled for life in 1989, to secure release of Israeli agents arrested in Amman (Jordan) after attempted assassination of another Hamas leader on 25 Sept.
6 British PM Blair in Moscow for day-long talks with President Yeltsin.
In Nepal, King Birendra appointed Surya Bahadur Thapa to form new government following resignation of PM Lokendra Bahadur Chand.
7 HM Queen Elizabeth II and Prince Philip began two-week state visit to India and Pakistan, marking 50th anniversary of independence on sub-continent.
8 In N. Korea, Kim Jong Il, son of late leader Kim Il Sung, named general secretary of ruling Workers' Party of Korea.
9 In Mexico, some 400 died when hurricane Pauline struck Pacific resort of Acapulco.
10 Leaders of 40 European nations attended Council of Europe summit in Strasbourg, the second summit in organization's 48-year history.
Nobel Peace Prize awarded jointly to International Campaign to Ban Landmines and its US coordinator, Jody Williams (see 4 Dec.).

CHRONICLE OF PRINCIPAL EVENTS IN 1997 597

In Kazakhstan, President Nursultan Nazarbayev appointed Nurlan Balgimbayev PM following dismissal of cabinet of Akezhan Kazhageldin.
13 Tony Blair met Sinn Féin leader Gerry Adams in N. Ireland peace talks at Stormont, becoming first British PM to meet an Irish Republican leader for 76 years.
President Clinton began week-long tour of Brazil, Venezuela and Argentina.
14 In Congo, forces of General Denis Sassou-Nguesso, backed by Angolan troops, overran capital Brazzaville and deposed President Pascal Lissouba after five-month civil war; Sassou-Nguesso was sworn in as President on 25 Oct.
15 In Algeria, reports of a further massacre by Islamic militants brought to 75,000 estimates of death toll in six-year civil war.
In Sri Lanka, 18 died in massive bomb blast in Colombo, believed the work of Tamil Tigers.
20 In Yugoslav republic of Montenegro, PM Milo Djukanović claimed victory in presidential election, amid allegations of ballot-rigging by his opponent President Momir Bulatović.
22 President Mandela of S. Africa held talks in Tripoli with Col. Qadafi in effort to mediate in Libya's dispute with UK and US governments over extradition of two men suspected of 1988 Lockerbie bombing.
23 In Hong Kong, Hang Seng share index crashed by more than 10 per cent: it had lost nearly 25 per cent of its value in a week.
24 Commonwealth heads of government meeting opened in Edinburgh, ending 27 Oct.; delegates approved the Edinburgh Declaration, an agreement on Commonwealth role in promotion of trade and investment, and guidelines for admission of new members.
A peace agreement was signed in Conakry, Guinea, to end five months of fighting in Sierra Leone between supporters of military coup and ECOWAS intervention force and to reinstate President Kabba.
27 In UK, Chancellor Brown delivered statement to House of Commons, setting out terms for joining European Monetary Union (EMU) but ruling out entry before next election.
President Jiang Zemin began eight-day state visit to USA, holding talks with President Clinton in Washington on 29 Oct.
In New York, Dow Jones share index suffered its largest-ever one day fall; London shares also suffered record fall on 28 Oct. amid continuing volatility in world markets in response to Hong Kong's share-price collapse and crisis in other Asian economies.
28 Talks, chaired by Kenya, opened in Nairobi with the aim of ending 14-year war in southern Sudan which had cost more than one million lives.
31 Mary McAleese won landslide victory in Ireland's presidential election; she was sworn in on 11 November.

NOVEMBER

2 French lorry drivers, demanding higher wages, began week-long blockade of roads, border crossings and fuel depots, causing widespread chaos.
3 In New Zealand, Jim Bolger was ousted as PM by opponents in ruling National Party; he was succeeded by Jenny Shipley on 8 Dec.
4 In Jordan, elections were held for 80-seat legislature; pro-government candidates loyal to King Husain made substantial gains to dominate lower house in poll boycotted by Islamist opposition.
5 Indonesia secured IMF loan pledges totalling $10,140 million in return for a promise to reform its ailing economy.
6 Gen. Chaovalit Yongchaiyut resigned as PM of Thailand; Chuan Leekpai formed new government on 13 Nov.
At least 30 died in violent storms and flooding in Spain and Portugal.
7 President Chirac and PM Jospin of France held talks at London's Canary Wharf with British PM Blair.
8 Chinese leaders attended completion of damming of River Yangtse, marking start of £15 billion Three Gorges Dam project to create 400-mile lake; one of world's largest hydro-electric

projects, it was due to be completed in 2009 and involved evacuation of 1.2 million people.
9 President Yeltsin on three-day visit to China; a declaration was signed defining joint 2,800-mile disputed border.
10 Israeli PM Binyamin Netanyahu on four-day visit to London for talks on Middle East peace process.

In USA, British au pair Louise Woodward freed from gaol after judge had reduced her conviction by a jury of murder of baby Matthew Eappen to one of manslaughter; case had caused international controversy.
13 President Geidar Aliyev attended ceremony to mark start of Azerbaijan's extraction of oil from Caspian basin with opening of first offshore oil pipeline.
17 In Egypt, 58 foreign tourists died in attack by Islamic militants at Luxor.
20 Iraq, which had been threatening to shoot down US U2 planes carrying UN weapons inspectors, agreed to allow resumption of weapons inspections following UN Security Council's adoption on 12 Nov. of resolution tightening sanctions against it.

In UK, following disputed two-vote general election victory, Liberal Democrats gained 21,000-vote majority over Conservatives in Winchester by-election; Conservatives held Beckenham with reduced majority.

HM Queen Elizabeth II and Prince Philip attended service at Westminster Abbey to mark 50th anniversary of their marriage.

EU heads of government held special two-day summit in Luxembourg to discuss employment policy.
21 In Malaysia, a National Economic Action Council was created to oversee efforts to overcome economic crisis.
24 In Japan, Yamaichi Securities collapsed with losses of £15,000 million (Y3.2 billion); it was country's biggest financial failure since World War II.

In UK, new British Library at St Pancras, London, opened to readers; it had cost £511 million and had been some 30 years under construction.
25 In UK, Chancellor Brown delivered a pre-budget statement to House of Commons; he announced £400 million heating bonus for pensioners, setting-up of after-school clubs for one million children and abolition of advance corporation tax.
28 In UK, second reading of a private member's bill to ban hunting with dogs was carried in the House of Commons by 411 votes to 151 on a free vote.
29 In India, government led by PM Inder Kumar Gujral resigned.
30 Czech PM Vaclav Klaus resigned: his three-party coalition had collapsed over party funding scandal.

At elections in Honduras, ruling Liberal Party of Honduras gained comfortable victory; in presidential contest its candidate Carlos Roberto Flores Facussé defeated National Party of Honduras candidate Alba Nova Gunera de Melar.

DECEMBER

2 A three-day international conference on wartime trade in Jewish gold plundered by Nazis during Holocaust opened in London.

President Farooq Ahmad Leghari of Pakistan resigned over power struggle with PM Nawaz Sharif; Muhammad Rafiq Tarar was elected as his successor on 31 Dec.
3 South Korea, in deep financial crisis, was granted IMF pledges totalling $57,000 million.

President Fernando Cardoso of Brazil on three-day state visit to Britain.
4 At Ottawa, Canada, 125 nations signed UN convention banning use, production, transfer and stockpiling of anti-personnel landmines; USA, China and Russia were among states refusing to sign.
9 In UK, government published White Paper, *The New NHS-Modern, Dependable*; proposals included abolition of internal market and reduction in bureaucracy.

In Zimbabwe, trade unions held national strike and day of protest over proposed tax increases; government threatened to shoot demonstrators.

10 At end of UN Conference on Climate Control in Kyoto, Japan, delegates of industrial nations adopted protocol binding them to reduction of greenhouse gas emissions by early 21st century in effort to prevent global warming.

11 In UK, Sinn Féin leaders Gerry Adams and Martin McGuinness in London for talks with PM Blair, first Irish Republican leaders to visit Downing Street since 1921.

In UK, royal yacht *Britannia* decommissioned after 45 years in ceremony at Portsmouth attended by HM Queen Elizabeth II.

14 Largest-ever regional summit of SE Asian nations opened in Kuala Lumpur, with regional economic crisis top of the agenda: delegates from ASEAN countries, Japan, China and S. Korea attended.

In Yugoslav republic of Serbia, former Foreign Minister Milan Milutinović defeated extreme nationalist candidate Vojislav Seselj in run-off poll for presidency.

15 President Clinton visited Sarajevo and US troops serving in Bosnia.

18 At presidential election in S. Korea, Kim Dae Jung, opposition pro-democracy campaigner, defeated ruling party candidate Lee Hoi Chang.

19 At general election in Jamaica, ruling PNP, led by Percival Patterson, gained third consecutive victory.

104 died when Singapore SilkAir Boeing 737–300 crashed en route from Jakarta to Singapore.

22 In southern Mexico, 45 Indian peasants died in attack by paramilitary gunmen in Chiapas state.

24 13 died when hurricane-force winds swept Britain, causing widespread destruction and power failures.

25 In Zambia, former President Kenneth Kaunda detained for alleged complicity in failed October coup; he was later released and placed under house arrest.

29 At elections in Kenya, President Daniel Arap Moi, in office for 19 years, and his ruling KANU party, returned to power amid opposition allegations of ballot-rigging and calls for new poll.

In Hong Kong, government officials began compulsory cull of all region's 1¼ million poultry amid fears over transmission to humans of an avian flu virus which had killed four people.

President Niyazov of Turkmenistan and President Khatami of Iran attended opening of 125-mile natural gas pipeline linking Iranian and Turkmen gas fields.

30 In Algeria, 412 massacred in western province of Relizan; some 850 civilians had died in attacks by Islamic militants in past fortnight.

INDEX

Page references in bold indicate location of main coverage.

Abacha, Gen. Sani, 250, 251, 253, 427
Abdou, Ahmed, 323
Abdullah ibn Abdul Aziz, Crown Prince, 220, 400
Abiola, Chief M.K.O., 252
Abkhazia, 144, **389**
Abu Dhabi, 304
Abu Musa & Tunbs Islands, 220, **424**
Adamkus, Valdas, 107, 108
Adams, Gerry, 19, 28, 29, 43, 45, 46, 47, 597, 599
Adams, John, 490, 492
Adcock, Fleur, 520
Adisa, Maj.-Gen. Abdulkarim, 253
Adonis, Andrew, 10
Afewerki, Issaias, 230, 240, 242
Afghanistan, 34, 98, **295–7**, 300, 302, 313, 400, 401
African Economic Community (EAC), 427
African Organizations and Conferences, 282–4, **425–8**
Agama, G.K., 250
Agard, John, 520
Agboyigbo, Yaovi, 261
Agius, Francis, 93
Agyemen-Rawlings, Nana Konadu, 249
Ahern, Bertie, 43, 44, 45, 46, 47, 65, 67, 68, 593
Ahmar, Shaikh Abdullah bin Hussain al-, 223
Ahmed, Shahabuddin, 313
Ahtisaari, Martti, 76, 77
AIDS/HIV, 248, 279, 458
Ailey, Alvin, 495
Aitchison, Craigie, 510
Aitken, Jonathan, 482, 593
Akayesu, Jean-Paul, 473
Akayev, Askar, 298, 300, 304
Akhmatova, Anna, 575
Akihito, Emperor Tsugu no Miya, 356
Alanis of Urgel, Bishop Joan Martí, 83
Alarcón Rivera, Fabián, 173, 590
Albania, 60, 78, **122–5**, 131, 132, 135, 388, 394, 400, 411, 412, 414, 415, 416, 586, 590, 593, 594
Albee, Edward, 500
Albert II, King, 61
Albert, Prince, 84
Albery, Tim, 488
Albright, Madeleine K., 43, 95, 100, 159, 160, 181, 207, 208, 216, 226, 230, 241, 308, 313, 327, 330, 337, 346, 352, 431, 573, 590, 593, 596
Alderdice, Lord (John), 41, 44
Alemán Lacayo, Arnoldo, 181, 182, 589
Alesana, Tofilau Eti, 377, 379
Alex, David, 333
Alexis II, Patriarch, 449
Alfi, Gen. Mohammed al, 209

Algeria, 56, **234–6**, 451, 593, 595, 596, 597, 599
Alho, Arja, 29, 77
Aliyev, Geidar, 143, 144, 598
Allen, George, 153
Allford, David, 516
Almunia, Joaquín, 87
Althorp, Viscount, 577
Alvarez, Aida, 573
Alvarez, Carlos, 167
Amamou, Mohammed, 423
Amato, Giuliano, 61
American Organizations, **432–5**
American Samoa, 379
Amis, Kingsley, 521
Amis, Martin, 517, 519
Amnesty International, 51, 221, 232, 233
Amnuay Virawan, 327
Amory, Vance, 195
Amoudi, Mohammed al, 241
Amour, Salmin, 246
an-Nibari, Abdullah, 227
an-Nuaimi, Najib Mohamed, 227
an-Nuri, Anwar Abdullah, 227
Anand, Mulk Raj, 518
Ananiashvili, Nina, 495
Ancram, Michael, 27, 42
Andean Community (CA), 433, **434–5**
Andersen, Hans, 490
Anderson, Jon Lee, 520
Anderson, Reid, 495
Andersson, Claes, 76
Ando, Tadao, 514
Andorra, **83, 84**
Andrews, David, 47, 68
Andriessen, Louis, 490, 491
Angola, 4, 85, 92, 266, 268, **275–7**, 279, 387, 396, 591
Anguilla, **196**, 197
Anguita, Julio, 87
Ani, Anthony, 251
Annan, Justice D.F., 249
Annan, Kofi, 85, 98, 239, 380, 381, 382, 402, 423, 426, 589
Antarctica, 465
Anthony, Kenny D., 194, 195, 196
Antigua & Barbuda, 190, **194–5**
Anton, Abel, 523
Anwar Ibrahim, 329
Anyaoku, Chief Emeka, 391, 393
Applewhite, Marshall, 158
Aptidon, Hassan Gouled, 243
Aquino, Corazon, 335

INDEX

Arab League, 219, 231, 398, 399, **423**
Arab Maghreb Union (AMU), 423
Arab Organizations, **423–4**
Arab States of the Gulf, 224–8
Arab, Brig. Hussain Muhammad, 223
Arabi, Rija'a al, 210
Arafat, Yassir, 206, 207, 208, 400, 589
Aragona, Giancarlo, 413
Arancibia, Vice-Adm. Horacio Patricio, 170
Araujo, Miguel, 182
Archer, Lord (Jeffrey), 30
Architecture, 512–16
Arctic Council, 418
Arena, Franca, 370
Argaña, Luís María, 174
Argentina, 35, 85, **166–7**, 300, 434, 534, 597
Armenia, 121, **143–4**, 304, 401, 412
Armitage, Simon, 520
Arms Control, see Defence, Disarmament and Security
Aronson, Theo, 520
Arsenis, Gerasimos, 97
Art, see Visual Arts
Arteaga, Rosalía, 173
Arthur, Owen, 190
Aruba, 200
Arzú Irigoyen, Alvaro, 180, 181
Asad, Bashir al-, 214
Asad, Hafiz al-, 213, 214
Asahara, Shoko, 358
Asamoah, Obed, 250
Åsbrink, Erik, 74
Asfa Wossen, Crown Prince, 241, 574 (obit.)
Asgrímsson, Halldór, 71
Ashdown, Paddy, 11, 13, 26, 29, 38
Ashton, Frederick, 495, 577
Asia-Europe Meeting (ASEM), 431
Asia-Pacific Economic Cooperation (APEC), 160, 373, **428–30**
Asia-Pacific Organizations, 428–32
Asian Development Bank (ADB), 328, 366
Asmal, Kader, 292
Assiseh, Vincent, 249
Association of Caribbean States (ACS), 433, 435
Association of South-East Asian Nations (ASEAN), 326, 327, 330, 338, 357, **428**, 468
Asylmuratova, Altynai, 493
Atherton, Mike, 526
Athulathmudali, Srimani, 320
Atkins, Eileen, 500
Atkinson, Kate, 519
Atkinson, Rowan, 502
Ato, Osman Ali, 242
Attenborough, Michael, 498
Attlee, Clement, 500
Aun, Michel, 216
Austen, Jane, 517
Australia, 202, 328, 330, **367–71**, 372, 393, 431, 432, 469, 575
Austria, 60, **78–80**, 124, 132, 230, 414, 421, 446, 588, 589

Awdry, Rev Wilbert Vere, 574 (obit.)
Axworthy, Lloyd, 163, 178
Aydid, Hussein, 242
Ayers, Gillian, 510
Ayrey, Craig, 493
Azerbaijan, 121, **143, 144**, 302, 303, 304, 400, 401, 412, 598
Azika, Major-Gen. Patrick, 253
Azimov, Yahya, 298
Aziz, Sartaj, 312
Aziz, Tariq, 218
Aznar López, José María, 86, 87, 88

Babbitt, Bruce, 573
Babbitt, Milton, 492
Badawi, Abdullah Ahmad, 332, 430
Badawi, Dr Zaki, 452
Bagabandi, Natsagiin, 364, 365, 592
Bagaza, Jean-Baptiste, 272
Bah, Hamat, 15, 254
Bahamas, The, 193, 200, 350
Bahrain, 225, 226, 304, 380, 400
Bailey, Donovan, 522
Baing, Andrew, 372
Bajramović, Miro, 130
Baker, James, 239, 388
Balanchine, George, 493, 495, 576
Balasuriya, Fr Tissa, 448, 449
Balcerowicz, Leszek, 105
Balconi, Gen. Julio, 181
Baldeosingh, Kevin, 519
Baldwin, Mark, 496
Balendra, Ken, 320
Balgimbayev, Nurlan, 298, 299, 597
Ballesteros, Severiano, 527
Ballet & Dance, 493–6
Baltic Council, 418, 419–20
Banda, Dr Hastings Kamuzu, 279, 574 (obit.)
Bandaranaike, Sirimavo, 318
Bang Van Le, 338
Bangladesh, 307, **313–5**, 325, 401, 432
Banks, Iain, 519
Banville, John, 519
Bánzer Suárez, Gen. Hugo, 168, 595
Bao Dai, 338, 574 (obit.)
Barak, Ehud, 206, 593
Barbados, 190–1, 392, 435
Barco Vargas, Virgilio, 574–5 (obit.)
Barenboim, Daniel, 491
Barker, Harley Granville, 500
Baron, Roni, 205
Barrios Zelada, Gen. Héctor, 182
Barry, Sebastian, 500
Barshefsky, Charlene, 537, 573
Barwick, Sir Garfield, 370, 575 (obit.)
Baryshnikov, Mikhail, 493
Barzani, Mustafa, 103
Basescu, Traian, 118
Bashir, Omar Hasan Ahmed al-, 228, 229
Basri, Driss, 237, 238

Bassolino, Antonio, 60
Baston, Lewis, 520
Bauch, Pina, 495
Bauer, Lord, 10
Bawden, Nina, 519
Bayer, Paul, 460
Baykal, Deniz, 102
Bayley, Stephen, 513
Bays, Daniel, 453
Beatrix, Queen, 63
Beckett, Margaret, 20, 572
Bedoya Pizzaro, Gen. Haroldo, 172
Beebeejaun, Rashid, 321
Beethoven, Ludwig van, 488
Begin, Benny, 203, 205
Begin, Menachem, 203, 580
Beilin, Yossi, 206
Belarus, 140, 141, 412, 414, 416, 420, 591
Belgium, 53, **61–2**, 64, 269, 271, 383, 395, 417, 446
Béliz, Gustavo, 166
Belize, 191–2
Belka, Marek, 104
Bell, Martin, 17
Bellow, Saul, 516, 519
Ben Ali, Zayn al-Abdin, 233, 234
Ben Ami, Shlomo, 206
Benhamouda, Abdelhak, 234
Benin, 257, 261, 394, 395
Benn, Tony, 13, 27
Bensalah, Abdelkader, 234
Bérenger, Paul, 320, 321
Berger, Samuel D., 573
Bergreen, Laurence, 520
Berisha, Sali, 123, 124, 590, 594
Berlin, Sir Isaiah, 575 (obit.)
Berlusconi, Silvio, 59, 60
Bermuda, 196, 197, 591
Berri, Nabih, 216, 217
Bertini, Catherine, 363
Besson, Luc, 502
Bhattarai, Krishna Prasad, 317
Bheenick, Rundheersing, 321
Bhumibol Adulyadej (Rama IX), King, 327
Bhutan, 317–8, 432
Bhutto, Benazir, 311, 589
Bhutto, Murtaza, 311
Bicakčić, Edhem, 125
Bid, Mohammed al-, 223
Bidouane, Nezhe, 523
Bing, Sir Rudolf, 575 (obit.)
Bildt, Carl, 74, 75, 126, 593
Bin, Zachary, 251
Bintley, David, 495
Bird, Lester, 190, 194, 195
Bird, Vere, Jr., 195
Birendra Bir Bikram Shah Deva, King, 316, 596
Birkavs, Valdis, 109
Birtwistle, Harrison, 490
Biryukov, Vadim, 138
Bishara, Abdullah, 227
Bishop, Maurice, 192

Biwott, Nicholas, 245
Biya, Paul, 262, 264
Bizet, Georges, 488
Bizimungu, Pasteur, 271
Black Sea, 119, 142, 302, 470
Black Sea Economic Cooperation (BSEC), 420, 422
Blackburn, Robin, 521
Blair, Tony (UK Prime Minister), cabinet, 20, 27, 572; devolution, 29, 38; election victory, 4, 15–18, 592; European Union, 24, 31, 32, 403, 406, 593; external affairs, 35, 36, 37, 352, 391, 446, 596; home affairs, 9, 11, 12, 13, 29, 30, 33, 513, 522; N. Ireland, 28, 29, 43–7, 67, 597, 599; royal family, 5, 6, 7
Blanchard, James Ulysses, III, 275
Blanco, Miguel Angel, 88
Bland, Sir Christopher, 506
Blaskić, Tihomir, 474
Blewett, Greg, 525
Bloch, Felix, 584
Blunkett, David, 16, 20, 22, 27, 33, 572
Bošić, Boro, 125
Boal, Peter, 493
Bojars, Juris, 107
Bojaxhiu, Agnes, 586
Bolger, Dermot, 519
Bolger, Jim, 373, 374, 375, 376, 597
Bolivia, 168, 434, 595
Bolkiah, Prince Jafi Jefri, 330, 331
Bolkiah, Sultan Sir Hassanal, 330
Bond, Samantha, 498
Bondevik, Kjell Magne, 72, 596
Bonev, Bogomil, 121
Bongo, Omar, 263, 265
Bonham-Carter, Helena, 502
Bonino, Emma, 410
Bonnet, Manuel José, 172
Booker Prize, 516
Booth, Mark, 505
Boothroyd, Betty, 44
Borer, Thomas, 81
Born, Georgina, 493
Bosnia & Hercegovina, 36, 74, 80, 98, **125–8**, 149, 389, 399, 400, 401, 412, 414, 415, 416, 421, 449, 473, 474, 594, 599
Boswell, Laurence, 498
Botchwey, Kwesi, 249
Botha, P.W., 290
Botswana, 282, 283, 284–5, 392, 393, 469
Bouchard, Lucien, 164
Bougainville, 371, 372, 374, 378, 393, 431
Boula, Rhissa Ag, 262
Boulahya, Ismail, 233
Boulez, Pierre, 490
Bourguiba, Habib, 233
Bourhane, Nourdine, 322, 324
Bourne, Matthew, 494
Bouterse, Desi, 199
Boutros-Ghali, Dr Boutros, 393, 395, 589

Boutros-Ghali, Yusuf, 210
Bowie, David, 511
Bowker, John, 453
Bowles, Erskine, 573
Boxer, Major Charles, 579
Boyd, Michael, 497
Boyle, James, 506
Bozhkov, Aleksandur, 120
Brady, Archbishop Sean, 595
Bragaglia, Carlo, 503
Brahimi, Lakhdar, 218, 297
Branagh, Kenneth, 502
Branco, Rafael, 396
Brand, Juliana, 493
Brandstrup, Kim, 495
Brandt, David, 197, 198
Branson, Richard, 506
Braque, Georges, 511
Brazauskas, Algirdas, 107, 108
Brazil, 85, 92, 93, 167, **168–70**, 380, 396, 434, 469, 534, 597, 598
Breeze, Jean Binta, 520
Brennan, Justice William, 575 (obit.)
Brezhnev, Leonid, 587
Briguera, Sergei, 529
Brincat, Leo, 94
British Virgin Islands, 196, 197
Brittan, Sir Leon, 31, 410, 537
Britten, Benjamin, 487, 584
Broadcasting, see Television & Radio
Brookner, Anita, 519
Brown, Colin, 520
Brown, George Mackay, 520
Brown, Gordon, 8, 9, 11, 12, 13, 15, 17, 20, 21, 25, 26, 31, 32, 33, 38, 393, 406, 407, 408, 572, 573, 592, 593, 597, 598
Brown, Nicole, see Simpson, Nicole Brown
Browner, Carol, 573
Browning, Dolly, 153
Brownjohn, Alan, 519
Browse & Darby, 511
Bruce, Steve, 453
Brunei, 330–1, 431, 468
Bruton, John, 66
BSE (bovine spongiform encephalopathy), 13, 21, 34, 66, 411, 457
Bubka, Sergey, 523
Bucaram Ortiz, Abdala, 173, 590
Bulatović, Momir, 134, 135, 597
Bulgaria, 119–22, 215, 408, 421, 534, 589, 591
Bunwaree, Vasant, 321
Burek, Jerzy, 596
Burke, Ray, 47, 68
Burkina Faso, 257, 261, 266, 467
Burma, see Myanmar
Burnham, Forbes, 581
Burnside, John, 520
Burrell, Sir William, 509
Burroughs, William S., 512, 576 (obit.)
Burundi, 247, **271–2**, 427
Bush, George, 526

Bush, McKeeva, 198
Bussotti, Sylvano, 490
Butler, Richard, 218
Buyoya, Pierre, 271, 272
Buzek, Jerzy, 104, 105
Byars, James Lee, 512

Cabezas, José Luis, 166
Caddick, Andy, 526
Cage, Nicolas, 501
Cairns, Lord, 392, 562
Calder, Jenni, 517, 520
Calderón Sol, Armando, 180
Caldera Rodríguez, Rafael, 177, 190
Callas, Maria, 500
Calvin, Prof. Melvin, 576 (obit.)
Camacho Solís, Manuel, 184
Camargo, Gen. Sergio, 181
Cambodia, 338–40, 430, 431, 594, 595
Camdessus, Michel, 532, 538
Cameron, James, 502
Cameroon, 262, 264, 392
Cammerata, Joseph, 152
Campbell, Donovan, 152
Campos, Rueben, 191
Campos, Torres, 91
Canada, 85, 112, **160–6**, 178, 184, 188, 191, 212, 220, 226, 230, 252, 302, 303, 304, 319, 383, 394, 429, 443, 593, 598
Canary Islands, 88
Canterbury, Archbishop of (Dr George Carey), 4, 8, 447, 448
Cape Verde, 274, 396
Cárdenas Solórzano, Cuauhtemoc, 184
Cardoso e Cunha, António, 91
Cardoso, Fernando Henrique, 85, 168, 169, 598
Carey, Jim, 501
Carey, Peter, 519
Carey, Ron, 159
Caribbean Basin Initiative (CBI), 434
Caribbean Community (Caricom), 190, 196, 199, 433, 435
Caribbean Development Bank (CDB), 199, 435
Caribbean Organizations, 534–5
Carl XVI Gustav, King, 74
Carlisle, Sir James B., 194
Carlot Korman, Maxime, 379
Caroline and Stephanie, Princesses, 84
Carrera, Elsa, 176
Carrillo Fuentes, Amado, 184
Carrington, Edward, 433
Carter, Angela, 521
Carter, Elliott, 492
Carter, Jimmy, 172, 581
Carter, Martin, 187
Caruana, Peter, 89
Carver, Raymond, 520
Caso, José Luis, 88
Casper, Billy, 527
Caspian Sea, 300, 301 (*map of oil pipelines*)
Cassese, Judge Antonio, 473
Castelli, Leo, 582

Castillo Meza, Gen. Tomás, 176
Castro Ruz, Fidel, 178, 179, 583
Castro Ruz, Raúl, 179
Cato, Vincent, 196
Cattaneo, Peter, 502
Caurier, Patrice, 488
Causley, Charles, 517, 520
Cavallo, Domingo, 166, 167
Cayman Islands, 196, 197–8
Cecil, Henry, 530
Celant, Germano, 509
Cem, Ismail, 102
Central African Republic, 56, **263, 266–7**, 386–7
Central America, 180–3
Central European Free Trade Association (CEFTA), 420, 421
Central European Initiative (CEI), 420, 421
Cerpa Cartolini, Néstor, 175
Chad, 262–4, 266
Chadlington, Lord, 488
Chambers, Colin, 520
Chambers, George, 190
Chamoiseau, Patrick, 519
Chan, Anson, 350
Chan, Sir Julius, 371, 372, 393, 591
Chand, Lokendra Bahadur, 316, 590, 596
Chandra, Vikram, 519
Chang Hsiao-yen, 355
Chang Sung Kil, 363
Chaovalit Yongchaiyut, Gen., 328, 597
Charest, Jean, 162
Charles, Carson, 189
Charles, Prince of Wales, 1, 4, 5, 7, 12, 352, 391, 392, 514, 577
Chatichai Choonhaven, 327
Chaudhuri, Nirad C., 518
Chávez Frías, Lt.-Gen. (retd.) Hugo, 177
Chechenya, 414, 419, 420, 589
Chen Yifei, 512
Chernomyrdin, Viktor, 109, 135, 142, 304, 337, 366, 446, 590
Chettiar, Angidi, 321
Cheyo, John, 246
Chiam See Tong, 331
Chidambaram, Palaniappan, 309
Chile, 167, **170–1**, 380, 385, 434, 470, 534
Chiluba, Frederick, 277, 279, 427
China, 34, 36, 93, 136, 139, 148, 150, 166, 183, 193, 219, 230, 231, 290, 295, 297, 300, 302, 304, 308, 312, 328, 336, 337, **341–53**, 354–5, 357, 362, 365–6, 370, 382, 393, 399, 429, 431, 435, 442, 452, 470, 471, 475, 535, 537, 577, 590, 591, 592, 593, 598, 599
Chinyata, Kasasa Mutati, 425
Chirac, Jacques, 52, 53, 54, 56, 83, 337, 349, 394, 395, 403, 406, 592, 593, 597
Chisholm, Sam, 505
Chissano, Joaquim Alberto, 274, 427
Chrétien, Jean, 160, 161, 162, 163, 165, 395, 593
Chronicle of 1997, 589–99
Chu, Steven, 460

Chuan Leekpai, 327, 328, 597
Chubais, Anatolii, 136, 138, 590
Chun Doo Hwan, 362
Chung Tai Soo, 360
Chung, Johnny, 149
Churchett, Stephen, 500
Churchill, Carol, 500
Churchill, Randolph, 579
Çiller, Tansu, 101, 102
Cimabue, Giovanni, 508
Cimarosa, Domenico, 489
Cimoszewicz, Wlodzimierz, 105
Cindoruk, Hüsamettin, 102
Cinema, 501–3
Ciorbea, Victor, 116, 117
Cissé, Amadou Boubacar, 262
Cissé, Gen. Lamine, 259
Ciubuc, Ion, 141
Clair, Jean, 509, 510
Clapp, Susannah, 520
Clark, Alan, 10
Clark, David, 572
Clark, Glen, 165
Clark, Helen, 373
Clark, James, 157
Clarke, Arthur C., 519
Clarke, Darren, 528
Clarke, Kenneth, 11, 12, 23, 24, 31, 39, 593
Clerides, Glafkos, 97, 99, 100
Cline, Sally, 520
Clinton, Bill (US President), cabinet, 149–50, 573; environment, 465, 466; external affairs, 35, 44, 70, 98, 100, 103, 139, 148, 159–60, 165, 167, 171, 184, 196, 206, 207, 212, 214, 230, 304, 308, 314, 343, 346, 347, 357, 410, 434, 440, 443, 465, 466, 533, 589, 591, 592, 597, 599; home affairs, 145, 146–9, 150–4, 157, 158, 533, 589; scandals, 145, 146, 147, 148–9, 150–3; State of the Union, 147–8
Clodumar, Kinza, 376, 378
Coard, Phyllis, 192
Cobb, Michael, 368
Coe, Jonathan, 519
Coe, Sebastian, 523
Coen brothers, 501
Coetzee, J.M., 520
Cohen, William S., 573
Colić, Gen. Pero, 127
Collett, Glenna, 588
Colombia, 171–3, 183, 435, 445, 446, 574
Colston, Mal, 369
Common Market for Eastern and Southern Africa (COMESA), 288, **425**, 427
Commonwealth, The, 1, 2, 35, 36, 37, 92, 199, 231, 250, 252, 255, 264, 290, 314, 320, 373, 379, **391–3**, 394, 395, 396, 435, 561–4, 597
Community of Portuguese-Speaking Countries (CPLP), 92, **393**, **396**
Comoros, 322, 323–4, 595
Compaoré, (Capt.) Blaise, 257, 261
Compton, Denis, 576 (obit.)

Coney, Miranda, 494
Congo, Democratic Republic of the, 56, 248, 266, **268–71**, 272, 273, 276, 282, 283, 290, 394, 428, 583, 592
Congo, Republic of, 56, **263**, **265–6**, 269, 276, 597
Connon, Bryan, 520
Conradi, Peter, 521
Constantine, ex-King, 96
Constantinescu, Emil, 116, 117
Conté, (Gen.) Lansana, 257, 260
Cook Islands, 377–8, 432
Cook, Robin, 17, 20, 28, 34, 35, 36, 37, 89, 221, 313, 572
Cooke, Sir Howard, 186
Cookson, Catherine, 516
Coombs, Herbert Cole ('Nugget'), 370
Cooper, Adam, 494
Copland, Aaron, 490
Copley, Terence, 453
Coppen, Nathan, 494
Córdovez, Diego, 98
Corigliano, John, 492
Correia, Carlos, 273, 274
Costa Rica, 181, 183, 380, 397, 399, 434, 469
Costanza, Robert, 471
Costello, Peter, 367
Côte d'Ivoire, 257, 260, 402, 426, 428, 469
Cotton, Fran, 530
Coulthard, David, 528
Council of Europe, 125, 141, **411–13**, 414, 446, 475, **559–61**, 596
Council of the Baltic Sea States (CBSS), 418
Cousteau, Jacques-Yves, 576 (obit.)
Coxon, Raymond, 512
Cragg, Tony, 511
Craig, Charles, 489
Cranko, John, 495
Cravinho, João, 92
Crick, Michael, 520
Cristina de Borbón, Infanta, 86
Cristo, Jorge, 172
Croatia, 36, **129–30**, 389, 390, 414, 415, 421, 591, 593
Cruz León, Raúl Ernesto, 179
Crvenovski, Branko, 131
Cuba, 85, **178–9**, 187, 192, 195, 410, 435
Cunningham, Jack, 572
Cuomo, Andrew M., 573
Curnow, Allen, 520
Curry, David, 31
Cusack, Catherine, 500
Cusk, Rachel, 519
Cutileiro, José, 437
Cyprus, 95, 96, **97–101**, 102, 390, 401, 408, 420
Czech Republic, 85, **110–12**, 114, 139, 408, 419, 421–2, 438, 534, 592, 594, 598

da Gama, Vasco, 91
da Silva ('Lula'), Luis Inácio, 169
D'Aguiar, Fred, 517, 519
Dahanayake, Wijayananda, 576 (obit.)
Dalai Lama, 349, 452
Daldry, Stephen, 500
D'Alema, Massimo, 58, 59
Daley, William M., 573
D'Amato, Alfonse, 231
Damiens, Alain, 492
Daniel, Paul, 488
Daniel, Yuli, 585
Daniels, Ron, 498
Danilova, Alexandra, 576–7 (obit.)
Darboe, Oussainou, 254
Darling, Alistair, 33, 572
Dash-Yondon, Büdragchaagiyn, 364
Dashbalbar, Ochirbatyn, 365
David Cohen Literature Prize, 516
David, Catherine, 510
David, Hugh, 521
Davie, Donald, 520
Davies, Caitlin, 285
Davies, Hilary, 520
Davies, Howard, 498
Davies, Howard, 488
Davies, Ron, 41, 572
Davies, Nick, 10
Davies, Sir Peter Maxwell, 492
Davis, Andrew, 488
Davis, Gilbert, 152
Dawson, Matt, 530
de Botton, Alain, 521
de Chastelain, Gen. John, 47
de Klerk, F.W., 289, 595
de Kooning, Willem, 512, 577 (obit.)
de Lange, Nicholas, 453
de Larosière, Jacques, 416, 417
de Melgar, Alba Nora Gunera, 183
de Monchaux, Cathy, 511
de Selliers, Guy, 417
de Sousa Franco, António, 92
de Venecia, José, 335
de Villa, Gen. Renato, 335, 336
de Vroe, Richter, 490
Deane, Sir William, 367
Dear, Sir John, 191
Dearing, Sir Ron, 594
Debono, Miriam Spiteri, 93
Déby, Col. Idriss, 262
Defence, Disarmament and Security, 436–45;
arms control, 139, 440–3; defence expenditure and procurement, 443–5; landmines, 4, 85, 165–6, 384, 442–3, **566–8**; NATO and European security, 436–40; NATO-Russia Founding Act, 138–9, 439, **555–9**; non-traditional threats, 445–6
Degas, Edgar, 511
Dehaene, Jean-Luc, 61, 62
Dehaybe, Roger, 395
Delacroix, Eugène, 511
Delalić, Zejnil, 474
Delamuraz, Jean-Pascal, 81
Delbrück, Max, 579
Delclaux, Cosme, 88
Delić, Hazim, 474

Delibes, Leo, 494
Delport, Tertius, 290
Demirel, Süleyman, 98, 101, 103, 304, 401, 593
Dench, Dame Judi, 498, 502
Deng Xiaoping, 341, 342, 343, 352, 353, 354, 577 (obit.), 590
Denis, Hervé, 180
Denktash, Rauf, 49, 97, 98, 99
Denmark, 69–70, 71, 404, 405, 413, 414, 416
Dennis, Ferdinand, 517, 519
Denniston, Patrick, 488
Deri, Aryeh, 205
Dettori, Frankie, 530
Deuba, Sher Bahadur, 316, 590
Deutch, John M., 149
Developing Eight (D-8), 401
Dewar, Donald, 20, 34, 38, 572
Dexter, Sally, 499
Di Mateo, Roberto, 525
Di Pietro, Antonio, 59, 60
Diaderas, Gen. Fernando, 175
Diaghilev, Serge, 576
Diana, Princess of Wales, 1, 4, 29, 165, 277, 443, 447, 489, 507, 517, 577–8 (obit.), 595
Díaz Delmas, Gen. Oscar Rodrígo, 175
Dieng, Ousmane Tanor, 258
Dietrich, Marlene, 586
Digby, Lord, 579
Dimbleby, Jonathan, 521
Dimitrov, Filip, 120
Ding Guangen, 341
Dini, Ahmed, 243
Dini, Lamberto, 57, 60, 61
Dion, Stéphane, 163
Diouf, Abdou, 256, 258
Disasters and Accidents (see also Environmental Questions), Australia, 595; Belize, 192; Brazil, 170; Chile, 171; Guam, 378, 595; Haiti, 180; Indonesia, 596; Iran, 592; Israel, 202; Mexico, 185; Saudi Arabia, 231; Singapore, 599; Spain, 591, 597; UK, 10, 596, 599; USA, 145–6; Venezuela, 178
Diski, Jenny, 520
Diya, Lt.-Gen. Oladipo, 253
Djibouti, 226, **240, 243**
Djukanović, Milo, 133, 134, 135, 597
Dlamini, Sibusiso Barnabas, 282
Do Muoi, 337
Dobin, Tony, 529
Dobrev, Nikolay, 120
Dobson, Frank, 572
Documents and Reference, 555–73
Dogan, Ahmed, 122
Dolly, the cloned sheep, 457
Dolmetsch, Arnold, 578
Dolmetsch, Carl, 492, 578 (obit.)
Dominica, 194, 195, 394
Dominican Republic, 179, 180, 435
Donleavy, J.P., 519
Doran, Gregory, 498
Dorligjav, Dambiyn, 366

Dorrell, Stephen, 11, 23, 24, 37
dos Santos, José Eduardo, 266, 275
Dostam, Gen. Abdul Rashid, 296, 297
Douglas, Denzil, 194
Downey, Sir Gordon, 16
Drašković, Vuk, 134
Dreyfus, Laurence, 493
Driberg, Tom, 500
Drnovšek, Janez, 132
Dromgoole, Dominic, 500
Drosnin, Michael, 453
Dudinskaya, Natalya, 495
Duffey, Joseph, 573
Dugan, Angel Serafin Seriche, 263
Duhalde, Eduardo, 166
Duhalde, Hilda, 167
Duisenberg, Wim, 406
Dun, Bob, 428
Duncan, Daniel Kablan, 257, 260
Duncan, Lindsay, 498
Dunmore, Helen, 519, 520
Durán, Juan Carlos, 168
Dusapin, Pascal, 491
Dvorak, Tomas, 523
Dyer, Geoff, 521
Dyulgerov, Asen, 122

Eappen, Deborah, 155
Eappen, Matthew, 154, 598
East African Commission (EAC), 425, 427
East Timor, 35, 93, 290, 333, 370, 396, 430
Easton, Carol, 520
Ebb, Fred, 496
Ebert, Carl, 575
Ecclestone, Bernie, 522
Ecevit, Bülent, 99, 102
Echeverri Mejía, Gilberto, 172
Economic and Social Affairs, 532–54; East Asian crisis, **535–7**; G-7 summit, **537**; institutions, 537–9; international survey, **532–5**; statistical tables, **540–54**
Economic Community of Central African States (CEEAC), 425, 427
Economic Community of West African States (ECOWAS), 250, 254, 256, 387, **425**, 426, **427**, 597
Economic Cooperation Organization (ECO), 304
Ecuador, 98, **173–4**, 435, 590
Eddery, Pat, 530
Edinburgh, Duke of, 366
Edlinger, Rudolf, 79
Edwards, Jonathan, 523
Egal, Mohammed Ibrahim, 243
Eggert, Moritz, 490
Egypt, 203, 207, **209–11**, 213, 225, 226, 229, 230, 232, 241, 363, 380, 395, 401, 451, 452, 463, 592, 596, 598
Einstein, Albert, 455
Eizenstat, Stuart, 81
Ek, Mats, 494
Ekeus, Rolf, 218
El Guerrouj, Hicham, 523

INDEX

El Salvador, 180, 182
Elgar, Edward, 492
Elizabeth I, Queen of England etc., 4, 6–7, 89, 160, 186, 190, 191, 192, 193, 194, 352, 367, 371, 373, 377, 379, 391, 392, 451, 499, 596, 598, 599
Ellis, Marc, 453
Elroy, James, 502
Els, Ernie, 527, 528
Elton, Ben, 498
Eman, Jan Hendrick (Henny), 200
Emin, Tracy, 511
Engell, Hans, 69
Enhbayar, Nambaryn, 364, 365
Enhsayhan, Mendsayhany, 364
Environmental Questions, 464–71; Earth Summit II, 385, 465; El Niño, 185, 287, 334, 372, 468 (*map*), 469; forest fires in Asia, 467; Kyoto climate conference, 374, 466–7, **569–71**
Equatorial Guinea, 263, 267
Erbakan, Necmettin, 101, 102, 401, 593
Eritrea, 223, 229, 230, **240, 242,** 399
Eroglu, Dervis, 100
Ershad, Mohammed, 314
Erundina, Luiza, 169
Esquivel, Manuel, 191
Essy, Amara, 426
Estonia, 77, **106–8,** 109, 408, 416, 419, 591
Estrada, Joseph, 336
Estrada, Raul, 467
Etete, Dan, 252
Ethiopia, 229, **240–2,** 243, 574
European Bank for Reconstruction and Development (EBRD), 300, **416–17,** 422
European Community Law, 476–7
European Court of Human Rights (ECHR), 96, 475
European Court of Justice (ECJ), 79, 477
European Economic Area (EEA), 71, 73, 420, 421
European Free Trade Association (EFTA), 420–1
European Union (see also European Community Law), **402–11;** Albania, 123–4, 411; Americas, 178, 198, 200; Amsterdam Treaty, 403–5, 476–8; Asia, 327, 431; BSE, 34, 410–11; economic and monetary union, 9, 11, 13, 14, 16–19, 21, 24, 31, 32, 49–50, 51, 53, 55, 56, 57, 61, 62, 63, 64–5, 66, 69–70, 75, 76–7, 78, 79, 86, 87, 88, 91, 92, 402, 405–7; EEA, 420–1; EFTA states, 73, 82, 418, 420–1; enlargement, 35, 92, 98, 102, 104, 106, 107, 108, 109, 110, 112, 113, 114, 116, 118, 119, 121, 132–3, 136, 408, 409 (map), 422; single market, 411; South Africa, 283, 285, 290–1; trade relations, 410; Turkey, 95, 99, 101, 102
Evangelisti, Franco, 491
Evans, Chris, 506
Everist, Mark, 493
Evert, Miltiades, 96
Extracts from Past Volumes, xvi
Eyadema, Gen. Gnassingbé, 257, 261
Eyre, Richard (Theatre), 487, 498, 499
Eyre, Richard (TV), 505

Eysenck, Hans J., 578 (obit.)

Fabre, Brett, 531
Facetti, Carlos, 174
Fahd ibn Abdul Aziz, King, 220, 221
Fainlight, Ruth, 520
Faldo, Nick, 527
Falkland Islands/Malvinas, 35, 167
Fallon, Kieran, 530
Fan, Rita, 350
Faroe Islands, 71
Farrell, Andy, 531
Farrow, Mia, 517, 520
Fassino, Piero, 421
Fasslabend, Werner, 80
Fayed, Dodi, 4, 5, 447, 578
Fayed, Mohammed al-, 5
Fearon, Ray, 498
Feinstein, Diane, 149, 158
Feldman, Morton, 492
Feldstein, Martin, 536
Fenech Adami, Dr Eddie, 94
Ferguson, Alex, 524
Fernández Mejide, Gracela, 167
Fernández, Atilio R., 174
Fernández, Leonel, 179
Fernández, Roque, 166
Ferrand, Robert W., 126
Ferrer Costa, Eduardo, 176
Ferrero, Lorenzo, 489
Ferro, Marc, 521
Fielding, David, 488
Fiennes, Ralph, 501
Figueres, José María, 181, 183
Figueroa, Salvador, 181
Fiji, 376, 378, **379,** 391, 431
Filali, Abdellatif, 237, 239
Finland, 76–7, 349, 404, 419, 471
Fino, Bashkim, 123, 590
Fischer, Tibor, 519
Fischler, Franz, 410
Fisher, Mark, 515
Flaherty, Robert, 499
Fleischman, Lawrence, 578 (obit.)
Fletcher, Christine, 374
Fleury, Michel, 493
Flores Facussé, Carlos Roberto, 181, 183, 598
Flowers, Gennifer, 153
Fo, Daniel, 516
Fonda, Henry, 586
Food and Agriculture Organization (FAO), 272, 396
Forbes, Grania, 520
Forné Molne, Marc, 83, 84
Forsyth, Michael, 20, 24
Fortier, Michael, 154
Foster, Sir Norman, 513, 514
Foster, R.F., 517, 520
Foster, Vincent, 148, 151
Foulkes, George, 198
Fowler, Sir Norman, 23
Fox, Edward, 500

Fox, Sir Marcus, 20
Fraga, Manuel, 87
France, 5, 34, **52–7**, 85, 88, 92, 106, 158, 164, 215, 218, 232, 234, 236, 238, 243, 259, 262, 265, 266, 267, 269, 277, 295, 299, 303, 323, 337, 338, 349, 363, 382, 383, 394, 395, 402, 403, 404, 405, 406, 417, 426, 446, 462, 533, 576, 579, 591, 593, 595, 597
Francesconi, Luca, 491
Franco, Itamar, 169
Francophone Agency, 395
Francophone Community, 393–5, 396, 565–6
Frank, Anne, 520
Frank, Charles, 417
Franklin, John Hope, 151
Fraser, Malcolm, 393
Free Trade Area of the Americas (FTAA), 434
Freeh, Louis, 147
Freeman, Ron, 300, 417
Frei, Eduardo, 170
French Polynesia, 378
French, Patrick, 521
Freud, Esther, 519
Frick, Mario, 83, 84
Frímannsdóttir, Margrét, 71
Frlec, Boris, 132
Frowick, Robert, 415
Fryer, Jonathan, 520
Fujimori, Alberto Keinya, 85, 175, 176
Fukuyama, Francis, 10
Fulani, Ifeona, 517, 519
Fuller, John, 517, 520
Fuller, Sam, 503
Funar, Gheorghe, 115

Gabon, 263, 265, 266, 380
Gagnan, Emile, 576
Gairy, Sir Eric, 578 (obit.)
Galtieri, Leopoldo, 167
Gambia, The, 254–5, 380, 589
Gambon, Michael, 500
Gandhi, Mahatma, 450
Gandhi, Rajiv, 306
Gandhi, Sonia, 306
Ganzuri, Kamal Ahmad, 209, 210
Garang, Col. John, 229
García Belaunde, José Antonio, 433
Gardiner, Sir George, 15
Gates, Bill, 507
Gauguin, Paul, 511
Gaulieder, Frantisek, 113
Gaviria Trujillo, César, 432
Gayoom, Maumoun Abdul, 322, 324
Gbezera-Bria, Michel, 263, 267
Gear, William, 512
Gedda, Nicolai, 487
Gehry, Frank, 508, 514
Geingob, Hage, 282, 287
Georgescu, Costin, 117
Georgia, 143, 144, 302, 304, 389, 412, 422
Gephardt, Richard, 146, 149
Geremek, Bronislaw, 105

Gergiev, Valery, 495
Germany, 9, 15, 31, **49–52**, 61, 64, 75, 79, 80, 81, 100, 106, 112, 139, 157, 188, 214, 231, 232, 261, 294–5, 304, 309, 314, 331, 380, 383, 403, 404, 405, 422, 443, 444, 446, 464, 533, 591, 595
Gesualdo, 491
Ghafurzai, Abdorrahim, 297
Ghana, 249–50, 261, 426, 589
Ghanem, Faraj Said bin, 222, 223
Ghosaibi, Ghazi al-, 221
Ghurburrun, Rabindranath, 321
Gibraltar, 34, 88, **89–90**, 579
Gidada, Negaso, 240
Gifford, Frank, 221
Gifford, Paul, 453
Gifford, Yvonne, 220
Gilheno, John, 591
Gilmore, James, 153
Gingrich, Newt, 146, 149, 151
Ginsberg, Allen, 518, 578–9 (obit.)
Giscard d'Estaing, Valéry, 55, 164
Giuliani, Rudolph, 153, 159
Giusti, Carlos, 175
Glass, Philip, 492
Glenister, Robert, 497
Glickman, Dan, 573
Gligorov, Kiro, 131
Gobardhan, Tjan, 199
Godwin, David, 516
Goh Chok Tong, 331, 332, 336
Goldenthal, Elliot, 495
Goldman, Ronald, 153, 590
Goldsmith, Sir James, 18
Goldsworthy, Andy, 494
Golota, Andrzej, 525
Gombojav, Jambyn, 364
Gomes, Ciro, 169
Gómez Mendez, Alfonso, 173
Göncz, Arpád, 114, 118
González, Felipe, 87
González Insfran, Sebastián, 175
González Maldonado, Gen. Evaristo, 175
González Mosquera, Guillermo, 171
Good, Andrew, 155
Goosen, Retief, 527
Gorbachev, Mikhail, 517, 520
Gordon, Pamela, 196, 197, 591
Gore, Al, 149, 151, 573
Gorky, Arshile, 577
Gorriarán Merlo, Enrique, 167
Gough, Darren, 525
Gouled Aptidon, Hassan, 240
Gourad Hamadou, Barkat, 240
Gowda, H.D. Deve, 306, 308, 591
Grade, Michael, 504
Graffin, Guillaume, 495
Graham, Gordon, 516
Graham, Katherine, 520
Grappelli, Stephane, 579 (obit.)
Gray, Nicolette, 512

INDEX

Gray, Simon, 516, 519
Greece, 95–7, 99, 125, 405, 408
Green, Squad.-Leader Andy, 528, 596
Greene, Maurice, 522
Greenfield, Susan, 521
Greenland, 71
Greenspan, Alan, 533
Grenada, 192–3, 578
Grimshaw, Nicholas, 515
Grímsson, Ólafur Ragnar, 70
Grossman, Edith, 521
Group of 77, 397–9
Group of Seven (G-7), 56, 139, 357, **537**, 538
Gryn, Rabbi Hugo, 451
Guérin, Isabelle, 493
Guam, 378
Guarini, Guarino, 507
Guatemala, 180, 181–2, 191, 388
Guelendouksia, Nassour Owaido, 262
Guerra, Alfonso, 87
Guevara, Ernesto 'Che', 179
Guig, Mohammed Lemine Ould, 256, 259
Guinea, 257, 260, 428, 476, 597
Guinea-Bissau, 92, 258, **273–4**, 380, 427
Gujral, Inder Kumar, 305, 306, 307, 308, 312, 591, 598
Gukasyan, Arkadii, 144
Gulf Cooperation Council (GCC), 214, 223, 226, 227, 400, **423–4**
Gullit, Ruud, 524
Gunera de Melar, Alba Nova, 598
Guscott, Jeremy, 530
Gusmão, José, 333
Guterres, António, 90
Gutiérrez Rebolledo, Gen. Jesús, 184
Guyana, 187–8, 392, 580, 590
Gyatso, Palden, 452

Haas, Bishop Wolfgang, 449
Habibi, Dr Hassan, 293
Hachani, Abdelkader, 236
Hackett, Gen. Sir John, 579 (obit.)
Haeggman, Joachim, 527
Hagen, Carl, 72
Hague, William, 23, 24, 25, 26, 27, 29, 30, 31, 32, 33, 38, 41, 593
Hahn, Emily, 579 (obit.)
Haider, Dr Jörg, 78
Haile Gebrselassie, 523
Haile Selassie, Emperor, 241
Hailey, Christopher, 493
Haiti, 179, 180, 193, 388, 434, 435, 596
Haiveta, Chris, 372
Hakkinen, Mikka, 528
Hall, Aleksander, 104
Hall, Sir Peter, 499, 500
Hall, Tony, 363
Hama, Amadou, 262
Hamad bin Khalifa al-Thani, Shaikh, 225
Hamadou, Barkat Gourad, 243
Hamburger, Michael, 520
Handel, George Frideric, 487

Hamed, 'Prince' Naseem, 525
Hamilton, James, 520
Hamilton, Neil, 16, 27, 32
Hampson, Christopher, 494
Hamutenya, Hidipo, 287
Hamzik, Pavol, 112
Hanegbi, Tzachi, 205
Hannay, Sir David, 98
Hans Adam II, Prince, 83, 85
Hanson, Curtis, 502
Hanson, Pauline, 367
Haq, Admiral Mansoorul, 311
Harald V, King, 72
Hardie Boys, Sir Michael, 373
Hardy, Billy, 525
Hare, David, 498
Harewood, David, 499
Hariri, Rafiq, 215, 217
Harman, Harriet, 9, 22, 572
Harney, Mary, 67
Harpur, James, 520
Harrell, Lynn, 491
Harriman, Averell, 579
Harriman, Pamela, 579 (obit.)
Harrison, Lou, 494
Harry, Prince, see William and Henry (Harry), Princes
Harvey, Marcus, 510
Hasan, Naeem ul-, 429
Hasan ibn Talal, Crown Prince, 203, 212
Hashimoto, Ryutaro, 175, 348, 349, 356, 357, 358, 359, 429
Hasina Wajed, Sheikh, 313, 314, 315
Hassan II, King, 237, 238
Hassan, Sir Joshua, 90, 579 (obit.)
Hattersley, Roy, 9, 27, 521
Haughey, Charles, 68
Havel, Václav, 110, 111
Havergal, Giles, 488
Haydn, Joseph, 489
Hayward, Leland, 579
Heaney, Seamus, 520
Heath, Sir Edward, 14, 28, 584
Heath, Roy, 519
Heathcoat Amory, Lady, 588
Heathcoat Amory, Sir John, 588
Heelas, Paul, 453
Helfgott, David, 501
Helms, Jesse, 150
Henderson, Doug, 21
Henman, Tim, 529
Henze, Hans Werner, 490, 496
Hermoza Ríos, Gen. Nicolás, 176
Hersh, Seymour, 145
Hershey, Alfred, 579–80 (obit.)
Herzog, Chaim, 206, 580 (obit.)
Herzog, Roman, 49
Heseltine, Michael, 18, 20, 23, 31, 33, 513
Heyliger, Hugh, 195
Hibbert, Christopher, 520
Higgins, Clare, 500

Higgins, Rita Ann, 520
Hill, Damon, 528
Hill, Selima, 520
Hill, Tobias, 519
Hillier, Paul, 492
Hindley, Myra, 510
Hinds, Ciaran, 499
Hinds, Sam, 187, 590
Hiney, Tom, 520
Hingis, Martina, 529
Hiro, Dilip, 521
Hirst, Damien, 510
Hirst, Sir Michael, 38
Hjelm-Wallén, Lena, 75
Ho Chi Minh, 338, 394
Hobsbawm, Eric, 521
Hoch, Scott, 526, 527
Hoddle, Glenn, 523, 524
Hodgkin, Howard, 494
Hoengen, Elisabeth, 489
Hoffa, James, Jr., 159
Hoffa, Jimmy, 159
Hoffman, Dustin, 52
Hogan, Ben, 580 (obit.)
Hogg, Douglas, 13
Hokama Tokashiki, Daniel, 176
Holbrooke, Richard, 98, 128
Holler, York, 491
Holm, Ian, 499
Holmes Trujillo, Carlos, 172
Holomisa, Bantu, 289
Holy See, see Vatican
Holyfield, Evander, 186, 525
Holyoake, Adam, 526
Honduras, 181, 182–3, 598
Hong Kong, 24, 31, 34, 36, 93, 312, 328, 342, 343, 346, 347, 349, **350–3**, 354, 355, 356, 358, 393, 479, 535, 537, 538, 539, 593, 597, 599
Hoover, J. Edgar, 581
Hope, Christopher, 519
Hopkins, Sir Michael, 514
Horn, Gyula, 114
Hossain, Anwar, 314
Housman, A.E., 498
Howard, Alan, 500
Howard, Desmond, 531
Howard, John, 367, 368, 369, 370
Howard, Michael, 7, 8, 23, 24, 446
Howley, Rob, 530
Hoyte, Desmond, 188
Hrawi, Elias, 215
Hu Jintao, 341
Hu Yaobang, 342
Hu, Richard, 332
Huang, John, 147, 148, 151, 152
Hübbe, Nikolaj, 494
Hubbell, Webster, 148
Huber, Klaus, 491
Hudson, Richard, 487
Huebler, Douglas, 512
Hughes, Hubert, 196, 197

Hughes, Malcolm, 512
Hughes, Pat, 580 (obit.)
Hughes, Ted, 517, 520
Hujilan, Jameel al-, 423
Hume, Cardinal Basil, 448
Hume, John, 43, 45, 46
Humphreys, John, 506
Hun Sen, 338, 339, 594
Hungary, 112, 113, **114–6**, 118, 139, 304, 408, 419, 422, 438, 472–3, 534, 582, 585, 592
Hunter, Robert, 110
Hurd, Lord (Douglas), 7, 31
Hurtado, Osvaldo, 174
Husain ibn Talal, King, 203, 204, 206, 207, 211, 212, 591, 597
Husain, Saddam, see Saddam Husain
Husain, Uday, 219
Husbands, Sir Clifford, 190
Hussein, Nasser, 525
Hutchence, Michael, 370
Hutton, Will, 521
Huxley, Elspeth, 518
Hwang Chang Yop, 363
Hynd, Ronald, 495

Iakovou, George, 100
Ibero-American Summit, 435
Ibrahim, Abdallah, 323
Ibuka, Masaru, 580 (obit.)
Iceland, 70–1, 355, 420, 421
Ickes, Harold, 149
Ienaga, Saburo, 358
Ikeda, Masuo, 512
Iliescu, Ion, 117
Inderfurth, Karl, 297
India, 3, 37, 92, **305–9**, 312, 313, 315, 317, 325, 383, 432, 441, 442, 450, 475, 534–5, 586, 589, 591, 592, 594, 595, 596, 598
Indian Ocean Rim Association for Regional Cooperation (IORARC), 321, 323, **429**, **432**
Indonesia, 35, 93, 199, 314, 330, **332–5**, 370, 396, 401, 429, 431, 468, 535, 537, 538, 590, 595, 596, 597
Information Technology, 460–4
Ingraham, Hubert, 193
Inter-Governmental Authority on Development (IGAD), 229
Inter-Parliamentary Union, 314
International Atomic Energy Agency (IAEA), 441
International Court of Justice (ICJ), 113, 115, 119, 231, 472–3
International Development Association (IDA), 538–9
International Labour Organization (ILO), 216
International Monetary Fund (IMF), 36, 103, 122, 129, 130, 131, 222, 223, 230, 237, 245, 247, 259, 260, 261, 278, 280, 281, 286, 312, 325, 327, 328, 329, 332, 334, 336, 361, 397, 398, 405, 411, 422, 429, **532**, 535, 536, **537–8**, 539
International Whaling Commission (IWC), 469

INDEX

Iran, 35, 149, 215, 219, 220, 230, **293–5**, 297, 299, 302, 303, 304, 325, 363, 400, 401, 410, 432, 590, 592, 599
Iraq, 37, 93, 160, 211, 213, **217–9**, 225, 226, 230, 386, 400, 401, 424, 470, 581, 598
Ireland, Northern, see Northern Ireland
Ireland, Republic of, 33, 44, 45, 46, 47, 48, **65–8**, 85, 215, 404, 469, 533, 585, 593, 595, 596, 597
Iriani, Abd al-Karim, 223
Irvine of Lairg, Lord, 20, 480, 572
Isa bin Sulman al-Khalifah, Shaikh, 225
Islamic Conference Organization, see Organization of the Islamic Conference
Islamic Development Bank (IDB), 214, 231
Ismail, Eyad, 154
Ismail, Razali, 384
Israel, 85, 101, 159, 160, **202–6**, 207, 208, 209, 210, 211, 212, 213, 214, 215, 216, 220, 226, 232, 234, 238, 295, 384, 398, 399, 401, 423, 424, 442, 444, 451, 580, 589, 590, 591, 592, 595, 596, 598
Issing, Otmar, 50
Issoufou, Mamadou, 262
Italy, 32, **57–61**, 79, 119, 125, 132, 234, 241, 304, 383, 405, 406, 421, 422, 444, 446, 533, 585, 587, 591, 594, 596
Ivanić, Mladen, 127
Izetbegović, Alija, 125
Izurieta, Maj.-Gen. Ricardo, 170

Jabir al-Ahmad al-Jabir al-Sabah, Shaikh, 224
Jack, Sir David, 194
Jackson, Colin, 523
Jackson, Michael, 505
Jacobs, Helen, 580 (obit.)
Jaffe, Susan, 495
Jagan, Cheddi, 187, 580–1 (obit.), 590
Jagan, Janet, 187, 188, 580, 581, 590
Jagland, Thorbjørn, 72
Jalloud, Major Abdel Salam, 232
Jamaica, **186–7**, 190, 199, 392, 583
Jamali, Mohammed Fadhil, 219, 581 (obit.)
James, Edison, 194
James, Henry, 502
James, P.D., 519
Jammeh, Yahya, 254, 255, 589
Janacek, Leos, 488
Janzen, Lee, 527
Japan, 1, 36, 61, 140, 175, 228, 270, 300, 309, 314, 320, 328, 331, 334, 342, 348–9, 355, **356–60**, 363, 364, 366, 379, 380, 383, 429, 431, 467, 469, 536, 537, 580, 591, 596, 598, 599
Jassan, Elías, 167
Jean, Grand Duke, 64
Jenkins of Hillhead, Lord, 14, 29
Jenkins, Ffion, 41
Jenkins, Neil, 530
Jennings, Alex, 497
Jennings, Elizabeth, 520
Jeyaretnam, J.B, 332
Jiang Zemin, 139, 308, 341, 342, 343, 346, 347, 348, 349, 352, 429, 591, 597
Jifri, Abd ul-Rahman Ali al-, 223

Jigme Singye Wangchuk, Dragon King, 317
Job, Morgan, 189
Joffe, Michael, 512
Jóhannsson, Kjartan, 420
Johansson, Per-Ulrik, 527
John Paul II, Pope, 83, 85, 182, 444, 448, 449, 521, 591, 592, 593, 595
John XXIII, Pope, 581, 587
John, Elton, 489
Johnson, Italia, 193
Johnson, Linton Kwesi, 520
Johnson, Martin, 530
Johnson, Paul, 520
Johnson, Tom, 525
Johnston, Donald, 532
Jolley, Elizabeth, 519
Jones, Allen, 523
Jones, Bill T., 496
Jones, Della, 488
Jones, Gwyn, 42
Jones, Marilyn, 494
Jones, Marion, 522
Jones, Paula, 145, 146, 150, 151, 152, 153
Jones, Prof. R.V., 581 (obit.)
Jonson, Ben, 498
Jordan, 1, 202, 203, 204, 207, 208, **211–13**, 219, 226, 420, 591, 597
Jordan, Michael, 531
Jordán, Servando, 170
Joseph, Jenny, 520
Joseph, Molwyn, 195
Josephs, Wilfred, 492
Jospin, Lionel, 52, 54, 55, 56, 238, 402, 403, 404, 405, 406, 593, 597
Juan Carlos, King, 86, 87
Jumagulov, Apas, 298
Juncker, Jean-Claude, 64
Junor, John, 186
Juppé, Alain, 52, 53, 54, 55

Ka, Djibo, 258
Kabariti, Abdul Karim, 211, 212
Kabba, Alhaji Ahmed Tejan, 253, 254, 391, 425, 426, 592, 597
Kabila, Laurent, 248, 265, 266, 268, 269, 270, 276, 283, 394, 583, 592
Kabua, Amata, 378
Kabua, Imata, 376, 378
Kaczynski, Theodore, 155
Kaempfer, Steven, 417
Kaganne, Gen. Paul, 272, 273
Kagel, Mauricio, 491
Kain, Karen, 495
Kalpokas, Donald, 378
Kama, Laity, 473
Kamil, Husain, 219
Kamougue, Abdelkader Wadal, 263
Kander, John, 496
Kang Kyung Shik, 361
Kansi, Aimal, 313
Kant, Krishan, 305

Karadžić, Radovan, 126, 127, 128, 474
Karadayi, Gen. Ismail, 95
Karamanlis, Costas, 96
Karamanlis, Konstantinos, 96
Karamat, Gen. Jahangir, 311
Karimov, Islam, 298, 304
Kashmir, 307–8, 313
Kasparov, Garry, 460
Kaufman, Gerald, 489
Kaunda, Kenneth, 278, 599
Kazakkstan, 121, **298–304**, 348, 597
Kazhageldin, Akezhan, 299, 597
Keating, Paul, 369
Keats, John, 517
Keay, John, 521
Kebzabo, Saleh, 263
Kedikilwe, Ponatshego, 284
Keita, Ibrahim Boubakar, 257, 260
Kelley, Clarence, 581 (obit.)
Kelley, Kevin, 525
Kelly, Ellsworth, 511
Kelly, John, 197
Kelly, Linda, 520
Kemp, Edward, 498
Kendrew, Sir John, 581 (obit.)
Kennedy, A.L., 519
Kennedy, Judge Ian, 482
Kennedy, John F., 145
Kennedy, John F., Jr., 145
Kennedy, Joseph, 145
Kennedy, Michael, 145
Kennedy, Robert F., 145
Kennett, Jeff, 369
Kenny, Anthony, 520
Kenny, Mary, 453
Kenya, 229, 241, **244–5**, 247, 380, 452, 469, 597, 599
Kérékou, Mathieu, 257
Kernot, Cheryl, 370
Kerr, Sir John, 575
Kershaw, Alex, 520
Kesri, Sitaram, 305, 306
Khaddam, Abdul Khaliq, 214
Khalfallah, Mohammed Ali, 233
Khalid, Meraj, 310
Khalifa bin Sulman al-Khalifa, Shaikh, 225, 226
Khamenei, Ayatollah Seyed Ali, 293, 294, 400
Khamtay Siphandon, Gen., 340
Khan, Gohar Ayub, 307
Khan, Meyer, 292
Kharrazi, Dr Kamal, 293
Khatami, Mohammed, 225, 293, 294, 400, 424, 592, 599
Khieu Samphan, 339
Khin Nyunt, Lieut.-Gen., 326
Khouna, Ould Mohammed, 259
Khuwaiter, Abdulaziz bin Abdullah al-, 220
Kibaki, Mwai, 244, 245
Kilać, Dragan, 127
Kim Dae Jung, 360, 361, 599
Kim Hyun Chul, 360

Kim Il Sung, 362, 363, 596
Kim Jong Il, 362, 364, 596
Kim Yong Nam, 362
Kim Young Sam, 360
King, Martin Luther, 147
Kingsley, Ben, 500
Kinkel, Klaus, 100, 108
Kipketer, Wilson Boit, 523
Kippenberger, Martin, 512
Kiptanui, Moses, 523
Kiribati, **376**, 432
Kite, Tom, 526
Klaus, Vaclav, 110, 111, 112, 114, 598
Klestil, Thomas, 78
Klima, Viktor, 78, 79, 589
Klutse, Kouassi, 257, 261
Koch, Ursula, 82
Kocharyan, Robert, 143, 144
Kodjo, Edem, 261
Koh Kon, 360, 429, 590
Kohl, Helmut, 49, 50, 51, 52, 57, 112, 139, 331, 404, 591, 593
Kok, Wim, 63, 370
Kokkos, Yannis, 488
Kolelas, Bernard, 265, 266
Koller, Arnold, 80, 81
Konan Bédié, Henri, 257, 260
Konaré, Alpha Oumar, 257, 259, 260
Kong Muni, 339
Kontić, Radoje, 133
Koolman, Olindo, 200
Kordić, Dario, 130
Korea, Democratic People's Republic of (North Korea), 148, 319, 358, **362–4**, 596
Korea, Republic of (South Korea), 160, 165, 228, 242, 304, 348, **360–2**, 363, 366, 370, 380, 399, 429, 431, 441, 443, 535, 538, 590, 594, 598, 599
Koroma, Lt.-Col. Johnny Paul, 253, 391, 592
Korowi, Wiwa, 371
Korzhakov, Alexander, 137
Kosit Panpiamrat, 328
Kosovo, 134, 135, 416
Kostov, Ivan, 120, 121, 591
Kosygin, Aleksei, 587
Kouyate, Lansana, 425
Kovác, Michal, 112, 113
Kovalev, Valentin, 136
Krajci, Gustav, 112
Krajisnik, Momčilo, 127
Kramer, Lottie, 520
Kramplova, Zdenka, 112
Krasts, Guntars, 106, 107, 419
Krens, Thomas, 508
Krenz, Egon, 51, 595
Kristopans, Vilis, 107
Kromah, Alhaji, 255
Kučan, Milan, 132, 422
Kuchma, Leonid, 140, 142
Kuerten, Gustavo, 529
Kulenty, Hanna, 490
Kulikov, Anatoliy, 446

INDEX

Kumaratunga, Chandrika Bandaranaike, 318, 319, 320
Küng, Hans, 449
Kurdistan, 103, 217, 218, **475–6**
Kureishi, Hanif, 519
Kurosawa, Akira, 503
Kusa, Musa, 232
Kuwait, 93, 210, 211, 213, 218, 221, **224, 226–7**, 230, 304, 424, 444
Kwasniewski, Aleksander, 104, 106
Kwelagobe, Daniel, 284
Kyd, Thomas, 497
Kylian, Jiri, 496
Kyrgyzstan, 298–304

Lachenmann, Helmut, 490, 491
Lacotte, Pierre, 493
Laho, Marc, 488
Lahud, Gen., 216
Laing, Stewart, 488
Laíno, Domingo, 174
Lake, Anthony, 149
Lamari, Gen. Mohamed, 236
Lamont, Norman, 24
Landzo, Esad, 474
Langer, Bernhard, 527
Laos, 340–1, 430
Laraki, Azeddine, 399
Latvia, 77, **106, 107**, 108, 109, 408, 416, 419, 421
Laurier, Sir Wilfrid, 162
Law and Legal Affairs, 476–86; European Community Law, **476–9**; international law, **472–6**; UK law, **479–83**; US law, **153–8, 484–6**
Lazarenko, Pavlo, 142
le Blanc, Bart, 417
Le Duc Anh, Gen., 337
Le Kha Phieu, Gen., 337
Le Pen, Jean-Marie, 56
Le Riche, Nicolas, 493
Leach, Janet, 512
Leakey, Richard, 245
Lebanon, 85, 202, 204, **205**, 211, **215–7**, 390, 420
Lebed, Alexander, 137, 138
LeBlanc, Roméo, 160
Lebrecht, Norman, 492
Ledezma, Antonio, 177
Lee Hoi Chang, 361, 599
Lee Hsien Loong, 332
Lee Kuan Yew, 330, 331, 332
Lee Soo Sung, 360, 590
Lee Teng-hui, 349, 353, 354, 355
Lee, Bill Lann, 153
Lee, Laurie, 518, 582 (obit.)
Lee, Martin, 352
Leghari, Farooq Ahmad, 311, 598
Legris, Manuel, 493
Lehar, Franz, 487
Leiferkus, Sergei, 487
Leigh, Mike, 502
Leiser, Moshe, 488
Leka Zogu, 124
Lenin, Vladimir Ilyich, 81

Leonard, Justin, 527, 528
Léotard, François, 55
Lesotho, 283, 284, **286–7**
Lessing, Doris, 520
Lestrade, Swinburne, 433
Letsie III, King, 282, 286
Lévêque, Michel, 84
Levi, Noel, 429, 432
Levi, Peter, 520
Levy, David, 205, 207
Lewenstein, Oscar, 582 (obit.)
Lewis, Derek, 23
Lewis, Geoffrey, 520
Lewis, Jeremy, 520
Lewis, Lennox, 525
Lewis, Vaughan, 195
Leye Lenelgau, Jean-Marie, 377
Li Lanqing, 341
Li Pen, 349
Li Peng, 304, 341, 344, 345, 346, 348, 352, 358
Li Ruihuan, 341
Liberia, 255–6, 387, 427, 594
Libeskind, Daniel, 515
Libya, 85, 94, 208, 210, 230, **231–2**, 234, 250, 386, 398, 401, 410, 423, 427, 589, 597
Lichtenstein, Roy, 512, 582 (obit.)
Liddell, Helen, 22
Lieberman, Avigdor, 205
Liechtenstein, 1, **83, 84–5**, 420, 421
Lien Chan, 85, 354, 355
Lifschutz Davidson, 515
Ligeti, György, 490
Lilić, Zoran, 134
Lilley, Peter, 24, 31
Lim Chang Yul, 361
Lim, Kim, 512
Lindberg, Magnus, 492
Lineger, Jerry, 455
Ling, Syargey, 140, 141
Lipponen, Paavo, 76, 119
Lissouba, Pascal, 26, 265, 266, 276, 597
Listowel, Earl of, 582 (obit.)
Literature, 516–21
Lithuania, 77, **107, 108**, 109, 408, 419, 421
Livesey, Richard, 41
Livingstone, Ken, 30
Lobb Partnership, 515
Lohani, Prakash Chandra, 316
Lombardy, Vincent, 531
London Club, 131
López, Almabeatriz Rengifo, 171
Lopez, Lourdez, 494
Lorant, Stefan, 582–3 (obit.)
Lorenzetti, Ambrogio, 508
Louima, Abner, 159
Louisy, Perlette, 194, 195
Love, Davis, III, 527
Lovell, Terry, 453
Lowery, Nigel, 487
Lowry, L.S., 515
Lowry, Michael, 68

Lubovitch, Lar, 495
Luce, Sir Richard, 89, 90
Lucinschi, Petru, 141, 142, 422
Lucky, Judge Anthony, 189
Luhrmann, Buz, 503
Lukashenka, Alyaksandr, 140, 141, 591, 592
Lumumba, Patrice, 269, 583
Lundberg, Mark, 488
Lungu, Capt. Steven, 278
Luo Gan, 341
LuPone, Patti, 500
Luria, Salvador, 579
Lutoslawski, Witold, 491
Luxembourg, 32, **64–5**, 101, 102, 106, 133, 405, 406, 407, 408, 598

Maar, Dora, 512
Macao, 93
McAleese, Mary, 65, 68, 597
McAslan, John, 514
McBarnette, Colville (Kamau), 192
McCall, Oliver, 525
Macapagal Arroyo, Gloria, 336
Macapagal, Diosdado, 583 (obit.)
McCartney, Bill, 158
McCartney, Robert, 44, 46
McCowen, Alec, 500
McCoy, Tony, 529
McCreevy, Charlie, 67
McDonagh, Martin, 499
MacDonald, Anthony, 488
McDonald, Gabrielle Kirk, 473
McDonough, Alexa, 162
McDormand, Frances, 501
McDougal, James, 150
Macedonia, 96, 125, **131–2**, 390, 394, 414, 421
McEwan, Ian, 517, 519
McGaughey, Bobbi, 159
McGrath, Glen, 525, 526
McGreevey, James, 153
MacGregor, Neil, 509
McGuinness, Martin, 43, 46, 47, 499, 599
Machado, Manuela, 523
Machar, Riak, 229
Macintosh, Cameron, 497
McKellen, Sir Ian, 499
McKendrick, Jamie, 520
Mackerras, Sir Charles, 488
MacKilligin, David, 196
McKinney, Gene, 156
McKinnon, Don, 374
McLaren, Richard, 158
McLauchlan, Lucille, 220, 221
MacLaverty, Bernard, 519
McLellan, Anne, 162
Macmillan, Harold, 500
McNamara, Robert, 538
McPherson, Conor, 500
MacSweeney, Barry, 520
McVeigh, Timothy, 154, 593
'Mad Cow Disease', see BSE
Madagascar, 325, 589

Madani, Abassi, 236
Madi, Abdou, 324
Madikizela-Mandela, Winnie, 289, 290
Maggert, Jeff, 527
Maginness, Alban, 44
Maguire, Sarah, 520
Magureanu, Virgil, 117
Mahamane, Ousmane, 262
Mahathir Mohamad, 304, 329, 330, 366, 431, 467
Mahdi, Sadiq al-, 242
Mahon, Sir Denis, 509
Maigari, Bello Bouba, 264
Mainassara, Brig.-Gen. Ibrahim Barre, 258, 262
Maiyaki, Ibrahim Assane, 258, 262
Majali, Abdul Salam, 211, 591
Majoli, Eva, 529
Major, John, 10, 11, 12, 13, 14, 15, 16, 17, 18, 20, 24, 522, 589, 591, 592
Makhakhe, Tseliso, 286
Makower, Frances, 520
Maktoum bin Rashid al-Maktoum, Shaikh, 224
Malainine, Ould Cheikh, 259
Malawi, 229, **279**, 428, 574
Malaysia, 35, 230, 295, 304, 328, **329–30**, 331, 334, 355, 366, 384, 401, 429, 430, 431, 468, 470, 535, 538, 596, 598
Malcolm, George, 492
Maldives, 312, 314, **322**, **324–5**, 432
Malecela, John, 246
Malevich, Casimir, 508
Mali, 257, **259–60**, 266
Mallary, Robert, 512
Malott, John, 330
Malta, 93–4, 232
Maluf, Paulo, 169
Mandela, Nelson, 93, 229, 231, 269, 283, 284, 288, 289, 290, 333
Mandelson, Peter, 9, 20, 30, 513
Manet, Edouard, 511
Manley, Michael, 187, 583 (obit.)
Manley, Norman W., 583
Manning, Patrick, 189
Manning, Preston, 161
Manqoush, Mohammed Ahmed al-, 231, 232
Manuella, Sir Tulaga, 377
Mao Zedong, 341, 343
Maope, Kelebone, 286
Marín, Gen. Guillermo, 170
Mara, Ratu Sir Kamisese, 376
Mara, Tim, 512
Marber, Patrick, 499
Marcos, Ferdinand, 335, 583
Margrethe II, Queen, 69
Marjanović, Mirko, 133
Marković, Mirjana, 134
Marquez, Gabriel Garcia, 521
Marshall Islands, 376, **378**
Martínez Busch, Adm. Jorge, 170
Martínez, Alfredo, 191
Martin, Angel, 527
Martin, David, 453

INDEX

Martin, Paul, 163, 164
Martinu, Bohuslav, 488
Marufu, Reward, 280
Marwa, Col. Muhammad, 251
Marx, Karl, 518, 575
Mas Canosa, Jorge, 179
Masefield, Thorold, 196, 197
Masha'al, Khalid, 204, 212
Masire, Sir Quett Ketumile, 282, 284
Maskhadov, Aslan, 138, 589
Massenet, Jules, 488
Massera, Adm. (retd.) Emilio, 167
Massie, Allan, 519
Massine, Léonide, 495
Masud, Gen. Ahmed Shah, 296
Matesa, Zlatko, 129
Mathews, Ted, 370
Matliauskas, Rolands, 108
Matos Azócar, Luis Raúl, 178
Matutes, Abel, 90
Mauritania, 226, **256, 259**
Mauritius, 320–1, 393, 394, 432
Maxwell, James Clarke, 455
Maxwell, Robert, 25
May, Judge, 481
Mayhew, Sir Patrick, 42
Mazza, Luigi, 84
Mbeki, Thabo, 283, 289, 290
Mbuende, Kaire, 425
Meciar, Vladimir, 112, 114
Medellín Becerra, Carlos, 171
Medical Research, see Scientific, Medical and Industrial Research
Mégret, Catherine, 53
Meguid, Ahmad Esmat Abdel, 423
Meier, Richard, 508, 514
Mejdani, Rexhep, 122, 124, 594
Meksi, Alexander, 123, 590
Melanesian Spearhead Group, 431
Melescanu, Teodor, 117
Melville, Pauline, 517, 519
Mendes, Sam, 499
Menem, Carlos Saúl, 85, 166, 167, 434
Mengistu Haile-Mariam, 241
Menotti, Gian-Carlo, 489
Mensah, J.H., 249
Menuhin, Yehudi, 579
Merchant, Piers, 16, 17, 32
Mercosur, see Southern Common Market
Meri, Lennart, 106, 108, 109
Meridor, Dan, 205
Merrem, Gerd-Dietrich, 299
Merton, Robert, 539
Mexico, 150, **183–5**, 534, 592, 594, 596
Meyer, Roelf, 289
Michael, King, 118
Michelini, Rafael, 177
Michell, Roger, 498
Michener, James, 583 (obit.)
Micronesia, Federated States of, 376, **378**, 399
Middleton, Stanley, 519

Mifsud Bonnici, Ugo, 93
Mifune, Toshiro, 503
Mihaylova, Nadezhda, 121
Millares, Edgar, 168
Mills, Iain, 12
Milošević, Slobodan, 128, 133, 134, 415, 590, 594
Milutinović, Milan, 133, 134, 599
Minghella, Anthony, 501
Mintoff, Dom, 93
Mirghani, Sayyid Muhammed Osman al-, 229
Miroshnicho, Alexei, 495
Mirvishes, 500
Misuari, Nur, 336
Mitchell, Adrian, 520
Mitchell, George, 46, 48
Mitchell, Katie, 498
Mitchell, Keith, 192
Mitchell, L.G., 520
Mitchell, Sir James F., 194, 196
Mitchison, Naomi, 517, 518
Mitchum, Robert, 503, 583 (obit.)
Mitterrand, François, 394, 395
Mkapa, Benjamin, 246
Mladić, Gen. Ratko, 128, 474
Mobutu Sese Seko, 56, 268, 269, 273, 276, 583–4 (obit.), 592
Mockus, Antanas, 173
Moco, Marcolino, 393, 396
Mocumbi, Pascoal, 274
Mogae, Festus, 284
Moggach, Deborah, 519
Mohajerani, Ataollah, 293
Mohammed, Ali Mahdi, 242
Mohammed, Nizam, 189
Moi, Daniel Arap, 244, 599
Mokhehle, Ntsu, 282, 286
Moldova, 141, **142–3**, 416, 422
Molina Duarte, Simón, 433
Molins, Joaquim, 86
Moller, Per Stig, 69
Monaco, 1, **84**
Mondrian, Piet, 511
Mongolia, 348, **364–6**, 592
Montazeri, Ayatollah, 294
Monteiro, Antonio Mascarenhas, 274, 385
Montenegro, Yugoslav Republic of, 133, 134, 474, 597
Montesinos, Vladimir, 176
Montgomerie, Colin, 526, 527
Montserrat, 34, 194, **197, 198**, 595
Moody, Helen Wills, 580
Moore, Brian, 519
Moore, Demi, 501
Moore, Henry, 510, 512
Moran, Commandante Rolando, 181
Morer, Michael, 525
Morgan, Kenneth O., 520
Morita, Akio, 580
Morocco, 237–8, 239, 268, 269, 400, 592
Morris, Mark, 493, 494

Morrison, Blake, 521
Morton, Andrew, 517
Mosbacher, Emil (Bus), 584 (obit.)
Mosisili, Pakalitha, 286
Motion, Andrew, 517, 520
Moto, Severo, 267
Motpan, Dumitru, 422
Mouada, Mohamed, 233
Moussavi, Hossein, 294
Mowlam, Marjorie (Mo), 19, 20, 44, 45, 47, 48, 67, 572
Moya, Carlos, 529
Mozaffar, Hossein, 293
Mozambique, 92, 229, **274–5**, 291, 427
Mozart, Wolfgang Amadeus, 488, 496
Mswati III, King, 282
Muñoz Ledo, Porfirio, 185
Mubarak, Mohammed Husni, 203, 207, 209, 210, 229, 592
Mucio, Zdravko, 474
Mudavadi, Musalia, 245
Mugabe, Robert, 229, 280, 284, 426
Muluzi, Bakili, 279
Mungomba, Dean, 278
Mungra, Motilal, 199
Munyarrun, Djakapuura, 493
Murdoch, Iris, 521
Murdoch, Rupert, 505, 507,
Murerwa, Herbert, 281
Murillo, Javier, 168
Murrow, Edward, 579
Museveni, Yoweri, 229, 247, 248
Music, 489–93
Musoke, Kintu, 247
Musonge, Peter Mafany, 262
Mutharika, Bingo wa, 425
Myanmar (Burma), 35, **326–7**, 340, 430, 431
Myer, Valerie Grosvenor, 520

Nagorno-Karabakh, 144, 414, 416
Najafabadi, Dorri, 293
Namazi, Dr Hossein, 293
Namdar-Zanganeh, Bijan, 293
Namibia, 282, 284, 285, **287–8**, 427, 469
Nano, Fatos, 122, 123, 124, 135, 415, 594
Narayan, R.K., 518
Narayanan, Kocheril Raman, 305, 594
Nauru, 376, 378
Navarro, Carlos, 89
Nazarbayev, Nursultan, 298, 299, 304, 348, 597
McNally, Terrence, 500
Ndadaye, Melchior, 272
Ndi, Fru, 264
Ndimira, Pascal-Firmin, 271
Ne Win, 326
Neate, Kenneth, 489
Nelson, Richard, 498
Nemtsov, Boris, 136, 140
Nena, Jacob, 376, 378
Nepal, 307, **316–7**, 325, 432, 590, 596
Netanyahu, Binyamin, 15, 85, 158, 159, 202, 203, 205, 206, 207, 208, 212, 214, 216, 238, 591, 592, 598
Netherlands Antilles, 200
Netherlands, The, 63–4, 136, 188, 199, 370, 383, 403, 417
Neto, Raul Bragança, 274
Neuhaus, Heinrich, 584
Neumeier, John, 494
New Brunswick, 394
New Caledonia, 431
New Zealand, 372, **373–6**, 379, 432, 590, 597
Newby, P.H., 518
Newland, Courttia, 517, 519
Newton, Eddie, 525
Ngilu, Charity, 245
Nicaragua, 181, 182–3, 589
Nicholas, Alison, 528
Nichols, Terry, 154
Nicholson, Harold, 157
Nicholson, Nigel, 520
Nicholson, Pamela, 189
Niger, 258, 262, 467
Nigeria, 36, **250–3**, 256, 261, 392, 401, 427, 591
Niinistö, Sauli, 76
Nikula, Paavo, 77
Nirmala, Sister, 450
Nitescu, Adina, 488
Nixon, Richard M., 581
Niyazov, Gen. Saparmurad, 298, 300, 599
Nkangi, Mayanja, 248
Nkrumah, Kwame, 582
Nobel Prizes, chemistry, **460**; economics, **539**; literature, **516**, 517; medicine, **460**; peace, 165–6, 374, 430, **443**; physics, **460**
Noble, Adrian, 497, 498
Noble, Richard, 528
Non-Aligned Movement (NAM), 94, **397–9**
Nono, Luigi, 490
Nooteboom, Cees, 519
Nordic Council, 418, 419
Norodom Ranariddh, Prince, see Ranariddh, Prince Norodom
North American Free Trade Agreement (NAFTA), 434
North Atlantic Treaty Organization (NATO), 24, 35, 36, 37, 70, 71, 75, 79, 80, 88, 90, 95, 99, 106, 108, 109, 110, 113, 114, 115, 116, 118, 119, 121, 126, 128, 132, 136, 138, 142, 144, 148, 159, 167, 232, 415, 420, 421, 422, **436–40, 555–9**
Northern Ireland, 14, 20, 28–9, 35, 36, **42–8**
Northern Marianas, 378
Norway, 71, **72–3**, 165, 188, 226, 418, 420, 421, 443, 469, 586, 596
Nouhak Phoumsavan, 340
Nouri, Abdullah, 293
Novotna, Jana, 529
Nujoma, Sam, 282, 287
Nunn, Trevor, 499
Nuri, Said Abdullo, 299

Obame-Nguema, Paulin, 263

Obiang Nguema Mbasogo, Brig.-Gen. Teodoro, 263
Obituaries, 574–88
O'Brian, Patrick, 519
Obst, Michael, 490
Ochirbat, Punsalmaagiyn, 364, 592
Ochring, Helmut, 491
Oddsson, Davíd, 70
Odinga, Raila, 245
Odlum, George, 195
O'Driscoll, Dennis, 520
Okri, Ben, 521
Olarenwaju, Maj.-Gen. Tajudeen, 253
Olarreaga, Manuel, 433
Oldman, Gary, 502
Olsen, John, 369
Olter, Bailey, 378
Oman, 224, 226, **227**, 228, 304, 444
Omar, Abu Hassan, 330
Omar, Mohammad, 295
Ona, Francis, 372
O'Neal, Ralph, 196
Onyszkiewicz, Janusz, 105
Opera, 487–9
Opie, Alan, 488
Organization for Economic Cooperation and Development (OECD), 15, 399, **532–3**
Organization for Security and Cooperation in Europe (OSCE), 124, 127, 129, 133, 144, 411, 412, **413–6**, 439
Organization of African Unity (OAU), 231, 239, 250, 323, 324, 398, **425–7**
Organization of American States (OAS), 186, 190, **432–4**
Organization of Eastern Caribbean States (OECS), 433, 435
Organization of the Islamic Conference (OIC), 103, 208, 219, 220, 225, 295, 304, **399–402**
Organization of the Petroleum Exporting Countries (OPEC), 220, 221, 227
Ortega Saavedra, Daniel, 182
Ortega, José Antonio, 88
Osborne, Bertrand, 198
Osborne, John, 582
Oscar Awards, 501
Ostrovsky, Yacov, 473
O'Sullevan, Peter, 529
O'Toole, Fintan, 520
Otto, Robert, 158
Ouédraogo, Kadre Désiré, 257, 261
Ouyahia, Ahmed, 234, 235, 593
Oviedo Silva, Gen. Lino César, 174, 175
Owen, Clive, 499
Owen, John, 196
Owusu, Theresa, 250
Ozawa, Ichiro, 360

Pacific Community, Secretariat of (SPC), 428, 431–2
Pacific Island States, 376–9
Paeniu, Bikenibeu, 377
Pahad, Aziz, 284
Pahlawan, Gen. Malik, 296, 297
Paisley, Dr Ian, 29, 44, 46
Pakistan, 34, 37, 297, 300, 305, 307, 308, **310–13**, 317, 383, 392, 399, 400, 401, 432, 441, 442, 451, 452, 471, 475, 589, 595, 596, 598
Palacios Alcocer, Mariano, 185
Palauskas, Arturas, 108
Palestinian Entity, 160, 202–4, **206–8**, 212, 232, 392, 400, 401, 589, 595, 596
Palme, Olof, 75
Palmer, William, 519
Pamungkas, Sri Bintang, 333
Panama, 181, 183
Panday, Basdeo, 189, 190
Pandolfi Arbulu, Alberto, 175, 176
Pangalos, Theodoros, 96
Papandreou, Andreas, 96
Papandreou, Georgios, 96
Papariga, Aleka, 96
Papon, Maurice, 56
Papua New Guinea, 370, **371–2**, 374, 378, 392, 393, 431, 432, 591, 594
Paraga, Dobroslav, 130
Paraguay, 174–5, 434, 585
Paris Club, 188, 213
Parizeau, Jacques, 164
Parker-Bowles, Camilla, 4
Parnevik, Jesper, 528
Parrinello, Danilo, 181
Parry, Deborah, 220
Partnership for Peace, 75, 80, 144, **437, 439**
Pasternak, Boris, 575, 585
Patassé, Ange-Félix, 263, 267
Paterson, Don, 517, 520
Patten, Chris, 24, 30, 36, 350
Patterson, Percival J., 186, 187, 599
Paxman, Jeremy, 506
Payne, Nicholas, 487
Peña Gómez, José Francisco, 180
Peñalosa, Enrique, 173
Pearce, Joanne, 497
Pedrosa, Ivan, 523
Pena, Federico, 573
Peng Zhen, 343
Pepreh, Kwame, 249
Peratikos, Costas, 97
Peres, Shimon, 205, 207, 593
Pérez Balladares, Ernesto, 181, 183
Pérez de Cuellar, Javier, 176
Peronansky, Georges, 520
Perron, Marc, 184
Perry, Fred, 580
Persson, Göran, 74
Peru, 85, 174, **175–6**, 357, 430, 434, 591
Perutz, Max, 581
Peslier, Olivier, 530
Peters, Winston, 374, 375
Petersen, Niels Helveg, 413, 414, 416
Peterson, Douglas 'Pete', 338
Petit, Roland, 493
Pettersson, Christer, 75
Pettifer, James, 453

INDEX

Pfitzner, Hans, 487
Phaladi, Letswetswe, 285
Phan Van Khai, 337
Philip, Prince (Duke of Edinburgh), 6, 391, 596, 598
Philippines, 314, **335–6**, 430, 431, 468, 535, 583, 594
Phillips, Caryl, 517, 519
Phillips, William, 460
Picasso, Pablo, 512
Pierre, Eric, 180
Piks, Rihards, 107
Pilip, Ivan, 111
Pindling, Sir Lynden, 193
Pinochet Ugarte, Gen. Augusto, 170
Pinter, Harold, 498
Pintussevich, Zana, 522
Pioline, Cedric, 529
Pipe, Martin, 529
Piper, John, 512
Piper, Myfanwy, 512
Pitakaka, Moses Puibangara, 377
Pitt the Younger, 593
Pitta, Celso, 169
Pitts, Edwin, 157
Platel, Elisabeth, 493
Plavšić, Biljana, 125, 126, 127
Plesu, Andrei, 118
Podobnik, Marijan, 132
Pol Pot, 339, 594
Poland, 85, **104–6**, 112, 139, 380, 394, 408, 414, 419, 422, 438, 534, 590, 592, 593, 594, 596
Pollard, Stephen, 10
Poole, Alan, 196
Porter, Peter, 520
Portillo, Michael, 20, 24, 30
Portugal, **90–3**, 222, 349, 380, 385, 396, 597
Pountney, David, 488
Pourier, Miguel, 200
Powell, Gen. Colin, 186
Préval, René, 179, 180
Prescott, John, 20, 23, 29, 30, 515, 572
Pressler, Mirjam, 520
Pretaapnarain Radhakishum, 198
Previti, Cesare, 60
Primakov, Yevgenii, 139
Pritchett, Sir Victor (V.S.), 518, 584 (obit.)
Prodi, Romano, 57, 58
Prokofiev, Serge, 494
Prusiner, Stanley, 460
Puccini, Giacomo, 498
Puerto Rico, 201
Pujol, Jordi, 86
Purcell, Edward, 584 (obit.)
Purryag, Rajkeswur, 321
Pustovoytenko, Valery, 140, 142
Puttnam, David, 521
Pynchon, Thomas, 519

Q, 517, 519
Qaboos bin Said, Shaikh, 224, 227
Qadafi, Col. Muammar, 231, 232, 597
Qarwi, Hamid, 233, 234

Qatar, 160, **225**, 226, 227, 230, 234, 402, 444
Qaud, Abd al-Majid al-, 232
Qhobela, Molapo, 286
Qian Qichen, 346, 347, 352
Qiao Shi, 342
Qin Jiwei, 343
Quebec, 161–4, 394
Quesada, Yeolvis, 523
Quinn, Ruairi, 67

Rabassa, Gregory, 519
Rabbani, Mohammad, 295
Rabe, David, 500
Rabin, Yitzhak, 202
Rabuka, Maj.-Gen. Sitiveni, 376, 379, 391
Radix, Roger, 192
Rafsanjani, Hashemi, 294
Rafter, Patrick, 529
Raines, Franklin D., 573
Rainha, José, 170
Rainier III, Prince, 84
Rakhmanov, Imamali, 298, 299, 304
Rakotomavo, Pascal, 325
Ralston, Gen. Joseph, 156
Ramírez, Miguel Angel, 174
Ramírez, Ricardo, 181, 182
Ramadan, Taha Yassin, 400
Ramaphosa, Cyril, 392, 562
Rame, Franca, 516
Rameau, Jean Philippe, 487
Ramgoolam, Navin, 320, 321, 432
Ramos, Fidel, 335
Ramoutar, Donald, 187
Ramsay, John, 155
Ramsay, JonBenet, 155
Ranariddh, Prince Norodom, 338, 339, 594, 595
Ransmayr, Christoph, 519
Rao, P.V. Narasimha, 305, 592
Rao, Raja, 518
Rasizade, Artur, 143
Rasmussen, Poul Nyrup, 69
Ratsiraka, Didier, 325, 589
Rattle, Sir Simon, 491
Ratzinger, Cardinal Joseph, 448
Rauschenberg, Robert, 511
Rawlings, Jerry, 249, 261
Rawsthorne, Alan, 492
Rayfield, Donald, 520
Read, Piers Paul, 519
Reading, Peter, 520
Reagan, Ronald, 434
Rebelo de Sousa, Marcelo, 92
Redmond, Siobhan, 497
Redwood, John, 24
Rees-Mogg, William, 30
Reich, Steve, 492
Reiffel, Paul, 526
Reina Idiaquez, Carlos Roberto, 181
Reinhart, Django, 579
Rejouis, Rose-Myriam, 519
Religion, 51–2, **447–53**
René, France-Albert, 322

Reno, Janet, 150, 151, 152, 220, 573
Rerngchai Marakanond, 328
Rezai, Mohsen, 294
Rhys, Paul, 498
Richard of Ammanford, Lord, 572
Richardson, Bill, 573
Richardson, Desmond, 495
Richler, Mordecai, 519
Richter, Svyatoslav, 492, 584 (obit.)
Rickson, Ian, 500
Ridderbusch, Karl, 489
Riedl, Lars, 522
Riegger, Wallingford, 492
Rifkind, Malcolm, 11, 20, 24, 35, 197
Riley, Bridget, 511
Riley, Richard W., 573
Rilke, Ina, 519
Rincón Bravo, Vice-Adm. Tito Manglio, 177
Rio Group, 433, 434
Rippon of Hexham, Lord (Geoffrey), 584–5 (obit.)
Ritchie, Harvey, 521
Rizq, Abu, 216
Robbe, Hervé, 496
Robbins, Jerome, 494
Roberts, Michele, 519
Robertson, George, 37, 572
Robertson, Robin, 520
Robinson, Arthur N.R., 189
Robinson, Mary, 68, 273, 596
Robson, Bobby, 524
Robson, Brian, 525
Rocca, Constantino, 527
Rock, David, 514
Rodionov, Gen. Igor, 136, 592
Rodríguez, Gen. Andres, 585 (obit.)
Rodríguez Maradiaga, Oscar Andrés, 182
Rodríguez Orejuela, Gilberto, 171
Rodríguez Orejuela, Manuel, 171
Rogers, Lord, 513
Rogers, Sir Richard, 513
Roh Tae Woo, 362
Rojas Parra, Freddy, 178
Rojo, Tamara, 494
Rokhlin, Gen. (retd.) Lev, 136
Roman, Petru, 422
Romania, 115, **116–9**, 139, 408, 422, 470, 534
Romanow, Roy, 163
Romiti, Cesare, 57
Roosevelt, Franklin D., 589
Rose, David, 10
Rosen, Albert, 492, 585 (obit.)
Rosenthal, Norman, 511
Ross, Dennis, 159, 206, 214
Ross, Ronald, 458
Rossello, Pedro, 201
Rossi, Aldo, 516, 585 (obit.)
Rossi, Guido, 58
Rossini, Gioacchino, 487, 488
Roth, Philip, 519
Rowntree, Kenneth, 512
Rowse, Afred Leslie (A.L.), 585 (obit.)

Roy, Arundhati, 516, 519
Rubens, Bernice, 517, 519
Rubin, Robert E., 573
Rubinstein, Elyakim, 205
Ruggiero, Renato, 532
Rühe, Volker, 51
Ruml, Jan, 111
Rusedski, Greg, 529
Rush, Richard, 501
Rushdie, Salman, 517, 590
Russell Beale, Simon, 499
Russian Federation, 37, 75, 77, 98, 103, 109, 110, 121, **135–40**, 141, 142, 157, 159, 166, 195, 218, 219, 230, 231, 295, 297, 299, 302, 303, 304, 308, 333, 342, 343, 347–8, 358–9, 364, 366, 382, 383, 386, 420, 430, 436, 437, 439, 440, 441, 442, 444, 446, 449, 465, 473, 475, 532, 534, 537, 555–9, 576, 585, 590, 591, 592, 593, 598
Rutaganda, Georges, 473
Rwanda, 248, 268, 269, 279, **271**, **272–3**, 392, 473, 591
Rwigyema, Pierre-Célestin, 271
Ryan, Willie, 530

Saad al-Abdullah as-Salim as-Sabah, Crown Prince, 224
Saatchi, Charles, 510, 511
Sachs, Jeffrey, 536
Sacks, Dr Jonathan, 451
Saddam Husain, 217, 218, 219, 401
Saint-Saens, Camille, 488
Saitoti, George, 245
Sala, Josep Maria, 89
Saleh, Ali Abdullah, 222
Saleh, Jaime M., 200
Salih, Al-Zubair Mohammed, 230
Salim, Salim Ahmed, 425, 426
Salinas de Gortari, Carlos, 184
Salinger, Pierre, 155
Salmond, Alex, 39
Sam Rangsi, 339
Samoa, 377, 379
Sampa, Chitalu, 278
Sampaio, Jorge, 90
Samper Pizano, Ernesto, 171, 172, 397
Sampras, Pete, 529
Sampson, Anthony, 521
Samsova, Galina, 495
San Marino, 84
Sandle, Michael, 510
Sangma, Purno A., 306
Sanguinetti, Julio María, 177
Sankara, Thomas, 261
Sankoh, Foday, 254
Sant, Alfred, 93, 94
Santacruz Londoño, José, 171
Santer, Jacques, 402, 410, 594
Santos, Juan Manuel, 172
São Tomé & Príncipe, 274, 396
Saramago, José, 519
Sarkissian, Armen, 143

Sassou-Nguesso, Gen. Denis, 263, 265, 266, 276, 597
Sato, Koko, 359
Saucedo Sánchez, Gen. César, 175, 176
Saud al-Faisal, Prince, 221
Saudi Arabia, 1, 208, 214, 218, **220–2**, 223, 225, 226, 297, 300, 304, 400, 424, 444, 591
Saul, David, 197, 591
Saul, Nigel, 520
Savage, Frank J., 197
Savary, Jerome, 488
Savimbi, Jonas, 275, 276, 277, 279
Sayegh, Hani Abd al-Rahim al-, 220
Scalfaro, Oscar Luigi, 57, 58, 241, 304
Scavone, Ubaldo, 174
Schüssel, Wolfgang, 78
Schäuble, Wolfgang, 51
Scheck, Barry, 155
Schickel, Richard, 520
Schmidt, Michael, 520
Schneider, Roy, 201
Scholes, Myron, 539
Schonzeler, Hans-Hubert, 492
Schrader, Paul, 501
Schumacher, Michael, 528
Schwebel, Judge Stephen, 473
Scientific, Medical and Industrial Research, 454–60
Scioli, Daniel, 167
Scotland, 5, 8, 14, 20, 27, 29, 34, **37–40**, 391, 412, 592
Scott Thomas, Kristin, 501
Sebastian, Sir Cuthbert, 194
Sebba, Anne, 453, 520
Sebron, Carolyn, 488
Security Issues, see Defence, Disarmament and Security
Sedivy, Jaroslav, 111
Seeger, Norbert, 85
Séguin, Philippe, 55
Seldon, Anthony, 520
Seleznev, Gennadii, 141
Self, Will, 519
Senegal, 256, 258–9, 394, 473
Senna, Ayrton, 528
Serbia, Yugoslav Republic of, 133, 134–5, 474, 589, 590, 594, 599
Sergeev, Gen. Igor, 136
Sergeyev, Konstantin, 495
Serpa Uribe, Horacio, 172
Serpents' Island, 119
Seselj, Vojislav, 134, 599
Setshwaelo, Ephraim, 284
Severin, Adrian, 118
Severino, Rodolfo C., 428, 430
Seychelles, 282, **322–3**, 394, 428, 432
Seymour, Lynn, 494
Shadley, Maj.-Gen. Robert, 156
Shah, Sajjad Ali, 311
Shalala, Donna E., 573
Shalikashvili, Gen. John, 156

Sharif, Mian Nawaz, 307, 310, 311, 312, 314, 589, 598
Sharma, Shankar Dayal, 305
Sharon, Ariel, 207
Sheen, Michael, 498
Sheng, Bright, 492
Sher, Antony, 498
Sherry, Nick, 369
Shevardnadze, Eduard, 143, 144, 304
Shields, Carol, 519
Shipley, Jenny, 373, 374, 597
Short, Clare, 36, 198, 572
Short, Justice Emile, 250
Shustari, Esmail, 293
Sierra Leone, 251, **253–4**, 256, 387, 391, 426, 592
Siew, Vincent, 353, 355
Sihanouk, King Norodom, 338, 339
Siimann, Mart, 106, 107, 591
Silajdzic, Haris, 125
Sillitoe, Alan, 519
Silva, Héctor, 182
Simbeye, Gen. Nobby, 278
Simitis, Kostas, 95, 96
Simon of Highbury, Lord, 28
Simon, Neil, 500
Simon, Sir David, 20
Simonsen, Torkil, 69
Simpson, Nicole Brown, 153, 590
Simpson, O.J., 153, 155, 590
Simpson, Robert, 492
Sin, Cardinal Jaime, 335
Sinclair, Iain, 521
Singapore, 317, 328, 330, **331–2**, 334, 336, 355, 430, 431, 462, 468, 535, 589
Singherok, Brig.-Gen. Jerry, 371
Sinyavsky, Andrei, 518, 585 (obit.)
Sivanandan, A., 519
Skate, Bill, 371, 372, 594
Skele, Andris, 107
Skinner, Claire, 499
Skou, Jen, 460
Slater, Andrew, 489
Slater, Rodney E., 573
Slezevicius, Adolfas, 108
Slovakia, 112–4, 115, 408, 422, 438, 472, 534
Slovenia, 132–3, 139, 380, 408, 419, 421, 422, 534
Small Island States, 431
Smarth, Rosny, 180
Smith, Chris, 487, 515, 572
Smith, Dame Maggie, 500
Smith, Iain Crichton, 520
Smith, Tim, 16
Smith, Walter, 525
Snegur, Mircea, 142
Sneh, Ephraim, 206
Sodano, Cardinal Angelo, 83
Sofía, Queen, 87
Sofiyanski, Stefan, 120, 121
Softley, Iain, 502
Sokurov, Aleksandr, 503
Solana, Javier, 80, 415, 436, 592

Soljic, Vladimir, 125
Solomon Islands, 372, **377, 378**, 431
Solti, Sir Georg, 489, 492, 585–6 (obit.)
Solzhenitsyn, Alexander, 521
Somalia, 240, 241, **242–3**, 589
Somaliland, 240, 243
Somavia, Juan, 385
Son Sen, 339
Soong, James, 355
Sope, Barak, 379
Sorhaindo, Crispin, 194
Sotomeyor, Jan, 522
Souflias, Georgios, 96
South Africa, 92, 93, 124, 157, 214, 227, 229, 231, 242, 269, 270, 275, 278, 283, 284, 286, **289–92**, 333, 371, 392, 399, 469, 535, 595, 597
South Asian Association for Regional Cooperation (SAARC), 307, 312, 314, 324, **429, 432**
South Pacific Commission (SPC), 431
South Pacific Forum (SPF), 429, 432
Southern African Development Community (SADC), 282–4, 288, 291, **425, 428**
Southern Common Market (Mercosur), 433, 434
Soyinka, Wole, 251, 517, 521, 591
Space Research, see Scientific, Medical and Industrial Research
Spahlinger, Mathias, 490
Spain, 2, 5, 34, 35, **86–9**, 90, 211, 234, 238, 267, 304, 383, 405, 406, 444, 533, 591, 594, 597
Spalding, Frances, 521
Spalding, Julian, 509
Spark, Dame Muriel, 516
Spencer, Earl, 5
Spenser, Edmund, 499
Sperling, Gene, 573
Spice Girls, The, 504
Spicer, Tim, 371
Spielberg, Steven, 501
Spitaels, Guy, 62
Spiteri, Lino, 94
Sport, 32, 42, 97, 202, 370–1, 375, **522–31**
Spring, Dick, 67
Squillacote, Theresa, 157
Sri Lanka, 307, **318–20**, 325, 432, 448, 473, 576, 597
St Kitts & Nevis, 194, 195
St Lucia, 194, 195–6, 394
St Vincent & the Grenadines, 194, 196, 476
Staats, Leo, 495
Stand, Kurt, 157
Starr, Kenneth, 148, 150
Statistical Tables, 540–54
Stephanopoulos, Kostas, 95
Stevenson, Anne, 517, 520
Stevenson, Ben, 495
Stewart, Allan, 38
Stewart, James, 503, 586 (obit.)
Steyn, Mark, 492
Stich, Michael, 529
Stirling, Jim, 514
Stockhausen, Karlheinz, 491

Stojičić, Radovan, 134
Stokes, Prof. Donald, 586 (obit.)
Stone, Oliver, 52
Stone, Shane, 368
Stoppard, Tom, 498
Stoute, Michael, 530
Stoyanov, Petar, 119, 120, 121, 589
Strang, Gavin, 572
Strauss, Johann, 488
Strauss, Richard, 489
Stravinsky, Igor, 491, 495
Straw, Jack, 7, 8, 20, 572
Stroessner, Alfredo, 585
Suchocka, Hanna, 106
Sudan, 228–31, 241, 242, 248, 290, 452
Sudjatmiko, Budiman, 333
Suharto, Gen. (retd.), 326, 332, 333, 334
Sujuki, Hirami, 523
Sukarno, Gen., 333
Sukarnoputri, Megawati, 333
Sultonov, Otkir, 298
Sumaye, Frederick, 246
Sundqvist, Ulf, 77
Sundström, Anders, 75
Supple, Tim, 496
Suriname, 198–9
Susak, Gojko, 130
Suu Kyi, Aung San, 326, 430
Swaziland, 6, **282**, 284, **288**, 291
Sweden, 21, **74–5**, 126, 140, 188, 380, 404, 405
Switzerland, 80–3, 98, 413, 414, 446, 449, 590, 592
Syria, 211, **213–5**, 218, 220, 230, 363, 401
Syse, John, 586 (obit.)

Ta Mok, 14, 339
Tabai, Ieremia, 432
Tadić, Dušan, 128, 473, 474
Tagliaventi & Associates, 515
Taib, Muhammad Muhammad, 330
Taiwan, 85, 183, 192, 193, 274, 290, 331, 342, 347, 349–50, **353–6**, 358, 388
Tajikistan, 297, **298–304**, 389
Taki Abdoulkarim, Mohammed, 322, 323, 324
Talbott, Strobe, 341
Talibani, Jallal, 103
Tamrat Layne, 241
Tamraz, Roger, 150
Tan Dun, 492
Tandja, Mamadou, 262
Tang Liang Hong, 331, 332
Tanumafili II, Susuga Malietoa, 377
Tanzania, 229, **246–7**, 272, 273, 397, 426, 473
Tarar, Mohammed Rafiq, 310, 311, 598
Tarkovsky, Andrei, 511
Tarrin Nimmanahaeminda, 328
Tarschys, Daniel, 411
Taruskin, Richard, 493
Tate, James, 520
Taufa'ahua Tupou IV, King, 377
Tavener, John, 492
Taya, Col. Maaouiya Ould Sidi Mohammed, 256, 259

Taylor, Ann, 572
Taylor, Charles Ghankay, 255, 256, 594
Taylor, Derek H., 197
Taylor, Elisabeth Russell, 519
Taylor, Ian, 31
Taylor, Mark, 525
Taylor of Gosforth, Lord, 586 (obit.)
Television & Radio, 504–7
Temple-Morris, Peter, 32
Tenet, George, 150, 573
Tenorio, Friolan C., 378
Tenorio, Pedro P., 378
ter Schiphorst, Iris, 491
Ter-Petrosyan, Levon, 143
Teresa of Calcutta, Mother, 447, 450, 586–7 (obit.), 596
Terreblanche, Eugene, 290
Tetley, Glen, 495
Thailand, 227, **327–9**, 332, 340, 370, 429, 431, 432, 468, 535, 538, 594, 597
Thaler, Goran, 132
Than Shwe, Gen., 326
Thani, Shaikh Hamid bin Jassim bin Jabr al-, 24, 225
Thanong Bidaya, 327, 328
Thapa, Surya Bahadur, 316, 317, 596
Tharp, Twyla, 493, 495
Thatcher of Finchley, Baroness, 10, 15, 16, 18, 23, 24, 39
Thayer, Nate, 339
Theatre, 496–500
Thiam, Habib, 256
Thomas, Adrian, 492
Thomas, George, 587
Thomas, R.S., 521
Thompson, Fred, 151, 152
Thompson, William, 46
Thomson, Andrew, 492
Thorpe, Graham, 525, 526
Thwaite, Anthony, 520
Tibet, 345, 349
Tick, Judith, 492
Tietmeyer, Hans, 405
Tikhonov, Nikolai, 587 (obit.)
Tin Oo, Lt.-Gen., 327
Tinnoudji, Claude Cohen, 460
Tito, Teburoro, 376
Todd, Lord, 587 (obit.)
Todorović, Zoran, 134
Togo, 257, **261**, 266, 268, 400
Toibin, Colm, 519
Tokelau, 379
Toller, Owen, 492
Tomasson, Helgi, 493
Tonga, **377**, 378, **379**
Tonypandy, Viscount (George Thomas), 587 (obit.)
Tosovsky, Josef, 110, 111
Touré, Gen. Amadou Toumani, 266
Touré, Sidya, 257
Tran Duc Luong, 337
Travolta, John, 501
Tremain, Rose, 517, 519

Trichet, Jean-Claude, 406
Trimble, David, 43, 44, 46, 47, 48, 595
Trinidad & Tobago, 188, **189–90**
Trovoada, Miguel, 274
Tsang, Steve Yui-sang, 521
Tsedenbal, Yumjaagiyn, 365
Tshisekedi, Etienne, 269
Tsibilyev, Vasily, 455
Tsikata, Kojo, 250
Tsokhatsopoulos, Akis, 95
Tuckey, Raymond, 580
Tudela, Francisco, 176
Tudjman, Franjo, 129, 130, 593
Tudor, Antony, 495
Tufnell, Phil, 526
Tulio Espinosa, Gen. Marco, 182
Tung Chee-hwa, 350, 352, 353, 593
Tunisia, 226, 232, **233–4**, 420
Turkey, 95, 96, 98, 99, **101–3**, 144, 214, 218, 219, 220, 232, 303, 304, 401, 408, 422, 424, 470, 475–6, 478, 593
Turkish Republic of Northern Cyprus (TRNC), 97–101, 102, 400
Turkmenistan, 121, 297, **298–304**, 599
Turks & Caicos Islands, 197, 198
Turner, Ted, 384
Turnquest, Sir Orville, 193
Tutu, Desmond, 290
Tutuola, Amos, 518
Tuvalu, 377
Tyson, Mike, 525

U Kyaw Din, 326
U Ohn Gyaw, 431
U Tin Shwe, 326
Uganda, 229, **247–6**, 270, 392
Uglow, Euan, 511
Uglow, Jenny, 521
Ukraine, 106, 119, **140**, **141–2**, 380, 421, 438, 439, 471, 478, 584, 587, 593
Ulmanis, Guntis, 106
Ulufa'alu, Bartholomew, 377, 378
Ung Huot, 338, 339, 595
United Arab Emirates (UAE), 220, **224**, 225, **227–8**, 230, 400, 424
United Kingdom (see also Northern Ireland, Scotland, Wales), **4–48**; arts, 487–521; Bank of England, 21–2; broadcasting, 10, 504–7; cabinet, 20, 27, **572**; devolution, 13–14, 29, 34, 38–9, 40–1; Diana, death of, 1–2, 4–7, 447, 577–8; European Union, 11, 14, 16, 17, 21, 24, 31, 32–3, 35–6, 349, 350–3, 354, 402, 403, 476–7; Gen. election, 4, 14, 15–20; Hong Kong, 24, 31, 34, 36, 343, 404–8; international relations, 34–7, 188, 195, 209, 217, 218, 220–1, 223, 231, 250, 295, 313, 366, 380, 391, 431–2; Millennium Exhibition, 12; National Lottery, 22–3; obituaries, 574ff; press, 18; religion, 447–8; sleaze, 16–17, 19, 27–8, 32; social policy, 7–10, 22–3; sport, 522–31
United Nations, 380–90; Albania, 60, 123, 388; Arab-Israeli dispute, 206, 215, 390; budget and

arrears, 148, 382–4; Africa, 242, 265, 270, 277, 386–7; Americas, 178, 183, 388; Asia, 297, 299, 314, 318, 330, 338, 346, 363, 389; Cyprus, 98, 100, 390; environment, 374, 385, 464–6, 569–71; ex-Yugoslavia, 128, 129, 132, 389–90; Iraq, 214, 217–8, 219, 225, 227, 231, 386, 424; Libya, 386, 398, 423; reform process, 61, 132–3, 255, 308–9, 381–2, 397–8, 427; war crimes tribunals, 128, 273, 473–4; Western Sahara, 239, 388
United States of America, 45–60; Africa, 241, 243, 426; Americas, 168, 172, 178, 181, 183–4, 186–7, 188, 190, 197, 197, 198, 201, 434–5; Arab world, 206, 207, 208, 212, 213, 214, 216, 217, 220, 223, 226, 227, 230, 231–2, 236, 239; Asian relations, 297, 303–4, 308, 313, 327, 330, 331, 333, 337, 341, 353, 361, 362, 363–4, 429, 430; cabinet, **573**; Canada, 164–5; China, 342, 346–7, 348, 352; disasters, 145–6, 155–6; economy, 148, 151; European relations, 43, 46, 52, 70, 81, 100, 109–10, 128, 129–30; intelligence services, 157; Iran, 294, 400; Japan, 357, 358; obituaries, 575ff; political affairs, 146–53; scandals, 145, 146, 147, 148–9, 150–1; social and legal affairs, 153–9, **484–6**; sport, 527, 528, 529, 531; Unabomber, 155; Woodward case, 154–5
Urdangarín, Iñaki, 87
Uruguay, 177
US Virgin Islands, 201
Uteem, Cassam, 320, 321
Uzbekistan, 121, 296, 297, **298–304**

Vaea, Baron, 377
Vagnorius, Gediminas, 107, 108
Vähi, Tiit, 107
Vakil, Ardashir, 519
Valdiveso Sarmiento, Alfonso, 172
Valencia Vivas, Gen. Pedro Nicolas, 177
van den Broek, Hans, 108
van der Stoel, Max, 416
van der Veer, Walter, 179
van Dunem, Fernando José da França Dias, 275, 591
van Schalkwyk, Marthinus, 289
Vanuatu, 377, 378–9, 431
Varga, Bálint Andras, 492
Varsavsky, Tatiana, 520
Vasarely, Victor, 512
Vassallo, Francis, 94
Vatican, 83, 85–6, 126, 179, 231, 448–9, 451
Védrine, Hubert, 57, 234, 238
Veiga Simão, Prof. José, 92
Veiga, Carlos, 274
Vella, George, 93, 94
Venables, Terry, 524
Venezuela, 177–8, 190, 435, 597
Venizelos, Evangelos, 97
Verdi, Giuseppe, 487, 488
Versace, Gianni, 587 (obit.), 594
Vick, Graham, 487, 488
Vidal, Gore, 52
Videnov, Zhan, 119, 122
Vieira, João Bernardo, 273

Vietnam, 337–8, 340, 394, 395, 430, 431, 574, 593
Viljoen, Constand, 290
Villanueva Ruesta, Gen. José, 176
Villanueva, Humberto Roque, 185
Villeneuve, Jacques, 528
Villoresi, Luigi, 587–8 (obit.)
Vinokurow, Val, 519
Visegrad Group, 112, 438
Visual Arts, 507–12
Vitorino, António, 92
Vo Van Kiet, 337
Vohor, Serge, 11, 377, 378, 379
Volcker, Paul, 81
von Einem, Gottfried, 488
von Trier, Lars, 503
Vonnegut, Kurt, 519
Voss, Philip, 498
Vranitzky, Franz, 60, 78, 124, 414, 415, 589
Vulkan, Ersoy, 422

Waddington, Lord, 197
Wade, Abdoulaye, 258
Wagner, Richard, 488, 489
Waigel, Theo, 49, 50, 405
Waites, Zoë, 498
Wajed Miah, M.A., 314
Walcott, Derek, 517, 520
Wales, 5, 29, **40–2**
Wales, Prince of, see Charles, Prince of Wales
Wales, Princess of, see Diana, Princess of Wales
Walker, John, 460
Walker, Liza, 499
Wallenberg, Raoul, 451
Wallström, Margot, 75
Wamalwa, Michael, 245
Wangchuk, Jigme Singye, 317
Warchus, Matthew, 488, 497
Ward, Anthony, 498, 499
Warioba, Joseph, 246
Warne, Shane, 525, 526
Wasmosy, Juan Carlos, 174
Waterhouse, Sir Ronald, 42
Watkins, Roderick, 490
Wedgwood, Josiah, 588
Wedgwood, Dame Veronica, 588 (obit.)
Weeramantry, Christopher, 473
Wei Jianxing, 341
Wei Jingsheng, 346
Weight, Carel, 512
Weintraub, Stanley, 521
Weiss, Birthe, 69
Weizman, Ezer, 202, 590
Welch, Damien, 494
Welch, Stanton, 494
Weld, William, 150
Weldon, Fay, 519
Wen Jiabao, 341
Wenström, Anders, 418
Wesker, Arnold, 498
Wesley, Samuel, 492
West African Economic and Monetary Union (UEMOA), 425, 427–8

West, Richard, 521
Westendorp, Carlos, 126, 128, 593
Western European Union (WEU), 75, 404, 411, 437
Western Sahara, 238, **239**, 388
Wethered, Joyce, 588 (obit.)
Wheatley, Willard, 197
Wheeldon, Christopher, 494
Whelan, Peter, 498
White, Edmund, 519
Whitemore, Hugh, 500
Whiteread, Rachel, 510
Whitlam, Gough, 575
Whitman, Christine, 153
Whittleton, Jack A., 428
Wicks, Susan, 520
Widdecombe, Ann, 23
Wijdenbosch, Jules, 198, 199
Wilde, Oscar, 498
Wildor, Sarah, 494
Wilecki, Gen. Tadeusz, 105
Wiles, Prof. Peter, 588
Wilford, Michael, 514, 515
Wilkinson, Chris, 515
Willi, Dr Andrea, 85
William and Henry (Harry), Princes, 4, 5, 6, 577
Williams, C.K., 520
Williams, Ellis, 515
Williams, Eric, 190
Williams, Frank, 528
Williams, Jody, 165, 443, 596
Williams, Margaret, 149
Williams, Sir Daniel, 192
Wilson, A.N., 521
Wilson, Colin St John, 514, 518
Wilson, Pete, 158
Wilson, Snoo, 500
Windsor, Duke of, 500
Windward & Leeward Islands, **194–6**
Winterson, Jeanette, 517, 519
Wlaschiha, Ekkehard, 487
Wolf, Marcus, 51
Wolf-Ferrari, Ermanno, 489
Wolfensohn, James D., 465, 538, 532
Wolpert, Stanley, 521
Woo, John, 501
Wood, John, 498
Woodbridge, Tod, 529
Woodforde, Mark, 529
Woodham, Luke, 158
Woods, John E., 519
Woods, Tiger, 527, 528
Woodward, Bob, 148
Woodward, Louise, 154, 155, 598
Workman, Charles, 488
World Bank, 129, 166, 214, 217, 223, 224, 228, 230, 237, 242, 247, 259, 260, 261, 270, 280, 281, 291, 309, 325, 328, 397, 398, 411, 470, **532**, **537–8**, 539
World Trade Organization (WTO), 178, 284, 342, 347, 366, 410, 430, **532**, **537**

Wright, Billy, 48
Wright, Frank Lloyd, 508
Wright, Glyn, 520
Wyatt, Will, 504

Xenakis, Iannis, 491

Yadav, Laloo Prasad, 306
Yadav, Rabri Devi, 306
Yar'Adua, Gen. Shehu Musa, 253
Yasin, Shaikh Ahmad, 204, 212, 596
Yazdi, Ibrahim, 294
Yeats, W.B., 517
Yellin, Janet L., 573
Yeltsin, Boris, 36, 109, 135, 136, 137, 138, 139, 140, 141, 142, 143, 144, 159, 299, 343, 347, 358, 366, 440, 450, 590, 591, 592, 593, 596, 598
Yemen, 221, **222–4**, 226, 230, 392
Yentob, Alan, 505
Yeré, Pierre, 323
Yilmaz, Mesut, 95, 99, 100, 101, 102, 103, 593
Yo-Yo Ma, 492
Yona, Daniel, 247
Young, Sir Colville, 191
Young, Kirsty, 504
Yousef, Ramzi Ahmed, 154
Yugoslavia, Federal Republic of, 125, 126, 130, **133–5**, 390, 414, 470, 589, 594

Zafy, Albert, 589
Zaimov, Martin, 122
Zaïre, see Congo, Democratic Republic of the
Zambia, **277–9**, 284, 427, 599
Zanotti, Marino, 84
Zanzibar & Pemba, 246
Zao Wou Ki, 512
Zardari, Asif Ali, 311
Zayad bin Sultan al-Nahayyan, Shaikh, 224, 230
Zebiri, Kate, 453
Zedillo Ponce de León, Ernesto, 183, 184, 185
Zemeckis, Robert, 501
Zeng Qinghong, 341
Zephaniah, Benjamin, 520
Zéroual, Brig.-Gen. Liamine, 234, 235, 593
Zhang Wannian, 341
Zhelev, Zhelyu, 589
Zhivkov, Todor, 122
Zhou Enlai, 342
Zhu Rongji, 341
Zia, Begum Khaleda, 315
Zieleniec, Josef, 111
Zimbabwe, 229, 241, **280–2**, 284, 285, 426, 428, 469, 535, 599
Zinnemann, Fred, 588 (obit.)
Zinsou, Emile Derlin, 395
Zobel, Hiller, 155
Zola, Gianfranco, 524
Zuabi, Mahmud, 213
Zuma, Jacob, 289